CONSTITUTIONAL LAW

CIVIL LIBERTY

AND

INDIVIDUAL RIGHTS

SIXTH EDITION

By

WILLIAM COHEN
C. Wendell and Edith M. Carlsmith
Professor Emeritus, Stanford Law School

DAVID J. DANELSKI
Mary Lou and George Boone Centennial Professor Emeritus
Stanford University

DAVID A. YALOF
Associate Professor of Political Science
The University of Connecticut

FOUNDATION PRESS
2007

© 1976, 1982, 1994, 1997, 2002 FOUNDATION PRESS
© 2007 By FOUNDATION PRESS
        395 Hudson Street
        New York, NY 10014
        Phone Toll Free 1–877–888–1330
        Fax (212) 367–6799
        foundation–press.com
Printed in the United States of America

ISBN 978–1–59941–170–5

TEXT IS PRINTED ON 10% POST CONSUMER RECYCLED PAPER

For Nancy and Jill

*

PREFACE

This volume, which is for undergraduate courses, focuses on the individual rights necessary for democracy and self-realization. These rights are freedom of thought and belief, freedom of speech and press, freedom of association, freedom of religion (including freedom from religious establishment), privacy, equality, due process, and the right to vote.

We approach these rights institutionally, doctrinally, historically, and realistically.

We begin by considering four constitutional institutions in relation to each other—the Bill of Rights (broadly considered), federalism, the judiciary, and judicial review. Because of the Supreme Court's importance in the American judiciary and in defining and guaranteeing individual rights, we explain and illustrate the six steps in the Court's decisionmaking process: (1) preliminary case selection, (2) oral argument, (3) conference discussion and voting, (4) opinion assignment, (5) opinion writing and circulation, and (6) public announcement of decisions and delivery of opinions.

The justices' opinions—majority, dissenting, and concurring—almost invariably reflect constitutional or legal doctrine. Such doctrine consists of theories, principles, rules, tests, and policies that are often used to justify future decisions in similar cases. We report, examine, clarify, trace the growth, and at times raise questions as to the soundness and consistency of judicial doctrine.

The individual rights covered in this volume must be approached historically because most of those rights antedate the making of the Constitution in 1787 and the Bill of Rights in 1791, and their interpretation has changed over time. In addition, we stress this approach because law-school courses in constitutional law typically do not emphasize it, apparently because those courses assume that law students had studied constitutional history as undergraduates.

Our presentation of material from court members' working papers—*certiorari* memos, conference notes, voting data in docket books, draft opinions, and intra-Court communications—provides a realistic dimension in understanding Supreme Court decisionmaking, for such materials sometimes show that the reasons for the Court's decisions are not those given in its opinions. In other words, opinions are often justifications (or rationalizations) for decisions reached on some other basis. It is not uncommon for ideologically-based decisions to be justified on the basis of doctrine that satisfies a majority. And it is not uncommon for a doctrinal shift and even doctrinal abandonment to occur when there is a change of personnel in the Court following a change of ideology in the nation reflected in the presidency and Congress.

Consistent with our realistic approach, we report, where evidence is available, the political and social impact of principal cases in this volume. We do so for three reasons—(1) to show that Supreme Court decisions are not self-executing and that compliance varies, (2) to show that the consequences of decisions sometimes constitute feedback in the Court, and (3) to show that Supreme Court decisionmaking often plays a part in the nation's socio-political process.

We hope that this volume will be interesting and enjoyable for students. In an effort to make it interesting and to show the human side of the Supreme Court, we have presented biographies of all justices who wrote opinions reported in this volume. The data in the biographies include the Court member's social class, education, religion, party affiliation, appointing president, and confirmation vote. The biographies and notes also report relevant facts that often fall between the cracks—for example, Oliver Wendell Holmes, Jr., rereading Mill's *On Liberty* just before writing his opinion in *Schenk v. United States* (1919), which established the clear and present danger test; John Marshall Harlan I deliberately using the same pen and inkwell in writing his dissenting opinion in *The Civil Rights Cases* (1883) that Chief Justice Taney had used to write the Court's opinion in *Dred Scott v. Stanford* (1857); and William J. Brennan, Jr., asking Thurgood Marshall, when *Regents of the University of California v. Bakke* (1978) was before the Court, whether he thought it was proper for one of his sons to be accorded special consideration in the medical admissions process because of race and Marshall answering: "Damn right. They owe us."

WILLIAM COHEN
DAVID J. DANELSKI
DAVID A. YALOF

ABOUT THE AUTHORS

William Cohen clerked for Justice William O. Douglas after graduation from UCLA Law School. He has been a member of the law faculties
at Minnesota, UCLA, and Stanford. He is the author or co-author of several casebooks on constitutional law.

David J. Danelski, a lawyer and political scientist with a Ph.D. from
the University of Chicago, has taught undergraduate and graduate courses in constitutional law and civil liberties at Yale, Cornell, Stanford, and
other universities. He has served as pro bono counsel to the ACLU and
several civil rights groups. He has also written widely on the Supreme
Court.

David A. Yalof is an associate professor of political science at the University of Connecticut. His first book, *Pursuit of Justices*, won the 1999
American Political Science Association's Richard Neustadt prize as the
best book published on presidential studies. A graduate of The University of Virginia Law School (J.D. 1991) and the Johns Hopkins University
(Ph.D. 1997), Dr. Yalof has authored numerous articles about various aspects of constitutional law inter-branch relations.

*

SUMMARY OF CONTENTS

SUMMARY OF CONTENTS

TABLE OF CONTENTS

TABLE OF CONTENTS

TABLE OF CONTENTS

Page

TABLE OF CONTENTS

TABLE OF CONTENTS

TABLE OF CONTENTS

*

TABLE OF CASES

Principal cases are in bold type. Non-principal cases are in roman type. References are to Pages.

TABLE OF CASES

*

CONSTITUTIONAL LAW

CIVIL LIBERTY

AND

INDIVIDUAL RIGHTS

*

Part One

INSTITUTIONAL CONTEXT

Chapter I

THE BILL OF RIGHTS

I. PRELUDE*

What is a bill of rights? In the popular sense it is any document setting forth the liberties of the people. I prefer to think of our Bill of Rights as including all provisions of the original Constitution and Amendments** that protect individual liberty by barring government from acting in a particular area or from acting except under certain prescribed procedures.

. . .

Today most Americans seem to have forgotten the ancient evils which forced their ancestors to flee to this new country and to form a government stripped of old powers used to oppress them. But the Americans who supported the Revolution and the adoption of our Constitution knew firsthand the dangers of tyrannical governments. They were familiar with the long existing practice of English persecutions of people wholly because of their religious or political beliefs. They knew that many accused of such offenses had stood, helpless to defend themselves, before biased legislators and judges.

John Lilburne, a Puritan dissenter, is a conspicuous example. He found out the hard way that a citizen of England could not get a court and jury trial under English law if Parliament wanted to try and punish him in some kind of summary and unfair method of its own. Time and time again, when his religious or political activities resulted in criminal charges against him, he had demanded jury trials under the "law of the

---

 * Hugo L. Black, The Bill of Rights. New York University Law Review, 1960, vol. 35, pp. 865–869. Reprinted with permission.

 ** These provisions are (1) Article I, § 10, and Article II § 9, which prohibit the United States and the States from enacting *ex post facto* laws (laws that make conduct criminal after it occurred) and bills of attainder (legislative action finding person guilty of crimes), (2) Article I, § 9, which limits suspension of *habeas corpus*, (3) Article III, which requires trial by jury in all federal criminal cases and also that such trial be held in the State in which the alleged crime occurred, and which requires the testimony of two witnesses to the same overt act or a confession in open court for a conviction of treason, and (4) Article 6, § 3, which prohibits any religious test for federal office.

land" but had been refused. Due to "trials" either by Parliament, its legislative committees, or courts subservient to the King or to Parliament, against all of which he vigorously protested as contrary to "due process" or "the law of the land," Lilburne had been whipped, put in the pillory, sent to prison, heavily fined and banished from England, all its islands and dominions, under penalty of death should he return. This last sentence was imposed by a simple Act of Parliament without any semblance of a trial. Upon his defiant return he was arrested and subjected to an unfair trial for his life. His chief defense was that the Parliamentary conviction was a nullity, as a denial of "due process of law," which he claimed was guaranteed under Magna Charta, the 1628 Petition of Right, and statutes passed to carry them out.... Lilburne repeatedly and vehemently contended that he was entitled to notice, an indictment, and court trial by jury under the known laws of England; that he had a right to be represented by counsel; that he had a right to have witnesses summoned in his behalf and be confronted by the witnesses against him; that he could not be compelled to testify against himself. When Lilburne finally secured a jury, it courageously acquitted him, after which the jury itself was severely punished by the court.

Prompted largely by the desire to save Englishmen from such legislative mockeries of fair trials, Lilburne and others strongly advocated adoption of an "Agreement of the People" which contained most of the provisions of our present Bill of Rights. That Agreement would have done away with Parliamentary omnipotence. Lilburne pointed out that the basic defect of Magna Charta and statutes complementing it was that they were not binding on Parliament since "that which is done by one Parliament, as a Parliament, may be undone by the next Parliament: but an Agreement of the People begun and ended amongst the People can never come justly within the Parliament's cognizance to destroy." The proposed "Agreement of the People," Lilburne argued, could be changed only by the people and would bind Parliament as the supreme "law of the land." This same idea was picked up before the adoption of our Federal Constitution by Massachusetts and New Hampshire, which adopted their constitutions only after popular referendums. Our Federal Constitution is largely attributable to the same current of thinking.

NOTE

Witch-hunts, both literal and figurative, were not unknown in America. Migration to avoid persecution, such as that of Roger Williams, was not uncommon. In Virginia, Baptists went to jail for their preaching. In New England, Quakers suffered death for their faith. And in several of the colonies, test oaths were used to bar any but Christians from holding office.

During and after the Revolution, seven states took steps to protect the liberties of their citizens by written guarantee. As noted in the excerpt above, the influence of Lilburne's "Agreement of the People" can be seen in the constitutions of New Hampshire and Massachusetts. Virginia's Declaration of Rights owed more to the genius of George Mason, while Pennsylvania's provisions were largely copies from the Declaration of Independence. Delaware, Maryland, and North Carolina had bills of rights as well. Clearly, the founders of the republic were no more interested in a home-grown autocracy than they were in the imported variety. As Thomas Jefferson emphasized when Virginia framed its constitution of 1776, the establishment of a satisfactory political system was the "whole object" of the rebellion, "for should a bad government be instituted for us in the future, it had been as well to have accepted at first the bad one offered to us from beyond the water without the risk and expense of contest."

It may seem odd, then, that the Constitution of the United States drawn up in 1787 at Philadelphia contained no bill of rights. Of course, the framers were creating a strikingly new form of government—one national in its operation but (theoretically) limited in its objects. We may reasonably ask whether they appreciated, or could have appreciated, the enormous powers that their creation would come in time to wield.

We can only speculate. The records of the constitutional convention are fragmentary. We do know that on September 12, 1787, shortly before the close of proceedings, "It was moved and seconded to appoint a Committee to prepare a Bill of Rights." According to Mason of Virginia, the author of the Virginia Declaration and the chief proponent of a similar guarantee by the national government, a bill of rights "might be prepared in a few hours" and "would give great quiet to the people." The convention apparently thought such an effort too much trouble or simply unnecessary, however, and the motion went down to defeat without the favorable vote of a single state.

The stage was set for the great debate on the necessity of a bill of rights.

II.   THE GREAT DEBATE

A.   HAMILTON'S AND WILSON'S VIEWS*

In Federalist No 84, Alexander Hamilton wrote:

> It has been several times truly remarked, that Bills of Rights are, in their origin, stipulations between kings and their subjects, ... reservations of rights not surrendered to the prince.... It is evident, therefore, that, according to their primitive signification, they have no application to Constitutions professedly founded upon the power of the People, and executed by their immediate representatives and servants. Here, in strictness, the People surrender nothing; and as they retain everything, they have no need of particular reservations....
>
> . . .
>
> I go further, and affirm, that Bills of Rights, in the sense and to the extent in which they are contended for, are not only unnecessary in the proposed Constitution, but would even be dangerous. They would contain various exceptions to powers not granted; and on this very account, would afford a colorable

* Henry B. Dawson, ed., The Federalist (#84), Charles Scribner, New York, 1864, p. 597.

pretext to claim more than were granted. For why declare that things shall not be done which there is no power to do? Why, for instance, should it be said, that the liberty of the press shall not be restrained, when no power is given by which restrictions may be imposed? I will not contend that such a provision would confer a regulating power; but it is evident that it would furnish, to men disposed to usurp, a plausible pretence for claiming that power. They might urge with a semblance of reason, that the Constitution ought not to be charged with the absurdity of providing against the abuse of an authority, which was not given, and that the provision against restraining the liberty of the press afforded a clear implication, that a power to prescribe proper regulations concerning it was intended to be vested in the National Government. This may serve as a specimen of the numerous handles which would be given to the doctrine of constructive powers, by the indulgence of an injudicious zeal for Bills of Rights.

James Wilson, a delegate to the Constitutional Convention from Pennsylvania, expressed a similar view at his State's ratifying convention:**

> Whence comes this notion, that in the United States there is no security without a bill of rights? Have the citizens of South Carolina no security for their liberties? They have no bill of rights....
>
> The state of New Jersey has no bill of rights. The state of New York has no bill of rights. The states of Connecticut and Rhode Island have no bill of rights.
>
> [T]his enumeration, sir, will serve to show by experience, as well as principle, that, even in single governments, a bill of rights is not an essential or necessary measure. But in a government consisting of enumerated powers, such as is proposed for the United States, a bill of rights would not only be unnecessary, but, in my humble judgment, highly imprudent. In all societies, there are many powers and rights which cannot be particularly enumerated. A bill of rights annexed to a constitution is *an enumeration of the powers* reserved. If we attempt an enumeration, every thing that is not enumerated is presumed to be given. The consequence is, that an imperfect enumeration would throw all implied power into the scale of the government, and the rights of the people would be rendered incomplete. On the other hand, an imperfect enumeration of the powers of government reserves all implied power to the people; and by that means the constitution becomes incomplete. But of the two, it is much safer to run the risk on the side of the constitution; for an omission in the enumeration of the powers of government is neither so dangerous nor important as an omission in the enumeration of the rights of the people.

** Jonathan Elliot, ed., The Debates in the Several State Conventions on the Adoption of the Federal Constitution, J.B. Lippincott & Co., 2nd ed., 1863, vol. 2, pp. 436–437.

B. JEFFERSON'S VIEW

THOMAS JEFFERSON—Born on April 13, 1743, in Shadwell, Virginia, son of a surveyor, cartographer, and landowner. Democratic–Republican. Did not belong to a church, but wrote in 1816: "... I am a *real Christian,* that is to say, a disciple of the doctrines of Jesus." Attended William and Mary, 1760–1762. Studied law with George Wythe, 1762–1765. Member of Virginia House of Burgesses, 1769–1776. Drafted the Declaration of Independence, 1776. Also wrote a draft constitution for Virginia (which was not adopted) that limited slavery and guaranteed freedom of religion, freedom of press, and equal inheritance for males and females. Virginia governor, 1779–1781. Submitted in 1779 a bill for establishing religious freedom, which was enacted by the Virginia legislature in 1786. U.S. minister to France, 1785–1789. Urged James Madison and others in 1787 to include a bill of rights in the Constitution. Washington's secretary of state, 1790–1794; vice-president, 1796–1801. Wrote Kentucky Resolutions declaring the Alien and Sedition laws unconstitutional, 1798. U.S. president, 1801–1809; appointed three justices to the Supreme Court— William Johnson (1804), Henry Brockholst Livingston (1807), and Thomas Todd (1807). Died at Monticello on July 4, 1826. Although Jefferson's image in history is that of an apostle of liberty, historians have noted "a darker side" that included support for loyalty oaths and prosecutions of seditious libel. "His lapses, which were abundant," wrote Leonard W. Levy, "did not result from hypocrisy or meanness of spirit. His darker side derived, rather, in some instances from the fact that he was simply not as libertarian as later Americans liked to believe; in others, from the fact that circumstances seemed to him to require a course that sacrificed libertarian considerations for even larger ends." *Jefferson and Civil Liberties: The Darker Side,* Quadrangle/The New York Times Book Co., 1973, p. 20.

Writing from Paris on December 20, 1787, Thomas Jefferson told James Madison that one of the things he did not like about the Constitution was "the omission of a bill of rights providing clearly and without the aid of sophisms for freedom of religion, freedom of the press, protection against standing armies, restriction against monopolies, the eternal and unremitting force of the habeas corpus laws, and trials by jury in all matters of fact triable by the laws of the land and not by the law of Nations. To say, as Mr. Wilson does, that a bill of rights was not necessary because all is reserved in the case of the general government which is not given, while in the particular ones all is given which is not reserved, might do for the audience to whom it was addressed, but is surely a gratis dictum, opposed by strong inferences from the body of the instrument, as well as from the omission of the clause of our present confederation which had declared that in express terms.... Let me add that a bill of rights is what the people are entitled to against every government on earth, general or particular, and what no just government should refuse, or rest on inferences."*

On March 15, 1789, Jefferson again wrote Madison about the necessity for a bill of rights:

> ... The Declaration of rights is like all other human blessings alloyed with some inconveniences, and not accomplishing fully its object. But the good in this instance vastly overweighs the evil. I cannot refrain from making short answers to the objections which your letter states to have been raised. 1. That the rights in question are reserved by the manner in which the federal powers are granted. Answer. A constitutive act may certainly be so formed as to need no declaration of rights. The act itself has the force of a declaration as far as it goes; and if it goes to all material points nothing more is wanting. In the draught of a constitution which I had once a thought of proposing in Virginia, & printed afterwards, I endeavored to reach all the great objects of public liberty, and did not mean to add a declaration of rights. Probably the object was imperfectly executed; but the deficiencies would have been supplied by others, in the course of discussion. But in a constitutive act which leaves some precious articles unnoticed, and raises implications against others, a declaration of rights becomes necessary by way of supplement. This is the case of our new federal constitution. This instrument forms us into one state as to certain objects, and gives us a legislative & executive body for these objects. It should therefore guard us against their abuses of power within the field submitted to them. 2. A positive declaration of some essential rights could not be obtained in the requisite latitude. Answer. Half a loaf is better than no bread. If we cannot secure all our rights, let us secure what we can. 3. The limited powers of the federal government & jealousy of the subordinate governments afford a security which exists in no other instance. Answer. The first member of this seems resolvable into the first objection before stated. The jealousy of the subordinate governments is a precious reliance. But observe that those governments are only agents. They must have principles furnished them whereon to found their opposition. The declaration of rights will be the text whereby they will try all the acts of the federal government. In this view it is necessary to the federal government also; as by the same text they may try the opposition of the subordinate governments. 4. Experience proves the inefficacy of a bill of rights. True. But tho it is not absolutely efficacious under all circumstances, it is of great potency always, and rarely inefficacious. A brace the more will often keep up the building which would have fallen with that brace the less. There is a remarkable difference between the characters of the Inconveniences which attend a Declaration of rights, & those which attend the want of it. The inconveniences of the Declaration are that it may cramp government in its useful exertions. But the evil of this is short-lived, trivial & reparable. The inconven-

---

* James Madison Papers, Library of Congress, Series 1, Microfilm Reel 3.

iences of the want of a Declaration are permanent, afflicting & irreparable. They are in constant progression from bad to worse.*

Which argument in this great debate is the most persuasive? Why?

III. RATIFICATION AT A PRICE**

Delaware, the first state to consider the Constitution, discussed it four days and ratified unanimously. In Pennsylvania, ... the convention voted two to one to join the union. The New Jersey convention was in session only seven days and gave unanimous endorsement of an un-amended Constitution. The Georgia delegates met on Christmas Day, 1787, and approved unanimously on the second day of the new year. In Connecticut debate lasted less than seven days. On being assured by Lieutenant–Governor Oliver Wolcott that the Constitution was so well guarded that "it seems impossible that the rights either of the States or of the people should be destroyed," the delegates voted 128 to 40 in favor of ratification.

The Constitution first encountered powerful opposition in Massa-chusetts. For a while it seemed doubtful that enough votes in favor could be mustered.

. . .

John Hancock, initially inclined to be negative, finally supplied the formula that won acquiescence: "I give my assent to the Constitution, in full confidence that the amendments proposed will soon become a part of the system." Recommendatory, not "conditional amendments" was the price exacted. ... Meanwhile, Maryland and South Carolina ratified with comfortable margins. New Hampshire became the ninth to ratify by vote of 57 to 47.

The [Massachusetts] procedure had worked so well that Madison now advocated its use wherever the vote promised to be close ...

The Massachusetts formula caught on. Thereafter the issue was no longer "what the constitution is, but what degree of probability there is that the amendments will hereafter be incorporated...." "My idea is," Virginia delegate Francis Corbin observed, "that we should go hand in hand with Massachusetts; adopt it first, and then propose amend-ments...." Jefferson, who had earlier urged that ratification be delayed until a bill of rights could be added, now surrendered. "[T]he plan of Massachusetts is far preferable," he agreed, "and will I hope be followed by those who are yet to decide." "It will be more difficult, if we lose this instrument, to recover what is good in it, than to correct what is bad after we shall have adopted it."

Virginia posed the most crucial hurdle. Even if enough states ratified to put the Constitution into effect, no one entertained the slightest hope for its success without New York and Virginia, where the

---

* Ibid.

** Alpheus T. Mason, The States Rights Debate, 2d ed., Oxford University Press, 1972, pp. 91–93. Reprinted with permission.

Bill of Rights issue was most hotly and narrowly contested. In Virginia, the Constitution, at first, had evoked great enthusiasm. Then the tide took "a sudden and strong turn in the opposite direction." Nowhere was the opposition so well organized or so well led. Patrick Henry, George Mason, and Richard Henry Lee constituted a formidable trio. It was said that Patrick Henry's purpose was to amend the Constitution and "leave the fate of the measures to depend on all the other States conforming to the will of Virginia," the theory being that "other States cannot do without us...."

George Wythe of Virginia took a decisive step on June 24, 1788, when he admitted the Constitution's imperfections, and "the propriety of some amendments." Wythe then proposed "that whatsoever amendments might be deemed necessary, should be recommended to consideration of the congress which should first assemble under the constitution...." Notwithstanding misgivings as to their efficacy, Madison finally acquiesced. Two days earlier—on June 22—he had written Rufus King that rather than incur the dangers implicit in a temporary adjournment, which he thought the Henry-led Antifederalist forces were seeking, he would support a Bill of Rights. "It has been judged prudent," he wrote,

> ... to maintain so exemplary a fairness on our part, (and even in some points to give way to unreasonable pretensions) as will withhold every pretext for so rash a step. Madison was adamant in his opposition to *prior* amendments or to *any* amendments which would materially alter the structure of the new government.

In the end, the issue which clinched victory in Virginia did not concern "recommendatory" versus "conditional" amendments. It was the one Governor Randolph stated in his final dramatic appeal:

> ... *I went to the federal Convention,* with the strongest affection for the union; ... I acted there, in full conformity with this affection: ... *I refused to subscribe, because I had as I still have objections to the Constitution,* and wished a free inquiry into its merits; and ... the accession of eight states reduced our *deliberations* to the single question of *union or no union.*

The decision for union stood 89 to 79.

In New York, the Antifederalists, led by Governor Clinton, were strong. Success was by no means assured. During the last days of the convention word came that New Hampshire and Virginia had ratified. It was now certain that the Constitution would be given a trial.

While news of Virginia gladdened the hearts of the Federalists, it served only to harden Antifederalist opposition. Enemies of the new Constitution now proposed conditional ratification—ratification with the right of withdrawal if amendments were not adopted. Alarmed by this move, Hamilton insisted on *recommendatory* amendments only. The Federalists would only "concur in rational recommendations." To stall the Antifederalist drive for prior amendments, Federalists moved for temporary adjournment. Being outvoted, 40–22, they had no recourse but to debate the issue. The situation looked grim. Hamilton, having just received a propitious reply from Madison, repulsed the opposition by apt quotation:

> My opinion is, that a reservation of a right to withdraw, if amendments be not decided on under the form of the constitution within a certain time, is a *conditional* ratification; that it does not make New York a member of the new union, and, consequently, that she could not be received on that plan. The constitution requires an adoption *in toto* and *forever*. It has been so adopted by the other states. An adoption for a limited time would be as defective as an adoption of some of the articles only. In short, any *condition* whatever must vitiate the ratification.

In New York, as in Virginia, the vote, though close (30 to 27), was for union. Eleven states had now ratified; the new system of government would be put in operation.

IV. TRIUMPH OF THE BILL OF RIGHTS

The clamor for a bill of rights became irresistible. Madison, faced in his campaign for a seat in the First Congress with the accusation of having abandoned the cause of religious freedom, announced his conversion. "Under this change of circumstances [ratification], it is my sincere opinion that the Constitution ought to be revised, and that the First Congress meeting under it ought to prepare and recommend to the States ... the most satisfactory provision for all essential rights." In agreeing to a bill of rights to protect individual liberties, however, Madison had no intention of acquiescing in changes in the Constitution which might sap the energy of the new government. Therefore, upon assuming his new office and learning that others were eager to take the initiative in proposing amendments damaging to national authority, he served notice that on June 8, 1789, he would place his own proposals before the House of Representatives.

THE BIRTH OF THE BILL OF RIGHTS*

Madison believed the amendment issue could wait no longer.... [H]e asked the House to resolve itself into a Committee of the Whole to consider amendments "as contemplated in the fifth article of the Constitution." Instead of rushing to support his proposals, Madison's fellow congressmen seemed to be in no hurry to take up the topic which had so recently stirred the Republic ... Let us wait until the government is organized, [they] said, and not risk disrupting the harmony which now prevailed in the House. Madison answered that ... he considered further delay impolitic. He added that if the subject of amendments were postponed ... "it may occasion suspicions, which, though not well founded, may tend to inflame or prejudice the public mind against our decisions." ...

* Robert A. Rutland, The Birth of the Bill of Rights, 1776–1791, University of North Carolina Press and the Institute of Early American History and Culture, 1955, pp. 200–215. Reprinted with permission.

Roger Sherman, who had opposed a bill of rights in the Federal Convention, followed Madison. His state, Connecticut, wanted no amendments. What the people everywhere wanted was a stable government. Sherman said he was ready to see amendments introduced as a matter of form, but not as an interruption of the really important business at hand....

Madison did not consider his duty so lightly discharged, however.... Many who had opposed the Constitution were ready to support the new government. Their only price was an explicit declaration of the great rights of mankind.... As long as a great number of citizens thought these securities necessary it would be an injustice to ignore their desires. These safeguards could be added to the Constitution without endangering the worthwhile features of the new government.

Madison then read to the House his plan of amendment. His proposals covered all of the ten articles which eventually formed the federal Bill of Rights. Even his phraseology was preserved in the final draft in numerous cases.... In drafting the proposals Madison had leaned heavily on the Virginia Declaration of Rights, but he had also incorporated additional features adopted by the ratifying conventions. He followed a reading of the amendments with a lengthy speech.... After canvassing the whole field of objections to a bill of rights, he declared that a specific declaration of rights would be worth while because it offered "tranquillity of the public mind, and the stability of the Government." Madison alluded to Jefferson's striking observation that the "independent tribunals of justice will consider themselves in a peculiar manner the guardians of those rights ... [and] resist every encroachment upon rights expressly stipulated ... by the declaration of rights."

JAMES MADISON—Born on March 16, 1751, in Port Conway, Virginia, son of a leading Virginia landowner and squire. Democratic–Republican. Unitarian. Graduated from the College of New Jersey (Princeton University) in 1771, having completed a four-year course in two years. Overwork precipitated epileptoid hysteria and premonitions of early death. While recovering at the family estate— Montpelier—he studied public law, government, and politics, and advocated independence of England. Elected in 1776 to the Virginia Revolutionary Convention, where he supported adoption of a bill of rights. Served on the governor's council and went to the Continental Congress in 1780. Returning to the Virginia legislature in 1784, he helped defeat Patrick Henry's bill to provide aid to Christian teachers, and supported disestablishing the Anglican church. Member of the Constitutional Convention in Philadelphia in 1787, at which he took notes of the debates. Wrote, with Alexander Hamilton and John Jay, *The Federalist,* 1787–1788. Elected in 1789 to the U.S. House of Representatives, where he sponsored the Bill of Rights, emphasizing in debate freedom of religion, speech, and press. Jefferson's secretary of state, 1801–1809; U.S. president, 1809–1817. Appointed two justices to the Supreme Court— Gabriel Duvall (1811) and Joseph Storey (1811). Died at Montpelier on June 28, 1836.

Madison concluded that these changes could not "endanger the beauty of the Government in any one important feature, even in the eyes of its most sanguine admirers." The alterations would go far toward making "the constitution better in the opinion of those who are opposed to it, without weakening its frame or abridging its usefulness, in the judgment of those who are attached to it, [and] we act the part of wise and liberal men who make such alterations as shall produce that effect."

. . .

Reactions to Madison's amendments were mixed. . . . Fisher Ames of Massachusetts called them "the fruit of much labor and research." Ames reported that Madison had "hunted up all grievances and complaints of newspapers, all the articles of conventions, and the small talk of their debates," in compiling his propositions. He was inclined to think that Madison had tried to cover too much ground but added that "it may do some good towards quieting men, who attend to sounds only, and may get the mover some popularity, which he wishes." William Grayson sent word of Madison's proposals to [Patrick] Henry, objecting to the great overemphasis on personal liberty and slight attention for the judiciary, direct taxation, and other issues. . . .

. . .

Madison's willingness to become the legislative champion of amendments indicated that he, though young in years, was an experienced hand at practical politics. He candidly confessed . . . that his proposals were limited to issues which would excite the least exertions of the opposition. "Nothing of a controvertible nature ought to be hazarded by those who are sincere in wishing for the approbation of ⅔ of each House, and ¾ of the State Legislatures," he explained. Among the most zealous Federalists there was an undercurrent of opinion decidedly unfavorable to amendments, principally on the ground that hastily enacted alterations would demolish the effectiveness of the Constitution. Madison was caught between this faction and his own campaign pledge, which, if fulfilled, would allay not only the doubts of many of his constituents, but a large portion of citizens throughout the Republic. To a man of Madison's talents and temperament the situation offered an ideal opportunity. He played off Scylla against Charybdis instead of trying to go between them. He had to apologize to his home constituents because more could not be gained. To the anti-amendment group in the House he was forced to defend the lengths he had gone in safeguarding the personal rights of citizens. To his neighbors and his colleagues Madison counseled the need for compromise. His task called for political tight-rope walking, and he performed the feat with the skill of a veteran.

On July 21, [1789] six weeks after his first discussion of amendments, Madison reintroduced the subject to the House . . .

The amendment question was debated for over a week in the Committee of the Whole. Madison still favored alterations in the main text of the Constitution rather than a separate list of amendments. Other congressmen agreed with Roger Sherman, who moved for separate amendments and declared that Madison's proposal placed contradictory articles side by side....

"[O]n the question, Mr. SHERMAN'S motion was carried by two-thirds of the House: in consequence it was agreed to."

The contents of the Madison proposals were thoroughly examined in the House when it sat as a Committee of the Whole. A simple statement about the nature of government, offered as an additional clause to the preamble, threatened to involve the House in a wearisome debate over abstractions. Proposals for apportioning representation and fixing the pay of legislators were subjects of sharp controversy. On the other hand, the guarantees of individual rights in matters of speech, religion, petitions, and a free press provoked less discussion although they formed the nucleus of the amendments....

The ... report survived the debate and on August 24 it was forwarded to the Senate as seventeen proposed amendments to the Constitution.

. . .

Since the Senate debates were at this time not open to the public, the twenty-two members were able to discuss the amendments more freely than the members of the House of Representatives. With a majority of the senators convinced that some amendments must go forth from Congress, the group set about the task of editing the House version. They slashed out wordiness with a free hand....

The Senate rejected that amendment which Madison said he prized above all the others, the one that prohibited the states from infringing on personal rights....

After the Senate had completed its revision of the seventeen House proposals twelve amendments remained. These revised articles of amendment then were sent back to the House of Representatives for concurrence.

. . .

When the House took up the proposed changes in the amendments on September 19, it was obvious that only a conference could resolve the differences created by the Senate revision.... The Conference committee [of which Madison was a member] rapidly smoothed over the rough spots objected to by their colleagues.... A preamble was drafted to explain that the amendments were being submitted to the states in answer to the expressed desire of certain ratifying conventions "that further declaratory and restrictive clauses should be added." By September 25, [1789] both houses had approved the twelve amendments which emerged from the joint conference. These were forwarded to the President for transmission to the states.

NOTE

A majority of states received with enthusiasm what we know today as the first ten amendments. Nine legislatures gave their approval during the next year. Only one more state had to approve to achieve the required three-fourths majority. Virginia's Senate, dominated by hard-core opponents of a strong federal government, stalled for nearly two years in hopes of deleting the most popular amendments and adding one to restrict the power of Congress to levy direct taxes. Finally, chastened by popular opinion and election returns, the Senate gave way and brought the amendments originally submitted into force on December 15, 1791.

Two other proposed amendments, which apparently had little support, were not ratified in 1789. One would have limited the size of Congressional districts to 50,000 persons—a measure that would now produce a house with 50,000 members. The other proposed amendment was ratified by a thirty-eighth state in 1992. Despite the passage of more than 200 years since the Amendment's submission for ratification, on May 21, 1992, Congress by joint resolution declared it to be effective as the 27th amendment to the Constitution! The amendment forbids a Congressional pay raise or cut to take effect until after the next election.

V. APPLICABILITY OF THE BILL OF RIGHTS TO THE STATES

As the previous material shows, the original Bill of Rights operated only as a restriction upon the power of the national government. The Supreme Court confirmed that view in an opinion by Chief Justice Marshall in Barron v. Baltimore, 7 Pet. 243 (1833). The Bill of Rights of the United States Constitution became an important restriction on the powers of state governments only after the adoption of the Fourteenth Amendment in 1868. The first case to apply a guarantee of the Bill of Rights to the states was *Chicago, Burlington, & Quincy R.R. v. Chicago,* 166 U.S. 226 (1897), which held that the takings clause of the Fifth Amendment restricted state action through the Due Process Clause of the Fourteenth Amendment. Twenty-eight years later the Supreme Court acknowledged by way of dictum in Gitlow v. New York (1925), that the guarantees of freedom of speech and press also applied to the states through the Fourteenth Amendment.

A. HUGHES ON THE EARLY APPLICATION OF BILL OF RIGHTS GUARANTEES

Soon after Charles Evans Hughes retired from the Supreme Court in 1941, he wrote the following in a memorandum:*

> [I]n *Gitlow* ... the Court had the question whether the New York statute against "criminal anarchy" violated the due process clause of the Fourteenth Amendment. For the purposes

---

* David J. Danelski and Joseph S. Tulchin, eds., The Autobiographical Notes of Charles Evans Hughes, Harvard University Press, 1973, pp. 340–342. Reprinted with permission.

of the decision, the Court assumed ... that the Fourteenth Amendment did protect freedom of speech and of the press. . . . The Court said: "For present purposes we may and do assume that freedom of speech and of the press—which are protected by the First Amendment from abridgement by Congress—are among the fundamental personal rights and 'liberties' protected by the due process clause of the Fourteenth Amendment from impairment by the States. We do not regard the incidental statement in Prudential Ins. Co. v. Cheek, 259 U.S. 530, 543, that the Fourteenth Amendment imposes no restrictions on the States concerning freedom of speech, as determinative of this question."

The New York statute was sustained. Justice Holmes wrote a dissenting opinion, in which Justice Brandeis concurred, holding that the judgment should be reversed. He said: "The general principle of free speech, it seems to me, must be taken to be included in the Fourteenth Amendment, in view of the scope that has been given to the word 'liberty' as there used, although perhaps it may be accepted with a somewhat larger latitude of interpretation than is allowed to Congress by the sweeping language that governs or ought to govern the laws of the United States."

What was assumed by the majority in the *Gitlow* case was evidently regarded as the law in Whitney v. California, 274 U.S. 357 (1927), and the validity of the "Criminal Syndicalism Act" of California was sustained over the contention that it violated the due process clause of the Fourteenth Amendment (p. 371). Justice Brandeis, concurring, said: "Despite arguments to the contrary which had seemed to me persuasive, it is settled that the due process clause of the Fourteenth Amendment applies to matters of substantive law as well as to matters of procedure. Thus all fundamental rights comprised within the term 'liberty' are protected by the Federal Constitution from invasion by the States. The right of free speech, the right to teach and the right of assembly are, of course, fundamental rights" (p. 373). Justice Holmes concurred in Justice Brandeis' opinion. Then in the next case, Fiske v. Kansas, 274 U.S. 380 (1927), the Court unanimously reversed the conviction of the plaintiff in error under the "Criminal Syndicalism Act" of Kansas, holding that the Act as applied in that instance was "repugnant to the due process clause of the Fourteenth Amendment."

It fell to my lot as Chief Justice, in 1930, to write the opinions for the Court in Stromberg v. California, 283 U.S. 359 (1931), and in Near v. Minnesota, 283 U.S. 697 (1931), holding that freedom of speech and of the press was embraced in the concept of liberty protected against state action by the Fourteenth Amendment.

Near v. Minnesota dealt with freedom of the press as curtailed by a Minnesota statute directed at "alleged defamatory newspapers." The Court held that the statute was not aimed at the redress of individual or private wrongs but at the continued publication by newspapers and periodicals of charges against public officers of corruption, malfeasance in office or serious neglect of duty, and that the statute operated not only to suppress the offending newspaper or periodical but to put the publisher under a form of censorship. (See Chafee Free Speech in the United States, 1941, pp. 375–381.)

The final decision as to the application of the Fourteenth Amendment has had two important general results, apart from their immediate application. As Justice Brandeis pointed out in his concurring opinion in Whitney v. California, it is recognized as settled that the due process clause of the Fourteenth Amendment applies to matters of substantive law as well as to matters of procedure. The contention that it was limited to matters of procedure was widely held by those who endeavored to restrict the application of the due process clause when it was considered in relation to property rights. The conclusion that the clause covered matters of substantive law has always seemed to me to be in accord with the original intention when the Fifth Amendment was adopted. As I have pointed out in my Columbia lectures on the Supreme Court (p. 187), Madison, who probably drafted the Fifth Amendment, said that under it the judicial tribunals would be "an impenetrable bulwark against every assumption of power in the Legislative or Executive."

Another result has been that the right to "liberty," in relation to freedom of speech and of the press, has received a broader interpretation under the Fourteenth Amendment than has been given to the right of property, although the due process clause makes no such distinction. The suggestion of Justice Holmes in the *Gitlow* case that the States "might be allowed a somewhat larger latitude of interpretation" than is allowed to Congress by the sweeping language of the First Amendment, has not been followed. On the contrary, the scope of freedom of speech and of the press under the Fourteenth Amendment has been regarded as quite as broad as that which obtains under the First Amendment.

B. CARDOZO'S RATIONALE FOR SELECTIVE APPLICATION OF THE BILL OF RIGHTS

In Palko v. Connecticut, 302 U.S. 319 (1937), the Supreme Court held that the Fifth Amendment guarantee against double jeopardy did not apply to the states through the Fourteenth Amendment for the same reason that the Sixth Amendment guarantee of jury trial did not apply and that the Fifth Amendment guarantee of indictment by grand jury did not apply. Writing for the Court, Justice Cardozo gave this rationale for selective application of the Bill of Rights:

... The right to trial by jury and the immunity from prosecution except as the result of an indictment may have value and importance. Even so, they are not of the very essence of a scheme of ordered liberty. To abolish them is not to violate a "principle of justice so rooted in the traditions and conscience of our people as to be ranked as fundamental." ... Few would be so narrow or provincial as to maintain that a fair and enlightened system of justice would be impossible without them. What is true of jury trials and indictments is true also, as the cases show, of the immunity from compulsory self-incrimination.... This too might be lost, and justice still be done. Indeed, today as in the past there are students of our penal system who look upon the immunity as a mischief rather than a benefit, and who would limit its scope, or destroy it altogether. No doubt there would remain the need to give protection against torture, physical or mental.... Justice, however, would not perish if the accused were subject to a duty to respond to orderly inquiry. The exclusion of these immunities and privileges from the privileges and immunities protected against the action of the states has not been arbitrary or casual. It has been dictated by a study and appreciation of the meaning, the essential implications, of liberty itself.

We reach a different plane of social and moral values when we pass to the privileges and immunities that have been taken over from the earlier articles of the federal bill of rights and brought within the Fourteenth Amendment by a process of absorption. These in their origin were effective against the federal government alone. If the Fourteenth Amendment has absorbed them, the process of absorption has had its source in the belief that neither liberty nor justice would exist if they were sacrificed.

C. SELECTIVE INCORPORATION PLUS

Three opinions in Adamson v. California, 332 U.S. 46 (1947), contributed to the present application of the Bill of Rights to the states. Adamson, a defendant in a murder case, elected not to testify in his behalf, and both the prosecutor and judge in his case called this fact to the attention of the jury, which California law permitted. In federal trials such comments violated the Fifth Amendment's privilege against self-incrimination. After being convicted, Adamson appealed to the Supreme Court, which, by a five-to-four vote, rejected his claim that the Fifth Amendment privilege not to incriminate himself applied to California through the Fourteenth Amendment.

Justice Black dissented, saying:

[I]n my judgment, ... history conclusively demonstrates that the language of the first section of the Fourteenth Amendment, taken as a whole, was by those responsible for its submission to the people, and by those who opposed its submission, is sufficiently explicit to guarantee thereafter that no state could deprive its citizens of the privileges and protections of the Bill of Rights.

Black's position, which is know as "total incorporation," contains two premises: (1) the Fourteenth Amendment applies the entire Bill of Rights to the states; (2) the guarantees in the Bill of Rights apply identically to both the state and federal governments. Justices Douglas, Murphy, and Rutledge agreed with Black's position in *Adamson*.

Justice Frankfurter, who completely disagreed with Black's position, wrote in a concurring opinion:

> [T]he issue is not whether an infraction of one specific provision of the first eight amendments is disclosed in the record. The relevant question is whether the criminal proceedings which resulted in conviction deprived the accused of due process of law to which the United States Constitution entitled him. Judicial review of that guaranty of the Fourteenth Amendment inescapably imposes upon this Court an exercise of judgment upon the whole course of the proceeding in order to ascertain whether they offend those canons of decency and fair play which express the notions of justice of English-speaking peoples even toward those charged with the most heinous offenses. These standards of justice are not authoritatively formulated anywhere as though they were prescriptions in a pharmacopoeia. But neither does the application of the Due Process Clause imply that judges are wholly at large. The judicial judgment in applying the Due Process clause must move within the limits of accepted notions of justice and is not to be based upon the idiosyncracies of merely personal judgment.

Thus Frankfurter's position was that the Due Process Clause may or may not protect specific rights in the Bill of Rights, and further, the Due Process Clause may protect rights that are not in the Bill of Rights.*

Though it would seem impossible to agree with both Justices Black and Frankfurter on the application of the Bill of Rights to the states, Justice Murphy to some extent did so. In his *Adamson* dissenting opinion, he wrote:

> I agree that the specific guarantees of the Bill of Rights should be carried over intact into the first section of the Fourteenth Amendment. But I am not prepared to say that the latter is entirely and necessarily limited by the Bill of Rights. Occasions may arise where a proceeding falls so short of conforming to fundamental standards of procedure as to warrant constitutional condemnation in terms of a lack of due process despite the absence of a specific provision in the Bill of Rights.

Justice Rutledge joined Murphy's opinion. Murphy's position is known as "total incorporation plus."

The Supreme Court never completely adopted the approaches of Justices Black, Frankfurter, or Murphy. But from 1947 to 1969, the Court, by a process of "selective incorporation," incorporated almost all

---

* The Frankfurter passage quoted above refers to procedural rights, but he viewed substantive rights, for example, freedom of association, the same way. See page 539 below.

of the important guarantees of the Bill of Rights through the Due Process Clause of the Fourteenth Amendment.

1947: Separation of Church and State

1948: Public trial

1961: No unreasonable searches and seizures

1963: Counsel in criminal cases

1964: No self-incrimination

1966: Trial by an impartial jury

1967: Speedy trial

1969: No double jeopardy

The Supreme Court, adopting the "plus" part of Murphy's position, also selectively incorporated unenumerated rights. Those unenumerated rights have been both procedural (e.g., the right to proof beyond a reasonable doubt in a criminal trial)* and substantive (e.g., the right to privacy).**

---

* *In re Winship*, 397 U.S. 358 (1970).

** *Roe v. Wade*, 410 U.S. 113 (1973).

Chapter II

THE JUDICIARY

Two related premises underlie the Bill of Rights—Locke's premise that law is a condition for liberty and Jefferson's and Madison's premise that the Bill of Rights gives the judiciary legal check on the legislative and executive branches of government. On March 15, 1789, Jefferson wrote Madison saying that an argument "of great weight" to him for the adoption of the Bill of Rights was "the legal check which it puts into the hands of the judiciary." "This is a body," Jefferson added, "which if rendered independent and kept strictly to their own department, merits great confidence for their learning and integrity. In fact what degree of confidence would be too much for a body composed of such men as Wythe, Blair and Pendleton?"* Later the same year, Madison said in the debate on the Bill of Rights in the House of Representatives: "If [individual rights] are incorporated into the Constitution, independent tribunals of justices will consider themselves in a peculiar manner the guardians of these rights; they will be an impenetrable bulwark against every assumption of power in the Legislature or Executive; they will be naturally led to resist every encroachment upon rights expressly stipulated in the Constitution by the declaration of rights."** Madison's statement indicates that he expected judges to exercise judicial review to protect individual rights. Alexander Hamilton also took that position in *Federalist* No. 78. So did Chief Justice John Marshall in Marbury v. Madison, 1 Cranch 137 (1803), which established judicial review.

Despite the Bill of Rights' premises, the Supreme Court seldom exercised judicial review to protect individual rights during its first 140 years. It was not until the 1930s that the Court began to protect individual rights actively, and it was not until 1938 that it laid a theoretical foundation for granting individual rights greater judicial protection than economic rights. Curiously, that theory was set forth in a footnote.

* Madison Papers, Library of Congress, Series 1, Microfilm Reel 3. Jefferson had studied law with George Wythe, who was a member of the Continental Congress and a signer of the Declaration of Independence. John Blair was a member of Virginia's first Supreme Court of Appeals and later U.S. Supreme Court associate justice appointed by George Washington. Edmund Pendleton was the presiding judge of Virginia's first Supreme Court of Appeals. Pendleton, Wythe, and Jefferson had worked together to revise the laws of Virginia in 1779.

** Quoted in Leonard W. Levy, Judicial Review and the Supreme Court, Harper & Row, 1967, p. 5.

FOOTNOTE FOUR IN UNITED STATES
v. CAROLENE PRODUCTS CO.

The issue in United States v. Carolene Products Co., 304 U.S. 144 (1938), was whether a congressional statute prohibiting the shipment in interstate commerce of "filled" milk (i.e., skimmed milk compounded with fat or oil) violated the commerce clause or the due process clause of the Fifth Amendment. A lower federal court had held the statute unconstitutional. The Supreme Court reversed the lower court by a vote of six to one. In the Court's opinion, Justice Stone wrote that Congress' characterization of "filled" milk as injurious to health and a fraud on the public was a legislative finding that supported and justified the exertion of legislative power, "aiding informed judicial review ... by revealing the rationale of the legislation. Even in the absence of such aids the existence of facts supporting the legislative judgment is to be presumed, for regulatory legislation affecting ordinary commercial transactions is not to be pronounced unconstitutional unless in the light of the facts made known or generally assumed it is of such a character as to preclude the assumption that it rests upon some rational basis within the knowledge and experience of the legislators." At that point in his opinion, Justice Stone appended his famous Footnote Four:*

> There may be narrower scope for operation of the presumption of constitutionality when legislation appears on its face to be within a specific prohibition of the Constitution, such as those of the first ten amendments, which are deemed equally specific when held to be embraced within the Fourteenth. See Stromberg v. California, 283 U.S. 359, 369–370 [1931]; Lovell v. Griffin, 303 U.S. 444, 452 [1938].

> It is unnecessary to consider now whether legislation which restricts those political processes which can ordinarily be expected to bring about repeal of undesirable legislation, is to be subjected to more exacting judicial scrutiny under the general prohibitions of the Fourteenth Amendment than are most other types of legislation. On restrictions upon the right to vote, see Nixon v. Herndon, 273 U.S. 536 [1927]; Nixon v. Condon, 286 U.S. 73 [1932]; on restraints upon the dissemination of information, see Near v. Minnesota ex rel. Olson, 283 U.S. 697, 712–714, 718–720, 722 [1931]; Grosjean v. American Press Co., 297 U.S. 233 [1936]; Lovell v. Griffin, supra; on interferences with political organizations, see Stromberg v. California, supra, 369; Fiske v. Kansas, 274 U.S. 380 [1927]; Whitney v. California, 274 U.S. 357, 373–378 [1927]; Herndon v. Lowry, 301 U.S. 242 [1937]; and see Holmes, J., in Gitlow v. New York, 268 U.S. 652 [1925]; as to prohibition of peaceable assembly, see DeJonge v. Oregon, 299 U.S. 353, 365 [1937].

> Nor need we enquire whether similar considerations enter into the review of statutes directed at particular religions,

---

* 304 U.S. at 152–153. Justice Stone drafted the first paragraph at Chief Justice Hughes' suggestion. Hughes to Stone, April 18, 1938; Stone to Hughes, April 19, 1938; Harlan Fiske Stone Papers, Library of Congress, Box 63. Louis Lusky, Justice Stone's law clerk, drafted the other two paragraphs.

Pierce v. Society of Sisters, 268 U.S. 510 [1925], or national, Meyer v. Nebraska, 262 U.S. 390 [1923]; Bartels v. Iowa, 262 U.S. 404 [1923]; Farrington v. Tokushige, 273 U.S. 284 [1927], or racial minorities, Nixon v. Herndon, supra; Nixon v. Condon, supra: whether prejudice against discrete and insular minorities may be a special condition, which tends seriously to curtail the operation of those political processes ordinarily to be relied upon to protect minorities, and which may call for a correspondingly more searching judicial inquiry. Compare McCulloch v. Maryland, 4 Wheat. 316, 428 [1819]; South Carolina v. Barnwell Bros., 303 U.S. 177, 184, n. 2 [1938] and cases cited.

NOTES

1. The three paragraphs in Footnote Four, wrote Alpheus T. Mason, contain "a corresponding number of ideas. The first suggests that when legislation, on its face, contravenes the specific constitutional negatives set out in the Bill of Rights, the usual presumption of constitutionality may be curtailed or even waived. The second paragraph indicates that the judiciary has a special responsibility as defender of those liberties prerequisite to the purity of political processes. The Court thus becomes the ultimate guardian against abuses that would poison the primary check on government—the ballot box. It must protect those liberties on which the democratic effectiveness of political action depends. The third paragraph suggests a special role for the Court as protector of minorities and of unpopular groups peculiarly helpless at the polls in the face of discriminatory or repressive assault."*

2. Footnote Four suggests a double standard for judicial review—a strict standard in cases involving basic democratic rights and a looser standard in other cases. It also suggests the idea of "preferred freedoms." Both ideas surfaced a year later in Schneider v. New Jersey, 308 U.S. 147, 161 (1939), in which Justice Roberts wrote: "In every case ... where legislative abridgment of [fundamental personal rights and liberties] is asserted, the courts should be astute to examine the effect of the challenged legislation. Mere legislative preferences or beliefs respecting matters of public convenience may well support regulation directed at other personal activities, but be insufficient to justify such as diminishes the exercise of rights so vital to the maintenance of democratic institutions. And so, as cases arise, the delicate and difficult task falls upon the courts to weigh the circumstances and to appraise the substantiality of the reasons advanced in support of the regulation of the free enjoyment of the rights."

3. Footnote Four has been used often in discussions in support of theories of judicial review. Louis Lusky, who, as Stone's law clerk, participated in drafting the Footnote, wrote in 1975 that it contained the germs of two theories that justify the Court's role in protecting individual liberties. One is the implied power theory, which stems from paragraphs two and three of the Footnote, and is based on the Court's unique fitness to reach definable goals, which are essential in keeping

---

* Alpheus Thomas Mason, Harlan Fiske Stone: Pillar of the Law, Viking, 1955, pp. 514–515. Reprinted with permission.

the democratic process and assuring fairness, particularly to insular minorities. It is a rational theory, says Lusky, because "it calls for measurement of the Court's performance against the objective standards." The other theory stems from the first sentence of the Footnote. This theory is the preferred position theory, and it "affirms that certain rights are in some sense more important than others—so important that the Court should protect them against impairment by any governmental organ—and that the Court's power to select them is limited only by its ability to manipulate words contained in the Constitution. It dispenses with the need for justification in terms of explained necessity, and assumes that any meaning the Court chooses to ascribe to the sacred text will be accepted as authentic revelation."* Obviously, Lusky supports only the first theory. Similarly, John Hart Ely has drawn on Footnote Four in formulating his theory of judicial review. He views the first paragraph as "pure interpretivism," which has its place but is not as interesting as the second and third paragraphs, which seek to protect popular control and egalitarianism. These themes, he writes, "are concerned with participation: they ask us to focus not on whether this substantive value is unusually important or fundamental, but rather on whether the opportunity to participate either in the political processes by which values are appropriately identified and accommodated, or in the accommodation those processes have reached, has been unduly restricted."**

THE FIRST FLAG–SALUTE CASE—1940

In November, 1935, the Board of Education of Minersville, Pennsylvania, passed a resolution requiring teachers and pupils to salute the American flag while reciting the pledge of allegiance. Lillian Gobitis, aged twelve, and her brother William, aged ten—both Jehovah's Witnesses—refused to participate in the flag ceremony on religious grounds, and for that reason they were expelled from school. Prior to his expulsion, William, who was known as Billy, wrote the following statement to the members of the school board, explaining why he would not salute the flag:

* Louis Lusky, By What Right, Michie Co., 1975, pp. 111–112.

** John Hart Ely, Democracy and Distrust, Harvard University Press, 1980, p. 77.

Dear Sirs

I do not salute the flag because I have promised to do the will of God. That means that I must not worship anything out of harmony with God's law. In the twentieth chapter of Exodus it is stated, "Thou shalt not make unto thee any graven image, nor bow down to them nor serve them for I the Lord thy God am a jealous God visiting the iniquity of the fathers upon the children unto the third and fourth generation of them that hate me. I am a true follower of Christ. I do not salute the flag because I do not love my country but I love my country and I love God more and I must obey His commandments.

Your Pupil,
Billy Gobitas *

---

* Gobitas Papers, Library of Congress. Because of a typographical error, the children's family name was misspelled "Gobitis" in the Court records. As a result, their case was known thereafter as the *Gobitis* Case and the petitioners have been known as the Gobitises.

His sister wrote a similar statement. Walter Gobitis, their father, sought to enjoin the school authorities for exacting the participation in the flag salute ceremony as a condition for school attendance. A federal district court issued the injunction, and the Court of Appeals affirmed. The Minersville School District filed a petition for a writ of certiorari to the Supreme Court.

Gobitis was one of approximately a thousand cases in which petitioners sought discretionary review by the Supreme Court in the 1939 term.*

---

* Today, more than 6,000 applications for review come to the Court each year. Using a unanimous-consent procedure devised by Chief Justice Hughes in the 1930s, the Court dismisses a large number of these applications without discussion or vote by the justices.

Then, as now, the Supreme Court operated under the "Rule of Four" in exercising its discretionary jurisdiction: the votes of four justices are necessary for a case to be reviewed. Although only a small percentage of the certiorari cases receive the necessary four votes, the vote for review in *Gobitis* was unanimous.** After being informed that the Court had granted a petition for certiorari, counsel for the Minersville School District filed a brief on the merits. The Watchtower Bible and Tract Society filed a brief for the Gobitises, and the Bill of Rights Committee of the American Bar Association and the American Civil Liberties Union, with permission of the Court, filed briefs as amici curiae.

The Supreme Court heard oral arguments in *Gobitis* on April 25, 1940. Joseph Henderson, counsel for the Minersville School District, stressed in his argument that several state courts had upheld the constitutionality of the flag salute and that the Supreme Court had dismissed the appeals in those cases. "Judge" Joseph F. Rutherford, a lawyer who was also a leader of the Jehovah's Witnesses, represented the Gobitises. He shared his time for argument with Harvard Professor George K. Gardner, who represented the ABA Bill of Rights Committee. Rutherford, who had not been asked any questions from the bench, focused entirely on theological arguments against the flag salute requirement. In arguing in support of the Gobitises' claims, Professor Gardner "received very rough treatment from the justices, and ... most of his trouble came from Associate Justice Felix Frankfurter, himself a former professor at Harvard Law School." At the conclusion of the arguments, Henderson w satisfied with his presentation. Rutherford was disappointed that the justices had not asked him any questions. Gardner was crushed by the treatment he had received from Frankfurter; years later he recalled the argument "with undisguised disgust."†

The chief justice determines which applications will be discussed and voted upon in conference. Any case may be added to the discussion list at the request of any justice.

** Chief Justice Hughes gave his views on the Minersville School District's petition for certiorari first; his colleagues in order of seniority then gave their views. They voted in inverse order of seniority. Today the procedure is the somewhat different. S. Sidney Ulmer, whose source was Chief Justice William H. Rehnquist, has written: "When considering petitions for certiorari, the person who put the case on the discuss list goes first, then the vote to grant or deny is taken up in order of seniority." S. Sidney Ulmer, Book Review, American Political Science Review, vol. 86, 1992, p. 811.

† David Manwarring, Render Unto Caesar, University of Chicago Press, 1961, pp. 131–132.

William, Walter, and Lillian Gobitis seen after they filed
their case. Photo from the Library of Congress

On Saturday afternoon, April 27, the justices discussed *Gobitis* in conference.* "I come up to this case like a skittish horse to a brass band," Chief Justice Hughes said as he began his presentation of the case.** He told his colleagues that the threshold issue in the case was religious freedom. If Minersville's requirement had been aimed at religion, he said that it would be unconstitutional. But he thought that the requirement was secular in character; hence there was no constitutional violation. The next issue the Chief Justice raised was the reasonableness of the flag salute: was the requirement rationally related to a legitimate object of government? In other words, he used the rational-basis test. "As I see it," he said, "the state can insist on inculcation of loyalty. It would be extraordinary if in this country the state could not provide for respect for the flag of our land."†

After Chief Justice Hughes finished his presentation, the justices, in order of seniority, had an opportunity to give their views. None of the justices opposed the chief justice's views. Justice Frankfurter strongly supported Hughes' conclusions in a moving statement about public schools instilling love of country in a pluralistic society. There is no record of what the others had said. The most junior justice—Frank

* Today, the Court meets at 10 a.m. on Friday following oral argument.

** Justice Murphy's notes of Hughes' remarks, Frank Murphy Papers, Bentley Historical Library, University of Michigan, Box 63.

† Ibid.

Murphy—was the first to vote. Though uncertain of his position, he voted to reverse. The other Court members—William O. Douglas, Frankfurter, Stanley Reed, Hugo L. Black, Owen J. Roberts, Harlan Fiske Stone, James C. McReynolds, and Hughes—then voted in inverse order of seniority.* Douglas recorded their votes in his docket book as follows:**

518   ACTION TAKEN ON CASES, MOTIONS, CERTIFICATES, AND MISCELLANEOUS MATTERS

April 25, 1940	Argued
	, 19___	Submitted
	, 19___	Voted on
June 3, 1940	Announced

No. 690

	, 19___	Recommitted
	, 19___	Reallotted
	, 19___	Passed
	, 19___	___

Minersville School District, Board of Education of Minersville School District, Et al.

vs.

Walter Gobitis, Individually and Lillian Gobitis and William Gobitis, Minors, Etc.

2-1-40 Petition for certiorari to U.S.C.C.A., 3d Circuit

3-4-40 Certiorari granted

4-27-40 Reverse (Frankfurter, J.)

	MERITS		DISMISS		QUESTION			REQUEST FOR RULE		DISCHARGE—RULE		S. D.		P. TO M.		Absent	Not Voting	REMARKS
	Af.	Rev.	Yes	No	Yes	No	Yes	No	Grant	Refuse	Yes	No	Yes	No	Yes	No			
Murphy, J		/																	
Douglas, J.		/																	
Frankfurter, J.		/																	
Reed, J.		/																	
Black, J.	pass																		
Roberts, J.		/																	
Stone, J.	pass																		
Butler, J.																			
McReynolds, J.	/																		
Hughes, C. J.	/																		

---

* Today, the Court has a different conference procedure. Each Court member beginning with the Chief Justice and ending with the most junior justice gives his or her views and vote at the same time.

** Douglas Papers, Library of Congress.

The vote was 7–0 with Justices Black and Stone passing, which meant they would later indicate their votes, most likely after reading a draft of the Court's opinion.

Because Chief Justice Hughes was in the majority, he had the power of assignment of the Court's opinion, and he assigned it to Justice Frankfurter.* If Hughes had not voted with the majority, the senior associate justice would have assigned the opinion.

Justice Frankfurter was not the only justice to begin an opinion in *Gobitis*. Although Justice Murphy had voted to reverse, he began drafting a dissenting opinion. Justice Stone remained undecided weeks after the *Gobitis* conference. By that time, Justice Frankfurter had circulated his opinion, which won warm praise from many of his colleagues. Chief Justice Hughes wrote on the back of Justice Frankfurter's opinion: "I agree. You have accomplished most admirably a very difficult task—the Court is indebted to you." Justice Douglas wrote: "This is a powerful moving document of incalculable contemporary and (I believe) historic value. I congratulate you on a statesmanlike job." Upon recirculation of the opinion, he added, "You have done a magnificent job on a subject which defied, because of the host of intangibles, conventional legal treatment." Justice Roberts said that Frankfurter's opinion was "among the best ever prepared by a judge of this Court." Justice Murphy, reflecting some indecisiveness, wrote: "This has been a Gethsemane for me. But after all the institution presupposes a government that will nourish and protect itself and therefore I join your beautifully expressed opinion."**

Justices Stone and Black, who had passed in conference, had not responded to Justice Frankfurter's opinion. Believing that Stone intended to dissent, Frankfurter tried to dissuade him. On May 27, 1940, he sent Stone the following letter:†

> Were No. 690 [*Gobitis*] an ordinary case, I should let the opinion speak for itself. But that you should entertain doubts has naturally stirred me to an anxious re-examination of my own views, even though I can assure you that nothing has weighed as much on my conscience, since I have come on this Court, as has this case. Your doubts have stirred me to a reconsideration of the whole matter, because I am not happy that you should entertain doubts that I cannot share or meet in

* According to Merlo J. Pusey, as the justices were leaving the conference room, one of them said that Hughes ought to write the Court's opinion in *Gobitis*. At Roberts' suggestion, Frankfurter turned back and repeated the idea to Hughes. "No," the Chief Justice replied emphatically, "I'm going to assign it to you." Pusey, Charles Evans Hughes, Macmillan Co., 1952, vol. 2, p. 729. In an interview in 1961, Douglas said that he doubted Pusey's account. "No one," he added, "would ever suggest to Hughes that Hughes assign [an] opinion to one person or another. Hughes was very severe. Frankfurter was very brash, but even Frankfurter would have never ... dared to do that." According to Douglas, Frankfurter told him that he wanted to write the Court's opinion in *Gobitis* and had asked Douglas to mention it to Hughes. Douglas said that he refused. Transcript of interview of William O. Douglas by Walter F. Murphy, Seeley G. Mudd Manuscript Library, Princeton University, pp. 47–48.

** Felix Frankfurter Papers, Harvard Law School, Box 10.

† Ibid.

a domain where constitutional power is on one side and my private notions of liberty and toleration and good sense are on the other. After all, the vulgar intrusion of law in the domain of conscience is for me a very sensitive area.

. . .

But no one has more clearly in his mind than you, that even when it comes to these ultimate civil liberties, insofar as they are protected by the Constitution, we are not in the domain of absolutes. Here, also, we have an illustration of what the Greeks thousands of years ago recognized as a tragic issue, namely, the clash of rights, not the clash of wrongs. For resolving such clash we have no calculus. But there is for me, and I know also for you, a great makeweight for dealing with this problem, namely, that we are not the primary resolvers of the clash. We are not exercising an independent judgment; we are sitting in judgment upon the judgment of the legislature. I am aware of the important distinction which you so skillfully adumbrated in your footnote 4 (particularly the second paragraph of it) in the *Carolene Products Co.* case. I agree with that distinction; I regard it as basic. I have taken over that distinction in its central aspect, however inadequately, in the present opinion by insisting on the importance of keeping open all those channels of free expression by which undesirable legislation may be removed, and keeping unobstructed all forms of protest against what are deemed invasions of conscience, however much the invasion may be justified on the score of the deepest interests of national wellbeing.

What weighs with me strongly in this case is my anxiety that, while we lean in the direction of the libertarian aspect, we do not exercise our judicial power unduly, and as though we ourselves were legislators by holding with too tight a rein the organs of popular government. In other words, I want to avoid the mistake comparable to that made by those whom we criticized when dealing with the control of property. I hope I am aware of the different interests that are compendiously summarized by opposing "liberty" to "property." But I also know that the generalizations implied in these summaries are also inaccurate and hardly correspond to the complicated realities of an advanced society. I cannot rid myself of the notion that it is not fantastic, although I think foolish and perhaps worse, for school authorities to believe—as the record in this case explicitly shows the school authorities to have believed—that to allow exemption to some of the children goes far towards disrupting the whole patriotic exercise. And since certainly we must admit the general right of the school authorities to have such flag-saluting exercises, it seems to me that we do not trench on an undebatable territory of libertarian immunity to permit the school authorities a judgment as to the effect of this exemption in the particular setting of our time and circumstances.

. . .

For my intention—and I hope my execution did not lag too far behind—was to use this opinion as a vehicle for preaching the true democratic faith of not relying on the Court for the impossible task of assuring a vigorous, mature, self-protecting and tolerant democracy by bringing the responsibility for a combination of firmness and toleration directly home where it belongs—to the people and their representatives themselves.

"I am truly sorry not to go along with you," Stone responded. "The case is peculiarly one of the relative weight of imponderables and I cannot overcome the feeling that the Constitution tips the scale in favor of religion."* Justice Frankfurter still awaited Justice Black's response. Two days before the Court announced the opinion, Black came to Frankfurter's chambers and said: "Like you, I don't like this kind of law and wish we could stop it, but I doubt there is anything in the due process clause that possibly can enable us to hold this [unconstitutional]." At Black's request, Frankfurter made some changes in his opinion and Black then agreed to it.** Thus the final vote in *Gobitis* was 8 to 1. All of the majority justices, except McReynolds, had joined Justice Frankfurter's opinion.

MINERSVILLE SCHOOL DISTRICT v. GOBITIS

Supreme Court of the United States, 1940.
310 U.S. 586, 60 S.Ct. 1010, 84 L.Ed. 1375.

JUSTICE FRANKFURTER delivered the opinion of the Court.

A grave responsibility confronts this Court whenever in course of litigation it must reconcile the conflicting claims of liberty and authority. But when the liberty invoked is liberty of conscience, and the authority is authority to safeguard the nation's fellowship, judicial conscience is put to its severest test. Of such a nature is the present controversy.

. . .

We must decide whether the requirement of participation in [the flag-salute] ceremony, exacted from a child who refuses upon sincere religious grounds, infringes without due process of law the liberty guaranteed by the Fourteenth Amendment.

Certainly the affirmative pursuit of one's convictions about the ultimate mystery of the universe and man's relation to it is placed beyond the reach of law. Government may not interfere with organized or individual expression of belief or disbelief. Propagation of belief—or even of disbelief—in the supernatural is protected, whether in church or chapel, mosque or synagogue, tabernacle or meeting-house. Likewise the

* Ibid.
** Handwritten note by Justice Frankfurter, ibid.

FELIX FRANKFURTER—Born on November 15, 1882, in Vienna, Austria, son of the owner of a small business. Emigrated to the United States at the age of 12. Independent. Jewish. Initially lived in New York's Lower East Side but later moved to a better but still modest neighborhood in the East Seventies. Although he knew no English when he arrived in New York, he quickly learned the language—in six weeks according to one report. City College of New York, A.B., 1902, graduating third in his class; Harvard, LL.B., 1906, graduating first in his class. Assistant U.S. attorney, Southern District of New York, 1906–1910; law officer, Bureau of Insular Affairs, War Department, 1911–1914; Harvard law professor, 1914–1939. Nominated associate justice by President Franklin D. Roosevelt on January 5, 1939, to replace Benjamin N. Cardozo. Confirmed by the Senate on April 4, 1938, by a voice vote. Informally advised F.D.R. before and after joining the Court. Though reputed to be a liberal prior to his appointment, he often voted with conservative justices, usually arguing that judicial restraint required him to do so. Suffered a stroke at the Supreme Court and retired on August 28, 1962. Died on February 22, 1965.

Constitution assures generous immunity to the individual from imposition of penalties for offending, in the course of his own religious activities, the religious views of others, be they a minority or those who are dominant in government. . . .

But the manifold character of man's relations may bring his conception of religious duty into conflict with the secular interests of his fellowmen. When does the constitutional guarantee compel exemption from doing what society thinks necessary for the promotion of some great common end, or from a penalty for conduct which appears dangerous to the general good? To state the problem is to recall the truth that no single principle can answer all of life's complexities. The right to freedom of religious belief, however dissident and however obnoxious to the cherished beliefs of others—even of a majority—is itself the denial of an absolute. But to affirm that the freedom to follow conscience has itself no limits in the life of a society would deny that very plurality of principles which, as a matter of history, underlies protection of religious toleration.

. . .

Situations like the present are phases of the profoundest problem confronting a democracy—the problem which Lincoln cast in memorable dilemma: "Must a government of necessity be too *strong* for the liberties of its people, or too *weak* to maintain its own existence?" No mere textual reading or logical talisman can solve the dilemma. And when the issue demands judicial determination, it is not the personal notion of judges of what wise adjustment requires which must prevail.

Unlike the instances we have cited, the case before us is not concerned with an exertion of legislative power for the promotion of some specific need or interest of secular society—the protection of the family, the promotion of health, the common defense, the raising of public revenues to defray the cost of government. But all these specific activities of government presuppose the existence of an organized political society. The ultimate foundation of a free society is the binding tie of cohesive sentiment. Such a sentiment is fostered by all those agencies of the mind and spirit which may serve to gather up the traditions of a people, transmit them from generation to generation, and thereby create that continuity of a treasured common life which constitutes a civilization. "We live by symbols." The flag is the symbol of our national unity, transcending all internal differences, however large, within the framework of the Constitution. This Court has had occasion to say that "... the flag is the symbol of the Nation's power, the emblem of freedom in its truest, best sense. . . . [I]t signifies government resting on the consent of the governed; liberty regulated by law; the protection of the weak against the strong; security against the exercise of arbitrary power; and absolute safety for free institutions against foreign aggression." ...

The case before us must be viewed as though the legislature of Pennsylvania had itself formally directed the flag-salute for the children of Minersville; had made no exemption for children whose parents were possessed of conscientious scruples like those of the Gobitis family; and had indicated its belief in the desirable ends to be secured by having its public school children share a common experience at those periods of development when their minds are supposedly receptive to its assimilation, by an exercise appropriate in time and place and setting, and one designed to evoke in them appreciation of the nation's hopes and dreams, its sufferings and sacrifices. The precise issue, then, for us to decide is whether the legislatures of the various states and the authorities in a thousand counties and school districts of this country are barred from determining the appropriateness of various means to evoke that unifying sentiment without which there can ultimately be no liberties, civil or religious. To stigmatize legislative judgment in providing for this universal gesture of respect for the symbol of our national life in the setting of the common school as a lawless inroad on that freedom of conscience which the Constitution protects, would amount to no less than the pronouncement of pedagogical and psychological dogma in a field where courts possess no marked and certainly no controlling competence. The influences which help toward a common feeling for the common country are manifold. Some may seem harsh and others no doubt are foolish. Surely, however, the end is legitimate. And the effective means for its attainment are still so uncertain and so unauthenticated by science as to preclude us from putting the widely prevalent belief in flag-saluting beyond the pale of legislative power. It mocks reason and denies our whole history to find in the allowance of a requirement to salute our flag on fitting occasions the seeds of sanction for obeisance to a leader.

. . .

Judicial review, itself a limitation on popular government, is a fundamental part of our constitutional scheme. But to the legislature no less than to courts is committed the guardianship of deeply-cherished liberties.... Where all the effective means of inducing political changes are left free from interference, education in the abandonment of foolish legislation is itself a training in liberty. To fight out the wise use of legislative authority in the forum of public opinion and before legislative assemblies rather than to transfer such a contest to the judicial arena, serves to vindicate the self-confidence of a free people.

Reversed.

[Justice McReynolds concurred in the result.]

JUSTICE STONE, dissenting:

HARLAN FISKE STONE—Born on October 11, 1872, in Chesterfield, New Hampshire, son of a school teacher and farmer. Republican. Congregationalist. Amherst, B.S., Phi Beta Kappa, 1894; M.A., 1897; Columbia, LL.B., 1898. Law practice, 1898–1905, 1923–1924; Columbia law professor and dean, 1902–1923; U.S. attorney general, 1924–1925. Nominated associate justice by President Calvin Coolidge on January 5, 1925, to replace Joseph McKenna. Confirmed by the Senate on February 5, 1925, by a 71–6 vote. Nominated chief justice by President Franklin D. Roosevelt on June 12, 1941, to replace Charles Evans Hughes. Confirmed by the Senate on June 27, 1941, by voice vote. Stricken on the bench, he died on April 22, 1946.

I think the judgment below should be affirmed.

. . .

The law which is thus sustained is unique in the history of Anglo–American legislation. It does more than suppress freedom of speech and more than prohibit the free exercise of religion, which concededly are forbidden by the First Amendment and are violations of the liberty guaranteed by the Fourteenth. For by this law the state seeks to coerce these children to express a sentiment which, as they interpret it, they do not entertain, and which violates their deepest religious convictions. It is not denied that such compulsion is a prohibited infringement of personal liberty, freedom of speech and religion, guaranteed by the Bill of Rights, except in so far as it may be justified and supported as a proper exercise of the state's power over public education. Since the state, in competition with parents, may through teaching in the public schools indoctrinate the minds of the young, it is said that in aid of its undertaking to inspire loyalty and devotion to constituted authority and the flag which symbolizes it, may coerce the pupil to make affirmation contrary to his belief and in violation of his religious faith. And, finally, it is said that since the Minersville School Board and others are of the opinion that the country will be better served by conformity than by the observance of religious liberty which the Constitution prescribes, the courts are not free to pass judgment on the Board's choice.

. . .

The guaranties of civil liberty are but guaranties of freedom of the human mind and spirit and of reasonable freedom and opportunity to express them. They presuppose the right of the individual to hold such opinions as he will and to give them reasonably free expression, and his freedom, and that of the state as well, to teach and persuade others by the communication of ideas. The very essence of the liberty which they guaranty is the freedom of the individual from compulsion as to what he shall think and what he shall say, at least where the compulsion is to bear false witness to his religion. If these guaranties are to have any meaning they must, I think, be deemed to withhold from the state any authority to compel belief or the expression of it where that expression violates religious convictions, whatever may be the legislative view of the desirability of such compulsion.

History teaches us that there have been but few infringements of personal liberty by the state which have not been justified, as they are here, in the name of righteousness and the public good, and few which have not been directed, as they are now, at politically helpless minorities. The framers were not unaware that under the system which they created most governmental curtailments of personal liberty would have the support of a legislative judgment that the public interest would be better served by its curtailment than by its constitutional protection. I cannot conceive that in prescribing, as limitations upon the powers of government, the freedom of the mind and spirit secured by the explicit guaranties of freedom of speech and religion, they intended or rightly could have left any latitude for a legislative judgment that the compulsory expression of belief which violates religious convictions would better serve the public interest than their protection. The Constitution may well elicit expressions of loyalty to it and to the government which it created, but it does not command such expressions or otherwise give any indication that compulsory expressions of loyalty play any such part in our scheme of government as to override the constitutional protection of freedom of speech and religion. And while such expressions of loyalty, when voluntarily given, may promote national unity, it is quite another matter to say that their compulsory expression by children in violation of their own and their parents' religious convictions can be regarded as playing so important a part in our national unity as to leave school boards free to exact it despite the constitutional guarantee of freedom of religion. The very terms of the Bill of Rights preclude, it seems to me, any reconciliation of such compulsions with the constitutional guaranties by a legislative declaration that they are more important to the public welfare than the Bill of Rights.

But even if this view be rejected and it is considered that there is some scope for the determination by legislatures whether the citizen shall be compelled to give public expression of such sentiments contrary to his religion, I am not persuaded that we should refrain from passing upon the legislative judgment "as long as the remedial channels of the democratic process remain open and unobstructed." This seems to me no less than the surrender of the constitutional protection of the liberty of small minorities to the popular will. We have previously pointed to the importance of a searching judicial inquiry into the legislative judgment in situations where prejudice against discrete and insular minorities may tend to curtail the operation of those political processes ordinarily to be relied on to protect minorities. See United States v. Carolene Products Co., 304 U.S. 144, 152, note 4 (1938). And until now we have not hesitated similarly to scrutinize legislation restricting the civil liberty of racial and religious minorities although no political process was affected. Meyer v. Nebraska, 262 U.S. 390 (1923); Pierce v. Society of Sisters, supra; Farrington v. Tokushige, 273 U.S. 284 (1927). Here we have such a small minority entertaining in good faith a religious belief, which is such a departure from the usual course of human conduct, that most persons are disposed to regard it with little toleration or concern. In such circumstances careful scrutiny of legislative efforts to secure conformity of belief and opinion by a compulsory affirmation of the desired belief, is especially needful if civil rights are to receive any protection. Tested by this standard, I am not prepared to say that the right of this small and helpless minority, including children having a strong religious conviction, whether they understand its nature or not, to refrain from an expression obnoxious to their religion, is to be overborne by the interest of the state in maintaining discipline in the schools.

The Constitution expresses more than the conviction of the people that democratic processes must be preserved at all costs. It is also an expression of faith and a command that freedom of mind and spirit must be preserved, which government must obey, if it is to adhere to that justice and moderation without which no free government can exist. For this reason it would seem that legislation which operates to repress the religious freedom of small minorities, which is admittedly within the scope of the protection of the Bill of Rights, must at least be subject to the same judicial scrutiny as legislation which we have recently held to infringe the constitutional liberty of religious and racial minorities.

With such scrutiny I cannot say that the inconveniences which may attend some sensible adjustment of school discipline in order that the religious convictions of these children may be spared, presents a problem so momentous or pressing as to outweigh the freedom from compulsory violation of religious faith which has been thought worthy of constitutional protection.

NOTES AND QUESTIONS

1. What influenced Justice Frankfurter's vote in *Gobitis*? After reading a draft of Justice Frankfurter's opinion, Justice Douglas wrote in his diary on June 1, 1940: "One thing influencing F.F., I suspect, is his early experience as an immigrant. He told me with what exhilaration he as a lad had to salute the flag in his school in N.Y.C. It was the symbol of a new life for him. Those early experiences had a powerful pull, I believe, in this Gobitis case. In conference, when he discussed it, F.F. was under obvious emotional strain.... I think F.F. had a feeling also that a contrary decision, in view of the great Nazi propaganda in this country, would have a powerful, disintegrating effect." What influenced Justice Douglas's vote? This is his answer in the same diary entry: "It has been a most difficult [case] to decide. I had doubts about F.F.'s decision, as did Hugo [Black] & Frank M[urphy]. We decided to go along,

tho it was very close in our minds. I talked it over with Brandeis, [who had retired the previous year]. He was very clear that F.F. was right—he had not doubts. That influenced me." Philip E. Urofsky, ed. "Diary of Wm. O. Douglas," *Journal of the Supreme Court History* (1995), p. 94.

2.   Did Justice Stone rely in his dissenting opinion on the second paragraph of Footnote Four in *Carolene Products* as Justice Frankfurter assumed in his letter, or did Stone rely on the third paragraph of the Footnote? Does it make any difference?

3.   Murphy's indecisiveness in *Gobitis* illustrates what Supreme Court scholars have called "freshman effect." Typically, freshmen justices, when uncertain or cross-pressured, vote with the majority, as Murphy did in *Gobitis*.

THE IMPACT OF GOBITIS

Law review comment on the Court's opinion in *Gobitis* was highly critical; so was newspaper editorial comment. Further, there were also many reports of harassment of and violence to Jehovah's Witnesses soon after the Court decided the case. The papers of the justices indicated that they were aware of the press reports and criticisms. Justice Frankfurter recorded the following conversation he had with Justice Douglas in late September of 1940:

Douglas: Hugo [Black] tells me now he wouldn't go with you in the *Gobitis* case.

FF: Has Hugo been re-reading the Constitution during the summer?

Douglas: No—he has been reading the papers.*

In fact, Black, Murphy, and Douglas concluded that they had erred in deciding the *Gobitis* case, and they said so two years later when they dissented in Jones v. Opelika, 316 U.S. 584, 623 (1942).

THE SECOND FLAG–SALUTE CASE—1943

Two months after the Supreme Court's decision in Jones v. Opelika, the Jehovah's Witnesses challenged the constitutionality of the flag-salute law in West Virginia before a three-judge federal court, which held the West Virginia law unconstitutional, explaining that it had not followed *Gobitis* for the following reasons:**

Ordinarily we would feel constrained to follow an unre-versed decision of the Supreme Court of the United States, whether we agree with it or not. It is true that decisions are but evidences of the law and not the law itself; but the decisions of the Supreme Court must be accepted by the lower courts as binding upon them if any orderly administration of justice is to be attained. The developments with respect to the Gobitis case, however, are such that we do not feel that it is incumbent upon

* Frankfurter Papers, Harvard Law School, Box 10.

** Barnette v. West Virginia State Board of Education, 47 F.Supp. 251, 252–253 (S.D.W.Va.1942).

us to accept it as binding authority. Of the seven justices now members of the Supreme Court who participated in that decision, four have given public expression to the view that it is unsound, the present Chief Justice in his dissenting opinion rendered therein and three other justices in a special dissenting opinion in Jones v. City of Opelika.

WEST VIRGINIA STATE BOARD OF EDUCATION v. BARNETTE

Supreme Court of the United States, 1943.
319 U.S. 624, 63 S.Ct. 1178, 87 L.Ed. 1628.

JUSTICE JACKSON delivered the opinion of the Court.

. . .

This case calls upon us to reconsider a precedent decision, as the Court throughout its history often has been required to do. Before turning to the *Gobitis* case, however, it is desirable to notice certain characteristics by which this controversy is distinguished.

ROBERT H. JACKSON—Born on February 13, 1892, in Spring Creek, Pennsylvania, son of a farmer who bred and raced horses. Democrat. Episcopalian. Attended Albany Law School, 1911–1912. Practiced law in Jamestown, New York, 1913–1935; Bureau of Internal Revenue general counsel, 1934–1936; assistant U.S. attorney general, 1936–1938; U.S. solicitor general, 1938–1940; U.S. attorney general, 1940–1941. Nominated associate justice by President Franklin D. Roosevelt on June 12, 1941, to replace Harlan Fiske Stone, who had been promoted to the chief justiceship. Confirmed by the Senate on July 7, 1941, by voice vote. Chief U.S. prosecutor at Nuremberg war crimes trial while on leave from the Supreme Court, 1945–1946. Served on the Supreme Court until his death on October 9, 1954. He was one of the Court's most gifted writers.

. . .

The *Gobitis* opinion reasoned that this is a field "where courts possess no marked and certainly no controlling competence," that it is committed to the legislatures as well as the courts to guard cherished liberties and that it is constitutionally appropriate to "fight out the wise use of legislative authority in the forum of public opinion and before legislative assemblies rather than to transfer such a contest to the judicial arena," since all the "effective means of inducing political changes are left free." . . .

The very purpose of a Bill of Rights was to withdraw certain subjects from the vicissitudes of political controversy, to place them beyond the reach of majorities and officials and to establish them as legal principles to be applied by the courts. One's right to life, liberty, and property, to free speech, a free press, freedom of worship and assembly, and other fundamental rights may not be submitted to vote; they depend on the outcome of no elections.

In weighing arguments of the parties it is important to distinguish between the due process clause of the Fourteenth Amendment as an instrument for transmitting the principles of the First Amendment and those cases in which it is applied for its own sake. The test of legislation which collides with the Fourteenth Amendment, because it also collides with the principles of the First, is much more definite than the test when only the Fourteenth is involved. Much of the vagueness of the due process clause disappears when the specific prohibitions of the First become its standard. The right of a State to regulate, for example, a public utility may well include, so far as the due process test is concerned, power to impose all of the restrictions which a legislature may have a "rational basis" for adopting. But freedoms of speech and of press, of assembly, and of worship may not be infringed on such slender grounds. They are susceptible of restriction only to prevent grave and immediate danger to interests which the State may lawfully protect. It is important to note that while it is the Fourteenth Amendment which bears directly upon the State it is the more specific limiting principles of the First Amendment that finally govern this case.

Nor does our duty to apply the Bill of Rights to assertions of official authority depend upon our possession of marked competence in the field where the invasion of rights occurs. True, the task of translating the majestic generalities of the Bill of Rights, conceived as part of the pattern of liberal government in the eighteenth century, into concrete restraints on officials dealing with the problems of the twentieth century, is one to disturb self-confidence. These principles grew in soil which also produced a philosophy that the individual was the center of society, that his liberty was attainable through mere absence of governmental restraints, and that government should be entrusted with few controls and only the mildest supervision over men's affairs. We must transplant these rights to a soil in which the *laissez-faire* concept or principle of non-interference has withered at least as to economic affairs, and social advancements are increasingly sought through closer integration of society and through expanded and strengthened governmental controls. These changed conditions often deprive precedents of reliability and cast us more than we would choose upon our own judgment. But we act in these matters not by authority of our competence but by force of our commissions. We cannot, because of modest estimates of our competence in such specialties as public education, withhold the judgment that history authenticates as the function of this Court when liberty is infringed.

Lastly, and this is the very heart of the *Gobitis* opinion, it reasons that "National unity is the basis of national security," that the authorities have "the right to select appropriate means for its attainment," and hence reaches the conclusion that such compulsory measures toward "national unity" are constitutional. Id. at 595. Upon the verity of this assumption depends our answer in this case.

National unity as an end which officials may foster by persuasion and example is not in question. The problem is whether under our Constitution compulsion as here employed is a permissible means for its achievement.

Struggles to coerce uniformity of sentiment in support of some end thought essential to their time and country have been waged by many good as well as by evil men. Nationalism is a relatively recent phenomenon but at other times and places the ends have been racial or territorial security, support of a dynasty or regime, and particular plans for saving souls. As first and moderate methods to attain unity have failed, those bent on its accomplishment must resort to an ever-increasing severity. As governmental pressure toward unity becomes greater, so strife becomes more bitter as to whose unity it shall be. Probably no deeper division of our people could proceed from any provocation than from finding it necessary to choose what doctrine and whose program public educational officials shall compel youth to unite in embracing. Ultimate futility of such attempts to compel coherence is the lesson of every such effort from the Roman drive to stamp out Christianity as a disturber of its pagan unity, the Inquisition, as a means to religious and dynastic unity, the Siberian exiles as a means to Russian unity, down to the fast failing efforts of our present totalitarian enemies. Those who begin coercive elimination of dissent soon find themselves exterminating dissenters. Compulsory unification of opinion achieves only the unanimity of the graveyard.

It seems trite but necessary to say that the First Amendment to our Constitution was designed to avoid these ends by avoiding these beginnings. There is no mysticism in the American concept of the State or of the nature or origin of its authority. We set up government by consent of the governed, and the Bill of Rights denies those in power any legal opportunity to coerce that consent. Authority here is to be controlled by public opinion, not public opinion by authority.

The case is made difficult not because the principles of its decision are obscure but because the flag involved is our own. Nevertheless, we apply the limitations of the Constitution with no fear that freedom to be intellectually and spiritually diverse or even contrary will disintegrate the social organization. To believe that patriotism will not flourish if patriotic ceremonies are voluntary and spontaneous instead of a compulsory routine is to make an unflattering estimate of the appeal of our institutions to free minds. We can have intellectual individualism and the rich cultural diversities that we owe to exceptional minds only at the price of occasional eccentricity and abnormal attitudes. When they are so harmless to others or to the State as those we deal with here, the price is not too great. But freedom to differ is not limited to things that do not matter much. That would be a mere shadow of freedom. The test of its substance is the right to differ as to things that touch the heart of the existing order.

If there is any fixed star in our constitutional constellation, it is that no official, high or petty, can prescribe what shall be orthodox in politics, nationalism, religion, or other matters of opinion or force citizens to confess by word or act their faith therein. If there are any circumstances which permit an exception, they do not now occur to us.

We think the action of the local authorities in compelling the flag salute and pledge transcends constitutional limitations on their power and invades the sphere of intellect and spirit which it is the purpose of the First Amendment to our Constitution to reserve from all official control.

[The concurring opinions of Justices Black, Douglas, and Murphy are omitted.]

JUSTICE FRANKFURTER, dissenting:

One who belongs to the most vilified and persecuted minority in history is not likely to be insensible to the freedoms guaranteed by our Constitution. Were my purely personal attitude relevant I should whole-heartedly associate myself with the general libertarian views in the Court's opinion, representing as they do the thought and action of a lifetime. But as judges we are neither Jew nor Gentile, neither Catholic nor agnostic. We owe equal attachment to the Constitution and are equally bound by our judicial obligations whether we derive our citizen-ship from the earliest or the latest immigrants to these shores. As a member of this Court I am not justified in writing my private notions of policy into the Constitution, no matter how deeply I may cherish them or how mischievous I may deem their disregard. The duty of a judge who must decide which of two claims before the Court shall prevail, that of a State to enact and enforce laws within its general competence or that of an individual to refuse obedience because of the demands of his con-science, is not that of the ordinary person. It can never be emphasized too much that one's own opinion about the wisdom or evil of a law should be excluded altogether when one is doing one's duty on the bench. The only opinion of our own even looking in that direction that is material is our opinion whether legislators could in reason have enacted such a law. In the light of all the circumstances, including the history of this question in this Court, it would require more daring than I possess to deny that reasonable legislators could have taken the action which is before us for review. Most unwillingly, therefore, I must differ from my brethren with regard to legislation like this. I cannot bring my mind to believe that the "liberty" secured by the Due Process Clause gives this Court authority to deny to the State of West Virginia the attainment of that which we all recognize as a legitimate legislative end, namely, the promotion of good citizenship, by employment of the means here chosen.

Not so long ago we were admonished that "the only check upon our own exercise of power is our own sense of self-restraint. For the removal of unwise laws from the statute books appeal lies not to the courts but to the ballot and to the processes of democratic government." . . . We have been told that generalities do not decide concrete cases. But the intensity with which a general principle is held may determine a particular issue, and whether we put first things first may decide a specific controversy.

The admonition that judicial self-restraint alone limits arbitrary exercise of our authority is relevant every time we are asked to nullify legislation. The Constitution does not give us greater veto power when dealing with one phase of "liberty" than with another, or when dealing with grade school regulations than with college regulations that offend conscience, as was the case in Hamilton v. Regents, 293 U.S. 245. In neither situation is our function comparable to that of a legislature or are we free to act as though we were a super-legislature. Judicial self-restraint is equally necessary whenever an exercise of political or legislative power is challenged. There is no warrant in the constitutional basis of this Court's authority for attributing different roles to it depending upon the nature of the challenge to the legislation. Our power does not vary according to the particular provision of the Bill of Rights which is invoked. The right not to have property taken without just compensation has, so far as the scope of judicial power is concerned, the same constitutional dignity as the right to be protected against unreasonable searches and seizures, and the latter has no less claim than freedom of the press or freedom of speech or religious freedom. In no instance is this Court the primary protector of the particular liberty that is invoked. This Court has recognized, what hardly could be denied, that all the provisions of the first ten Amendments are "specific" prohibitions, United States v. Carolene Products Co., 304 U.S. 144, 152, n. 4. But each specific Amendment, in so far as embraced within the Fourteenth Amendment, must be equally respected, and the function of this Court does not differ in passing on the constitutionality of legislation challenged under different Amendments.

When Justice Holmes, speaking for this Court, wrote that "it must be remembered that legislatures are ultimate guardians of the liberties and welfare of the people in quite as great a degree as the courts, . . ." he went to the very essence of our constitutional system and the democratic conception of our society. He did not mean that for only some phases of civil government this Court was not to supplant legislatures and sit in judgment upon the right or wrong of a challenged measure. He was stating the comprehensive judicial duty and role of this Court in our constitutional scheme whenever legislation is sought to be nullified on any ground, namely, that responsibility for legislation lies with legislatures, answerable as they are directly to the people, and this Court's only and very narrow function is to determine whether within the broad grant of authority vested in legislatures they have exercised a judgment for which reasonable justification can be offered.

The framers of the federal Constitution might have chosen to assign an active share in the process of legislation to this Court. They had before them the well-known example of New York's Council of Revision, which had been functioning since 1777. After stating that "laws inconsistent with the spirit of this constitution, or with the public good, may be hastily and unadvisedly passed," the state constitution made the judges of New York part of the legislative process by providing that "all bills which have passed the senate and assembly shall, before they become laws," be presented to a Council of which the judges constituted a majority, "for their revisal and consideration." Art. III, New York Constitution of 1777. Judges exercised this legislative function in New York for nearly fifty years. . . . They chose instead to insulate the judiciary from the legislative function. They did not grant to this Court supervision over legislation.

The reason why from the beginning even the narrow judicial authority to nullify legislation has been viewed with a jealous eye is that it serves to prevent the full play of the democratic process. The fact that it may be an undemocratic aspect of our scheme of government does not call for its rejection or its disuse. But it is the best of reasons, as this Court has frequently recognized, for the greatest caution in its use.

. . .

One's conception of the Constitution cannot be severed from one's conception of a judge's function in applying it. The Court has no reason for existence if it merely reflects the pressures of the day. Our system is built on the faith that men set apart for this special function, freed from the influences of immediacy and from the deflections of worldly ambition, will become able to take a view of longer range than the period of responsibility entrusted to Congress and legislatures. We are dealing with matters as to which legislators and voters have conflicting views. Are we as judges to impose our strong convictions on where wisdom lies? That which three years ago had seemed to five successive Courts to lie within permissible areas of legislation is now outlawed by the deciding shift of opinion of two Justices. What reason is there to believe that they or their successors may not have another view a few years hence? Is that which was deemed to be of so fundamental a nature as to be written into the Constitution to endure for all times to be the sport of shifting winds of doctrine? Of course, judicial opinions, even as to questions of constitutionality, are not immutable. As has been true in the past, the Court will from time to time reverse its position. But I believe that never before these Jehovah's Witnesses cases (except for minor deviations subsequently retraced) has this Court overruled decisions so as to restrict the powers of democratic government. Always heretofore, it has withdrawn narrow views of legislative authority so as to authorize what formerly it had denied.

. . .

Of course patriotism can not be enforced by the flag salute. But neither can the liberal spirit be enforced by judicial invalidation of illiberal legislation. Our constant preoccupation with the constitutionality of legislation rather than with its wisdom tends to preoccupation of the American mind with a false value. The tendency of focusing attention on constitutionality is to make constitutionality synonymous with wisdom, to regard a law as all right if it is constitutional. Such an attitude is a great enemy of liberalism. Particularly in legislation affecting freedom of thought and freedom of speech much which should offend a free-spirited society is constitutional. Reliance for the most precious interests of civilization, therefore, must be found outside of their vindication in courts of law. Only a persistent positive translation of the faith of a free society into the convictions and habits and actions of a community is the ultimate reliance against unabated temptations to fetter the human spirit.

[Justices Roberts and Reed also dissented, saying they adhered to the views expressed in the Court's opinion in *Gobitis*.]

NOTES AND QUESTIONS

1. Justice Frankfurter's opening sentence in his dissenting opinion in *Barnette*—"One who belongs to the most vilified and persecuted minorities is not likely to be insensitive to the freedoms guaranteed by our Constitution"—is one of the most personal statements written by a justice in a Supreme Court opinion. Why did he do it? A recent oral history memoir by his law clerk, Philip Elman, provides an answer. Upon reading the sentence, Elman said to Frankfurter, "You're not going to put that in the opinion." Elman argued that it was inconsistent with Frankfurter's later statement: "As judges we are neither Jew nor Gentile, neither Catholic nor agnostic." "[I]f you're going to say that it makes no difference whether you are Jew or Gentile," said Elman, "you don't remind people you're a Jew." After listening to Elman, Frankfurter said: "Phil, I heard enough. This is my opinion, not yours." Elman agreed and said no more. Yet he wondered why Frankfurter put that opening sentence in his opinion. Years later, he gave the answer: "He put it in because of Mrs. Roosevelt and others with the same feeling as hers. They had said to him, in effect, after *Gobitis*, 'You of all people, how can you ...' They didn't say, 'You as a Jew ...' They didn't say, 'Felix, you out of all people, you are a Jew ...' They'd say, 'You Felix Frankfurter, sensitive as you are to being singled out on religious grounds, as sensitive as you are to civil liberties,' et cetera. But he knew that was in their minds, and he wanted people to know and not forget that he was a Jew and that he didn't come out that way because he was personally in favor of the action ..."* Because of the personal character of Frankfurter's remarks, Justices Roberts and Reed, who had also dissented in *Barnette*, did not join his opinion, though they agreed with it. In a note to Frankfurter, Reed wrote "Your W.Va. Bd. Dissent is perfect. I know that its teaching is a real basis of our judicial authority. The opinion, however, is quite personal ... I think it better simply to note a dissent."†

2. Why did the Supreme Court overrule *Gobitis*? Was it because of new appointments to the Court? Robert H. Jackson and Wiley Rutledge had been appointed to the Court between 1940 and 1943. Justice Douglas explained his change of position in the flag-salute cases this way: "Every Justice I have known feels in retrospect that he made mistakes in his early years. The problems sometimes come so fast that the uninitiated is drawn into channels from which he later wants to retreat. That happened ... to Hugo Black, Frank Murphy and me when the first flag-salute case ... was argued on April 25, 1940. In those days Felix Frankfurter was our hero. He was indeed learned in constitutional law and we were inclined to take him at face value."*

---

* Norman J. Silber, ed., With All Deliberate Speed: The Life of Philip Elman, An Oral History and Memoir, University of Michigan Press, 2004, p. 113.

† Stanley Reed to Felix Frankfurter, n.d., Paige Box 10, Felix Frankfurter Papers, Harvard Law School.

* William O. Douglas, The Court Years, Random House, 1980, pp. 43–44.

Part Two

FREEDOM OF THOUGHT, BELIEF, SPEECH, PRESS, AND ASSOCIATION

Chapter III

FREEDOM OF THOUGHT AND BELIEF

Freedom of thought is the right of individuals to form and hold opinions whether or not those opinions are expressed or acted upon. Freedom of thought and freedom of belief are virtually synonymous. The Constitution does not expressly guarantee these rights; courts have implied them from First Amendment guarantees of free speech and press and free exercise of religion and have accorded them great protection. Justice Holmes' dissenting views in United States v. Schwimmer, 279 U.S. 644, 654–655 (1929) are now universally accepted. "[I]f there is any principle of the Constitution that imperatively calls for attachment more than any other," wrote Holmes, "it is the principle of free thought—not free thought for those who agree with us but freedom for the thought that we hate." In Cantwell v. Connecticut, 310 U.S. 296, 303–304 (1940), Justice Roberts wrote for a unanimous Court that the First Amendment "embraces two concepts, freedom to believe and freedom to act. The first is absolute, but, in the nature of things, the second cannot be. Conduct remains subject to regulation for the protection of society."

AMERICAN COMMUNICATIONS ASSOCIATION v. DOUDS

Supreme Court of the United States, 1950.
339 U.S. 382, 70 S.Ct. 674, 94 L.Ed. 925.

[One of the issues in *Douds* was whether Section 9(h) of the National Labor Relations Act violated rights to freedom of belief and association. Section 9(h) provided that no union could avail itself of the services of the National Labor Relations Board unless each of its officers filed an affidavit stating "that he is not a member of the Communist Party or affiliated with such party, and that he does not believe in, and is not a member of or supports any organization that believes in or teaches, the overthrow of the United States Government by force or any illegal or unconstitutional method." The Court of Appeals for the Seventh Circuit, by a divided vote, had upheld the provisions of the six

justices who participated in the Court's decision of the case, three of them—Justices Frankfurter, Jackson, and Black—held that the belief provision violated freedom of belief. Chief Justice Vinson and Justices Reed and Burton held that the provision did not violate freedom of belief. Justices Frankfurter and Jackson agreed with Chief Justice Vinson and Justices Reed and Burton that Section 9(h) did not violate freedom of association. Because the Court had divided equally on the belief issue and voted five to one on the association issue, Section 9(h) was held constitutional. The excerpts that follow deal with the constitutionality of the belief provision in Section 9(h).]

CHIEF JUSTICE VINSON delivered the opinion of the Court.

FRED M. VINSON—Born in Louisa, Kentucky, on January 22, 1890, son of a small-town jailer. Democrat. Methodist. Centre College, A.B., 1909; LL.B., 1911, graduating first in his class. Law practice, 1911–1921; commonwealth attorney, 1921–1924; member of U.S. House of Representatives, 1923–1929, 1931–1938; U.S. Court of Appeals judge (D.C. Circuit), 1938–1943; director of the Office of Economic Stabilization, 1943–1945; federal loan administrator, 1945; director of the War Mobilization and Reconversion Board, 1945; secretary of the treasury, 1945–1946. Nominated chief justice by President Harry S. Truman on June 6, 1946, to replace Harlan Fiske Stone. Confirmed by the Senate on June 20, 1946, by voice vote. Informally advised President Truman while on the Court. Served on the Court until his death on September 8, 1953. Except in the area of civil rights, he was ideologically conservative. The consensus of historians is that he was the weakest chief justice in the Court's history.

... Of course we agree that one may not be imprisoned or executed because he holds particular beliefs. But to attack the straw man of "thought control" is to ignore the fact that the sole effect of the statute upon one who believes in overthrow of the Government by force and violence—and does not deny his belief—is that he may be forced to relinquish his position as a union leader.

If the principle that one may under no circumstances be required to state his beliefs on any subject nor suffer the loss of any right or privilege because of his beliefs be a valid one, its application in other possible situations becomes relevant. Suppose, for example, that a federal statute provides that no person may become a member of the Secret Service force assigned to protect the President unless he swears that he does not believe in assassination of the President. Is this beyond the power of Congress, whatever the need revealed by its investigations? An affirmative answer hardly commends itself to reason unless, indeed, the Bill of Rights has been converted into a "suicide pact." ... Yet the example chosen is far-fetched only because of the manifest absurdity of reliance upon an oath in such a situation. One can have no doubt that the screening process in the selection of persons to occupy such positions probes far deeper than mere oathtaking can possibly do.

To hold that such an oath is permissible, on the other hand, is to admit the circumstances under which one is asked to state his belief and the consequences which flow from his refusal to do so or his disclosure of a particular belief make a difference.... First, the loss of a particular position is not the loss of life or liberty. We have noted that the distinction is one of degree, and it is for this reason that the effect of the statute in proscribing beliefs—like its effect in restraining speech or freedom of association—must be carefully weighed by the courts in determining whether the balance struck by Congress comports with the dictates of the Constitution. But it is inaccurate to speak of Section 9(h) as "punishing" or "forbidding" the holding of beliefs, any more than it punishes or forbids membership in the Communist Party.

Second, the public interest at stake in ascertaining one's beliefs cannot automatically be assigned at zero without consideration of the circumstances of the inquiry. If it is admitted that beliefs are springs to action, it becomes highly relevant whether the person who is asked whether he believes in overthrow of the Government by force is a general with five hundred thousand men at his command or a village constable. To argue that because the latter may not be asked his beliefs the former must *necessarily* be exempt is to make a fetish of beliefs. The answer to the implication that if this statute is upheld "then the power of government over beliefs is as unlimited as its power over conduct and the way is open to force disclosure of attitudes on all manner of social, economic, moral and political issues," is that result does not follow "while this Court sits." The circumstances giving rise to the inquiry, then, are likewise factors to be weighed by the courts, giving due weight, of course, to the congressional judgment concerning the need. In short, the problem of balancing the conflicting individual and national interests involved is no different from the problem presented by proscriptions based upon political affiliations.

We conclude that Section 9(h) of the National Labor Relations Act, as amended by the Labor–Management Relations Act, 1947, as herein construed, is compatible with the Federal Constitution and may stand. The judgments of the courts below are therefore affirmed.

JUSTICE FRANKFURTER, dissenting in part.

... In order to curb a mischief Congress cannot be so indefinite in its requirements that effort to meet them raises hazards unfair to those who seek obedience or involves surrender of freedoms which exceeds what may fairly be exacted. These restrictions on the broad scope of legislative discretion are merely the law's application of the homely saws that one should not throw out the baby with the bath or burn the house in order to roast the pig.

In my view Congress has cast its net too indiscriminately in some of the provisions of Section 9(h). To ask avowal that one "does not believe in, and is not a member of or supports any organization that believes in ... the overthrow of the United States Government ... by any illegal or unconstitutional methods" is to ask assurances from men regarding matters that open the door too wide to mere speculation or uncertainty.

[P]robing into men's thoughts trenches on those aspects of individual freedom which we rightly regard as the most cherished aspects of Western civilization. The cardinal article of faith of our civilization is the inviolate character of the individual. A man can be regarded as an individual and not as a function of the state only if he is protected to the largest possible extent in his thoughts and in his beliefs as the citadel of his person. Entry into that citadel can be justified, if at all, only if strictly confined so that the belief that a man is asked to reveal is so denied as to leave no fair room for doubt that he is not asked to disclose what he has a right to withhold.

No one could believe more strongly than I do that every rational indulgence should be made in favor of the constitutionality of an enactment by Congress. I deem it my duty to go to the farthest possible limits in so construing legislation as to avoid a finding that Congress has exceeded the limits of its powers.

If I possibly could, to avoid questions of unconstitutionality I would construe the requirements of Section 9(h) to be restricted to disavowal of actual membership in the Communist Party, or in an organization that is in fact a controlled cover for that Party, or of active belief, as a matter of present policy, in the overthrow of the Government of the United States by force. But what Congress has written does not permit such a gloss nor deletion of what it has written. . . . I cannot deem it within the rightful authority of Congress to probe into opinions that involve only an argumentative demonstration of some coincidental parallelism of belief with some of the beliefs of those who direct the policy of the Communist Party, though without any allegiance to it. To require oaths as to matters that open up such possibilities invades the inner life of men whose compassionate thought or doctrinaire hopes may be as far removed from any dangerous kinship with the Communist creed as were those of the founders of the present orthodox political parties in this country.

JUSTICE JACKSON, dissenting in part.

. . . It is a strange paradox if one may be forbidden to have an idea in mind that he is free to put into execution. But apart from this, efforts to weed erroneous beliefs from the minds of men have always been supported by the argument which the Court invokes today, that beliefs are springs to action, that evil thoughts tend to become forbidden deeds. Probably so. But if power to forbid acts includes power to forbid contemplating them, then the power of government over beliefs is as unlimited as its power over conduct and the way is open to force disclosure of attitudes on all manner of social, economic, moral and political issues.

These suggestions may be discounted as fanciful and farfetched. But we must not forget that in our country are evangelists and zealots of many different political, economic and religious persuasions whose fanatical conviction is that all thought is divinely classified into two kinds— that which is their own and that which is false and dangerous. Communists are not the only faction which would put us all in mental strait jackets. Indeed all ideological struggles, religious or political, are primarily battles for dominance over the minds of people. It is not to be supposed that the age-old readiness to try to convert minds by pressure or suppression, instead of reason and persuasion, is extinct. Our protection against all kinds of fanatics and extremists, none of whom can be trusted with unlimited power over others, lies not in their forbearance but in the limitations of our Constitution.

[W]hile I think Congress may make it a crime to take one overt step to use or to incite violence or force against our Government, I do not see how in the light of our history, a mere belief that one has a natural right under some circumstances to do so can subject an American to prejudice any more than possession of any other erroneous belief. Can we say that men of our time must not even think about the propositions on which our own revolution was justified?

While the Governments, State and Federal, have expansive powers to curtail action, and some small powers to curtail speech or writing, I think neither has any power, on any pretext, directly or indirectly to attempt foreclosure of any line of thought. Our forefathers found the evils of free thinking more to be endured than the evils of inquest or suppression. They gave the status of almost absolute individual rights to the outward means of expressing belief. I cannot believe that they left open a way for legislation to embarrass or impede the mere intellectual processes by which those expressions of belief are examined and formulated. This is not only because individual thinking presents no danger to society, but because thoughtful, bold and independent minds are essential to wise and considered self-government.

Progress generally begins in skepticism about accepted truths. Intellectual freedom means the right to re-examine much that has been long taken for granted. A free man must be a reasoning man, and he must dare to doubt what a legislative or electoral majority may most passionately assert. The danger that citizens will think wrongly is serious, but less dangerous than atrophy from not thinking at all. Our Constitution relies on our electorate's complete ideological freedom to nourish independent and responsible intelligence and preserve our democracy from that submissiveness, timidity and herd-mindedness of the masses which would foster a tyranny of mediocrity. The priceless heritage of our society is the unrestricted constitutional right of each member to think as he will. Thought control is a copyright of totalitarianism, and we have no claim to it. It is not the function of our Government to keep the citizen from falling into error; it is the function of the citizen to keep the Government from falling into error. We could justify any censorship only when the censors are better shielded against error than the censored.

I think that under our system, it is time enough for the law to lay hold of the citizen when he acts illegally, or in some rare circumstances when his thoughts are given illegal utterance. I think we must let his mind alone.

JUSTICE BLACK, dissenting.

HUGO L. BLACK—Born in Harlan, Alabama, on February 27, 1886, son of a rural storekeeper who had joined the Confederate army at 14. Democrat. Baptist. Attended Birmingham Medical College, 1903–1904; University of Alabama, LL.B., 1906. Embarked on a self-study program that included reading Greek and Roman classics, history, philosophy, and the writings of Jefferson and Madison. Law practice, 1906–1910; police court judge 1910–1911; county solicitor, 1915–1917; captain, U.S. army, 1917–1919; U.S. senator, 1927–1937. Ku Klux Klan member, 1923–1925. Nominated associate justice by President Franklin D. Roosevelt, on August 12, 1937, to replace Willis Van Devanter. Confirmed by the Senate on August 17, 1937, by a 63–16 vote. Former Klan membership disclosed publicly soon after confirmation. In a radio address, refused to resign and affirmed his belief in religious freedom. Retired on September 17, 1971. Died on September 25, 1971. Jurisprudentially a legal positivist and ideologically a liberal, he is best remembered for his absolutist interpretation of the First Amendment.

We have said that "Freedom to think is absolute of its own nature; the most tyrannical government is powerless to control the inward workings of the mind." But people can be, and in the less democratic countries have been, made to suffer for their admitted or conjectured thoughts. Blackstone recalls that Dionysus is "recorded to have executed a subject barely for dreaming that he had killed him; which was held sufficient proof that he had thought thereof in his waking hours." Such a result, while too barbaric to be tolerated in our nation, is not illogical if a government can tamper within the realm of thought and penalize "belief" on the ground that it might lead to illegal conduct. Individual freedom and governmental thought-probing cannot live together. As the Court admits even today, under the First Amendment "Beliefs are inviolate."

Since Section 9(h) was passed to exclude certain beliefs from one arena of the national economy, it was quite natural to utilize the test oath as a weapon. History attests the efficacy of that instrument for inflicting penalties and disabilities on obnoxious minorities. It was one of the major devices used against the Huguenots in France, and against "heretics" during the Spanish Inquisition. It helped English rulers identify and outlaw Catholics, Quakers, Baptists, and Congregationalists—groups considered dangerous for political as well as religious reasons. And wherever the test oath was in vogue, spies and informers found rewards far more tempting than truth. Painful awareness of the evils of thought espionage made such oaths "an abomination to the founders of this nation." Whether religious, political, or both, test oaths are implacable foes of free thought. By approving their imposition, this Court has injected compromise into a field where the First Amendment forbids compromise.

... [P]enalties should be imposed only for a person's own conduct, not for his beliefs or for the conduct of others with whom he may associate. Guilt should not be imputed solely from association or affiliation with political parties or any other organization, however much we abhor the ideas which they advocate. Like anyone else, individual Communists who commit overt acts in violation of valid laws can and should be punished. But the postulate of the First Amendment is that our free institutions can be maintained without proscribing or penalizing political belief, speech, press assembly, or party affiliation. This is a far bolder philosophy than despotic rulers can afford to follow. It is the heart of the system on which our freedom depends.

Fears of alien ideologies have frequently agitated the nation and inspired legislation aimed at suppressing advocacy of those ideologies. At such times the fog of public excitement obscures the ancient landmarks set up in our Bill of Rights.... Speaking through Chief Justice Hughes [in De Jonge v. Oregon], a unanimous Court calmly announced time-honored principles that should govern this Court today: "The greater the importance of safeguarding the community from incitements to the overthrow of our institutions by force and violence, the more imperative is the need to preserve constitutional rights of free speech, free press and free assembly in order to maintain the opportunity for free political discussion, to the end that government may be responsive to the will of the people and that changes, if desired, may be obtained by peaceful means. Therein lies the security of the Republic, the very foundation of constitutional government."

NOTES AND QUESTIONS

1.　When the Supreme Court heard *Douds,* Justice Minton had been nominated but not yet sworn in, and Justice Douglas was recovering from a serious injury. With Justices Douglas' and Minton's votes, counsel for the Association believed that the Court might grant their petition for rehearing and reverse. The Court, however, denied the petition. Justice Douglas voted with Justices Black, Frankfurter, and Jackson, and Justice Minton voted with Chief Justice Vinson and Justices Reed and Burton. Justice Clark did not participate because he had been attorney general when the case had been litigated. Justices Black, Frankfurter, Douglas and Jackson had been appointed by Franklin Roosevelt. Of the remaining justices, all but Justice Reed had been appointed by Harry Truman. Are these facts of any significance in explaining the justices' votes in *Douds*?

2.　In an unpublished opinion in *Douds,* Justice Reed wrote: "A government need not supinely await open attack. Not only may it punish overt acts of sedition but also it may demand declarations of loyalty.... Though [the First Amendment] assures open discussion directed toward changing the Constitution by peaceful means, it would abuse that right to twist its guarantee into a cover under which preparations for the overthrow of our constitutional democracy may be carried forward with impunity. Individual beliefs and concerted activities can derive from the First Amendment no greater immunity than it affords to speech and the press."* Does Justice Reed maintain that persons may be constitutionally punished for their beliefs? Is he correct in asserting that individual beliefs have no greater protection under the Constitution than speech or press?

* Stanley Reed Papers, University of Kentucky, Box 126.

3.   After reading Chief Justice Vinson's draft opinion in *Douds,* Justice Frankfurter wrote to him on January 19, 1950, urging that the Court's opinion be written on the broadest ground of agreement possible. "As I understand it," Frankfurter wrote, "no matter how the opinion is written there will be a far-flung dissent by Black. I have no doubt it will be a powerful dissent because it has been long in preparation and enlists deep feelings in him. The issues are bound to stir public feeling. When considering how a result should be stated rather than what a result should be, the repercussion upon public feeling becomes relevant. Not only public feeling but the effect on legislative opinion throughout the country is relevant. To me it is very important not to justify, let alone still further excite, what I regard as a prevailing un-American fear and hysteria—not to encourage still further what seem to me unworthy 'loyalty programs' and heresy-hunting. With Black appealing to and evoking, as he will, the traditional American feelings about tolerance and freedom and the rest, it seems to me profoundly important that the opinion of the Court, particularly when expressed through the Chief Justice, be as detached as possible toward the claim of intrinsic danger from Communist infiltration."** Did Justice Frankfurter accurately predict the nature of Justice Black's dissent? Do you believe that Chief Justice Vinson's opinion satisfied Justice Frankfurter?

THE IMPACT OF DOUDS

Two kinds of unions had challenged Section 9(h) of the Taft–Hartley Law—Communist controlled unions and unions representing miners and steelworkers. The former thought that the issue would rally popular support. The latter were so strong that loss of the NLRB benefits hardly mattered. The Communists had miscalculated. Soon after the *Douds* decision, AFL and CIO units, whose leaders signed the affidavits, moved in and took over the Communist-controlled unions. In time, the dissenters' opinions in *Douds* apparently also had an impact, for the government brought no further prosecutions under Section 9(h), and in 1959 Congress repealed it.

** Frankfurter Papers, Library of Congress, Box 218.

Chapter IV

FREEDOM OF SPEECH AND PRESS:
HISTORICAL BACKGROUND

I. THE PHILOSOPHY OF FREE SPEECH AND PRESS

ON LIBERTY*

This, then, is the appropriate region of human liberty. It comprises
. . . the inward domain of consciousness, demanding liberty of conscience
in the most comprehensive sense, liberty of thought and feeling, absolute
freedom of opinion and sentiment on all subjects, practical or speculative, scientific, moral, or theological. The liberty of expressing and
publishing opinions may seem to fall under a different principle, since it
belongs to that part of the conduct of an individual which concerns other
people, but, being almost of as much importance as the liberty of thought
itself and resting in great part on the same reasons, is practically
inseparable from it. . . .

. . . The beliefs which we have most warrant for, have no safeguard
to rest on, but a standing invitation to the whole world to prove them
unfounded. If the challenge is not accepted, or is accepted and the
attempt fails, we are far enough from certainty still; but we have done
the best that the existing state of human reason admits of; we have
neglected nothing that could give the truth a chance of reaching us: if
the lists are kept open, we may hope that if there be a better truth, it
will be found when the human mind is capable of receiving it; and in the
mean time we may rely on having attained such approach to truth, as is
possible in our own day. This is the amount of certainty attainable by a
fallible being, and this the sole way of attaining it.

Strange it is, that men should admit the validity of the arguments
for free discussion, but object to their being "pushed to an extreme;" not
seeing that unless the reasons are good for an extreme case, they are not
good for any case. Strange that they should imagine that they are not
assuming infallibility when they acknowledge that there should be free
discussion on all subjects which can possibly be *doubtful,* but think that
some particular principle or doctrine should be forbidden to be questioned because it is *so certain,* that is, because *they are certain* that it is
certain. To call any proposition certain, while there is any one who
would deny its certainty if permitted, but who is not permitted, is to
assume that we ourselves, and those who agree with us, are the judges of
certainty, and judges without hearing the other side.

---

* John Stuart Mill, On Liberty, Bobbs–Merrill Co., Inc., 1956, pp. 16, 26–27. Reprinted
with permission.

A CONTEMPORARY ANALYSIS OF FREEDOM OF SPEECH*

What are the effects on a total society of providing the right of free speech? There are three basic effects which philosophers have tended to emphasize. First, in matters of empirical science, free speech allows the truth to have a better chance of getting accepted. The suppression of Galileo and his observation that the earth revolves around the sun rather than vice versa is a case in point.

Second, in matters of normative policy, free speech allows the most effective means toward given ends to have a better chance of getting accepted. For example, suppression of the slavery abolitionists delayed the improved labor productivity per labor expense and the improved capital equipment which free labor promoted.

Third, free speech provides a check on corrupt and inefficient leadership and administrative personnel. Even dictatorships recognize the value of encouraging critics of administrative inefficiency even though they do not encourage criticism of top national officials or fundamental government policy.

Free speech is indirectly responsible for higher standards of living to the extent that free speech promotes scientific discovery and dissemination, more effective means toward given societal goals, and more efficient governmental personnel. This partly explains why [there is] a positive correlation between the level of free speech permissiveness and the level of modernity.... Some of the positive correlation is also due to the reciprocal fact that higher standards of living create a more tolerant middle class which allows still more freedom of speech.

Some critics of free speech argue that it leads to political instability and revolution. The empirical data tend to show just the opposite relation. [There is] a positive correlation between being a country that has a permissive free speech policy and being a country that has a high degree of stability. This relation is partly attributable to the fact that free speech facilitates non-violent change, particularly by providing more peaceful outlets through which potential revolutionaries can make themselves heard and win converts without resorting to revolution. The positive relation between free speech and non-violent change is also partly attributable to the fact that free speech and non-violent change are partly co-effects of having a large tolerant middle class. The correlation between permissiveness and stability is, however, not as high as the correlation between permissiveness and modernity.

NOTE AND QUESTION

Mill's classic defense of freedom of expression argues that all ideas, no matter how abhorrent, must be protected. While that may sound congenial to twentieth century American ears, we must remember that Mill was speaking in the mid-nineteenth century. Does the English and American history as set out in this chapter establish that Framers of the First Amendment intended to reflect arguments similar to Mill's, or did

* Stuart S. Nagel, Improving the Legal Process, Lexington Books, 1975, pp. 42, 44. Reprinted with permission.

the Framers intend that the arguments for freedom of expression not be "pushed to an extreme"?

II. FREEDOM OF SPEECH AND PRESS IN ENGLAND*

Historical Trends

The law of speech and press as it existed in England and America at the time of the American Revolution was the result of a historical development of long duration. From the beginning concern for the security of the state and the preservation of the public peace motivated whatever measures were adopted, whether by legislative enactment or by judicial interpretation, however oppressive the measures happened to be. . . .

The era . . . [of] development . . . was turbulent. During much of it neither organized police nor standing armies existed and private war was not unknown. To a considerable extent, severity of law and of punishment were relied on for the preservation of the public peace.

At the time of the adoption of the American Constitution, the only guarantee of freedom of speech that existed in England was that of freedom of speech and debate in Parliament. But even this was established only after a long struggle between the Crown and Parliament. . . .

To trace the history of . . . [the law of speech and press] in England the starting point is the statute *De Scandalis Magnatum* enacted in 1275 which was political in nature and had as its object the preservation of the realm rather than the redress of private wrong. It provided for imprisonment of anyone who should disseminate false news or "tales" from which discord might result between the king and his people. The statute was re-enacted in 1378 to include peers, prelates, justices, and various other officials. . . . [Later] re-enactments . . . added "seditious words" to the statute. With this new provision, vague or general words that could not support an action at common law could support such an action under the statute if spoken of a "magnate." The truth could not be pleaded as a defense.

The statute *De Scandalis Magnatum* is significant. It was a criminal law which punished political scandal. It was administered by the Court of Star Chamber once its administration by the Common Law Courts was considered ineffectual.

The Court of Star Chamber was originally that part of the King's Council which sat in the "starred chambre" at Westminster to handle administrative and judicial matters, as distinguished from that part of the Council which followed the King. . . .

To a great extent the Star Chamber was responsible for the evolution of censorship and the law of seditious libel. Its intervention was largely due to the invention of printing, and it was to preserve order that it undertook to suppress defamation likely to endanger the safety of the government. . . .

---

* Edward Gerard Hudon, Freedom of Speech and Press in America, Public Affairs Press, 1963, pp. 8–15. Reprinted with permission.

During the reign of Elizabeth the Star Chamber effectively controlled printing and publishing by censorship, a measure that was thought essential for the peace and security of the state. Its ordinance of 1585 required a special license to print a book and it established a monopoly of printing in the Stationers' Company composed of ninety-seven London stationers. This company was empowered to seize all publications by outsiders; offenders were brought before the Star Chamber. In 1637 printing was further regulated by another ordinance which limited the number of printers, presses, and apprentices....

As the law was administered by the Court of Star Chamber the security of the state was regarded as imperilled by seditious libel against the rulers of the state. Moreover, the maintenance of peace was considered threatened by libels on individuals, especially if they were influential.... Some measure of control was necessary: "*If it be against a private man it deserves a severe punishment,* for although the libel be made against one, yet it incites all those of the same family, kindred, or society to revenge, and so tends *per consequens* to quarrels and breach of the peace, and may be the cause of shedding of blood, and of great inconvenience: *if it be against a magistrate, or other public person, it is a greater offence;* for it concerns not only the breach of the peace, but also the scandal of government; for what greater scandal of government can there be than to have corrupt or wicked magistrates to be appointed and constituted by the King to govern his subjects under him? And greater imputation to the state cannot be, than to suffer such corrupt men to sit in the sacred seat of justice, or to have any meddling in or concerning the administration of justice."

The Star Chamber was so efficient in its prosecution of libels that in one case an author was fined £10,000, given a sentence of life imprisonment, branded on the forehead, his nose slit and his ears cut off. His crime consisted of having expressed a dislike for actors and acting in a book. This was looked upon as directed against the Queen who had recently taken part in a play, and therefore against the government.... With the abolition of the Star Chamber in 1641 the Common Law Courts assumed or inherited the position of *custos moram** of the realm and absorbed the entire jurisdiction over defamation. At first, these courts were hampered by the necessity of establishing a malicious intent, a finding of fact by a jury. But seditious libels affected the state and it became accepted that the intentional publication of a document, seditious or defamatory in character, constituted the offense. The jury merely determined the fact of intentional publication, the court decided as a question of law whether or not the publication was seditious or defamatory.

When it is realized that during this era it was treason to so much as imagine the King's death, it can readily be understood why political libels were the order of the day. And these were carried to such limits that in 1684 Sir Samuel Barnardiston was tried, convicted, and fined for expressing political opinions in a private letter written to a friend.

* Guardian of the morals.

In 1731 Richard Francklin was tried for publishing "A letter from the Hague" in his newspaper, *The Craftsman*. This was an opposition paper and the letter was critical of the government's foreign policy. An offer to prove the truth of the matter published was rejected by Lord Chief Justice Raymond. He said, "It is my opinion, that it is not material whether the facts charged in a libel be true or false, ..." The Chief Justice then pointed out the serious nature of libels against private individuals, and the even more serious nature of libels against public officials. These were said "to sow sedition, and disturb the peace of the Kingdom." ...

The law of the press as it existed in England at the end of the eighteenth century was probably best summarized by Blackstone as follows: "The liberty of the press is indeed essential to the nature of a free state; but this consists in laying no *previous* restraints upon publications, and not in freedom from censure for criminal matter when published. Every freeman has an undoubted right to lay what sentiments he pleases before the public; to forbid this, is to destroy the freedom of the press: but if he publishes what is improper, mischievous, or illegal, he must take the consequences of his own temerity."

Only after the Constitution of the United States and its First Amendment had been adopted did the Fox Libel Act become law in England.... [T]his act of 1792 enlarged the scope of the jury's function in libel cases and authorized a general verdict of guilty or not guilty upon the whole matter put in issue. The jury could no longer be directed by the presiding judge to find the defendant guilty merely upon proof of publication.

But even after the passage of the Fox Libel Act, trials for political and seditious libel continued. Indeed, they were as common as before, if not more so. In fact, on December 18, 1792, subsequent to the passage of the act, the prosecution of Thomas Paine for publishing *The Rights of Man* took place. As soon as the defense had been presented in the case, Paine was convicted by a jury that expressed the desire to hear neither reply nor summing-up. In effect, the Fox Libel Act substituted the jury for the judge and as late as 1914 Dicey could assert that "Freedom of discussion is then, in England, little else than the right to write or say anything which a jury, consisting of twelve shopkeepers, think it expedient should be said or written."

III. FREEDOM OF SPEECH AND PRESS
IN COLONIAL AMERICA*

... Colonial America was the scene of the most extraordinary diversity of opinion on religion, politics, social structure, and other vital subjects, but every community, particularly outside of the few "cities," tended to be a tight little island clutching its own respective orthodoxy and too eager to banish or extralegally punish unwelcome dissidents. As John P. Roche says so strikingly, "Colonial America was an open society

* Leonard W. Levy, Legacy of Suppression, Harvard University Press, 1960, pp. 18–21, 141–142, 164, 179–80, 187. Reprinted with permission.

dotted with closed enclaves, and one could generally settle with his co-believers in safety and comfort and exercise the right of oppression."

Where vigorously expressed nonconformist opinions were suffered to exist by the community, they were likely to run afoul of the law. In colonial America, as in England, the common law of criminal libel was strung out like a chicken wire of constraint against the captious and the chancy, making the open discussion of public issues hazardous, if not impossible, except when public opinion opposed administration policy. However, the judiciary in America, particularly in the eighteenth century, was not the agency that menaced those who would disturb an acquiescent public opinion. . . .

The traditionally maligned judges were, as a matter of fact, virtually angels of self-restraint when compared with the intolerance of community opinion or the tyranny of the governors who, acting in a quasi-judicial capacity with their Councils, were a much more dreaded and active instrument of suppression than the common-law courts. Yet the most suppressive body by far, . . . was that acclaimed bastion of the people's liberties: the popularly elected Assembly. . . . The law of seditious libel, particularly in the eighteenth century, was enforced in America chiefly by the provincial legislatures exercising their power of punishing alleged breaches of parliamentary privilege, secondly, by the executive officers in concert with the upper houses, and lastly, a poor third, by the common-law courts. The latter gathered a very few seditious scalps and lost as many to acquittals; but the Assemblies, like the House of Commons which they emulated, needing no grand jury to indict and no petty jury to convict, racked up a far larger score.

Zealously pursuing its prerogative of being immune to criticism, an Assembly might summon, interrogate, and fix criminal penalties against anyone who had supposedly libeled its members, proceedings, or the government generally. Any words, written, printed, or spoken, which were imagined to have a tendency of impeaching an Assembly's behavior, questioning its authority, derogating from its honor, affronting its dignity, or defaming its members, individually or together, were regarded as a seditious scandal against the government, punishable as a breach of privilege. The historian of *Parliamentary Privilege in the American Colonies* concludes, in guarded understatement, "Literally scores of persons, probably hundreds, throughout the colonies were tracked down by the various messengers and sergeants and brought into the house to make inglorious submission for words spoken in the heat of anger or for writings which intentionally or otherwise had given offense."

In 1753, the colonial understanding of the scope of free expression was . . . revealed by an editorial in *The Independent Reflector,* the voice of the New York "Triumvirate," William Livingston, John Morin Scott, and William Smith, young lawyers with republican ideas and a passion to be heard. When an opposition paper refused to publish a rejoinder composed by one of them, they published a credo on liberty of the press:

> A Printer ought not to publish every Thing that is offered to him; but what is conducive of general Utility, he should not refuse, be the Author a Christian, Jew, Turk or Infidel. Such

Refusal is an immediate abridgement of the Freedom of the Press. When on the other Hand, he prostitutes his Art by the Publication of any Thing injurious to his Country, it is criminal.... It is high Treason against the State. The usual Alarm rung in such Cases, the common Cry of an Attack upon the LIBERTY OF THE PRESS, is groundless and trifling. The Press neither has, nor can have such a Liberty, and whenever it is assumed, the Printer should be punished.

The revolutionary controversy with England did wonders for the expansion and vitality of the colonial press, because the patriot leaders discovered the secret of propaganda. The press, along with pulpit, platform, and parliamentary forum, became an enormously effective vehicle for advertising the Whig position, and so long as England maintained control of the situation, the revolutionary journalists, whose newspapers doubled in number between 1763 and 1775, unceasingly urged the value of open debate.... The royal judges and their common law of seditious libel were identified with Star Chamber tyranny on the slightest suggestion that patriot propagandists were licentiously abusing their privileges of free speech and press....

[However] John Adams' writings suggest the manner in which the patriots did somersaults with the common law of seditious libel. Back in 1765, when the British were in control, Adams had written an essay for the *Boston Gazette* in which he addressed his publishers, Edes and Gill, in the following brave words:

The stale, impudent insinuations of slander and sedition, with which the gormandizers of power have endeavored to discredit your paper, are so much the more to your honor; for the jaws of power are always stretched out, if possible, to destroy the freedom of thinking, speaking, and writing.... Be not intimidated, therefore, by any terrors, from publishing with the utmost freedom *whatever* can be warranted by the laws of your country....

By 1774, when the "jaws of power" were beginning to grow American incisors, Adams began to sound more like [Thomas Hutchinson, Chief Justice of the royal court in Massachusetts].... [Hutchinson] and Adams were in agreement on the fundamental principle that abuse of the press, as each respectively understood it, was a thing apart from the true liberty of the press. By early 1776 Adams ... proposed that making adherence to the independence movement the legal test of loyalty would have the beneficial result of stopping "unfriendly" papers. Then, "the presses will produce no more seditious or traitorous speculations. Slanders upon public men and measures will be lessened."

The evidence forces the conclusion that Chief Justice Hutchinson had accurately summarized the situation when he acidly observed that the Adamses and their supporters were "contending for an unlimited Freedom of Thought and Action, which they would confine wholly to themselves." Free speech for one side only is not free speech at all, or at best is an extraordinarily narrow concept of it. That, indeed, is the whole point: during the entire colonial period, from the time of the first settlements to the Revolutionary War and the framing of the first bills of rights, America had very little experience with freedom of speech or press as a meaningful condition of life.

QUESTIONS

1. Is the story of colonial repression already familiar to you? Why do you suppose that Levy is painting this rather vivid portrait? In order to contrast it later on with the equally familiar, greatly more enlightened era ushered in by the Declaration of Independence?

2. Are you at all bothered by John Adams' "somersault"?

IV. THE MIND OF THE REVOLUTIONARY GENERATION*

Our main task, therefore, is to ascertain the nature and scope of the policy which finds expression in the First Amendment to the United States Constitution. . . .

One theory construes the First Amendment as enacting Blackstone's statement that "the liberty of the press . . . consists in laying no *previous* restraints upon publications and not in freedom from censure for criminal matter when published." The line where legitimate suppression begins is fixed chronologically at the time of publication. The government cannot interfere by a censorship or injunction *before* the words are spoken or printed, but can punish them as much as it pleases *after* publication, no matter how harmless or essential to the public welfare the discussion may be. . . .

This Blackstonian theory dies hard, but it ought to be knocked on the head once for all. In the first place, Blackstone was not interpreting a constitution, but trying to state the English law of his time, which had no censorship and did have extensive libel prosecutions. Whether or not he stated that law correctly, an entirely different view of the liberty of the press was soon afterwards enacted in Fox's Libel Act, . . . so that Blackstone's view does not even correspond to the English law of the last hundred and twenty-five years. . . .

The framers of the First Amendment make it plain that they regarded freedom of speech as very important; "absolutely necessary" is Luther Martin's phrase. But they say very little about its exact meaning. That should not surprise us . . . [since] [m]en rarely define their inspirations until they are forced into doing so by sharp antagonism. Therefore, it is not until the Sedition Law of 1798 made the limits of liberty of the press a concrete and burning issue that we get much helpful expression of opinion on our problem. Before that time, however, we have a few important pieces of evidence to show that the words were used in the Constitution in a wide and liberal sense.

On October 26, 1774, the Continental Congress issued an address to the inhabitants of Quebec, declaring that the English colonists had five invaluable rights, representative government, trial by jury, liberty of the person, easy tenure of land, and freedom of the press:

* Zechariah Chafee, Free Speech in the United States, Harvard University Press, 1941, pp. 7, 16–19. Reprinted with permission.

The last right we shall mention regards the freedom of the press. The importance of this consists, besides the advancement of truth, science, morality and arts in general, in its diffusion of liberal sentiment on the administration of government, its ready communication of thoughts between subjects, and its consequential promotion of union among them, whereby oppressive officials are shamed or intimidated into more honorable and just modes of conducting affairs.

In 1785 Virginia, which was the first state to insert a clause protecting the liberty of the press in its constitution (1776), enacted a statute drawn by Jefferson for Establishing Religious Freedom. This opened with a very broad principle of toleration: "Whereas, Almighty God hath created the mind free: that all attempts to influence it by temporal punishments or burthens, or by civil incapacitations, tend only to beget habits of hypocrisy and meanness." Though this relates specifically to religion, it shows the trend of men's thoughts, and the meaning which "liberty" had to Jefferson long before the bitter controversy of 1798.

Benjamin Franklin, in discussing the brief "freedom of speech" clause in the Pennsylvania Constitution of 1776, said in 1789 that if by the liberty of the press were to be understood merely the liberty of discussing the propriety of public measures and political opinions, let us have as much of it as you please. On the other hand, if it means liberty to calumniate another, there ought to be some limit.

The reason given by the Maryland convention of 1788 to the people for including a free speech clause in the proposed federal Bill of Rights was: "In prosecutions in the federal courts, for libels, the constitutional preservation of this great and fundamental right may prove invaluable."

The contemporaneous evidence in the passages just quoted shows that in the years before the First Amendment freedom of speech was conceived as giving a wide and genuine protection for all sorts of discussion of public matters. These various statements are, of course, absolutely inconsistent with any Blackstonian theory that liberty of the press forbids nothing except censorship. The men of 1791 went as far as Blackstone, and much farther.

All through the eighteenth century, however, there existed beside this definite legal meaning of liberty of the press, a definite popular meaning: the right of unrestricted discussion of public affairs. There can be no doubt that this was in a general way what freedom of speech meant to the framers of the Constitution. Thus Madison, who drafted the First Amendment, bases his explanation of it in 1799 on "the essential difference between the British Government and the American constitutions." In the United States the people and not the government possess the absolute sovereignty, and the legislature as well as the executive is under limitations of power. Hence, Congress is not free to punish anything which was criminal at English common law. A government which is "elective, limited and responsible" in all its branches may well be supposed to require "a greater freedom of animadversion" than might be tolerated by one that is composed of an irresponsible hereditary king and upper house, and an omnipotent legislature.

This contemporary testimony corroborates the conclusions of Professor Schofield:

> One of the objects of the Revolution was to get rid of the English common law on liberty of speech and of the press.... Liberty of the press as declared in the First Amendment, and the English common-law crime of sedition, cannot co-exist.

NOTE

The historical analysis provided by Chafee is widely, but not universally, accepted. Levy argues for a different interpretation of the historical evidence. He puts his case as follows:*

> We may even have to confront the possibility that the intentions of the Framers were not the most libertarian and their insights on the subject of freedom of expression not the most edifying. But this should be expected since the Framers were nurtured on the crabbed historicism of Coke and the narrow conservatism of Blackstone. The ways of thought of a lifetime are not easily broken. The Declaration of Independence severed the political connection with England but the American states continued the English common-law system.
>
> A long war for independence is scarcely a propitious time for the birth and nurturing of freedom of expression or any civil liberties. Everywhere there was unlimited liberty to praise the American cause; criticism of it brought the zealots of patriotism with tar and feathers. Even on the rare occasion when some revolutionist might ritualistically reaffirm devotion to freedom of expression, there was a tacit understanding that "liberty of speech," as Professor Schlesinger has so aptly said, "belonged solely to those who spoke the speech of liberty."

Some of the evidence used by Levy is the same as that presented in the Chafee excerpt. Concerning the Quebec declaration quoted by Chafee, Levy states:*

> But the noble libertarianism of the Quebec declaration of 1774 was not for home consumption, since its most significant phrase stressed the diffusion of "liberal sentiments." Illiberal, that is, loyalist sentiments were simply suppressed.... Its true meaning, ... was revealed by Congress itself just fifteen months later in a recommendation to the states that they take appropriate measures against "erroneous opinions."

One of the greatest burdens on free expression was the imported English common law of seditious libel. Chafee contended, quoting with approval the view of Professor Schofield, that "One of the objects of the

---

* Levy, Legacy of Suppression, pp. 3, 176.

* Ibid., pp. 177, 188.

Revolution was to get rid of the English common law on liberty of speech
and of the press." Levy disputes this statement.**

>　In the decade between the cessation of hostilities and the
> ratification of the First Amendment (1781–1791), independence
> and peace brought America its first opportunity to develop a
> legal system and a society in which all men were free to express
> their opinions, however unpopular, on any subject, short of
> direct and immediate incitement to crime.... [However] [w]hat
> is significant is the fact that the American states, with the
> possible exceptions of Virginia and Pennsylvania, did not take
> the opportunity of abandoning or seriously limiting the oppres-
> sive common law of seditious libel.

... If it was an object of the Revolution to repudiate *in toto* the well-
known and infamous Blackstone–Mansfield exposition of the common
law's restrictions on freedom of expression, how very strange it is that
Americans of the revolutionary generation did not say so.

Levy also contended that Benjamin Franklin was not as libertarian
as Chafee made him out to be. Concerning Franklin's remark on freedom
of expression quoted in the Chafee excerpt, Levy wrote:†

> He [Benjamin Franklin] did not express himself, however, on
> the legal remedy for calumny against the government, except to
> remark, in the same article, that as to writers who affront the
> government's reputation, "we should in moderation, content
> ourselves with tarring and feathering and tossing them in a
> blanket." ... Whatever Franklin intended by the remark, it had
> ugly overtones. More than likely his endorsement of unlimited
> discussion was understood to be hedged by the qualification that
> verbal criticisms of the government must be guided by modera-
> tion, truth, and good motives....

In conclusion Levy wrote:*

>　No one can say for certain what the Framers had in mind,
> for although the evidence all points in one direction there is not
> enough of it to justify cocksure conclusions. It is not even
> certain that the Framers themselves knew what they had in
> mind; that is, at the time of the drafting and ratification of the
> First Amendment, few among them if any at all clearly under-
> stood what they meant by the free speech-and-press clause, and
> it is perhaps doubtful that those few agreed except in a general-
> ized way and equally doubtful that they represented a consen-
> sus....
>
>　What is clear is that there exists no evidence to suggest an
> understanding that a constitutional guarantee of free speech or
> press meant the impossibility of future prosecutions of seditious
> utterances. The traditional libertarian interpretation of the

** Ibid., pp. 182, 190.

† Ibid., p. 187.

* Ibid., p. 236.

original meaning of the First Amendment is surely subject to the Scottish verdict: not proven.

There is a considerable historical debate taking place between Chafee and Levy. Many of the pieces of evidence used by each author are common to both readings, but the conclusions drawn from them are quite different.

Levy clearly does *not* view the Revolutionary Era as greatly more enlightened than colonial times. Indeed, his point is that the ideas and practices of the earlier period, far from being repudiated, were embraced by the Founders. In arguing thus, he takes direct aim at Chafee and other "traditionalists."

James Morton Smith responded to Levy as follows:**

> Most writers, revisionists or not, seem to agree that 1798 was a turning point in libertarian theorizing, and the chief disagreement seems to be over the pace of the switchover from the restrictive Blackstonian principles to the "new libertarianism." Did the new theory, as Levy contends, suddenly erupt in America in 1798 like an underwater volcano thrusting upward from the ocean floor to form "a new promontory of libertarian thought jutting out of a stagnant Blackstonian sea"? Or was it the culmination of a prolonged exploration of the meaning of self-government, the working out of the implication of the concept that government rests on the consent of the governed?

> By identifying dissent with disaffection and disloyalty, the Federalists in 1794 clearly marked out the path they were to follow in their alien and sedition system of 1798; by defending the rights of a free press—even the rights of allegedly seditious libelers—the Republicans sketched the basis of the libertarian theory which they elaborated in 1798–1800. Nothing, Madison asserted, could be more indefensible in reason or more dangerous in practice than the proposition that "the Government may stifle all censure whatever on its misdoings; for if it be itself the Judge, it will never allow any censures to be just; and if it can suppress censures flowing from one lawful source, it may those flowing from any other—from the press and from individuals, as well as from Societies, etc."

> Essentially, what Madison and his Republican colleagues did in 1794 and later in 1798, as the Federalists had done in the Confederation period, was to argue against the principle of legislative sovereignty as the sole reflection of the people. By emphasizing the sovereignty of the people, they fragmented the monolithic concept of the people into individuals; by stressing the power of the public in a republic, they put a premium on opinion expressed by the people at large, who could comment on the constituted authorities—individually or in self-constituted

---

** James Morton Smith, Freedom's Fetters: The Alien and Sedition Laws and American Civil Liberties. Cornell University Press, 1966, pp. x–xi, xiv–xv. Reprinted with permission.

societies, orally or in newspapers and pamphlets—without running the risk of prosecution for sedition.

The "new libertarian" theory of 1794 and 1798 was not a sudden breakthrough in American political thought. It was tied inextricably to the altered relation of the people and government worked out between 1760 and 1776; only gradually did legal theory and practice catch up with the cataclysmic and unexpected changes wrought in American political thought by the Revolution.

Which view is more convincing? Why? What difference does it make if a Supreme Court justice accepts the traditional interpretation or the revisionist interpretation?

V. FIRST TEST OF THE FOUNDERS' INTENT: THE SEDITION ACT OF 1798

One of the most important events in the history of the First Amendment occurred seven years after ratification. The Sedition Act of 1798, passed largely in response to the seeming imminence of war with France, punished, among other things, false, scandalous and malicious writings against the Government of the United States. This law, patterned after the English law of seditious libel, never reached the United States Supreme Court because the Court did not at that time have jurisdiction to review convictions in federal criminal cases. However, a number of Supreme Court justices, sitting as trial judges, enforced the law with considerable vigor against critics of the Federalist administration. Is the Sedition Act evidence that the First Amendment meant to leave government wide-ranging powers to punish dangerous critics? Or was the Sedition Act a model of the kind of law that violates freedom of speech and freedom of the press?

"AN ACT FOR THE PUNISHMENT OF CERTAIN CRIMES AGAINST THE UNITED STATES"

1 Stat. 596, July 14, 1798.

Sec. 2. *And be it further enacted,* That if any person shall write, print, utter or publish, or shall cause to procure to be written, printed, uttered or published, or shall knowingly and willingly assist or aid in writing, printing, uttering or publishing any false, scandalous and malicious writing or writings against the government of the United States, or either house of the Congress of the United States, or the President of the United States, with intent to defame the said government, or either house of the said Congress, or the said President, or to bring them, or either of them, into contempt or disrepute; or to excite against them, or either or any of them, the hatred of the good people of the United States, or to stir up sedition within the United States, or to excite any unlawful combination therein, for opposing or resisting any law of the United States, or any act of the President of the United States, done in pursuance of any such law, or of the powers in him vested by the constitution of the United States, or to resist, oppose, or defeat any such law or act, or to aid, encourage or abet any hostile designs of any foreign nation against the United States, their people or government, then such person, being thereof convicted before any court of the United States having jurisdiction thereof, shall be punished by a fine not exceeding two thousand dollars, and by imprisonment not exceeding two years.

Sec. 3. *And be it further enacted and declared,* That if any person shall be prosecuted under this act, for the writing or publishing any libel aforesaid, it shall be lawful for the defendant, upon the trial of the cause, to give in evidence in his defence, the truth of the matter contained in the publication charged as a libel. And the jury who shall try the cause, shall have a right to determine the law and the fact, under the direction of the court, as in other cases.

RESOLUTIONS OF VIRGINIA OF DECEMBER 21, 1798 AND MADISON'S REPORT THEREON*

Resolved, ... that the General Assembly doth particularly protest against the palpable and alarming infractions of the Constitution, in the ... case of the "... sedition-act," passed at the last session of Congress, ... which act exercises ... a power not delegated by the Constitution, but on the contrary expressly and positively forbidden by one of the amendments thereto; a power which more than any other ought to produce universal alarm, because it is levelled against that right of freely examining public characters and measures, and of free communication among the people thereon, which has ever been justly deemed the only effectual guardian of every other right.

Let the question be asked, then, whether the power over the press, exercised in the "sedition-act," be found among the powers expressly vested in the Congress? This is not pretended.

Is there any express power, for executing which it is a necessary and proper power?

The power which has been selected, as least remote, in answer to this question, is that "of suppressing insurrections;" which is said to imply a power to prevent insurrections, by punishing whatever may lead or tend to them. But, it surely cannot, with the least plausibility, be said, that a regulation of the press, and a punishment of libels, are exercises of a power to suppress insurrections.

... [T]he construction employed to justify the "sedition-act," would exhibit a phenomenon, without a parallel in the political world. It would exhibit a number of respectable states, as denying first that any power over the press was delegated by the Constitution; as proposing next, that an amendment to it, should explicitly declare that no such power was delegated; and finally, as concurring in an amendment actually recognizing or delegating such a power.

Is then the federal government, it will be asked, destitute of every authority for restraining the licentiousness of the press, and for shielding itself against the libellous attacks which may be made on those who administer it?

* Elliot's Debates, J.B. Lippincott & Co., 1861, vol. 4, pp. 528–529, 568, 572–73.

The Constitution alone can answer this question. If no such power be expressly delegated, and if it be not both necessary and proper to carry into execution an express power; above all if it be expressly forbidden, by a declaratory amendment to the Constitution,—the answer must be, that the federal government is destitute of all such authority.

REPUBLICAN OPPOSITION TO THE FEDERAL SEDITION ACT*

Even though the war with France stubbornly refused to burst into open flame, the domestic caldron was seething ominously. For, in their efforts to suppress "Jacobinism" at home, the Federalists kindled a fire which gravely menaced freedom of speech and of the press.

The so-called American Reign of Terror, unlike that of France, was the work of conservatives bent upon upholding the established order. One of the principal benefits the Federalists expected to derive from all-out war with France was the proscription of the "internal enemies" of the government—in which category they placed most of the leaders of the Republican party. It was these "servile minions of France," they asserted, who had encouraged the Directory to believe that Americans were alienated from their own government, who tormented discord between the United States and Great Britain, and who strove "to immolate the independence and welfare of their country at the shrine of France." Under the name of liberty, the Federalists complained, these "democrats, mobocrats & all other kinds of rats" opposed the war effort and heaped obloquy and contempt upon the highest officers of the government. "Even the Nursery is not exempt from the unremitting efforts of these disturbers of the human race," exclaimed an agitated Federalist. Through the medium of childrens' books, the Jacobins were making "a truly diabolical effort to corrupt the minds of the Rising Generation, to make them imbibe, with their very milk, as it were, the poison of atheism and disaffection."

So eager were the Federalists to take action against their political enemies that during June–July, 1798, without waiting for a formal declaration of war, they pushed through Congress four acts which imposed curbs upon freedom of speech and of the press and curtailed the liberty of foreigners in the United States....

The Act for the Punishment of Certain Crimes, popularly known as the Sedition Act, passed the House of Representatives by a narrow sectional majority; the vote was forty-four to forty-one and only two members from south of the Potomac voted aye.... While the act in its final form prescribed heavy fines and imprisonment for those judged guilty of writing, publishing, or speaking anything of "a false, scandalous and malicious" nature against the government or any officer of the government, it actually ameliorated several of the oppressive rules established by the common law. Under the common law, truth was not a defense, malicious intent need not be proved, and it was given to the judge to decide whether the matter was libelous. The Sedition Act made

* Abridged from John C. Miller, The Federalist Era 1789–1801, Harper & Row, 1960, pp. 228–237. Reprinted with permission.

truth a defense, made the jury judge of the fact of libel, and required proof of malicious intent.

The Sedition Act was not as harsh as the British Treasonable Practices Act passed in 1795 immediately after the King had been attacked on his way to Parliament. By that law, drastic restrictions were imposed upon the press and the right of assemblage and even legitimate forms of party activity were proscribed. Instead, the Federalist lawmakers sought to eliminate from the Sedition Act "those elements in English law to which objections had been persistently made on both sides of the Atlantic during the eighteenth century." For this reason, it was asserted that the Sedition Act was "remarkable for its lenity and humanity: No honest man need to dread such laws as these."

In July, 1798, when the Sedition Act was adopted, few Federalists doubted that the country would soon be involved in a declared war with France. In that sense, it was a war measure designed to supplement the acts for strengthening the armed forces of the country. . . . [I]n the Alien and Sedition Acts, as viewed by Federalists, the national government was doing no more than self-preservation required. Because of this overriding necessity, the Bill of Rights, by the Federalists' reckoning, could not debar the Federal government from imposing restraints upon freedom of speech and of the press. Harrison Gray Otis succinctly defined the attitude of his party when he declared in Congress that "to punish licentiousness and sedition is not a restraint or abridgment of the freedom of speech or of the press"; there was no absolute right, he observed, to publish whatever one pleased. Certainly it was never intended, a Federalist newspaper pointed out, that freedom of speech should cover "the most groundless and malignant lies, striking at the safety and existence of the nation. . . . It never was intended that the right to side with the enemies of one country in slandering and vilifying the government, and dividing the people should be protected under the name of the Liberty of the Press." When the country was beset by enemies, said Judge Addison of the Pennsylvania Supreme Court, Americans could not afford the luxury of discussing both sides of a question: "Truth," he remarked "has but one side, and listening to error and falsehood is indeed a strange way to discover truth." In the opinion of this Federalist jurist, "all truths are not useful or proper for publication: therefore all truths are not to be written, printed or published."

Even without the sanction of a wartime emergency, the Sedition Act was constitutional because, according to Federalist theory, the Federal Constitution endowed the national government with cognizance over all cases arising under the common law. Seditious and defamatory speaking or writing being a crime at common law, it followed that in the Sedition Act the Federal government was not overstepping its constitutional mandate. In every state of the Union the government and its officials were protected by statute or common law against the practices which the Sedition Act laid under duress. No Federalist was willing to admit that in this regard the states possessed larger powers than did the Federal government.

Acting upon the maxim that "Government should be a terror to evil doers," the Federalist administration brought fifteen indictments under the Sedition Act. Of these only ten resulted in conviction and punishment. The four leading Republican newspapers—the *General Advertiser,* the New York *Argus,* the Richmond *Examiner,* and the Boston *Independent Chronicle*—were attacked and three of the most prominent Republican editors—Thomas Cooper, James Callender, and William Duane—were convicted of violating the law. The moving spirit behind many of these prosecutions was Secretary of State Timothy Pickering, vigorously abetted by Justice Samuel Chase of the United States Supreme Court. Chase's grossly partisan conduct as a presiding judge served as the basis for the impeachment proceedings later brought against him by the Jeffersonian Republicans. Truth did not prove to be an effective defense to Republican journalists accused of violating the Sedition Act because their charges were for the most part palpable falsehoods.

Among the most conspicuous victims of the Sedition Act was Matthew Lyon, the "Spitting Lyon" from Vermont. . . .

In July, 1798, at the instigation of his political enemies in Vermont Lyon was indicted on the charge of having published in the Vermont *Journal* libelous statements against President John Adams (a rehash of the strictures he had passed upon Adams from the floor of Congress), together with a letter from Joel Barlow, a Connecticut Yankee who had gone to Paris and turned revolutionist. At his trial, held in Rutland, Vermont, in the summer of 1798, Lyon based his defense upon the unconstitutionality of the Sedition Act. But Justice Paterson of the United States Supreme Court refused to admit this line of argument and the jury found Lyon guilty as charged. . . . [T]he judge sentenced Lyon to four months' imprisonment and imposed a fine of $1,000. . . .

The Federalists hailed Lyon's downfall as a memorable victory of government over "the licentiousness of the press" and the "unbridled spirit of opposition to government." In actuality, however, they had succeeded only in making Lyon a Republican martyr to the cause of freedom of the press. From his cell, Lyon wrote letters and articles which were widely reprinted in Republican newspapers and thereby drew national attention to the kind of rough justice meted out by Federalist-dominated courts. As a result, in December, 1798, he was re-elected to Congress even though he was still serving a prison term under a Federal offense. He took his seat in Congress, where, it was observed, he looked "remarkably well for a gentleman just out of jail." A few years later, he had his revenge upon his persecutors: in the election of 1801 he cast the decisive vote which made Thomas Jefferson President of the United States.

The Alien and Sedition Acts were denounced as "the most diabolical laws that were ever attempted to be imposed on a free and enlightened people" and they gave substance to the Republicans' charge that the Federalists made war upon liberty. Nevertheless, while opposing the exercise of power by the Federal government, the Republicans did not question the principle that government must punish libels—they merely demanded that such prosecutions be undertaken by the states rather than by the Federal government. Accordingly, when they came into power, the Republicans transferred these trials from Federal to state courts, where the common law was enforced in all its rigor.

NOTES AND QUESTIONS

1. However sincere Jefferson may have been in his opposition to *federal* sedition laws, he could be astute in urging *state* prosecutions when irritated with the press. Thus, in 1803, while he was President, he wrote to Governor McKean of Pennsylvania:*

> The federalists having failed in destroying the freedom of press by their gag-law, seem to have attacked it in an opposite form, that is by pushing it's licentiousness & it's lying to such a degree of prostitution as to deprive it of all credit. And the fact is that so abandoned are the tory presses in this particular that even the least informed of the people have learnt that nothing in a newspaper is to be believed. This is a dangerous state of things, and the press ought to be restored to its credibility if possible. The restraints provided by the laws of the states are sufficient for this if applied. And I have therefore long thought that a few prosecutions of the most prominent offenders would have a wholesome effect in restoring the integrity of the presses. Not a general prosecution, for that would look like persecution: but a selected one.... If the same thing be done in some other of the states it will place the whole band more on their guard.

Jefferson enclosed a copy of an offending newspaper—to illustrate his point.

2. The Sedition Act was consistent with the reforms in English law accomplished by Fox's Libel Act (1792). The Libel Act allowed the jury to determine questions of both law and fact, and permitted evidence of truth as a defense—but it did nothing to change the theory of seditious libel. Indeed, in England, as in America, a wave of prosecutions followed the adoption of such rules.

3. Like the historians, the United States Supreme Court has experienced some difficulty in ascertaining the "original" meaning of the First Amendment. For example, Justice Holmes, on first encountering the problem, thought that the Constitution forbade "all such *previous restraints* upon publication as had been practiced by other governments" but not "the subsequent punishment of such as may be deemed contrary to the public welfare."* Twelve years later, and perhaps under the influence of his good friend, Chafee, Holmes recanted:**

> I wholly disagree with the argument of the Government that the First Amendment left the common law as to seditious libel in force. History seems to me against the notion. I had conceived that the United States through many years had shown its repentance for the Sedition Act of 1798, by repaying

---

* Paul L. Ford, ed., The Writings of Thomas Jefferson, G.P. Putnam's Sons, 1897, vol. 8, pp. 218–219.

* Patterson v. Colorado, 205 U.S. 454, 462 (1907).

** Abrams v. United States, 250 U.S. 616, 630–631 (1919).

fines that it imposed. Only the emergency that makes it immediately dangerous to leave the correction of evil counsels to time
warrants making any exception to the sweeping command,
"Congress shall make no law ... abridging the freedom of
speech." ... I regret that I cannot put into more impressive
words my belief that in their conviction upon this indictment
the defendants were deprived of their rights under the Constitution of the United States.

The latter view, which Holmes advanced in dissent, has since received
the imprimatur of a majority of the Court:[†]

> Although the Sedition Act was never tested in this Court,
> the attack upon its validity has carried the day in the court of
> history. Fines levied in its prosecution were repaid by Act of
> Congress on the ground that it was unconstitutional. Calhoun,
> reporting to the Senate on February 4, 1836, assumed that its
> invalidity was a matter "which no one now doubts." Jefferson,
> as President, pardoned those who had been convicted and
> sentenced under the Act and remitted their fines, stating: "I
> discharged every person under punishment or prosecution un-
> der the sedition law, because I considered, and now consider,
> that law to be a nullity, as absolute and as palpable as if
> Congress had ordered us to fall down and worship a golden
> image." The invalidity of the Act has also been assumed by
> Justices of this Court.... These views reflect a broad consensus
> that the Act, because of the restraint it imposed upon criticism
> of government and public officials, was inconsistent with the
> First Amendment.

> There is no force in respondent's argument that the consti-
> tutional limitations implicit in the history of the Sedition Act
> apply only to Congress and not to the States. It is true that the
> First Amendment was originally addressed only to action by the
> Federal Government, and that Jefferson, for one, while denying
> the power of Congress "to controul the freedom of the press,"
> recognized such a power in the States. But this distinction was
> eliminated with the adoption of the Fourteenth Amendment and
> the application to the States of the First Amendment's restric-
> tions.

Can this debate over the original intentions of the founders ever be
resolved with certainty? If not, is the problem the impossibility of
mustering the relevant evidence? Of weighing it? Or do our troubles
arise from the studied imprecision of the Framers, who phrased the
Constitution in generalized (almost tentative) terms so that, like Martin
Chuzzlewit's grandnephew, it has no more than "the first idea and
sketchy notion of a face"—and can grow?

And why believe that the Framers possessed the ultimate wisdom
concerning freedom of expression? Suppose that Levy is right about the
meaning of the First Amendment. Would that mean that Congress
should decree, the Executive enforce, courts ratify, or citizens tolerate,

---

† New York Times Co. v. Sullivan, 376 U.S. 254, 276–277 (1964).

new limitations on freedom of expression? In certain circumstances, e.g., actual wartime?

VI. A SURVEY OF FREE SPEECH AND PRESS FROM THE SEDITION ACT THROUGH WORLD WAR I

The expiration of the Alien and Sedition Acts by no means represented a final victory for freedom of expression. The new nation was far too large and diverse for that. Rather, periods of relative freedom alternated with crises in which Federal or state legal action or often simply illegal mob violence acted as major limitations on free expression.

THE WAR OF 1812*

Though the expression of press opinion is always hampered in war times, the Federalist opposition to the Second War with England was remarkably outspoken, especially in New England. Benjamin Russell wrote in the *Columbian Centinel* again and again of the "waste of blood and property" in a "useless and unnecessary war," and other Federalist papers followed his lead. Their news columns might exult in Yankee victories, but their editorials still spoke of the "bloody hands" of Democratic leaders.

In the states where the war was more popular, however, such boldness was not always permitted to the opposition. In Baltimore, where the *Federal Republican* had protested strongly against the declaration of war, a mob stormed the printshop, wrecked the presses, and tore down the building. The editor retreated to Georgetown, where, with the encouragement of a group of friends, he printed another edition and brought the papers down to Baltimore to distribute them from his house in that city. Meantime the mob had been running wild, destroying property, assaulting bold Federalists, and overawing the city government; and the friends of the *Federal Republican,* knowing the editor's house would be visited by the mob, fortified it for a siege. Two veteran generals of the Revolution were among the defenders.** The mob came promptly. After its first efforts to take the house were driven off, it brought up a cannon and prepared to blow the place up. City authorities then intervened and obtained the promise of the mob leaders to disperse if the garrison would surrender and go to jail. As soon as the men were marched off to the jail, however, the mob destroyed the house, and then stormed the jail and killed all the prisoners they could lay hands upon.

This bloody assault upon the liberty of the press roused a fury of partisan denunciation of Baltimore officials, the Democratic party, and "Madison's War," which died down only as other events of the war crowded the incident out of men's minds.

* Frank Luther Mott, American Journalism. Macmillan Co., 1950, p. 174. Reprinted with permission.

** "Light Horse Harry" Lee and General J.M. Lingan. The former was crippled and the latter killed in the fight.

AFTER THE WAR OF 1812[†]

As Americans after 1815 settled into a stable domestic world, their attitudes and actions demonstrated the value they placed upon freedom of expression. For well over a hundred years, they continued to treat the explicit First Amendment guarantee as a presumption. Their federal government made no move to enact the sort of legislation the amendment proscribed, so that court cases and legal definition were unnecessary. Their state constitutions, unlike Pennsylvania's of 1776 (which had designated freedom of speech as a "right"), generally proscribed only legislation which might limit the practice. The paucity of cases which required judges to explicitly define the extent of permissible expression implied that the controlling forces over dangerous words were those mechanisms within an open society that ensured that improper concepts would fail before convincingly expressed truths.

Americans in the middle period of the 1830s and 1840s placed a high priority upon the power of sheer communication. The oratory of a Daniel Webster or a Henry Clay had the power to convince Supreme Court justices and backwoods constituents alike. Hell-fire religion or sophisticated theological theorizing was best propagated by the words of the revivalist preacher, or the lecturing transcendentalist. Oral persuasion was the medium for reform movements from temperance and women's rights to abolitionism and Fourierism. "So long as a man was confident that the truth of his own doctrines could not fail of acceptance, as soon as they won sufficient circulation, he would not fear diversity of opinion or even the freedom of others to propagate patent falsehoods."

Josiah Warren, the American forerunner of Proudhon and Marx, published a weekly anarchist newspaper, the *Peaceful Revolutionist,* and held meetings in which his unorthodox ideas about everything from education to the futility of capitalist economics were discussed, drawing only occasional murmurs of public protest. Robert Dale Owen, free-thinking son of the patron of the New Harmony experiment, and Frances Wright, brilliant champion of a dozen unpopular causes ranging from black equality to anticlericalism, were absorbed by the tolerant spirit of their day.

Yet subtle restrictions on complete freedom of expression stemmed from the assumptions and values of the society. The theory that free discussion by free men was salutary to truth raised the question of who was a free man. In nineteenth-century America, the answer was one who was master of his own destiny, a man of some substance. As Daniel Webster once put it: "Property ... is the fund out of which the means of protecting life and liberty are usually furnished. We have no experience that teaches us, that any other rights are safe, where property is not safe." John C. Calhoun put it even more directly: "Liberty, equality and freedom are all in a sense dependent on the ownership of property." Or, as certain twentieth-century libertarians liked to remind the public, "those who have power have civil rights."

† From Paul L. Murphy, The Meaning of Freedom of Speech: First Amendment Freedoms from Wilson to FDR, Greenwood Press, 1972, pp. 13–16. Reprinted with permission.

This, however, implied two basic and converse assumptions. Those who did not have power, being without its corollary, property, were to confine their activities to gaining a place within the system. For as Mark Twain remarked: "The American people enjoy three great blessings— free speech, free press and the good sense not to use either." If, however, they unwisely insisted upon speaking out prematurely, they were to do so openly so that their concepts could quickly be rebutted.

Hence, even in the ebullient middle period, certain types of expression elicited censorship by either formal restraint or informal pressures. Americans drew the line when the value of freedom of expression seemed outweighed by the danger to more essential values. The fundamental sanctity of the family, of the essentially Christian establishment, and of the Union were shielded from expression which might undermine them. The story of Mormon persecution and expulsion was frequently appalling. When freedom of conscience led to the advocacy or defense of actions which a popular majority could not sanction, suppression followed.

Restrictions on those who, by speech as well as action, endangered the order found concrete expression as abolitionist strength and raucousness alarmed the South. "To retain political and economic control of the South, the slaveholders felt it necessary that no deep-seated criticism of slavery be tolerated." Every southern state except Kentucky passed laws authorizing public control of speech, press, and discussion, and Andrew Jackson demanded federal censorship of abolitionist literature.

Yet even here a tolerance factor was present. The first application of any of these laws, the arrest in 1839 of Lysander Barrett on a charge of distributing "incendiary publications" in violation of a Virginia statute of 1836, led to acquittal. And in subsequent cases the record of conviction was minimal. Jackson's censorship law, which failed to pass, drew fire from abolitionists and southerners alike. Anti–Slavery Society leaders defiantly told the President, "We never intend to surrender the liberty of speech, or of press, or of conscience—blessings we have inherited from our fathers, and which we mean, so far as we are able, to transmit unimpaired to our children." Only with the emergence of a younger generation of southern judges in the 1850s were legal restrictions formally enforced, although the compelling pressure of public disapprobation was felt early.

Anti–Mason, anti-Mormon, and anti-Catholic crusades by a variety of nativist groups sought less to curtail free expression of supposed enemies than to force them to live by the American norms of an open society. All patriotic participants were to lay their ideas open to the cleansing currents of public opinion. These groups operated in secrecy, and their leaders deluded the membership so that their capacity for weighing true doctrine was blunted. Hence, in order for truth to prevail, it was necessary to break down isolation and uniqueness and force their ideas into the forum where they could be sifted. One end, then, of such assaults on suspect autonomous groups was the preservation of liberty. Those who did not play by the accepted free-speech code surrendered the right to play by their own.

In the realm of less hortatory and more informal forms of communication, especially in relation to coexistence within a stable nineteenth-century community, certain patterns regarding the permissibility of free expression emerge. Deviation in personal beliefs and their expression was sanctioned for those orthodox in their personal life, and, conversely, deviation in personal life was possible by those orthodox as to beliefs. But deviation in both by the same individual could not be tolerated. Certainly the ideas of Ralph Waldo Emerson were startling, as were those of the freethinking agnostic, Robert Ingersoll. Yet Emerson's personal life represented the height of nineteenth-century respectability, and Ingersoll frequently partook at the tables of the rich. The Reverend Henry Ward Beecher, whose ideas were certainly orthodox, was allowed a considerable degree of deviation in his personal morals. Yet the Mormon or Shaker leader who was religiously, politically, and morally unorthodox could not be assimilated by the average community with equanimity. He was too great a threat to the existing order and to its value orientation. His freedom was the freedom to withdraw from the immediate society and either live with those of his kind in isolated communities or seek the anonymity of the city.

THE SLAVERY CONTROVERSY*

Long before the Civil War, public controversy over slavery led to both official and unofficial repressive actions against the abolitionist press. During the Jackson administration Postmaster General Amos Kendall called antislavery papers "most flagitious" and privately advised Southern postmasters to intercept all such matter in the future and to deliver it only to those who would come forward and identify themselves as bona fide subscribers.

The chief weapon against abolitionist freedom of expression, however, was private intimidation, often officially condoned. William Lloyd Garrison was attacked by a mob in Boston in 1835. That same year the office of the Utica *Standard and Democrat* was sacked. James G. Birney's *Philanthropist*, another abolitionist paper, was driven out of Kentucky. He moved it to Cincinnati, where it was mobbed three times in the late 1830s.

Alton, Illinois, in 1837 was the scene of one of the worst outrages against the abolitionist press. The Reverend Elijah P. Lovejoy had engaged in journalism in St. Louis, had entered the Presbyterian ministry, and then established the *Observer,* a religious newspaper with antislavery leanings. As a border slave state, Missouri at the time was often gripped by mob psychology generated in those areas by the slavery question. Lovejoy deplored the disregard for law. In 1836 he quarreled editorially with Judge Luke E. Lawless of St. Louis over the latter's condoning of mob violence against a Negro. Shortly afterward he moved his press across the river to Alton, Illinois, where he hoped to find greater liberty to oppose slavery. But mobs in the free state of Illinois destroyed his press and threw it in the river three times in one year.

* John Lofton, Justice and the Press, Beacon Press, 1966, pp. 19–20. Reprinted with permission.

Meeting under the chairmanship of the attorney general of Illinois, the citizens of Alton proclaimed their "sacred regard for the great principles contained in our Bill of Rights." Yet in the same resolution they warned Lovejoy to give up his press and leave town. The editor responded that he would stay in Alton and "insist on protection" in the exercise of his rights. If the civil authorities refused to protect him, he said: "I must look to God, and if I die, I have determined to make my grave in Alton." On November 7, 1837, he was attacked and killed by a mob as he defended a new printing press that had just arrived. He died in Alton, as he had pledged, a martyr in the cause of freedom of the press and of abolition. Abolitionist papers continued to speak out and to suffer the consequences of popular retribution as long as slavery lasted.

THE CIVIL WAR*

During the Civil War Congress passed only two Acts that permitted civil prosecution of persons disloyal to the Union: the Conscription Act, which related solely to resistance to the draft, and the Treason Act, which was never claimed to apply to published statements. On the contrary, utterances that were considered detrimental to the Union or that might directly assist the South, were regulated by limiting the privileges of war correspondents through army regulations and through control of the telegraph by the Treasury, War and State Departments. This latter resulted in such violent protests from the newspapers that an agreement was reached between the press and the government by which the press was not to publish dispatches that might "give aid and comfort to the enemy." That arrangement also proved to be unsatisfactory. The Secretary of War, under orders from the President, established a drastic censorship over the telegraph, but this censorship operated so unfairly that Congress passed a statute giving the President power to take over entire control of the telegraph system.

The only control exercised over the press was by restricting its mailing privilege. Newspapers that published articles that were considered detrimental to the interests of the government or as hindering its military operations were barred from the mails. A committee of the Senate investigated the Postmaster General, who justified his right with the following statement:

> "The freedom of the Press is secured by a high constitutional sanction. But it is freedom and not license that is guaranteed. It is to be used only for lawful purposes. It cannot aim blows at the existence of the Government, the Constitution, and the Union, and at the same time claim its protection.... While, therefore, this department neither enjoyed nor claimed the power to suppress such treasonable publications but left them free to publish what it pleased, it could not be called upon to give them circulation. It could not and would not interfere with the freedom secured by law, but it could and did obstruct the dissemination of that which was without the pale of it."

* Giles J. Patterson, Free Speech and a Free Press. Little, Brown and Company, 1939, pp. 143–144.

Numerous controversies arose between the press and the military authorities. One of the best known occurred in Chicago when General Burnside ordered suppression of the Chicago Times. Twenty thousand citizens denounced this act and President Lincoln rescinded the order and rebuked the General.

Congress passed no Act during this period similar to the Espionage Act,* but the number of persons arrested by the military authorities was very large. Apparently there was no thought in the mind of the administration that it had power to re-enact the Sedition Act even during war time and it depended largely upon military power, the proper limits of the exercise of which were never definitely determined by the courts.

THE REASONS FOR THE CIVIL WAR SUPPRESSIONS**

Some historians ... imply that the justifications for restraints were patently evident and the degree of suppression was rather mild, from this vantage point. The military crisis was almost constant until the last period, and opposition to the war was open and widespread. Understandably, there were many southern sympathizers by kinship and friendship, particularly in the border states and the southern portion of the midwestern states. Nationality groups, particularly the Irish and even many of the pro-Republican Germans, were openly hostile. Newspapers not only criticized the administration and asked for immediate peace, but in effect some also took the southern side, declaring that the federal government could not keep states in the Union by force. Some of the leadership of the Democratic party, particularly in the Midwest, assumed some or all of these positions. Conscription efforts were often met with armed violence, including murder. Secret organizations assisted the southern cause and even planned a rebellion in the North. In other words, the need for an unprecedented national mobilization, the maintenance of the political system under which it operated, and the legitimacy of the political authorities were subject to extensive, continuing challenges in the midst of a very uncertain military situation.

Except for the arbitrary acts of military detention, the legal suppression, however, appears to have been comparatively limited. There were "private" acts against dissenters, particularly violence against the opposition press, frequently by Union soldiers on furlough. But there were few prosecutions of opposition publications and politicians whose utterances might, under other situations, be readily interpreted as inciting sedition. Apparently, only those directly involved in conspiracies—from helping deserters to forceful opposition to conscription to quixotic plans for armed rebellion—were prosecuted, and sentences were generally mild. As already indicated, the end of one of the most violent internal armed conflicts in human history terminated the suppressive atmosphere.

* Of 1917 (See Chapter 5, p. 86.)

** William Spinrad. Civil Liberties, Quadrangle, 1970, pp. 41–42. Reprinted with permission.

WORDS ON TRIAL[†]

The cessation of military conflict did not necessarily mean peace for the press. In the South during the Reconstruction era, newspapers on both sides were manipulated by pressure, forced to speak softly or suspend. During the 1880s labor organizational activities and printed pleas for better wages and working conditions brought harsh interference with what was then an unfamiliar voice. When workers held meetings, marched in picket lines, distributed literature, or otherwise exercised their constitutional rights of freedom of speech and of the press, they were frequently met with injunctions and, if they persisted in their activity, they were thrown into jail without jury trials.

During the Spanish–American War military censorship was unusually lenient, though a censor was appointed in New York and tried to curb the disclosures of some of the correspondents. General William Shafter on one occasion banished all Hearst men from captured Santiago.

While official and collective private attacks on the press might have been most prevalent during periods of war and tension, individual assaults with the club, the horsewhip, or the dueling pistol came at many unexpected times, especially during the first part of the nineteenth century.

Editors in the South and West were frequently involved in man-to-man fighting over the contents of their papers, a phenomenon which led Mark Twain to write his sketch of "Journalism in Tennessee." In it he portrayed the old editor, who has just shot one man and leaves his new assistant in charge of the office with the following instructions:

> Jones will be here at three—cowhide him. Gillespie will call earlier, perhaps—throw him out of the window. Ferguson will be along about four—kill him. That is all for today, I believe. If you have any odd time, you may write a blistering article on the police. The cowhides are under the table, weapons in the drawer, ammunition there in the corner, lint and bandages up there in the pigeonholes. In case of accident, go to Lancet, the surgeon, downstairs. He advertises; we take it out in trade.

THE RADICAL CHALLENGE*

The comparative "tranquility" that followed [the Civil War] at least as far as civil liberties issues are concerned, did not last too long. A new legitimacy crisis emerged with its attendant suppressions, involving labor and "radical" organizations, which represented a form of self-assertion by the "downtrodden."

The curtailment of the civil liberties of labor organizations, the suppression of their rights of association, remained a significant civil liberties problem until well into the 1930s.... The difficulties of radical organizations were different at different times. Some labor leaders might object to the identification of labor and "radical" groups so closely together, but their respective struggles for the right to exist without

† Lofton, Justice and the Press, pp. 21–22.

* Spinrad, Civil Liberties, pp. 35–38.

legal and extralegal harassment tended to be joined until the post-World War II period.

All branches of government participated in the process, and many extralegal and nonlegal tactics were applied. The courts assisted by regularly issuing "injunctions," which could make various types of union action in contempt of court. The executive branch was most involved. Action ranged from that of President Cleveland in calling out federal troops, which, in effect, broke the Pullman strike in 1894, to local police running labor organizers out of town. Legislative acts were, at least officially, more concerned with radicalism and will be later discussed.

But the suppressions by the "private government" of employers were even more persuasive. In some "company towns," the company made the laws and its private police force enforced them. Freedom of expression and association essentially was by their sufferance. There were also economic weapons available—the "blacklisting" of those who joined unions or even spoke to unionists and the "Yellow Dog" contract by which a prospective worker promised never to join a union. Extralegal violence, including murder, could come from public or private police or any unofficial group of citizens.... It may be difficult to accept this history from a contemporary vantage point, to appreciate to what extent the assertion of labor's right to organize was of central concern to libertarians for a long time. The American Civil Liberties Union devoted much of its effort in its earliest days to that goal. As a lingering manifestation of this tendency, the Congress of Industrial Organizations (CIO) was not permitted to hold a public meeting in Jersey City until the Supreme Court ruled such denials unconstitutional in 1939.

Although civil libertarians have been firm in their defense of the right of labor to organize, the various techniques to thwart those rights have not only been a result of the recalcitrant power of vested interests. They, too, have been able to make appeals in value terms. By nature, unions are opposed to the notion of individual contracts, a time-honored American value frequently sanctified by the Supreme Court. Unions are frequently organized by "outsiders," seem to disturb the apparent social peace, have been identified with "foreign" ideas and were, at least in the early stages, frequently disproportionately supported by immigrant groups. Violence on both sides was a frequent concomitant of labor struggles.

All of this was even more true of "radicals." The first to be involved were the anarchists. The historic event that set off the campaign against them was the famous Haymarket Square bomb explosion in Chicago in 1886, which actually occurred during a labor rally. President McKinley was assassinated by a man publicly identified as a presumed "anarchist." As a result, New York State passed the first state anti-sedition law under the heading of a "criminal anarchy" law. The law stated that it was a criminal offense to advocate either by speech or writing the doctrine that organized government should be overthrown by force or violence, or by assassination or any unlawful means. It was also unlawful to join any organization or attend the meeting of any organization that advocated overthrow of the government. In 1903, Congress passed a law excluding even "peaceable" anarchists from entry into the country. Several other states followed the example of New York shortly thereafter, although there was little prosecution under such legislation for some time. For instance, the New York law was not applied for almost twenty years until it became very appropriate to the atmosphere of World War I.

The difficulties of the anarchists were compounded in the case of the "revolutionary syndicalist" labor organization, the Industrial Workers of the World. Its members were physically assaulted by both police and private groups, arrested for fictitious offenses, and denied procedures of due process.

THE SYNDICALISM LAWS*

Beginning in 1902, with the enactment of a law by the New York legislature, the states moved to curb discussion by anarchists and others whose political and economic views were distasteful to the majority of citizens. As defined by new state statutes, the offense of "criminal syndicalism" consisted of violence or the advocacy of violence or other illicit means to bring about political change. Publications inciting to violence and the overthrow of government were thus made criminal. Laws against criminal syndicalism multiplied during and immediately after World War I until some thirty-three states had them, with many of the acts being uniform in wording. Chief targets of criminal syndicalism prosecutions were members of the Industrial Workers of the World and others who, under the intolerance of wartime emotion, were deemed guilty of radical, socialist, or "bolshevik" tendencies. The Kentucky law provided that the mere expression of radical opinion constituted evidence of a plot to overthrow the government. Thus the states in effect joined forces with the federal government in the effort to stamp out sedition. While criminal syndicalism acts soon became a dead letter in most states, California continued to enforce its law. In the five years after its enactment in 1919, 504 persons were arrested and held for bail of $15,000 each, and 264 were actually tried. When juries eventually began to refuse to convict, the California attorney general secured a court injunction under which IWW organizers could be tried for contempt of court without juries for merely soliciting new members.

* Lofton, Justice and the Press, pp. 23–24.

Chapter V

FREEDOM OF SPEECH–ADVOCACY
OF VIOLATION OF LAW

———

I. INTRODUCTION

ON LIBERTY*

... No one pretends that actions should be as free as opinions. On the contrary, even opinions lose their immunity when the circumstances in which they are expressed are such as to constitute their expression a positive instigation to some mischievous act. An opinion that corn-dealers are starvers of the poor, or that private property is robbery, ought to be unmolested when simply circulated through the press, but may justly incur punishment when delivered orally to an excited mob assembled before the house of a corn-dealer, or when handed about among the same mob in the form of a placard. Acts of whatever kind, which without justifiable cause do harm to others may be, and in the more important cases absolutely require to be, controlled by the unfavorable sentiments, and, when needful, by the active interference of mankind.

NOTE

It is significant that Mill's classic defense of freedom of speech (see p. 51) also recognized that, in some circumstances, those who advocated the violation of law could be punished. From the corn-dealers example that Mill uses, can you restate exactly what his exception is? Can everyone who urges another to violate the criminal law be punished? If someone does not urge violation of the law, can he be punished because his speech creates some danger that others will violate the law?

In the United States, those questions have not arisen in a vacuum. As the material in the previous chapter shows, freedom of speech issues in this country have been crucial during wartime, and in post-war periods when there has been public concern about disloyalty. The cases discussed in the following materials deal with free speech problems that arose during the First and Second World Wars and during the periods of concern about subversion which followed those conflicts. The defendants in these cases include those who urged the violation of the draft laws and those who preached revolutionary doctrine advocating violent overthrow of existing government.

* John Stuart Mill, On Liberty, Bobbs–Merrill Co., Inc., 1956, p. 67. Reprinted with permission.

The term "clear and present danger" appears often in the opinions. Consider, when you encounter it, whether this is what Mill meant in his corn-dealer example.

WAR, FEAR AND SPEECH*

[At the moment of its entry into the First World War, America found itself faced simultaneously with the necessity of deciding afresh what principles of community should dominate its national life.] The old bases of community founded on a rural, white, Protestant society of farmers and small businessmen had been sapped at their foundations by urban, industrial, Catholic, and immigrant explosions. An old society, to paraphrase Arnold Bennett, was dying, and a new society was powerless to be born. Community values were in flux and the old sense of security in jeopardy—and into this anomic, disturbed universe came the ultimate disruption: the fear of treason. At the time of the Hungarian Revolution against Soviet tyranny in 1956, a young freedom fighter was asked why, after years of oppression, he and his comrades had suddenly dared to raise the banner of revolt. Why had they not remained intimidated and cowed by the regime? He replied simply: "One day, for the first time, we trusted each other and we trusted our neighbors." Forty years earlier, the people of the United States lived through the converse situation: one day they awoke and distrusted their neighbors. In the same way that the Hungarians—alas so briefly—discovered a sense of community and trusted, the Americans lost their identity and hated.

The pressure for Americanization and an end to "hyphenated Americanism" had been growing; with the United States in the war, it overflowed all restraints. Moreover, since sentiments of this sort are seldom accompanied by logic, the internal enemy was visualized as one compact category which included German–Americans, Socialists, Wobblies, pacifists (known commonly as "slackers"), and militant trade unionists....

Harold Hyman and others have chronicled the shambles of civil rights in detail. However, certain aspects of the situation should be limned, particularly for purposes of comparison with World War II. First of all, the *positive* oppressive role of the federal government was limited: only 877 people were actually convicted under the Espionage Act of 1917, though indictments were lodged against 1,956. The real crime of the federal authorities was one of omission. They stood aside and permitted, where they did not encourage, the domination of the United States by one vast vigilante organization. The Department of Justice, led by an Attorney General who stated publicly the view that opponents of war should ask mercy from God "for they need expect none from an outraged people and an avenging Government," officially sponsored the largest of the vigilante groups, the American Protective League. Equipped with badges and calling themselves "Secret Service," 250,000 members of the APL were on the snoop by 1918. The quest for juvenile sedition was in the capable hands of the Boy Spies of America.

---

* John P. Roche, The Quest for the Dream, The Development of Civil Rights and Human Relations in Modern America, Macmillan Co., New York, 1963, pp. 39–47. Reprinted with permission.

Wilson became disturbed by the mob-rule aspects of the APL and asked Attorney General Gregory if it should not be curbed, but the latter stood his ground, maintained his support, and the President dropped the matter. But Wilson's intuition was correct; the APL was nothing less than a government-sponsored lynch mob which proudly took the law into its own hands in summary and brutal fashion. Its specialty was not arrest and trial in courts duly appointed for that purpose; it specialized in direct prophylaxis: tar and feathers, beatings, and flag-kissing. (No one seemed to sense the irony of forcing suspects on their hands and knees to kiss the symbol of American freedom.) The official apology for the APL, Emerson Hough's *The Web,* claimed—with perhaps some exaggeration—that the league "brought to judgment three million cases of disloyalty." This has to be glossed, however, to read that the APL used direct action against three million people whom it defined, by whatever processes of deduction or divination, as "disloyal."

With the APL, and a dozen or more similar organizations (the Sedition Slammers and the Terrible Threateners were, with the Anti–Yellow Dog League, the most picturesque) whooping up the search for disloyalty, with the conviction spreading that German spies and saboteurs were everywhere, with Theodore Roosevelt shrieking for the blood of "half-hidden traitors," and the circumspect Elihu Root announcing that there were men on the New York streets "who ought to be taken out at sunrise tomorrow and shot for treason," it was not surprising that the American people simply went mad. And it was not long before any who opposed the spy hunt on libertarian or common-sense grounds were themselves automatically consigned to the category of the disloyal. The constitutional right not to speak became the protection of the astute at a time when a federal judge could in deadly earnest define freedom of speech as protecting only "criticism which is made friendly to the government, friendly to the war, friendly to the policies of the government." And even then suspects were on occasion forced to kiss the flag for showing insufficient enthusiasm, i.e., for keeping their mouths shut.

First to be engulfed by the great wave were the residual evidences of German culture. As towns changed their names, streets were rebaptized, and hamburgers became liberty sandwiches, many patriots celebrated July 4, 1917, by consigning German books to bonfires. German opera was banned, and not only was the speaking of German in public forbidden in many areas, but state legislators set to work to bar the teaching of that tongue in public or private schools. . . .

It would be pointless to continue a bill of particulars which could fill several volumes. The suppression of dissent affected every sector of American life: books, films, newspapers were censored and banned; teachers and ministers were disciplined or dismissed; lawful opposition to conscription was extirpated by methods both legal and illegal. . . .

[In light of this extensive repression of speech and opinion, one must wonder what role the Constitution, as interpreted by the Supreme Court, could and did play in protecting freedom of speech.]

It should be recalled that at that time, indeed, until 1925, the Supreme Court refused to exercise constitutional oversight in the area of state intrusions into freedom of speech or opinion. Thus there was no basis for appealing most state actions to the high tribunal; the state courts, generally composed of elected judges, had the last word on wartime infringements of individual rights and rarely stood firm against the sentiments of King Mob. . . .

Consequently the important civil liberty cases of the war period were all concerned with the power of the national government to limit freedom of opinion; the question was the scope of the protection guaranteed to the citizen by the First Amendment's seemingly absolute pronouncement that "Congress shall make no law ... abridging the freedom of speech, or of the press; or the right of the people peaceably to assemble, and to petition the Government for a redress of grievances."

II. THE WORLD WAR I CASES

MASSES PUBLISHING CO. v. PATTEN

U.S. District Court Southern District New York, 1917.
244 Fed. 535.

(BILLINGS) LEARNED HAND—Born on January 27, 1872, in Albany, New York, into an upper-class family. His father, a successful appellate lawyer and briefly an appellate judge, aspired to become a member of the U.S. Supreme Court. Progressive. Agnostic. Harvard, A.B., 1893; A.M., 1894; LL.B., 1896. Law practice, 1897–1909. Appointed U.S. District Judge for the Southern District of New York, 1909. Considered for appointment to the U.S. Supreme Court in 1922 but opposed by Chief Justice Taft. "[Hand] is an able judge and a hard worker," wrote Taft to President Harding. "I appointed him [to the U.S. District Court] on [Attorney General] Wickersham's recommendation, but he turned out to be a wild Roosevelt man and a progressive, and though on the Bench, he went into the campaign. If promoted to our Bench, he would most certainly herd with Brandeis and be a dissenter. I think it would be risking too much to appoint him." Earlier Hand aspired to an appointment on the Court of Appeals for the Second Circuit. In 1918, he was denied the appointment in part because of the unpopularity of his decision in *Masses*. In 1924, with Taft's warm support, he was promoted to the Second Circuit. For the next 19 years, he aspired to an appointment to the U.S. Supreme Court. In 1943, Justice Frankfurter conducted an aggressive campaign to persuade F.D.R. to appoint Hand, but Hand's age at the time—71—and strong support from Attorney General Francis Biddle and Justices Black and Douglas for another candidate—Wiley Rutledge—were too much to overcome. Hand's major contributions to Supreme Court free speech jurisprudence were his incitement test in *Masses*, which the Court essentially adopted in Brandenburg v. Ohio, and his reinterpretation of the clear and present danger test, which Chief Justice Vinson adopted in Dennis v. United States. He retired from regular active service as a judge in 1951. He died on August 18, 1961.

[Soon after the United States entered World War I, Congress passed the Espionage Act of 1917. Despite its title, only some of its provisions concerned espionage. The Act punished, among other things, false statements intended to interfere with military operations, attempts to cause insubordination, disloyalty, or mutiny, and obstruction of recruitment or enlistment. Further, it banned from the mails written and graphic matter that violated the act or advocated treason or forcible resistance to the law. In the summer of 1917, Thomas G. Patten, postmaster of New York City, banned the August issue of *The Masses*, a radical magazine. He objected to four cartoons, a poem that described Emma Goldman and Alexander Berkman, who were then in jail for resisting the draft, as "elemental forces," and three articles that praised conscientious objectors as self-sacrificing and Goldman and Berkman as "friends of American freedom." The Post Office Department considered one of the cartoons "the worst thing in the magazine." Entitled "Conscription," the cartoon is shown below. Counsel for *The Masses* sought to enjoin Patten from banning the issue from the U.S. mails.]

Drawn by Henry J. Glintenkamp, August 1917

Conscription

. . .

LEARNED HAND, DISTRICT JUDGE, delivered the following opinion.

... One may not counsel or advise others to violate the law as it stands. Words are not only the keys of persuasion, but the triggers of action, and those which have no purport but to counsel the violation of law cannot by any latitude of interpretation be a part of that public opinion which is the final source of government in a democratic state.... To counsel or advise a man to an act is to urge upon him either that it is his interest or his duty to do it. While, of course, this may be accomplished as well by indirection as expressly, since words carry the meaning that they impart, the definition is exhaustive, I think, and I shall use it. Political agitation, by the passions it arouses or the convictions it engenders, may in fact stimulate men to the violation of law. Detestation of existing policies is easily transformed into forcible resistance of the authority which puts them in execution, and it would be folly to disregard the causal relation between the two. Yet to assimilate agitation, legitimate as such, with direct incitement to violent resistance, is to disregard the tolerance of all methods of political agitation which in normal times is a safeguard of free government. The distinction is not a scholastic subterfuge, but a hard-bought acquisition in the fight for freedom, and the purpose to disregard it must be evident when the power exists. If one stops short of urging upon others that it is their duty or their interest to resist the law, it seems to me one should not be held to have attempted to cause its violation. If that be not the test, I can see no escape from the conclusion that under this section every political agitation which can be shown to be apt to create a seditious temper is illegal. I am confident that by such language Congress had not such revolutionary purpose in view.

It seems to me, however, quite plain that none of the language and none of the cartoons in this paper can be thought directly to counsel or advise insubordination or mutiny, without a violation of their meaning quite beyond any tolerable understanding. I come, therefore, to the third phrase of the section, which forbids any one from willfully obstructing the recruiting or enlistment service of the United States. I am not prepared to assent to the plaintiff's position that this only refers to acts other than words, nor that the act thus defined must be shown to have been successful. One may obstruct without preventing, and the mere obstruction is an injury to the service for it throws impediments in its way. Here again, however, since the question is of the expression of opinion, I construe the sentence, so far as it restrains public utterance, as I have construed the other two, and as therefore limited to the direct advocacy of resistance to the recruiting and enlistment service. If so, the inquiry is narrowed to the question whether any of the challenged matter may be said to advocate resistance to the draft, taking the meaning of the words with the utmost latitude which they can bear.

As to the cartoons it seems to me quite clear that they do not fall within such a test. Certainly the nearest is that entitled "Conscription," and the most that can be said of that is that it may breed such animosity to the draft as will promote resistance and strengthen the determination of those disposed to be recalcitrant. There is no intimation that, however hateful the draft may be, one is in duty bound to resist it, certainly not that such resistance is to one's interest. I cannot, therefore, even with the limitations which surround the power of the court, assent to the assertion that any of the cartoons violate the act.

The text offers more embarrassment. The poem to Emma Goldman and Alexander Berkman, at most, goes no further than to say that they are martyrs in the cause of love among nations. Such a sentiment hold them up to admiration, and hence their conduct to possible emulation. The paragraph in which the editor offers to receive funds for their appeal also expresses admiration for them, but goes no further. The paragraphs upon conscientious objectors are of the same kind. They go no further than to express high admiration for those who have held and are holding out for their convictions even to the extent of resisting the law. It is plain enough that the paper has the fullest sympathy for these people, that it admires their courage, and that it presumptively approves their conduct. Indeed, in the earlier numbers and before the draft went into effect the editor urged resistance. Since I must interpret the language in the most hostile sense, it is fair to suppose, therefore, that these passages go as far as to say:

> "These men and women are heroes and worthy of a free-man's admiration. We approve their conduct; we will help to secure them their legal rights. They are working for the betterment of mankind through their obdurate consciences."

Moreover, these passages, it must be remembered, occur in a magazine which attacks with the utmost violence the draft and the war. That such comments have a tendency to arouse emulation in others is clear enough, but that they counsel others to follow these examples is not so plain. Literally at least they do not, and while, as I have said, the words are to be taken, not literally, but according to their full import, the literal meaning is the starting point for interpretation. One may admire and approve the course of a hero without feeling any duty to follow him. There is not the least implied intimation in these words that others are under a duty to follow. The most that can be said is that, if others do follow, they will get the same admiration and the same approval. Now, there is surely an appreciable distance between esteem and emulation; and unless there is here some advocacy of such emulation, I cannot see how the passages can be said to fall within the law. If they do, it would follow that, while one might express admiration and approval for the Quakers or any established sect which is excused from the draft, one could not legally express the same admiration and approval for others who entertain the same conviction, but do not happen to belong to the Society of Friends. It cannot be that the law means to curtail such expressions merely, because the convictions of the class within the draft are stronger than their sense of obedience to the law. There is ample evidence in history that the Quaker is as recalcitrant to legal compulsion as any man; his obstinacy has been regarded in the act, but his disposition is as disobedient as that of any other conscientious objector. Surely, if the draft had not excepted Quakers, it would be too strong a doctrine to say that any who openly admire their fortitude or even approved their conduct was willfully obstructing the draft. . . .

SCHENCK v. UNITED STATES

Supreme Court of the United States, 1919.
249 U.S. 47, 39 S.Ct. 247, 63 L.Ed. 470.

[Charles Schenck, general secretary of the Socialist Party in Philadelphia, was convicted under the Espionage Act of 1917 Act for mailing to prospective draftees anti-war circulars that claimed the draft to be unconstitutional and, in veiled terms, urged resistance to it. "A conscript," Schenck's circular read, "is little better than a convict. . . . ASSERT YOUR RIGHTS." A unanimous Supreme Court affirmed the conviction, with Justice Holmes writing the opinion. The jury had found that Schenck intended to obstruct the draft, and the Court agreed that the leaflet had a tendency to produce that result. Answering Schenck's argument that his distribution of the leaflet was protected by the First Amendment, Justice Holmes set forth the clear and present danger test.]

JUSTICE HOLMES delivered the opinion of the Court.

OLIVER WENDELL HOLMES, JR.—Born on March 8, 1841, in Boston, Massachusetts, son of a physician, poet, and essayist. Republican. Unitarian. Harvard, A.B., 1861; LL.B., 1866. Knew Ralph Waldo Emerson and was a college friend of William James. Served as a Union officer in the Civil War and was wounded three times (twice almost fatally). Author of *The Common Law,* originally the Lowell lectures delivered in 1880. Practiced law, 1867–1870, 1873–1882; editor of the *American Law Review,* 1870–1873; Harvard law professor, 1882; associate justice of the Massachusetts Supreme Judicial Court, 1882–1899; chief justice, 1899–1902. Nominated associate justice on December 2, 1902, by President Theodore Roosevelt to replace Horace Gray. Confirmed by the Senate on December 4, 1902, by voice vote. Retired on January 12, 1932, at the age of 91. Died on March 6, 1935. Holmes is one of the few American judges to emerge as a culture hero. Known as the Magnificent Yankee, there are many stories about him—most of them apocryphal. Stories about Holmes often concern either his ribald side or his military service. He regularly attended the Gaiety burlesque theatre in Washington, D.C., and once slapped the knee of the man seated next to him saying, "I thank God I'm a man of low tastes." Silas Bent, *Justice Oliver Wendell Holmes,* Vanguard Press, 1932, p. 19. In the defense of Washington during the Civil War, Holmes—then a twenty-three year old captain—saw a tall civilian in a stove-pipe hat standing on a parapet watching the puffs of smoke from the rifles of snipers. Appalled by the danger the civilian had exposed himself to, Holmes shouted, "Get down you damn fool, before you get shot." The civilian was Holmes' commander-in-chief, Abraham Lincoln, who reacted with amusement and obeyed the young officer. Shelby Foote, *The Civil War: A Narrative,* Random House, 1974, pp. 458–459.

. . .

It well may be that the prohibition of laws abridging the freedom of speech is not confined to previous restraints, although to prevent them may have been the main purpose.... We admit that in many places and in ordinary times the defendants in saying all that was said in the circular would have been within their constitutional rights. But the character of every act depends upon the circumstances in which it is done.... The most stringent protection of free speech would not protect a man in falsely shouting fire in a theatre and causing a panic.... The question in every case is whether the words used are used in such circumstances and are of such a nature as to create a clear and present danger that they will bring about the substantive evils that Congress has a right to prevent. It is a question of proximity and degree. When a nation is at war many things that might be said in time of peace are such a hindrance to its effort that their utterance will not be endured so long as men fight and that no Court could regard them as protected by any constitutional right....

THE FROHWERK AND DEBS CASES

During the same term the Supreme Court decided *Schenck*, it also decided Frohwerk v. United States, 249 U.S. 204 (1919), and Debs v. U.S., 249 U.S. 211 (1919). Both cases involved convictions under the Espionage Act of 1917.

Frohwerk, the editor of the *Missouri Staats–Zeitung*, was convicted of publishing articles on the constitutionality and merits of the draft and on the purpose of the war. He was sentenced to a fine and 10 years imprisonment. Writing for a unanimous Court, Holmes acknowledged that even in wartime, Frohwerk's words were not in themselves punishable. "We do not lose our right to condemn either measures or men because the country is at war," said Holmes, "But we take the case on the record as it is, and on that record [a jury might have] found that circulation of the paper was in quarters where a little breath would be enough to kindle a flame and the fact was known and relied on by those who sent that paper out." 249 U.S. at 208–09. In other words, a jury might have found in the circumstances of the case that Frohwerk's articles created a clear and present danger and for that reason were not constitutionally protected.

Eugene V. Debs was convicted of attempting to cause insubordination in the Army and obstruct recruiting because of statements he made at a Socialist convention. Although Debs had not directly asked his listeners to resist the draft, he did say, "You need to know that you are fit for something better than slavery and cannon fodder." Further, he told the jury, "I abhor war. I would oppose it if I stood alone. When I think of a cold, glittering steel bayonet being plunged in the white, quivering flesh of a human being, I recoil." As in *Frohwerk*, the Supreme

Court unanimously affirmed Deb's conviction, and Holmes again wrote for the Court, but without enthusiasm. He later wrote to a friend:

> I had a disagreeable task in writing a decision against Debs, the agitator, for obstructing recruiting by speech—found by a jury to have been made with that intent. There is no doubt in my mind about the law but I wondered that the Government should have pressed the case to a hearing—as it enables knaves, fools and the ignorant to say that he was really condemned as a dangerous agitator.*

ABRAMS v. UNITED STATES

Supreme Court of the United States, 1919.
250 U.S. 616, 40 S.Ct. 17, 63 L.Ed. 1173.

[Early one morning in August, 1918, a flurry of leaflets descended from an upper story of a manufacturing building in New York City. They were in both English and Yiddish. The English versions began:

THE

HYPOCRISY

OF THE

UNITED STATES

AND HER ALLIES

> "Our" President Wilson, with his beautiful phraseology, has hypnotized the people of America to such an extent that they do not see his hypocrisy.

The leaflet then went on to say that the president was afraid to tell the American people of the U.S. intervention in Russia and in an effort "to crush the Russian Revolution." "WORKERS OF THE WORLD AWAKE," it continued. "RISE! PUT DOWN YOUR ENEMY AND MINE." A postscript added, "It is absurd to call us pro-German. We hate and despise German militarism more than your hypocritical tyrants. We have more reasons for denouncing German militarism that the coward in the White House," The Yiddish leaflet, entitled "WORKERS—WAKE UP," stated:

> Workers in the ammunition factories, you are producing bullets, bayonets, cannon, to murder not only the Germans, but also your dearest, best, who are in Russia and are fighting for freedom.

The leaflet called for a general strike and concluded with these words:

> Do not let the Government scare you with their wild punishment in prisons, hanging and shooting. We must not and will not betray the splendid fighters of Russia. Workers, [rise] up to fight.

. . .

* Quoted in Sheldon M. Novick, The Life of Oliver Wendell Holmes. Little, Brown & Co., 1989, pp. 327–328.

Three hundred years had the Romanoff dynasty taught us how to fight. Let all rulers remember this, from the smallest to the biggest despot, that the hand of revolution will not shiver in a fight.

Woe unto those who will be in the way of progress. Let solidarity live!

(signed)

THE REBELS

Military intelligence police who had observed the descent of the leaflets sent two sergeants into the building to determine who was throwing them out of the window. On the fourth floor the sergeants arrested Hyman Rosansky, a young radical who worked in the building. Rosansky admitted throwing out the leaflets, and he named several other young radicals at whose behest he said he had acted. Rosansky and four others he had named—Jacob Abrams, Hyam Lackowsky, Samuel Libman, and Mollie Steamer—were charged, convicted, and sentenced under a 1918 amendment to the Espionage Act of 1917, which some have called the Sedition Act because it punished speech critical of the government. The precise charges against Abrams and his fellow radicals are set forth in the following excerpt from the Supreme Court's opinion in the case.]

JUSTICE CLARKE delivered the opinion of the Court.

JOHN HESSIN CLARKE—Born on September 18, 1857, in New Lisbon, Ohio, the son of Irish immigrants. His father was a lawyer. Democrat. Protestant. He received an A.B. Phi Beta Kappa, Western Reserve College 1877. After studying law in his father's office, he passed the Ohio bar examination with honors. Practiced corporate law, 1888–1914. Politically progressive, he supported women suffrage, civil service, public disclosure of campaign expenditures, and direct election of U.S. senators, and he twice ran unsuccessfully for the U.S. Senate. U.S. District Judge for the Southern District of Ohio, 1914–1916. Nominated to the Supreme Court by Woodrow Wilson on July 14, 1916, to replace Charles Evans Hughes, who had resigned to run for the presidency. Confirmed by the Senate 10 days later by voice vote. He usually voted with Brandeis, which irked McReynolds. As a result, McReynolds made life on the Court unpleasant for Clarke, which played a part in his decision to resign on September 18, 1922, only six years after his appointment. He had a long retirement. In 1937, at the age of 80, he endorsed F.D.R.'s court-packing plan in a radio address. He died on March 22, 1945.

On a single indictment, containing four counts, the five plaintiffs in error, hereinafter designated the defendants, were convicted of conspiring to violate provisions of the Espionage Act of Congress (§ 3, Title 1, of Act approved June 15, 1917, as amended May 16, 1918, 40 Stat. 553).

Each of the first three counts charged the defendants with conspiring, when the United States was at war with the Imperial Government of Germany, to unlawfully utter, print, write and publish: In the first count, "disloyal, scurrilous and abusive language about the form of Government of the United States;" in the second count, language "intended to bring the form of Government of the United States into contempt, scorn, contumely and disrepute;" and in the third count, language "intended to incite, provoke and encourage resistance to the United States in said war." The charge in the fourth count was that the defendants conspired "when the United States was at war with the Imperial German Government, . . . unlawfully and wilfully, by utterance, writing, printing and publication, to urge, incite and advocate curtailment of production of things and products, to wit, ordnance and ammunition, necessary and essential to the prosecution of the war." The offenses were charged in the language of the act of Congress.

It was charged in each count of the indictment that it was a part of the conspiracy that the defendants would attempt to accomplish their unlawful purpose by printing, writing and distributing in the City of New York many copies of a leaflet or circular, printed in the English language, and of another printed in the Yiddish language. . . .

All of the five defendants were born in Russia. They were intelligent, had considerable schooling, and at the time they were arrested they had lived in the United States terms varying from five to ten years but none of them had applied for naturalization. Four of them testified as witnesses in their own behalf and of these, three frankly avowed that they were "rebels," "revolutionists," "anarchists," that they did not believe government in any form, and they declared that they had no interest whatever in the Government of the United States. The fourth defendant testified that he was a "socialist" and believed in "a proper kind of government, not capitalistic," but in his classification the Government of the United States was "capitalistic."

It was admitted on the trial that the defendants had united to print and distribute the described circulars and that five thousand of them had been printed and distributed about the 22d day of August, 1918. The group had a meeting place in New York City, in rooms rented by defendant Abrams, under an assumed name, and there the subject of printing the circulars was discussed about two weeks before the defendants were arrested. The defendant Abrams, although not a printer, on July 27, 1918, purchased the printing outfit with which the circulars were printed and installed it in a basement room where the work was done at night. The circulars were distributed some by throwing them from a window of a building where one of the defendants was employed and others secretly, in New York City.

The defendants pleaded "not guilty," and the case of the Government consisted in showing the facts we have stated, and in introducing in evidence copies of the two printed circulars attached to the indictment, a sheet entitled "Revolutionists Unite for Action," written by the defendant Lipman, and found on him when he was arrested, and another paper, found at the headquarters of the group, and for which Abrams assumed responsibility.

Thus the conspiracy and the doing of the overt acts charged were largely admitted and were fully established.

On the record thus described it is argued, somewhat faintly, that the acts charged against the defendants were not unlawful because within the protection of that freedom of speech and of the press which is guaranteed by the first amendment to the Constitution of the United States, and that the entire Espionage Act is unconstitutional because in conflict with that Amendment.

This contention is sufficiently discussed and is definitely negatived in Schenck v. United States and Baer v. United States, 239 U.S. 47; and in Frohwerk v. United States, 249 U.S. 204.

. . .

[The leaflets distributed] sufficiently show, that while the immediate occasion for this particular outbreak of lawlessness, on the part of the defendant alien anarchists, may have been resentment caused by our Government sending troops to Russia as a strategic operation against the Germans on the eastern battle front, yet the plain purpose of their propaganda was to excite, at the supreme crisis of the war, disaffection, sedition, riots, and, as they hoped, revolution, in this country for the purpose of embarrassing and if possible defeating the military plans of the Government in Europe. A technical distinction may perhaps be taken between disloyal and abusive language applied to the *form* of our government or language intended to bring the *form* of our government into contempt and disrepute, and language of like character and intended to produce like results directed against the President and Congress, the agencies through which that form of government must function in time of war. But it is not necessary to a decision of this case to consider whether such distinction is vital or merely formal, for the language of these circulars was obviously intended to provoke and to encourage resistance to the United States in a war, as the third count runs, and, the defendants, in terms, plainly urged and advocated a resort to a general strike of workers in ammunition factories for the purpose of curtailing the production of ordnance and munitions necessary and essential to the prosecution of the war was is charged in the fourth count. Thus it is clear not only that some evidence but that much persuasive evidence was before the jury tending to prove that the defendants were guilty as charged in both the third and fourth counts of the indictment and under the long established rule of law hereinbefore stated the judgment of the District Court must be affirmed.

JUSTICE HOLMES dissenting.

. . .

I have never seen any reason to doubt that the questions of law that alone were before this Court in the cases of *Schenck*, *Frohwerk*, and *Debs*, . . . were rightly decided. I do not doubt for a moment that by the same reasoning that would justify punishing persuasion to murder, the United States constitutionally may punish speech that produces or is intended to produce a clear and imminent danger that it will bring about forthwith certain substantive evils that the United States constitutionally may seek to prevent. The power undoubtedly is greater in time of war than in time of peace because war opens dangers that do not exist at other times.

But as against dangers peculiar to war, as against others, the principle of the right to free speech is always the same. It is only the present danger of immediate evil or an intent to bring it about that warrants Congress in setting a limit to the expression of opinion where private rights are not concerned. Congress certainly cannot forbid all effort to change the mind of the country. Now nobody can suppose that the surreptitious publishing of a silly leaflet by an unknown man, without more, would present any immediate danger that its opinions would hinder the success of the government arms or have any appreciable tendency to do so. Publishing those opinions for the very purpose of obstructing however, might indicate a greater danger and at any rate would have the quality of an attempt. So I assume that the second leaflet if published for the purposes alleged ... might be punishable. But it seems pretty clear to me that nothing less than that would bring these papers within the scope of this law....

I do not see how anyone can find the intent required by the statute in any of the defendants' words. The second leaflet is the only one that affords even a foundation for the charge, and there, without invoking the hatred of German militarism expressed in the former one, it is evident from the beginning to the end that the only object of the paper is to help Russia and stop American intervention there against the popular government—not to impede the United States in the war that it was carrying on. To say that two phrases taken literally might import a suggestion of conduct that would have interference with the war as an indirect and probably undesired effect seems to me by no means enough to show an attempt to produce that effect....

In this case sentences of twenty years imprisonment have been imposed for the publishing of two leaflets that I believe the defendants had as much right to publish as the Government has to publish the Constitution of the United States now vainly invoked by them. Even if I am technically wrong and enough can be squeezed from these poor and puny anonymities to turn the color of legal litmus paper; I will add, even if what I think the necessary intent were shown; the most nominal punishment seems to me all that possibly could be inflicted, unless the defendants are to be made to suffer not for what the indictment alleges but for the creed that they avow—a creed that I believe to be the creed of ignorance and immaturity when honestly held, as I see no reason to doubt that it was held here, but which although made the subject of examination at the trial, no one has a right even to consider in dealing with the charges before the Court.

Persecution for the expression of opinions seems tome perfectly logical. If you have no doubt of your premises or your power and want a certain result with all your heart you naturally express your wishes in law and sweep away all opposition. To allow opposition by speech seems to indicate that you think the speech impotent, as when a man says that he has squared the circle, or that you do not care whole-heartedly for the result, or that you doubt either your power or your premises. But when men have realized that time has upset many fighting faiths, they may come to believe even more than they believe the very foundations of their own conduct that the ultimate good desired is better reached by free trade in ideas—that the best test of truth is the power of the thought to get itself accepted in the competition of the market, and that truth is the only ground upon which their wishes safely can be carried out. That at any rate is the theory of our Constitution. It is an experiment, as all life is an experiment. Every year if not every day we have to wager our salvation upon some prophecy based upon imperfect knowledge. While that experiment is part of our system I think that we should be eternally vigilant against attempts to check the expression of opinions that we loathe and believe to be fraught with death, unless they so imminently threaten immediate interference with the lawful and pressing purposes of the law that an immediate check is required to save the country. I wholly disagree with the argument of the Government that the First Amendment left the common law as to seditious libel in force. History seems to me against the notion. I had conceived that the United States through many years had shown its repentance for the Sedition Act of 1798, by repaying fines that it imposed. Only the emergency that makes it immediately dangerous to leave the correction of evil counsels to time warrants making any exception to the sweeping command, "Congress shall make no law ... abridging the freedom of speech." Of course I am speaking only of expressions of opinion and exhortations, which were all that were uttered here, but I regret that I cannot put into more impressive words my belief that in their conviction upon this indictment the defendants were deprived of their rights under the Constitution of the United States.

JUSTICE BRANDEIS concurs with the foregoing opinion.

NOTES

1. The similarity between Mill's defense of freedom of speech (quoted at the beginning of this chapter) and Holmes' clear and present danger test is more than a coincidence. Three days before the *Schenck* decision, Holmes wrote Harold Laski that he had recently reread Mill's *On Liberty*.* There is also a similarity between Holmes' test and a passage in his 1880 Lowell lectures that were later published under the title, *The Common Law*. Discussing the law of criminal attempts, Holmes wrote: "The accompanying intent ... renders the otherwise innocent act harmful, because it raises the probability that it will be followed by such other acts and events that will result in harm.... The law does not punish every act which is done with the intent to bring about a crime.... Eminent judges have been puzzled where to draw the line, or even to state the principle on which it should be drawn.... But the principle is believed to be similar to that on which all other lines are drawn by the law. Public policy, that is to say, legislative considerations,

* Holmes to Laski, Feb. 28, 1919. Mark De Wolfe Howe, ed., Holmes–Laski Letters, Harvard University Press, 1953, vol. 1, p. 187.

are at the bottom of the matter; the considerations being ... the nearness of the danger, the greatness of the harm, and the degree of apprehension felt"**

2. Since the Court held that writings such as Schenck's satisfied the clear and present danger test, the test did not impose significant limits on efforts by government to punish speech that advocates breaking the law. All that seemed to be required was that the speech have a "tendency" to induce violation of the law, and that the speaker intended that result. Any antiwar speech could be prosecuted successfully under such a lose standard.

3. The *Abrams* dissent is one of Holmes' most famous opinions. But, as is so often true of Holmes opinions, the force of his literate style (particularly of his last paragraph, which has been quoted over and over again) only makes it more difficult to find his analytical point. He is still saying that it is no violation of the First Amendment to punish a man for advocating the violation of law, so long as there is sufficient danger or the speaker has the requisite intent. His unease with punishing speakers for "intent" alone is demonstrated by his statement that only a nominal punishment could be imposed. That trial balloon has never been followed up in a later case.

Abrams differed from *Schenck* and *Debs* in two respects. First, Holmes is no longer willing to infer an intent that the law be broken if it were very unlikely that anyone listening would violate the law. Second, through the use of words such as "forthwith" and "immediate," Holmes has introduced the concept of immediacy—that the crime advocated follow closely upon the speech.

4. It is instructive to compare Holmes' views in *Abrams* with Hand's views in *Masses*. Hand's distinction between advocating specific violation of the law and general political doctrine would have produced different results in *Abrams*, in which Holmes dissented. It would also have produced a different result in *Debs,* and possibly also in *Schenck,* in which Holmes wrote the Court's opinions. Nevertheless, Hand found it clear that the Constitution did not protect one who "counseled" or "advised" others to violate the law at a specific time and place no matter how remote the danger.

Hand by letter urged his friend Holmes that the *Masses* standard was much more appropriate and easier to administer than "clear and present danger." Indeed though Holmes gradually, in part through this correspondence with Hand, became much more sensitive to the problems in the free speech area, the *Masses* standard received virtually no acceptance or recognition for about 40 years. Before his death and even longer before his standard was accepted into constitutional doctrine (see pp. 126–127), Learned Hand himself had given up on it. Probably the clearest statement by Hand as to why he preferred the *Masses* standard is contained in a letter to Professor Zechariah Chafee in 1920.*

** Oliver Wendell Holmes, The Common Law (Mark De Wolfe Howe, ed.), Little, Brown & Co., 1963, p. 56.

* Gunther, Learned Hand and the Origins of Modern First Amendment Doctrine: Some Fragments of History, Stanford Law Review, 1975, vol. 27, p. 766.

There could be no objection to the rule of the Supreme Court, tendency plus a purpose to produce the evil, even though the words did not come to the objective standard, if one were sure of the result in practical administration.... My own objection to the rule rests in the fact that it exposes all who discuss heated questions to an inquiry before a jury as to their purposes. That inquiry necessarily is of the widest scope and if their general attitude is singular and intransigent, my own belief is that a jury is an insufficient protection. I think it is precisely at those times when alone the freedom of speech becomes important as an institution, that the protection of a jury on such an issue is illusory. The event seems to me to have proved this.

Therefore, to be a real protection to the expression of egregious opinion in times of excitement, I own I cannot see any escape from construing the privilege as absolute, so long as the utterance, objectively regarded, can by any fair construction be held to fall short of counselling violence. That much actually sinister utterance will pass, is undoubtedly true, but the whole institution presupposes a balance of evils....

5. Holmes's dissenting opinion in *Abrams* troubled some of the majority justices. Three of them called on Holmes at his home in an effort to persuade him not to publish the dissent. "They laid before him their request that in this case, which they thought affected the safety of the country, he should, like the old soldier he had once been, close ranks and forego individual predilections. Mrs. Holmes agreed. The tone of the discussion was at all times friendly, even affectionate. The Justice regretted that he could not do as they wished. They did not press."[*]

6. With only a couple of exceptions, the defendants in the cases covered in this section initially received stiff sentences—Abrams, Lackowsky, and Lipman, each 20 years; Steamer, 15 years; Debs, 10 years; and Frohwerk, 10 years. Rosansky, who had turned state's evidence in *Abrams,* received three years, and Schenck received only six months. Holmes' statement in his *Abrams* dissent that the defendants in such cases merited no more than nominal punishment even if guilty may have influenced executive clemency. Warren Harding commuted the sentences for all the defendants mentioned, except Schenck, who was out of jail before Harding's election. The commutation of the sentences of Steamer, Abrams, Lackowsky, and Lipman had been on the condition they accept deportation to Russia.

III. THE 1920'S "RED SCARE" CASES

PEACE, BUT NO END TO FEAR[**]

With the Armistice in November, 1918, and the subsequent surrender of the Central Powers, one might assume that the frenzy would have abated, that a return to sanity would have left the American people, like the victim of a hangover, with a feeling of sheepish guilt. Yet, for reasons

* Dean Acheson, Morning and Noon, Houghton Mifflin Co., p. 119.

** John P. Roche, The Quest for the Dream, The Development of Civil Rights and Human Relations in Modern America, Macmillan Co., New York, 1963, pp. 66–68. Reprinted with permission.

which have never been adequately probed, the opposite was the case. The antiradical sentiments of the wartime years became, if anything, more intense after the Armistice and reached a somber climax of indignity in the Palmer Raids of 1919 and 1920.

The background of the Great Red Scare was provided by a number of objective historical factors—the Bolshevik Revolution and formation of the Comintern; a wave of vicious bombings or attempts at assassination of public officials attributed to the "Reds"[†]; a tremendous surge of strikes as labor abandoned the restraints of wartime and attempted to have wages catch up with prices; demobilization and accompanying uncertainty . . .; the constitutional absurdity of the Eighteenth Amendment [Prohibition], the Maginot Line of moribund Puritanism; a depression in which everything dropped but prices (in 1919, 2.3 percent of the work force was unemployed; by 1921, this had leaped to 11.9 percent); a reunited Republican Party savagely mauling President Wilson (who collapsed under the strain) and employing the motif of disillusionment with the war to castigate the whole reform tradition. These are the main threads the historian can trace, but there was a deeper social basis for the madness of the immediate postwar years: a generalized but largely unarticulated recognition that the country and the world had been transformed, and an equally widespread inability to comprehend the premises of the new, emerging social order. It was, in the phrase of the time, "a cockeyed world," but only the Dadaists and a few other artists of extraordinary cultural sensitivity faced up to the fact and tried to adjust their standards to the reality.

Most Americans simply got frightened and looked for the villains, the daemonic agents of insecurity who had destroyed the nice, comfortable world of 1914. Some rushed to eliminate strong drink, others saw jazz, or modernistic theology, or Darwinian biology, or the League of Nations as the enemy. But the simplest answer, one which fitted neatly into a long tradition of nativism, was to blame foreign influence, and specifically the impending conquest of America by foreign radicals. This attack, of course, meshed beautifully with the antiradical campaign of the war years, but was potentially far more inclusive. American Jews, for example, who had distinguished themselves in supporting the war effort, could be netted by the equation of Jews and Bolshevism; the American Federation of Labor could be lambasted along with the IWW as a radical, foreign conspiracy against the freedom of the American workingman.

GITLOW v. PEOPLE OF NEW YORK

Supreme Court of the United States, 1925.
268 U.S. 652, 45 S.Ct. 625, 69 L.Ed. 1138.

Justice Sanford delivered the opinion of the Court.

Benjamin Gitlow was indicted in the Supreme Court of New York, with three others, for the statutory crime of criminal anarchy. New

---

[†] On June 21, 1919, "a bomb wrecked the residence of Attorney General Palmer, archfoe of the Reds, in Washington; a man thought to be the bearer of the bomb was blown to pieces. The homes of Mayor Davis of Cleveland and Justice Albert F. Hayden of Roxbury, Mass., were dynamited at the same hour. A bomb partially destroyed the residence of Judge C. C. Mott in New York City." Mark Sullivan, Our Times, Scribners, 1936, vol. 6, pp. 170–71.

EDWARD TERRY SANFORD—Born on July 23, 1865, into a wealthy family in Knoxville, Tennessee. His father was a highly successful lumber dealer and wholesale drug merchant. Tennessee, A.B., and Ph. B., first in his class and Phi Beta Kappa, 1883. Two years later, he received a second A.B. at Harvard, where he was elected Class Day orator. After studying and travelling in Europe for a year before enrolling in the Harvard Law School, he served on the inaugural editorial board of the *Harvard Law Review* and received his LL.B. in 1889. Law practice in Knoxville, 1890–1906. Special assistant to U.S. attorney general 1905. Assistant U.S. attorney general, 1907–1908; U.S. district judge for the eastern and middle districts of Tennessee, 1908–1923. Taught law at the University of Tennessee, 1897–1916. Nominated to the Supreme Court on January 24, 1923, by Warren G. Harding upon the recommendation of Chief Justice Taft, to replace Mahlon Pitney, and confirmed by voice vote in the Senate on January 29, 1923. Urbane, genial, and courtly, Sanford was, in Justice Holmes' words, "born to charm." En route to Justice Holmes' 89th birthday party on March 8, 1930, Sanford stopped at his dentist's office to have a tooth extracted. Immediately thereafter he collapsed and died. Chief Justice Taft died the same day.

York Penal Laws, §§ 160, 161. He was separately tried, convicted, and sentenced to imprisonment. The judgment was affirmed by the Appellate Division and by the Court of Appeals....

The contention here is that the Statute, by its terms and as applied in this case, is repugnant to the due process clause of the Fourteenth Amendment. Its material provisions are:

§ 160. *Criminal anarchy defined.* Criminal anarchy is the doctrine that organized government should be overthrown by force or violence, or by assassination of the executive head or of any of the executive official of government, or by any unlawful means. The advocacy of such doctrine either by word of mouth or writing is a felony.

§ 161. *Advocacy of criminal anarchy.* Any person who:

1. By word of mouth or writing advocates, advises or teaches the duty, necessity or propriety of overthrowing or overturning organized government by force or violence, or by assassination of the executive head or of any of the executive officials of government, or by any unlawful means; or,

2. Prints, publishes, edits, issues or knowingly circulates, sells, distributes or publicly displays any book, paper, document, or written or printed matter in any form, containing or advocating, advising or teaching the doctrine that organized govern-

ment should be overthrown by force, violence, or any unlawful means. . . .

The following facts were established on the trial by undisputed evidence and admissions: The defendant is a member of the Left Wing Section of the Socialist Party, a dissenting branch or faction of that party formed in opposition to its dominant policy of "moderate Socialism." Membership in both is open to aliens as well as citizens. The Left Wing Section was organized nationally at a conference in New York City in June, 1919, attended by ninety delegates from twenty different States. The conference elected a National Council, of which the defendant was a member, and left to it the adoption of a "Manifesto." This was published in The Revolutionary Age, the official organ of the Left Wing. The defendant was on the board of managers of the paper and was its business manager. He arranged for the printing of the paper and took to the printer the manuscript of the first issue which contained the Left Wing Manifesto, and also a Communist Program and a Program of the Left Wing that had been adopted by the conference. Sixteen thousand copies were printed, which were delivered at the premises in New York City used as the office of the Revolutionary Age and the headquarters of the Left Wing, and occupied by the defendant and other officials. These copies were paid for by the defendant, as business manager of the paper. Employees of this office wrapped and mailed out copies of the paper under the defendant's direction; and copies were sold from this office. . . .

There was no evidence of any effect resulting from the publication and circulation of the Manifesto.

No witnesses were offered in behalf of the defendant.

. . . Coupled with a review of the rise of Socialism [the Manifesto] condemned the dominant "moderate Socialism" for its recognition of the necessity of the democratic parliamentary state; repudiated its policy of introducing Socialism by legislative measures; and advocated, in plain and unequivocal language, the necessity of accomplishing the "Communist Revolution" by a militant and "revolutionary Socialism", based on "the class struggle" and mobilizing the "power of the proletariat in action", through mass industrial revolts developing into mass political strikes and "revolutionary mass action," for the purpose of conquering and destroying the parliamentary state and establishing in its place, through a "revolutionary dictatorship of the proletariat", the system of Communist Socialist. The then recent strikes in Seattle and Winnipeg were cited as instances of a development already verging on revolutionary action and suggestive of proletarian dictatorship, in which the strike-workers were "trying to usurp the functions of municipal government"; and revolutionary Socialism, it was urged, must use these mass industrial revolts to broaden the strike, make it general and militant, and develop it into mass political strikes and revolutionary mass action for the annihilation of the parliamentary state. . . .

The Court of Appeals held that the Manifesto "advocated the overthrow of this government by violence, or by unlawful means."

... The sole contention here is, essentially, that as there was no evidence of any concrete result flowing from the publication of the Manifesto or of circumstances showing the likelihood of such result, the statute as construed and applied by the trial court penalized the mere utterance, as such, of "doctrine" having no quality of incitement, without regard either to the circumstances of its utterance or to the likelihood of unlawful sequences; and that, as the exercise of the right of free expression with relation to government is only punishable "in circumstances involving likelihood of substantive evil," the statute contravenes the due process clause of the Fourteenth Amendment. The argument in support of this contention rests primarily upon the following propositions: 1st, That the "liberty" protected by the Fourteenth Amendment includes the liberty of speech and of the press; and 2nd, That while liberty of expression "is not absolute," it may be restrained "only in circumstances where its exercise bears a causal relation with some substantive evil, consummated, attempted, or likely," and as the statute "takes no account of circumstances," it unduly restrains this liberty and is therefore unconstitutional.

The precise question presented, and the only question which we can consider under this writ of error, then is, whether the statute, as construed and applied in this case by the state courts, deprived the defendant of his liberty of expression in violation of the due process clause of the Fourteenth Amendment. . . .

For present purposes we may and do assume that freedom of speech and of the press—which are protected by the First Amendment from abridgment by Congress—are among the fundamental personal rights and "liberties" protected by the due process clause of the Fourteenth Amendment from impairment by the states. . . .

It is a fundamental principle, long established, that the freedom of speech and of the press which is secured by the Constitution, does not confer an absolute right to speak or publish, without responsibility, whatever one my choose, or an unrestricted and unbridled license that gives immunity for every possible use of language and prevents the punishment of those who abuse this freedom. . . . That a State in the exercise of its police power may punish those who abuse this freedom by utterances inimical to the public welfare, tending to corrupt public morals, incite to crime, or disturb the public peace, is not open to question. . . . And, for yet more imperative reasons, a State may punish utterances endangering the foundations of organized government and threatening its overthrow by unlawful means. These imperil its own existence as a constitutional State. Freedom of speech and press, said Story . . . does not protect disturbances to the public peace or the attempt to subvert the government. . . .

By enacting the present statute the State has determined, through its legislative body, that utterances advocating the overthrow of organized government by force, violence and unlawful means, are so inimical to the general welfare and involve such danger of substantive evil that they may be penalized in the exercise of its police power. That determination must be given great weight. Every presumption is to be indulged in favor of the validity of the statute. . . . And the case is to be considered "in the light of the principle that the state is primarily the judge of regulations required in the interest of public safety and welfare;" and that its police "statutes may only be declared unconstitutional where they are arbitrary or unreasonable attempts to exercise authority vested in the State in the public interest." Great Northern Ry. v. Clara City, 246 U.S. 434, 439. That utterances inciting to the overthrow of organized government by unlawful means, present a sufficient danger of substantive evil to bring their punishment within the range of legislative discretion, is clear. Such utterances, by their very nature, involve danger to the public peace and to the security of the State. They threaten breaches of the peace and ultimate revolution. And the immediate danger is none the less real and substantial, because the effect of a given utterance cannot be accurately foreseen. The State cannot reasonably be required to measure the danger from every such utterance in the nice balance of a jeweler's scale. A single revolutionary spark may kindle a fire that, smouldering for a time, may burst into a sweeping and destructive conflagration. It cannot be said that the State is acting arbitrarily or unreasonably when in the exercise of its judgment as to the measures necessary to protect the public peace and safety, it seeks to extinguish the spark without waiting until it has enkindled the flame or blazed into the conflagration. It cannot reasonably be required to defer the adoption of measures for its own peace and safely until the revolutionary utterances lead to actual disturbances of the public peace or imminent and immediate danger of its own destruction; but it may, in the exercise of its judgment, suppress the threatened danger in its incipiency.

· · ·

JUSTICE HOLMES, dissenting.

Justice Brandeis and I are of opinion that this judgment should be reversed. The general principle of free speech, it seems to me, must be taken to be included in the Fourteenth Amendment, in view of the scope that has been given to the word "liberty" as there used, although perhaps it may be accepted with a somewhat larger latitude of interpretation than is allowed to Congress by the sweeping language that governs or ought to govern the laws of the United States. If I am right, then I think that the criterion sanctioned by the full Court in Schenck v. United States, 249 U.S. 47, 52, applies. "The question in every case is whether the words used are used in such circumstances and are of such a nature as to create a clear and present danger that they will bring about the substantive evils that [the State] has a right to prevent." It is true that in my opinion this criterion was departed from in Abrams v. United States, 251 U.S. 616, but the convictions that I expressed in that case are too deep for it to be possible for me as yet to believe that it and Schaefer v. United States, 251 U.S. 466, have settled the law. If what I think the correct test is applied, it is manifest that there was no present danger of an attempt to overthrow the government by force on the part of the admittedly small minority who shared the defendant's views. It is said that this manifesto was more than a theory, that it was an incitement. Every idea is an incitement. It offers itself for belief and if believed it is acted on unless some other belief outweighs it or some failure of energy stifles the movement at its birth. The only difference between the expression of an opinion and an incitement in the narrower sense is the speaker's enthusiasm for the result. Eloquence may set fire to reason. But whatever may be thought of the redundant discourse before us it had no chance of starting a present conflagration. If in the long run the beliefs expressed in proletarian dictatorship are destined to be accepted by the dominant forces of the community, the only meaning of free speech is that they should be given their chance and have their way.

If the publication of this document had been laid as an attempt to induce an uprising against government at once and not at some indefinite time in the future it would have presented a different question. The object would have been one with which the law might deal, subject to the doubt whether there was any danger that the publication could produce any result, or in other word, whether it was not futile and too remote from possible consequences. But the indictment alleges the publication and nothing more.

WHITNEY v. CALIFORNIA

274 U.S. 357, 47 S.Ct. 641, 71 L.Ed. 1095 (1927).

[Charlotte Anita Whitney, Chafee reported, "was a woman nearing sixty, a Wellesley graduate long distinguished in philanthropic work. She joined the Socialist Party, and in 1919 when her 'local' participated in the Left Wing secession at Chicago she became a temporary member of the new Communist Labor Party and went as a delegate to a convention at Oakland ... for organizing a California branch.... The convention was openly held, reporters were present, and its deliberations were described in the next issues of the press. Miss Whitney vigorously supported a resolution that the new state party should aim to capture political power through the ballot. The convention voted this down, and adopted in its place the Chicago program of the national party, which ... urged the seizure of power by revolutionary industrial unionism.... Miss Whitney remained at the convention and did not resign from the party."* Three weeks later, she was arrested and charged with violating the following California statute: "Any person who ... organizes or assists in organizing, or is or knowingly becomes a member of any organization, society, group or assemblage of persons organized or assembled to advocate, teach, or aid and abet criminal syndicalism ... is guilty of a felony." A California statute defined "criminal syndicalism" as a doctrine that supports "the commission of crimes, sabotage ... or unlawful acts of force or violence or unlawful methods of terrorism as a means of accomplishing a change in industrial ownership or control, or affecting any political change." A jury convicted her of organizing and joining an association prohibited by the statute. The judge sentenced her to San Quentin Prison for a term of from one to 14 years. The California Court of Appeals affirmed the conviction and sentence.]

* Zechariah Chafee, Jr., Free Speech in the United States, 1941, pp. 343–44.

Justice Sanford delivered the opinion of the Court.

... [F]reedom of speech ... secured by the Constitution does not confer an absolute right to speak, without responsibility, whatever one may choose, or an unrestricted and unbridled license giving immunity for every possible use of language and preventing the punishment of those who abuse this freedom; and that a state in the exercise of its police power may punish those who abuse this freedom by utterances inimical to the public welfare, tending to incite in crime, disturb the public peace, or endanger the foundations of organized government and threaten its overthrow by unlawful means, is not open to question. Gitlow v. New York, ...

By enacting the provisions of the Syndicalism Act the state has declared, through its legislative body, that to knowingly be or become a member of or assist in organizing an association to advocate, teach or aid and abet the commission of crimes or unlawful acts of force, violence or terrorism as a means of accomplishing industrial or political changes, involves such danger to the public peace and the security of the state, that these acts should be penalized in the exercise of its police power. That determination must be given great weight....

The essence of the offense denounced by the act is the combining with others in an association for the accomplishment of the desired ends through the advocacy and use of criminal and unlawful methods. It partakes of the nature of a criminal conspiracy.... That such united and joint action involves even greater danger to the public peace and security than the isolated utterances and acts of individuals, is clear. We cannot hold that, as here applied, the act is an unreasonable or arbitrary exercise of the police power of the state, unwarrantably infringing any right of free speech, assembly, or association, or that those persons are protected from punishment by the due process clause who abuse such rights by joining and furthering an organization thus menacing the peace and welfare of the state.

We find no repugnancy in the Syndicalism Act as applied in this case to either the due process or equal protection clause of the 14th Amendment, on any of the grounds upon which its validity has been here challenged.

The order dismissing the writ of error will be vacated and set aside, and the judgment of the Court of Appeal affirmed.

Justice Brandeis wrote the following concurring opinion in which Justice Holmes joined.

[A]lthough the rights of free speech and assembly are fundamental, they are not in their nature absolute. Their exercise is subject to restriction, if the particular restriction proposed is required in order to protect the State from destruction or from serious injury, political, economic or moral. That the necessity which is essential to a valid restriction does not exist unless speech would produce, or is intended to produce, a clear and imminent danger of some substantive evil which

 LOUIS D. BRANDEIS—Born on November 13, 1856, in Louisville, Kentucky, to prosperous immigrants from Bohemia. Democrat. Jewish. Early education in Dresden, Germany. Harvard, LL.B., 1877, graduating first in his class with the highest average up to that time. Practiced law, 1878–1916. Called "the people's attorney" because of his *pro bono* legal work. Author of *Other People's Money* (1914) and *Business—A Profession* (1914). Introduced the "Brandeis brief," which presented economic and social data as well as legal arguments. Nominated associate justice on January 28, 1916, by President Woodrow Wilson, a political ally, to replace Joseph R. Lamar. First Jewish nominee to the Court. Confirmed by the Senate over strenuous opposition (some of it anti-Semitic) on June 1, 1916, by a 47–22 vote. Informally advised Woodrow Wilson and Franklin D. Roosevelt while on the Court. Retired on February 13, 1939. Died on October 5, 1941.

the State constitutionally may seek to prevent has been settled. See Schenck v. United States, 249 U.S. 47, 52 (1919).

This Court has not yet fixed the standard by which to determine when a danger shall be deemed clear; how remote the danger may be and yet be deemed present; and what degree of evil shall be deemed sufficiently substantial to justify resort to abridgement of free speech and assembly as the means of protection. To reach sound conclusions on these matters, we must bear in mind why a State is, ordinarily, denied the power to prohibit dissemination of social, economic and political doctrine which a vast majority of its citizens believes to be false and fraught with evil consequence.

Those who won our independence believed that the final end of the State was to make men free to develop their faculties; and that in its government the deliberative forces should prevail over the arbitrary. They valued liberty both as an end and as a means. They believed liberty to be the secret of happiness and courage to be the secret of liberty. They believed that freedom to think as you will and to speak as you think are means indispensable to the discovery and spread of political truth; that without free speech and assembly discussion would be futile; that with them, discussion affords ordinarily adequate protection against the dissemination of noxious doctrine; that the greatest menace to freedom is an inert people; that public discussion is a political duty; and that this should be a fundamental principle of the American government.[1] They recognized the risks to which all human institutions are subject. But they knew that order cannot be secured merely through fear of punishment for its infraction; that it is hazardous to discourage thought, hope and imagination; that fear breeds repression; that repression breeds

---

1. Compare Thomas Jefferson: "We have nothing to fear from the demoralizing reasonings of some, if others are left free to demonstrate their errors and especially when the law stands ready to punish the first criminal act produced by the false reasonings; these are safer corrections than the conscience of the judge." Quoted by Charles A. Beard, The Nation, July 7, 1926, vol. 123, p. 8. Also in first Inaugural Address: "If there be any among us who would wish to dissolve this union or change its republican form, let them stand undisturbed as monuments of the safety with which error of opinion may be tolerated where reason is left free to combat it."

hate; that hate menaces stable government; that the path of safety lies in the opportunity to discuss freely supposed grievances and proposed remedies; and that the fitting remedy for evil counsels is good ones. Believing in the power of reason as applied through public discussion, they eschewed silence coerced by law—the argument of force in its worst form. Recognizing the occasional tyrannies of governing majorities, they amended the Constitution so that free speech and assembly should be guaranteed.

Fear of serious injury cannot alone justify suppression of free speech and assembly. Men feared witches and burnt women. It is the function of speech to free men from the bondage of irrational fears. To justify suppression of free speech there must be reasonable ground to fear that serious evil will result if free speech is practiced. There must be reasonable ground to believe that the danger apprehended is imminent. There must be reasonable ground to believe that the evil to be prevented is a serious one. Every denunciation of existing law tends in some measure to increase the probability that there will be violation of it. Condonation of a breach enhances the probability. Expressions of approval add to the probability. Propagation of the criminal state of mind by teaching syndicalism increases it. Advocacy of law-breaking heightens it still further. But even advocacy of violation, however reprehensible morally, is not a justification for denying free speech where the advocacy falls short of incitement and there is nothing to indicate that the advocacy would be immediately acted on. The wide difference between advocacy and incitement, between preparation and attempt, between assembling and conspiracy, must be borne in mind. In order to support a finding of clear and present danger it must be shown either that immediate serious violence was to be expected or was advocated, or that the past conduct furnished reason to believe that such advocacy was then contemplated.

Those who won our independence by revolution were not cowards. They did not fear political change. They did not exalt order at the cost of liberty. To courageous, self-reliant men, with confidence in the power of free and fearless reasoning applied through the processes of popular government, no danger flowing from speech can be deemed clear and present, unless the incidence of the evil apprehended is so imminent that it may befall before there is opportunity for full discussion. If there be time to expose through discussion the falsehood and fallacies, to avert the evil by the processes of education, the remedy to be applied is more speech, not enforced silence. Only an emergency can justify repression. Such must be the rule if authority is to be reconciled with freedom. Such, in my opinion, is the command of the Constitution. It is therefore always open to Americans to challenge a law abridging free speech and assembly by showing that there was no emergency justifying it.

Moreover, even imminent danger cannot justify resort to prohibition of these functions essential to effective democracy, unless the evil apprehended is relatively serious. Prohibition of free speech and assembly is a measure so stringent that it would be inappropriate as the means for averting a relatively trivial harm to society. A police measure may be unconstitutional merely because the remedy, although effective as means of protection, is unduly harsh or oppressive. Thus, a State might, in the exercise of its police power, make any trespass upon the land of another a crime, regardless of the results or of the intent or purpose of the trespasser. It might, also, punish an attempt, a conspiracy, or an incitement to commit the trespass. But it is hardly conceivable that this Court would hold constitutional a statute which punished as a felony the mere voluntary assembly with a society formed to teach that pedestrians had the moral right to cross unenclosed, unposted, waste lands and to advocate their doing so, even if there was imminent danger that advocacy would lead to a trespass. The fact that speech is likely to result in some violence or in destruction of property is not enough to justify its suppression. There must be the probability of serious injury to the State. Among free men, the deterrents ordinarily to be applied to prevent crime are education and punishment for violations of the law, not abridgment of the rights of free speech and assembly.

THE IMPACT OF BRANDEIS' OPINION IN WHITNEY

Soon after the Court's decision in *Whitney,* Governor C.C. Young of California pardoned Anita Whitney. Repeatedly referring to Justice Brandeis' opinion, Young concluded that there was no clear and present danger to justify Whitney's conviction. "The Communist Labor Party," he wrote in pardoning her, "has practically disappeared, not only in California, but also in other states where no criminal syndicalism law existed. It was a visionary attempt to plant European radicalism upon an American soil, where it simply could not thrive. I am unable to learn of any activities of this party, in California, at least, and possibly in America, which ever rendered it a danger to the state or a menace to our institutions."*

NOTES AND QUESTIONS

1.   Justice Sanford's opinion in *Gitlow* is important for two reasons. First, it acknowledged for the first time that the free speech and press guarantees of the First Amendment apply to the States as "liberty" protected by the due process clause of the Fourteenth Amendment. Second, it illustrates the bad tendency test which prevailed during the nineteenth century and well into the twentieth century. Under that test, the danger need not be immediate. As Sanford wrote: "A simple revolutionary spark my kindle a fire that, smouldering for a time, may burst into a sweeping and destructive conflagration."

2.   Justice Brandeis' separate opinion in the *Whitney* case is a concurrence and not a dissent. That means that he agreed with the result reached by the majority, which was to affirm the conviction. His reasons were procedural. Normally, the Supreme Court will not consider issues that have not been raised in the courts below and are presented, for the first time, when the case reaches the Supreme Court. Miss Whitney had not raised the "clear and present danger issue" in the California courts, and thus Justices Brandeis and Holmes concluded that her conviction could not be upset on the ground that there was no clear and present danger. Significantly, Justice Brandeis stated that "there

---

* Quoted in Zachariah Chafee, Jr., Free Speech in the United States, Harvard University Press, 1941, p. 353.

was evidence on which the court or jury might have found that such danger existed." Evidently, he concluded that there was evidence that showed that the Communist Labor Party of California had engaged in advocacy of illegal acts under circumstances where a "clear and present danger," even as he defined that term, might exist. There was, however, no evidence that Miss Whitney engaged in that kind of advocacy. Although she did not resign when her efforts failed, she had sought to channel the party in a direction that would have relied on the political processes to seek change. Would there still be a free speech issue if it were concluded that (1) the Party advocated violence under circumstances where that advocacy could be made a crime; (2) Miss Whitney disagreed with what was advocated and did not personally participate in that kind of advocacy; and (3) Miss Whitney remained an active member of the Party, knowing of the Party's illegal advocacy?

3.   Under the Brandeis test, could someone be punished for giving a speech saying that when governments cease to represent the people, the people have the right to revolt? Would that depend on whether conditions were so unsettled that violent revolution was a real possibility in the near future? Is it paradoxical to allow speech only when it is so unpopular as not to present a "clear and present danger?" If the same speech finds enough acceptance in the marketplace of ideas as to present a "clear and present danger," can we then disallow it?

4.   One reason that Brandeis' concurring opinion does not seem to fit the Whitney facts is that originally it had been written for another case—Ruthenberg v. Michigan, 273 U.S. 782 (1927), which had been dismissed because the appellant had died while the case was on appeal. In a draft of the *Ruthenberg* opinion, which shows the influence of Chafee's *Freedom of Speech* (1920), Brandeis wrote: "[A]dvocacy of violation, however reprehensible morally, is not a justification for denying free speech, where, as here, the advocacy falls short of incitement. Here, there is nothing to indicate that the advocacy would be immediately acted on. To support a finding of clear and present danger, it would have to be shown either that immediate violence was, in fact, advocated, or that the past conduct of Ruthenberg or other delegates furnished reason to believe that such advocacy was then contemplated."*

IV.   THE POST WORLD WAR II CASES

DENNIS v. UNITED STATES

Supreme Court of the United States, 1951.
341 U.S. 494, 71 S.Ct. 857, 95 L.Ed. 1137.

[In July of 1948, top leaders of the Communist Party of the United States were indicted under a federal criminal statute, the Smith Act, which had been enacted in 1940, prior to the United States' entry into the Second World War. It was similar, in substance, to the New York Criminal Anarchy Act of 1902, under which Gitlow had been convicted in the 1920s. The defendants were charged with conspiracy to advocate the violent overthrow of the government of the United States, and with

---

* Louis D. Brandeis Papers, Harvard Law School, Microfilm Reel 34, p. 322.

organizing the Communist Party to advocate violent overthrow of the government. After a lengthy and turbulent trial, the defendants were convicted in July, 1949. Their conviction was affirmed by the United States Court of Appeals, with Chief Judge Learned Hand writing the opinion for the majority. The government proved its case primarily by showing, through the use of classic Marxist–Leninist materials, that the Communist Party was committed to a policy of violent revolution and that the defendants were principal officers of the Party. During the trial, there was little or no proof that any defendant had personally advocated any specific act of violence or that the Party had laid specific plans for revolution. When it agreed to review the case, the Supreme Court declined to consider whether the evidence against the defendants was sufficient to sustain their convictions. The issues argued before the Court were limited to whether the Smith Act was constitutional. The government's arguments to the Supreme Court relied squarely on the *Gitlow* case, which stood for the proposition that statutes outlawing the advocacy of violent revolution did not violate the First Amendment. The defendants relied on Holmes' dissent in *Gitlow* and Brandeis' concurrence in *Whitney*. Specifically, they pointed out that there was no charge or proof that they had advocated an immediate revolution.]

CHIEF JUSTICE VINSON announced the judgment of the Court and an opinion in which JUSTICE REED, JUSTICE BURTON and JUSTICE MINTON join.*

. . .

The obvious purpose of the statute is to protect existing Government, not from change by peaceable, lawful and constitutional means, but from change by violence, revolution and terrorism. That it is within the *power* of the Congress to protect the Government of the United States from armed rebellion is a proposition which requires little discussion. Whatever theoretical merit there may be to the argument that there is a "right" to rebellion against dictatorial governments is without force where the existing structure of the government provides for peaceful and orderly change. We reject any principle of governmental helplessness in the face of preparation for revolution, which principle, carried to its logical conclusion, must lead to anarchy. No one could conceive that it is not within the power of Congress to prohibit acts intended to overthrow the Government by force and violence. The question with which we are concerned here is not whether Congress has such *power*, but

---

* If a majority of the Justices who participated in the decision all join one opinion, it is the opinion of "the Court." It happens sometimes, that a majority of the Justices agree to a particular result but not to a particular rationale for the decision. The opinion that commands the most votes of those in the majority is often referred to as a plurality opinion. In *Dennis*, eight Justices participated. (Justice Clark, who had been United States Attorney General while the case was in the lower courts, took himself out of the case.) The plurality opinion of Chief Justice Vinson had the votes of three other Justices. Technically, nothing said in the plurality opinion can be counted on as the position of "the Court." One must take into account the other opinions and engage in the complex process of deciding what points were agreed to be a majority. (In this case, there are separate concurrences by Justices Frankfurter and Jackson, and dissents by Justices Black and Douglas.) Nevertheless, subsequent cases, while they have substantially modified the law, have treated the plurality opinion in *Dennis* much as they would have treated it if it had been the opinion for "the Court."

whether the *means* which it has employed conflict with the First and Fifth Amendments to the Constitution.

One of the bases for the contention that the means which Congress has employed are invalid takes the form of an attack on the face of the statute on the grounds that by its terms it prohibits academic discussion of the merits of Marxism–Leninism, that it stifles ideas and is contrary to all concepts of a free speech and a free press. Although we do not agree that the language itself has that significance, we must bear in mind that it is the duty of the federal courts to interpret federal legislation in a manner not inconsistent with the demands of the Constitution. . . .

The very language of the Smith Act negates the interpretation which petitioners would have us impose on that Act. It is directed at advocacy, not discussion. Thus, the trial judge properly charged the jury that they could not convict if they found that petitioners did "no more than pursue peaceful studies and discussions or teaching and advocacy in the realm of ideas." He further charged that it was not unlawful "to conduct in an American college or university a course explaining the philosophical theories set forth in the books which have been placed in evidence." Such a charge is in strict accord with the statutory language, and illustrates the meaning to be placed on those words. Congress did not intend to eradicate the free discussion of political theories, to destroy the traditional rights of Americans to discuss and evaluate ideas without fear of governmental sanction. Rather Congress was concerned with the very kind of activity in which the evidence showed these petitioners engaged.

Although no case subsequent to *Whitney* and *Gitlow* has expressly overruled the majority opinions in those cases, there is little doubt that subsequent opinions have inclined toward the Holmes–Brandeis rationale. . . . But . . . neither Justice Holmes nor Justice Brandeis ever envisioned that a shorthand phrase should be crystalized into a rigid rule to be applied inflexibly without regard to the circumstances of each case. Speech is not an absolute, above and beyond control by the legislature when its judgment, subject to review here, is that certain kinds of speech are so undesirable as to warrant criminal sanction. Nothing is more certain in modern society than the principle that there are no absolutes, that a name, a phrase, a standard has meaning only when associated with the considerations which gave birth to the nomenclature. To those who would paralyze our Government in the face of impending threat by encasing it in a semantic straitjacket we must reply that all concepts are relative.

In this case we are squarely presented with the application of the "clear and present danger" test, and must decide what that phrase imports. We first note that many of the cases in which this Court has reversed convictions by use of this or similar tests have been based on the fact that the interest which the State was attempting to protect was itself too insubstantial to warrant restriction of speech. Overthrow of the Government by force and violence is certainly a substantial enough interest for the Government to limit speech. Indeed, this is the ultimate value of any society, for if a society cannot protect its very structure from armed internal attack, it must follow that no subordinate value can be protected. If, then, this interest may be protected, the literal problem which is presented is what has been meant by the use of the phrase "clear and present danger" of the utterances bringing about the evil within the power of Congress to punish.

Obviously, the words cannot mean that before the Government may act, it must wait until the *putsch* is about to be executed, the plans have been laid and the signal is awaited. If Government is aware that a group aiming at its overthrow is attempting to indoctrinate its members and to commit them to a course whereby they will strike when the leaders feel the circumstances permit, action by the Government is required. The argument that there is no need for Government to concern itself, for Government is strong, it possesses ample powers to put down a rebellion, it may defeat the revolution with ease needs no answer. For that is not the question. Certainly an attempt to overthrow the Government by force, even though doomed from the outset because of inadequate numbers or power of the revolutionists, is a sufficient evil for Congress to prevent. The damage which such attempts create both physically and politically to a nation makes it impossible to measure the validity in terms of the probability of success, or the immediacy of a successful attempt. In the instant case the trial judge charged the jury that they could not convict unless they found that petitioners intended to over-throw the Government "as speedily as circumstances would permit." This does not mean, and could not properly mean, that they would not strike until there was certainty of success. What was meant was that the revolutionists would strike when they thought the time was ripe. We must therefore reject the contention that success or probability of success is the criterion.

The situation with which Justices Holmes and Brandeis were con-cerned in *Gitlow* was a comparatively isolated event, bearing little relation in their minds to any substantial threat to the safety of the community. They were not confronted with any situation comparable to the instant one—the development of an apparatus designed and dedicat-ed to the overthrow of the Government, in the context of world crisis after crisis.

Chief Judge Learned Hand, writing for the majority below, inter-preted the phrase as follows: "In each case [courts] must ask whether the gravity of the 'evil,' discounted by its improbability, justifies such invasion of free speech as is necessary to avoid the danger." We adopt this statement of the rule. As articulated by Chief Judge Hand, it is as succinct and inclusive as any other we might devise at this time. It takes into consideration those factors which we deem relevant, and relates their significances. More we cannot expect from words.

Likewise, we are in accord with the court below, which affirmed the trial court's finding that the requisite danger existed. The mere fact that from the period 1945 to 1948 petitioners' activities did not result in an attempt to overthrow the Government by force and violence is of course no answer to the fact that there was a group that was ready to make the attempt. The formation by petitioners of such a highly organized conspiracy, with rigidly disciplined members subject to call when the leaders, these petitioners, felt that the time had come for action, coupled with the inflammable nature of world conditions, similar uprisings in other countries, and the touch-and-go nature of our relations with countries with whom petitioners were in the very least ideologically attuned, convince us that their convictions were justified on this score. And this analysis disposes of the contention that a conspiracy to advocate, as distinguished from the advocacy itself, cannot be constitutionally restrained, because it comprises only the preparation. It is the existence of the conspiracy which creates the danger. If the ingredients of the reaction are present, we cannot bind the Government to wait until the catalyst is added.

We hold that ... the Smith Act [does] not inherently, or as construed or applied in the instant case, violate the First Amendment ... Petitioners intended to overthrow the Government of the United States as speedily as the circumstances would permit. Their conspiracy to organize the Communist Party and to teach and advocate the overthrow of the Government of the United States by force and violence created a "clear and present danger" of an attempt to overthrow the Government by force and violence. They were properly and constitutionally convicted.

Affirmed.

JUSTICE CLARK took no part in the consideration or decision of this case.

JUSTICE FRANKFURTER concurring in the affirmance of the judgment.

... The First Amendment categorically demands the "Congress shall make no law respecting an establishment of religion, or prohibiting the free exercise thereof; or abridging the freedom of speech, or of the press; or the right of the people peaceably to assemble, and to petition the Government for a redress of grievances." The right of a man to think what he pleases, to write what he thinks, and to have his thoughts made available for others to hear or read has an engaging ring of universality. The Smith Act and this conviction under it no doubt restrict the exercise of free speech and assembly. Does that, without more, dispose of the matter? ...

Absolute rules would inevitably lead to absolute exceptions, and such exceptions would eventually corrode the rules. The demands of free speech in a democratic society as well as the interest in national security are better served by candid and informed weighing of the competing interests, within the confines of the judicial process, than by announcing dogmas too inflexible for the non-Euclidian problems to be solved.

But how are competing interests to be assumed? Since they are not subject to quantitative ascertainment, the issue necessarily resolves itself into asking, who is to make the adjustment?—who is to balance the relevant factors and ascertain which interest is in the circumstances to prevail? Full responsibility for the choice cannot be give to the courts. Courts are not representative bodies. They are not designed to be a good reflex of a democratic society. Their judgment is best informed, and therefore most dependable, within narrow limits. Their essential quality is detachment, founded on independence. History teaches that the independence of the judiciary is jeopardized when courts become embroiled in the passions of the day and assume primary responsibility in choosing between competing political, economic and social pressures.

Primary responsibility for adjusting the interest which compete in the situation before us of necessity belongs to the Congress. The nature of the power to be exercised by this Court has been delineated in decisions not charged with the emotional appeal of the situations such as that now before us. We are to set aside the judgment of those whose duty it is to legislate only if there is no reasonable basis for it.

. . . Some members of the Court—and at times a majority—have done more. They have suggested that our function in reviewing statutes restricting freedom of expression differs sharply from our normal duty in sitting in judgment of legislation. It has been said that such statutes "must be justified by clear public interest, threatened not doubtfully or remotely, but by clear and present danger. The rational connection between the remedy provided and the evil to be curbed, which in other contexts might support legislation against attack on due process grounds, will not suffice." Thomas v. Collins, 323 U.S. 516, 530. It has been suggested, with the casualness of a footnote, that such legislation is not presumptively valid, see United States v. Carolene Products Co., 304 U.S. 144, 152, n. 4, and it has been weightily reiterated that freedom of speech as a "preferred position" among constitutional safeguards. Kovacs v. Cooper, 336 U.S. 77,88.

The precise meaning intended to be conveyed by these phrases need not now be pursued. It is enough to note that they have recurred in the Court's opinions, and their cumulative force has, not without justification, engendered belief that there is a constitutional principle, expressed by those attractive but imprecise words, prohibiting restriction upon utterance unless it creates a situation of "imminent" peril against which legislation may guard. It is on this body of the Court's pronouncements that the defendants' argument here is based. . . .

I must leave to others the ungrateful task of trying to reconcile all these decisions. . . . In other instances we weighted the interest in free speech so heavily that we permitted essential conflicting values to be destroyed. Bridges v. California. . . . Viewed as a whole, however, the decisions express an attitude toward the judicial function and a standard of values which for me are decisive of the case before us.

Free-speech cases are not an exception to the principle that we are not legislators, that direct policy-making is not our province. How best to reconcile competing interests is the business of legislatures, and the balance they strike is a judgment not to be displaced by ours, but to be respected unless outside the pale of fair judgment.

On occasion we have strained to interpret legislation in order to limit its effect on interest protected by the first Amendment. Schneiderman v. United States, *supra;* Bridges v. Wixon, *supra.* In some instances we have denied to States the deference to which I think they are entitled. Bridges v. California, *supra;* Craig v. Harney, *supra.* Once in this recent course of decisions the Court refused to permit a jury to draw inferences which seemed to me obviously reasonable. Hartzel v. United States, *supra.*

But in no case has a majority of this Court held that a legislative judgment, even as to freedom of utterance, may be overturned merely because the Court would have made a different choice between the competing interests had the initial legislative judgment been for it to make. . . .

One of the judges below rested his affirmance on the *Gitlow* decision, and the defendants do not attempt to distinguish the case. They place their argument squarely on the ground that the case has been overruled by subsequent decisions. It has not been explicitly overruled. But it would be disingenuous to deny that the dissent in *Gitlow* has been treated with the respect usually accorded to a decision.

The result of the *Gitlow* decision was to send a left-wing socialist to jail for publishing a Manifesto expressing Marxist exhortations. It requires excessive tolerance of the legislative judgment to suppose that the *Gitlow* publication in the circumstances could justify serious concern.

In contrast, there is ample justification for a legislative judgment that the conspiracy now before us is a substantial threat to national order and security. If the Smith Act is justified at all, it is justified precisely because it may serve to prohibit the type of conspiracy for which these defendants were convicted. The court below properly held that as a matter of separability the Smith Act may be limited to those situations to which it can constitutionally be applied. Our decision today certainly does not mean that the Smith Act can constitutionally be applied to facts like those in Gitlow v. New York. While reliance may properly be placed on the attitude of judicial self-restraint which the *Gitlow* decision reflects, it is not necessary to depend on the facts or the full extent of the theory of that case in order to find that the judgment of Congress, as applied to the facts of the case now before us, is not in conflict with the First Amendment. . . .

Throughout our decisions there has recurred a distinction between the statement of an idea which may prompt its hearers to take unlawful action, and advocacy that such action be taken. . . .

It is true that there is no divining rod by which we may locate "advocacy." Exposition of ideas readily merges into advocacy. The same Justice who gave currency to application of the incitement doctrine in this field dissented four times from what he thought was its misapplication. As he said in the *Gitlow* dissent, "Every idea is an incitement." 268 U.S. at 673. Even though advocacy of overthrow deserves little protection, we should hesitate to prohibit it if we thereby inhibit the interchange of rational ideas so essential to representative government and free society.

But there is underlying validity in the distinction between advocacy and the interchange of ideas, and we do not discard a useful tool because it may be misused. That distinction could be used unreasonably by those in power against hostile or unorthodox views does not negate the fact that it may be used reasonably against an organization wielding the power of the centrally controlled international Communist movement. The object of the conspiracy before is so clear that the chance of error in saying that the defendants conspired to advocate rather than to express ideas is slight. Justice Douglas quite properly points out that the conspiracy before us is not a conspiracy to overthrow the Government. But it would be equally wrong to treat it as a seminar in political theory.

Of course no government can recognize a "right" of revolution or a "right" to incite revolution if the incitement has no other purpose or effect. But speech is seldom restricted to a single purpose, and its effects may be manifold. A public interest is not wanting in granting freedom to speak their minds even to those who advocate the overthrow of the Government by force. For, as the evidence in this case abundantly illustrates, coupled with such advocacy is criticism of defects in our society.... It is a commonplace that there may be a grain of truth in the most uncouth doctrine, however false and repellent the balance may be. Suppressing advocates of overthrow inevitably will also silence critics who do not advocate overthrow but fear that their criticism may be so construed. No matter how clear we may be that the defendants now before us are preparing to overthrow our Government at the propitious moment, it is self-delusion to think that we can punish them for their advocacy without adding to the risks run by loyal citizens who honestly believe in some of the reforms these defendants advance. It is a sobering fact that in sustaining the convictions before us we can hardly escape restriction on the interchange of ideas....

It is not for us to decide how we would adjust the clash of interests which this case presents were the primary responsibility for reconciling it ours. Congress has determined that the danger created by advocacy of overthrow justifies the ensuing restriction on freedom of speech. The determination was made after due deliberation, and the seriousness of the congressional purpose is attested by the volume of legislation passed to effectuate the same ends....

To make validity of legislation depend on judicial reading of events still in the womb of time—a forecast, that is, of the outcome of forces at best appreciated only with knowledge of the topmost secrets of nations— is to charge the judiciary with duties beyond its equipment....

All the Court says is that Congress was not forbidden by the Constitution to pass this enactment and that a prosecution under it may be brought against a conspiracy such as the one before us....

JUSTICE JACKSON, concurring.

. . .

The "clear and present danger" test was an innovation by Justice Holmes in the *Schenck* case, reiterated and refined by him and Justice Brandeis in later cases, all arising before the era of World War II revealed the subtlety and efficacy of modernized revolutionary techniques used by totalitarian parties.

I would save it, unmodified, for application as a "rule of reason" in the kind of case for which it was devised. When the issue is criminality of a hot-headed speech on a street corner, or circulation of a few incendiary pamphlets, or parading by some zealots behind a red flag, or refusal of a handful of school children to salute our flag, it is not beyond the capacity of the judicial process to gather, comprehend, and weigh the necessary materials for decision whether it is a clear and present danger of substantive evil or a harmless letting off of steam. . . .

In more recent times these problems have been complicated by the intervention between the state and the citizen of permanently organized, well-financed, semisecret and highly disciplined political organizations. Totalitarian groups here and abroad perfected the technique of creating private paramilitary organizations to coerce both the public government and its citizens. These organizations assert as against our Government all of the constitutional rights and immunities of individuals and at the same time exercise over their followers much of the authority which they deny to the Government. The Communist Party realistically is a state within a state, an authoritarian dictatorship within a republic. It demands these freedoms, not for its members, but for the organized party. It denies to its own members at the same time the freedom to dissent, to debate, to deviate from the party line, and enforces its authoritarian rule by crude purges, if nothing more violent.

The law of conspiracy has been the chief means at the Government's disposal to deal with the growing problems created by such organizations. I happen to think it is an awkward and inept remedy, but I find no constitutional authority for taking this weapon from the Government. There is no constitutional right to "gang up" on the Government

While I think there was power in Congress to enact this statute and that, as applied in this case, it cannot be held unconstitutional, I add that I have little faith in the long-range effectiveness of this conviction to stop the rise of the Communist movement. . . .

JUSTICE BLACK, dissenting.

At the outset I want to emphasize what the crime involved in this case is, and what it is not. These petitioners were not charged with an attempt to overthrow the Government. They were not charged with overt acts of any kind designed to overthrow the Government. They were not even charged with saying anything or writing anything designed to overthrow the Government. The charge was that they agreed to assemble and to talk and publish certain ideas at a later date: The indictment is that they conspired to organize the Communist Party and to use speech or newspapers and other publications in the future to teach and advocate the forcible overthrow of the Government. No matter how it is worded, this is a virulent form of prior censorship of speech and press, which I believe the First Amendment forbids. I would hold § 3 of the Smith Act authorizing this prior restraint unconstitutional on its face and as applied.

. . . The opinions for affirmance indicate that the chief reason for jettisoning the rule [of clear and present danger] is the expressed fear that advocacy of Communist doctrine endangers the safety of the Republic. Undoubtedly, a governmental policy of unfettered communication of ideas does entail dangers. To the Founders of this Nation, however, the benefits derived from free expression were worth the risk. They embodied this philosophy in the First Amendment's command that "Congress shall make no law ... abridging the freedom of speech, or of the press...." I have always believed that the First Amendment is the keystone of our Government, that the freedoms it guarantees provide the best insurance against destruction of all freedom. At least as to speech in the realm of public matters, I believe that the "clear and present danger" test does not "mark the furthermost constitutional boundaries of protected expression" but does "no more than recognize a minimum compulsion of the Bill of Rights." Bridges v. California, 314 U.S. 252, 263 (1941).

So long as this Court exercises the power of judicial review of legislation, I cannot agree that the First Amendment permits us to sustain laws suppressing freedom of speech and press on the basis of Congress' or our own notions of mere "reasonableness." Such a doctrine waters down the First Amendment so that it amounts to little more than an admonition to Congress. The Amendment as so construed is not likely to protect any but those "safe" or orthodox views which rarely need its protection....

Public opinion being what it now is, few will protest the conviction of these Communist petitioners. There is hope, however, that in calmer times, when present pressures, passions and fears subside, this or some later Court will restore the First Amendment liberties to the high preferred place where they belong in a free society.

JUSTICE DOUGLAS, dissenting.

WILLIAM O. DOUGLAS—Born on October 16, 1898, in Maine, Minnesota, son of a Presbyterian home missionary who died when Douglas was five. Democrat. Presbyterian. Grew up in genteel poverty in Yakima, Washington. Served as a private in the U.S. army in 1918. Whitman, B.A., Phi Beta Kappa, 1920. High school teacher, 1920–1922. Attended Columbia Law School, from which he received an LL.B. in 1925, graduating second in his class. Practiced law, 1925–1927; Columbia law faculty, 1925–1928; Yale law faculty, 1928–1934; 1928–1934; director of protective committee study, Securities and Exchange Commission, 1934–1936; S.E.C. commissioner and chairman, 1936–1939. Author of numerous legal and popular books. Nominated associate justice on March 20, 1939, by President Franklin D. Roosevelt, with whom he regularly played poker, to replace Louis D. Brandeis. Confirmed on April 4, 1939, by a 62–4 vote. Suffered a stroke and retired on November 12, 1975. Died on January 19, 1980. Holds the record for longest service on the Supreme Court.

If this were a case where those who claimed protection under the First Amendment were teaching the techniques of sabotage, the assassination of the President, the filching of documents from public files, the planting of bombs, the art of street warfare, and the like, I would have no doubts. The freedom to speak is not absolute; the teaching of methods of terror and other seditious conduct should be beyond the pale along with obscenity and immorality. This case was argued as if those were the facts. The argument imported much seditious conduct into the record. That is easy and it has popular appeal, for the activities of Communists in plotting and scheming against the free world are common knowledge. But the fact is that no such evidence was introduced at the trial.... It may well be that indoctrination in the techniques of terror to destroy the Government would be indictable under either statute. But the teaching which is condemned here is of a different character.

So far as the present record is concerned, what petitioners did was to organize people to teach and themselves teach the Marxist–Leninist doctrine contained chiefly in four books: Stalin, Foundations of Leninism (1924); Marx and Engels, Manifesto of the Communist Party (1848); Lenin, The State and Revolution (1917); History of the Communist Party of the Soviet Union (B.) (1939).

Those books are to Soviet Communism what Mein Kampf was to Nazism. If they are understood, the ugliness of Communism is revealed, its deceit and cunning are exposed, the nature of its activities becomes apparent, and the chances of its success less likely. That is not, of course, the reason why petitioners chose these books for their classrooms. They are fervent Communists to whom these volumes are gospel. They preached the creed with the hope that some day it would be acted upon.

The opinion of the Court does not outlaw these texts nor condemn them to the fire, as the Communists do literature offensive to their creed. But if the books themselves are not outlawed, if they can lawfully remain on library shelves, by what reasoning does their use in a classroom become a crime? It would not be a crime under the Act to introduce these books to a class, though that would be teaching what the creed of violent overthrow of the Government is. The Act, as construed, requires the element of intent—that those who teach the creed believe in it. The crime then depends not on what is taught but on who the teacher is. That is to make freedom of speech turn not on *what is said,* but on the *intent* with which it is said. Once we start down that road we enter territory dangerous to the liberties of every citizen.

There was a time in England when the concept of constructive treason flourished. Men were punished not for raising a hand against the king but for thinking murderous thoughts about him. The Framers of the Constitution were alive to that abuse and took steps to see that the practice would not flourish here. Treason was defined to require overt acts—the evolution of a plot against the country into an actual project. The present case is not one of treason. But the analogy is close when the illegality is made to turn on intent, not on the nature of the act. We then start probing men's minds for motive and purpose; they become entangled in the law not for what they did but *for what they thought;* they get convicted not for what they said but for the purpose with which they said it.

Intent, of course, often makes the difference in the law. An act otherwise excusable or carrying minor penalties may grow to an abhorrent thing if the evil intent is present. We deal here, however, not with ordinary acts but with speech, to which the Constitution has given a special sanction.

The vice of treating speech as the equivalent of overt acts of a treasonable or seditious character is emphasized by a concurring opinion, which by invoking the law of conspiracy makes speech do service for deeds which are dangerous to society.... [W]e deal here with speech alone, not with speech *plus* acts of sabotage or unlawful conduct. Not a single seditious act is charged in the indictment. To make a lawful speech unlawful because two men conceive it is to raise the law of conspiracy to appalling proportions. That course is to make a radical break with the past and to violate one of the cardinal principles of our constitutional scheme.

There comes a time when even speech loses its constitutional immunity. Speech innocuous one year may at another time fan such destructive flames that it must be halted in the interests of the safety of the Republic. That is the meaning of the clear and present danger test. When conditions are so critical that there will be no time to avoid the evil that the speech threatens, it is time to call a halt. Otherwise, free speech which is the strength of the Nation will be the cause of its destruction.

Yet free speech is the rule, not the exception. The restraint to be constitutional must be based on more than fear, on more than passionate opposition against the speech, on more than a revolted dislike for its contents. There must be some immediate injury to society that is likely if speech is allowed....

The nature of Communism as a force on the world scene would, of course, be relevant to the issue of clear and present danger of petitioners' advocacy within the United States. But the primary consideration is the strength and tactical position of petitioners and their converts in this country. On that there is no evidence in the record. If we are to take judicial notice of the threat of Communists within the Nation, it should not be difficult to conclude that *as a political party* they are of little consequence. Communists in this country have never made a respectable or serious showing in any election. I would doubt that there is a village, let alone a city or county or state, which the Communists could carry. Communism in the world scene is no bogeyman, but Communism as a political faction or party in this country plainly is. Communism has been so thoroughly exposed in this country that it has been crippled as a political force. Free speech has destroyed it as an effective political party. It is inconceivable that those who went up and down this country preaching the doctrine of revolution which petitioners espouse would have any success. In days of trouble and confusion, when bread lines were long, when the unemployed walked the streets, when people were starving, the advocates of a short-cut by revolution might have a chance to gain adherents. But today there are no such conditions. The country is not in despair; the people know Soviet Communism; the doctrine of Soviet revolution is exposed in all of its ugliness and the American people want none of it.

How it can be said that there is a clear and present danger that this advocacy will succeed is, therefore, a mystery. Some nations less resilient than the United States, where illiteracy is high and where democratic traditions are only budding, might have to take drastic steps and jail these men for merely speaking their creed. But in America they are miserable merchants of unwanted ideas; their wares remain unsold. The fact that their ideas are abhorrent does not make them powerful.

The political impotence of the Communists in this country does not, of course, dispose of the problem. Their numbers; their positions in industry and government; the extent to which they have in fact infiltrated the police, the armed services, transportation, stevedoring, power plants, munitions works, and other critical places—these facts all bear on the likelihood that their advocacy of the Soviet theory of revolution will endanger the Republic. But the record is silent on these facts. If we are to proceed on the basis of judicial notice, it is impossible for me to say that the Communists in this country are so potent or so strategically deployed that they must be suppressed for their speech. I could not so hold unless I were willing to conclude that the activities in recent years of committees of Congress, of the Attorney General, of labor unions, of state legislatures, and of Loyalty Boards were so futile as to leave the country on the edge of grave peril. To believe that petitioners and their following are placed in such critical positions as to endanger the Nation is to believe the incredible. It is safe to say that the followers of the creed of Soviet Communism are known to the F.B.I.; that in case of war with Russia they will be picked up overnight as were all prospective saboteurs at the commencement of World War II; that the invisible army of petitioners is the best known, the most beset, and the least thriving of any fifth column in history. Only those held by fear and panic could think otherwise.

This is my view if we are to act on the basis of judicial notice. But the mere statement of the opposing views indicates how important it is that we know the facts before we act. Neither prejudice nor hate nor senseless fear should be the basis of this solemn act. Free speech—the glory of our system of government—should not be sacrificed on anything less than plain and objective proof of danger that the evil advocated is imminent. On this record no one can say that petitioners and their converts are in such a strategic position as to have even the slightest chance of achieving their aims.

The First Amendment provides that "Congress shall make no law ... abridging the freedom of speech." The Constitution provides no exception. This does not mean, however, that the Nation need hold its hand until it is in such weakened condition that there is no time to protect itself from incitement to revolution. Seditious conduct can always be punished. But the command of the First Amendment is so clear that we should not allow Congress to call a halt to free speech except in the extreme case of peril from the speech itself. The First Amendment makes confidence in the common sense of our people and in their maturity of judgment the great postulate of our democracy. Its philosophy is that violence is rarely, if ever, stopped by denying civil liberties to those advocating resort to force. The First Amendment reflects the philosophy of Jefferson "that it is time enough for the rightful purposes of civil government, for its officers to interfere when principles break out into overt acts against peace and good order." The political censor has no place in our public debates. Unless and until extreme and necessitous circumstances are shown, our aim should be to keep speech unfettered and to allow the processes of law to be invoked only when the provocateurs among us move from speech to action.

Vishinsky wrote in 1938 in The Law of the Soviet State, "In our state, naturally, there is and can be no place for freedom of speech, press, and so on for the foes of socialism."

Our concern should be that we accept no such standard for the United States. Our faith should be that our people will never give support to these advocates of revolution, so long as we remain loyal to the purposes for which our Nation was founded.

JUSTICE DOUGLAS ON THE DENNIS CONFERENCE

Justice Douglas took the following notes of the Court's conference discussion in *Dennis* on December 9, 1950:*

CJ—affirms (practically no discussion).

Black—clear and present danger test not satisfied—reverses.

Reed—affirms.

FF— (1) status of clear and present since Gitlow.
(2) how imminent must the substantive evil be?
(3) should the clear and present danger be submitted to the jury? In Holmes and Brandeis opinions it is a question of fact.
(4) can we take judicial notice of the evil and danger?

(he indicates he would affirm)

WOD—(agrees with Black—reverses)

RHJ—US can protect against activity—can stop some things because they are inherently dangerous without reference to clear and present danger—he has not made up his mind (but indicates he will affirm).

HB—clear and probable danger rather than clear and present danger is the test—affirms—can take judicial knowledge of the danger.

SM affirms.

(The amazing thing about the conference on this important case was the brief nature of the discussion—those wanting to affirm had minds closed to argument or persuasion. The conference discussion was largely *pro forma*. It was all the more amazing because of the drastic revision of the "clear and present danger" test which affirmance requires.)

THE IMPACT OF DENNIS

Dennis had a devastating impact on the Communist Party. It drove approximately 2,000 party members underground. Party members, wrote

* Douglas Papers, Library of Congress, Box 164.

Vivian Gornick, "thought fascism was coming to America: that American Communists in wholesale lots would be arrested, imprisoned, exiled, perhaps even killed." For years following the Court's decision in *Dennis,* Gornick continued, "these 2,000 experienced a life which—until the 1960s—was unknown in America: the life of an entire subpopulation on the political run from its own government, living in eerie exile."*

THE YATES, SCALES AND NOTO CASES

In the aftermath of affirmance of the convictions in *Dennis,* the government began prosecutions in a number of places throughout the country against second-level leadership of the Communist Party. The first of these cases to be decided by the United States Supreme Court was Yates v. United States, 354 U.S. 298 (1957). The *Yates* case involved the conviction of 14 top officers of the Communist Party in California. The charges against the defendants, and the proof introduced at the trial, followed the pattern of the *Dennis* case. A significant difference was that, in agreeing to review the decision, the Supreme Court agreed to decide all issues in the case, including whether the evidence was sufficient to sustain the convictions. When the Court discussed the case in conference, Justice Douglas recorded Justice Black as saying: "This was a political trial. [I do] not know what the crime is—teaching is not a crime." All the other justices participating agreed that either the trial judge's charge was defective or the evidence was inadequate.*

The Court's opinion, written by Justice Harlan, left undisturbed the constitutional law decided in *Dennis.* The First Amendment did not require the government to prove that there was imminent danger that the Communist Party would succeed in overthrowing the government, or that the danger existed at any time other than the indefinite future. But, in construing what the Smith Act meant, the Court held that it required proof that the defendants had advocated "unlawful action" as opposed to "abstract doctrine."** No defendant could be convicted unless he was proved to have advocated specific unlawful conduct. It was not enough to show that a defendant was a Communist Party official and that the Party adhered to classic Marxist doctrine that included general advocacy of violent overthrow of existing government. The distinction, in other words, was similar to that which Learned Hand had discussed in his *Masses* opinion (see above, pp. 82–86) forty years earlier—a distinction between "political agitation" and "incitement" to violation of the law.

Four years later, the Court decided a pair of cases dealing with another provision of the Smith Act. That provision, the "membership clause", like the 1902 New York Criminal Anarchy law and the California statute under which Anita Whitney had been convicted, punished "knowing" membership in an organization which advocated violent

---

* Vivian Gornick, The Romance of American Communism, Basic Books, 1977, p. 158.

* Douglas Papers, Library of Congress, Box 1176.

** The trial judge in the *Dennis* case had instructed the jury that the government must prove advocacy of action rather than abstract doctrine. The trial judge in the *Yates* case refused to so instruct the jury, because he interpreted the *Dennis* case's rejection of the "immediacy" requirement of clear and present danger as inconsistent with a distinction between advocating "action" rather than "abstract doctrine."

overthrow of government. The Court upheld the membership clause, and the conviction of the defendant, in Scales v. United States, 367 U.S. 203 (1961). It again insisted that no one could be convicted if the organization's only advocacy was of abstract doctrine. (The conviction in Noto v. United States, 367 U.S. 290 [1961], decided the same day, was reversed because there was insufficient proof that the Party engaged in advocacy of illegal action.) Moreover, the Court insisted that there be proof that the defendant was an "active member" and that he had a "specific intent" to accomplish the Party's unlawful objectives. Notice that the "active member" and "specific intent" requirements go beyond the requirements of Justice Brandeis' opinion in the *Whitney* case. Even if the Party was proved to have engaged in some unlawful advocacy of specific acts of violence and sabotage, it was not enough to prove that the defendant was a member of the Party and knew of the advocacy—it was necessary to prove that the defendant participated in the unlawful advocacy in some meaningful way.

The requirement of the *Yates* case that, before a defendant can be punished, he must advocate relatively specific acts which violate the law, would have required reversal of all the convictions in the cases from *Schenck* through *Dennis,* since all those defendants had advocated violence or breaking the law in the most general terms. The requirement of the *Scales* and *Noto* cases that the defendant be proved to have the "specific intent" to accomplish illegal purposes would have required crediting the defense of Anita Whitney that, although she remained a member, she was attempting to turn the organization in the direction of accomplishing its ends by lawful means. Two very important qualifications remain. All three cases are not technically constitutional law decisions. They reached their results by construing the Smith Act. That left open the possibility that Congress could amend the law and permit conviction on less proof than the cases insisted upon. Second, even if the decisions are treated as stating a constitutional rule, they—like Hand's *Masses* opinion—leave open the possibility of conviction of those who advocate specific unlawful acts, even if the advocacy is of conduct in the indefinite future or if there is little danger the results will come about.

The process of converting the interpretation of the Smith Act in *Yates, Scales* and *Noto* into an interpretation of the First Amendment began in Elfbrandt v. Russell, 384 U.S. 11 (1966). This was a case involving a loyalty oath for government employees that effectively disqualified members of the Communist Party or other organizations having for "one of its purposes" violent overthrow of government. In the 5–4 decision, the Court held the oath requirement to be unconstitutional because it did not include the element of "specific intent." Justice Douglas' opinion, for the Court, said:

> We recognized in Scales v. United States that "quasi-political parties or other groups ... may embrace both legal and illegal aims." We noted that a "blanket prohibition of association with a group having both legal and illegal aims" would pose "a real danger that legitimate political expression or association would be impaired." The statute with which we dealt in *Scales,* the so-called "membership clause" of the Smith Act, was found

not to suffer from this constitutional infirmity because, as the Court construed it, the statute reached only "active" membership with the "specific intent" of assisting in achieving the unlawful ends of the organization. . . .

Those who join an organization but do not share its unlawful purposes and who do not participate in its unlawful activities surely pose no threat, either as citizens or as public employees. Laws such as this which are not restricted in scope to those who join with the "specific intent" to further illegal action impose, in effect, a conclusive presumption that the member shares the unlawful aims of the organization.

BRANDENBURG v. OHIO

Supreme Court of the United States, 1969.
395 U.S. 444, 89 S.Ct. 1827, 23 L.Ed.2d 430.

PER CURIAM.*

The appellant, a leader of a Ku Klux Klan group, was convicted under the Ohio Criminal Syndicalism statute for "advocat[ing] . . . the duty, necessity, or propriety of crime, sabotage, violence, or unlawful methods of terrorism as a means of accomplishing industrial or political reform" and for "voluntarily assembl[ing] with any society, group, or assemblage of persons formed to teach or advocate the doctrines of criminal syndicalism." . . . The appellant challenged the constitutionality of the criminal syndicalism statute under the First and Fourteenth Amendments to the United States Constitution, but the intermediate appellate court of Ohio affirmed his conviction without opinion. The Supreme Court of Ohio dismissed his appeal, . . . "for the reason that no substantial constitutional question exists herein." . . . We reverse.

The record shows that a man, identified at trial as the appellant, telephoned an announcer-reporter on the staff of a Cincinnati television station and invited him to come to a Ku Klux Klan "rally" to be held at a farm in Hamilton County. With the cooperation of the organizers, the reporter and a cameraman attended the meeting and filmed the events. Portions of the films were later broadcast on the local station and on a national network.

* *Per curiam* is Latin for "by the court." Most significant decisions of the United States Supreme Court are "signed" opinions. Their captions would read "Mr. Justice X delivered the opinion of the Court." That means that the named justice had written the opinion, and enough Justices had agreed to join the opinion to constitute a majority of the Court. A *per curiam* opinion is unsigned, but it has no more and no less force than one that is signed. The *per curiam* device is often used in cases which are disposed of without oral argument, or in cases that are easily resolved, or cases with extremely brief opinions. The *Brandenburg* opinion was written originally by Justice Fortas, who resigned from the Court a few days before the Court delivered its opinion. Justice Brennan edited the opinion to meet certain concerns of Justice Black. Earlier, Justice Black had asked Justice Fortas to note that he (Black) only concurred in the result because he did not subscribe to the clear and present test. Justice Fortas answered that though he had referred to the Holmes–Brandeis statement of clear and present danger, his reference did not indicate his agreement with the doctrine. Black to Fortas, April 15, 1969; Fortas to Black, April 30, 1969. Hugo L. Black Papers, Library of Congress, Box 404. The test articulated at the end of the opinion was Brennan's contribution.

The prosecution's case rested on the films and on testimony identifying the appellant as the person who communicated with the reporter and who spoke at the rally. The State also introduced into evidence several articles appearing in the film, including a pistol, a rifle, a shotgun, ammunition, a Bible, and a red hood worn by the speaker in the films.

One film showed 12 hooded figures, some of whom carried firearms. They were gathered around a large wooden cross, which they burned. No one was present other than the participants and the newsmen who made the film. Most of the words uttered during the scene were incomprehensible when the film was projected, but scattered phrases could be understood that were derogatory of Negroes and, in one instance, of Jews.* Another scene on the same film showed the appellant, in Klan regalia, making a speech. The speech, in full, was as follows:

"This is an organizers" meeting. We have had quite a few members here today which are—we have hundreds, hundreds of members throughout the State of Ohio. I can quote from a newspaper clipping from the Columbus, Ohio, Dispatch, five weeks ago Sunday morning. The Klan has more members in the State of Ohio than does any other organization. We're not a revengent organization, but if our President, our Congress, our Supreme Court, continues to suppress the white, Caucasian race, it's possible that there might have to be some revengeance taken.

"We are marching on Congress July the Fourth, four hundred thousand strong. From there we are dividing into two groups, one group to march on St. Augustine, Florida, the other group to march into Mississippi. Thank you."

The second film showed six hooded figures one of whom, later identified as the appellant, repeated a speech very similar to that recorded on the first film. The reference to the possibility of "revengeance" was omitted, and one sentence was added: "Personally, I believe the nigger should be returned to Africa, the Jew returned to Israel." Though some of the figures in the films carried weapons, the speaker did not.

* The significant portions that could be understood were:

"How far is the nigger going to—yeah."

"This is what we are going to do to niggers."

"A dirty nigger."

"Send the Jews back to Israel."

"Let's give them back to the dark garden."

"Save America."

"Let's go back to constitutional betterment."

"Bury the niggers."

"We intend to do our part."

"Give us our state rights."

"Freedom for the whites."

"Nigger will have to fight for every inch he gets from now on."

... In 1927, this Court sustained the constitutionality of California's Criminal Syndicalism Act, the text of which is quite similar to that of the laws of Ohio. Whitney v. California, 274 U.S. 357 (1927). The Court upheld the statute on the ground that, without more, "advocating" violent means to effect political and economic change involves such danger to the security of the State that the State may outlaw it. But *Whitney* has been thoroughly discredited by later decisions. See Dennis v. United States, 341 U.S. 494, at 507 (1951). These later decisions have fashioned the principle that the constitutional guarantees of free speech and free press do not permit a State to forbid or proscribe advocacy of the use of force or of law violation except where such advocacy is directed to inciting or producing imminent lawless action and is likely to incite or produce such action.* As we said in Noto v. United States, 367 U.S. 290, 297–298 (1961), "the mere abstract teaching ... of the moral propriety or even moral necessity for a resort to force and violence, is not the same as preparing a group for violent action and steeling it to such action." A statute which fails to draw this distinction impermissibly intrudes upon the freedoms guaranteed by the First and Fourteenth Amendments. It sweeps within its condemnation speech which our Constitution has immunized from governmental control. Cf. Yates v. United States, 354 U.S. 298 (1957).

Measured by this test, Ohio's Criminal Syndicalism Act cannot be sustained. The Act punishes persons who "advocate or teach the duty, necessity, or propriety" of violence "as a means of accomplishing industrial or political reform"; or who publish or circulate or display any book or paper containing such advocacy; or who "justify" the commission of violent acts "with intent to exemplify, spread or advocate the propriety of the doctrines of criminal syndicalism"; or who "voluntarily assemble" with a group formed "to teach or advocate the doctrines of criminal syndicalism." Neither the indictment nor the trial judge's instructions to the jury in any way refined the statute's bald definition of the crime in terms of mere advocacy not distinguished from incitement to imminent lawless action.

Accordingly, we are here confronted with a statute which, by its own words and as applied, purports to punish mere advocacy and to forbid, on pain of criminal punishment, assembly with others merely to advocate the described type of action. Such a statute falls within the condemnation of the First and Fourteenth Amendments. The contrary teaching of Whitney v. California, supra, cannot be supported, and that decision is therefore overruled.

Reversed.

---

* It was on the theory that the Smith Act embodied such a principle and that it had been applied only in conformity with it that this Court sustained the Act's constitutionality. Dennis v. United States, 341 U.S. 494 (1951). That this was the basis for *Dennis* was emphasized in Yates v. United States, 354 U.S. 298, 320–324 (1957), in which the Court overturned convictions for advocacy of the forcible overthrow of the Government under the Smith Act, because the trial judge's instructions had allowed conviction for mere advocacy, unrelated to its tendency to produce forcible action.

JUSTICE BLACK, concurring.

I agree with the views expressed by Justice Douglas in his concurring opinion in this case that the "clear and present danger" doctrine should have no place in the interpretation of the First Amendment. I join the Court's opinion, which, as I understand it, simply cites Dennis v. United States, 341 U.S. 494 (1951), but does not indicate any agreement on the Court's part with the "clear and present danger" doctrine on which *Dennis* purported to rely.

JUSTICE DOUGLAS, concurring.

While I join the opinion of the Court, I desire to enter a *caveat*.

The "clear and present danger" test was adumbrated by Mr. Justice Holmes in a case arising during World War I—a war "declared" by the Congress, not by the Chief Executive. The case was Schenck v. United States, 249 U.S. 47, 52, where the defendant was charged with attempts to cause insubordination in the military and obstruction of enlistment.

[T]he World War I cases put the gloss of "clear and present danger" on the First Amendment. Whether the war power—the greatest leveler of them all—is adequate to sustain that doctrine is debatable.... Though I doubt if the "clear and present danger" test is congenial to the First Amendment in time of a declared war, I am certain it is not reconcilable with the First Amendment in days of peace.

... I see no place in the regime of the First Amendment for any "clear and present danger" test, whether strict and tight as some would make it, or free-wheeling as the Court in *Dennis* rephrased it.

When one reads the opinions closely and sees when and how the "clear and present danger" test has been applied, great misgivings are aroused. First, the threats were often loud but always puny and made serious only by judges so wedded to the *status quo* that critical analysis made them nervous. Second, the test was so twisted and perverted in *Dennis* as to make the trial of those teachers of Marxism an all-out political trial which was part and parcel of the cold war that has eroded substantial parts of the First Amendment.

The line between what is permissible and not subject to control and what may be made impermissible and subject to regulation is the line between ideas and overt acts.

The example usually given by those who would punish speech is the case of one who falsely shouts fire in a crowded theatre.

This is, however, a classic case where speech is brigaded with action. They are indeed inseparable and a prosecution can be launched for the overt acts actually caused. Apart from rare instances of that kind, speech is, I think, immune from prosecution. Certainly there is no constitutional line between advocacy of abstract ideas as in *Yates* and advocacy of political action as in *Scales*. The quality of advocacy turns on the depth of the conviction; and government has no power to invade that sanctuary of belief and conscience.

NOTES AND QUESTIONS

1. The *Brandenburg* case obviously converts *Yates'* distinction between advocacy of belief and advocacy of action to an interpretation of

the First Amendment. Does it do more than that? Lawyers distinguish between "holdings" and "dicta." A "holding" is the core of a court's decision—those things that had to be decided in order to reach the court's result. "Dicta" are the extraneous statements that were not necessary to the decision. The "holding" of a case is "law," binding on other courts and government officials; "dicta" are persuasive but, in theory, do not have the force of "law." As lawyers, the authors are slow to denigrate a distinction that has kept so many members of the legal profession gainfully employed, but we admit that the distinction between "holding" and "dicta" is treacherous in practice. Notice that the Court in *Brandenburg,* in restating the rule of clear and present danger *twice* uses the word "imminent." In saying that it is following the rule of the *Dennis* case, which in fact rejected any requirement of imminence, has the Court overruled it? One commentator* has asserted:

> [I]n Brandenburg v. Ohio, the Warren Court built on *Yates* and *Scales* to produce its clearest and most protective standard under the first amendment. And *Brandenburg* continues to be adhered to by the Burger Court.8** *Brandenburg* rests ultimately on the insight Learned Hand urged without success at the end of World War I. The *Brandenburg* per curiam emphasized that laws affecting first amendment rights "must observe the established distinction between mere advocacy and incitement to imminent lawless action." That was hardly an "established" distinction. Indeed, that was precisely the distinction Holmes has sought to discredit in the *Gitlow* dissent with the deprecating comment: "Every idea is an incitement." An incitement-nonincitement distinction had only fragmentary and ambiguous antecedents in the pre-*Brandenburg* era; it was *Brandenburg* that really "established" it; and, it was essentially an establishment of the legacy of Learned Hand.

> In one sense, *Brandenburg* combines the most protective ingredients of the *Masses* incitement emphasis with the most useful elements of the clear and present danger heritage. As the Court summarized first amendment principles in *Brandenburg*—purporting to restate, but in fact creating—:

>> [T]he constitutional guarantees of free speech and free press do not permit a State to forbid or proscribe advocacy of the use of force or of law violation except where such advocacy is directed to inciting or producing imminent lawless action and is likely to incite or produce such action.

* Gerald Gunther, Learned Hand and the Origins of Modern First Amendment Doctrine: Some Fragments of History, Stanford Law Review, 1975, vol. 27, pp. 754–755.

** See Hess v. Indiana, 414 U.S. 105 (1973) (per curiam reversal of disorderly conduct conviction of demonstrator who had said: "We'll take the fucking street later [or again]"); the reversal eschews overbreadth and vagueness grounds and relies primarily on the failure to meet the *Brandenburg* incitement requirements: "At best, ... the statement could be taken as counsel for present moderation; at worst, it amounted to nothing more than advocacy of illegal action at some indefinite future time."

The incitement emphasis is Hand's; the reference to "imminent" reflects a limited influence of Holmes, combined with later experience; and the "likely to incite or produce such action" addition in the *Brandenburg* standard is the only reference to the need to guess about future consequences of speech, so central to the *Schenck* approach. Under *Brandenburg,* probability of harm is no longer the central criterion for speech limitations. The inciting language of the speaker—the Hand focus on "objective" words—is the major consideration. And punishment of the harmless inciter is prevented by the *Schenck*-derived requirement of a likelihood of dangerous consequences.

2.   Can someone be punished if he counsels or advocates that others do specific acts which are serious crimes, if the criminal acts are to be performed in some indefinite future time? And, how specific does advocacy have to be to move over the line that separates advocacy of belief and advocacy of action? Suppose the defendants are opposed to a war and prepare, sign and broadly distribute a circular that reads:

> We believe every free man has a legal right and a moral duty to exert every effort to end this war, to avoid collusion with it, and to encourage others to do the same. Young men in the armed forces or threatened with the draft face the most excruciating choices. For them various forms of resistance risk separation from their families and their country, destruction of their careers, loss of their freedom and loss of their lives. Each must choose the course of resistance dictated by his conscience and circumstances. Some are resisting openly and paying a heavy penalty, some are organizing more resistance within the United States and some have sought sanctuary in other countries. We believe that each of these forms of resistance against illegitimate authority is courageous and justified. Open resistance to the war and the draft is the course of action most likely to strengthen the moral resolve with which all of us can oppose the war.

> We will continue to lend our support to those who undertake resistance to this war. We will raise funds to organize draft resistance unions, to supply legal defense and bail, to support families and otherwise aid resistance to the war in whatever ways may seem appropriate.

Would conviction of the defendants for counseling Selective Service registrants to evade military service violate the First Amendment? Compare United States v. Spock, 416 F.2d 165 (1st Cir.1969).

3.   A large angry crowd is gathered on a college campus during a war protest. Speaker gives a vehement speech for ten minutes, arguing the university's complicity with the war effort. At the end, he says: "It's time to stop talking. Let's take over the physics labs." The crowd suddenly surges toward the physics laboratories, a five minute walk. At the entrance to the building, five minutes are consumed taking a vote as to whether to enter the building. After the lopsided vote, most of the crowd surges into the building and remains there until ejected by the

police the next day. Considerable equipment has been smashed, and the building is a shambles. Was Speaker's speech protected by the First Amendment?

4. Under the applicable constitutional standard can the state punish someone who:

(a) believing that there is a fire, shouts "Fire" in a crowded theater? (Does it matter whether anyone gets hurt in the ensuing panic? Would it even matter if there were a fire?)

(b) asks a friend to kill his wife?

(c) asks a friend to kill her husband when he is released from prison in five years?

(d) offers to sell someone the Brooklyn Bridge for $500?

V. ON "BALANCING" AND "ABSOLUTES"

Criticism of the clear and present danger rule has come from two sides, as indicated by the opinions in the previous section. On the one side is the criticism that clear and present danger is a wooden rule, too protective of speech. That position is represented by Justice Frankfurter's concurring opinion in the *Dennis* case. On the other side, as shown by Justice Douglas' concurring opinion in the *Brandenburg* case, is the view that the rule is not protective enough. The controversy has usually been put as one between "balancing" and "absolutes." This controversy will be seen over and over again in the chapters to follow. Justice Frankfurter was the leading proponent of balancing. His most comprehensive statement in support of that approach is his concurring opinion in *Dennis*. See pages 110–113. Justice Black was the leading proponent of the absolute position. His most comprehensive statement was his dissenting opinion in Konigsberg v. California State Bar, 366 U.S. 36 (1961), in which he wrote:

I recognize, of course, that the "clear and present danger test," though itself a great advance toward individual liberty over some previous notions of the protections afforded by the First Amendment, does not go as far as my own views as to the protection that should be accorded these freedoms. I agree with Justices Holmes and Brandeis, however, that a primary purpose of the First Amendment was to insure that all ideas would be allowed to enter the "competition of the market." But I fear that the creation of "tests" by which speech is left unprotected under certain circumstances is a standing invitation to abridge it. This is nowhere more clearly indicated than by the sudden transformation of the "clear and present danger test" in Dennis v. United States. In that case, this Court accepted Judge Learned Hand's "restatement" of the "clear and present danger test": "In each case [courts] must ask whether the gravity of the 'evil,' discounted by its improbability, justifies such invasion of free speech as is necessary to avoid the danger." After the "clear and present danger test" was diluted and weakened by being recast in terms of this "balancing" formula, there seems to me to be much room to doubt that Justices Holmes and Brandeis would even have recognized their test. And the reliance upon that weakened "test" by the majority here, without even so much as an attempt to find either a "clear" or a "present" danger, is only another persuasive reason for rejecting all such "tests" and enforcing the First Amendment according to its terms.

The Court suggests that a "literal reading of the First Amendment" would be totally unreasonable because it would invalidate many widely accepted laws. I do not know to what extent this is true. I do not believe, for example, that it would invalidate laws resting upon the premise that where speech is an integral part of unlawful conduct that is going on at the time, the speech can be used to illustrate, emphasize and establish the unlawful conduct. On the other hand, it certainly would invalidate all laws that abridge the right of the people to discuss matters of religious or public interest, in the broadest meaning of those terms, for it is clear that a desire to protect this right was the primary purpose of the First Amendment. Some people have argued, with much force, that the freedoms guaranteed by the First Amendment are limited to somewhat broad areas like those.* But I believe this Nation's security and tranquility can best be served by giving the First Amendment the same broad construction that all Bill of Rights guarantees deserve.

... The Court, by stating unequivocally that there are no "absolutes" under the First Amendment, necessarily takes the position that even speech that is admittedly protected by the First Amendment is subject to the "balancing test" and that therefore no kind of speech is to be protected if the Government can assert an interest of sufficient weight to induce this Court to uphold its abridgement. In my judgment, such a sweeping denial of the existence of any inalienable right to speak undermines the very foundation upon which the First Amendment, the Bill of Rights, and, indeed, our entire structure of government rest. The Founders of this Nation attempted to set up a limited government which left certain rights in the people—rights that could not be taken away without amendment of the basic charter of government. The majority's "balancing test" tells us that this is not so. It tells us that no right to think, speak or publish exists in the people that cannot be taken away if the Government finds it sufficiently imperative or expedient to do so. Thus, the "balancing test" turns our "Government of the people, by the people and for the people" into a government over the people.

NOTE

Whatever one thinks of the clear and present danger rule as a way of resolving cases where the speaker is advocating violence or violation of

---

* See, e.g., Alexander Meiklejohn, What Does the First Amendment Mean?, 20 U. of Chi.L.Rev., pp. 461, 464.

law, it is obviously not an all-purpose solution for free speech problems. Where community interests other than preventing law violation are at stake—as they are in cases involving false commercial advertising or defamation of character—clear and present danger may simply not be a relevant standard. But if "balancing" or an "absolute" are the alternatives to clear and present danger, both the "balancers" and the "absolutists" must face difficult problems.

If a balance is to be struck, how is one to define the competing interests? Do we balance the interest of the government in survival against the defendant's right to say whatever he pleases? Do we balance the interest in freedom of speech against the trivial danger to public order in a particular case? Is any balance struck by a legislature within the leeway given by the First Amendment so long as it is not very unreasonable?

If speech may not be made a crime at all, how are we to distinguish between "speech" and "conduct?" Is a deliberately misleading advertisement for a commercial product protected speech, or is it part of an attempt to defraud? Would the absolute protection for speech mean that the deliberate character assassin, who knowingly, falsely destroys a reputation, cannot even be required to pay damages to his victim?

Consider these problems of the polar positions in the chapters that follow. Is there a viable middle ground?

Chapter VI

THE PUBLIC FORUM

THE CONCEPT*

... I suggest three interrelated propositions for examination. First, that in an open democratic society the streets, the parks, and other public places are an important facility for public discussion and political process. They are in brief a public forum that the citizen can commandeer; the generosity and empathy with which such facilities are made available is an index of freedom. Second, that only confusion can result from distinguishing sharply between "speech pure" and "speech plus." And, third, that what is required is in effect a set of Robert's Rules of Order for the new uses of the public forum, albeit the designing of such rules poses a problem of formidable practical difficulty....

. . .

The initial questions are whether the citizen using the street as a forum and not as a passageway is making an anomalous use of it, and whether he is, in a sense, always out of place and out of order when he chooses the streets for his meeting place. Certainly it is easy to think of public places, swimming pools, for example, so clearly dedicated to recreational use that talk of their use as a public forum would in general be totally unpersuasive. Is the street, however, a kind of public hall, a public communication facility?

One would have thought the theoretical issue had been put to rest a generation ago by the collision of dicta in Davis v. Massachusetts and Hague v. C.I.O. *Davis,* it will be recalled, was one of the less admired efforts of Justice Holmes, then still on the Massachusetts Supreme Judicial Court. In reviewing a conviction for speaking on the Boston Common without a permit, in violation of an ordinance inhibiting many varieties of uses of the Common including "the discharge of cannon" thereon, Justice Holmes observed: "For the Legislature absolutely or conditionally to forbid public speaking in a highway or public park is no more an infringement of rights of a member of the public than for the owner of a private house to forbid it in the house."

When the case reached the United States Supreme Court, the Court endorsed the Holmes decision and its rationale. Said Chief Justice White: "The right to absolutely exclude all right to use, necessarily includes the authority to determine under what circumstances such use may be availed of, as the greater power contains the lesser." This position has at

---

* Harry Kalven, Jr., The Concept of the Public Forum: Cox v. Louisiana, The Supreme Court Review, University of Chicago Press, 1965, pp. 1, 11–13. Reprinted with permission.

least the virtue of clarity. The citizen uses the streets for political purposes at the sufferance of the state; his use is anomalous and marginal and can be terminated whenever and for whatever reason the state decides.

This view survived until 1937 when Mayor Hague of Jersey City got into an argument, not with Jehovah's Witnesses, but with the CIO, then seeking energetically to organize New Jersey labor. In a complicated lawsuit, the Court passed on the city's claim that its ordinance requiring a permit for an open air meeting was justified by the plenary power rationale of the *Davis* case. In rejecting the point, Justice Roberts uttered the counter dictum:

> Wherever the title of streets and parks may rest, they have immemorially been held in trust for the use of the public and time out of mind, have been used for purposes of assembly, communicating thoughts between citizens, and discussing public questions. Such use of the streets and public places has from ancient times, been a part of the privileges, immunities, rights, and liberties of citizens.

On this view the matter is perhaps not quite so clear, but there is the aura of a large democratic principle. When the citizen goes to the street, he is exercising an immemorial right of a free man, a kind of First–Amendment easement. If so generous a statement of principle does not tell us exactly when his privileges may be curtailed in the interest of other speech or other uses of the street, it does give us a good starting point for the argument.

I. SPEECH ON PUBLIC PROPERTY

A. STREETS AND PARKS

The government has an affirmative obligation to make some forms of public property available as a public forum. This harks back to Justice Roberts' statement that "streets and parks . . . have immemorially been held in trust for the use of the public and time out of mind, have been used for the purpose of assembly, communicating thoughts between citizens, and discussing public questions." The streets and the parks are the "poor man's printing press," available to speakers who have no access to privately-owned auditoriums or the media.

If particular public property is closed entirely, or at specified times, it is necessary to weigh the governmental interest in closing the property against the interest in maintaining a public forum. Thus in some cases, a "time, place and manner" rule will be upheld if there are reasons strong enough to outweigh the interests in the public forum. Balancing of competing interests presents real problems in striking the balance. For example, suppose a small city has only one park, and decides to set the park off as a place of peace and quiet. Should a rule banning all speeches and meetings in the park be unconstitutional?

THE SOUND TRUCK CASES

In Saia v. New York, 334 U.S. 558 (1948), the Supreme Court dealt, for the first time, with a city ordinance controlling the use of sound trucks. By a vote of 5–4 the Court held that the ordinance was unconstitutional because the local police chief was given uncontrolled discretion whether to issue a license permitting particular sound trucks to operate. Thus, while there was no evidence in the *Saia* case that a license had been refused for any reason other than noise, the licensing ordinance was unconstitutional "on its face" because it permitted the police chief to grant or deny a license for any reason, or no reason at all. Justice Douglas' majority opinion also suggested that a flat ban on *all* sound trucks would be as unconstitutional as a flat ban on all handbills. In Kovacs v. Cooper, 336 U.S. 77 (1949), only a year later, however, the Court upheld an ordinance banning all sound trucks emitting "loud and raucous noises." The Court was so fragmented, there was no opinion signed by a majority of the justices. (See Chapter 5, footnote on p. 107.) Since the *Kovacs* decision, constitutional law experts have debated the question whether a flat ban on all outdoor loudspeakers or on all sound trucks within a city would be constitutional. What do you think? An ordinance of the City of Palm Springs, California, prohibited the use of "stationary" sound-trucks. The California Supreme Court thought the ordinance was not valid. Wollam v. City of Palm Springs, 59 Cal.2d 276, 29 Cal.Rptr. 1, 379 P.2d 481 (1963). Do you agree?

PICKETING THE UNITED STATES SUPREME COURT

In United States v. Grace, 461 U.S. 171 (1983), the Court decided that it was unconstitutional to bar *all* picketing, sign-carrying and leafleting on the sidewalks surrounding the United States Supreme Court. The United States had argued that, since speech related to pending court cases could be curtailed, the only persons affected by the ban were those who wanted to address issues *unrelated* to the Court, and they were free to make their point on the sidewalks across the street. In *Grace,* the Court left for another day a decision whether the ban on picketing etc., on the steps and in the court building, was valid. Do you think it is? What about a law that prohibits all picketing in the halls and on the steps of a state capitol?

The two cases that follow consider the standards governing "content-neutral," "viewpoint-neutral," and "viewpoint-based" regulations of speech in the public streets—the paradigm "traditional public forum."

FRISBY v. SCHULTZ

Supreme Court of the United States, 1988.
487 U.S. 474, 108 S.Ct. 2495, 101 L.Ed.2d 420.

JUSTICE O'CONNOR delivered the opinion of the Court.

Brookfield, Wisconsin, has adopted an ordinance that completely bans picketing "before or about" any residence. This case presents a facial First Amendment challenge to that ordinance.

I

Brookfield, Wisconsin, is a residential suburb of Milwaukee with a population of approximately 4,300. The appellees, Sandra C. Schultz and

Robert C. Braun, are individuals strongly opposed to abortion and wish to express their views on the subject by picketing on a public street outside the Brookfield residence of a doctor who apparently performs abortions at two clinics in neighboring towns. Appellees and others engaged in precisely that activity, assembling outside the doctor's home on at least six occasions between April 20, 1985, and May 20, 1985, for periods ranging from one to one and a half hours. The size of the group varied from 11 to more than 40. The picketing was generally orderly and peaceful; the town never had occasion to invoke any of its various ordinances prohibiting obstruction of the streets, loud and unnecessary noises, or disorderly conduct. Nonetheless, the picketing generated substantial controversy and numerous complaints.

SANDRA DAY O'CONNOR—Born on March 26, 1930, in El Paso, Texas. Grew up in southeastern Arizona on a very large ranch, which her grandfather had pioneered, and in El Paso, where she lived with her grandmother while attending school. Republican. Episcopalian. Graduated from high school at 16 and completed undergraduate study and law school in six years. Stanford, A.B. in economics with great distinction, 1950; Stanford, LL.B. Order of the Coif and law review editor, 1952. William H. Rehnquist graduated from the Stanford Law School the same year. Had difficulty finding a job after graduation because of discrimination against women seeking legal positions. San Mateo deputy county attorney, 1952–1954; civilian attorney, Q.M. Market Center, Frankfurt am Main, West Germany, 1954–1957; practiced law, 1959–1965; Arizona assistant attorney general (first woman to hold the position), 1965–1969; Arizona state senator, 1969–1975; Arizona senate majority leader (first woman to hold the position), 1973–1974; Maricopa County superior court judge, 1975–1979; Arizona court of appeals judge, 1979–1981. Nominated associate justice by President Ronald Reagan on August 19, 1981, to replace Potter Stewart. Confirmed by the Senate on September 21, 1981, by a 99–0 vote. First woman appointed to the U.S. Supreme Court. Provided the crucial swing vote on many hot-button issues during her final years on the Rehnquist Court. Announced her intention to retire on July 1, 2005. Her retirement became effective upon the confirmation of her successor, Samuel Alito, on January 31, 2006.

The Town Board therefore resolved to enact an ordinance to restrict the picketing.... [The ordinance provided:]

"It is unlawful for any person to engage in picketing before or about the residence or dwelling of any individual in the Town of Brookfield."

· · ·

II

The antipicketing ordinance operates at the core of the First Amendment by prohibiting appellees from engaging in picketing on an issue of public concern.... [W]e have traditionally subjected restrictions on public issue picketing to careful scrutiny....

To ascertain what limits, if any, may be placed on protected speech, we have often focused on the "place" of that speech, considering the nature of the forum the speaker seems to employ....

... [W]e have repeatedly referred to public streets as the archetype of a traditional public forum.... [The City argues, however,] that the streets of Brookfield should be considered a nonpublic forum. Pointing to the physical narrowness of Brookfield's streets as well as to their residential character, appellants contend that such streets have not by tradition or designation been held open for public communication.

We reject this suggestion. Our prior holdings make clear that a public street does not lose its status as a traditional public forum simply because it runs through a residential neighborhood....

... [O]ur decisions identifying public streets and sidewalks as traditional public fora are not accidental invocations of a "cliche" but recognition that "[w]herever the title of streets and parks may rest, they have immemorially been held in trust for the use of the public." Hague v. CIO, [307 U.S.] at 515 (Roberts, J.). No particularized inquiry into the precise nature of a specific street is necessary; all public streets are held in the public trust and are properly considered traditional public fora. Accordingly, the streets of Brookfield are traditional public fora. The residential character of those streets may well inform the application of the relevant test, but it does not lead to a different test; the antipicketing ordinance must be judged against the stringent standards we have established for restrictions on speech in traditional public fora:

> "In these quintessential public for[a], the government may not prohibit all communicative activity. For the State to enforce a content-based exclusion it must show that its regulation is necessary to serve a compelling state interest and that it is narrowly drawn to achieve that end.... The State may also enforce regulations of the time, place, and manner of expression which are content-neutral, are narrowly tailored to serve a significant government interest, and leave open ample alternative channels of communication."

... [T]he appropriate level of scrutiny is initially tied to whether the statute distinguishes between prohibited and permitted speech on the basis of content.... [W]e accept the lower courts' conclusion that the Brookfield ordinance is content-neutral. Accordingly, we turn to consider whether the ordinance is "narrowly tailored to serve a significant government interest" and whether it "leave[s] open ample alternative channels of communication."

Because the last question is so easily answered, we address it first. Of course, before we are able to assess the available alternatives, we must consider more carefully the reach of the ordinance. The precise scope of the ban is not further described within the text of the ordinance, but in our view the ordinance is readily subject to a narrowing construction that avoids constitutional difficulties.... General marching through residential neighborhoods, or even walking a route in front of an entire block of houses, is not prohibited by this ordinance.... [O]nly focused picketing taking place solely in front of a particular residence is prohibited.

... [T]he limited nature of the prohibition makes it virtually self-evident that ample alternatives remain:

> "Protestors have not been barred from the residential neighborhoods. They may enter such neighborhoods, alone or in groups, even marching.... They may go door-to-door to proselytize their views. They may distribute literature in this manner ... or through the mails. They may contact residents by telephone, short of harassment."

We readily agree that the ordinance preserves ample alternative channels of communication and thus move on to inquire whether the ordinance serves a significant government interest. We find that such an interest is identified within the text of the ordinance itself: the protection of residential privacy.

. . .

One important aspect of residential privacy is protection of the unwilling listener. Although in many locations, we expect individuals simply to avoid speech they do not want to hear, the home is different.... [A] special benefit of the privacy all citizens enjoy within their own walls, which the State may legislate to protect, is an ability to avoid intrusions. Thus, we have repeatedly held that individuals are not required to welcome unwanted speech into their own homes and that the government may protect this freedom.

This principle is reflected even in prior decisions in which we have invalidated complete bans on expressive activity, including bans operating in residential areas. See, e.g., Schneider v. State, 308 U.S. 147, 162–163 (1939) (handbilling); Martin v. Struthers, 319 U.S. 141 (1943) (door-to-door solicitation). In all such cases, we have been careful to acknowledge that unwilling listeners may be protected when within their own homes. In *Schneider,* for example, in striking down a complete ban on handbilling, we spoke of a right to distribute literature only "to one willing to receive it." Similarly, when we invalidated a ban on door-to-door solicitation in *Martin,* we did so on the basis that the "home owner could protect himself from such intrusion by an appropriate sign 'that he is unwilling to be disturbed.' " ... There simply is no right to force speech into the home of an unwilling listener.

It remains to be considered, however, whether the Brookfield ordinance is narrowly tailored to protect only unwilling recipients of the communications. A statute is narrowly tailored if it targets and eliminates no more than the exact source of the "evil" it seeks to remedy....

... The type of focused picketing prohibited by the Brookfield ordinance is fundamentally different from more generally directed means of communication that may not be completely banned in residential areas.... Here, in contrast, the picketing is narrowly directed at the household, not the public. The type of picketers banned by the Brookfield ordinance generally do not seek to disseminate a message to the general public, but to intrude upon the targeted resident, and to do so in an especially offensive way. Moreover, even if some such picketers have a broader communicative purpose, their activity nonetheless inherently and offensively intrudes on residential privacy. The devastating effect of targeted picketing on the quiet enjoyment of the home is beyond doubt....

In this case, for example, appellees subjected the doctor and his family to the presence of a relatively large group of protestors on their doorstep in an attempt to force the doctor to cease performing abortions. But the actual size of the group is irrelevant; even a solitary picket can invade residential privacy. The offensive and disturbing nature of the form of the communication banned by the Brookfield ordinance thus can scarcely be questioned.

... The resident is figuratively, and perhaps literally, trapped within the home, and because of the unique and subtle impact of such picketing is left with no ready means of avoiding the unwanted speech.... Accordingly, the Brookfield ordinance's complete ban of that particular medium of expression is narrowly tailored.

.   .   .

Because the picketing prohibited by the Brookfield ordinance is speech directed primarily at those who are presumptively unwilling to receive it, the State has a substantial and justifiable interest in banning it. The nature and scope of this interest make the ban narrowly tailored. The ordinance also leaves open ample alternative channels of communication and is content-neutral. Thus, [the ordinance is constitutional.]

Justice White, concurring in the judgment.

.   .   .

... In my view, if the ordinance were construed to forbid all picketing in residential neighborhoods, [it would be unconstitutional.] ... I would ... sustain the ordinance as applied in this case, which the Court ... does, and await further developments.

Justice Brennan, with whom Justice Marshall joins, dissenting.

The Court today sets out the appropriate legal tests and standards governing the question presented, and proceeds to apply most of them correctly. Regrettably, though, the Court errs in the final step of its analysis, and approves an ordinance banning significantly more speech than is necessary to achieve the government's substantial and legitimate goal. Accordingly, I must dissent.

.   .   .

Without question there are many aspects of residential picketing that, if unregulated, might easily become intrusive or unduly coercive. Indeed, some of these aspects are illustrated by this very case. As the District Court found, before the ordinance took effect up to 40 sign-carrying, slogan-shouting protestors regularly converged on Dr. Victoria's home and, in addition to protesting, warned young children not to go near the house because Dr. Victoria was a "baby killer." Further, the throng repeatedly trespassed onto the Victorias' property and at least once blocked the exits to their home. Surely it is within the government's power to enact regulations as necessary to prevent such intrusive and coercive abuses. Thus, for example, the government could constitutionally regulate the number of residential picketers, the hours during which a residential picket may take place, or the noise level of such a picket. In short, substantial regulation is permitted to neutralize the intrusive or unduly coercive aspects of picketing around the home. But to say that picketing may be substantially regulated is not to say that it may be prohibited in its entirety. Once size, time, volume, and the like have been controlled to ensure that the picket is no longer intrusive or coercive, only the speech itself remains, conveyed perhaps by a lone, silent individual, walking back and forth with a sign. Such speech, which no longer implicates the heightened governmental interest in residential privacy, is nevertheless banned by the Brookfield law. Therefore, the ordinance is not narrowly tailored.

· · ·

JUSTICE STEVENS, dissenting.

· · ·

I do not believe we advance the inquiry by rejecting ... the ... "argument that residential streets are something less than public fora." The streets in a residential neighborhood that has no sidewalks are quite obviously a different type of forum than a stadium or a public park. Attaching the label "public forum" to the area in front of a single family dwelling does not help us decide whether the town's interest in the safe and efficient flow of traffic or its interest in protecting the privacy of its citizens justifies denying picketers the right to march up and down the streets at will.

· · ·

In this case ... the town will probably not enforce its ban against friendly, innocuous, or even brief unfriendly picketing.... The scope of the ordinance gives the town officials far too much discretion in making enforcement decisions.... [I]t is a simple matter for the town to amend its ordinance and to limit the ban to conduct that unreasonably interferes with the privacy of the home and does not serve a reasonable communicative purpose....

NOTES AND QUESTIONS

1. The Court first inquires whether the ordinance bans all picketing in residential neighborhoods, or all picketing near residences, and concludes that it does not. If it did so, would it be constitutional?

2. Would the ordinance have been valid if it banned picketing only if the "targeted resident" considered its message to be offensive? Does the ordinance instead bar all picketing directed at a residence? (Would it punish someone carrying a placard outside Doctor Victoria's house congratulating him for his service to the community? Is Justice Stevens

right that, in any event, the ordinance is likely to be enforced only when the resident concludes that the message is offensive?)

3. Usually, if the government denies speech access to a "traditional public forum" on the basis of a rule that is "content-based," the "most exacting scrutiny" means that the denial of access will be unconstitutional. In Burson v. Freeman, 504 U.S. 191 (1992), however, the Court sustained a Tennessee law that prohibited the solicitation of votes and the display or distribution of campaign materials within 100 feet of the entrance to a polling place. The Court conceded that the rule operated to limit speech on streets and sidewalks, the traditional public forum, and that whether one violated the rule depended on the content of speech. A majority of the Court, however, concluded that the rule was justified to serve a compelling interest in preventing voter intimidation and election fraud.

HILL v. COLORADO

Supreme Court of the United States, 2000.
530 U.S. 703, 120 S.Ct. 2480, 147 L.Ed.2d 597.

JUSTICE STEVENS delivered the opinion of the Court.

At issue is the constitutionality of a 1993 Colorado statute that regulates speech-related conduct within 100 feet of the entrance to any health care facility. The specific section of the statute that is challenged ... makes it unlawful within the regulated areas for any person to "knowingly approach" within eight feet of another person, without that person's consent, "for the purpose of passing a leaflet or handbill to, displaying a sign to, or engaging in oral protest, education, or counseling with such other person...." Although the statute prohibits speakers from approaching unwilling listeners, it does not ... place any restriction on the content of any message that anyone may wish to communicate to anyone else, either inside or outside the regulated areas. It does, however, make it more difficult to give unwanted advice, particularly in the form of a handbill or leaflet, to persons entering or leaving medical facilities.

The question is whether the First Amendment rights of the speaker are abridged by the protection the statute provides for the unwilling listener.

.   .   .

II

... A brief review of both sides of the dispute reveals that each has legitimate and important concerns.

The First Amendment interests of petitioners are clear and undisputed. As a preface to their legal challenge, petitioners emphasize three propositions. First, ... the areas protected by the statute encompass all the public ways within 100 feet of every entrance to every health care facility everywhere in the State of Colorado ... even though the legislative history makes it clear that its enactment was primarily motivated by activities in the vicinity of abortion clinics. Second, ... their leafleting, sign displays, and oral communications are protected by the First Amendment.... Third, the public sidewalks, streets, and ways affected by the statute are "quintessential" public forums for free speech....

On the other hand, petitioners do not challenge the legitimacy of the state interests that the statute is intended to serve. It is a traditional exercise of the States' "police powers to protect the health and safety of their citizens." ... That interest may justify a special focus on unimpeded access to health care facilities and the avoidance of potential trauma to patients associated with confrontational protests....

It is also important when conducting this interest analysis to recognize the significant difference between state restrictions on a speaker's right to address a willing audience and those that protect listeners from unwanted communication....

. . .

... None of our decisions has minimized the enduring importance of "the right to be free" from persistent "importunity, following and dogging" after an offer to communicate has been declined.... It is that right, as well as the right of "passage without obstruction," that the Colorado statute legitimately seeks to protect....

... [O]ur cases have repeatedly recognized the interests of unwilling listeners in situations where "the degree of captivity makes it impractical for the unwilling viewer or auditor to avoid exposure...." ...

III

... It is ... appropriate to comment on the "content neutrality" of the statute....

... [T]he statute's "restrictions apply equally to all demonstrators, regardless of viewpoint, and the statutory language makes no reference to the content of the speech." ... [T]he State's interests in protecting access and privacy, and providing the police with clear guidelines, are unrelated to the content of the demonstrators' speech....

Petitioners nevertheless argue that the statute is not content neutral insofar as it applies to some oral communication. The statute applies to all persons who "knowingly approach" within eight feet of another for the purpose of leafleting or displaying signs; for such persons, the content of their oral statements is irrelevant. With respect to persons who are neither leafletters nor sign carriers, however, the statute does not apply unless their approach is "for the purpose of ... engaging in oral protest, education, or counseling." Petitioners contend that an individual near a health care facility who knowingly approaches a pedestrian to say "good morning" or to randomly recite lines from a novel would not be subject to the statute's restrictions. Because the content of the oral statements made by an approaching speaker must sometimes be examined to determine whether the knowing approach is covered by the statute, petitioners argue that the law is "content-based"
. . .

. . .

It is common in the law to examine the content of a communication to determine the speaker's purpose. Whether a particular statement constitutes a threat, blackmail, an agreement to fix prices, a copyright violation, a public offering of securities, or an offer to sell goods often depends on the precise content of the statement. We have never held, or suggested, that it is improper to look at the content of an oral or written statement in order to determine whether a rule of law applies to a course of conduct. With respect to the conduct that is the focus of the Colorado statute, it is unlikely that there would often be any need to know exactly what words were spoken in order to determine whether "sidewalk counselors" are engaging in "oral protest, education, or counseling" rather than pure social or random conversation.

Theoretically, of course, cases may arise in which it is necessary to review the content of the statements made by a person approaching within eight feet of an unwilling listener to determine whether the approach is covered by the statute. But that review need be no more extensive than a determination of whether a general prohibition of "picketing" or "demonstrating" applies to innocuous speech.... [W]e have never suggested that the kind of cursory examination that might be required to exclude casual conversation from the coverage of a regulation of picketing would be problematic.

. . .

... [A] statute that restricts certain categories of speech only lends itself to invidious use if there is a significant number of communications, raising the same problem that the statute was enacted to solve, that fall outside the statute's scope, while others fall inside.... The statute does not distinguish among speech instances that are similarly likely to raise the legitimate concerns to which it responds. Hence, the statute cannot be struck down for failure to maintain "content neutrality," ...

Also flawed is Justice Kennedy's theory that a statute restricting speech becomes unconstitutionally content based because of its application "to the specific locations where that discourse occurs." A statute prohibiting solicitation in airports that was motivated by the aggressive approaches of Hari–Krishnas does not become content based solely because its application is confined to airports ...

Similarly, the contention that a statute is "viewpoint based" simply because its enactment was motivated by the conduct of the partisans on one side of a debate is without support....

... The statute is not limited to those who oppose abortion.... It applies to all "protest," to all "counseling," and to all demonstrators whether or not the demonstration concerns abortion, and whether they oppose or support the woman who has made an abortion decision. That is the level of neutrality that the Constitution demands.

. . .

IV

... [The statute] is a valid time, place, and manner regulation ...

The three types of communication regulated ... are the display of signs, leafletting, and oral speech. The 8–foot separation between the speaker and the audience should not have any adverse impact on the readers' ability to read signs displayed by demonstrators....

With respect to oral statements, the distance certainly can make it more difficult for a speaker to be heard.... [T]his 8–foot zone allows the speaker to communicate at a "normal conversational distance." ... Additionally, the statute allows the speaker to remain in one place, and other individuals can pass within eight feet of the protester without causing the protester to violate the statute. Finally, here there is a "knowing" requirement that protects speakers "who thought they were keeping pace with the targeted individual" at the proscribed distance from inadvertently violating the statute....

· · ·

The burden on the ability to distribute handbills is more serious because it seems possible that an 8–foot interval could hinder the ability of a leafletter to deliver handbills to some unwilling recipients. The statute does not, however, prevent a leafletter from simply standing near the path of oncoming pedestrians and proffering his or her material, which the pedestrians can easily accept.... [T]he regulation primarily burdened the distributors' ability to communicate with unwilling readers.... [T]he First Amendment protects the right of every citizen to "reach the minds of willing listeners and to do so there must be opportunity to win their attention." ... The Colorado statute adequately protects those rights.

· · ·

Persons who are attempting to enter health care facilities—for any purpose—are often in particularly vulnerable physical and emotional conditions. The State of Colorado has responded to its substantial and legitimate interest in protecting these persons from unwanted encounters, confrontations, and even assaults by enacting an exceedingly modest restriction on the speakers' ability to approach.

... [T]he statute takes a prophylactic approach; it forbids all unwelcome demonstrators to come closer than eight feet. We recognize that by doing so, it will sometimes inhibit a demonstrator whose approach in fact would have proved harmless. But the statute's prophylactic aspect is justified by the great difficulty of protecting, say, a pregnant woman from physical harassment with legal rules that focus exclusively on the individual impact of each instance of behavior, demanding in each case an accurate characterization (as harassing or not harassing) of each individual movement within the 8–foot boundary. Such individualized characterization of each individual movement is often difficult to make accurately. A bright-line prophylactic rule may be the best way to provide protection, and, at the same time, by offering clear guidance and avoiding subjectivity, to protect speech itself.

· · ·

JUSTICE SOUTER, with whom JUSTICE O'CONNOR, JUSTICE GINSBURG, and JUSTICE BREYER join, concurring.

I join the opinion of the Court and add this further word. . . .

. . .

. . . There is always a correlation with subject and viewpoint when the law regulates conduct that has become the signature of one side of a controversy. But that does not mean that every regulation of such distinctive behavior is content based as First Amendment doctrine employs that term. The correct rule, rather, is captured in the formulation that a restriction is content based only if it is imposed because of the content of the speech, . . . and not because of offensive behavior identified with its delivery.

. . .

. . . [S]ubsection (3) simply does not forbid the statement of any position on any subject. . . . What it forbids, and all it forbids, is approaching another person closer than eight feet (absent permission) to deliver the message. . . .

. . . The question is simply whether the ostensible reason for regulating the circumstances is really something about the ideas. Here, the evidence indicates that the ostensible reason is the true reason. . . . What is prohibited is a close encounter when the person addressed does not want to get close. . . . Hence the implausibility of any claim that an antiabortion message, not the behavior of protesters, is what is being singled out.

. . .

JUSTICE SCALIA, with whom JUSTICE THOMAS joins, dissenting.

. . .

. . . What is before us, after all, is a speech regulation directed against the opponents of abortion, and it therefore enjoys the benefit of the "ad hoc nullification machine" that the Court has set in motion to push aside whatever doctrines of constitutional law stand in the way of that highly favored practice. . . . Having deprived abortion opponents of the political right to persuade the electorate that abortion should be restricted by law, the Court today continues and expands its assault upon their individual right to persuade women contemplating abortion that what they are doing is wrong. . . .

I

. . . Whether a speaker must obtain permission before approaching within eight feet—and whether he will be sent to prison for failing to do so—depends entirely on what he intends to say when he gets there. I have no doubt that this regulation would be deemed content-based in an instant if the case before us involved antiwar protesters, or union members seeking to "educate" the public about the reasons for their strike.... But the jurisprudence of this Court has a way of changing when abortion is involved.

. . .

In sum, it blinks reality to regard this statute, in its application to oral communications, as anything other than a content-based restriction upon speech in the public forum. As such, it must survive that stringent mode of constitutional analysis our cases refer to as "strict scrutiny,"
. . .

II

. . .

I turn now to the real state interest at issue here [is] the preservation of unimpeded access to health care facilities.... In subsection (3), however, the State of Colorado has prohibited a vast amount of speech that cannot possibly be thought to correspond to that evil.

. . .

... For those who share an abiding moral or religious conviction ... that abortion is the taking of a human life, there is no option but to persuade women, one by one, not to make that choice. And as a general matter, the most effective place, if not the only place, where that persuasion can occur, is outside the entrances to abortion facilities. By upholding these restrictions on speech in this place the Court ratifies the State's attempt to make even that task an impossible one.

... [T]hose who would accomplish their moral and religious objectives by peaceful and civil means, by trying to persuade individual women of the rightness of their cause, will be deterred; and that is not a good thing in a democracy....

. . .

JUSTICE KENNEDY, dissenting.

. . .

I

... Colorado's statute is a textbook example of a law which is content based.

A

... The law imposes content-based restrictions on speech by reason of the terms it uses, the categories it employs, and the conditions for its enforcement. It is content based, too, by its predictable and intended operation. Whether particular messages violate the statute is determined by their substance. The law is a prime example of a statute inviting screening and censoring of individual speech; and it is serious error to hold otherwise.

. . .

After the Court errs in finding the statute content neutral, it compounds the mistake by finding the law viewpoint neutral. Viewpoint-based rules are invidious speech restrictions, yet the Court approves this one. The purpose and design of the statute—as everyone ought to know and as its own defenders urge in attempted justification—are to restrict speakers on one side of the debate: those who protest abortions. The statute applies only to medical facilities, a convenient yet obvious mask for the legislature's true purpose and for the prohibition's true effect. One need read no further than the statute's preamble to remove any doubt about the question. . . .

. . .

. . . One of the arguments by the proponents of abortion, I had thought, was that a young woman might have been so uninformed that she did not know how to avoid pregnancy. The speakers in this case seek to ask the same uninformed woman, or indeed any woman who is considering an abortion, to understand and to contemplate the nature of the life she carries within her. To restrict the right of the speaker to hand her a leaflet, to hold a sign, or to speak quietly is for the Court to deny the neutrality that must be the first principle of the First Amendment. . . .

. . .

QUESTION

Justice Scalia's dissent in *Hill* argues that the Court's result is dictated more by the abortion controversy than free speech doctrine. ("What is before us, after all, is a speech regulation directed against the opponents of abortion . . .") Was that true in *Frisby* also?

B. PROPERTY OTHER THAN PARKS AND STREETS

What are the appropriate questions to be asked when a speaker claims a constitutional right of access to government property other than the streets and parks? Some cases assert that, when access is denied by a "content neutral" rule, the issue is always to be decided by a balancing of competing interests. In Grayned v. City of Rockford, 408 U.S. 104 (1972), the Court sustained a law that forbad noisy demonstrations near schools when classes were in session. Justice Marshall's opinion for the Court said that the issues were whether the law was "narrowly tailored to further Rockford's interest in having an undisrupted school session" and whether it "unnecessarily interfere[d] with First Amendment Rights." Other cases, however, seem to say that an initial question is whether the place to which access is sought has been a traditional place for free public assembly and communication. (If *not,* then there is no access right, no matter how competing interests are balanced.) That was the approach taken when Benjamin Spock, a presidential candidate for the People's Party in 1972, was denied permission to speak and distribute literature at Fort Dix, a military post located in a rural area of New Jersey. Military authorities had banned all speeches and demonstrations of a partisan political nature on the post. A divided Court sustained the ban, with Justice Stewart's opinion for the Court reasoning that a military post was not a traditional public forum. Greer v. Spock, 424 U.S. 828 (1976). Does the case that follows resolve the confusion?

INTERNATIONAL SOCIETY FOR KRISHNA CONSCIOUSNESS, INC. v. LEE

Supreme Court of the United States, 1992.
505 U.S. 672, 112 S.Ct. 2701, 120 L.Ed.2d 541.

CHIEF JUSTICE REHNQUIST delivered the opinion of the Court.

In this case we consider whether an airport terminal operated by a public authority is a public forum and whether a regulation prohibiting solicitation in the interior of an airport terminal violates the First Amendment.

. . . International Society for Krishna Consciousness, Inc. (ISKCON) is a not-for-profit religious corporation whose members perform a ritual known as sankirtan. The ritual consists of " 'going into public places, disseminating religious literature and soliciting funds to support the religion.' " The primary purpose of this ritual is raising funds for the movement.

. . .

The Port Authority [which owns and operates three major airports in the greater New York City area] has adopted a regulation forbidding within the terminals the repetitive solicitation of money or distribution of literature. The regulation states:

"1. The following conduct is prohibited within the interior areas of buildings or structures at an air terminal if conducted by a person to or with passers-by in a continuous or repetitive manner:

"(a) The sale or distribution of any merchandise, including but not limited to jewelry, food stuffs, candles, flowers, badges and clothing.

"(b) The sale or distribution of flyers, brochures, pamphlets, books or any other printed or written material.

"(c) Solicitation and receipt of funds."

The regulation governs only the terminals; the Port Authority permits solicitation and distribution on the sidewalks outside the terminal buildings. The regulation effectively prohibits petitioner from performing sankirtan in the terminals. . . .

. . .

. . . [T]he government need not permit all forms of speech on property that it owns and controls. . . . Where the government is acting as a proprietor, managing its internal operations, rather than acting as lawmaker with the power to regulate or license, its action will not be subjected to the heightened review to which its actions as a lawmaker may be subject. . . . Thus, we have upheld a ban on political advertisements in city-operated transit vehicles, Lehman v. City of Shaker Heights, 418 U.S. 298 (1974), even though the city permitted other types of advertising on those vehicles. Similarly, we have permitted a school district to limit access to an internal mail system used to communicate with teachers employed by the district. Perry Education Assn. v. Perry Local Educators' Assn., 460 U.S. 37 (1983).

These cases reflect, either implicitly or explicitly, a "forum-based" approach for assessing restrictions that the government seeks to place on the use of its property.... Under this approach, regulation of speech on government property that has traditionally been available for public expression is subject to the highest scrutiny. Such regulations survive only if they are narrowly drawn to achieve a compelling state interest.... The second category of public property is the designated public forum, whether of a limited or unlimited character—property that the state has opened for expressive activity by part or all of the public.... Regulation of such property is subject to the same limitations as that governing a traditional public forum.... Finally, there is all remaining public property. Limitations on expressive activity conducted on this last category of property must survive only a much more limited review. The challenged regulation need only be reasonable, as long as the regulation is not an effort to suppress the speaker's activity due to disagreement with the speaker's view....

... [W]e conclude that the terminals are nonpublic fora and that the regulation reasonably limits solicitation.

· · ·

... [A] traditional public forum is property that has as "a principal purpose ... the free exchange of ideas." ... Moreover, consistent with the notion that the government—like other property owners—"has power to preserve the property under its control for the use to which it is lawfully dedicated," ... the government does not create a public forum by inaction. Nor is a public forum created "whenever members of the public are permitted freely to visit a place owned or operated by the Government." ... The decision to create a public forum must instead be made "by intentionally opening a nontraditional forum for public discourse." ... Finally, we have recognized that the location of property also has bearing because separation from acknowledged public areas may serve to indicate that the separated property is a special enclave, subject to greater restriction....

[A]irport terminals are [not] public fora.... [G]iven the lateness with which the modern air terminal has made its appearance, it hardly qualifies for the description of having "immemorially ... time out of mind" been held in the public trust and used for purposes of expressive activity.... Moreover, even within the rather short history of air transport, it is only "[i]n recent years [that] it has become a common practice for various religious and non-profit organizations to use commercial airports as a forum for the distribution of literature, the solicitation of funds, the proselytizing of new members, and other similar activities." ... Thus, the tradition of airport activity does not demonstrate that airports have historically been made available for speech activity. Nor

can we say that these particular terminals, or airport terminals generally, have been intentionally opened by their operators to such activity; the
frequent and continuing litigation evidencing the operators' objections
belies any such claim. In short, there can be no argument that society's
time-tested judgment, expressed through acquiescence in a continuing
practice, has resolved the issue in petitioner's favor.

Petitioner attempts to circumvent the history and practice governing airport activity by pointing our attention to the variety of speech
activity that it claims historically occurred at various "transportation
nodes" such as rail stations, bus stations, wharves, and Ellis Island.
Even if we were inclined to accept petitioner's historical account describing speech activity at these locations, an account respondent contests, we
think that such evidence is of little import for two reasons. First, much
of the evidence is irrelevant to public fora analysis, because sites such as
bus and rail terminals traditionally have had private ownership.... The
practices of privately held transportation centers do not bear on the
government's regulatory authority over a publicly owned airport.

Second, the relevant unit for our inquiry is an airport, not "transportation nodes" generally. When new methods of transportation develop, new methods for accommodating that transportation are also likely
to be needed. And with each new step, it therefore will be a new inquiry
whether the transportation necessities are compatible with various kinds
of expressive activity. To make a category of "transportation nodes,"
therefore, would unjustifiably elide what may prove to be critical differences of which we should rightfully take account. The "security magnet," for example, is an airport commonplace that lacks a counterpart in
bus terminals and train stations. And public access to air terminals is
also not infrequently restricted.... To blithely equate airports with
other transportation centers, therefore, would be a mistake. The differences among such facilities are unsurprising since ... airports are
commercial establishments funded by users fees and designed to make a
regulated profit, and where nearly all who visit do so for some travel
related purpose. As commercial enterprises, airports must provide services attractive to the marketplace. In light of this, it cannot fairly be
said that an airport terminal has as a principal purpose "promoting the
free exchange of ideas." ... To the contrary, ... Port Authority management considers the purpose of the terminals to be the facilitation of
passenger air travel, not the promotion of expression.... Even if we look
beyond the intent of the Port Authority to the manner in which the
terminals have been operated, the terminals have never been dedicated
(except under the threat of court order) to ... the solicitation of
contributions and the distribution of literature.

The terminals here are far from atypical. Airport builders and
managers focus their efforts on providing terminals that will contribute
to efficient air travel.... Although many airports have expanded their
function beyond merely contributing to efficient air travel, few have
included among their purposes the designation of a forum for solicitation
and distribution activities. Thus, we think that neither by tradition nor
purpose can the terminals be described as satisfying the standards we
have previously set out for identifying a public forum.

The restrictions here challenged, therefore, need only satisfy a requirement of reasonableness.... We have no doubt that under this standard the prohibition on solicitation passes muster.

We have on many prior occasions noted the disruptive effect that solicitation may have on business. "Solicitation requires action by those who would respond: The individual solicited must decide whether or not to contribute (which itself might involve reading the solicitor's literature or hearing his pitch), and then, having decided to do so, reach for a wallet, search it for money, write a check, or produce a credit card." ... Passengers who wish to avoid the solicitor may have to alter their path, slowing both themselves and those around them. The result is that the normal flow of traffic is impeded.... This is especially so in an airport, where "air travelers, who are often weighted down by cumbersome baggage ... may be hurrying to catch a plane or to arrange ground transportation." Delays may be particularly costly in this setting, as a flight missed by only a few minutes can result in hours worth of subsequent inconvenience.

· · ·

The Port Authority has concluded that its interest in monitoring the activities can best be accomplished by limiting solicitation and distribution to the sidewalk areas outside the terminals. This sidewalk area is frequented by an overwhelming percentage of airport users. Thus the resulting access of those who would solicit the general public is quite complete. In turn we think it would be odd to conclude that the Port Authority's terminal regulation is unreasonable despite the Port Authority having otherwise assured access to an area universally traveled.

· · ·

JUSTICE KENNEDY, with whom JUSTICE BLACKMUN, JUSTICE STEVENS, and JUSTICE SOUTER join as to Part I, concurring in the judgment.

While I concur in the judgment affirming in this case, my analysis differs in substantial respects from that of the Court. In my view the airport corridors and shopping areas outside of the passenger security zones, areas operated by the Port Authority, are public forums, and speech in those places is entitled to protection against all government regulation inconsistent with public forum principles. The Port Authority's blanket prohibition on the distribution or sale of literature cannot meet those stringent standards, and I agree it is invalid under the First and Fourteenth Amendments. The Port Authority's rule disallowing in-person solicitation of money for immediate payment, however, is in my view a narrow and valid regulation of the time, place, and manner of protected speech in this forum, or else is a valid regulation of the nonspeech element of expressive conduct. I would sustain the Port Authority's ban on solicitation and receipt of funds.

I

An earlier opinion expressed my concern that "[i]f our public forum jurisprudence is to retain vitality, we must recognize that certain objective characteristics of Government property and its customary use by the public may control" the status of the property. United States v. Kokinda, 497 U.S. 720, 737 (1990) (Kennedy, J., concurring in judgment). The case before us does not heed that principle. Our public forum doctrine ought not to be a jurisprudence of categories rather than ideas or convert what was once an analysis protective of expression into one which grants the government authority to restrict speech by fiat. I believe that the Court's public forum analysis in this case is inconsistent with the values underlying the speech and press clauses of the First Amendment.

Our public forum ... cases describe a three part analysis to designate government-owned property as either a traditional public forum, a designated public forum, or a nonpublic forum.... The Court today holds that traditional public forums are limited to public property which have as " 'a principal purpose ... the free exchange of ideas' "; and that this purpose must be evidenced by a long-standing historical practice of permitting speech. The Court also holds that designated forums consist of property which the government intends to open for public disclosure. All other types of property are, in the Court's view, nonpublic forums (in other words, not public forums), and government-imposed restrictions of speech in these places will be upheld so long as reasonable and viewpoint-neutral. Under this categorical view the application of public forum analysis to airport terminals seems easy. Airports are of course public spaces of recent vintage, and so there can be no time-honored tradition associated with airports of permitting free speech. And because governments have often attempted to restrict speech within airports, it follows a fortiori under the Court's analysis that they cannot be so-called "designated" forums. So, the Court concludes, airports must be nonpublic forums, subject to minimal First Amendment protection.

This analysis is flawed at its very beginning. It leaves the government with almost unlimited authority to restrict speech on its property by doing nothing more than articulating a non-speech-related purpose for the area, and it leaves almost no scope for the development of new public forums absent the rare approval of the government. The Court's error lies in its conclusion that the public forum status of public property depends on the government's defined purpose for the property, or on an explicit decision by the government to dedicate the property to expressive activity. In my view, the inquiry must be an objective one, based on the actual, physical characteristics and uses of the property....

... [U]nder the Court's view the authority of the government to control speech on its property is paramount, for in almost all cases the critical step in the Court's analysis is a classification of the property that turns on the government's own definition or decision, unconstrained by an independent duty to respect the speech its citizens can voice there....

The Court's approach is contrary to the underlying purposes of the public forum doctrine.... Public places are of necessity the locus for discussion of public issues, as well as protest against arbitrary government action. At the heart of our jurisprudence lies the principle that in a free nation citizens must have the right to gather and speak with other persons in public places. The recognition that certain government-owned property is a public forum provides open notice to citizens that their freedoms may be exercised there without fear of a censorial government, adding tangible reinforcement to the idea that we are a free people.

. . .

The Court's answer to these objections appears to be a recourse to history as justifying its recognition of streets, parks, and sidewalks, but apparently no other types of government property, as traditional public forums.... In my view the policies underlying the doctrine cannot be given effect unless we recognize that open, public spaces and thoroughfares which are suitable for discourse may be public forums, whatever their historical pedigree and without concern for a precise classification of the property.... In a country where most citizens travel by automobile, and parks all too often become locales for crime rather than social intercourse, our failure to recognize the possibility that new types of government property may be appropriate forums for speech will lead to a serious curtailment of our expressive activity.

... In my view, our public forum doctrine must recognize this reality, and allow the creation of public forums which do not fit within the narrow tradition of streets, sidewalks, and parks....

I agree with the Court that government property of a type which by history and tradition has been available for speech activity must continue to be recognized as a public forum. In my view, however, constitutional protection is not confined to these properties alone. Under the proper circumstances I would accord public forum status to other forms of property, regardless of its ancient or contemporary origins and whether or not it fits within a narrow historic tradition. If the objective, physical characteristics of the property at issue and the actual public access and uses which have been permitted by the government indicate that expressive activity would be appropriate and compatible with those uses, the property is a public forum. The most important considerations in this analysis are whether the property shares physical similarities with more traditional public forums, whether the government has permitted or acquiesced in broad public access to the property, and whether expressive activity would tend to interfere in a significant way with the uses to which the government has as a factual matter dedicated the property.... The possibility of some theoretical inconsistency between expressive activities and the property's uses should not bar a finding of a public forum, if those inconsistencies can be avoided through simple and permitted regulations.

. . .

Under this analysis, it is evident that the public spaces of the Port Authority's airports are public forums. First, ... the public spaces in the airports are broad, public thoroughfares full of people and lined with stores and other commercial activities. An airport corridor is of course not a street, but that is not the proper inquiry. The question is one of physical similarities, sufficient to suggest that the airport corridor should be a public forum for the same reasons that streets and sidewalks have been treated as public forums by the people who use them.

Second, the airport areas involved here are open to the public without restriction. Plaintiffs do not seek access to the secured areas of the airports, nor do I suggest that these areas would be public forums....

Third, and perhaps most important, it is apparent from the record, and from the recent history of airports, that when adequate time, place, and manner regulations are in place, expressive activity is quite compatible with the uses of major airports.... [T]he logical consequence of Port Authority's congestion argument is that the crowded streets and sidewalks of major cities cannot be public forums. These problems have been dealt with in the past, and in other settings, through proper time, place, and manner restrictions; and the Port Authority does not make any showing that similar regulations would not be effective in its airports....

. . .

II

It is my view, however, that the Port Authority's ban on the "solicitation and receipt of funds" within its airport terminals should be upheld under the standards applicable to speech regulations in public forums. The regulation may be upheld as either a reasonable time, place, and manner restriction, or as a regulation directed at the nonspeech element of expressive conduct. The two standards have considerable overlap in a case like this one.

. . .

... If the Port Authority's solicitation regulation prohibited all speech which requested the contribution of funds, I would conclude that it was a direct, content-based restriction of speech in clear violation of the First Amendment. The Authority's regulation does not prohibit all solicitation, however; it prohibits the "solicitation and receipt of funds." I do not understand this regulation to prohibit all speech that solicits funds. It reaches only personal solicitations for immediate payment of money....

So viewed, I believe the Port Authority's rule survives our test for speech restrictions in the public forum. In-person solicitation of funds, when combined with immediate receipt of that money, creates a risk of fraud and duress which is well recognized, and which is different in kind from other forms of expression or conduct.... [R]equests for immediate payment of money create a strong potential for fraud or undue pressure, in part because of the lack of time for reflection....

Because the Port Authority's solicitation ban is directed at these abusive practices and not at any particular message, idea, or form of speech, the regulation is a content-neutral rule serving a significant government interest....

. . .

... [T]he Port Authority has left open ample alternative channels for the communication of the message which is an aspect of solicitation.... Requests for money continue to be permitted, and in the course of requesting money solicitors may explain their cause, or the purposes of their organization, without violating the regulation. It is only if the solicitor accepts immediate payment that a violation occurs....

Much of what I have said about the solicitation of funds may seem to apply to the sale of literature, but the differences between the two activities are of sufficient significance to require they be distinguished for constitutional purposes. The Port Authority's flat ban on the distribution or sale of printed material must, in my view, fall in its entirety. The application of our time, place, and manner test to the ban on sales leads to a result quite different from the solicitation ban. For one, the government interest in regulating the sales of literature is not as powerful as in the case of solicitation. The danger of a fraud arising from such sales is much more limited than from pure solicitation, because in the case of a sale the nature of the exchange tends to be clearer to both parties.... And perhaps most important, the flat ban on sales of literature leaves open fewer alternative channels of communication than the Port Authority's more limited prohibition on the solicitation and receipt of funds. Given the practicalities and ad hoc nature of much expressive activity in the public forum, sales of literature must be completed in one transaction to be workable. Attempting to collect money at another time or place is a far less plausible option in the context of a sale than when soliciting donations....

. . .

JUSTICE O'CONNOR, concurring....

. . .

I ... agree that publicly owned airports are not public fora. Unlike public streets and parks, both of which our First Amendment jurisprudence has identified as "traditional public fora," airports do not count among their purposes the "free exchange of ideas," ...

For these reasons, the Port Authority's restrictions on solicitation and leafletting within the airport terminals do not qualify for the strict scrutiny that applies to restriction of speech in public fora. That airports are not public fora, however, does not mean that the government can restrict speech in whatever way it likes.... The determination that airports are not public fora thus only begins our inquiry.

... In this case, the "special attributes" and "surrounding circumstances" of the airports operated by the Port Authority are determinative. Not only has the Port Authority chosen not to limit access to the airports under its control, it has created a huge complex open to travelers and nontravelers alike.... The International Arrivals Building at JFK Airport even has two branches of Bloomingdale's.

... [T]he Port Authority is operating a shopping mall as well as an airport. The reasonableness inquiry, therefore, is not whether the restrictions on speech are "consistent with ... preserving the property" for air travel, ... but whether they are reasonably related to maintaining the multipurpose environment that the Port Authority has deliberately created.

Applying that standard, I agree with the Court ... that the ban on solicitation is reasonable....

In my view, however, the regulation banning leafletting—or, in the Port Authority's words, the "continuous or repetitive ... distribution of ... printed or written material"—cannot be upheld as reasonable on this record. I therefore concur in the judgment ... striking down that prohibition....

· · ·

... Because I cannot see how peaceful pamphleteering is incompatible with the multipurpose environment of the Port Authority airports, I cannot accept that a total ban on that activity is reasonable without an explanation as to why such a restriction "preserv[es] the property" for the several uses to which it has been put....

· · ·

JUSTICE SOUTER, with whom JUSTICE BLACKMUN and JUSTICE STEVENS, join, concurring ... and dissenting....

I

I join in Part I of Justice Kennedy's opinion.... The designation of a given piece of public property as a traditional public forum must not merely state a conclusion that the property falls within a static category including streets, parks, sidewalks and perhaps not much more, but must represent a conclusion that the property is no different in principle from such examples....

· · ·

I also agree with Justice Kennedy's statement of the public forum principle: we should classify as a public forum any piece of public property that is "suitable for discourse" in its physical character, where expressive activity is "compatible" with the use to which it has actually been put....

II

From the Court's conclusion ... sustaining the total ban on solicitation of money for immediate payment, I respectfully dissent....

· · ·

... Since there is here no evidence of any type of coercive conduct, over and above the merely importunate character of the open and public solicitation, that might justify a ban, ... the regulation cannot be sustained to avoid coercion.

... [Government cannot] ban solicitation just because it could be fraudulent.... The evidence of fraudulent conduct here is virtually nonexistent....

Even assuming a governmental interest adequate to justify some regulation, the present ban would fall when subjected to the requirement of narrow tailoring. . . .

Finally, I do not think the Port Authority's solicitation ban leaves open the "ample" channels of communication required of a valid content-neutral time, place and manner restriction.

NOTES AND QUESTIONS

1. In a companion case, Lee v. International Society for Krishna Consciousness, the Court held that the ban on distribution of literature was invalid under the First Amendment. The Court's per curiam opinion stated that affirmance was "[f]or the reasons expressed in the opinions of Justice O'Connor, Justice Kennedy, and Justice Souter in International Society for Krishna Consciousness v. Lee." Justice Rehnquist's dissent, joined by Justices White, Scalia and Thomas, also relied on his opinion in that case. He said, in addition:

> The risks and burdens posed by leafletting are quite similar to those posed by solicitation. The weary, harried, or hurried traveler may have no less desire and need to avoid the delays generated by having literature foisted upon him than he does to avoid delays from a financial solicitation. And while a busy passenger perhaps may succeed in fending off a leafletter with minimal disruption to himself by agreeing simply to take the proffered material, this does not completely ameliorate the dangers of congestion flowing from such leafletting. Others may choose not simply to accept the material but also to stop and engage the leafletter in debate, obstructing those who follow. Moreover, those who accept material may often simply drop it on the floor once out of the leafletter's range, creating an eyesore, a safety hazard, and additional clean-up work for airport staff.

2. The Court has consistently refused to classify any property other than streets, sidewalks and parks as a traditional public forum. If the government denies speech access to public property that is not a public forum for reasons that are unrelated to hostility to the speaker's point of view, the Court has almost always sustained that denial. (Before the decision in *Lee*, the one exception was in Board of Airport Comm'rs of Los Angeles v. Jews for Jesus, Inc., 482 U.S. 569 (1987), where a regulation prohibited "all First Amendment activities" in the Los Angeles International Airport. That regulation literally forbade reading and talking!) For example, in Heffron v. International Society for Krishna Consciousness, Inc., 452 U.S. 640 (1981), the Court upheld a rule of the Minnesota State Fair prohibiting distribution of literature or the solicitation of funds, except from fixed-location rented booths. In United States Postal Service v. Council of Greenburgh Civic Associations, 453 U.S. 114 (1981), it upheld a federal statute which forbids putting unstamped "mailable material" in the letter boxes of private homes. In Cornelius v. NAACP Legal Defense and Educational Fund, Inc., 473 U.S. 788 (1985), it upheld a Presidential order excluding legal defense and "political advocacy" organizations from participating in the charity drive for

federal employees. (The Court conceded that the distinction drawn was based on subject matter and speaker identity, but emphasized that it was "viewpoint neutral.")

3. The principal case continues the pattern of limiting public forum status to streets, sidewalks, and parks. Does the companion case, which strikes down the viewpoint-neutral ban on distributing literature, break the pattern which sustains such bans on public property? Notice that four of the five Justices who vote to invalidate the ban do so on the ground that the airport should be classified as a public forum, and only Justice O'Connor invalidates the ban on the basis of the standards applicable to public property other than public fora. On the other hand, Justice O'Connor seems to emphasize some of the same concerns that Justice Kennedy does in asking whether the government's actual use of the property is compatible with speech. Is Justice O'Connor likely to find denials of speech access to be "unreasonable" in the same cases where Justice Kennedy is likely to conclude that the public property is a public forum?

II. SPEECH BY STUDENTS IN PUBLIC SCHOOLS

BOARD OF EDUCATION, ISLAND TREES UNION FREE SCHOOL DISTRICT NO. 26 v. PICO

Supreme Court of the United States, 1982.
457 U.S. 853, 102 S.Ct. 2799, 73 L.Ed.2d 435.

JUSTICE BRENNAN announced the judgment of the Court, and delivered an opinion in which JUSTICE MARSHALL and JUSTICE STEVENS joined, and in which JUSTICE BLACKMUN joined except for Part II–A–(1).

The principal question presented is whether the First Amendment imposes limitations upon the exercise by a local school board of its discretion to remove library books from high school and junior high school libraries.

I

. . .

[Three members of the Board of Education attended a meeting sponsored by a politically conservative organization, and were given a list of "objectionable" books. Five months later, the Board issued a directive that the listed books be removed from junior and senior high school library shelves because they were "anti-American, anti-Christian, anti-Semitic, and just plain filthy." (The books affected were Slaughter House Five, by Kurt Vonnegut, Jr.; The Naked Ape, by Desmond Morris; Down These Mean Streets, by Piri Thomas; Best Short Stories of Negro Writers, edited by Langston Hughes; Go Ask Alice, of anonymous authorship; Laughing Boy, by Oliver LaFarge; Black Boy, by Richard Wright; A Hero Ain't Nothing But A Sandwich, by Alice Childress; Soul On Ice, by Eldridge Cleaver; A Reader for Writers, edited by Jerome Archer; and The Fixer, by Bernard Malamud.)

Suit was brought in a federal trial court to set aside the Board's decision, alleging a violation of the First Amendment in that the books were removed "because particular passages ... offended [the board's] social, political and moral tastes and not because the books, taken as a whole, were lacking in educational value." The trial court dismissed the suit without a trial, concluding that the Board was entitled to remove the books based on its "conservative educational philosophy" and its belief that the books were "irrelevant, vulgar, immoral, and in bad taste." The federal appeals court reversed, sending the case back to the trial court to give the plaintiffs a chance to prove "that the ostensible justifications" for removing the books "were simply pretexts for the suppression of free speech." It was at this point that the Supreme Court agreed to review the case, to decide whether it should be dismissed or sent back to the trial court for a trial.]

II

We emphasize at the outset the limited nature of the substantive question presented by the case before us. Our precedents have long recognized certain constitutional limits upon the power of the State to control even the curriculum and classroom. For example, Meyer v. Nebraska, 262 U.S. 390 (1923), struck down a state law that forbade the teaching of modern foreign languages in public and private schools, and Epperson v. Arkansas, 393 U.S. 97 (1968), declared unconstitutional a state law that prohibited the teaching of the Darwinian theory of evolution in any state-supported school. But the current action does not require us to re-enter this difficult terrain, which *Meyer* and *Epperson* traversed without apparent misgiving. For as this case is presented to us, it does not involve textbooks, or indeed any books that Island Trees students would be required to read. Respondents do not seek in this Court to impose limitations upon their school board's discretion to prescribe the curricula of the Island Trees Schools. On the contrary, the only books at issue in this case are *library* books, books that by their nature are optional rather than required reading. Our adjudication of the present case thus does not intrude into the classroom, or into the compulsory courses taught there. Furthermore, even as to library books, the action before us does not involve the *acquisition* of books. Respondents have not sought to compel their school board to add to the school library shelves any books that students desire to read. Rather, the only action challenged in this case is the *removal* from school libraries of books originally placed there by the school authorities, or without objection from them.

. . .

In sum, the issue before us in this case is a narrow one.... [D]oes the First Amendment impose *any* limitations upon the discretion of petitioners to remove library books from the Island Trees High School and Junior High School? ...

A

(1)

The Court has long recognized that local school boards have broad discretion in the management of school affairs.... We are therefore in full agreement with petitioners that local school boards must be permitted "to establish and apply their curriculum in such a way as to transmit community values," and that "there is a legitimate and substantial community interest in promoting respect for authority and traditional values be they social, moral, or political."

At the same time, however, we have necessarily recognized that the discretion of the States and local school boards in matters of education must be exercised in a manner that comports with the transcendent imperatives of the First Amendment. In West Virginia State Board of Education v. Barnette, 319 U.S. 624 (1943), we held that under the First Amendment a student in a public school could not be compelled to salute the flag.... Later cases have consistently followed this rationale. Thus Epperson v. Arkansas invalidated a State's anti-evolution statute as violative of the Establishment Clause, and reaffirmed the duty of federal courts "to apply the First Amendment's mandate in our educational system where essential to safeguard the fundamental values of freedom of speech and inquiry." And Tinker v. Des Moines School Dist. held that a local school board had infringed the free speech rights of high school and junior high school students by suspending them from school for wearing black armbands in class as a protest against the Government's policy in Vietnam....

... In short, "First Amendment rights, applied in light of the special characteristics of the school environment, are available to ... students."

Of course, courts should not "intervene in the resolution of conflicts which arise in the daily operation of school systems" unless "basic constitutional values" are "directly and sharply implicate[d]" in those conflicts. But we think that the First Amendment rights of students may be directly and sharply implicated by the removal of books from the shelves of a school library. Our precedents have focused "not only on the role of the First Amendment in fostering individual self-expression but also on its role in affording the public access to discussion, debate, and the dissemination of information and ideas." And we have recognized that "the State may not, consistently with the spirit of the First Amendment, contract the spectrum of available knowledge." In keeping with this principle, we have held that in a variety of contexts "the Constitution protects the right to receive information and ideas." This right is an inherent corollary of the rights of free speech and press that are explicitly guaranteed by the Constitution, in two senses. First, the right to receive ideas follows ineluctably from the *sender's* First Amendment right to send them....

More importantly, the right to receive ideas is a necessary predicate to the *recipient's* meaningful exercise of his own rights of speech, press, and political freedom. Madison admonished us:

"A popular Government, without popular information, or the means of acquiring it, is but a Prologue to a Farce or a Tragedy; or, perhaps both. Knowledge will forever govern ignorance: And a people who mean to be their own Governors, must arm

themselves with the power which knowledge gives." 9 Writings
of James Madison 103 (G. Hunt ed. 1910).

As we recognized in *Tinker,* students too are beneficiaries of this
principle.... In sum, just as access to ideas makes it possible for citizens
generally to exercise their rights of free speech and press in a meaningful
manner, such access prepares students for active and effective participation in the pluralistic, often contentious society in which they will
soon be adult members. Of course all First Amendment rights accorded
to students must be construed "in light of the special characteristics of
the school environment." But the special characteristics of the school
library make that environment especially appropriate for the recognition
of the First Amendment rights of students.

   ... Petitioners emphasize the inculcative function of secondary
education, and argue that they must be allowed *unfettered* discretion to
"transmit community values" through the Island Trees schools. But that
sweeping claim overlooks the unique role of the school library. It appears
from the record that use of the Island Trees school libraries is completely
voluntary on the part of students. Their selection of books from these
libraries is entirely a matter of free choice; the libraries afford them an
opportunity at self-education and individual enrichment that is wholly
optional. Petitioners might well defend their claim of absolute discretion
in matters of *curriculum* by reliance upon their duty to inculcate
community values. But we think that petitioners' reliance upon that
duty is misplaced where, as here, they attempt to extend their claim of
absolute discretion beyond the compulsory environment of the classroom, into the school library and the regime of voluntary inquiry that
there holds sway.

(2)

   In rejecting petitioners' claim of absolute discretion to remove books
from their school libraries, we do not deny that local school boards have
a substantial legitimate role to play in the determination of school
library content. We thus must turn to the question of the extent to
which the First Amendment places limitations upon the discretion of
petitioners to remove books from their libraries....

   ... Petitioners rightly possess significant discretion to determine
the content of their school libraries. But that discretion may not be
exercised in a narrowly partisan or political manner. If a Democratic
school board, motivated by party affiliation, ordered the removal of all
books written by or in favor of Republicans, few would doubt that the
order violated the constitutional rights of the students denied access to
those books. The same conclusion would surely apply if an all-white
school board, motivated by racial animus, decided to remove all books
authored by blacks or advocating racial equality and integration. Our
Constitution does not permit the official suppression of *ideas.* Thus
whether petitioners' removal of books from their school libraries denied
respondents their First Amendment rights depends upon the motivation
behind petitioners' actions. If petitioners *intended* by their removal
decision to deny respondents access to ideas with which petitioners
disagreed, and if this intent was the decisive factor in petitioners'

decision, then petitioners have exercised their discretion in violation of the Constitution. To permit such intentions to control official actions would be to encourage the precise sort of officially prescribed orthodoxy unequivocally condemned in *Barnette.* On the other hand, respondents implicitly concede that an unconstitutional motivation would *not* be demonstrated if it were shown that petitioners had decided to remove the books at issue because those books were pervasively vulgar. And again, respondents concede that if it were demonstrated that the removal decision was based solely upon the "educational suitability" of the books in question, then their removal would be "perfectly permissible." In other words, in respondents' view such motivations, if decisive of petitioners' actions, would not carry the danger of an official suppression of ideas, and thus would not violate respondents' First Amendment rights.

As noted earlier, nothing in our decision today affects in any way the discretion of a local school board to choose books to *add* to the libraries of their schools. Because we are concerned in this case with the suppression of ideas, our holding today affects only the discretion to *remove* books. In brief, we hold that local school boards may not remove books from school library shelves simply because they dislike the ideas contained in those books and seek by their removal to "prescribe what shall be orthodox in politics, nationalism, religion, or other matters of opinion." Such purposes stand inescapably condemned by our precedents.

B

We now turn to the remaining question presented by this case: Do the evidentiary materials that were before the District Court, when construed most favorably to respondents, raise a genuine issue of material fact whether petitioners exceeded constitutional limitations in exercising their discretion to remove the books from the school libraries? We conclude that the materials do raise such a question, which forecloses summary judgment in favor of petitioners.

. . .

Affirmed.

JUSTICE BLACKMUN, concurring in part and concurring in the judgment.

While I agree with much in today's plurality opinion, and while I accept the standard laid down by the plurality to guide proceedings on remand, I write separately because I have a somewhat different perspective on the nature of the First Amendment right involved.

I

To my mind, this case presents a particularly complex problem because it involves two competing principles of constitutional stature. On the one hand, as the dissenting opinions demonstrate, and as we all can agree, the Court has acknowledged the importance of the public schools "in the preparation of individuals for participation as citizens, and in the preservation of the values on which our society rests."

Because of the essential socializing function of schools, local education officials may attempt "to promote civic virtues," and to "awake[n] the child to cultural values." Indeed, the Constitution presupposes the existence of an informed citizenry prepared to participate in governmental affairs, and these democratic principles obviously are constitutionally incorporated into the structure of our government. It therefore seems entirely appropriate that the State use "public schools [to] ... inculcat[e] fundamental values necessary to the maintenance of a democratic political system."

On the other hand, as the plurality demonstrates, it is beyond dispute that schools and school boards must operate within the confines of the First Amendment....

. . .

In combination with more generally applicable First Amendment rules, most particularly the central proscription of content-based regulations of speech, the cases yield a general principle: the State may not suppress exposure to ideas—for the sole *purpose* of suppressing exposure to those ideas—absent sufficiently compelling reasons.... Surely this is true in an extreme case: as the plurality notes, it is difficult to see how a school board, consistent with the First Amendment, could refuse for political reasons to buy books written by Democrats or by Negroes, or books that are "anti-American" in the broadest sense of that term. Indeed, Justice Rehnquist appears "cheerfully [to] concede" this point.

In my view, then, the principle involved here is both narrower and more basic than the "right to receive information" identified by the plurality.... And I do not believe, as the plurality suggests, that the right at issue here is somehow associated with the peculiar nature of the school library; if schools may be used to inculcate ideas, surely libraries may play a role in that process. Instead, I suggest that certain forms of state discrimination *between* ideas are improper. In particular, our precedents command the conclusion that the State may not act to deny access to an idea simply because state officials disapprove of that idea for partisan or political reasons.

. . .

II

. . .

As I view it, this is a narrow principle. School officials must be able to choose one book over another, without outside interference, when the first book is deemed more relevant to the curriculum, or better written, or when one of a host of other politically neutral reasons is present. These decisions obviously will not implicate First Amendment values. And even absent space or financial limitations, First Amendment principles would allow a school board to refuse to make a book available to students because it contains offensive language, or because it is psychologically or intellectually inappropriate for the age group, or even, perhaps, because the ideas it advances are "manifestly inimical to the public welfare." And, of course, school officials may choose one book over another because they believe that one subject is more important, or is more deserving of emphasis.

. . .

Concededly, a tension exists between the properly inculcative purposes of public education and any limitation on the school board's absolute discretion to choose academic materials. But that tension demonstrates only that the problem here is a difficult one, not that the problem should be resolved by choosing one principle over another. . . .

. . .

Because I believe that the plurality has derived a standard similar to the one compelled by my analysis, I join all but Part II–A(1) of the plurality opinion.

JUSTICE WHITE, concurring in the judgment.

. . .

The plurality seems compelled to ... issue a dissertation on the extent to which the First Amendment limits the discretion of the school board to remove books from the school library. I see no necessity for doing so at this point. When findings of fact and conclusions of law are made by the District Court, that may end the case. If, for example, the District Court concludes after a trial that the books were removed for their vulgarity, there may be no appeal. In any event, if there is an appeal, if there is dissatisfaction with the subsequent Court of Appeals' judgment, and if certiorari is sought and granted, there will be time enough to address the First Amendment issues that may then be presented.

. . .

... We should not decide constitutional questions until it is necessary to do so, or at least until there is better reason to address them than are evident here. I therefore concur in the judgment of affirmance.

CHIEF JUSTICE BURGER, with whom JUSTICE POWELL, JUSTICE REHNQUIST, and JUSTICE O'CONNOR join, dissenting.

The First Amendment, as with other parts of the Constitution, must deal with new problems in a changing world. In an attempt to deal with a problem in an area traditionally left to the states, a plurality of the Court, in a lavish expansion going beyond any prior holding under the First Amendment, expresses its view that a school board's decision concerning what books are to be in the school library is subject to federal court review. Were this to become the law, this Court would come perilously close to becoming a "super censor" of school board library decisions. Stripped to its essentials, the issue comes down to two important propositions: *first,* whether local schools are to be administered by elected school boards, or by federal judges and teenage pupils; and *second,* whether the values of morality, good taste, and relevance to education are valid reasons for school board decisions concerning the contents of a school library. . . .

. . .

Whatever role the government might play as a conduit of information, schools in particular ought not be made a slavish courier of the material of third parties. The plurality pays homage to the ancient verity that in the administration of the public schools " 'there is a legitimate and substantial community interest in promoting respect for authority and traditional values be they social, moral, or political.' " If, as we have held, schools may legitimately be used as vehicles for "inculcating fundamental values necessary to the maintenance of a democratic political system," school authorities must have broad discretion to fulfill that obligation. Presumably all activity within a primary or secondary school involves the conveyance of information and at least an implied approval of the worth of that information. How are "fundamental values" to be inculcated except by having school boards make content-based decisions about the appropriateness of retaining materials in the school library and curriculum. In order to fulfill its function, an elected school board *must* express its views on the subjects which are taught. . . .

. . .

. . . Today the plurality suggests that the *Constitution* distinguishes between school libraries and school classrooms, between *removing* unwanted books and *acquiring* books. Even more extreme, the plurality concludes that the Constitution *requires* school boards to justify to its teenage pupils the decision to remove a particular book from a school library. I categorically reject this notion that the Constitution dictates that judges, rather than parents, teachers, and local school boards, must determine how the standards of morality and vulgarity are to be treated in the classroom.

JUSTICE POWELL, dissenting.

The plurality opinion today rejects a basic concept of public school education in our country: that the States and locally elected school boards should have the responsibility for determining the educational policy of the public schools. After today's decision any junior high school student, by instituting a suit against a school board or teacher, may invite a judge to overrule an educational decision by the official body designated by the people to operate the schools.

. . .

JUSTICE REHNQUIST, with whom THE CHIEF JUSTICE and JUSTICE POWELL join, dissenting.

. . .

In the course of his discussion, Justice Brennan states:

"Petitioners rightly possess significant discretion to determine the content of their school libraries. But that discretion may not be exercised in a narrowly partisan or political manner. If a Democratic school board, motivated by party affiliation, ordered the removal of all books written by or in favor of Republicans, few would doubt that the order violated the constitutional rights of the students.... The same conclusion would surely apply if an all-white school board, motivated by racial animus, decided to remove all books authored by blacks or advocating racial equality and integration. Our Constitution does not permit the official suppression of *ideas.*"

I can cheerfully concede all of this, but as in so many other cases the extreme examples are seldom the ones that arise in the real world of constitutional litigation.... I would save for another day—feeling quite confident that that day will not arrive—the extreme examples posed in Justice Brennan's opinion.

Considerable light is shed on the correct resolution of the constitutional question in this case by examining the role played by petitioners. Had petitioners been the members of a town council, I suppose all would agree that, absent a good deal more than is present in this record, they could not have prohibited the sale of these books by private booksellers within the municipality. But we have also recognized that the government may act in other capacities than as sovereign, and when it does the First Amendment may speak with a different voice....

... When it acts as an educator, at least at the elementary and secondary school level, the government is engaged in inculcating social values and knowledge in relatively impressionable young people. Obviously there are innumerable decisions to be made as to what courses should be taught, what books should be purchased, or what teachers should be employed.... In the very course of administering the many-faceted operations of a school district, the mere decision to purchase some books will necessarily preclude the possibility of purchasing others. The decision to teach a particular subject may preclude the possibility of teaching another subject. A decision to replace a teacher because of ineffectiveness may by implication be seen as a disparagement of the subject matter taught. In each of these instances, however, the book or the exposure to the subject matter may be acquired elsewhere. The managers of the school district are not proscribing it as to the citizenry in general, but are simply determining that it will not be included in the curriculum or school library. In short, actions by the government as educator do not raise the same First Amendment concerns as actions by the government as sovereign.

. . .

Education consists of the selective presentation and explanation of ideas. The effective acquisition of knowledge depends upon an orderly exposure to relevant information. Nowhere is this more true than in elementary and secondary schools, where, unlike the broad-ranging inquiry available to university students, the courses taught are those thought most relevant to the young students' individual development. Of necessity, elementary and secondary educators must separate the relevant from the irrelevant, the appropriate from the inappropriate. Determining what information *not* to present to the students is often as important as identifying relevant material. This winnowing process necessarily leaves much information to be discovered by students at another time or in another place, and is fundamentally inconsistent with any constitutionally required eclecticism in public education.

. . .

... [E]lementary and secondary schools are inculcative in nature. The libraries of such schools serve as supplements to this inculcative role. Unlike university or public libraries, elementary and secondary school libraries are not designed for freewheeling inquiry; they are tailored, as the public school curriculum is tailored, to the teaching of basic skills and ideas. Thus, Justice Brennan cannot rely upon the nature of school libraries to escape the fact that the First Amendment right to receive information simply has no application to the one public institution which, by its very nature, is a place for the selective conveyance of ideas.

After all else is said, however, the most obvious reason that petitioners' removal of the books did not violate respondents' right to receive information is the ready availability of the books elsewhere....

Justice Brennan's own discomfort with the idea that students have a right to receive information from their elementary or secondary schools is demonstrated by the artificial limitations which he places upon the right—limitations which are supported neither by logic nor authority and which are inconsistent with the right itself. The attempt to confine the right to the library is one such limitation, the fallacies of which have already been demonstrated.

As a second limitation, Justice Brennan distinguishes the act of removing a previously acquired book from the act of refusing to acquire the book in the first place.... If Justice Brennan truly has found a "right to receive ideas," however, this distinction between acquisition and removal makes little sense. The failure of a library to acquire a book denies access to its contents just as effectively as does the removal of the book from the library's shelf. As a result of either action the book cannot be found in the "principal locus" of freedom discovered by Justice Brennan.

The justification for this limiting distinction is said by Justice Brennan to be his concern in this case with "the suppression of ideas." Whatever may be the analytical usefulness of this appealing sounding phrase, the suppression of ideas surely is not the identical twin of the denial of access to information. Not every official act which denies access to an idea can be characterized as a suppression of the idea. Thus unless the "right to receive information" and the prohibition against "suppression of ideas" are each a kind of Mother–Hubbard catch phrase for whatever First Amendment doctrines one wishes to cover, they would not appear to be interchangeable.

Justice Brennan's reliance on the "suppression of ideas" to justify his distinction between acquisition and removal of books has additional logical pitfalls. Presumably the distinction is based upon the greater visibility and the greater sense of conscious decision thought to be involved in the removal of a book, as opposed to that involved in the refusal to acquire a book. But if "suppression of ideas" is to be the talisman, one would think that a school board's public announcement of its refusal to acquire certain books would have every bit as much impact on public attention as would an equally publicized decision to remove the books. And yet only the latter action would violate the First Amendment under Justice Brennan's analysis.

The final limitation placed by Justice Brennan upon his newly discovered right is a motive requirement. . . .

It is difficult to tell from Justice Brennan's opinion just what motives he would consider constitutionally impermissible. I had thought that the First Amendment proscribes content-based restrictions on the marketplace of ideas. Justice Brennan concludes, however, that a removal decision based solely upon the "educational suitability" of a book or upon its perceived vulgarity is " 'perfectly permissible.' " But such determinations are based as much on the content of the book as determinations that the book espouses pernicious political views.

Moreover, Justice Brennan's motive test is difficult to square with his distinction between acquisition and removal. If a school board's removal of books might be motivated by a desire to promote favored political or religious views, there is no reason that its acquisition policy might not also be so motivated. And yet the "pall of orthodoxy" cast by a carefully executed book-acquisition program apparently would not violate the First Amendment under Justice Brennan's view.

. . .

The inconsistencies and illogic of the limitations placed by Justice Brennan upon his notion of the right to receive ideas in school are not here emphasized in order to suggest that they should be eliminated. They are emphasized because they illustrate that the right itself is misplaced in the elementary and secondary school setting. Likewise, the criticism of Justice Brennan's newly found prohibition against the "suppression of ideas" is by no means intended to suggest that the Constitution permits the suppression of ideas; it is rather to suggest that such a vague and imprecise phrase, while perhaps wholly consistent with the First Amendment, is simply too diaphanous to assist careful decision of cases such as this one.

I think the Court will far better serve the cause of First Amendment jurisprudence by candidly recognizing that the role of government as sovereign is subject to more stringent limitations than is the role of government as employer, property owner, or educator. It must also be recognized that the government as educator is subject to fewer strictures when operating an elementary and secondary school system than when operating an institution of higher learning. With respect to the education of children in elementary and secondary schools, the school board may properly determine in many cases that a particular book, a particular course, or even a particular area of knowledge is not educationally suitable for inclusion within the body of knowledge which the school seeks to impart. Without more, this is not a condemnation of the book or the course. . . .

. . .

JUSTICE O'CONNOR, dissenting.

. . .

I do not personally agree with the board's action with respect to some of the books in question here, but is not the function of the courts to make the decisions that have been properly relegated to the elected members of school boards. It is the school board that must determine educational suitability, and it has done so in this case. I therefore join The Chief Justice's dissent.

NOTES AND QUESTIONS

1. Notice that, on the merits, there is a flat 4–4 tie, since Justice White refuses to say how the First Amendment issues should be resolved at the trial. Thus the *Pico* decision does not resolve the issues discussed at length in Justice Brennan's plurality opinion. (There was never a trial in the *Pico* case, since the case was settled after the Court's decision.)

2. Once Justice Brennan concedes the right of a school board to "promote respect for authority and traditional values be they social, moral or political," how is it possible to challenge the Board's decision to remove the books? Does it make sense to distinguish a school board's decisions as to the content of classroom textbooks and its decisions as to library books? Does Justice Brennan's emphasis on students' First Amendment rights to receive information justify his further distinctions: between a decision not to place a book on the shelves and a decision to remove it? between decisions to remove books that are "vulgar" or "educationally unsuitable," and decisions to remove books to deny students access to their ideas?

3. Would the dissenters' position permit school boards to tailor the public school library and curriculum to an express goal of inculcating the principles of the Democratic or Republican parties? We will return to the difficult question of the application of the First Amendment to the public schools in connection with the discussion of Epperson v. Arkansas, which appears in Chapter 19, at page 718.

TINKER v. DES MOINES INDEPENDENT COMMUNITY SCHOOL DIST.

Supreme Court of the United States, 1969.
393 U.S. 503, 89 S.Ct. 733, 21 L.Ed.2d 731.

[The report in this case appears at page 281]

BETHEL SCHOOL DISTRICT NO. 403 v. FRASER

Supreme Court of the United States, 1986.
478 U.S. 675, 106 S.Ct. 3159, 92 L.Ed.2d 549.

CHIEF JUSTICE BURGER delivered the opinion of the Court.

We granted certiorari to decide whether the First Amendment prevents a school district from disciplining a high school student for giving a lewd speech at a school assembly.

I

A

On April 26, 1983, respondent Matthew N. Fraser, a student at Bethel High School in Pierce County, Washington, delivered a speech nominating a fellow student for student elective office. Approximately 600 high school students, many of whom were 14–year–olds, attended the assembly....

[Fraser said:

"I know a man who is firm—he's firm in his pants, he's firm in his shirt, his character is firm—but most ... of all, his belief in you, the students of Bethel, is firm.

"Jeff Kuhlman is a man who takes his point and pounds it in. If necessary, he'll take an issue and nail it to the wall. He doesn't attack things in spurts—he drives hard, pushing and pushing until finally—he succeeds.

"Jeff is a man who will go to the very end—even the climax, for each and every one of you.

"So vote for Jeff for A.S.B. vice-president—he'll never come between you and the best our high school can be."]

. . .

During Fraser's delivery of the speech, a school counselor observed the reaction of students to the speech. Some students hooted and yelled; some by gestures graphically simulated the sexual activities pointedly alluded to in respondent's speech. Other students appeared to be bewildered and embarrassed by the speech. One teacher reported that on the day following the speech, she found it necessary to forgo a portion of the scheduled class lesson in order to discuss the speech with the class.

A Bethel High School disciplinary rule prohibiting the use of obscene language in the school provides:

"Conduct which materially and substantially interferes with the educational process is prohibited, including the use of obscene, profane language or gestures."

The morning after the assembly, the Assistant Principal called Fraser into her office and notified him that the school considered his speech to have been a violation of this rule.... Fraser was ... suspended for three days, and ... his name was removed from the list of candidates for graduation speaker at the school's commencement exercises.

. . . Fraser served two days of his suspension, and was allowed to return to school on the third day.

B

Respondent, by his father as guardian ad litem, then brought this action in [a federal court, alleging] a violation of his First Amendment right to freedom of speech. . . .

II

This Court acknowledged in Tinker v. Des Moines Independent Community School Dist. that students do not "shed their constitutional rights to freedom of speech or expression at the schoolhouse gate." . . . [T]he use of lewd and obscene speech in order to make what the speaker considered to be a point in a nominating speech for a fellow student [is not] the same as the wearing of an armband in *Tinker* as a form of protest or the expression of a political position.

The[re is a] marked distinction between the political "message" of the armbands in *Tinker* and the sexual content of respondent's speech in this case. . . . In upholding the students' right to engage in a nondisruptive, passive expression of a political viewpoint in *Tinker*, this Court was careful to note that the case did "not concern speech or action that intrudes upon the work of the schools or the rights of other students."
. . .

. . .

III

The role and purpose of the American public school system were well described by two historians, who stated: "[p]ublic education must prepare pupils for citizenship in the Republic. . . . It must inculcate the habits and manners of civility as values in themselves conducive to happiness and as indispensable to the practice of self-government in the community and the nation." C. Beard & M. Beard, New Basic History of the United States 228 (1968). . . .

These fundamental values of "habits and manners of civility" essential to a democratic society must, of course, include tolerance of divergent political and religious views, even when the views expressed may be unpopular. But these "fundamental values" must also take into account consideration of the sensibilities of others, and, in the case of a school, the sensibilities of fellow students. The undoubted freedom to advocate unpopular and controversial views in schools and classrooms must be balanced against the society's countervailing interest in teaching students the boundaries of socially appropriate behavior. Even the most heated political discourse in a democratic society requires consideration for the personal sensibilities of the other participants and audiences.

In our Nation's legislative halls, where some of the most vigorous political debates in our society are carried on, there are rules prohibiting the use of expressions offensive to other participants in the debate. . . .

Can it be that what is proscribed in the halls of Congress is beyond the reach of school officials to regulate?

The First Amendment guarantees wide freedom in matters of adult public discourse. A sharply divided Court upheld the right to express an antidraft viewpoint in a public place, albeit in terms highly offensive to most citizens. See Cohen v. California, 403 U.S. 15 (1971). It does not follow, however, that simply because the use of an offensive form of expression may not be prohibited to adults making what the speaker considers a political point, the same latitude must be permitted to children in a public school. . . .

Surely it is a highly appropriate function of public school education to prohibit the use of vulgar and offensive terms in public discourse. Indeed, the "fundamental values necessary to the maintenance of a democratic political system" disfavor the use of terms of debate highly offensive or highly threatening to others. Nothing in the Constitution prohibits the states from insisting that certain modes of expression are inappropriate and subject to sanctions. The inculcation of these values is truly the "work of the schools." *Tinker*, 393 U.S., at 508. The determination of what manner of speech in the classroom or in school assembly is inappropriate properly rests with the school board.

The process of educating our youth for citizenship in public schools is not confined to books, the curriculum, and the civics class; schools must teach by example the shared values of a civilized social order. Consciously or otherwise, teachers—and indeed the older students— demonstrate the appropriate form of civil discourse and political expression by their conduct and deportment in and out of class. Inescapably, like parents, they are role models. The schools, as instruments of the state, may determine that the essential lessons of civil, mature conduct cannot be conveyed in a school that tolerates lewd, indecent, or offensive speech and conduct such as that indulged in by this confused boy.

The pervasive sexual innuendo in Fraser's speech was plainly offensive to both teachers and students—indeed to any mature person. By glorifying male sexuality, and in its verbal content, the speech was acutely insulting to teenage girl students. The speech could well be seriously damaging to its less mature audience, many of whom were only 14 years old and on the threshold of awareness of human sexuality. Some students were reported as bewildered by the speech and the reaction of mimicry it provoked.

. . . [I]n addressing the question whether the First Amendment places any limit on the authority of public schools to remove books from a public school library, all Members of the Court, otherwise sharply divided, acknowledged that the school board has the authority to remove books that are vulgar. Board of Education v. Pico, 457 U.S. 853. . . .

We have also recognized an interest in protecting minors from exposure to vulgar and offensive spoken language. In FCC v. Pacifica Foundation, 438 U.S. 726 (1978), we dealt with the power of the Federal Communications Commission to regulate a radio broadcast described as "indecent but not obscene." . . .

We hold that petitioner School District acted entirely within its permissible authority in imposing sanctions upon Fraser in response to his offensively lewd and indecent speech. Unlike the sanctions imposed on the students wearing armbands in *Tinker,* the penalties imposed in this case were unrelated to any political viewpoint. The First Amendment does not prevent the school officials from determining that to permit a vulgar and lewd speech such as respondent's would undermine the school's basic educational mission. A high school assembly or classroom is no place for a sexually explicit monologue directed towards an unsuspecting audience of teenage students. Accordingly, it was perfectly appropriate for the school to disassociate itself to make the point to the pupils that vulgar speech and lewd conduct is wholly inconsistent with the "fundamental values" of public school education....

IV

Respondent contends that the circumstances of his suspension violated due process because he had no way of knowing that the delivery of the speech in question would subject him to disciplinary sanctions. This argument is wholly without merit.... Given the school's need to be able to impose disciplinary sanctions for a wide range of unanticipated conduct disruptive of the educational process, the school disciplinary rules need not be as detailed as a criminal code which imposes criminal sanctions....

· · ·

JUSTICE BLACKMUN concurs in the result.

JUSTICE BRENNAN concurring in the judgment.

· · ·

The Court, referring to [Fraser's] remarks as "obscene," "vulgar," "lewd," and "offensively lewd," concludes that school officials properly punished respondent for uttering the speech. Having read the full text of respondent's remarks, I find it difficult to believe that it is the same speech the Court describes. To my mind, the most that can be said about respondent's speech—and all that need be said—is that in light of the discretion school officials have to teach high school students how to conduct civil and effective public discourse, and to prevent disruption of school educational activities, it was not unconstitutional for school officials to conclude, under the circumstances of this case, that respondent's remarks exceeded permissible limits. Thus, while I concur in the Court's judgment, I write separately to express my understanding of the breadth of the Court's holding.

The Court today reaffirms the unimpeachable proposition that students do not "shed their constitutional rights to freedom of speech or expression at the schoolhouse gate." If respondent had given the same speech outside of the school environment, he could not have been penalized simply because government officials considered his language to be inappropriate, see Cohen v. California, 403 U.S. 15 (1971).... Moreover, despite the Court's characterizations, the language respondent used is far removed from the very narrow class of "obscene" speech which the Court has held is not protected by the First Amendment.... It is true, however, that the State has interests in teaching high school students how to conduct civil and effective public discourse and in avoiding disruption of educational school activities. Thus, the Court holds that under certain circumstances, high school students may properly be reprimanded for giving a speech at a high school assembly which school officials conclude disrupted the school's educational mission. Respondent's speech may well have been protected had he given it in school but under different circumstances, where the school's legitimate interests in teaching and maintaining civil public discourse were less weighty.

In the present case, school officials sought only to ensure that a high school assembly proceed in an orderly manner. There is no suggestion that school officials attempted to regulate respondent's speech because they disagreed with the views he sought to express. Cf. *Tinker,* supra. Nor does this case involve an attempt by school officials to ban written materials they consider "inappropriate" for high school students, ... or to limit what students should hear, read, or learn about. Thus, the Court's holding concerns only the authority that school officials have to restrict a high school student's use of disruptive language in a speech given to a high school assembly.

The authority school officials have to regulate such speech by high school students is not limitless. Under the circumstances of this case, however, I believe that school officials did not violate the First Amendment in determining that respondent should be disciplined for the disruptive language he used while addressing a high school assembly. Thus, I concur in the judgment reversing the decision of the Court of Appeals.

JUSTICE MARSHALL, dissenting.

I agree with the principles that Justice Brennan sets out in his opinion concurring in the judgment. I dissent from the Court's decision, however, because in my view the School District failed to demonstrate that respondent's remarks were indeed disruptive....

JUSTICE STEVENS, dissenting.

"Frankly, my dear, I don't give a damn."

When I was a high school student, the use of those words in a public forum shocked the Nation. Today Clark Gable's four-letter expletive is less offensive than it was then. Nevertheless, I assume that high school administrators may prohibit the use of that word in classroom discussion and even in extracurricular activities that are sponsored by the school and held on school premises. For I believe a school faculty must regulate the content as well as the style of student speech in carrying out its educational mission. It does seem to me, however, that if a student is to be punished for using offensive speech, he is entitled to fair notice of the scope of the prohibition and the consequences of its violation....

* * *

The fact that the speech may not have been offensive to his audience—or that he honestly believed that it would be inoffensive—does not mean that he had a constitutional right to deliver it. For the school—not the student—must prescribe the rules of conduct in an educational institution. But it does mean that he should not be disciplined for speaking frankly in a school assembly if he had no reason to anticipate punitive consequences.

. . .

It seems fairly obvious that respondent's speech would be inappropriate in certain classroom and formal social settings. On the other hand, in a locker room or perhaps in a school corridor the metaphor in the speech might be regarded as a rather routine comment. If this be true, and if respondent's audience consisted almost entirely of young people with whom he conversed on a daily basis, can we—at this distance— confidently assert that he must have known that the school administration would punish him for delivering it?

QUESTIONS

1. What is the difference between *Tinker* and *Fraser*? Is it the difference in the content of their messages, or the place and circumstances in which they were delivered? Is it both?

2. When the Court in *Tinker* announced that students do not "shed their constitutional rights to freedom of speech or expression at the schoolhouse gate," was it assuming that school authorities had no more authority to control student speech than did any other government authority? Suppose Fraser had given the same speech he gave to exactly the same audience, but not in a public school setting. Does the Court's opinion in *Fraser* suggest that he could have been punished for that? Could he have been suspended if he had said exactly the same things to a large group of students on the school grounds during lunch hour?

HAZELWOOD SCHOOL DISTRICT v. KUHLMEIER

Supreme Court of the United States, 1988.
484 U.S. 260, 108 S.Ct. 562, 98 L.Ed.2d 592.

JUSTICE WHITE delivered the opinion of the Court.

This case concerns the extent to which educators may exercise editorial control over the contents of a high school newspaper produced as part of the school's journalism curriculum.

I

. . . [F]ormer Hazelwood East [High School] students who were staff members of Spectrum, the school newspaper . . . contend that school officials violated their First Amendment rights by deleting two pages of articles from the May 13, 1983, issue of Spectrum.

Spectrum was written and edited by the Journalism II class at Hazelwood East. . . .

. . .

The practice at Hazelwood East during the spring 1983 semester was for the journalism teacher to submit page proofs of each Spectrum issue to Principal Reynolds for his review prior to publication. Emerson [the journalism teacher] delivered the proofs of the May 13 edition to Reynolds, who objected to two of the articles scheduled to appear in that edition. One of the stories described three Hazelwood East students' experiences with pregnancy; the other discussed the impact of divorce on students at the school.

Reynolds was concerned that, although the pregnancy story used false names "to keep the identity of these girls a secret," the pregnant students still might be identifiable from the text. He also believed that the article's references to sexual activity and birth control were inappropriate for some of the younger students at the school. In addition, Reynolds was concerned [with] a student identified by name in the divorce story. . . .

Reynolds believed that there was no time to make the necessary changes in the stories before the scheduled press run and that the newspaper would not appear before the end of the school year if printing were delayed to any significant extent. He concluded that his only options under the circumstances were to publish a four-page newspaper instead of the planned six-page newspaper, eliminating the two pages on which the offending stories appeared, or to publish no newspaper at all. . . .

. . .

II

Students in the public schools do not "shed their constitutional rights to freedom of speech or expression at the schoolhouse gate." *Tinker* . . .

We have nonetheless recognized that the First Amendment rights of students in the public schools "are not automatically coextensive with the rights of adults in other settings," Bethel School District No. 403 v. Fraser. . . .

A

We deal first with the question whether Spectrum may appropriately be characterized as a forum for public expression. . . . [S]chool facilities may be deemed to be public forums only if school authorities have "by policy or by practice" opened those facilities "for indiscriminate use by the general public," or by some segment of the public, such as student organizations. If the facilities have instead been reserved for other intended purposes, "communicative or otherwise," then no public forum has been created. . . .

The policy of school officials toward Spectrum was reflected in Hazelwood School Board Policy . . . that "[s]chool sponsored publications are developed within the adopted curriculum and its educational implications in regular classroom activities." The Hazelwood East Curriculum Guide described the Journalism II course as a "laboratory situation in which the students publish the school newspaper applying skills they have learned in Journalism I." ... Students received grades and academic credit for their performance in the course.

School officials did not deviate in practice from their policy that production of Spectrum was to be part of the educational curriculum and a "regular classroom activit[y]." ...

... Accordingly, school officials were entitled to regulate the contents of Spectrum in any reasonable manner.... It is this standard, rather than our decision in *Tinker,* that governs this case.

B

The question whether the First Amendment requires a school to tolerate particular student speech—the question that we addressed in *Tinker*—is different from the question whether the First Amendment requires a school affirmatively to promote particular student speech. The former question addresses educators' ability to silence a student's personal expression that happens to occur on the school premises. The latter question concerns educators' authority over school-sponsored publications, theatrical productions, and other expressive activities that students, parents, and members of the public might reasonably perceive to bear the imprimatur of the school. These activities may fairly be characterized as part of the school curriculum, whether or not they occur in a traditional classroom setting, so long as they are supervised by faculty members and designed to impart particular knowledge or skills to student participants and audiences.

Educators are entitled to exercise greater control over this second form of student expression to assure that participants learn whatever lessons the activity is designed to teach, that readers or listeners are not exposed to material that may be inappropriate for their level of maturity, and that the views of the individual speaker are not erroneously attributed to the school. Hence, a school may in its capacity as publisher of a school newspaper or producer of a school play "disassociate itself," ... from speech that is, for example, ungrammatical, poorly written, inadequately researched, biased or prejudiced, vulgar or profane, or unsuitable for immature audiences. A school must be able to set high standards for the student speech that is disseminated under its auspices—standards that may be higher than those demanded by some newspaper publishers or theatrical producers in the "real" world—and may refuse to disseminate student speech that does not meet those standards. In addition, a school must be able to take into account the emotional maturity of the intended audience in determining whether to disseminate student speech on potentially sensitive topics, which might range from the existence of Santa Claus in an elementary school setting to the particulars of teenage sexual activity in a high school setting. A school must also retain the authority to refuse to sponsor student speech that might reasonably be perceived to advocate drug or alcohol use, irresponsible sex, or conduct otherwise inconsistent with "the shared values of a civilized social order," *Fraser,* or to associate the school with any position other than neutrality on matters of political controversy....

Accordingly, we conclude that the standard articulated in *Tinker* for determining when a school may punish student expression need not also be the standard for determining when a school may refuse to lend its name and resources to the dissemination of student expression. Instead, we hold that educators do not offend the First Amendment by exercising editorial control over the style and content of student speech in school-sponsored expressive activities so long as their actions are reasonably related to legitimate pedagogical concerns.

. . .

III

We also conclude that Principal Reynolds acted reasonably in requiring the deletion from the May 13 issue of Spectrum of the pregnancy article, the divorce article, and the remaining articles that were to appear on the same pages of the newspaper.

. . .

In sum, we cannot reject as unreasonable Principal Reynolds' conclusion that neither the pregnancy article nor the divorce article was suitable for publication in Spectrum.... Accordingly, no violation of First Amendment rights occurred.

. . .

JUSTICE BRENNAN, with whom JUSTICE MARSHALL and JUSTICE BLACKMUN join, dissenting.

. . .

In my view the principal ... violated the First Amendment's prohibitions against censorship of any student expression that neither disrupts classwork nor invades the rights of others, and against any censorship that is not narrowly tailored to serve its purpose.

I

. . .

Free student expression undoubtedly sometimes interferes with the effectiveness of the school's pedagogical functions. Some brands of student expression do so by directly preventing the school from pursuing its pedagogical mission: The young polemic who stands on a soapbox during calculus class to deliver an eloquent political diatribe interferes with the legitimate teaching of calculus.... Likewise, the student newspaper that, like Spectrum, conveys a moral position at odds with the school's official stance might subvert the administration's legitimate inculcation of its own perception of community values.

. . .

[The Court has never] intimated a distinction between personal and school-sponsored speech in any other context. Particularly telling is this Court's heavy reliance on *Tinker* in two cases of First Amendment infringement on state college campuses. See Papish v. University of

Missouri Board of Curators, 410 U.S. 667, 671, n. 6 (1973) (per curiam); Healy v. James, 408 U.S. 169, 180, 189, and n. 18, 191 (1972). One involved the expulsion of a student for lewd expression in a newspaper that she sold on campus pursuant to university authorization, see *Papish,* supra, at 667–668, and the other involved the denial of university recognition and concomitant benefits to a political student organization, see *Healy,* supra, at 174, 176, 181–182. Tracking *Tinker*'s analysis, the Court found each act of suppression unconstitutional. In neither case did this Court suggest the distinction, which the Court today finds dispositive, between school-sponsored and incidental student expression.

II

Even if we were writing on a clean slate, I would reject the Court's rationale for abandoning *Tinker* in this case. . . .

. . .

. . . The educator may, under *Tinker,* constitutionally "censor" poor grammar, writing, or research because to reward such expression would "materially disrup[t]" the newspaper's curricular purpose.

The same cannot be said of official censorship designed to shield the *audience* or dissociate the *sponsor* from the expression. Censorship so motivated might well serve some other school purpose. But it in no way furthers the curricular purposes of a student *newspaper* . . . unless one believes that the purpose of the school newspaper is to teach students that the press ought never report bad news, express unpopular views, or print a thought that might upset its sponsors. Unsurprisingly, Hazelwood East claims no such pedagogical purpose.

NOTES AND QUESTIONS

1. If city officials ordered the editors of a local newspaper not to print articles on teenage pregnancy and divorce, there is no doubt that this would violate the First Amendment. Is that this case? Suppose the editors of a local newspaper planned to print articles on teenage pregnancy and divorce, but the articles were deleted by the owner of the newspaper. Is that this case? Does it make a difference whether the "owner" of a newspaper is a private person or some level of government?

2. Is it important that the Hazelwood East High School newspaper was published as a project of a journalism class? Would the result have been any different if the high school newspaper were an extracurricular activity? Would the result have been different if the principal had banned circulation of any "underground newspaper" on the high school grounds? Does the rationale of this case apply to censorship of a student newspaper at a public university?

BOARD OF REGENTS OF THE UNIVERSITY OF WISCONSIN SYSTEM v. SOUTHWORTH

Supreme Court of the United States, 2000.
529 U.S. 217, 120 S.Ct. 1346, 146 L.Ed.2d 193.

JUSTICE KENNEDY delivered the opinion of the Court.

For the second time in recent years, we consider constitutional questions arising from a program designed to facilitate extracurricular student speech at a public university. Respondents are a group of students at the University of Wisconsin. They brought a First Amendment challenge to a mandatory student activity fee imposed by petitioner Board of Regents of the University of Wisconsin and used in part by the University to support student organizations engaging in political or ideological speech. Respondents object to the speech and expression of some of the student organizations. Relying upon our precedents which protect members of unions and bar associations from being required to pay fees used for speech the members find objectionable, both the District Court and the Court of Appeals invalidated the University's student fee program. The University contends that its mandatory student activity fee and the speech which it supports are appropriate to further its educational mission.

We reverse. The First Amendment permits a public university to charge its students an activity fee used to fund a program to facilitate extracurricular student speech if the program is viewpoint neutral. We do not sustain, however, the student referendum mechanism of the University's program, which appears to permit the exaction of fees in violation of the viewpoint neutrality principle. As to that aspect of the program, we remand for further proceedings.

I

. . .

The responsibility for governing the University of Wisconsin System is vested by law with the board of regents.... The same law empowers the students to share in aspects of the University's governance. One of those functions is to administer the student activities fee program.... The program the University maintains to support the extracurricular activities undertaken by many of its student organizations is the subject of the present controversy.

It seems that, since its founding, the University has required full-time students enrolled at its Madison campus to pay a nonrefundable activity fee.... For the 1995–1996 academic year, when this suit was commenced, the activity fee amounted to $331.50 per year. The fee is segregated from the University's tuition charge.... The fees are drawn upon by the University to support various campus services and extracurricular student activities....

The board of regents classifies the segregated fee into allocable and nonallocable portions....

The allocable portion of the fee supports extracurricular endeavors pursued by the University's registered student organizations or RSO's. To qualify for RSO status, students must organize as a not-for-profit group, limit membership primarily to students, and agree to undertake activities related to student life on campus.... During the 1995–1996 school year, 623 groups had RSO status on the Madison campus.... To name but a few, RSO's included the Future Financial Gurus of America; the International Socialist Organization; the College Democrats; the College Republicans; and the American Civil Liberties Union Campus Chapter. As one would expect, the expressive activities undertaken by RSO's are diverse in range and content, from displaying posters and circulating newsletters throughout the campus to hosting campus debates and guest speakers and to what can best be described as political lobbying.

RSO's may obtain a portion of the allocable fees in one of three ways. Most do so by seeking funding from the Student Government Activity Fund (SGAF), administered by the ASM. SGAF moneys may be issued to support an RSO's operations and events, as well as travel expenses "central to the purpose of the organization." ... As an alternative, an RSO can apply for funding from the General Student Services Fund (GSSF), administered through the ASM's finance committee. During the 1995–1996 academic year, 15 RSO's received GSSF funding. These RSO's included a campus tutoring center, the student radio station, a student environmental group, a gay and bisexual student center, a community legal office, an AIDS support network, a campus women's center, and the Wisconsin Student Public Interest Research Group (WISPIRG).... The University acknowledges that, in addition to providing campus services (e.g., tutoring and counseling), the GSSF-funded RSO's engage in political and ideological expression....

The GSSF as well as the SGAF consist of moneys originating in the allocable portion of the mandatory fee. The parties have stipulated that, with respect to SGAF and GSSF funding, "[t]he process for reviewing and approving allocations for funding is administered in a viewpoint-neutral fashion," ... and that the University does not use the fee program for "advocating a particular point of view,"....

A student referendum provides a third means for an RSO to obtain funding.... While the record is sparse on this feature of the University's program, the parties inform us that the student body can vote either to approve or to disapprove an assessment for a particular RSO. One referendum resulted in an allocation of $45,000 to WISPIRG during the 1995–1996 academic year. At oral argument, counsel for the University acknowledged that a referendum could also operate to defund an RSO or to veto a funding decision of the ASM. In October, 1996, for example, the student body voted to terminate funding to a national student organization to which the University belonged.... Both parties confirmed at oral argument that their stipulation regarding the program's viewpoint neutrality does not extend to the referendum process....

II

It is inevitable that government will adopt and pursue programs and policies within its constitutional powers but which nevertheless are contrary to the profound beliefs and sincere convictions of some of its citizens. The government, as a general rule, may support valid programs and policies by taxes or other exactions binding on protesting parties. Within this broader principle it seems inevitable that funds raised by the government will be spent for speech and other expression to advocate and defend its own policies.... The case we decide here, however, does not raise the issue of the government's right, or, to be more specific, the state-controlled University's right, to use its own funds to advance a particular message. The University's whole justification for fostering the challenged expression is that it springs from the initiative of the students, who alone give it purpose and content in the course of their extracurricular endeavors.

... If the challenged speech here were financed by tuition dollars and the University and its officials were responsible for its content, the case might be evaluated on the premise that the government itself is the speaker. That is not the case before us.

The University of Wisconsin exacts the fee at issue for the sole purpose of facilitating the free and open exchange of ideas by, and among, its students. We conclude the objecting students may insist upon certain safeguards with respect to the expressive activities which they are required to support. Our public forum cases are instructive here by close analogy. This is true even though the student activities fund is not a public forum in the traditional sense of the term, and despite the circumstance that those cases most often involve a demand for access, not a claim to be exempt from supporting speech.... The standard of viewpoint neutrality found in the public forum cases provides the standard we find controlling. We decide that the viewpoint neutrality requirement of the University program is in general sufficient to protect the rights of the objecting students. The student referendum aspect of the program for funding speech and expressive activities, however, appears to be inconsistent with the viewpoint neutrality requirement.

We must begin by recognizing that the complaining students are being required to pay fees which are subsidies for speech they find objectionable, even offensive. The *Abood* and *Keller* cases, then, provide the beginning point for our analysis. Abood v. Detroit Bd. of Ed., 431 U.S. 209 (1977); Keller v. State Bar of Cal., 496 U.S. 1 (1990). While those precedents identify the interests of the protesting students, the means of implementing First Amendment protections adopted in those decisions are neither applicable nor workable in the context of extracurricular student speech at a university.

In *Abood*, some nonunion public school teachers challenged an agreement requiring them, as a condition of their employment, to pay a service fee equal in amount to union dues.... The objecting teachers alleged that the union's use of their fees to engage in political speech violated their freedom of association guaranteed by the First and Fourteenth Amendments.... The Court agreed, and held that any objecting teacher could "prevent the Union's spending a part of their required service fees to contribute to political candidates and to express political views unrelated to its duties as exclusive bargaining representative".... The principles outlined in *Abood* provided the foundation for our later decision in *Keller*. There, we held that lawyers admitted to practice in California could be required to join a state bar association and to fund activities "germane" to the association's mission of "regulating the legal profession and improving the quality of legal services." ... The lawyers could not, however, be required to fund the bar association's own political expression....

The proposition that students who attend the University cannot be required to pay subsidies for the speech of other students without some First Amendment protection follows from the *Abood* and Keller cases.... Yet recognition must be given as well to the important and substantial purposes of the University, which seeks to facilitate a wide range of speech.

In *Abood* and *Keller*, the constitutional rule took the form of limiting the required subsidy to speech germane to the purposes of the union or bar association. The standard of germane speech as applied to student speech at a university is unworkable, however, and gives insufficient protection both to the objecting students and to the University program itself....

The speech the University seeks to encourage in the program before us is distinguished not by discernable limits, but by its vast, unexplored bounds. To insist upon asking what speech is germane would be contrary to the very goal the University seeks to pursue. It is not for the Court to say what is or is not germane to the ideas to be pursued in an institution of higher learning.

Just as the vast extent of permitted expression makes the test of germane speech inappropriate for intervention, so too does it underscore the high potential for intrusion on the First Amendment rights of the objecting students. It is all but inevitable that the fees will result in subsidies to speech which some students find objectionable and offensive to their personal beliefs. If the standard of germane speech is inapplicable, then it might be argued the remedy is to allow each student to list those causes which he or she will or will not support. If a university decided that its students' First Amendment interests were better protected by some type of optional or refund system, it would be free to do so. We decline to impose a system of that sort as a constitutional requirement, however. The restriction could be so disruptive and expensive that the program to support extracurricular speech would be ineffective. The First Amendment does not require the University to put the program at risk.

The University may determine that its mission is well served if students have the means to engage in dynamic discussions of philosophical, religious, scientific, social, and political subjects in their extracurricular campus life outside the lecture hall. If the University reaches this conclusion, it is entitled to impose a mandatory fee to sustain an open dialogue to these ends.

The University must provide some protection to its students' First Amendment interests, however. The proper measure, and the principal standard of protection for objecting students, we conclude, is the requirement of viewpoint neutrality in the allocation of funding support.... [V]iewpoint neutrality is the justification for requiring the student to pay the fee in the first instance, and for ensuring the integrity of the program's operation once the funds have been collected. We conclude that the University of Wisconsin may sustain the extracurricular dimensions of its programs by using mandatory student fees with viewpoint neutrality as the operational principle.

. . .

III

It remains to discuss the referendum aspect of the University's program. While the record is not well developed on the point, it appears that, by majority vote of the student body, a given RSO may be funded or defunded. It is unclear to us what protection, if any, there is for viewpoint neutrality in this part of the process. To the extent the referendum substitutes majority determinations for viewpoint neutrality, it would undermine the constitutional protection the program requires. The whole theory of viewpoint neutrality is that minority views are treated with the same respect as are majority views. Access to a public forum, for instance, does not depend upon majoritarian consent. That principle is controlling here. A remand is necessary and appropriate to resolve this point, and the case in all events must be reexamined in light of the principles we have discussed.

. . .

Justice Souter, with whom Justice Stevens and Justice Breyer join, concurring in the judgment.

... I agree that the University's scheme is permissible, but do not believe that the Court should take the occasion to impose a cast-iron viewpoint neutrality requirement to uphold it.... Instead, I would hold that the First Amendment interest claimed by the student respondents ... here is simply insufficient to merit protection by anything more than the viewpoint neutrality already accorded by the University, and I would go no further....

III. SPEECH BY RECIPIENTS OF GOVERNMENT SUBSIDIES

Government is permitted to be a partisan, and is usually not required to be neutral on controversial issues, when it communicates. The Religion Clauses of the First Amendment forbid the government from taking positions on issues of religious doctrine. (The implications of that principle will be the subject of Chapter 17, below.) Religious issues to one side, however, government, as a speaker, need not always be neutral or present all sides of the debate on controversial issues. For example, one of the challenges to the Federal Election Campaign Act of 1971, was that it used public money to finance partisan political debate. The Supreme Court rejected the argument that the Speech and Press

Clauses of the First Amendment required the same government neutrality on political issues that the Establishment Clause required for religious issues. Buckley v. Valeo, 424 U.S. 1, 92–93 (1976). But if government can take sides when it speaks, can it not also insist that those it pays to speak for it hew the government line?

The analytical problem present when government library finances the media was involved in Federal Communications Commission v. League of Women Voters, 468 U.S. 364 (1984). The Public Broadcasting Amendments Act of 1981 provided that any educational broadcaster receiving a grant from the Corporation for Public Broadcasting was forbidden to "engage in editorializing." The Court's majority held the prohibition invalid, for the most part treating the case as one where government was placing restrictions on the private media, and concluding that there were insufficient reasons for the prohibition. The four dissenters viewed the issue very differently—as involving Congressional power to decide how its subsidy to public broadcasting should be spent. (On this point, the majority responded that public broadcasters received only a minor fraction of their income from CPB grants; since the prohibition applied to all broadcasts, it did more than tell the broadcaster how to spend its federal subsidy.)

Whether government can limit speech by recipients of public funds remains a controversial question. In Rust v. Sullivan, 500 U.S. 173 (1991), a 5–4 majority of the Court sustained a federal regulation which prohibited the staff of federally funded family planning clinics to provide clients information regarding abortion. The majority concluded that this was not a case of government "suppressing a dangerous idea," but a case of funding "one activity to the exclusion of another." Ten years later, another 5–4 majority distinguished *Rust* and struck down a federal statute forbidding federally funded lawyers in welfare cases to challenge the constitutionality of existing welfare laws. Legal Services Corporation v. Velazquez, 531 U.S. 533 (2001). The majority distinguished *Rust* as a case where the government was speaking through its grantees. (The government need not be neutral when it is the speaker.) The advice from an attorney to a client, and the advocacy by an attorney in court, "cannot be classified as governmental speech even under a generous understanding of the concept." The dissent contended that *Rust* was controlling. The distinction between the speech of doctors in *Rust* and the lawyers in *Velazquez* was "an improper special solicitude for our own profession."

UNITED STATES v. AMERICAN LIBRARY ASSOCIATION, INC.

539 U.S. 194, 123 S.Ct. 2297, 156 L.Ed.2d 221 (2003).

CHIEF JUSTICE REHNQUIST announced the judgment of the Court and delivered an opinion, in which JUSTICE O'CONNOR, JUSTICE SCALIA, and JUSTICE THOMAS joined.

... Under [the Children's Internet Protection Act (CIPA)], a public library may not receive federal assistance to provide Internet access unless it installs software to block images that constitute obscenity or child pornography, and to prevent minors from obtaining access to material that is harmful to them. The District Court held these provisions facially invalid on the ground that they induce public libraries to violate patrons' First Amendment rights. We now reverse.

To help public libraries provide their patrons with Internet access, Congress offers two forms of federal assistance. First, the E-rate program established by the Telecommunications Act of 1996 entitles qualifying libraries to buy Internet access at a discount.... In the year ending June 30, 2002, libraries received $58.5 million in such discounts.... Second, pursuant to the Library Services and Technology Act (LSTA), ... the Institute of Museum and Library Services makes grants to state library administrative agencies to "electronically lin[k] libraries with educational, social, or information services," "assis[t] libraries in accessing information through electronic networks," and "pa[y] costs for libraries to acquire or share computer systems and telecommunications technologies.".... In fiscal year 2002, Congress appropriated more than $149 million in LSTA grants. These programs have succeeded greatly in bringing Internet access to public libraries: By 2000, 95% of the Nation's libraries provided public Internet access. ...

By connecting to the Internet, public libraries provide patrons with a vast amount of valuable information. But there is also an enormous amount of pornography on the Internet, much of which is easily obtained. The accessibility of this material has created serious problems for libraries, which have found that patrons of all ages, including minors, regularly search for online pornography. Some patrons also expose others to pornographic images by leaving them displayed on Internet terminals or printed at library printers.

Upon discovering these problems, Congress became concerned that the E-rate and LSTA programs were facilitating access to illegal and harmful pornography. ...Congress learned that adults "us[e] library computers to access pornography that is then exposed to staff, passersby, and children," and that "minors acces[s] child and adult pornography in libraries."

But Congress also learned that filtering software that blocks access to pornographic Web sites could provide a reasonably effective way to prevent such uses of library resources. ... By 2000, before Congress enacted CIPA, almost 17% of public libraries used such software on at least some of their Internet terminals, and 7% had filters on all of them. ... A library can set such software to block categories of material, such as "Pornography" or "Violence." When a patron tries to view a site that falls within such a category, a screen appears indicating that the site is blocked. ... But a filter set to block pornography may sometimes block other sites that present neither obscene nor pornographic material, but that nevertheless trigger the filter. To minimize this problem, a library can set its software to prevent the blocking of material that falls into categories like "Education," "History," and "Medical." ... A library may also add or delete specific sites from a blocking category and anyone can ask companies that furnish filtering software to unblock particular sites. . . .

. . . CIPA . . . provides that a library may not receive E-rate or LSTA assistance unless it has "a policy of Internet safety for minors that includes the operation of a technology protection measure . . . that protects against access" by all persons to "visual depictions" that constitute "obscen[ity]" or "child pornography," and that protects against access by minors to "visual depictions" that are "harmful to minors." . . . The statute defines a "[t]echnology protection measure" as "a specific technology that blocks or filters Internet access to material covered by" CIPA. . . . CIPA also permits the library to "disable" the filter "to enable access for bona fide research or other lawful purposes." . . . Under the E-rate program, disabling is permitted "during use by an adult." . . . Under the LSTA program, disabling is permitted during use by any person.

Appellees are a group of libraries, library associations, library patrons, and Web site publishers, including the American Library Association (ALA) and the Multnomah County Public Library in Portland, Oregon. . . .

Congress has wide latitude to attach conditions to the receipt of federal assistance in order to further its policy objectives. South Dakota v. Dole, 483 U.S. 203, 206 (1987). But Congress may not "induce" the recipient "to engage in activities that would themselves be unconstitutional." . . . To determine whether libraries would violate the First Amendment by employing the filtering software that CIPA requires, we must first examine the role of libraries in our society.

. . . To fulfill their traditional missions, public libraries must have broad discretion to decide what material to provide to their patrons. Although they seek to provide a wide array of information, their goal has never been to provide "universal coverage." . . . Instead, public libraries seek to provide materials "that would be of the greatest direct benefit or interest to the community." . . . To this end, libraries collect only those materials deemed to have "requisite and appropriate quality." . . .

We have held in two analogous contexts that the government has broad discretion to make content-based judgments in deciding what private speech to make available to the public. In Arkansas Ed. Television Comm'n v. Forbes, 523 U.S. 666, 672–673 (1998), we held that public forum principles do not generally apply to a public television station's editorial judgments regarding the private speech it presents to its viewers. "[B]road rights of access for outside speakers would be antithetical, as a general rule, to the discretion that stations and their editorial staff must exercise to fulfill their journalistic purpose and statutory obligations." . . .

Similarly, in National Endowment for Arts v. Finley, 524 U.S. 569 (1998), we upheld an art funding program that required the National Endowment for the Arts (NEA) to use content-based criteria in making funding decisions. We explained that "[a]ny content-based considerations that may be taken into account in the grant-making process are a consequence of the nature of arts funding." *Id.*, at 585. In particular, "[t]he very assumption of the NEA is that grants will be awarded according to the 'artistic worth of competing applicants,' and absolute neutrality is simply inconceivable." . . .

The principles underlying *Forbes* and *Finley* also apply to a public library's exercise of judgment in selecting the material it provides to its patrons. Just as forum analysis and heightened judicial scrutiny are incompatible with the role of public television stations and the role of the NEA, they are also incompatible with the discretion that public libraries must have to fulfill their traditional missions. Public library staffs necessarily consider content in making collection decisions and enjoy broad discretion in making them.

. . . [P]ublic forum principles . . . are out of place in the context of this case. Internet access in public libraries is neither a "traditional" nor a "designated" public forum. . . . First, this resource—which did not exist until quite recently—has not "immemorially been held in trust for the use of the public and, time out of mind, . . . been used for purposes of assembly, communication of thoughts between citizens, and discussing public questions." . . . We have "rejected the view that traditional public forum status extends beyond its historic confines." . . . The doctrines surrounding traditional public forums may not be extended to situations where such history is lacking.

Nor does Internet access in a public library satisfy our definition of a "designated public forum." To create such a forum, the government must make an affirmative choice to open up its property for use as a public forum. . . . The government does not create a public forum by inaction or by permitting limited discourse, but only by intentionally opening a non-traditional forum for public discourse. . . .

. . . A public library does not acquire Internet terminals in order to create a public forum for Web publishers to express themselves, any more than it collects books in order to provide a public forum for the authors of books to speak. It provides Internet access . . . for the same reasons it offers other library resources: to facilitate research, learning, and recreational pursuits by furnishing materials of requisite and appropriate quality. . . .

. . . A library's failure to make quality-based judgments about all the material it furnishes from the Web does not somehow taint the judgments it does make. . . . Most libraries already exclude pornography from their print collections because they deem it inappropriate for inclusion. We do not subject these decisions to heightened scrutiny; it would make little sense to treat libraries' judgments to block online pornography any differently, when these judgments are made for just the same reason.

Moreover, because of the vast quantity of material on the Internet and the rapid pace at which it changes, libraries cannot possibly segregate, item by item, all the Internet material that is appropriate for inclusion from all that is not. While a library could limit its Internet collection to just those sites it found worthwhile, it could do so only at the cost of excluding an enormous amount of valuable information that it lacks the capacity to review. . . .

... [T]he dissents fault the tendency of filtering software to "over-block"—that is, to erroneously block access to constitutionally protected speech that falls outside the categories that software users intend to block. Due to the software's limitations, "[m]any erroneously blocked [Web] pages contain content that is completely innocuous for both adults and minors, and that no rational person could conclude matches the filtering companies' category definitions, such as 'pornography' or 'sex.'" Assuming that such erroneous blocking presents constitutional difficulties, any such concerns are dispelled by the ease with which patrons may have the filtering software disabled. When a patron encounters a blocked site, he need only ask a librarian to unblock it or (at least in the case of adults) disable the filter. As the District Court found, libraries have the capacity to permanently unblock any erroneously blocked site, and the Solicitor General stated at oral argument that a "library may ... eliminate the filtering with respect to specific sites ... at the request of a patron." ... The Solicitor General confirmed that a "librarian can, in response to a request from a patron, unblock the filtering mechanism altogether," and further explained that a patron would not "have to explain ... why he was asking a site to be unblocked or the filtering to be disabled." ... [S]ome patrons may be too embarrassed to request them. But the Constitution does not guarantee the right to acquire information at a public library without any risk of embarrassment.

Appellees urge us to affirm the District Court's judgment on the alternative ground that CIPA imposes an unconstitutional condition on the receipt of federal assistance. Under this doctrine, "the government may not deny a benefit to a person on a basis that infringes his constitutionally protected ... freedom of speech" even if he has no entitlement to that benefit. ...Appellees argue that CIPA imposes an unconstitutional condition on libraries ... by requiring them, as a condition on their receipt of federal funds, to surrender their First Amendment right to provide the public with access to constitutionally protected speech.

We need not decide this question because, even assuming that appellees may assert an "unconstitutional conditions" claim, this claim would fail on the merits. Within broad limits, "when the Government appropriates public funds to establish a program it is entitled to define the limits of that program." ... In *Rust* [v. Sullivan, 500 U.S. 173 (1991)], Congress had appropriated federal funding for family planning services and forbidden the use of such funds in programs that provided abortion counseling. ...Recipients of these funds challenged this restriction, arguing that it impermissibly conditioned the receipt of a benefit on the relinquishment of their constitutional right to engage in abortion counseling. ... We rejected that claim, recognizing that "the Government [was] not denying a benefit to anyone, but [was] instead simply insisting that public funds be spent for the purposes for which they were authorized." ...

The same is true here. The E-rate and LSTA programs were intended to help public libraries fulfill their traditional role of obtaining material of requisite and appropriate quality for educational and infor-

mational purposes.... Especially because public libraries have traditionally excluded pornographic material from their other collections, Congress could reasonably impose a parallel limitation on its Internet
assistance programs....

Justice Stevens asserts the premise that "[a] federal statute penalizing a library for failing to install filtering software on every one of its
Internet-accessible computers would unquestionably violate [the First]
Amendment." ... But—assuming again that public libraries have First
Amendment rights—CIPA does not "penalize" libraries that choose not
to install such software, or deny them the right to provide their patrons
with unfiltered Internet access. Rather, CIPA simply reflects Congress'
decision not to subsidize their doing so....

Appellees mistakenly contend, in reliance on Legal Services Corporation v. Velazquez, 531 U.S. 533 (2001), that CIPA's filtering conditions
"[d]istor[t] the [u]sual [f]unctioning of [p]ublic [l]ibraries." In *Velazquez*,
the Court concluded that a Government program of furnishing legal aid
to the indigent differed from the program in *Rust* "[i]n th [e] vital
respect" that the role of lawyers who represent clients in welfare
disputes is to advocate *against* the Government, and there was thus an
assumption that counsel would be free of state control. ... The Court
concluded that the restriction on advocacy in such welfare disputes
would distort the usual functioning of the legal profession and the
federal and state courts before which the lawyers appeared. Public
libraries, by contrast, have no comparable role that pits them against the
Government, and there is no comparable assumption that they must be
free of any conditions that their benefactors might attach to the use of
donated funds or other assistance.

Because public libraries' use of Internet filtering software does not
violate their patrons' First Amendment rights, CIPA does not induce
libraries to violate the Constitution, and is a valid exercise of Congress'
spending power. Nor does CIPA impose an unconstitutional condition on
public libraries. Therefore, the judgment of the District Court for the
Eastern District of Pennsylvania is

Reversed.

JUSTICE KENNEDY, concurring in the judgment.

If, on the request of an adult user, a librarian will unblock filtered
material or disable the Internet software filter without significant delay,
there is little to this case. The Government represents this is indeed the
fact.

. . .

If some libraries do not have the capacity to unblock specific Web
sites or to disable the filter or if it is shown that an adult user's election
to view constitutionally protected Internet material is burdened in some
other substantial way, that would be the subject for an as-applied
challenge, not the facial challenge made in this case.

The interest in protecting young library users from material inappropriate for minors is legitimate, and even compelling, as all Members

of the Court appear to agree. Given this interest, and the failure to show that the ability of adult library users to have access to the material is burdened in any significant degree, the statute is not unconstitutional on its face. For these reasons, I concur in the judgment of the Court.

JUSTICE BREYER, concurring in the judgment.

. . . I reach the plurality's ultimate conclusion in a different way.

In ascertaining whether the statutory provisions are constitutional, I would apply a form of heightened scrutiny, examining the statutory requirements in question with special care. The Act directly restricts the public's receipt of information. . . . And it does so through limitations imposed by outside bodies (here Congress) upon two critically important sources of information—the Internet as accessed via public libraries. . . . [W]e should not examine the statute's constitutionality as if it raised no special First Amendment concern—as if, like tax or economic regulation, the First Amendment demanded only a "rational basis" for imposing a restriction. Nor should we accept the Government's suggestion that a presumption in favor of the statute's constitutionality applies.

At the same time, in my view, the First Amendment does not here demand application of the most limiting constitutional approach—that of "strict scrutiny." The statutory restriction in question is, in essence, a kind of "selection" restriction (a kind of editing). It affects the kinds and amount of materials that the library can present to its patrons. And libraries often properly engage in the selection of materials, either as a matter of necessity (*i.e.*, due to the scarcity of resources) or by design (*i.e.*, in accordance with collection development policies). . . . "[S]trict scrutiny" implies too limiting and rigid a test for me to believe that the First Amendment requires it in this context.

Instead, I would examine the constitutionality of the Act's restrictions here as the Court has examined speech-related restrictions in other contexts where circumstances call for heightened, but not "strict," scrutiny—where, for example, complex, competing constitutional interests are potentially at issue or speech-related harm is potentially justified by unusually strong governmental interests. Typically the key question in such instances is one of proper fit. . . .

In such cases the Court has asked whether the harm to speech-related interests is disproportionate in light of both the justifications and the potential alternatives. It has considered the legitimacy of the statute's objective, the extent to which the statute will tend to achieve that objective, whether there are other, less restrictive ways of achieving that objective, and ultimately whether the statute works speech-related harm that, in relation to that objective, is out of proportion. . . . This approach does not substitute a form of "balancing" for less flexible, though more speech-protective, forms of "strict scrutiny." Rather, it *supplements* the latter with an approach that is more flexible but nonetheless provides the legislature with less than ordinary leeway in light of the fact that constitutionally protected expression is at issue. . . .

The Act's restrictions satisfy these constitutional demands. . . . [T]he software filters both "overblock," screening out some perfectly legitimate material, and "underblock," allowing some obscene material to escape detection by the filter. But no one has presented any clearly superior or better fitting alternatives.

At the same time, the Act contains an important exception that limits the speech-related harm that "overblocking" might cause ... [allowing] libraries to permit any adult patron access to an "over-blocked" Web site; the adult patron need only ask a librarian to unblock the specific Web site or, alternatively, ask the librarian, "Please disable the entire filter."

. . .

Given the comparatively small burden that the Act imposes upon the library patron seeking legitimate Internet materials, I cannot say that any speech-related harm that the Act may cause is disproportionate when considered in relation to the Act's legitimate objectives. I therefore agree with the plurality that the statute does not violate the First Amendment, and I concur in the judgment.

JUSTICE STEVENS, dissenting.

... I agree with the plurality that it is neither inappropriate nor unconstitutional for a local library to experiment with filtering software as a means of curtailing children's access to Internet Web sites displaying sexually explicit images. I also agree with the plurality that the 7% of public libraries that decided to use such software on *all* of their Internet terminals in 2000 did not act unlawfully. Whether it is constitutional for the Congress of the United States to impose that requirement on the other 93%, however, raises a vastly different question. Rather than allowing local decisionmakers to tailor their responses to local problems, the Children's Internet Protection Act (CIPA) operates as a blunt nationwide restraint on adult access to "an enormous amount of" ... constitutionally protected speech. In my view, this restraint is unconstitutional.

I

The unchallenged findings of fact made by the District Court reveal fundamental defects in the filtering software that is now available or that will be available in the foreseeable future. Because the software relies on key words or phrases to block undesirable sites, it does not have the capacity to exclude a precisely defined category of images. ...

The effect of the overblocking is the functional equivalent of a host of individual decisions excluding hundreds of thousands of individual constitutionally protected messages from Internet terminals located in public libraries throughout the Nation. ...

. . .

... The plurality ... relies on the Solicitor General's assurance that the statute permits individual librarians to disable filtering mechanisms whenever a patron so requests. In my judgment, that assurance does not cure the constitutional infirmity in the statute.

Until a blocked site or group of sites is unblocked, a patron is unlikely to know what is being hidden and therefore whether there is any point in asking for the filter to be removed. It is as though the statute required a significant part of every library's reading materials to be kept in unmarked, locked rooms or cabinets, which could be opened only in response to specific requests. Some curious readers would in time obtain access to the hidden materials, but many would not. Inevitably, the interest of the authors of those works in reaching the widest possible audience would be abridged.

II

The plurality incorrectly argues that the statute does not impose "an unconstitutional condition on public libraries." On the contrary, it impermissibly conditions the receipt of Government funding on the restriction of significant First Amendment rights.

. . .

... [W]e have always assumed that libraries have discretion when making decisions regarding what to include in, and exclude from, their collections. ... Given our Nation's deep commitment "to safeguarding academic freedom" and to the "robust exchange of ideas," ... a library's exercise of judgment with respect to its collection is entitled to First Amendment protection.

A federal statute penalizing a library for failing to install filtering software on every one of its Internet-accessible computers would unquestionably violate that Amendment. ... I think it equally clear that the First Amendment protects libraries from being denied funds for refusing to comply with an identical rule. An abridgment of speech by means of a threatened denial of benefits can be just as pernicious as an abridgment by means of a threatened penalty.

Our cases holding that government employment may not be conditioned on the surrender of rights protected by the First Amendment illustrate the point. . . .

The issue in this case does not involve governmental attempts to control the speech or views of its employees. It involves the use of its treasury to impose controls on an important medium of expression. In an analogous situation, we specifically held that when "the Government seeks to use an existing medium of expression and to control it, in a class of cases, in ways which distort its usual functioning," the distorting restriction must be struck down under the First Amendment. . . .

The plurality argues that the controversial decision in Rust v. Sullivan ... requires rejection of appellees' unconstitutional conditions claim. But, as subsequent cases have explained, *Rust* only involved and only applies to instances of governmental speech—that is, situations in which the government seeks to communicate a specific message. ... These programs thus are designed to provide access, particularly for individuals in low-income communities, ... to a vast amount and wide variety of private speech. They are not designed to foster or transmit any particular governmental message.

. . .

The plurality's reliance on National Endowment for Arts v. Finley ... is also misplaced. That case involved a challenge to a statute setting forth the criteria used by a federal panel of experts administering a federal grant program. Unlike this case, the Federal Government was not seeking to impose restrictions on the administration of a nonfederal program. ... *Rust* would appear to permit restrictions on a federal program such as the NEA arts grant program at issue in *Finley*.

Further, like a library, the NEA experts in *Finley* had a great deal of discretion to make judgments as to what projects to fund. But unlike this case, *Finley* did not involve a challenge by the NEA to a governmental restriction on its ability to award grants. Instead, the respondents were performance artists who had applied for NEA grants but were denied funding. ... If this were a case in which library patrons had challenged a library's decision to install and use filtering software, it would be in the same posture as *Finley*. Because it is not, *Finley* does not control this case.

Also unlike *Finley*, the Government does not merely seek to control a library's discretion with respect to computers purchased with Government funds or those computers with Government-discounted Internet access. ... [I]f a library attempts to provide Internet service for even *one* computer through an E-rate discount, that library must put filtering software on *all* of its computers with Internet access, not just the one computer with E-rate discount.

This Court should not permit federal funds to be used to enforce this kind of broad restriction of First Amendment rights, particularly when such a restriction is unnecessary to accomplish Congress' stated goal. ... The abridgment of speech is equally obnoxious whether a rule like this one is enforced by a threat of penalties or by a threat to withhold a benefit.

. . .

JUSTICE SOUTER, with whom JUSTICE GINSBURG joins, dissenting.

I agree in the main with Justice Stevens that the blocking requirements of the Children's Internet Protection Act ... impose an unconstitutional condition on the Government's subsidies to local libraries for providing access to the Internet. I also agree with the library appellees on a further reason to hold the blocking rule invalid in the exercise of the spending power under Article I, § 8: the rule mandates action by recipient libraries that would violate the First Amendment's guarantee of free speech if the libraries took that action entirely on their own. I respectfully dissent on this further ground.

I

Like the other Members of the Court, I have no doubt about the legitimacy of governmental efforts to put a barrier between child patrons of public libraries and the raw offerings on the Internet otherwise available to them there, and if the only First Amendment interests raised here were those of children, I would uphold application of the Act. . . .

Nor would I dissent if I agreed with the majority of my colleagues, that an adult library patron could, consistently with the Act, obtain an unblocked terminal simply for the asking. I realize the Solicitor General represented this to be the Government's policy, and if that policy were communicated to every affected library as unequivocally as it was stated to us at argument, local librarians might be able to indulge the unblocking requests of adult patrons to the point of taking the curse off the statute for all practical purposes. But the Federal Communications Commission, in its order implementing the Act, pointedly declined to set a federal policy on when unblocking by local libraries would be appropriate under the statute. . . .

In any event, we are here to review a statute, and the unblocking provisions simply cannot be construed, even for constitutional avoidance purposes, to say that a library must unblock upon adult request, no conditions imposed and no questions asked. . . .

We therefore have to take the statute on the understanding that adults will be denied access to a substantial amount of nonobscene material harmful to children but lawful for adult examination, and a substantial quantity of text and pictures harmful to no one. . . .

We likewise have to examine the statute on the understanding that the restrictions on adult Internet access have no justification in the object of protecting children. Children could be restricted to blocked terminals, leaving other unblocked terminals in areas restricted to adults and screened from casual glances. And of course the statute could simply have provided for unblocking at adult request, with no questions asked. . . .

The question for me, then, is whether a local library could itself constitutionally impose these restrictions on the content otherwise available to an adult patron through an Internet connection, at a library terminal provided for public use. The answer is no. A library that chose to block an adult's Internet access to material harmful to children (and whatever else the undiscriminating filter might interrupt) would be imposing a content-based restriction on communication of material in the library's control that an adult could otherwise lawfully see. This would simply be censorship. . . .

II

The Court's plurality does not treat blocking affecting adults as censorship, but chooses to describe a library's act in filtering content as simply an instance of the kind of selection from available material that every library . . . must perform. . . . But this position does not hold up.

A

Public libraries are indeed selective in what they acquire to place in their stacks, as they must be. There is only so much money and so much shelf space ... Selectivity is thus necessary and complex, and these two characteristics explain why review of a library's selection decisions must be limited....

At every significant point, however, the Internet blocking here defies comparison to the process of acquisition. Whereas traditional scarcity of money and space require a library to make choices about what to acquire, and the choice to be made is whether or not to spend the money to acquire something, blocking is the subject of a choice made after the money for Internet access has been spent or committed. Since it makes no difference to the cost of Internet access whether an adult calls up material harmful for children or the Articles of Confederation, blocking (on facts like these) is not necessitated by scarcity of either money or space. In the instance of the Internet, what the library acquires is electronic access, and the choice to block is a choice to limit access that has already been acquired. Thus, deciding against buying a book means there is no book (unless a loan can be obtained), but blocking the Internet is merely blocking access purchased in its entirety and subject to unblocking if the librarian agrees. The proper analogy therefore is not to passing up a book that might have been bought; it is either to buying a book and then keeping it from adults lacking an acceptable "purpose," or to buying an encyclopedia and then cutting out pages with anything thought to be unsuitable for all adults.

B

... The plurality ... argues ... that the traditional responsibility of public libraries has called for denying adult access to certain books, or bowdlerizing the content of what the libraries let adults see. But, in fact, the plurality's conception of a public library's mission has been rejected by the libraries themselves. And no library that chose to block adult access in the way mandated by the Act could claim that the history of public library practice in this country furnished an implicit gloss on First Amendment standards, allowing for blocking out anything unsuitable for adults.

Institutional history of public libraries in America discloses an evolution toward a general rule, now firmly rooted, that any adult entitled to use the library has access to any of its holdings. To be sure, this freedom of choice was apparently not within the inspiration for the mid–19th century development of public libraries ... [There] was a growing understanding that a librarian's job was to guarantee that "all people had access to all ideas," ...

By the time McCarthyism began its assaults, appellee American Library Association had developed a Library Bill of Rights against censorship ... and an Intellectual Freedom Committee to maintain the position that beyond enforcing existing laws against obscenity, "there is no place in our society for extra-legal efforts to coerce the taste of others, to confine adults to the reading matter deemed suitable for adolescents, or to inhibit the efforts of writers to achieve artistic expression." ... So far as I have been able to tell, this statement expressed the prevailing ideal in public library administration after World War II, and it seems fair to say as a general rule that libraries by then had ceased to deny requesting adults access to any materials in their collections. . . .

. . .

. . . [I]n 1973, the ALA adopted a policy opposing the practice . . . of keeping certain books off the open shelves, available only on specific request. . . . The statement conceded that "closed shelf," "locked case," "adults only," or "restricted shelf" collections were "common to many libraries in the United States." . . . The ALA nonetheless came out against it, in these terms: "While the limitation differs from direct censorship activities, such as removal of library materials or refusal to purchase certain publications, it nonetheless constitutes censorship, albeit a subtle form." . . .

Amidst these and other ALA statements from the latter half of the 20th century, however, one subject is missing. There is not a word about barring requesting adults from any materials in a library's collection . . . The silence bespeaks an American public library that gives any adult patron any material at hand, and a history without support for the plurality's reading of the First Amendment as tolerating a public library's censorship of its collection against adult enquiry.

C

. . . Quite simply, we can smell a rat when a library blocks material already in its control, just as we do when a library removes books from its shelves for reasons having nothing to do with wear and tear, obsolescence, or lack of demand. Content-based blocking and removal tell us something that mere absence from the shelves does not.

. . .

After a library has acquired material . . ., the variety of possible reasons that might legitimately support an initial rejection are no longer in play. Removal of books or selective blocking by controversial subject matter is not a function of limited resources and less likely than a selection decision to reflect an assessment of esthetic or scholarly merit. Removal (and blocking) decisions being so often obviously correlated with content, they tend to show up for just what they are, and because such decisions tend to be few, courts can examine them without facing a deluge. The difference between choices to keep out and choices to throw out is thus enormous, a perception that underlay the good sense of the plurality's conclusion in Board of Ed., Island Trees Union Free School Dist. No. 26 v. Pico, 457 U.S. 853 (1982), that removing classics from a school library in response to pressure from parents and school board members violates the Speech Clause.

. . .

RUMSFELD v. FORUM FOR ACADEMIC AND INSTITUTIONAL RIGHTS, INC.

___ U.S. ___, 126 S.Ct. 1297, 164 L.Ed.2d 156 (2006).

CHIEF JUSTICE ROBERTS delivered the opinion of the Court.

When law schools began restricting the access of military recruiters to their students because of disagreement with the Government's policy on homosexuals in the military, Congress responded by enacting the Solomon Amendment. That provision specifies that if any part of an institution of higher education denies military recruiters access equal to that provided other recruiters, the entire institution would lose certain federal funds. The law schools responded by suing, alleging that the Solomon Amendment infringed their First Amendment freedoms of speech and association. The District Court disagreed but was reversed by a divided panel of the Court of Appeals for the Third Circuit, which ordered the District Court to enter a preliminary injunction against enforcement of the Solomon Amendment. We granted certiorari.

JOHN G. ROBERTS, Jr.—Born in Buffalo, New York, on January 27, 1955, son of an executive with Bethlehem Steel. Republican. Roman Catholic. Harvard, A.B., summa cum laude, 1976; Harvard J.D., magna cum laude, 1979, law review managing editor. Law clerk to Justice William Rehnquist, 1980–81. Special Assistant to U.S. Attorney General William French Smith, 1981–82; Associate Counsel to the President, White House Counsel's Office, 1982–86; Practiced law, 1986–89; Principal Deputy Solicitor General, 1989–93; Partner at Hogan & Hartson, 1993–2003. U.S. Court of Appeals Judge (D.C. Circuit), 2003–2005. Nominated to associate justice by President George W. Bush on July 19, 2005, to replace Sandra Day O'Connor, who had announced her intention to retire; renominated to be chief justice by President George W. Bush on September 6, 2005, to replace the late William H. Rehnquist. Confirmed by the Senate on September 29, 2005, by a 78–22 vote.

I

Respondent Forum for Academic and Institutional Rights, Inc. (FAIR) is an association of law schools and law faculties. App. 5. Its declared mission is "to promote academic freedom, support educational institutions in opposing discrimination and vindicate the rights of institutions of higher education." FAIR members have adopted policies expressing their opposition to discrimination based on, among other factors, sexual orientation. They would like to restrict military recruiting on their campuses because they object to the policy Congress has adopted with respect to homosexuals in the military. (Under [the] policy, a person generally may not serve in the Armed Forces if he has engaged in homosexual acts, stated that he is a homosexual, or married a person of the same sex). Respondents do not challenge that policy in this litigation. The Solomon Amendment, however, forces institutions to choose between enforcing their nondiscrimination policy against military recruiters in this way and continuing to receive specified federal funding.

In 2003, FAIR sought a preliminary injunction against enforcement of the Solomon Amendment, which at that time ... prevented the Department of Defense (DOD) from providing specified federal funds to any institution of higher education "that either prohibits, or in effect prevents" military recruiters "from gaining entry to campuses." FAIR considered the DOD's interpretation of this provision particularly objectionable. Although the statute required only "entry to campuses," the Government—after the terrorist attacks on September 11, 2001— adopted an informal policy of " 'require[in] universities to provide military recruiters access to students equal in quality and scope to that provided to other recruiters.' " Prior to the adoption of this policy, some law schools sought to promote their nondiscrimination policies while still complying with the Solomon Amendment by having military recruiters interview on the undergraduate campus. But under the equal access policy, military recruiters had to be permitted to interview at the law schools, if other recruiters did so.

FAIR argued that this forced inclusion and equal treatment of military recruiters violated the law schools' First Amendment freedoms of speech and association. According to FAIR, the Solomon Amendment was unconstitutional because it forced law schools to choose between exercising their First Amendment right to decide whether to disseminate or accommodate a military recruiter's message, and ensuring the availability of federal funding for their universities.

III

The Constitution grants Congress the power to "provide for the common Defense," "[t]o raise and support Armies," and "[t]o provide and maintain a Navy." Art. I, § 8, cols. 1, 12–13. Congress' power in this area "is broad and sweeping," *United States v. O'Brien,* 391 U.S., at 377, and there is no dispute in this case that it includes the authority to require campus access for military recruiters. That is, of course, unless Congress exceeds constitutional limitations on its power in enacting such legislation. See *Roster v. Goldberg,* 453 U.S. 57, 67 (1981). But the fact that legislation that raises armies is subject to First Amendment constraints does not mean that we ignore the purpose of this legislation when determining its constitutionality; as we recognized in *Roster,* "judicial deference ... is at its apogee" when Congress legislates under its authority to raise and support armies. *Id.,* at 70.

Although Congress has broad authority to legislate on matters of military recruiting, it nonetheless chose to secure campus access for military recruiters indirectly, through its Spending Clause power. The Solomon Amendment gives universities a choice: Either allow military recruiters the same access to students afforded any other recruiter or forgo certain federal funds. Congress' decision to proceed indirectly does not reduce the deference given to Congress in the area of military affairs. Congress' choice to promote its goal by creating a funding condition deserves at least as deferential treatment as if Congress had imposed a mandate on universities.

Congress' power to regulate military recruiting under the Solomon Amendment is arguably greater because universities are free to decline the federal funds.... Other decisions, however, recognize a limit on Congress' ability to place conditions on the receipt of funds. We recently held that " 'the government may not deny a benefit to a person on a basis that infringes his constitutionally protected ... freedom of speech even if he has no entitlement to that benefit.' " *United States v. American Library Assn., Inc.,* 539 U.S. 194, 210 (2003) ...

A

The Solomon Amendment neither limits what law schools may say nor requires them to say anything. Law schools remain free under the statute to express whatever views they may have on the military's congressionally mandated employment policy, all the while retaining eligibility for federal funds. ...As a general matter, the Solomon Amendment regulates conduct, not speech. It affects what law schools must *do*—afford equal access to military recruiters—not what they may or may not *say*....

Some of this Court's leading First Amendment precedents have established the principle that freedom of speech prohibits the government from telling people what they must say. In *West Virginia Bd. of Ed. v. Barnett,* 319 U.S. 624, 642 (1943), we held unconstitutional a state law requiring schoolchildren to recite the Pledge of Allegiance and to salute the flag. And in *Wooly v. Maynard,* 430 U.S. 705, 717 (1977), we held unconstitutional another that required New Hampshire motorists to display the state motto—"Live Free or Die"—on their license plates.

The Solomon Amendment does not require any similar expression by law schools. Nonetheless, recruiting assistance provided by the schools often includes elements of speech. For example, schools may send e-mails or post notices on bulletin boards on an employer's behalf. ... Law schools offering such services to other recruiters must also send e-mails and post notices on behalf of the military to comply with the Solomon Amendment ... This sort of recruiting assistance, however, is a far cry from the compelled speech in *Barnett* and *Wooly.* The Solomon Amendment, unlike the laws at issue in those cases, does not dictate the content of the speech at all, which is only "compelled" if, and to the extent, the school provides such speech for other recruiters. There is nothing in this case approaching a Government-mandated pledge or motto that the school must endorse.

The compelled speech to which the law schools point is plainly incidental to the Solomon Amendment's regulation of conduct, and "it has never been deemed an abridgment of freedom of speech or press to make a course of conduct illegal merely because the conduct was in part initiated, evidenced, or carried out by means of language, either spoken, written, or printed." ... Compelling a law school that sends scheduling e-mails for other recruiters to send one for a military recruiter is simply not the same as forcing a student to pledge allegiance, or forcing a

Jehovah's Witness to display the motto "Live Free or Die," and it trivializes the freedom protected in *Barnett* and *Wooley* to suggest that it is....

... Our compelled-speech cases are not limited to the situation in which an individual must personally speak the government's message. We have also in a number of instances limited the government's ability to force one speaker to host or accommodate another speaker's message.... The compelled-speech violation in each of our prior cases, however, resulted from the fact that the complaining speaker's own message was affected by the speech it was forced to accommodate.... In this case, accommodating the military's message does not affect the law schools' speech, because the schools are not speaking when they host interviews and recruiting receptions. Unlike a parade organizer's choice of parade contingents, a law school's decision to allow recruiters on campus is not inherently expressive. Law schools facilitate recruiting to assist their students in obtaining jobs. A law school's recruiting services lack the expressive quality of a parade, a newsletter, or the editorial page of a newspaper; its accommodation of a military recruiter's message is not compelled speech because the accommodation does not sufficiently interfere with any message of the school.

The schools respond that if they treat military and nonmilitary recruiters alike in order to comply with the Solomon Amendment, they could be viewed as sending the message that they see nothing wrong with the military's policies, when they do. ... Nothing about recruiting suggests that law schools agree with any speech by recruiters, and nothing in the Solomon Amendment restricts what the law schools may say about the military's policies ...

Having rejected the view that the Solomon Amendment impermissibly regulates *speech*, we must still consider whether the expressive nature of the *conduct* regulated by the statute brings that conduct within the First Amendment's protection. In *O'Brien*, we recognized that some forms of " 'symbolic speech' " were deserving of First Amendment protection. 391 U.S., at 376. But we rejected the view that "conduct can be labeled 'speech' whenever the person engaging in the conduct intends thereby to express an idea." *Ibid.* Instead, we have extended First Amendment protection only to conduct that is inherently expressive. In *Texas v. Johnson,* 491 U.S. 397, 406 (1989), for example, we applied *O'Brien* and held that burning the American flag was sufficiently expressive to warrant First Amendment protection.

Unlike flag burning, the conduct regulated by the Solomon Amendment is not inherently expressive. Prior to the adoption of the Solomon Amendment's equal-access requirement, law schools "expressed" their disagreement with the military by treating military recruiters differently from other recruiters. But these actions were expressive only because the law schools accompanied their conduct with speech explaining it. For example, the point of requiring military interviews to be conducted on the undergraduate campus is not "overwhelmingly apparent." *Johnson, supra,* at 406. An observer who sees military recruiters interviewing away from the law school has no way of knowing whether the law school is expressing its disapproval of the military, all the law school's interview rooms are full, or the military recruiters decided for reasons of their own that they would rather interview someplace else.

The expressive component of a law school's actions is not created by the conduct itself but by the speech that accompanies it. The fact that such explanatory speech is necessary is strong evidence that the conduct at issue here is not so inherently expressive that it warrants protection under *O'Brien*. If combining speech and conduct were enough to create expressive conduct, a regulated party could always transform conduct into "speech" simply by talking about it. For instance, if an individual announces that he intends to express his disapproval of the Internal Revenue Service by refusing to pay his income taxes, we would have to apply *O'Brien* to determine whether the Tax Code violates the First Amendment. Neither *O'Brien* nor its progeny supports such a result.

. . . We have held that "an incidental burden on speech is no greater than is essential, and therefore is permissible under *O'Brien*, so long as the neutral regulation promotes a substantial government interest that would be achieved less effectively absent the regulation." . . . The Solomon Amendment clearly satisfies this requirement. Military recruiting promotes the substantial Government interest in raising and supporting the Armed Forces—an objective that would be achieved less effectively if the military were forced to recruit on less favorable terms than other employers.

B

. . . The Solomon Amendment therefore does not violate a law school's First Amendment rights. A military recruiter's mere presence on campus does not violate a law school's right to associate, regardless of how repugnant the law school considers the recruiter's message.

* * *

. . . In this case, FAIR has attempted to stretch a number of First Amendment doctrines well beyond the sort of activities these doctrines protect. The law schools object to having to treat military recruiters like other recruiters, but that regulation of conduct does not violate the First Amendment. To the extent that the Solomon Amendment incidentally affects expression, the law schools' effort to cast themselves as just like the schoolchildren in *Barnette* . . . plainly overstates the expressive nature of their activity and the impact of the Solomon Amendment on it, while exaggerating the reach of our First Amendment precedents.

Because Congress could require law schools to provide equal access to military recruiters without violating the schools' freedoms of speech or association, the Court of Appeals erred in holding that the Solomon Amendment likely violates the First Amendment. We therefore reverse the judgment of the Third Circuit and remand the case for further proceedings consistent with this opinion. It is so ordered.

JUSTICE ALITO took no part in the consideration or decision of this case.

NOTE

Nor does the First Amendment offer much of a safe haven for public employees to exercise their free speech rights on the job. Consider *Garcetti v. Ceballos*, ___ U.S. ___, 126 S.Ct. 1951 (2006), in which the Supreme Court by a narrow 5–4 majority held that the First Amendment did not protect a deputy district attorney from reprisals after he testified for the defense about a memo he wrote alleging government misrepresentations in the attainment of a warrant. According to the Court, when public employees make statements pursuant to their official duties, the Constitution does not safeguard their communications from employer discipline. Writing for the Court, Justice Kennedy was joined by Chief Justice Roberts, and Justices Scalia, Thomas and Alito.

IV. HECKLERS—HECKLER'S VETO AND THE CONSTITUTIONAL RIGHT TO HECKLE

FEINER v. NEW YORK

Supreme Court of the United States, 1951.
340 U.S. 315, 71 S.Ct. 303, 95 L.Ed. 295.

CHIEF JUSTICE VINSON delivered the opinion of the Court.

. . .

On the evening of March 8, 1949, petitioner Irving Feiner was addressing an open-air meeting at the corner of South McBride and Harrison Streets in the City of Syracuse. At approximately 6:30 p.m., the police received a telephone complaint concerning the meeting, and two officers were detailed to investigate. One of these officers went to the scene immediately, the other arriving some twelve minutes later. They found a crowd of about seventy-five or eighty people, both Negro and white, filling the sidewalk and spreading out into the street. Petitioner, standing on a large wooden box on the sidewalk, was addressing the crowd through a loud-speaker system attached to an automobile. Although the purpose of his speech was to urge his listeners to attend a meeting to be held that night in the Syracuse Hotel, in its course he was making derogatory remarks concerning President Truman, the American Legion, the Mayor of Syracuse, and other local political officials.

The police officers made no effort to interfere with petitioner's speech, but were first concerned with the effect of the crowd on both pedestrian and vehicular traffic. They observed the situation from the opposite side of the street, noting that some pedestrians were forced to walk in the street to avoid the crowd. Since traffic was passing at the time, the officers attempted to get the people listening to petitioner back on the sidewalk. The crowd was restless and there was some pushing, shoving and milling around. One of the officers telephoned the police station from a nearby store, and then both policemen crossed the street and mingled with the crowd without any intention of arresting the speaker.

At this time, petitioner was speaking in a "loud, high-pitched voice." He gave the impression that he was endeavoring to arouse the Negro people against the whites, urging that they rise up in arms and fight for equal rights. The statements before such a mixed audience "stirred up a little excitement." Some of the onlookers made remarks to the police about their inability to handle the crowd and at least one threatened violence if the police did not act. There were others who appeared to be favoring petitioner's arguments. Because of the feeling that existed in the crowd both for and against the speaker, the officers finally "stepped in to prevent it from resulting in a fight." One of the officers approached the petitioner, not for the purpose of arresting him, but to get him to break up the crowd. He asked petitioner to get down off the box, but the latter refused to accede to his request and continued talking. The officer waited for a minute and then demanded that he cease talking. Although the officer had thus twice requested petitioner to stop over the course of several minutes, petitioner not only ignored him but continued talking. During all this time, the crowd was pressing closer around petitioner and the officer. Finally, the officer told petitioner he was under arrest and ordered him to get down from the box, reaching up to grab him. Petitioner stepped down, announcing over the microphone that "the law has arrived, and I suppose they will take over now." In all, the officer had asked petitioner to get down off the box three times over a space of four or five minutes. Petitioner had been speaking for over a half hour.

On these facts, petitioner was specifically charged with ["refus[ing] to move on when ordered by the police;...."] ... The bill of particulars, demanded by petitioner and furnished by the State, gave in detail the facts upon which the prosecution relied to support the charge of disorderly conduct. Paragraph C is particularly pertinent here: "By ignoring and refusing to heed and obey reasonable police orders issued at the time and place mentioned in the Information to regulate and control said crowd and to prevent a breach or breaches of the peace and to prevent injury to pedestrians attempting to use said walk, and being forced into the highway adjacent to the place in question, and prevent injury to the public generally."

We are not faced here with blind condonation by a state court of arbitrary police action. Petitioner was accorded a full, fair trial. The trial judge heard testimony supporting and contradicting the judgment of the police officers that a clear danger of disorder was threatened. After weighing this contradictory evidence, the trial judge reached the conclusion that the police officers were justified in taking action to prevent a breach of the peace. The exercise of the police officers' proper discretionary power to prevent a breach of the peace was thus approved by the trial court and later by two courts on review. The courts below recognized petitioner's right to hold a street meeting at this locality, to make use of loud-speaking equipment in giving his speech, and to make derogatory remarks concerning public officials and the American Legion. They found that the officers in making the arrest were motivated solely by a proper concern for the preservation of order and protection of the general welfare, and that there was no evidence which could lend color to a claim that the acts of the police were a cover for suppression of petitioner's views and opinions. Petitioner was thus neither arrested nor convicted for the making or the content of his speech. Rather, it was the reaction which it actually engendered.

We are well aware that the ordinary murmurings and objections of a hostile audience cannot be allowed to silence a speaker, and are also mindful of the possible danger of giving overzealous police officials complete discretion to break up otherwise lawful public meetings. "A State may not unduly suppress free communication of views, religious or other, under the guise of conserving desirable conditions." But we are not faced here with such a situation. It is one thing to say that the police cannot be used as an instrument for the suppression of unpopular views, and another to say that, when as here the speaker passes the bounds of argument or persuasion and undertakes incitement to riot, they are powerless to prevent a breach of the peace. Nor in this case can we condemn the considered judgment of three New York courts approving the means which the police, faced with a crisis, used in the exercise of their power and duty to preserve peace and order. The findings of the state courts as to the existing situation and the imminence of greater disorder coupled with petitioner's deliberate defiance of the police officers convince us that we should not reverse this conviction in the name of free speech.

Affirmed.

[A concurring opinion of Justice Frankfurter is omitted.]

Justice Black, dissenting.

The record before us convinces me that petitioner, a young college student, has been sentenced to the penitentiary for the unpopular views he expressed on matters of public interest while lawfully making a street-corner speech in Syracuse, New York. . . .

. . . Even accepting every "finding of fact" below, I think this conviction makes a mockery of the free speech guarantees of the First and Fourteenth Amendments. The end result of the affirmance here is to approve a simple and readily available technique by which cities and states can with impunity subject all speeches, political or otherwise, on streets or elsewhere, to the supervision and censorship of the local police. I will have no part or parcel in this holding which I view as a long step toward totalitarian authority.

. . . Both officers swore they did not intend to make an arrest when they started, and the trial court accepted their statements. They also said, and the court believed, that they heard and saw "angry mutterings," "pushing," "shoving and milling around" and "restlessness." Petitioner spoke in a "loud, high pitched voice." He said that colored people "don't have equal rights and they should rise up *in arms* and fight for them." One man who heard this told the officers that if they did not take that "S . . . O . . . B . . ." off the box, he would. The officers then approached petitioner for the first time. One of them first "asked" petitioner to get off the box, but petitioner continued urging his audience to attend Rogge's speech. The officer next "told" petitioner to get down, but he did not. The officer finally "demanded" that petitioner get down, telling him he was under arrest. Petitioner then told the crowd that "the law had arrived and would take over" and asked why he was arrested. The officer first replied that the charge was "unlawful assembly" but later changed the ground to "disorderly conduct."

The Court's opinion apparently rests on this reasoning: The police-man, under the circumstances detailed, could reasonably conclude that serious fighting or even riot was imminent; therefore he could stop petitioner's speech to prevent a breach of peace; accordingly, it was "disorderly conduct" for petitioner to continue speaking in disobedience of the officer's request. As to the existence of a dangerous situation on the street corner, it seems far-fetched to suggest that the "facts" show any imminent threat of riot or uncontrollable disorder. It is neither unusual nor unexpected that some people at public street meetings mutter, mill about, push, shove, or disagree, even violently, with the speaker. Indeed, it is rare where controversial topics are discussed that an outdoor crowd does not do some or all of these things. Nor does one isolated threat to assault the speaker forebode disorder. Especially should the danger be discounted where, as here, the person threatening was a man whose wife and two small children accompanied him and who, so far as the record shows, was never close enough to petitioner to carry out the threat.

Moreover, assuming that the "facts" did indicate a critical situation, I reject the implication of the Court's opinion that the police had no obligation to protect petitioner's constitutional right to talk. The police of course have power to prevent breaches of the peace. But if, in the name of preserving order, they ever can interfere with a lawful public speaker, they first must make all reasonable efforts to protect him. Here the policemen did not even pretend to try to protect petitioner. Accord-ing to the officers' testimony, the crowd was restless but there is no showing of any attempt to quiet it; pedestrians were forced to walk into the street, but there was no effort to clear a path on the sidewalk; one person threatened to assault petitioner but the officer did nothing to discourage this when even a word might have sufficed. Their duty was to protect petitioner's right to talk, even to the extent of arresting the man who threatened to interfere. Instead, they shirked that duty and acted only to suppress the right to speak.

Finally, I cannot agree with the Court's statement that petitioner's disregard of the policeman's unexplained request amounted to such "deliberate defiance" as would justify an arrest or conviction for disor-derly conduct. On the contrary, I think that the policeman's action was a "deliberate defiance" of ordinary official duty as well as of the constitu-tional right of free speech. For at least where time allows, courtesy and explanation of commands are basic elements of good official conduct in a democratic society. Here petitioner was "asked" then "told" then "com-manded" to stop speaking, but a man making a lawful address is certainly not required to be silent merely because an officer directs it. Petitioner was entitled to know why he should cease doing a lawful act. Not once was he told. I understand that people in authoritarian coun-tries must obey arbitrary orders. I had hoped that there was no such duty in the United States.

In my judgment, today's holding means that as a practical matter, minority speakers can be silenced in any city. Hereafter, despite the First and Fourteenth Amendments, the policeman's club can take heavy toll of a current administration's public critics. Criticism of public officials will be too dangerous for all but the most courageous....

. . .

JUSTICE DOUGLAS, with whom JUSTICE MINTON concurs, dissenting.

. . .

Public assemblies and public speech occupy an important role in American life. One high function of the police is to protect these lawful gatherings so that the speakers may exercise their constitutional rights. When unpopular causes are sponsored from the public platform, there will commonly be mutterings and unrest and heckling from the crowd. When a speaker mounts a platform it is not unusual to find him resorting to exaggeration, to vilification of ideas and men, to the making of false charges. But those extravagances, ... do not justify penalizing the speaker by depriving him of the platform or by punishing him for his conduct.

A speaker may not, of course, incite a riot any more than he may incite a breach of the peace by the use of "fighting words." But this record shows no such extremes. It shows an unsympathetic audience and the threat of one man to haul the speaker from the stage. It is against that kind of threat that speakers need police protection. If they do not receive it and instead the police throw their weight on the side of those who would break up the meetings, the police become the new censors of speech. Police censorship has all the vices of the censorship from city halls which we have repeatedly struck down.

THE FEINER CONFERENCE

Justice Douglas took the following notes in the Feiner conference:[1]

CJ—need not wait until explosion took place—simple breach of the peace case—police may have been wrong—but jury convicted him—speaker has the right to be protected whether he overstepped—affirms.

Black—reverses.

Reed—affirms.

FF—affirms—this is a unanimous decision of NY court—did peace officer have entertainable grounds for believing that if he does not arrest the man all hell could break loose?

RHJ—affirms—he may change his vote in *Kunz* if this case is written in the right way.

HB—not trying the cop—goal for cop is peace—speaker was going too far until law stopped him.

---

1. Douglas Papers, Library of Congress, Box 203.

TC—one man can cause trouble to start a riot—cop was patient—he affirms.

SM—reverses—cop can't tell a speaker when to quit when he is making a speech in the place he lawfully is present.

Justice Jackson's conference notes for *Feiner* show Chief Justice Vinson saying that Feiner was in a place where he had a right to be, but he had committed a "[b]reach of the peace in presence of [an] officer," and Justice Douglas as saying that the officer "[a]rrested [the] wrong fellow."[2]

JUSTICE JACKSON ON HECKLERS AND THE PUBLIC FORUM

In Kunz v. New York, 340 U.S. 290 (1951)—decided the same day as *Feiner*—the Court reversed the conviction of a Baptist preacher who had held a public worship meeting without obtaining a permit from the Police Commissioner, as required by a New York City ordinance. Earlier Kunz's meetings had brought "a flood of complaints" to the city authorities because of his scurrilous attacks on Catholics and Jews, and, as a result, the Commissioner revoked his permit and refused to approve his application for a new permit. The Court held that the New York permit requirement was an unconstitutional prior restraint on speech. Dissenting, Justice Jackson wrote (340 U.S. at 311–312):

> The purpose of the Court is to enable those who feel a call to proselytize to do so by street meetings. The means is to set up a private right to speak in the city streets without asking permission. Of course, if Kunz may speak without a permit, so may anyone else. If he may speak whenever and wherever he may elect, I know of no way in which the City can silence the heckler, the interrupter, the dissenter, the rivals with missionary fervor, who have an equal right at the same time and place to lift their voices. And, of course, if the City may not stop Kunz from uttering insulting and "fighting" words, neither can it stop his adversaries and the discussion degenerates to a name-calling contest without social value and, human nature being what it is, to a fight or perhaps a riot. The end of the Court's method is chaos.

> But if the Court conceives, as *Feiner* indicates, that upon uttering insulting, provocative or inciting words the policeman on the beat may stop the meeting, then its assurance of free speech in this decision is "a promise to the ear to be broken to the hope," if the patrolman on the beat happens to have prejudices of his own.

An earlier version of Justice Jackson's dissenting opinion applying both to *Kunz* and *Feiner* sets forth in more detail his views on the public forum, as well as his reasons for upholding Feiner's conviction. In that unpublished opinion, he wrote:[3]

2. Jackson Papers, Library of Congress, Box 167.
3. Ibid.

These cases, we must bear in mind, relate only to street meetings, and not to meetings held on private property. The different relations of these to public peace and order places them in separate categories. The audience attends voluntarily at a meeting on private property. Generally, it is attracted to attend by sympathy with the speaker, but if one finds himself insulted it is something that he has more or less brought on his own head. But those who go into the highways and byways, with loudspeakers or high-pitched voice, assail the ears of what in a sense is a captive audience. The speaker, to impose his message upon them, takes advantage of their presence on the streets where their rights are quite as great as his. Persons of all colors, races, religion, shades of opinion, degrees of education and national origin, are subjected to this uninvited verbal aggression, merely because they go upon the streets and not infrequently resent the impertinence of it even apart from the sentiments expressed. There is thus a world of difference between the relations of the two types of meeting to the public peace and order. It is at this type of street meeting that the minority clearly declares the city must not only tolerate, but, in effect, sponsor the language of these speakers. The first question before us is whether the Constitution protects this kind of language in the environment of the street meeting.

If there are any words or ideas so inherently anti-social that, independently of the reactions they cause, their serious public utterance is beyond constitutional protection, language which advises, incites or encourages the commission of a crime must be such. If for acting out his exhortation men may be jailed, it does not seem to me that the constitution protects the instigator. Feiner's statement to colored people in a colored neighborhood that the colored should rise up in arms and fight is a literal invitation to violence. Apologists for him may read it as "theoretical" or say that it shows no "extremes." Perhaps so in the scale of values that prevail in some quarters, but to me it was "rhetoric" of naked incitement to violence. I cannot believe that such lawless discourse ever enjoys constitutional protection.

NOTES AND QUESTIONS

1. Note the different versions of the facts in the *Feiner* majority and dissenting opinions. Justice Frankfurter relied on the New York trial judge's findings of fact and indirectly questioned the dissenters' reexamination of the facts. "A state court," Justice Frankfurter wrote, "cannot of course preclude review of due process questions merely by phrasing its opinion in terms of an ultimate standard which in itself satisfies due process. But this Court should not re-examine determinations of the State courts on those matters which are usually termed issues of fact. And it should not overturn a fair appraisal of facts made by State courts in the light of their knowledge of local conditions." (340 U.S. at 289) What apparently troubled the dissenters were statements by

the trial judge, which were part of the record. The following excerpts illustrate those statements:[4]

> He [referring to Rabbi Friedman, whose address on free speech the trial judge approved] maintains that people who advocate change by violence, and who divide a nation to conquer, and pit man against man, and class against class, and race against race, and color against color, and religion against religion, should be denied the right of freedom of speech.... I think that is a good, sound, sensible philosophy. I think our citizens should be permitted to exercise those liberties Rabbi Friedman spoke about; the freedom of speech and the numerous other freedoms you have heard a good deal about, subject however, to some regard for the rights of others; subject to other people's convenience; subject to the people's wishes. (R. 272–3)

> The Officers say, and they so testified, that they stood there during this period of time on the opposite side of the street, and they heard you call Mayor Costello, and Mayor O'Dwyer and President Truman the names you heard testified to.

> Now it is conceded by your Counsel, that that might be considered bad taste; that might be disrespectful, even though, so far as the exercise of that particular right is concerned, to call people names, we will assume you had a right to do it. I don't think that was the sensible or the proper or the decent way in which a good citizen should operate. Of course that is disputed by you, but I am inclined to go along with the Officers, because what they say is in so many respects so close to what your witnesses have testified to that I am impressed by that fact. (R. 275–7)

> The Officers acted on these appeals at the last stage, after hearing you stress the inequalities and the unfair things you claim you were disturbed about. They then heard you appeal to these people to stand up, and in arms or with arms, and to fight.

> Now, under these circumstances I think the officers were fully justified in feeling that a situation was developing which could very, very easily result in serious disorder. I think the officers were very patient up to that time. I think that on the basis of the evidence here that you deliberately agitated and that in every way that you could, you goaded these officers to action. They were right there on the opposite side of the street; you knew they were there.... And you kept right on talking about racial inequalities, with this muttering; this angry muttering, which according to the Officers, made them feel that a situation was developing and which, they finally decided called for some action. (R. 278–9)

> I have just as much respect for you as for anyone else, but I haven't much respect for the philosophy you endorse or for the remarks you made on that night in question. I think that talk of

---

4. Quoted in certiorari memo, Douglas Papers, Library of Congress, Box 203.

yours was designed to do the very things that Rabbi Friedman has spoken about: to line up class against class and race against race, and that philosophy of yours will never prevail in this country. (R. 281)

2.   Justice Jackson justified his vote to affirm Feiner's conviction on the fighting-words and clear and present danger doctrines. Were Feiner's statements "fighting words"? Did they create a clear and present danger? If so, what was the danger? Who was in danger?

3.   Justice Jackson suggested that speech is entitled to more constitutional protection in the private forum than in the public forum? Do you agree?

4.   Justice Jackson suggested that licensing public gatherings is an appropriate way to deal with the heckler problem. Do you agree? What constitutional rights do hecklers have?

5.   Suppose a member of the American Nazi party steps in front of a synagogue, as a crowd is leaving at the end of religious services. He puts on a swastika armband, and begins to praise Hitler's extermination of Jews. As cries of rage come from the crowd, the speaker's voice becomes louder and his anti-Semitic remarks become more pointed. Finally, the crowd begins to surge forward and violence erupts. The lone policeman on the scene restores order by dragging the protesting speaker away and placing him in his squad car. Have the speaker's constitutional rights been violated? Could he be punished, constitutionally, for breach of the peace?

Chapter VII

THE PRIVATE FORUM

I. ACCESS TO PRIVATE PROPERTY

WATCHTOWER BIBLE AND TRACT SOCIETY OF NEW YORK v. VILLAGE OF STRATTON

536 U.S. 150, 122 S.Ct. 2080, 153 L.Ed.2d 205 (2002).

Justice Stevens delivered the opinion of the Court.

Petitioners contend that a village ordinance making it a misdemeanor to engage in door-to-door advocacy without first registering with the mayor and receiving a permit violates the First Amendment. Through this facial challenge, we consider the door-to-door canvassing regulation not only as it applies to religious proselytizing, but also to anonymous political speech and the distribution of handbills.

I

Petitioner Watchtower Bible and Tract Society of New York, Inc., coordinates the preaching activities of Jehovah's Witnesses throughout the United States and publishes Bibles and religious periodicals that are widely distributed. Petitioner Wellsville, Ohio, Congregation of Jehovah's Witnesses, Inc., supervises the activities of approximately 59 members in a part of Ohio that includes the Village of Stratton (Village). Petitioners offer religious literature without cost to anyone interested in reading it. They allege that they do not solicit contributions or orders for the sale of merchandise or services, but they do accept donations.

Petitioners brought this action against the Village and its mayor in the United States District Court for the Southern District of Ohio, seeking an injunction against the enforcement of several sections of Ordinance No. 1998–5 regulating uninvited peddling and solicitation on private property in the Village. Petitioners' complaint alleged that the ordinance violated several constitutional rights, including the free exercise of religion, free speech, and the freedom of the press. The District Court conducted a bench trial at which evidence of the administration of the ordinance and its effect on petitioners was introduced.

Section 116.01 prohibits "canvassers" and others from "going in and upon" private residential property for the purpose of promoting any "cause" without first having obtained a permit pursuant to § 116.03. That section provides that any canvasser who intends to go on private property to promote a cause, must obtain a "Solicitation Permit" from the office of the mayor; there is no charge for the permit, and apparently one is issued routinely after an applicant fills out a fairly detailed

"Solicitor's Registration Form." The canvasser is then authorized to go upon premises that he listed on the registration form, but he must carry the permit upon his person and exhibit it whenever requested to do so by a police officer or by a resident. The ordinance sets forth grounds for the denial or revocation of a permit, but the record before us does not show that any application has been denied or that any permit has been revoked. Petitioners did not apply for a permit.

A section of the ordinance that petitioners do not challenge establishes a procedure by which a resident may prohibit solicitation even by holders of permits. If the resident files a "No Solicitation Registration Form" with the mayor, and also posts a "No Solicitation" sign on his property, no uninvited canvassers may enter his property, unless they are specifically authorized to do so in the "No Solicitation Registration Form" itself. Only 32 of the Village's 278 residents filed such forms. Each of the forms in the record contains a list of 19 suggested exceptions; on one form, a resident checked 17 exceptions, thereby excluding only "Jehovah's Witnesses" and "Political Candidates" from the list of invited canvassers. Although Jehovah's Witnesses do not consider themselves to be "solicitors" because they make no charge for their literature or their teaching, leaders of the church testified at trial that they would honor "no solicitation" signs in the Village. They also explained at trial that they did not apply for a permit because they derive their authority to preach from Scripture. "For us to seek a permit from a municipality to preach we feel would almost be an insult to God."

Petitioners introduced some evidence that the ordinance was the product of the mayor's hostility to their ministry, but the District Court credited the mayor's testimony that it had been designed to protect the privacy rights of the Village residents, specifically to protect them "from 'flim flam' con artists who prey on small town populations." Nevertheless, the court concluded that the terms of the ordinance applied to the activities of petitioners as well as to "business or political canvassers."

The District Court ... held the ordinance constitutionally valid as applied to petitioners and dismissed the case.

The Court of Appeals for the Sixth Circuit affirmed....

. . .

We granted certiorari to decide the following question: "Does a municipal ordinance that requires one to obtain a permit prior to engaging in the door-to-door advocacy of a political cause and to display upon demand the permit, which contains one's name, violate the First Amendment protection accorded to anonymous pamphleteering or discourse?"

II

For over 50 years, the Court has invalidated restrictions on door-to-door canvassing and pamphleteering. It is more than historical accident that most of these cases involved First Amendment challenges brought by Jehovah's Witnesses, because door-to-door canvassing is mandated by their religion. As we noted in *Murdock v. Pennsylvania*, 319 U.S. 105,

108 (1943), the Jehovah's Witnesses "claim to follow the example of Paul, teaching 'publicly, and from house to house.' ... In doing so they believe that they are obeying a commandment of God." ...

Although our past cases involving Jehovah's Witnesses, most of which were decided shortly before and during World War II, do not directly control the question we confront today, they provide both a historical and analytical backdrop for consideration of petitioners' First Amendment claim that the breadth of the Village's ordinance offends the First Amendment. Those cases involved petty offenses that raised constitutional questions of the most serious magnitude—questions that implicated the free exercise of religion, the freedom of speech, and the freedom of the press. From these decisions, several themes emerge that guide our consideration of the ordinance at issue here.

First, the cases emphasize the value of the speech involved. For example, in *Murdock v. Pennsylvania*, the Court noted that "hand distribution of religious tracts is an age-old form of missionary evangelism—as old as the history of printing presses.... It has the same claim to protection as the more orthodox and conventional exercises of religion. It also has the same claim as the others to the guarantees of freedom of speech and freedom of the press." ...

In addition, the cases discuss extensively the historical importance of door-to-door canvassing and pamphleteering as vehicles for the dissemination of ideas. In *Schneider v. State (Town of Irvington)*, 308 U.S. 147 (1939), the petitioner was a Jehovah's Witness who had been convicted of canvassing without a permit based on evidence that she had gone from house to house offering to leave books or booklets. Writing for the Court, Justice Roberts stated that "pamphlets have proved most effective instruments in the dissemination of opinion.... To require a censorship through license which makes impossible the *free and unhampered* distribution of pamphlets strikes at the very heart of the constitutional guarantees." ...

Despite the emphasis on the important role that door-to-door canvassing and pamphleteering has played in our constitutional tradition of free and open discussion, these early cases also recognized the interests a town may have in some form of regulation, particularly when the solicitation of money is involved. In *Cantwell v. Connecticut*, 310 U.S. 296 (1940), the Court held that an ordinance requiring Jehovah's Witnesses to obtain a license before soliciting door to door was invalid because the issuance of the license depended on the exercise of discretion by a city official. Our opinion recognized that "a State may protect its citizens from fraudulent solicitation by requiring a stranger in the community, before permitting him publicly to solicit funds for any purpose, to establish his identity and his authority to act for the cause which he purports to represent." *Id.*, at 306. Similarly, in Martin v. City of Struthers, the Court recognized crime prevention as a legitimate interest served by these ordinances and noted that "burglars frequently pose as canvassers, either in order that they may have a pretense to discover whether a house is empty and hence ripe for burglary, or for the purpose of spying out the premises in order that they may return later."

319 U.S., at 144. Despite recognition of these interests as legitimate, our precedent is clear that there must be a balance between these interests and the effect of the regulations on First Amendment rights. . . .

Finally, the cases demonstrate that efforts of the Jehovah's Witnesses to resist speech regulation have not been a struggle for their rights alone. In *Martin*, after cataloging the many groups that rely extensively upon this method of communication, the Court summarized that "[d]oor to door distribution of circulars is essential to the poorly financed causes of little people." 319 U.S., at 144–146.

That the Jehovah's Witnesses are not the only "little people" who face the risk of silencing by regulations like the Village's is exemplified by our cases involving nonreligious speech. . . . In *Thomas* [v. Collins, 323 U.S. 516 (1945)], the issue was whether a labor leader could be required to obtain a permit before delivering a speech to prospective union members. After reviewing the Jehovah's Witnesses cases discussed above, the Court observed:

"As a matter of principle a requirement of registration in order to make a public speech would seem generally incompatible with an exercise of the rights of free speech and free assembly. . . .

. . .

"If the exercise of the rights of free speech and free assembly cannot be made a crime, we do not think this can be accomplished by the device of requiring previous registration as a condition for exercising them and making such a condition the foundation for restraining in advance their exercise and for imposing a penalty for violating such a restraining order. So long as no more is involved than exercise of the rights of free speech and free assembly, it is immune to such a restriction. If one who solicits support for the cause of labor may be required to register as a condition to the exercise of his right to make a public speech, so may he who seeks to rally support for any social, business, religious or political cause. We think a requirement that one must register before he undertakes to make a public speech to enlist support for a lawful movement is quite incompatible with the requirements of the First Amendment." *Id.*, at 539–540.

Although these World War II-era cases provide guidance for our consideration of the question presented, they do not answer one preliminary issue that the parties adamantly dispute. That is, what standard of review ought we use in assessing the constitutionality of this ordinance. We find it unnecessary, however, to resolve that dispute because the breadth of speech affected by the ordinance and the nature of the regulation make it clear that the Court of Appeals erred in upholding it.

III

The Village argues that three interests are served by its ordinance: the prevention of fraud, the prevention of crime, and the protection of residents' privacy. We have no difficulty concluding, in light of our precedent, that these are important interests that the Village may seek to safeguard through some form of regulation of solicitation activity. We must also look, however, to the amount of speech covered by the ordinance and whether there is an appropriate balance between the affected speech and the governmental interests that the ordinance purports to serve.

The text of the Village's ordinance prohibits "canvassers" from going on private property for the purpose of explaining or promoting any "cause," unless they receive a permit and the residents visited have not opted for a "no solicitation" sign. Had this provision been construed to apply only to commercial activities and the solicitation of funds, arguably the ordinance would have been tailored to the Village's interest in protecting the privacy of its residents and preventing fraud. Yet, even though the Village has explained that the ordinance was adopted to serve those interests, it has never contended that it should be so narrowly interpreted. To the contrary, the Village's administration of its ordinance unquestionably demonstrates that the provisions apply to a significant number of noncommercial "canvassers" promoting a wide variety of "causes." Indeed, on the "No Solicitation Forms" provided to the residents, the canvassers include "Camp Fire Girls," "Jehovah's Witnesses," "Political Candidates," "Trick or Treaters during Halloween Season," and "Persons Affiliated with Stratton Church." The ordinance unquestionably applies, not only to religious causes, but to political activity as well. It would seem to extend to "residents casually soliciting the votes of neighbors," or ringing doorbells to enlist support for employing a more efficient garbage collector.

The mere fact that the ordinance covers so much speech raises constitutional concerns. It is offensive—not only to the values protected by the First Amendment, but to the very notion of a free society—that in the context of everyday public discourse a citizen must first inform the government of her desire to speak to her neighbors and then obtain a permit to do so. Even if the issuance of permits by the mayor's office is a ministerial task that is performed promptly and at no cost to the applicant, a law requiring a permit to engage in such speech constitutes a dramatic departure from our national heritage and constitutional tradition. Three obvious examples illustrate the pernicious effect of such a permit requirement.

First, as our cases involving distribution of unsigned handbills demonstrate, there are a significant number of persons who support causes anonymously.[1] ... The Court of Appeals erred in concluding that the ordinance does not implicate anonymity interests.... The badge requirement that we invalidated in *Buckley* [v. American Constitutional Law Foundation, Inc., 525 U.S. 182 (1999)] applied to petition circulators seeking signatures in face-to-face interactions.... In the Village, strangers to the resident certainly maintain their anonymity, and the ordi-

---

1. Although the Jehovah's Witnesses do not themselves object to a loss of anonymity, they bring this facial challenge in part on the basis of overbreadth. We may, therefore, consider the impact of this ordinance on the free speech rights of individuals who are deterred from speaking because the registration provision would require them to forgo their right to speak anonymously....

nance may preclude such persons from canvassing for unpopular causes. Such preclusion may well be justified in some situations—for example, by the special state interest in protecting the integrity of a ballot-initiative process, see *ibid.*, or by the interest in preventing fraudulent commercial transactions. The Village ordinance, however, sweeps more broadly, covering unpopular causes unrelated to commercial transactions or to any special interest in protecting the electoral process.

Second, requiring a permit as a prior condition on the exercise of the right to speak imposes an objective burden on some speech of citizens holding religious or patriotic views. As our World War II-era cases dramatically demonstrate, there are a significant number of persons whose religious scruples will prevent them from applying for such a license. There are no doubt other patriotic citizens, who have such firm convictions about their constitutional right to engage in uninhibited debate in the context of door-to-door advocacy, that they would prefer silence to speech licensed by a petty official.

Third, there is a significant amount of spontaneous speech that is effectively banned by the ordinance. A person who made a decision on a holiday or a weekend to take an active part in a political campaign could not begin to pass out handbills until after he or she obtained the required permit. Even a spontaneous decision to go across the street and urge a neighbor to vote against the mayor could not lawfully be implemented without first obtaining the mayor's permission. . . .

The breadth and unprecedented nature of this regulation does not alone render the ordinance invalid. . . . [I]t is not tailored to the Village's stated interests. Even if the interest in preventing fraud could adequately support the ordinance insofar as it applies to commercial transactions and the solicitation of funds, that interest provides no support for its application to petitioners, to political campaigns, or to enlisting support for unpopular causes. The Village, however, argues that the ordinance is nonetheless valid because it serves the two additional interests of protecting the privacy of the resident and the prevention of crime.

With respect to the former, it seems clear that § 107 of the ordinance, which provides for the posting of "No Solicitation" signs and which is not challenged in this case, coupled with the resident's unquestioned right to refuse to engage in conversation with unwelcome visitors, provides ample protection for the unwilling listener. *Schaumburg*, 444 U.S., at 639 ("[T]he provision permitting homeowners to bar solicitors from their property by posting [no solicitation] signs . . . suggest[s] the availability of less intrusive and more effective measures to protect privacy"). The annoyance caused by an uninvited knock on the front door is the same whether or not the visitor is armed with a permit.

With respect to the latter, it seems unlikely that the absence of a permit would preclude criminals from knocking on doors and engaging in conversations not covered by the ordinance. They might, for example, ask for directions or permission to use the telephone, or pose as surveyers or census takers. Or they might register under a false name with impunity because the ordinance contains no provision for verifying an applicant's identity or organizational credentials. Moreover, the Village did not assert an interest in crime prevention below, and there is an absence of any evidence of a special crime problem related to door-to-door solicitation in the record before us.

The rhetoric used in the World War II-era opinions that repeatedly saved petitioners' co-religionists from petty prosecutions reflected the Court's evaluation of the First Amendment freedoms that are implicated in this case. The value judgment that then motivated a united democratic people fighting to defend those very freedoms from totalitarian attack is unchanged. It motivates our decision today.

The judgment of the Court of Appeals is reversed, and the case is remanded for further proceedings consistent with this opinion.

It is so ordered.

JUSTICE BREYER, with whom JUSTICE SOUTER and JUSTICE GINSBURG join, concurring.

While joining the Court's opinion, I write separately to note that the dissent's "crime prevention" justification for this ordinance is not a strong one. For one thing, there is no indication that the legislative body that passed the ordinance considered this justification. . . .

. . . I can only conclude that if the village of Stratton thought preventing burglaries and violent crimes was an important justification for this ordinance, it would have said so.

· · ·

JUSTICE SCALIA, with whom JUSTICE THOMAS joins, concurring in the judgment.

I concur in the judgment, for many but not all of the reasons set forth in the opinion for the Court. I do not agree, for example, that one of the causes of the invalidity of Stratton's ordinance is that some people have a religious objection to applying for a permit . . .

· · ·

As for the Court's fairy-tale category of "patriotic citizens," who would rather be silenced than licensed in a manner that the Constitution (but for their "patriotic" objection) would permit: If our free-speech jurisprudence is to be determined by the predicted behavior of such crackpots, we are in a sorry state indeed.

CHIEF JUSTICE REHNQUIST, dissenting.

Stratton is a village of 278 people located along the Ohio River where the borders of Ohio, West Virginia, and Pennsylvania converge. It is strung out along a multilane highway connecting it with the cities of East Liverpool to the north and Steubenville and Weirton, West Virginia, to the south. One may doubt how much legal help a village of this size has available in drafting an ordinance such as the present one, but even if it had availed itself of a battery of constitutional lawyers, they would have been of little use in the town's effort. For the Court today ignores the cases on which those lawyers would have relied, and comes up with newly fashioned doctrine. . . .

More than half a century ago we recognized that canvassers, "whether selling pots or distributing leaflets, may lessen the peaceful enjoyment of a home," and that "burglars frequently pose as canvassers, either in order that they may have a pretense to discover whether a house is empty and hence ripe for burglary, or for the purpose of spying out the premises in order that they may return later." *Martin v. City of Struthers,* 319 U.S. 141, 144 (1943). These problems continue to be associated with door-to-door canvassing, as are even graver ones.

. . .

The town had little reason to suspect that the negligible burden of having to obtain a permit runs afoul of the First Amendment. For over 60 years, we have categorically stated that a permit requirement for door-to-door canvassers, which gives no discretion to the issuing authority, is constitutional. The District Court and Court of Appeals, relying on our cases, upheld the ordinance. The Court today, however, abruptly changes course and invalidates the ordinance.

. . . Our early decisions in this area expressly sanction a law that merely requires a canvasser to register. In *Cantwell v. Connecticut,* 310 U.S. 296, 306 (1940), we stated that "[w]ithout doubt a State may protect its citizens from fraudulent solicitation by requiring a stranger in the community, before permitting him publicly to solicit funds for any purpose, to establish his identity and his authority to act for the cause which he purports to represent." In *Murdock v. Pennsylvania,* 319 U.S. 105, 116 (1943), we contrasted the license tax struck down in that case with "merely a registration ordinance calling for an identification of the solicitors so as to give the authorities some basis for investigating strangers coming into the community." And *Martin, supra,* at 148, states that a "city can punish those who call at a home in defiance of the previously expressed will of the occupant and, in addition, can by identification devices control the abuse of the privilege by criminals posing as canvassers."

It is telling that Justices Douglas and Black, perhaps the two Justices in this Court's history most identified with an expansive view of the First Amendment, authored, respectively, *Murdock* and *Martin.* Their belief in the constitutionality of the permit requirement that the Court strikes down today demonstrates just how far the Court's present jurisprudence has strayed from the core concerns of the First Amendment.

. . .

The Stratton ordinance suffers from none of the defects deemed fatal in these earlier decisions. The ordinance does not prohibit door-to-door canvassing; it merely requires that canvassers fill out a form and receive a permit. Cf. *Martin, supra.* The mayor does not exercise any discretion in deciding who receives a permit; approval of the permit is automatic upon proper completion of the form. Cf. *Cantwell, supra.* And petitioners do not contend in this Court that the ordinance is vague. . . .

Just as troubling . . . is the difficulty of discerning from the Court's opinion what exactly it is about the Stratton ordinance that renders it unconstitutional. It is not clear what test the Court is applying, or under which part of that indeterminate test the ordinance fails.... Under a straightforward application of the applicable First Amendment framework, however, the ordinance easily passes muster.

There is no support in our case law for applying anything more stringent than intermediate scrutiny to the ordinance. The ordinance is content neutral and does not bar anyone from going door-to-door in Stratton. It merely regulates the manner in which one must canvass: A canvasser must first obtain a permit.... Earlier this Term, the Court reaffirmed that this test applies to content-neutral time, place, or manner restrictions on speech in public forums. See Thomas v. Chicago Park Dist., 534 U.S. 316 (2002).

... [I]t would be puzzling if regulations of speech taking place on *another citizen's* private property warranted greater scrutiny than regulations of speech taking place in public forums. Common sense and our precedent say just the opposite....

. . .

The next question is whether the ordinance serves the important interests of protecting privacy and preventing fraud and crime. With respect to the interest in protecting privacy, the Court concludes that "[t]he annoyance caused by an uninvited knock on the front door is the same whether or not the visitor is armed with a permit." True, but that misses the key point: the permit requirement results in fewer uninvited knocks. Those who have complied with the permit requirement are less likely to visit residences with no trespassing signs, as it is much easier for the authorities to track them down.

The Court also fails to grasp how the permit requirement serves Stratton's interest in preventing crime. We have approved of permit requirements for those engaging in protected First Amendment activity because of a common-sense recognition that their existence both deters and helps detect wrongdoing....

The ordinance prevents and detects serious crime by making it a crime not to register....

Of course, the Stratton ordinance does not guarantee that no canvasser will ever commit a burglary or violent crime.... In order to survive intermediate scrutiny, however, a law need not solve the crime problem, it need only further the interest in preventing crime. Some deterrence of serious criminal activity is more than enough to survive intermediate scrutiny.

. . .

... A discretionless permit requirement for canvassers does not violate the First Amendment. Today, the Court elevates its concern with what is, at most, a negligible burden on door-to-door communication above this established proposition. Ironically, however, today's decision may result in less of the door-to-door communication that the Court extols. As the Court recognizes, any homeowner may place a "No Solicitation" sign on his or her property, and it is a crime to violate that sign. In light of today's decision depriving Stratton residents of the degree of accountability and safety that the permit requirement provides, more and more residents may decide to place these signs in their yards and cut off door-to-door communication altogether.

PRUNEYARD SHOPPING CENTER v. ROBINS

Supreme Court of the United States, 1980.
447 U.S. 74, 100 S.Ct. 2035, 64 L.Ed.2d 741.

JUSTICE REHNQUIST delivered the opinion of the Court.

[T]he important federal constitutional questions ... presented ... are whether state constitutional provisions, which permit individuals to exercise free speech and petition rights on the property of a privately owned shopping center to which the public is invited, violate the shopping center owner's property rights under the Fifth and Fourteenth Amendments or his free speech rights under the First and Fourteenth Amendments.

I

Appellant PruneYard is a privately owned shopping center in the city of Campbell, Cal. It covers approximately 21 acres—five devoted to parking and 16 occupied by walkways, plazas, sidewalks, and buildings that contain more than 65 specialty shops, 10 restaurants, and a movie theater. The PruneYard is open to the public for the purpose of encouraging the patronizing of its commercial establishments. It has a policy not to permit any visitor or tenant to engage in any publicly expressive activity, including the circulation of petitions, that is not directly related to its commercial purposes. This policy has been strictly enforced in a nondiscriminatory fashion. The PruneYard is owned by appellant Fred Sahadi.

Appellees are high school students who sought to solicit support for their opposition to a United Nations resolution against "Zionism." On a Saturday afternoon they set up a card table in a corner of PruneYard's central courtyard. They distributed pamphlets and asked passersby to sign petitions, which were to be sent to the President and Members of Congress. Their activity was peaceful and orderly and so far as the record indicates was not objected to by PruneYard's patrons.

Soon after appellees had begun soliciting signatures, a security guard informed them that they would have to leave because their activity violated PruneYard regulations. The guard suggested that they move to the public sidewalk at the PruneYard's perimeter. Appellees immediately left the premises and later filed this lawsuit in the California Superior Court of Santa Clara County. They sought to enjoin appellants from denying them access to the PruneYard for the purpose of circulating their petitions.

· · ·

The California Supreme Court [held] that the California Constitution protects "speech and petitioning, reasonably exercised, in shopping centers even when the centers are privately owned." 23 Cal.3d 899, 910

(1979). It concluded that appellees are entitled to conduct their activity on PruneYard property....

. . .

IV

Appellants contend that a right to exclude others underlies the Fifth Amendment guarantee against the taking of property without just compensation and the Fourteenth Amendment guarantee against the deprivation of property without due process of law.

It is true that one of the essential sticks in the bundle of property rights is the right to exclude others. And here there has literally been a "taking" of that right to the extent that the California Supreme Court has interpreted the state constitution to entitle its citizens to exercise free expression and petition rights on shopping center property. But it is well-established that "not every destruction or injury to property by governmental action has been held to be a 'taking' in the constitutional sense." Rather, the determination whether a state law unlawfully infringes a land owner's property in violation of the Taking Clause requires an examination of whether the restriction on private property "forc[es] some people alone to bear public burdens which, in all fairness and justice, should be borne by the public as a whole." ...

Here the requirement that appellants permit appellees to exercise state-protected rights of free expression and petition on shopping center property clearly does not amount to an unconstitutional infringement of appellants' property rights under the Taking Clause. There is nothing to suggest that preventing appellants from prohibiting this sort of activity will unreasonably impair the value or use of their property as a shopping center....

. . .

There is also little merit to appellants' argument that they have been denied their property without due process of law. In Nebbia v. New York, 291 U.S. 502 (1934), this Court stated that

"[Neither] property rights nor contract rights are absolute;....
Equally fundamental with the private right is that of the public
to regulate it in the common interest...."

V

Appellants finally contend that a private property owner has a First Amendment right not to be forced by the State to use his property as a forum for the speech of others. They state that in Wooley v. Maynard, 430 U.S. 705 (1977), this Court concluded that a State may not constitutionally require an individual to participate in the dissemination of an ideological message by displaying it on his private property in a manner and for the express purpose that it be observed and read by the public. This rationale applies here, they argue, because the message of Wooley is that the State may not force an individual to display any message at all.

Wooley, however, was a case in which the government itself prescribed the message, required it to be displayed openly on appellee's personal property that was used "as part of his daily life," and refused to permit him to take any measures to cover up the motto even though the Court found that the display of the motto served no important state interest. Here, by contrast, there are a number of distinguishing factors. Most important, the shopping center by choice of its owner is not limited to the personal use of appellants. It is instead a business establishment that is open to the public to come and go as they please. The views expressed by members of the public in passing out pamphlets or seeking signatures for a petition thus will not likely be identified with those of the owner. Second, no specific message is dictated by the State to be displayed on appellants' property. There consequently is no danger of governmental discrimination for or against a particular message. Finally, as far as appears here appellants can expressly disavow any connection with the message by simply posting signs in the area where the speakers or handbillers stand. Such signs, for example, could disclaim any sponsorship of the message and could explain that the persons are communicating their own messages by virtue of state law.

Appellants also argue that their First Amendment rights have been infringed in light of West Virginia State Board of Education v. Barnette, 319 U.S. 624 (1943) and Miami Herald Publishing Co. v. Tornillo, 418 U.S. 241 (1974). *Barnette* is inapposite because it involved the compelled recitation of a message containing an affirmation of belief. This Court held such compulsion unconstitutional because it "require[d] the individual to communicate by word and sign his acceptance" of government dictated political ideas, whether or not he subscribed to them. 319 U.S., at 633. Appellants are not similarly being compelled to affirm their belief in any governmentally prescribed position or view, and they are free to publicly dissociate themselves from the views of the speakers or handbillers.

Tornillo struck down a Florida statute requiring a newspaper to publish a political candidate's reply to criticism previously published in that newspaper. It rests on the principle that the State cannot tell a newspaper what it must print. The Florida statute contravened this principle in that it "exact[ed] a penalty on the basis of the content of a newspaper." There also was a danger in *Tornillo* that the statute would "dampen the vigor and limit the variety of public debate" by deterring editors from publishing controversial political statements that might trigger the application of the statute. Thus, the statute was found to be an "intrusion into the function of editors." These concerns obviously are not present here.

We conclude that neither appellants' federally recognized property rights nor their First Amendment rights have been infringed by the California Supreme Court's decision recognizing a right of appellees to exercise state protected rights of expression and petition on appellants' property. The judgment of the Supreme Court of California is therefore

Affirmed.

. . .

Justice Powell, with whom Justice White joins, concurring in part and in the judgment.

Although I join the judgment, I do not agree with all of the reasoning in Part V of the Court's opinion....

. . .

I

... I agree that the owner of this shopping center has failed to establish a cognizable First Amendment claim in this case. But some of the language in the Court's opinion is unnecessarily and perhaps confusingly broad. In my view, state action that transforms privately owned property into a forum for the expression of the public's views could raise serious First Amendment questions.

The State may not compel a person to affirm a belief he does not hold....

As the Court observes, this case involves only a state-created right of limited access to a specialized type of property. But even when no particular message is mandated by the State, First Amendment interests are affected by state action that forces a property owner to admit third-party speakers. In many situations, a right of access is no less intrusive than speech compelled by the State itself. For example, a law requiring that a newspaper permit others to use its columns imposes an unacceptable burden upon the newspaper's First Amendment right to select material for publication.... As such, it is tantamount to compelled affirmation and, thus, presumptively unconstitutional.

.... If a state law mandated public access to the bulletin board of a freestanding store, hotel, office, or small shopping center, customers might well conclude that the messages reflect the view of the proprietor. The same would be true if the public were allowed to solicit or pamphleteer in the entrance area of a store or in the lobby of a private building. The property owner or proprietor would be faced with a choice: he either could permit his customers to receive a mistaken impression or he could disavow the messages. Should he take the first course, he effectively has been compelled to affirm someone else's belief. Should he choose the second, he has been forced to speak when he would prefer to remain silent. In short, he has lost control over his freedom to speak or not to speak on certain issues. The mere fact that he is free to dissociate himself from the views expressed on his property, cannot restore his "right to refrain from speaking at all."

A property owner also may be faced with speakers who wish to use his premises as a platform for views that he finds morally repugnant. Numerous examples come to mind. A minority-owned business confronted with leafleteers from the American Nazi Party or the Ku Klux Klan, a church-operated enterprise asked to host demonstrations in favor of abortion, or a union compelled to supply a forum to right-to-work advocates could be placed in an intolerable position if state law requires it to make its private property available to anyone who wishes to speak.

The strong emotions evoked by speech in such situations may virtually compel the proprietor to respond.

.   .   .

II

One easily can identify other circumstances in which a right of access to commercial property would burden the owner's First and Fourteenth Amendment right to refrain from speaking. But appellants have identified no such circumstance. Nor did appellants introduce evidence that would support a holding in their favor under either of the legal theories outlined above.

.   .   .

Appellants have not alleged that they object to the ideas contained in the appellees' petitions. Nor do they assert that some groups who reasonably might be expected to speak at the PruneYard will express views that are so objectionable as to require a response even when listeners will not mistake their source. The record contains no evidence concerning the numbers or types of interest groups that may seek access to this shopping center, and no testimony showing that the appellants strongly disagree with any of them.

Because appellants have not shown that the limited right of access held to be afforded by the California Constitution burdened their First and Fourteenth Amendment rights in the circumstances presented, I join the judgment of the Court. I do not interpret our decision today as a blanket approval for state efforts to transform privately owned commercial property into public forums. Any such state action would raise substantial federal constitutional questions not present in this case.

NOTES AND QUESTIONS

1. Notice carefully the issue that is *not* involved in the *PruneYard* case. Earlier Supreme Court cases had focused on the question of whether the First Amendment required private property owners to give the same access to their property as would be required if the government owned the property. The difficulty here is that the Constitution's guarantees of individual liberty place restrictions on actions by the government only and do not control the action of private parties. A complex body of law deals with the question of whether private parties are so interconnected with the government, or exercise government-like powers, that they become bound by the Constitution's limitations on government action. (See pp. 1027–1029, below.) The particular problem, here, is whether large shopping centers, although they are privately owned, should be treated as the functional equivalent of the more traditional business district where the streets and sidewalks are publicly owned.

The Supreme Court's first encounter with that problem came many years ago in Marsh v. Alabama, 326 U.S. 501 (1946). A Jehovah's Witness had been convicted of trespass for distributing religious literature in the "business block" of the town of Chickasaw, Alabama. Chickasaw was a company town, entirely owned by the Gulf Shipbuilding Co. Justice Black's opinion for the Court stated the issue as being whether "those people who live in or come to Chickasaw [can] be denied freedom of press and religion simply because a single company has legal title to all the town." Putting the issue that way, he answered it by deciding that the company's property interests did not control. Balancing property rights against the rights of the residents of the town to be informed, he concluded that Alabama could not permit the company to govern a community of citizens "so as to restrict their fundamental liberties."

More than twenty years later, the issue was whether the principle in the *Marsh* case applied when a single company owned a large shopping center, but did not own or manage the surrounding town. Amalgamated Food Employees Union v. Logan Valley Plaza, 391 U.S. 308 (1968). Labor pickets were ordered by a state court to cease picketing in the parking lot behind a supermarket. A majority of the Supreme Court held that the pickets had the same First Amendment rights to picket within the shopping center that they had on public streets. Justice Marshall's opinion for the Court stated: "We see no reason why access to a business district in a company town for the purpose of exercising First Amendment rights should be constitutionally required, while access for the same purpose to property functioning as a business district should be limited simply because the property surrounding the 'business district' is not under the same ownership." The core of his argument was: that picketing, leafletting and speaking on public streets in conventional shopping centers was an important avenue of communication; that population movements to the suburbs, accompanied by the advent of the modern privately owned shopping center, would close that avenue of communication; that the owners could not be permitted, simply because the property was private rather than public, to create "a *cordon sanitaire* of parking lots around their stores." Justice Black, one of three dissenters, vigorously opposed the extension of his own opinion in *Marsh*, arguing that a shopping center, no matter how large, simply was not a town. (Recall that his opinion in *Marsh* had emphasized the rights of the people who *lived* in Chickasaw.) "To hold that store owners are compelled by law to supply picketing areas for pickets to drive store customers away is to create a court-made law wholly disregarding the constitutional basis on which private ownership of property rests in this country."

The *Logan Valley* principle was to prove short lived. When the question arose again, only four years later in Lloyd Corp. v. Tanner, 407 U.S. 551 (1972), private property rights prevailed. (The Court's membership had changed, and only five of the Justices who had participated in the *Logan Valley* decision remained. Justice White, who had dissented, joined the four new Justices in the *Lloyd* majority. The four other Justices, who had been in the *Logan Valley* majority, dissented in *Lloyd*.) The Court held that persons distributing anti-war literature could be ejected from a large privately owned shopping center. Justice Powell's opinion emphasized that the First Amendment only applied to the conduct of governments, and not to decisions made by owners of private property. Interestingly, he attempted to distinguish *Logan Valley* on its facts, rather than overrule it. In Hudgens v. National Labor Relations Bd., 424 U.S. 507 (1976), however, the Court stated: "[W]e make clear now, if it was not clear before, that the rationale of *Logan Valley* did not survive the Court's decision in the *Lloyd* case."

2.   The line of cases discussed in the previous note seems to have settled the question whether the United States Constitution gives speakers any right of access to private property. With the possible example of situations that are nearly identical to the company owned town in *Marsh*, the answer is no. The company town is a vanishing phenomenon in this country, so that the Court may never be called upon to decide whether company towns are still subject to the First Amendment. (Query. Is a large, residential, private university like a company town?) Large shopping malls, however, are replacing older business sections for most urban Americans. Was the Court right when it concluded that the United States Constitution places no restrictions on the right of their owners to eject speakers, leafleteers and pickets?

3.   The California Supreme Court's majority, in its *PruneYard* opinion, in reasoning that followed Justice Marshall's *Logan Valley* opinion, concluded that the United States Supreme Court had been wrong when it decided that a shopping center owner should have the same right to exclude speakers as the owner of a house or a single store. How is that possible? It was not possible for the California court to overrule the United States Supreme Court concerning the meaning of the United States Constitution. State courts, however, have the last word on the meaning of State law, including State Constitutions. Most state constitutions have Bills of Rights, with provisions identical to or parallel to those in the United States Constitution. In general, a state court remains free to give an entirely contrary construction to its own Bill of Rights. Thus, many constitutional issues which are apparently settled by United States Supreme Court decisions can remain very much alive in the States.

The California Constitution provides:

[Art. I, § 2(a).] "Every person may freely speak, write and publish his or her sentiments on all subjects, being responsible for the abuse of this right. A law may not restrain or abridge liberty of speech or press."

[Art. I, § 3.] "[P]eople have the right to ... petition government for redress of grievances...."

Like the United States Constitution, the California Constitution's guarantees of speech, press and petition are directed only at government. The California Supreme Court, however, emphasized that suburban privately-owned shopping centers were much more ubiquitous in California, that the process of gathering signatures for ballot measures was most often carried out where people shop, and that recognizing a shopping center's absolute right to eject speakers, leafleteers, and people seeking signatures on petitions, would seriously dilute rights of speech and petition. Do you prefer California's "First Amendment"?

4.   When the United States Supreme Court reviews a state court decision interpreting state law, it cannot determine whether that inter-

pretation is abstractly right or wrong. The only issue open is whether state law, as interpreted, violates federal law or federal rights. Normally, no federal law forbids the state from giving its citizens broader protections against state government than the United States Constitution does. The California court's decision, however, had given one group rights against another group of private parties. That raised the question whether the California Constitution, as construed, denied the federal constitutional rights of the owners of shopping centers. That brings us, at long last, to the issues that *are* involved in the *PruneYard* case.

5. A major issue concerns whether required access violates the shopping center owner's constitutional guarantees of property. The Fourteenth Amendment provides that a state shall not deny "life, liberty or property" without due process of law. The Fifth Amendment provides that private property shall not "be taken for public use, without just compensation." After the *PruneYard* decision, are there any cases where a landowner can successfully contend that state law requiring access of speakers to his property denies his federally-protected property rights? (It should be emphasized again that other state courts can interpret their constitutions to require protection of property rather than speech rights in situations like *Logan Valley, Lloyd* and *PruneYard*.)

6. It appears from the concurring opinions that a more serious problem of the owner's rights emerges from the argument that compelled access violates the owner's own First Amendment rights. The argument was premised on two groups of earlier Supreme Court decisions. First are those cases that hold that it is unconstitutional for government to require someone to profess a belief. (See West Virginia State Bd. of Educ. v. Barnette, a case invalidating compulsory flag salutes for public school pupils, Chapter 2, p. 36, and Wooley v. Maynard, Chapter 16, page 573. The case involving rights of access to newspapers, which involves different problems—Miami Herald Pub. Co. v. Tornillo—appears on page 238, below.) Another case, decided after *PruneYard*, is Hurley v. Irish–American Gay, Lesbian and Bisexual Group of Boston, 515 U.S. 557 (1995), which is summarized on pp. 555–556.

A second line of cases is represented by Abood v. Detroit Bd. of Educ., 431 U.S. 209 (1977), which is cited in Justice Powell's concurring opinion, but not mentioned in the Court's opinion. In that case, high school teachers argued that is was unconstitutional to require them to pay dues to a union to which they were ideologically opposed. The Court held that it was permissible to require the employee to contribute to the union's expenses relating to the bargaining process, administering the collective bargaining agreement, and adjusting grievances. The First Amendment, however, forbad the State to require teachers to support the union's ideological causes. The teachers were thus entitled either to an order forbidding union expenditures from compulsory dues money for ideological causes, or to a refund of a portion of their dues. The Court reasons that compelling people to make contributions for political purposes with which they disagree violated a right "at the heart of the First Amendment"—"that an individual should be free to believe as he will, and that in a free society one's beliefs should be shaped by his mind and his conscience rather than coerced by the State."

7. Has the Court's opinion in *PruneYard* resolved the issues of the shopping center owner's free speech rights? What if the PruneYard's owner was offended by the Zionist pamphlets, and had announced that everyone could distribute leaflets in the shopping center except Zionists? Would it make sense to restrict state law protection of leafleteers most in those cases where the property owner's restrictions are deliberately designed to censor content? Suppose the owner of the shopping center had testified that he imposed a flat ban on all leaflets because he wanted to avoid having to pick and choose, but that many people had distributed leaflets whose views he passionately and vehemently resented, and he wanted to avoid subsidizing the people whose causes he opposed. Would that have changed the result?

II. PRIVATE COMMUNICATIONS MEDIA

COLUMBIA BROADCASTING SYSTEM, INC. v. DEMOCRATIC NATIONAL COMMITTEE

Supreme Court of the United States, 1973.
412 U.S. 94, 93 S.Ct. 2080, 36 L.Ed.2d 772.

CHIEF JUSTICE BURGER delivered the opinion of the Court (Parts I, II, and IV) together with an opinion (Part III), in which JUSTICE STEWART and JUSTICE REHNQUIST joined.

. . .

[Two organizations, plaintiffs in this case, approached radio station WTOP in Washington D.C. to purchase advertisements opposing the war in Vietnam.]

... WTOP, in common with many, but not all, broadcasters, followed a policy of refusing to sell time for spot announcements to individuals and groups who wished to expound their views on controversial issues. WTOP took the position that since it presented full and fair coverage of important public questions, including the Vietnam conflict, it was justified in refusing to accept editorial advertisements. WTOP also submitted evidence showing that the station had aired the views of critics of our Vietnam policy on numerous occasions.

[The organizations then complained to the Federal Communications Commission, which rejected the complaints.]

. . .

I

Justice White's opinion for the Court in Red Lion Broadcasting Co. v. FCC, 395 U.S. 367 (1969), makes clear that the broadcast media pose unique and special problems not present in the traditional free speech case. Unlike other media, broadcasting is subject to an inherent physical limitation. Broadcast frequencies are a scarce resource; they must be portioned out among applicants. All who possess the financial resources and the desire to communicate by television or radio cannot be satisfactorily accommodated....

Because the broadcast media utilize a valuable and limited public resource, there is also present an unusual order of First Amendment values....

. . .

II

This Court has on numerous occasions recounted the origins of our modern system of broadcast regulation....

. . .

... Congress intended to permit private broadcasting to develop with the widest journalistic freedom consistent with its public obligations. Only when the interests of the public are found to outweigh the private journalistic interests of the broadcasters will government power be asserted within the framework of the [Communications] Act. License renewal proceedings, in which the listening public can be heard, are a principal means of such regulation.

Subsequent developments in broadcast regulation illustrate how this regulatory scheme has evolved. Of particular importance, in light of Congress' flat refusal to impose a "common carrier" right of access for all persons wishing to speak out on public issues, is the Commission's "Fairness Doctrine," which evolved gradually over the years spanning federal regulation of the broadcast media....

Since it is physically impossible to provide time for all viewpoints, however, the right to exercise editorial judgment was granted to the broadcaster. The broadcaster, therefore, is allowed significant journalistic discretion in deciding how best to fulfill the Fairness Doctrine obligations, although that discretion is bounded by rules designed to assure that the public interest in fairness is furthered....

Thus, under the Fairness Doctrine broadcasters are responsible for providing the listening and viewing public with access to a balanced presentation of information on issues of public importance. The basic principle underlying that responsibility is "the right of the public to be informed, rather than any right on the part of the Government, any broadcast licensee or any individual member of the public to broadcast his own particular views on any matter...." ...

With this background in mind, we next proceed to consider whether a broadcaster's refusal to accept editorial advertisements is governmental action violative of the First Amendment.

III

That "Congress shall make no law ... abridging the freedom of speech, or of the press" is a restraint on government action, not that of private persons. The Court has not previously considered whether the action of a broadcast licensee such as that challenged here is "governmental action" for purposes of the First Amendment.

. . .

As we have seen, with the advent of radio a half century ago, Congress was faced with a fundamental choice between total Government ownership and control of the new medium—the choice of most other countries—or some other alternative. Long before the impact and potential of the medium was realized, Congress opted for a system of private broadcasters licensed and regulated by Government. . . .

. . .

. . . We do not reach the question whether the First Amendment or the [Communications] Act can be read to preclude the Commission from determining that in some situations the public interest requires licensees to re-examine their policies with respect to editorial advertisements. The Commission has not yet made such a determination; it has, for the present at least, found the policy to be within the sphere of journalistic discretion which Congress has left with the licensee.

Thus, it cannot be said that the Government is a "partner" to the action of the broadcast licensee complained of here, nor is it engaged in a "symbiotic relationship" with the licensee, profiting from the invidious discrimination of its proxy. The First Amendment does not reach acts of private parties in every instance where the Congress or the Commission has merely permitted or failed to prohibit such acts.

. . .

Were we to read the First Amendment to spell out governmental action in the circumstances presented here, few licensee decisions on the content of broadcasts or the processes of editorial evaluation would escape constitutional scrutiny. In this sensitive area so sweeping a concept of governmental action would go far in practical effect to undermine nearly a half century of unmistakable congressional purpose to maintain—no matter how difficult the task—essentially private broadcast journalism held only broadly accountable to public interest standards. To do this Congress, and the Commission as its agent, must remain in a posture of flexibility to chart a workable "middle course" in its quest to preserve a balance between the essential public accountability and the desired private control of the media.

More profoundly, it would be anomalous for us to hold, in the name of promoting the constitutional guarantees of free expression, that the day-to-day editorial decisions of broadcast licensees are subject to the kind of restraints urged by respondents. To do so in the name of the First Amendment would be a contradiction. Journalistic discretion would in many ways be lost to the rigid limitations that the First Amendment imposes on Government. Application of such standards to broadcast licensees would be antithetical to the very ideal of vigorous, challenging debate on issues of public interest. Every licensee is already held accountable for the totality of its performance of public interest obligations.

The concept of private, independent broadcast journalism, regulated by Government to assure protection of the public interest, has evolved slowly and cautiously over more than 40 years and has been nurtured by processes of adjudication. That concept of journalistic independence could not co-exist with a reading of the challenged conduct of the licensee as governmental action. Nor could it exist without administrative flexibility to meet changing needs and swift technological developments. We therefore conclude that the policies complained of do not constitute governmental action violative of the First Amendment.

IV

There remains for consideration the question whether the "public interest" standard of the Communications Act requires broadcasters to accept editorial advertisements or, whether, assuming governmental action, broadcasters are required to do so by reason of the First Amendment. . . .

. . .

The Commission was justified in concluding that the public interest in providing access to the marketplace of "ideas and experiences" would scarcely be served by a system so heavily weighted in favor of the financially affluent, or those with access to wealth. Even under a first-come-first-served system, proposed by the dissenting Commissioner in these cases, the views of the affluent could well prevail over those of others, since they would have it within their power to purchase time more frequently. Moreover, there is the substantial danger, as the Court of Appeals acknowledged, that the time allotted for editorial advertising could be monopolized by those of one political persuasion.

These problems would not necessarily be solved by applying the Fairness Doctrine . . . to editorial advertising. If broadcasters were required to provide time, free when necessary, for the discussion of the various shades of opinion on the issue discussed in the advertisement, the affluent could still determine in large part the issues to be discussed. . . .

If the Fairness Doctrine were applied to editorial advertising, there is also the substantial danger that the effective operation of that doctrine would be jeopardized. To minimize financial hardship and to comply fully with its public responsibilities a broadcaster might well be forced to make regular programming time available to those holding a view different from that expressed in an editorial advertisement. . . . The result would be a further erosion of the journalistic discretion of broadcasters in the coverage of public issues . . .

. . .

. . . . The [lower] court relied on decisions holding that state-supported school newspapers and public transit companies were prohibited by the First Amendment from excluding controversial editorial advertisements in favor of commercial advertisements. The court also attempted to analogize this case to some of our decisions holding that States may not constitutionally ban certain protected speech while at the same time permitting other speech in public areas. . . .

Those decisions provide little guidance, however, in resolving the question whether the First Amendment requires the Commission to mandate a private right of access to the broadcast media. In none of those cases did the forum sought for expression have an affirmative and independent statutory obligation to provide full and fair coverage of public issues, such as Congress has imposed on all broadcast licensees. In short, there is no "discrimination" against controversial speech present in this case. The question here is not whether there is to be discussion of controversial issues of public importance on the broadcast media, but rather who shall determine what issues are to be discussed by whom, and when.

. . .

Conceivably at some future date Congress or the Commission—or the broadcasters—may devise some kind of limited right of access that is both practicable and desirable. Indeed, the Commission noted in these proceedings that the advent of cable television will afford increased opportunities for the discussion of public issues. In its proposed rules on cable television the Commission has provided that cable systems in major television markets

> "shall maintain at least one specially designated, noncommercial public access channel available on a first-come non-discriminatory basis. The system shall maintain and have available for public use at least the minimal equipment and facilities necessary for the production of programming for such a channel."

. . .

JUSTICE STEWART, concurring.

While I join Parts I and II of the Court's opinion, and the opinion in Part III, my views closely approach those expressed by Justice Douglas concurring in the judgment.

. . .

In Red Lion Broadcasting Co. v. FCC ... this Court held that, despite the First Amendment, the Commission may impose a so-called Fairness Doctrine upon broadcasters, requiring them to present balanced coverage of various and conflicting views on issues of public importance. I agreed with the Court in *Red Lion,* although with considerable doubt, because I thought that that much Government regulation of program content was within the outer limits of First Amendment tolerability. Were the Commission to require broadcasters to accept some amount of editorial advertising as part of the public interest mandate upon which their licenses are conditional, the issue before us would be in the same posture as was the Fairness Doctrine itself in *Red Lion,* and we would have to determine whether this additional governmental control of broadcasters was consistent with the statute and tolerable under the First Amendment. Here, however, the Commission imposed no such requirement ...

. . .

The First Amendment protects the press *from* governmental interference; it confers no analogous protection *on* the Government. To hold that broadcaster action is governmental action would thus simply strip broadcasters of their own First Amendment rights. They would be obligated to grant the demands of all citizens to be heard over the air, subject only to reasonable regulations as to "time, place and manner." If, as the dissent today would have it, the proper analogy is to public forums—that is, if broadcasters are Government for First Amendment purposes—then broadcasters are inevitably drawn to the position of common carriers. For this is precisely the status of Government with respect to public forums—a status mandated by the First Amendment.

To hold that broadcaster action is governmental action would thus produce a result wholly inimical to the broadcasters' own First Amendment rights, and wholly at odds with the broadcasting system established by Congress and with our many decisions approving those legislative provisions....

· · ·

This Court was persuaded in *Red Lion* to accept the Commission's view that a so-called Fairness Doctrine was required by the unique electronic limitations of broadcasting, at least in the then-existing state of the art. Rightly or wrongly, we there decided that broadcasters' First Amendment rights were "abridgeable." But surely this does not mean that those rights are nonexistent. And even if all else were in equipoise, and the decision of the issue before us were finally to rest upon First Amendment "values" alone, I could not agree with the Court of Appeals. For if those "values" mean anything, they should mean at least this: If we must choose whether editorial decisions are to be made in the free judgment of individual broadcasters, or imposed by bureaucratic fiat, the choice must be for freedom.

JUSTICE WHITE, concurring.

I join Parts I, II, and IV of the Court's opinion and its judgment. I do not, however, concur in the Part III opinion.

· · ·

... I am not ready to conclude, as is done in the Part III opinion, that the First Amendment may be put aside for lack of official action necessary to invoke its proscriptions.... Given the constitutionality of the Fairness Doctrine, and accepting Part IV of the Court's opinion, I have little difficulty in concluding that statutory and regulatory recognition of broadcaster freedom and discretion to make up their own programs and to choose their method of compliance with the Fairness Doctrine is consistent with the First Amendment.

JUSTICE BLACKMUN, with whom JUSTICE POWELL joins, concurring.

... The Court's conclusion that the First Amendment does not compel the result reached by the Court of Appeals demonstrates that the governmental action issue does not affect the outcome of this case. I therefore refrain from deciding it.

JUSTICE DOUGLAS, concurring in the judgment.

While I join the Court in reversing the judgment below, I do so for quite different reasons.

My conclusion is that TV and radio stand in the same protected position under the First Amendment as do newspapers and magazines. The philosophy of the First Amendment requires that result, for the fear that Madison and Jefferson had of government intrusion is perhaps even more relevant to TV and radio than it is to newspapers and other like publications. That fear was founded not only on the spectre of a lawless government but of government under the control of a faction that desired to foist its views of the common good on the people....

. . .

Red Lion Broadcasting Co. v. FCC, 395 U.S. 367, in a carefully written opinion that was built upon predecessor cases, put TV and radio under a different regime. I did not participate in that decision and, with all respect, would not support it. The Fairness Doctrine has no place in our First Amendment regime. It puts the head of the camel inside the tent and enables administration after administration to toy with TV or radio in order to serve its sordid or its benevolent ends. In 1973—as in other years—there is clamoring to make TV and radio emit the messages that console certain groups. There are charges that these mass media are too slanted, too partisan, too hostile in their approach to candidates and the issues.

The same cry of protest has gone up against the newspapers and magazines. When Senator Joseph McCarthy was at his prime, holding in his hand papers containing the names of 205 "Communists" in the State Department (R. Feuerlicht, Joe McCarthy and McCarthyism 54 (1972)), there were scarcely a dozen papers in this Nation that stood firm for the citizen's right to due process and to First Amendment protection. That, however, was no reason to put the saddle of the federal bureaucracy on the backs of publishers. Under our Bill of Rights people are entitled to have extreme ideas, silly ideas, partisan ideas.

The same is true, I believe, of TV and radio. At times they have a nauseating mediocrity. At other times they show the dazzling brilliance of a Leonard Bernstein; and they very often bring humanistic influences of faraway people into every home.

Both TV and radio news broadcasts frequently tip the news one direction or another and even try to turn a public figure into a character of disrepute. Yet so do the newspapers and the magazines and other segments of the press. The standards of TV, radio, newspapers, or magazines—whether of excellence or mediocrity—are beyond the reach of Government...

. . .

The Court in National Broadcasting Co. v. United States, 319 U.S. 190, 226, said, "Unlike other modes of expression, radio inherently is not available to all. That is its unique characteristic, and that is why, unlike other modes of expression, it is subject to governmental regulation."

That uniqueness is due to engineering and technical problems. But the press in a realistic sense is likewise not available to all. Small or "underground" papers appear and disappear; and the weekly is an established institution. But the daily papers now established are unique in the sense that it would be virtually impossible for a competitor to enter the field due to the financial exigencies of this era. The result is that in practical terms the newspapers and magazines, like TV and radio, are available only to a select few. Who at this time would have the folly to think he could combat the New York Times or Denver Post by building a new plant and becoming a competitor? That may argue for a redefinition of the responsibilities of the press in First Amendment terms. But I do not think it gives us carte blanche to design systems of supervision and control or empower Congress to read the mandate in the First Amendment that "Congress shall make no law ... abridging the freedom ... of the press" to mean that Congress may, acting directly or through any of its agencies such as the FCC make "some" laws "abridging" freedom of the press.

· · ·

What kind of First Amendment would best serve our needs as we approach the 21st century may be an open question. But the old-fashioned First Amendment that we have is the Court's only guideline; and one hard and fast principle which it announces is that Government shall keep its hands off the press. That principle has served us through days of calm and eras of strife and I would abide by it until a new First Amendment is adopted. That means, as I view it, that TV and radio, as well as the more conventional methods for disseminating news, are all included in the concept of "press" as used in the First Amendment and therefore are entitled to live under the laissez-faire regime which the First Amendment sanctions.

· · ·

JUSTICE BRENNAN, with whom JUSTICE MARSHALL concurs, dissenting.

· · ·

... I would ... affirm the determination of the Court of Appeals that the challenged broadcaster policy is violative of the First Amendment.

I

· · ·

... [T]he public nature of the airwaves, the governmentally created preferred status of broadcast licensees, the pervasive federal regulation of broadcast programming, and the Commission's specific approval of the challenged broadcaster policy combine in this case to bring the promulgation and enforcement of that policy within the orbit of constitutional imperatives.

· · ·

II

Radio and television have long been recognized as forms of communication "affected by a First Amendment interest" and, indeed, it can

hardly be doubted that broadcast licensees are themselves protected by
that Amendment. Recognition of this fact does not end our inquiry,
however, for it is equally clear that the protection of the First Amendment in this context is not limited solely to broadcasters. On the
contrary, at least one set of competing claims to the protection of that
Amendment derives from the fact that, because of the limited number of
broadcast frequencies available and the potentially pervasive impact of
the electronic media, "the people as a whole retain their interest in free
speech by radio and their collective right to have the medium function
consistently with the ends and purposes of the First Amendment." Red
Lion Broadcasting Co. v. FCC, supra, at 390.

. . .

... [T]he Court ... upholds the absolute ban on editorial advertising because, in its view, the Commission's Fairness Doctrine, in and of
itself, is sufficient to satisfy the First Amendment interests of the public.
I cannot agree.

... [T]he Fairness Doctrine does not in any sense require broadcasters to allow "non-broadcaster" speakers to use the airwaves to express
their own views on controversial issues of public importance. On the
contrary, broadcasters may meet their fairness responsibilities through
presentation of carefully edited news programs, panel discussions, interviews, and documentaries. As a result, broadcasters retain almost exclusive control over the selection of issues and viewpoints to be covered, the
manner of presentation, and, perhaps most important, who shall speak.
Given this doctrinal framework, I can only conclude that the Fairness
Doctrine, standing alone, is insufficient—in theory as well as in practice—to provide the kind of "uninhibited, robust, and wide-open" exchange of views to which the public is constitutionally entitled.

As a practical matter, ... even under the Fairness Doctrine, broadcasters generally tend to permit only established—or at least moderat-
ed—views to enter the broadcast world's "marketplace of ideas."

. . .

The Fairness Doctrine's requirement of full and fair coverage of
controversial issues is, beyond doubt, a commendable and, indeed, essential tool for effective regulation of the broadcast industry. But, standing
alone, it simply cannot eliminate the need for a further, complementary
airing of controversial views through the limited availability of editorial
advertising. . . .

III

Moreover, a proper balancing of the competing First Amendment
interests at stake in this controversy must consider, not only the
interests of broadcasters and of the listening and viewing public, but also
the independent First Amendment interest of groups and individuals in
effective self-expression. . . .

. . .

[W]ith the assistance of the Federal Government, the broadcast industry has become what is potentially the most efficient and effective "marketplace of ideas" ever devised.... [I]n light of the current dominance of the electronic media as the most effective means of reaching the public, any policy that *absolutely* denies citizens access to the airwaves necessarily renders even the concept of "full and free discussion" practically meaningless.

. . .

IV

. . .

... [T]he Court hypothesizes three potential sources of difficulty: (1) the availability of editorial advertising might, in the absence of adjustments in the system, tend to favor the wealthy; (2) application of the Fairness Doctrine to editorial advertising might adversely affect the operation of that doctrine; and (3) regulation of editorial advertising might lead to an enlargement of Government control over the content of broadcast discussion. These are, of course, legitimate and, indeed, important concerns. But, at the present time, they are concerns—not realities. We simply have no sure way of knowing whether, and to what extent, if any, these potential difficulties will actually materialize....

NOTES AND QUESTIONS

1. In Red Lion Broadcasting Co. v. FCC, 395 U.S. 367 (1969) the Court was faced with a challenge to one aspect of the Federal Communications Commissions "Fairness Doctrine." The Broadcasting Company had carried a personal attack by the Reverend Billy James Hargis upon Journalist Fred J. Cook. Cook demanded free time to reply to the attack.

The Court, rebuffing a challenge to the FCC regulations which granted Cook such a right, held that the regulations "enhance rather than abridge the freedoms of speech and press protected by the First Amendment." The opinion for eight Justices (Justice Douglas did not participate) was written by Justice White and constituted a broad endorsement of the Fairness Doctrine policy "that issues be presented and presented with coverage of competing views."

As described by Justice White, the "Fairness Doctrine" operates as follows:

> There is a twofold duty laid down by the FCC's decisions and described by the 1949 Report on Editorializing by Broadcast Licensees. The broadcaster must give adequate coverage to public issues, and coverage must be fair in that it accurately reflects the opposing views. This must be done at the broadcaster's own expense if sponsorship is unavailable.

Justice White's opinion concluded that the Fairness Doctrine did not violate the First Amendment for the following reasons:

> Rather than confer frequency monopolies on a relatively small number of licensees, in a Nation of 200,000,000, the Government could surely have decreed that each frequency

should be shared among all or some of those who wish to use it, each being assigned a portion of the broadcast day or the broadcast week. The ruling and regulations at issue here do not go quite so far. They assert that under specified circumstances, a licensee must offer to make available a reasonable amount of broadcast time to those who have a view different from that which has already been expressed on his station. The expression of a political endorsement, or of a personal attack while dealing with a controversial public issue, simply triggers this time sharing. As we have said, the First Amendment confers no right on licensees to prevent others from broadcasting on "their" frequencies and no right to an unconditional monopoly of a scarce resource which the Government has denied others the right to use.

2.   Changes in the membership of the Court between the time of two decisions are not always the whole story. Eight Justices participated in the *Red Lion* opinion. Only four of the eight (Justices Brennan, Stewart, White and Marshall) were still on the Court when *CBS* was decided in 1973. Three of the four indicate quite clearly that they continue to adhere to the language in the *Red Lion* case which hints that the fairness doctrine, or some version of it, is *required* by the First Amendment. But Justice Stewart in *CBS* says that he joined the *Red Lion* opinion with "considerable doubt," and announces that his present views "closely approach" those of Justice Douglas who thinks the fairness doctrine is *prohibited* by the First Amendment. Oversimplified, the issue in *Red Lion* was whether First Amendment values of free and robust debate can best be accomplished by subjecting broadcasters to government regulation or by freeing broadcasters of government regulation. Did anything happen from 1969 to 1973 that explains Justice Stewart's shift from reliance on governmental regulation?

3.   It might help, in thinking through the problems in both *Red Lion* and *CBS* to draw two polar models for radio and television broadcasting. (1) The Common Carrier Model. This model analogizes broadcasters to "common carriers." Common carriers, such as railroads, can't pick and choose their customers, but have to serve all comers (or, at least, those who can pay the freight charges), usually under tight government regulation. Under this model, stations would continue to be licensed as they are today, and would be required by the government to provide access to all groups who wanted to use the media. (2) The Newspaper Model. Under this model, broadcast licenses would become private property. (They could be sold by the government to the highest bidder.) Government control would be limited to protecting the "private property" rights of each broadcaster to his part of the broadcast spectrum. Individual stations could have their own editorial policies, and there would be no obligation to provide any particular form of programs, to be fair or to provide equal time or access to anyone. Does either model hold promise for opening broadcasting to the fullest exposition of conflicting views on important public issues?

4.   Early radio pioneers had a noble vision of radio broadcasting as an important public service medium. If television and radio broadcasting

today is a "vast wasteland," what is the source of the problem? Is it the failure of the Federal Communications Commission to use its existing regulatory powers to require that broadcasters operate in the public interest? Or, is it a misconception that government regulation is the way to make broadcasters operate in the public interest?

5.   One of the difficulties with the *CBS* case is the great complexity introduced by the wide divisions in the views of individual justices. Notice carefully the division on one issue. Suppose Congress were to repeal the "Fairness Doctrine" in its entirety. Would the First Amendment require broadcast licensees to provide access in some cases on the ground that the broadcaster is like the company town in Marsh v. Alabama? Of the nine justices, four answered "no"—Chief Justice Burger and Justices Douglas, Stewart and Rehnquist. Two answered "yes"— Justices Brennan and Marshall. Justice White, who wrote the *Red Lion* opinion, hints some agreement with Justices Brennan and Marshall on this point. Two justices, Blackmun and Powell, argue that the issue doesn't affect the outcome of the *CBS* case and they don't have to decide. Would it be constitutional to allow broadcast licensees to editorialize without giving free time to opposing views?

MIAMI HERALD PUBLISHING CO. v. TORNILLO

Supreme Court of the United States, 1974.
418 U.S. 241, 94 S.Ct. 2831, 41 L.Ed.2d 730.

CHIEF JUSTICE BURGER delivered the opinion of the Court.

The issue in this case is whether a state statute granting a political candidate a right to equal space to reply to criticism and attacks on his record by a newspaper violates the guarantees of a free press.

I

In the fall of 1972, appellee, Executive Director of the Classroom Teachers Association, apparently a teachers' collective-bargaining agent, was a candidate for the Florida House of Representatives. On September 20, 1972, and again on September 29, 1972, appellant printed editorials critical of appellee's candidacy.[2] In response to these editorials appellee

2.   The text of the September 20, 1972, editorial is as follows:

"The State's Laws And Pat Tornillo

"LOOK who's upholding the law!

"Pat Tornillo, boss of the Classroom Teachers Association and candidate for the State Legislature in the Oct. 3 runoff election, has denounced his opponent as lacking 'the knowledge to be a legislator, as evidenced by his failure to file a list of contributions to and expenditures of his campaign as required by law.'

"Czar Tornillo calls 'violation of this law inexcusable.'

"This is the same Pat Tornillo who led the CTA strike from February 19 to March 11, 1968, against the school children and taxpayers of Dade County. Call it whatever you will, it was an illegal act against the public interest and clearly prohibited by the statutes.

"We cannot say it would be illegal but certainly it would be inexcusable of the voters if they sent Pat Tornillo to Tallahassee to occupy the seat for District 103 in the House of Representatives."

The text of the September 29, 1972, editorial is as follows:

demanded that appellant print verbatim his replies, defending the role of the Classroom Teachers Association and the organization's accomplishments for the citizens of Dade County. Appellant declined to print the appellee's replies, and appellee brought suit in Circuit Court, Dade County, seeking declaratory and injunctive relief and actual and punitive damages in excess of $5,000. The action was premised on Florida Statute § 104.38 (1973), a "right of reply" statute which provides that if a candidate for nomination or election is assailed regarding his personal character or official record by any newspaper, the candidate has the right to demand that the newspaper print, free of cost to the candidate, any reply the candidate may make to the newspaper's charges. The reply must appear in as conspicuous a place and in the same kind of type as the charges which prompted the reply, provided it does not take up more space than the charges. Failure to comply with the statute constitutes a first-degree misdemeanor.

. . .

... [T]he Florida Supreme Court [decided] that § 104.38 did not violate constitutional guarantees. It held that free speech was enhanced and not abridged by the Florida right-of-reply statute, which in that court's view, furthered the "broad societal interest in the free flow of information to the public." ...

. . .

The challenged statute creates a right to reply to press criticism of a candidate for nomination or election. The statute was enacted in 1913 and this is only the second recorded case decided under its provisions.

. . .

The appellee and supporting advocates of an enforceable right of access to the press vigorously argue that government has an obligation to ensure that a wide variety of views reach the public.... It is urged that at the time the First Amendment to the Constitution was enacted in 1791 as part of our Bill of Rights the press was broadly representative of the people it was serving. While many of the newspapers were intensely partisan and narrow in their views, the press collectively presented a broad range of opinions to readers. Entry into publishing was inexpensive; pamphlets and books provided meaningful alternatives to the

"FROM the people who brought you this—the teacher strike of '68—come now instructions on how to vote for responsible government, i.e., against Crutcher Harrison and Ethel Beckham, for Pat Tornillo. The tracts and blurbs and bumper stickers pile up daily in teachers' school mailboxes amidst continuing pouts that the School Board should be delivering all this at your expense. The screeds say the strike is not an issue. We say maybe it wouldn't be were it not a part of a continuation of disregard of any and all laws the CTA might find aggravating. Whether in defiance of zoning laws at CTA Towers, contracts and laws during the strike, or more recently state prohibitions against soliciting campaign funds amongst teachers, CTA says file and try and sue us—what's good for CTA is good for CTA and that is natural law. Tornillo's law, maybe. For years now he has been kicking the public shin to call attention to his shakedown statesmanship. He and whichever acerbic prexy is in alleged office have always felt their private ventures so chock-full of public weal that we should leap at the chance to nab the tab, be it half the Glorious Leader's salary or the dues checkoff or anything else except perhaps mileage on the staff hydrofoil. Give him public office, says Pat, and he will no doubt live by the Golden Rule. Our translation reads that as more gold and more rule."

organized press for the expression of unpopular ideas and often treated events and expressed views not covered by conventional newspapers. A true marketplace of ideas existed in which there was relatively easy access to the channels of communication.

Access advocates submit that although newspapers of the present are superficially similar to those of 1791 the press of today is in reality very different from that known in the early years of our national existence.

The elimination of competing newspapers in most of our large cities, and the concentration of control of media that results from the only newspaper's being owned by the same interests which own a television station and a radio station, are important components of this trend toward concentration of control of outlets to inform the public.

. . .

The obvious solution, which was available to dissidents at an earlier time when entry into publishing was relatively inexpensive, today would be to have additional newspapers. But the same economic factors which have caused the disappearance of vast numbers of metropolitan newspapers, have made entry into the marketplace of ideas served by the print media almost impossible. It is urged that the claim of newspapers to be "surrogates for the public" carries with it a concomitant fiduciary obligation to account for that stewardship. From this premise it is reasoned that the only effective way to insure fairness and accuracy and to provide for some accountability is for government to take affirmative action. The First Amendment interest of the public in being informed is said to be in peril because the "marketplace of ideas" is today a monopoly controlled by the owners of the market.

Proponents of enforced access to the press take comfort from language in several of this Court's decisions which suggests that the First Amendment acts as a sword as well as a shield, that it imposes obligations on the owners of the press in addition to protecting the press from government regulation. . . .

. . .

However much validity may be found in these arguments, at each point the implementation of a remedy such as an enforceable right of access necessarily calls for some mechanism, either governmental or consensual. If it is governmental coercion, this at once brings about a confrontation with the express provisions of the First Amendment and the judicial gloss on that Amendment developed over the years.

. . .

. . . [T]he Court has expressed sensitivity as to whether a restriction or requirement constituted the compulsion exerted by government on a newspaper to print that which it would not otherwise print. The clear implication has been that any such a compulsion to publish that which " 'reason' tells them should not be published" is unconstitutional. A responsible press is an undoubtedly desirable goal, but press responsibility is not mandated by the Constitution and like many other virtues it cannot be legislated.

Appellee's argument that the Florida statute does not amount to a restriction of appellant's right to speak because "the statute in question here has not prevented the *Miami Herald* from saying anything it wished" begs the core question. Compelling editors or publishers to publish that which " 'reason' tells them should not be published" is what is at issue in this case. The Florida statute operates as a command in the same sense as a statute or regulation forbidding appellant to publish specified matter. Governmental restraint on publishing need not fall into familiar or traditional patterns to be subject to constitutional limitations on governmental powers.... The Florida statute exacts a penalty on the basis of the content of a newspaper. The first phase of the penalty resulting from the compelled printing of a reply is exacted in terms of the cost in printing and composing time and materials and in taking up space that could be devoted to other material the newspaper may have preferred to print. It is correct, as appellee contends, that a newspaper is not subject to the finite technological limitations of time that confront a broadcaster but it is not correct to say that, as an economic reality, a newspaper can proceed to infinite expansion of its column space to accommodate the replies that a government agency determines or a statute commands the readers should have available.

Faced with the penalties that would accrue to any newspaper that published news or commentary arguably within the reach of the right-of-access statute, editors might well conclude that the safe course is to avoid controversy. Therefore, under the operation of the Florida statute, political and electoral coverage would be blunted or reduced. Government-enforced right of access inescapably "dampens the vigor and limits the variety of public debate,"....

Even if a newspaper would face no additional costs to comply with a compulsory access law and would not be forced to forgo publication of news or opinion by the inclusion of a reply, the Florida statute fails to clear the barriers of the First Amendment because of its intrusion into the function of editors. A newspaper is more than a passive receptacle or conduit for news, comment, and advertising. The choice of material to go into a newspaper, and the decisions made as to limitations on the size and content of the paper, and treatment of public issues and public officials—whether fair or unfair—constitute the exercise of editorial control and judgment. It has yet to be demonstrated how governmental regulation of this crucial process can be exercised consistent with First Amendment guarantees of a free press as they have evolved to this time....

· · ·

[Concurring opinions by Justice Brennan (joined by Justice Rehnquist) and Justice White are omitted.]

NOTES AND QUESTIONS

1. Aren't the "penalties" on newspapers exacted by the Florida reply law exactly those imposed on broadcasters by the fairness doctrine? Notice that the only reference to broadcasting in the opinion is a concession that it is somewhat *easier* for a newspaper to provide equal time or access than it is for a broadcaster because a broadcaster has a finite period of time available.

2. Note that the challenged statute required the newspaper to provide free space to a political candidate it had attacked—but that the Court's opinion expressly stated that a requirement that a newspaper sell an advertisement to the victim of its attack would be equally unconstitutional. Should this be true?

3. Can the scarcity of broadcast channels continue to justify the distinction between broadcasters and newspaper publishers? Notice the concession in *Miami Herald* that there is considerably more monopoly in newspapers than broadcasting. In most major cities, aren't there many more radio and television "channels" available than major newspaper "channels?" Notice that the Court's opinion concedes that there are newspaper monopolies but that the First Amendment precludes compelled access as the solution to the problem. Can the distinction between broadcasters and newspaper publisher then be justified solely on the ground that the airwaves are in the "public domain" or are "publicly owned?" On the ground that newspaper publishers and broadcasters serve different functions?

4. The Court rejected a scarcity rationale for restricting speech in Consolidated Edison Co. v. Public Service Comm'n, 447 U.S. 530 (1980). A regulatory commission ordered a private electric company to stop enclosing inserts promoting nuclear power, or discussing other controversial public issues, with its bills to customers. The Court held that the utility's First Amendment rights had been violated. The commission argued that billing envelopes could hold only a limited amount of information, and political messages shouldn't take the place of inserts that promoted conservation or advised consumers of their rights. The Court replied that envelopes sent through the mails were not a scarce resource, and, even if they were, the commission hadn't shown that the envelopes had become so full that other information could not be included.

Interestingly, in the *Consolidated Edison* case, the commission had adopted its unconstitutional flat ban on political message inserts after an anti-nuclear group had asked the commission to order the utility to enclose that group's rebuttal in its next billing. Suppose the commission had ordered the utility to open its billing envelopes to contrasting views replying to the utility's political messages. The California Commission issued such an order, requiring the company to include messages from a consumer group in its billing envelope four times a year. In Pacific Gas and Electric Co. v. Public Utilities Commission of California, 475 U.S. 1 (1986), the Court concluded that this order, too, violated the First Amendment. The Court relied on *Tornillo,* concluding that its principle applied beyond the institutional press. In a footnote, *Red Lion* was again distinguished on the ground that broadcasters can be required to obtain licenses because they used "a scarce, publicly owned resource."

5. In both *Consolidated Edison* and *Pacific Gas and Electric,* the Court noted that broadcasters were different from other speakers because they could be required to obtain a government license, while those who sent materials through the mails, or distributed books and newspapers, could not be constitutionally required to obtain government permission in advance. Does the analogy to broadcasting apply to other media? That was the issue in Los Angeles v. Preferred Communications, Inc., 476 U.S. 488 (1986). A federal statute, passed in 1984, allows municipalities to grant exclusive franchises to cable television operators to construct and operate cable systems. A lower federal court concluded that it was unconstitutional for a city to grant a single, exclusive, license to only one cable operator to construct a cable system. The lower court reasoned that it was physically possible to have more than one set of cables, and concluded that cable television operators were more like newspapers than broadcasters. (Everyone conceded that it would be unconstitutional for a city to give an exclusive franchise to one newspaper to have newspaper racks on the city streets.) The Supreme Court agreed that cable television involved an activity that implicated "First Amendment interests." However, it sent the case back to the lower federal courts for further factual development to learn more about the implications of the decision, and expressed no view concerning whether the city's exclusive franchise violated the First Amendment. Does it help to think about the question in terms of whether cable television is more like broadcasting or more like newspaper publishing? Is it more like a telephone company?

The Supreme Court returned to the issue of the First Amendment status of cable broadcasting in Turner Broadcasting System, Inc. v. Federal Communications Commission, 512 U.S. 622 (1994). Turner challenged a 1992 federal statute that required cable television systems to devote a portion of their channels to transmission of local broadcasting stations. The Court rejected the government's argument that the regulation of cable television was governed by the same First Amendment standards as the regulation of broadcast television. The justification for the broadcast rules turned on the limits of the electromagnetic spectrum—physical limitations not applicable to cable television. The Court also rejected an argument that the must-carry rules were designed to favor speech with particular content. Instead, they were subject to the more relaxed standards governing "content-neutral" regulation. Ultimately, however, the Court did not decide whether or not the must-carry rules violated the First Amendment—the case was sent back to the lower court to decide whether the rules sufficiently served the government's interest in preserving local broadcasting. Four Justices dissented, concluding that the must-carry rules were "content based" because Congress wanted to preserve local broadcasters precisely because they offered a different point of view than national broadcasters.

RENO v. AMERICAN CIVIL LIBERTIES UNION

Supreme Court of the United States, 1997.
521 U.S. 844, 117 S.Ct. 2329, 138 L.Ed.2d 874.

JUSTICE STEVENS delivered the opinion of the Court.

At issue is the constitutionality of two statutory provisions enacted to protect minors from "indecent" and "patently offensive" communications on the Internet. Notwithstanding the legitimacy and importance of the congressional goal of protecting children from harmful materials, we agree with the three-judge District Court that the statute abridges "the freedom of speech" protected by the First Amendment.

I

. . .

Internet

The Internet is an international network of interconnected computers ... that, eventually linking with each other, now enable tens of millions of people to communicate with one another and to access vast amounts of information from around the world. The Internet is "a unique and wholly new medium of worldwide human communication."

. . .

Anyone with access to the Internet may take advantage of a wide variety of communication and information retrieval methods.... [T]hose most relevant to this case are electronic mail ("e-mail"), automatic mailing list services ("mail exploders," sometimes referred to as "list-servs"), "newsgroups," "chat rooms," and the "World Wide Web." All of these methods can be used to transmit text; most can transmit sound, pictures, and moving video images. Taken together, these tools constitute a unique medium—known to its users as "cyberspace"—located in no particular geographical location but available to anyone, anywhere in the world, with access to the Internet.

. . .

The best known category of communication over the Internet is the World Wide Web, which allows users to search for and retrieve information stored in remote computers, as well as, in some cases, to communicate back to designated sites. In concrete terms, the Web consists of a vast number of documents stored in different computers all over the world. Some of these documents are simply files containing information. However, more elaborate documents, commonly known as Web "pages," are also prevalent....

... A particular Web page may contain the information sought by the "surfer," or, through its links, it may be an avenue to other documents located anywhere on the Internet. Users generally explore a given Web page, or move to another, by clicking a computer "mouse" on one of the page's icons or links.... The Web is thus comparable, from the readers' viewpoint, to both a vast library including millions of readily available and indexed publications and a sprawling mall offering goods and services.

From the publishers' point of view, it constitutes a vast platform from which to address and hear from a world-wide audience of millions of readers, viewers, researchers, and buyers. Any person or organization with a computer connected to the Internet can "publish" information ..... "No single organization controls any membership in the Web, nor is there any centralized point from which individual Web sites or services can be blocked from the Web." ...

Sexually Explicit Material

Sexually explicit material on the Internet includes text, pictures, and chat and "extends from the modestly titillating to the hardest-core." ...

Though such material is widely available, users seldom encounter such content accidentally. "A document's title or a description of the document will usually appear before the document itself ... and in many cases the user will receive detailed information about a site's content before he or she need take the step to access the document. Almost all sexually explicit images are preceded by warnings as to the content." ... A child requires some sophistication and some ability to read to retrieve material and thereby to use the Internet unattended.

Systems have been developed to help parents control the material that may be available on a home computer with Internet access. A system may either limit a computer's access to an approved list of sources that have been identified as containing no adult material, it may block designated inappropriate sites, or it may attempt to block messages containing identifiable objectionable features. "Although parental control software currently can screen for certain suggestive words or for known sexually explicit sites, it cannot now screen for sexually explicit images." Nevertheless, the evidence indicates that "a reasonably effective method by which parents can prevent their children from accessing sexually explicit and other material which parents may believe is inappropriate for their children will soon be available."

Age Verification

The problem of age verification differs for different uses of the Internet. The District Court categorically determined that there "is no effective way to determine the identity or the age of a user who is accessing material through e-mail, mail exploders, newsgroups or chat rooms." The Government offered no evidence that there was a reliable way to screen recipients and participants in such fora for age. Moreover, even if it were technologically feasible to block minors' access to newsgroups and chat rooms containing discussions of art, politics or other subjects that potentially elicit "indecent" or "patently offensive" contributions, it would not be possible to block their access to that material and "still allow them access to the remaining content, even if the overwhelming majority of that content was not indecent."

Technology exists by which an operator of a Web site may condition access on the verification of requested information such as a credit card number or an adult password. Credit card verification is only feasible, however, either in connection with a commercial transaction in which the card is used, or by payment to a verification agency. Using credit card possession as a surrogate for proof of age would impose costs on non-commercial Web sites that would require many of them to shut down. For that reason, at the time of the trial, credit card verification was "effectively unavailable to a substantial number of Internet content providers.". Moreover, the imposition of such a requirement "would completely bar adults who do not have a credit card and lack the resources to obtain one from accessing any blocked material."

Commercial pornographic sites that charge their users for access have assigned them passwords as a method of age verification. The record does not contain any evidence concerning the reliability of these technologies. Even if passwords are effective for commercial purveyors of indecent material, the District Court found that an adult password requirement would impose significant burdens on noncommercial sites, both because they would discourage users from accessing their sites and because the cost of creating and maintaining such screening systems would be "beyond their reach."

In sum, the District Court found: "Even if credit card verification or adult password verification were implemented, the Government presented no testimony as to how such systems could ensure that the user of the password or credit card is in fact over 18. The burdens imposed by credit card verification and adult password verification systems make them effectively unavailable to a substantial number of Internet content providers."

II

The Telecommunications Act of 1996 ... was an unusually important legislative enactment.... Title V—known as the "Communications Decency Act of 1996" (CDA)—contains provisions that were either added in executive committee after the hearings were concluded or as amendments offered during floor debate on the legislation. An amendment offered in the Senate was the source of the two statutory provisions challenged in this case. They are informally described as the "indecent transmission" provision and the "patently offensive display" provision.

The first, 47 U.S.C.A. § 223(a) ... prohibits the knowing transmission of obscene or indecent messages to any recipient under 18 years of age. It provides in pertinent part:

> "Whoever ... in interstate or foreign communications ... by means of a telecommunications device knowingly makes, creates, or solicits, and ... initiates the transmission of, ... any comment, request, suggestion, proposal, image, or other communication which is obscene or indecent, knowing that the recipient of the communication is under 18 years of age, regardless of whether the maker of such communication placed the call or initiated the communication; ... [or] knowingly permits any

telecommunications facility under his control to be used for any [such] activity ... with the intent that it be used for such activity, shall be fined under Title 18, or imprisoned not more than two years, or both."

The second provision, § 223(d), prohibits the knowing sending or displaying of patently offensive messages in a manner that is available to a person under 18 years of age. It provides:

"(d) Whoever ... in interstate or foreign communications knowingly ... uses an interactive computer service to send to a specific person or persons under 18 years of age, or ... uses any interactive computer service to display in a manner available to a person under 18 years of age, ... any comment, request, suggestion, proposal, image, or other communication that, in context, depicts or describes, in terms patently offensive as measured by contemporary community standards, sexual or excretory activities or organs, regardless of whether the user of such service placed the call or initiated the communication; or ... knowingly permits any telecommunications facility under such person's control to be used for an activity prohibited by paragraph (1) with the intent that it be used for such activity, ... shall be fined under Title 18, or imprisoned not more than two years, or both."

The breadth of these prohibitions is qualified by two affirmative defenses. One covers those who take "good faith, reasonable, effective, and appropriate actions" to restrict access by minors to the prohibited communications. § 223(e)(5)(A). The other covers those who restrict access to covered material by requiring certain designated forms of age proof, such as a verified credit card or an adult identification number or code. § 223(e)(5)(B).

III

On February 8, 1996, immediately after the President signed the statute, 20 plaintiffs filed suit against the Attorney General of the United States and the Department of Justice challenging the constitutionality of §§ 223(a)(1) and 223(d)....

. . .

The judgment of the District Court enjoins the Government from enforcing the prohibitions in § 223(a)(1)(B) insofar as they relate to "indecent" communications, but expressly preserves the Government's right to investigate and prosecute the obscenity or child pornography activities prohibited therein. The injunction against enforcement of §§ 223(d)(1) and (2) is unqualified because those provisions contain no separate reference to obscenity or child pornography.

... In its appeal, the Government argues that the District Court erred in holding that the CDA violated ... the First Amendment because it is overbroad ... [W]e conclude that the judgment should be affirmed ...

IV

In arguing for reversal, the Government contends that the CDA is plainly constitutional under three of our prior decisions: (1) Ginsberg v. New York, 390 U.S. 629 (1968); (2) FCC v. Pacifica Foundation, 438 U.S. 726 (1978); and (3) Renton v. Playtime Theatres, Inc., 475 U.S. 41 (1986). A close look at these cases, however, raises—rather than re-lieves—doubts concerning the constitutionality of the CDA.

In *Ginsberg*, we upheld the constitutionality of a New York statute that prohibited selling to minors under 17 years of age material that was considered obscene as to them even if not obscene as to adults....

In four important respects, the statute upheld in *Ginsberg* was narrower than the CDA. First, we noted in *Ginsberg* that "the prohibi-tion against sales to minors does not bar parents who so desire from purchasing the magazines for their children." ... Under the CDA, by contrast, neither the parents' consent—nor even their participation—in the communication would avoid the application of the statute. Second, the New York statute applied only to commercial transactions, ... whereas the CDA contains no such limitation. Third, the New York statute cabined its definition of material that is harmful to minors with the requirement that it be "utterly without redeeming social importance for minors." ... The CDA fails to provide us with any definition of the term "indecent" ... and, importantly, omits any requirement that the "patently offensive" material covered by § 223(d) lack serious literary, artistic, political, or scientific value. Fourth, the New York statute defined a minor as a person under the age of 17, whereas the CDA, in applying to all those under 18 years, includes an additional year of those nearest majority.

In *Pacifica*, we upheld a declaratory order of the Federal Communi-cations Commission, holding that the broadcast of a recording of a 12–minute monologue entitled "Filthy Words" that had previously been delivered to a live audience "could have been the subject of administra-tive sanctions." ...

. . .

As with the New York statute at issue in *Ginsberg*, there are significant differences between the order upheld in *Pacifica* and the CDA. First, the order in *Pacifica*, issued by an agency that had been regulating radio stations for decades, targeted a specific broadcast that represented a rather dramatic departure from traditional program con-tent in order to designate when—rather than whether—it would be permissible to air such a program in that particular medium. The CDA's broad categorical prohibitions are not limited to particular times and are not dependent on any evaluation by an agency familiar with the unique characteristics of the Internet. Second, unlike the CDA, the Commis-sion's declaratory order was not punitive.... Finally, the Commission's order applied to a medium which as a matter of history had "received the most limited First Amendment protection," ..., in large part be cause warnings could not adequately protect the listener from unexpect-ed program content. The Internet, however, has no comparable history.

Moreover, the District Court found that the risk of encountering indecent material by accident is remote because a series of affirmative steps is required to access specific material.

In *Renton*, we upheld a zoning ordinance that kept adult movie theatres out of residential neighborhoods. The ordinance was aimed, not at the content of the films shown in the theaters, but rather at the "secondary effects"—such as crime and deteriorating property values— that these theaters fostered.... [T]he purpose of the CDA is to protect children from the primary effects of "indecent" and "patently offensive" speech, rather than any "secondary" effect of such speech....

These precedents, then, surely do not require us to uphold the CDA and are fully consistent with the application of the most stringent review of its provisions.

V

 ... [S]ome of our cases have recognized special justifications for regulation of the broadcast media that are not applicable to other speakers.... In these cases, the Court relied on the history of extensive government regulation of the broadcast medium, ... the scarcity of available frequencies at its inception, ... and its "invasive" nature ...

Those factors are not present in cyberspace. Neither before nor after the enactment of the CDA have the vast democratic fora of the Internet been subject to the type of government supervision and regulation that has attended the broadcast industry. Moreover, the Internet is not as "invasive" as radio or television. The District Court specifically found that "[c]ommunications over the Internet do not 'invade' an individual's home or appear on one's computer screen unbidden. Users seldom encounter content 'by accident.' " It also found that "[a]lmost all sexually explicit images are preceded by warnings as to the content," and cited testimony that " 'odds are slim' that a user would come across a sexually explicit sight by accident."

. . .

Finally, unlike the conditions that prevailed when Congress first authorized regulation of the broadcast spectrum, the Internet can hardly be considered a "scarce" expressive commodity. It provides relatively unlimited, low-cost capacity for communication of all kinds. The Government estimates that "[a]s many as 40 million people use the Internet today, and that figure is expected to grow to 200 million by 1999.".... As the District Court found, "the content on the Internet is as diverse as human thought." ...

VI

 ... [T]he many ambiguities concerning the scope of [the] coverage [of the CDA] render it problematic for purposes of the First Amendment. For instance, each of the two parts of the CDA uses a different linguistic form. The first uses the word "indecent," ... while the second speaks of material that "in context, depicts or describes, in terms patently offensive as measured by contemporary community standards, sexual or excretory activities or organs,".... Given the absence of a definition of either term, this difference in language will provoke uncertainty among speakers about how the two standards relate to each other and just what they mean....

. . .

The Government argues that the statute is no more vague than the obscenity standard this Court established in Miller v. California, 413 U.S. 15 (1973) ..... Because the CDA's "patently offensive" standard (and, we assume arguendo, its synonymous "indecent" standard) is one part of the three-prong *Miller* test, the Government reasons, it cannot be unconstitutionally vague.

. . .

The Government's reasoning is ... flawed. Just because a definition including three limitations is not vague, it does not follow that one of those limitations, standing by itself, is not vague....

In contrast to *Miller* and our other previous cases, the CDA thus presents a greater threat of censoring speech that, in fact, falls outside the statute's scope. Given the vague contours of the coverage of the statute, it unquestionably silences some speakers whose messages would be entitled to constitutional protection. That danger provides further reason for insisting that the statute not be overly broad. The CDA's burden on protected speech cannot be justified if it could be avoided by a more carefully drafted statute.

VII

... [T]he CDA effectively suppresses a large amount of speech that adults have a constitutional right to receive and to address to one another. That burden on adult speech is unacceptable if less restrictive alternatives would be at least as effective in achieving the legitimate purpose that the statute was enacted to serve.

. . .

In arguing that the CDA does not so diminish adult communication, the Government relies on the incorrect factual premise that prohibiting a transmission whenever it is known that one of its recipients is a minor would not interfere with adult-to-adult communication.... [T]his premise is untenable. Given the size of the potential audience for most messages, in the absence of a viable age verification process, the sender must be charged with knowing that one or more minors will likely view it. Knowledge that, for instance, one or more members of a 100–person chat group will be minor—and therefore that it would be a crime to send the group an indecent message—would surely burden communication among adults.

... [A]t the time of trial existing technology did not include any effective method for a sender to prevent minors from obtaining access to its communications on the Internet without also denying access to adults.... By contrast, the District Court found that "[d]espite its limitations, currently available user-based software suggests that a reasonably effective method by which parents can prevent their children from accessing sexually explicit and other material which parents may believe is inappropriate for their children will soon be widely available."

. . .

The breadth of the CDA's coverage is wholly unprecedented. . . . The general, undefined terms "indecent" and "patently offensive" cover large amounts of nonpornographic material with serious educational or other value. Moreover, the "community standards" criterion as applied to the Internet means that any communication available to a nation-wide audience will be judged by the standards of the community most likely to be offended by the message. . . .

. . . Under the CDA, a parent allowing her 17–year–old to use the family computer to obtain information on the Internet that she, in her parental judgment, deems appropriate could face a lengthy prison term . . . . . Similarly, a parent who sent his 17–year–old college freshman information on birth control via e-mail could be incarcerated even though neither he, his child, nor anyone in their home community, found the material "indecent" or "patently offensive," if the college town's community thought otherwise.

The breadth of this content-based restriction of speech imposes an especially heavy burden on the Government to explain why a less restrictive provision would not be as effective as the CDA. It has not done so. . . . Particularly in the light of the absence of any detailed findings by the Congress, or even hearings addressing the special problems of the CDA, we are persuaded that the CDA is not narrowly tailored if that requirement has any meaning at all.

. . .

XI

. . . [T]he Government asserts that—in addition to its interest in protecting children—its "[e]qually significant" interest in fostering the growth of the Internet provides an independent basis for upholding the constitutionality of the CDA. The Government apparently assumes that the unregulated availability of "indecent" and "patently offensive" material on the Internet is driving countless citizens away from the medium because of the risk of exposing themselves or their children to harmful material.

We find this argument singularly unpersuasive. The dramatic expansion of this new marketplace of ideas contradicts the factual basis of this contention. The record demonstrates that the growth of the Internet has been and continues to be phenomenal. As a matter of constitutional tradition, in the absence of evidence to the contrary, we presume that governmental regulation of the content of speech is more likely to interfere with the free exchange of ideas than to encourage it. The interest in encouraging freedom of expression in a democratic society outweighs any theoretical but unproven benefit of censorship.

. . .

JUSTICE O'CONNOR with whom THE CHIEF JUSTICE joins, concurring in the judgment in part and dissenting in part.

I write separately to explain why I view the Communications Decency Act of 1996 (CDA) as little more than an attempt by Congress to create "adult zones" on the Internet. Our precedent indicates that the creation of such zones can be constitutionally sound. Despite the soundness of its purpose, however, portions of the CDA are unconstitutional because they stray from the blueprint our prior cases have developed for constructing a "zoning law" that passes constitutional muster.

. . .

I

Our cases make clear that a "zoning" law is valid only if adults are still able to obtain the regulated speech. . . . If the law does not unduly restrict adults' access to constitutionally protected speech, however, it may be valid. . . .

The Court in *Ginsberg* concluded that the New York law created a constitutionally adequate adult zone simply because, on its face, it denied access only to minors. . . . [T]he twin characteristics of geography and identity enable the establishment's proprietor to prevent children from entering the establishment, but to let adults inside.

The electronic world is fundamentally different. . . . [I]t is not currently possible to exclude persons from accessing certain messages on the basis of their identity.

. . .

. . . I agree with the Court that the "display" provision cannot pass muster. . . .

The "indecency transmission" and "specific person" provisions present a closer issue, for they are not unconstitutional in all of their applications. . . .

. . . [B]oth provisions are constitutional as applied to a conversation involving only an adult and one or more minors—e.g., when an adult speaker sends an e-mail knowing the addressee is a minor, or when an adult and minor converse by themselves or with other minors in a chat room. In this context, these provisions are no different from the law we sustained in *Ginsberg*.

The analogy to *Ginsberg* breaks down, however, when more than one adult is a party to the conversation. If a minor enters a chat room otherwise occupied by adults, the CDA effectively requires the adults in the room to stop using indecent speech. . . . The CDA is therefore akin to a law that makes it a crime for a bookstore owner to sell pornographic magazines to anyone once a minor enters his store. . . .

. . . I agree with the Court that the provisions are overbroad in that they cover any and all communications between adults and minors, regardless of how many adults might be part of the audience to the communication.

This conclusion does not end the matter, however.... I would ... sustain the "indecency transmission" and "specific person" provisions to the extent they apply to the transmission of Internet communications where the party initiating the communication knows that all of the recipients are minors.

NOTE

Justice Souter, concurring in Denver Area Educational Telecommunications Consortium, Inc. v. Federal Communications Commission, 518 U.S. 727 (1996), warned about the difficulty of applying old concepts to new technologies. "In my own ignorance I have to accept the real possibility that 'if we had to decide today ... just what the First Amendment should mean in cyberspace, ... we would get it fundamentally wrong'."

ASHCROFT v. ACLU–I

535 U.S. 564, 122 S.Ct. 1700, 152 L.Ed.2d 771 (2002).

JUSTICE THOMAS announced the judgment of the Court and delivered the opinion of the Court with respect to Parts I, II, and IV, an opinion with respect to Parts III–A, III–C, and III–D, in which THE CHIEF JUSTICE and JUSTICE SCALIA join, and an opinion with respect to Part III–B, in which THE CHIEF JUSTICE, JUSTICE O'CONNOR, and JUSTICE SCALIA join.

This case presents the narrow question whether the Child Online Protection Act's (COPA or Act) use of "community standards" to identify "material that is harmful to minors" violates the First Amendment. We hold that this aspect of COPA does not render the statute facially unconstitutional.

I

... While "surfing" the World Wide Web, ... individuals can access material about topics ranging from aardvarks to Zoroastrianism. One can use the Web to read thousands of newspapers published around the globe, purchase tickets for a matinee at the neighborhood movie theater, or follow the progress of any Major League Baseball team on a pitch-by-pitch basis.

The Web also contains a wide array of sexually explicit material, including hardcore pornography.... In 1998, for instance, there were approximately 28,000 adult sites promoting pornography on the Web.... [C]hildren may discover this pornographic material either by deliberately accessing pornographic Web sites or by stumbling upon them....

Congress first attempted to protect children from exposure to pornographic material on the Internet by enacting the Communications Decency Act of 1996 (CDA) ... The CDA prohibited the knowing transmission over the Internet of obscene or indecent messages to any recipient under 18 years of age.... It also forbade any individual from knowingly sending over or displaying on the Internet certain "patently offensive" material in a manner available to persons under 18 years of age.... The prohibition specifically extended to "any comment, request, suggestion, proposal, image, or other communication that, in context, depict[ed] or describ[ed], in terms patently offensive as measured by contemporary community standards, sexual or excretory activities or organs." ...

The CDA provided two affirmative defenses to those prosecuted under the statute. The first protected individuals who took "good faith, reasonable, effective, and appropriate actions" to restrict minors from accessing obscene, indecent, and patently offensive material over the Internet.... The second shielded those who restricted minors from accessing such material "by requiring use of a verified credit card, debit account, adult access code, or adult personal identification number." ...

Notwithstanding these affirmative defenses, in Reno v. American Civil Liberties Union, [521 U.S. 844 (1997),] we held that the CDA's regulation of indecent transmissions, ... and the display of patently offensive material, ... ran afoul of the First Amendment. We concluded that "the CDA lack[ed] the precision that the First Amendment requires when a statute regulates the content of speech" because, "[i]n order to deny minors access to potentially harmful speech, the CDA effectively suppress[ed] a large amount of speech that adults ha[d] a constitutional right to receive and to address to one another." ...

Our holding was based on three crucial considerations. First, "existing technology did not include any effective method for a sender to prevent minors from obtaining access to its communications on the Internet without also denying access to adults." ... Second, "[t]he breadth of the CDA's coverage [was] wholly unprecedented." ... "Its open-ended prohibitions embrace[d]," not only commercial speech or commercial entities, but also "all nonprofit entities and individuals posting indecent messages or displaying them on their own computers in the presence of minors." *Ibid.* In addition, because the CDA did not define the terms "indecent" and "patently offensive," the statute "cover[ed] large amounts of nonpornographic material with serious educational or other value." ... As a result, regulated subject matter under the CDA extended to "discussions about prison rape or safe sexual practices, artistic images that include nude subjects, and arguably the card catalog of the Carnegie Library." ... Third, we found that neither affirmative defense set forth in the CDA "constitute[d] the sort of 'narrow tailoring' that [would] save an otherwise patently invalid unconstitutional provision." ... Consequently, only the CDA's ban on the knowing transmission of obscene messages survived scrutiny because obscene speech enjoys no First Amendment protection....

After our decision in Reno v. American Civil Liberties Union, Congress explored other avenues for restricting minors' access to pornographic material on the Internet. In particular, Congress passed and the President signed into law the Child Online Protection Act, 112 Stat. 2681–736 (codified in 47 U.S.C. § 231 (1994 ed., Supp. V)). COPA prohibits any person from "knowingly and with knowledge of the character of the material, in interstate or foreign commerce by means of the World Wide Web, mak[ing] any communication for commercial purposes that is available to any minor and that includes any material that is harmful to minors." 47 U.S.C. § 231(a)(1).

Apparently responding to our objections to the breadth of the CDA's coverage, Congress limited the scope of COPA's coverage in at least three ways. First, while the CDA applied to communications over the Internet as a whole, including, for example, e-mail messages, COPA applies only to material displayed on the World Wide Web. Second, unlike the CDA, COPA covers only communications made "for commercial purposes." ... And third, while the CDA prohibited "indecent" and "patently offensive" communications, COPA restricts only the narrower category of "material that is harmful to minors." ...

Drawing on the three-part test for obscenity set forth in *Miller v. California,* 413 U.S. 15, 93 S.Ct. 2607, 37 L.Ed.2d 419 (1973), COPA defines "material that is harmful to minors" as

"any communication, picture, image, graphic image file, article, recording, writing, or other matter of any kind that is obscene or that—

"(A) the average person, applying contemporary community standards, would find, taking the material as a whole and with respect to minors, is designed to appeal to, or is designed to pander to, the prurient interest;

"(B) depicts, describes, or represents, in a manner patently offensive with respect to minors, an actual or simulated sexual act or sexual contact, an actual or simulated normal or perverted sexual act, or a lewd exhibition of the genitals or post-pubescent female breast; and

"(C) taken as a whole, lacks serious literary, artistic, political, or scientific value for minors." 47 U.S.C. § 231(e)(6).

Like the CDA, COPA also provides affirmative defenses to those subject to prosecution under the statute. An individual may qualify for a defense if he, "in good faith, has restricted access by minors to material that is harmful to minors—(A) by requiring the use of a credit card, debit account, adult access code, or adult personal identification number; (B) by accepting a digital certificate that verifies age; or (C) by any other reasonable measures that are feasible under available technology." § 231(c)(1). Persons violating COPA are subject to both civil and criminal sanctions. A civil penalty of up to $50,000 may be imposed for each violation of the statute. Criminal penalties consist of up to six months in prison and/or a maximum fine of $50,000. An additional fine of $50,000 may be imposed for any intentional violation of the statute. § 231(a).

One month before COPA was scheduled to go into effect, respondents filed a lawsuit challenging the constitutionality of the statute in the United States District Court for the Eastern District of Pennsylvania. Respondents are a diverse group of organizations, most of which maintain their own Web sites. While the vast majority of content on their Web sites is available for free, respondents all derive income from their sites. Some, for example, sell advertising that is displayed on their Web sites, while others either sell goods directly over their sites or charge artists for the privilege of posting material. All respondents either post or have members that post sexually oriented material on the Web.

Respondents' Web sites contain "resources on obstetrics, gynecology, and sexual health; visual art and poetry; resources designed for gays and lesbians; information about books and stock photographic images offered for sale; and online magazines."

In their complaint, respondents alleged that, although they believed that the material on their Web sites was valuable for adults, they feared that they would be prosecuted under COPA because some of that material "could be construed as 'harmful to minors' in some communities." ...

The District Court granted respondents' motion for a preliminary injunction, barring the Government from enforcing the Act until the merits of respondents' claims could be adjudicated....

... The United States Court of Appeals for the Third Circuit affirmed....

We ... now vacate the Court of Appeals' judgment.

II

. . .

Ending over a decade of turmoil, this Court in *Miller* set forth the governing three-part test for assessing whether material is obscene and thus unprotected by the First Amendment ...

... The Court preserved the use of community standards in formulating the *Miller* test, explaining that they furnish a valuable First Amendment safeguard: "[T]he primary concern ... is to be certain that ... [material] will be judged by its impact on an average person, rather than a particularly susceptible or sensitive person—or indeed a totally insensitive one." ...

III

The Court of Appeals, however, concluded that this Court's prior community standards jurisprudence "has no applicability to the Internet and the Web" because "Web publishers are currently without the ability to control the geographic scope of the recipients of their communications." We therefore must decide whether this technological limitation renders COPA's reliance on community standards constitutionally infirm.

A

In addressing this question, the parties first dispute the nature of the community standards that jurors will be instructed to apply when assessing, in prosecutions under COPA, whether works appeal to the prurient interest of minors and are patently offensive with respect to minors. Respondents contend that jurors will evaluate material using "local community standards," while petitioner maintains that jurors will not consider the community standards of any particular geographic area, but rather will be "instructed to consider the standards of the adult community as a whole, without geographic specification."

In the context of this case, which involves a facial challenge to a statute that has never been enforced, we do not think it prudent to engage in speculation as to whether certain hypothetical jury instructions would or would not be consistent with COPA, and deciding this case does not require us to do so. It is sufficient to note that community standards need not be defined by reference to a precise geographic area....

B

Because juries would apply different standards across the country, and Web publishers currently lack the ability to limit access to their sites on a geographic basis, the Court of Appeals feared that COPA's "community standards" component would effectively force all speakers on the Web to abide by the "most puritan" community's standards.

In evaluating the constitutionality of the CDA, this Court expressed a similar concern over that statute's use of community standards to identify patently offensive material on the Internet. We noted that "the 'community standards' criterion as applied to the Internet means that any communication available to a nationwide audience will be judged by the standards of the community most likely to be offended by the message." *Reno*, ...

The CDA's use of community standards to identify patently offensive material, however, was particularly problematic in light of that statute's unprecedented breadth and vagueness. The statute covered communications depicting or describing "sexual or excretory activities or organs" that were "patently offensive as measured by contemporary community standards"—a standard somewhat similar to the second prong of *Miller*'s three-prong test. But the CDA did not include any limiting terms resembling *Miller*'s additional two prongs.... It neither contained any requirement that restricted material appeal to the prurient interest nor excluded from the scope of its coverage works with serious literary, artistic, political, or scientific value.... The tremendous breadth of the CDA magnified the impact caused by differences in community standards across the country, restricting Web publishers from openly displaying a significant amount of material that would have constituted protected speech in some communities across the country but run afoul of community standards in others.

COPA, by contrast, does not appear to suffer from the same flaw because it applies to significantly less material than did the CDA and defines the harmful-to-minors material restricted by the statute in a manner parallel to the *Miller* definition of obscenity. To fall within the scope of COPA, works must not only "depic[t], describ[e], or represen[t], in a manner patently offensive with respect to minors," particular sexual acts or parts of the anatomy, they must also be designed to appeal to the prurient interest of minors and "taken as a whole, lac[k] serious literary, artistic, political, or scientific value for minors." ...

These additional two restrictions substantially limit the amount of material covered by the statute. Material appeals to the prurient interest, for instance, only if it is in some sense erotic.... Of even more significance, however, is COPA's exclusion of material with serious value for minors. . . . In *Reno*, we emphasized that the serious value "requirement is particularly important because, unlike the 'patently offensive' and 'prurient interest' criteria, it is not judged by contemporary community standards." . . .

C

When the scope of an obscenity statute's coverage is sufficiently narrowed by a "serious value" prong and a "prurient interest" prong, we have held that requiring a speaker disseminating material to a national audience to observe varying community standards does not violate the First Amendment. . . . Hamling v. United States, 418 U.S. 87 (1974) . . .

Like respondents here, the dissenting opinion in *Hamling* argued that it was unconstitutional for a federal statute to rely on community standards to regulate speech. . . .

This Court, however, rejected Justice Brennan's argument that the federal mail statute unconstitutionally compelled speakers choosing to distribute materials on a national basis to tailor their messages to the least tolerant community . . .

Fifteen years later, *Hamling*'s holding was reaffirmed in Sable Communications of Cal., Inc. v. FCC, 492 U.S. 115 (1989). *Sable* addressed the constitutionality of . . . a statutory provision prohibiting the use of telephones to make obscene or indecent communications for commercial purposes. The petitioner in that case, a "dial-a-porn" operator, challenged, in part, that portion of the statute banning obscene phone messages. Like respondents here, the "dial-a-porn" operator argued that reliance on community standards to identify obscene material impermissibly compelled "message senders . . . to tailor all their messages to the least tolerant community." . . . Relying on *Hamling*, however, this Court once again rebuffed this attack on the use of community standards in a federal statute of national scope: "There is no constitutional barrier under *Miller* to prohibiting communications that are obscene in some communities under local standards even though they are not obscene in others. *If Sable's audience is comprised of different communities with different local standards, Sable ultimately bears the burden of complying with the prohibition on obscene messages.*" . . . (emphasis added).

The Court of Appeals below concluded that *Hamling* and *Sable* "are easily distinguished from the present case" because in both of those cases "the defendants had the ability to control the distribution of controversial material with respect to the geographic communities into which they released it" whereas "Web publishers have no such comparable control." In neither *Hamling* nor *Sable*, however, was the speaker's ability to target the release of material into particular geographic areas integral to the legal analysis. In *Hamling*, the ability to limit the distribution of material to targeted communities was not mentioned, let alone relied upon, and in *Sable*, a dial-a-porn operator's ability to screen incoming calls from particular areas was referenced only as a supplemental point.... In the latter case, this Court made no effort to evaluate how burdensome it would have been for dial-a-porn operators to tailor their messages to callers from thousands of different communities across the Nation, instead concluding that the burden of complying with the statute rested with those companies....

While Justice Kennedy and Justice Stevens question the applicability of this Court's community standards jurisprudence to the Internet, we do not believe that the medium's "unique characteristics" justify adopting a different approach than that set forth in *Hamling* and *Sable*. If a publisher chooses to send its material into a particular community, this Court's jurisprudence teaches that it is the publisher's responsibility to abide by that community's standards. The publisher's burden does not change simply because it decides to distribute its material to every community in the Nation.... If a publisher wishes for its material to be judged only by the standards of particular communities, then it need only take the simple step of utilizing a medium that enables it to target the release of its material into those communities.

Respondents offer no other grounds upon which to distinguish this case from *Hamling* and *Sable*. While those cases involved obscenity rather than material that is harmful to minors, we have no reason to believe that the practical effect of varying community standards under COPA, given the statute's definition of "material that is harmful to minors," is significantly greater than the practical effect of varying community standards under federal obscenity statutes.... [I]f we were to hold COPA unconstitutional *because of* its use of community standards, federal obscenity statutes would likely also be unconstitutional as applied to the Web ...

D

... Because Congress has narrowed the range of content restricted by COPA in a manner analogous to *Miller*'s definition of obscenity, we conclude, consistent with our holdings in *Hamling* and *Sable*, that any variance caused by the statute's reliance on community standards is not substantial enough to violate the First Amendment.

IV

The scope of our decision today is quite limited. We hold only that COPA's reliance on community standards to identify "material that is harmful to minors" does not *by itself* render the statute substantially overbroad for purposes of the First Amendment. We do not express any view as to whether COPA suffers from substantial overbreadth for other reasons, whether the statute is unconstitutionally vague, or whether the District Court correctly concluded that the statute likely will not survive strict scrutiny analysis once adjudication of the case is completed below. While respondents urge us to resolve these questions at this time, prudence dictates allowing the Court of Appeals to first examine these difficult issues.

Petitioner does not ask us to vacate the preliminary injunction entered by the District Court, and in any event, we could not do so without addressing matters yet to be considered by the Court of Appeals. As a result, the Government remains enjoined from enforcing COPA absent further action by the Court of Appeals or the District Court.

. . .

JUSTICE O'CONNOR, concurring in part and concurring in the judgment.

I agree with the plurality that even if obscenity on the Internet is defined in terms of local community standards, respondents have not shown that the Child Online Protection Act (COPA) is overbroad solely on the basis of the variation in the standards of different communities. Like Justice Breyer, however, I write separately to express my views on the constitutionality and desirability of adopting a national standard for obscenity for regulation of the Internet.

The plurality's opinion argues that, even under local community standards, the variation between the most and least restrictive communities is not so great with respect to the narrow category of speech covered by COPA as to, alone, render the statute substantially overbroad. I agree, given respondents' failure to provide examples of materials that lack literary, artistic, political, and scientific value for minors, which would nonetheless result in variation among communities judging the other elements of the test. . . .

But respondents' failure to prove substantial overbreadth on a facial challenge in this case still leaves open the possibility that the use of local community standards will cause problems for regulation of obscenity on the Internet, for adults as well as children, in future cases. In an as-applied challenge, for instance, individual litigants may still dispute that the standards of a community more restrictive than theirs should apply to them. And in future facial challenges to regulation of obscenity on the Internet, litigants may make a more convincing case for substantial overbreadth. Where adult speech is concerned, for instance, there may in fact be a greater degree of disagreement about what is patently offensive or appeals to the prurient interest.

Nor do I think such future cases can be resolved by application of the approach we took in *Hamling* . . . and *Sable* . . . I agree with Justice Kennedy that, given Internet speakers' inability to control the geographic location of their audience, expecting them to bear the burden of controlling the recipients of their speech, as we did in *Hamling* and *Sable,* may be entirely too much to ask, and would potentially suppress an inordinate amount of expression. For these reasons, adoption of a national standard is necessary in my view for any reasonable regulation of Internet obscenity.

. . .

While I would prefer that the Court resolve the issue before it by explicitly adopting a national standard for defining obscenity on the Internet, given respondents' failure to demonstrate substantial overbreadth due solely to the variation between local communities, I join Parts I, II, III–B, and IV of Justice Thomas' opinion and the judgment.

JUSTICE BREYER, concurring in part and concurring in the judgment.

I write separately because I believe that Congress intended the statutory word "community" to refer to the Nation's adult community taken as a whole, not to geographically separate local areas. The statutory language does not explicitly describe the specific "community" to which it refers. It says only that the "average person, applying contemporary community standards" must find that the "material as a whole and with respect to minors, is designed to appeal to, or is designed to pander to, the prurient interest...." ...

. . .

... [T]his view of the statute avoids the need to examine the serious First Amendment problem that would otherwise exist.... To read the statute as adopting the community standards of every locality in the United States would provide the most puritan of communities with a heckler's Internet veto affecting the rest of the Nation. The technical difficulties associated with efforts to confine Internet material to particular geographic areas make the problem particularly serious....

... I do not join Part III of Justice Thomas' opinion, although I agree with much of the reasoning set forth in Parts III–B and III–D, insofar as it explains ... that variation reflecting application of the same national standard by different local juries does not violate the First Amendment.

JUSTICE KENNEDY, with whom JUSTICE SOUTER and JUSTICE GINSBURG join, concurring in the judgment.

I

... COPA is a major federal statute, enacted in the wake of our previous determination that its predecessor violated the First Amendment.... Congress and the President were aware of our decision, and we should assume that in seeking to comply with it they have given careful consideration to the constitutionality of the new enactment. For these reasons, even if this facial challenge appears to have considerable merit, the Judiciary must proceed with caution and identify overbreadth with care before invalidating the Act.

. . .

... To observe only that community standards vary across the country is to ignore the antecedent question: community standards as to what? Whether the national variation in community standards produces overbreadth requiring invalidation of COPA, ... depends on the breadth of COPA's coverage and on what community standards are being invoked. Only by identifying the universe of speech burdened by COPA is it possible to discern whether national variation in community standards renders the speech restriction overbroad....

... Some examination of the group of covered speakers and the categories of covered speech is necessary in order to comprehend the extent of the alleged overbreadth.

... I join the judgment of the Court vacating the opinion of the Court of Appeals and remanding for consideration of the statute as a whole. Unlike Justice Thomas, however, I would not assume that the Act is narrow enough to render the national variation in community standards unproblematic. Indeed, if the District Court correctly construed the statute across its other dimensions, then the variation in community standards might well justify enjoining enforcement of the Act. I would leave that question to the Court of Appeals in the first instance.

II

... The nub of the problem is, as the Court has said, that "the 'community standards' criterion as applied to the Internet means that any communication available to a nationwide audience will be judged by the standards of the community most likely to be offended by the message." ... This observation was the linchpin of the Court of Appeals' analysis, and we must now consider whether it alone suffices to support the holding below.

The quoted sentence from *Reno* was not casual dicta; rather, it was one rationale for the holding of the case.... Variation in community standards rendered the statute broader than the scope of the Government's own expressed compelling interest.

It is true, as Justice Thomas points out, that requiring a speaker addressing a national audience to meet varying community standards does not always violate the First Amendment. See *Hamling* ...; *Sable* ... These cases, however, are of limited utility in analyzing the one before us, because each mode of expression has its own unique characteristics ... Indeed, when Congress purports to abridge the freedom of a new medium, we must be particularly attentive to its distinct attributes ... The economics and the technology of each medium affect both the burden of a speech restriction and the Government's interest in maintaining it.

... [I]n upholding a ban on obscene phone messages, we emphasized that the speaker could "hire operators to determine the source of the calls or engag[e] with the telephone company to arrange for the screening and blocking of out-of-area calls or fin[d] another means for providing messages compatible with community standards." ... And if we did not make the same point in *Hamling*, that is likely because it is so obvious that mailing lends itself to geographic restriction....

The economics and technology of Internet communication differ in important ways from those of telephones and mail. Paradoxically, as the District Court found, it is easy and cheap to reach a worldwide audience on the Internet, but expensive if not impossible to reach a geographic subset. A Web publisher in a community where avant garde culture is the norm may have no desire to reach a national market; he may wish only to speak to his neighbors; nevertheless, if an eavesdropper in a more traditional, rural community chooses to listen in, there is nothing the publisher can do. As a practical matter, COPA makes the eavesdropper the arbiter of propriety on the Web. And it is no answer to say that the speaker should "take the simple step of utilizing a [different] medium." . . .

. . .

. . . [W]e need not decide whether the statute invokes local or national community standards to conclude that vacatur and remand are in order. If the statute does incorporate some concept of national community standards, the actual standard applied is bound to vary by community nevertheless, as the Attorney General concedes.

For this reason the Court of Appeals was correct to focus on COPA's incorporation of varying community standards; and it may have been correct as well to conclude that in practical effect COPA imposes the most puritanical community standard on the entire country. . . . In striking down COPA's predecessor, the *Reno* Court identified this precise problem, and if the *Hamling* and *Sable* Courts did not find the problem fatal, that is because those cases involved quite different media. The national variation in community standards constitutes a particular burden on Internet speech.

III

The question that remains is whether this observation *"by itself"* suffices to enjoin the Act. I agree with the Court that it does not. We cannot know whether variation in community standards renders the Act substantially overbroad without first assessing the extent of the speech covered and the variations in community standards with respect to that speech.

. . . As this case comes to us, once it is accepted that we cannot strike down the Act based merely on the phrase "contemporary community standards," we should go no further than to vacate and remand for a more comprehensive analysis of the Act.

. . .

JUSTICE STEVENS, dissenting.

Appeals to prurient interests are commonplace on the Internet, as in older media. Many of those appeals lack serious value for minors as well as adults. Some are offensive to certain viewers but welcomed by others. For decades, our cases have recognized that the standards for judging their acceptability vary from viewer to viewer and from community to community. Those cases developed the requirement that communications should be protected if they do not violate contemporary community standards. In its original form, the community standard provided a shield for communications that are offensive only to the least tolerant members of society. . . . In the context of the Internet, however, community standards become a sword, rather than a shield. If a prurient appeal is offensive in a puritan village, it may be a crime to post it on the World Wide Web.

. . .

We have ... repeatedly rejected the position that the free speech rights of adults can be limited to what is acceptable for children. See ... *Butler v. Michigan*, 352 U.S. 380, 383 (1957).

... Like the ... ban against selling adult books found impermissible in *Butler*, COPA seeks to limit protected speech that is not targeted at children, simply because it can be obtained by them while surfing the Web. In evaluating the overbreadth of such a statute, we should be mindful of Justice Frankfurter's admonition not to "burn the house to roast the pig," *Butler*, 352 U.S., at 383.

COPA not only restricts speech that is made available to the general public, it also covers a medium in which speech cannot be segregated to avoid communities where it is likely to be considered harmful to minors....

If the material were forwarded through the mails, as in *Hamling*, or over the telephone, as in *Sable*, the sender could avoid destinations with the most restrictive standards.... In light of this fundamental difference in technologies, the rules applicable to the mass mailing of an obscene montage or to obscene dial-a-porn should not be used to judge the legality of messages on the World Wide Web.

. . .

Justice Thomas points to several other provisions in COPA to argue that any overbreadth will be rendered insubstantial by the rest of the statute. These provisions afford little reassurance, however, as they only marginally limit the sweep of the statute....

. . .

Justice Kennedy makes a similar misstep when he ties the overbreadth inquiry to questions about the scope of the other provisions of the statute.... These other provisions may reduce the absolute number of Web pages covered by the statute, but even the narrowest version of the statute abridges a substantial amount of protected speech that many communities would not find harmful to minors. Because Web speakers cannot limit access to those specific communities, the statute is substantially overbroad regardless of how its other provisions are construed.

Justice Thomas acknowledges, and petitioner concedes, that juries across the country will apply different standards and reach different conclusions about whether particular works are harmful to minors....

... Because communities differ widely in their attitudes toward sex, particularly when minors are concerned, the Court of Appeals was correct to conclude that, regardless of how COPA's other provisions are construed, applying community standards to the Internet will restrict a substantial amount of protected speech that would not be considered harmful to minors in many communities.

Whether that consequence is appropriate depends, of course, on the content of the message. The kind of hard-core pornography involved in *Hamling*, which I assume would be obscene under any community's standard, does not belong on the Internet. Perhaps "teasers" that serve no function except to invite viewers to examine hardcore materials, or the hidden terms written into a Web site's "metatags" in order to dupe unwitting Web surfers into visiting pornographic sites, deserve the same fate. But COPA extends to a wide range of prurient appeals in advertisements, online magazines, Web-based bulletin boards and chat rooms, stock photo galleries, Web diaries, and a variety of illustrations encompassing a vast number of messages that are unobjectionable in most of the country and yet provide no "serious value" for minors. It is quite wrong to allow the standards of a minority consisting of the least tolerant communities to regulate access to relatively harmless messages in this burgeoning market.

. . . I would affirm the judgment of the Court of Appeals . . .

. . .

ASHCROFT v. ACLU–II

542 U.S. 656, 124 S.Ct. 2783, 159 L.Ed.2d 690 (2004).

JUSTICE KENNEDY delivered the opinion of the Court.

This case presents a challenge to a statute enacted by Congress to protect minors from exposure to sexually explicit materials on the Internet, the Child Online Protection Act (COPA). 112 Stat. 2681–736, codified at 47 U.S.C. § 231. We must decide whether the Court of Appeals was correct to affirm a ruling by the District Court that enforcement of COPA should be enjoined because the statute likely violates the First Amendment.

In enacting COPA, Congress gave consideration to our earlier decisions on this subject, in particular the decision in *Reno v. American Civil Liberties Union*, 521 U.S. 844, 117 S.Ct. 2329, 138 L.Ed.2d 874 (1997). . . . The imperative of according respect to the Congress, however, does not permit us to depart from well-established First Amendment principles. Instead, we must hold the Government to its constitutional burden of proof.

Content-based prohibitions, enforced by severe criminal penalties, have the constant potential to be a repressive force in the lives and thoughts of a free people. To guard against that threat the Constitution demands that content-based restrictions on speech be presumed invalid . . . and that the Government bear the burden of showing their constitutionality. . . . This is true even when Congress twice has attempted to find a constitutional means to restrict, and punish, the speech in question.

This case comes to the Court on certiorari review of an appeal from the decision of the District Court granting a preliminary injunction. . . . The Government has failed, at this point, to rebut the plaintiffs' contention that there are plausible less restrictive alternatives to the statute. Substantial practical considerations, furthermore, argue in favor of upholding the injunction and allowing the case to proceed to trial. For those reasons, we affirm the decision of the Court of Appeals upholding the preliminary injunction, and we remand the case so that it may be returned to the District Court for trial on the issues presented.

I

A

COPA is the second attempt by Congress to make the Internet safe for minors by criminalizing certain Internet speech. . . .

In response to the Court's decision in *Reno,* Congress passed COPA. COPA imposes criminal penalties of a $50,000 fine and six months in prison for the knowing posting, for "commercial purposes," of World Wide Web content that is "harmful to minors." § 231(a)(1). Material that is "harmful to minors" is defined as:

"any communication, picture, image, graphic image file, article, recording, writing, or other matter of any kind that is obscene or that—

"(A) the average person, applying contemporary community standards, would find, taking the material as a whole and with respect to minors, is designed to appeal to, or is designed to pander to, the prurient interest;

"(B) depicts, describes, or represents, in a manner patently offensive with respect to minors, an actual or simulated sexual act or sexual contact, an actual or simulated normal or perverted sexual act, or a lewd exhibition of the genitals or post-pubescent female breast; and

"(C) taken as a whole, lacks serious literary, artistic, political, or scientific value for minors." § 231(e)(6).

"Minors" are defined as "any person under 17 years of age." § 231(e)(7). A person acts for "commercial purposes only if such person is engaged in the business of making such communications." . . .

While the statute labels all speech that falls within these definitions as criminal speech, it also provides an affirmative defense to those who employ specified means to prevent minors from gaining access to the prohibited materials on their Web site. A person may escape conviction under the statute by demonstrating that he

"has restricted access by minors to material that is harmful to minors—

"(A) by requiring use of a credit card, debit account, adult access code, or adult personal identification number;

"(B) by accepting a digital certificate that verifies age, or

"(C) by any other reasonable measures that are feasible under available technology." § 231(c)(1).

Since the passage of COPA, Congress has enacted additional laws regulating the Internet in an attempt to protect minors. For example, it has enacted a prohibition on misleading Internet domain names, . . . in order to prevent Web site owners from disguising pornographic Web sites in a way likely to cause uninterested persons to visit them. See Brief for Petitioner 7 (giving, as an example, the Web site "whitehouse.com"). It has also passed a statute creating a "Dot Kids" second-level Internet domain, the content of which is restricted to that which is fit for minors under the age of 13. . . .

. . .

II

A

This Court, like other appellate courts, has always applied the abuse of discretion standard on the review of a preliminary injunction. . . . If the underlying constitutional question is close, therefore, we should uphold the injunction and remand for trial on the merits. Applying this mode of inquiry, we agree with the Court of Appeals that the District Court did not abuse its discretion in entering the preliminary injunction. . . .

. . . When plaintiffs challenge a content-based speech restriction, the burden is on the Government to prove that the proposed alternatives will not be as effective as the challenged statute. . . .

The purpose of the test is to ensure that speech is restricted no further than necessary to achieve the goal, for it is important to assure that legitimate speech is not chilled or punished. For that reason, the test does not begin with the status quo of existing regulations, then ask whether the challenged restriction has some additional ability to achieve Congress' legitimate interest. Any restriction on speech could be justified under that analysis. Instead, the court should ask whether the challenged regulation is the least restrictive means among available, effective alternatives.

In deciding whether to grant a preliminary injunction stage, a district court must consider whether the plaintiffs have demonstrated that they are likely to prevail on the merits. . . . As the Government bears the burden of proof on the ultimate question of COPA's constitutionality, respondents must be deemed likely to prevail unless the Government has shown that respondents' proposed less restrictive alternatives are less effective than COPA. Applying that analysis, the District Court concluded that respondents were likely to prevail. . . . That conclusion was not an abuse of discretion, because on this record there are a number of plausible, less restrictive alternatives to the statute.

The primary alternative considered by the District Court was blocking and filtering software. Blocking and filtering software is an alternative that is less restrictive than COPA, and, in addition, likely more effective as a means of restricting children's access to materials harmful to them. The District Court, in granting the preliminary injunction, did so primarily because the plaintiffs had proposed that filters are a less restrictive alternative to COPA and the Government had not shown it would be likely to disprove the plaintiffs' contention at trial.

Filters are less restrictive than COPA. They impose selective restrictions on speech at the receiving end, not universal restrictions at the source. Under a filtering regime, adults without children may gain access to speech they have a right to see without having to identify themselves or provide their credit card information. Even adults with children may obtain access to the same speech on the same terms simply by turning off the filter on their home computers. Above all, promoting the use of filters does not condemn as criminal any category of speech, and so the potential chilling effect is eliminated, or at least much diminished. All of these things are true, moreover, regardless of how broadly or narrowly the definitions in COPA are construed.

Filters also may well be more effective than COPA. First, a filter can prevent minors from seeing all pornography, not just pornography posted to the Web from America. ... COPA does not prevent minors from having access to those foreign harmful materials. That alone makes it possible that filtering software might be more effective in serving Congress' goals. Effectiveness is likely to diminish even further if COPA is upheld, because the providers of the materials that would be covered by the statute simply can move their operations overseas. It is not an answer to say that COPA reaches some amount of materials that are harmful to minors; the question is whether it would reach more of them than less restrictive alternatives. In addition, the District Court found that verification systems may be subject to evasion and circumvention, for example by minors who have their own credit cards. Finally, filters also may be more effective because they can be applied to all forms of Internet communication, including e-mail, not just communications available via the World Wide Web.

. . .

One argument to the contrary is worth mentioning—the argument that filtering software is not an available alternative because Congress may not require it to be used. That argument carries little weight, because Congress undoubtedly may act to encourage the use of filters. We have held that Congress can give strong incentives to schools and libraries to use them. It could also take steps to promote their development by industry, and their use by parents. It is incorrect, for that reason, to say that filters are part of the current regulatory status quo. The need for parental cooperation does not automatically disqualify a proposed less restrictive alternative. In enacting COPA, Congress said its goal was to prevent the "widespread availability of the Internet" from providing "opportunities for minors to access materials through the World Wide Web in a manner that can frustrate parental supervision or control." ... COPA presumes that parents lack the ability, not the will, to monitor what their children see. By enacting programs to promote use of filtering software, Congress could give parents that ability without subjecting protected speech to severe penalties.

The closest precedent on the general point is our decision in *Playboy Entertainment Group. Playboy Entertainment Group*, like this case, involved a content-based restriction designed to protect minors from viewing harmful materials. The choice was between a blanket speech restriction and a more specific technological solution that was available to parents who chose to implement it. ...Absent a showing that the proposed less restrictive alternative would not be as effective, we concluded, the more restrictive option preferred by Congress could not survive strict scrutiny.... In the instant case, too, the Government has failed to show, at this point, that the proposed less restrictive alternative will be less effective. The reasoning of *Playboy Group Entertainment*, and the holdings and force of our precedents require us to affirm the preliminary injunction. To do otherwise would do less than the first amendment commands. "The starch of our constitutional standards cannot be sacrificed to accommodate the enforcement choices of the Government." [529 U.S.] at 830 (Thomas, J., concurring).

B

There are also important practical reasons to let the injunction stand pending a full trial on the merits. First, the potential harms from reversing the injunction outweigh those of leaving it in place by mistake....

Second, there are substantial factual disputes remaining in the case. As mentioned above, there is a serious gap in the evidence as to the effectiveness of filtering software. ... By allowing the preliminary injunction to stand and remanding for trial, we require the Government to shoulder its full constitutional burden of proof respecting the less restrictive alternative argument, rather than excuse it from doing so.

Third, and on a related point, the factual record does not reflect current technological reality—a serious flaw in any case involving the Internet. The technology of the Internet evolves at a rapid pace. Yet the factfindings of the District Court were entered in February 1999, over five years ago. Since then, certain facts about the Internet are known to have changed. ... It is reasonable to assume that other technological developments important to the First Amendment analysis have also occurred during that time. More and better filtering alternatives may exist than when the District Court entered its findings. Indeed, we know that after the District Court entered its factfindings, a congressionally appointed commission issued a report that found that filters are more effective than verification screens.

. . .

Remand will also permit the District Court to take account of a changed legal landscape. Since the District Court made its factfindings, Congress has passed at least two further statutes that might qualify as less restrictive alternatives to COPA—a prohibition on misleading domain names, and a statute creating a minors-safe "Dot Kids" domain. See *supra*, at 4. Remanding for trial will allow the District Court to take into account those additional potential alternatives.

Justice Stevens, with whom Justice Ginsburg joins, concurring.

When it first reviewed the constitutionality of the Child Online Protection Act (COPA), the Court of Appeals held that the statute's use of "contemporary community standards" to identify materials that are "harmful to minors" was a serious, and likely fatal, defect. ...I continue to believe that the Government may not penalize speakers for making available to the general World Wide Web audience that which the least tolerant communities in America deem unfit for their children's consumption, but COPA's use of community standards is not the statute's only constitutional defect. Today's decision points to another: that, as far as the record reveals, encouraging deployment of user-based controls, such as filtering software, would serve Congress' interest in protecting minors from sexually explicit Internet materials as well or better than attempting to regulate the vast content of the World Wide Web at its source, and at a far less significant cost to First Amendment values. Because implementation of the various adult-verification mechanisms described in the statute provides only an affirmative defense, ... even full compliance with COPA cannot guarantee freedom from prosecution. Speakers who dutifully place their content behind age screens may nevertheless find themselves in court, forced to prove the lawfulness of their speech on pain of criminal conviction....

Criminal prosecutions are, in my view, an inappropriate means to regulate the universe of materials classified as "obscene," ... [E]ven with Justice Breyer's guidance, I find it impossible to identify just how far past the already ill-defined territory of "obscenity" he thinks the statute extends. Attaching criminal sanctions to a mistaken judgment about the contours of the novel and nebulous category of "harmful to minors" speech clearly imposes a heavy burden....

. . .

JUSTICE SCALIA, dissenting. I agree with Justice Breyer's conclusion that the Child Online Protection Act (COPA), 47 U.S.C. § 231, is constitutional. See *post,* at 14 (dissenting opinion). Both the Court and Justice Breyer err, however, in subjecting COPA to strict scrutiny. Nothing in the First Amendment entitles the type of material covered by COPA to that exacting standard of review. ...

There is no doubt that the commercial pornography covered by COPA fits this description. The statute applies only to a person who, "as a regular course of such person's trade or business, with the objective of earning a profit," ... and "with knowledge of the character of the material," § 231(a)(1), communicates material that depicts certain specified sexual acts and that "is designed to appeal to, or is designed to pander to, the prurient interest," ... Since this business could, consistent with the First Amendment, be banned entirely, COPA's lesser restrictions raise no constitutional concern.

Justice Breyer, with whom the Chief Justice and Justice O'Connor join, dissenting.

. . .

... [T]he Court is wrong. I cannot accept its conclusion that Congress could have accomplished its statutory objective—protecting children from commercial pornography on the Internet—in other, less restrictive ways.

1

... [T]he Act, properly interpreted, imposes a burden on protected speech that is no more than modest.

A

The Act's definitions limit the material it regulates to material that does not enjoy First Amendment protection, namely legally obscene material, and very little more. A comparison of this Court's definition of unprotected, "legally obscene," material with the Act's definitions makes this clear. . . .

B

The Act does not censor the material it covers. Rather, it requires providers of the "harmful to minors" material to restrict minors' access to it by verifying age. They can do so by inserting screens that verify age using a credit card, adult personal identification number, or other similar technology. See § 231(c)(1). In this way, the Act requires creation of an internet screen that minors, but not adults, will find difficult to bypass.

. . .

In addition to the monetary cost, and despite strict requirements that identifying information be kept confidential, . . . the identification requirements inherent in age-screening may lead some users to fear embarrassment. Both monetary costs and potential embarrassment can deter potential viewers and, in that sense, the statute's requirements may restrict access to a site. But this Court has held that in the context of congressional efforts to protect children, restrictions of this kind do not automatically violate the Constitution. And the Court has approved their use. . . .

In sum, the Act at most imposes a modest additional burden on adult access to legally obscene material, perhaps imposing a similar burden on access to some protected borderline obscene material as well.

II

I turn next to the question of "compelling interest," that of protecting minors from exposure to commercial pornography. No one denies that such an interest is "compelling." . . . Rather, the question here is whether the Act, given its restrictions on adult access, significantly advances that interest. In other words, is the game worth the candle?

The majority argues that it is not, because of the existence of "blocking and filtering software." The majority refers to the presence of that software as a "less restrictive alternative." But that is a misnomer—a misnomer that may lead the reader to believe that all we need do is look to see if the blocking and filtering software is less restrictive; and to believe that, because in one sense it is (one can turn off the software), that is the end of the constitutional matter.

But such reasoning has no place here. Conceptually speaking, the presence of filtering software is not an *alternative* legislative approach to the problem of protecting children from exposure to commercial pornography. Rather, it is part of the status quo, *i.e.*, the backdrop against which Congress enacted the present statute. It is always true, by definition, that the status quo is less restrictive than a new regulatory law. It is always less restrictive to do *nothing* than to do *something*. But "doing nothing" does not address the problem Congress sought to address—namely that, despite the availability of filtering software, children were still being exposed to harmful material on the Internet.

Thus, the relevant constitutional question is not the question the Court asks: Would it be less restrictive to do nothing? Of course it would be. Rather, the relevant question posits a comparison of (a) a status quo that includes filtering software with (b) a change in that status quo that adds to it an age-verification screen requirement. Given the existence of filtering software, does the problem Congress identified remain significant? Does the Act help to address it? These are questions about the relation of the Act to the compelling interest. Does the Act, compared to the status quo, significantly advance the ball? . . .

The answers to these intermediate questions are clear: Filtering software, as presently available, does not solve the "child protection" problem. It suffers from four serious inadequacies that prompted Congress to pass legislation instead of relying on its voluntary use. First, its filtering is faulty, allowing some pornographic material to pass through without hindrance. . . .[I]n the absence of words, the software alone cannot distinguish between the most obscene pictorial image and the Venus de Milo. . . .

Second, filtering software costs money. Not every family has the $40 or so necessary to install it.

. . .

Third, filtering software depends upon parents willing to decide where their children will surf the Web and able to enforce that decision. As to millions of American families, that is not a reasonable possibility. More than 28 million school age children have both parents or their sole parent in the work force, at least 5 million children are left alone at home without supervision each week, and many of those children will spend afternoons and evenings with friends who may well have access to computers and more lenient parents. . . .

Chapter VIII

SYMBOLIC SPEECH

I. THE SPEECH–CONDUCT DISTINCTION

SYMBOLIC CONDUCT*

Symbolic conduct is an exceptionally vivid means of communication. It is more intensely emotional than the spoken or written word or the traditional cool art forms. Its dramatic effect is a substitute for the protester's lack of access to the more traditional mass media. The illegal act of burning draft cards, done at mass rallies in a city park, creates news and assures press and television coverage for the "speaker's" views. The same voice would be lost in obscurity if its only outlet were mimeographed pamphlets....

The challenge to those who interpret our Constitution is to accommodate the symbolic act—often denominated symbolic speech—without treading on the government's right to resist civil disobedience and mass interference with the rights of other citizens....

Obviously not all conduct is protected by the first amendment. The amendment protects that which is necessary to free expression and communication and most conduct has little if any connection with this purpose. One would expect, then, that in discussing symbolic speech the courts would be careful to establish criteria for identifying conduct which has communicative value and for which first amendment protection is required. Such, however, has not been the case. The courts have instead substituted for a refined definition of symbolic speech a balancing process weighted in favor of state interest and applied indiscriminately to all conduct arguably related to speech.

The Medium is the Message**

... The electric light is pure information. It is a medium without a message, as it were, unless it is used to spell out some verbal ad or name. This fact, characteristic of all media, means that the "content" of any medium is always another medium. The content of writing is speech, just as the written word is the content of print, and print is the content of the telegraph. If it is asked, "What is the content of speech?," it is necessary to say, "It is an actual process of thought, which is in itself nonverbal." An abstract painting represents direct manifestation of creative thought processes as they might appear in computer designs.

---

* Note, Symbolic Conduct, Columbia Law Review, 1968, vol. 68, p. 1091.

** From Marshall McLuhan, Understanding Media, McGraw–Hill Book Company, 1964, p. 8. Reprinted with permission.

NOTE

On December 3, 1968, Justice Hugo Black appeared on a televised CBS News Special, entitled "Justice Black and the Bill of Rights." During the course of the one hour program, Justice Black was asked by Eric Sevareid to define the distinction between "action and speech as protest." He answered: "The only way they have ever been able to define it as to this Amendment, where they said it with reference to the Mormons." [Justice Black was referring to Reynolds v. United States, 98 U.S. 145 (1878), discussed in Chapter 18, at p. 610.] The Mormons had a perfectly logical argument, if conduct is the same as speech. They said, "But this expresses our religious views. We're protesting because the Federal Government is passing a law suppressing our right to have a dozen wives." Well, the Court said, "That won't do, that's conduct not speech." Of course it involves speech—partially. Before you get to it, before you get a dozen wives, you've got to do some talking. But that doesn't mean the Constitution protects their right to have a dozen wives. The two are separate. Of course there are places where you cannot sharply draw a boundary.

UNITED STATES v. O'BRIEN

Supreme Court of the United States, 1968.
391 U.S. 367, 88 S.Ct. 1673, 20 L.Ed.2d 672.

CHIEF JUSTICE WARREN delivered the opinion of the Court.

EARL WARREN—Born on March 19, 1891, in Los Angeles, California, into a Scandinavian immigrant family. Grew up in Bakersfield, California, where his father was a railroad repairman. Republican. Protestant. In his *Memoirs* (1977), Warren wrote that he "was not an inspired student. I did well in the subjects I liked, ... but was lackadaisical in the others, to my lasting regret." California, Berkeley, B.L., 1912; J.D., 1914. Practiced law, 1915–1919; Oakland deputy city attorney, 1919–1920; Alameda County deputy assistant district attorney, 1920–1923; chief deputy district attorney, 1923–1925; district attorney, 1925–1939; California attorney general, 1939–1943; California governor, 1943–1953. U.S. vice presidential candidate, 1944. As California attorney general during World War II, he supported the Japanese Relocation, which he acknowledged near the end of this life was a serious mistake. Provided significant support for Dwight Eisenhower's presidential candidacy in 1952; as a result, Eisenhower promised to nominate him to the first vacancy on the Supreme Court. Nominated chief justice by President Eisenhower on September 30, 1953, to succeed Fred M. Vinson, who died in office. Confirmed by the Senate on March 1, 1954, by voice vote. Initially he tended to vote with Justice Frankfurter, but soon he increasingly voted with Justices Black and Douglas. His chief ally on the Court was Justice Brennan. In addition to his regular duties as chief justice, he chaired the Warren Commission, which investigated the assassination of President John F. Kennedy. Retired on June 23, 1969. Died on July 9, 1974.

On the morning of March 31, 1966, David Paul O'Brien and three companions burned their Selective Service registration certificates on the steps of the South Boston Courthouse. A sizable crowd, including several agents of the Federal Bureau of Investigation, witnessed the event.[1] ...

For this act, O'Brien was indicted, tried, convicted, and sentenced[2] in the United States District Court for the District of Massachusetts.... [The statute under which he was convicted punished anyone] "who forges, alters, *knowingly destroys, knowingly mutilates,* or in any manner changes ..." a draft card. (Italics supplied.) [On appeal, the Court of Appeals for the First Circuit held this provision unconstitutional as applied.]

[A draft card, or "registration certificate" is a] ... small white card ... approximately 2 by 3 inches [that] ... specifies the name of the registrant, the date of registration, and the number and address of the local board with which he is registered. Also inscribed upon it are the date and place of the registrant's birth, his residence at registration, his physical description, his signature, and his Selective Service number. The Selective Service number itself indicates his State of registration, his local board, his year of birth, and his chronological position in the local board's classification record.

... [T]he registration ... certificate bears notices that the registrant must notify his local board in writing of every change in address, physical condition, and occupational, marital, family, dependency, and military status, and of any other fact which might change his classification.... [It] also contain[s] ... a notice that the registrant's Selective Service number should appear on all communications to his local board.

By the 1965 Amendment, Congress added to ... the 1948 Act the provision here at issue, subjecting to criminal liability not only one who "forges, alters, or in any manner changes" but also one who "knowingly destroys, [or] knowingly mutilates" a certificate. We note at the outset that the 1965 Amendment plainly does not abridge free speech on its face, and we do not understand O'Brien to argue otherwise.... [O]n its face [it] deals with conduct having no connection with speech. It prohibits the knowing destruction of certificates issued by the Selective Service System, and there is nothing necessarily expressive about such conduct. The Amendment does not distinguish between public and private destruction, and it does not punish only destruction engaged in for the purpose of expressing views. A law prohibiting destruction of Selective Service certificates no more abridges free speech on its face than a motor vehicle law prohibiting the destruction of drivers' licenses, or a tax law prohibiting the destruction of books and records.

1. At the time of the burning, the agents knew only that O'Brien and his three companions had burned small white cards. They later discovered that the card O'Brien burned was his registration certificate, and the undisputed assumption is that the same is true of his companions.

2. He was sentenced under the Youth Corrections Act, 18 U.S.C.A. § 5010(b), to the custody of the Attorney General for a maximum period of six years for supervision and treatment.

O'Brien nonetheless argues that the 1965 Amendment is unconstitutional in its application to him, and is unconstitutional as enacted because what he calls the "purpose" of Congress was "to suppress freedom of speech." We consider these arguments separately.

O'Brien first argues that the 1965 Amendment is unconstitutional as applied to him because his act of burning his registration certificate was protected "symbolic speech" within the First Amendment. His argument is that the freedom of expression which the First Amendment guarantees includes all modes of "communication of ideas by conduct," and that his conduct is within this definition because he did it in "demonstration against the war and against the draft."

We cannot accept the view that an apparently limitless variety of conduct can be labeled "speech" whenever the person engaging in the conduct intends thereby to express an idea. However, even on the assumption that the alleged communicative element in O'Brien's conduct is sufficient to bring into play the First Amendment, it does not necessarily follow that the destruction of a registration certificate is constitutionally protected activity. This Court has held that when "speech" and "nonspeech" elements are combined in the same course of conduct, a sufficiently important governmental interest in regulating the nonspeech element can justify incidental limitations on First Amendment freedoms. To characterize the quality of the governmental interest which must appear, the Court has employed a variety of descriptive terms: compelling; substantial; subordinating; paramount; cogent; strong. Whatever imprecision inheres in these terms, we think it clear that a government regulation is sufficiently justified if it is within the constitutional power of the Government; if it furthers an important or substantial governmental interest; if the governmental interest is unrelated to the suppression of free expression; and if the incidental restriction on alleged First Amendment freedoms is no greater than is essential to the furtherance of that interest. We find that the 1965 Amendment . . . meets all of these requirements, and consequently that O'Brien can be constitutionally convicted for violating it.

The constitutional power of Congress to raise and support armies and to make all laws necessary and proper to that end is broad and sweeping. The power of Congress to classify and conscript manpower for military service is "beyond question." Pursuant to this power, Congress may establish a system of registration for individuals liable for training and service, and may require such individuals within reason to cooperate in the registration system. The issuance of certificates indicating the registration and eligibility classification of individuals is a legitimate and substantial administrative aid in the functioning of this system. And legislation to insure the continuing availability of issued certificates serves a legitimate and substantial purpose in the system's administration.

O'Brien's argument to the contrary is necessarily premised upon his unrealistic characterization of Selective Service certificates. He essentially adopts the position that such certificates are so many pieces of paper designed to notify registrants of their registration or classification, to be retained or tossed in the wastebasket according to the convenience or taste of the registrant. Once the registrant has received notification, according to this view, there is no reason for him to retain the certificates. O'Brien notes that most of the information on a registration certificate serves no notification purpose at all; the registrant hardly needs to be told his address and physical characteristics. We agree that the registration certificate contains much information of which the registrant needs no notification. This circumstance, however, does not lead to the conclusion that the certificate serves no purpose, but that, like the classification certificate, it serves purposes in addition to initial notification. Many of these purposes would be defeated by the certificates' destruction or mutilation. Among these are:

1. The registration certificate serves as proof that the individual described thereon has registered for the draft.... Voluntarily displaying the ... certificate is an easy and painless way for a young man to dispel a question as to whether he might be delinquent in his Selective Service obligations. Correspondingly, the availability of the certificates for such display relieves the Selective Service System of the administrative burden it would otherwise have in verifying the registration and classification of all suspected delinquents. Further, since [the] certificates are in the nature of "receipts" attesting that the registrant has done what the law requires, it is in the interest of the just and efficient administration of the system that they be continually available, in the event, for example, of a mix-up in the registrant's file. Additionally, in a time of national crisis, reasonable availability to each registrant of the ... cards assures a rapid and uncomplicated means for determining his fitness for immediate induction, no matter how distant in our mobile society he may be from his local board.

2. The information supplied on the certificates facilitates communication between registrants and local boards, simplifying the system and benefiting all concerned. To begin with, each certificate bears the address of the registrant's local board, an item unlikely to be committed to memory. Further, each card bears the registrant's Selective Service number, and a registrant who has his number readily available so that he can communicate it to his local board when he supplies or requests information can make simpler the board's task in locating his file. Finally, a registrant's inquiry, particularly through a local board other than his own, concerning his eligibility status is frequently answerable simply on the basis of his classification certificate; whereas, if the certificate were not reasonably available and the registrant were uncertain of his classification, the task of answering his questions would be considerably complicated.

3. The certificate carries continual reminders that the registrant must notify his local board of any change of address, and other specified changes in his status. The smooth functioning of the system requires that local boards be continually aware of the status and whereabouts of registrants, and the destruction of certificates deprives the system of a potentially useful notice device.

4.   The regulatory scheme involving Selective Service certificates includes clearly valid prohibitions against the alteration, forgery, or similar deceptive misuse of certificates. The destruction or mutilation of certificates obviously increases the difficulty of detecting and tracing abuses such as these. Further, a mutilated certificate might itself be used for deceptive purposes.

The many functions performed by Selective Service certificates established beyond doubt that Congress has a legitimate and substantial interest in preventing their wanton and unrestrained destruction and assuring their continuing availability by punishing people who knowingly and wilfully destroy or mutilate them. And we are unpersuaded that the pre-existence of the nonpossession regulations in any way negates this interest.

In conclusion, we find that because of the Government's substantial interest in assuring the continuing availability of issued Selective Service certificates, because [the statute] is an appropriately narrow means of protecting this interest and condemns only the independent noncommunicative impact of conduct within its reach, and because the noncommunicative impact of O'Brien's act of burning his registration certificate frustrated the Government's interest, a sufficient governmental interest has been shown to justify O'Brien's conviction.

O'Brien finally argues that the 1965 Amendment is unconstitutional as enacted because what he calls the "purpose" of Congress was "to suppress freedom of speech." We reject this argument because under settled principles the purpose of Congress, as O'Brien uses that term, is not a basis for declaring this legislation unconstitutional.

It is a familiar principle of constitutional law that this Court will not strike down an otherwise constitutional statute on the basis of an alleged illicit legislative motive. . . .

Inquiries into congressional motives or purposes are a hazardous matter. When the issue is simply the interpretation of legislation, the Court will look to statements by legislators for guidance as to the purpose of the legislature, because the benefit to sound decision-making in this circumstance is thought sufficient to risk the possibility of misreading Congress' purpose. It is entirely a different matter when we are asked to void a statute that is, under well-settled criteria, constitutional on its face, on the basis of what fewer than a handful of Congressmen said about it. What motivates one legislator to make a speech about a statute is not necessarily what motivates scores of others to enact it, and the stakes are sufficiently high for us to eschew guesswork. We decline to void essentially on the ground that it is unwise legislation which Congress had the undoubted power to enact and which could be reenacted in its exact form if the same or another legislator made a "wiser" speech about it.

We think it not amiss, in passing, to comment upon O'Brien's legislative-purpose argument. . . . It is principally on the basis of the statements by three Congressmen that O'Brien makes his congressional-"purpose" argument. We note that if we were to examine legislative purpose in the instant case, we would be obliged to consider not only these statements but also the more authoritative reports of the Senate and House Armed Services Committees.... While both reports make clear a concern with the "defiant" destruction of so-called "draft cards" and with "open" encouragement to others to destroy their cards, both reports also indicate that this concern stemmed from an apprehension that unrestrained destruction of cards would disrupt the smooth functioning of the Selective Service System.

JUSTICE HARLAN, concurring.

The crux of the Court's opinion, which I join, is of course its general statement, that:

> "a government regulation is sufficiently justified if it is within the constitutional power of the Government; if it furthers an important or substantial governmental interest; if the governmental interest is unrelated to the suppression of free expression; and if the incidental restriction on alleged First Amendment freedoms is no greater than is essential to the furtherance of that interest."

I wish to make explicit my understanding that this passage does not foreclose consideration of First Amendment claims in those rare instances when an "incidental" restriction upon expression, imposed by a regulation which furthers an "important or substantial" governmental interest and satisfies the Court's other criteria, in practice has the effect of entirely preventing a "speaker" from reaching a significant audience with whom he could not otherwise lawfully communicate. This is not such a case, since O'Brien manifestly could have conveyed his message in many ways other than by burning his draft card.

[Justice Douglas' dissent was limited to the point that the case should be reargued to decide the question whether a "peacetime" draft (that is, a draft not occurring during a time of declared war) violated the Constitution, and did not address the question whether O'Brien's conviction violated the First Amendment. However, a year later in Brandenburg v. Ohio, 395 U.S. 444 (1969), (see Chapter 5, p. 122), Justice Douglas argued that O'Brien was protected by the First Amendment. On that point, Justice Douglas' concurring opinion in the *Brandenburg* case said:

> Action is often a method of expression and within the protection of the First Amendment.
>
> Suppose one tears up his own copy of the Constitution in eloquent protest to a decision of this Court. May he be indicted?
>
> Suppose one rips his own Bible to shreds to celebrate his departure from one "faith" and his embrace of atheism. May he be indicted?
>
> ... O'Brien was not prosecuted for not having his draft card available when asked for by a federal agent. He was indicted, tried, and convicted for burning the card. And this Court's affirmance of that conviction was not, with all respect, consistent with the First Amendment.]

NOTE

With Justice Marshall not participating, seven justices voted in conference to reverse, including Justice Douglas. Justice Stewart voted "pass." Assigning himself the Court's opinion, Chief Justice Warren circulated a draft that characterized O'Brien's burning of his draft card as a nonverbal communicative act unprotected by the First Amendment. According to the draft, "an act unrelated to the employment of language or other inherently expressive symbols is not speech within the First Amendment if as a matter of fact the act has an immediate harmful impact not completely apart from any impact arising by virtue of the claimed communication itself."*

The basis for this new "test" was set forth in a memo to the chief justice by one of his clerks. The memo stated that one of two approaches had to be followed to reach the result the Court wanted in *O'Brien*. The Court either had to concede that draft-card burning was unprotected speech, or it had to hold that it simply was not speech. The latter was the approach Chief Justice Warren initially wanted to take. The problem with that approach was that the Court had held in other cases that conduct like O'Brien's that expressed ideas was protected. So the clerk concluded that it was necessary "to try to draw a line which the court has never before drawn—a line which is consistent with the previous case and which separates conduct from speech."** The memo considered using the clear and present danger test, but rejected it because several members of the Court disliked that approach and because it led to the "wrong result." The memo also considered Professor Emerson's approach but rejected it because it was "inconsistent with many cases decided by this Court ... and, in any event, would probably lead to the wrong result in *O'Brien*."† Finally, the memo considered the approach taken in *Chaplinsky* and *Roth* but rejected it because, unlike the expression in those cases, the communicative value of O'Brien's expression was "not at all low, and correspondingly, the govt's interest in preventing the destruction of draft cards is not very high."

So the memo proposed a new approach in *O'Brien*—the narrowest rule imaginable, one that would be "expressly inapplicable whenever the conduct in question is the utterance of language or other inherently expressive symbolic communication or is a means of circulating any such communication. Further, even as to the limited class of cases where the rule becomes applicable, the rule is so hedged with qualifying clauses that the Court should have great flexibility under it." The memo then

---

* Warren Papers, Library of Congress, Box 625.

** Ibid.

† The memo did not explain Emerson's approach because it "is rather complicated." The critical question for Emerson is "whether expression or action is the dominant element." Further, "the concept of expression must be related to the fundamental purposes of the system and dynamics of its operation." For Emerson, the main purposes of the American system of freedom of expression are (1) "individual self-fulfillment," (2) "advancement of knowledge and discovering truth," (3) "participation in decision making by all members of society," and (4) "achieving a more acceptable, and hence a more stable community, of maintaining a precarious balance between healthy cleavage and necessary consensus." Thomas I. Emerson, The System of Freedom of Expression, Random House, 1970, pp. 6–7, 17–18.

restated the "guts of the rule" underlining the qualifying clauses: "if as a *matter of fact* [upon which this Court has the ultimate say ...] the act has an *immediate harmful* impact *completely apart* from any impact arising by virtue of the claimed communication itself."

The approach taken in Warren's draft opinion disturbed some of the justices, particularly Harlan and Brennan. Harlan circulated a concurring opinion taking issue with Warren's approach. Justice Brennan tried to get Warren to accept the compelling state interest test that Brennan had articulated in N.A.A.C.P. v. Button, 371 U.S. 415 (1963). Chief Justice Warren's revised draft, wrote Schwartz, "embodied much of the approach that Brennan has suggested. It recognized that the communicative element in O'Brien's conduct brought the First Amendment into play. But it found the government had a *substantial* interest (not the *compelling* interest Brennan had urged was necessary) in assuring the continued availability of draft cards which justified the law prohibiting their destruction."*

TINKER v. DES MOINES INDEPENDENT COMMUNITY SCHOOL DIST.

Supreme Court of the United States, 1969.
393 U.S. 503, 89 S.Ct. 733, 21 L.Ed.2d 731.

JUSTICE FORTAS delivered the opinion of the Court.

Petitioner John F. Tinker, 15 years old, and petitioner Christopher Eckhardt, 16 years old, attended high schools in Des Moines, Iowa. Petitioner Mary Beth Tinker, John's sister, was a 13–year–old student in junior high school.

In December 1965, a group of adults and students in Des Moines held a meeting at the Eckhardt home. The group determined to publicize their objections to the hostilities in Vietnam and their support for a truce by wearing black armbands during the holiday season and by fasting on December 16 and New Year's Eve. Petitioners and their parents had previously engaged in similar activities, and they decided to participate in the program.

The principals of the Des Moines schools became aware of the plan to wear armbands. On December 14, 1965, they met and adopted a policy that any student wearing an armband to school would be asked to remove it, and if he refused he would be suspended until he returned without the armband. Petitioners were aware of the regulation that the school authorities adopted.

On December 16, Mary Beth and Christopher wore black armbands to their schools. John Tinker wore his armband the next day. They were all sent home and suspended from school until they would come back without their armbands. They did not return to school until after the planned period for wearing armbands had expired—that is, until after New Year's Day.

* Bernard Schwartz, Super Chief, New York University Press, 1983, pp. 684–685.

ABE FORTAS—Born on June 19, 1910, in Memphis, Tennessee, son of Eastern Europeans who had lived in England before coming to the U.S. His father was the owner of a small business. Democrat. Jewish. Learned to play the violin as a boy and gave lessons to neighborhood children; later in life, he would play chamber music with Isaac Stern and other leading musicians on Sunday evenings at his home. A brilliant student, he won a scholarship to Southwestern, a small Presbyterian college, from which he graduated first in his class in 1930. He then went to the Yale Law School, where he studied with Professors William O. Douglas and Thurman Arnold. He was editor in chief of the law journal, and graduated second in his class in 1933. Yale law faculty member, 1933–1938. Held various positions at the Department of Agriculture, 1933–1934, and the Securities and Exchange Commission, 1934–1939; Public Works Administration, 1939–1940; Interior Department, 1940–1946 (under-secretary, 1942–1946). Founded a Washington law firm with Thurman Arnold and Paul Porter and practiced law, 1946–1965. Argued pro bono Durham v. U.S. (1954) and Gideon v. Wainwright (1963), which established respectively a modern definition of insanity and the right to counsel in state prosecutions. Nominated associate justice by President Lyndon B. Johnson, who was a close friend, on July 28, 1965, to replace Arthur J. Goldberg. Confirmed by the Senate on August 11, 1965, by voice vote. Informally advised President Johnson while on the Court. Nominated chief justice of the U.S. by Johnson in 1968 when Chief Justice Warren said he intended to retire. Johnson withdrew the nomination because of a successful filibuster. During the controversy, the press published a report that Justice Fortas had received $15,000 to teach a course at a local university. Later the press revealed that he had an agreement to advise a charitable foundation controlled by the family of an indicted stock manipulator. Denying any wrongdoing, Fortas resigned on May 14, 1969. Practiced law from 1969 until his death on April 5, 1982.

[The three students brought suit in a federal court to obtain a court order prohibiting school officials from disciplining them. The District Court decided that the school authorities had not violated the Constitution, and dismissed their complaint.]

The District Court recognized that the wearing of an armband for the purpose of expressing certain views is the type of symbolic act that is within the Free Speech Clause of the First Amendment.

As we shall discuss, the wearing of armbands in the circumstances of this case was entirely divorced from actually or potentially disruptive conduct by those participating in it. It was closely akin to "pure speech" which, we have repeatedly held, is entitled to comprehensive protection under the First Amendment.

First Amendment rights, applied in light of the special characteristics of the school environment, are available to teachers and students. It can hardly be argued that either students or teachers shed their constitutional rights to freedom of speech or expression at the schoolhouse gate. This has been the unmistakable holding of this Court for almost 50 years. In Meyer v. Nebraska, 262 U.S. 390 (1923), and Bartels v. Iowa,

262 U.S. 404 (1923), this Court, in opinions by Justice McReynolds, held that the Due Process Clause of the Fourteenth Amendment prevents States from forbidding the teaching of a foreign language to young students. Statutes to this effect, the Court held, unconstitutionally interfere with the liberty of teacher, student, and parent.[1]

... On the other hand, the Court has repeatedly emphasized the need for affirming the comprehensive authority of the States and of school officials, consistent with fundamental constitutional safeguards, to prescribe and control conduct in the schools. Our problem lies in the area where students in the exercise of First Amendment rights collide with the rules of the school authorities.

The problem posed by the present case does not relate to regulation of the length of skirts or the type of clothing, to hair style, or deportment. It does not concern aggressive, disruptive action or even group demonstrations. Our problem involves direct, primary First Amendment rights akin to "pure speech."

The school officials banned and sought to punish petitioners for a silent, passive expression of opinion, unaccompanied by any disorder or disturbance on the part of petitioners. There is here no evidence whatever of petitioners' interference, actual or nascent with the schools' work or of collision with the rights of other students to be secure and to be let alone. Accordingly, this case does not concern speech or action that intrudes upon the work of the schools or the rights of other students.

Only a few of the 18,000 students in the school system wore the black armbands.... There is no indication that the work of the schools or any class was disrupted. Outside the classrooms, a few students made hostile remarks to the children wearing armbands, but there were no threats or acts of violence on school premises.

The District Court concluded that the action of the school authorities was reasonable because it was based upon their fear of a disturbance from the wearing of the armbands. But, in our system, undifferentiated fear or apprehension of disturbance is not enough to overcome the right to freedom of expression. Any departure from absolute regimentation may cause trouble. Any variation from the majority's opinion may inspire fear. Any word spoken, in class, in the lunchroom, or on the campus, that deviates from the views of another person may start an argument or cause a disturbance. But our Constitution says we must take this risk; and our history says that it is this sort of hazardous freedom—this kind of openness—that is the basis of our national strength and of the independence and vigor of Americans who grow up and live in this relatively permissive, often disputatious, society.

---

1. Hamilton v. Regents of University of California, 293 U.S. 245 (1934), is sometimes cited for the broad proposition that the State may attach conditions to attendance at a state university that require individuals to violate their religious convictions. The case involved dismissal of members of a religious denomination from a land grant college for refusal to participate in military training. Narrowly viewed, the case turns upon the Court's conclusion that merely requiring a student to participate in school training in military "science" could not conflict with his constitutionally protected freedom of conscience. The decision cannot be taken as establishing that the State may impose and enforce any conditions that it chooses upon attendance at public institutions of learning, however violative they may be of fundamental constitutional guarantees.

In order for the State in the person of school officials to justify prohibition of a particular expression of opinion, it must be able to show that its action was caused by something more than a mere desire to avoid the discomfort and unpleasantness that always accompany an unpopular viewpoint. Certainly where there is no finding and no showing that engaging in the forbidden conduct would "materially and substantially interfere with the requirements of appropriate discipline in the operation of the school," the prohibition cannot be sustained.

It is also relevant that the school authorities did not purport to prohibit the wearing of all symbols of political or controversial significance. The record shows that students in some of the schools wore buttons relating to national political campaigns, and some even wore the Iron Cross, traditionally a symbol of Nazism. The order prohibiting the wearing of armbands did not extend to these. Instead, a particular symbol—black armbands worn to exhibit opposition to this Nation's involvement in Vietnam—was singled out for prohibition. Clearly, the prohibition of expression of one particular opinion, at least without evidence that it is necessary to avoid material and substantial interference with schoolwork or discipline, is not constitutionally permissible.

In our system, state-operated schools may not be enclaves of totalitarianism. . . .

Under our Constitution, free speech is not a right that is given only to be so circumscribed that it exists in principle but not in fact. Freedom of expression would not truly exist if the right could be exercised only in an area that a benevolent government has provided as a safe haven for crackpots. . . .

If a regulation were adopted by school officials forbidding discussion of the Vietnam conflict, or the expression by any student of opposition to it anywhere on school property except as part of a prescribed classroom exercise, it would be obvious that the regulation would violate the constitutional rights of students, at least if it could not be justified by a showing that the students' activities would materially and substantially disrupt the work and discipline of the school. In the circumstances of the present case, the prohibition of the silent, passive "witness of the armbands," as one of the children called it, is no less offensive to the Constitution's guarantees.

JUSTICE STEWART, concurring.

Although I agree with much of what is said in the Court's opinion, and with its judgment in this case, I cannot share the Court's uncritical assumption that, school discipline aside, the First Amendment rights of children are co-extensive with those of adults. I continue to hold the view [that]: "[A] State may permissibly determine that, at least in some precisely delineated areas, a child—like someone in a captive audience— is not possessed of that full capacity for individual choice which is the presupposition of First Amendment guarantees."

JUSTICE WHITE, concurring.

While I join the Court's opinion, I deem it appropriate to note, first, that the Court continues to recognize a distinction between communicating by words and communicating by acts or conduct which sufficiently impinges on some valid state interest. . . .

Justice Black, dissenting.

The Court's holding in this case ushers in what I deem to be an entirely new era in which the power to control pupils by the elected "officials of state supported public schools . . ." in the United States is in ultimate effect transferred to the Supreme Court. . . .

Assuming that the Court is correct in holding that the conduct of wearing armbands for the purpose of conveying political ideas is protected by the First Amendment, the crucial remaining questions are whether students and teachers may use the schools at their whim as a platform for the exercise of free speech—"symbolic" or "pure"—and whether the courts will allocate to themselves the function of deciding how the pupils' school day will be spent. While I have always believed that under the First and Fourteenth Amendments neither the State nor the Federal Government has any authority to regulate or censor the content of speech, I have never believed that any person has a right to give speeches or engage in demonstrations where he pleases and when he pleases. . . .

While the record does not show that any of these armband students shouted, used profane language, or were violent in any manner, detailed testimony by some of them shows their armbands caused comments, warnings by other students, the poking of fun at them, and a warning by an older football player that other, nonprotesting students had better let them alone. There is also evidence that a teacher of mathematics had his lesson period practically "wrecked" chiefly by disputes with Mary Beth Tinker, who wore her armband for her "demonstration." Even a casual reading of the record shows that this armband did divert students' minds from their regular lessons, and that talk, comments, etc., made John Tinker "self-conscious" in attending school with his armband. While the absence of obscene remarks or boisterous and loud disorder perhaps justifies the Court's statement that the few armband students did not actually "disrupt" the classwork, I think the record overwhelmingly shows that the armbands did exactly what the elected school officials and principals foresaw they would, that is, took the students' minds off their classwork and diverted them to thoughts about the highly emotional subject of the Vietnam war. And I repeat that if the time has come when pupils of state-supported schools, kindergartens, grammar schools, or high schools, can defy and flout orders of school officials to keep their minds on their own schoolwork, it is the beginning of a new revolutionary era of permissiveness in this country fostered by the judiciary. . . .

Justice Harlan, dissenting.

I certainly agree that state public school authorities in the discharge of their responsibilities are not wholly exempt from the requirements of the Fourteenth Amendment respecting the freedoms of expression and association. At the same time I am reluctant to believe that there is any disagreement between the majority and myself on the proposition that school officials should be accorded the widest authority in maintaining discipline and good order in their institutions. To translate that proposition into a workable constitutional rule, I would, in cases like this, cast upon those complaining the burden of showing that a particular school measure was motivated by other than legitimate school concerns—for example, a desire to prohibit the expression of an unpopular point of view, while permitting expression of the dominant opinion.

THE TINKER CONFERENCE

Justice Douglas took the following notes during the *Tinker* conference:*

CJ reverses on narrow ground of equal protection—B[oar]d singles out a particular brand of conduct and ideas—schools can abolish all badges etc. but here there was discrimination.

HLB affirms on a broad ground, as broad as possible.

WOD reverses—will go on equal protection.

JMH affirms.

WJB reverses—agrees with CJ.

PS [reverses—] School authorities should have power to discipline.

BW inclined to reverse—not sure of equal protection[.] [I]f you are going to protect discipline, the school must have power to ban labels that arouse violence etc.—or the badge may be too competitive with the teacher—but they did not ban the badge only from the classroom but from the entire school—

AF reverses—closer to BW than to CJ—school authorities can and should control the school—justification must be in terms of school functions, not equality—

TM agrees with AF and BW [—] reverses.

CJ would go along with BW.

WOD Could the students be required to take off their Klan hoods?

TM They could ban all political buttons if some buttons cause problems—they should make a showing—

HLB The schools are in great trouble—children need discipline—the country is going to ruin because of it. [T]his is no 1st Amendment problem—question is whether the rule is reasonable.

CJ BW's ground is the narrowest.

NOTES AND QUESTIONS

1. In *O'Brien*, the burning of a draft card is characterized as "conduct" that could be punished despite an "incidental restriction on alleged First Amendment freedoms." In *Tinker*, on the other hand, the wearing of black armbands is described as "akin to 'pure speech'" and

* Douglas Papers, Library of Congress, Box 1430.

as a "silent, passive expression of opinion." Can it really be argued that what the three students were "doing" in *Tinker* is very different from what O'Brien "did"? Is it possible to distinguish conduct and symbolic speech simply by asking whether the actor's purpose was to communicate?

2. The real distinction between *Tinker* and *O'Brien,* if it does not lie in differences between the dangerousness of the actors' conduct, or whether conduct was intended primarily as communication, must lie in the differences between the rules being enforced. The objective of the selective service law in *O'Brien* was said not to be the suppression of O'Brien's views, but rather to enforce the requirement of registration for the draft. In *Tinker,* on the other hand, the objective of the rule barring black armbands was said to be the suppression of a particular opinion because it might cause controversy. That suggests that in symbolic speech cases, it may be more important to decide whether the objective of the rule being enforced is to punish communication than whether the actor's purpose is to communicate.

3. If the objective of the rule being enforced is not to punish communication, the problem presented is similar if not identical to the problems of "time, place and manner" regulation of speech. There are two issues. First, if the objective of the law is not to prevent communication, is that the end of the matter? As applied to the *O'Brien* case, once it is decided that the objective of the law was to enforce registration for the draft and not to punish communication of opposition to the draft, is it significant that O'Brien intended to communicate opposition to the draft? Or, should the government's interest in enforcing the law be weighed against the restriction on the defendant's ability to communicate his views? Did the Court balance competing interests in O'Brien's case or did it simply conclude that the law was valid once it was decided that the law's objective was to enforce draft registration? Second, if there is to be balancing, how would you strike the balance? The government's interest in keeping people from destroying their draft cards is pretty trivial isn't it, especially if it is conceded that registrants could still be punished for not having their cards available when requested by a federal agent? (Did O'Brien's "conduct" justify a six year sentence?) Or, is the key to the *O'Brien* decision (as Justice Harlan argues) that there was little restriction on communicating opposition to the war or the draft, since so many other channels of protest were left open?

4. Does *Tinker* suggest that, if the objective of the rule being enforced is to prevent communication, symbolic speech is protected in the same way and to the same extent as "pure" speech? That question will be explored further in the next section of the Chapter, particularly in connection with cases dealing with flag desecration laws.

5. In any event, if discovering the objective of the rule being enforced is so important in symbolic speech cases, how does one go about discovering the objective? It is often said that there is an important distinction between the "governmental interest," or "objective" of a rule on the one hand, and the "motives" of those who promulgated the rule on the other hand. The objective of a rule is said to be determined by

looking to what the rule does—its effects. Motive, on the other hand, has to do with the subjective thought processes of those who promulgated the rule. Using this distinction, even if all the federal legislators who voted for the draft card burning statute subjectively wanted to punish those who expressed opposition to the war in this form, the objective of the rule would still be to enforce registration for the draft because preventing people from burning their draft cards is logically related to that end. Unfortunately, the distinction is hard to apply in practice. Is the distinction illusory, especially in cases where a rule might have several objectives? Is the "objective" of a rule simply a motive that is clearly proved or admitted? (Notice how much easier it is to find out what was going through the minds of the Des Moines school authorities, who can be called to the stand and asked why they forbade wearing of the armbands, than it is to plumb the consciences of 435 Members of the Congress and 100 Senators.) Would it have made a difference if the House and Senate Armed Service Committee reports referred to in *O'Brien,* had stated that their only purpose was to punish opposition to the Vietnamese war?

6. Discovering the legislature's objective, and deciding whether that objective was to punish communication were the central issues in Barnes v. Glen Theatre, Inc., 501 U.S. 560 (1991). Indiana has a "public indecency" statute that makes it a crime to appear nude in public. A lower federal court decided that the statute was unconstitutional insofar as it prohibited nude dancing in a bar and a theatre. A bare majority of the Supreme Court disagreed. Justice Rehnquist, joined by Justices O'Connor and Kennedy, conceded that nude dancing was expressive conduct. The statute, however, banned all public nudity "to protect morals and public order." Justice Rehnquist said:

> The perceived evil ... is not erotic dancing but public nudity. The appearance of people of all shapes, sizes, and ages in the nude at a beach, for example, would convey little if any erotic message, yet the state still seeks to prevent it. Public nudity is the evil the state seeks to prevent, whether or not it is combined with expressive activity.

Concurring, Justice Scalia argued that the communication of offense to other people was not the objective for a prohibition of public nudity. Indiana had decided that public nudity was simply immoral behavior.

> The purpose of Indiana's nudity law would be violated, I think, if 60,000 fully consenting adults crowded into the Hoosierdome to display their genitals to one another, even if there were not an offended innocent in the crowd.... The purpose of the Indiana statute ... is to enforce the traditional moral belief that people should not expose their private parts indiscriminately, regardless of whether those who see them are disedified.

Justice White's dissenting opinion, joined by Justices Marshall, Blackmun and Stevens, agreed with Justice Scalia that offensiveness to observers could not be the purpose for applying the law to public performances before adult audiences. Instead, the purpose of the proscription in these contexts is to protect the viewers from what the State believes is the harmful message that nude dancing communicates.... As the State now tells us, ... the State's goal is 'deterrence of prostitution, sexual assaults, criminal activity, degradation of women, and other activities which break down family structure.' The attainment of these goals, however, depends on preventing an expressive activity.

7. With the Court split 4–4 on the question whether the reason for forbidding public nudity was to prevent its erotic message, Justice Souter cast the deciding vote, and said that his decision was not based "on the possible sufficiency of society's moral views" concerning public nudity. Rather, the permissible objective was to control "prostitution, sexual assault, and other criminal behavior" that might be associated with "adult" entertainment, without reference to the thoughts communicated to the spectators. Justice Souter conceded, however, that it was doubtful whether controlling these "secondary effects" of adult entertainment was the legislature's "actual purpose," and that it had not been proved that these effects would be less serious if the dancers were partially clothed.

8. How would you apply the analysis developed in the previous notes to these situations? (a) A high school dress code prohibits long hair on males, as well as beards and mustaches. (Notice that the Court in *Tinker* takes pains to point out that the problem in the case "does not relate" to public school dress and hair length regulations. Should the issue be treated as one involving the First Amendment rights of students? Or, if not, should "unreasonable" hair length and dress regulations be invalidated as an invasion of students' rights to "privacy"? [As to the latter concept, see Chapter 22, below.]) (b) A zoning law requires houses to be set so many feet back from sidewalks, and prohibits clotheslines in front yards. Defendant sets up a temporary clothesline in his front yard, and hangs his wash from it, to protest the action of the city council in raising property taxes. (Do "esthetic zoning" laws—laws that regulate unsightly uses of property—invoke the First Amendment because their objective is to prohibit "communication" by unsightly buildings?) (c) Actors and actresses appear nude in a live stage performance that is not obscene under applicable obscenity standards. (See Chapter 11, infra.) They are arrested and charged under laws that generally prohibit public nudity or indecent exposure.

9. Would it make more sense to analyze symbolic speech cases primarily with reference to whether the defendant's mode of communication is protected by the First Amendment and pay less attention to the nature of the rule that is being enforced? Would such a theory result in a net gain or net loss of the freedom to communicate by symbolic speech?

10. Why was equal protection initially a more appealing ground for deciding *Tinker* for Chief Justice Warren and Justices Douglas, Brennan, and Stewart? Why did the Court abandon that ground for decision?

II. FLAGS—THEIR DISPLAY, DESECRATION
AND DESTRUCTION

STROMBERG v. CALIFORNIA

Supreme Court of the United States, 1931.
283 U.S. 359, 51 S.Ct. 532, 75 L.Ed. 1117.

CHIEF JUSTICE HUGHES delivered the opinion of the Court.

The appellant was convicted in the Superior Court of San Bernardino County, California, for violation ... [of a California criminal statute that] provides:

"Any person who displays a red flag, banner or badge or any flag, badge, banner, or device of any color or form whatever in any public place or in any meeting place or public assembly, or from or on any house, building or window as a sign, symbol or emblem of opposition to organized government or as an invitation or stimulus to anarchistic action or as an aid to propaganda that is of a seditious character is guilty of a felony."

... It appears that the appellant, a young woman of nineteen, a citizen of the United States by birth, was one of the supervisors of a summer camp for children, between ten and fifteen years of age, in the foothills of the San Bernardino mountains. Appellant led the children in their daily study, teaching them history and economics. "Among other things, the children were taught class consciousness, the solidarity of the workers, and the theory that the workers of the world are of one blood and brothers all." Appellant was a member of the Young Communist League, an international organization affiliated with the Communist Party. The charge against her concerned a daily ceremony at the camp, in which the appellant supervised and directed the children in raising a red flag, "a camp-made reproduction of the flag of Soviet Russia, which was also the flag of the Communist Party in the United States." In connection with the flag-raising, there was a ritual at which the children stood at salute and recited a pledge of allegiance "to the worker's red flag, and to the cause for which it stands; one aim throughout our lives, freedom for the working class." ...

We are ... brought to the question whether any one of the three clauses, as construed by the state court, is upon its face repugnant to the Federal Constitution so that it could not constitute a lawful foundation for a criminal prosecution.... We have no reason to doubt the validity of the second and third clauses of the statute as construed by the state court to relate to ... incitements to violence.

The question is thus narrowed to that of the validity of the first clause, that is, with respect to the display of the flag "as a sign, symbol or emblem of opposition to organized government," and the construction which the state court has placed upon this clause removes every element of doubt. The state court recognized the indefiniteness and ambiguity of the clause. The court considered that it might be construed as embracing conduct which the State could not constitutionally prohibit. Thus it was said that the clause "might be construed to include the peaceful and orderly opposition to a government as organized and controlled by one political party by those of another political party equally high minded and patriotic, which did not agree with the one in power. It might also be construed to include peaceful and orderly opposition to government by legal means and within constitutional limitations." The maintenance of the opportunity for free political discussion to the end that government may be responsive to the will of the people and that changes may be obtained by lawful means, an opportunity essential to the security of the Republic, is a fundamental principle of our constitutional system. A statute which upon its face, and as authoritatively construed, is so vague and indefinite as to permit the punishment of the fair use of this opportunity is repugnant to the guaranty of liberty contained in the Fourteenth Amendment. The first clause of the statute being invalid upon its face, the conviction of the appellant, which so far as the record discloses may have rested upon that clause exclusively, must be set aside.

[Dissenting opinions of Justices McReynolds and Butler are omitted.]

A FLAG BURNS IN NEW YORK*

Despite my eventual misgivings, I got out of the war experience a new sense of pride in our flag which was to stay with me through the years. When it rippled in the wind, I was always deeply affected. Years later I was sick at heart when another kind of mob, a crowd that was marching to object to one of our overseas commitments, burned an American flag in New York City. I understood these people who were opposed to the war in Vietnam, but I was shocked when they actually destroyed the flag.

The burning of an American flag is a crime under certain laws, but it has a more sinister aspect than most violations of law. Our flag is not just a piece of cloth, nor is it the personal emblem of the party in power. The American flag does not belong solely to whoever may be in the White House. The American flag is symbolic of all of the free institutions represented by our way of life.

Under our Bill of Rights every person is guaranteed the right peacefully to assemble and peacefully to petition his government for the redress of grievances. It gives the citizen the privilege of parading and making known his protests. This First Amendment privilege is unknown in most parts of the world. In many countries the right to assemble, to parade and to petition are subject to the whim and caprice of the man or the party in power, who decides who shall and who shall not speak up.

The American flag to me is symbolic of the right to assemble and the right to petition our government for the redress of grievances. It signifies equal justice under law and the right to a fair trial. It stands for the right of any person—whatever the color of his skin or whatever his creed or national origin—to enjoy the public facilities of our nation. It repre-

* William O. Douglas, Go East Young Man, Random House, 1974, pp. 93–95. Reprinted with permission.

sents free elections and an independent judiciary. It is symbolic of all civil liberties that the American tradition honors and respects.

These were my thoughts that day in New York when the flag was burned in public.

When I expressed these sentiments in a Washington, D.C., drawing room, the hostess smiled rather dryly and said, "But you taught them that disrespect." What she referred to was the second Flag Salute case in the 1940's when the Supreme Court held that schoolchildren, when motivated by religious scruples prohibiting "worship" of any secular symbol, need not salute the flag. But there is, of course, no tolerable religious dogma that would sanction flag burning or flag desecration any more than it would sanction human sacrifice.

QUESTION

What does the above statement suggest as to Justice Douglas' views as to the constitutionality of flag burning as a means of political protest?

A FLAG BURNS IN BROOKLYN

On June 6, 1966, civil rights leader James Meredith was shot by a sniper in Mississippi. Street heard the report of the shooting on his radio in his Brooklyn apartment. Street said to himself: "They didn't protect him." He then took a neatly folded 48–star American flag, which he kept to display on national holidays, and went to the nearby intersection of James Place and Lafayette Avenue. He stood on the street corner, lit the flag with a match, and dropped the flag to the pavement as it began to burn. A police officer arrived, saw the burning flag, and saw Street talking to a group of people across the street. As the officer approached, Street was saying: "We don't need no damn flag." The officer asked Street whether he had burned the flag. He replied: "Yes, that is my flag; I burned it. If they let that happen to Meredith we don't need an American flag." Street was arrested, convicted, and given a suspended sentence under a New York law which makes it a misdemeanor to "mutilate, deface, defile, or defy, trample upon, or cast contempt" on an American flag "either by words or act."

A majority of the Court concluded, in an opinion by Justice Harlan, that Street had been convicted, at least in part, for his "words" rather than his "act." Street's conviction was reversed because convicting him for his words violated his First Amendment rights to freedom of speech. Street v. New York, 394 U.S. 576 (1969).* That disposition of the case made it unnecessary to decide whether the First Amendment protected Street's "act" of burning the flag. The four dissenting Justices (Chief Justice Warren, and Justices Black, White and Fortas) argued that Street had been convicted for his "conduct" in burning the flag, and that his conviction should be sustained. Justice Fortas' dissent went to the greatest length, of the four dissenting opinions, to elaborate on the

---

* In an effort to get Justice Harlan to clarify the holding in *Street,* Justice Brennan wrote to him on Dec. 12, 1968: "I personally doubt that any governmental interest can ever justify punishment of mere words that are only provocative and not inciting, obscene, defamatory, or an invasion of privacy." Harlan Papers, Princeton University, Box 334.

argument that it did not violate the constitution to punish someone who burned or otherwise desecrated an American flag.

"[T]he States and the Federal Government have the power to protect the flag from acts of desecration committed in public.

"If the national flag were nothing more than a chattel, subject only to the rules governing the use of private personalty, its use would nevertheless be subject to certain types of state regulation. For example, regulations concerning the use of chattels which are reasonably designed to avoid danger to life or property, or impingement upon the rights of others to the quiet use of their property and of public facilities, would unquestionably be a valid exercise of police power. They would not necessarily be defeated by a claim that they conflicted with the rights of the owner of the regulated property. . . .

"If a state statute provided that it is a misdemeanor to burn one's shirt or trousers or shoes on the public thoroughfare, it could hardly be asserted that the citizen's constitutional right is violated. If the arsonist asserted that he was burning his shirt or trousers or shoes as a protest against the Government's fiscal policies, for example, it is hardly possible that his claim to First Amendment shelter would prevail against the State's claim of a right to avert danger to the public and to avoid obstruction to traffic as a result of the fire. This is because action, even if clearly for serious protest purposes, is not entitled to the pervasive protection that is given to speech alone. It may be subjected to reasonable regulation that appropriately takes into account the competing interests involved.

"The test that is applicable in every case where conduct is restricted or prohibited is whether the regulation or prohibition is reasonable, due account being taken of the paramountcy of First Amendment values. If, as I submit, it is permissible to prohibit the burning of personal property on the public sidewalk, there is no basis for applying a different rule to flag burning. And the fact that the law is violated for purposes of protest does not immunize the violator.

"Beyond this, however, the flag is a special kind of personalty. Its use is traditionally and universally subject to special rules and regulations. As early as 1907, this Court affirmed the constitutionality of a state statute making it a crime to use a representation of the United States flag for purposes of advertising. Halter v. Nebraska, 205 U.S. 34 (1907). Statutes prescribe how the flag may be displayed; how it may lawfully be disposed of; when, how, and for what purposes it may and may not be used. A person may "own" a flag, but ownership is subject to special burdens and responsibilities. A flag may be property, in a sense; but it is property burdened with peculiar obligations and restrictions. Certainly, as Halter v. Nebraska held, these special conditions are not *per se* arbitrary or beyond governmental power under our Constitution.

"One may not justify burning a house, even if it is his own, on the ground, however sincere, that he does so as a protest. One may not justify breaking the windows of a government building on that basis. Protest does not exonerate lawlessness. And the prohibition against flag burning on the public thoroughfare being valid, the misdemeanor is not excused merely because it is an act of flamboyant protest."

Originally Justice Fortas had voted with the majority in *Street* but later withdrew his vote with an "apology to Brother HARLAN for inconstancy!"*

Justice Douglas originally voted "pass" in the *Street* conference. In an unpublished opinion, which he did not circulate, he said that *O'Brien* strongly supported affirmance in *Street*, but he had not reached the issue decided by the majority in *O'Brien*. If he had, he would have dissented. He later inserted that portion of the opinion in his *Brandenburg* concurring opinion. The rest of his unpublished opinion addressed the constitutionality of flag burning. Excerpts of the opinion follow:*

The flag of one's country is a symbol by which many of us live. It is therefore charged with emotions and not always easy to discuss in wholly rational terms.

[The second] Flag Salute case [Board of Education v. Barnette, Chapter 2, p. 36, supra] seems to me to be the starting point for the disposition of this case. For the present petitioner in denouncing and bemoaning the death of James Meredith was plainly exercising a First Amendment right. And the question is whether burning his *own flag* was a protected form of "expression" within the meaning of the First Amendment.

Certainly one could be prosecuted for burning or destroying or despoiling the flag of another person. The flag that flies over the courthouse or school or hospital or private home, like other private property, can be protected against all forms of vandalism. And one who defends on the ground that he hauled down and burned the city's flag in protest to corruption in the city's government may not stretch the First Amendment that far.

Yet what one does with his own property seems to me to be his own business, so long as he does not imperil the lives or property of other people or use it to produce a riot.

When this petitioner burned his own flag he was expressing disapproval and discontent with a society that allowed the Meredith tragedy to happen. If he had bought a tract denouncing Meredith or extolling the Ku Klux Klan and torn it to bits before a street audience, he would in essence have done the same symbolic act that he did when he burned his own flag.

There is, of course, a disrespect that is implicit in what he did. But that was also true in the *Flag Salute* case. The present case is even stronger, as the harm inflicted was on this man's own flag, not on school discipline and a public ceremony in which others were participating. The First Amendment that gave shelter there should *a fortiori* give shelter here.

* Douglas Papers, Library of Congress, Box 1441.
* Ibid.

SPENCE v. WASHINGTON

Supreme Court of the United States, 1974.
418 U.S. 405, 94 S.Ct. 2727, 41 L.Ed.2d 842.

PER CURIAM.

Appellant displayed a United States flag, which he owned, out of the window of his apartment. Affixed to both surfaces of the flag was a large peace symbol fashioned of removable tape. Appellant was convicted under a Washington statute forbidding the exhibition of a United States flag to which is attached or superimposed figures, symbols, or other extraneous material. The Supreme Court of Washington affirmed appellant's conviction.... We reverse on the ground that as applied to appellant's activity the Washington statute impermissibly infringed protected expression.

I

On May 10, 1970, appellant, a college student, hung his United States flag from the window of his apartment on private property in Seattle, Washington. The flag was upside down, and attached to the front and back was a peace symbol (i.e., a circle enclosing a trident) made of removable black tape. The window was above the ground floor. The flag measured approximately three by five feet and was plainly visible to passersby. The peace symbol occupied roughly half of the surface of the flag.

Three Seattle police officers observed the flag and entered the apartment house. They were met at the main door by appellant, who said, "I suppose you are here about the flag. I didn't know there was anything wrong with it. I will take it down." Appellant permitted the officers to enter his apartment, where they seized the flag and arrested him. Appellant cooperated with the officers. There was no disruption or altercation.

Appellant was not charged under Washington's flag-desecration statute.[1] Rather, the State relied on the so-called "improper use" statute. This statute provides, in pertinent part:

"No person shall, in any manner, for exhibition or display:

"(1) Place or cause to be placed any word, figure, mark, picture, design, drawing or advertisement of any nature upon any flag, standard, color, ensign or shield of the United States or of this state ... or

"(2) Expose to public view any such flag, standard, color, ensign or shield upon which shall have been printed, painted or otherwise produced, or to which shall have been attached, appended, affixed or annexed any such word, figure, mark, picture, design, drawing or advertisement...."

---

1. This statute provides in part:

"No person shall knowingly cast contempt upon any flag, standard, color, ensign or shield ... by publicly mutilating, defacing, defiling, burning, or trampling upon said flag, standard, color, ensign or shield."

The State based its case on the flag itself and the testimony of the three arresting officers, who testified that they had observed the flag displayed from appellant's window and that on the flag was superimposed what they identified as a peace symbol. Appellant took the stand in his own defense. He testified that he put a peace symbol on the flag and displayed it to public view as a protest against the invasion of Cambodia and the killings at Kent State University, events which occurred a few days prior to his arrest. He said that his purpose was to associate the American flag with peace instead of war and violence:

> "I felt there had been so much killing and that this was not what America stood for. I felt that the flag stood for America and I wanted people to know that I thought America stood for peace."

Appellant further testified that he chose to fashion the peace symbol from tape so that it could be removed without damaging the flag. The State made no effort to controvert any of appellant's testimony.

The trial court instructed the jury in essence that the mere act of displaying the flag with the peace symbol attached, if proved beyond a reasonable doubt, was sufficient to convict. There was no requirement of specific intent to do anything more than display the flag in that manner. The jury returned a verdict of guilty. The court sentenced appellant to 10 days in jail, suspended, and to a $75 fine....

II

A number of factors are important in the instant case. First, this was a privately owned flag. In a technical property sense it was not the property of any government. We have no doubt that the state or national governments constitutionally may forbid anyone from mishandling in any manner a flag that is public property. But this is a different case. Second, appellant displayed his flag on private property. He engaged in no trespass or disorderly conduct. Nor is this a case that might be analyzed in terms of reasonable time, place, or manner restraints on access to a public area. Third, the record is devoid of proof of any risk of breach of the peace. It was not appellant's purpose to incite violence or even stimulate a public demonstration. There is no evidence that any crowd gathered or that appellant made any effort to attract attention beyond hanging the flag out of his own window. Indeed, on the facts stipulated by the parties there is no evidence that anyone other than the three police officers observed the flag.

Fourth, the State concedes, as did the Washington Supreme Court, that appellant engaged in a form of communication. Although the stipulated facts fail to show that any member of the general public viewed the flag, the State's concession is inevitable on this record. The undisputed facts are that appellant "wanted people to know that I thought America stood for peace." To be sure, appellant did not choose to articulate his views through printed or spoken words. It is therefore necessary to determine whether his activity was sufficiently imbued with elements of communication to fall within the scope of the First and Fourteenth Amendments, for as the Court noted in United States v.

O'Brien, "[w]e cannot accept the view that an apparently limitless variety of conduct can be labeled 'speech' whenever the person engaging in the conduct intends thereby to express an idea." But the nature of appellant's activity, combined with the factual context and environment in which it was undertaken, lead to the conclusion that he engaged in a form of protected expression.

... In this case, appellant's activity was roughly simultaneous with and concededly triggered by the Cambodian incursion and the Kent State tragedy, also issues of great public moment. A flag bearing a peace symbol and displayed upside down by a student today might be interpreted as nothing more than bizarre behavior, but it would have been difficult for the great majority of citizens to miss the drift of appellant's point at the time that he made it.

It may be noted, further, that this was not an act of mindless nihilism. Rather, it was a pointed expression of anguish by appellant about the then-current domestic and foreign affairs of his government. An intent to convey a particularized message was present, and in the surrounding circumstances the likelihood was great that the message would be understood by those who viewed it.

We are confronted then with a case of prosecution for the expression of an idea through activity.... Accordingly, we must examine with particular care the interests advanced by appellee to support its prosecution.

... Presumably, this interest might be seen as an effort to prevent the appropriation of a revered national symbol by an individual, interest group, or enterprise where there was a risk that association of the symbol with a particular product or viewpoint might be taken erroneously as evidence of governmental endorsement.[2] Alternatively, it might be argued that the interest asserted by the state court is based on the uniquely universal character of the national flag as a symbol. For the great majority of us, the flag is a symbol of patriotism, of pride in the history of our country, and of the service, sacrifice, and valor of the millions of Americans who in peace and war have joined together to build and to defend a Nation in which self-government and personal liberty endure. It evidences both the unity and diversity which are America. For others the flag carries in varying degrees a different message.... It might be said that we all draw something from our national symbol, for it is capable of conveying simultaneously a spectrum of meanings. If it may be destroyed or permanently disfigured, it could be argued that it will lose its capability of mirroring the sentiments of all who view it.

2. Undoubtedly such a concern underlies that portion of the improper-use statute forbidding the utilization of representations of the flag in a commercial context.... There is no occasion in this case to address the application of the challenged statute to commercial behavior. Cf. Halter v. Nebraska, 205 U.S. 34 (1907). The dissent places major reliance on *Halter*, ... despite the fact that *Halter* was decided nearly 20 years before the Court concluded that the First Amendment applies to the States by virtue of the Fourteenth Amendment. See Gitlow v. New York, 268 U.S. 652 (1925).

But we need not decide in this case whether the interest advanced by the court below is valid.[3] We assume, *arguendo,* that it is. The statute is nonetheless unconstitutional as applied to appellant's activity. There was no risk that appellant's acts would mislead viewers into assuming that the Government endorsed his viewpoint. To the contrary, he was plainly and peacefully protesting the fact that it did not. Appellant was not charged under the desecration statute, see n. 1, supra, nor did he permanently disfigure the flag or destroy it. He displayed it as a flag of his country in a way closely analogous to the manner in which flags have always been used to convey ideas. Moreover, his message was direct, likely to be understood, and within the contours of the First Amendment. Given the protected character of his expression and in light of the fact that no interest the State may have in preserving the physical integrity of a privately owned flag was significantly impaired on these facts, the conviction must be invalidated.[4]

JUSTICE DOUGLAS, concurring.

I would affirm the judgment for substantially the same reasons given by the Iowa Supreme Court in State v. Kool, 212 N.W.2d 518. In that case the defendant hung a peace symbol made of cardboard and wrapped in tinfoil in the window of his home and hung a replica of the United States flag behind the peace symbol but in an upsidedown position. The state statute made it a crime to "cast contempt upon, satirize, deride or burlesque [the] flag," Iowa Code § 32.1.

The court held that defendant's conduct constituted "symbolic speech." The court, in reversing the conviction, said:

"Someone in Newton might be so intemperate as to disrupt the peace because of this display. But if absolute assurance of tranquility is required, we may as well forget about free speech. Under such a requirement, the only 'free' speech would consist of platitudes. That kind of speech does not need constitutional protection."

That view is precisely my own. Hence I concur in reversing this judgment of conviction.

CHIEF JUSTICE BURGER, dissenting.

If the constitutional role of this Court were to strike down unwise laws or restrict unwise application of some laws, I could agree with the result reached by the Court. That is not our function, however, and it should be left to each State and ultimately the common sense of its people to decide how the flag, as a symbol of national unity, should be protected.

JUSTICE REHNQUIST, with whom THE CHIEF JUSTICE and JUSTICE WHITE join, dissenting.

---

3. If this interest is valid, we note that it is directly related to expression in the context of activity like that undertaken by appellant. For that reason and because no other governmental interest unrelated to expression has been advanced or can be supported on this record, the four-step analysis of United States v. O'Brien, 391 U.S. 367, 377 (1968), is inapplicable.

4. The similarity of our holding to that of the Iowa Supreme Court in State v. Kool, 212 N.W.2d 518 (1973), merits note. . . .

The Court holds that a Washington statute prohibiting persons from attaching material to the American flag was unconstitutionally applied to appellant. Although I agree with the Court that appellant's activity was a form of communication, I do not agree that the First Amendment prohibits the State from restricting this activity in furtherance of other important interests. And I believe the rationale by which the Court reaches its conclusion is unsound.

Since a State concededly may impose some limitations on speech directly, it would seem to follow *a fortiori* that a State may legislate to protect important state interests even though an incidental limitation on free speech results. Virtually any law enacted by a State, when viewed with sufficient ingenuity, could be thought to interfere with some citizen's preferred means of expression. But no one would argue, I presume, that a State could not prevent the painting of public buildings simply because a particular class of protesters believed their message would best be conveyed through that medium. Had appellant here chosen to tape his peace symbol to a federal courthouse, I have little doubt that he could be prosecuted under a statute properly drawn to protect public property.

The statute under which appellant was convicted is no stranger to this Court, a virtually identical statute having been before the Court in Halter v. Nebraska, 205 U.S. 34 (1907). In that case the Court held that the State of Nebraska could enforce its statute to prevent use of a flag representation on beer bottles, stating flatly that "a State will be wanting in care for the well-being of its people if it ignores the fact that they regard the flag as a symbol of their country's power and prestige...." The Court then continued: "Such an use tends to degrade and cheapen the flag in the estimation of the people, as well as to defeat the object of maintaining it as an emblem of National power and National honor." ...

... [I]f the Court is suggesting that *Halter* would now be decided differently, and that the State's interest in the flag falls before any speech which is "direct, likely to be understood, and within the contours of the First Amendment," that view would mean the flag could be auctioned as a background to anyone willing and able to buy or copy one. I find it hard to believe the Court intends to presage that result.

The true nature of the State's interest in this case is not only one of preserving "the physical integrity of the flag," but also one of preserving the flag as "an important symbol of nationhood and unity." Although the Court treats this important interest with a studied inattention, it is hardly one of recent invention and has previously been accorded considerable respect by this Court....

... [The Washington statute] simply withdraws a unique national symbol from the roster of materials that may be used as a background for communications. Since I do not believe the Constitution prohibits Washington from making that decision, I dissent.

QUESTIONS

1. Why was it crucial that Spence displayed the flag to convey an idea? O'Brien burned his draft card to express an idea, didn't he?

2. The Court in the *Spence* case emphasizes that Spence was not charged under the flag desecration statute, and he did not disfigure or destroy a flag. After the *Spence* case, is it constitutional to punish someone under a flag desecration statute for burning his own American flag? Would the governmental interests in preventing flag desecration be different from those advanced for a misuse law? Would the flag burner's actions be more conduct and less symbolic speech?

TEXAS v. JOHNSON

Supreme Court of the United States, 1989.
491 U.S. 397, 109 S.Ct. 2533, 105 L.Ed.2d 342.

JUSTICE BRENNAN delivered the opinion of the Court.

After publicly burning an American flag as a means of political protest, Gregory Lee Johnson was convicted of desecrating a flag in violation of Texas law. This case presents the question whether his conviction is consistent with the First Amendment. We hold that it is not.

I

While the Republican National Convention was taking place in Dallas in 1984, respondent Johnson participated in a political demonstration dubbed the "Republican War Chest Tour." As explained in literature distributed by the demonstrators and in speeches made by them, the purpose of this event was to protest the policies of the Reagan administration and of certain Dallas-based corporations. The demonstrators marched through the Dallas streets, chanting political slogans and stopping at several corporate locations to stage "die-ins" intended to dramatize the consequences of nuclear war. On several occasions they spray-painted the walls of buildings and overturned potted plants, but Johnson himself took no part in such activities. He did, however, accept an American flag handed to him by a fellow protestor who had taken it from a flag pole outside one of the targeted buildings.

The demonstration ended in front of Dallas City Hall, where Johnson unfurled the American flag, doused it with kerosene, and set it on fire. While the flag burned, the protestors chanted, "America, the red, white, and blue, we spit on you." After the demonstrators dispersed, a witness to the flag-burning collected the flag's remains and buried them in his backyard. No one was physically injured or threatened with injury, though several witnesses testified that they had been seriously offended by the flag-burning.

Of the approximately 100 demonstrators, Johnson alone was charged with a crime. The only criminal offense with which he was charged was the desecration of a venerated object....[1] After a trial, he

---

1. Tex.Penal Code Ann. section 42.09 (1989) provides in full:

was convicted, sentenced to one year in prison, and fined $2,000. The Court of Appeals for the Fifth District of Texas at Dallas affirmed Johnson's conviction, ... but the Texas Court of Criminal Appeals reversed....

　　... We ... affirm.

II

Johnson was convicted of flag desecration for burning the flag rather than for uttering insulting words. This fact somewhat complicates our consideration of his conviction under the First Amendment. We must first determine whether Johnson's burning of the flag constituted expressive conduct, permitting him to invoke the First Amendment in challenging his conviction. See, e.g., Spence v. Washington, 418 U.S. 405, 409–411 (1974). If his conduct was expressive, we next decide whether the State's regulation is related to the suppression of free expression.... If the State's regulation is not related to expression, then the less stringent standard we announced in United States v. O'Brien for regulations of noncommunicative conduct controls.... If it is, then we are outside of *O'Brien*'s test, and we must ask whether this interest justifies Johnson's conviction under a more demanding standard.[3] ... A third possibility is that the State's asserted interest is simply not implicated on these facts, and in that event the interest drops out of the picture....

The First Amendment literally forbids the abridgement only of "speech," but we have long recognized that its protection does not end at the spoken or written word....

In deciding whether particular conduct possesses sufficient communicative elements to bring the First Amendment into play, we have asked whether "[a]n intent to convey a particularized message was present, and [whether] the likelihood was great that the message would be understood by those who viewed it." Hence, we have recognized the expressive nature of students' wearing of black armbands to protest American military involvement in Vietnam, Tinker v. Des Moines Independent Community School Dist., 393 U.S. 503, 505 (1969); of a sit-in by blacks in a "whites only" area to protest segregation, Brown v. Louisiana, 383 U.S. 131, 141–142 (1966); of the wearing of American military uniforms in a dramatic presentation criticizing American involvement in Vietnam, Schacht v. United States, 398 U.S. 58 (1970); and of picketing about a wide variety of causes, see, e.g., Food Employees v. Logan Valley

---

Section 42.09. Desecration of Venerated Object. (a) A person commits an offense if he intentionally or knowingly desecrates: (1) a public monument; (2) a place of worship or burial; or (3) a state or national flag. (b) For purposes of this section, "desecrate" means deface, damage, or otherwise physically mistreat in a way that the actor knows will seriously offend one or more persons likely to observe or discover his action....

3. Although Johnson has raised a facial challenge to Texas' flag-desecration statute, we choose to resolve this case on the basis of his claim that the statute as applied to him violates the First Amendment. Section 42.09 regulates only physical conduct with respect to the flag, not the written or spoken word.... A tired person might, for example, drag a flag through the mud, knowing that this conduct is likely to offend others, and yet have no thought of expressing any idea.... Because the prosecution of a person who had not engaged in expressive conduct would pose a different case, and because we are capable of disposing of this case on narrower grounds, we address only Johnson's claim that section 42.09 as applied to political expression like his violates the First Amendment.

Plaza, Inc., 391 U.S. 308, 313–314 (1968); United States v. Grace, 461 U.S. 171, 176 (1983).

Especially pertinent to this case are our decisions recognizing the communicative nature of conduct relating to flags. Attaching a peace sign to the flag, *Spence,* supra, at 409–410; saluting the flag, *Barnette,* 319 U.S., at 632; and displaying a red flag, Stromberg v. California, 283 U.S. 359, 368–369 (1931), we have held, all may find shelter under the First Amendment.... That we have had little difficulty identifying an expressive element in conduct relating to flags should not be surprising. The very purpose of a national flag is to serve as a symbol of our country....

We have not automatically concluded, however, that any action taken with respect to our flag is expressive. Instead, in characterizing such action for First Amendment purposes, we have considered the context in which it occurred. In *Spence,* for example, we emphasized that Spence's taping of a peace sign to his flag was "roughly simultaneous with and concededly triggered by the Cambodian incursion and the Kent State tragedy." ... The State of Washington had conceded, in fact, that Spence's conduct was a form of communication....

The State of Texas conceded for purposes of its oral argument in this case that Johnson's conduct was expressive conduct, and this concession seems to us as prudent as was Washington's in Spence. Johnson burned an American flag as part—indeed, as the culmination— of a political demonstration that coincided with the convening of the Republican Party and its renomination of Ronald Reagan for President. The expressive, overtly political nature of this conduct was both intentional and overwhelmingly apparent.... In these circumstances, Johnson's burning of the flag was conduct "sufficiently imbued with elements of communication," ... to implicate the First Amendment.

III

The Government generally has a freer hand in restricting expressive conduct than it has in restricting the written or spoken word.... It may not, however, proscribe particular conduct *because* it has expressive elements.... It is ... not simply the verbal or nonverbal nature of the expression, but the governmental interest at stake, that helps to determine whether a restriction on that expression is valid.

... [W]e have limited the applicability of O'Brien's relatively lenient standard to those cases in which "the governmental interest is unrelated to the suppression of free expression." ...

In order to decide whether *O'Brien's* test applies here, therefore, we must decide whether Texas has asserted an interest in support of Johnson's conviction that is unrelated to the suppression of expression.... The State offers two separate interests to justify this conviction: preventing breaches of the peace, and preserving the flag as a symbol of nationhood and national unity. We hold that the first interest is not implicated on this record and that the second is related to the suppression of expression.

A

Texas claims that its interest in preventing breaches of the peace justifies Johnson's conviction for flag desecration. However, no disturbance of the peace actually occurred or threatened to occur because of Johnson's burning of the flag. Although the State stresses the disruptive behavior of the protestors during their march toward City Hall, it admits that "no actual breach of the peace occurred at the time of the flagburning or in response to the flagburning." . . . The only evidence offered by the State at trial to show the reaction to Johnson's actions was the testimony of several persons who had been seriously offended by the flag-burning.

The State's position, therefore, amounts to a claim that an audience that takes serious offense at particular expression is necessarily likely to disturb the peace and that the expression may be prohibited on this basis. . . .

[W]e have not permitted the Government to assume that every expression of a provocative idea will incite a riot, but have instead required careful consideration of the actual circumstances surrounding such expression. . . . Texas' [argument is] that it need only demonstrate "the potential for a breach of the peace," and that every flag-burning necessarily possesses that potential . . . [The argument is rejected.]

Nor does Johnson's expressive conduct fall within that small class of "fighting words" that are "likely to provoke the average person to retaliation, and thereby cause a breach of the peace." Chaplinsky v. New Hampshire, 315 U.S. 568, 574 (1942). No reasonable onlooker would have regarded Johnson's generalized expression of dissatisfaction with the policies of the Federal Government as a direct personal insult or an invitation to exchange fisticuffs. . . .

We thus conclude that the State's interest in maintaining order is not implicated on these facts. . . .

B

The State also asserts an interest in preserving the flag as a symbol of nationhood and national unity. In *Spence,* we acknowledged that the Government's interest in preserving the flag's special symbolic value "is directly related to expression in the context of activity" such as affixing a peace symbol to a flag. . . . We are equally persuaded that this interest is related to expression in the case of Johnson's burning of the flag. The State, apparently, is concerned that such conduct will lead people to believe either that the flag does not stand for nationhood and national unity, but instead reflects other, less positive concepts, or that the concepts reflected in the flag do not in fact exist, that is, we do not enjoy unity as a Nation. These concerns blossom only when a person's treatment of the flag communicates some message, and thus are related "to the suppression of free expression" within the meaning of *O'Brien.* We are thus outside of *O'Brien*'s test altogether.

IV

It remains to consider whether the State's interest in preserving the flag as a symbol of nationhood and national unity justifies Johnson's conviction.

As in *Spence,* "[w]e are confronted with a case of prosecution for the expression of an idea through activity," and "[a]ccordingly, we must examine with particular care the interests advanced by [petitioner] to support its prosecution." ... Johnson was not, we add, prosecuted for the expression of just any idea; he was prosecuted for his expression of dissatisfaction with the policies of this country, expression situated at the core of our First Amendment values....

Moreover, Johnson was prosecuted because he knew that his politically charged expression would cause "serious offense." If he had burned the flag as a means of disposing of it because it was dirty or torn, he would not have been convicted of flag desecration under this Texas law.... The Texas law is thus not aimed at protecting the physical integrity of the flag in all circumstances, but is designed instead to protect it only against impairments that would cause serious offense to others....

Whether Johnson's treatment of the flag violated Texas law thus depended on the likely communicative impact of his expressive conduct....

... Johnson's political expression was restricted because of the content of the message he conveyed. We must therefore subject the State's asserted interest in preserving the special symbolic character of the flag to "the most exacting scrutiny." Boos v. Barry, 485 U.S., at 321.[8]

Texas argues that its interest in preserving the flag as a symbol of nationhood and national unity survives this close analysis.... [T]he State's claim is that it has an interest in preserving the flag as a symbol of *nationhood* and *national unity,* a symbol with a determinate range of meanings. According to Texas, if one physically treats the flag in a way that would tend to cast doubt on either the idea that nationhood and national unity are the flag's referents or that national unity actually exists, the message conveyed thereby is a harmful one and therefore may be prohibited.

If there is a bedrock principle underlying the First Amendment, it is that the Government may not prohibit the expression of an idea simply because society finds the idea itself offensive or disagreeable....

We have not recognized an exception to this principle even where our flag has been involved. In Street v. New York, 394 U.S. 576 (1969),

---

8. Our inquiry is, of course, bounded by the particular facts of this case and by the statute under which Johnson was convicted. There was no evidence that Johnson himself stole the flag he burned, nor did the prosecution or the arguments urged in support of it depend on the theory that the flag was stolen.... [N]othing in our opinion should be taken to suggest that one is free to steal a flag so long as one later uses it to communicate an idea. We also emphasize that Johnson was prosecuted *only* for flag desecration—not for trespass, disorderly conduct, or arson.

we held that a State may not criminally punish a person for uttering words critical of the flag....

... In *Spence,* we held that the same interest asserted by Texas here was insufficient to support a criminal conviction under a flag-misuse statute for the taping of a peace sign to an American flag....

In short, nothing in our precedents suggests that a State may foster its own view of the flag by prohibiting expressive conduct relating to it.[10] To bring its argument outside our precedents, Texas attempts to convince us that even if its interest in preserving the flag's symbolic role does not allow it to prohibit words or some expressive conduct critical of the flag, it does permit it to forbid the outright destruction of the flag. The State's argument cannot depend here on the distinction between written or spoken words and nonverbal conduct. That distinction, we have shown, is of no moment where the nonverbal conduct is expressive, as it is here, and where the regulation of that conduct is related to expression, as it is here. In addition, both *Barnette* and *Spence* involved expressive conduct, not only verbal communication, and both found that conduct protected.

Texas' focus on the precise nature of Johnson's expression, moreover, misses the point of our prior decisions: their enduring lesson, that the Government may not prohibit expression simply because it disagrees with its message, is not dependent on the particular mode in which one chooses to express an idea. If we were to hold that a State may forbid flag-burning wherever it is likely to endanger the flag's symbolic role, but allow it wherever burning a flag promotes that role—as where, for example, a person ceremoniously burns a dirty flag—we would be saying that when it comes to impairing the flag's physical integrity, the flag itself may be used as a symbol ... only in one direction.

We never before have held that the Government may ensure that a symbol be used to express only one view of that symbol or its referents....

There is, moreover, no indication—either in the text of the Constitution or in our cases interpreting it—that a separate juridical category exists for the American flag alone.... The First Amendment does not guarantee that other concepts virtually sacred to our Nation as a whole—such as the principle that discrimination on the basis of race as odious and destructive—will go unquestioned in the marketplace of ideas.... We decline, therefore, to create for the flag an exception to the joust of principles protected by the First Amendment.

It is not the State's ends, but its means, to which we object. It cannot be gainsaid that there is a special place reserved for the flag in this Nation, and thus we do not doubt that the Government has a legitimate interest in making efforts to "preserv[e] the national flag as

---

10. Our decision in Halter v. Nebraska, 205 U.S. 34 (1907), addressing the validity of a state law prohibiting certain commercial uses of the flag, is not to the contrary. That case was decided "nearly 20 years before the Court concluded that the First Amendment applies to the States by virtue of the Fourteenth Amendment." Spence v. Washington, 418 U.S. 405, 413, n. 7 (1974). More important, as we continually emphasized in *Halter* itself, that case involved purely commercial rather than political speech....

an unalloyed symbol of our country." *Spence,* 418 U.S., at 412.... To say that the Government has an interest in encouraging proper treatment of the flag, however, is not to say that it may criminally punish a person for burning a flag as a means of political protest....

We are fortified in today's conclusion by our conviction that forbidding criminal punishment for conduct such as Johnson's will not endanger the special role played by our flag or the feelings it inspires....

... [T]he flag's deservedly cherished place in our community will be strengthened, not weakened, by our holding today. Our decision is a reaffirmation of the principles of freedom and inclusiveness that the flag best reflects, and of the conviction that our toleration of criticism such as Johnson's is a sign and source of our strength....

... We do not consecrate the flag by punishing its desecration, for in doing so we dilute the freedom that this cherished emblem represents.

V

Johnson was convicted for engaging in expressive conduct. The State's interest in preventing breaches of the peace does not support his conviction because Johnson's conduct did not threaten to disturb the peace. Nor does the State's interest in preserving the flag as a symbol of nationhood and national unity justify his criminal conviction for engaging in political expression. The judgment of the Texas Court of Criminal Appeals is therefore

Affirmed.

CHIEF JUSTICE REHNQUIST, with whom JUSTICE WHITE and JUSTICE O'CONNOR join, dissenting.

In holding this Texas statute unconstitutional, the Court ignores Justice Holmes' familiar aphorism that "a page of history is worth a volume of logic." New York Trust Co. v. Eisner, 256 U.S. 345, 349 (1921). For more than 200 years, the American flag has occupied a unique position as the symbol of our Nation, a uniqueness that justifies a governmental prohibition against flag burning in the way respondent Johnson did here.

[At this point, Chief Justice Rehnquist's opinion contains several pages of the history of the importance of the flag—from the Revolutionary War to the Vietnamese War.]

[In Chaplinsky v. New Hampshire, 315 U.S. 568 (1942),] [t]he Court upheld Chaplinsky's conviction....

Here it may equally well be said that the public burning of the American flag by Johnson was no essential part of any exposition of ideas, and at the same time it had a tendency to incite a breach of the peace. Johnson was free to make any verbal denunciation of the flag that he wished; indeed, he was free to burn the flag in private. He could publicly burn other symbols of the Government or effigies of political leaders. He did lead a march through the streets of Dallas, and conducted a rally in front of the Dallas City Hall. He engaged in a "die-in" to protest nuclear weapons. He shouted out various slogans during the march, including: "Reagan, Mondale which will it be? Either one means

World War III" "Ronald Reagan, killer of the hour, Perfect example of U.S. power"; and "red, white and blue, we spit on you, you stand for plunder, you will go under." . . .

The Court could not, and did not, say that Chaplinsky's utterances were not expressive phrases. . . . The same may be said of Johnson's public burning of the flag in this case; it obviously did convey Johnson's bitter dislike of his country. But his act, like Chaplinsky's provocative words, conveyed nothing that could not have been conveyed and was not conveyed just as forcefully in a dozen different ways. As with "fighting words," so with flag burning, for purposes of the First Amendment: It is "no essential part of any exposition of ideas, and [is] of such slight social value as a step to truth that any benefit that may be derived from [it] is clearly outweighed" by the public interest in avoiding a probable breach of the peace. . . .

. . . The Texas statute deprived Johnson of only one rather inarticulate symbolic form of protest—a form of protest that was profoundly offensive to many—and left him with a full panoply of other symbols and every conceivable form of verbal expression to express his deep disapproval of national policy. Thus, in no way can it be said that Texas is punishing him because his hearers—or any other group of people—were profoundly opposed to the message that he sought to convey. Such opposition is no proper basis for restricting speech or expression under the First Amendment. It was Johnson's use of this particular symbol, and not the idea that he sought to convey by it or by his many other expressions, for which he was punished.

Our prior cases dealing with flag desecration statutes have left open the question that the Court resolves today. In Street v. New York . . . [t]he Court . . . expressly reserved the question of whether a defendant could constitutionally be convicted for burning the flag. . . .

In Spence v. Washington, . . . there was no risk of a breach of the peace, no one other than the arresting officers saw the flag, and the defendant owned the flag in question. The Court was careful to note, however, that the defendant "was not charged under the desecration statute, nor did he permanently disfigure the flag or destroy it." . . .

. . . The Court decides that the American flag is just another symbol, about which not only must opinions pro and con be tolerated, but for which the most minimal public respect may not be enjoined. The government may conscript men into the Armed Forces where they must fight and perhaps die for the flag, but the government may not prohibit the public burning of the banner under which they fight. I would uphold the Texas statute as applied in this case.

JUSTICE STEVENS, dissenting.

As the Court analyzes this case, it presents the question whether the State of Texas, or indeed the Federal Government, has the power to prohibit the public desecration of the American flag. The question is unique. In my judgment rules that apply to a host of other symbols, such as state flags, armbands, or various privately promoted emblems of political or commercial identity, are not necessarily controlling. Even if flag burning could be considered just another species of symbolic speech under the logical application of the rules that the Court has developed in its interpretation of the First Amendment in other contexts, this case has an intangible dimension that makes those rules inapplicable.

NOTES AND QUESTIONS

1. The Court's footnote 3 states that it reserves the question whether the Texas flag desecration statute would be unconstitutional in all of its applications, deciding only that it is unconstitutional as applied to Johnson. The footnote suggests that the statute might be constitutional if it were applied to someone who "intentionally or knowingly desecrates" a flag, but does not intend to express an idea. The example that the Court gives of this is a person dragging the flag through the mud, knowing his conduct is offensive, but not expressing any idea. Do you think that a flag desecration conviction could rest on the proposition that the defendant knew that desecration of the flag expressed an offensive idea, but at the same time he did not intend to identify himself with that idea?

2. Note Chief Justice Rehnquist's reliance on Chaplinsky v. New Hampshire in his dissenting opinion in *Johnson*. Compare Chafee's discussion of the constitutionality of flag abuse, Chapter 10, pp. 355–357, supra.

THE IMPACT OF JOHNSON

After the decision in Texas v. Johnson, Congress passed the Flag Protection Act of 1989, which provided:

> "(a)(1) Whoever knowingly mutilates, defaces, physically defiles, burns, maintains on the floor or ground, or tramples upon any flag of the United States shall be fined under this title or imprisoned for not more than one year, or both.

> "(2) This subsection does not prohibit any conduct consisting of the disposal of a flag when it has become worn or soiled.

> "(b) As used in this section, the term 'flag of the United States' means any flag of the United States, or any part thereof, made of any substance, of any size, in a form that is commonly displayed."

Senator Biden, the sponsor of the legislation, explained that it differed from the Texas statute, and the previous Federal flag desecration statute, because it was not tied to the "communicative impact" of flag desecration and was "more neutral." By the same 5–4 division of the Justices as in *Johnson*, the Court held that the Act was unconstitutional. United States v. Eichman, 496 U.S. 310 (1990). Justice Brennan's opinion for the Court rejected the argument that a conviction under the new federal law could be upheld because the law did not expressly make the actor's motive, or the likely effect on onlookers, relevant. The law still rested on the objective of preserving the flag as a symbol—an interest that was implicated only when mistreatment of the flag communicated a message inconsistent with national ideals.

The decision in the *Eichman* case predictably led to serious proposals to amend the Constitution to add a proviso to the First Amendment that would permit punishment for desecrating the American flag. During each session of Congress from 1995 through 2006, the proposed amendment was approved by two-thirds of the House of Representatives, but then fell short in the Senate of the two-thirds approval necessary to send the amendment on to the states. Would you favor such an amendment if it were carefully limited, so that it would change nothing in the First Amendment except for its permission of punishment for flag desecration? Would it also make sense to change the First Amendment to permit punishment of other expression that is deeply offensive, anti-social or dangerous?

Chapter IX

COMMERCIAL SPEECH

VIRGINIA STATE BOARD OF PHARMACY v. VIRGINIA
CITIZENS CONSUMER COUNCIL, INC.

Supreme Court of the United States, 1976.
425 U.S. 748, 96 S.Ct. 1817, 48 L.Ed.2d 346.

JUSTICE BLACKMUN delivered the opinion of the Court.

HARRY A. BLACKMUN—Born on November 12, 1908, in Nashville, Illinois, son of a grocery store owner. Republican. Methodist. Grew up in a working-class neighborhood in St. Paul, Minnesota, where he was a boyhood friend of Warren Burger. Harvard, B.A., 1929, Phi Beta Kappa and summa cum laude in mathematics; Harvard, LL.B., 1932. Law clerk, U.S. Court of Appeals (8th Circuit), 1932–1933; law practice, 1935–1950. Taught law part-time, St. Paul College of Law, 1935–1941; University of Minnesota Law School, 1945–1947. Resident counsel, Mayo Clinic, 1950–1959; U.S. Court of Appeals judge (8th Circuit), 1959–1970. Nominated associate justice by President Richard M. Nixon on April 14, 1970, to replace Abe Fortas, who resigned. Nomination followed President Nixon's unsuccessful attempts to appoint Judges Clement F. Haynsworth and G. Harrold Carswell. Confirmed by the Senate on May 12, 1970, by a 94–0 vote. Initially voted with Chief Justice Burger—hence dubbed a "Minnesota Twin" by the press—but later moved leftward across the ideological spectrum. When he retired on June 30, 1994, he was known as a liberal. Died on March 4, 1999.

[A Virginia statute forbad pharmacists to advertise prices or credit terms for prescription drugs. Consumer groups brought suit in a federal court to enjoin enforcement of the law.]

. . .

Inasmuch as only a licensed pharmacist may dispense prescription drugs in Virginia, advertising or other affirmative dissemination of prescription drug price information is effectively forbidden in the State. Some pharmacies refuse even to quote prescription drug prices over the telephone. The Board's position, however, is that this would not constitute an unprofessional publication. It is clear, nonetheless, that all advertising of such prices, in the normal sense, is forbidden. The prohibition does not extend to nonprescription drugs but neither is it confined to prescriptions that the pharmacist compounds himself. Indeed, about 95% of all prescriptions now are filled with dosage forms prepared by the pharmaceutical manufacturer.

. . .

... The plaintiffs are an individual Virginia resident who suffers from diseases that require her to take prescription drugs on a daily basis, and two nonprofit organizations. Their claim is that the First Amendment entitles the user of prescription drugs to receive information that pharmacists wish to communicate to them through advertising and other promotional means, concerning the prices of such drugs.

Certainly that information may be of value. Drug prices in Virginia, for both prescription and nonprescription items, strikingly vary from outlet to outlet even within the same locality. It is stipulated, for example, that in Richmond "the cost of 40 Achromycin tablets ranges from $2.59 to $6.00, a difference of 140% [sic]," and that in the Newport News–Hampton area the cost of tetracycline ranges from $1.20 to $9.00, a difference of 650%.

. . .

The question first arises whether, even assuming that First Amendment protection attaches to the flow of drug price information, it is a protection enjoyed by the appellees as recipients of the information, and not solely, if at all, by the advertisers themselves who seek to disseminate that information.

Freedom of speech presupposes a willing speaker. But where a speaker exists, as is the case here, the protection afforded is to the communication, to its source and to its recipients both. This is clear from the decided cases. In Lamont v. Postmaster General, 381 U.S. 301 (1965), the Court upheld the First Amendment rights of citizens to receive political publications sent from abroad.... And in Procunier v. Martinez, 416 U.S. 396 (1974), where censorship of prison inmates' mail was under examination, we thought it unnecessary to assess the First Amendment rights of the inmates themselves, for it was reasoned that such censorship equally infringed the rights of non-inmates to whom the correspondence was addressed....

The appellants contend that the advertisement of prescription drug prices is outside the protection of the First Amendment because it is "commercial speech." There can be no question that in past decisions the Court has given some indication that commercial speech is unprotected. In Valentine v. Chrestensen, the Court upheld a New York statute that prohibited the distribution of any "handbill, circular ... or other advertising matter whatsoever in or upon any street." The Court concluded that, although the First Amendment would forbid the banning of all communication by handbill in the public thoroughfares, it imposed "no such restraint on government as respects purely commercial advertising." ...

. . .

Last Term, in Bigelow v. Virginia, 421 U.S. 809 (1975), the notion of unprotected "commercial speech" all but passed from the scene.... *Chrestensen's* continued validity was questioned and its holding was described as "distinctly a limited one" that merely upheld "a reasonable regulation of the manner in which commercial advertising could be distributed." ...

Some fragment of hope for the continuing validity of a "commercial speech" exception arguably might have persisted because of the subject matter of the advertisement in *Bigelow*. We noted that in announcing the availability of legal abortions in New York, the advertisement "did more than simply propose a commercial transaction. It contained factual material of clear 'public interest.' " ...

Here, in contrast, the question whether there is a First Amendment exception for "commercial speech" is squarely before us. Our pharmacist does not wish to editorialize on any subject, cultural, philosophical, or political. He does not wish to report any particularly newsworthy fact, or to make generalized observations even about commercial matters. The "idea" he wishes to communicate is simply this: "I will sell you the X prescription drug at the Y price." Our question, then, is whether this communication is wholly outside the protection of the First Amendment.

· · ·

If there is a kind of commercial speech that lacks all First Amendment protection, ... it must be distinguished by its content. Yet the speech whose content deprives it of protection cannot simply be speech on a commercial subject. No one would contend that our pharmacist may be prevented from being heard on the subject of whether, in general, pharmaceutical prices should be regulated, or their advertisement forbidden. Nor can it be dispositive that a commercial advertisement is uneditorial, and merely reports a fact. Purely factual matter of public interest may claim protection.

· · ·

Focusing first on the individual parties to the transaction that is proposed in the commercial advertisement, we may assume that the advertiser's interest is a purely economic one. That hardly disqualifies him for protection under the First Amendment....

As to the particular consumer's interest in the free flow of commercial information, that interest may be as keen, if not keener by far, than his interest in the day's most urgent political debate. Appellees' case in this respect is a convincing one. Those whom the suppression of prescription drug price information hits the hardest are the poor, the sick, and particularly the aged. A disproportionate amount of their income tends to be spent on prescription drugs; yet they are the least able to learn, by shopping from pharmacist to pharmacist, where their scarce dollars are best spent. When drug prices vary as strikingly as they do, information as to who is charging what becomes more than a convenience. It could mean the alleviation of physical pain or the enjoyment of basic necessities.

Generalizing, society also may have a strong interest in the free flow of commercial information. Even an individual advertisement, though entirely "commercial," may be of general public interest....

Moreover, ... no line between publicly "interesting" or "important" commercial advertising and the opposite kind could ever be drawn. Advertising, however tasteless and excessive it sometimes may seem, is nonetheless dissemination of information as to who is producing and selling what product, for what reason, and at what price. So long as we preserve a predominantly free enterprise economy, the allocation of our resources in large measure will be made through numerous private economic decisions. It is a matter of public interest that those decisions, in the aggregate, be intelligent and well informed. To this end, the free flow of commercial information is indispensable. And if it is indispensable to the proper allocation of resources in a free enterprise system, it is also indispensable to the formation of intelligent opinions as to how that system ought to be regulated or altered. Therefore, even if the First Amendment were thought to be primarily an instrument to enlighten public decision-making in a democracy, we could not say that the free flow of information does not serve that goal.

Arrayed against these substantial individual and societal interests are a number of justifications for the advertising ban. These have to do principally with maintaining a high degree of professionalism on the part of licensed pharmacists. Indisputably, the State has a strong interest in maintaining that professionalism....

Price advertising, it is argued, will place in jeopardy the pharmacist's expertise and, with it, the customer's health. It is claimed that the aggressive price competition that will result from unlimited advertising will make it impossible for the pharmacist to supply professional services in the compounding, handling, and dispensing of prescription drugs.... It is further claimed that advertising will lead people to shop for their prescription drugs among the various pharmacists who offer the lowest prices, and the loss of stable pharmacist-customer relationships will make individual attention—and certainly the practice of monitoring—impossible. Finally, it is argued that damage will be done to the professional image of the pharmacist. This image, that of a skilled and specialized craftsman, attracts talent to the profession and reinforces the better habits of those who are in it. Price advertising, it is said, will reduce the pharmacist's status to that of a mere retailer.

... [W]e cannot discount the Board's justifications entirely. The Court [has] regarded justifications of this type sufficient to sustain ... advertising bans challenged on due process and equal protection grounds.

The challenge now made, however, is based on the First Amendment. This casts the Board's justifications in a different light, for on close inspection it is seen that the State's protectiveness of its citizens rests in large measure on the advantages of their being kept in ignorance....

. . .

There is, of course, an alternative to this highly paternalistic approach. That alternative is to assume that this information is not in itself harmful, that people will perceive their own best interests if only they are well enough informed, and that the best means to that end is to open the channels of communication rather than to close them.... It is precisely this kind of choice, between the dangers of suppressing information, and the dangers of its misuse if it is freely available, that the First Amendment makes for us. Virginia is free to require whatever professional standards it wishes of its pharmacists; it may subsidize them or protect them from competition in other ways. But it may not do so by keeping the public in ignorance of the entirely lawful terms that competing pharmacists are offering. In this sense, the justifications Virginia has offered for suppressing the flow of prescription drug price information, far from persuading us that the flow is not protected by the First Amendment, have re-enforced our view that it is. We so hold.

In concluding that commercial speech, like other varieties, is protected, we of course do not hold that it can never be regulated in any way. Some forms of commercial speech regulation are surely permissible. We mention a few only to make clear that they are not before us and therefore are not foreclosed by this case.

There is no claim, for example, that the prohibition on prescription drug price advertising is a mere time, place, and manner restriction.... Whatever may be the proper bounds of time, place, and manner restrictions on commercial speech, they are plainly exceeded by this Virginia statute, which singles out speech of a particular content and seeks to prevent its dissemination completely.

Nor is there any claim that prescription drug price advertisements are forbidden because they are false or misleading in any way. Untruthful speech, commercial or otherwise, has never been protected for its own sake. Obviously, much commercial speech is not provably false, or even wholly false, but only deceptive or misleading. We foresee no obstacle to a State's dealing effectively with this problem....

Also, there is no claim that the transactions proposed in the forbidden advertisements are themselves illegal in any way. Finally, the special problems of the electronic broadcast media are likewise not in this case.

What is at issue is whether a State may completely suppress the dissemination of concededly truthful information about entirely lawful activity, fearful of that information's effect upon its disseminators and its recipients.... [W]e conclude that the answer ... is in the negative.

· · ·

Justice Rehnquist, dissenting.

The logical consequences of the Court's decision in this case, a decision which elevates commercial intercourse between a seller hawking his wares and a buyer seeking to strike a bargain to the same plane as has been previously reserved for the free marketplace of ideas, are far reaching indeed....

· · ·

... Here, the only group truly restricted by this statute, the pharmacists, have not even troubled to join in this litigation and may well feel that the expense and competition of advertising is not in their interest.

Thus the issue on the merits is not, as the Court phrases it, whether "[o]ur pharmacist" may communicate the fact that he "will sell you the X prescription drug at the Y price." No pharmacist is asserting any such claim to so communicate. The issue is rather whether appellee consumers may override the legislative determination that pharmacists should not advertise even though the pharmacists themselves do not object....

... While there is ... much to be said for the Court's observation as a matter of desirable public policy, there is certainly nothing in the United States Constitution which requires the Virginia Legislature to hew to the teachings of Adam Smith in its legislative decisions regulating the pharmacy profession.

As Justice Black, writing for the Court, observed in Ferguson v. Skrupa, 372 U.S. 726, 730 (1963).

> "The doctrine ... that due process authorizes courts to hold laws unconstitutional when they believe the legislature has acted unwisely has long since been discarded. We have returned to the original constitutional proposition that courts do not substitute their social and economic beliefs for the judgment of legislative bodies who are elected to pass law."

Similarly in Williamson v. Lee Optical Co., 348 U.S. 483 (1955), the Court, in dealing with a state prohibition against the advertisement of eyeglass frames, held "We see no constitutional reason why a State may not treat all who deal with the human eye as members of a profession who should use no merchandising methods for obtaining customers." ...

. . .

There are undoubted difficulties with an effort to draw a bright line between "commercial speech" on the one hand and "protected speech" on the other, and the Court does better to face up to these difficulties than to attempt to hide them under labels. In this case, however, the Court has unfortunately substituted for the wavering line previously thought to exist between commercial speech and protected speech a no more satisfactory line of its own—that between "truthful" commercial speech, on the one hand, and that which is "false and misleading" on the other. The difficulty with this line is not that it wavers, but on the contrary that it is simply too Procrustean to take into account the congeries of factors which I believe could, quite consistently with the First and Fourteenth Amendments, properly influence a legislative decision with respect to commercial advertising....

In the case of "our" hypothetical pharmacist, he may now presumably advertise not only the prices of prescription drugs, but may attempt to energetically promote their sale so long as he does so truthfully. Quite consistently with Virginia law requiring prescription drugs to be available only through a physician, "our" pharmacist might run any of the following representative advertisements in a local newspaper:

"Pain getting you down? Insist that your physician prescribe Demerol. You pay a little more than for aspirin, but you get a lot more relief."

"Can't shake the flu? Get a prescription for Tetracycline from your doctor today."

"Don't spend another sleepless night. Ask your doctor to prescribe Seconal without delay."

Unless the State can show that these advertisements are either actually untruthful or misleading, it presumably is not free to restrict in any way commercial efforts on the part of those who profit from the sale of prescription drugs to put them in the widest possible circulation. But such a line simply makes no allowance whatever for what appears to have been a considered legislative judgment in most States that while prescription drugs are a necessary and vital part of medical care and treatment, there are sufficient dangers attending their widespread use that they simply may not be promoted in the same manner as hair creams, deodorants, and toothpaste. The very real dangers that general advertising for such drugs might create in terms of encouraging, even though not sanctioning, illicit use of them by individuals for whom they have not been prescribed, or by generating patient pressure upon physicians to prescribe them, are simply not dealt with in the Court's opinion. If prescription drugs may be advertised, they may be advertised on television during family viewing time. Nothing we know about the acquisitive instincts of those who inhabit every business and profession to a greater or lesser extent gives any reason to think that such persons will not do everything they can to generate demand for these products in much the same manner and to much the same degree as demand for other commodities has been generated.

Both Congress and state legislatures have by law sharply limited the permissible dissemination of information about some commodities because of the potential harm resulting from those commodities, even though they were not thought to be sufficiently demonstrably harmful to warrant outright prohibition at their sale. Current prohibitions on television advertising of liquor and cigarettes are prominent in this category, but apparently under the Court's holding so long as the advertisements are not deceptive they may no longer be prohibited.

... I do not believe that the First Amendment mandates the Court's "open door policy" toward such commercial advertising.

NOTES AND QUESTIONS

1. Suppose that Virginia had attempted to maintain the professionalism of licensed pharmacists by setting *minimum* prices for prescription drugs. Wouldn't that law be subject to most of the objections directed to Virginia's ban on prescription drug price advertising? If prices are too high, those hit the hardest would be the poor, the sick, and the aged, who might lack the means to buy essential drugs. (And if prices were set, there would be no chance of finding a pharmacist willing to sell at a lower price.) Decisions to purchase drugs would cease to be regulated by private economic decisions to the extent that prices were set, not by the

marketplace, but by government fiat. There would be alternatives to "this highly paternalistic approach" for maintaining the professionalism of pharmacists that most people would find wiser and less restrictive of individual freedom. Would the price maintenance law then be unconstitutional under the Due Process and Equal Protection Clauses of the Fourteenth Amendment? The Court's opinion, as well as the dissent of Justice Rehnquist, make it reasonably clear that the answer to that question is no. Does that surprise you? Are there good reasons for giving constitutional protection to a marketplace for "ideas," while denying all constitutional protection for a marketplace in "goods"? Is it a sufficient answer that the text of the Constitution protects a free market in ideas, through the First Amendment, but there is no mention of a free market in goods?

2.　There was a time, prior to the 1930s, when the Supreme Court read the Due Process Clauses of the Fifth and Fourteenth Amendments to protect a free market in goods. Laws that controlled hours of work, wages of workers, or prices, were in most cases declared unconstitutional. In a classic dissent to one of the earliest of these cases, which struck down a New York law setting a maximum ten hour day for bakers, Justice Holmes argued that the wisdom of economic regulatory laws was not a question for courts to decide.

> This case is decided upon an economic theory which a large part of the country does not entertain. If it were a question whether I agreed with that theory, I should desire to study it further and long before making up my mind. But I do not conceive that to be my duty, because I strongly believe that my agreement or disagreement has nothing to do with the right of a majority to embody their opinions in law.... Some ... laws embody convictions or prejudices which judges are likely to share. Some may not. But a constitution is not intended to embody a particular economic theory, whether of paternalism and the organic relation of the citizen to the state or of laissez faire. It is made for people of fundamentally differing views....

Lochner v. New York, 198 U.S. 45, 75–76 (1905).

For over four decades, the United States Supreme Court has been following the theory of Justice Holmes' dissent, that a law is not unconstitutional because it "unreasonably" interferes with a free market for goods. One case illustrating the approach is Williamson v. Lee Optical Co., 348 U.S. 483 (1955). The Oklahoma legislature forbad dispensing opticians to make lenses or fit them in a frame without a prescription from an ophthalmologist or optometrist. The opticians argued that the restriction did not protect the public, since they could duplicate lenses or fit them in frames without a prescription, but had been designed by the Oklahoma legislature to give the lion's share of the prescription eyeglass business to their competitors, the optometrists and ophthalmologists. The Court unanimously sustained the law, Justice Douglas observing for the Court:

> The day is gone when this Court uses the Due Process Clause of the Fourteenth Amendment to strike down state laws, regulato-

ry of business and industrial conditions, because they may be unwise, improvident, or out of harmony with a particular school of thought.

3. Significantly, one of the restrictions imposed by the Oklahoma legislature in the *Williamson* case was a ban on all advertising of "frames, mountings ... or any other optical appliances." The Due Process attack on the advertising restriction was answered in a single sentence. "We see no constitutional reason why a State may not treat all who deal with the human eye as members of a profession who should use no merchandising methods for obtaining customers." In *Williamson,* the argument was not even made that the advertising restriction violated the First Amendment. Should it have made a difference if the argument had been advanced? Is it anomalous that Oklahoma is free under the Constitution to enact all kinds of "unreasonable" laws that unnecessarily burden both opticians and the public, but that the public's right to receive "information" would now apparently strike down the advertising ban? What good is a right to receive information about eyeglasses if there is no right to receive the eyeglasses?

CENTRAL HUDSON GAS & ELECTRIC CORPORATION v. PUBLIC SERVICE COMMISSION OF NEW YORK

Supreme Court of the United States, 1980.
447 U.S. 557, 100 S.Ct. 2343, 65 L.Ed.2d 341.

JUSTICE POWELL delivered the opinion of the Court.

This case presents the question whether a regulation of the Public Service Commission of the State of New York violates the First and Fourteenth Amendments because it completely bans promotional advertising by an electrical utility.

I

In December 1973, the Commission, appellee here, ordered electric utilities in New York State to cease all advertising that "promot[es] the use of electricity." The order was based on the Commission's finding that "the interconnected utility system in New York State does not have sufficient fuel stocks or sources of supply to continue furnishing all customer demands for the 1973–1974 winter."

Three years later, when the fuel shortage had eased, the Commission requested comments from the public on its proposal to continue the ban on promotional advertising. Central Hudson Gas & Electric Corp., the appellant in this case, opposed the ban on First Amendment grounds. After reviewing the public comments, the Commission extended the prohibition in a Policy Statement issued on February 25, 1977.

The Policy Statement divided advertising expenses "into two broad categories—promotional—advertising intended to stimulate the purchase of utility services—and institutional and informational, a broad category inclusive of all advertising not clearly intended to promote sales." The Commission declared all promotional advertising contrary to the national policy of conserving energy. It acknowledged that the ban is not a perfect vehicle for conserving energy. For example, the Commission's order prohibits promotional advertising to develop consumption during periods when demand for electricity is low. By limiting growth in "off-peak" consumption, the ban limits the "beneficial side effects" of such growth in terms of more efficient use of existing powerplants.... And since oil dealers are not under the Commission's jurisdiction and thus remain free to advertise, it was recognized that the ban can achieve only "piecemeal conservationism." Still, the Commission adopted the restriction because it was deemed likely to "result in some dampening of unnecessary growth" in energy consumption....

The Commission's order explicitly permitted "informational" advertising designed to encourage *"shifts* of consumption" from peak demand times to periods of low electricity demand. Informational advertising would not seek to increase aggregate consumption, but would invite a leveling of demand throughout any given 24–hour period. The agency offered to review "specific proposals by the companies for specifically described [advertising] programs that meet these criteria." ...

Appellant challenged the order in state court, arguing that the Commission had restrained commercial speech in violation of the First and Fourteenth Amendments. The Commission's order was upheld by the trial court and at the intermediate appellate level. The New York Court of Appeals affirmed. We noted probable jurisdiction, and now reverse.

II

The Commission's order restricts only commercial speech, that is, expression related solely to the economic interests of the speaker and its audience. The First Amendment, as applied to the States through the Fourteenth Amendment, protects commercial speech from unwarranted governmental regulation. *Virginia Pharmacy Board*, 425 U.S., at 761–762. Commercial expression not only serves the economic interest of the speaker, but also assists consumers and furthers the societal interest in the fullest possible dissemination of information. In applying the First Amendment to this area, we have rejected the "highly paternalistic" view that government has complete power to suppress or regulate commercial speech. [P]eople will perceive their own best interests if only they are well enough informed, and ... the best means to that end is to open the channels of communication, rather than to close them.... Even when advertising communicates only an incomplete version of the relevant facts, the First Amendment presumes that some accurate information is better than no information at all.

Nevertheless, our decisions have recognized "the 'commonsense' distinction between speech proposing a commercial transaction, which occurs in an area traditionally subject to government regulation, and other varieties of speech." The Constitution therefore accords a lesser protection to commercial speech than to other constitutionally guaranteed expression....

The First Amendment's concern for commercial speech is based on the informational function of advertising.... Consequently, there can be no constitutional objection to the suppression of commercial messages that do not accurately inform the public about lawful activity. The government may ban forms of communication more likely to deceive the public than to inform it, or commercial speech related to illegal activity, Pittsburgh Press Co. v. Human Relations Comm'n, 413 U.S. 376, 388 (1973).

If the communication is neither misleading nor related to unlawful activity, the government's power is more circumscribed. The State must assert a substantial interest to be achieved by restrictions on commercial speech. Moreover, the regulatory technique must be in proportion to that interest. The limitation on expression must be designed carefully to achieve the State's goal. Compliance with this requirement may be measured by two criteria. First, the restriction must directly advance the state interest involved; the regulation may not be sustained if it provides only ineffective or remote support for the government's purpose. Second, if the governmental interest could be served as well by a more limited restriction on commercial speech, the excessive restrictions cannot survive.

Under the first criterion, the Court has declined to uphold regulations that only indirectly advance the state interest involved. In both *Bates* and *Virginia Pharmacy Board,* the Court concluded that an advertising ban could not be imposed to protect the ethical or performance standards of a profession. The Court noted in *Virginia Pharmacy Board* that "[t]he advertising ban does not directly affect professional standards one way or the other." ...

The second criterion recognized that the First Amendment mandates that speech restrictions be "narrowly drawn." *In re* Primus, 436 U.S. 412, 438 (1978). The regulatory technique may extend only as far as the interest it serves. The State cannot regulate speech that poses no danger to the asserted state interest, nor can it completely suppress information when narrower restrictions on expression would serve its interest as well. For example, in *Bates* the Court explicitly did not "foreclose the possibility that some limited supplementation, by way of warning or disclaimer or the like, might be required" in promotional materials. 433 U.S., at 384. See *Virginia Pharmacy Board,* at 773. And in Carey v. Population Services International, 431 U.S. 678, 701–702 (1977), we held that the State's "arguments ... do not justify the total suppression of advertising concerning contraceptives." This holding left open the possibility that the State could implement more carefully drawn restrictions. ...

In commercial speech cases, then, a four-part analysis has developed. At the outset, we must determine whether the expression is protected by the First Amendment. For commercial speech to come within that provision, it at least must concern lawful activity and not be misleading. Next, we ask whether the asserted governmental interest is substantial. If both inquiries yield positive answers, we must determine whether the regulation directly advances the governmental interest asserted, and whether it is not more extensive than is necessary to serve that interest.

III

We now apply this four-step analysis for commercial speech to the Commission's arguments in support of its ban on promotional advertising.

The Commission does not claim that the expression at issue either is inaccurate or relates to unlawful activity. . . .

The Commission offers two state interests as justifications for the ban on promotional advertising. The first concerns energy conservation. Any increase in demand for electricity—during peak or off-peak periods—means greater consumption of energy. The Commissions argues, and the New York court agreed, that the State's interest in conserving energy is sufficient to support suppression of advertising designed to increase consumption of electricity. In view of our country's dependence on energy resources beyond our control, no one can doubt the importance of energy conservation. Plainly, therefore, the state interest asserted is substantial.

The Commission also argues that promotional advertising will aggravate inequities caused by the failure to base the utilities' rates on marginal cost. The utilities argued to the Commission that if they could promote the used of electricity in periods of low demand, they would improve their utilization of generating capacity. The Commission responded that promotion of off-peak consumption also would increase consumption during peak periods. If peak demand were to rise, the absence of marginal cost rates would mean that the rates charged for the additional power would not reflect the true costs of expanding production. Instead, the extra costs would be borne by all consumers through higher overall rates. Without promotional advertising, the Commission stated, this inequitable turn of events would be less likely to occur. The choice among rate structures involves difficult and important questions of economic supply and distributional fairness. The State's concern that rates be fair and efficient represents a clear and substantial governmental interest.

. . . The link between the advertising prohibition and appellant's rate structure is, at most, tenuous. The impact of promotional advertising on the equity of appellant's rates is highly speculative. Advertising to increase off-peak usage would have to increase peak usage, while other factors that directly affect the fairness and efficiency of appellant's rates remained constant. Such conditional and remote eventualities simply cannot justify silencing appellant's promotional advertising.

In contrast, the State's interest in energy conservation is directly advanced by the Commission order at issue here. There is an immediate connection between advertising and demand for electricity. Central Hudson would not contest the advertising ban unless it believed that promotion would increase its sales. Thus, we find a direct link between the state's interest in conservation and the Commission's order.

. . . [T]he critical inquiry in this case [is] whether the Commission's complete suppression of speech ordinarily protected by the First Amendment is no more extensive than necessary to further the State's interest in energy conservation. The Commission's order reaches all promotional advertising, regardless of the impact of the touted service on overall energy use. But the energy conservation rationale, as important as it is, cannot justify suppressing information about electric devices or services that would cause no net increase in total energy use. In addition, no showing has been made that a more limited restriction on the content of promotional advertising would not serve adequately the State's interest.

Appellant insists that but for the ban, it would advertise products and services that use energy efficiently. These include the "heat pump," which both parties acknowledge to be a major improvement in electric heating, and the use of electric heat as a "backup" to solar and other heat sources. Although the Commission has questioned the efficiency of electric heating before this Court, neither the Commission's Policy Statement nor its order denying rehearing made findings on this issue. In the absence of authoritative findings to the contrary, we must credit as within the realm of possibility the claim that electric heat can be an efficient alternative in some circumstances.

The Commission's order prevents appellant from promoting electric services that would reduce energy use by diverting demand from less efficient sources, or that would consume roughly the same amount of energy as do alternative sources. In neither situation would the utility's advertising endanger conservation or mislead the public. To the extent that the Commission's order suppresses speech that in no way impairs the State's interest in energy conservation, the Commission's order violates the First and Fourteenth Amendments and must be invalidated, . . .

The Commission also has not demonstrated that its interest in conservation cannot be protected adequately by more limited regulation of appellant's commercial expression. To further its policy of conservation, the Commission could attempt to restrict the format and content of Central Hudson's advertising. It might, for example, require that the advertisements include information about the relative efficiency and expense of the offered service, both under current conditions and for the foreseeable future. . . .

[T]he judgment of the New York Court of Appeals is

Reversed.

JUSTICE BRENNAN's concurring opinion is omitted.

JUSTICE BLACKMUN, with whom JUSTICE BRENNAN joins, concurring in the judgment.

I agree with the Court that the Public Service Commission's ban on promotional advertising of electricity by public utilities is inconsistent with the First and Fourteenth Amendments. I concur only in the Court's judgment, however, because I believe the test now evolved and applied by the Court is not consistent with our prior cases and does not provide adequate protection for truthful, nonmisleading, noncoercive commercial speech.

. . . I agree with the Court that this level of intermediate scrutiny is appropriate for a restraint on commercial speech designed to protect consumers from misleading or coercive speech, or a regulation related to the time, place, or manner of commercial speech. I do not agree, however, that the Court's four-part test is the proper one to be applied when a State seeks to suppress information about a product in order to manipulate a private economic decision that the State cannot or has not regulated or outlawed directly . . . .

No differences between commercial speech and other protected speech justify suppression of commercial speech in order to influence public conduct through manipulation of the availability of information . . .

It appears that the Court would permit the State to ban all direct advertising of air conditioning, assuming that a more limited restriction on such advertising would not effectively deter the public from cooling its homes. In my view, our cases do not support this type of suppression. If a governmental unit believes that use or overuse of air conditioning is a serious problem, it must attack that problem directly by prohibiting air conditioning or regulating thermostat levels. Just as the Commonwealth of Virginia may promote professionalism of pharmacists directly, so too New York may *not* promote energy conservation "by keeping the public in ignorance." *Virginia Pharmacy Board,* 425, U.S., at 770.

The concurring opinion of JUSTICE STEVENS, in which JUSTICE BRENNAN joined, is omitted.

JUSTICE REHNQUIST's dissenting opinion is omitted.

44 LIQUORMART, INC. v. RHODE ISLAND

Supreme Court of the United States, 1996.
517 U.S. 484, 116 S.Ct. 1495, 134 L.Ed.2d 711.

JUSTICE STEVENS announced the judgment of the Court and delivered the opinion of the Court with respect to Parts I, II, VII, and VIII, an opinion with respect to Parts III and V, in which JUSTICE KENNEDY, JUSTICE SOUTER, and JUSTICE GINSBURG join, an opinion with respect to Part VI, in which JUSTICE KENNEDY, JUSTICE THOMAS, and JUSTICE GINSBURG join, and an opinion with respect to Part IV, in which JUSTICE KENNEDY and JUSTICE GINSBURG join.

Last Term we held that a federal law abridging a brewer's right to provide the public with accurate information about the alcoholic content of malt beverages is unconstitutional. Rubin v. Coors Brewing Co., 514 U.S. 476, 491 (1995). We now hold that Rhode Island's statutory prohibition against advertisements that provide the public with accurate information about retail prices of alcoholic beverages is also invalid. Our holding rests on the conclusion that such an advertising ban is an abridgment of speech protected by the First Amendment and that it is not shielded from constitutional scrutiny by the Twenty-first Amendment.

I

In 1956, the Rhode Island Legislature enacted two separate prohibitions against advertising the retail price of alcoholic beverages. The first applies to vendors licensed in Rhode Island as well as to out-of-state manufacturers, wholesalers, and shippers. It prohibits them from "advertising in any manner whatsoever" the price of any alcoholic beverage offered for sale in the State; the only exception is for price tags or signs displayed with the merchandise within licensed premises and not visible from the street. The second statute applies to the Rhode Island news media. It contains a categorical prohibition against the publication or broadcast of any advertisements—even those referring to sales in other States—that "make reference to the price of any alcoholic beverages."

II

Petitioners 44 Liquormart, Inc. (44 Liquormart), and Peoples Super Liquor Stores, Inc. (Peoples), are licensed retailers of alcoholic beverages. Petitioner 44 Liquormart operates a store in Rhode Island and petitioner Peoples operates several stores in Massachusetts that are patronized by Rhode Island residents. Peoples uses alcohol price advertising extensively in Massachusetts, where such advertising is permitted, but Rhode Island newspapers and other media outlets have refused to accept such ads.

Complaints from competitors about an advertisement placed by 44 Liquormart in a Rhode Island newspaper in 1991 generated enforcement proceedings that in turn led to the initiation of this litigation. The advertisement did not state the price of any alcoholic beverages. Indeed, it noted that "State law prohibits advertising liquor prices." The ad did, however, state the low prices at which peanuts, potato chips, and Schweppes mixers were being offered, identify various brands of packaged liquor, and include the word "WOW" in large letters next to pictures of vodka and rum bottles. Based on the conclusion that the implied reference to bargain prices for liquor violated the statutory ban on price advertising, the Rhode Island Liquor Control Administrator assessed a $400 fine.

After paying the fine, 44 Liquormart, joined by Peoples, filed this action against the administrator in the Federal District Court seeking a declaratory judgment that the two statutes ... violate the First Amendment ...

III

In Central Hudson Gas & Elec. Corp. v. Public Serv. Comm'n of N.Y., 447 U.S. 557 (1980), we ... considered a regulation "completely" banning all promotional advertising by electric utilities.... Our decision acknowledged the special features of commercial speech but identified the serious First Amendment concerns that attend blanket advertising prohibitions that do not protect consumers from commercial harms.

Five Members of the Court recognized that the state interest in the conservation of energy was substantial, and that there was "an immediate connection between advertising and demand for electricity." ... Nevertheless, they concluded that the regulation was invalid because the Commission had failed to make a showing that a more limited speech regulation would not have adequately served the State's interest....

In reaching its conclusion, the majority explained that although the special nature of commercial speech may require less than strict review of its regulation, special concerns arise from "regulations that entirely suppress commercial speech in order to pursue a nonspeech-related policy." . . . In those circumstances, "a ban on speech could screen from public view the underlying governmental policy.". . . . As a result, the Court concluded that "special care" should attend the review of such blanket bans, and it pointedly remarked that "in recent years this Court has not approved a blanket ban on commercial speech unless the speech itself was flawed in some way, either because it was deceptive or related to unlawful activity." . . .

IV

When a State regulates commercial messages to protect consumers from misleading, deceptive, or aggressive sales practices, or requires the disclosure of beneficial consumer information, the purpose of its regulation is consistent with the reasons for according constitutional protection to commercial speech and therefore justifies less than strict review. However, when a State entirely prohibits the dissemination of truthful, nonmisleading commercial messages for reasons unrelated to the preservation of a fair bargaining process, there is far less reason to depart from the rigorous review that the First Amendment generally demands.

Sound reasons justify reviewing the latter type of commercial speech regulation more carefully. Most obviously, complete speech bans, unlike content-neutral restrictions on the time, place, or manner of expression, . . . are particularly dangerous because they all but foreclose alternative means of disseminating certain information.

Our commercial speech cases have recognized the dangers that attend governmental attempts to single out certain messages for suppression. . . .

The special dangers that attend complete bans on truthful, nonmisleading commercial speech cannot be explained away by appeals to the "commonsense distinctions" that exist between commercial and noncommercial speech. Regulations that suppress the truth are no less troubling because they target objectively verifiable information, nor are they less effective because they aim at durable messages. As a result, neither the "greater objectivity" nor the "greater hardiness" of truthful, nonmisleading commercial speech justifies reviewing its complete suppression with added deference. . . .

It is the State's interest in protecting consumers from "commercial harms" that provides "the typical reason why commercial speech can be subject to greater governmental regulation than noncommercial speech." . . . Yet bans that target truthful, nonmisleading commercial messages rarely protect consumers from such harms. Instead, such bans often serve only to obscure an "underlying governmental policy" that could be implemented without regulating speech. . . . In this way, these commercial speech bans not only hinder consumer choice, but also impede debate over central issues of public policy. . . .

Precisely because bans against truthful, nonmisleading commercial speech rarely seek to protect consumers from either deception or over-reaching, they usually rest solely on the offensive assumption that the public will respond "irrationally" to the truth.... The First Amendment directs us to be especially skeptical of regulations that seek to keep people in the dark for what the government perceives to be their own good. That teaching applies equally to state attempts to deprive consumers of accurate information about their chosen products: "The commercial market-place, like other spheres of our social and cultural life, provides a forum where ideas and information flourish." Some of the ideas and information are vital, some of slight worth. But the general rule is that the speaker and the audience, not the government, assess the value of the information presented. Thus, even a communication that does no more than propose a commercial transaction is entitled to the coverage of the First Amendment....

V

In this case, there is no question that Rhode Island's price advertising ban constitutes a blanket prohibition against truthful, nonmisleading speech about a lawful product. There is also no question that the ban serves an end unrelated to consumer protection. Accordingly, we must review the price advertising ban with "special care," ... mindful that speech prohibitions of this type rarely survive constitutional review....

The State argues that the price advertising prohibition should nevertheless be upheld because it directly advances the State's substantial interest in promoting temperance, and because it is no more extensive than necessary.... Although there is some confusion as to what Rhode Island means by temperance, we assume that the State asserts an interest in reducing alcohol consumption.

In evaluating the ban's effectiveness in advancing the State's interest, we note that a commercial speech regulation "may not be sustained if it provides only ineffective or remote support for the government's purpose." *Central Hudson*, 447 U.S., at 564. For that reason, the State bears the burden of showing not merely that its regulation will advance its interest, but also that it will do so "to a material degree." ... The need for the State to make such a showing is particularly great given the drastic nature of its chosen means—the wholesale suppression of truthful, nonmisleading information. Accordingly, we must determine whether the State has shown that the price advertising ban will significantly reduce alcohol consumption.

We can agree that common sense supports the conclusion that a prohibition against price advertising ... will tend to mitigate competition and maintain prices at a higher level.... [W]e can even agree ... that it is reasonable to assume that demand, and hence consumption throughout the market, is somewhat lower whenever a higher, noncompetitive price level prevails. However, ... we cannot agree with the assertion that the price advertising ban will significantly advance the State's interest in promoting temperance.

Although ... the price advertising ban may have some impact on the purchasing patterns of temperate drinkers of modest means, ... the abusive drinker will probably not be deterred by a marginal price increase, and ... the true alcoholic may simply reduce his purchases of other necessities.

... As is evident, any conclusion that elimination of the ban would significantly increase alcohol consumption would require us to engage in the sort of "speculation or conjecture" that is an unacceptable means of demonstrating that a restriction on commercial speech directly advances the State's asserted interest....

The State also cannot satisfy the requirement that its restriction on speech be no more extensive than necessary. It is perfectly obvious that alternative forms of regulation that would not involve any restriction on speech would be more likely to achieve the State's goal of promoting temperance. As the State's own expert conceded, higher prices can be maintained either by direct regulation or by increased taxation. Per capita purchases could be limited as is the case with prescription drugs. Even educational campaigns focused on the problems of excessive, or even moderate, drinking might prove to be more effective.

As a result, even under the less than strict standard that generally applies in commercial speech cases, the State has failed to establish a "reasonable fit" between its abridgment of speech and its temperance goal.... It necessarily follows that the price advertising ban cannot survive the more stringent constitutional review that *Central Hudson* itself concluded was appropriate for the complete suppression of truthful, nonmisleading commercial speech.

VI

The State responds by arguing that it merely exercised appropriate "legislative judgment" in determining that a price advertising ban would best promote temperance. Relying on the *Central Hudson* analysis set forth in Posadas de Puerto Rico Associates v. Tourism Co. of P. R., 478 U.S. 328 (1986), and United States v. Edge Broadcasting Co., 509 U.S. 418 (1993), Rhode Island first argues that, because expert opinions as to the effectiveness of the price advertising ban "go both ways," the Court of Appeals correctly concluded that the ban constituted a "reasonable choice" by the legislature.... The State next contends that precedent requires us to give particular deference to that legislative choice because the State could, if it chose, ban the sale of alcoholic beverages outright. Finally, the State argues that deference is appropriate because alcoholic beverages are so-called "vice" products.... We consider each of these contentions in turn.

The State's first argument fails to justify the speech prohibition at issue. Our commercial speech cases recognize some room for the exercise of legislative judgment.... However, Rhode Island errs in concluding that *Edge* and *Posadas* establish the degree of deference that its decision to impose a price advertising ban warrants.

In *Edge*, we upheld a federal statute that permitted only those broadcasters located in States that had legalized lotteries to air lottery advertising. The statute was designed to regulate advertising about an activity that had been deemed illegal in the jurisdiction in which the broadcaster was located. 509 U.S., at 433–434. Here, by contrast, the commercial speech ban targets information about entirely lawful behavior.

Posadas is more directly relevant. There, a five-Member majority held that, under the *Central Hudson* test, it was "up to the legislature" to choose to reduce gambling by suppressing in-state casino advertising rather than engaging in educational speech.... Rhode Island argues that this logic demonstrates the constitutionality of its own decision to ban price advertising in lieu of raising taxes or employing some other less speech-restrictive means of promoting temperance.

The reasoning in *Posadas* does support the State's argument, but, on reflection, we are now persuaded that *Posadas* erroneously performed the First Amendment analysis. The casino advertising ban was designed to keep truthful, nonmisleading speech from members of the public for fear that they would be more likely to gamble if they received it. As a result, the advertising ban served to shield the State's antigambling policy from the public scrutiny that more direct, nonspeech regulation would draw....

Given our longstanding hostility to commercial speech regulation of this type, *Posadas* clearly erred in concluding that it was "up to the legislature" to choose suppression over a less speech-restrictive policy. The *Posadas* majority's conclusion on that point cannot be reconciled with the unbroken line of prior cases striking down similarly broad regulations on truthful, nonmisleading advertising when non-speech-related alternatives were available....

Because the 5-to-4 decision in *Posadas* marked such a sharp break from our prior precedent, and because it concerned a constitutional question about which this Court is the final arbiter, we decline to give force to its highly deferential approach. Instead, in keeping with our prior holdings, we conclude that a state legislature does not have the broad discretion to suppress truthful, nonmisleading information for paternalistic purposes that the *Posadas* majority was willing to tolerate....

We also cannot accept the State's second contention, which is premised entirely on the "greater-includes-the-lesser" reasoning endorsed toward the end of the majority's opinion in *Posadas*. There, the majority stated that "the greater power to completely ban casino gambling necessarily includes the lesser power to ban advertising of casino gambling." ... It went on to state that "because the government could have enacted a wholesale prohibition of [casino gambling] it is permissible for the government to take the less intrusive step of allowing the conduct, but reducing the demand through restrictions on advertising." ... The majority concluded that it would "surely be a strange constitutional doctrine which would concede to the legislature the authority to totally ban a product or activity, but deny to the legislature the authority to forbid the stimulation of demand for the product or activity through advertising on behalf of those who would profit from such increased demand." Ibid. On the basis of these statements, the State reasons that its undisputed authority to ban alcoholic beverages must include the power to restrict advertisements offering them for sale.

In Rubin v. Coors Brewing Co., 514 U.S. at 483 (1995), the United States advanced a similar argument as a basis for supporting a statutory prohibition against revealing the alcoholic content of malt beverages on product labels. We rejected the argument, noting that the statement in the *Posadas* opinion was made only after the majority had concluded that the Puerto Rican regulation "survived the *Central Hudson* test." ... Further consideration persuades us that the "greater-includes-the-lesser" argument should be rejected for the additional and more important reason that it is inconsistent with both logic and well-settled doctrine.

Although we do not dispute the proposition that greater powers include lesser ones, we fail to see how that syllogism requires the conclusion that the State's power to regulate commercial activity is "greater" than its power to ban truthful, nonmisleading commercial speech. Contrary to the assumption made in *Posadas,* we think it quite clear that banning speech may sometimes prove far more intrusive than banning conduct. As a venerable proverb teaches, it may prove more injurious to prevent people from teaching others how to fish than to prevent fish from being sold. Similarly, a local ordinance banning bicycle lessons may curtail freedom far more than one that prohibits bicycle riding within city limits. In short, we reject the assumption that words are necessarily less vital to freedom than actions, or that logic somehow proves that the power to prohibit an activity is necessarily "greater" than the power to suppress speech about it.

As a matter of First Amendment doctrine, the *Posadas* syllogism is even less defensible. The text of the First Amendment makes clear that the Constitution presumes that attempts to regulate speech are more dangerous than attempts to regulate conduct. That presumption accords with the essential role that the free flow of information plays in a democratic society. As a result, the First Amendment directs that government may not suppress speech as easily as it may suppress conduct, and that speech restrictions cannot be treated as simply another means that the government may use to achieve its ends.

These basic First Amendment principles clearly apply to commercial speech.... Thus, it is no answer that commercial speech concerns products and services that the government may freely regulate.... [A] State's regulation of the sale of goods differs in kind from a State's regulation of accurate information about those goods....

Thus, just as it is perfectly clear that Rhode Island could not ban all obscene liquor ads except those that advocated temperance, we think it equally clear that its power to ban the sale of liquor entirely does not include a power to censor all advertisements that contain accurate and nonmisleading information about the price of the product. As the entire Court apparently now agrees, the statements in the *Posadas* opinion on which Rhode Island relies are no longer persuasive.

Finally, we find unpersuasive the State's contention that, under *Posadas* and *Edge,* the price advertising ban should be upheld because it targets commercial speech that pertains to a "vice" activity. The appellees premise their request for a so-called "vice" exception to our commercial speech doctrine on language in Edge which characterized gambling as a "vice"....

... [T]he scope of any "vice" exception to the protection afforded by the First Amendment would be difficult, if not impossible, to define. Almost any product that poses some threat to public health or public morals might reasonably be characterized by a state legislature as relating to "vice activity". Such characterization, however, is anomalous when applied to products such as alcoholic beverages, lottery tickets, or playing cards, that may be lawfully purchased on the open market. The recognition of such an exception would also have the unfortunate consequence of either allowing state legislatures to justify censorship by the simple expedient of placing the "vice" label on selected lawful activities, or requiring the federal courts to establish a federal common law of vice.... For these reasons, a "vice" label that is unaccompanied by a corresponding prohibition against the commercial behavior at issue fails to provide a principled justification for the regulation of commercial speech about that activity.

VII

From 1919 until 1933, the Eighteenth Amendment to the Constitution totally prohibited "the manufacture, sale, or transportation of intoxicating liquors" in the United States and its territories. Section 1 of the Twenty-first Amendment repealed that prohibition, and § 2 delegated to the several States the power to prohibit commerce in, or the use of, alcoholic beverages....

As is clear, the text of the Twenty-first Amendment supports the view that, while it grants the States authority over commerce that might otherwise be reserved to the Federal Government, it places no limit whatsoever on other constitutional provisions....

... [T]he Twenty-first Amendment does not qualify the constitutional prohibition against laws abridging the freedom of speech embodied in the First Amendment. The Twenty-first Amendment, therefore, cannot save Rhode Island's ban on liquor price advertising.

VIII

Because Rhode Island has failed to carry its heavy burden of justifying its complete ban on price advertising, we conclude that [the challenged statutes] abridge speech in violation of the First Amendment as made applicable to the States by the Due Process Clause of the Fourteenth Amendment. The judgment of the Court of Appeals is therefore reversed.

It is so ordered.

JUSTICE SCALIA, concurring in part and concurring in the judgment.

I share Justice Thomas's discomfort with the *Central Hudson* test, which seems to me to have nothing more than policy intuition to support it. I also share Justice Stevens' aversion towards paternalistic governmental policies that prevent men and women from hearing facts that might not be good for them. On the other hand, it would also be paternalism for us to prevent the people of the States from enacting laws that we consider paternalistic, unless we have good reason to believe that the Constitution itself forbids them. I will take my guidance as to what the Constitution forbids, with regard to a text as indeterminate as the First Amendment's preservation of "the freedom of speech," and where the core offense of suppressing particular political ideas is not at issue, from the long accepted practices of the American people....

The briefs and arguments of the parties in the present case provide no illumination on that point ...

Since I do not believe we have before us the wherewithal to declare *Central Hudson* wrong—or at least the wherewithal to say what ought to replace it—I must resolve this case in accord with our existing jurisprudence, which all except Justice Thomas agree would prohibit the challenged regulation. I am not disposed to develop new law, or reinforce old, on this issue, and accordingly I merely concur in the judgment of the Court....

JUSTICE THOMAS, concurring in Parts I, II, VI, and VII, and concurring in the judgment.

CLARENCE THOMAS—Born on July 23, 1948, in Pin Point, Georgia, into a poor African–American family. Brought up by a strict grandfather who was an ardent Catholic, loyal Democrat, and member of the National Association for the Advancement of Colored People (NAACP). Republican. Born a Baptist, raised a Catholic, and became an Episcopalian. After studying in a Catholic seminary, he went to Holy Cross, where he received a B.A. with honors in English in 1968. Yale, J.D., 1974. Assistant attorney general, Missouri, 1974–1977. Attorney, Monsano Co., 1977–1979. Legislative assistant to Senator John Danforth, 1979–1981. Assistant secretary for civil rights, Department of Education, 1981–1982. Director, Equal Employment Opportunity Commission (EEOC), 1982–1990. Judge, U.S. Court of Appeals (D.C.Cir.), 1990–91. Nominated associate justice on July 1, 1991, by President George Bush to replace Thurgood Marshall. Charged with sexual harassment by Anita Hill in confirmation hearing. Confirmed by the Senate on October 15, 1991, by a 52–48 vote. Usually votes with Justice Scalia and almost never asks questions of counsel during oral arguments before the Court.

In cases such as this, in which the government's asserted interest is to keep legal users of a product or service ignorant in order to manipulate their choices in the marketplace, the balancing test adopted in Central Hudson Gas & Elec. Corp. v. Public Serv. Comm'n of N.Y., 447 U.S. 557 (1980), should not be applied, in my view. Rather, such an "interest" is per se illegitimate and can no more justify regulation of "commercial" speech than it can justify regulation of "noncommercial" speech.

I

... I do not join the principal opinion's application of the *Central Hudson* balancing test because I do not believe that such a test should be applied to a restriction of "commercial" speech, at least when, as here, the asserted interest is one that is to be achieved through keeping would-be recipients of the speech in the dark....

... I would adhere to the doctrine adopted in *Virginia Pharmacy Bd.* and in Justice Blackmun's *Central Hudson* concurrence, that all attempts to dissuade legal choices by citizens by keeping them ignorant are impermissible.

... The courts, including this Court, have found the *Central Hudson* "test" to be, as a general matter, very difficult to apply with any uniformity. This may result in part from the inherently nondeterminative nature of a case-by-case balancing "test" unaccompanied by any categorical rules, and the consequent likelihood that individual judicial preferences will govern application of the test. Moreover, the second prong of *Central Hudson*, as applied to the facts of that case and to those here, apparently requires judges to delineate those situations in which citizens cannot be trusted with information, and invites judges to decide whether they themselves think that consumption of a product is harmful enough that it should be discouraged. In my view, the *Central Hudson* test asks the courts to weigh incommensurables—the value of knowledge versus the value of ignorance—and to apply contradictory premises—that informed adults are the best judges of their own interests, and that they are not....

JUSTICE O'CONNOR, with whom THE CHIEF JUSTICE, JUSTICE SOUTER, and JUSTICE BREYER join, concurring in the judgment.

... I agree with the Court that Rhode Island's price-advertising ban is invalid. I would resolve this case more narrowly, however, by applying our established *Central Hudson* test to determine whether this commercial-speech regulation survives First Amendment scrutiny.

Under that test, we first determine whether the speech at issue concerns lawful activity and is not misleading, and whether the asserted governmental interest is substantial. If both these conditions are met, we must decide whether the regulation "directly advances the governmental interest asserted, and whether it is not more extensive than is necessary to serve that interest." ...

Given the means by which this regulation purportedly serves the State's interest, our conclusion is plain: Rhode Island's regulation fails First Amendment scrutiny.

Both parties agree that the first two prongs of the *Central Hudson* test are met. Even if we assume arguendo that Rhode Island's regulation also satisfies the requirement that it directly advance the governmental interest, Rhode Island's regulation fails the final prong; that is, its ban is more extensive than necessary to serve the State's interest.

. . . Rhode Island offers one, and only one, justification for its ban on price advertising. . . . The higher cost of obtaining alcohol, Rhode Island argues, will lead to reduced consumption.

The fit between Rhode Island's method and this particular goal is not reasonable. If the target is simply higher prices generally to discourage consumption, the regulation imposes too great, and unnecessary, a prohibition on speech in order to achieve it. The State has other methods at its disposal-methods that would more directly accomplish this stated goal without intruding on sellers' ability to provide truthful, nonmisleading information to customers. Indeed, Rhode Island's own expert conceded that " 'the objective of lowering consumption of alcohol by banning price advertising could be accomplished by establishing minimum prices and/or by increasing sales taxes on alcoholic beverages'." A tax, for example, is not normally very difficult to administer and would have a far more certain and direct effect on prices, without any restriction on speech. The principal opinion suggests further alternatives, such as limiting per capita purchases or conducting an educational campaign about the dangers of alcohol consumption. The ready availability of such alternatives—at least some of which would far more effectively achieve Rhode Island's only professed goal, at comparatively small additional administrative cost—demonstrates that the fit between ends and means is not narrowly tailored. Too, this regulation prevents sellers of alcohol from communicating price information anywhere but at the point of purchase. No channels exist at all to permit them to publicize the price of their products.

Respondents point for support to Posadas de Puerto Rico Associates v. Tourism Co. of P. R., 478 U.S. 328 (1986), where, applying the *Central Hudson* test, we upheld the constitutionality of a Puerto Rico law that prohibited the advertising of casino gambling aimed at residents of Puerto Rico, but permitted such advertising aimed at tourists.

. . . It is true that *Posadas* accepted as reasonable, without further inquiry, Puerto Rico's assertions that the regulations furthered the government's interest and were no more extensive than necessary to serve that interest. Since *Posadas*, however, this Court has examined more searchingly the State's professed goal, and the speech restriction put into place to further it, before accepting a State's claim that the speech restriction satisfies First Amendment scrutiny. . . . The closer look that we have required since *Posadas* comports better with the purpose of the analysis set out in *Central Hudson*, by requiring the State to show that the speech restriction directly advances its interest and is narrowly tailored. Under such a closer look, Rhode Island's price-advertising ban clearly fails to pass muster.

Because Rhode Island's regulation fails even the less stringent standard set out in *Central Hudson*, nothing here requires adoption of a new analysis for the evaluation of commercial speech regulation. . . .

NOTES AND QUESTIONS

1. It is settled that commercial advertising can be regulated in ways that might be inappropriate for noncommercial speech. Commercial speech that is false, deceptive, or misleading can be prohibited. Moreover, advertising can be prohibited if the transaction it proposes is itself illegal. Thus, if Rhode Island had set minimum prices for liquor sold in the State, 44 Liquormart could have been fined for advertising that it would sell below those prices. What has been contentious is the question whether the government can control advertising to reduce demand for products that it is lawful to buy.

2. A case decided six years later seemed to signal that extensive control of advertising of liquor, tobacco and gambling would be permissible under that *Central Hudson* test. Posadas de Puerto Rico Associates v. Tourism Co. of P. R., 478 U.S. 328 (1986). Puerto Rico had prohibited advertisement, in Puerto Rico, of Puerto Rico casinos. Justice Rehnquist's opinion for a bare majority concluded that Puerto Rico could have forbidden gambling by Puerto Rico residents. That "greater power" necessarily included the "lesser power" to ban advertising. That broad rationale does not survive the decision in *44 Liquormart*. Only four Justices joined part VI of the Stevens opinion, where the plurality rebuted and rejected the *Posadas* opinion. The four Justices who joined the O'Connor opinion (including Chief Justice Rehnquist) concede that the "Court has examined more searchingly the State's professed goal, and the speech restriction put into place to further it" in later cases, and that a "closer look that we have required since *Posadas* comports better" with free speech theory. No Justice challenged the conclusion in the Stevens opinion that "the entire Court apparently now agrees" that the statements in the *Posadas* opinion "are no longer persuasive."

3. 18 U.S.C. § 1304 prohibits radio and television broadcasts of advertisements for any lottery or gambling enterprise. Subsequent to the provision's original adoption, Congress modified it by enacting several exceptions, among them fishing contests, state lotteries, gaming by Indian tribes, and lotteries run by nonprofit organizations. In Greater New Orleans Broadcasting Association, Inc. v. United States, 527 U.S. 173 (1999), petitioners, an association of broadcasters in Louisiana, challenged the constitutionality of § 1304 as applied to broadcasts of private casino gambling in Louisiana, where such gambling is legal. Those broadcasts, however, are heard in Texas and Arkansas, where such gambling is unlawful. In an opinion by Justice Stevens, the Supreme Court held § 1304 unconstitutional as applied because it failed to satisfy every part of the *Central Hudson* test. (1) The content of the broadcast was not misleading and concerned lawful activities. (2) The government's asserted interests—reducing the social costs of gambling and assisting the states within their own boundaries—were not substantial, particularly in view of § 1304's many exceptions. (3) The speech restrictions in § 1304 did not materially advance the government's asserted interest. (4) The speech restrictions were more extensive than necessary to serve the government's asserted interests. "Had the Federal Government adopted a more coherent policy or accommodated the rights of speakers in states that have legalized the underlying conduct," wrote

Justice Stevens, "... this might be a different case. But under current federal law, as applied to petitioners and the messages that they wish to convey, the broadcast prohibition in § 1304 violates the First Amendment." The entire Court, except Justice Thomas, joined Stevens' opinion. Thomas concurred in the Court's judgment. "I continue to adhere to my view," he wrote, "that ... *Central Hudson* should not be applied because [it] can no more justify regulation of 'commercial speech' than it can justify regulation of 'noncommercial speech.' "

LORILLARD TOBACCO CO. v. REILLY

Supreme Court of the United States, 2001.
533 U.S. 525, 121 S.Ct. 2404, 150 L.Ed.2d 532.

Justice O'Connor delivered the opinion of the Court.

In January 1999, the Attorney General of Massachusetts promulgated comprehensive regulations governing the advertising and sale of cigarettes, smokeless tobacco, and cigars.... Petitioners, a group of cigarette, smokeless tobacco, and cigar manufacturers and retailers, filed suit in Federal District Court claiming that the regulations violate federal law and the United States Constitution. In large measure, the District Court determined that the regulations are valid and enforceable. The United States Court of Appeals for the First Circuit affirmed in part and reversed in part, concluding that the regulations are not pre empted by federal law and do not violate the First Amendment. The first question presented for our review is whether certain cigarette advertising regulations are pre-empted by the Federal Cigarette Labeling and Advertising Act (FCLAA), ... 15 U. S. C. § 1331 et seq. The second question presented is whether certain regulations governing the advertising and sale of tobacco products violate the First Amendment.

I

In November 1998, Massachusetts, along with over 40 other States, reached a landmark agreement with major manufacturers in the cigarette industry. The signatory States settled their claims against these companies in exchange for monetary payments and permanent injunctive relief.... At the press conference covering Massachusetts' decision to sign the agreement, then-Attorney General Scott Harshbarger announced that as one of his last acts in office, he would create consumer protection regulations to restrict advertising and sales practices for tobacco products. He explained that the regulations were necessary in order to "close holes" in the settlement agreement and "to stop Big Tobacco from recruiting new customers among the children of Massachusetts.".

In January 1999, pursuant to his authority to prevent unfair or deceptive practices in trade, ... the Massachusetts Attorney General (Attorney General) promulgated regulations governing the sale and advertisement of cigarettes, smokeless tobacco, and cigars.... The regulations have a broader scope than the master settlement agreement, reaching advertising, sales practices, and members of the tobacco industry not covered by the agreement. The regulations place a variety of restrictions on outdoor advertising, point-of-sale advertising, retail sales transactions, transactions by mail, promotions, sampling of products, and labels for cigars.

. . .

II

[The Court held that the State's outdoor and point-of-sale advertising regulations for cigarettes were pre-empted.]

III

By its terms, the FCLAA's pre-emption provision only applies to cigarettes. Accordingly, we must evaluate the smokeless tobacco and cigar petitioners' First Amendment challenges to the State's outdoor and point-of-sale advertising regulations. The cigarette petitioners did not raise a pre-emption challenge to the sales practices regulations. Thus, we must analyze the cigarette as well as the smokeless tobacco and cigar petitioners' claim that certain sales practices regulations for tobacco products violate the First Amendment.

A

. . .

Petitioners urge us to reject the *Central Hudson* analysis and apply strict scrutiny. . . . But here, as in Greater New Orleans Broadcasting Assn., Inc. v. United States, 527 U. S. 173, 184 (1999)., we see "no need to break new ground. *Central Hudson*, as applied in our more recent commercial speech cases, provides an adequate basis for decision." . . .

Only the last two steps of *Central Hudson*'s four-part analysis are at issue here. The Attorney General has assumed for purposes of summary judgment that petitioners' speech is entitled to First Amendment protection. With respect to the second step, none of the petitioners contests the importance of the State's interest in preventing the use of tobacco products by minors.

The third step of *Central Hudson* concerns the relationship between the harm that underlies the State's interest and the means identified by the State to advance that interest. . . .

The last step of the *Central Hudson* analysis . . . requires a reasonable " 'fit between the legislature's ends and the means chosen to accomplish those ends, . . . a means narrowly tailored to achieve the desired objective.' " . . . Focusing on the third and fourth steps of the *Central Hudson* analysis, we first address the outdoor advertising and point-of-sale advertising regulations for smokeless tobacco and cigars. We then address the sales practices regulations for all tobacco products.

B

The outdoor advertising regulations prohibit smokeless tobacco or cigar advertising within a 1,000–foot radius of a school or playground. . . .

1

The smokeless tobacco and cigar petitioners contend that the Attorney General's regulations do not satisfy *Central Hudson*'s third step. They maintain that although the Attorney General may have identified a problem with underage cigarette smoking, he has not identified an equally severe problem with respect to underage use of smokeless tobacco or cigars. . . . The cigar petitioners catalogue a list of differences between cigars and other tobacco products, including the characteristics of the products and marketing strategies. . . . The petitioners finally contend that the Attorney General cannot prove that advertising has a causal link to tobacco use such that limiting advertising will materially alleviate any problem of underage use of their products.

In previous cases, we have acknowledged the theory that product advertising stimulates demand for products, while suppressed advertising may have the opposite effect. . . . The Attorney General cites numerous studies to support this theory in the case of tobacco products.

. . .

Our review of the record reveals that the Attorney General has provided ample documentation of the problem with underage use of smokeless tobacco and cigars. In addition, we disagree with petitioners' claim that there is no evidence that preventing targeted campaigns and limiting youth exposure to advertising will decrease underage use of smokeless tobacco and cigars. On this record and in the posture of summary judgment, we are unable to conclude that the Attorney General's decision to regulate advertising of smokeless tobacco and cigars in an effort to combat the use of tobacco products by minors was based on mere "speculation [and] conjecture." . . .

2

Whatever the strength of the Attorney General's evidence to justify the outdoor advertising regulations, however, we conclude that the regulations do not satisfy the fourth step of the *Central Hudson* analysis. The final step of the *Central Hudson* analysis, the "critical inquiry in this case," requires a reasonable fit between the means and ends of the regulatory scheme. . . . The Attorney General's regulations do not meet this standard. The broad sweep of the regulations indicates that the Attorney General did not "carefully calculat[e] the costs and benefits associated with the burden on speech imposed" by the regulations. . . .

The outdoor advertising regulations prohibit any smokeless tobacco or cigar advertising within 1,000 feet of schools or playgrounds. . . . [T]he Court of Appeals concluded that the regulations prohibit advertising in a substantial portion of the major metropolitan areas of Massachusetts. . . .

The substantial geographical reach of the Attorney General's outdoor advertising regulations is compounded by other factors. "Outdoor" advertising includes not only advertising located outside an establishment, but also advertising inside a store if that advertising is visible from outside the store. The regulations restrict advertisements of any size and the term advertisement also includes oral statements. . . .

In some geographical areas, these regulations would constitute nearly a complete ban on the communication of truthful information about smokeless tobacco and cigars to adult consumers. The breadth and scope of the regulations, and the process by which the Attorney General adopted the regulations, do not demonstrate a careful calculation of the speech interests involved.

First, the Attorney General did not seem to consider the impact of the 1,000–foot restriction on commercial speech in major metropolitan areas. . . . The uniformly broad sweep of the geographical limitation demonstrates a lack of tailoring.

In addition, the range of communications restricted seems unduly broad. For instance, it is not clear from the regulatory scheme why a ban on oral communications is necessary to further the State's interest. Apparently that restriction means that a retailer is unable to answer inquiries about its tobacco products if that communication occurs outdoors. Similarly, a ban on all signs of any size seems ill suited to target the problem of highly visible billboards, as opposed to smaller signs. To the extent that studies have identified particular advertising and promotion practices that appeal to youth, tailoring would involve targeting those practices while permitting others. As crafted, the regulations make no distinction among practices on this basis.

. . .

The State's interest in preventing underage tobacco use is substantial, and even compelling, but it is no less true that the sale and use of tobacco products by adults is a legal activity. We must consider that tobacco retailers and manufacturers have an interest in conveying truthful information about their products to adults, and adults have a corresponding interest in receiving truthful information about tobacco products. . . . As the State protects children from tobacco advertisements, tobacco manufacturers and retailers and their adult consumers still have a protected interest in communication. . . .

. . .

. . . [A] retailer in Massachusetts may have no means of communicating to passersby on the street that it sells tobacco products because alternative forms of advertisement, like newspapers, do not allow that retailer to propose an instant transaction in the way that onsite advertising does. The ban on any indoor advertising that is visible from the outside also presents problems in establishments like convenience stores, which have unique security concerns that counsel in favor of full visibility of the store from the outside. It is these sorts of considerations that the Attorney General failed to incorporate into the regulatory scheme.

We conclude that the Attorney General has failed to show that the outdoor advertising regulations for smokeless tobacco and cigars are not more extensive than necessary to advance the State's substantial interest in preventing underage tobacco use. Justice Stevens urges that the Court remand the case for further development of the factual record. We believe that a remand is inappropriate in this case because the State had ample opportunity to develop a record with respect to tailoring (as it had to justify its decision to regulate advertising), and additional evidence would not alter the nature of the scheme before the Court.

A careful calculation of the costs of a speech regulation does not mean that a State must demonstrate that there is no incursion on legitimate speech interests, but a speech regulation cannot unduly impinge on the speaker's ability to propose a commercial transaction and the adult listener's opportunity to obtain information about products. After reviewing the outdoor advertising regulations, we find the calculation in this case insufficient for purposes of the First Amendment.

C

Massachusetts has also restricted indoor, point-of-sale advertising for smokeless tobacco and cigars. Advertising cannot be "placed lower than five feet from the floor of any retail establishment which is located within a one thousand foot radius of" any school or playground. . . .

We conclude that the point-of-sale advertising regulations fail both the third and fourth steps of the *Central Hudson* analysis. . . . [T]he State's goal is to prevent minors from using tobacco products and to curb demand for that activity by limiting youth exposure to advertising. The 5 foot rule does not seem to advance that goal. Not all children are less than 5 feet tall, and those who are certainly have the ability to look up and take in their surroundings.

By contrast to Justice Stevens, we do not believe this regulation can be construed as a mere regulation of conduct under United States v. O'Brien, 391 U. S. 367 (1968). To qualify as a regulation of communicative action governed by the scrutiny outlined in *O'Brien*, the State's regulation must be unrelated to expression. . . . Here, Massachusetts' height restriction is an attempt to regulate directly the communicative impact of indoor advertising.

Massachusetts may wish to target tobacco advertisements and displays that entice children, much like floor-level candy displays in a convenience store, but the blanket height restriction does not constitute a reasonable fit with that goal. . . . There is no de minimis exception for a speech restriction that lacks sufficient tailoring or justification. We conclude that the restriction on the height of indoor advertising is invalid under *Central Hudson*'s third and fourth prongs.

D

The Attorney General also promulgated a number of regulations that restrict sales practices by cigarette, smokeless tobacco, and cigar manufacturers and retailers. Among other restrictions, the regulations bar the use of self-service displays and require that tobacco products be placed out of the reach of all consumers in a location accessible only to salespersons. Two of the cigarette petitioners . . . , petitioner U. S. Smokeless Tobacco Company, and the cigar petitioners challenge the sales practices regulations on First Amendment grounds. The cigar petitioners additionally challenge a provision that prohibits sampling or promotional giveaways of cigars or little cigars. . . .

. . .

. . . As we read the regulations, they basically require tobacco retailers to place tobacco products behind counters and require customers to have contact with a salesperson before they are able to handle a tobacco product.

The cigarette and smokeless tobacco petitioners contend that "the same First Amendment principles that require invalidation of the outdoor and indoor advertising restrictions require invalidation of the display regulations at issue in this case." The cigar petitioners contend that self-service displays for cigars cannot be prohibited because each brand of cigar is unique and customers traditionally have sought to handle and compare cigars at the time of purchase.

We reject these contentions. Assuming that petitioners have a cognizable speech interest in a particular means of displaying their products, . . . these regulations withstand First Amendment scrutiny.

Massachusetts' sales practices provisions regulate conduct that may have a communicative component, but Massachusetts seeks to regulate the placement of tobacco products for reasons unrelated to the communication of ideas . . . . . We conclude that the State has demonstrated a substantial interest in preventing access to tobacco products by minors and has adopted an appropriately narrow means of advancing that interest. . . .

. . . Unattended displays of tobacco products present an opportunity for access without the proper age verification required by law. Thus, the State prohibits self-service and other displays that would allow an individual to obtain tobacco products without direct contact with a salesperson. It is clear that the regulations leave open ample channels of communication. The regulations do not significantly impede adult access to tobacco products. Moreover, retailers have other means of exercising any cognizable speech interest in the presentation of their products. We presume that vendors may place empty tobacco packaging on open display, and display actual tobacco products so long as that display is only accessible to sales personnel. As for cigars, there is no indication in the regulations that a customer is unable to examine a cigar prior to purchase, so long as that examination takes place through a salesperson.

. . .

We conclude that the sales practices regulations withstand First Amendment scrutiny. The means chosen by the State are narrowly tailored to prevent access to tobacco products by minors, are unrelated to expression, and leave open alternative avenues for vendors to convey information about products and for would-be customers to inspect products before purchase.

IV

. . .

To the extent that federal law and the First Amendment do not prohibit state action, States and localities remain free to combat the problem of underage tobacco use by appropriate means. . . .

JUSTICE KENNEDY, with whom JUSTICE SCALIA joins, concurring in part and concurring in the judgment.

The obvious overbreadth of the outdoor advertising restrictions suffices to invalidate them under the fourth part of the test in *Central Hudson*. . . . As a result, in my view, there is no need to consider whether the restrictions satisfy the third part of the test, a proposition about which there is considerable doubt. Neither are we required to consider whether Central Hudson should be retained in the face of the substantial objections that can be made to it. My continuing concerns that the test gives insufficient protection to truthful, nonmisleading commercial speech require me to refrain from expressing agreement with the Court's application of the third part of *Central Hudson*. . . . With the exception of Part III–B–1, then, I join the opinion of the Court.

JUSTICE THOMAS, concurring in part and concurring in the judgment.

I join the opinion of the Court (with the exception of Part III–B–1) because ... I would subject all of the advertising restrictions to strict scrutiny and would hold that they violate the First Amendment.

I

. . .

... In my view, an asserted government interest in keeping people ignorant by suppressing expression "is per se illegitimate and can no more justify regulation of 'commercial' speech than it can justify regulation of 'noncommercial' speech." ... That is essentially the interest asserted here, and, adhering to the views I expressed in *44 Liquormart*, I would subject the Massachusetts regulations to strict scrutiny.

B

Even if one accepts the premise that commercial speech generally is entitled to a lower level of constitutional protection than are other forms of speech, it does not follow that the regulations here deserve anything less than strict scrutiny. . . . Even when speech falls into a category of reduced constitutional protection, the government may not engage in content discrimination for reasons unrelated to those characteristics of the speech that place it within the category. . . .

. . .

C

. . .

Viewed as an effort to proscribe solicitation to unlawful conduct, these regulations clearly fail the *Brandenburg* test. A State may not "forbid or proscribe advocacy of the use of force or of law violation except where such advocacy is directed to inciting or producing imminent lawless action and is likely to incite or produce such action." ... Even if Massachusetts could prohibit advertisements reading, "Hey kids, buy cigarettes here," these regulations sweep much more broadly than that. They cover "any ... statement or representation ... the purpose or effect of which is to promote the use or sale" of tobacco products, whether or not the statement is directly or indirectly addressed to minors.... On respondents' theory, all tobacco advertising may be limited because some of its viewers may not legally act on it.

· · ·

At bottom, respondents' theory rests on the premise that an indirect solicitation is enough to empower the State to regulate speech, and that, as petitioners put it, even an advertisement directed at adults "will give any children who may happen to see it the wrong idea and therefore must be suppressed from public view." ...

... Even if Massachusetts has a valid interest in regulating speech directed at children—who, it argues, may be more easily misled, and to whom the sale of tobacco products is unlawful—it may not pursue that interest at the expense of the free speech rights of adults.

· · ·

We have held consistently that speech "cannot be suppressed solely to protect the young from ideas or images that a legislative body thinks unsuitable for them." ... To be sure, in FCC v. Pacifica Foundation, 438 U.S. 726 (1978), we upheld the Federal Communications Commission's power to regulate indecent but nonobscene radio broadcasts. But *Pacifica* relied heavily on what it considered to be the "special justifications for regulation of the broadcast media that are not applicable to other speakers." ...

Outside of the broadcasting context, we have adhered to the view that "the governmental interest in protecting children from harmful materials" does not "justify an unnecessarily broad suppression of speech addressed to adults." ...

II

Under strict scrutiny, the advertising ban may be saved only if it is narrowly tailored to promote a compelling government interest.... If that interest could be served by an alternative that is less restrictive of speech, then the State must use that alternative instead.... Applying this standard, the regulations here must fail.

A

Massachusetts asserts a compelling interest in reducing tobacco use among minors. Applied to adults, an interest in manipulating market choices by keeping people ignorant would not be legitimate, let alone compelling. But assuming that there is a compelling interest in reducing underage smoking, and that the ban on outdoor advertising promotes this interest, I doubt that the same is true of the ban on point-of-sale advertising below five feet.... Far from serving a compelling interest, the ban on displays below five feet seems to lack even a minimally rational relationship to any conceivable interest.

There is also considerable reason to doubt that the restrictions on cigar and smokeless tobacco outdoor advertising promote any state interest. Outdoor advertising for cigars, after all, is virtually nonexistent. Cigar makers use no billboards in Massachusetts, and in fact their nationwide outdoor advertising budget is only about $50,000 per year. To the extent outdoor advertising exists, there is no evidence that it is targeted at youth or has a significant effect on youth .....

Much the same is true of smokeless tobacco. Here respondents place primary reliance on evidence that, in the late 1960's, the U. S. Smokeless Tobacco Company increased its sales through advertising targeted at young males. But this does nothing to show that advertising affecting minors is a problem today....

B

In any case, even assuming that the regulations advance a compelling state interest, they must be struck down because they are not narrowly tailored. The Court is correct, that the arbitrary 1,000–foot radius demonstrates a lack of narrow tailoring, but the problem goes deeper than that. A prohibited zone defined solely by circles drawn around schools and playgrounds is necessarily overinclusive, regardless of the radii of the circles. Consider, for example, a billboard located within 1,000 feet of a school but visible only from an elevated freeway that runs nearby. Such a billboard would not threaten any of the interests respondents assert, but it would be banned anyway, because the regulations take no account of whether the advertisement could even be seen by children. The prohibited zone is even more suspect where, as here, it includes all but 10 percent of the area in the three largest cities in the State.

The loose tailoring of the advertising ban is displayed not only in its geographic scope but also in the nature of the advertisements it affects. The regulations define "advertisement" very broadly; the term includes any "written ... statement or representation, made by" a person who sells tobacco products, "the purpose or effect of which is to promote the use or sale of the product." ... Almost everything a business does has the purpose of promoting the sale of its products, so this definition would cover anything a tobacco retailer might say. Some of the prohibited speech would not even be commercial. If a store displayed a sign promoting a candidate for Attorney General who had promised to repeal the tobacco regulations if elected, it probably would be doing so with the long-term purpose of promoting sales, and the display of such a sign would be illegal.

Even if the definition of "advertisement" were read more narrowly so as to require a specific reference to tobacco products, it still would have Draconian effects. It would, for example, prohibit a tobacconist from displaying a sign reading "Joe's Cigar Shop." ... Respondents assert no interest in cigar retailer anonymity, and it is difficult to conceive of any other interest to which this rule could be said to be narrowly tailored.

The regulations fail the narrow tailoring inquiry for another, more fundamental reason. In addition to examining a narrower advertising ban, the State should have examined ways of advancing its interest that do not require limiting speech at all. Here, respondents had several alternatives. Most obviously, they could have directly regulated the conduct with which they were concerned.... Massachusetts already prohibits the sale of tobacco to minors, but it could take steps to enforce that prohibition more vigorously. It also could enact laws prohibiting the purchase, possession, or use of tobacco by minors. And, if its concern is that tobacco advertising communicates a message with which it disagrees, it could seek to counteract that message with "more speech, not enforced silence," Whitney v. California, 274 U. S. 357, 377 (1927) (Brandeis, J., concurring).

III

Underlying many of the arguments of respondents and their amici is the idea that tobacco is in some sense sui generis—that it is so special, so unlike any other object of regulation, that application of normal First Amendment principles should be suspended.... [T]o uphold the Massachusetts tobacco regulations would be to accept a line of reasoning that would permit restrictions on advertising for a host of other products.

. . .

Respondents have identified no principle of law or logic that would preclude the imposition of restrictions on fast food and alcohol advertising similar to those they seek to impose on tobacco advertising. In effect, they seek a "vice" exception to the First Amendment. No such exception exists.... If it did, it would have almost no limit....

No legislature has ever sought to restrict speech about an activity it regarded as harmless and inoffensive.... It is therefore no answer for the State to say that the makers of cigarettes are doing harm: perhaps they are. But in that respect they are no different from the purveyors of other harmful products, or the advocates of harmful ideas. When the State seeks to silence them, they are all entitled to the protection of the First Amendment.

JUSTICE STEVENS, with whom JUSTICE GINSBURG and JUSTICE BREYER join, and with whom JUSTICE SOUTER joins as to Part I, concurring in part, concurring in the judgment in part, and dissenting in part.

Because I strongly disagree with the Court's conclusion that the Federal Cigarette Labeling and Advertising Act of 1965 (FCLAA or Act) ... precludes States and localities from regulating the location of cigarette advertising, I dissent from Parts II–A and II–B of the Court's opinion. On the First Amendment questions, I agree with the Court both that the outdoor advertising restrictions imposed by Massachusetts serve legitimate and important state interests and that the record does not indicate that the measures were properly tailored to serve those interests. Because the present record does not enable us to adjudicate the merits of those claims on summary judgment, I would vacate the decision upholding those restrictions and remand for trial on the constitutionality of the outdoor advertising regulations. Finally, because I do not believe that either the point-of-sale advertising restrictions or the sales practice restrictions implicate significant First Amendment concerns, I would uphold them in their entirety.

. . .

II

On the First Amendment issues raised by petitioners, my disagreements with the majority are less significant. I would, however, reach different dispositions as to the 1,000–foot rule and the height restrictions for indoor advertising, and my evaluation of the sales practice restrictions differs from the Court's.

The 1,000–Foot Rule

. . . [N]oble ends do not save a speech-restricting statute whose means are poorly tailored.

. . .

. . . I share the majority's concern as to whether the 1,000–foot rule unduly restricts the ability of cigarette manufacturers to convey lawful information to adult consumers. This, of course, is a question of line-drawing. . . .

. . . Finding the appropriate balance is no easy matter. Though many factors plausibly enter the equation when calculating whether a child-directed location restriction goes too far in regulating adult speech, one crucial question is whether the regulatory scheme leaves available sufficient "alternative avenues of communication." . . . Because I do not think the record contains sufficient information to enable us to answer that question, I would vacate the award of summary judgment upholding the 1,000–foot rule and remand for trial on that issue. . . .

. . . The dearth of reliable statistical information as to the scope of the ban is problematic.

. . . More importantly, the Court lacks sufficient qualitative information as to the areas where cigarette advertising is prohibited and those where it is permitted . . . . .

Finally, the Court lacks information as to other avenues of communication available to cigarette manufacturers and retailers. . . .

. . . While the ultimate question before us is one of law, the answer to that question turns on complicated factual questions relating to the practical effects of the regulations. As the record does not reveal the answer to these disputed questions of fact, the court should have denied summary judgment to both parties and allowed the parties to present further evidence.

. . .

The Sales Practice and Indoor Advertising Restrictions

... I ... write separately on this issue to make two brief points.

First, ... the sales practice restrictions are best analyzed as regulating conduct, not speech. See 218 F. 3d, at 53. While the decision how to display one's products no doubt serves a marginal communicative function, the same can be said of virtually any human activity performed with the hope or intention of evoking the interest of others. This Court has long recognized the need to differentiate between legislation that targets expression and legislation that targets conduct for legitimate non-speech-related reasons but imposes an incidental burden on expression. See, e.g., United States v. O'Brien, 391 U. S. 367 (1968). However difficult that line may be to draw, it seems clear to me that laws requiring that stores maintain items behind counters and prohibiting self-service displays fall squarely on the conduct side of the line. Restrictions as to the accessibility of dangerous or legally-restricted products are a common feature of the regulatory regime governing American retail stores. I see nothing the least bit constitutionally problematic in requiring individuals to ask for the assistance of a salesclerk in order to examine or purchase a handgun, a bottle of penicillin, or a package of cigarettes.

Second, though I admit the question is closer, I would, for similar reasons, uphold the regulation limiting tobacco advertising in certain retail establishments to the space five feet or more above the floor. When viewed in isolation, this provision appears to target speech.... Nonetheless, I am ultimately persuaded that the provision is unobjectionable because it is little more than an adjunct to the other sales practice restrictions. As the Commonwealth of Massachusetts can properly legislate the placement of products and the nature of displays in its convenience stores, I would not draw a distinction between such restrictions and height restrictions on related product advertising. I would accord the Commonwealth some latitude in imposing restrictions that can have only the slightest impact on the ability of adults to purchase a poisonous product and may save some children from taking the first step on the road to addiction.

· · ·

THOMPSON v. WESTERN STATES MEDICAL CENTER
535 U.S. 357, 122 S.Ct. 1497, 152 L.Ed.2d 563 (2002).

JUSTICE O'CONNOR delivered the opinion of the Court.

Section 503A of the Food and Drug Administration Modernization Act of 1997 (FDAMA or Act), 111 Stat. 2328, 21 U.S.C. § 353a, exempts "compounded drugs" from the Food and Drug Administration's standard drug approval requirements as long as the providers of those drugs abide by several restrictions, including that they refrain from advertising or promoting particular compounded drugs. Respondents, a group of licensed pharmacies that specialize in compounding drugs, sought to enjoin enforcement of the subsections of the Act dealing with advertising and solicitation, arguing that those provisions violate the First Amendment's free speech guarantee. The District Court agreed with respondents and granted their motion for summary judgment ...

The Court of Appeals for the Ninth Circuit affirmed ... We conclude, as did the courts below, that § 503A's provisions regarding advertisement and promotion amount to unconstitutional restrictions on commercial speech, and we therefore affirm.

I

Drug compounding is a process by which a pharmacist or doctor combines, mixes, or alters ingredients to create a medication tailored to the needs of an individual patient. Compounding is typically used to prepare medications that are not commercially available, such as medication for a patient who is allergic to an ingredient in a mass-produced product. It is a traditional component of the practice of pharmacy ... Pharmacists may provide compounded drugs to patients only upon receipt of a valid prescription from a doctor or other medical practitioner licensed to prescribe medication....

. . .

For approximately the first 50 years ... the FDA generally left regulation of compounding to the States.... The FDA eventually became concerned, however, that some pharmacists were manufacturing and selling drugs under the guise of compounding, thereby avoiding the FDCA's new drug requirements. In 1992, in response to this concern, the FDA issued a Compliance Policy Guide.... It stated that the "FDA believes that an increasing number of establishments with retail pharmacy licenses are engaged in manufacturing, distributing, and promoting unapproved new drugs for human use in a manner that is clearly outside the bounds of traditional pharmacy practice and that constitute violations of the [FDCA]." ...

... [T]he Guide announced that it was FDA policy to permit pharmacists to compound drugs after receipt of a valid prescription for an individual patient or to compound drugs in "very limited quantities" before receipt of a valid prescription if they could document a history of receiving valid prescriptions "generated solely within an established professional practitioner-patient-pharmacy relationship" ...

Congress turned portions of this policy into law when it enacted the FDAMA in 1997. The FDAMA ... exempts compounded drugs from the FDCA's "new drug" requirements and other requirements provided the drugs satisfy a number of restrictions.... [M]ost relevant for this litigation, the prescription must be "unsolicited," § 353a(a), and the pharmacy, licensed pharmacist, or licensed physician compounding the drug may "not advertise or promote the compounding of any particular drug, class of drug, or type of drug." § 353a(c). The pharmacy, licensed pharmacist, or licensed physician may, however, "advertise and promote the compounding service." *Ibid.*

Respondents are a group of licensed pharmacies that specialize in drug compounding. They have prepared promotional materials that they distribute by mail and at medical conferences to inform patients and physicians of the use and effectiveness of specific compounded drugs. . . .

. . .

II

The parties agree that the advertising and soliciting prohibited by the FDAMA constitute commercial speech. . . .

. . .

Neither party has challenged the appropriateness of applying the *Central Hudson* framework to the speech-related provisions at issue here. . . .

III

The Government does not attempt to defend the FDAMA's speech-related provisions under the first prong of the *Central Hudson* test; *i.e.*, it does not argue that the prohibited advertisements would be about unlawful activity or would be misleading. Instead, the Government argues that the FDAMA satisfies the remaining three prongs of the *Central Hudson* test.

The Government asserts that three substantial interests underlie the FDAMA. The first is an interest in "preserv[ing] the effectiveness and integrity of the FDCA's new drug approval process and the protection of the public health that it provides." The second is an interest in "preserv[ing] the availability of compounded drugs for those individual patients who, for particularized medical reasons, cannot use commercially available products that have been approved by the FDA." Finally, the Government argues that "[a]chieving the proper balance between those two independently compelling but competing interests is itself a substantial governmental interest."

Explaining these interests, the Government argues that the FDCA's new drug approval requirements are critical to the public health and safety. . . .

. . . [T]he Government also acknowledges that "because obtaining FDA approval for a new drug is a costly process, requiring FDA approval of all drug products compounded by pharmacies for the particular needs of an individual patient would, as a practical matter, eliminate the practice of compounding, and [that this] would be undesirable because compounding is sometimes critical to the care of patients with drug allergies, patients who cannot tolerate particular drug delivery systems, and patients requiring special drug dosages."

. . . [T]he Government needs to be able to draw a line between small-scale compounding and large-scale drug manufacturing. That line must distinguish compounded drugs produced on such a small scale that they could not undergo safety and efficacy testing from drugs produced and sold on a large enough scale that they could undergo such testing and therefore must do so.

The Government argues that the FDAMA's speech-related provisions provide just such a line, *i.e.*, that, in the terms of *Central Hudson*, they "directly advanc[e] the governmental interest[s] asserted." ... The Government argues that advertising ... is "a fair proxy for actual or intended large-scale manufacturing," ...

... [T]he Government has failed to demonstrate that the speech restrictions are "not more extensive than is necessary to serve [those] interest[s]." ...

Several non-speech-related means of drawing a line between compounding and large-scale manufacturing might be possible here. First, it seems that the Government could use the very factors the FDA relied on to distinguish compounding from manufacturing in its 1992 Compliance Policy Guide. For example, the Government could ban the use of "commercial scale manufacturing or testing equipment for compounding drug products." It could prohibit pharmacists from compounding more drugs in anticipation of receiving prescriptions than in response to prescriptions already received. It could prohibit pharmacists from "[o]ffering compounded drugs at wholesale to other state licensed persons or commercial entities for resale." Alternately, it could limit the amount of compounded drugs, either by volume or by numbers of prescriptions, that a given pharmacist or pharmacy sells out of State. Another possibility not suggested by the Compliance Policy Guide would be capping the amount of any particular compounded drug, either by drug volume, number of prescriptions, gross revenue, or profit that a pharmacist or pharmacy may make or sell in a given period of time. It might even be sufficient to rely solely on the non-speech-related provisions of the FDAMA, such as the requirement that compounding only be conducted in response to a prescription or a history of receiving a prescription, ... and the limitation on the percentage of a pharmacy's total sales that out-of-state sales of compounded drugs may represent ...

... Nowhere in the legislative history of the FDAMA or petitioners' briefs is there any explanation of why the Government believed forbidding advertising was a necessary as opposed to merely convenient means of achieving its interests. ... If the First Amendment means anything, it means that regulating speech must be a last—not first—resort. Yet here it seems to have been the first strategy the Government thought to try.

... The dissent describes another governmental interest—an interest in prohibiting the sale of compounded drugs to "patients who may not clearly need them," ... Nowhere in its briefs, however, does the Government argue that this interest motivated the advertising ban. Although, for the reasons given by the dissent, Congress conceivably could have enacted the advertising ban to advance this interest, we have generally only sustained statutes on the basis of hypothesized justifications when reviewing statutes merely to determine whether they are rational. ... The *Central Hudson* test is significantly stricter than the rational basis test, however, requiring the Government not only to identify specifically "a substantial interest to be achieved by [the] restrictio[n] on commercial speech," ... but also to prove that the regulation "directly advances" that interest and is "not more extensive than is necessary to serve that interest," ...

Even if the Government had argued that the FDAMA's speech-related restrictions were motivated by a fear that advertising compounded drugs would put people who do not need such drugs at risk by causing them to convince their doctors to prescribe the drugs anyway, that fear would fail to justify the restrictions. Aside from the fact that this concern rests on the questionable assumption that doctors would prescribe unnecessary medications (an assumption the dissent is willing to make based on one magazine article and one survey, neither of which was relied upon by the Government), this concern amounts to a fear that people would make bad decisions if given truthful information about compounded drugs. We have previously rejected the notion that the Government has an interest in preventing the dissemination of truthful commercial information in order to prevent members of the public from making bad decisions with the information....

Even if the Government had asserted an interest in preventing people who do not need compounded drugs from obtaining those drugs, the statute does not directly advance that interest.... Although the advertising ban may reduce the demand for compounded drugs from those who do not need the drugs, it does nothing to prevent such individuals from obtaining compounded drugs other than requiring prescriptions. But if it is appropriate for the statute to rely on doctors to refrain from prescribing compounded drugs to patients who do not need them, it is not clear why it would not also be appropriate to rely on doctors to refrain from prescribing compounded drugs to patients who do not need them in a world where advertising was permitted.

· · ·

If the Government's failure to justify its decision to regulate speech were not enough to convince us that the FDAMA's advertising provisions were unconstitutional, the amount of beneficial speech prohibited by the FDAMA would be.... It would prevent pharmacists with no interest in mass-producing medications, but who serve clienteles with special medical needs, from telling the doctors treating those clients about the alternative drugs available through compounding. For example, a pharmacist serving a children's hospital where many patients are unable to swallow pills would be prevented from telling the children's doctors about a new development in compounding that allowed a drug that was previously available only in pill form to be administered another way.... The fact that the FDAMA would prohibit such seemingly useful speech even though doing so does not appear to directly further any asserted governmental objective confirms our belief that the prohibition is unconstitutional.

· · ·

JUSTICE THOMAS, concurring.

I concur because I agree with the Court's application of the test set forth in *Central Hudson* ... I continue, however, to adhere to my view that cases such as this should not be analyzed under the *Central Hudson* test. . . .

JUSTICE BREYER, with whom THE CHIEF JUSTICE, JUSTICE STEVENS, and JUSTICE GINSBURG join, dissenting.

. . .

. . . I believe that the Court seriously undervalues the importance of the Government's interest in protecting the health and safety of the American public.

I

In my view, the advertising restriction "directly advances" the statute's important safety objective . . . to confine the sale of untested, compounded, drugs to where they are medically needed. But to do so the statute must exclude from the area of permitted drug sales *both* (1) those drugs that traditional drug manufacturers might supply after testing— typically drugs capable of being produced in large amounts, *and* (2) those compounded drugs sought by patients who may not clearly need them— including compounded drugs produced in small amounts.

The . . . statute, in seeking to confine distribution of untested tailored drugs, must look both at the amount supplied (to help decide whether ordinary manufacturers might provide a tested alternative) and at the nature of demand (to help separate genuine need from simple convenience). . . .

This second intermediate objective is logically related to Congress' primary end—the minimizing of safety risks. The statute's basic exemption from testing requirements inherently creates risks simply by placing untested drugs in the hands of the consumer. Where an individual has a specific medical need for a specially tailored drug those risks are likely offset. But where an untested drug is a convenience, not a necessity, that offset is unlikely to be present.

That presumably is why neither the Food and Drug Administration (FDA) nor Congress anywhere suggests that all that matters is the total *amount* of a particular drug's sales. . . . That is why the statute itself, as well as the FDA policy that the statute reflects, lists several distinguishing factors, of which advertising is one. . . .

. . .

And that, in part, is why federal and state authorities have long permitted pharmacists to advertise the fact that they compound drugs, while forbidding the advertisement of individual compounds. . . .

These policies and statutory provisions reflect the view that individualized consideration is more likely present, and convenience alone is more likely absent, when demand for a compounding prescription originates with a doctor, not an advertisement. The restrictions try to assure that demand is generated doctor-to-patient-to-pharmacist, not pharmacist-to-advertisement-to-patient-to-doctor. And they do so in order to diminish the likelihood that those who do not genuinely need untested compounded drugs will not receive them.

There is considerable evidence that the relevant means—the advertising restrictions—directly advance this statutory objective....

... [C]ompounded drugs carry with them special risks. After all, compounding is not necessarily a matter of changing a drug's flavor, but rather it is a matter of combining different ingredients in new, untested ways, say, adding a pain medication to an antihistamine to counteract allergies or increasing the ratio of approved ingredients in a salve to help the body absorb it at a faster rate. And the risks associated with the untested combination of ingredients or the quicker absorption rate or the working conditions necessary to change an old drug into its new form can, for some patients, mean infection, serious side effects, or even death....

There is considerable evidence that consumer oriented advertising will create strong consumer-driven demand for a particular drug....

And there is strong evidence that doctors will often respond affirmatively to a patient's request for a specific drug that the patient has seen advertised....

In these circumstances, Congress could reasonably conclude that doctors will respond affirmatively to a patient's request for a compounded drug even if the doctor would not normally prescribe it. When a parent learns that a child's pill can be administered in liquid form, when a patient learns that a compounded skin cream has an enhanced penetration rate, or when an allergy sufferer learns that a compounded anti-inflammatory allergy medication can alleviate a sinus headache without the sedative effects of antihistamines, that parent or patient may well ask for the desired prescription. And the doctor may well write the prescription even in the absence of special need—at least if any risk likely to arise from lack of testing is so small that only *scientific testing,* not anecdote or experience, would reveal it....

Of course, the added risks in any such individual case may be small. But those individual risks added together can significantly affect the public health. At least, the FDA and Congress could reasonably reach that conclusion. And that fact, along with the absence of any significant evidence that the advertising restrictions have prevented doctors from learning about, or obtaining, compounded drugs, means that the FDA and Congress could also conclude that the advertising restrictions "directly advance" the statute's safety goal.... There is no reason for this Court, as a matter of constitutional law, to reach a different conclusion.

II

I do not believe that Congress could have achieved its safety objectives in significantly less restrictive ways. Consider the several alternatives the Court suggests....

. . .

The Court adds that "[t]he Government has not offered any reason why these possibilities, alone or in combination, would be insufficient." The Government's failure to do so may reflect the fact that only the Court, not any of the respondents, has here suggested that these "alternatives," alone or in combination, would prove sufficient. In fact, the FDA's Compliance Policy Guide, from which the Court draws its first four alternatives, specifically warned that these alternatives alone were insufficient to successfully distinguish traditional compounding from unacceptable manufacturing....

III

The Court responds to the claim that advertising compounded drugs causes people to obtain drugs that do not promote their health, by finding it implausible given the need for a prescription and by suggesting that it is not relevant. The First Amendment, it says, does not permit the Government to control the content of advertising, where doing so flows from "fear" that "people would make bad decisions if given truthful information about compounded drugs." This response ... fails to take account of considerations that make the claim more than plausible (if properly stated); and it is inconsistent with this Court's interpretation of the Constitution.

It is an oversimplification to say that the Government "fear[s]" that doctors or patients "would make bad decisions if given truthful information." Rather, the Government fears the safety consequences of multiple compound-drug prescription decisions initiated not by doctors but by pharmacist-to-patient advertising. Those consequences flow from the adverse cumulative effects of multiple individual decisions each of which may seem perfectly reasonable considered on its own. The Government fears that, taken together, these apparently rational individual decisions will undermine the safety testing system, thereby producing overall a net balance of harm ... Consequently, the Government leaves pharmacists free to explain through advertisements what compounding is, to advertise that they engage in compounding, and to advise patients to discuss the matter with their physicians. And it forbids advertising the specific drug in question, not because it fears the "information" the advertisement provides, but because it fears the systematic effect ... of advertisements that will not fully explain the complicated risks at issue. And this latter fear is more than plausible.

I do not deny that the statute restricts the circulation of some truthful information.... Nonetheless, this Court has not previously held that commercial advertising restrictions automatically violate the First Amendment. Rather, the Court has applied a more flexible test. It has examined the restriction's proportionality, the relation between restriction and objective, the fit between ends and means.... It has done so because it has concluded that, from a constitutional perspective, commercial speech does not warrant application of the Court's strictest speech-protective tests. And it has reached this conclusion in part because restrictions on commercial speech do not often repress individual self-expression; they rarely interfere with the functioning of democratic political processes; and they often reflect a democratically determined governmental decision to regulate a commercial venture in order to protect, for example, the consumer, the public health, individual safety, or the environment....

... The Court, in my view, gives insufficient weight to the Government's regulatory rationale, and too readily assumes the existence of practical alternatives. It thereby applies the commercial speech doctrine too strictly....

... [A]n overly rigid "commercial speech" doctrine will transform what ought to be a legislative or regulatory decision about the best way to protect the health and safety of the American public into a constitutional decision prohibiting the legislature from enacting necessary protections. As history in respect to the Due Process Clause shows, any such transformation would involve a tragic constitutional misunderstanding....

. . .

Chapter X

THE MULTI–LEVEL THEORY OF FREE SPEECH

Although the First Amendment's guarantee of free speech makes no distinctions among levels of speech, the Supreme Court has recognized different levels and has protected some levels more than others. As the preceding chapters have shown, spoken or written political speech receives more protection than symbolic speech or commercial speech. The former receives strict scrutiny while the latter receives heightened scrutiny. Below those two levels is a third level that receives at most the rational-basis test. Examples of speech at that lowest level are obscenity, fighting words, and defamation, which are considered in the next three chapters.

Justice Murphy, writing for a unanimous Court in Chaplinsky v. New Hampshire, 315 U.S. 568, 571–572 (1942), explained why third-level speech received virtually no protection. He wrote:

> Allowing the broadest scope to the language and purpose of the Fourteenth Amendment, it is well understood that the right of free speech is not absolute at all times and under all circumstances. There are certain well-defined and narrowly limited classes of speech, the prevention and punishment of which have never been thought to raise any Constitutional problem. These include the lewd and obscene, the profane, the libelous, and insulting or "fighting" words—those which by their very utterance inflict injury or tend to incite an immediate breach of the peace. It has been well observed that such utterances are no essential part of any exposition of ideas, and are of such slight social value as a step to truth that any benefit that may be derived from them is clearly outweighed by the social interest in order and morality.

The *Chaplinsky* dictum has two sources. The first is Cantwell v. Connecticut, 310 U.S. 296, 309–310 (1940), in which Justice Roberts wrote: "Resort to epithets or personal abuse is not in any proper sense communication of information or opinion safeguarded by the Constitution, and its punishment as a criminal act would raise no question under that instrument." The second is Chafee's *Free Speech in the United States,* in which he argued that generally speech was entitled to constitutional protection unless it created a clear and present danger of harm, but he acknowledged that there were certain verbal crimes that could be constitutionally punished whether or not they created a clear and present danger. He wrote:*

---

* Zechariah Chafee, Jr., Free Speech in the United States, Harvard University Press, 1941, pp. 149–152. Reprinted with permission.

[T]he normal criminal law is interested in preventing crimes and certain non-criminal interferences with governmental functions like refusals to enlist or subscribe to bonds. It is directed primarily against actual injuries. Such injuries are usually committed by acts, but the law also punishes a few classes of words like obscenity, profanity, and gross libels upon individuals, because the very utterance of such words is considered to inflict a present injury upon listeners, readers, or those defamed, or else to render highly probable an immediate breach of the peace. This is a very different matter from punishing words because they are thought to cause a future danger to the State.

... [These verbal crimes] are too-well recognized to question their constitutionality, but I believe that if they are properly limited they fall outside the protection of the free speech clauses as I have defined them. My reason is not that they existed at common law before the constitutions, for a similar argument would apply to the crime of sedition, which was abolished by the First Amendment. The existence of a verbal crime at common law shows the presence of a social interest which must be weighed in the balance, but the free speech guaranties, as I have argued at length, enact a countervailing social interest in the attainment and dissemination of truth, which was insufficiently recognized by common law. Nor do I base my conclusion on the historical fact that the framers of the constitutions wanted to safeguard political discussion, because their own statements of freedom of speech in the address to the people of Quebec, the Virginia Toleration Statute, and the opening clause of the First Amendment itself, prove that they also wanted to safeguard scientific and religious freedom, both of which would be greatly restricted by a sweeping application of the common law of obscenity and blasphemy. The true explanation is that profanity and indecent talk and pictures, which do not form an essential part of any exposition of ideas, have a very slight social value as a step toward truth, which is clearly outweighed by the social interests in order, morality, the training of the young, and the peace of mind of those who hear and see. Words of this type offer little opportunity for the usual process of counter-argument. The harm is done as soon as they are communicated, or is liable to follow almost immediately in the form of retaliatory violence. The only sound explanation of the punishment of obscenity and profanity is that the words are criminal, not because of the ideas they communicate, but like acts because of their immediate consequences to the five senses. The man who swears in a street car is as much of a nuisance as the man who smokes there. Insults are punished like a threatening gesture, since they are liable to provoke a fight. Adulterated candy is no more poisonous to children than some books. Grossly unpatriotic language may be punished for the same reasons. The man who talks scurrilously about the flag commits a crime, not because the implications of his ideas tend to weaken the Federal Government, but because the effect resembles that of an injurious act such as trampling on the flag, which would be a public nuisance and a breach of the peace. This is a state but not a federal crime, for the United States has no criminal jurisdiction over offenses against order and good manners, although Congress may possibly have power to regulate the use of the national emblem. It is altogether different from sedition.

The absurd and unjust holdings in some of these prosecutions for the use of indecent or otherwise objectionable language furnish a sharp warning against any creation of new verbal crimes. Thus, the test of obscenity is very vague, and many decisions have utterly failed to distinguish nasty talk or the sale of unsuitable books to the young from the serious discussion of topics of great social significance. . . . When the law supplies no definite standard of criminality, a judge in deciding what is indecent or profane may consciously disregard the sound test of present injury, and proceeding upon an entirely different theory may condemn the defendant because his words express ideas which are thought liable to cause bad future consequences. Thus musical comedies enjoy almost unbridled license, while a problem play is often forbidden because opposed to our views of marriage. In the same way, the law of blasphemy has been used against Shelley's *Queen Mab* and the decorous promulgation of pantheistic ideas, on the ground that to attack religion is to loosen the bonds of society and endanger the state. This is simply a roundabout modern method to make heterodoxy in sex matters and even in religion a crime. A Washington decision punishing a man for a newspaper article tending to defame George Washington is a serious restriction on historical writing. Those of us who feel strongly that faith in the teachings of Christ means a better world must still recognize that others deplore the evils of superstition, and concede that the value of Christianity is one of the very questions which ought to be freely debated. Hence the authorities should be very reluctant to punish the contrary-minded, even though the prosecution be rested on some non-religious ground like the offensiveness of the defendant's irreligious language or the tendency of blasphemy to produce a breach of the peace.

This breach of the peace theory is peculiarly liable to abuse when applied against unpopular expressions and practices. It makes a man a criminal simply because his neighbors have no self-control and cannot refrain from violence. . . . A man does not become a criminal because someone else assaults him, unless his own conduct is in itself illegal or may be reasonably considered a direct provocation to violence.

Thus all these crimes of injurious words must be kept within very narrow limits if they are not to give excessive opportunities for outlawing heterodox ideas.

NOTES AND QUESTIONS

1.   Chafee would narrowly limit the definitions of obscenity, profanity, and fighting words. What are his principles of limitation?

2.   Does Chafee believe that burning the American flag is not entitled to constitutional protection under the First and Fourteenth Amendments? Compare Justice Rehnquist's dissenting opinion in Johnson v. Texas, supra, p. 306.

Chapter XI

OBSCENITY

I. EARLY HISTORY OF THE LAW OF OBSCENITY*

EARLY BEGINNINGS IN ENGLAND

Censorship for political and religious reasons dates back, at least, to Greek and Roman times. In both cultures, however, sexual licentiousness was tolerated in drama (a principal means of popular entertainment) and was often combined with religious themes. During medieval times, bawdiness was apparently quite acceptable in ballads (again, frequently mixed with religious themes) and even in religious works. The Exeter Book, for example, a largely devotional work which is the earliest example of Anglo–Saxon literature, contains explicit sexual riddles which were collected by a monk.

The printing of books increased greatly in England in the 15th Century. Royal censorship began in England in 1538 through a licensing system established by Henry VIII. Like earlier manifestations of governmental censorship in other cultures, however, English censorship at this time was not directed toward sexual content, but only against seditious and heretical works. Subsequently, the strong influence of Puritanism in England in the first half of the 17th Century led to authorization of proceedings against the use of profanity by actors on stage in 1605 and the total abolition of the play houses by Parliament in 1642. The licensing system may have been used to prohibit sexual explicitness during this time. After the Restoration in 1660, however, licensing was again limited to suppressing sedition and heresy in printed works, and the play houses were revived.

The only prosecution in England prior to the 18th Century which somewhat related to what was later deemed to be "obscenity" was King v. Sedley in 1663. Sir Charles Sedley, an intimate of Charles II, became drunk with two friends at a tavern. They climbed to the balcony of the tavern, which overlooked Covent Garden, and removed their clothes. Sedley thereupon gave a speech which included profanities and poured bottles of urine down upon his audience. A riot followed. Sedley was given a substantial fine and committed to jail for a week for breaking the peace. The case is often referred to as the first reported obscenity case, apparently because it showed that common-law courts would, even in the absence of a statute, penalize conduct which is grossly offensive to the public. Sedley's case, however, did not concern the distribution of sexual materials, but involved both a physical assault upon others and the

* Report of the Commission on Obscenity and Pornography, 1970, pp. 297–301.

public broadcasting of profanity and nudity upon unwilling recipients. It has little direct relationship with the offense of distributing sexual works to consenting recipients which was later evolved by the law.

The end of the 17th Century in England brought the beginning of long-term governmental concern with the morals of the public in the sexual area which culminated in the Victorian period. Puritan repression of stage plays was renewed. A Society for the Reformation of Manners, which blacklisted persons guilty of "vice," was formed under Royal patronage and Queen Anne issued a proclamation denouncing vice. On the other hand, the Licensing Act was allowed to lapse by Parliament in 1695 because of practical considerations. This, coupled with the spread of literacy and the increased popularity of reading, led to a new class of "popular" literature which often had sexual content and which caused concern because of its attraction for lower-class readers. Nevertheless, in 1708 a man named Read was acquitted for writing a book called *The Fifteen Plagues of a Maidenhead.* The book was held by the court to be "bawdy stuff," but since it libelled no one, did not reflect upon the government and did not attack religion, it was held to be "punishable only in the spiritual court."

THE DEVELOPMENT OF THE ENGLISH LAW OF OBSCENITY

In the 1720s one, Curl, was prosecuted for "obscene libel" for publishing a book entitled *Venus in the Cloister or the Nun in her Smock.* The judges were troubled by the *Read* decision and by the fact that, previously, the common law had not recognized as crimes acts which did not tend to a breach of the peace, as Curl's book did not. However, after several continuances a conviction was rendered in 1727. As shown by its title, the work in issue in *Curl's* case was not offensive solely because of its sexual content, but because of its anti-religious content as well. An early report of the case states that the court found there to be an offense because "religion was part of the common law; and therefore whatever is an offense against that is evidently an offense against the common law."

Eighteenth Century legal writers treated the offense of obscene libel created by *Curl* as an offense against God. Eighteenth Century obscenity cases which followed *Curl* similarly limited themselves to sexual material in the context of anti-religious works. In fact, some very sexually explicit books and pamphlets of the type often referred to today as hard-core pornography circulated quite freely in England throughout the 18th Century, apparently because their lack of anti-religious content kept them outside the law's proscription.

Near the beginning of the 19th Century, the common law appears to have evolved by degrees in England to where it began to be applied in some cases to prohibit purely sexual works which did not attack or libel religious institutions. It has been estimated that there were about three obscenity prosecutions per year in England between 1802 and 1857. Obscenity legislation was first enacted in England as part of the Vagrancy Act of 1824, which prohibited exposing an obscene book or print in public places. In 1853, a statute, apparently aimed at French postcards, was passed to prohibit the importation of obscene materials and in 1857 the so-called Lord Campbell's Act, generally prohibiting the dissemination of obscenity, was enacted.

Lord Campbell's Act did not contain a definition of what was deemed "obscene." In 1868, in Queen v. Hicklin an authoritative judicial definition was adopted. The *Hicklin* case involved an anti-religious pamphlet with sexual content entitled, *The Confession Unmasked, showing the depravity of the Roman Priesthood, the iniquity of the Confessional and the questions put to females in confession*. The opinion of the court, however, did not expressly limit itself to material with anti-religious content. It held instead that the test of obscenity was

> whether the tendency of the matter charged as obscenity is to deprave and corrupt those whose minds are open to such immoral influences, and into whose hands a publication of this sort may fall.

Hicklin thus made it clear in England, for the first time, that publications might be prohibited as "obscene" solely because of their sexual content, and not because of their attack upon the government or upon religious institutions.

THE DEVELOPMENT OF OBSCENITY LAW IN THE UNITED STATES

There appears to have been no common-law development in the American colonies, during the 18th Century, of the offense of anti-religious obscenity which was recognized in England in *Curl's* case in 1727. Only in the Massachusetts colony were there statutes in the area. The Puritan authorities in Massachusetts early prohibited offenses against religion, such as blasphemy (which was punishable by death until 1697 and by boring through the tongue with a hot iron thereafter), and possession of writings containing Quaker opinions. A strict general censorship system was instituted in 1662, but was not aimed at sexual materials. In 1711, however, apparently because of the appearance in the colony of sexual materials imported from England, a statute was passed which recited that "evil communication, wicked, profane, impure, filthy and obscene songs, composures, writings or prints do corrupt the mind and are incentives to all manner of impieties and debaucheries, more especially when digested, composed or uttered in imitation or in mimicking of preaching, or any other part of divine worship" and which prohibited the "composing, writing, printing or publishing of any filthy, obscene or profane song, pamphlet, libel or mock-sermon, in imitation of preaching, or any other part of divine worship." This statute, although closely related to anti-religious material, was apparently potentially applicable to solely sexual material as well.... All the other colonies appear to have left sexual materials entirely unregulated by the criminal law, although some such materials were in circulation in the colonies.

The first obscenity case in the United States occurred in 1815 in Pennsylvania. There the court found the private showing for profit of a picture of a man and woman in an "indecent posture" to be a common-law offense because it was in violation of the public decency. In 1821, the publisher of *Fanny Hill* was found guilty in Massachusetts under both the colonial statute and the common law. Subsequent state-law development was statutory. In 1821, Vermont became the first state to pass an obscenity statute. A Connecticut statute followed in 1834, and in 1835 Massachusetts amended and broadened its statute, lessened its tie to anti-religious works, and defined the obscene to be works "manifestly tending to the corruption of the morals of youth." Subsequent state statutes also typically emphasized a purpose of protecting youth. The proliferation of state obscenity statutes coincided with an increase in literacy among the American population, the beginnings of free universal education, and a decline in the direct influence of the Church over community life.

II. LATER HISTORY OF THE LAW OF OBSCENITY

COMSTOCK'S INFLUENCE*

In 1872, Anthony Comstock [1844–1915] began a crusade to strengthen anti-obscenity laws. With financial backing from the upper-class businessmen on the board of the YMCA, Comstock tirelessly lobbied state and federal legislatures. He also founded the New York Society for the Suppression of Vice to support his work. Through the Society, Comstock enforced existing obscenity laws; he seized and handed over to the police "bad books" and "articles made of rubber for immoral purposes, and used by both sexes." Comstock's major political victory came in 1873, when the U.S. Congress passed, without debate, "An Act for the Suppression of Trade in, and Circulation of Obscene Literature and Articles of Immoral Use." This revision of the federal postal law forbade the mailing of obscene, lewd, lascivious, and indecent writing or advertisements, including articles that aided contraception or abortion.

Throughout the 1880s and 1890s, Congress strengthened the so-called Comstock law, and the courts upheld its constitutionality. Comstock himself supervised enforcement. As an unpaid U.S. postal inspector, he almost single-handedly prosecuted those who wrote, published, and sold literature or art that he considered obscene. In 1875 alone, his vigilance led to forty-seven arrests, twenty-eight convictions (aggregating thirty years in prison), and ... [a large number of] fines. That year the New York Society for the Suppression of Vice seized twelve hundred pounds of books and destroyed over twenty-nine thousand sexually explicit photos, songs, leaflets, rubber goods, and circulars. The objects of Comstock's attack ranged from penny postcards sold on the Bowery to fine arts exhibited in Fifth Avenue galleries depicting the nude body, from dime novels of seduction to Leo Tolstoy's *Kreutzer Sonata....* The conviction rate under the Comstock Act—as high as ninety percent of those accused—attested to Comstock's boundless (some claimed prurient) interest in suppressing vice.

Comstock could not have managed his campaign without broader public support. While he set about enforcing anti-obscenity postal stat-

---

* John D. Emilio and Estelle B. Freedman, Intimate Matters: A History of Sexuality in America. Harper & Row, 1988, pp. 159–160, 277–278. Reprinted with permission.

utes, the social purity and suffrage movements also voiced concerns about the danger of vicious literature. In 1883 the WCTU established a Department for the Suppression of Impure Literature. In the 1890s, local women successfully campaigned for the removal of a painting depicting a nude from the bar of a Cincinnati restaurant, and the WCTU kept the sculpture *Bacchante and Infant* from being displayed at the Boston Public Library. Eventually, both the WCTU and the *Woman's Journal* became critical of Comstock's methods of intimidation and entrapment, and he in turn attacked the suffragists. In the meantime, however, Comstock had consolidated extensive support from wealthy urban businessmen who formed local societies to suppress vice. In Rochester, Providence, Detroit, Toledo, San Francisco, Portland, and Cincinnati, local elites organized chapters of the Society for the Suppression of Vice. A New England branch, founded in 1882, declared itself the Watch and Ward Society in 1891. Fueled by Comstock's Boston counterpart Godfrey Lowell Cabot (who privately wrote lascivious sexual fantasies in letters to his wife), the Watch and Ward succeeded in strengthening the Massachusetts anti-obscenity law to imprison publishers and to fine news dealers who sold any literature that might corrupt the morals of the young. By the end of the century, at least seven states had passed "Little Comstock Acts" to regulate newsstand sales of lascivious literature, and almost every state eventually joined their ranks. Meanwhile, respectable publishers imposed self-censorship to avoid conflict with the anti-vice societies.

... The Comstock law of 1873, with its proscription against the mailing of contraceptive information and devices, had also included stringent provisions about obscenity. From the 1930s onward, however, the courts in the United States steadily narrowed the definition of obscenity until, by the mid–1960s, they had virtually removed the barriers against the forthright presentation of sexual matters in literature and other media. The veil of nineteenth-century reticence was torn away, as sex was put on display.

Until the 1930s, American judges had applied the broadest possible interpretation to the obscenity provisions of the Comstock Act. The courts adopted the standard enunciated in a nineteenth-century English case, *Queen v. Hicklin:* "The test of obscenity is this, whether the tendency of the matter ... is to deprave and corrupt those whose minds are open to such immoral influences." Isolated passages became the criteria for censorship, while the innocence of youth served as the yardstick for determining a work's potential to corrupt. With state laws and local purity societies buttressing the Comstock statute, censorship forces exerted a chilling effect on publishers and bookdealers well into the 1920s. Self-policing became common practice, as editors and retailers struggled to avoid costly legal entanglements. The activity of censors extended not only to contemporary writing but also to classics; customs officials regularly seized shipments of books, from Petronius to Boccaccio, deemed dangerous to the nation's morals.

Throughout this period, however, a double standard reigned in the definition of obscenity. Law-enforcement officials selectively applied the law. Anti-vice crusaders of the Progressive era had little trouble in publishing tracts that exposed the existence of commercialized prostitution or the horrors of white slavery, even though many of these works had all the trappings of soft-core pornography and undoubtedly titillated quite a number of readers. Similarly, social hygienists, who wrote about sexual matters for the purpose of shoring up the decaying civilized morality of the middle class, escaped legal difficulties.

... Comstock had represented the dominant middle-class view in the late nineteenth century. By the 1950s, the mores of the middle class had shifted profoundly, while purity crusaders acted from outside the mainstream. Then, too, zealous law-enforcement efforts to suppress pornography provoked wave after wave of litigation. By the late 1950s, obscenity cases were reaching the Supreme Court in such large numbers that the justices were forced to examine carefully the complicated constitutional issues that changing sexual mores posed. Finally, purity advocates themselves recognized that the material they targeted no longer stood so obviously outside the realm of the permissible.

THE ROTH CASE

The Supreme Court first defined obscenity in Roth v. United States, 354 U.S. 476 (1957). Samuel Roth, a publisher and distributor of erotic literature, prided himself in being the first American to publish excerpts of James Joyce's *Ulysses.* Later he distributed an unexpurgated edition of the entire work, for which he received a 60–day jail sentence in 1930. Undeterred by the punishment, he continued to publish and distribute erotic works after he gained his freedom. In the 1930s, he served another 90–day sentence for selling *The Perfumed Garden,* one of Boccaccio's works, and some figure drawings considered obscene by the leader of the New York Society for the Suppression of Vice, John Summer, who was Anthony Comstock's successor. In 1935, Roth received a three-year sentence for sending obscene books in the U.S. mail. Among the books listed in evidence were *The Perfumed Garden* and D.H. Lawrence's *Lady Chatterley's Lover.* Other similar prosecutions followed into the 1940s and 1950s. In 1955, Senator Estes Kefauver, who headed a subcommittee investigating pornography and juvenile delinquency, scheduled a public hearing in New York and subpoenaed Roth to testify.

Gay Talese described Roth's testimony before the subcommittee, his subsequent indictment, and trial as follows:*

> [Senator Kefauver] was very accusatory toward Roth, whose business he called "slime," and whose influence he partly blamed for the existence of juvenile delinquency in America.

> Roth denied this, alluding to the fact that his own children, who were not delinquents, had grown up around him and had worked in his office, and he suggested that juvenile delinquents as a group were perhaps the least affected by books because they rarely read them. While Roth had a cogent reply for every question, his self-assured manner and his retorts delivered in his mild British accent suggested a tone of condescension that irritated Kefauver. After Roth had attributed literary value to

* Gay Talese, Thy Neighbor's Wife, Doubleday & Co., 1980, pp. 104–105.

most of what he had published, Kefauver noted that Roth had once tried to negotiate a contract with the prostitute Pat Ward of the Mickey Jelke case.

"Why would you like to have a book about a person who had just been in a notorious trial?" Kefauver asked.

"I believe," Roth said, "that the New Testament rotates around just that kind of woman."

Kefauver paused, but soon recovered; and in his concluding remarks he repeated that Roth's business was "reprehensible," an opinion seconded by Senator William Langer. Then Kefauver permitted Roth to have a final word before the committee.

"I believe the people who have criticized me are wrong," Roth said; and looking at Kefauver: "I believe you are a great deal more wrong than they are, because you are sitting in judgment on me, and I believe that I will someday within the very near future convince you that you are wrong."

"It will take a good deal of convincing," Kefauver said.

"I will do it," insisted Roth.

Roth thought he had done quite well before the subcommittee. Of course, Roth knew that one did not insult a United States senator without paying for it, but even he was surprised when the government indicted him on twenty-six counts of sending obscene materials through the mails. One of the counts charged him with mailing a single copy of *American Aphrodite* that had reprinted Aubrey Beardsley's illustrated classic, "Venus and Tannhauser," a work that could be found in university libraries.

Although Roth did not think a jury would be offended by the materials he had been charged with mailing, he and his lawyer carefully prepared for trial. Roth called Dr. Alfred Kinsey to testify in his behalf, but Kinsey refused because he said that he did not support obscenity. Roth nevertheless presented testimony of others who said that Roth was a defender of individual rights and that he appreciated literature. The trial took nine days. After twelve hours of deliberation, the jury found Roth guilty of four counts—one for mailing Beardsley's "Venus and Tannhauser" and three for mailing sexually suggestive advertising circulars. Although Roth was disappointed, he did not expect a severe sentence—perhaps ninety days. His lawyer told him to prepare himself for something worse because of what he had heard from people at the Justice Department. "You are an old offender," he said. "And your enemies include a member of the United States Senate." On February 5, 1956, Roth was sentenced to five years in a penitentiary and a fine of $5,000.*

Before the United States Supreme Court, Roth's lawyers argued that the federal obscenity statute under which Roth had been convicted—the Comstock Act of 1873—violated the First Amendment. Three justices—Black, Douglas, and Harlan—agreed. A majority of the justices,

* *Ibid.*, p. 106.

however, disagreed. In an opinion by Justice Brennan, they held, quoting the *Chaplinsky* dictum, see page 355, that obscenity was unprotected by the First Amendment. They then adopted the following definition of obscenity: "Whether to the average person, applying contemporary community standards, the dominant theme of the material taken as a whole appeals to the prurient interest." Roth v. United States, 354 U.S. 476, 489 (1957). Justice Brennan's opinion also contained the following statement: "All ideas having even the slightest redeeming social importance—unorthodox ideas, controversial ideas, even ideas hateful to the prevailing climate of opinion—have the full protection of the guaranties, unless excludable because they encroach upon the limited area of more important interest." Id., 484.

III. OVERVIEW OF THE LAW OF OBSCENITY

PARIS ADULT THEATRE v. SLATON

Supreme Court of the United States, 1973.
413 U.S. 49, 93 S.Ct. 2628, 37 L.Ed.2d 446.

Excerpt from the dissenting opinion of JUSTICE BRENNAN.

In Roth v. United States, 354 U.S. 476 (1957), the Court held that obscenity, although expression, falls outside the area of speech or press constitutionally protected under the First and Fourteenth Amendments against state or federal infringement. But at the same time we emphasized in *Roth* that "sex and obscenity are not synonymous," and that matter which is sexually oriented but not obscene is fully protected by the Constitution. For we recognized that "[s]ex, a great and mysterious

WILLIAM J. BRENNAN, JR.—Born on April 25, 1906, in Newark, New Jersey, second of eight children, to Irish immigrants. His father worked in a brewery and later became a labor leader and an elected public official. "Every-thing I am," he said, "I am because of my father." Democrat. Roman Catholic. Grew up in Newark, New Jersey. Pennsylvania, B.S., 1928, with honors; Harvard, LL.B., 1931, where he studied with Felix Frankfurter, was president of the Legal Aid Society, and graduated in the top ten percent of his class. Practiced law, 1931–1949, with a break for military service during World War II. New Jersey trial and appellate judge, 1949–1956. Nominated associate justice on October 15, 1956, in the midst of the presidential election campaign, by President Dwight D. Eisenhower to replace Sherman Minton. Confirmed by the Senate (over the opposition of Senator Joseph McCarthy) on March 19, 1957, by voice vote. Served from 1956 to 1962 with Justice Frankfurter, who once said of him: "I always wanted my students to think for themselves, but Brennan goes too far." A master of the Court's internal politics, he was known as "a play maker," i.e., a justice skilled in obtaining majorities. Architect of many Warren Court liberal decisions, his contributions to civil liberties jurisprudence rank him with Holmes and Brandeis. Retired on July 20, 1990. Died on July 24, 1997.

motive force in human life, has indisputably been a subject of absorbing interest to mankind through the ages; it is one of the vital problems of human interest and public concern." *Roth* rested, in other words, on what has been termed a two-level approach to the question of obscenity. While much criticized, that approach has been endorsed by all but two members of this Court who have addressed the question since *Roth*. Yet our efforts to implement that approach demonstrate that agreement on the existence of something called "obscenity" is still a long and painful step from agreement on a workable definition of the term.

Recognizing that "the freedoms of expression ... are vulnerable to gravely damaging yet barely visible encroachments," we have demanded that "sensitive tools" be used to carry out the "separation of legitimate from illegitimate speech." The essence of our problem in the obscenity area is that we have been unable to provide "sensitive tools" to separate obscenity from other sexually oriented but constitutionally protected speech, so that efforts to suppress the former do not spill over into the suppression of the latter. The attempt, as the late Justice Harlan observed, has only "produced a variety of views among the members of the Court unmatched in any other course of constitutional adjudication."

To be sure, five members of the Court did agree in *Roth* that obscenity could be determined by asking "whether to the average person, applying contemporary community standards, the dominant theme of the material taken as a whole appeals to prurient interest." But agreement on that test—achieved in the abstract and without reference to the particular material before the Court—was, to say the least, short lived. By 1967 the following views had emerged: Justice Black and Justice Douglas consistently maintained that government is wholly powerless to regulate any sexually oriented matter on the ground of its obscenity. Justice Harlan, on the other hand, believed that the Federal Government in the exercise of its enumerated powers could control the distribution of "hard core" pornography, while the States were afforded more latitude to "[ban] any material which, taken as a whole, has been reasonably found in state judicial proceedings to treat with sex in a fundamentally offensive manner, under rationally established criteria for judging such material." Justice Stewart regarded "hard core" pornography as the limit of both federal and state power.

The view that, until today, enjoyed the most, but not majority, support was an interpretation of *Roth* .... We expressed the view that Federal or State Governments could control the distribution of material where "three elements ... coalesce: it must be established that (a) the dominant theme of the material taken as a whole appeals to a prurient interest in sex; (b) the material is patently offensive because it affronts contemporary community standards relating to the description or representation of sexual matters; and (c) the material is utterly without redeeming social value." Even this formulation, however, concealed differences of opinion. [These include: whether community standards are local or whether material is obscene if it is intended to appeal to a deviant sexual group; whether slight "social value" redeemed patently offensive material.]

In the face of this divergence of opinion the Court began the practice in Redrup v. New York, 386 U.S. 767 (1967), of *per curiam* reversals of convictions for the dissemination of materials that at least five members of the Court, applying their separate tests, deemed not to be obscene....

... [T]he *Redrup* approach ... resolves cases as between the parties, but offers only the most obscure guidance to legislation, adjudication by other courts, and primary conduct. By disposing of cases through summary reversal or denial of certiorari we have deliberately and effectively obscured the rationale underlying the decisions.

NOTE

In the preceding excerpt, Justice Brennan summarizes the Supreme Court's obscenity decisions through 1967. With the exception of Justices Black and Douglas (who argued that all obscenity laws were unconstitutional), disagreement among the Justices centered around the definition of obscenity, and the standards by which materials were to be judged to decide whether they were obscene. Seven Justices seemed to agree, however, that if obscenity could be identified, it was not a violation of the First Amendment to punish those who disseminated obscene materials to willing adults.

Two developments after 1967 suggested the possibility of a different approach. In 1969, in Stanley v. Georgia, 394 U.S. 557, a majority of the Court decided that it violated the First Amendment to punish the private possession of obscene material, no matter how obscenity was defined. As Justice Marshall's Opinion for the Court put the matter:

> Whatever may be the justifications for other statutes regulating obscenity, we do not think they reach into the privacy of one's own home. If the First Amendment means anything, it means that a State has no business telling a man, sitting alone in his own house, what books he may read or what films he may watch. Our whole constitutional heritage rebels at the thought at giving government the power to control men's minds.

Stanley, of course, raised the additional question whether, if the government had no business telling a person what books he may read, the government had any business punishing someone who sold him the book.

In 1970, the United States Commission on Obscenity and Pornography concluded that government, indeed, had no business punishing those who disseminated obscenity to willing adults. The Commission recommended that obscenity laws should be modified to limit them to punishing the display of offensive material before unwilling adults, and to the protection of children. Some lawyers and scholars argued that the Commission's legislative recommendations also provided the appropriate constitutional standard in the obscenity area. Whether that was so, and whether the Constitution prohibited the punishment of disseminators of obscene material to willing adults, were the issues in a series of cases decided by the Court in 1973.

MILLER v. CALIFORNIA

Supreme Court of the United States, 1973.
413 U.S. 15, 93 S.Ct. 2607, 37 L.Ed.2d 419.

CHIEF JUSTICE BURGER delivered the opinion of the Court.

WARREN E. BURGER—Born on September 17, 1907, in St. Paul, Minnesota, into a family of modest means. Republican. Protestant. Worked selling insurance while attending the University of Minnesota from 1925–1927 and the St. Paul College of Law (now the William Mitchell College of Law), from which he received an LL.B., magna cum laude, in 1931. Practiced law, 1931–1953; taught law part-time at the William Mitchell College of Law, 1931–1948; assistant U.S. attorney general, 1953–1956; U.S. Court of Appeals judge (D.C. Circuit), 1956–1969. Nominated chief justice on May 21, 1969, by President Richard M. Nixon to replace Earl Warren. Confirmed by the Senate on June 9, 1969, by a 74–3 vote. Retired on September 26, 1986. Died on June 25, 1995.

This is one of a group of "obscenity-pornography" cases being reviewed by the Court in a re-examination of standards enunciated in earlier cases involving what Justice Harlan called "the intractable obscenity problem."

Appellant conducted a mass mailing campaign to advertise the sale of illustrated books, euphemistically called "adult" material. After a jury trial, he was convicted of violating California Penal Code § 311.2(a), a misdemeanor, by knowingly distributing obscene matter, . . .

This much has been categorically settled by the Court, that obscene material is unprotected by the First Amendment.... We acknowledge, however, the inherent dangers of undertaking to regulate any form of expression. State statutes designed to regulate obscene materials must be carefully limited.... As a result, we now confine the permissible scope of such regulation to works which depict or describe sexual conduct. That conduct must be specifically defined by the applicable state law, as written or authoritatively construed. A state offense must also be limited to works which, taken as a whole, appeal to the prurient interest in sex, which portray sexual conduct in a patently offensive way, and which, taken as a whole, do not have serious literary, artistic, political, or scientific value.

The basic guidelines for the trier of fact must be: (a) whether "the average person, applying contemporary community standards" would find that the work, taken as a whole, appeals to the prurient interest; (b) whether the work depicts or describes, in a patently offensive way, sexual conduct specifically defined by the applicable state law; and (c) whether the work, taken as a whole, lacks serious literary, artistic, political, or scientific value. We do not adopt as a constitutional standard the "*utterly* without redeeming social value" test of Memoirs v. Massachusetts, 383 U.S., at 419; that concept has never commanded the adherence of more than three Justices at one time. If a state law that regulates obscene material is thus limited, as written or construed, the First Amendment values applicable to the States through the Fourteenth Amendment are adequately protected by the ultimate power of appellate courts to conduct an independent review of constitutional claims when necessary.

We emphasize that it is not our function to propose regulatory schemes for the States. That must await their concrete legislative efforts. It is possible, however, to give a few plain examples of what a state statute could define for regulation . . .:

(a) Patently offensive representations or descriptions of ultimate sexual acts, normal or perverted, actual or simulated.

(b) Patently offensive representations or descriptions of masturbation, excretory functions, and lewd exhibition of the genitals.

Sex and nudity may not be exploited without limit by films or pictures exhibited or sold in places of public accommodation any more than live sex and nudity can be exhibited or sold without limit in such public places. At a minimum, prurient, patently offensive depiction or description of sexual conduct must have serious literary, artistic, political, or scientific value to merit First Amendment protection. For example, medical books for the education of physicians and related personnel necessarily use graphic illustrations and descriptions of human anatomy. In resolving the inevitably sensitive questions of fact and law, we must continue to rely on the jury system, accompanied by the safeguards that judges, rules of evidence, presumption of innocence, and other protective features provide, as we do with rape, murder, and a host of other offenses against society and its individual members.

It is certainly true that the absence, since *Roth*, of a single majority view of this Court as to proper standards for testing obscenity has placed a strain on both state and federal courts. But today, for the first time since *Roth* was decided in 1957, a majority of this Court has agreed on concrete guidelines to isolate "hard core" pornography from expression protected by the First Amendment. Now we may . . . attempt to provide positive guidance to federal and state courts alike.

This may not be an easy road, free from difficulty. But no amount of "fatigue" should lead us to adopt a convenient "institutional" rationale—an absolutist, "anything goes" view of the First Amendment— because it will lighten our burdens.

Under a National Constitution, fundamental First Amendment limitations on the powers of the States do not vary from community to community, but this does not mean that there are, or should or can be, fixed, uniform national standards of precisely what appeals to the "prurient interest" or is "patently offensive." These are essentially questions of fact, and our Nation is simply too big and too diverse for this Court to reasonably expect that such standards could be articulated for all 50 States in a single formulation, even assuming the prerequisite consensus exists. When triers of fact are asked to decide whether "the average person, applying contemporary community standards" would consider certain materials "prurient," it would be unrealistic to require that the answer be based on some abstract formulation. The adversary system, with lay jurors as the usual ultimate factfinders in criminal prosecutions, has historically permitted triers of fact to draw on the standards of their community, guided always by limiting instructions on the law. To require a State to structure obscenity proceedings around evidence of a *national* "community standard" would be an exercise in futility.

It is neither realistic nor constitutionally sound to read the First Amendment as requiring that the people of Maine or Mississippi accept public depiction of conduct found tolerable in Las Vegas, or New York City....

The dissenting Justices sound the alarm of repression. But, in our view, to equate the free and robust exchange of ideas and political debate with commercial exploitation of obscene material demeans the grand conception of the First Amendment and its high purposes in the historic struggle for freedom. It is a "misuse of the great guarantees of free speech and free press...." The First Amendment protects works which, taken as a whole, have serious literary, artistic, political, or scientific value, regardless of whether the government or a majority of the people approve of the ideas these works represent. "The protection given speech and press was fashioned to assure unfettered interchange of *ideas* for the bringing about of political and social changes desired by the people," Roth v. United States (emphasis added). But the public portrayal of hard-core sexual conduct for its own sake, and for the ensuing commercial gain, is a different matter.

There is no evidence, empirical or historical, that the stern 19th century American censorship of public distribution and display of material relating to sex ... in any way limited or affected expression of serious literary, artistic, political, or scientific ideas. On the contrary, it is beyond any question that the era following Thomas Jefferson to Theodore Roosevelt was an "extraordinarily vigorous period," not just in economics and politics, but in *belles lettres* and in "the outlying fields of social and political philosophies." We do not see the harsh hand of censorship of ideas—good or bad, sound or unsound—and "repression" of political liberty lurking in every state regulation of commercial exploitation of human interest in sex.

Justice Brennan finds "it is hard to see how state-ordered regimentation of our minds can ever be forestalled." These doleful anticipations assume that courts cannot distinguish commerce in ideas, protected by the First Amendment, from commercial exploitation of obscene material. Moreover, state regulation of hard-core pornography so as to make it unavailable to nonadults, a regulation which Justice Brennan finds constitutionally permissible, has all the elements of "censorship" for adults; indeed even more rigid enforcement techniques may be called for with such dichotomy of regulation. One can concede that the "sexual revolution" of recent years may have had useful byproducts in striking layers of prudery from a subject long irrationally kept from needed ventilation. But it does not follow that no regulation of patently offensive "hard core" materials is needed or permissible; civilized people do not allow unregulated access to heroin because it is a derivative of medicinal morphine.

In sum, we (a) reaffirm the *Roth* holding that obscene material is not protected by the First Amendment; (b) hold that such material can be regulated by the States, subject to the specific safeguards enunciated above, without a showing that the material is "*utterly* without redeeming social value"; and (c) hold that obscenity is to be determined by applying "contemporary community standards," not "national standards."

[Justices Douglas, Brennan, Stewart and Marshall dissented. Justice Douglas argued that all obscenity laws violate the First Amendment. Justice Brennan had written the Court's first opinion on the law of obscenity in 1957 in the *Roth* case, and a number of important opinions since then elaborating on the definition of obscenity. Now, in his dissenting opinion in the *Miller* case (an opinion joined by Justices Stewart and Marshall), he concluded that he had been in error: "Our experience with the *Roth* approach has certainly taught us that the outright suppression of obscenity cannot be reconciled with the fundamental principles of the First and Fourteenth Amendments." He now argued for a constitutional standard similar to that of the U.S. Commission on Obscenity and Pornography.*]

IV. THE PROBLEM OF DEFINITION

ESQUIRE, INC. v. WALKER

United States Court of Appeals, District of Columbia, 1945.
80 U.S.App.D.C. 145, 151 F.2d 49, 52.

The first source of ... confusion is, of course, the age old question when a scantily clad lady is art, and when she is highly improper. Some refined persons are hopeful that an answer to this vexing riddle may some day be found. Others are pessimistic. But whichever school eventually proves correct it is clear from the following cross-examination of one of the expert witnesses for the Post Office that the problem had not yet been solved when the record in this case went to press:

"Q. ... [C]ould you tell me in your opinion whether that picture is decent or indecent? A. Well, taking the expression of the picture and who the person is and what her attitude in life is, I think it is decent. I think the purpose for which you do things in life has a great deal to do with it. It is the motive in those pictures which is harmful.

"Q. Will you look at this Exhibit 133, and tell me if this picture is decent or indecent? A. I think I am being trapped, Your Honor.

"Q. You found that out, haven't you? A. Yes. I knew I was going to be trapped when I came here and I know I shall be in every column tomorrow.

* See, also, Justice Brennan's concurring opinion in Jenkins v. Georgia, below at p. 374.

"Q. Now, just where and how are you being trapped? A. I am trying to be made a prude. I am not a prude.

"Q. Well, would you mind telling me if that picture is decent or indecent? A. If I had a daughter I shouldn't like to have her photograph in that costume. I have no daughter, I have only sons.

"Q. Is that your criterion for decency, Madam? A. My criterion for decency is anything that is proper, in order, certainly not harmful to human dignity. This woman is evidently by the ocean. I see the ocean there. She has probably come in and out of the ocean and if she stays there all right for me, but I do not wish to see that picture displayed except where it belongs. I believe in suitability, suitability; I don't like the picture. It is not pleasing to me and to my eye because I don't believe in such poses.

"Now, I am going to be raked, I know, over the coals by those people over there for being a prude. No, I am not a prude. I know I am not a prude; I am a dignified woman who believes in life being lived for a purpose.

"Have you ever been to the headquarters of the National Education Society and seen the statute of Horace Mann: "Be not afraid to die unless you have won some victory for humanity". Do you think this sort of thing is winning a victory? I don't.

"Q. Well, do you think it is decent or indecent? A. I think it is indecent. You force me to an answer. I say it is indecent for a picture, not for the beach. You asked we [sic] about the picture. Now, I don't know that young lady. On the beach I think it would be all right, but not as a picture to be published in a magazine."

A VIEW THAT OBSCENITY IS CAPABLE OF DEFINITION*

If priorities are to be assigned in the battle against indecency, laws protecting the young and statutes safeguarding community sensibilities against offensive displays, are more urgently needed than are those imposing restrictions on adult off-the-street behavior. But if there are to be laws in this area of adult indecency, they should strive to avoid the absurdities that generally mock present-day anti-obscenity provisions.

First, insofar as is possible, a proper law should shun today's imprecise vocabulary. The words and phrases "obscene," "patently offensive," "hard-core," "redeeming social importance," and "appeals to prurient interests," emphasize personal *tastes,* not legislative *standards.* Testifying in Britain in 1909, in opposition to the Lord Chamberlain's authority to censor plays ..., but favoring some controls, George Bernard Shaw said:

> I strongly protest against anything that is not quite definite. You may make any law you like defining what is an incentive to sexual vice, but to lay down a general law ... with regard to unspecified incentives to sexual vice is going too far, when the mere fact of a woman washing her face and putting on decent

* Kuh, Richard H., Foolish Figleaves, Macmillan Co., New York, 1967, pp. 290–292, 294. Reprinted with permission.

clothes, or anything of the kind, may possibly cause somebody in the street who passes to admire her, and to say, "I have been incited to sexual vice." These definitions are too dangerous. I do not think that any lawyer should tolerate them.

Second, the law should recognize that there is a vast gulf between what one does or sees in private and what is done or seen in public. *Private* entertainment, ranging from reading through *dolce vita* private parties, should be largely immune to regulation. Such activities are, essentially, one's own business. Quite different are those entertainments that take place at the "publick house." Inns and theaters have always been subject to regulation, and publicly advertised entertainments held in them are not private in any meaningful sense of the word. All adults for whom there is space and who can pay the price of admission are admitted, and the shows play to audiences of strangers—strangers both to each other and to the performers. The impact of the public show is likely to radiate far beyond these immediate audiences. Such shows, for continued life, depend on their financial success; that, in turn, depends upon the critical and popular splash the show makes. It is not sufficient that the first audience approves. The community outside must be informed, in the hopes that more of it will attend in the future. . . . Obviously, the mere fact that an admission may have been charged does not make it private, if that word is to have other than economic significance. The gulf, then, between the truly private and what realistically considered is public should be acknowledged in any proper adult anti-obscenity statute.

Third, any new statute should build on the differences among those media through which seeming pornography is presented. Statutes too commonly lump together books, motion pictures, live shows, and other means of presenting the possibly offensive, applying the same language in testing each for obscenity. Yet sex, sexual intercourse or oral-genital contact for example, staged as *live* entertainment for third persons, strains at depravity; it is a far greater affront to community mores than would be *pictured* sex. And *pictured* sex, in turn, is appreciably more shocking than *literary* sex.

Fourth, a wise adult obscenity law must take stock of the particular audience at whom the disputed items are directed. Not only is there a difference between adolescents and adults, but there may be differences between varying adults.

If the obscenity standard is to be a variable one, with numerous decisions being made that classify media, audiences, advertising, and the items that may or may not be portrayed, it is more fitting that it be legislatively designed than relegated by legislative inaction to the courts. Legislators, elected for limited terms, are necessarily in close touch with community standards. Besides, line drawing should be, in the first instance, a legislative and not a judicial function. "I recognize without hesitation," said Justice Oliver Wendell Holmes, "that judges do and must legislate, but they can do so only interstitially; they are confined from molar to molecular motions." Creative legislation can do far more.

It can effectively construct new standards, and can do so explicitly and in advance of the sheer exhaustion that litigation entails.

 POTTER STEWART—Born on January 23, 1915, in Jackson, Michigan, into an affluent family. His father was a lawyer who became mayor of Cincinnati and later an Ohio Supreme Court Justice. Republican. Episcopalian. A graduate of Hotchkiss, he went to Yale, where he received his B.A., cum laude and Phi Beta Kappa, in 1935. Yale, LL.B., cum laude, 1941. Practiced law, 1941–1942, 1945–1954. Served as a naval officer during World War II. Member of Cincinnati City Council, 1950–1953; vice mayor of Cincinnati, 1952–1953; U.S. Court of Appeals judge (6th Circuit), 1954–1958. Nominated associate justice on October 14, 1958, by President Dwight D. Eisenhower to replace Harold H. Burton. Confirmed by the Senate on May 5, 1959, by a 70–17 vote. Best known for his statement defining obscenity: "I know it when I see it." Retired on June 3, 1981. Died on December 5, 1985.

A VIEW THAT OBSCENITY IS INCAPABLE OF DEFINITION*

Henry Miller, author of the controversial *Tropic of Cancer,* has reflected on the single overriding problem which confronts those attempting to regulate books, films, and plays through general obscenity statutes:

> To discuss the nature and meaning of obscenity is almost as difficult as to talk about God.... If one begins with etymology one is immediately aware that lexicographers are bamboozlers every bit as much as jurists, moralists and politicians. To begin with, those who have seriously attempted to track down the meaning of the term are obliged to confess that they have arrived nowhere.

If one traces the word "obscene" in a dictionary, he encounters a seemingly endless list of wholly subjective descriptive terms. Its modern English meaning is "offensive to modesty or decency; expressing or suggesting lewd thoughts." "Lewd" means "lascivious, unchaste." "Lascivious" means "inclined to lust, lewd, wanton." "Chaste" means "pure from unlawful sexual intercourse; continent, virtuous; ... decent; free from indecency or offensiveness." Historically, the definition of obscenity has invoked the substitution of interchangeable synonyms. The net result is that, conceptually, obscenity is defined differently by everyone. Justice Stewart's frank (and famous) concurrence in *Jacobellis* is exemplary of this problem:

> I have reached the conclusion, which I think is confirmed at least by negative implication in the Court's decisions since *Roth* ..., that under the First and Fourteenth Amendments criminal laws in this area are constitutionally limited to hard-core por-

---

* Obscenity: Prosecutorial Techniques, UCLA Law Review, vol. 21, 1973, pp. 197–200, 234–235. Reprinted with permission.

nography. I shall not today attempt further to define the kinds of material I understand to be embraced within that shorthand description; and perhaps I could never succeed in intelligibly doing so. *But I know it when I see it, and the motion picture involved in this case is not that.*

Justice Stewart joined in Justice Brennan's dissenting opinions in the five 1973 cases, apparently giving up the attempt to define obscenity.

The definitional problems are especially acute in the case of visual entertainment. In sexually oriented films and plays, dialogue is often relegated to a subordinate role in developing the theme, idea, or plot. The producer has little opportunity—other than in the minds of the beholders—to vouch for the socially important intentions he may have. Since the various adjectives used to define obscenity are subject to many differing interpretations, those involved in the production of a sexually oriented theatrical work really cannot successfully predict whether the production will be considered artistic, enlightened, educational, dramatic, or worthless.[1] Such a prediction is made most difficult by the fact that visual obscenity is indeed a concept that acquires meaning only in its effect on the viewer. There may not even be such a thing as an obscene act until an observer evaluates it as obscene.

If general obscenity statutes continue to be the means of regulating conduct on stage and in films, Smith's desire to see a "dirty" movie will forever be weighed against Jones' concern that such things be kept as far from his children as the law will permit. One might take the position that the law, like constitutional doctrine, is flexible and must change to fit the temper of the times. But the temper of the times seems impossible to measure for purposes of applying obscenity law. It is difficult to know what "community standards," "appeal to prurient interest," and "social importance" really are.

The prospects for achieving any kind of workable standard within present obscenity concepts are bleak. In view of the wide-ranging alternative prosecutorial techniques which may result, it is suggested that the current obscenity laws be repealed, at least insofar as they are applicable to theatrical presentations and films. The sexual conduct which the legislators wish to proscribe should then be the subject of statutory prohibitions which state the time, place, and manner in which a given

---

1. Speaking in his capacity as an attorney and acting associate professor of law at the University of California Law School, Berkeley, Robert O'Neil told the 1963 Assembly committee hearings on obscenity that "a given book can never mean exactly the same thing to two different people. At one pole I recall Judge Jerome Frank's wry suggestion some years ago that even the contents of the seed catalog would arouse lascivious thoughts in some peculiarly susceptible readers. At the other pole, there's no better illustration than the comment on Lady Chatterly's [sic] Lover by a book reviewer in Field and Stream Magazine about three years ago. He wrote:

"This fictional account of the day-by-day life of an English gamekeeper is still of considerable interest to outdoor minded readers, as it certainly contains many passages on pheasant raising, and apprehending of poachers, ways to control vermin and other chores and duties of the professional gamekeeper. Unfortunately, one is obliged to wade through many pages of extraneous material in order to discover and savor these sidelights on the management of a midland shooting estate. In this reviewer's opinion, this book cannot take the place of J.R. Miller's Practical Gamekeeper. So, it would seem it all depends on who is reading it and for what purpose!"

act is illegal. These prohibitions should also alleviate the inconsistency and unfairness which result from the imposition of varied penalties that depend upon the statute under which an "obscenity" prosecution is brought.

Recent obscenity formulations, as has been noted by many critics, do not give film makers or prosecutors advance notice of what is obscene and what is not. Consequently, those judges who are asked to decide obscenity cases are confronted, not so much with questions of whether a defendant committed the act charged, as with a philosophical appraisal of the Supreme Court standards. As has been discussed, the lack of objectivity in these standards is undesirable from the standpoint of all the potential parties to actions concerning "pornographic" films and plays. Specific statutory statements embodying a practical consensus of existing obscenity law would be a useful guide to all parties. This Comment suggests that sex acts on stage or screen should either be expressly forbidden or permitted by statute. Deciding the issue de novo on the basis of general obscenity doctrine consumes time, encourages disparity among courts, and lacks predictability.

JENKINS v. GEORGIA

Supreme Court of the United States, 1974.
418 U.S. 153, 94 S.Ct. 2750, 41 L.Ed.2d 642.

JUSTICE REHNQUIST delivered the opinion of the Court.

WILLIAM H. REHNQUIST—Born on October 1, 1924, in Milwaukee, Wisconsin. His father was a salesman for a paper company. Grew up in a suburb of the city. Republican. Lutheran. Attended Kenyon for a year and then served three years in the air force during World War II. Stanford, B.A., Phi Beta Kappa, 1948; M.A., 1949. Did graduate work in government at Harvard, and received an M.A. in 1950. Returned to Stanford to study law. Classmate of Sandra Day O'Connor. Graduated from Stanford with an LL.B., Order of the Coif and first in his class, 1952. Law clerk to Justice Robert H. Jackson. Practiced law, 1953–1969; assistant U.S. attorney general, Office of Legal Counsel, 1969–1971. Nominated associate justice on October 21, 1971, by President Richard M. Nixon to replace John Marshall Harlan. Confirmed by the Senate on December 10, 1971, by a 68–26 vote. Nominated chief justice June 20, 1986, by President Ronald Reagan to replace Warren E. Burger. Confirmed by the Senate on September 17, 1986, by a 65–33 vote. Died on September 3, 2005; first member of the Supreme Court to die while in office since Justice Robert H. Jackson in 1954. Succeeded as chief justice by his former law clerk, John Roberts.

Appellant was convicted in Georgia of the crime of distributing obscene material. His conviction, in March 1972, was for showing the film "Carnal Knowledge" in a movie theater in Albany, Georgia.

We agree with the Supreme Court of Georgia's implicit ruling that the Constitution does not require that juries be instructed in state obscenity cases to apply the standards of a hypothetical statewide community. *Miller* approved the use of such instructions; it did not mandate their use. What *Miller* makes clear is that state juries need not be instructed to apply "national standards." We also agree with the Supreme Court of Georgia's implicit approval of the trial court's instructions directing jurors to apply "community standards" without specifying what "community." *Miller* held that it was constitutionally permissible to permit juries to rely on the understanding of the community from which they came as to contemporary community standards, and the States have considerable latitude in framing statutes under this element of the *Miller* decision. A State may choose to define an obscenity offense in terms of "contemporary community standards" as defined in *Miller* without further specification, as was done here, or it may choose to define the standards in more precise geographic terms, as was done by California in *Miller*.

We now turn to the question of whether appellant's exhibition of the film was protected by the First and Fourteenth Amendments, ...

There is little to be found in the record about the film "Carnal Knowledge" other than the film itself.[1] However, appellant has supplied a variety of information and critical commentary, the authenticity of which appellee does not dispute. The film appeared on many "Ten Best" lists for 1971, the year in which it was released. Many but not all of the reviews were favorable. We believe that the following passage from a review which appeared in the Saturday Review is a reasonably accurate description of the film:

"[It is basically a story] of two young college men, roommates and lifelong friends forever preoccupied with their sex lives. Both first met as virgins. Nicholson is the more knowledgeable and attractive of the two; speaking colloquially, he is a burgeoning bastard. Art Garfunkel is his friend, the nice but troubled guy straight out of those early Feiffer cartoons, but *real*. He falls in love with the lovely Susan (Candice Bergen) and unknowingly shares her with his college buddy. As the 'safer' one of the two, he is selected by Susan for marriage.

"The time changes. Both men are in their thirties, pursuing successful careers in New York. Nicholson has been running through an average of a dozen women a year but has never managed to meet the right one, the one with the full bosom, the good legs, the properly rounded bottom. More than that, each and every one is a threat to his malehood and peace of mind, until at last, in a bar, he finds Ann–Margret, an aging bachelor girl with striking cleavage and, quite obviously, something of a past. 'Why don't we shack up?' she suggests. They do and a horrendous relationship ensues, complicated mainly by her paranoidal desire to marry. Meanwhile, what of Garfunkel? The

---

1. Appellant testified that the film was "critically acclaimed as one of the ten best pictures of 1971 and Ann–Margret has received an Academy Award nomination for her performance in the picture." He further testified that "Carnal Knowledge" had played in 29 towns in Georgia and that it was booked in 50 or 60 more theaters for spring and summer showing.

sparks have gone out of his marriage, the sex has lost its savor, and Garfunkel tries once more. And later, even more foolishly, again."

Miller states that the questions of what appeals to the "prurient interest" and what is "patently offensive" under the obscenity test which it formulates are "essentially questions of fact."

But ... this does not lead us to agree with the Supreme Court of Georgia's apparent conclusion that the jury's verdict against appellant virtually precluded all further appellate review of appellant's assertion that his exhibition of the film was protected by the First and Fourteenth Amendments. Even though questions of appeal to the "prurient interest" or of patent offensiveness are "essentially questions of fact," it would be a serious misreading of *Miller* to conclude that juries have unbridled discretion in determining what is "patently offensive." ...

We ... took pains in *Miller* to "give a few plain examples of what a state statute could define for regulation under ... the requirement of patent offensiveness. These examples included 'representations or descriptions of ultimate sexual acts, normal or perverted, actual or simulated,' and 'representations or descriptions of masturbation, excretory functions, and lewd exhibition of the genitals.' " While this did not purport to be an exhaustive catalog of what juries might find patently offensive, it was certainly intended to fix substantive constitutional limitations, deriving from the First Amendment, on the type of material subject to such a determination. It would be wholly at odds with this aspect of *Miller* to uphold an obscenity conviction based upon a defendant's depiction of a woman with a bare midriff, even though a properly charged jury unanimously agreed on a verdict of guilty.

Our own viewing of the film satisfies us that "Carnal Knowledge" could not be found under the *Miller* standards to depict sexual conduct in a patently offensive way. Nothing in the movie falls within either of the two examples given in *Miller* of material which may constitutionally be found to meet the "patently offensive" element of those standards, nor is there anything sufficiently similar to such material to justify similar treatment. While the subject matter of the picture is, in a broader sense, sex, and there are scenes in which sexual conduct including "ultimate sexual acts" is to be understood to be taking place, the camera does not focus on the bodies of the actors at such times. There is no exhibition whatever of the actors' genitals, lewd or otherwise, during these scenes. There are occasional scenes of nudity, but nudity alone is not enough to make material legally obscene under the *Miller* standards.

Appellant's showing of the film "Carnal Knowledge" is simply not the "public portrayal of hard core sexual conduct for its own sake, and for the ensuing commercial gain" which we said was punishable in *Miller*. We hold that the film could not, as a matter of constitutional law, be found to depict sexual conduct in a patently offensive way, and that it is therefore not outside the protection of the First and Fourteenth Amendments because it is obscene. No other basis appearing in the record upon which the judgment of conviction can be sustained, we reverse the judgment of the Supreme Court of Georgia.

Reversed.

Justice Douglas, being of the view that any ban on obscenity is prohibited by the First Amendment, made applicable to the States through the Fourteenth, concurs in the reversal of this conviction. See Paris Adult Theatre I v. Slaton, 413 U.S. 49, 70–73 (1973) (Douglas J., dissenting).

JUSTICE BRENNAN, with whom JUSTICE STEWART and JUSTICE MARSHALL join, concurring in the result.

... Today's decision confirms my observation in Paris Adult Theatre I v. Slaton, 413 U.S. 49 (1973), that the Court's new formulation does not extricate us from the mire of case-by-case determinations of obscenity. I there noted, in dissent, that:

> "Ultimately, the reformulation must fail because it still leaves in this Court the responsibility of determining in each case whether the materials are protected by the First Amendment. The Court concedes that even under its restated formulation, the First Amendment interests at stake require 'appellate courts to conduct an independent review of constitutional claims when necessary,' Miller v. California[, 413 U.S. 15, 25], citing Justice Harlan's opinion in *Roth,* where he stated, 'I do not understand how the Court can resolve the constitutional problems now before it without making its own independent judgment upon the character of the material upon which these convictions were based.' Thus, the Court's new formulation will not relieve us of 'the awesome task of making case by case at once the criminal and the constitutional law.' And the careful efforts of state and lower federal courts to apply the standard will remain an essentially pointless exercise, in view of the need for an ultimate decision by this Court. In addition, since the status of sexually oriented material will necessarily remain in doubt until final decision by this Court, the new approach will not diminish the chill on protected expression that derives from the uncertainty of the underlying standard. I am convinced that a definition of obscenity in terms of physical conduct cannot provide sufficient clarity to afford fair notice, to avoid a chill on protected expression, and to minimize the institutional stress, so long as that definition is used to justify the outright suppression of any material that is asserted to fall within its terms."

> ...

After the Court's decision today, there can be no doubt that *Miller* requires appellate courts—including this Court—to review independently the constitutional fact of obscenity. Moreover, the Court's task is not limited to reviewing a jury finding under part (c) of the *Miller* test that "the work, taken as a whole, lack[ed] serious literary, artistic, political, or scientific value." *Miller* also requires independent review of a jury's determination under part (b) of the *Miller* test that "the work depicts or describes, in a patently offensive way, sexual conduct specifically defined by the applicable state law."

In order to make the review mandated by *Miller,* the Court was required to screen the film "Carnal Knowledge" and make an independent determination of obscenity *vel non.* Following that review, the Court holds that "Carnal Knowledge" "could not, as a matter of constitutional law, be found to depict sexual conduct in a patently offensive way, and that it is therefore not outside the protection of the First and Fourteenth Amendments because it is obscene."

Thus, it is clear that as long as the *Miller* test remains in effect "one cannot say with certainty that material is obscene until at least five members of this Court, applying inevitably obscure standards, have pronounced it so." Paris Adult Theatre I v. Slaton, 413 U.S., at 92 (Brennan, J., dissenting). Because of the attendant uncertainty of such a process and its inevitable institutional stress upon the judiciary, I continue to adhere to my view that, "at least in the absence of distribution to juveniles or obtrusive exposure to unconsenting adults, the First and Fourteenth Amendments prohibit the State and Federal Governments from attempting wholly to suppress sexually oriented materials on the basis of their allegedly 'obscene' contents." It is clear that, tested by that constitutional standard, the Georgia obscenity statutes under which appellant Jenkins was convicted are constitutionally overbroad and therefore facially invalid. I therefore concur in the Court's judgment reversing Jenkins' conviction.

NOTES AND QUESTIONS

1. Justice Brennan is clearly telling the Court's majority "I told you so." One of his major points, as in his dissents in the 1973 cases, is that the impossibility of defining obscenity leaves no alternative but for the Court to view each disputed film or book, and make case-by-case judgments on the basis of standards that really can't be articulated. Wouldn't that be a problem, too, under Justice Brennan's approach where adults were offended by public displays or material was distributed to juveniles? Does the First Amendment permit punishment of someone who continues to display *any* kind of material after being informed it offended a majority of people in the community, or would it be necessary to decide whether the display was, in some sense, obscene?

2. One way out of the vagueness dilemma is to describe rather specifically the kinds of materials that are prohibited. Ironically, if the prohibition is really specific, it is likely to be struck down on the ground that it is "overbroad," (see Chapter 12, page 424, note 1) since it includes constitutionally protected material in its definition of the obscene. An illustration of the problems that arise if obscenity laws get too specific is Erznoznik v. City of Jacksonville, 422 U.S. 205 (1975). A Jacksonville city ordinance prohibited showing, in drive-in movies whose screens were visible from public streets or other public places, of movies that showed "the human male or female bare buttocks, human female bare breasts, or human bare pubic areas." Erznoznik was prosecuted for showing, in the drive-in theatre he managed, "Class of '74," an "R" rated motion picture. "Class of '74" was not claimed to be obscene, but did include pictures of uncovered female breasts and buttocks. Erznoznik was certainly given explicit directions by the Jacksonville city ordinance

as to the kinds of films that could not be shown in his drive-in. But, as a majority of the Court pointed out, "it would bar a film containing a picture of a baby's buttocks, the nude body of a war victim, or scenes from a culture where nudity is indigenous. The ordinance also might prohibit newsreel scenes of the opening of an art exhibit as well as shots of bathers on a beach." The ordinance was held unconstitutional.

3.   The Supreme Court has decided that people who sell or display materials to juveniles can be punished even if the material would not be obscene if sold or displayed to adults. Ginsberg v. New York, 390 U.S. 629 (1968). But, even here, it is necessary to develop some kind of definition as to what is obscene as to minors. One of the arguments in the *Erznoznik* case was that it was necessary to protect minors who viewed the movies from public streets and public places. The Court responded that "clearly all nudity cannot be deemed obscene even as to minors."

4.   Jacksonville also argued that its drive-in ordinance was designed to protect unwilling watchers from films that were offensive to them. The Court concluded that since the "offended viewer readily can avert his eyes," the city could not protect him from movies which were not obscene. Why should not offended viewers or listeners be shielded from material that falls somewhat short of the obscene?

5.   The final argument made in the unsuccessful attempt to uphold the Jacksonville ordinance was that it was necessary as a traffic safety measure. As Chief Justice Burger, joined by Justice Rehnquist, argued in dissent, "it is not unreasonable for lawmakers to believe that public nudity on a giant screen, visible at night to hundreds of drivers of automobiles, may have a tendency to divert attention from their task and cause accidents." The problem with the argument, according to the Court majority, was that nudity was singled out as the only traffic distraction, while movies which might be equally distracting (such as those with scenes of gory violence) could be shown. And, under the First Amendment, "even a traffic regulation cannot discriminate on the basis of content unless there are clear reasons for the distinctions." Would it be possible to list all of the kinds of movie scenes that would be distracting to motorists if seen on a drive-in's giant screen?

6.   In Marks v. United States, 430 U.S. 188 (1977), a separate opinion by Justice Stevens stated:

> There are three reasons which, in combination, persuade me that this criminal prosecution is constitutionally impermissible. First, as the Court's opinion recognizes, this "statute regulates expression and implicates First Amendment values." However distasteful these materials are to some of us, they are nevertheless a form of communication and entertainment acceptable to a substantial segment of society; otherwise, they would have no value in the marketplace. Second, the statute is predicated on the somewhat illogical premise that a person may be prosecuted criminally for providing another with material he has a constitutional right to possess. Third, the present consti-

tutional standards, both substantive and procedural,[1] which apply to these prosecutions are so intolerably vague that even-handed enforcement of the law is a virtual impossibility. Indeed, my brief experience on the Court has persuaded me that grossly disparate treatment of similar offenders is a characteristic of the criminal enforcement of obscenity law.

7. In Young v. American Mini Theatres, Inc., 427 U.S. 50 (1976), the Court upheld the use of the zoning power to control sexually explicit motion pictures. Detroit had decided that theatres exhibiting those movies should not be concentrated in a limited section of the city, but should be dispersed. A theatre showing sexually explicit movies could not be located within 500 feet of a residential area, or within 1,000 feet of any two "regulated uses." (The latter term included adult book stores, taverns, hotels, pool halls and dance halls.) Justice Stevens concluded that:

> Since what is ultimately at stake is nothing more than a limitation on the place where adult films may be exhibited, even though the determination of whether a particular film fits that characterization turns on the nature of its content, we conclude that the city's interest in the present and future character of its neighborhoods adequately supports its classification of motion pictures.

There were four dissenters. Justice Stewart's opinion stressed that the Detroit ordinance turned on film content, and thus involved selective interference with speech based on its content. Justice Blackmun's dissent emphasized the problem of vagueness—he doubted that any theatre owner could know whether the films he showed brought him within the ordinance. Is Justice Stevens' majority opinion consistent with his conclusion in the *Marks* case that obscenity laws are "intolerably vague"? Is Justice Blackmun's dissent consistent with the *Miller* decision, which he joined, and which concluded that the definition of obscenity was sufficiently precise?

AFTERWORD*

It is at this point that Mr. [Thurman] Arnold enters with the appropriate last word. Having been engaged as counsel for the defense in a prosecution in Vermont for the sale of an allegedly obscene magazine, he submitted a brief to the Vermont Supreme Court which must rank as one of the more extraordinary briefs ever filed. The main point is advice to the Vermont court on how to handle the issue before it sensibly and diplomatically. Mr. Arnold purports to get his rule of judicial prudence from the United States Supreme Court. The rule is simple: the court should hold the items before it not obscene unless they amount to hard-core pornography, and should, after rendering a decision, shut up. In Mr. Arnold's view, any fool can quickly recognize hard-core pornography, but

---

1. How, for example, can an appellate court intelligently determine whether a jury has properly identified the relevant community standards?

* Harry Kalven, Jr., Metaphysics of the Law of Obscenity, The Supreme Court Review, 1960, pp. 42–45.

it is a fatal trap for judicial decorum and judicial sanity to attempt thereafter to write an opinion explaining why:

> As William James, the great psychologist, said: "Such discussions are tedious—not as hard subjects like physics or mathematics are tedious, but as throwing feathers endlessly hour after hour is tedious."

THE IMPACT OF MILLER**

Despite the Court's adherence to *Miller*, the availability of pornography has continued to grow. "Since 1973 ... the nature and extent of pornography in the United States has changed dramatically. The materials that are available today are more sexually explicit and portray more violence than those available before 1970. The production, distribution and sale of pornography has become a large, well-organized and highly profitable industry." Furthermore, the few studies available show that the number of prosecutions and appeals of obscenity convictions nationwide have declined rather than increased since *Miller*, at least until the mid–1980s. The 1986 Attorney General's commission appears to have encouraged greater enforcement efforts in some localities, according to press reports, but this effect may not persist.

Why then has there not been greater carrythrough on *Miller?* Several reasons have been offered:

1. Low priority has been given to obscenity cases by prosecutors because of the scarcity of resources, prosecutors' unfavorable attitudes, and greater concern for other crimes.

2. Relative public tolerance of freedom of choice in this area reinforces similar attitudes on the parts of juries and judges.

3. Confusion over the meaning of key parts of the *Miller* test— "prurience," "serious value," "patently offensive," "community standards"—make prosecutors reluctant to prosecute and juries reluctant to convict, especially given the need to find guilt "beyond a reasonable doubt." Complex laws and judicial instructions confuse juries, making them less inclined to convict, and few laws are more confusing and complex than obscenity laws.

4. The vagaries of political pressure.

5. Under-complaining by the public to the police, under-investigation by police, and under-sentencing by judges.

6. Attorneys involved in obscenity cases pointed out another reason: many jury members are sexually aroused by the material presented and are therefore loathe to declare it obscene on the grounds that it appeals to unhealthy, abnormal ("prurient") interests!

7. Finally, pornographers are seasoned litigants who manipulate the factors mentioned above and consider court battles a part of doing business. Prosecutors have won many battles but often lose the war.

** Donald Alexander Downs, The New Politics of Pornography, University of Chicago Press, 1989, pp. 20–21. Reprinted with permission.

V. THE RATIONALE OF THE LAW OF OBSCENITY: ITS IMPLICATIONS FOR THE FIRST AMENDMENT

It is possible to become so bemused with the anomalies and difficulties of the law of obscenity that one loses sight of the general First Amendment implications of obscenity decisions. Putting to one side the intractable problem of defining obscenity, the Supreme Court has said it does not violate the First Amendment to punish the disseminator of obscenity to willing adults. If the First Amendment requires the balancing of free speech values against competing societal interests, what are the competing interests that justify suppression of the obscene? Are any of them sufficiently strong to justify obscenity laws? Finally, what implications do the obscenity decisions have for First Amendment problems in other areas? The preceding materials indicate that the First Amendment issues are not as easily resolved as the *Chaplinsky* dictum, quoted at the beginning of Chapter 10, would indicate. Are the obscenity decisions a water-tight compartment with no implications for control of speech in other areas? Or do they indicate the rationale for controlling speech that is not obscene?

The materials that follow examine the three rationales most often given to justify punishing purveyors of obscenity—the control of anti-social behavior, protecting community moral standards, and eliminating material which is offensive to the community. Do any of these rationales justify obscenity laws? If obscenity laws are constitutional, could similar arguments justify suppression of material that is not sexually explicit?

A. CONTROLLING ANTI–SOCIAL BEHAVIOR

A VIEW THAT PREVENTION OF ANTI–SOCIAL BEHAVIOR IS AMONG THE REASONS FOR CONTROL OF OBSCENITY*

Certain it is that most legislatures which debated or considered statutes forbidding dissemination of pornographic materials operated on the theory that such materials were especially harmful to children and adolescents. Whatever the particular or specific motivation, all the legislatures concerned with this problem regarded the mephitic outpourings of venal scatologists as a social evil threatening perils to the individual and society.

Now it is true that most, if not all, legislatures which dealt with the problem of legislation on this subject did not call for extensive legislative hearings and did not invite the testimony and statistics of sociologists. In this respect they operated much as they do with respect to other moral evils. They needed no sociological research to determine that rape or murder or large-scale unemployment were evils which clamored for mitigation or suppression. Nor, in the main, were legislators living in the illusion that laws could be perfectly efficient instruments for the extirpation of any of the evil factors whose character as evil they took for granted, or explicitly recognized. The point is that all of the legislatures

---

* Godfrey P. Schmidt, A Justification of Statutes Barring Pornography from the Mail, Fordham Law Review, 1957, vol. 26, pp. 70, 83–84. Reprinted with permission.

in the Anglo–American tradition more or less took for granted certain basic principles of the Judeo–Christian tradition with respect to sex—the Sixth and Ninth Commandments and their religious and ethical commentary.

Yet the fundamentals of this tradition with respect to sex were not transplanted into our jurisprudence indiscriminately. Legislators realized that laws operate only in the external forum and that thought control by law is quite impossible. But printed promulgation of pornographic material is not mere thought. It is, rather, thought reduced to objective and unmistakable act and fact.

... Surely, legislatures considering this matter ... could, with a decent respect for free speech, seek to repress lurid sexological materials whose publication is corrupting, and is prompted only by prurient venality. They could have the legislative purposes of: (1) preventing detriment to the characters of citizens, young or old, normal or abnormal; (2) obstructing the development of unhealthy attitudes toward sex and marriage; (3) disciplining, by pedagogic effects of legislation, the citizen's inclinations and tendencies, such as the strong passion and instinct of sex might easily arouse, and thus seek to limit the occasions when they run amuck; (4) to prevent stimulation of sex maniacs and others toward crime and perversion; and (5) to restrict the evil activities of those who deliberately set out to tempt, in the manner of an *agent provocateur,* others toward immorality, such as prostitution, perversion, seduction, etc.

AN EMPIRICAL STUDY*

... [A] reasonable exposure to erotica, particularly during adolescence, reflects a high degree of sexual interest and curiosity that coincides with adult patterns of acceptable heterosexual interest and practice. Contrary to our expectations, and those of many popular writers, less-than-average adolescent exposure to pornography reflects either active avoidance of heterosexual stimuli, or limitation to an environment where such materials are unavailable. It appears that the amount of exposure to pornography is a surface manifestation of the total pattern of sexual development. If sexual development proceeds along an unorthodox track, then unorthodox patterns of sexual behavior will result, including either underexposure to pornography or an obsessive interest in it.

... [A]dults are less likely to find their contacts with erotica educational than they did as adolescents. If these contacts do serve an educational function, it is to introduce the person to more exotic types of sexual relations. The most prominent reaction to erotica as adults is sexual arousal, experienced pleasurably by the controls and more ambivalently by the sex offenders. There is no clear-cut pattern of sexual activity following this arousal, and performance of specific antisocial sexual acts suggested or elicited by this heightened state of arousal is rarely reported by the sex offenders. The pattern of sexual behavior

* Michael J. Goldstein, Harold Sanford Kant, Pornography and Sexual Deviance, University of California Press, 1973, pp. 70, 108–109. Reprinted with permission.

manifested appears to be a response to a highly complex set of stimuli of which erotica is but one factor. Lowered inhibitions via alcohol, rejection of wives or lovers ("I came home one night and wanted to have sexual relations with my wife. She hadn't let me make love to her for months and she wasn't any different that night. I lay there frustrated, furious and wild with desire. I finally got disgusted and went downtown and raped this woman who I followed home. All through the rape, I fantasied that I was making love to my wife"), or associations with peer groups advocating deviant sexual patterns ("I was going with this group who were all into the sadomasochism thing. I was tremendously turned on by the whole idea and couldn't think of anything but rape for weeks until finally I seemed to go out of control and did rape somebody myself") seemed highly significant in releasing antisocial sexual behavior.

Still we cannot deny completely the role of erotica in stimulating thoughts and desires of sexual relations. It does seem that the intentions of the creator of the erotic stimulus do not always parallel the reaction produced. For example, *The Boston Strangler* hardly qualifies as erotica, yet the violence was stimulating to the rapist quoted above. The genre of motorcycle gang movies, so common a few years ago, is more directly sexual in intent, and once again a rapist in our sample found the violence stimulating. But, what of the description of a rape by a house-wife in the *Ladies' Home Journal?* Would anyone suggest that this was meant to constitute an erotic stimulus likely to activate desires of rape? Hardly, so we must consider that sex offenders are highly receptive to suggestions of sexual behavior congruent with their previously formed desires and will interpret the material at hand to fit their needs. It is true, however, that while few, if any, sex offenders suggest that erotica played a role in the commission of sex crimes, stimuli expressing brutali-ty, with or without concomitant sexual behavior, were often mentioned as disturbing, by rapists in particular. This raises the question of whether the stimulus most likely to release antisocial sexual behavior is one representing sexuality, or one representing aggression.

CONCLUSIONS OF THE PRESIDENT'S COMMISSION*

The Commission believes that there is no warrant for continued governmental interference with the full freedom of adults to read, obtain or view whatever such material they wish. Our conclusion is based upon the following considerations:

> 1. Extensive empirical investigation, both by the Commis-sion and by others, provides no evidence that exposure to or use of explicit sexual materials play a significant role in the causa-tion of social or individual harms such as crime, delinquency, sexual or nonsexual deviancy or severe emotional disturbances. This research and its results are described in detail in the Report of the Effects Panel of the Commission.... Empirical investigation thus supports the opinion of a substantial majority of persons professionally engaged in the treatment of deviancy,

* Report of the Commission on Obscenity and Pornography, 1970, pp. 52–53.

delinquency and antisocial behavior, that exposure to sexually explicit materials has no harmful causal role in these areas.

Studies show that a number of factors, such as disorganized family relationships and unfavorable peer influences, are intimately related to harmful sexual behavior or adverse character development. Exposure to sexually explicit materials, however, cannot be counted as among these determinative factors. Despite the existence of widespread legal prohibitions upon the dissemination of such materials, exposure to them appears to be a usual and harmless part of the process of growing up in our society and a frequent and nondamaging occurrence among adults. Indeed, a few Commission studies indicate that a possible distinction between sexual offenders and other people, with regard to experience with explicit sexual materials, is that sex offenders have seen markedly *less* of such materials while maturing.

This is not to say that exposure to explicit sexual materials has no effect upon human behavior. A prominent effect of exposure to sexual materials is that persons tend to talk more about sex as a result of seeing such materials. In addition, many persons become temporarily sexually aroused upon viewing explicit sexual materials and the frequency of their sexual activity may, in consequence, increase for short periods. Such behavior, however, is the type of sexual activity already established as usual activity for the particular individual.

In sum, empirical research designed to clarify the question has found no evidence to date that exposure to explicit sexual materials plays a significant role in the causation of delinquent or criminal behavior among youth or adults.

2. On the positive side, explicit sexual materials are sought as a source of entertainment and information by substantial numbers of American adults. At times, these materials also appear to serve to increase and facilitate constructive communication about sexual matters within marriage. The most frequent purchaser of explicit sexual materials is a college-educated, married male, in his thirties or forties, who is of above average socio-economic status. Even where materials are legally available to them, young adults and older adolescents do not constitute an important portion of the purchasers of such materials.

NOTES AND QUESTIONS

1. Assume, for the sake of argument, that there is a correlation between exposure to explicit sexual materials and sexual behavior it is appropriate to control. Would it follow that the First Amendment is not violated by prohibiting the general dissemination of that sort of material? Would it ever be possible to satisfy the standards of proof required by Brandenburg v. Ohio, Chapter 5, page 122. Should that be the applicable constitutional standard?

2. The link between literature and behavior was central in New York v. Ferber, 458 U.S. 747 (1982). A lower court struck down a state law prohibiting distribution of materials depicting sexual performances by children under 16. The lower court reasoned that the statute could not constitutionally be applied to materials that were not "obscene," as that term had been defined by the Supreme Court. The Supreme Court disagreed, concluding that the advertising and selling of "child pornography" could be prohibited to control the exploitation of children in the initial production of the material. Notice that the focus here is not on the behavior of the viewer. Would the rationale of the *Ferber* decision justify laws forbidding photographs and motion pictures that depict cruelty to animals? That depict sexual intercourse?

B. PROTECTING COMMUNITY MORAL STANDARDS

DISSENTS FROM CONCLUSIONS OF THE PRESIDENT'S COMMISSION*

The Commission's majority report is a Magna Carta for the pornographer.

The Commission has deliberately and carefully avoided coming to grips with the basic underlying issue. The government interest in regulating pornography has always related primarily to the prevention of moral corruption and *not* to prevention of overt criminal acts and conduct, or the protection of persons from being shocked and/or offended.

The basic question is whether and to what extent society may establish and maintain certain moral standards. If it is conceded that society has a legitimate concern in maintaining moral standards, it follows logically that government has a legitimate interest in at least attempting to protect such standards against any source which threatens them.

The Commission report simply ignores this issue, and relegates government's interest to little more than a footnote—passing it off with the extremist cliche that it is "unwise" for government to attempt to legislate morality. Obscenity law in no way legislates individual morality, but provides protection for public morality. The Supreme Court itself has never denied society's interest in maintaining moral standards, but has instead ruled for the protection of the "social interest in order and morality."

... Pornography is not new. But for centuries its invidious effects upon individuals and upon nations has been held in reasonable control by law.

There is good reason for such law, as Reo M. Christenson in an article "Censorship of Pornography? Yes" (*The Progressive,* September, 1970) writes:

> ... *Sex and Culture* by former Oxford Professor J.D. Unwin, whose massive studies in eighty primitive and civilized

* Report of The Commission on Obscenity and Pornography, 1970, pp. 385–386, 513–514.

societies reveal a distinct correlation between increasing sexual freedom and social decline. The more sexually permissive a society becomes, Unwin says, the less creative energy it exhibits and the slower its movement toward rationality, philosophical speculation, and advanced civilization.

Harvard sociologist Pitirim Sorokin agrees with Unwin that sexual restraints promote cultural progress; in *The American Sexual Revolution* he contends that immoral and anti-social behavior increased with cultural permissiveness toward the erotic sub-arts. In an article in *The New York Times* magazine entitled "Why I Dislike Western Civilization," May 10, 1964, Arnold Toynbee argued that a culture which postpones rather than stimulates sexual experience in young adults is a culture most prone to progress.

In another article in *The New York Times* magazine, Bruno Bettelheim, the noted psychoanalyst, recently observed: "If a society does not taboo sex, children will grow up in relative sex freedom. But so far, history has shown that such a society cannot create culture or civilization; it remains primitive." Sorokin asserts "... there is no example of a community which has retained its high position on the cultural scale after less rigorous sexual customs have replaced more restricting ones."

Against the general background of the history of nations and against the specific background of the history of the United States, it is apparent that the laws prohibiting obscenity and pornography have played an important role in the creativity and excellence of our system and our society—these laws have played an important part in our people coming so far and achieving so much.

A VIEW THAT OBSCENITY LAWS PROTECT COMMUNITY MORALS*

The ACLU has not a single doubt. Any statute that interferes with our traditional freedoms should be "held unconstitutional regardless of the merit or the taste of the particular publication under scrutiny."

It might be urged that [*Headquarters Detective*] cannot be classified with the literary forms given as illustration [the Bible and the works of Shakespeare]. It is submitted, however, that any differences are those of taste.

To say nothing of the reference to the Bible as a "literary form," a statement of this sort can be made only by persons who are insensitive to the subject on which they pretend to speak with authority. Their opinion can be justified only on the basis of absolute proof that the distinction between Shakespeare and the author of "Bargains in Bodies" is of no importance to the American society and that the law can be indifferent to what Americans, including young Americans, read. Their insistence, furthermore, that the American Constitution must look with equal benevolence on what is praiseworthy and on the most malicious

---

* Walter Berns, Freedom, Virtue and the First Amendment, Louisiana State University Press, 1957, pp. 22–23, 46, 250, 255. Reprinted with permission.

trash can be justified only on the basis of real proof that censorship involves dangers so excessive that it can never be condoned. But what proof of these propositions is offered? How can libertarians be so dogmatically certain that their policy is correct?

... The First Amendment does not stand in isolation; it is but one part of the Constitution. And the Constitution is a charter of *government,* whose purposes are specified in the Preamble: "... a more perfect Union ... justice ... domestic tranquility ... the common defense ... the general Welfare, and ... the Blessings of Liberty...." The problem of the First Amendment is not one merely of protecting freedom of speech, press, religion, and political opinion, but is inseparable from the problem of governing, of establishing justice, the central political virtue....

... [J]udges are not and cannot be aloof from moral considerations. Judges cannot be amoral because law is not amoral. Amoral law is bad law. Law that attempts to regulate the distribution of power without regard to the use to which that power is put is law for automatons, not people. One cannot say that a law that grants people the freedom to speak is a good law unless he examines what people do with that freedom. Or, a legal principle that defines justice as the maximum amount of personal freedom compatible with security ignores, what common sense does not ignore, that a secure nation may not be worth living in—no matter how much freedom exists.

The problem we have discussed in these pages is not really the problem of free speech at all; it is the problem of virtue. Under the influence of liberal theory, we have denied or overlooked what ancient wisdom declares to be the primary function of law; the formation of character. For, not only are the liberal efforts to devise legal formulas, such as the clear and present danger test, ignorant of the dimensions of the problem, but liberalism compounds the error by attempting to deny the law of its primary function.

ASHCROFT v. THE FREE SPEECH COALITION

535 U.S. 234, 122 S.Ct. 1389, 152 L.Ed.2d 403 (2002).

JUSTICE KENNEDY delivered the opinion of the Court.

We consider in this case whether the Child Pornography Prevention Act of 1996 (CPPA), 18 U.S.C. § 2251 et seq., abridges the freedom of speech. The CPPA extends the federal prohibition against child pornography to sexually explicit images that appear to depict minors but were produced without using any real children. The statute prohibits, in specific circumstances, possessing or distributing these images, which may be created by using adults who look like minors or by using computer imaging. The new technology, according to Congress, makes it possible to create realistic images of children who do not exist....

By prohibiting child pornography that does not depict an actual child, the statute goes beyond New York v. Ferber, 458 U.S. 747 (1982), which distinguished child pornography from other sexually explicit speech because of the State's interest in protecting the children exploited by the production process.... As a general rule, pornography can be banned only if obscene, but under *Ferber*, pornography showing minors can be proscribed whether or not the images are obscene under the definition set forth in Miller v. California....

While we have not had occasion to consider the question, we may assume that the apparent age of persons engaged in sexual conduct is relevant to whether a depiction offends community standards. Pictures of young children engaged in certain acts might be obscene where similar depictions of adults, or perhaps even older adolescents, would not. The CPPA, however, is not directed at speech that is obscene.... Like the law in *Ferber*, the CPPA seeks to reach beyond obscenity, and it makes no attempt to conform to the *Miller* standard. For instance, the statute would reach visual depictions, such as movies, even if they have redeeming social value.

The principal question to be resolved, then, is whether the CPPA is constitutional where it proscribes a significant universe of speech that is neither obscene under *Miller* nor child pornography under *Ferber*.

I

Before 1996, Congress defined child pornography as the type of depictions at issue in *Ferber*, images made using actual minors.... The CPPA retains that prohibition at 18 U.S.C. § 2256(8)(A) and adds three other prohibited categories of speech, of which the first, § 2256(8)(B), and the third, § 2256(8)(D), are at issue in this case. Section 2256(8)(B) prohibits "any visual depiction, including any photograph, film, video, picture, or computer or computer-generated image or picture" that "is, or appears to be, of a minor engaging in sexually explicit conduct." The prohibition on "any visual depiction" does not depend at all on how the image is produced. The section captures a range of depictions, sometimes called "virtual child pornography," which include computer-generated images, as well as images produced by more traditional means. For instance, the literal terms of the statute embrace a Renaissance painting depicting a scene from classical mythology, a "picture" that "appears to be, of a minor engaging in sexually explicit conduct." The statute also prohibits Hollywood movies, filmed without any child actors, if a jury believes an actor "appears to be" a minor engaging in "actual or simulated ... sexual intercourse." § 2256(2).

These images do not involve, let alone harm, any children in the production process; but Congress decided the materials threaten children in other, less direct, ways. Pedophiles might use the materials to encourage children to participate in sexual activity.... Furthermore, pedophiles might "whet their own sexual appetites" with the pornographic images, "thereby increasing the creation and distribution of child pornography and the sexual abuse and exploitation of actual children." ... Under these rationales, harm flows from the content of the images, not from the means of their production. In addition, Congress identified another problem created by computer-generated images: Their existence can make it harder to prosecute pornographers who do use real minors.... As imaging technology improves, Congress found, it becomes more difficult to prove that a particular picture was produced using actual children....

Section 2256(8)(C) prohibits a more common and lower tech means of creating virtual images, known as computer morphing. Rather than creating original images, pornographers can alter innocent pictures of real children so that the children appear to be engaged in sexual activity. Although morphed images may fall within the definition of virtual child pornography, they implicate the interests of real children and are in that sense closer to the images in *Ferber*. Respondents do not challenge this provision, and we do not consider it.

Respondents do challenge § 2256(8)(D). Like the text of the "appears to be" provision, the sweep of this provision is quite broad. Section 2256(8)(D) defines child pornography to include any sexually explicit image that was "advertised, promoted, presented, described, or distributed in such a manner that conveys the impression" it depicts "a minor engaging in sexually explicit conduct." One Committee Report identified the provision as directed at sexually explicit images pandered as child pornography.... The statute is not so limited in its reach, however, as it punishes even those possessors who took no part in pandering. Once a work has been described as child pornography, the taint remains on the speech in the hands of subsequent possessors, making possession unlawful even though the content otherwise would not be objectionable.

Fearing that the CPPA threatened the activities of its members, respondent Free Speech Coalition and others challenged the statute in the United States District Court for the Northern District of California. The Coalition, a California trade association for the adult-entertainment industry, alleged that its members did not use minors in their sexually explicit works, but they believed some of these materials might fall within the CPPA's expanded definition of child pornography. The other respondents are Bold Type, Inc., the publisher of a book advocating the nudist lifestyle; Jim Gingerich, a painter of nudes; and Ron Raffaelli, a photographer specializing in erotic images. Respondents alleged that the "appears to be" and "conveys the impression" provisions are overbroad and vague, chilling them from producing works protected by the First Amendment. The District Court disagreed and granted summary judgment to the Government....

The Court of Appeals for the Ninth Circuit reversed....

. . .

II

... [A] law imposing criminal penalties on protected speech is a stark example of speech suppression. The CPPA's penalties are indeed severe. A first offender may be imprisoned for 15 years.... A repeat offender faces a prison sentence of not less than 5 years and not more than 30 years in prison.... While even minor punishments can chill protected speech, ... this case provides a textbook example of why we permit facial challenges to statutes that burden expression. With these severe penalties in force, few legitimate movie producers or book publishers, or few other speakers in any capacity, would risk distributing images in or near the uncertain reach of this law. The Constitution gives significant protection from overbroad laws that chill speech within the First Amendment's vast and privileged sphere. Under this principle, the CPPA is unconstitutional on its face if it prohibits a substantial amount of protected expression. . . .

. . .

. . . [S]peech may not be prohibited because it concerns subjects offending our sensibilities. . . .

As a general principle, the First Amendment bars the government from dictating what we see or read or speak or hear. The freedom of speech has its limits; it does not embrace certain categories of speech, including defamation, incitement, obscenity, and pornography produced with real children. . . . While these categories may be prohibited without violating the First Amendment, none of them includes the speech prohibited by the CPPA. . . .

As we have noted, the CPPA is much more than a supplement to the existing federal prohibition on obscenity. . . . The CPPA . . ., extends to images that appear to depict a minor engaging in sexually explicit activity without regard to the *Miller* requirements. . . . Any depiction of sexually explicit activity, no matter how it is presented, is proscribed. The CPPA applies to a picture in a psychology manual, as well as a movie depicting the horrors of sexual abuse. . . .

. . . The statute proscribes the visual depiction of an idea—that of teenagers engaging in sexual activity—that is a fact of modern society and has been a theme in art and literature throughout the ages. Under the CPPA, images are prohibited so long as the persons appear to be under 18 years of age. This is higher than the legal age for marriage in many States, as well as the age at which persons may consent to sexual relations. . . .

. . . Both themes—teenage sexual activity and the sexual abuse of children—have inspired countless literary works. William Shakespeare created the most famous pair of teenage lovers, one of whom is just 13 years of age. . . . The work has inspired no less than 40 motion pictures, some of which suggest that the teenagers consummated their relationship. . . .

Contemporary movies pursue similar themes. Last year's Academy Awards featured the movie, *Traffic*, which was nominated for Best Picture. . . . The film portrays a teenager, identified as a 16–year-old, who becomes addicted to drugs. The viewer sees the degradation of her addiction, which in the end leads her to a filthy room to trade sex for drugs. The year before, *American Beauty* won the Academy Award for Best Picture. . . . In the course of the movie, a teenage girl engages in sexual relations with her teenage boyfriend, and another yields herself to the gratification of a middle-aged man. . . .

. . . Whether or not the films we mention violate the CPPA, they explore themes within the wide sweep of the statute's prohibitions. If these films, or hundreds of others of lesser note that explore those subjects, contain a single graphic depiction of sexual activity within the statutory definition, the possessor of the film would be subject to severe punishment without inquiry into the work's redeeming value. This is inconsistent with an essential First Amendment rule: The artistic merit of a work does not depend on the presence of a single explicit scene....

The Government seeks to address this deficiency by arguing that speech prohibited by the CPPA is virtually indistinguishable from child pornography, which may be banned without regard to whether it depicts works of value.... *Ferber* recognized that the State had an interest in stamping it out without regard to any judgment about its content.... The production of the work, not its content, was the target of the statute. The fact that a work contained serious literary, artistic, or other value did not excuse the harm it caused to its child participants....

... First, as a permanent record of a child's abuse, the continued circulation itself would harm the child who had participated. Like a defamatory statement, each new publication of the speech would cause new injury to the child's reputation and emotional well-being.... Second, because the traffic in child pornography was an economic motive for its production, the State had an interest in closing the distribution network.... Under either rationale, the speech had what the Court in effect held was a proximate link to the crime from which it came.

Later, in Osborne v. Ohio, 495 U.S. 103 (1990), the Court ruled that these same interests justified a ban on the possession of pornography produced by using children.... It did not suggest that, absent this concern, other governmental interests would suffice....

... [T]he CPPA prohibits speech that records no crime and creates no victims by its production. Virtual child pornography is not "intrinsically related" to the sexual abuse of children, as were the materials in *Ferber*.... While the Government asserts that the images can lead to actual instances of child abuse, ... the causal link is contingent and indirect. The harm does not necessarily follow from the speech, but depends upon some unquantified potential for subsequent criminal acts.

The Government says these indirect harms are sufficient because, as *Ferber* acknowledged, child pornography rarely can be valuable speech.... This argument, however, suffers from two flaws. First, *Ferber*'s judgment about child pornography was based upon how it was made, not on what it communicated. ...

The second flaw in the Government's position is that *Ferber* did not hold that child pornography is by definition without value. On the contrary, the Court recognized some works in this category might have significant value, ... but relied on virtual images—the very images prohibited by the CPPA—as an alternative and permissible means of expression ... *Ferber*, then, not only referred to the distinction between actual and virtual child pornography, it relied on it as a reason supporting its holding. *Ferber* provides no support for a statute that eliminates the distinction and makes the alternative mode criminal as well.

III

... The Government ... argues that the CPPA is necessary because pedophiles may use virtual child pornography to seduce children.... The

Government, of course, may punish adults who provide unsuitable materials to children, see Ginsberg v. New York, 390 U.S. 629 (1968), and it may enforce criminal penalties for unlawful solicitation. The precedents establish, however, that speech within the rights of adults to hear may not be silenced completely in an attempt to shield children from it. . . .

Here, the Government wants to keep speech from children not to protect them from its content but to protect them from those who would commit other crimes. The principle, however, remains the same: The Government cannot ban speech fit for adults simply because it may fall into the hands of children. The evil in question depends upon the actor's unlawful conduct, conduct defined as criminal quite apart from any link to the speech in question. This establishes that the speech ban is not narrowly drawn. The objective is to prohibit illegal conduct, but this restriction goes well beyond that interest by restricting the speech available to law-abiding adults.

The Government submits further that virtual child pornography whets the appetites of pedophiles and encourages them to engage in illegal conduct. This rationale cannot sustain the provision in question. The mere tendency of speech to encourage unlawful acts is not a sufficient reason for banning it. . . . First Amendment freedoms are most in danger when the government seeks to control thought or to justify its laws for that impermissible end. The right to think is the beginning of freedom, and speech must be protected from the government because speech is the beginning of thought.

. . . There is here no attempt, incitement, solicitation, or conspiracy. The Government has shown no more than a remote connection between speech that might encourage thoughts or impulses and any resulting child abuse. Without a significantly stronger, more direct connection, the Government may not prohibit speech on the ground that it may encourage pedophiles to engage in illegal conduct.

The Government next argues that its objective of eliminating the market for pornography produced using real children necessitates a prohibition on virtual images as well. Virtual images, the Government contends, are indistinguishable from real ones; they are part of the same market and are often exchanged. In this way, it is said, virtual images promote the trafficking in works produced through the exploitation of real children. The hypothesis is somewhat implausible. If virtual images were identical to illegal child pornography, the illegal images would be driven from the market by the indistinguishable substitutes. Few pornographers would risk prosecution by abusing real children if fictional, computerized images would suffice.

In the case of the material covered by *Ferber*, the creation of the speech is itself the crime of child abuse; the prohibition deters the crime by removing the profit motive. . . . [H]ere, there is no underlying crime at all. Even if the Government's market deterrence theory were persuasive in some contexts, it would not justify this statute.

Finally, the Government says that the possibility of producing images by using computer imaging makes it very difficult for it to prosecute those who produce pornography by using real children. Experts, we are told, may have difficulty in saying whether the pictures were made by using real children or by using computer imaging. The necessary solution, the argument runs, is to prohibit both kinds of images. The argument, in essence, is that protected speech may be banned as a means to ban unprotected speech. This analysis turns the First Amendment upside down.

The Government may not suppress lawful speech as the means to suppress unlawful speech. Protected speech does not become unprotected merely because it resembles the latter. The Constitution requires the reverse.... The overbreadth doctrine prohibits the Government from banning unprotected speech if a substantial amount of protected speech is prohibited or chilled in the process.

To avoid the force of this objection, the Government would have us read the CPPA not as a measure suppressing speech but as a law shifting the burden to the accused to prove the speech is lawful. In this connection, the Government relies on an affirmative defense under the statute, which allows a defendant to avoid conviction for nonpossession offenses by showing that the materials were produced using only adults and were not otherwise distributed in a manner conveying the impression that they depicted real children....

The Government raises serious constitutional difficulties by seeking to impose on the defendant the burden of proving his speech is not unlawful.... If the evidentiary issue is a serious problem for the Government, as it asserts, it will be at least as difficult for the innocent possessor....

We need not decide, however, whether the Government could impose this burden on a speaker. Even if an affirmative defense can save a statute from First Amendment challenge, here the defense is incomplete and insufficient, even on its own terms.... A defendant charged with possessing, as opposed to distributing, proscribed works may not defend on the ground that the film depicts only adult actors.... So while the affirmative defense may protect a movie producer from prosecution for the act of distribution, that same producer, and all other persons in the subsequent distribution chain, could be liable for possessing the prohibited work. Furthermore, the affirmative defense provides no protection to persons who produce speech by using computer imaging, or through other means that do not involve the use of adult actors who appear to be minors.... In these cases, the defendant can demonstrate no children were harmed in producing the images, yet the affirmative defense would not bar the prosecution. For this reason, the affirmative defense cannot save the statute, for it leaves unprotected a substantial amount of speech not tied to the Government's interest in distinguishing images produced using real children from virtual ones.

. . .

IV

Respondents challenge § 2256(8)(D) as well. This provision bans depictions of sexually explicit conduct that are "advertised, promoted, presented, described, or distributed in such a manner that conveys the impression that the material is or contains a visual depiction of a minor engaging in sexually explicit conduct." . . .

. . . The CPPA prohibits sexually explicit materials that "conve[y] the impression" they depict minors. While that phrase may sound like the "appears to be" prohibition in § 2256(8)(B), it requires little judgment about the content of the image. Under § 2256(8)(D), the work must be sexually explicit, but otherwise the content is irrelevant. Even if a film contains no sexually explicit scenes involving minors, it could be treated as child pornography if the title and trailers convey the impression that the scenes would be found in the movie. The determination turns on how the speech is presented, not on what is depicted. . . .

The Government does not offer a serious defense of this provision . . . The materials, for instance, are not likely to be confused for child pornography in a criminal trial. The Court has recognized that pandering may be relevant, as an evidentiary matter, to the question whether particular materials are obscene. See Ginzburg v. United States, 383 U.S. 463, 474 (1966) . . .

. . . Section 2256(8)(D), however, prohibits a substantial amount of speech that falls outside Ginzburg's rationale. Materials falling within the proscription are tainted and unlawful in the hands of all who receive it, though they bear no responsibility for how it was marketed, sold, or described. The statute, furthermore, does not require that the context be part of an effort at "commercial exploitation." . . . § 2256(8)(D) is substantially overbroad . . .

V

. . . [T]he prohibitions of §§ 2256(8)(B) and 2256(8)(D) are overbroad and unconstitutional. . . .

The judgment of the Court of Appeals is affirmed.

. . .

JUSTICE THOMAS, concurring in the judgment.

In my view, the Government's most persuasive asserted interest in support of the [CCPA] is the prosecution rationale—that persons who possess and disseminate pornographic images of real children may escape conviction by claiming that the images are computer-generated, thereby raising a reasonable doubt as to their guilt. At this time, however, the Government asserts only that defendants raise such defenses, not that they have done so successfully. In fact, the Government points to no case in which a defendant has been acquitted based on a "computer-generated images" defense. While this speculative interest cannot support the broad reach of the CPPA, technology may evolve to the point where it becomes impossible to enforce actual child pornography laws because the Government cannot prove that certain pornographic images are of real children. In the event this occurs, the Government should not be foreclosed from enacting a regulation of virtual child pornography that contains an appropriate affirmative defense or some other narrowly drawn restriction.

... [I]f technological advances thwart prosecution of "unlawful speech," the Government may well have a compelling interest in barring or otherwise regulating some narrow category of "lawful speech" in order to enforce effectively laws against pornography made through the abuse of real children. . . .

JUSTICE O'CONNOR, with whom THE CHIEF JUSTICE and JUSTICE SCALIA join as to Part II, concurring in the judgment in part and dissenting in part.

. . .

This litigation involves a facial challenge to the CPPA's prohibitions of pornographic images that "appea[r] to be . . . of a minor" and of material that "conveys the impression" that it contains pornographic images of minors. While I agree with the Court's judgment that the First Amendment requires that the latter prohibition be struck down, I disagree with its decision to strike down the former prohibition in its entirety. . . . I would strike down the prohibition of pornography that "appears to be" of minors only insofar as it is applied to the class of youthful-adult pornography.

I

. . . The Government . . . requests that the Court exclude youthful-adult and virtual-child pornography from the protection of the First Amendment.

I agree with the Court's decision not to grant this request. . . . [W]hat the Government asks this Court to rule is that it may . . . prohibit youthful-adult and virtual-adult pornography that is merely indecent. . . . Although such pornography looks like the material at issue in New York v. Ferber, . . . no children are harmed in the process of creating such pornography. . . . Therefore, Ferber does not support the Government's ban on youthful-adult and virtual-child pornography. . . . The Court correctly concludes that the causal connection between pornographic images that "appear" to include minors and actual child abuse is not strong enough to justify withdrawing First Amendment protection for such speech.

I also agree with the Court's decision to strike down the CPPA's ban on material presented in a manner that "conveys the impression" that it contains pornographic depictions of actual children ("actual-child pornography"). . . . The Court concludes that § 2256(8)(D) is overbroad, but its reasoning also persuades me that the provision is not narrowly tailored. The provision therefore fails strict scrutiny. . . .

Finally, I agree with Court that that the CPPA's ban on youthful-adult pornography is overbroad. The Court provides several examples of movies that, although possessing serious literary, artistic or political value and employing only adult actors to perform simulated sexual conduct, fall under the CPPA's proscription . . .

II

I disagree with the Court, however, that the CPPA's prohibition of virtual-child pornography is overbroad. Before I reach that issue, there are two preliminary questions: whether the ban on virtual-child pornography fails strict scrutiny and whether that ban is unconstitutionally vague. I would answer both in the negative.

... [G]iven the rapid pace of advances in computer-graphics technology, the Government's concern is reasonable....

Respondents argue that, even if the Government has a compelling interest to justify banning virtual-child pornography, the "appears to be ... of a minor" language is not narrowly tailored to serve that interest.... They assert that the CPPA would capture even cartoon-sketches or statues of children that were sexually suggestive. Such images surely could not be used, for instance, to seduce children. I agree. A better interpretation of "appears to be ... of" is "virtually indistinguishable from"—an interpretation that would not cover the examples respondents provide....

Reading the statute only to bar images that are virtually indistinguishable from actual children would not only assure that the ban on virtual-child pornography is narrowly tailored, but would also assuage any fears that the "appears to be ... of a minor" language is vague....

The Court concludes that the CPPA's ban on virtual-child pornography is overbroad.... Respondents provide no examples of films or other materials that are wholly computer-generated and contain images that "appea[r] to be ... of minors" engaging in indecent conduct, but that have serious value or do not facilitate child abuse. Their overbreadth challenge therefore fails.

III

Although in my view the CPPA's ban on youthful-adult pornography appears to violate the First Amendment, the ban on virtual-child pornography does not. It is true that both bans are authorized by the same text.... Invalidating a statute due to overbreadth, however, is an extreme remedy, one that should be employed "sparingly and only as a last resort." ...

Heeding this caution, I would strike the "appears to be" provision only insofar as it is applied to the subset of cases involving youthful-adult pornography....

... Drawing a line around, and striking just, the CPPA's ban on youthful-child pornography ... preserves the CPPA's prohibition of the material that Congress found most dangerous to children.

· · ·

CHIEF JUSTICE REHNQUIST, with whom JUSTICE SCALIA joins in part, dissenting.

I agree with Part II of Justice O'Connor's opinion ... Congress has a compelling interest in ensuring the ability to enforce prohibitions of actual child pornography, and we should defer to its findings that rapidly advancing technology soon will make it all but impossible to do so. . . .

I also agree with Justice O'Connor that serious First Amendment concerns would arise were the Government ever to prosecute someone for simple distribution or possession of a film with literary or artistic value, such as "Traffic" or "American Beauty." I write separately, however, because the . . . (CPPA) . . . need not be construed to reach such materials.

We normally do not strike down a statute on First Amendment grounds "when a limiting instruction has been or could be placed on the challenged statute." . . .

Other than computer generated images that are virtually indistinguishable from real children engaged in sexually explicitly conduct, the CPPA can be limited so as not to reach any material that was not already unprotected before the CPPA. . . .

Indeed, we should be loath to construe a statute as banning film portrayals of Shakespearian tragedies, without some indication—from text or legislative history—that such a result was intended. . . .

. . .

AMERICAN BOOKSELLERS ASSOCIATION, INC. v. HUDNUT

United States Court of Appeals, Seventh Circuit, 1985.
771 F.2d 323.

Before CUDAHY and EASTERBROOK, CIRCUIT JUDGES, and SWYGERT, SENIOR CIRCUIT JUDGE.

EASTERBROOK, CIRCUIT JUDGE.

Indianapolis enacted an ordinance defining "pornography" as a practice that discriminates against women. "Pornography" is to be redressed through the administrative and judicial methods used for other discrimination. The City's definition of "pornography" is considerably different from "obscenity," which the Supreme Court has held is not protected by the First Amendment.

To be "obscene" under Miller v. California, 413 U.S. 15 (1973), "a publication must, taken as a whole, appeal to the prurient interest, must contain patently offensive depictions or descriptions of specified sexual conduct, and on the whole have no serious literary, artistic, political, or scientific value." Brockett v. Spokane Arcades, Inc., 472 U.S. 491 (1985). Offensiveness must be assessed under the standards of the community. Both offensiveness and an appeal to something other than "normal, healthy sexual desires" are essential elements of "obscenity."

"Pornography" under the ordinance is "the graphic sexually explicit subordination of women, whether in pictures or in words, that also includes one or more of the following:

(1) Women are presented as sexual objects who enjoy pain or humiliation; or

(2) Women are presented as sexual objects who experience sexual pleasure in being raped; or

(3) Women are presented as sexual objects tied up or cut up or mutilated or bruised or physically hurt, or as dismembered or truncated or fragmented or severed into body parts; or

(4) Women are presented as being penetrated by objects or animals; or

(5) Women are presented in scenarios of degradation, injury, abasement, torture, shown as filthy or inferior, bleeding, bruised, or hurt in a context that makes these conditions sexual; or

(6) Women are presented as sexual objects for domination, conquest, violation, exploitation, possession, or use, or through postures or positions of servility or submission or display." ...

The statute provides that the "use of men, children, or transsexuals in the place of women in paragraphs (1) through (6) above shall also constitute pornography under this section." The ordinance as passed in April 1984 defined "sexually explicit" to mean actual or simulated intercourse or the uncovered exhibition of the genitals, buttocks or anus. An amendment in June 1984 deleted this provision, leaving the term undefined.

The Indianapolis ordinance does not refer to the prurient interest, to offensiveness, or to the standards of the community. It demands attention to particular depictions, not to the work judged as a whole. It is irrelevant under the ordinance whether the work has literary, artistic, political, or scientific value. The City and many amici point to these omissions as virtues. They maintain that pornography influences attitudes, and the statute is a way to alter the socialization of men and women rather than to vindicate community standards of offensiveness. And as one of the principal drafters of the ordinance has asserted, "if a woman is subjected, why should it matter that the work has other value?" Catharine A. MacKinnon, Pornography, Civil Rights, and Speech, 20 Harv.Civ.Rts.—Civ.Lib.L.Rev. 1, 21 (1985).

Civil rights groups and feminists have entered this case as amici on both sides. Those supporting the ordinance say that it will play an important role in reducing the tendency of men to view women as sexual objects, a tendency that leads to both unacceptable attitudes and discrimination in the workplace and violence away from it. Those opposing the ordinance point out that much radical feminist literature is explicit and depicts women in ways forbidden by the ordinance and that the ordinance would reopen old battles. It is unclear how Indianapolis would treat works from James Joyce's *Ulysses* to Homer's *Iliad;* both depict women as submissive objects for conquest and domination.

We do not try to balance the arguments for and against an ordinance such as this. The ordinance discriminates on the ground of the content of the speech. Speech treating women in the approved way—in sexual encounters "premised on equality" (MacKinnon, supra, at 22)—is lawful no matter how sexually explicit. Speech treating women in the

disapproved way—as submissive in matters sexual or as enjoying humiliation—is unlawful no matter how significant the literary, artistic, or
political qualities of the work taken as a whole. The state may not ordain
preferred viewpoints in this way. The Constitution forbids the state to
declare one perspective right and silence opponents.

I

The ordinance contains four prohibitions. People may not "traffic"
in pornography, "coerce" others into performing in pornographic works,
or "force" pornography on anyone. Anyone injured by someone who has
seen or read pornography has a right of action against the maker or
seller.

Trafficking is defined ... as the "production, sale, exhibition, or
distribution of pornography." The offense excludes exhibition in a public
or educational library, but a "special display" in a library may be sex
discrimination. [The ordinance] provides that the trafficking paragraph
"shall not be construed to make isolated passages or isolated parts
actionable."

"Coercion into pornographic performance" is defined ... as
"[c]oercing, intimidating or fraudulently inducing any person ... into
performing for pornography...." The ordinance specifies that proof of
any of the following "shall not constitute a defense: I. That the person is
a woman; ... VI. That the person has previously posed for sexually
explicit pictures ... with anyone ...; ... VIII. That the person actually
consented to a use of the performance that is changed into pornography;
... IX. That the person knew that the purpose of the acts or events in
question was to make pornography; ... XI. That the person signed a
contract, or made statements affirming a willingness to cooperate in the
production of pornography; XII. That no physical force, threats, or
weapons were used in the making of the pornography; or XIII. That the
person was paid or otherwise compensated."

"Forcing pornography on a person" ... is the "forcing of pornography on any woman, man, child, or transsexual in any place of employment, in education, in a home, or in any public place." The statute does
not define forcing, but one of its authors states that the definition
reaches pornography shown to medical students as part of their education or given to language students for translation. MacKinnon, supra,
at 40–41.

[The ordinance] defines as a prohibited practice the "assault, physical attack, or injury of any woman, man, child, or transsexual in a way
that is directly caused by specific pornography."

For purposes of all four offenses, it is generally "not ... a defense
that the respondent did not know or intend that the materials were
pornography...." But the ordinance provides that damages are unavailable in trafficking cases unless the complainant proves "that the respondent knew or had reason to know that the materials were pornography."
It is a complete defense to a trafficking case that all of the materials in
question were pornography only by virtue of category (6) of the definition of pornography. In cases of assault caused by pornography, those

who seek damages from "a seller, exhibitor or distributor" must show that the defendant knew or had reason to know of the material's status as pornography. By implication, those who seek damages from an author need not show this.

A woman aggrieved by trafficking in pornography may file a complaint "as a woman acting against the subordination of women" with the office of equal opportunity. A man, child, or transsexual also may protest trafficking "but must prove injury in the same way that a woman is injured...." [The ordinance] also provides, however, that "any person claiming to be aggrieved" by trafficking, coercion, forcing, or assault may complain against the "perpetrators." ...

II

The plaintiffs are a congeries of distributors and readers of books, magazines, and films. The American Booksellers Association comprises about 5,200 bookstores and chains. The Association for American Publishers includes most of the country's publishers. Video Shack, Inc., sells and rents video cassettes in Indianapolis. Kelly Bentley, a resident of Indianapolis, reads books and watches films. There are many more plaintiffs. Collectively the plaintiffs (or their members, whose interests they represent) make, sell, or read just about every kind of material that could be affected by the ordinance, from hard-core films to W.B. Yeats's poem "Leda and the Swan" (from the myth of Zeus in the form of a swan impregnating an apparently subordinate Leda), to the collected works of James Joyce, D.H. Lawrence, and John Cleland.

III

"If there is any fixed star in our constitutional constellation, it is that no official, high or petty, can prescribe what shall be orthodox in politics, nationalism, religion, or other matters of opinion or force citizens to confess by word or act their faith therein." West Virginia State Board of Education v. Barnette, 319 U.S. 624, 642 (1943). Under the First Amendment the government must leave to the people the evaluation of ideas. Bald or subtle, an idea is as powerful as the audience allows it to be. A belief may be pernicious—the beliefs of Nazis led to the death of millions, those of the Klan to the repression of millions. A pernicious belief may prevail. Totalitarian governments today rule much of the planet, practicing suppression of billions and spreading dogma that may enslave others. One of the things that separates our society from theirs is our absolute right to propagate opinions that the government finds wrong or even hateful.

The ideas of the Klan may be propagated. Brandenburg v. Ohio, 395 U.S. 444 (1969). Communists may speak freely and run for office. DeJonge v. Oregon, 299 U.S. 353 (1937). The Nazi Party may march through a city with a large Jewish population. Collin v. Smith, 578 F.2d 1197 (7th Cir.), cert. denied, 439 U.S. 916 (1978).... People may teach religions that others despise. People may seek to repeal laws guaranteeing equal opportunity in employment or to revoke the constitutional amendments granting the vote to blacks and women. They may do this because "above all else, the First Amendment means that government has no power to restrict expression because of its message [or] its ideas...." Police Department v. Mosley, 408 U.S. 92, 95 (1972). See also Geoffrey R. Stone, Content Regulation and the First Amendment, 25 William & Mary L.Rev. 189 (1983); Paul B. Stephan, The First Amendment and Content Discrimination, 68 Va.L.Rev. 203, 233–36 (1982).

Under the ordinance graphic sexually explicit speech is "pornography" or not depending on the perspective the author adopts. Speech that "subordinates" women and also, for example, presents women as enjoying pain, humiliation, or rape, or even simply presents women in "positions of servility or submission or display" is forbidden, no matter how great the literary or political value of the work taken as a whole. Speech that portrays women in positions of equality is lawful, no matter how graphic the sexual content. This is thought control. It establishes an "approved" view of women, of how they may react to sexual encounters, of how the sexes may relate to each other. Those who espouse the approved view may use sexual images; those who do not, may not.

Indianapolis justifies the ordinance on the ground that pornography affects thoughts. Men who see women depicted as subordinate are more likely to treat them so. Pornography is an aspect of dominance. It does not persuade people so much as change them. It works by socializing, by establishing the expected and the permissible. In this view pornography is not an idea; pornography is the injury.

There is much to this perspective. Beliefs are also facts. People often act in accordance with the images and patterns they find around them. People raised in a religion tend to accept the tenets of that religion, often without independent examination. People taught from birth that black people are fit only for slavery rarely rebelled against that creed; beliefs coupled with the self-interest of the masters established a social structure that inflicted great harm while enduring for centuries. Words and images act at the level of the subconscious before they persuade at the level of the conscious. Even the truth has little chance unless a statement fits within the framework of beliefs that may never have been subjected to rational study.

Therefore we accept the premises of this legislation. Depictions of subordination tend to perpetuate subordination. The subordinate status of women in turn leads to affront and lower pay at work, insult and injury at home, battery and rape on the streets. In the language of the legislature, "[p]ornography is central in creating and maintaining sex as a basis of discrimination. Pornography is a systematic practice of exploitation and subordination based on sex which differentially harms women. The bigotry and contempt it produces, with the acts of aggression it fosters, harm women's opportunities for equality and rights [of all kinds]." Indianapolis Code § 16–1(a)(2).

Yet this simply demonstrates the power of pornography as speech. All of these unhappy effects depend on mental intermediation. Pornography affects how people see the world, their fellows, and social relations. If pornography is what pornography does, so is other speech.... The Alien and Sedition Acts passed during the administration of John Adams rested on a sincerely held belief that disrespect for the government leads to social collapse and revolution—a belief with support in the history of many nations. Most governments of the world act on this empirical regularity, suppressing critical speech. In the United States, however, the strength of the support for this belief is irrelevant. . . .

Racial bigotry, anti-Semitism, violence on television, reporters' biases—these and many more influence the culture and shape our socialization. None is directly answerable by more speech, unless that speech too finds its place in the popular culture. Yet all is protected as speech, however insidious. Any other answer leaves the government in control of all of the institutions of culture, the great censor and director of which thoughts are good for us.

Sexual responses often are unthinking responses, and the association of sexual arousal with the subordination of women therefore may have a substantial effect. But almost all cultural stimuli provoke unconscious responses. Religious ceremonies condition their participants. Teachers convey messages by selecting what not to cover; the implicit message about what is off limits or unthinkable may be more powerful than the messages for which they present rational argument. Television scripts contain unarticulated assumptions. People may be conditioned in subtle ways. If the fact that speech plays a role in a process of conditioning were enough to permit governmental regulation, that would be the end of freedom of speech.

It is possible to interpret the claim that the pornography is the harm in a different way. Indianapolis emphasizes the injury that models in pornographic films and pictures may suffer. The record contains materials depicting sexual torture, penetration of women by red-hot irons and the like. These concerns have nothing to do with written materials subject to the statute, and physical injury can occur with or without the "subordination" of women. As we discuss in Part IV, a state may make injury in the course of producing a film unlawful independent of the viewpoint expressed in the film.

The more immediate point, however, is that the image of pain is not necessarily pain. In *Body Double,* a suspense film directed by Brian DePalma, a woman who has disrobed and presented a sexually explicit display is murdered by an intruder with a drill. The drill runs through the woman's body. The film is sexually explicit and a murder occurs—yet no one believes that the actress suffered pain or died. In *Barberella* a character played by Jane Fonda is at times displayed in sexually explicit ways and at times shown "bleeding, bruised, [and] hurt in a context that makes these conditions sexual"—and again no one believes that Fonda was actually tortured to make the film. In *Carnal Knowledge* a woman grovels to please the sexual whims of a character played by Jack Nicholson; no one believes that there was a real sexual submission, and the Supreme Court held the film protected by the First Amendment. Jenkins v. Georgia, 418 U.S. 153 (1974). And this works both ways. The description of women's sexual domination of men in *Lysistrata* was not real dominance. Depictions may affect slavery, war, or sexual roles, but a book about slavery is not itself slavery, or a book about death by poison a murder.

Much of Indianapolis's argument rests on the belief that when speech is "unanswerable," and the metaphor that there is a "market-place of ideas" does not apply, the First Amendment does not apply either. The metaphor is honored; Milton's *Aeropagitica* and John Stewart Mill's *On Liberty* defend freedom of speech on the ground that the truth will prevail, and many of the most important cases under the First Amendment recite this position. The Framers undoubtedly believed it. As a general matter it is true. But the Constitution does not make the dominance of truth a necessary condition of freedom of speech. To say that it does would be to confuse an outcome of free speech with a necessary condition for the application of the amendment.

A power to limit speech on the ground that truth has not yet prevailed and is not likely to prevail implies the power to declare truth. At some point the government must be able to say (as Indianapolis has said): "We know what the truth is, yet a free exchange of speech has not driven out falsity, so that we must now prohibit falsity." If the government may declare the truth, why wait for the failure of speech? Under the First Amendment, however, there is no such thing as a false idea, Gertz v. Robert Welch, Inc., 418 U.S. 323, 339 (1974), so the government may not restrict speech on the ground that in a free exchange truth is not yet dominant.

At any time, some speech is ahead in the game; the more numerous speakers prevail. Supporters of minority candidates may be forever "excluded" from the political process because their candidates never win, because few people believe their positions. This does not mean that freedom of speech has failed.

We come, finally, to the argument that pornography is "low value" speech, that it is enough like obscenity that Indianapolis may prohibit it. Some cases hold that speech far removed from politics and other subjects at the core of the Framers' concerns may be subjected to special regulation. E.g., FCC v. Pacifica Foundation, 438 U.S. 726 (1978); Young v. American Mini Theatres, Inc., 427 U.S. 50, 67–70 (1976) (plurality opinion); Chaplinsky v. New Hampshire, 315 U.S. 568, 571–72 (1942). These cases do not sustain statutes that select among viewpoints, however. In *Pacifica* the FCC sought to keep vile language off the air during certain times. The Court held that it may; but the Court would not have sustained a regulation prohibiting scatological descriptions of Republicans but not scatological descriptions of Democrats, or any other form of selection among viewpoints. . . .

At all events, "pornography" is not low value speech within the meaning of these cases. Indianapolis seeks to prohibit certain speech because it believes this speech influences social relations and politics on a grand scale, that it controls attitudes at home and in the legislature. This precludes a characterization of the speech as low value. True, pornography and obscenity have sex in common. But Indianapolis left out of its definition any reference to literary, artistic, political, or scientific value. The ordinance applies to graphic sexually explicit subordination in works great and small.[1] The Court sometimes balances the

---

1. Indianapolis briefly argues that Beauharnais v. Illinois, 343 U.S. 250 (1952), which allowed a state to penalize "group libel," supports the ordinance. In Collin v. Smith, 578

value of speech against the costs of its restriction, but it does this by category of speech and not by the content of particular works.... Indianapolis has created an approved point of view and so loses the support of these cases.

Any rationale we could imagine in support of this ordinance could not be limited to sex discrimination. Free speech has been on balance an ally of those seeking change. Governments that want stasis start by restricting speech. Culture is a powerful force of continuity; Indianapolis paints pornography as part of the culture of power. Change in any complex system ultimately depends on the ability of outsiders to challenge accepted views and the reigning institutions. Without a strong guarantee of freedom of speech, there is no effective right to challenge what is.

IV

The definition of "pornography" is unconstitutional. No construction or excision of particular terms could save it. The offense of trafficking in pornography necessarily falls with the definition. We express no view on the district court's conclusions that the ordinance is vague and that it establishes a prior restraint. Neither is necessary to our judgment. We also express no view on the argument presented by several amici that the ordinance is itself a form of discrimination on account of sex.

NOTES AND QUESTIONS

1.   What are the differences between the term "pornography" used in the Indianapolis ordinance, and the term "obscenity"? Can you think of books or movies that would constitute "pornography" but would not be obscene? Would Judge Easterbrook's rationale have been applicable if the ordinance had defined "pornography" in exactly the way the United States Supreme Court has defined obscenity? Why wasn't it written that way?

2.   Judge Easterbrook accepted "the premises" of the Indianapolis ordinance—that depictions in literature of the subordination of women perpetuates that subordination, leading in turn to "lower pay at work, insult and injury at home, battery and rape on the streets." Is that so? If it is, how can he then conclude that the ordinance is unconstitutional? Do you agree?

3.   At the time of the decision in this case, decisions of lower federal courts holding state or local statutes unconstitutional could be reviewed by the Supreme Court on appeal. (Most other decisions of lower federal courts could only be reviewed by certiorari—meaning the Supreme Court

F.2d at 1205, we concluded that cases such as New York Times v. Sullivan had so washed away the foundations of *Beauharnais* that it could not be considered authoritative. If we are wrong in this, however, the case still does not support the ordinance. It is not clear that depicting women as subordinate in sexually explicit ways, even combined with a depiction of pleasure in rape, would fit within the definition of a group libel. The well received film *Swept Away* used explicit sex, plus taking pleasure in rape, to make a political statement, not to defame. Work must be an insult or slur for its own sake to come within the ambit of *Beauharnais,* and a work need not be scurrilous at all to be "pornography" under the ordinance.

had discretion whether or not to hear the case. The provision for appeals in cases holding state statutes unconstitutional has now been amended to provide for discretionary review by certiorari in those cases as well.) The Court of Appeals decision that the ordinance was unconstitutional was appealed to the United States Supreme Court. The Supreme Court affirmed the decision, without hearing argument or writing an opinion. 475 U.S. 1001 (1986). (Three justices—Chief Justice Burger and Justices Rehnquist and O'Connor dissented from the Court's failure to schedule the case for argument. Under the Supreme Court's practices, it takes four votes to schedule a case for argument.) Supreme Court affirmance, on appeal, of a lower federal court's decision, unlike a discretionary refusal to hear a case, is a precedent binding lower courts. The precedent is ambiguous, however, since the affirmance without opinion does not necessarily approve what the lower court said, or even the rationale for its decision.

4. The trial court awarded counsel for the plaintiffs in *Hudnut* more than $90,000 in legal fees. Total legal costs paid by Indianapolis exceeded $200,000. As a result, Indianapolis leaders, according to Downs, "were wary of adopting any new radical approaches to pornography. For the time, at least, enthusiasm for the politics of pornography was at a low ebb." As one city official said: "I doubt that we'll spend that kind of money again.... There will be more weighing of costs ... in the future.... At least we're a community that tried."*

C. OFFENSIVENESS

ON OBSCENITY, MORALS AND ESTHETICS**

The civil libertarian position on obscenity is that if we forget about it, it will go away. We aren't told to admire the king's beautiful cloak. We are told not to care whether he has one or not. Walter Berns[†] is the little boy who said the king is naked, and added that it makes a hell of a difference.

Never mind whether books get girls pregnant, or whether sexy or violent movies turn men to crime. Assume that they do not, or that, at any rate, there are plenty of other efficient causes of pregnancy and crime. Assume further that we must protect privacy; that government, therefore, properly has no business punishing anyone for amusing himself obscenely in his home, and must ignore the means by which he may have obtained his obscene materials, if all it knows is that he uses them at home; assume, in other words, that the Supreme Court was right in Stanley v. Georgia, in 1969, when it held: "Whatever may be the justifications for other statutes regulating obscenity, we do not think they reach into the privacy of one's own home. If the First Amendment means anything, it means that a State has no business telling a man,

---

* Downs, The New Politics of Pornography, p. 140. Reprinted with permission.

** Alexander Bickel, On Pornography: II, Dissenting and Concurring Opinions, The Public Interest, 1971, vol. 22, pp. 25–28. Reprinted with permission.

† See p. 390.

sitting alone in his house, what books he may read or what films he may watch."

Take these assumptions, and still you are left with at least one problem of large proportions. It concerns the tone of the society, the mode, or to use terms that have perhaps greater currency, the style and quality of life, now and in the future. A man may be entitled to read an obscene book in his room, or expose himself indecently there, or masturbate, or flog himself, if that is possible, or what have you. We should protect his privacy. But if he demands a right to obtain the books and pictures he wants in the market, and to foregather in public places— discreet, if you will, but accessible to all—with others who share his tastes, then to grant him his right is to affect the world about the rest of us, and to impinge on other privacies. Even supposing that each of us can, if he wishes, effectively avert the eye and stop the ear (which, in truth, we cannot), what is commonly read and seen and heard and done intrudes upon us all, want it or not. As Berns says, how is a parent who would teach his children the impropriety of certain forms of speech going "to overcome the power of common usage and the idea of propriety it implies?"

Now, not only books and pictures and speech, but all sorts of behavior and artifacts—architecture, fashions in clothes and in other aspects of personal appearance, habits such as smoking and drinking, overt public homosexuality—all affect the mode and quality of life, all impinge unavoidably on the privacy of each of us. Yet each of us cannot but tolerate a very great deal that violates our freedom and privacy in these senses, because the alternative is to let government, acting perhaps in behalf of a majority, control it all; and that is tyranny—massive tyranny, if it works, selective or occasional and random tyranny if, as is more likely, it does not work very well.

So, as Berns is well aware, to identify the problem of obscenity truly is to expose its intractability. But to lapse into total permissiveness about obscenity, to equate it with smoking and drinking and the miniskirt, is not the sole option left to us. The problem is no less intractable as it is raised by the physical environment, or by extremities of fashion which are called indecent exposure, or by extremities of behavior, such as boisterous drunkenness or open lovemaking, hetero or homo. Yet the same Supreme Court which during the past decade has decreed virtually unlimited permissiveness with regard to obscenity has not construed the Constitution so as to forbid the placing of legal restraints on architectural designs, for example, or on indecencies of public behavior, and is not likely to do so. Nor is the Court very likely to tell us that fostering heterosexual marriage while not countenancing homosexual unions— which is what the legal order does, of course—is unconstitutional. The reason cannot be that the First Amendment throws special safeguards around speech and other forms of communication, which are relevant to obscenity. That is not even a significant technical point, because the relevant protections are drawn as much from the Due Process Clause of the Fourteenth Amendment as from the First. And in substance, the point is absurd. There is no bright line between communication and conduct. The effect, in the segment of both that we are here considering, is the same. What is *Oh, Calcutta* ? Communication or conduct?

Law which attempts to come to grips with the problem of obscenity—or aesthetics in the physical environment, or drinking, or exposure of the body, or drug-taking, or offensive or assaultive speech—is a different kind of instrument, running greater risks and expecting to attain a rather more remote approximation of its ends, than the law which forbids murder and theft, or defines the rights and obligations of a property-owner, or governs the relations between General Motors and the United Automobile Workers of America.

Very little of what is called law achieves its ends always or precisely. But much of it tries to, because it is fully confident of the validity of its ends, which it can and does define intelligibly and with some precision. A law attempting to regulate obscenity, however, has to exist in a peculiar tension. It must avoid tyrannical enforcement of supposed majority tastes, while providing visible support for the diffuse private endeavors of an overwhelming majority of people to sustain the style and quality of life minimally congenial to them. This sort of law, . . . necessarily accepts a certain ambiguity about its ends.

The short of it, then, is that its very existence, and occasional but steady enforcement in aggravated cases for the sake of making itself visible, is the real and virtually sole purpose of a law against obscenity. Its role is supportive, tentative, even provisional. It walks a tight-rope, and runs high risks. Every so often in some corner of the country, some idiot finds Chaucer obscene or the lower female leg indecent. For this reason, the federal government itself, as Justice Harlan has long argued, and as Chief Justice Burger agrees, should stay out of the business of censorship altogether, because its idiocies, when they occur, affect the whole country. But the Supreme Court, while exercising procedural oversight, ought to let state and local governments run the risks if they wish. For the stakes, . . . are high.

QUESTIONS

Is Professor Bickel directing his attention to moral or esthetic concerns? Is there much of a difference?

EXCERPT FROM A DISSENTING OPINION
BY JUSTICE DOUGLAS*

People are, of course, offended by many offerings made by merchants in this area. They are also offended by political pronouncements, sociological themes, and by stories of official misconduct. The list of activities and publications and pronouncements that offend someone is endless. Some of it goes on in private; some of it is inescapably public, as when a government official generates crime, becomes a blatant offender of the moral sensibilities of the people, engages in burglary, or breaches the privacy of the telephone, the conference room, or the home. Life in this crowded modern technological world creates many offensive state-

---

* Paris Adult Theatre I v. Slaton, 413 U.S. 49, 70, 71–73 (1973).

ments and many offensive deeds. There is no protection against offensive ideas, only against offensive conduct.

"Obscenity" at most is the expression of offensive ideas. There are regimes in the world where ideas "offensive" to the majority (or at least to those who control the majority) are suppressed. There life proceeds at a monotonous pace. Most of us would find that world offensive. One of the most offensive experiences in my life was a visit to a nation where bookstalls were filled only with books on mathematics and books on religion.

I am sure I would find offensive most of the books and movies charged with being obscene. But in a life that has not been short, I have yet to be trapped into seeing or reading something that would offend me. I never read or see the materials coming to the Court under charges of "obscenity," because I have thought the First Amendment made it unconstitutional for me to act as a censor. I see ads in bookstores and neon lights over theaters that resemble bait for those who seek vicarious exhilaration. As a parent or a priest or as a teacher I would have no compunction in edging my children or wards away from the books and movies that did no more than excite man's base instincts. But I never supposed that government was permitted to sit in judgment on one's tastes or beliefs—save as they involved action within the reach of the police power of government.

When man was first in the jungle he took care of himself. When he entered a societal group, controls were necessarily imposed. But our society—unlike most in the world—presupposes that freedom and liberty are in a frame of reference that makes the individual, not government, the keeper of his tastes, beliefs, and ideas. That is the philosophy of the First Amendment; and it is the article of faith that sets us apart from most nations in the world.

QUESTIONS

Is offensiveness, after all is said, *the* justification for First Amendment standards that permit control of obscenity? Would the obscenity decisions then support control of other forms of offensive speech? (For the answer to the latter question, turn to the next chapter.)

Chapter XII

FIGHTING WORDS AND OFFENSIVE SPEECH

CHAPLINSKY v. NEW HAMPSHIRE

Supreme Court of the United States, 1942.
315 U.S. 568, 62 S.Ct. 766, 86 L.Ed. 1031.

JUSTICE MURPHY delivered the opinion of the Court.

FRANK MURPHY—Born on April 13, 1890, in Sand Beach, Michigan, son of a country lawyer. Democrat. Roman Catholic. Michigan, A.B., 1912; LL.B., 1914. After serving as an army officer in World War I, studied briefly at Lincoln's Inn, London, and Trinity College, Dublin. Practiced law, 1916–1917, 1920–1923; chief assistant U.S. attorney, Eastern District of Michigan, 1920–1923; taught law part-time at the University of Detroit, 1922–1927; judge, Detroit Recorder's Court 1923–1930; Detroit mayor, 1930–1933; U.S. high commissioner and governor general of the Philippines, 1935–1936; Michigan governor, 1936–1938; U.S. attorney general, 1939–1940. Nominated associate justice on January 4, 1939, by President Franklin D. Roosevelt to replace Pierce Butler. Confirmed by the Senate on January 15, 1940, by voice vote. Murphy was one of the most liberal justices in the Court's history. In 1944, Frankfurter passed him a note while they were on the bench that said: "F.M.'s clients: Reds, Whores, Crooks, Indians and all other Colored people, Longshoremen, M'grs and all other Debtors, R.R. employees, Pacifists, Traitors, Japs, Women, Children, Most men." Murphy probably took the note as a compliment. He once said that members of minority groups were what he had "instead of children," and he would do all that he could to protect them. Died in office on July 19, 1949.

Appellant, a member of the sect known as Jehovah's Witnesses, was convicted in the municipal court of Rochester, New Hampshire, for violation of Chapter 378, § 2, of the Public Laws of New Hampshire:

"No person shall address any offensive, derisive or annoying word to any other person who is lawfully in any street or other public place, nor call him by any offensive or derisive name, nor make any noise or exclamation in his presence and hearing with intent to deride, offend or annoy him, or to prevent him from pursuing his lawful business or occupation."

The complaint charged that appellant, "with force and arms, in a certain public place in said city of Rochester, to wit, on the public sidewalk on the easterly side of Wakefield Street, near unto the entrance of the City Hall, did unlawfully repeat, the words following, addressed to the complainant, that is to say, 'You are a God damned racketeer' and 'a damned Fascist and the whole government of Rochester are Fascists or agents of Fascists,' the same being offensive, derisive and annoying words and names."

He was found guilty and the judgment of conviction was affirmed by the Supreme Court of the State.

... [A]ppellant raised the questions that the statute was invalid under the Fourteenth Amendment of the Constitution of the United States, in that it placed an unreasonable restraint on freedom of speech, freedom of the press, and freedom of worship, and because it was vague and indefinite.

There is no substantial dispute over the facts. Chaplinsky was distributing the literature of his sect on the streets of Rochester on a busy Saturday afternoon. Members of the local citizenry complained to the City Marshal, Bowering, that Chaplinsky was denouncing all religion as a "racket." Bowering told them that Chaplinsky was lawfully engaged, and then warned Chaplinsky that the crowd was getting restless. Some time later, a disturbance occurred and the traffic officer on duty at the busy intersection started with Chaplinsky for the police station, but did not inform him that he was under arrest or that he was going to be arrested. On the way, they encountered Marshal Bowering, who had been advised that a riot was under way and was therefore hurrying to the scene. Bowering repeated his earlier warning to Chaplinsky, who then addressed to Bowering the words set forth in the complaint.

Allowing the broadest scope to the language and purpose of the Fourteenth Amendment, it is well understood that the right of free speech is not absolute at all times and under all circumstances. There are certain well-defined and narrowly limited classes of speech, the prevention and punishment of which have never been thought to raise any Constitutional problem. These include the lewd and obscene, the profane, the libelous, and the insulting or "fighting" words—those which by their very utterance inflict injury or tend to incite an immediate breach of the peace. It has been well observed that such utterances are no essential part of any exposition of ideas, and are of such slight social value as a step to truth that any benefit that may be derived from them is clearly outweighed by the social interest in order and morality. "Resort to epithets or personal abuse is not in any proper sense communication of information or opinion safeguarded by the Constitution, and its punishment as a criminal act would raise no question under that instrument." Cantwell v. Connecticut, 310 U.S. 296, 309–310.

On the authority of its earlier decisions, the state court declared that the statute's purpose was to preserve the public peace, no words being "forbidden except such as have a direct tendency to cause acts of violence by the persons to whom, individually, the remark is addressed." ... The statute, as construed, does no more than prohibit the face-to-face words plainly likely to cause a breach of the peace by the addressee, words whose speaking constitutes a breach of the peace by the speaker—

including "classical fighting words", words in current use less "classical" but equally likely to cause violence, and other disorderly words, including profanity, obscenity and threats.

We are unable to say that the limited scope of the statute as thus construed contravenes the Constitutional right of free expression. It is a statute narrowly drawn and limited to define and punish specific conduct lying within the domain of state power, the use in a public place of words likely to cause a breach of the peace....

Nor can we say that the application of the statute to the facts disclosed by the record substantially or unreasonably impinges upon the privilege of free speech. Argument is unnecessary to demonstrate that the appellations "damned racketeer" and "damned Fascist" are epithets likely to provoke the average person to retaliation, and thereby cause a breach of the peace.

NOTES AND QUESTIONS

1.   Since Justice Murphy said there was no substantial dispute over the facts, Chaplinsky's version of the events leading up to his arrest merits quotation:*

> While appellant was ... engaged in his [religious] work, a mob formed around him on the sidewalk, a tumultuous crowd of about fifty or sixty persons objected to his work and threatened him with violence if he did not discontinue. While the crowd was still around him, City Marshal Bowering, accompanied by a man named Bowman, came through the crowd and accosted appellant, and Bowman assaulted the appellant, catching him by the throat with his left hand and struck at him with his right fist, whereupon appellant wrenched himself free and turned to Marshal Bowering and said, "Marshal, I want you to arrest this man," and Bowering answered, "I will if I feel like it."

> The Marshal walked away with Bowman and the appellant continued his work of offering the magazines containing the message of God's Kingdom for distribution on the sidewalk. In about four or five minutes appellant looked down South Main Street and saw Bowman coming rapidly down the street with a staff and flag in his hand, with the staff pointed towards appellant. As Bowman came within about ten feet of appellant, he made a terrific lunge at appellant with the flagstaff as a spear in an effort to plunge the flagstaff through appellant, who avoided the blow, but was pushed by Bowman into the gutter against an automobile as he passed appellant. Bowman then walked to the corner and gave the flag to another man and came back toward appellant and caught him by the collar and said, "You son of a bitch—." Bowman then asked the appellant, "Will you salute the flag?"

> The Marshal, Officer Lapierre and two others picked him up from the ground and started him along Wakefield Street

* Appellant's Brief, Chaplinsky v. New Hampshire, pp. 3–4.

toward the City Hall, shoving him along roughly. While so doing, the appellant turned to the Marshal and asked, "Will you please arrest the ones who started this fight?" and the Marshal replied, "Shut up, you damn bastard, and come along," where-upon appellant said to him, "You are a damn Fascist and a racketeer."

Under these facts, did Chaplinsky's statement inflict injury? If so, what was the injury and whom did it injure? Was the statement likely to cause a breach of the peace? If so, who would have been incited? Bowering? An average person? Did Chaplinsky's statement contain any ideas? Was the statement a political protest? If it contained ideas or was a political protest, could it still be labeled fighting words? See Chafee's discussion on pages 355–357, supra.

2.   Note that Justice Black, who took an absolutist position on free speech, joined Justice Murphy's opinion in *Chaplinsky*. Yarbrough gives two explanations for Black joining the *Chaplinsky* opinion—(1) Justice Black had not yet formulated his absolutist stance, and (2) "the speech in question was merely part of a course of conduct."* Which is the better explanation?

THE IMPACT OF CHAPLINSKY

After *Chaplinsky*, the Supreme Court never upheld another conviction punishing "fighting words." Indeed, over time, the Court narrowed this category of unprotected expression. But state courts have used the precedent to justify the punishment of such expression, and universities have used it to justify their anti-harassment speech codes.

COHEN v. CALIFORNIA

Supreme Court of the United States, 1971.
403 U.S. 15, 91 S.Ct. 1780, 29 L.Ed.2d 284.

JUSTICE HARLAN delivered the opinion of the Court.

This case may seem at first blush too inconsequential to find its way into our books, but the issue it presents is of no small constitutional significance.

Appellant Paul Robert Cohen was convicted in the Los Angeles Municipal Court of violating that part of California Penal Code § 415 which prohibits "maliciously and willfully disturb[ing] the peace or quiet of any neighborhood or person ... by ... offensive conduct...." He was given 30 days' imprisonment. The facts upon which his conviction rests are detailed in the opinion of the Court of Appeal of California, Second Appellate District, as follows:

---

* Tinsley Yarbrough, Mr. Justice Black and His Critics, Duke University Press, 1988, p. 165.

JOHN MARSHALL HARLAN II—Born on May 20, 1899, in Chicago, Illinois, grandson of Supreme Court Justice John Marshall Harlan and son of a prominent lawyer and reform politician. Republican. Episcopalian. Princeton, B.A., 1920; Oxford, Rhodes Scholar, B.A., 1923; New York Law School, LL.B., 1924. Assistant U.S. attorney, Southern District, New York, 1925–1927; special assistant N.Y. attorney general, 1928–1930, 1951–1953; practiced law, 1931–1943, 1945–1954. Served as an air force colonel in England during World War II and was a member of a committee that planned the occupation of Germany. Chief counsel, New York Crime Commission, 1951–1953; U.S. Court of Appeals judge (Second Circuit), 1954–1955. Nominated associate justice on November 8, 1954, by President Dwight D. Eisenhower to replace Robert H. Jackson. Confirmed by the Senate on March 16, 1955, by a 71–11 vote. Retired on September 23, 1971. Died on December 29, 1971.

"On April 26, 1968, the defendant was observed in the Los Angeles County Courthouse in the corridor outside of division 20 of the municipal court wearing a jacket bearing the words 'Fuck the Draft' which were plainly visible. There were women and children present in the corridor. The defendant was arrested. The defendant testified that he wore the jacket knowing that the words were on the jacket as a means of informing the public of the depth of his feelings against the Vietnam War and the draft.

"The defendant did not engage in, nor threaten to engage in, nor did anyone as the result of his conduct in fact commit or threaten to commit any act of violence. The defendant did not make any loud or unusual noise, nor was there any evidence that he uttered any sound prior to his arrest."

In affirming the conviction the Court of Appeal held that "offensive conduct" means "behavior which has a tendency to provoke *others* to acts of violence or to in turn disturb the peace," and that the State had proved this element because, on the facts of this case, "[i]t was certainly reasonably foreseeable that such conduct might cause others to rise up to commit a violent act against the person of the defendant or attempt to forceably remove his jacket." . . .

In order to lay hands on the precise issue which this case involves, it is useful first to canvass various matters which this record does *not* present.

The conviction quite clearly rests upon the asserted offensiveness of the *words* Cohen used to convey his message to the public. The only "conduct" which the State sought to punish is the fact of communication. Thus, we deal here with a conviction resting solely upon "speech," . . . Further, the State certainly lacks power to punish Cohen for the underlying content of the message the inscription conveyed. At least so long as there is no showing of an intent to incite disobedience to or disruption of the draft, Cohen could not, consistently with the First and Fourteenth Amendments, be punished for asserting the evident position on the inutility or immorality of the draft his jacket reflected.

Appellant's conviction, then, rests squarely upon his exercise of the "freedom of speech" protected from arbitrary governmental interference by the Constitution and can be justified, if at all, only as a valid regulation of the manner in which he exercised that freedom, not as a permissible prohibition on the substantive message it conveys. This does not end the inquiry, of course, for the First and Fourteenth Amendments have never been thought to give absolute protection to every individual to speak whenever or wherever he pleases, or to use any form of address in any circumstances that he chooses. In this vein, too, however, we think it important to note that several issues typically associated with such problems are not presented here.

In the first place, Cohen was tried under a statute applicable throughout the entire State. Any attempt to support this conviction on the ground that the statute seeks to preserve an appropriately decorous atmosphere in the courthouse where Cohen was arrested must fail in the absence of any language in the statute that would have put appellant on notice that certain kinds of otherwise permissible speech or conduct would nevertheless, under California law, not be tolerated in certain places. No fair reading of the phrase "offensive conduct" can be said sufficiently to inform the ordinary person that distinctions between certain locations are thereby created.[1]

In the second place, as it comes to us, this case cannot be said to fall within those relatively few categories of instances where prior decisions have established the power of government to deal more comprehensively with certain forms of individual expression simply upon a showing that such a form was employed. This is not, for example, an obscenity case. Whatever else may be necessary to give rise to the States' broader power to prohibit obscene expression, such expression must be, in some significant way, erotic. Roth v. United States, 354 U.S. 476 (1957). It cannot plausibly be maintained that this vulgar allusion to the Selective Service System would conjure up such psychic stimulation in anyone likely to be confronted with Cohen's crudely defaced jacket.

This Court has also held that the States are free to ban the simple use, without a demonstration of additional justifying circumstances, of so-called "fighting words," those personally abusive epithets which, when addressed to the ordinary citizen, are, as a matter of common knowledge, inherently likely to provoke violent reaction. Chaplinsky v. New Hampshire, 315 U.S. 568 (1942). While the four-letter word displayed by Cohen in relation to the draft is not uncommonly employed in a personally provocative fashion, in this instance it was clearly not "directed to the person of the hearer." Cantwell v. Connecticut, 310 U.S. 296, 309 (1940). No individual actually or likely to be present could reasonably have regarded the words on appellant's jacket as a direct personal insult. Nor do we have here an instance of the exercise of the State's police power to prevent a speaker from intentionally provoking a

---

1. It is illuminating to note what transpired when Cohen entered a courtroom in the building. He removed his jacket and stood with it folded over his arm. Meanwhile, a policeman sent the presiding judge a note suggesting that Cohen be held in contempt of court. The judge declined to do so and Cohen was arrested by the officer only after he emerged from the courtroom.

given group to hostile reaction. Cf. Feiner v. New York, 340 U.S. 315 (1951); Terminiello v. Chicago, 337 U.S. 1 (1949). There is, as noted above, no showing that anyone who saw Cohen was in fact violently aroused or that appellant intended such a result.

Finally, in arguments before this Court much has been made of the claim that Cohen's distasteful mode of expression was thrust upon unwilling or unsuspecting viewers, and that the State might therefore legitimately act as it did in order to protect the sensitive from otherwise unavoidable exposure to appellant's crude form of protest. Of course, the mere presumed presence of unwitting listeners or viewers does not serve automatically to justify curtailing all speech capable of giving offense.

In this regard, persons confronted with Cohen's packet were in a quite different posture than, say, those subjected to the raucous emissions of sound trucks blaring outside their residences. Those in the Los Angeles courthouse could effectively avoid further bombardment of their sensibilities simply by averting their eyes. And, while it may be that one has a more substantial claim to a recognizable privacy interest when walking through a courthouse corridor than, for example, strolling through Central Park, surely it is nothing like the interest in being free from unwanted expression in the confines of one's own home....

Against this background, the issue flushed by this case stands out in bold relief. It is whether California can excise, as "offensive conduct," one particular scurrilous epithet from the public discourse, either upon the theory of the court below that its use is inherently likely to cause violent reaction or upon a more general assertion that the States, acting as guardians of public morality, may properly remove this offensive word from the public vocabulary.

The rationale of the California court is plainly untenable. At most it reflects an "undifferentiated fear or apprehension of disturbance [which] is not enough to overcome the right to freedom of expression." Tinker v. Des Moines Indep. Community School Dist., 393 U.S. 503, 508 (1969). We have been shown no evidence that substantial numbers of citizens are standing ready to strike out physically at whoever may assault their sensibilities with execrations like that uttered by Cohen.

Admittedly, it is not so obvious that the First and Fourteenth Amendments must be taken to disable the States from punishing public utterance of this unseemly expletive in order to maintain what they regard as a suitable level of discourse within the body politic. We think, however, that examination and reflection will reveal the shortcomings of a contrary viewpoint.

At the outset, we cannot overemphasize that, in our judgment, most situations where the State has a justifiable interest in regulating speech will fall within one or more of the various established exceptions, discussed above but not applicable here, to the usual rule that governmental bodies may not prescribe the form or content of individual expression. Equally important to our conclusion is the constitutional backdrop against which our decision must be made. The constitutional right of free expression is powerful medicine in a society as diverse and populous as ours. It is designed and intended to remove governmental restraints from the arena of public discussion, putting the decision as to what views shall be voiced largely into the hands of each of us, in the hope that use of such freedom will ultimately produce a more capable citizenry and more perfect polity and in the belief that no other approach would comport with the premise of individual dignity and choice upon which our political system rests.

To many, the immediate consequence of this freedom may often appear to be only verbal tumult, discord, and even offensive utterance. These are, however, within established limits, in truth necessary side effects of the broader enduring values which the process of open debate permits us to achieve. That the air may at times seem filled with verbal cacophony is, in this sense not a sign of weakness but of strength. . . .

Against this perception of the constitutional policies involved, we discern certain more particularized considerations that peculiarly call for reversal of this conviction. First, the principle contended for by the State seems inherently boundless. How is one to distinguish this from any other offensive word? Surely the State has no right to cleanse public debate to the point where it is grammatically palatable to the most squeamish among us. Yet no readily ascertainable general principle exists for stopping short of that result were we to affirm the judgment below. For, while the particular four-letter word being litigated here is perhaps more distasteful than most others of its genre, it is nevertheless often true that one man's vulgarity is another's lyric. Indeed, we think it is largely because governmental officials cannot make principled distinctions in this area that the Constitution leaves matters of taste and style so largely to the individual.

Additionally, we cannot overlook the fact, because it is well illustrated by the episode involved here, that much linguistic expression serves a dual communicative function: it conveys not only ideas capable of relatively precise, detached explication, but otherwise inexpressible emotions as well. In fact, words are often chosen as much for their emotive as their cognitive force. We cannot sanction the view that the Constitution, while solicitous of the cognitive content of individual speech, has little or no regard for that emotive function which, practically speaking, may often be the more important element of the overall message sought to be communicated. . . .

Finally, and in the same vein, we cannot indulge the facile assumption that one can forbid particular words without also running a substantial risk of suppressing ideas in the process. Indeed, governments might soon seize upon the censorship of particular words as a convenient guise for banning the expression of unpopular views. We have been able, as noted above, to discern little social benefit that might result from running the risk of opening the door to such grave results.

It is, in sum, our judgment that, absent a more particularized and compelling reason for its actions, the State may not, consistently with the First and Fourteenth Amendments, make the simple public display here involved of this single four-letter expletive a criminal offense.

JUSTICE BLACKMUN, with whom THE CHIEF JUSTICE and JUSTICE BLACK join.

I dissent . . .

Cohen's absurd and immature antic, in my view, was mainly conduct and little speech. The California Court of Appeal appears so to have described it, and I cannot characterize it otherwise. Further, the case appears to me to be well within the sphere of Chaplinsky v. New Hampshire, 315 U.S. 568 (1942), where Justice Murphy, a known champion of First Amendment freedoms, wrote for a unanimous bench. As a consequence, this Court's agonizing over First Amendment values seems misplaced and unnecessary.

NOTES AND QUESTIONS

1.   Justice Harlan's opinion in *Cohen* has been called "balancing, at its best." Note that he weighs the advantages and disadvantages of prohibiting this kind of speech, together with First Amendment values, and freedom of speech does not lose. Do you think he is correct, however?

2.   In a footnote to his opinion in *Cohen,* Justice Harlan indicates that after Cohen entered the courtroom, "[h]e removed his jacket and stood with it folded over his arm. Meanwhile, a policeman sent the presiding judge a note suggesting that Cohen be held in contempt of court. The judge declined to do so and Cohen was arrested by the officer only after he emerged from the courtroom." Would Cohen's rights under the First Amendment have been infringed if he had been held in contempt of court? Suppose he had been asked by the judge to fold his jacket so other people couldn't see its message, and he had refused.

3.   Suppose Cohen had been convicted for violating a statute that punished the public display of "obscenity." Would the conviction have been a violation of his constitutional rights? Suppose that Cohen's jacket had a picture on it illustrating the verb on his jacket. Can the *Cohen* decision be reconciled with the Court's decisions on obscenity?

4.   Justice Black, who, as we have seen, argued that the First Amendment is "absolute," joined in Justice Blackmun's dissent. The clue to his agreement may be the opening sentence that what Cohen did "was mainly conduct and little speech." Would it be "conduct" if Cohen was carrying a sign? Would it have been conduct if Cohen had said the words on his jacket? (He would be moving his lips?)

5.   On May 25, 1971, Chief Justice Burger circulated a dissenting opinion, which he said was "the most restrained utterance" he could manage. In that opinion, which he later decided not to publish, he wrote: "I, too, join in a word of protest that this Court's limited resources of time should be devoted to such a case as this. It is a measure of a lack of a sense of priorities and with all deference I submit that Mr. Justice Harlan's 'first blush' was the correct reaction. It is nothing short of absurd nonsense that juvenile delinquents and their emotionally unstable outbursts should command the attention of this Court." Do you agree? William J. Brennan Papers, Library of Congress, Box 242.

GOODING, WARDEN v. WILSON

Supreme Court of the United States, 1972.
405 U.S. 518, 92 S.Ct. 1103, 31 L.Ed.2d 408.

JUSTICE BRENNAN delivered the opinion of the Court.

[Wilson was one of a group of people picketing a building in which an army headquarters was located. When police tried to remove the demonstrators, a scuffle ensued. Wilson was convicted of assault and battery on two arresting police officers, but that conviction was not before the Supreme Court. The issue before the Court concerned Wilson's use of this language to the arresting officers: "White son of a bitch, I'll kill you" and "You son of a bitch, I'll choke you to death." In addition to his assault and battery conviction, Wilson had been convicted of using "opprobrious words or abusive language, tending to cause a breach of the peace."]

[The Georgia statute] punishes only spoken words. It can therefore withstand appellee's attack upon its facial constitutionality only if, as authoritatively construed by the Georgia courts, it is not susceptible of application to speech, although vulgar or offensive, that is protected by the First and Fourteenth Amendments.... It matters not that the words appellee used might have been constitutionally prohibited under a narrowly and precisely drawn statute....

The constitutional guarantees of freedom of speech forbid the States to punish the use of words or language not within "narrowly limited classes of speech." Chaplinsky v. New Hampshire, 315 U.S. 568, 571 (1942).... [T]he statute must be carefully drawn or be authoritatively construed to punish only unprotected speech and not be susceptible of application to protected expression....

Appellant does not challenge these principles but contends that the Georgia statute is narrowly drawn to apply only to a constitutionally unprotected class of words—"fighting" words—"those which by their very utterance inflict injury or tend to incite an immediate breach of the peace." Chaplinsky v. New Hampshire, supra, at 572....

... Our decisions since Chaplinsky have continued to recognize state power constitutionally to punish "fighting" words under carefully drawn statutes not also susceptible of application to protected expression. We reaffirm that proposition today.

Appellant argues that the Georgia appellate courts have by construction limited the proscription of § 26–6303 to "fighting" words, as the New Hampshire Supreme Court limited the New Hampshire statute.... We have ... made our own examination of the Georgia cases, both those cited and others discovered in research. That examination brings us to the conclusion, in agreement with the courts below, that the Georgia appellate decisions have not construed [the law] to be limited in application, as in *Chaplinsky,* to words that "have a direct tendency to cause acts of violence by the person to whom, individually, the remark is addressed."

The dictionary definitions of "opprobrious" and "abusive" give them greater reach than "fighting" words. Webster's Third New International Dictionary (1961) defined "opprobrious" as "conveying or intended to convey disgrace," and "abusive" as including "harsh insulting language." Georgia appellate decisions have construed [the law] to apply to utterances that, although within these definitions, are not "fighting" words as *Chaplinsky* defines them. In Lyons v. State, 94 Ga.App. 570, 95 S.E.2d 478 (1956), a conviction under the statute was sustained for awakening 10 women scout leaders on a camp-out by shouting, "Boys, this is where we are going to spend the night." "Get the G—d—bed rolls out ... let's see how close we can come to the G—d—tents." ...

Moreover, in Samuels v. State, 103 Ga.App. 66, 67, 118 S.E.2d 231, 232 (1961), the Court of Appeals, in applying another statute, adopted from a textbook the common-law definition of "breach of the peace."

> "The term 'breach of the peace' is generic, and includes all violations of the public peace or order, or decorum; in other words, it signifies the offense of disturbing the public peace or tranquility enjoyed by the citizens of a community. By 'peace,' as used in this connection, is meant the tranquility enjoyed by the citizens of a municipality or a community where good order reigns among its members."

This definition makes it a "breach of peace" merely to speak words offensive to some who hear them, and so sweeps too broadly.

Justice Powell and Justice Rehnquist took no part in the consideration or decision of this case.

Justice Blackmun, with whom The Chief Justice joins, dissenting.

It seems strange, indeed, that in this day a man may say to a police officer, who is attempting to restore access to a public building, "White son of a bitch, I'll kill you" and "You son of a bitch, I'll choke you to death," and say to an accompanying officer, "You son of a bitch, if you ever put your hands on me again, I'll cut you all to pieces," and yet constitutionally cannot be prosecuted and convicted under a state statute that makes it a misdemeanor to "use to or of another, and in his presence ... opprobrious words or abusive language, tending to cause a breach of the peace...." This, however, is precisely what the Court pronounces as the law today.

For me, Chaplinsky v. New Hampshire, 315 U.S. 568 (1942), was good law when it was decided and deserves to remain as good law now. A unanimous Court, including among its members Chief Justice Stone and Justices Black, Reed, Douglas, and Murphy, obviously thought it was good law. But I feel that by decisions such as this one and, indeed, Cohen v. California, 403 U.S. 15 (1971), the Court, despite its protestations to the contrary, is merely paying lip service to *Chaplinsky*. As the appellee states in a footnote to his brief, p. 14, "Although there is no doubt that the state can punish 'fighting words' this appears to be about all that is left of the decision in *Chaplinsky*." If this is what the overbreadth doctrine means, and if this is what it produces, it urgently needs re-examination. The Court has painted itself into a corner from which it, and the States, can extricate themselves only with difficulty.

NOTES AND QUESTIONS

1.   We hesitate to inflict the "overbreadth" doctrine on our readers. Unfortunately, some understanding of this rather technical rule of law is necessary to an understanding of the *Gooding* case. If a person is convicted for the use of language, there are two different possible reasons for upsetting his conviction. One reason would be that his words were protected by the Constitution, and he couldn't be punished under *any* statute. The second reason would be that, whether or not his words were protected by the Constitution, the statute under which he was convicted violated the Constitution. That is what happened in the *Gooding* case, the Court deciding that since the statute was invalid for "overbreadth," no one could be punished for violating it.

Most simply stated, the overbreadth doctrine requires that a statute be invalidated if it is fairly capable of being applied to punish people for constitutionally protected speech. The argument is that people who fear prosecution and punishment will try to "steer clear" and that constitutionally protected speech will be deterred by an "overbroad" statute. Thus, even someone who could be punished under a "narrowly drawn" statute is allowed to raise the argument that other people's constitutional rights to freedom of speech might be infringed by the law. The Court noted that the statute under which Gooding was convicted had been applied in the past to punish all forms of offensive speech, much of which would be constitutionally protected. Since the statute could be applied to deny constitutional rights in other situations, whether or not Gooding could be punished for his "fighting words," his conviction under that statute was invalid.

The overbreadth doctrine presents questions of degree. The controversial issue is how far a court should search out possible unconstitutional applications of a law to upset the conviction of someone whose speech could be punished if the law had been more carefully worded. It has sometimes been argued that courts use the overbreadth doctrine (and some similar rules) as "devices" to avoid hard questions as to whether the defendant's speech is constitutionally protected. Do you think this was the case in *Gooding* ?

2.   Suppose defendant is arrested at his home by a police officer, who is executing an arrest warrant for some outstanding traffic offenses. Defendant does not resist arrest, but calls the arresting officer a "white son of a bitch." Would it be a denial of the defendant's constitutional rights to convict him under a criminal statute limited to punishing "fighting words"?

3.   In a situation identical to that of the previous questions, suppose the defendant calls the policeman a "God damned racketeer" and a "damned Fascist." Would it violate the constitution to punish him for fighting words?

4.   In Lewis v. City of New Orleans, 408 U.S. 913 (1972), the defendant called a police officer a "g—d——m——f——" policeman.

(The quote is taken verbatim from Justice Powell's opinion.) The case was remanded for reconsideration in light of Gooding v. Wilson. Justice Powell, concurring, said:

> If these words had been addressed by one citizen to another, face to face and in a hostile manner, I would have no doubt they would be 'fighting words.' But the situation may be different where such words are addressed to a police officer trained to exercise a higher degree of restraint than the average citizen.

5. The New Orleans ordinance in *Lewis* was not limited to "fighting words", and was specifically directed at people who "cursed" or "reviled" a police officer. When the case returned to the Supreme Court, the ordinance was held unconstitutional. Lewis v. New Orleans, 415 U.S. 130 (1974). In his concurring opinion in the second *Lewis* case, Justice Powell expressed concern that it was the kind of law that was usually invoked "only where there is no other valid basis for arresting an objectionable or suspicious person."

6. The Court relied on *Lewis* to hold unconstitutional a Houston ordinance that made it a crime to "oppose, molest, abuse or interrupt any policeman in the execution of his duty." City of Houston v. Hill, 482 U.S. 451 (1987). Wayne Hill had been arrested for violating the ordinance after he shouted at police who were questioning another man on the street. (Hill shouted: "Why don't you pick on somebody your own size?" After the officer asked whether Hill was interrupting him in his "official capacity as a Houston police officer," Hill replied: "Yes, why don't you pick on somebody my size?" The officer obliged and arrested him.) Although Hill was acquitted by a jury, he then brought suit in a federal court to have the law held unconstitutional. Justice Brennan's opinion for the Court noted that the statute was even more sweeping than that involved in *Lewis*—it reached all language that "in any manner interrupts an officer" and it neither required "fighting words" nor was limited to "obscene or opprobrious language." A municipality could enact laws punishing people who failed to disperse in response to a valid police order, created traffic hazards, or physically obstructed an officer's investigation. But "freedom of individuals verbally to oppose or challenge police action without thereby risking arrest is one of the principal characteristics by which we distinguish a free nation from a police state."

7. Justice Powell had narrower reasons for finding that the Houston ordinance was unconstitutional. (Hill proved that, in other Houston prosecutions under the ordinance, people had been charged with such crimes as "failure to remain silent and stationary," "refusing to remain silent," and "talking.") While he agreed that the First Amendment protected speech simply criticizing a police officer, he suggested that a law could be drafted to punish some speech, even if it was not "fighting words," where the speaker's purpose was to interfere with performance of the officer's functions. (He gave two examples: a person insisting on engaging an officer in conversation while the officer was busy directing traffic; a person running alongside, and shouting at an officer chasing a fleeing felon.)

FEDERAL COMMUNICATIONS COMMISSION
v. PACIFICA FOUNDATION

Supreme Court of the United States, 1978.
438 U.S. 726, 98 S.Ct. 3026, 57 L.Ed.2d 1073.

JUSTICE STEVENS delivered the opinion of the Court (Parts I, II, III, and IV–C) and an opinion in which THE CHIEF JUSTICE and JUSTICE REHNQUIST joined (Parts IV–A and IV–B).

This case requires that we decide whether the Federal Communications Commission has any power to regulate a radio broadcast that is indecent but not obscene.

A satiric humorist named George Carlin recorded a 12–minute monologue entitled "Filthy Words" before a live audience in a California theater. He began by referring to his thoughts about "the words you couldn't say on the public, ah, airwaves, um, the ones you definitely wouldn't say, ever." He proceeded to list those words and repeat them over and over again in a variety of colloquialisms. The transcript of the recording, which is appended to this opinion, indicates frequent laughter from the audience.

JOHN PAUL STEVENS—Born on April 20, 1920, in Chicago, Illinois, into an affluent and socially prominent family. His father, a law graduate, was owner and manager of the Stevens (later Conrad Hilton) Hotel in Chicago. Republican. Protestant. Chicago, A.B., Phi Beta Kappa, 1941; Northwestern, J.D., 1942, graduating first in his class. Served in the U.S. Navy during World War II and awarded the Bronze Star. Law clerk to Justice Wiley Rutledge, 1947–1948; practiced law, 1948–1970; associate counsel, House Subcommittee on the Study of Monopoly Power, 1951; taught law part-time at Northwestern and Chicago, 1953–1955; U.S. Court of Appeals judge (Seventh Circuit), 1970–1975. Nominated associate justice on November 28, 1975, by President Gerald Ford to replace William O. Douglas. Confirmed by the Senate on December 17, 1975, by a 98–0 vote.

At about 2 o'clock in the afternoon on Tuesday, October 30, 1973, a New York radio station owned by respondent, Pacifica Foundation, broadcast the "Filthy Words" monologue. A few weeks later a man, who stated that he had heard the broadcast while driving with his young son, wrote a letter complaining to the Commission. He stated that, although he could perhaps understand the "record's being sold for private use, I certainly cannot understand the broadcast of same over the air that, supposedly, you control."

The complaint was forwarded to the station for comment. In its response, Pacifica explained that the monologue had been played during a program about contemporary society's attitude toward language and that immediately before its broadcast listeners had been advised that it included "sensitive language which might be regarded as offensive to some." Pacifica characterized George Carlin as "a significant social satirist" who "like Twain and Sahl before him, examines the language of ordinary people. . . . Carlin is not mouthing obscenities, he is merely using words to satirize as harmless and essentially silly our attitudes towards those words." Pacifica stated that it was not aware of any other complaints about the broadcast.

On February 21, 1975, the Commission issued a Declaratory Order granting the complaint and holding that Pacifica "could have been the subject of administrative sanctions." The Commission did not impose formal sanctions, but it did state that the order would be "associated with the station's license file, and in the event that subsequent complaints are received, the Commission will then decide whether it should utilize any of the available sanctions it has been granted by Congress."

[W]e must decide: (1) whether the scope of judicial review encompasses more than the Commission's determination that the monologue was indecent "as broadcast"; (2) whether the Commission's order was a form of censorship forbidden by § 326; (3) whether the broadcast was indecent within the meaning of § 1464; and (4) whether the order violates the First Amendment of the United States Constitution.

I

. . . [T]he focus of our review must be on the Commission's determination that the Carlin monologue was indecent as broadcast.

II

The relevant statutory questions are whether the Commission's action is forbidden "censorship" within the meaning of 47 U.S.C. § 326 and whether speech that concededly is not obscene may be restricted as "indecent" under the authority of 18 U.S.C. § 1464. The questions are not unrelated, for the two statutory provisions have a common origin. Nevertheless, we analyze them separately.

Section 29 of the Radio Act of 1927 provided:

> "Nothing in this Act shall be understood or construed to give the licensing authority the power of censorship over the radio communications or signals transmitted by any radio station, and no regulation or condition shall be promulgated or fixed by the licensing authority which shall interfere with the right of free speech by means of radio communications. No person within the jurisdiction of the United States shall utter any obscene, indecent, or profane language by means of radio communication." 44 Stat. 1172.

The prohibition against censorship unequivocally denies the Commission any power to edit proposed broadcasts in advance and to excise material considered inappropriate for the airwaves. The prohibition, however, has never been construed to deny the Commission the power to review the content of completed broadcasts in the performance of its regulatory duties.

We conclude, therefore, that § 326 does not limit the Commission's authority to impose sanctions on licensees who engage in obscene, indecent, or profane broadcasting.

III

The only other statutory question presented by this case is whether the afternoon broadcast of the "Filthy Words" monologue was indecent within the meaning of § 1464. Even that question is narrowly confined by the arguments of the parties.

. . . Pacifica does not quarrel with the conclusion that this afternoon broadcast was patently offensive. Pacifica's claim that the broadcast was not indecent within the meaning of the statute rests entirely on the absence of prurient appeal.

The plain language of the statute does not support Pacifica's argument. The words "obscene, indecent, or profane" are written in the disjunctive, implying that each has a separate meaning. Prurient appeal is an element of the obscene, but the normal definition of "indecent" merely refers to nonconformance with accepted standards of morality.

IV

Pacifica makes two constitutional attacks on the Commission's order. First, it argues that the Commission's construction of the statutory language broadly encompasses so much constitutionally protected speech that reversal is required even if Pacifica's broadcast of the "Filthy Words" monologue is not itself protected by the First Amendment. Second, Pacifica argues that inasmuch as the recording is not obscene, the Constitution forbids any abridgment of the right to broadcast it on the radio.

A

The first argument fails because our review is limited to the question whether the Commission has the authority to proscribe this particular broadcast. . . .

It is true that the Commission's order may lead some broadcasters to censor themselves. At most, however, the Commission's definition of indecency will deter only the broadcasting of patently offensive references to excretory and sexual organs and activities.* While some of these references may be protected they surely lie at the periphery of First Amendment concern.

B

When the issue is narrowed to the facts of this case, the question is whether the First Amendment denies government any power to restrict the public broadcast of indecent language in any circumstances. For if the government has any such power, this was an appropriate occasion for its exercise.

---

* A requirement that indecent language be avoided will have its primary effect on the form, rather than the content, of serious communication. There are few, if any, thoughts that cannot be expressed by the use of less offensive language.

The words of the Carlin monologue are unquestionably "speech" within the meaning of the First Amendment. It is equally clear that the Commission's objections to the broadcast were based in part on its content. The order must therefore fall if, as Pacifica argues, the First Amendment prohibits all governmental regulation that depends on the content of speech. Our past cases demonstrate, however, that no such absolute rule is mandated by the Constitution.

The question in this case is whether a broadcast of patently offensive words dealing with sex and excretion may be regulated because of its content. Obscene materials have been denied the protection of the First Amendment because their content is so offensive to contemporary moral standards. But the fact that society may find speech offensive is not a sufficient reason for suppressing it. Indeed, if it is the speaker's opinion that gives offense, that consequence is a reason for according it constitutional protection. For it is a central tenet of the First Amendment that the government must remain neutral in the marketplace of ideas. If there were any reason to believe that the Commission's characterization of the Carlin monologue as offensive could be traced to its political content—or even to the fact that it satirized contemporary attitudes about four letter words—First Amendment protection might be required. But that is simply not this case. These words offend for the same reasons that obscenity offends. Their place in the hierarchy of First Amendment values was aptly sketched by Justice Murphy when he said, "such utterances are no essential part of any exposition of ideas, and are of such slight social value as a step to truth that any benefit that may be derived from them is clearly outweighed by the social interest in order and morality." Chaplinsky v. New Hampshire, 315 U.S. 568, 572.

Although these words ordinarily lack literary, political, or scientific value, they are not entirely outside the protection of the First Amendment. Some uses of even the most offensive words are unquestionably protected. Indeed, we may assume, arguendo, that this monologue would be protected in other contexts. Nonetheless, the constitutional protection accorded to a communication containing such patently offensive sexual and excretory language need not be the same in every context. It is a characteristic of speech such as this that both its capacity to offend and its "social value," to use Justice Murphy's term, vary with the circumstances. Words that are commonplace in one setting are shocking in another. To paraphrase Justice Harlan, one occasion's lyric is another's vulgarity. Cf. Cohen v. California, 403 U.S. 15, 25.*

* The importance of context is illustrated by the *Cohen* case. That case arose when Paul Cohen entered a Los Angeles courthouse wearing a jacket emblazoned with the words "Fuck the Draft." After entering the courtroom, he took the jacket off and folded it. So far as the evidence showed, no one in the courtroom was offended by his jacket. Nonetheless, when he left the courtroom, Cohen was arrested, convicted of disturbing the peace, and sentenced to 30 days in prison.

In holding that criminal sanctions could not be imposed on Cohen for his political statement in a public place, the Court rejected the argument that his speech would offend unwilling viewers: it noted that "there was no evidence that persons powerless to avoid [his] conduct did in fact object to it." In contrast, in this case the Commission was responding to a listener's strenuous complaint, and Pacifica does not question its determination that this afternoon broadcast was likely to offend listeners. It should be noted that the Commission imposed a far more moderate penalty on Pacifica than the state court

In this case it is undisputed that the content of Pacifica's broadcast was "vulgar," "offensive," and "shocking." Because content of that character is not entitled to absolute constitutional protection under all circumstances, we must consider its context in order to determine whether the Commission's action was constitutionally permissible.

C

We have long recognized that each medium of expression presents special First Amendment problems. And of all forms of communication, it is broadcasting that has received the most limited First Amendment protection. Thus, although other speakers cannot be licensed except under laws that carefully define and narrow official discretion, a broadcaster may be deprived of his license and his forum if the Commission decides that such an action would serve "the public interest, convenience, and necessity." Similarly, although the First Amendment protects newspaper publishers from being required to print the replies of those whom they criticize, Miami Herald Publishing Co. v. Tornillo, 418 U.S. 241, it affords no such protection to broadcasters; on the contrary, they must give free time to the victims of their criticism. Red Lion Broadcasting Co., Inc. v. FCC, 395 U.S. 367.

The reasons for these distinctions are complex, but two have relevance to the present case. First, the broadcast media have established a uniquely pervasive presence in the lives of all Americans. Patently offensive, indecent material presented over the airwaves confronts the citizen, not only in public, but also in the privacy of the home, where the individual's right to be let alone plainly outweighs the First Amendment rights of an intruder. Because the broadcast audience is constantly tuning in and out, prior warnings cannot completely protect the listener or viewer from unexpected program content. To say that one may avoid further offense by turning off the radio when he hears indecent language is like saying that the remedy for an assault is to run away after the first blow. One may hang up on an indecent phone call, but that option does not give the caller a constitutional immunity or avoid a harm that has already taken place.*

Second, broadcasting is uniquely accessible to children, even those too young to read. Although Cohen's written message might have been incomprehensible to a first grader, Pacifica's broadcast could have enlarged a child's vocabulary in an instant. Other forms of offensive expression may be withheld from the young without restricting the expression at its source. Bookstores and motion picture theaters, for example, may be prohibited from making indecent material available to children.... The ease with which children may obtain access to broadcast material, ... recognized in *Ginsberg,* amply justif[ies] special treatment of indecent broadcasting.

imposed on Cohen. Even the strongest civil penalty at the Commission's command does not include criminal prosecution.

* Outside the home, the balance between the offensive speaker and the unwilling audience may sometimes tip in favor of the speaker, requiring the offended listener to turn away. See Erznoznik v. Jacksonville, 422 U.S. 205....

It is appropriate, in conclusion, to emphasize the narrowness of our holding. This case does not involve a two-way radio conversation between a cab driver and a dispatcher, or a telecast of an Elizabethan comedy. We have not decided that an occasional expletive in either setting would justify any sanction or, indeed, that this broadcast would justify a criminal prosecution. The Commission's decision rested entirely on a nuisance rationale under which context is all-important. The concept requires consideration of a host of variables. The time of day was emphasized by the Commission. The content of the program in which the language is used will also affect the composition of the audience, and differences between radio, television, and perhaps closed-circuit transmissions, may also be relevant. As Justice Sutherland wrote, a "nuisance may be merely a right thing in the wrong place—like a pig in the parlor instead of the barnyard." Euclid v. Ambler Realty Co., 272 U.S. 365, 388. We simply hold that when the Commission finds that a pig has entered the parlor, the exercise of its regulatory power does not depend on proof that the pig is obscene.

JUSTICE POWELL, with whom JUSTICE BLACKMUN joins, concurring. . . .

I . . . agree with much that is said in Part IV of Justice Stevens' opinion, and with its conclusion that the Commission's holding in this case does not violate the First Amendment. Because I do not subscribe to all that is said in Part IV, however, I state my views separately.

I

It is conceded that the monologue at issue here is not obscene in the constitutional sense. Nor, in this context, does its language constitute "fighting words" within the meaning of Chaplinsky v. New Hampshire, 315 U.S. 568 (1942). Some of the words used have been held protected by the First Amendment in other cases and contexts. I do not think Carlin, consistently with the First Amendment, could be punished for delivering the same monologue to a live audience composed of adults who, knowing what to expect, chose to attend his performance. And I would assume that an adult could not constitutionally be prohibited from purchasing a recording or transcript of the monologue and playing or reading it in the privacy of his own home.

But it also is true that the language employed is, to most people, vulgar and offensive. It was chosen specifically for this quality, and it was repeated over and over as a sort of verbal shock treatment. The Commission did not err in characterizing the narrow category of language used here as "patently offensive" to most people regardless of age.

The issue, however, is whether the Commission may impose civil sanctions on a licensee radio station for broadcasting the monologue at two o'clock in the afternoon. The Commission's primary concern was to prevent the broadcast from reaching the ears of unsupervised children who were likely to be in the audience at that hour. In essence, the Commission sought to "channel" the monologue to hours when the fewest unsupervised children would be exposed to it. In my view, this consideration provides strong support for the Commission's holding.

The Commission's holding does not prevent willing adults from purchasing Carlin's record, from attending his performances, or, indeed, from reading the transcript reprinted as an appendix to the Court's opinion. On its face, it does not prevent respondent from broadcasting the monologue during late evening hours when fewer children are likely to be in the audience, nor from broadcasting discussions of the contemporary use of language at any time during the day. The Commission's holding, and certainly the Court's holding today, does not speak to cases involving the isolated use of a potentially offensive word in the course of a radio broadcast, as distinguished from the verbal shock treatment administered by respondent here. In short, I agree that on the facts of this case, the Commission's order did not violate respondent's First Amendment rights.

II

As the foregoing demonstrates, my views are generally in accord with what is said in Part IV(C) of Justice Stevens' opinion. I therefore join that portion of his opinion. I do not join Part IV(B), however, because I do not subscribe to the theory that the Justices of this Court are free generally to decide on the basis of its content which speech protected by the First Amendment is most "valuable" and hence deserving of the most protection, and which is less "valuable" and hence deserving of less protection. In my view, the result in this case does not turn on whether Carlin's monologue, viewed as a whole, or the words that comprise it, have more or less "value" than a candidate's campaign speech. This is a judgment for each person to make, not one for the judges to impose upon him.

The result turns instead on the unique characteristics of the broadcast media, combined with society's right to protect its children from speech generally agreed to be inappropriate for their years, and with the interest of unwilling adults in not being assaulted by such offensive speech in their homes. Moreover, I doubt whether today's decision will prevent any adult who wishes to receive Carlin's message in Carlin's own words from doing so, and from making for himself a value judgment as to the merit of the message and words. These are the grounds upon which I join the judgment of the Court as to Part IV.

JUSTICE BRENNAN, with whom JUSTICE MARSHALL joins, dissenting.

I

... This majority apparently believes that the FCC's disapproval of Pacifica's afternoon broadcast of Carlin's "Dirty Words" recording is a permissible time, place, and manner regulation. Kovacs v. Cooper, 336 U.S. 77 (1949). Both the opinion of my Brother Stevens and the opinion of my Brother Powell rely principally on two factors in reaching this conclusion: (1) the capacity of a radio broadcast to intrude into the unwilling listener's home, and (2) the presence of children in the listening audience. Dispassionate analysis, removed from individual notions as to what is proper and what is not, starkly reveals that these justifications, whether individually or together, simply do not support even the professedly moderate degree of governmental homogenization of radio communications—if, indeed, such homogenization can ever be moderate given the pre-eminent status of the right of free speech in our constitutional scheme—that the Court today permits.

A

Without question, the privacy interests of an individual in his home are substantial and deserving of significant protection. In finding these interests sufficient to justify the content regulation of protected speech, however, the Court commits two errors. First, it misconceives the nature of the privacy interests involved where an individual voluntarily chooses to admit radio communications into his home. Second, it ignores the constitutionally protected interests of both those who wish to transmit and those who desire to receive broadcasts that many—including the FCC and this Court—might find offensive.

... I believe that an individual's actions in switching on and listening to communications transmitted over the public airways and directed to the public at-large do not implicate fundamental privacy interests, even when engaged in within the home. Instead, because the radio is undeniably a public medium, these actions are more properly viewed as a decision to take part, if only as a listener, in an ongoing public discourse. Although an individual's decision to allow public radio communications into his home undoubtedly does not abrogate all of his privacy interests, the residual privacy interests he retains vis-à-vis the communication he voluntarily admits into his home are surely no greater than those of the people present in the corridor of the Los Angeles courthouse in *Cohen* who bore witness to the words "Fuck the Draft" emblazoned across Cohen's jacket. Their privacy interests were held insufficient to justify punishing Cohen for his offensive communication.

Even if an individual who voluntarily opens his home to radio communications retains privacy interests of sufficient moment to justify a ban on protected speech if those interests are "invaded in an essentially intolerable manner," Cohen v. California, supra, at 21, the very fact that those interests are threatened only by a radio broadcast precludes any intolerable invasion of privacy; for unlike other intrusive models of communication, such as sound trucks, "[t]he radio can be turned off,"— and with a minimum of effort.... Whatever the minimal discomfort suffered by a listener who inadvertently tunes into a program he finds offensive during the brief interval before he can simply extend his arm and switch stations or flick the "off" button, it is surely worth the candle to preserve the broadcaster's right to send, and the right of those interested to receive, a message entitled to full First Amendment protection....

The Court's balance, of necessity, fails to accord proper weight to the interests of listeners who wish to hear broadcasts the FCC deems offensive. It permits majoritarian tastes completely to preclude a protected message from entering the homes of a receptive, unoffended minority....

B

Most parents will undoubtedly find understandable as well as commendable the Court's sympathy with the FCC's desire to prevent offensive broadcasts from reaching the ears of unsupervised children. Unfortunately, the facial appeal of this justification for radio censorship masks its constitutional insufficiency....

In concluding that the presence of children in the listening audience provides an adequate basis for the FCC to impose sanctions for Pacifica's broadcast of the Carlin monologue, the opinions of my Brother Powell, and my Brother Stevens, both stress the time-honored right of a parent to raise his child as he sees fit—a right this Court has consistently been vigilant to protect. See Wisconsin v. Yoder, 406 U.S. 205 (1972); Pierce v. Society of Sisters, 268 U.S. 510 (1925). Yet this principle supports a result directly contrary to that reached by the Court. *Yoder* and *Pierce* hold that parents, *not* the government, have the right to make certain decisions regarding the upbringing of their children. As surprising as it may be to individual Members of this Court, some parents may actually find Mr. Carlin's unabashed attitude towards the seven "dirty words" healthy, and deem it desirable to expose their children to the manner in which Mr. Carlin defuses the taboo surrounding the words. Such parents may constitute a minority of the American public, but the absence of great numbers willing to exercise the right to raise their children in this fashion does not alter the right's nature or its existence. Only the Court's regrettable decision does that.

II

The absence of any hesitancy in the opinions of my Brothers Powell and Stevens to approve the FCC's censorship of the Carlin monologue on the basis of two demonstrably inadequate grounds is a function of their perception that the decision will result in little, if any, curtailment of communicative exchanges protected by the First Amendment....

My Brother Stevens, in reaching a result apologetically described as narrow, takes comfort in his observation that "[a] requirement that indecent language be avoided will have its primary effect on the form, rather than the content, of serious communication," and finds solace in his conviction that "[t]here are few, if any, thoughts that cannot be expressed by the use of less offensive language." The idea that the content of a message and its potential impact on any who might receive it can be divorced from the words that are the vehicle for its expression is transparently fallacious. A given word may have a unique capacity to capsule an idea, evoke an emotion, or conjure up an image....

The Court apparently believes that the FCC's actions here can be analogized to the zoning ordinances upheld in Young v. American Mini Theatres, 427 U.S. 50 (1976). For two reasons, it is wrong. First, the zoning ordinances found to pass constitutional muster in *Young* had valid goals other than the channeling of protected speech. No such goals are present here. Second, ...—the ordinances did not restrict the access of distributors or exhibitors to the market or impair the viewing public's access to the regulated material. Again, this is not the situation here.

Both those desiring to receive Carlin's message over the radio and those wishing to send it to them are prevented from doing so by the Commission's actions. Although, as my Brethren point out, Carlin's message may be disseminated or received by other means, this is of little consolation to those broadcasters and listeners who, for a host of reasons, not least among them financial, do not have access to, or cannot take advantage of, these other means.

Moreover, it is doubtful that even those frustrated listeners in a position to follow my Brother Powell's gratuitous advice and attend one of Carlin's performances or purchase one of his records would receive precisely the same message Pacifica's radio station sent its audience. The airways are capable not only of carrying a message, but also of transforming it. A satirist's monologue may be most potent when delivered to a live audience; yet the choice whether this will in fact be the manner in which the message is delivered and received is one the First Amendment prohibits the government from making.

III

... [T]here runs throughout the opinions of my Brothers Powell and Stevens another vein I find equally disturbing: a depressing inability to appreciate that in our land of cultural pluralism, there are many who think, act, and talk differently from the Members of this Court, and who do not share their fragile sensibilities. It is only an acute ethnocentric myopia that enables the Court to approve the censorship of communications solely because of the words they contain.

Today's decision will thus have its greatest impact on broadcasters desiring to reach, and listening audiences comprised of, persons who do not share the Court's view as to which words or expressions are acceptable and who, for a variety of reasons, including a conscious desire to flout majoritarian conventions, express themselves using words that may be regarded as offensive by those from different socio-economic backgrounds. In this context, the Court's decision may be seen for what, in the broader perspective, it really is: another of the dominant culture's inevitable efforts to force those groups who do not share its mores to conform to its way of thinking, acting, and speaking.

Pacifica, in response to an FCC inquiry about its broadcast of Carlin's satire on "the words you couldn't say on the public ... airwaves," explained that "Carlin is not mouthing obscenities, he is merely using words to satirize as harmless and essentially silly our attitudes towards those words." In confirming Carlin's prescience as a social commentator by the result it reaches today, the Court evinces an attitude towards the "seven dirty words" that many others besides Mr. Carlin and Pacifica might describe as "silly." Whether today's decision will similarly prove "harmless" remains to be seen. One can only hope that it will.

Justice Stewart, with whom Justice Brennan, Justice White, and Justice Marshall join, dissenting.

... I think that "indecent" should properly be read as meaning no more than "obscene." Since the Carlin monologue concededly was not "obscene," I believe that the Commission lacked statutory authority to ban it. Under this construction of the statute, it is unnecessary to address the difficult and important issue of the Commission's constitutional power to prohibit speech that would be constitutionally protected outside the context of electronic broadcasting.

NOTES AND QUESTIONS

1. After this case, can you say whether the First Amendment prohibits punishing people who use profanity in public places? Does it matter whether someone, other than the police officer who arrested the speaker, complained? Whether the speaker continued to use the words after someone complained and he was asked to stop? Whether the words were used repeatedly? Whether there were children in the audience?

2. Is it possible this decision is limited entirely to the electronic broadcast media, and has no relationship to speech in other public places? (For consideration of the special First Amendment problems connected with broadcast media, see Chapter 7, p. 227 et seq.)

3. Two features of the Court's decision in the *Pacifica Foundation* case make it difficult to answer the questions posed above. One is that Justice Stevens' opinion emphasizes "the narrowness of our holding" and mentions that its application turns on "a host of variables." Second is the fact that Justices Powell and Blackmun deliberately disassociate themselves from much that Justice Stevens says about the First Amendment.

In an earlier case, Justice Powell spoke more directly to the issue of offensive speech in public places. Rosenfeld v. New Jersey, 408 U.S. 901 (1972), involved these facts, according to Justice Powell's dissenting opinion.

> Appellant addressed a school board meeting attended by about 150 people, approximately 40 of whom were children and 25 of whom were women. In the course of his remarks he used the adjective "m——f——" on four occasions, to describe the teachers, the school board, the town and his own country.

The Court's disposition of the case did not decide whether Rosenfeld's speech was protected by the First Amendment. Justice Powell, however, was clear that it was not. He said, in part:

> The preservation of the right to free and robust speech is accorded high priority in our society and under the Constitution. Yet, there are other significant values. One of the hallmarks of a civilized society is the level and quality of discourse. We have witnessed in recent years a disquieting deterioration in standards of taste and civility in speech. For the increasing number of persons who derive satisfaction from vocabularies dependent upon filth and obscenities, there are abundant opportunities to gratify their debased tastes. But our free society must be flexible enough to tolerate even such a debasement provided it occurs without subjecting unwilling audiences to the type of verbal nuisance committed in this case. The shock and

sense of affront, and sometimes the injury to mind and spirit, can be as great from words as from some physical attacks.

I conclude in this case that appellant's utterances ... are not protected by the First Amendment.

4.   Is the problem presented in the *Pacifica Foundation* case one of controlling the *location* of offensive speech rather than its content? You might consider two cases from the previous chapter that could also be described that way. Young v. American Mini Theatres, Inc., 427 U.S. 50 (1976) (page 383, supra), sustained an ordinance controlling the location of theatres showing sexually explicit motion pictures. Erznoznik v. City of Jacksonville, 422 U.S. 205 (1975) (page 381, supra), invalidated an ordinance prohibiting the showing of sexually explicit motion pictures in drive-in theatres whose screens were visible from public streets. Can you formulate a principle that will reflect the results of all three cases?

5.   If profanity can be prohibited in some locations and at some times, what exactly is the rationale for doing so? Is that rationale limited to profanity? Suppose an American Nazi deliberately praises Hitler's extermination of Jews before a largely Jewish audience. Could a law be drafted that would constitutionally control that kind of offensive speech?

6.   In Bolger v. Youngs Drug Products Corp., 463 U.S. 60 (1983), the Court unanimously decided that a 19th century federal statute forbidding mailing of contraceptive advertisements violated the First Amendment. In one part of its opinion, the Court said that an interest in protecting people from material offensive to them could not justify the statute. "At least where obscenity is not involved, we have consistently held that the fact that protected speech may be offensive to some does not justify its suppression." Even where a captive audience was involved, offensiveness did not permit suppression if the audience could avoid the offensive speech. Concurring in the result, Justice Stevens argued that the essential distinction was between material offensive in its ideas, and that offensive in its "style." While offensiveness in the first sense could never justify suppression, offensiveness in the second sense could permit regulations of "form and context," after balancing the speaker's and the government's interests. Does Justice Stevens' rationale explain the results in the cases in this chapter, and the previous one? Does it provide a coherent test?

7.   In Sable Communications of California, Inc. v. Federal Communications Commission, 492 U.S. 115 (1989), the Court held that a federal statute forbidding "indecent" commercial telephone messages was unconstitutional. The Court distinguished FCC v. Pacifica Foundation, describing that decision as a "narrow" ruling. *Pacifica* did not involve a total ban on broadcasting "indecent" material. Moreover, *Pacifica* dealt with radio broadcasting which was "unique" in intruding on the privacy of the home without prior warning, whereas adult telephone services required listeners to take affirmative steps to receive the communications. The statute in *Sable* was unconstitutional because it had "the invalid effect of limiting the content of adult telephone conversations to that which is suitable for children to hear."

THE IMPACT OF PACIFICA FOUNDATION

After the Supreme Court's decision in *Pacifica Foundation,* the FCC's regulation banning "indecent" material applied only to broadcasts prior to 10 p.m. In 1987, the Commission considered extending the ban to midnight. Congress wanted even more and added the following rider to a 1989 appropriation bill: "By January 31, 1989, the Federal Communications Commission shall promulgate regulations in accordance with section 1464, title 18, United States Code, to *enforce the provisions of such section on a 24 hour per day basis.*" The FCC then promulgated a new rule prohibiting all broadcasts of indecent materials. The Court of Appeals for the D.C. circuit held that such a sweeping rule violated the First Amendment rights of adults. Action for Children's Television v. FCC, 932 F.2d 1504 (D.C.Cir.1991). When the Supreme Court decided not to hear the FCC's application for review, the *Washington Post* published an editorial on March 4, 1992, that argued the principle at stake "goes far beyond the right of individual adults to listen to Mr. Carlin's chatter, to yuk it up with bathroom jokes or watch pornographic movies in their own homes. Not everyone wants to do any of the above. But every adult counts on the courts to protect his free speech rights from assault by the government. If some regulator in Washington can decide what's indecent and therefore banned from the airwaves, the Constitution is violated whether the material at issue is pornography or politics. If by a quick vote in each house, Congress can prohibit the use of certain words on television or telephone, sooner or later that list of words will grow and free expression will be diminished."

VIRGINIA v. BLACK

538 U.S. 343, 123 S.Ct. 1536, 155 L.Ed.2d 535 (2003).

JUSTICE O'CONNOR announced the judgment of the Court and delivered the opinion of the Court with respect to Parts I, II, and III, and an opinion with respect to Parts IV and V, in which THE CHIEF JUSTICE, JUSTICE STEVENS, and JUSTICE BREYER join.

In this case we consider whether the Commonwealth of Virginia's statute banning cross burning with "an intent to intimidate a person or group of persons" violates the First Amendment. Va.Code Ann. § 18.2–423 (1996). We conclude that while a State, consistent with the First Amendment, may ban cross burning carried out with the intent to intimidate, the provision in the Virginia statute treating any cross burning as prima facie evidence of intent to intimidate renders the statute unconstitutional in its current form.

I

Respondents Barry Black, Richard Elliott, and Jonathan O'Mara were convicted separately of violating Virginia's cross-burning statute, § 18.2–423. That statute provides:

"It shall be unlawful for any person or persons, with the intent of intimidating any person or group of persons, to burn, or cause to be burned, a cross on the property of another, a highway or other public place. Any person who shall violate any provision of this section shall be guilty of a Class 6 felony.

"Any such burning of a cross shall be prima facie evidence of an intent to intimidate a person or group of persons."

On August 22, 1998, Barry Black led a Ku Klux Klan rally in Carroll County, Virginia. Twenty-five to thirty people attended this gathering, which occurred on private property with the permission of the owner, who was in attendance. The property was located on an open field just off Brushy Fork Road (State Highway 690) in Cana, Virginia.

When the sheriff of Carroll County learned that a Klan rally was occurring in his county, he went to observe it from the side of the road. During the approximately one hour that the sheriff was present, about 40 to 50 cars passed the site, a "few" of which stopped to ask the sheriff what was happening on the property. Eight to ten houses were located in the vicinity of the rally. Rebecca Sechrist ... "sat and watched to see wha[t][was] going on" from the lawn of her in-laws' house. She looked on as the Klan prepared for the gathering and subsequently conducted the rally itself. During the rally, Sechrist heard Klan members speak about "what they were" and "what they believed in." The speakers "talked real bad about the blacks and the Mexicans." One speaker told the assembled gathering that "he would love to take a .30/.30 and just random[ly] shoot the blacks." The speakers also talked about "President Clinton and Hillary Clinton," and about how their tax money "goes to ... the black people." Sechrist testified that this language made her "very ... scared."

At the conclusion of the rally, the crowd circled around a 25–to 30–foot cross. The cross was between 300 and 350 yards away from the road. According to the sheriff, the cross "then all of a sudden ... went up in a flame." As the cross burned, the Klan played Amazing Grace over the loudspeakers. Sechrist stated that the cross burning made her feel "awful" and "terrible."

... The sheriff ... entered the rally, and asked "who was responsible for burning the cross." ... Black responded, "I guess I am because I'm the head of the rally." ...

Black was charged with burning a cross with the intent of intimidating a person or group of persons, in violation of § 18.2–423. At his trial, the jury was instructed that "intent to intimidate means the motivation to intentionally put a person or a group of persons in fear of bodily harm. Such fear must arise from the willful conduct of the accused rather than from some mere temperamental timidity of the victim." The trial court also instructed the jury that "the burning of a cross by itself is sufficient evidence from which you may infer the required intent." ... The Court of Appeals of Virginia affirmed Black's conviction.

On May 2, 1998, respondents Richard Elliott and Jonathan O'Mara, as well as a third individual, attempted to burn a cross on the yard of James Jubilee. Jubilee, an African–American, was Elliott's next-door neighbor in Virginia Beach, Virginia. Four months prior to the incident, Jubilee and his family had moved from California to Virginia Beach.

Before the cross burning, Jubilee spoke to Elliott's mother to inquire about shots being fired from behind the Elliott home. Elliott's mother explained to Jubilee that her son shot firearms as a hobby, and that he used the backyard as a firing range.

On the night of May 2, respondents drove a truck onto Jubilee's property, planted a cross, and set it on fire. Their apparent motive was to "get back" at Jubilee for complaining about the shooting in the backyard. Respondents were not affiliated with the Klan. The next morning, as Jubilee was pulling his car out of the driveway, he noticed the partially burned cross approximately 20 feet from his house. After seeing the cross, Jubilee was "very nervous" because he "didn't know what would be the next phase," and because "a cross burned in your yard ... tells you that it's just the first round."

Elliott and O'Mara were charged with attempted cross burning and conspiracy to commit cross burning. O'Mara pleaded guilty to both counts, reserving the right to challenge the constitutionality of the cross-burning statute. The judge sentenced O'Mara to 90 days in jail and fined him $2,500. The judge also suspended 45 days of the sentence and $1,000 of the fine.

At Elliott's trial, the judge originally ruled that the jury would be instructed "that the burning of a cross by itself is sufficient evidence from which you may infer the required intent." At trial, however, the court instructed the jury that the Commonwealth must prove that "the defendant intended to commit cross burning," that "the defendant did a direct act toward the commission of the cross burning," and that "the defendant had the intent of intimidating any person or group of persons." ... The jury found Elliott guilty of attempted cross burning and acquitted him of conspiracy to commit cross burning. It sentenced Elliott to 90 days in jail and a $2,500 fine. The Court of Appeals of Virginia affirmed the convictions of both Elliott and O'Mara.

Each respondent appealed to the Supreme Court of Virginia, arguing that § 18.2–423 is facially unconstitutional. The Supreme Court of Virginia consolidated all three cases, and held that the statute is unconstitutional on its face. It held that the Virginia cross-burning statute "is analytically indistinguishable from the ordinance found unconstitutional in *R.A.V.* [*v. St. Paul,* 505 U.S. 377 (1992)]." ...

. . .

II

. . .

Often, the Klan used cross burnings as a tool of intimidation and a threat of impending violence....

. . .

Throughout the history of the Klan, cross burnings have also remained potent symbols of shared group identity and ideology....

At Klan gatherings across the country, cross burning became the climax of the rally or the initiation....

... In short, a burning cross has remained a symbol of Klan ideology and of Klan unity.

... [W]hile cross burning sometimes carries no intimidating message, at other times the intimidating message is the *only* message conveyed. For example, when a cross burning is directed at a particular person not affiliated with the Klan, the burning cross often serves as a message of intimidation, designed to inspire in the victim a fear of bodily harm. Moreover, the history of violence associated with the Klan shows that the possibility of injury or death is not just hypothetical. The person who burns a cross directed at a particular person often is making a serious threat, meant to coerce the victim to comply with the Klan's wishes unless the victim is willing to risk the wrath of the Klan. Indeed, as the cases of respondents Elliott and O'Mara indicate, individuals without Klan affiliation who wish to threaten or menace another person sometimes use cross burning because of this association between a burning cross and violence.

In sum, while a burning cross does not inevitably convey a message of intimidation, often the cross burner intends that the recipients of the message fear for their lives. And when a cross burning is used to intimidate, few if any messages are more powerful.

III

A

. . .

... The First Amendment permits "restrictions upon the content of speech in a few limited areas, which are 'of such slight social value as a step to truth that any benefit that may be derived from them is clearly outweighed by the social interest in order and morality.'" R.A.V. v. City of St. Paul, *supra,* at 382–383, (quoting Chaplinsky v. New Hampshire, [313 U.S. 568] at 572).

... [T]he First Amendment ... permits a State to ban a "true threat." ... ("[T]hreats of violence are outside the First Amendment"); Madsen v. Women's Health Center, Inc., 512 U.S. 753 (1994); Schenck v. Pro–Choice Network of Western N.Y., 519 U.S. 357, 373 (1997).

"True threats" encompass those statements where the speaker means to communicate a serious expression of an intent to commit an act of unlawful violence to a particular individual or group of individuals. ...The speaker need not actually intend to carry out the threat. Rather, a prohibition on true threats "protect[s] individuals from the fear of violence" and "from the disruption that fear engenders," in addition to protecting people "from the possibility that the threatened violence will occur." ... Intimidation in the constitutionally proscribable sense of the word is a type of true threat, where a speaker directs a threat to a person or group of persons with the intent of placing the victim in fear of bodily harm or death. Respondents do not contest that some cross burnings fit within this meaning of intimidating speech, and rightly so. As noted in Part II, *supra,* the history of cross burning in this country shows that cross burning is often intimidating, intended to create a pervasive fear in victims that they are a target of violence.

B

... It is true, as the Supreme Court of Virginia held, that the burning of a cross is symbolic expression. The reason why the Klan burns a cross at its rallies, or individuals place a burning cross on someone else's lawn, is that the burning cross represents the message that the speaker wishes to communicate. Individuals burn crosses as opposed to other means of communication because cross burning carries a message in an effective and dramatic manner.

The fact that cross burning is symbolic expression, however, does not resolve the constitutional question. The Supreme Court of Virginia relied upon R.A.V. v. City of St. Paul, *supra,* to conclude that once a statute discriminates on the basis of this type of content, the law is unconstitutional. We disagree.

In *R.A.V.,* we held that a local ordinance that banned certain symbolic conduct, including cross burning, when done with the knowledge that such conduct would " 'arouse anger, alarm or resentment in others on the basis of race, color, creed, religion or gender' " was unconstitutional ... We held that the ordinance did not pass constitutional muster because it discriminated on the basis of content by targeting only those individuals who "provoke violence" on a basis specified in the law. ... The ordinance did not cover "[t]hose who wish to use 'fighting words' in connection with other ideas—to express hostility, for example, on the basis of political affiliation, union membership, or homosexuality." ... This content-based discrimination was unconstitutional because it allowed the city "to impose special prohibitions on those speakers who express views on disfavored subjects." ...

We did not hold in *R.A.V.* that the First Amendment prohibits *all* forms of content-based discrimination within a proscribable area of speech. Rather, we specifically stated that some types of content discrimination did not violate the First Amendment:

> "When the basis for the content discrimination consists entirely of the very reason the entire class of speech at issue is proscribable, no significant danger of idea or viewpoint discrimination exists. Such a reason, having been adjudged neutral enough to support exclusion of the entire class of speech from First Amendment protection, is also neutral enough to form the basis of distinction within the class." ...

Indeed, we noted that it would be constitutional to ban only a particular type of threat: "[T]he Federal Government can criminalize only those threats of violence that are directed against the President ... since the reasons why threats of violence are outside the First Amendment ... have special force when applied to the person of the President." ... And a State may "choose to prohibit only that obscenity which is the most patently offensive *in its prurience—i.e.,* that which involves the most lascivious displays of sexual activity." ... Consequently, while the holding of *R.A.V.* does not permit a State to ban only obscenity based on "offensive *political* messages," or "only those threats against the President that mention his policy on aid to inner cities," the First Amendment permits content discrimination "based on the very reasons why the particular class of speech at issue . . . is proscribable," . . .

Similarly, Virginia's statute does not run afoul of the First Amendment insofar as it bans cross burning with intent to intimidate. Unlike the statute at issue in *R.A.V.,* the Virginia statute does not single out for opprobrium only that speech directed toward "one of the specified disfavored topics." . . . It does not matter whether an individual burns a cross with intent to intimidate because of the victim's race, gender, or religion, or because of the victim's "political affiliation, union membership, or homosexuality." Moreover, as a factual matter it is not true that cross burners direct their intimidating conduct solely to racial or religious minorities. . . . Indeed, in the case of Elliott and O'Mara, it is at least unclear whether the respondents burned a cross due to racial animus. . . .

The First Amendment permits Virginia to outlaw cross burnings done with the intent to intimidate because burning a cross is a particularly virulent form of intimidation. Instead of prohibiting all intimidating messages, Virginia may choose to regulate this subset of intimidating messages in light of cross burning's long and pernicious history as a signal of impending violence. Thus, just as a State may regulate only that obscenity which is the most obscene due to its prurient content, so too may a State choose to prohibit only those forms of intimidation that are most likely to inspire fear of bodily harm. A ban on cross burning carried out with the intent to intimidate is fully consistent with our holding in *R.A.V.* and is proscribable under the First Amendment.

IV

The Supreme Court of Virginia ruled in the alternative that Virginia's cross-burning statute was unconstitutionally overbroad due to its provision stating that "[a]ny such burning of a cross shall be prima facie evidence of an intent to intimidate a person or group of persons." . . . In this Court, as in the Supreme Court of Virginia, respondents do not argue that the prima facie evidence provision is unconstitutional as applied to any one of them. Rather, they contend that the provision is unconstitutional on its face.

The Supreme Court of Virginia has not ruled on the meaning of the prima facie evidence provision. It has, however, stated that "the act of burning a cross alone, with no evidence of intent to intimidate, will nonetheless suffice for arrest and prosecution and will insulate the Commonwealth from a motion to strike the evidence at the end of its case-in-chief." The jury in the case of Richard Elliott did not receive any instruction on the prima facie evidence provision, and the provision was not an issue in the case of Jonathan O'Mara because he pleaded guilty. The court in Barry Black's case, however, instructed the jury that the provision means: "The burning of a cross, by itself, is sufficient evidence from which you may infer the required intent." . . .

The prima facie evidence provision, as interpreted by the jury instruction, renders the statute unconstitutional. Because this jury instruction is the Model Jury Instruction, and because the Supreme Court of Virginia had the opportunity to expressly disavow the jury instruction, the jury instruction's construction of the prima facie provision "is a ruling on a question of state law that is as binding on us as though the precise words had been written into" the statute. . . . As construed by the jury instruction, the prima facie provision strips away the very reason why a State may ban cross burning with the intent to intimidate. The prima facie evidence provision permits a jury to convict in every cross-burning case in which defendants exercise their constitutional right not to put on a defense. And even where a defendant like Black presents a defense, the prima facie evidence provision makes it more likely that the jury will find an intent to intimidate regardless of the particular facts of the case. The provision permits the Commonwealth to arrest, prosecute, and convict a person based solely on the fact of cross burning itself.

It is apparent that the provision as so interpreted " 'would create an unacceptable risk of the suppression of ideas.' " . . . The act of burning a cross may mean that a person is engaging in constitutionally proscribable intimidation. But that same act may mean only that the person is engaged in core political speech. The prima facie evidence provision in this statute blurs the line between these two meanings of a burning cross. As interpreted by the jury instruction, the provision chills constitutionally protected political speech because of the possibility that a State will prosecute—and potentially convict—somebody engaging only in lawful political speech at the core of what the First Amendment is designed to protect.

As the history of cross burning indicates, a burning cross is not always intended to intimidate. Rather, sometimes the cross burning is a statement of ideology, a symbol of group solidarity. It is a ritual used at Klan gatherings, and it is used to represent the Klan itself. . . . Indeed, occasionally a person who burns a cross does not intend to express either a statement of ideology or intimidation. Cross burnings have appeared in movies such as Mississippi Burning, and in plays such as the stage adaptation of Sir Walter Scott's The Lady of the Lake.

The prima facie provision makes no effort to distinguish among these different types of cross burnings. It does not distinguish between a cross burning done with the purpose of creating anger or resentment and a cross burning done with the purpose of threatening or intimidating a victim. It does not distinguish between a cross burning at a public rally or a cross burning on a neighbor's lawn. It does not treat the cross burning directed at an individual differently from the cross burning directed at a group of like-minded believers. . . . I agree with Justice Souter that the prima facie evidence provision can "skew jury deliberations toward conviction in cases where the evidence of intent to intimidate is relatively weak and arguably consistent with a solely ideological reason for burning."

It may be true that a cross burning, even at a political rally, arouses a sense of anger or hatred among the vast majority of citizens who see a burning cross. But this sense of anger or hatred is not sufficient to ban all cross burnings. As Gerald Gunther has stated, "The lesson I have drawn from my childhood in Nazi Germany and my happier adult life in this country is the need to walk the sometimes difficult path of denouncing the bigot's hateful ideas with all my power, yet at the same time challenging any community's attempt to suppress hateful ideas by force of law." Casper, Gerry, 55 Stan. L.Rev. 647, 649 (2002) (internal quotation marks omitted). The prima facie evidence provision in this case ignores all of the contextual factors that are necessary to decide whether a particular cross burning is intended to intimidate. The First Amendment does not permit such a shortcut.

For these reasons, the prima facie evidence provision, as interpreted through the jury instruction and as applied in Barry Black's case, is unconstitutional on its face. ...Unlike Justice Scalia, we refuse to speculate on whether *any* interpretation of the prima facie evidence provision would satisfy the First Amendment. Rather, all we hold is that because of the interpretation of the prima facie evidence provision given by the jury instruction, the provision makes the statute facially invalid at this point. We also recognize the theoretical possibility that the court, on remand, could interpret the provision in a manner different from that so far set forth in order to avoid the constitutional objections we have described. We leave open that possibility. We also leave open the possibility that the provision is severable, and if so, whether Elliott and O'Mara could be retried under § 18.2–423.

V

With respect to Barry Black, we agree with the Supreme Court of Virginia that his conviction cannot stand, and we affirm the judgment of the Supreme Court of Virginia. With respect to Elliott and O'Mara, we vacate the judgment of the Supreme Court of Virginia, and remand the case for further proceedings.*

. . .

JUSTICE SCALIA, with whom JUSTICE THOMAS joins as to Parts I and II, concurring in part, concurring in the judgment in part, and dissenting in part.

I agree with the Court that, under our decision in *R.A.V. v. St. Paul*, 505 U.S. 377 (1992), a State may, without infringing the First Amendment, prohibit cross burning carried out with the intent to intimidate. Accordingly, I join Parts I–III of the Court's opinion. I also agree that we should vacate and remand the judgment of the Virginia Supreme Court so that that Court can have an opportunity authoritatively to construe the prima-facie-evidence provision ... I write separately, however, to describe what I believe to be the correct interpretation of § 18.2–423, and to explain why I believe there is no justification for the plurality's apparent decision to invalidate that provision on its face.

_____
* A concurring opinion by Justice Stevens is omitted.

I

Section 18.2–423 provides that the burning of a cross in public view "shall be prima facie evidence of an intent to intimidate." In order to determine whether this component of the statute violates the Constitution, it is necessary, first, to establish precisely what the presentation of prima facie evidence accomplishes.

· · ·

The established meaning in Virginia, then, of the term "prima facie evidence" appears to be perfectly orthodox: It is evidence that suffices, on its own, to establish a particular fact. But ... this is true only to the extent that the evidence goes unrebutted....

· · ·

It is important to note that the Virginia Supreme Court did not suggest (as did the trial court's jury instructions in respondent Black's case) that a jury may, in light of the prima-facie-evidence provision, ignore any rebuttal evidence that has been presented and, solely on the basis of a showing that the defendant burned a cross, find that he intended to intimidate. Nor, crucially, did that court say that the presentation of prima facie evidence is always sufficient to get a case to a jury ... That is, presentation of evidence that a defendant burned a cross in public view is automatically sufficient, on its own, to support an inference that the defendant intended to intimidate *only until* the defendant comes forward with some evidence in rebuttal.

II

The question presented, then, is whether, given this understanding of the term "prima facie evidence," the cross-burning statute is constitutional....

... We have never held that the mere threat that individuals who engage in protected conduct will be subject to arrest and prosecution suffices to render a statute overbroad. Rather, our overbreadth jurisprudence has consistently focused on whether *the prohibitory terms* of a particular statute extend to protected conduct; that is, we have inquired whether individuals who engage in protected conduct can be *convicted* under a statute, not whether they might be subject to arrest and prosecution....

· · ·

... [T]he plurality cannot claim that improper convictions will result from the operation of the prima-facie-evidence provision *alone*. As the plurality concedes, the only persons who might impermissibly be convicted by reason of that provision are those who adopt a particular trial strategy, to wit, abstaining from the presentation of a defense.

· · ·

Conceding (quite generously, in my view) that this class of persons exists, it cannot possibly give rise to a viable facial challenge, not even with the aid of our First Amendment overbreadth doctrine. For this

Court has emphasized repeatedly that "where a statute regulates expressive conduct, the scope of the statute does not render it unconstitutional unless its overbreadth is not only real, but *substantial* as well, judged in relation to the statute's plainly legitimate sweep." Osborne v. Ohio, 495 U.S. 103, 112 (1990)....

. . .

... [T]he plurality holds out the possibility that the Virginia Supreme Court will offer some saving construction of the statute. It should go without saying that if a saving construction of § 18.2–423 is possible, then facial invalidation is inappropriate. ...So, what appears to have happened is that the plurality has facially invalidated not § 18.2–423, but its own hypothetical interpretation of § 18.2–423, and has then remanded to the Virginia Supreme Court to learn the *actual* interpretation of § 18.2–423. Words cannot express my wonderment at this virtuoso performance.

III

... I believe the prima-facie-evidence provision in Virginia's cross-burning statute is constitutionally unproblematic. Nevertheless, because the Virginia Supreme Court has not yet offered an authoritative construction of § 18.2–423, I concur in the Court's decision to vacate and remand the judgment with respect to respondents Elliott and O'Mara. I also agree that respondent Black's conviction cannot stand. ... Because I believe the constitutional defect in Black's conviction is rooted in a jury instruction and not in the statute itself, I would not dismiss the indictment and would permit the Commonwealth to retry Black if it wishes to do so....

JUSTICE SOUTER, with whom JUSTICE KENNEDY and JUSTICE GINSBURG join, concurring in the judgment in part and dissenting in part.

I agree with the majority that the Virginia statute makes a content-based distinction within the category of punishable intimidating or threatening expression, the very type of distinction we considered in R.A.V. v. St. Paul, 505 U.S. 377 (1992). I disagree that any exception should save Virginia's law from unconstitutionality under the holding in *R.A.V.* or any acceptable variation of it.

The ordinance struck down in *R.A.V.,* as it had been construed by the State's highest court, prohibited the use of symbols (including but not limited to a burning cross) as the equivalent of generally proscribable fighting words, but the ordinance applied only when the symbol was provocative " 'on the basis of race, color, creed, religion or gender.' " Although the Virginia statute in issue here contains no such express "basis of" limitation on prohibited subject matter, the specific prohibition of cross burning with intent to intimidate selects a symbol with particular content from the field of all proscribable expression meant to intimidate....

... [T]he *R.A.V.* ... opinion called an exception for content discrimination on a basis that "consists entirely of the very reason the entire class of speech at issue is proscribable." *R.A.V., supra,* at 388, 112 S.Ct.

2538. This is the exception the majority speaks of here as covering statutes prohibiting "particularly virulent" proscribable expression.

I do not think that the Virginia statute qualifies for this virulence exception as *R.A.V.* explained it. The statute fits poorly with the illustrative examples given in *R.A.V.,* none of which involves communication generally associated with a particular message....

II

... I thus read *R.A.V.* ... as covering prohibitions that are not clearly associated with a particular viewpoint, and that are consequently different from the Virginia statute. On that understanding of things, I necessarily read the majority opinion as treating *R.A.V.*'s virulence exception in a more flexible, pragmatic manner....

III

My concern here, in any event, is not with the merit of a pragmatic doctrinal move. For whether or not the Court should conceive of exceptions to *R.A.V.*'s general rule in a more practical way, no content-based statute should survive even under a pragmatic recasting of *R.A.V.* without a high probability that no "official suppression of ideas is afoot," *R.A.V., supra,* at 390. I believe the prima facie evidence provision stands in the way of any finding of such a high probability here.

. . .

As I see the likely significance of the evidence provision, its primary effect is to skew jury deliberations toward conviction in cases where the evidence of intent to intimidate is relatively weak and arguably consistent with a solely ideological reason for burning. an initiation ceremony or political rally visible to the public. In such a case, if the factfinder is aware of the prima facie evidence provision, as the jury was in respondent Black's case, the provision will have the practical effect of tilting the jury's thinking in favor of the prosecution. What is significant is not that the provision permits a factfinder's conclusion that the defendant acted with proscribable and punishable intent without any further indication, because some such indication will almost always be presented. What is significant is that the provision will encourage a factfinder to err on the side of a finding of intent to intimidate when the evidence of circumstances fails to point with any clarity either to the criminal intent or to the permissible one....

To the extent the prima facie evidence provision skews prosecutions, then, it skews the statute toward suppressing ideas....

. . .

JUSTICE THOMAS, dissenting.

In every culture, certain things acquire meaning well beyond what outsiders can comprehend. That goes for both the sacred, see Texas v. Johnson, 491 U.S. 397, 422–429 (1989) (Rehnquist, C. J., dissenting) (describing the unique position of the American flag in our Nation's 200 years of history), and the profane. I believe that cross burning is the paradigmatic example of the latter.

I

... I believe that the majority errs in imputing an expressive component to the activity in question. In my view, whatever expressive value cross burning has, the legislature simply wrote it out by banning only intimidating conduct undertaken by a particular means. A conclusion that the statute prohibiting cross burning with intent to intimidate sweeps beyond a prohibition on certain conduct into the zone of expression overlooks not only the words of the statute but also reality.

A

... To me, the majority's brief history of the Ku Klux Klan only reinforces this common understanding of the Klan as a terrorist organization, which, in its endeavor to intimidate, or even eliminate those its dislikes, uses the most brutal of methods.

Such methods typically include cross burning—"a tool for the intimidation and harassment of racial minorities, Catholics, Jews, Communists, and any other groups hated by the Klan." ... For those not easily frightened, cross burning has been followed by more extreme measures, such as beatings and murder. ...As the Solicitor General points out, the association between acts of intimidating cross burning and violence is well documented in recent American history....

But the perception that a burning cross is a threat and a precursor of worse things to come is not limited to blacks. Because the modern Klan expanded the list of its enemies beyond blacks and "radical[s]," to include Catholics, Jews, most immigrants, and labor unions, a burning cross is now widely viewed as a signal of impending terror and lawlessness....

In our culture, cross burning has almost invariably meant lawlessness and understandably instills in its victims well—grounded fear of physical violence.

B

. . .

It strains credulity to suggest that a state legislature that adopted a litany of segregationist laws self-contradictorily intended to squelch the segregationist message. Even for segregationists, violent and terroristic conduct, the Siamese twin of cross burning, was intolerable. The ban on cross burning with intent to intimidate demonstrates that even segregationists understood the difference between intimidating and terroristic conduct and racist expression. It is simply beyond belief that, in passing the statute now under review, the Virginia legislature was concerned with anything but penalizing conduct it must have viewed as particularly vicious.

Accordingly, this statute prohibits only conduct, not expression. And, just as one cannot burn down someone's house to make a political point and then seek refuge in the First Amendment, those who hate cannot terrorize and intimidate to make their point. In light of my conclusion that the statute here addresses only conduct, there is no need to analyze it under any of our First Amendment tests.

II

Even assuming that the statute implicates the First Amendment, in my view, the fact that the statute permits a jury to draw an inference of intent to intimidate from the cross burning itself presents no constitutional problems. Therein lies my primary disagreement with the plurality.

. . .

B

... The plurality fears the chill on expression because, according to the plurality, the inference permits "the Commonwealth to arrest, prosecute and convict a person based solely on the fact of cross burning itself." First, it is, at the very least, unclear that the inference comes into play during arrest and initiation of a prosecution, that is, prior to the instructions stage of an actual trial. Second, ... the inference is rebuttable and, as the jury instructions given in this case demonstrate, Virginia law still requires the jury to find the existence of each element, including intent to intimidate, beyond a reasonable doubt.

Moreover, even in the First Amendment context, the Court has upheld such regulations where conduct that initially appears culpable, ultimately results in dismissed charges. A regulation of pornography is one such example. ... [P]ornographers trafficking in images of adults who look like minors, may be not only deterred but also arrested and prosecuted for possessing what a jury might find to be legal materials. This "chilling" effect has not, however, been a cause for grave concern with respect to overbreadth of such statutes among the members of this Court.

That the First Amendment gives way to other interests is not a remarkable proposition. What is remarkable is that, under the plurality's analysis, the determination of whether an interest is sufficiently compelling depends not on the harm a regulation in question seeks to prevent, but on the area of society at which it aims. For instance, in Hill v. Colorado, 530 U.S. 703 (2000), the Court upheld a restriction on protests near abortion clinics, explaining that the State had a legitimate interest, which was sufficiently narrowly tailored, in protecting those seeking services of such establishments "from unwanted advice" and "unwanted communication" ... In so concluding, the Court placed heavy reliance on the "vulnerable physical and emotional conditions" of patients. ...Thus, when it came to the rights of those seeking abortions, the Court deemed restrictions on "unwanted advice," which, notably, can be given only from a distance of at least 8 feet from a prospective patient, justified by the countervailing interest in obtaining abortion. Yet, here, the plurality strikes down the statute because one day an individual might wish to burn a cross, but might do so without an intent to intimidate anyone. That cross burning subjects its targets, and, some-times, an unintended audience, ... to extreme emotional distress, and is virtually never viewed merely as "unwanted communication," but rath-er, as a physical threat, is of no concern to the plurality. Henceforth, under the plurality's view, physical safety will be valued less than the right to be free from unwanted communications.

III

Because I would uphold the validity of this statute, I respectfully dissent.

Chapter XIII

DEFAMATION AND MEDIA INVASION
OF PRIVACY

———

I. DEFAMATION

A. GROUP LIBEL

BEAUHARNAIS v. ILLINOIS

Supreme Court of the United States, 1952.
343 U.S. 250, 72 S.Ct. 725, 96 L.Ed. 919.

[Beauharnais was president of the White Circle League in Chicago. In January of 1950, he organized the distribution of leaflets on downtown Chicago street corners. The leaflets complained of blacks moving into white neighborhoods. The leaflets called for "[o]ne million self-respecting white people in Chicago to unite," and said further: "If persuasion and the need to prevent the white race from becoming mongrelized by the negro will not unite us, then the aggressions ... rapes, robberies, knives, guns and marijuana of the negro, surely will." Beauharnais was prosecuted under Illinois' "group libel" law. That law punishes the exhibition of publications which portray "depravity, criminality, unchastity, or lack of virtue of a class of citizens, of any race, color, creed or religion" and which exposes them to "contempt, derision, or obloquy or which is productive of breach of the peace or riots...." After conviction he sought review in the United States Supreme Court. Justice Douglas' docket book for the 1951 Term shows that Justices Black, Reed, Douglas, and Burton were in the minority when the justices voted in conference. After Chief Justice Vinson assigned the Court's opinion to Justice Frankfurter, Justices Jackson and Burton changed their votes, but since they had been on opposite sides, there was still a majority upholding the constitutionality of the Illinois "group libel" law. Justice Clark later had doubts about his vote, for when the Court received a petition for rehearing, Justice Douglas recorded in his docket book: "Clark indicated he was in error in voting to affirm." Justice Clark, nonetheless, voted to deny the petition for rehearing.]

JUSTICE FRANKFURTER delivered the opinion of the Court.

The Illinois Supreme Court tells us that § 224a [the law under which Beauharnais was convicted] "is a form of criminal libel law."

Libel of an individual was a common-law crime, and thus criminal in the colonies. Indeed, at common law, truth or good motives was no defense. In the first decades after the adoption of the Constitution, this was changed by judicial decision, statute or constitution in most States, but nowhere was there any suggestion that the crime of libel be abolished. Today, every American jurisdiction—the forty-eight States, the District of Columbia, Alaska, Hawaii and Puerto Rico—punish libels directed at individuals. "There are certain well-defined and narrowly limited classes of speech, the prevention and punishment of which have never been thought to raise any Constitutional problem. These include the lewd and obscene, the profane, the libelous, and the insulting or 'fighting' words—those which by their very utterance inflict injury or tend to incite an immediate breach of the peace...." Such were the views of a unanimous Court in Chaplinsky v. New Hampshire.

No one will gainsay that it is libelous falsely to charge another with being a rapist, robber, carrier of knives and guns, and user of marijuana. The precise question before us, then, is whether the protection of "liberty" in the Due Process Clause of the Fourteenth Amendment prevents a State from punishing such libels—as criminal libel has been defined, limited and constitutionally recognized time out of mind—directed at designated collectivities and flagrantly disseminated. There is even authority, however dubious, that such utterances were also crimes at common law. It is certainly clear that some American jurisdictions have sanctioned their punishment under ordinary criminal libel statutes. We cannot say, however, that the question is concluded by history and practice. But if an utterance directed at an individual may be the object of criminal sanctions, we cannot deny to a State power to punish the same utterance directed at a defined group, unless we can say that this is a wilful and purposeless restriction unrelated to the peace and well-being of the State.

Illinois did not have to look beyond her own borders or await the tragic experience of the last three decades to conclude that wilful purveyors of falsehood concerning racial and religious groups promote strife and tend powerfully to obstruct the manifold adjustments required for free, ordered life in a metropolitan, polyglot community. From the murder of the abolitionist Lovejoy in 1837 to the Cicero riots of 1951, Illinois has been the scene of exacerbated tension between races, often flaring into violence and destruction. In many of these outbreaks, utterances of the character here in question, so the Illinois legislature could conclude, played a significant part. The law was passed on June 29, 1917, at a time when the State was struggling to assimilate vast numbers of new inhabitants, as yet concentrated in discrete racial or national or religious groups—foreign-born brought to it by the crest of the great wave of immigration, and Negroes attracted by jobs in war plants and the allurements of northern claims....

In the face of this history and its frequent obligato of extreme racial and religious propaganda, we would deny experience to say that the Illinois legislature was without reason in seeking ways to curb false or malicious defamation of racial and religious groups, made in public places and by means calculated to have a powerful emotional impact on those to whom it was presented....

It may be argued, and weightily, that this legislation will not help matters; that tension and on occasion violence between racial and religious groups must be traced to causes more deeply embedded in our society than the rantings of modern Know–Nothings. Only those lacking responsible humility will have a confident solution for problems as intractable as the frictions attributable to differences of race, color or religion. This being so, it would be out of bounds for the judiciary to deny the legislature a choice of policy, provided it is not unrelated to the problem and not forbidden by some explicit limitation on the State's power. That the legislative remedy might not in practice mitigate the evil, or might itself raise new problems, would only manifest once more the paradox of reform. It is the price to be paid for the trial-and-error inherent in legislative efforts to deal with obstinate social issues. . . .

. . . It is not within our competence to confirm or deny claims of social scientists as to the dependence of the individual on the position of his racial or religious group in the community. It would, however, be arrant dogmatism, quite outside the scope of our authority in passing on the powers of a State, for us to deny that the Illinois legislature may warrantably believe that a man's job and his educational opportunities and the dignity accorded him may depend as much on the reputation of the racial and religious group to which he willy-nilly belongs, as on his own merits. . . .

We are warned that the choice open to the Illinois legislature here may be abused, that the law may be discriminatorily enforced; prohibiting libel of a creed or of a racial group, we are told, is but a step from prohibiting libel of a political party. Every power may be abused, but the possibility of abuse is a poor reason for denying Illinois the power to adopt measures against criminal libels sanctioned by centuries of Anglo–American law. "While this Court sits" it retains and exercises authority to nullify action which encroaches on freedom of utterance under the guise of punishing libel. Of course discussion cannot be denied and the right, as well as the duty, of criticism must not be stifled.

Libelous utterances not being within the area of constitutionally protected speech, it is unnecessary, either for us or for the State courts, to consider the issues behind the phrase "clear and present danger." Certainly no one would contend that obscene speech, for example, may be punished only upon a showing of such circumstances. Libel, as we have seen, is in the same class.

We find no warrant in the Constitution for denying to Illinois the power to pass the law here under attack. But it bears repeating— although it should not—that our finding that the law is not constitutionally objectionable carries no implication of approval of the wisdom of the legislation or of its efficacy. These questions may raise doubts in our minds as well as in others. It is not for us, however, to make the legislative judgment. We are not at liberty to erect those doubts into fundamental law.

Affirmed.

JUSTICE BLACK, with whom JUSTICE DOUGLAS concurs, dissenting.

The Court's holding here and the constitutional doctrine behind it leave the rights of assembly, petition, speech and press almost completely at the mercy of state legislative, executive, and judicial agencies.... My own belief is that no legislature is charged with the duty or vested with the power to decide what public issues Americans can discuss. In a free country that is the individual's choice, not the state's. State experimentation in curbing freedom of expression is startling and frightening doctrine in a country dedicated to self-government by its people. I reject the holding that either state or nation can punish people for having their say in matters of public concern.

... However tagged, the Illinois law is not that criminal libel which has been "defined, limited and constitutionally recognized time out of mind."

The Court's reliance on Chaplinsky v. New Hampshire, 315 U.S. 568, is also misplaced. New Hampshire had a state law making it an offense to direct insulting words at an *individual* on a public street. Chaplinsky had violated that law by calling a man vile names "face-to-face." We pointed out in that context that the use of such "fighting" words was not an essential part of exposition of ideas. Whether the words used in their context here are "fighting" words in the same sense is doubtful, but whether so or not they are not addressed to or about *individuals*. Moreover, the leaflet used here was also the means adopted by an assembled group to enlist interest in their efforts to have legislation enacted. And the fighting words were but a part of arguments on questions of wide public interest and importance. Freedom of petition, assembly, speech and press could be greatly abridged by a practice of meticulously scrutinizing every editorial, speech, sermon or other printed matter to extract two or three naughty words on which to hang charges of "group libel." The *Chaplinsky* case makes no such broad inroads on First Amendment freedoms. Nothing Justice Murphy wrote for the Court in that case or in any other case justifies any such inference.

Unless I misread history the majority is giving libel a more expansive scope and more respectable status than it was ever accorded even in the Star Chamber. For here it is held to be punishable to give publicity to any picture, moving picture, play, drama or sketch, or any printed matter which a judge may find unduly offensive to any race, color, creed or religion. In other words, in arguing for or against the enactment of laws that may differently affect huge groups, it is now very dangerous indeed to say something critical of one of the groups. And any "person, firm or corporation" can be tried for this crime. "Person, firm or corporation" certainly includes a book publisher, newspaper, radio or television station, candidate or even a preacher.

It is easy enough to say that none of this latter group have been proceeded against under the Illinois Act. And they have not—yet. But emotions bubble and tempers flare in racial and religious controversies, the kind here involved. It would not be easy for any court, in good conscience, to narrow this Act so as to exclude from it any of those I have mentioned....

This Act sets up a system of state censorship which is at war with the kind of free government envisioned by those who forced adoption of our Bill of Rights. The motives behind the state law may have been to do good. But the same can be said about most laws making opinions punishable as crimes. History indicates that urges to do good have led to the burning of books and even to the burning of "witches."

No rationalization on a purely legal level can conceal the fact that state laws like this one present a constant overhanging threat to freedom of speech, press and religion. Today Beauharnais is punished for publicly expressing strong views in favor of segregation. Ironically enough, Beauharnais, convicted of crime in Chicago, would probably be given a hero's reception in many other localities, if not in some parts of Chicago itself. Moreover, the same kind of state law that makes Beauharnais a criminal for advocating segregation in Illinois can be utilized to send people to jail in other states for advocating equality and nonsegregation. What Beauharnais said in his leaflet is mild compared with usual arguments on both sides of racial controversies.

We are told that freedom of petition and discussion are in no danger "while this Court sits." This case raises considerable doubt. Since those who peacefully petition for changes in the law are not to be protected "while this Court sits," who is? ... I think the First Amendment, with the Fourteenth, "absolutely" forbids such laws without any "ifs" or "buts" or "whereases." Whatever the danger, if any, in such public discussions, it is a danger the Founders deemed outweighed by the danger incident to the stifling of thought and speech. The Court does not act on this view of the Founders. It calculates what it deems to be the danger of public discussion, holds the scales are tipped on the side of state suppression, and upholds state censorship. This method of decision offers little protection to First Amendment liberties "while this Court sits."

If there be minority groups who hail this holding as their victory, they might consider the possible relevancy of this ancient remark:

"Another such victory and I am undone."

[The separate dissents of Justices Reed, Douglas and Jackson are omitted.]

NOTES AND QUESTIONS

1. Is the Illinois law valid simply because the state legislature reasonably concluded that group libel could lead to violence? Suppose a community decides that advocates of school integration have produced violence and stress. Could a valid law be passed, then, that would make public advocacy of school integration a crime?

2. Notice that Justice Black's dissent does not take issue with Justice Frankfurter's assumption that the traditional law of libel is constitutional. Instead, he argues that the Illinois law goes beyond the law of libel. If a group libel law is valid, wouldn't it follow that there are no constitutional problems with the ancient law of libel which has been "defined, limited and constitutionally recognized time out of mind"?

3. There has been considerable controversy in recent times about the free speech rights of a handful of academics who have argued that

certain racial groups are genetically less intelligent than whites. Would a speech before a University audience advocating that theory be a crime under the Illinois law? Would the speech be protected by the First Amendment?

4. Ten years before *Beauharnais,* a distinguished sociologist, David Riesman, supporting "group libel" laws, wrote:*

> In part, the assumption of some courts and writers is that as the number of the libelled group expands the extravagance of the defendant's statements—or his obvious misanthropy—will discredit him without the need for legal interference. This is much too rationalistic; it might be so where "other things are equal," as they never are. On the contrary, where the defendant is engaged in exploiting the anxieties or the sadism of his audience and can count on built-in prejudice, he may increase his credibility as he increases the scope and violence of his lies. The more daring the lie, the more simple it is to comprehend, the more satisfying as an "explanation" and the more impressive the speaker—if the political and social context provide fuel, and the object of the lies is already held in fear and suspicion. Indeed, all the "general" rules concerned in this aspect of libel and slander run into difficulty because of failure to take adequate account of this occasional—at times and for periods, perennial—bearing of the social and political context.

> Lawyers, trained in a tradition of distinction drawing and eschewing generalities, may find it difficult to recognize, or to admit, these "nonlogical" factors in communication, although their training also teaches them the varying meanings which emotion may attach to words. Even their day-to-day experience in practice bears out the contention that statements such as Salmond's example of "all lawyers are dishonest" cause harm to lawyers as a group, and a derivative harm to every individual lawyer. The legal profession has suffered in esteem and influence from such reiterated remarks (it is noteworthy that Hollywood usually portrays lawyers as obfuscators or crooks, while doctors and clergymen are spotless), and its members have directly suffered in pocket, for many persons are deterred, as we all know, from resorting to lawyers out of fear of excessive fees and other sharp practices. And the devastating harm caused to racial or cultural minorities—to Negroes, to Jews, to American Indians, to Poles—as a result of systematic defamation needs no underscoring here; no member of these groups escapes some psychic or material hurt as a consequence of the attacks upon the groups with which he is voluntarily or involuntarily identified. Of course, there is more involved in the issue of group libel than this question of damage.... But we can at least eliminate as over-optimistic the belief that statements which defame large groups are mere idle blathering and do no harm to individuals.

* David Riesman, Democracy and Defamation: Control of Group Libel, Columbia Law Review, 1942, vol. 42, pp. 770–771. Reprinted with permission.

This belief is the adult variant of the child's "Sticks and stones can break my bones, but names can never hurt me"—a song never sung by any child who was not smarting under the hurt.

If you agree with Riesman that libel of groups can be extremely harmful to members of the group, does it follow that states should make it a crime to defame racial and religious groups? What about libel of other groups, such as doctors and lawyers? Law professors?

5. The soundness of the *Beauharnais* decision has been questioned in recent years. See Collin v. Smith, 578 F.2d 1197 (7th Cir.1978), and Judge Easterbrook's comments in American Booksellers Association, Inc. v. Hudnut in the note on pp. 407–408, Chapter 11. Justice Blackmun noted, however, in a dissenting opinion in which Justice Rehnquist joined: "Beauharnais has never been overruled or formally limited." Smith v. Collin, 436 U.S. 953 (1978).

B. PRIOR RESTRAINT OF DEFAMATION

NEAR v. MINNESOTA EX REL. OLSON

Supreme Court of the United States, 1931.
283 U.S. 697, 51 S.Ct. 625, 75 L.Ed. 1357.

[In 1925, the Minnesota legislature enacted a public nuisance law that permitted judges, sitting without juries, to enjoin publication of newspapers and periodicals that regularly and customarily published materials that were "obscene, lewd, and lascivious" or "malicious, scandalous, and defamatory." The regular daily newspapers in the state did not oppose the law's enactment. In 1927, a Minnesota court enjoined the publication of the *Saturday Press,* a small weekly Minneapolis newspaper, on the grounds that it had published malicious, scandalous, and defamatory material about the police chief, mayor, county attorney, and others. The injunction applied to all future issues of the newspaper. After the Minnesota Supreme Court upheld the law's constitutionality, Jay M. Near, the *Saturday Press's* editor, appealed to the Supreme Court.]

CHIEF JUSTICE HUGHES delivered the opinion of the Court.

Without attempting to summarize the contents of the voluminous exhibits attached to the complaint, we deem it sufficient to say that the articles charged in substance that a Jewish gangster was in control of gambling, bootlegging and racketeering in Minneapolis, and that law enforcing officers and agencies were not energetically performing their duties. Most of the charges were directed against the Chief of Police; he was charged with gross neglect of duty, illicit relations with gangsters, and with participation in graft. The County Attorney was charged with knowing the existing conditions and with failure to take adequate measures to remedy them. The Mayor was accused of inefficiency and dereliction. One member of the grand jury was stated to be in sympathy with the gangsters. A special grand jury and a special prosecutor were demanded to deal with the situation in general, and, in particular, to

CHARLES EVANS HUGHES—Born on April 11, 1862, in Glen Falls, New York, son of a Baptist minister and a former school teacher. Republican. Baptist. Grew up in upstate New York, Newark, and New York City. Precocious, he learned to read at the age of three and a half and studied the Bible, French, and German at the age of five. Refusing to go to school when he was six on the ground that it was a waste of time, he organized his own plan of study. He attended regular classes for only three and a half years, graduating from high school as salutatorian at the age of 13. Brown, A.B., Phi Beta Kappa, 1881; Columbia, LL.B., 1884, graduating first in his class. Passed the New York bar examination in 1884 with the highest grade given up to that time—99½ percent. Law practice, 1884–1891, 1893–1906; Cornell law professor, 1891–1893; New York governor, 1907–1910. Nominated associate justice on April 25, 1910, by President William Howard Taft to replace David J. Brewer. Confirmed by the Senate on May 2, 1910, by voice vote. Resigned June 10, 1916, to accept Republican presidential nomination. Narrowly defeated by Woodrow Wilson. Law practice, 1917–1921, 1925–1930; secretary of state, 1921–1925; judge, International Court of Justice, 1928–1930. Nominated chief justice of the United States on February 3, 1930, by President Herbert Hoover to replace William Howard Taft. Confirmed by the Senate on February 13, 1930, by a 52–26 vote. Retired on July 1, 1941. Died on August 27, 1948.

investigate an attempt to assassinate one Guilford, one of the original defendants, who, it appears from the articles, was shot by gangsters after the first issue of the periodical had been published. There is no question but that the articles made serious accusations against the public officers named and others in connection with the prevalence of crimes and the failure to expose and punish them.

This statute, for the suppression as a public nuisance of a newspaper or periodical, is unusual, if not unique, and raises questions of grave importance transcending the local interests involved in the particular action. It is no longer open to doubt that the liberty of the press, and of speech, is within the liberty safeguarded by the due process clause of the Fourteenth Amendment from invasion by state action. It was found impossible to conclude that this essential personal liberty of the citizen was left unprotected by the general guaranty of fundamental rights of person and property.... In maintaining this guaranty, the authority of the State to enact laws to promote the health, safety, morals and general welfare of its people is necessarily admitted. The limits of this sovereign power must always be determined with appropriate regard to the particular subject of its exercise.

If we cut through mere details of procedure, the operation and effect of the statute in substance is that public authorities may bring the owner or publisher of a newspaper or periodical before a judge upon a charge of conducting a business of publishing scandalous and defamatory matter—in particular that the matter consists of charges against public officers of official dereliction—and unless the owner or publisher is able and disposed to bring competent evidence to satisfy the judge that the charges are true and are published with good motives and for justifiable ends, his newspaper or periodical is suppressed and further publication is made punishable as a contempt. This is of the essence of censorship.

The question is whether a statute authorizing such proceedings in restraint of publication is consistent with the conception of the liberty of the press as historically conceived and guaranteed. In determining the extent of the constitutional protection, it has been generally, if not universally, considered that it is the chief purpose of the guaranty to prevent previous restraints upon publication. The struggle in England, directed against the legislative power of the licenser, resulted in renunciation of the censorship of the press. The liberty deemed to be established was thus described by Blackstone: "The liberty of the press is indeed essential to the nature of a free state; but this consists in laying no *previous* restraints upon publications, and not in freedom from censure for criminal matter when published. Every freeman has an undoubted right to lay what sentiments he pleases before the public; to forbid this, is to destroy the freedom of the press; but if he publishes what is improper, mischievous or illegal, he must take the consequence of his own temerity." 4 Bl.Com. 151, 152; see Story on the Constitution, §§ 1884, 1889. The distinction was early pointed out between the extent of the freedom with respect to censorship under our constitutional system and that enjoyed in England. Here, as Madison said, "the great and essential rights of the people are secured against legislative as well as against executive ambition. They are secured, not by laws paramount to prerogative, but by constitutions paramount to laws. This security of the freedom of the press requires that it should be exempt not only from previous restraint by the Executive, as in Great Britain, but from legislative restraint also." Report on the Virginia Resolutions, Madison's Works, vol. IV, p. 543. This Court said, in Patterson v. Colorado, 205 U.S. 454, 462: " . . . In the first place, the main purpose of such constitutional provisions is 'to prevent all such *previous restraints* upon publications as had been practiced by other governments,' and they do not prevent the subsequent punishment of such as may be deemed contrary to the public welfare. . . . The preliminary freedom extends as well to the false as to the true; the subsequent punishment may extend as well to the true as to the false. This was the law of criminal libel apart from statute in most cases, if not in all. . . . "

The criticism upon Blackstone's statement has not been because immunity from previous restraint upon publication has not been regarded as deserving of special emphasis, but chiefly because that immunity cannot be deemed to exhaust the conception of the liberty guaranteed by state and federal constitutions. The point of criticism has been "that the mere exemption from previous restraints cannot be all that is secured by the constitutional provisions"; and that "the liberty of the press might be rendered a mockery and a delusion, and the phrase itself a by-word, if, while every man was at liberty to publish what he pleased, the public authorities might nevertheless punish him for harmless publications." 2 Cooley, Const.Lim., 8th ed., p. 885. But it is recognized that punishment for the abuse of the liberty accorded to the press is essential to the protection of the public, and that the common law rules that subject the libeler to responsibility for the public offense, as well as for the private injury, are not abolished by the protection extended in our constitutions. *id.* pp. 883, 884. The law of criminal libel rests upon that secure foundation. There is also the conceded authority of courts to punish for contempt when publications directly tend to prevent the proper discharge of judicial functions. In the present case, we have no occasion to inquire as to the permissible scope of subsequent punishment. For whatever wrong the appellant has committed or may commit, by his publications, the State appropriately affords both public and private redress by its libel laws. As has been noted, the statute in question does not deal with punishments; it provides for no punishment, except in case of contempt for violation of the court's order, but for suppression and injunction, that is, for restraint upon publication.

The objection has also been made that the principle as to immunity from previous restraint is stated too broadly, if every such restraint is deemed to be prohibited. That is undoubtedly true; the protection even as to previous restraint is not absolutely unlimited. But the limitation has been recognized only in exceptional cases: "When a nation is at war many things that might be said in time of peace are such a hindrance to its effort that their utterance will not be endured so long as men fight and that no Court could regard them as protected by any constitutional right." Schenck v. United States, 249 U.S. 47, 52. No one would question but that a government might prevent actual obstruction to its recruiting service or the publication of the sailing dates of transports or the number and location of troops. On similar grounds, the primary requirements of decency may be enforced against obscene publications. The security of the community life may be protected against incitements to acts of violence and the overthrow by force of orderly government. The constitutional guaranty of free speech does not "protect a man from an injunction against uttering words that may have all the effect of force." ... These limitations are not applicable here. Nor are we now concerned with questions as to the extent of authority to prevent publications in order to protect private rights according to the principles governing the exercise of the jurisdiction of courts of equity. While reckless assaults upon public men, and efforts to bring obloquy upon those who are endeavoring faithfully to discharge official duties, exert a baleful influence and deserve the severest condemnation in public opinion, it cannot be said that this abuse is greater, and it is believed to be less, than that which characterized the period in which our institutions took shape. Meanwhile, the administration of government has become more complex, the opportunities for malfeasance and corruption have multiplied, crime has grown to most serious proportions, and the danger of its protection by unfaithful officials and of the impairment of the fundamental security of life and property by criminal alliances and official neglect, emphasizes the primary need of a vigilant and courageous press, especially in great cities. The fact that the liberty of the press may be abused by miscreant purveyors of scandal does not make any the less necessary the immunity of the press from previous restraint in dealing with official misconduct.

Subsequent punishment for such abuses as may exist is the appropriate remedy, consistent with constitutional privilege.

[The dissenting opinion of Justice Butler, in which Justices Van Devanter, McReynolds, and Sutherland joined, has been omitted.]

NOTES AND QUESTIONS

1. During the oral argument of *Near* in January, 1931, Chief Justice Hughes said to Minnesota's counsel: "You need not argue further whether or not freedom of press is a privilege or immunity under the Fourteenth Amendment."* The Chief Justice then asked counsel to address the issue of whether the Minnesota law "was an unconstitutional prior restraint so as to be a deprivation of liberty without due process." Apparently Chief Justice Hughes accepted Justice Sanford's dictum in Gitlow v. New York (1925) that the First Amendment's free speech and press provisions were applicable to the states through the provisions of the Fourteenth Amendment. See Chapter 1, pp. 13–15.

2. Was the injunction in *Near* a prior restraint or punishment for past behavior? Was it both? Often it is difficult to separate these two forms of government action infringing free speech and press. Fear of punishment may restrain expression, i.e., create "a chilling effect."

3. Freedom from prior restraints is, as Chief Justice Hughes wrote in *Near,* not absolute. He stated, however, that prior restraints are constitutionally permissible only in exceptional cases. One of those cases is obscenity. Does *Near,* unlike *Chaplinsky,* view libel and obscenity at different levels of expression? See Chapter 10, page 458. If so, are libel and obscenity entitled to different constitutional protection? Does the *Chaplinsky* dictum concerning libel weaken the holding in *Near?*

4. Like many litigants in civil liberties cases, Near did not have the resources to appeal his case to the Supreme Court. Initially the American Civil Liberties Union had agreed to represent him on appeal. Later, Colonel Robert B. McCormick, publisher of the *Chicago Tribune,* agreed to finance the appeal and engaged a leading Chicago law firm to represent Near. At that point, the ACLU withdrew from the case. Although McCormick obtained the support of the American Newspaper Publisher Association, he paid virtually all of Near's costs, which exceeded $24,000. Harry Chandler, president of the ANPA and publisher of the *Los Angeles Times,* disagreed with McCormick about appealing *Near.* He argued that it was better to let "sleeping dogs lie." "If we go to the Supreme Court now," he wrote to McCormick, "and that tribunal upholds that Minnesota Court, we will have stirred up the matter to a point strongly conducive to similar legislation in other states."* When *Near* reached the Supreme Court, its chances of reversal were not good. If the Court voted in *Near* as it had in *Gitlow* five years earlier, Chief Justice Taft and Justices Van Devanter, McReynolds, Sutherland, Butler, and Sanford would have voted for affirmance. Less than 18 months before the *Near* decision, Chief Justice Taft retired and Justice Stanford unexpectedly died. Their replacements—Charles Evans Hughes and

* Fred W. Friendly, Minnesota Rag, Random House, 1981, p. 129.

* Quoted, ibid., p. 88.

Owen J. Roberts—contributed the crucial votes for reversal. Justice Roberts' vote surprised Robert Tresler, his former Philadelphia law firm partner. "Knowing Roberts and the times and issues in Near v. Minnesota," Tresler later recalled, "I would have given a hundred-to-one odds that Roberts would have voted the other way. Well, maybe ten to one."**

THE IMPACT OF NEAR

Although *Near*'s immediate effect was to void the Minnesota law, the case appears to have stemmed the movement to enact similar state statutes. But *Near* had little immediate effect in the Twin Cities. The second anniversary of the *Near* decision was marked by the seizure of another paper, the *Pink Sheet*, edited and published by [Near's former partner,] Howard A. Guilford. The publication, which contained an attack on Mayor William A. Anderson, was seized by Chief W.J. Meehan. The police chief had unsuccessfully tried to justify his action by relying on the newspapers pre-registry law of 1931. He permitted the paper's circulation but warned Guilford: "The playing up of sensational criminal cases and sexual matters in heavy black faced type before the children of Minneapolis must stop."†

Near quickly became a landmark decision. Colonel McCormick had a portion of Chief Justice Hughes' opinion in the case chiselled on the wall of the *Chicago Tribune*'s lobby. The final sentence of the passage was: "The fact that the liberty of the press may be abused by miscreant purveyors of scandal does not make any less necessary the immunity of the press from previous restraint in dealing with official misconduct."

Near greatly influenced two important modern free-press cases— New York Times v. Sullivan, 376 U.S. 254 (1964), which the next section of this chapter considers, and New York Times v. United States (the Pentagon Papers case), 403 U.S. 713 (1971). The issue in the latter case was whether or not the *New York Times* and the *Washington Post* could be enjoined from publishing material from a U.S. government secret history of the Vietnam War. By a six-to-three vote, the Court held that the government had not satisfied *Near*'s requirements to justify a prior restraint. The justices wrote a total of nine opinions to explain their votes, and they cited *Near* ten times.

C. DEFAMATION OF PUBLIC OFFICIALS

NEW YORK TIMES v. SULLIVAN

United States Supreme Court, 1964.
376 U.S. 254, 84 S.Ct. 710, 11 L.Ed.2d 686.

JUSTICE BRENNAN delivered the opinion of the Court.

We are required in this case to determine for the first time the extent to which the constitutional protections for speech and press limit a State's power to award damages in a libel action brought by a public official against critics of his official conduct.

** Quoted, ibid., p. 171.

† Ibid., pp. 162, 164.

Respondent L.B. Sullivan is one of the three elected Commissioners of the City of Montgomery, Alabama. He testified that he was "Commissioner of Public Affairs and the duties are supervision of the Police Department, Fire Department, Department of Cemetery and Department of Scales." He brought this civil libel action against the four individual petitioners, who are Negroes and Alabama clergymen, and against petitioner the New York Times Company, a New York corporation which publishes the New York Times, a daily newspaper. A jury in the Circuit Court of Montgomery County awarded him damages of $500,000, the full amount claimed, against all the petitioners, and the Supreme Court of Alabama affirmed....

Respondent's complaint alleged that he had been libeled by statements in a full-page advertisement that was carried in the New York Times on March 29, 1960. Entitled "Heed Their Rising Voices," the advertisement [charged that peaceful demonstrations of Southern Negro students in behalf of their rights guaranteed by the Constitution] "... are being met by an unprecedented wave of terror by those who would deny and negate that document which the whole world looks upon as setting the pattern for modern freedom...." Succeeding paragraphs purported to illustrate the "wave of terror" by describing certain alleged events. The text concluded with an appeal for funds for three purposes: support of the student movement, "the struggle for the right-to-vote," and the legal defense of Dr. Martin Luther King, Jr., leader of the movement, against a perjury indictment then pending in Montgomery....

Of the 10 paragraphs of text in the advertisement, the third and a portion of the sixth were the basis of respondent's claim of libel. They read as follows:

Third paragraph:

"In Montgomery, Alabama, after students sang 'My Country, 'Tis of Thee' on the State Capitol steps, their leaders were expelled from school, and truckloads of police armed with shotguns and tear-gas ringed the Alabama State College Campus. When the entire student body protested to state authorities by refusing to re-register, their dining hall was padlocked in an attempt to starve them into submission."

Sixth paragraph:

"Again and again the Southern violators have answered Dr. King's peaceful protests with intimidation and violence. They have bombed his home almost killing his wife and child. They have assaulted his person. They have arrested him seven times—for 'speeding,' 'loitering' and similar 'offenses.' And now they have charged him with 'perjury'—a *felony* under which they could imprison him for *ten years....*"

Although neither of these statements mentions respondent by name, he contended that the word "police" in the third paragraph referred to him as the Montgomery Commissioner who supervised the Police Department, so that he was being accused of "ringing" the campus with police. He further claimed that the paragraph would be read as imputing to the police, and hence to him, the padlocking of the dining hall in order to starve the students into submission. As to the sixth paragraph, he contended that since arrests are ordinarily made by the police, the statement "They have arrested [Dr. King] seven times" would be read as referring to him; he further contended that the "They" who did the arresting would be equated with the "They" who committed the other described acts and with the "Southern violators." . . .

It is uncontroverted that some of the statements contained in the two paragraphs were not accurate descriptions of events which occurred in Montgomery. Although Negro students staged a demonstration on the State Capitol steps, they sang the National Anthem and not "My Country, 'Tis of Thee." Although nine students were expelled by the State Board of Education, this was not for leading the demonstration at the Capitol, but for demanding service at a lunch counter in the Montgomery County Courthouse on another day. Not the entire student body, but most of it, had protested the expulsion, not by refusing to register, but by boycotting classes on a single day; virtually all the students did register for the ensuing semester. The campus dining hall was not padlocked on any occasion, and the only students who may have been barred from eating there were the few who had neither signed a preregistration application nor requested temporary meal tickets. Although the police were deployed near the campus in large numbers on three occasions, they did not at any time "ring" the campus, and they were not called to the campus in connection with the demonstration on the State Capitol steps, as the third paragraph implied. Dr. King had not been arrested seven times, but only four; and although he claimed to have been assaulted some years earlier in connection with his arrest for loitering outside a courtroom, one of the officers who made the arrest denied that there was such an assault.

On the premise that the charges in the sixth paragraph could be read as referring to him, respondent was allowed to prove that he had not participated in the events described. Although Dr. King's home had in fact been bombed twice when his wife and child were there, both of these occasions antedated respondent's tenure as Commissioner, and the police were not only not implicated in the bombings, but had made every effort to apprehend those who were. Three of Dr. King's four arrests took place before respondent became Commissioner. Although Dr. King had in fact been indicted (he was subsequently acquitted) on two counts of perjury, each of which carried a possible five-year sentence, respondent had nothing to do with procuring the indictment.

Respondent made no effort to prove that he suffered actual pecuniary loss as a result of the alleged libel. One of his witnesses, a former employer, testified that if he had believed the statements, he doubted whether he "would want to be associated with anybody who would be a party to such things that are stated in that ad," and that he would not re-employ respondent if he believed "that he allowed the Police Department to do the things that the paper say he did." But neither this witness nor any of the others testified that he had actually believed the statements in their supposed reference to respondent. . . .

The trial judge submitted the case to the jury under instructions that the statements in the advertisement were "libelous per se" and were not privileged, so that petitioners might be held liable if the jury found that they had published the advertisement and that the statements were made "of and concerning" respondent. . . .

. . .

We reverse the judgment. We hold that the rule of law applied by the Alabama courts is constitutionally deficient for failure to provide the safeguards for freedom of speech and of the press that are required by the First and Fourteenth Amendments in a libel action brought by a public official against critics of his official conduct. We further hold that under the proper safeguards the evidence presented in this case is constitutionally insufficient to support the judgment for respondent. . . .

Under Alabama law as applied in this case, a publication is "libelous per se" if the words "tend to injure a person . . . in his reputation" or to "bring [him] into public contempt"; the trial court stated that the standard was met if the words are such as to "injure him in his public office, or impute misconduct to him in his office, or want of official integrity, or want of fidelity to a public trust. . . ." The jury must find that the words were published "of and concerning" the plaintiff, but where the plaintiff is a public official his place in the governmental hierarchy is sufficient evidence to support a finding that his reputation has been affected by statements that reflect upon the agency of which he is in charge. Once "libel per se" has been established, the defendant has no defense as to stated facts unless he can persuade the jury that they were true in all their particulars. . . . Unless he can discharge the burden of proving truth, general damages are presumed, and may be awarded without proof of pecuniary injury. . . .

The question before us is whether this rule of liability, as applied to an action brought by a public official against critics of his official conduct, abridges the freedom of speech and of the press that is guaranteed by the First and Fourteenth Amendments.

Respondent relies heavily, as did the Alabama courts, on statements of this Court to the effect that the Constitution does not protect libelous publications. Those statements do not foreclose our inquiry here. None of the cases sustained the use of libel laws to impose sanctions upon expression critical of the official conduct of public officials. . . . Like insurrection, contempt, advocacy of unlawful acts, breach of the peace, obscenity, solicitation of legal business, and the various other formulae for the repression of expression that have been challenged in this Court, libel can claim no talismanic immunity from constitutional limitations. It must be measured by standards that satisfy the First Amendment.

The general proposition that freedom of expression upon public questions is secured by the First Amendment has long been settled by our decisions. The constitutional safeguard, we have said, "was fashioned to assure unfettered interchange of ideas for the bringing about of political and social changes desired by the people." Roth v. United States, 354 U.S. 476, 484. . . .

Thus we consider this case against the background of a profound national commitment to the principle that debate on public issues should be uninhibited, robust, and wide-open, and that it may well include vehement, caustic, and sometimes unpleasantly sharp attacks on government and public officials. See Terminiello v. Chicago, 337 U.S. 1, 4; De Jonge v. Oregon, 299 U.S. 353, 365. The present advertisement, as an expression of grievance and protest on one of the major public issues of our time, would seem clearly to qualify for the constitutional protection. The question is whether it forfeits that protection by the falsity of some of its factual statements and by its alleged defamation of respondent.

Authoritative interpretations of the First Amendment guarantees have consistently refused to recognize an exception for any test of truth—whether administered by judges, juries, or administrative officials—and especially not one that puts the burden of proving truth on the speaker. . . .

Injury to official reputation affords no more warrant for repressing speech that would otherwise be free than does factual error. Where judicial officers are involved, this Court has held that concern for the dignity and reputation of the courts does not justify the punishment as criminal contempt of criticism of the judge or his decision. Bridges v. California, 314 U.S. 252. . . .

If neither factual error nor defamatory content suffices to remove the constitutional shield from criticism of official conduct, the combination of the two elements is no less inadequate. This is the lesson to be drawn from the great controversy over the Sedition Act of 1798 . . .

Although the Sedition Act was never tested in this Court, the attack upon its validity has carried the day in the court of history. . . . These views reflect a broad consensus that the Act, because of the restraint it imposed upon criticism of government and public officials, was inconsistent with the First Amendment.

. . .

What a State may not constitutionally bring about by means of a criminal statute is likewise beyond the reach of its civil law of libel. The fear of damage awards under a rule such as that invoked by the Alabama courts here may be markedly more inhibiting than the fear of prosecution under a criminal statute. . . . The judgment awarded in this case—without the need for any proof of actual pecuniary loss—was one thousand times greater than the maximum fine provided by the Alabama criminal statute, and one hundred times greater than that provided by the Sedition Act. And since there is no double-jeopardy limitation applicable to civil lawsuits, this is not the only judgment that may be awarded against petitioners for the same publication. Whether or not a newspaper can survive a succession of such judgments, the pall of fear and timidity imposed upon those who would give voice to public criticism is an atmosphere in which the First Amendment freedoms cannot survive. Plainly the Alabama law of civil libel is "a form of regulation that creates hazards to protected freedoms markedly greater than those that attend reliance upon the criminal law." Bantam Books, Inc. v. Sullivan, 372 U.S. 58, 70.

The state rule of law is not saved by its allowance of the defense of truth.... Allowance of the defense of truth, with the burden of proving it on the defendant, does not mean that only false speech will be deterred.... Under such a rule, would-be critics of official conduct may be deterred from voicing their criticism, even though it is believed to be true and even though it is in fact true, because of doubt whether it can be proved in court or fear of the expense of having to do so. They tend to make only statements which "steer far wider of the unlawful zone." ... The rule thus dampens the vigor and limits the variety of public debate. It is inconsistent with the First and Fourteenth Amendments.

The constitutional guarantees require, we think, a federal rule that prohibits a public official from recovering damages for a defamatory falsehood relating to his official conduct unless he proves that the statement was made with "actual malice"—that is, with knowledge that it was false or with reckless disregard of whether it was false or not....

· · ·

... We think the evidence against the Times supports at most a finding of negligence in failing to discover the misstatements, and is constitutionally insufficient to show the recklessness that is required for a finding of actual malice....

We also think the evidence was constitutionally defective in another respect: it was incapable of supporting the jury's finding that the allegedly libelous statements were made "of and concerning" respondent. Respondent relies on the words of the advertisement and the testimony of six witnesses to establish a connection between it and himself....

Reversed and remanded.

JUSTICE BLACK with whom JUSTICE DOUGLAS joins, concurring.

... "Malice," even as defined by the Court, is an elusive, abstract concept, hard to prove and hard to disprove. The requirement that malice be proved provides at best an evanescent protection for the right critically to discuss public affairs and certainly does not measure up to the sturdy safeguard embodied in the First Amendment. Unlike the Court, therefore, I vote to reverse exclusively on the ground that the Times and the individual defendants had an absolute, unconditional constitutional right to publish in the Times advertisement their criticisms of the Montgomery agencies and officials....

· · ·

JUSTICE GOLDBERG, with whom JUSTICE DOUGLAS joins (concurring in the result).

· · ·

In my view, the First and Fourteenth Amendments to the Constitution afford to the citizen and to the press an absolute, unconditional privilege to criticize official conduct despite the harm which may flow from excesses and abuses....

NOTES AND QUESTIONS

1. Why are the justices talking about the Sedition Act of 1798? For almost 200 years after that no one questioned the constitutionality of civil suits for libel. One commentator has written on this issue:*

We get a sense of difference between a legal theory of freedom of speech and a philosophic theory as we trace the career of seditious libel from seventeenth-century England through Fox's Libel Act through the Sedition Act to the *Times* case. It is one thing to assert that a vigorous criticism of the government must be permitted. It is another to choose among the calibrations of freedom that legal institutions and procedures can provide. Initially the great issue about seditious libel was whether judge or jury would have the final say as to what was defamatory of the government. The effect of Fox's Libel Act was simply to shift control from the judges to the juries, from the government and its judges to the people themselves. Then it became important to establish truth as a defense.[1] And, finally, in the *Times* case the critical area involves the degree of privilege to be afforded statements that are not true. We are reminded not only of how much more complex the legal debate over freedom of speech or over seditious libel can be, but again of the arresting problem how much freedom of speech in a legal system must depend on law's conscious distrust of its own processes to make needed discriminations.

The closing question, of course, is whether the treatment of seditious libel as the key concept for development of appropriate constitutional doctrine will prove germinal. It is not easy to predict what the Court will see in the *Times* opinion as the years roll by. It may regard the opinion as covering simply one pocket of cases, those dealing with libel of public officials, and not destructive of the earlier notions that are inconsistent only with the larger reading of the Court's action. But the invitation to follow a dialectic progression from public official to government policy to public policy to matters in the public domain, like art, seems to me to be overwhelming. If the Court accepts the invitation, it will slowly work out for itself the theory of free speech that Alexander Meiklejohn has been offering us for some fifteen years now.[2]

* Harry Kalven, The New York Times Case: A Note on "The Central Meaning of The First Amendment," The Supreme Court Review, 1964, pp. 220–221. Reprinted with permission.

1. It is an instructive quirk of history that the Sedition Act of 1798 has come down to us as odious legislation while Fox's Libel Act of 1792 is seen as a milestone on the march to liberty. Yet the Sedition Act followed Fox's Libel Act in providing jury trial and went further by affording the defendant the defense of truth. The fact that this liberalizing of the law of seditious libel was viewed so dimly in the United States suggests to my mind, some doubts about the validity of Dean Levy's thesis as to the common understanding prior to the Sedition Act crisis.

2. It is perhaps a fitting postscript to say that I had occasion this summer to discuss the *Times* case with Mr. Meiklejohn. Before I had disclosed my own views, I asked him for his

2.   The *New York Times* case does not formally overrule the *Beauharnais* decision. The pressure for enactment of group libel laws seems to have subsided, however, and those that are still on the books seem to have fallen into disuse since the *New York Times* case. After the *New York Times* decision, would it still be constitutional to apply a group libel law to facts like those in the *Beauharnais* case? To any set of facts?

D.   DEFAMATION OF PUBLIC AND NOT–SO–PUBLIC FIGURES

The "*New York Times* rule" applied only to defamatory statements about the official acts of public officials. It was clear, however, that the sweep of the Court's opinion would require reworking of the traditional rules of libel law in other cases as well. Three years later, a majority of five out of nine Justices agreed to extend the rule to statements about the public conduct of "public figures." Curtis Publishing Co. v. Butts and Associated Press v. Walker, reported together at 388 U.S. 130 (1967).

The *Butts* case grew out of a story in the *Saturday Evening Post* which claimed that the prominent coach of the University of Georgia football team had fixed a football game with the University of Alabama. The Georgia jury's verdict for $3,060,000 in damages was later cut by the Georgia courts to a more modest $460,000. The *Walker* case grew out of an Associated Press dispatch detailing the activities of General Walker, a well known campaigner against integration, during the riots which erupted on the University of Mississippi campus following the enrollment of James Meredith as the first Black student at the University. The Texas courts pared Walker's $800,000 verdict to $500,000.

The Supreme Court reversed the *Walker* decision outright. Ironically, the *Butts* decision was affirmed because Chief Justice Warren, who agreed that the *New York Times* rule applied to the *Butts* case, also concluded that the Saturday Evening Post *had* acted in "reckless disregard of truth." In presenting the case to the conference, the chief justice acknowledged that Butts was a public figure, but he added that the "mere fact a man is a public figure does not take away his right to have his character secure. Butts had not injected himself in any situation. The fact that a man is in [the] limelight or a star athlete does not make him any different so far as defamation is concerned from anyone else. Butts was minding his own business.... [I]n any event he has a case of 'malice' if anyone ever did ... affirm on 'malice'." (The Saturday Evening Post, its sales sagging, had attempted to stay in business by emphasizing "sophisticated muckraking." The Post editors made little effort to check the factual details of the story, even though the story made very serious charges against Coach Butts.)

The combination of the *New York Times*, *Butts* and *Walker* cases left for solution the problem of defamation of people who were neither "public officials" nor "public figures." That problem proved to be especially difficult to solve. The Supreme Court encountered the problem

judgment of the *Times* case. "It is," he said, "an occasion for dancing in the streets." As always I am inclined to think he is right.

for the first time in 1971, in Rosenbloom v. Metromedia, Inc., 403 U.S. 29 (1971). While the Court seemed to be in agreement in that case that the First Amendment required some modification of traditional libel law, at least when newspapers, radio and television were reporting newsworthy events, no opinion garnered more than three votes. In the case of private citizens, the issues concerned the same common law rules as were involved in *New York Times*—defendants were liable even if they had not been at fault, and substantial damages could be awarded even if the plaintiff introduced no evidence that he had, in fact, been hurt. It was finally settled that these ancient rules of the law of defamation must yield to the First Amendment in the following case.

GERTZ v. ROBERT WELCH, INC.

Supreme Court of the United States, 1974.
418 U.S. 323, 94 S.Ct. 2997, 41 L.Ed.2d 789.

JUSTICE POWELL delivered the opinion of the Court.

This Court has struggled for nearly a decade to define the proper accommodation between the law of defamation and the freedoms of speech and press protected by the First Amendment. With this decision we return to that effort. We granted certiorari to reconsider the extent of a publisher's constitutional privilege against liability for defamation of a private citizen. 410 U.S. 925 (1973).

I

In 1968 a Chicago policeman named Nuccio shot and killed a youth named Nelson. The state authorities prosecuted Nuccio for the homicide and ultimately obtained a conviction for murder in the second degree. The Nelson family retained petitioner Elmer Gertz, a reputable attorney, to represent them in civil litigation against Nuccio.

Respondent publishes American Opinion, a monthly outlet for the views of the John Birch Society. Early in the 1960's the magazine began to warn of a nationwide conspiracy to discredit local law enforcement agencies and create in their stead a national police force capable of supporting a Communist dictatorship. As part of the continuing effort to alert the public to this assumed danger, the managing editor of American Opinion commissioned an article on the murder trial of Officer Nuccio. For this purpose he engaged a regular contributor to the magazine. In March of 1969 respondent published the resulting article under the title "FRAME–UP: Richard Nuccio And The War On Police." The article purports to demonstrate that the testimony against Nuccio at his criminal trial was false and that his prosecution was part of the Communist campaign against the police.

In his capacity as counsel for the Nelson family in the civil litigation, petitioner attended the coroner's inquest into the boy's death and initiated actions for damages, but he neither discussed Officer Nuccio with the press nor played any part in the criminal proceeding. Notwithstanding petitioner's remote connection with the prosecution of Nuccio, respondent's magazine portrayed him as an architect of the "frame-up." According to the article, the police file on petitioner took "a big, Irish cop to lift." The article stated that petitioner had been an official of the "Marxist League for Industrial Democracy, originally known as the Intercollegiate Socialist Society, which has advocated the violent seizure of our government." It labelled Gertz a "Leninist" and a "Communist-fronter." It also stated that Gertz had been an officer of the National Lawyers Guild, described as a Communist organization that "probably did more than any other outfit to plan the Communist attack on the Chicago police during the 1968 Democratic convention."

These statements contained serious inaccuracies. The implication that petitioner had a criminal record was false. Petitioner had been a member and officer of the National Lawyers Guild some 15 years earlier, but there was no evidence that he or that organization had taken any part in planning the 1968 demonstrations in Chicago. There was also no basis for the charge that petitioner was a "Leninist" or a "Communist-fronter." And he had never been a member of the "Marxist League for Industrial Democracy" or the "Intercollegiate Socialist Society."

The managing editor of American Opinion made no effort to verify or substantiate the charges against petitioner. Instead, he appended an editorial introduction stating that the author had "conducted extensive research into the Richard Nuccio case." And he included in the article a photograph of petitioner and wrote the caption that appeared under it: "Elmer Gertz of Red Guild harasses Nuccio." Respondent placed the issue of American Opinion containing the article on sale at newsstands throughout the country and distributed reprints of the article on the streets of Chicago.

Petitioner filed a diversity action for libel in the United States District Court for the Northern District of Illinois....

. . .

... [T]he District Court concluded that the *New York Times* standard should govern this case even though petitioner was not a public official or public figure....

Petitioner appealed to contest the applicability of the *New York Times* standard to this case.... The Court of Appeals ... affirmed.... [W]e reverse.

II

. . .

Three years after *New York Times,* a majority of the Court agreed to extend the constitutional privilege to defamatory criticism of "public figures." This extension was announced in Curtis Publishing Co. v. Butts and its companion Associated Press v. Walker, 388 U.S. 130, 162 (1967). The first case involved the Saturday Evening Post's charge that Coach Wally Butts of the University of Georgia had conspired with Coach Bear Bryant of the University of Alabama to fix a football game between their respective schools. *Walker* involved an erroneous Associated Press account of former Major General Edwin Walker's participation in a University of Mississippi campus riot. Because Butts was paid by a private alumni association and Walker had resigned from the Army, neither could be classified as a "public official" under *New York Times*. Although Mr. Justice Harlan announced the result in both cases, a majority of the Court agreed with Mr. Chief Justice Warren's conclusion that the *New York Times* test should apply to criticism of "public figures" as well as "public officials." The Court extended the constitutional privilege announced in that case to protect defamatory criticism of nonpublic persons who "are nevertheless intimately involved in the resolution of important public questions or, by reason of their fame, shape events in areas of concern to society at large." . . .

. . .

III

We begin with the common ground. Under the First Amendment there is no such thing as a false idea. However pernicious an opinion may seem, we depend for its correction not on the conscience of judges and juries but on the competition of other ideas. But there is no constitutional value in false statements of fact. Neither the intentional lie nor the careless error materially advances society's interest in "uninhibited, robust, and wide-open" debate on public issues. . . .

Although the erroneous statement of fact is not worthy of constitutional protection, it is nevertheless inevitable in free debate. . . . And punishment of error runs the risk of inducing a cautious and restrictive exercise of the constitutionally guaranteed freedoms of speech and press. Our decisions recognize that a rule of strict liability that compels a publisher or broadcaster to guarantee the accuracy of his factual assertions may lead to intolerable self-censorship. Allowing the media to avoid liability only by proving the truth of all injurious statements does not accord adequate protection to First Amendment liberties. . . .

The need to avoid self-censorship by the news media is, however, not the only societal value at issue. If it were, this Court would have embraced long ago the view that publishers and broadcasters enjoy an unconditional and indefeasible immunity from liability for defamation. . . . Such a rule would indeed obviate the fear that the prospect of civil liability for injurious falsehood might dissuade a timorous press from the effective exercise of First Amendment freedoms. Yet absolute protection for the communications media requires a total sacrifice of the competing value served by the law of defamation.

The legitimate state interest underlying the law of libel is the compensation of individuals for the harm inflicted on them by defamatory falsehood. We would not lightly require the State to abandon this purpose. . . .

. . .

The *New York Times* standard defines the level of constitutional protection appropriate to the context of defamation of a public person. Those who, by reason of the notoriety of their achievements or the vigor and success with which they seek the public's attention, are properly classed as public figures and those who hold governmental office may recover for injury to reputation only on clear and convincing proof that the defamatory falsehood was made with knowledge of its falsity or with reckless disregard for the truth. This standard administers an extremely powerful antidote to the inducement to media self-censorship of the common law rule of strict liability for libel and slander. And it exacts a correspondingly high price from the victims of defamatory falsehood.... For the reasons stated below, we conclude that the state interest in compensating injury to the reputation of private individuals requires that a different rule should obtain with respect to them.

. . .

... [W]e have no difficulty in distinguishing among defamation plaintiffs. The first remedy of any victim of defamation is self-help— using available opportunities to contradict the lie or correct the error and thereby to minimize its adverse impact on reputation. Public officials and public figures usually enjoy significantly greater access to the channels of effective communication and hence have a more realistic opportunity to counteract false statements than private individuals normally enjoy. Private individuals are therefore more vulnerable to injury, and the state interest in protecting them is correspondingly greater.

More important than the likelihood that private individuals will lack effective opportunities for rebuttal, there is a compelling normative consideration underlying the distinction between public and private defamation plaintiffs. An individual who decides to seek governmental office must accept certain necessary consequences of that involvement in public affairs. He runs the risk of closer public scrutiny than might otherwise be the case. And society's interest in the officers of government is not strictly limited to the formal discharge of official duties....

Those classed as public figures stand in a similar position. Hypothetically, it may be possible for someone to become a public figure through no purposeful action of his own, but the instances of truly involuntary public figures must be exceedingly rare. For the most part those who attain this status have assumed roles of especial prominence in the affairs of society. Some occupy positions of such persuasive power and influence that they are deemed public figures for all purposes. More commonly, those classed as public figures have thrust themselves to the forefront of particular public controversies in order to influence the resolution of the issues involved. In either event, they invite attention and comment.

Even if the foregoing generalities do not obtain in every instance, the communications media are entitled to act on the assumption that public officials and public figures have voluntarily exposed themselves to increased risk of injury from defamatory falsehood concerning them. No such assumption is justified with respect to a private individual. He has not accepted public office nor assumed an "influential role in ordering society." Curtis Publishing Co. v. Butts, 388 U.S., at 164 (Warren, C.J., concurring in result). He has relinquished no part of his interest in the protection of his own good name, and consequently he has a more compelling call on the courts for redress of injury inflicted by defamatory falsehood. Thus, private individuals are not only more vulnerable to injury than public officials and public figures; they are also more deserving of recovery.

For these reasons we conclude that the States should retain substantial latitude in their efforts to enforce a legal remedy for defamatory falsehood injurious to the reputation of a private individual. The extension of the *New York Times* test proposed by the *Rosenbloom* plurality would abridge this legitimate state interest to a degree that we find unacceptable. . . .

We hold that, so long as they do not impose liability without fault, the States may define for themselves the appropriate standard of liability for a publisher or broadcaster of defamatory falsehood injurious to a private individual. This approach provides a more equitable boundary between the competing concerns involved here. It recognizes the strength of the legitimate state interest in compensating private individuals for wrongful injury to reputation, yet shields the press and broadcast media from the rigors of strict liability for defamation. At least this conclusion obtains where, as here, the substance of the defamatory statement "makes substantial danger to reputation apparent." This phrase places in perspective the conclusion we announce today. Our inquiry would involve considerations somewhat different from those discussed above if a State purported to condition civil liability on a factual misstatement whose content did not warn a reasonably prudent editor or broadcaster of its defamatory potential. Cf. Time, Inc. v. Hill, 385 U.S. 374 (1967). Such a case is not now before us, and we intimate no view as to its proper resolution.

IV

. . . For the reasons stated below, we hold that the States may not permit recovery of presumed or punitive damages, at least when liability is not based on a showing of knowledge of falsity or reckless disregard for the truth.

The common law of defamation is an oddity of tort law, for it allows recovery of purportedly compensatory damages without evidence of actual loss. Under the traditional rules pertaining to actions for libel, the existence of injury is presumed from the fact of publication. Juries may award substantial sums as compensation for supposed damage to reputation without any proof that such harm actually occurred. The largely uncontrolled discretion of juries to award damages where there is no loss unnecessarily compounds the potential of any system of liability for defamatory falsehood to inhibit the vigorous exercise of First Amendment freedoms. Additionally, the doctrine of presumed damages invites juries to punish unpopular opinion rather than to compensate individuals for injury sustained by the publication of a false fact. More to the point, the States have no substantial interest in securing for plaintiffs such as this petitioner gratuitous awards of money damages far in excess of any actual injury.

. . . It is necessary to restrict defamation plaintiffs who do not prove knowledge of falsity or reckless disregard for the truth to compensation for actual injury. We need not define "actual injury," as trial courts have wide experience in framing appropriate jury instructions in tort actions. Suffice it to say that actual injury is not limited to out-of-pocket loss. Indeed, the more customary types of actual harm inflicted by defamatory falsehood include impairment of reputation and standing in the community, personal humiliation, and mental anguish and suffering. Of course, juries must be limited by appropriate instructions, and all awards must be supported by competent evidence concerning the injury, although there need be no evidence which assigns an actual dollar value to the injury.

We also find no justification for allowing awards of punitive damages against publishers and broadcasters held liable under state-defined standards of liability for defamation. In most jurisdictions jury discretion over the amounts awarded is limited only by the gentle rule that they not be excessive. Consequently, juries assess punitive damages in wholly unpredictable amounts bearing no necessary relation to the actual harm caused. And they remain free to use their discretion selectively to punish expressions of unpopular views. Like the doctrine of presumed damages, jury discretion to award punitive damages unnecessarily exacerbates the danger of media self-censorship, but, unlike the former rule, punitive damages are wholly irrelevant to the state interest that justifies a negligence standard for private defamation actions. They are not compensation for injury. Instead, they are private fines levied by civil juries to punish reprehensible conduct and to deter its future occurrence. In short, the private defamation plaintiff who establishes liability under a less demanding standard than that stated by *New York Times* may recover only such damages as are sufficient to compensate him for actual injury.

V

Notwithstanding our refusal to extend the *New York Times* privilege to defamation of private individuals, respondent contends that we should affirm the judgment below on the ground that petitioner is either a public official or a public figure. There is little basis for the former assertion. Several years prior to the present incident, petitioner had served briefly on housing committees appointed by the mayor of Chicago, but at the time of publication he had never held any remunerative governmental position. Respondent admits this but argues that petitioner's appearance at the coroner's inquest rendered him a "de facto public official." Our cases recognize no such concept. Respondent's suggestion would sweep all lawyers under the *New York Times* rule as officers of the court and distort the plain meaning of the "public official" category beyond all recognition. We decline to follow it.

Respondent's characterization of petitioner as a public figure raises a different question. That designation may rest on either of two alternative bases. In some instances an individual may achieve such pervasive fame or notoriety that he becomes a public figure for all purposes and in all contexts. More commonly, an individual voluntarily injects himself or is drawn into a particular public controversy and thereby becomes a public figure for a limited range of issues. In either case such persons assume special prominence in the resolution of public questions.

Petitioner has long been active in community and professional affairs. He has served as an officer of local civic groups and of various professional organizations, and he has published several books and articles on legal subjects. Although petitioner was consequently well-known in some circles, he had achieved no general fame or notoriety in the community. None of the prospective jurors called at the trial had ever heard of petitioner prior to this litigation, and respondent offered no proof that this response was atypical of the local population. We would not lightly assume that a citizen's participation in community and professional affairs rendered him a public figure for all purposes. Absent clear evidence of general fame or notoriety in the community, and pervasive involvement in the affairs of society, an individual should not be deemed a public personality for all aspects of his life. It is preferable to reduce the public figure question to a more meaningful context by looking to the nature and extent of an individual's participation in the particular controversy giving rise to the defamation.

In this context it is plain that petitioner was not a public figure. He played a minimal role at the coroner's inquest, and his participation related solely to his representation of a private client. He took no part in the criminal prosecution of Officer Nuccio. Moreover, he never discussed either the criminal or civil litigation with the press and was never quoted as having done so. He plainly did not thrust himself into the vortex of this public issue, nor did he engage the public's attention in an attempt to influence its outcome. We are persuaded that the trial court did not err in refusing to characterize petitioner as a public figure for the purpose of this litigation.

We therefore conclude that the *New York Times* standard is inapplicable to this case and that the trial court erred in entering judgment for respondent. Because the jury was allowed to impose liability without fault and was permitted to presume damages without proof of injury, a new trial is necessary. We reverse and remand for further proceedings in accord with this opinion.

It is so ordered.

[The concurring opinion of JUSTICE BLACKMUN is omitted.]

[The dissenting opinions of CHIEF JUSTICE BURGER, and JUSTICES BRENNAN and WHITE are omitted.]

JUSTICE DOUGLAS dissenting.

The Court describes this case as a return to the struggle of "defin[ing] the proper accommodation between the law of defamation and the freedoms of speech and press protected by the First Amendment." It is indeed a struggle, once described by Mr. Justice Black as "the same quagmire" in which the Court "is now helplessly struggling in the field of obscenity." Curtis Publishing Co. v. Butts, 388 U.S. 130, 171 (concurring opinion). I would suggest that the struggle is a quite hopeless one, for, in light of the command of the First Amendment, no "accommodation" of its freedoms can be "proper" except those made by the Framers themselves.

. . .

Justice Brennan, dissenting.

... [W]e strike the proper accommodation between avoidance of media self-censorship and protection of individual reputations only when we require States to apply the ... knowing-or-reckless-falsity standard in civil libel actions concerning media reports of the involvement of private individuals in events of public or general interest.

· · ·

Justice White, dissenting.

· · ·

... As I see it, there are wholly insufficient grounds for scuttling the libel laws of the States in such wholesale fashion, to say nothing of deprecating the reputation interest of ordinary citizens and rendering them powerless to protect themselves. I do not suggest that the decision is illegitimate or beyond the bounds of judicial review, but it is an ill-considered exercise of the power entrusted to this Court, particularly when the Court has not had the benefit of briefs and argument addressed to most of the major issues which the Court now decides. I respectfully dissent.

E. MATTERS OF PRIVATE CONCERN

Dun & Bradstreet, Inc. v. Greenmoss Builders, Inc., 472 U.S. 749 (1985), was a defamation case that didn't involve the reputation of an individual, but of a company. Dun & Bradstreet is a credit reporting company, which falsely reported that a construction contractor had filed for bankruptcy. The Vermont Supreme Court decided that the construction contractor was entitled to recover presumed damages without proof of actual harm (fixed by the jury at $50,000), and punitive damages of $300,000. Dun & Bradstreet argued that this was inconsistent with the *Gertz* case because, while they had been negligent, it had not been proved that they acted with knowledge of falsity or with reckless disregard of the truth. The Vermont Supreme Court responded that *Gertz* (and *New York Times* as well) were cases of publications by mass media. The state court thought that the First Amendment rules laid down in those cases were limited to publications by the media.

A majority of the Justices of the United States Supreme Court rejected that argument. As Justice Brennan explained, the principles of *Gertz* and *New York Times* were designed to protect the speech rights of speakers and listeners. Thus, "in the context of defamation law, the rights of the institutional media are no greater and no less than those enjoyed by other individuals engaged in the same activities."

A different majority of the justices, however, affirmed the judgment imposing liability for another reason. A credit report involved "no issue of public concern." In striking a balance between state interests and first amendment interests, speech "of purely private concern" invoked a lesser first amendment interest, because it had nothing to do with a continuing dialogue about political and social changes. With a lesser first amendment interest in the balance, common law rules allowing liability for presumed damages and punitive damages could be applied. (Although Dun & Bradstreet was negligent in making its false credit report, presumably common law rules permitting the imposition of liability without fault could also be applied to speech "of private concern.") Four of the Justices disagreed with this new balance of competing interests, and also objected that the distinction between statements of "private" and "public" concern could be very difficult to apply in the future.

NOTES AND QUESTIONS

1.　One function traditionally served by the private defamation suit is vindication of reputation, although that function has been less clear in American law than it has been in English law. As one commentator has pointed out:[*]

> [T]here appears to be a genuine difference between the English and American attitude toward libel actions. Although in recent years we have seen Hiss sue Chambers, McCarthy sue Benton, and Quentin Reynolds sue Pegler, it is very doubtful that we regard the failure to sue for libel as an admission. But in England, as Mr. Dean's book confirms, the bringing of a libel action is quite respectable and in some situations the social compulsion to do so appears very strong. Mr. Dean's telling of the controversy between Gladstone's sons and Peter Wright, a writer, is an excellent instance. Wright having accused Gladstone, who was by then dead, of sexual irregularity and hypocrisy throughout his life, Gladstone's sons by publicly charging Wright with being a liar and a "foul fellow" were able to force him, as the author puts it, to "ordeal by trial." Wright, incidentally, lost the action and Gladstone's reputation as a pillar of respectability was saved. The Laski case appears to be another illustration. Did not Laski have to sue? There is in this national difference, as David Riesman suggested a decade ago, an excellent cue for a sociological exploration of the sources of the two national attitudes.

> This first point leads readily to a second. On the English view the law of defamation may be considered not so much a way of giving monetary recovery for loss occasioned by injury to reputation, as a way of securing an official and definitive determination of the truth of a charge.

Notice how the development of the rules from *New York Times* through *Gertz* make it even more difficult to view the law of defamation as primarily a vehicle for vindicating reputation. If the defamed person brings a lawsuit for libel, and then loses it, that can only underscore the harm of the original defamation. If the plaintiff is a private citizen, he can recover damages only if he proves actual harm to his reputation and that the publisher was negligent. (As we have seen, the proof of the publisher's fault is more difficult if the plaintiff is a public official or a public figure.) Thus, if the jury is convinced that the plaintiff has been

---

[*] Harry Kalven, Jr., Book Review of Hatred, Ridicule, or Contempt by Joseph Dean, University of Chicago Law Review, 1955, vol. 22, pp. 583–584.

libeled, and that there is not a grain of truth in the libelous statements, they can still return a verdict for the defendant if they find that the defendant was not negligent. (Moreover, in American law juries are seldom required to give the reasons for their verdicts.) Even under the traditional rules, there was often reluctance to sue a character assassin because the suits were expensive to bring, and the impact of losing the suit could only add to the injury to reputation. Will the new rules, with the requirement of proving the publisher at fault, further deter deserving libel plaintiffs from using the courts to repair their damaged reputations?

2. It is interesting to compare the constitutional law developments in the law of defamation with other developments in the law of torts. (The law of torts, of which defamation is a small part, is the body of law that permits individuals to sue for "wrongs.") Beginning in the nineteenth century, tort law centered around the notion that people ought not to be required to pay damages unless their conduct was, in some way, at fault—i.e., unless they intended injury or were negligent. Thus pedestrian A could not recover damages when he was run down by motorist B unless motorist B was driving carelessly. Much of the modification of tort law in the twentieth century has been in the direction of imposing liability without fault. Workers' compensation, for example, requires employers to pay workers injured on the job without reference to whether the employer or the worker was at fault. In the last ten years, American courts have begun to work out the rule that manufacturers of dangerously defective products are liable to people injured by those products without reference to fault. And, in the last few years, a number of states have enacted "no fault" automobile compensation acts.

Traditionally, the law of defamation was one exception to the general notion that defendants were not liable unless they were at fault. But, at the same time the fault principle is being discarded in other areas of tort law, the Supreme Court's interpretation of the First Amendment is turning defamation law in the opposite direction—insisting that defendants cannot be required to pay damages unless they are at fault.

3. Obviously, a very complex body of law has evolved from the simple statement in the First Amendment that: "Congress shall make no law ... abridging the freedom of speech, or of the press...." In the defamation area, among other complexities, there is the definition of "public official" and "public figure," the distinction between "recklessness" and "negligence," and the notion of "actual damage" to contend with. Consider this description of the role of the Supreme Court in deciding upon the constitutionality of laws:

> It is sometimes said that the court assumes a power to overrule or control the action of the people's representatives. This is a misconception. The Constitution is the supreme law of the land ordained and established by the people. All legislation must conform to the principles it lays down. When an act of Congress is appropriately challenged in the courts as not con-

forming to the constitutional mandate, the judicial branch of
the government has only one duty; to lay the article of the
Constitution which is invoked beside the statute which is challenged and to decide whether the latter squares with the former. (Justice Roberts, for the Court, in United States v. Butler,
297 U.S. 1, 62 [1936].)

Do you think that is a meaningful and accurate description of what the
Supreme Court does when it interprets and applies provisions of the Bill
of Rights? Of course, the law of defamation, being considered here, is not
an Act of Congress nor a statute passed by state legislatures. It is judge-
made law, developed by state courts and rooted in English common law
rules. Does that make a difference?

   4.   A possible explanation for, and a complication in explaining, the
complex law that has grown out of the First Amendment, is the American federal structure. Many nations in the world have federal structures
of government—a central government and local governments, each with
responsibility for passing different aspects of "law." The United States is
virtually unique in one respect, however. It does not have a unitary court
system. Most federal systems do not have distinct federal and state
courts, but a single court system.

   The law of defamation is, as has been noted, largely judge-made. If
the United States Supreme Court sat at the apex of a single court
system, it might have the last word on modifying and applying that
judge-made law. But, under our system, state courts have the last word
on the meaning of state law. And, defamation is an area that had been
controlled almost entirely by state law until the *New York Times* case.
The United States Supreme Court cannot upset state court decisions on
the meaning of state law simply because they are, in the Court's
judgment, wrong—those decisions stand unless they contravene a valid
federal statute or some provision of the United States Constitution. One
way of looking at the decisions discussed in this chapter is to conclude
that the law of defamation has been largely "federalized" through
interpretation of the First Amendment.

   Without reference to the content of the decisions, federalization of
the law of defamation is a happy development for the national media.
Before *New York Times, Butts, Walker* and *Gertz,* a national magazine or
television network had to cope with the possible application of the law of
defamation of 50 states. (It was even possible for a single person,
claiming he received a different injury in each state in which the
defamation was published, to bring suit in many states.) There are wide
disparities in the defamation law of individual states. And, if that is
possible, the law of "conflict of laws" (the rules for determining which
state law applies when the facts of the lawsuit have contact with more
than one state) in defamation cases was even more complex than the law
of defamation itself. In editing a national magazine, or preparing a
national broadcast, with view to the possible exposure to defamation
liability, it must be comforting to have a single rule to look to, no matter
what the rule is. Since Congress has never seen fit to pass a single

national law dealing with defamation, is it legitimate for the Supreme Court to use the First Amendment to accomplish that objective?

5. It should be obvious by now that there is no single doctrine in interpreting the First Amendment, but disparate doctrines for handling different problem areas. And, as we have seen, it is often difficult to reconcile the handling of different areas of First Amendment law. (Recall the problem of reconciling the treatment of obscenity and offensive speech.) In part that is because different areas have very different functional problems. In part, the rules are determined by the historical accident of the makeup of the Court and the doctrines in vogue when the problem is first presented to the Court.

Recall, also, the conflict among "absolutes," "balancing," and "clear and present danger" which was discussed in Chapter 5 at pp. 128–130. How would you characterize the libel decisions? Obviously, clear and present danger hasn't taken root in this area of free speech law. (Could it be applied? How would you define the "danger"? How would you decide whether it is "clear" or "present"?) In terms of the distinction between "absolutes" and "balancing," can you clearly categorize the libel decisions? One way to look at the decisions is as an exercise in "definitional balancing"—i.e. hard-and-fast rules (or limited absolutes) that themselves are the product of balancing competing considerations. (This is distinguished from "ad hoc" balancing—i.e. deciding *in each individual case* whether society has a sufficient interest to silence the speaker.)

It is helpful to recall some of the criticisms that were often leveled at the kind of balancing practiced by Justice Frankfurter in his concurring opinion in the *Dennis* case (in Chapter 5, at p. 110), and in his opinion for the Court in the *Beauharnais* case (in this chapter at pp. 452–454). First was the problem that weighing imponderables against each other gave very little guide to decision-making. If, in each individual case, the task was to weight the values of speech against the policies that justified silencing the speaker, a reasonable argument could usually be made that silence was to be preferred. Local judges often share a community's prejudices, and the balance might too often be struck in a way that punished the unpopular speaker for what he said.

Second, when Justice Frankfurter unpacked his scales to strike the balance, free speech often seemed to be the loser. Thus, even if the important cases reached the Supreme Court, the result of balancing seemed to be an interpretation of the First Amendment that allowed the speaker to be silenced whenever there was some respectable body of opinion that it was appropriate to do so. That was because Justice Frankfurter emphasized that legislatures rather than courts were the best places to weigh and decide between competing interests.

Arguably, "definitional balancing" has avoided both of these problems. The defamation cases show that free speech interests have not been lost in the balance. Indeed a body of law centuries old has been largely remade in the interest of freedom of expression. Moreover, since rules have emerged which do not just leave each case to be decided on its own peculiar facts, lower courts are not given unlimited discretion to silence unpopular speakers. There is still, obviously, the question of judging whether the balance has been properly struck. The several opinions in the libel cases show there is much room for argument whether the rules that have emerged give the press insufficient breathing room or whether they have given too little weight to the interest in personal reputation. No matter where a line is drawn in the course of "definitional balancing," there is likely to be such an argument. That is why Justice Douglas stubbornly stuck by his argument that the only safe course is to read the First Amendment as "absolute." Do you agree?

II. MEDIA INVASION OF PRIVACY

A. INTRODUCTION

WILLIAM L. PROSSER, PRIVACY*

In the year 1890 Mrs. Samuel D. Warren, a young matron of Boston, which is a large city in Massachusetts, held at her home a series of social entertainments on an elaborate scale. She was the daughter of Senator Bayard of Delaware, and her husband was a wealthy young paper manufacturer, who only the year before had given up the practice of law to devote himself to an inherited business. Socially Mrs. Warren was among the elite; and the newspapers of Boston, and in particular the *Saturday Evening Gazette,* which specialized in "blue blood" items, covered her parties in highly personal and embarrassing detail. It was the era of "yellow journalism," when the press had begun to resort to excesses in the way of prying that have become more or less commonplace today; and Boston was perhaps, of all of the cities in the country, the one in which a lady and a gentleman kept their names and their personal affairs out of the papers. The matter came to a head when the newspapers had a field day on the occasion of the wedding of a daughter, and Mr. Warren became annoyed. It was an annoyance for which the press, the advertisers and the entertainment industry of America were to pay dearly over the next seventy years.

Mr. Warren turned to his recent law partner, Louis D. Brandeis, who was destined not to be unknown to history. The result was a noted article, "The Right to Privacy," in the *Harvard Law Review,* upon which the two men collaborated. It has come to be regarded as the outstanding example of the influence of legal periodicals upon the American law. In the Harvard Law School class of 1877 the two authors had stood respectively second and first, and both of them were gifted with scholarship, imagination, and ability. Internal evidences of style, and the probabilities of the situation, suggest that the writing, and perhaps most of the research, was done by Brandeis; but it was undoubtedly a joint effort, to which both men contributed their ideas.

Piecing together old decisions in which relief had been afforded on the basis of defamation, or the invasion of some property right, or a breach of confidence or an implied contract, the article concluded that such cases were in reality based upon a broader principle which was entitled to separate recognition. This principle they called the right to

* California Law Review, 1960, vol. 48, pp. 383–384.

privacy; and they contended that the growing abuses of the press made a remedy upon such a distinct ground essential to the protection of private individuals against the outrageous and unjustifiable infliction of mental distress. This was the first of a long line of law review discussions of the right of privacy....

WARREN & BRANDEIS, THE RIGHT TO PRIVACY*

Of the desirability—indeed of the necessity—of some such protection, there can, it is believed, be no doubt. The press is overstepping in every direction the obvious bounds of propriety and of decency. Gossip is no longer the resource of the idle and of the vicious, but has become a trade, which is pursued with industry as well as effrontery. To satisfy a prurient taste the details of sexual relations are spread broadcast in the columns of the daily papers. To occupy the indolent, column upon column is filled with idle gossip, which can only be procured by intrusion upon the domestic circle. The intensity and complexity of life, attendant upon advancing civilization, have rendered necessary some retreat from the world, and man, under the refining influence of culture, has become more sensitive to publicity, so that solitude and privacy have become more essential to the individual; but modern enterprise and invention have, through invasions upon his privacy, subjected him to mental pain and distress, far greater than could be inflicted by mere bodily injury. Nor is the harm wrought by such invasions confined to the suffering of those who may be made the subjects of journalistic or other enterprise. In this, as in other branches of commerce, the supply creates the demand. Each crop of unseemly gossip, thus harvested, becomes the seed of more, and, in direct proportion to its circulation, results in a lowering of social standards and of morality. Even gossip apparently harmless, when widely and persistently circulated, is potent for evil. It both belittles and perverts. It belittles by inverting the relative importance of things, thus dwarfing the thoughts and aspirations of a people. When personal gossip attains the dignity of print, and crowds the space available for matters of real interest to the community, what wonder that the ignorant and thoughtless mistake its relative importance. Easy of comprehension, appealing to that weak side of human nature which is never wholly cast down by the misfortunes and frailties of our neighbors, no one can be surprised that it usurps the place of interest in brains capable of other things. Triviality destroys at once robustness of thought and delicacy of feeling. No enthusiasm can flourish, no generous impulse can survive under its blighting influence.

NOTE

In the years that followed the Warren and Brandeis article, American courts developed law giving a right to recover for invasion of privacy. This right protected four distinct interests. First the law protects against physical intrusion. This part of the law of privacy protects people whose telephones are tapped, who are spied upon with binoculars, who are shadowed by private detectives and the like. A second interest protected by the law of privacy has to do with commercial exploitation of the

* Harvard Law Review, 1890, vol. 4, p. 196.

names or personalities of famous people, such as the famous football star whose picture and name are put on a bubble gum card without his consent (and hence without paying him). These two aspects of the law of privacy will not be treated further here.

Two other aspects of the law of privacy, however, are of particular concern to the media, and are involved in the case of Time, Inc. v. Hill, 385 U.S. 374 (1967). One of these is the so-called "true" privacy action. That is what the Warren and Brandeis article was all about—media reporting of true events. Since truth has been a complete defense in civil actions for libel, that body of law will not protect the citizen if intimate details of his private life are printed in magazines and newspapers. Warren and Brandeis argued that the press ought not to be permitted to invade people's privacy by printing stories about their private lives. Ironically, very few cases have allowed recovery on a "true" privacy theory, despite the gallons of printer's ink that have been spilled by courts and commentators talking about the law of privacy. The catch here has been the concept of "newsworthiness." It is clear that, no matter how much someone is embarrassed by the media's disclosures concerning his private life, he can't complain if what was disclosed was "newsworthy." If newsworthiness were defined in the way Warren and Brandeis argued it should be—in terms of what was "decent" to print— the courts would be engaged in the uncomfortable role of overseeing what the press should be allowed to disclose to the public.

Actually, the overwhelming number of cases that have allowed people to recover for invasion of privacy have involved "false-light" invasions of privacy. Here, the gist of the person's complaint is not just that his privacy was invaded by what was disclosed, but that what was disclosed wasn't true at all—it put him in a false light. Here, the difficult problem is to reconcile the law of privacy with the law of libel. Libel has for a long time provided protection against some kinds of false reports by the media—those that injure "reputation." The question then is what kind of false stories belong to the complex rules of the ancient law of libel, and what kind of false stories invoke the newer law of privacy.

Until 1967, the law of privacy was developed, without reference to constitutional law, as part of the common law of torts. New York Times v. Sullivan, in 1964, raised the question whether the First Amendment rules that the Court had applied to libel cases would apply to privacy actions as well. That question was answered in 1967, in Time Inc. v. Hill, which follows.

B. "TRUE" PRIVACY

In September of 1952, the James Hill family—Hill, his wife and five children—were held hostage in their suburban, Whitemarsh, Pennsylvania home by three escaped convicts. After 19 hours, the family was released unharmed, and the convicts departed. The story was front-page news across the country. The notoriety was distasteful to the Hill family. They discouraged all attempts by the media to place them in a continuing spotlight—refusing interviews and television appearances. Soon after the incident, the Hills moved to Connecticut.

Joseph Hayes was moved by the Hill incident to write a novel called *The Desperate Hours* which depicted a family of four held hostage in a suburban home by three escaped convicts. The novel was made into a play, produced for the first time in 1955. *Life* magazine's story on the play posed the play's actors in the original Hill residence in Pennsylvania. The story accompanying the pictures recalled the Hills' ordeal two and one-half years earlier. After extremely complicated litigation in the New York courts, the Hills were awarded $30,000 for invasion of privacy. Time, Inc., the owner of *Life* magazine, took the case all the way to the Supreme Court, which reversed the decision and sent the case back for a new trial. Time, Inc. v. Hill, 385 U.S. 374 (1967). (The Hills' lawyer in the Supreme Court, by the way, was Richard M. Nixon, who was then practicing law in New York.)

Although the theory on which the Hills recovered was "invasion of privacy," their "true" privacy complaint was only a side issue in the case. The Hill family was the subject of a national news story, but that story had faded from public memory until the combination of the novel, the play and the *Life* magazine story once more brought them to public attention. This has some of the earmarks of a recurring problem in the law of privacy. A person is the subject of notoriety and national attention. He shuns the limelight, years pass, and he sinks into welcome obscurity. Then, years later, the media recall the past, bringing the long-forgotten events once more to public attention.

The Supreme Court held, however, that if the story about the Hills in *Life* had been scrupulously accurate,* the Hills could not recover. Justice Brennan's opinion, for the Court, argued that the media's privilege to print true, newsworthy stories was a minimum guarantee of the First Amendment.

> The guarantees for speech and press are not the preserve of political expression or comment upon public affairs, essential as those are to healthy government. One need only pick up any newspaper or magazine to comprehend the vast range of published matter which exposes persons to public view, both private citizens and public officials. Exposure of the self to others in varying degrees is a concomitant of life in a civilized community. The risk of this exposure is an essential incident of life in a society which places a primary value on freedom of speech and press. "Freedom of discussion, if it would fulfill its historic function in this nation, must embrace all issues about which information is needed or appropriate to enable the members of society to cope with the exigencies of their period."

It was, however, unnecessary to cope with the issue of the person once in the public eye who had become obscure. The subject of the *Life* article was the opening of a new play, and that was both something current and something of public interest. That made the Hills' experience, although years past, something of current interest too. It was therefore unnecessary to consider whether the First Amendment would permit recovery by

---

* The Court, however, held the story to have been inaccurate.

the Hills if the magazine had, in the absence of the novel or the play, lifted the Hills from their hard-won obscurity.

Time, Inc. v. Hill did elevate the newsworthiness privilege in "true" privacy actions to the status of a rule of constitutional law. It did little, however, to define the outer limits of the privilege, or the sweep of the media's rights to disclose true facts concerning "public affairs."

Time, Inc. v. Hill had been argued twice—in April, 1966, and again in October of the same year. Between the two arguments, the Court changed its position. In the April conference, a majority agreed to affirm in Hill's favor. Chief Justice Warren said: "It's a fictionalization of these people's experience and false and, in that circumstance, there's no First Amendment problem. In this limited application, I see no threat to a free press."** Justice Black disagreed. He said that "newspapers have the right to report and criticize plays. This is nothing but a statute prohibiting the press from publishing certain things."† Chief Justice Warren and Justices Clark, Harlan, Brennan, Stewart, and Fortas voted to affirm; Justices Black, Douglas, and White voted to reverse.

Chief Justice Warren assigned the Court's opinion to Justice Fortas, who circulated a 16-page opinion stressing the importance of the right of privacy. After summarizing the facts, Justice Fortas wrote: "The facts of this case are unavoidably distressing. Needless, heedless, wanton injury of the sort inflicted by Life's picture story is not an essential instrument of responsible journalism. Magazine writers and editors are not, by reason of their high office, relieved of the common obligation to avoid inflicting wanton and unnecessary injury. The prerogatives of the press—essential to our liberty—do not preclude reasonable care and thoughtfulness. They do not confer a license for pointless assault."* Justice Fortas then concluded.**

> The deliberate, callous invasion of the Hills' right to be let alone—this appropriation of a family's right not to be molested or to have its name exploited and its quiet existence invaded—cannot be defended on the ground that it is within the purview of a constitutional guarantee designed to protect the free exchange of ideas and opinions. This is exploitation, undertaken to titillate and excite, for commercial purposes. It was not a retelling of a newsworthy incident or of an event relating to a public figure. It was not such an account. It was not so designed. It was fiction: an invention, distorted and put to the uses of the promotion of Life magazine and of a play. Many difficult problems may arise under the right-to-privacy statute, but we conclude that the present case, on its facts and on the New York law as construed by the courts of that State, does not

** Quoted in Bernard Schwartz. Super Chief, New York, 1983, p. 643. Reprinted with permission.

† Ibid.

* Ibid.

** Bernard Schwartz, The Unpublished Opinions of the Warren Court, New York, pp. 263–264.

permit the appellant to claim immunity from liability because of
the First Amendment.

Justice Harlan wrote in a concurring opinion:[†]

> In defining the constitutional scope of free speech and press
> the decisions of this Court reflect a weighing process whereby
> relevant interests are taken into account in framing a solution
> for the case at hand. . . . or more rarely a guiding principle for
> the future. . . .
>
>   . . . The conflict between free press and privacy is so new to
> this Court, the possible fact situations so varied, and the inter-
> ests so elastic that I doubt whether it is now feasible to frame
> general rules that provide much guidance in hard cases. Howev-
> er, the present facts, to which I now turn, persuade me that the
> Life article is not privileged under the Constitution.

Justice Douglas and White wrote dissenting opinions. Justice White's
opinion was especially important. He asserted that the New York privacy
statute could be applied to true news accounts if commercially exploited.
Justice Fortas disagreed with that interpretation of New York law, but
White's view had raised such doubts among the justices that Fortas
himself proposed that the case be reargued.

The day before reargument of *Time Inc.,* Justice Black circulated a
memorandum that turned the Court around in the case. The heart of the
opinion was a critique of weighing values in deciding constitutional
issues. He wrote:[*]

> The use of the weighing process, which has here produced
> such divergent results, means simply to me that by legal leger-
> demain the First Amendment's promise of unequivocal press
> freedom, the freedom constitutionally promised, has been trans-
> muted into a debased alloy—transmuted into a freedom which
> will vacillate and grow weaker or stronger as the Court person-
> nel is shifted from time to time. This means that the scope of
> press freedom is not to be decided by what the Founders wrote,
> but by what a Court majority thinks they should have written
> had they been writing now. I prefer to have the people's liberty
> measured by the constitutional language the Founders wrote
> rather than by new views of new judges as to what liberty it is
> safe for the people to have. The weighing process makes it
> infinitely easier for judges to exercise their newly proclaimed
> power to curb the press. For under its aegis judges are no longer
> to be limited to their recognized power to make binding *inter-*
> *pretations* of the Constitution. That power, won after bitter
> constitutional struggles, has apparently become too prosaic and
> unexciting. So the judiciary now confers upon the judiciary the
> more "elastic" and exciting power to decide, under its value-
> weighing process, just how much freedom the courts will permit
> the press to have. And in making this decision the Court is to

---

† Ibid., p. 267.
* Ibid., pp. 274–275.

have important leeway, it seems, in order to make the Constitution the people adopted more adaptable to what the Court
deems to be modern needs. We, the judiciary, are no longer to
be crippled and hobbled by the old admonition that "We must
always remember it is a Constitution we are *expounding*," but
we are to work under the exhilarating new slogan that "We
must always remember that it is a Constitution we are *rewriting* to fit the times." I cannot join nor can I even acquiesce in
this doctrine which I firmly believe to be a violation of the
Constitution itself.

NOTES AND QUESTIONS

1. As previously indicated, there are relatively few cases that
permit recovery on a "true" privacy theory for the disclosure of true
facts by the media. Of the few cases that permit recovery, most were
decided before the *Hill* case. In the situations that follow, would recovery
on the basis of a "true" privacy theory violate the First Amendment?

(a) William James Sidis was a child prodigy, who lectured
mathematicians on the fourth dimension at the age of 11 and, at
16, graduated from Harvard. After his Harvard graduation,
however, Sidis developed a deep desire for obscurity and a
revulsion of his former notoriety. He disappeared from public
view, took a job as a bookkeeper, and in his non-working hours
collected street car transfers and studied the Okamakammessett
Indians. The *New Yorker* magazine published a sympathetic
account of his career, revealing where Sidis was now and what
he was doing. One can imagine the devastating effect on a
person who had, as Sidis had, so thoroughly sought obscurity
after his earlier notoriety. It was claimed that publication of the
article led to Sidis' early death. Sidis v. F–R Publishing Corp.,
113 F.2d 806 (2d Cir.1940) (no right of privacy).

(b) Gabrielle Darley was a prostitute who was charged with
a murder. She was acquitted of the charge after a sensational
trial. She left her profession, married a man named Melvin, and
lived a new life among friends who were unaware of her past life
and notoriety. Seven years after the trial, a movie was made
telling the true story of the trial. The movie, entitled "The Red
Kimono," used the name of Gabrielle Darley, and revealed her
past life to her friends. Melvin v. Reid, 112 Cal.App. 285, 297 P.
91 (1931) (right of privacy recognized).

(c) In December, 1956, Marvin Briscoe and another man
hijacked a truck in Danville, Kentucky. In 1967, *Reader's Digest*
published an article entitled "The Big Business of Hijacking,"
discussing truck thefts and the efforts made to stop them. One
sentence in the article said: "Typical of many beginners, Marvin
Briscoe and [another man] stole a 'valuable looking' truck in
Danville, Ky., and then fought a gun battle with the local police,
only to learn that they had hijacked four bowling-pin spotters."
Briscoe claimed he had not been involved in any criminal
activity since the 1956 hijacking, and had since lived an exem-

plary life. Briscoe v. Reader's Digest Ass'n, 4 Cal.3d 529, 93 Cal.Rptr. 866, 483 P.2d 34 (1971) (right of privacy recognized).

2.   Justice Douglas' concurring opinion in the *Hill* case suggests that once a person's activities become "news of the day," events pass into the "public domain" and there can be no liability for reviving public interest in those events. Do you agree? There has been lively controversy among commentators as to whether the newsworthiness privilege leaves anything of the "true" privacy action. Compare Kalven, *Privacy in Tort Law—Were Warren and Brandeis Wrong?* 31 Law & Contemp.Prob. 326 (1966) with Bloustein, *Privacy, Tort Law, and the Constitution: Is Warren and Brandeis' Tort Petty and Unconstitutional as Well?*, 46 Tex.L.Rev. 611 (1968).

3.   Authors of fiction often use people they know as models for their characters. If people who know the "model" recognize the similarities, has there been an invasion of privacy? Marjorie Kinnan Rawlings used an acquaintance as the prototype for the character "Zelma" in her novel, *Cross Creek*. The novel said this about Zelma:

> Zelma is an ageless spinster resembling an angry and efficient canary. She manages her orange grove and as much of the village and county as needs management or will submit to it. I cannot decide whether she should have been a man or a mother. She combines the more violent characteristics of both and those who ask for or accept her manifold ministrations think nothing of being cursed loudly at the very instant of being tenderly fed, clothed, nursed or guided through their troubles.

Assuming that Zelma's portrait is an accurate sketch of the plaintiff, and that Ms. Rawlings based Zelma on the plaintiff, has there been an invasion of privacy? Cason v. Baskin, 155 Fla. 198, 20 So.2d 243 (1944) (right of privacy recognized, but plaintiff's recovery limited to "nominal damages"—presumably one dollar).

4.   A few states had laws that made it unlawful for the news media to publish the name or identity of rape victims. One of those laws was before the Supreme Court in Cox Broadcasting Corp. v. Cohn, 420 U.S. 469 (1975). In that case, a Georgia television station had used the name of a rape victim in connection with a television news report of judicial proceedings in the cases of the persons accused of the crime. The Court decided that publication of the rape victim's name was protected by the First Amendment, despite the claim of invasion of her family's privacy (she had been killed in the rape). The decision was limited, however, by the fact that the name of the victim was included in the indictments charging the suspects in the crime. Under Georgia law, the indictments were public documents, open to inspection by anyone. The Court decided that the press had an absolute right to publish the contents of public official records. Suppose the State had taken pains to keep the victim's name from appearing in public records. Would it violate the First Amendment to criminally punish the newspaper for revealing her identity in news coverage?

5.   Consider, also, prohibitions on publishing the identity of juvenile criminal suspects. In Oklahoma Publishing Co. v. District Court, 430

U.S. 308 (1977), a state court order barring newspaper publication of the name or picture of an 11 year old charged with murder was held to violate the First Amendment. The limited ground of decision, however, was that, since reporters were allowed to be present during juvenile court hearings and to take pictures of the juvenile escorted from the courthouse, the newspaper had acquired the information lawfully and with the State's implicit approval. A state criminal law forbidding publication of names of juveniles subject to juvenile court proceedings was held to violate the First Amendment in Smith v. Daily Mail Publishing Co., 443 U.S. 97 (1979). That law, however, did not really protect juveniles' privacy since it permitted radio and television broadcasts of the same information. Suppose a state closes juvenile court hearings to the press, takes steps to prevent disclosure of the identity of juveniles charged with offenses, and forbids disclosure of juvenile suspects' identity in all media. Should it violate the First Amendment to punish a newspaper for revealing the identity of a juvenile charged with a serious crime?

6. In The Florida Star v. B.J.F., 491 U.S. 524 (1989), the Court decided the question it had left open in the *Cox Broadcasting* case discussed in note 4. Once again, a newspaper was sued for civil damages for publishing the name of a rape victim. This time, no prosecution had been begun, and the victim's name was not contained in a public record. The reporter, however, had obtained the victim's name by lawful means, and the Court concluded that imposing civil liability on the newspaper violated the First Amendment. The Court did not conclude that it would *always* violate the First Amendment to award damages for a truthful press report.

> [I]f a newspaper lawfully obtains truthful information about a matter of public significance then state officials may not constitutionally punish publication of the information, absent a need to further a state interest of the highest order.

In this case, the government had means other than controlling the press to keep rape victims' names confidential. Justice White's dissent argued that, in fact, the Court's standard would

> obliterate one of the most noteworthy legal inventions of the 20th–Century: the tort of the publication of private facts.... If the First Amendment prohibits wholly private persons (such as B.J.F.) from recovering for the publication of the fact that she was raped, I doubt that there remain any 'private facts' which persons may assume will not be published in the newspapers, or broadcast on television.

7. Bartnicki v. Vopper, 532 U.S. 514, 121 S.Ct. 1753 (2001) revisited the issue of damages of a true press report—this time the publication of the contents of an illegally intercepted cellular telephone conversation. Justice Stevens' opinion for the Court began by emphasizing that the case involved "a conflict between interests of the highest order—on the one hand, the interest in the full and free dissemination of information concerning public issues, and, on the other hand, the interest in individual privacy and, more specifically, in fostering private speech." Deciding

that, in this case, the interest in free dissemination prevailed, Justice Stevens said:

> [T]here are important interests to be considered on both sides of the constitutional calculus. In considering that balance, we acknowledge that some intrusions on privacy are more offensive than others, and that the disclosure of the contents of a private conversation can be an even greater intrusion on privacy than the interception itself. As a result, there is a valid independent justification for prohibiting such disclosures by persons who lawfully obtained access to the contents of an illegally intercepted message . . .

> We need not decide whether that interest is strong enough to justify the application of [the federal statute forbidding disclosure of illegally intercepted cellular telephone calls] to disclosures of trade secrets or domestic gossip or other information of purely private concern. . . . The enforcement of that provision in this case, however, implicates the core purposes of the First Amendment because it imposes sanctions on the publication of truthful information of public concern.

Justice Breyer's concurrence emphasized that the Court's holding was

> "narrow" . . . limited to the special circumstances present here: (1) the radio broadcasters acted lawfully (up to the time of final public disclosure); and (2) the information publicized involved a matter of unusual public concern, namely a threat of potential physical harm to others.

Chief Justice Rehnquist's dissent concluded:

> The Constitution should not protect the involuntary broadcast of personal conversations. Even where the communications involve public figures or concern public matters, the conversations are nonetheless private and worthy of protection. Although public persons may have forgone the right to live their lives screened from public scrutiny in some areas, it does not and should not follow that they also have abandoned their right to have a private conversation without fear of it being intentionally intercepted and knowingly disclosed.

C.　"FALSE LIGHT" PRIVACY

The bulk of the opinion in Time, Inc. v. Hill dealt with the problem of "false light" privacy. The *Life* story did not accurately relate what had happened to the Hills, but misrepresented that the play, "Desperate Hours," was an accurate portrayal of the Hill incident. Joseph Hayes, author of the book and the play, had not tried to recreate the Hills' experience, but had drawn his story from several incidents where convicts had held people hostage. The two pages of pictures in the *Life* story included an enactment of the son in the play being "roughed up" by a "brutish convict," a picture of the daughter biting a convict's hand to make him drop the gun, and one of the father throwing the gun through the door, described as a "brave try" to save his family. The convicts who had held the Hills had treated the family courteously, had not molested them, and had not been violent.

Justice Brennan's opinion for the Court held that the Hills could recover damages for invasion of privacy if the factual errors were made knowingly by *Life,* or were made with reckless disregard of truth. Excerpts from his opinion follow:

> Erroneous statement is no less inevitable in such a case than in the case of comment upon public affairs, and in both, if innocent or merely negligent, "... it must be protected if the freedoms of expression are to have the 'breathing space' that they 'need ... to survive'...." New York Times Co. v. Sullivan, ... at 271–272. As James Madison said, "Some degree of abuse is inseparable from the proper use of every thing; and in no instance is this more true than in that of the press." 4 Elliot's Debates on the Federal Constitution 571 (1876 ed.). We create a grave risk of serious impairment of the indispensable service of a free press in a free society if we saddle the press with the impossible burden of verifying to a certainty the facts associated in news articles with a person's name, picture or portrait, particularly as related to nondefamatory matter. Even negligence would be a most elusive standard, especially when the content of the speech itself affords no warning of prospective harm to another through falsity. A negligence test would place on the press the intolerable burden of guessing how a jury might assess the reasonableness of steps taken by it to verify the accuracy of every reference to a name, picture or portrait.

> In this context, sanctions against either innocent or negligent misstatement would present a grave hazard of discouraging the press from exercising the constitutional guarantees. Those guarantees are not for the benefit of the press so much as for the benefit of all of us....

> But the constitutional guarantees can tolerate sanctions against *calculated* falsehood without significant impairment of their essential function. We held in *New York Times* that calculated falsehood enjoyed no immunity in the case of alleged defamation of a public official concerning his official conduct. Similarly, calculated falsehood should enjoy no immunity in the situation here presented us....

> We find applicable here the standard of knowing or reckless falsehood, not through blind application of New York Times Co. v. Sullivan, relating solely to libel actions by public officials, but only upon consideration of the factors which arise in the particular context of the application of the New York statute in cases involving private individuals.... Were this a libel action, the distinction which has been suggested between the relative opportunities of the public official and the private individual to rebut defamatory charges might be germane. And the additional

state interest in the protection of the individual against damage to his reputation would be involved.

The Hills had presented sufficient evidence to the jury from which it might be concluded that the editors of *Life* had acted with reckless disregard of the truth. The first draft of the story did not contend that the play recreated the Hills' experience, stated that the Hill incident had only "sparked off" Hayes to write the novel, and stated that it was a "somewhat fictionalized" account. The final draft stated flatly that the play was a "re-enactment." Despite personal meetings with Hayes, Hayes was never asked the extent to which the book and play were based on the Hill incident. The Hills' $30,000 judgment was reversed, however, because the jury was not told that they must find *Life* guilty of knowing or reckless falsehood.

Justice Harlan, who dissented in part, argued that since the Hills were neither public officials nor public figures, they should be able to recover if the *Life* editors had been negligent—it should be unnecessary to show knowing or reckless disregard of truth. His reasons were similar to those in Justice Powell's majority opinion in the *Gertz* libel case (see above, p. 471) seven years later. An excerpt from his opinion follows:

> [T]here is a vast difference in the state interest in protecting individuals like Mr. Hill from irresponsibly prepared publicity and the state interest in similar protection for a public official. In *New York Times* we acknowledged public officials to be a breed from whom hardiness to exposure to charges, innuendoes, and criticisms might be demanded and who voluntarily assumed the risk of such things by entry into the public arena. But Mr. Hill came to public attention through an unfortunate circumstance not of his making rather than his voluntary actions and he can in no sense be considered to have "waived" any protection the State might justifiably afford him from irresponsible publicity. Not being inured to the vicissitudes of journalistic scrutiny such an individual is more easily injured and his means of self-defense are more limited. The public is less likely to view with normal skepticism what is written about him because it is not accustomed to seeing his name in the press and expects only a disinterested report.
>
> The coincidence of these factors in this situation leads me to the view that a State should be free to hold the press to a duty of making a reasonable investigation of the underlying facts and limiting itself to "fair comment" on the materials so gathered.

Justices Black and Douglas concurred in the reversal of the judgment, but once again expressed their belief in an "absolute" First Amendment. They said:

> [I]f the judicial balancing choice of constitutional changes is to be adopted by this Court, I could wish it had not started on the First Amendment. The freedoms guaranteed by that Amendment are essential freedoms in a government like ours. That Amendment was deliberately written in language designed

to put its freedoms beyond the reach of government to change while it remained unrepealed. If judges have, however, by their own fiat today created a right of privacy equal to or superior to the right of a free press that the Constitution created, then tomorrow and the next day and the next, judges can create more rights that balance away other cherished Bill of Rights freedoms. If there is any one thing that could strongly indicate that the Founders were wrong in reposing so much trust in a free press, I would suggest that it would be for the press itself not to wake up to the grave danger to its freedom, inherent and certain in this "weighing process." Life's conduct here was at most a mere understandable and incidental error of fact in reporting a newsworthy event. One does not have to be a prophet to foresee that judgments like the one we here reverse can frighten and punish the press so much that publishers will cease trying to report news in a lively and readable fashion as long as there is—and there always will be—doubt as to the complete accuracy of the newsworthy facts. Such a consummation hardly seems consistent with the clearly expressed purpose of the Founders to guarantee the press a favored spot in our free society.

Justice Fortas, joined by Chief Justice Warren and Justice Clark, would have affirmed the judgment. He complained that after 11 years of expensive litigation, the *Hill* judgment was being reversed and the case sent back to start all over because of a technicality—the words used to instruct the jury. He argued that in perspective the jury instructions were accurate enough. Justice Fortas also answered the argument of Justices Black and Douglas that the First Amendment should be read as an absolute in privacy cases. He said:

... I do not believe that whatever is in words, however much of an aggression it may be upon individual rights, is beyond the reach of the law, no matter how heedless of others' rights—how remote from public purpose, how reckless, irresponsible, and untrue it may be. I do not believe that the First Amendment precludes effective protection of the right of privacy—or, for that matter, an effective law of libel. I do not believe that we must or should, in deference to those whose views are absolute as to the scope of the First Amendment, be ingenious to strike down all state action, however circumspect, which penalizes the use of words as instruments of aggression and personal assault. There are great and important values in our society, none of which is greater than those reflected in the First Amendment, but which are also fundamental and entitled to this Court's careful respect and protection. Among these is the right to privacy, which has been eloquently extolled by scholars and members of this Court.... A distinct right of privacy is now recognized, either as a "common-law" right or by statute, in at least 35 States. Its exact scope varies in the respective jurisdictions. It is, simply stated, the right to be let alone; to live one's life as one chooses, free from assault, intrusion or invasion except as they can be justified by the clear needs of community living under a government of law. As Justice Brandeis said in his famous dissent in Olmstead v. United States, 277 U.S. 438, 478 (1928), the right of privacy is "the most comprehensive of rights and the right most valued by civilized men."

NOTES AND QUESTIONS

1. Were the Hills hurt any more by the fictionalized *Life* account than they would have been if *Life* had given the details of the Hills' experience and then accurately stated that the "Desperate Hours" events were quite different? The Court stated that if the Hills' story had been told accurately, the First Amendment would bar the award of damages for invasion of privacy. Even if the *Life* falsity was deliberate, why should it change the result? Is it because the privilege to discuss affairs of public interest, or newsworthy events, is only available to media representatives who are trying to tell the truth?

2. A New York case discussed at length in the *Hill* opinion involved an unauthorized biography of Warren Spahn. The New York courts conceded that a famous person could not recover damages because someone wrote an accurate unauthorized biography. Spahn was allowed to recover because the authors didn't want to pay Spahn for his cooperation, and lacking some detailed information about his personal life had "fictionalized" certain incidents. The book was designed for juvenile readers, and events involving Spahn's childhood, his relationship with his father, the courtship of his wife, and his military experience were simply made up to tell the story of Spahn's life in dramatic form. The fictionalized material was extensive, but none of the dramatization, imagined dialogue, fictionalized events or manipulated chronology reflected adversely on Spahn, but indeed was quite laudatory.

After lengthy litigation, Spahn recovered judgment in the New York courts. Spahn v. Julian Messner, Inc., 21 N.Y.2d 124, 286 N.Y.S.2d 832, 233 N.E.2d 840 (1967).

The Supreme Court agreed to review the case, perhaps to consider the kinds of falsity that would eliminate the First Amendment privilege to discuss the lives of famous persons. The parties, however, settled the case out of court, and the United States Supreme Court case was then dismissed. 393 U.S. 1046 (1969). Since none of the fictionalized material reflected adversely on Warren Spahn, should he be allowed to collect damages? Should famous people be paid when others write unauthorized biographies?

3. In a concurring opinion in Cox Broadcasting Corp. v. Cohn, 420 U.S. 469, 498, n. 2 (1975), Justice Powell wrote:

> ... The Court's abandonment [in *Gertz*] of the "matter of general or public interest" standard as the determining factor for deciding whether to apply the *New York Times* malice standard to defamation litigation brought by private individuals ... calls into question the conceptual basis of Time, Inc. v. Hill.

After quoting Justice Powell's view, Bernard Schwartz wrote in *The Unpublished Opinions of the Warren Court,* New York, 1985, p. 302:

> Since Time, Inc. v. Hill applies the *New York Times* standard to privacy suits, the *Gertz* modification of *New York Times* should also apply to such suits. Though the Supreme Court itself has stated that the question is still open, this means that an action such as that brought by Hill, under a false-light theory of invasion of privacy (which alleges publication of false and misleading information as well as invasion of privacy), would now be governed by a more relaxed standard of liability for the publisher than that laid down in both *New York Times* and Time, Inc. v. Hill. This appears to bring the law on the matter back to where it would have been if Time, Inc. v. Hill had been decided in accordance with the original opinion of the Court drafted by Justice Fortas.

Do you agree?

4. The combination of the *Hill* case and the *Gertz* case requires a careful distinction between libel cases and "false light" privacy cases. Under the *Gertz* case, if a private citizen is libeled, he can recover "actual damages" if the publisher is "negligent." He can recover nothing at all for "false light" invasion of privacy, under the *Hill* case, however, unless the publisher deliberately lied or acted with reckless disregard of truth.

Consider the facts of a famous case. Crawford Burton was a steeplechase rider who appeared, with his consent, in an advertisement for Camel cigarettes.

> Two photographs were inserted; the larger, a picture of the plaintiff in riding shirt and breeches, seated apparently outside a paddock with a cigarette in one hand and a cap and whip in the other. This contained the legend, "Get a lift with a Camel"; ... the legend may be read upon the other and offending photograph. That represented him coming from a race to be weighed in; he is carrying his saddle in front of him with his right hand under the pommel and his left under the cantle; the line of the seat is about twelve inches below his waist. Over the pommel hangs a stirrup; over the seat at his middle a white girth falls loosely in such a way that it seems to be attached to the plaintiff and not to the saddle. So regarded, the photograph becomes grotesque, monstrous, and obscene; and the legends, which without undue violence can be made to match ["when you feel 'all in'"; "Get a lift with a Camel."], reinforce the ribald interpretation.... The contrast between the drawn and serious face and the accompanying fantastic and lewd deformity was so extravagant that, though utterly unfair, it in fact made of the plaintiff a preposterously ridiculous spectacle; and the obvious mistake only added to the amusement. Burton v. Crowell Pub. Co., 82 F.2d 154 (2d Cir.1936).

Judge Learned Hand's opinion allowed recovery for libel. The defendant argued that no one thought the picture was a true representation of

Crawford Burton, and that it did not affect his reputation. Judge Learned Hand answered that anything that subjects a person to ridicule affects his reputation.

Obviously, the *Burton* case was decided years before the later constitutional law developments. But, an interesting controversy over the years has been whether the proper theory for recovery in *Burton* was libel or "false light" privacy (or some other theory). It was obvious that the offending photograph was not deliberate, but a mistake. Under the *Gertz* case, if Judge Hand was right that the picture was libelous, (and if we assume Burton was not a "public figure"), Burton could still recover "actual damages" for libel on a showing that there was negligence. On the other hand, if the theory is privacy, under the *Hill* case, the defendants would not be liable for invasion of privacy if they were "merely" negligent. Would Crawford Burton be able to recover "actual damages" if his case came up today? Does the *Gertz* decision, seven years later than Time v. Hill, require rethinking the earlier decision? Is it possible that *Gertz* overrules Time, Inc. v. Hill?

5.   Think now of the enormous complexity of the right to recover for invasion of one's privacy. One commentator has remarked:*

> All this is a most marvelous tree to grow from the wedding of the daughter of Mr. Samuel D. Warren. One is tempted to surmise that she must have been a very beautiful girl. Resembling, perhaps, that fabulous creature, the daughter of a Mr. Very, a confectioner in Regent Street, who was so wondrous fair that her presence in the shop caused three or four hundred people to assemble every day in the street before the window to look at her, so that her father was forced to send her out of town, and counsel was led to inquire whether she might not be indicted as a public nuisance. This was the face that launched a thousand lawsuits.

* Prosser, California Law Review, vol. 48, p. 423.

Chapter XIV

THE CONFLICT BETWEEN FREEDOM
OF THE PRESS AND THE RIGHT
TO A FAIR TRIAL

I. PUNISHING NEWSPAPERS FOR CRITICISM
OF JUDICIAL CONDUCT

BRIDGES v. CALIFORNIA

Supreme Court of the United States, 1941.
314 U.S. 252, 62 S.Ct. 190, 86 L.Ed. 192.

[This decision involved two unrelated cases from the California courts. In one case, the Los Angeles Times was fined $300 for contempt of court for publishing an editorial. Two labor union members had been found guilty of assaulting nonunion truck drivers, and were scheduled to be sentenced. The editorial referred to the defendants as "members of Dave Beck's* wrecking crew, entertainment committee, goon squad or gorillas" and urged, in strong language, that they should not be shown leniency or granted probation. The editorial concluded: "If Beck's thugs ... are made to realize that they face San Quentin when they are caught, it will tend to make their disreputable occupation unpopular. Judge A.A. Scott will make a serious mistake if he grants probation to Matthew Shannon and Kennan Holmes. This community needs the example of their assignment to the jute mill."

The other case involved the contempt conviction of Harry Bridges, the famous and controversial labor leader. In a case involving Bridges' union, the trial judge had rendered his decision against the union. The union had made a motion for a new trial, which was awaiting decision. Bridges sent a telegram to the United States Secretary of Labor which called the judge's original decision outrageous and concluded that his longshoremen's union did not "intend to allow state courts to override the majority vote of members in choosing its officers and representatives...." Bridges was held in contempt for "causing" or "acquiescing in" publication of the telegram in newspapers in Los Angeles and San Francisco. The state courts reasoned that the publications interfered with the fair administration of justice, and that freedom of the press was subordinated to the public interest in judicial impartiality and decorum. The Supreme Court reversed both convictions.]

JUSTICE BLACK delivered the opinion of the Court.

* National President of the Teamsters' union.

499

[T]he issue before us is of the very gravest moment. For free speech and fair trials are two of the most cherished policies of our civilization, and it would be a trying task to choose between them.

... [T]his Court has said that "it must necessarily be found, as an original question," that the specified publications involved created "such likelihood of bringing about the substantive evil as to deprive [them] of the constitutional protection." Gitlow v. New York, 268 U.S. 652, 671.

How much "likelihood" is another question, "a question of proximity and degree" that cannot be completely captured in a formula. In Schenck v. United States, however, this Court said that there must be a determination of whether or not "the words used are used in such circumstances and are of such a nature as to create a clear and present danger that they will bring about the substantive evils." We recognize that this statement, however helpful, does not comprehend the whole problem. As Mr. Justice Brandeis said in his concurring opinion in Whitney v. California, 274 U.S. 357, 374: "This Court has not yet fixed the standard by which to determine when a danger shall be deemed clear; how remote the danger may be and yet be deemed present."

Nevertheless, the "clear and present danger" language of the *Schenck* case has afforded practical guidance in a great variety of cases in which the scope of constitutional protections of freedom of expression was in issue. It has been utilized by either a majority or minority of this Court in passing upon the constitutionality of convictions under espionage acts, under a criminal syndicalism act, under an "anti-insurrection" act, and for breach of the peace at common law.

Moreover, the likelihood, however great, that a substantive evil will result cannot alone justify a restriction upon freedom of speech or the press. The evil itself must be "substantial," Brandeis, J., concurring in Whitney v. California, supra, 374; it must be "serious," Id. 376. And even the expression of "legislative preferences or beliefs" cannot transform minor matters of public inconvenience or annoyance into substantive evils of sufficient weight to warrant the curtailment of liberty of expression.

What finally emerges from the "clear and present danger" cases is a working principle that the substantive evil must be extremely serious and the degree of imminence extremely high before utterances can be punished. Those cases do not purport to mark the furthermost constitutional boundaries of protected expression, nor do we here. They do no more than recognize a minimum compulsion of the Bill of Rights. For the First Amendment does not speak equivocally. It prohibits any law "abridging the freedom of speech, or of the press." It must be taken as a command of the broadest scope that explicit language, read in the context of a liberty-loving society, will allow.

History affords no support for the contention that the criteria applicable under the Constitution to other types of utterances are not applicable, in contempt proceedings, to out-of-court publications pertaining to a pending case.

We may appropriately begin our discussion of the judgments below by considering how much, as a practical matter, they would affect liberty of expression. It must be recognized that public interest is much more likely to be kindled by a controversial event of the day than by a generalization, however penetrating, of the historian or scientist. Since they punish utterances made during the pendency of a case, the judgments below therefore produce their restrictive results at the precise time when public interest in the matters discussed would naturally be at its height. Moreover, the ban is likely to fall not only at a crucial time but upon the most important topics of discussion. Here, for example, labor controversies were the topics of some of the publications. Experience shows that the more acute labor controversies are, the more likely it is that in some aspect they will get into court. It is therefore the controversies that command most interest that the decisions below would remove from the arena of public discussion.

For these reasons we are convinced that the judgments below result in a curtailment of expression that cannot be dismissed as insignificant. If they can be justified at all, it must be in terms of some serious substantive evil which they are designed to avert. The substantive evil here sought to be averted has been variously described below. It appears to be double: disrespect for the judiciary; and disorderly and unfair administration of justice. The assumption that respect for the judiciary can be won by shielding judges from published criticism wrongly appraises the character of American public opinion. For it is a prized American privilege to speak one's mind, although not always with perfect good taste, on all public institutions. And an enforced silence, however limited, solely in the name of preserving the dignity of the bench, would probably engender resentment, suspicion, and contempt much more than it would enhance respect.

The other evil feared, disorderly and unfair administration of justice, is more plausibly associated with restricting publications which touch upon pending litigation. The very word "trial" connotes decisions on the evidence and arguments properly advanced in open court. Legal trials are not like elections, to be won through the use of the meeting-hall, the radio, and the newspaper. But we cannot start with the assumption that publications of the kind here involved actually do threaten to change the nature of legal trials, and that to preserve judicial impartiality, it is necessary for judges to have a contempt power by which they can close all channels of public expression to all matters which touch upon pending cases. We must therefore turn to the particular utterances here in question and the circumstances of their publication to determine to what extent the substantive evil of unfair administration of justice was a likely consequence, and whether the degree of likelihood was sufficient to justify summary punishment.

The Los Angeles Times Editorials . . . .

The basis for punishing the publication as contempt was by the trial court said to be its "inherent tendency" and by the Supreme Court its "reasonable tendency" to interfere with the orderly administration of justice in an action then before a court for consideration. In accordance with what we have said on the "clear and present danger" cases, neither "inherent tendency" nor "reasonable tendency" is enough to justify a restriction of free expression. But even if they were appropriate measures, we should find exaggeration in the use of those phrases to describe the facts here.

From the indications in the record of the position taken by the Los Angeles Times on labor controversies in the past, there could have been little doubt of its attitude toward the probation of Shannon and Holmes. In view of the paper's long-continued militancy in this field, it is inconceivable that any judge in Los Angeles would expect anything but adverse criticism from it in the event probation were granted. Yet such criticism after final disposition of the proceedings would clearly have been privileged. Hence, this editorial, given the most intimidating construction it will bear, did no more than threaten future adverse criticism which was reasonably to be expected anyway in the event of a lenient disposition of the pending case. To regard it, therefore, as in itself of substantial influence upon the course of justice would be to impute to judges a lack of firmness, wisdom, or honor,—which we cannot accept as a major premise.

The Bridges Telegram . . . .

It must be recognized that Bridges was a prominent labor leader speaking at a time when public interest in the particular labor controversy was at its height. The observations we have previously made here upon the timeliness and importance of utterances as emphasizing rather than diminishing the value of constitutional protection, and upon the breadth and seriousness of the censorial effects of punishing publications in the manner followed below, are certainly no less applicable to a leading spokesman for labor than to a powerful newspaper taking another point of view.

In looking at the reason advanced in support of the judgment of contempt, we find that here, too, the possibility of causing unfair disposition of a pending case is the major justification asserted. And here again the gist of the offense, according to the court below, is intimidation.

Let us assume that the telegram could be construed as an announcement of Bridges' intention to call a strike, something which, it is admitted, neither the general law of California nor the court's decree prohibited. With an eye on the realities of the situation, we cannot assume that Judge Schmidt was unaware of the possibility of a strike as a consequence of his decision. If he was not intimidated by the facts themselves, we do not believe that the most explicit statement of them could have sidetracked the course of justice. Again, we find exaggeration in the conclusion that the utterance even "tended" to interfere with justice. If there was electricity in the atmosphere, it was generated by the facts; the charge added by the Bridges telegram can be dismissed as negligible.

JUSTICE FRANKFURTER, with whom concurred the CHIEF JUSTICE, JUSTICE ROBERTS and JUSTICE BYRNES, dissenting.

Our whole history repels the view that it is an exercise of one of the civil liberties secured by the Bill of Rights for a leader of a large following or for a powerful metropolitan newspaper to attempt to over-awe a judge in a matter immediately pending before him. The view of the majority deprives California of means for securing to its citizens justice according to law—means which, since the Union was founded, have been the possession, hitherto unchallenged, of all the states. This sudden break with the uninterrupted course of constitutional history has no constitutional warrant. To find justification for such deprivation of the historic powers of the states is to misconceive the idea of freedom of thought and speech as guaranteed by the Constitution.

A trial is not a "free trade in ideas," nor is the best test of truth in a courtroom "the power of the thought to get itself accepted in the competition of the market." A court is a forum with strictly defined limits for discussion. It is circumscribed in the range of its inquiry and in its methods by the Constitution, by laws, and by age-old traditions. Its judges are restrained in their freedom of expression by historic compulsions resting on no other officials of government. They are so circumscribed precisely because judges have in their keeping the enforcement of rights and the protection of liberties which, according to the wisdom of the ages, can only be enforced and protected by observing such methods and traditions.

. . . The Fourteenth Amendment does not forbid a state to continue the historic process of prohibiting expressions calculated to subvert a specific exercise of judicial power. So to assure the impartial accomplishment of justice is not an abridgment of freedom of speech or freedom of the press, as these phases of liberty have heretofore been conceived even by the stoutest libertarians. In fact, these liberties themselves depend upon an untrammeled judiciary whose passions are not even unconsciously aroused and whose minds are not distorted by extra-judicial considerations.

Of course freedom of speech and of the press are essential to the enlightenment of a free people and in restraining those who wield power. Particularly should this freedom be employed in comment upon the work of courts, who are without many influences ordinarily making for humor and humility, twin antidotes to the corrosion of power. But the Bill of Rights is not self-destructive. Freedom of expression can hardly carry implications that nullify the guarantees of impartial trials. And since courts are the ultimate resorts for vindicating the Bill of Rights, a state may surely authorize appropriate historic means to assure that the process for such vindication be not wrenched from its rational tracks into the more primitive mêlée of passion and pressure. The need is great that courts be criticized, but just as great that they be allowed to do their duty.

NOTES AND QUESTIONS

1. *Bridges* and *Times–Mirror* had been argued twice. Justice Douglas' docket book for the 1941 Term shows that after the first argument, the conference vote was six to three—Chief Justice Hughes and Justices McReynolds, Stone, Roberts, Frankfurter, and Murphy voting to affirm

and Justices Black, Reed, and Douglas voting to reverse. Justice Frank-furter had already circulated his opinion for the Court when Justice McReynolds retired and Justice Murphy changed his vote, thus leaving the Court evenly divided. As a result, the Court ordered the cases reargued. The second conference vote was five to four—Justices Black, Reed, Douglas, Murphy, and Jackson (who replaced Justice Stone when he succeeded Chief Justice Hughes) voting to reverse and Chief Justice Stone and Justices Roberts, Frankfurter, and Byrnes (who replaced Justice McReynolds) voting to affirm. In a draft of his original opinion for the Court, Justice Frankfurter wrote that the contempt power of judges is

> deeply rooted in history. It is part and parcel of the Anglo–American system of administering justice.... It is believed that all the judicatures of the English-speaking world, including the courts of the United States and of the forty-eight states, have from time to time recognized and exercised the power....*

Responding to Justice Frankfurter's historical argument, Justice Black wrote in his draft dissent that

> the first and perhaps the basic fallacy of the Court's opinion is the assumption that the vitalizing liberties of the First Amend-ment can be abridged ... by reference to English judicial practice, either current, recent or remote.... In my judgment, to measure the scope of the liberties guaranteed by the First Amendment by the limitations that exist or have existed throughout the English-speaking world is to obtain a result directly opposite to that which the framers of the Amendment intended.... Perhaps no single purpose emerges more clearly from the history of our Constitution and Bill of Rights than that of giving far more security to the people of the United States with the respect to freedom of religion, conscience, expression, assembly, petition and press than the people of Great Britain had ever enjoyed.... The First Amendment is proof conclusive that the framers of our government were well aware of the suppression of conscience and expression that had been in-dulged in abroad, both in England and elsewhere, and intended by the First Amendment to see that they did not happen.**

Anthony Lewis has written that in Justices Frankfurter's and Black's disagreement about the meaning of history "we can see some-thing more profound: a conflict over the nature of the First Amendment. Justice Frankfurter saw the Amendment, as he saw much of the Consti-tution—as a natural development of English traditions, a part of a continuum. Justice Black saw the First Amendment as something very new and distinctively American. Benno Schmidt strikingly summed it up by saying that Justice Black's opinion in the *Bridges* case was a 'judicial

---

* Quoted in Anthony Lewis, "Justice Black and First Amendment," Tony Freyer. ed., Justice Hugo Black and Modern America, University of Alabama Press, 1990, p. 240.

** Quoted, ibid.

Declaration of Independence for the First Amendment, freeing it from English laws.' "*

2.   Notice that, although the Court's opinion is written by Justice Black, it doesn't speak of freedom of speech as being an absolute, but rather of "clear and present danger." The opinion insists, moreover, that the danger must be serious before a contempt conviction can be upheld. Is there also an implication that if the danger to judicial administration were serious enough, the First Amendment would not block conviction for contempt by publication?

3.   One possible explanation for the opinion's use of "clear and present danger" is that it was written in 1941, and Justice Black did not fully elaborate his "absolutist" position on the First Amendment until *after* the *Dennis* case (above, Chapter 5, p. 106), in 1951. A second explanation is that Justice Black was writing for a closely divided Court. A judge writing for the majority when the Court is divided has to be especially careful not to say anything that would cause any of the other justices who voted with him to disagree. Justice Black's earlier draft dissent in *Bridges* and *Times–Mirror* suggests the second explanation. He began that draft as follows: "First in the catalogue of human liberties essential to the life and growth of a government of, for, and by the people are those liberties written into the First Amendment to our Constitution. They are the pillars upon which popular government rests and without which a government of free men cannot survive. History persuades me that the moving forces which brought about the creation of the safeguards contained in the other sections of our Bill of Rights sprang from a resolute determination to place the liberties defined in the First Amendment in an area wholly safe and secure against *any* invasion."* (Emphasis supplied.)

4.   It has already been remarked (see above, p. 482, note 5) that free speech doctrine tends to develop in water-tight compartments. The discussion of contempt by publication in the *Bridges* case used the idiom of clear and present danger, and later cases continued to use it. In Pennekamp v. Florida, 328 U.S. 331 (1946), a newspaper engaged in an anti-vice crusade used cartoons and editorials to accuse judges of hindering prosecution of rape and gambling cases. And, in Craig v. Harney, 331 U.S. 367 (1947), a newspaper editorial referred to a judge's decision as "high handed" and a "travesty of justice [which] brought the wrath of public opinion upon his head." In both cases, the convictions for contempt were reversed by the Supreme Court, using the clear and present danger standard. And, much later, in 1962, in Wood v. Georgia, 370 U.S. 375 (1962), clear and present danger was again the standard for reversing the contempt conviction of a sheriff who criticized a judge in the press for ordering a grand jury to investigate election law violations. The sheriff had accused the judges of racial bias, hypocrisy, political intimidation, persecution and political naivete, and had compared the judges to the Ku Klux Klan.

---

* Ibid., pp. 240–241.

* Black Papers, Library of Congress, Box 258.

5.   No group of cases has used clear and present danger so consistently as the decision-making standard as have the contempt-by-publication cases. Most commentators and lower court judges, however, have concluded that clear and present danger, as used in these cases, is a synonym for an absolute prohibition—that is, those who criticize the actions of judges in the press, no matter when, where, or how virulent the criticism, can never be punished for contempt. No judge who bends before the force of a newspaper attack is likely to insist, at the same time, on punishing the newspaper for contempt; and, any judge angry enough to insist on punishing for contempt is just as likely to insist that he had the fortitude to resist. Can you imagine a case where the threat to a judge's impartiality would be so great that the media could be held in contempt?

II.   PUNISHMENT OF NEWSPAPERS FOR INTERFERENCE WITH IMPARTIAL JURY TRIALS

All of the cases in the previous section involved criticism of judges, so that the possibility of improperly influencing a jury decision played no part. Consider the implications of irresponsible newspaper activities before and during a jury trial for a serious crime. Would it be possible, despite the *Bridges–Pennekamp–Craig–Wood* line of cases, to hold the news media in contempt for denying a defendant a fair trial? Should it be possible?

NEBRASKA PRESS ASS'N v. STUART

Supreme Court of the United States, 1976.
427 U.S. 539, 96 S.Ct. 2791, 49 L.Ed.2d 683.

CHIEF JUSTICE BURGER ... delivered the opinion of the Court.

On the evening of October 18, 1975, local police found the six members of the Henry Kellie family murdered in their home in Sutherland, Neb., a town of about 850 people. Police released the description of a suspect, Erwin Charles Simants, to the reporters who had hastened to the scene of the crime. Simants was arrested and arraigned in Lincoln County Court the following morning, ending a tense night for this small rural community.

The crime immediately attracted widespread news coverage, by local, regional, and national newspapers, radio and television stations. Three days after the crime, the County Attorney and Simants' attorney joined in asking the County Court to enter a restrictive order relating to "matters that may or may not be publicly reported or disclosed to the public," because of the "mass coverage by news media" and the "reasonable likelihood of prejudicial news which would make difficult, if not impossible, the impaneling of an impartial jury and tend to prevent a fair trial." The County Court heard oral argument but took no evidence; no attorney for members of the press appeared at this stage. The County Court granted the prosecutor's motion for a restrictive order and entered it the next day, October 22. The order prohibited everyone in attendance from "releas[ing] or authoriz[ing] the release for public dissemination in any form or manner whatsoever any testimony given or evidence adduced"; the order also required members of the press to observe the Nebraska Bar–Press Guidelines.[1]

Simants' preliminary hearing was held the same day, open to the public but subject to the order. The County Court bound over the defendant for trial to the State District Court. The charges, as amended to reflect the autopsy findings, were that Simants had committed the murders in the course of a sexual assault.

Petitioners—several press and broadcast associations, publishers, and individual reporters—moved on October 23 for leave to intervene in the District Court, asking that the restrictive order imposed by the County Court be vacated. The District Court conducted a hearing, at which the County Judge testified and newspaper articles about the Simants case were admitted in evidence. The District Judge granted petitioners' motion to intervene and, on October 27, entered his own restrictive order. The judge found "because of the nature of the crimes charged in the complaint, that there is a clear and present danger that pre-trial publicity could impinge upon the defendant's right to a fair trial." The order applied only until the jury was impaneled, and specifically prohibited petitioners from reporting five subjects: (1) the existence or contents of a confession Simants had made to law enforcement officers, which had been introduced in open court at arraignment; (2) the fact or nature of statements Simants had made to other persons; (3) the contents of a note he had written the night of the crime; (4) certain aspects of the medical testimony at the preliminary hearing; and (5) the identity of the victims of the alleged sexual assault and the nature of the assault. It also prohibited reporting the exact nature of the restrictive order itself. Like the County Court's order, this order incorporated the Nebraska Bar–Press Guidelines. Finally, the order set out a plan for attendance, seating, and courthouse traffic control during the trial.

[On appeal from the state District Court] [t]he Nebraska Supreme Court balanced the "heavy presumption against . . . constitutional validity" that an order restraining publication bears, against the importance of the defendant's right to trial by an impartial jury. Both society and the individual defendant, the court held, had a vital interest in assuring that Simants be tried by an impartial jury. Because of the publicity surrounding the crime, the court determined that this right was in jeopardy. The court noted that Nebraska statutes required the District Court to try Simants within six months of his arrest, and that a change of venue could move the trial only to adjoining counties, which had been subject to essentially the same publicity as Lincoln County. The Nebras-

---

1. These Guidelines are voluntary standards adopted by members of the state bar and news media to deal with the reporting of crimes and criminal trials. They outline the matters of fact that may appropriately be reported, and also list what items are not generally appropriate for reporting, including confessions, opinions on guilt or innocence, statements that would influence the outcome of a trial, the results of tests or examinations, comments on the credibility of witnesses, and evidence presented in the jury's absence. The publication of an accused's criminal record should, under the Guidelines, be "considered very carefully." The Guidelines also set out standards for taking and publishing photographs, and set up a joint bar-press committee to foster cooperation in resolving particular problems that emerge.

ka Supreme Court held that "[u]nless the absolutist position of the [news media] was constitutionally correct, it would appear that the District Court acted properly."

The Nebraska Supreme Court rejected that "absolutist position," but modified the District Court's order to accommodate the defendant's right to a fair trial and the petitioners' interest in reporting pretrial events. The order as modified prohibited reporting of only three matters: (a) the existence and nature of any confessions or admissions made by the defendant to law enforcement officers, (b) any confessions or admissions made to any third parties, except members of the press, and (c) other facts "strongly implicative" of the accused. . . .

We granted certiorari to address the important issues raised by the District Court order as modified by the Nebraska Supreme Court. . . . We are informed by the parties that since we granted certiorari, Simants has been convicted of murder and sentenced to death. His appeal is pending in the Nebraska Supreme Court.

The problems presented by this case are almost as old as the Republic. Neither in the Constitution nor in contemporaneous writings do we find that the conflict between these two important rights was anticipated, yet it is inconceivable that the authors of the Constitution were unaware of the potential conflicts between the right to an unbiased jury and the guarantee of freedom of the press. The unusually able lawyers who helped write the Constitution and later drafted the Bill of Rights were familiar with the historic episode in which John Adams defended British soldiers charged with homicide for firing into a crowd of Boston demonstrators; they were intimately familiar with the clash of the adversary system and the part that passions of the populace sometimes play in influencing potential jurors. They did not address themselves directly to the situation presented by this case; their chief concern was the need for freedom of expression in the political arena and the dialogue in ideas. But they recognized that there were risks to private rights from an unfettered press. Jefferson, for example, writing from Paris in 1786 concerning press attacks on John Jay, stated:

> "In truth it is afflicting that a man who has past his life in serving the public . . . should yet be liable to have his peace of mind so much disturbed by any individual who shall think proper to arraign him in a newspaper. It is however an evil for which there is no remedy. Our liberty depends on the freedom of the press, and that cannot be limited without being lost. . . ."
> 9 Papers of Thomas Jefferson 239 (J. Boyd ed. 1954).

The Sixth Amendment in terms guarantees "trial, by an impartial jury . . ." in federal criminal prosecutions. Because "trial by jury in criminal cases is fundamental to the American scheme of justice," the Due Process Clause of the Fourteenth Amendment guarantees the same right in state criminal prosecutions.

In the overwhelming majority of criminal trials, pretrial publicity presents few unmanageable threats to this important right. But when the case is a "sensational" one tensions develop between the right of the accused to trial by an impartial jury and the rights guaranteed others by the First Amendment. The relevant decisions of this Court, even if not dispositive, are instructive by way of background.

In Irvin v. Dowd, for example, the defendant was convicted of murder following intensive and hostile news coverage. The trial judge had granted a defense motion for a change of venue, but only to an adjacent county, which had been exposed to essentially the same news coverage. At trial, 430 persons were called for jury service; 268 were excused because they had fixed opinions as to guilt. Eight of the 12 who served as jurors thought the defendant guilty, but said they could nevertheless render an impartial verdict. On review the Court vacated the conviction and death sentence and remanded to allow a new trial for, "[w]ith his life at stake, it is not requiring too much that petitioner be tried in an atmosphere undisturbed by so huge a wave of public passion. . . ."

Similarly, in Rideau v. Louisiana, 373 U.S. 723 (1963), the Court reversed the conviction of a defendant whose staged, highly emotional confession had been filmed with the cooperation of local police and later broadcast on television for three days while he was awaiting trial, saying "[a]ny subsequent court proceedings in a community so pervasively exposed to such a spectacle could be but a hollow formality." And in Estes v. Texas, 381 U.S. 532 (1965), the Court held that the defendant had not been afforded due process where the volume of trial publicity, the judge's failure to control the proceedings, and the telecast of a hearing and of the trial itself "inherently prevented a sober search for the truth."

In Sheppard v. Maxwell, 384 U.S. 333 (1966), the Court focused sharply on the impact of pretrial publicity and a trial court's duty to protect the defendant's constitutional right to a fair trial. With only Mr. Justice Black dissenting, and he without opinion, the Court ordered a new trial for the petitioner, even though the first trial had occurred 12 years before. Beyond doubt the press had shown no responsible concern for the constitutional guarantee of a fair trial; the community from which the jury was drawn had been inundated by publicity hostile to the defendant. But the trial judge "did not fulfill his duty to protect [the defendant] from the inherently prejudicial publicity which saturated the community and to control disruptive influences in the courtroom." The Court noted that "unfair and prejudicial news comment on pending trials has become increasingly prevalent," and issued a strong warning:

> "Due process requires that the accused receive a trial by an impartial jury free from outside influences. Given the pervasiveness of modern communications and the difficulty of effacing prejudicial publicity from the minds of the jurors, *the trial courts must take strong measures to ensure that the balance is never weighed against the accused* . . . . Of course, there is nothing that proscribes the press from reporting events that transpire in the courtroom. But where there is a reasonable likelihood that prejudicial news prior to trial will prevent a fair trial, the judge should *continue the case* until the threat abates, *or transfer it* to another county not so permeated with publicity.

In addition, *sequestration of the jury* was something the judge should have raised *sua sponte** with counsel. If publicity during the proceedings threatens the fairness of the trial, a new trial should be ordered. But we must remember that reversals are but palliatives; the cure lies in those remedial measures that will prevent the prejudice at its inception. The courts must take such steps by rule and regulation that will protect their processes from prejudicial outside interferences. *Neither prosecutors, counsel for defense, the accused, witnesses, court staff nor enforcement officers coming under the jurisdiction of the court should be permitted to frustrate its function.* Collaboration between counsel and the press as to information affecting the fairness of a criminal trial is not only subject to regulation, but is highly censurable and worthy of disciplinary measures." (Emphasis added).

Because the trial court had failed to use even minimal efforts to insulate the trial and the jurors from the "deluge of publicity," the Court vacated the judgment of conviction and a new trial followed, in which the accused was acquitted.

Cases such as these are relatively rare, and we have held in other cases that trials have been fair in spite of widespread publicity. In Stroble v. California, 343 U.S. 181 (1952), for example, the Court affirmed a conviction and death sentence challenged on the ground that pretrial news accounts, including the prosecutor's release of the defendant's recorded confession, were allegedly so inflammatory as to amount to a denial of due process. The Court disapproved of the prosecutor's conduct, but noted that the publicity had receded some six weeks before trial, that the defendant had not moved for a change of venue, and that the confession had been found voluntary and admitted in evidence at trial. The Court also noted the thorough examination of jurors on *voir dire* and the careful review of the facts by the state courts, and held that petitioner had failed to demonstrate a denial of due process.

Taken together, these cases demonstrate that pretrial publicity—even pervasive, adverse publicity—does not inevitably lead to an unfair trial. The capacity of the jury eventually impaneled to decide the case fairly is influenced by the tone and extent of the publicity, which is in part, and often in large part, shaped by what attorneys, police, and other officials do to precipitate news coverage. The trial judge has a major responsibility. What the judge says about a case, in or out of the courtroom, is likely to appear in newspapers and broadcasts. More important, the measures a judge takes or fails to take to mitigate the effects of pretrial publicity—the measures described in *Sheppard*—may well determine whether the defendant receives a trial consistent with the requirements of due process. That this responsibility has not always been properly discharged is apparent from the decisions just reviewed.

The First Amendment provides that "Congress shall make no law ... abridging the freedom ... of the press," and it is "no longer open to doubt that the liberty of the press, and of speech, is within the liberty

---

* On its own motion, i.e. without being asked.

safeguarded by the due process clause of the Fourteenth Amendment from invasion by state action." The Court has interpreted these guarantees to afford special protection against orders that prohibit the publication or broadcast of particular information or commentary—orders that impose a "previous" or "prior" restraint on speech. None of our decided cases on prior restraint involved restrictive orders entered to protect a defendant's right to a fair and impartial jury, but the opinions on prior restraint have a common thread relevant to this case.

In Near v. Minnesota ex rel. Olson, [283 U.S. 697 (1931),] the Court held invalid a Minnesota statute providing for the abatement as a public nuisance of any "malicious, scandalous and defamatory newspaper, magazine or other periodical." Near had published an occasional weekly newspaper described by the County Attorney's complaint as "largely devoted to malicious, scandalous and defamatory articles" concerning political and other public figures. Publication was enjoined pursuant to the statute. Excerpts from Near's paper, set out in the dissenting opinion of Justice Butler, show beyond question that one of its principal characteristics was blatant anti-Semitism.

Chief Justice Hughes, writing for the Court, noted that freedom of the press is not an absolute right, and the State may punish its abuses. He observed that the statute was "not aimed at the redress of individual or private wrongs." He then focused on the statute:

> "[T]he operation and effect of the statute in substance is that public authorities may bring the owner or publisher of a newspaper or periodical before a judge upon a charge of conducting a business of publishing scandalous and defamatory matter ... and unless the owner or publisher is able ... to satisfy the judge that the [matter is] true and ... published with good motives ... his newspaper or periodical is suppressed.... This is of the essence of censorship."

The Court relied on Patterson v. Colorado ex rel. Attorney General, 205 U.S. 454, 462 (1907): "[T]he main purpose of [the First Amendment] is 'to prevent all such *previous restraints* upon publications as had been practiced by other governments.'"

More recently in New York Times Co. v. United States, 403 U.S. 713 (1971), the Government sought to enjoin the publication of excerpts from a massive, classified study of this Nation's involvement in the Vietnam conflict, going back to the end of the Second World War. The dispositive opinion of the Court simply concluded that the Government had not met its heavy burden of showing justification for the prior restraint. Each of the six concurring Justices and the three dissenting Justices expressed his views separately, but "every member of the Court, tacitly or explicitly, accepted the *Near* and *Keefe* condemnation of prior restraints as presumptively unconstitutional." The Court's conclusion in *New York Times* suggests that the burden on the Government is not reduced by the temporary nature of a restraint; in that case the Government asked for a temporary restraint solely to permit it to study and assess the impact on national security of the lengthy documents at issue.

The thread running through all these cases is that prior restraints on speech and publication are the most serious and the least tolerable infringement on First Amendment rights. A criminal penalty or a judgment in a defamation case is subject to the whole panoply of protections afforded by deferring the impact of the judgment until all avenues of appellate review have been exhausted. Only after judgment has become final, correct or otherwise, does the law's sanction become fully operative.

A prior restraint, by contrast and by definition, has an immediate and irreversible sanction. If it can be said that a threat of criminal or civil sanctions after publication "chills" speech, prior restraint "freezes" it at least for the time.

The authors of the Bill of Rights did not undertake to assign priorities as between First Amendment and Sixth Amendment rights, ranking one as superior to the other. In this case, the petitioners would have us declare the right of an accused subordinate to their right to publish in all circumstances. But if the authors of these guarantees, fully aware of the potential conflicts between them, were unwilling or unable to resolve the issue by assigning to one priority over the other, it is not for us to rewrite the Constitution by undertaking what they declined to do. It is unnecessary, after nearly two centuries, to establish a priority applicable in all circumstances. Yet it is nonetheless clear that the barriers to prior restraint remain high unless we are to abandon what the Court has said for nearly a quarter of our national existence and implied throughout all of it.

We turn now to the record in this case to determine whether, as Learned Hand put it, "the gravity of the 'evil,' discounted by its improbability, justifies such invasion of free speech as is necessary to avoid the danger." United States v. Dennis, 183 F.2d 201, 212 (C.A.2 1950), aff'd, 341 U.S. 494 (1951). To do so, we must examine the evidence before the trial judge when the order was entered to determine (a) the nature and extent of pretrial news coverage; (b) whether other measures would be likely to mitigate the effects of unrestrained pretrial publicity; and (c) how effectively a restraining order would operate to prevent the threatened danger. The precise terms of the restraining order are also important. We must then consider whether the record supports the entry of a prior restraint on publication, one of the most extraordinary remedies known to our jurisprudence.

In assessing the probable extent of publicity, the trial judge had before him newspapers demonstrating that the crime had already drawn intensive news coverage, and the testimony of the County Judge, who had entered the initial restraining order based on the local and national attention the case had attracted. The District Judge was required to assess the probable publicity that would be given these shocking crimes prior to the time a jury was selected and sequestered. He then had to examine the probable nature of the publicity and determine how it would affect prospective jurors.

Our review of the pretrial record persuades us that the trial judge was justified in concluding that there would be intense and pervasive pretrial publicity concerning this case. He could also reasonably conclude, based on common human experience, that publicity might impair the defendant's right to a fair trial. He did not purport to say more, for he found only "a clear and present danger that pre-trial publicity *could* impinge upon the defendant's right to a fair trial." (Emphasis added.) His conclusion as to the impact of such publicity on prospective jurors was of necessity speculative, dealing as he was with factors unknown and unknowable.

We find little in the record that goes to another aspect of our task, determining whether measures short of an order restraining all publication would have insured the defendant a fair trial. Although the entry of the order might be read as a judicial determination that other measures would not suffice, the trial court made no express findings to that effect; the Nebraska Supreme Court referred to the issue only by implication.

Most of the alternatives to prior restraint of publication in these circumstances were discussed with obvious approval in Sheppard v. Maxwell: (a) change of trial venue to a place less exposed to the intense publicity that seemed imminent in Lincoln County; (b) postponement of the trial to allow public attention to subside; (c) searching questioning of prospective jurors, . . . to screen out those with fixed opinions as to guilt or innocence; (d) the use of emphatic and clear instructions on the sworn duty of each juror to decide the issues only on evidence presented in open court. Sequestration of jurors is, of course, always available. Although that measure insulates jurors only after they are sworn, it also enhances the likelihood of dissipating the impact of pretrial publicity and emphasizes the elements of the jurors' oaths.

This Court has outlined other measures short of prior restraints on publication tending to blunt the impact of pretrial publicity. Professional studies have filled out these suggestions, recommending that trial courts in appropriate cases limit what the contending lawyers, the police, and witnesses may say to anyone. See American Bar Association Project on Standards for Criminal Justice, Fair Trial and Free Press 2–15 (Approved Draft 1968).[2]

We have noted earlier that pretrial publicity, even if pervasive and concentrated, cannot be regarded as leading automatically and in every kind of criminal case to an unfair trial. The decided cases "cannot be made to stand for the proposition that juror exposure to information about a state defendant's prior convictions or to news accounts of the crime with which he is charged alone presumptively deprives the defendant of due process." . . .

We have therefore examined this record to determine the probable efficacy of the measures short of prior restraint on the press and speech. There is no finding that alternative measures would not have protected Simants' rights, and the Nebraska Supreme Court did no more than

2. Closing of pretrial proceedings with the consent of the defendant when required is also recommended in guidelines that have emerged from various studies. At oral argument petitioners' counsel asserted that judicially imposed restraints on lawyers and others would be subject to challenge as interfering with press rights to news sources. . . .

imply that such measures might not be adequate. Moreover, the record is lacking in evidence to support such a finding.

... [W]e note that the events disclosed by the record took place in a community of 850 people. It is reasonable to assume that, without any news accounts being printed or broadcast, rumors would travel swiftly by word of mouth. One can only speculate on the accuracy of such reports, given the generative propensities of rumors; they could well be more damaging than reasonably accurate news accounts. But plainly a whole community cannot be restrained from discussing a subject intimately affecting life within it.

Given these practical problems, it is far from clear that prior restraint on publication would have protected Simants' rights.

... We cannot say on this record that alternatives to a prior restraint on petitioners would not have sufficiently mitigated the adverse effects of pretrial publicity so as to make prior restraint unnecessary. Nor can we conclude that the restraining order actually entered would serve its intended purpose. Reasonable minds can have few doubts about the gravity of the evil pretrial publicity can work, but the probability that it would do so here was not demonstrated with the degree of certainty our cases on prior restraint require.

Of necessity our holding is confined to the record before us. But our conclusion is not simply a result of assessing the adequacy of the showing made in this case; it results in part from the problems inherent in meeting the heavy burden of demonstrating, in advance of trial, that without prior restraint a fair trial will be denied. The practical problems of managing and enforcing restrictive orders will always be present. In this sense, the record now before us is illustrative rather than exceptional. It is significant that when this Court has reversed a state conviction because of prejudicial publicity, it has carefully noted that some course of action short of prior restraint would have made a critical difference. However difficult it may be, we need not rule out the possibility of showing the kind of threat to fair trial rights that would possess the requisite degree of certainty to justify restraint. This Court has frequently denied that First Amendment rights are absolute and has consistently rejected the proposition that a prior restraint can never be employed.

Our analysis ends as it began, with a confrontation between prior restraint imposed to protect one vital constitutional guarantee and the explicit command of another that the freedom to speak and publish shall not be abridged. We reaffirm that the guarantees of freedom of expression are not an absolute prohibition under all circumstances, but the barriers to prior restraint remain high and the presumption against its use continues intact. We hold that, with respect to the order entered in this case prohibiting reporting or commentary on judicial proceedings held in public, the barriers have not been overcome; to the extent that this order restrained publication of such material, it is clearly invalid. To the extent that it prohibited publication based on information gained from other sources, we conclude that the heavy burden imposed as a condition to securing a prior restraint was not met and the judgment of the Nebraska Supreme Court is therefore

Reversed.

JUSTICE WHITE, concurring.

Technically there is no need to go farther than the Court does to dispose of this case, and I join the Court's opinion. I should add, however, that, for the reasons which the Court itself canvasses, there is grave doubt in my mind whether orders with respect to the press such as were entered in this case would ever be justifiable. It may be the better part of discretion, however, not to announce such a rule in the first case in which the issue has been squarely presented here. Perhaps we should go no farther than absolutely necessary until the federal courts, and ourselves, have been exposed to a broader spectrum of cases presenting similar issues. If the recurring result, however, in case after case is to be similar to our judgment today, we should at some point announce a more general rule and avoid the interminable litigation that our failure to do so would necessarily entail.

JUSTICE POWELL, concurring.

Although I join the opinion of the Court, in view of the importance of the case I write to emphasize the unique burden that rests upon the party, whether it be the State or a defendant, who undertakes to show the necessity for prior restraint on pretrial publicity.

In my judgment a prior restraint properly may issue only when it is shown to be necessary to prevent the dissemination of prejudicial publicity that otherwise poses a high likelihood of preventing, directly and irreparably, the impaneling of a jury meeting the Sixth Amendment requirement of impartiality. This requires a showing that (i) there is a clear threat to the fairness of trial, (ii) such a threat is posed by the actual publicity to be restrained, and (iii) no less restrictive alternatives are available. Notwithstanding such a showing, a restraint may not issue unless it also is shown that previous publicity or publicity from unrestrained sources will not render the restraint inefficacious.

[The concurring opinions of Justice Brennan (joined by Justices Stewart and Marshall) and of Justice Stevens are omitted.]

NOTES AND QUESTIONS

1. Justice Brennan argued in a concurring opinion that the First Amendment precluded any injunction against the press.

> [T]he press may be arrogant, tyrannical, abusive, and sensationalist, just as it may be incisive, probing, and informative. But at least in the context of prior restraints on publication, the decision of what, when, and how to publish is for editors, not judges.

Justice Stevens, who generally agreed with Justice Brennan, left that question open.

> Whether the same absolute protection would apply no matter how shabby or illegal the means by which the information is obtained, no matter how serious an intrusion on privacy might be involved, no matter how demonstrably false the information might be, no matter how prejudicial it might be to the interests

of innocent persons, and no matter how perverse the motivation for publishing it, is a question I would not answer without further argument.

Under the opinion of the Court in *Nebraska Press Association* are there still some cases where a trial judge could properly enjoin publication of material by a newspaper?

2. The Court talks at length about "prior restraints." Classically, prior restraint was a system where publication of a newspaper or book was illegal unless a government official approved of it in advance. One obvious vice of prior restraints was that a government official, simply by inaction, could prevent publication. It was all too easy for the censor, when in doubt, to say "no." Even if the censor was wrong, the publisher would have to bring a long and costly court proceeding to review the censor's negative decision. In the meantime, since he lacked permission to publish, the book or newspaper could not be published or sold.

Under this definition of prior restraint, does the order in Nebraska Press Association v. Stuart seem like a prior restraint? Is it enough that the order was issued *prior* to the threatened publication of any information and that it was a *restraint* in the sense that the newspaper knew it might be punished if it violated the Court's order?

The more particularly the publisher is told in advance what not to print, the more that looks like a prior restraint under the Court's use of the term. Could that problem be avoided by not deciding in advance what can be published and then punishing the press for contempt if publication actually interfered with a fair trial? Note that if the press is not told what it can and cannot print there is a problem of vagueness, which, in itself, exercises a "chilling" effect upon free speech. (Compare the discussion of the English rule of contempt, below at note 4.)

3. In one sense, the order in *Nebraska Press Association* has something in common with the classic prior restraint, under a doctrine that federal courts and many state courts have traditionally applied. That doctrine is that an order of a court with jurisdiction cannot be violated even if it is invalid. That is, the court order must be obeyed until it is reversed on appeal, as was the order in Nebraska Press Association v. Stuart. Note that application of this doctrine could put the trial judge in the position of a censor. That is, he might err on the side of unduly restricting the press, knowing that, before the matter could be published, the publisher would have to reverse the decision in a lengthy and expensive appeal. Does that suggest to you that the Court should adopt Justice Brennan's absolute rule that, no matter how irresponsibly it acts, the press should be immune from all injunctions against publication?

4. Many writers have argued that English law permitting the use of the contempt power against the press is superior to the present American rule. John Ely has written:*

> The English rule against contempt of court holds, fundamentally, that it is unlawful for a newspaper or other medium

---

* John Ely, Trial by Newspapers & Its Cures, Encounter, 1967, vol. 28, #3, pp. 80–81.

of communication to publish matter which tends to prejudice the course of justice in any pending litigation. In practice this means that once a man has been charged by the police, or a charge is imminent, papers cannot print matter which might incline a jury towards either convicting or acquitting him. This includes the evidence against him, his prior criminal record, and editorial speculation about his guilt. Whether the report is accurate is irrelevant. These are things papers simply cannot publish. The press must keep this silence until the committal proceeding—the hearing at which magistrates decide whether the prosecution has enough evidence to hold the accused for trial. Such proceedings are ordinarily conducted in public, and the press is free to report whatever transpires there. After the committal hearing, silence is again the order until the trial, which also can be fully reported. Even after a man is convicted, papers are not free to say whatever they like, for the contempt rule also bars the publication of anything which tends to prejudice the fair hearing of the appeal (although the rule is somewhat less stringent at this point than it is before trial). Should a newspaper overstep the line, it is liable to a fine and its editor may also be fined or even sent to prison. Whether a newspaper has committed contempt is decided by a judge sitting without a jury, and there is theoretically no limit to the amount of the fine or the term of imprisonment he can impose.

If we look only at its core effect—keeping from the jury factual data concerning the accused and editorial discussion of his guilt—the contempt rule makes much sense, for the English (and American) trial system is built upon the idea of a jury of twelve men who will make up their own minds, on the basis of the evidence produced before them in court. However, the rule has a number of side effects which are not so desirable, which should lead us to enquire whether the barn is not being burned to roast the pig.

Decisions as to whether it is legally safe to print a given item, like other journalistic judgments, must be made in a matter of minutes. And the penalty for a wrong guess is harsh. Thus contempt of court is an area in which particularly clear legal guide-lines are needed. However, the complaint about the law of contempt I heard most often during the year I spent in London talking to journalists and newspaper lawyers is that it is so vague as to be of essentially no assistance in many to-print-or-not-to-print situations. Despite repeated journalistic cries for help, the courts have extended little. Dealing only with the specific factual situations presented by the cases before them, judges have refused to lay down guide-lines for baffled editors and have contented themselves with warnings that crime reporting is a "perilous adventure." It is therefore not surprising that when there is a question as to whether an item can safely be printed, editors are inclined to err on the side of non-publication. The vagueness of the law of contempt thus gives it an "overkill" effect, deterring the publication of much which would not, if it ever came to court, be held to be within the rule's intendment. At first blush, overkill might appear a virtue, for is it not fortunate, one might ask, that the law makes papers steer far clear of prejudicing trials? That it is in fact *un*fortunate should become clear from an examination of the ways in which the vagueness of the contempt rule keep newspapers from providing valuable assistance, in the form of positive aid as well as constructive criticism, to the agencies charged with the detection of crime and the administration of justice.

III. PROTECTING FAIR TRIALS BY DENYING SOURCES OF INFORMATION TO THE PRESS

RICHMOND NEWSPAPERS, INC. v. VIRGINIA

Supreme Court of the United States, 1980.
448 U.S. 555, 100 S.Ct. 2814, 65 L.Ed.2d 973.

CHIEF JUSTICE BURGER announced the judgment of the Court and delivered an opinion in which JUSTICE WHITE and JUSTICE STEVENS joined.

The narrow question presented in this case is whether the right of the public and press to attend criminal trials is guaranteed under the United States Constitution.

I

In March 1976, one Stevenson was indicted for murder.... [For various reasons Stevenson's first three trials did not produce final judgments and, at the fourth trial, the judge, on motion of the defendant and with the acquiescence of the prosecution excluded the press. Appellant newspaper sought review of this decision in the Virginia Courts and having failed to prevail, appealed to the Supreme Court].

II

We begin consideration of this case by noting that the precise issue presented here has not previously been before this Court for decision. In Gannett Co., Inc. v. DePasquale, 443 U.S. 368 (1979), the Court was not required to decide whether a right of access to *trials,* as distinguished from hearings on *pre*trial motions, was constitutionally guaranteed. The Court held that the Sixth Amendment's guarantee to the accused of a public trial gave neither the public nor the press an enforceable right of access to a *pre*trial suppression hearing. One concurring opinion specifically emphasized that "a hearing on a motion before trial to suppress evidence is not a *trial....* " 443 U.S., at 394 (Burger, C.J., concurring). Moreover, the Court did not decide whether the First and Fourteenth Amendments guarantee a right of the public to attend trials, id., at 392, and n. 24: nor did the dissenting opinion reach this issue. Id., at 447 (Blackmun, J., dissenting).

In prior cases the Court has treated questions involving conflicts between publicity and a defendant's right to a fair trial; as we observed in Nebraska Press Assn. v. Stuart, 427 U.S. 539, 547 (1976), "[t]he

problems presented by this [conflict] are almost as old as the Republic.''
But here for the first time the Court is asked to decide whether a
criminal trial itself may be closed to the public upon the unopposed
request of a defendant, without any demonstration that closure is
required to protect the defendant's superior right to a fair trial, or that
some other overriding consideration requires closure.

A

The origins of the proceeding which has become the modern criminal trial in Anglo–American justice can be traced back beyond reliable
historical records. We need not here review all details of its development,
but a summary of that history is instructive. What is significant for
present purposes is that throughout its evolution, the trial has been open
to all who cared to observe.

In the days before the Norman Conquest, cases in England were
generally brought before moots, such as the local court of the hundred or
the county court, which were attended by the freemen of the community.
Pollock, English Law Before the Norman Conquest, in 1 Selected Essays
in Anglo–American Legal History 89 (1907). Somewhat like modern jury
duty, attendance at these early meetings was compulsory on the part of
the freemen, who were called upon to render judgment. Id., at 89–90; see
also 1 W. Holdsworth, A History of English Law, 10, 12 (1927).

With the gradual evolution of the jury system in the years after the
Norman Conquest, see, e.g., 1 Holdsworth, supra, at 316, the duty of all
freemen to attend trials to render judgment was relaxed, but there is no
indication that criminal trials did not remain public. When certain
groups were excused from compelled attendance, see The Statute of
Marleborough, 1267, 52 Hen. 3, c. 10; 1 Holdsworth, supra, at 79, and n.
4, the statutory exemption did not prevent them from attending; Lord
Coke observed that those excused "are not compellable to come, but left
to their own liberty." 2 E. Coke, Institutes of the Laws of England 121
(6th ed. 1681).

B

As we have shown, and as was shown in both the Court's opinion
and the dissent in *Gannett*, the historical evidence demonstrates conclusively that at the time when our organic laws were adopted, criminal
trials both here and in England had long been presumptively open. This
is no quirk of history; rather, it has long been recognized as an
indispensable attribute of an Anglo–American trial. Both Hale in the
17th century and Blackstone in the 18th saw the importance of openness
to the proper functioning of a trial; it gave assurance that the proceedings were conducted fairly to all concerned, and it discouraged perjury,
the misconduct of participants, and decisions based on secret bias or
partiality. See, e.g., M. Hale, The History of the Common Law of
England 343–345 (6th ed. 1820); 3 W. Blackstone, Commentaries *372–
373. Jeremy Bentham not only recognized the therapeutic value of open
justice but regarded it as the keystone:

"Without publicity, all other checks are insufficient: in comparison of publicity, all other checks are of small account. Recordation, appeal, whatever other institutions might present themselves in the character of checks, would be found to operate rather as cloaks than checks; as cloaks in reality, as checks only in appearance." 1 J. Bentham, Rationale of Judicial Evidence 524 (1827).

... The early history of open trials in part reflects the widespread acknowledgement, long before there were behavioral scientists, that public trials had significant community therapeutic value. Even without such experts to frame the concept in words, people sensed from experience and observation that, especially in the administration of criminal justice, the means used to achieve justice must have the support derived from public acceptance of both the process and its results.

When a shocking crime occurs, a community reaction of outrage and public protest often follows. See H. Weihofen, The Urge to Punish 130–131 (1956). Thereafter the open processes of justice serve an important prophylactic purpose, providing an outlet for community concern, hostility, and emotion. Without an awareness that society's responses to criminal conduct are underway, natural human reactions of outrage and protest are frustrated and may manifest themselves in some form of vengeful "self-help," as indeed they did regularly in the activities of vigilante "committees" on our frontiers. "The accusation and conviction or acquittal, as much perhaps as the execution of punishment, operat[e] to restore the imbalance which was created by the offense of public charge, to reaffirm the temporarily lost feeling of security, and, perhaps, to satisfy that latent 'urge to punish.'" Mueller, Problems Posed by Publicity to Crime and Criminal Proceedings, 110 U.Pa.L.Rev. 1, 6 (1961).

Civilized societies withdraw both from the victim and the vigilante the enforcement of criminal laws, but they cannot erase from people's consciousness the fundamental, natural yearning to see justice done—or even the urge for retribution. The crucial prophylactic aspects of the administration of justice cannot function in the dark; no community catharsis can occur if justice is "done in a corner [or] in any covert manner." It is not enough to say that results alone will satiate the natural community desire for "satisfaction." A result considered untoward may undermine public confidence, and where the trial has been concealed from public view an unexpected outcome can cause a reaction that the system at best has failed and at worst has been corrupted. To work effectively, it is important that society's criminal process "satisfy the appearance of justice," Offutt v. United States, 348 U.S. 11, 14 (1954), and the appearance of justice can best be provided by allowing people to observe it.

Looking back, we see that when the ancient "town meeting" form of trial became too cumbersome, twelve members of the community were delegated to act as its surrogates, but the community did not surrender its right to observe the conduct of trials. The people retained a "right of visitation" which enabled them to satisfy themselves that justice was in fact being done.

People in an open society do not demand infallibility from their institutions, but it is difficult for them to accept what they are prohibited from observing. When a criminal trial is conducted in the open, there is at least an opportunity both for understanding the system in general and its workings in a particular case:

> "The educative effect of public attendance is a material advantage. Not only is respect for the law increased and intelligent acquaintance acquired with the methods of government, but a strong confidence in judicial remedies is secured which could never be inspired by a system of secrecy." 6 Wigmore, supra, at 438. See also 1 Bentham, Rationale of Judicial Evidence, at 525.

III

A

The First Amendment, in conjunction with the Fourteenth, prohibits governments from "abridging the freedom of speech, or of the press; or the right of the people peaceably to assemble, and to petition the Government for a redress of grievances." These expressly guaranteed freedoms share a common core purpose of assuring freedom of communication on matters relating to the functioning of government. Plainly it would be difficult to single out any aspect of government of higher concern and importance to the people than the manner in which criminal trials are conducted; as we have shown, recognition of this pervades the centuries-old history of open trials and the opinions of this Court.

The Bill of Rights was enacted against the backdrop of the long history of trials being presumptively open. Public access to trials was then regarded as an important aspect of the process itself; the conduct of trials "before as many of the people as chuse to attend" was regarded as one of "the inestimable advantages of a free English constitution of government." 1 Journals of the Continental Congress, at 106, 107. In guaranteeing freedoms such as those of speech and press, the First Amendment can be read as protecting the right of everyone to attend trials so as to give meaning to those explicit guarantees. "[T]he First Amendment goes beyond protection of the press and the self-expression of individuals to prohibit government from limiting the stock of information from which members of the public may draw." First National Bank of Boston v. Bellotti, 435 U.S. 765, 783 (1978). Free speech carries with it some freedom to listen. "In a variety of contexts this Court has referred to a First Amendment right to 'receive information and ideas.'" Kleindienst v. Mandel, 408 U.S. 753, 762 (1972). What this means in the context of trials is that the First Amendment guarantees of speech and press, standing alone, prohibit government from summarily closing courtroom doors which had long been open to the public at the time that amendment was adopted. "For the First Amendment does not speak equivocally.... It must be taken as a command of the broadest scope that explicit language, read in the context of a liberty-loving society, will allow." Bridges v. California, 314 U.S. 252, 263 (1941).

It is not crucial whether we describe this right to attend criminal trials to hear, see, and communicate observations concerning them as a "right of access," cf. *Gannett,* supra, at 397 (Powell, J., concurring); Saxbe v. Washington Post Co., 417 U.S. 843 (1974); Pell v. Procunier, 417 U.S. 817 (1974), or a "right to gather information," for we have recognized that "without some protection for seeking out the news, freedom of the press could be eviscerated." Branzburg v. Hayes, 408 U.S. 665, 681 (1972). The explicit, guaranteed rights to speak and to publish concerning what takes place at a trial would lose much meaning if access to observe the trial could, as it was here, be foreclosed arbitrarily.

B

The right of access to places traditionally open to the public, as criminal trials have long been, may be seen as assured by the amalgam of the First Amendment guarantees of speech and press; and their affinity to the right of assembly is not without relevance. From the outset, the right of assembly was regarded not only as an independent right but also as a catalyst to augment the free exercise of the other First Amendment rights with which it was deliberately linked by the draftsmen. "The right of peaceable assembly is a right cognate to those of free speech and free press and is equally fundamental." DeJonge v. Oregon, 299 U.S. 353, 364 (1937). People assemble in public places not only to speak or to take action, but also to listen, observe, and learn; indeed, they may "assembl[e] for any lawful purpose," Hague v. C.I.O., 307 U.S. 496, 519 (1939) (opinion of Stone, J.). Subject to the traditional time, place, and manner restrictions, see, e.g., Cox v. New Hampshire, 312 U.S. 569 (1941); see also Cox v. Louisiana, 379 U.S. 559, 560–564 (1965) streets, sidewalks, and parks are places traditionally open, where First Amendment rights may be exercised, see Hague v. C.I.O., 307 U.S. 496, 515 (1939) (opinion of Roberts, J.); a trial courtroom also is a public place where the people generally—and representatives of the media—have a right to be present, and where their presence historically has been thought to enhance the integrity and quality of what takes place.

C

The State argues that the Constitution nowhere spells out a guarantee for the right of the public to attend trials, and that accordingly no such right is protected. The possibility that such a contention could be made did not escape the notice of the Constitution's draftsmen; they were concerned that some important rights might be thought disparaged because not specifically guaranteed. It was even argued that because of this danger no Bill of Rights should be adopted. See, e.g., A. Hamilton, The Federalist no. 84. In a letter to Thomas Jefferson in October of 1788, James Madison explained why he, although "in favor of a bill of rights," had "not viewed it in an important light" up to that time: "I conceive that in a certain degree ... the rights in question are reserved by the manner in which the federal powers are granted." He went on to state "there is great reason to fear that a positive declaration of some of the most essential rights could not be obtained in the requisite latitude." 5 Writings of James Madison 271 (Hunt ed. 1904).

But arguments such as the State makes have not precluded recognition of important rights not enumerated. Notwithstanding the appropriate caution against reading into the Constitution rights not explicitly defined, the Court has acknowledged that certain unarticulated rights are implicit in enumerated guarantees. For example, the rights of association and of privacy, the right to be presumed innocent and the right to be judged by a standard of proof beyond a reasonable doubt in a criminal trial, as well as the right to travel, appear nowhere in the Constitution or Bill of Rights. Yet these important but unarticulated rights have nonetheless been found to share constitutional protection in common with explicit guarantees. The concerns expressed by Madison and others have thus been resolved; fundamental rights, even though not expressly guaranteed, have been recognized by the Court as indispensable to the enjoyment of rights explicitly defined.

We hold that the right to attend criminal trials is implicit in the guarantees of the First Amendment; without the freedom to attend such trials, which people have exercised for centuries, important aspects of freedom of speech and "of the press could be eviscerated."

D

Having concluded there was a guaranteed right of the public under the First and Fourteenth Amendments to attend the trial of Stevenson's case, we return to the closure order challenged by appellants. The Court in *Gannett,* supra, made clear that although the Sixth Amendment guarantees the accused a right to a public trial, it does not give a right to a private trial. 443 U.S., at 382. Despite the fact that this was the fourth trial of the accused, the trial judge made no findings to support closure; no inquiry was made as to whether alternative solutions would have met the need to ensure fairness; there was no recognition of any right under the Constitution for the public or press to attend the trial. In contrast to the pretrial proceeding dealt with in *Gannett,* supra, there exist in the context of the trial itself various tested alternatives to satisfy the constitutional demands of fairness. There was no suggestion that any problems with witnesses could not have been dealt with by their exclusion from the courtroom or their sequestration during the trial. Nor is there anything to indicate that sequestration of the jurors would not have guarded against their being subjected to any improper information. All of the alternatives admittedly present difficulties for trial courts, but none of the factors relied on here was beyond the realm of the manageable. Absent an overriding interest articulated in findings, the trial of a criminal case must be open to the public. Accordingly, the judgment under review is

Reversed.

JUSTICE POWELL took no part in the consideration or decision of this case.

JUSTICE WHITE, concurring.

This case would have been unnecessary had Gannett Co. v. DePasquale, 443 U.S. 368 (1979), construed the Sixth Amendment to forbid excluding the public from criminal proceedings except in narrowly defined circumstances. But the Court there rejected the submission of four of us to this effect, thus requiring that the First Amendment issue involved here be addressed. On this issue, I concur in the opinion of The Chief Justice.

JUSTICE STEVENS, concurring.

This is a watershed case. Until today the Court has accorded virtually absolute protection to the dissemination of information or ideas, but never before has it squarely held that the acquisition of newsworthy matter is entitled to any constitutional protection whatsoever. An additional word of emphasis is therefore appropriate.

Twice before, the Court has implied that any governmental restriction on access to information, no matter how severe and no matter how unjustified, would be constitutionally acceptable so long as it did not single out the press for special disabilities not applicable to the public at large. In a dissent joined by Justice Brennan and Justice Marshall in Saxbe v. Washington Post Co., 417 U.S. 843, 850, Justice Powell unequivocally rejected the conclusion "that any governmental restriction on press access to information, so long as it is not discriminatory, falls outside the purview of First Amendment concern." Id., at 857 (emphasis in original). And in Houchins v. KQED, Inc., 438 U.S. 1, 19–40, I explained at length why Justice Brennan, Justice Powell, and I were convinced that "[a]n official prison policy of concealing ... knowledge from the public by arbitrarily cutting off the flow of information at its source abridges the freedom of speech and of the press protected by the First and Fourteenth Amendments to the Constitution." Id., at 38. Since Justice Marshall and Justice Blackmun were unable to participate in that case, a majority of the Court neither accepted nor rejected that conclusion or the contrary conclusion expressed in the prevailing opinions. Today, however, for the first time, the Court unequivocally holds that an arbitrary interference with access to important information is an abridgement of the freedoms of speech and of the press protected by the First Amendment.

JUSTICE BRENNAN, with whom JUSTICE MARSHALL joins, concurring in the judgment.

Gannett Co. v. DePasquale, 443 U.S. 368 (1979), held that the Sixth Amendment right to a public trial was personal to the accused, conferring no right of access to pretrial proceedings that is separately enforceable by the public or the press. The instant case raises the question whether the First Amendment, of its own force and as applied to the States through the Fourteenth Amendment, secures the public an independent right of access to trial proceedings. Because I believe that the First Amendment—of itself and as applied to the States through the Fourteenth Amendment—secures such a public right of access, I agree with those of my Brethren who hold that without more, agreement of the trial judge and the parties cannot constitutionally close a trial to the public.

I

While freedom of expression is made inviolate by the First Amendment, and, with only rare and stringent exceptions, may not be suppressed, the First Amendment has not been reviewed by the Court in all settings as providing an equally categorical assurance of the correlative freedom of access to information. Yet the Court has not ruled out a public access component to the First Amendment in every circumstance. Read with care and in context, our decisions must therefore be understood as holding only that any privilege of access to governmental information is subject to a degree of restraint dictated by the nature of the information and countervailing interests in security or confidentiality. These cases neither comprehensively nor absolutely deny that public access to information may at times be implied by the First Amendment and the principles which animate it.

The Court's approach in right of access cases simply reflects the special nature of a claim of First Amendment right to gather information. Customarily, First Amendment guarantees are interposed to protect communication between speaker and listener. When so employed against prior restraints, free speech protections are almost insurmountable. But the First Amendment embodies more than a commitment to free expression and communicative interchange for their own sakes; it has a *structural* role to play in securing and fostering our republican system of self-government. Implicit in this structural role is not only "the principle that debate on public issues should be uninhibited, robust, and wide-open," New York Times Co. v. Sullivan, 376 U.S. 254, 270 (1964), but the antecedent assumption that valuable public debate—as well as other civic behavior—must be informed. The structural model links the First Amendment to that process of communication necessary for a democracy to survive, and thus entails solicitude not only for communication itself, but for the indispensable conditions of meaningful communication.

IV

As previously noted, resolution of First Amendment public access claims in individual cases must be strongly influenced by the weight of historical practice and by an assessment of the specific structural value of public access in the circumstances. With regard to the case at hand, our ingrained tradition of public trials and the importance of public access to the broader purposes of the trial process, tip the balance strongly toward the rule that trials be open. What countervailing interests might be sufficiently compelling to reverse this presumption of openness need not concern us now, for the statute at stake here authorizes trial closures at the unfettered discretion of the judge and parties. Accordingly, Va.Code 19.2–266 violates the First and Fourteenth Amendments, and the decision of the Virginia Supreme Court to the contrary should be reversed.

JUSTICE STEWART, concurring in the judgment.

In Gannett Co. v. DePasquale, 443 U.S. 368, the Court held that the Sixth Amendment, which guarantees "the accused" the right to a public trial, does not confer upon representatives of the press or members of the general public any right of access to a trial. But the Court explicitly left open the question whether such a right of access may be guaranteed by other provisions of the Constitution, id., at 391–393. Justice Powell expressed the view that the First and Fourteenth Amendments do extend at least a limited right of access even to pretrial suppression hearings in criminal cases, id., at 397–403 (concurring opinion). Justice Rehnquist expressed a contrary view, id., at 403–406 (concurring opinion). The remaining members of the Court were silent on the question.

Whatever the ultimate answer to that question may be with respect to pretrial suppression hearings in criminal cases, the First and Fourteenth Amendments clearly give the press and the public a right of access to trials themselves, civil as well as criminal. As has been abundantly demonstrated in Part II of the opinion of The Chief Justice, in Justice Brennan's concurring opinion, and in Justice Blackmun's dissenting opinion last Term in the *Gannett* case, 443 U.S. at 406, it has for centuries been a basic presupposition of the Anglo–American legal system that trials shall be public trials. The opinions referred to also convincingly explain the many good reasons why this is so. With us, a trial is by very definition a proceeding open to the press and to the public.

In conspicuous contrast to a military base, a jail, or a prison, a trial courtroom is a public place. Even more than city streets, sidewalks, and parks as areas of traditional First Amendment activity, a trial courtroom is a place where representatives of the press and of the public are not only free to be, but where their presence serves to assure the integrity of what goes on.

But this does not mean that the First Amendment right of members of the public and representatives of the press to attend civil and criminal trials is absolute. Just as a legislature may impose reasonable time, place and manner restrictions upon the exercise of First Amendment freedoms, so may a trial judge impose reasonable limitations upon the unrestricted occupation of a courtroom by representatives of the press and members of the public. Much more than a city street, a trial courtroom must be a quiet and orderly place. Moreover, every courtroom has a finite physical capacity, and there may be occasions when not all who wish to attend a trial may do so. And while there exist many alternative ways to satisfy the constitutional demands of a fair trial, those demands may also sometimes justify limitations upon the unrestricted presence of spectators in the courtroom.

Since in the present case the trial judge appears to have given no recognition to the right of representatives of the press and members of the public to be present at the Virginia murder trial over which he was presiding, the judgment under review must be reversed.

It is upon the basis of these principles that I concur in the judgment.

JUSTICE BLACKMUN, concurring in the judgment.

My opinion and vote in partial dissent last Term in Gannett Co. v. DePasquale, 443 U.S. 368, 406 (1979), compels my vote to reverse the judgment of the Supreme Court of Virginia.

I

The decision in this case is gratifying for me for two reasons:

. . . It is gratifying to see the Court now looking to and relying upon legal history in determining the fundamental public character of the criminal trial. The partial dissent in *Gannett*, 443 U.S., at 419–433, took great pains in assembling—I believe adequately—the historical material and in stressing its importance to this area of the law. Although the Court in *Gannett* gave a modicum of lip service to legal history, 443 U.S., at 386, n. 15, it denied its obvious application when the defense and the prosecution, with no resistance by the trial judge, agreed that the proceeding should be closed.

The Court's return to history is a welcome change in direction.

II

The Court's ultimate ruling in *Gannett*, with such clarification as is provided by the opinions in this case today, apparently is now to the effect that there is no *Sixth* Amendment right on the part of the public— or the press—to an open hearing on a motion to suppress. I, of course, continue to believe that *Gannett* was in error, both in its interpretation of the Sixth Amendment generally, and in its application to the suppression hearing, for I remain convinced that the right to a public trial is to be found where the Constitution explicitly placed it—in the Sixth Amendment.

The Court, however, has eschewed the Sixth Amendment route. The plurality turns to other possible constitutional sources and invokes a veritable potpourri of them—the Speech Clause of the First Amendment, the Press Clause, the Assembly Clause, the Ninth Amendment, and a cluster of penumbral guarantees recognized in past decisions. This course is troublesome, but it is the route that has been selected and, at least for now, we must live with it. No purpose would be served by my spelling out at length here the reasons for my saying that the course is troublesome. I need do no more than observe that uncertainty marks the nature—and strictness—of the standard of closure the Court adopts.

Having said all this, and with the Sixth Amendment set to one side in this case, I am driven to conclude, as a secondary position, that the First Amendment must provide some measure of protection for public access to the trial. The opinion in partial dissent in *Gannett* explained that the public has an intense need and a deserved right to know about the administration of justice in general; about the prosecution of local crimes in particular; about the conduct of the judge, the prosecutor, defense counsel, police officers, other public servants, and all the actors in the judicial arena; and about the trial itself. It is clear and obvious to me, on the approach the Court has chosen to take, that, by closing this criminal trial, the trial judge abridged these First Amendment interests of the public.

I also would reverse, and I join the judgment of the Court.

JUSTICE REHNQUIST, dissenting.

In the Gilbert & Sullivan operetta *Iolanthe,* the Lord Chancellor recites:

"The Law is the true embodiment

of everything that's excellent,

It has no kind of fault or flaw,

And I, my lords, embody the law."

It is difficult not to derive more than a little of this flavor from the various opinions supporting the judgment in this case. . . .

We have at present 50 state judicial systems and one federal judicial system in the United States, and our authority to reverse a decision by the highest court of the State is limited to only those occasions when the state decision violates some provision of the United States Constitution. And that authority should be exercised with a full sense that the judges whose decisions we review are making the same effort as we to uphold the Constitution. As said by Justice Jackson, concurring in the result in Brown v. Allen, 344 U.S. 443, 540 (1953) "we are not final because we are infallible, but we are infallible only because we are final."

The proper administration of justice in any nation is bound to be a matter of the highest concern to all thinking citizens. But to gradually rein in, as this Court has done over the past generation, all of the ultimate decisionmaking power over how justice shall be administered, not merely in the federal system but in each of the 50 States, is a task that no Court consisting of nine persons, however gifted, is equal to. Nor is it desirable that such authority be exercised by such a tiny numerical fragment of the 220 million people who compose the population of this country. In the same concurrence just quoted, Justice Jackson accurately observed that "[t]he generalities of the Fourteenth Amendment are so indeterminate as to what state actions are forbidden that this Court has found it a ready instrument, in one field or another, to magnify federal, and incidentally its own, authority over the states." Id., at 534.

However high minded the impulses which originally spawned this trend may have been, and which impulses have been accentuated since the time Justice Jackson wrote, it is basically unhealthy to have so much authority concentrated in a small group of lawyers who have been appointed to the Supreme Court and enjoy virtual life tenure. Nothing in the reasoning of Chief Justice Marshall in Marbury v. Madison, 5 U.S. (1 Cranch) 137 (1803) requires that this Court through ever broadening use of the Supremacy Clause smother a healthy pluralism which would ordinarily exist in a national government embracing 50 States.

The issue here is not whether the "right" to freedom of the press conferred by the First Amendment to the Constitution overrides the defendant's "right" to a fair trial conferred by other amendments to the Constitution; it is instead whether any provision in the Constitution may fairly be read to prohibit what the trial judge in the Virginia state court system did in this case. Being unable to find any such prohibition in the

First, Sixth, Ninth, or any other Amendments to the United States Constitution, or in the Constitution itself, I dissent.

NOTES AND QUESTIONS

1. A major debate in constitutional law has concerned whether freedom of the press is a distinct constitutional guarantee, providing the media with constitutional protections additional to those provided by freedom of speech. Justice Potter Stewart has been among those who have argued that the free press guarantee is not synonymous with the guarantee of free speech. In an article he said:*

> [T]he Free Press guarantee is, in essence, a *structural* provision of the Constitution. Most of the other provisions in the Bill of Rights protect specific liberties or specific rights of individuals: freedom of speech, freedom of worship, the right to counsel, the privilege against compulsory self-incrimination, to name a few. In contrast, the Free Press Clause extends protection to an institution. The publishing business is, in short, the only organized private business that is given explicit constitutional protection.

> This basic understanding is essential, I think, to avoid an elementary error of constitutional law. It is tempting to suggest that freedom of the press means only that newspaper publishers are guaranteed freedom of expression. They *are* guaranteed that freedom, to be sure, but so are we all, because of the Free Speech Clause. If the Free Press guarantee meant no more than freedom of expression, it would be a constitutional redundancy.... By including both guarantees in the First Amendment, the Founders quite clearly recognized the distinction between the two.

> It is also a mistake to suppose that the only purpose of the constitutional guarantee of a free press is to insure that a newspaper will serve as a neutral forum for debate, a "market place for ideas," a kind of Hyde Park corner for the community. A related theory sees the press as a neutral conduit of information between the people and their elected leaders. These theories, in my view, again give insufficient weight to the institutional autonomy of the press that it was the purpose of the Constitution to guarantee.

> ... So far as the Constitution goes, the autonomous press may publish what it knows, and may seek to learn what it can.

> But this autonomy cuts both ways. The press is free to do battle against secrecy and deception in government. But the press cannot expect from the Constitution any guarantee that it will succeed. There is no constitutional right to have access to particular government information, or to require openness from the bureaucracy. The public's interest in knowing about its government is protected by the guarantee of a Free Press, but

* Potter Stewart, Or of the Press, Hastings Law Journal, 1975, vol. 26, p. 631, 633–34, 636.

the protection is indirect. The Constitution itself is neither a Freedom of Information Act nor an Official Secrets Act.

The Constitution, in other words, establishes the contest, not its resolution. Congress may provide a resolution, at least in some instances, through carefully drawn legislation. For the rest, we must rely, as so often in our system we must, on the tug and pull of the political forces in American society.

Justice Stewart's argument that freedom of the press means *more* than freedom of speech was challenged by Chief Justice Burger's concurring opinion in First National Bank of Boston v. Bellotti, 435 U.S. 765 (1978). He said, in part:

[T]he history of the Clause does not suggest that the authors contemplated a "special" or "institutional" privilege.

To conclude that the Framers did not intend to limit the freedom of the press to one select group is not necessarily to suggest that the Press Clause is redundant. The Speech Clause standing alone may be viewed as a protection of the liberty to express ideas and beliefs, while the Press Clause focuses specifically on the liberty to disseminate expression broadly and "comprehends every sort of publication which affords a vehicle of information and opinion." Yet there is no fundamental distinction between expression and dissemination. The liberty encompassed by the Press Clause, although complementary to and a natural extension of Speech Clause liberty, merited special mention simply because it had been more often the object of official restraints. . . .

Because the First Amendment was meant to guarantee freedom to express and communicate ideas, I can see no difference between the right of those who seek to disseminate ideas by way of a newspaper and those who give lectures or speeches and seek to enlarge the audience by publication and wide dissemination.

2.   The debate between Justice Stewart and Chief Justice Burger has been relevant to the question whether government can require reporters to disclose sources of news stories. That question will be explored in Chapter 12, Section III. The debate has also been relevant to the question whether the media have a constitutional right to access to information that is denied to the general public. In that context, however, resolution of the dispute about the meaning of the First Amendment's free press guarantee does not appear crucial. Notice, particularly, that Justice Stewart argues that freedom of the press is a distinct "structural" protection for media, but insists at the same time that "there is no constitutional right to have access to ... government information." In the companion cases of Pell v. Procunier, 417 U.S. 817 (1974) and Saxbe v. Washington Post Co., 417 U.S. 843 (1974), the Court sustained a prison regulation forbidding press interviews with inmates. Justice Stewart, writing for the Court, insisted that the Constitution imposed no obligation on government "to make available to journalists sources of information not available to the public generally." Nixon v.

Warner Communications, Inc., 435 U.S. 589 (1978), rejected a claim for media access to tape recordings of President Nixon's Watergate tapes. Justice Powell's opinion for the Court stated that the press "had no right of information about a trial superior to that of the general public," although his opinion also emphasized that in this case the public already had full information as to the content of the tapes.

3. In Houchins v. KQED, Inc., 438 U.S. 1 (1978), the issue was squarely put whether the press required access to a jail to inform the public. The press as well as the public were excluded by a local sheriff from certain portions of the jail despite a public controversy about jail conditions. Lower federal courts ordered that a television station be given access to those portions of the jail which were not open to the public. The Supreme Court reversed. Four of the seven Justices participating agreed with the principle that the press had no greater access to information than the public. The dissenting Justices argued that freedom of the press required greater access by the press when the lack of public access denied the public the full opportunity to observe jail conditions. There was no opinion for the Court in Houchins v. KQED. The crucial vote was Justice Stewart's, and he wrote a separate concurrence. The lower courts had also ordered the sheriff to allow press access at reasonable times to portions of the jail that were open at other times for public tours, and to allow the press to bring in camera and sound equipment. Justice Stewart agreed with the dissenting Justices (making a majority on this point) that this aspect of the lower court's order was required by the First Amendment. The principle was that the First Amendment required that the press be given *equal* access with the public. As he saw it, the rights of the press were not respected simply by allowing reporters to sign up for jail tours on the same terms as the public.

> [T]he concept of equal access must accommodate the practical distinctions between the press and the general public.

> When on assignment, a journalist does not tour a jail simply for his own edification. He is there to gather information to be passed on to others, and his mission is protected by the Constitution for very specific reasons. . . .

> . . . The Constitution requires sensitivity to that role, and to the special needs of the press in performing it effectively. A person touring Santa Rita Jail can grasp its reality with his own eyes and ears. But if a television reporter is to convey the jail's sights and sounds to those who cannot personally visit the place, he must use cameras and sound equipment. In short, terms of access that are reasonably imposed on individual members of the public may, if they impede effective reporting without sufficient justification, be unreasonable as applied to journalists who are there to convey to the general public what the visitors see.

Is it strange that the press should be given "effective" access to information only when the public already has some access? Should the case for press access have been stronger, not weaker, in those areas of the jail where the public had no access at all?

The initial conference vote in *Houchins* was four to three to affirm. The Court later reversed because Justice Stewart changed his vote. Bernard Schwartz reported the conference discussion in the case as follows:*

> The case for reversal was stated bluntly by Justice White, "I don't see any right of access for anyone or why, if [they] let the public in, [they] must let the press in with their cameras." On the other side, Justice Stevens asked, "Can a policy denying all access be constitutional? I think not." Stevens emphasized the public interest "as to how prisons are run."

> Of particular interest, in view of his position as the "swing vote," was the ambivalent statement of Justice Stewart. "The First Amendment," he declared, "does not give [the press] access superior to that of the general public. Moreover, there is no such thing as a constitutional right to know." Nevertheless, the Justice concluded, "Basically, I think the injunction here does not exceed [the permitted] bounds." Stewart also noted, "If the sheriff had not allowed public tours, he did not have to allow the press in."

4.   As indicated by several of the opinions in the *Richmond Newspapers* case, the 5–4 decision in Gannett Co. v. DePasquale, 443 U.S. 368 (1979), rejected a newspaper's constitutional attack on closing of pretrial criminal proceedings to the press. While it is true that the Court's majority noted a distinction between trials and pretrial proceedings, the rationale for rejecting a claim based on the public trial guarantee of the Sixth Amendment was that the public trial right was solely for the benefit of the accused. Thus, when the accused sought, or agreed to, closing proceedings to the public, the Sixth Amendment was irrelevant. Is Chief Justice Burger's plurality opinion in *Richmond Newspapers* nevertheless grounded in part on the Sixth Amendment? What is the Constitutional source of the public's right to attend criminal trials?

5.   Neither the majority nor the dissenting opinions in the *Gannett* case discussed the issue whether the First Amendment precluded closing proceedings in criminal cases to the press. Two members of the majority addressed that issue in separate concurrences. Justice Powell argued that, in the absence of findings that a fair trial was likely to be prejudiced by publicity, it would violate the First Amendment to close those proceedings to the press. Justice Rehnquist disagreed, pointing out that the Court had previously decided that the press never has a constitutional right to attend proceedings closed to the public.

6.   Some states provide that all preliminary hearings in criminal cases must be closed to press and public on request of the accused. Suppose a preliminary hearing is closed, on the defendant's request, without any inquiry whether an open hearing will interfere with a later

* Bernard Schwartz, The Unpublished Opinions of the Burger Court, Oxford University Press, 1988, p. 347.

fair trial. Does the *Gannett* case indicate that ordering the press from the hearing will be a violation of the Constitution? One way to read the case is that a majority of five Justices announced that there would be a constitutional violation. Four Justices, in dissent, read the Sixth Amendment as forbidding barring the press from pretrial proceedings in criminal cases unless irreparable damage to a fair trial would result. Justice Powell read the First Amendment as requiring press access unless a fair trial was "likely" to be prejudiced. There is, however, another way to read *Gannett,* as did Justice Rehnquist in his concurrence in that case. Since the majority in *Gannett* concluded there was no right of public access to pretrial proceedings, he said, there can be no right of press access. Has the *Richmond Newspapers* case resolved the question of closing pretrial hearings in criminal cases?

7.   Under the *Richmond Newspapers* decision, is it still possible to close criminal trials, or portions of them, to press and public? What would be the appropriate criteria for doing so? Does the decision have any implication for other press claims for access to public property or government information?

In Globe Newspaper Co. v. Superior Court, 457 U.S. 596 (1982), the Court considered the constitutionality of a Massachusetts statute that required the exclusion of the press and public during the testimony of the victims at criminal trials for sex offenses against minors.

The Court, in an opinion by Justice Brennan, regarded *Richmond Newspapers* as establishing a First Amendment right of public and press access to criminal trials. Although it granted that the state interest in protecting minor victims from the trauma of testifying in public would be sufficient in some cases to close that part of the trial, the Court said that such a decision required a careful consideration of the facts of each case. Since closing the courtroom in all such situations would bar press access even in cases where there was no need to protect minor witnesses, the Court held the Massachusetts statute unconstitutional.

The majority also rejected the state's second argument—that a law promising such a shield to victims who reported sexual offenses might reduce the underreporting of such crimes. Justice Brennan's opinion answered this argument in several ways. First, the state "has offered no empirical support for the claim that the rule of automatic closure . . . will lead to an increase in the number of minor sex victims coming forward and cooperating with state authorities;" secondly, since the press is not denied access to the transcript and other sources providing an account of the minor's testimony, the press could publicize the identity and substance of the victim's testimony anyway. And, finally, the encouragement-of-victims-to-come-forward argument proved too much, since it could be applied in all criminal cases in a way that would "run contrary to the very foundation of the right of access recognized in *Richmond Newspapers.*"

Chief Justice Burger, who wrote *Richmond Newspapers,* dissented in an opinion joined by Justice Rehnquist. His argument was that, unlike the case in *Richmond* where there was a "right of access to places traditionally open to the public . . . there is clearly a long history of exclusion of the public from trials involving sexual assault, particularly those against minors."

Is there any difference in the way the Court should have looked at the two arguments advanced by the state? What would be the result if the Massachusetts statute in question had simply required the judge to close the trial if the victim preferred not to testify in open court? What would be the result if the statute required the judge to close the trial if the victim would be traumatized by having to repeat the details of the crime in open court? What would be the result if the statute required the judge to close the court if the victim would be embarrassed by having to repeat the details of the crime in open court?

8.   Chief Justice Burger's opinion in Nebraska Press Ass'n v. Stuart suggested a number of alternatives to injunctions directed to the press. One was the "gag order," limiting by court injunction "what the contending lawyers, the police, and witnesses may say to anyone." In a footnote, he noted the contention that gagging trial participants interferes with press rights to news sources. On the basis of *Richmond Newspapers,* and the cases that preceded it, is there any substance to that contention? Do these orders raise any questions about the free speech rights of defendants' attorneys and independent witnesses?

Chapter XV

FREEDOM OF ASSOCIATION

Nowhere in the Constitution is there any mention of freedom of association, which is surprising, for Alexis de Tocqueville wrote in the early 1830s that the United States was the "only ... country on the face of the earth where the citizens enjoy unlimited freedom of association for political purposes," and "the only one ... where the continual exercise of the right of association has been introduced into civil life and where all advantages which civilization can confer are procured by means of it."* It is also surprising that the United States Supreme Court did not recognize freedom of association as a constitutionally protected right until 1958.

I. FREEDOM OF ASSOCIATION RECOGNIZED AS A CONSTITUTIONAL RIGHT

N.A.A.C.P. v. ALABAMA

Supreme Court of the United States, 1958.
357 U.S. 449, 78 S.Ct. 1163, 2 L.Ed.2d 1488.

[The National Association for the Advancement of Colored People chartered its first Alabama Branch in 1918. In 1951, the N.A.A.C.P. opened a regional office in Alabama, which employed three people. In 1956, when Southern "massive resistance" to the Supreme Court's school integration decisions was nearing its peak, the Attorney General of Alabama brought suit against the Association in a state court in Montgomery. He claimed that the Association had not complied with an Alabama law which requires out-of-state "corporations" to register with the Alabama Secretary of State before they "transact business" in Alabama. The trial judge entered a temporary order that the N.A.A.C.P. refrain from engaging in any further activities in Alabama. The Attorney General then demanded, on the ground that it was necessary in preparing for trial, that the Association produce its records, including its membership lists. The Association produced most of the information requested, but refused to produce its Alabama membership lists on the ground that public disclosure would subject its members to reprisals. The Association was held in contempt, and fined $100,000. The contempt citation also had the effect of preventing the N.A.A.C.P. from taking any steps to remove the "temporary" order which kept it from engaging in any activities in the State of Alabama. To complicate matters further, the Alabama Supreme Court refused to hear an appeal to overturn the

* Alexis de Tocqueville, Democracy in America, Phillips Bradley, ed., Vintage Books, 1945, II, p. 123.

contempt citation on the ground that the Association had followed the wrong procedures.

The N.A.A.C.P. then petitioned the U.S. Supreme Court for a writ of certiorari, which the Court granted. The organization's principal contention was that Alabama's action violated its members' rights to freedom of speech and association. Chief Justice Warren's docketbook for the 1957 Term shows that the Court voted unanimously in conference both to grant the N.A.A.C.P.'s petition for certiorari and to reverse the Alabama court. The justices agreed to state their reasons for reversal in a *per curiam* opinion. After working on the *per curiam* opinion, Justice Harlan concluded that it would reflect adversely on the Court to dispose of the case without a fully reasoned opinion. "In my view," he wrote his colleagues, on April 22, 1958, "the considerations here are quite different from those which have led us to *per cur* all of the cases in this field which have come to us since the original segregation cases were decided. Having found it impossible to write a satisfactory opinion within the normal compass of a *per curiam,* as originally proposed, I have ventured to prepare a full-scale opinion. In doing this, I have thought it important that the opinion should be written (1) with the utmost dispassion, (2) within an orthodox constitutional framework and (3) as narrowly as possible. You will be the judges of the extent to which these objectives have been attained."*]

JUSTICE HARLAN delivered the opinion of the Court.

. . .

III

. . .

The Association both urges that it is constitutionally entitled to resist official inquiry into its membership lists, and that it may assert, on behalf of its members, a right personal to them to be protected from compelled disclosure by the State of their affiliation with the Association as revealed by the membership lists. We think that petitioner argues more appropriately the rights of its members, [who are not of course parties to the litigation] and that its nexus with them is sufficient to permit that it act as their representative before this Court. . . .

. . .

We thus reach petitioner's claim that the production order in the state litigation trespasses upon fundamental freedoms protected by the Due Process Clause of the Fourteenth Amendment. Petitioner argues that in view of the facts and circumstances shown in the record, the effect of compelled disclosure of the membership lists will be to abridge the rights of its rank-and-file members to engage in lawful association in support of their common beliefs. It contends that governmental action which, although not directly suppressing association, nevertheless carries this consequence, can be justified only upon some overriding valid interest of the State.

* John Marshall Harlan Papers, Seely G. Mudd Manuscript Library, Princeton University, Box 495.

Effective advocacy of both public and private points of view, particularly controversial ones, is undeniably enhanced by group association, as this Court has more than once recognized by remarking upon the close nexus between the freedoms of speech and assembly. De Jonge v. Oregon, 299 U.S. 353, 364; Thomas v. Collins, 323 U.S. 516, 530. It is beyond debate that freedom to engage in association for the advancement of beliefs is an inseparable aspect of the "liberty" assured by the Due Process Clause of the Fourteenth Amendment, which embraces freedom of speech. See Gitlow v. New York . . . , Palko v. Connecticut. . . . Of course, it is immaterial whether the beliefs sought to be advanced by association pertain to political, economic, religious, or cultural matters, and State action which may have the effect of curtailing the freedom to associate is subject to the closest scrutiny.

The fact that Alabama, so far as is relevant to the validity of the contempt judgment presently under review, has taken no action . . . to restrict the right of petitioner's members to associate freely, does not end inquiry into the effect of the production orders. . . . The governmental action challenged may appear to be totally unrelated to protected liberties. Statutes imposing taxes upon rather than prohibiting particular activity have been struck down when perceived to have the consequence of unduly curtailing the liberty of freedom of press assured under the Fourteenth Amendment. Grosjean v. American Press Co., 297 U.S. 233; Murdock v. Pennsylvania, 319 U.S. 105.

It is hardly a novel perception that compelled disclosure of affiliation with groups engaged in advocacy may constitute as effective a restraint on freedom of association as the forms of governmental action in the cases above were thought likely to produce upon the particular constitutional rights there involved. . . . Inviolability of privacy in group association may in many circumstances be indispensable to preservation of freedom of association, particularly where a group espouses dissident beliefs. . . .

We think that the production order, in the respects here drawn in question, must be regarded as entailing the likelihood of a substantial restraint upon the exercise by petitioner's members of their right to freedom of association. Petitioner has made an uncontroverted showing that on past occasions revelation of the identity of its rank-and-file members has exposed these members to economic reprisal, loss of employment, threat of physical coercion, and other manifestations of public hostility. Under these circumstances, we think it apparent that compelled disclosure of petitioner's Alabama membership is likely to affect adversely the ability of petitioner and its members to pursue their collective effort to foster beliefs which they admittedly have the right to advocate, in that it may induce members to withdraw from the Association and dissuade others from joining it because of fear of exposure of their beliefs shown through their associations and of the consequences of this exposure.

· · ·

Whether there was "justification" in this instance turns solely on the substantiality of Alabama's interest in obtaining the membership lists. During the course of a hearing before the Alabama Circuit Court on a motion of petitioner to set aside the production order, the State Attorney General presented at length, under examination by petitioner, the State's reason for requesting the membership lists. The exclusive purpose was to determine whether petitioner was conducting intrastate business in violation of the Alabama foreign corporation registration statute, and the membership lists were expected to help resolve this question. The issues in the litigation ... were whether the character of petitioner and its activities in Alabama had been such as to make petitioner subject to the registration statute, and whether the extent of petitioner's activities without qualifying suggested its permanent ouster from the State. Without intimating the slightest view upon the merits of these issues, we are unable to perceive that the disclosure of the names of petitioner's rank-and-file members has a substantial bearing on either of them. As matters stand in the state court, petitioner (1) has admitted its presence and conduct of activities in Alabama since 1918; (2) has offered to comply in all respects with the state qualification statute, although preserving its contention that the statute does not apply to it; and (3) has apparently complied satisfactorily with the production order, except for the membership lists, by furnishing the Attorney General with varied business records, its charter and statement of purposes, the names of all of its directors and officers, and with the total number of its Alabama members and the amount of their dues. These last items would not on this record appear subject to constitutional challenge and have been furnished, but whatever interest the State may have in obtaining names of ordinary members has not been shown to be sufficient to overcome petitioner's constitutional objections to the production order.

From what has already been said, we think it apparent that Bryant v. Zimmerman, 278 U.S. 63, cannot be relied on in support of the State's position, for that case involved markedly different considerations in terms of the interest of the State in obtaining disclosure. There, this Court upheld, as applied to a member of a local chapter of the Ku Klux Klan, a New York statute requiring any unincorporated association which demanded an oath as a condition to membership to file with state officials copies of its "... constitution, by-laws, rules, regulations and oath of membership, together with a roster of its membership and a list of its officers for the current year." In its opinion, the Court took care to emphasize the nature of the organization which New York sought to regulate. The decision was based on the particular character of the Klan's activities, involving acts of unlawful intimidation and violence, which the Court assumed was before the state legislature when it enacted the statute, and of which the Court itself took judicial notice. Furthermore, the situation before us is significantly different from that in *Bryant,* because the organization there had made no effort to comply with any of the requirements of New York's statute but rather had refused to furnish the State with *any* information as to its local activities.

We hold that the immunity from state scrutiny of membership lists which the Association claims on behalf of its members is here so related to the right of the members to pursue their lawful private interests privately and to associate freely with others in so doing as to come within the protection of the Fourteenth Amendment. And we conclude that Alabama has fallen short of showing a controlling justification for the deterrent effect on the free enjoyment of the right to associate which disclosure of membership lists is likely to have. Accordingly, the judgment of civil contempt and the $100,000 fine which resulted from petitioner's refusal to comply with the production order in this respect must fall.

. . .

Reversed.

EVOLUTION OF THE COURT'S OPINION IN N.A.A.C.P. v. ALABAMA

The Court, viewing this case in the context of the Segregation Cases beginning with Brown v. Board of Education, made a special effort to speak unanimously. Justice Harlan initially grounded the Court's decision on the First Amendment's guarantees of freedom of speech and assembly as applied to the states by the due process clause of the Fourteenth Amendment, citing Gitlow v. New York and Palko v. Connecticut. In the course of his opinion, Justice Harlan also cited such First Amendment cases as Thomas v. Collins and Murdock v. Pennsylvania. Justice Frankfurter questioned Harlan's approach, arguing that the Fourteenth Amendment was by itself a sufficient ground for the decision. He put it this way in a letter to Justice Harlan written on April 24, 1958:*

> You seemed rather shocked last night when I suggested to you that "liberty" protected by the Fourteenth Amendment means my right to do as I damn please, unless what I am doing is properly outlawable by the state or calls for scrutiny by the state in support of interests of the state, by giving the state the broadest scope in asserting its interests and its means for safeguarding them. I still insist that my "liberty" includes my right to belong to any organization I please and the state can not forbid me—the state, mind you—unless the organization has aims which the state may outlaw or unless inquiry into my associations are relevant.... To say that such right of association is an ingredient of a person's "liberty" of which he cannot be deprived or in the exercise of which he cannot be limited, unless for a fairly statable justification of state control, seems to me a much more accurate and persuasive way of stating what is involved in the N.A.A.C.P. case, what would be involved if it were the American Philosophic Society, than to build up elaborate argumentation that somehow or other what Alabama has done affects free speech.

Persuaded by Justice Frankfurter, Justice Harlan revised Part III of his opinion. Justice Black, however, could not accept Justice Harlan's

---

* Frankfurter Papers, Library of Congress, Microfilm Reel 40.

reformulation. Justice Black explained his position in a letter to Justice Harlan written on May 2, 1958:*

> Part III is now written as though the First Amendment did not exist. In fact, this studious avoidance of any statement that might possibly imply a pertinency of the First Amendment leaves an impression on me that the basic provision of our Bill of Rights might be as contaminating as the leprosy. The avoidance of references to the First Amendment is emphasized by the cases that are cited in Part III and the cases that are not cited. Concurring opinions are relied on to support points that in my judgment could be much better supported by numerous Court opinions. Murdock v. Penna., 319 U.S. 105, and Thomas v. Collins, 323 U.S. 516, which partially rely on the First Amendment to prevent state abridgement of speech, press, etc. are relegated in this opinion to a "Cf. Grosjean v. American Press Co., 297 U.S. 233." There may be other reasons for this comparison but the only purpose that occurs to me is that the Court is repudiating the constitutional principles relied on in the *Murdock* and *Collins* cases.

> Without attempting to gather statistics as to the number of this Court's opinions that have drawn on the First Amendment to justify application of the Due Process Clause to safeguard First Amendment freedoms, it is sufficient to say that there are many of them, including Palko v. Conn., 302 U.S. at 324.

> As you know, I think unanimity is essential in opinions resolving problems in the field involved here. For that reason I am willing to go a long way to obtain such unanimity. If, however, agreement to Part III of your opinion is essential to get unanimous Court action, the price is greater than I am willing to pay. Personally, I do not believe that ignoring the First Amendment should be a *sine qua non* to unanimity here. If it is to be treated as having no effect in any cases, I believe it would be better to do so frankly, openly and without leaving anything to implication. I am not willing to do it either expressly or impliedly.

> There is one other basic objection I have to Part III. You have made additions relying on American Communications Association v. Douds, and other cases, which will justify state laws in abridging press, speech and association where there are rational grounds for believing that the state has an interest in such abridgement. I cannot go along with these additions.

Justice Harlan responded to Justice Black's concerns by restoring some of the citations in the initial opinion, and by making other changes. Justice Black then joined the opinion.

But matters did not end there. On June 25, 1958, just before the term's end, Justice Clark circulated a dissenting opinion in which he argued that since the Alabama Supreme Court had not passed on the

---

* Harlan Papers, Princeton University, Box 533.

constitutional issue decided by the Court, the case should be remanded for consideration of the issue rather than reversed. Justice Frankfurter urged Justice Clark not to break ranks with the rest of the Court. "Save your powder for [another] day," he wrote to Clark on June 25, 1958, "I hope it will never come, but it well may ..."* Five days later, Justice Clark withdrew his dissent.

NOTES AND QUESTIONS

1. Both Justices Frankfurter and Black agree that the Constitution protects freedom of association, but disagree on the source of that protection. Explain their difference. Whose view did Justice Harlan adopt—Frankfurter's or Black's? Did he adopt both views?

2. N.A.A.C.P. v. Alabama is an example of "ad hoc" balancing—that is, balancing *in the particular case* the interests of the state and the interests of freedom of speech or association. We have already seen that one of the problems with any form of balancing is the problem of assigning weights to the two sides of the equation. Notice that Justice Harlan's opinion resolved that problem by concluding that Alabama had shown no need for the membership list, indicating that there was nothing to balance against the free speech claim that disclosure would discourage membership in the N.A.A.C.P. A similar conclusion was drawn two years later, in another case involving N.A.A.C.P. membership lists. Bates v. Little Rock, 361 U.S. 516 (1960). The city of Little Rock, Arkansas had an ordinance imposing a license tax on businesses and professions. The tax ordinance required all organizations subject to the tax to file lists of persons contributing money. The N.A.A.C.P. claim of confidentiality of its list of contributors was sustained because the claim that the organization was subject to the tax was not plausible, and again no interest was shown that would require disclosure.

3. Balancing is more difficult if the state can show *some* interest in obtaining the information. How can anyone compare the strength of the state's interest in disclosure to the injury to First Amendment rights? That was the problem in Shelton v. Tucker, 364 U.S. 479 (1960). An Arkansas statute required that public school teachers file a list of every organization to which they belonged or to which they had contributed in the past five years. A teacher who was a member of the N.A.A.C.P. refused to file such an affidavit in 1959, and was advised by the Little Rock school board that he would not be re-employed. The Court's opinion conceded that the state had some interest in asking teachers about some of the organizations to which they belonged, and that membership in some organizations could be incompatible with the teacher's function. The Arkansas law was struck down, however, for "overbreadth"—it asked for all kinds of associational ties, including those that would have no bearing on the teacher's competence or fitness. This time, four Justices dissented. The dissenters argued that the state could have an interest in *all* organizations to which teachers belonged if, for no other reason, the teacher's extra-curricular activities were so extensive he or she had insufficient time to devote to teaching. Justice Harlan's

* Frankfurter Papers, Library of Congress, Microfilm Reel 45.

dissent argued that N.A.A.C.P. v. Alabama and Bates v. Little Rock were different, because they were cases "where the required disclosure bears no substantial relevance to a legitimate state interest." Does that mean, in this area of free speech law, balancing only works if there is nothing to be balanced on one side?

4.   The 1958 decision in N.A.A.C.P. v. Alabama did not end Alabama's efforts to enjoin the activities of the association in Alabama. The case dragged on for at least six more years. After two additional United States Supreme Court decisions, an Alabama trial court finally reached the merits of the case and permanently enjoined the N.A.A.C.P. from doing business in the State of Alabama. The Alabama Supreme Court dismissed an appeal from the order on the ground that the association's lawyers had argued "unrelated assignments of error" together, and some of them were without merit. In the fourth of the United States Supreme Court decisions in this case, a unanimous, and somewhat impatient, Court reversed. N.A.A.C.P. v. Alabama, 377 U.S. 288 (1964).

5.   While the combination of ad hoc balancing and overbreadth doctrines protected the N.A.A.C.P. from efforts of Southern states to destroy the organization through public exposure, the cases involving compelled disclosure of present and past membership in the Communist Party came out quite differently. For example, the California State Bar was sustained in denying admission to the bar (and thus denying the right to practice law) to an applicant who refused, on First Amendment grounds, to answer questions about his political associations and beliefs. Konigsberg v. State Bar of California, 366 U.S. 36 (1961). Justice Harlan's majority opinion (the court was divided 5–4) said:

> As regards the questioning of public employees relative to Communist Party membership it has already been held that the interest in not subjecting speech and association to the deterrence of subsequent disclosure is outweighed by the State's interest in ascertaining the fitness of the employee for the post he holds, and hence that such questioning does not infringe constitutional protections.... With respect to this same question of Communist Party membership, we regard the State's interest in having lawyers who are devoted to the law in its broadest sense, including not only its substantive provisions, but also its procedures for orderly change, as clearly sufficient to outweigh the minimal effect upon free association occasioned by compulsory disclosure in the circumstances here presented.

6.   Justice Black's dissent in the *Konigsberg* case disagreed with the balance struck by the majority. But, he also attacked the concept of balancing (see Chapter 5, pp. 128–129), reiterating his view that the First Amendment states an absolute. Do you think that the problem of compelled disclosure of political views and associations can be solved with an absolute? What is the absolute? That government can't question people about their beliefs and associations? Often during confirmation hearings in the Senate, Supreme Court nominees have been asked about beliefs they had previously expressed on civil rights issues. Did the

Senators who asked such questions violate the First Amendment rights of the nominees?

7.   Another group of cases, where government demands for information about political associations and belief prevailed, involved legislative investigations of subversion. Most of the cases involved the activities of the House UnAmerican Activities Committee. (HUAC. The Committee was later renamed the House Internal Security Committee, or HISC.) HUAC subcommittees met throughout the nation, investigating subversion in the movies, in education, and in other areas of human endeavor. Witnesses were asked questions ranging from Communist Party membership and other political activities in the 1930s to present Communist Party membership. Witnesses who had been members of the Communist Party in the 1930s when membership had been semi-respectable, or who had close friends or relatives who were members, were faced with a dilemma. They could become "friendly" witnesses, supplying the Committee with names of their associates of years ago. If the witness was "unfriendly," the choices were more limited. Truthful answers by the person who had been a Party member in the 1930s often meant loss of his job, and overwhelming difficulties in getting another. It also produced further questions as to who were the other members. Invoking the Fifth Amendment—claiming the privilege against self-incrimination—relieved the witness of the necessity of answering questions, but it just as often meant disgrace and the loss of his job. (This was a time when "Fifth Amendment Communist" was a term of ordinary speech.)

A few witnesses refused to answer questions on some basis other than the Fifth Amendment. They claimed that the Committee had no legitimate legislative purpose for asking about political activities that were remote in time, and was engaging in exposure for the sake of exposure. Thus, they argued, HUAC had little or no "legitimate" interest in asking the questions, and on the other hand there was a chilling effect on freedom of expression if people could be required to disclose past political associations years later when the organizations had become unpopular. (The Fifties were a time when many people refused to identify themselves with any organization for fear that, in some time in the future, the organization would be seen as dangerous or subversive, and their past association could ruin their career. So much for nostalgia.)

A typical case was Barenblatt v. United States, 360 U.S. 109 (1959). Barenblatt was a graduate student and teaching fellow at the University of Michigan from 1947 to 1950, and had gone on to become an instructor of psychology at Vassar. In June of 1954, he was called as a witness by a HUAC subcommittee investigating "Communists and Communist Activities within the field of education." Barenblatt refused to answer five questions, including whether he was now a Communist, whether he had ever been a member of the Communist Party, and whether he had been a member of the Haldane Club of the Communist Party while he had been at the University of Michigan. Barenblatt was sentenced to six months' imprisonment and a $250 fine for contempt of Congress.

The Supreme Court sustained Barenblatt's conviction by a vote of 5–4. Justice Harlan's opinion concluded that Congress had broad authority to investigate the activities of the Communist Party, which was not an "ordinary political party." Further, even if the Party was engaged in peaceful, lawful activities, or activities protected by the First Amendment, questions could be asked of those who participated because "the investigatory process must proceed step by step."

Justice Black's dissent again argued that Congressional Committees lacked power, because of the First Amendment, to investigate "in the realm of speech and association." Further, he argued, if there was to be balancing, the Court failed to place on the scales "the real interest in Barenblatt's silence, the interest of the people as a whole in being able to join organizations, advocate causes and make political 'mistakes' without later being subjected to governmental penalties for having dared to think for themselves."

8.   The existence of two lines of cases—one broadly protecting civil rights groups from compulsory disclosure by unfriendly Southern states, and the other broadly sustaining government power to ask about political associations in investigating subversion—was bound to produce a case that combined both elements. What would happen if there was an investigation into subversive infiltration of the N.A.A.C.P.?

II.   FROM AD HOC BALANCING TO COMPELLING STATE INTEREST

GIBSON v. FLORIDA LEGISLATIVE INVESTIGATION COMM.

Supreme Court of the United States, 1963.
372 U.S. 539, 83 S.Ct. 889, 9 L.Ed.2d 929.

[An investigating committee of the Florida legislature began in 1956 with the standard battle plan of forcing the Miami branch of the N.A.A.C.P. to furnish its membership list. The N.A.A.C.P. and the committee continued in a sparring match for three years, with the Florida courts deciding that the committee could not compel disclosure of the N.A.A.C.P.'s entire membership list. The charter of the committee was revised by the Florida Legislature in 1959, redefining the committee's purpose as the investigation of groups whose "principles or activities" included violence or violation of state laws. The last round of the sparring match ended in a strange deadlock.

Gibson, who was president of the Miami branch of the N.A.A.C.P., was called as a witness before the committee, and ordered to bring the membership records with him. Gibson appeared without the records, no doubt concerned that the committee had some new tactic up its sleeve which would end up with seizure or disclosure of the list. He was told by the committee that 14 persons had been identified by the committee as Communists or members of "Communist front or affiliated organizations." Gibson agreed to testify from memory whether any of those persons were N.A.A.C.P. members. He was assured by the committee that they would not ask him to turn over the membership records, but simply wanted him to bring the records with him so that Gibson could look at the records to see if any of 14 persons' names appeared on them. Gibson refused to do so, and was convicted for contempt of the committee. *Gibson* had been argued twice. After the first argument, the Court decided in conference, by a five-to-four vote, to affirm, with Justices Frankfurter, Clark, Harlan, White, and Stewart in the majority. Thereafter, when Justice Frankfurter became seriously ill and retired, the Court restored the case to the docket for reargument. Meanwhile, Arthur Goldberg filled Justice Frankfurter's vacancy. After the second argument, the conference vote was again five-to-four—but this time to reverse with Chief Justice Warren and Justices Black, Douglas, Brennan, and Goldberg in the majority.]

JUSTICE GOLDBERG delivered the opinion of the Court.

ARTHUR J. GOLDBERG—Born on August 8, 1908, in Chicago, Illinois, son of Russian immigrants. Democrat. Jewish. Northwestern, B.S.L., 1929; J.D., 1930, graduating first in his class. Practiced law from 1930 until World War II. Served in the Office of Strategic Service during the war. Continued in practice after the war and became special counsel of the AFL–CIO until his appointment as U.S. secretary of labor in 1961. Nominated associate justice by President John F. Kennedy on August 29, 1962, to replace Felix Frankfurter. Confirmed by the Senate on September 25, 1962, by voice vote. Persuaded by President Lyndon B. Johnson to resign from the Court on July 25, 1965, to become U.S. ambassador to the United Nations, where he served until 1968. "I left [the Court] because of vanity." Goldberg later said. "I thought I could influence the President to get [the U.S.] out of Vietnam." Johnson encouraged Goldberg's resignation largely to create a vacancy he could fill by appointing his close friend and advisor, Abe Fortas. Unsuccessful candidate for New York governorship in 1970. Died on January 19, 1990.

We are here called upon once again to resolve a conflict between individual rights of free speech and association and governmental interest in conducting legislative investigations. Prior decisions illumine the contending principles.

This Court has repeatedly held that rights of association are within the ambit of the constitutional protections afforded by the First and Fourteenth Amendments. N.A.A.C.P. v. Alabama, 357 U.S. 449; Bates v. Little Rock, 361 U.S. 516; Shelton v. Tucker, 364 U.S. 479....

The First and Fourteenth Amendment rights of free speech and free association are fundamental and highly prized, and "need breathing space to survive." ...

At the same time, however, this Court's prior holdings demonstrate that there can be no question that the State has power adequately to inform itself—through legislative investigation, if it so desires—in order to act and protect its legitimate and vital interest.... "The scope of the power of inquiry, in short, is as penetrating and far-reaching as the potential power to enact and appropriate under the Constitution." Barenblatt v. United States, 360 U.S. 109, 111. It is no less obvious, however, that the legislative power to investigate, broad as it may be, is not without limit. The fact that the general scope of the inquiry is authorized and permissible does not compel the conclusion that the investigatory body is free to inquire into or demand all forms of information. Validation of the broad subject matter under investigation does not necessarily carry with it automatic and wholesale validation of all individual questions, subpoenas, and documentary demands. When, as in this case, the claim is made that particular legislative inquiries and demands infringe substantially upon First and Fourteenth Amendment associational rights of individuals, the courts are called upon to, and must, determine the permissibility of the challenged actions. . . .

Significantly, the parties are in substantial agreement as to the proper test to be applied to reconcile the competing claims of government and individual and to determine the propriety of the Committee's demands. As declared by the respondent Committee in its brief to this Court, "Basically, this case hinges entirely on the question of whether the evidence before the Committee [was] . . . sufficient to show probable cause or nexus between the N.A.A.C.P. Miami Branch, and Communist activities." We understand this to mean—regardless of the label applied, be it "nexus," "foundation," or whatever—that it is an essential prerequisite to the validity of an investigation which intrudes into the area of constitutionally protected rights of speech, press, association and petition that the State convincingly show a substantial relation between the information sought and a subject of overriding and compelling state interest. Absent such a relation between the N.A.A.C.P. and conduct in which the State may have a compelling regulatory concern, the Committee has not "demonstrated so cogent an interest in obtaining and making public" the membership information sought to be obtained as to "justify the substantial abridgment of associational freedom which such disclosures will effect." Bates v. Little Rock, supra, 361 U.S., at 524. "Where there is a significant encroachment upon personal liberty, the State may prevail only upon showing a subordinating interest which is compelling." *Ibid.*

. . .

. . . The fact that governmental interest was deemed compelling in *Barenblatt,* . . . and held to support the inquiries there made into membership in the Communist Party does not resolve the issues here, where the challenged questions go to membership in an admittedly lawful organization.

. . .

In the absence of directly determinative authority, we turn . . . to consideration of the facts now before us. Obviously, if the respondent were still seeking discovery of the entire membership list, we could readily dispose of this case on the authority of Bates v. Little Rock, and N.A.A.C.P. v. Alabama; a like result would follow if it were merely attempting to do piecemeal what could not be done in a single step. Though there are indications that the respondent Committee intended to inquire broadly into the N.A.A.C.P. membership records, there is no need to base our decision today upon a prediction as to the course which the Committee might have pursued if initially unopposed by the petitioner. Instead, we rest our result on the fact that the record in this case is insufficient to show a substantial connection between the Miami branch of the N.A.A.C.P. and Communist *activities* which the respondent Committee itself concedes is an essential prerequisite to demonstrating the immediate, substantial, and subordinating state interest necessary to sustain its right of inquiry into the membership lists of the association.

. . .

This summary of the evidence discloses the utter failure to demonstrate the existence of any substantial relationship between the N.A.A.C.P. and subversive or Communist activities. In essence, there is here merely indirect, less than unequivocal, and mostly hearsay testimony that in years past some 14 people who were asserted to be, or to have been, Communists or members of Communist front or "affiliated organizations" attended occasional meetings of the Miami branch of the N.A.A.C.P. "and/or" were members of that branch, which had a total membership of about 1,000.

. . . The respondent Committee has laid no adequate foundation for its direct demands upon the officers and records of a wholly legitimate organization for disclosure of its membership; the Committee has neither demonstrated nor pointed out any threat to the State by virtue of the existence of the N.A.A.C.P. or the pursuit of its activities or the minimal associational ties of the 14 asserted Communists. The strong associational interest in maintaining the privacy of membership lists of groups engaged in the constitutionally protected free trade in ideas and beliefs may not be substantially infringed upon such a slender showing as here made by the respondent. While, of course, all legitimate organizations are the beneficiaries of these protections, they are all the more essential here, where the challenged privacy is that of persons espousing beliefs already unpopular with their neighbors and the deterrent and "chilling" effect on the free exercise of constitutionally enshrined rights of free speech, expression, and association is consequently the more immediate and substantial. . . .

Of course, a legislative investigation—as any investigation—must proceed "step by step," Barenblatt v. United States, supra, 360 U.S. at 130, but step by step or in totality, an adequate foundation for inquiry must be laid before proceeding in such a manner as will substantially intrude upon and severely curtail or inhibit constitutionally protected activities or seriously interfere with similarly protected associational rights. No such foundation has been laid here. The respondent Committee has failed to demonstrate the compelling and subordinating governmental interest essential to support direct inquiry into the membership records of the N.A.A.C.P.

Nothing we say here impairs or denies the existence of the underlying legislative right to investigate or legislate with respect to subversive activities by Communists or anyone else; our decision today deals only with the manner in which such power may be exercised and we hold simply that groups which themselves are neither engaged in subversive or other illegal or improper activities nor demonstrated to have any substantial connections with such activities are to be protected in their rights of free and private association. . . .

Reversed.

JUSTICE BLACK, concurring.

... In my view the constitutional right of association includes the privilege of any person to associate with Communists or anti-Communists, Socialists or anti-Socialists, or, for that matter, with people of all kinds of beliefs, popular or unpopular. I have expressed these views in many other cases and I adhere to them now. Since, as I believe, the National Association for the Advancement of Colored People and its members have a constitutional right to choose their own associates, I cannot understand by what constitutional authority Florida can compel answers to questions which abridge that right. Accordingly, I would reverse here on the ground that there has been a direct abridgment of the right of association of the National Association for the Advancement of Colored People and its members. . . .

JUSTICE DOUGLAS, concurring.

. . .

In my view, government is not only powerless to legislate with respect to membership in a lawful organization; it is also precluded from probing the intimacies of spiritual and intellectual relationships in the myriad of such societies and groups that exist in this country, regardless of the legislative purpose sought to be served. "[T]he provisions of the First Amendment ... of course reach and limit ... investigations." Barenblatt v. United States, 360 U.S. 109, 126. If that is not true, I see no barrier to investigation of newspapers, churches, political parties, clubs, societies, unions, and any other association for their political, economic, social, philosophical, or religious views. If, in its quest to determine whether existing laws are being enforced or new laws are needed, an investigating committee can ascertain whether known Communists or criminals are members of an organization not shown to be engaged in conduct properly subject to regulation, it is but a short and inexorable step to the conclusion that it may also probe to ascertain what effect they have had on the other members. For how much more "necessary and appropriate" this information is to the legislative purpose being pursued!

. . .

JUSTICE HARLAN, whom JUSTICE CLARK, JUSTICE STEWART, and JUSTICE WHITE join, dissenting.

The difficulties with this decision will become apparent once the case is deflated to its true size.

. . .

This Court rests reversal on its finding that the Committee did not have sufficient justification for including the Miami Branch of the N.A.A.C.P. within the ambit of its investigation—that, in the language of our cases an adequate "nexus" was lacking between the N.A.A.C.P. and the subject matter of the Committee's inquiry.

The Court's reasoning is difficult to grasp. I read its opinion as basically proceeding on the premise that the governmental interest in investigating Communist infiltration into admittedly nonsubversive organizations, as distinguished from investigating organizations themselves suspected of subversive activities, is not sufficient to overcome the countervailing right to freedom of association. On this basis "nexus" is seemingly found lacking because it was never claimed that the N.A.A.C.P. Miami Branch had itself engaged in subversive activity,....

But, until today, I had never supposed that any of our decisions relating to state or federal power to investigate in the field of Communist subversion could possibly be taken as suggesting any difference in the degree of governmental investigatory interest as between Communist infiltration *of* organizations and Communist activity *by* organizations.

Considering the number of congressional inquiries that have been conducted in the field of "Communist infiltration" since the close of World War II, affecting such diverse interests as "labor, farmer, veteran, professional, youth, and motion picture groups" (*Barenblatt*, 360 U.S. at 119), it is indeed strange to find the strength of state interest in the same type of investigation now impugned. And it is not amiss to recall that government evidence in Smith Act prosecutions has shown that the sensitive area of race relations has long been a prime target of Communist efforts at infiltration.

. . .

I also find it difficult to see how this case really presents any serious question as to interference with freedom of association. Given the willingness of the petitioner to testify from recollection as to individual memberships in the local branch of the N.A.A.C.P., the germaneness of the membership records to the subject matter of the Committee's investigation, and the limited purpose for which their use was sought—as an aid to refreshing the witness' recollection, involving their divulgence only to the petitioner himself ... what we are asked to hold here is that the petitioner had a constitutional right to give only partial or inaccurate testimony, and that indeed seems to me the true effect of the Court's holding today.

. . .

JUSTICE WHITE, dissenting.

In my view, the opinion of the Court represents a serious limitation upon the Court's previous cases dealing with this subject matter and upon the right of the legislature to investigate the Communist Party and its activities. Although one of the classic and recurring activities of the Communist Party is the infiltration and subversion of other organizations, either openly or in a clandestine manner, the Court holds that even where a legislature has evidence that a legitimate organization is under assault and even though that organization is itself sounding open and public alarm, an investigating committee is nevertheless forbidden to compel the organization or its members to reveal the fact, or not, of membership in that organization of named Communists assigned to the infiltrating task.

THE SIGNIFICANCE OF JUSTICE GOLDBERG'S APPOINTMENT

Goldberg's replacement of Frankfurter not only determined the liberal outcome in *Gibson*; it also determined the Supreme Court's ideological orientation during Goldberg's tenure. In the mid–1950s, Warren and Brennan joined Black and Douglas to form a liberal voting bloc in civil liberties cases. The bloc sometimes attracted a fifth vote to form a majority, but it was often in dissent. When Goldberg came to the Court in 1962, he gave the liberal bloc its crucial fifth vote, and the Warren Court's "Constitutional Revolution" began. Although Black's votes in civil liberties cases became more conservative in the mid–1960s, and Goldberg left the Court in 1965, the liberal bloc remained intact until Warren left the Court in 1969, for Abe Fortas, a liberal, replaced Goldberg, and Thurgood Marshall, another liberal, replaced Clark, a conservative.

NOTES AND QUESTIONS

1. In Justice Goldberg's first circulation of his *Gibson* opinion, he introduced the compelling-state-interest test in the following paragraph:

> Significantly, the parties are in substantial agreement as to the proper test to be applied to reconcile the competing claims of government and individual and to determine the propriety of the Committee's demands. As declared by the respondent Committee in its brief to this Court, "Basically, this case hinges entirely on the question of whether the evidence before the Committee [was] ... sufficient to show probable cause or nexus between the N.A.A.C.P. Miami Branch, and Communist activities." We agree with the respondent's statement of the issue. Absent such nexus or probable cause, the Committee has not "demonstrated so cogent an interest in obtaining and making public" the membership information sought to be obtained as to "justify the substantial abridgement of associational freedoms which such disclosure would effect. Where there is a significant encroachment upon personal liberty, the State may prevail only upon showing a subordinating interest which is compelling." Bates v. Little Rock, ... 361 U.S., at 524. If probable cause is present, if there is the suggested nexus, then the state interest is apparent, and may prevail over the right of associational privacy.*

Goldberg's final circulation contained the following revision of the above paragraph:

> Significantly, the parties are in substantial agreement as to the proper test to be applied to reconcile the competing claims of government and individual and to determine the propriety of

---

* Douglas Papers, Library of Congress, Box 1287.

the Committee's demands. As declared by the respondent Committee in its brief to this Court, "Basically, this case hinges entirely on the question of whether the evidence before the Committee [was] ... sufficient to show probable cause or nexus between the N.A.A.C.P. Miami Branch, and Communist activities." We understand this to mean—regardless of the label applied, be it "nexus, foundation," or whatever—that it is an essential prerequisite to the validity of an investigation which intrudes into the area of constitutionally protected rights of speech, press, association and petition that the State convincingly show a substantial relation between the information sought and a subject of overriding and compelling state interest. Absent such a relation between the N.A.A.C.P. and conduct in which the State may have a compelling regulatory concern, the Committee has not "demonstrated so cogent an interest in obtaining and making public" the membership information sought to be obtained as to "justify the substantial abridgement of association freedoms which such disclosure will effect." Bates v. Little Rock, ... 361 U.S., at 524. "Where there is a significant encroachment upon personal liberty, the State may prevail only upon showing a subordinating interest which is compelling."*

Which paragraph is more protective of freedom of association?

2. Is *Gibson*'s rationale consistent with that of the *Barenblatt* case? Is there a viable distinction between investigating Communist activity *by* organizations and Communist infiltration *of* organizations? If the N.A.A.C.P. had been thoroughly infiltrated by Communists, Justice Goldberg's opinion suggests that the cases dealing with investigation of Communists would apply. Why isn't the committee then allowed to ask whether particular persons thought to be Communists are members of the N.A.A.C.P.?

3. DeGregory v. Attorney General of New Hampshire, 383 U.S. 825 (1966), involved a man who refused to answer, in 1964, questions relating to Communist activities prior to 1957. Noting that DeGregory had been shown to be connected with the Communist Party only until 1953, a majority of the Court held that there was insufficient state interest to justify "intrusion into the realm of political and associational privacy protected by the First Amendment." The basis of the Court's decision in *DeGregory* was that there was insufficient state interest because the activities investigated were "stale" and not shown to have any relationship to the present. What if the witness is questioned about more recent activities?

4. The Supreme Court returned to the problem of the *Konigsberg* case (above, pp. 542–543, notes 5 and 6) in Baird v. State Bar of Arizona, 401 U.S. 1 (1971). On her application for admission to the Arizona Bar, Baird did answer one question which asked her to reveal all organizations with which she had been associated since the age of 16. She refused, however, to answer another question that asked whether she had ever been a member of the Communist Party or any other organiza-

* *Ibid.*

tion advocating forceful overthrow of the United States Government. Because she refused to answer the question, the Arizona Supreme Court refused to admit her to practice law. The Supreme Court reversed by a 5–4 vote, but there was no opinion for the Court.

Justice Black, joined by Justices Douglas, Brennan and Marshall urged reversal on the basis of the flat principle that "a State may not inquire about a man's views or associations solely for the purpose of withholding a right or benefit because of what he believes." Justice Stewart, who agreed that Ms. Baird should be admitted to the Arizona Bar, and who supplied the crucial fifth vote, decided the case on much more limited grounds. Innocent membership in such an organization could not be a basis for refusing someone the right to practice law (see the cases discussed in Chapter 5, particularly Brandenburg v. Ohio, p. 122). Here, the question was not limited to knowing membership. The dissenters—Justice Blackmun, Chief Justice Burger and Justices Harlan and White—argued that the result was inconsistent with the rationale of the *Konigsberg* case. Even if Arizona couldn't deny a license to practice law to innocent members of the Communist Party, it should have the unrestricted right to ask whether someone was a member in order to further inquire whether membership was innocent or not.

III. EXPRESSIVE ASSOCIATION

ROBERTS v. UNITED STATES JAYCEES

Supreme Court of the United States, 1984.
468 U.S. 609, 104 S.Ct. 3244, 82 L.Ed.2d 462.

[When the Minneapolis and St. Paul chapters of the Jaycees began to admit women as regular members, the national organization advised the chapters that their charters would be revoked. The chapters filed charges of discrimination with the Minnesota Department of Human Rights, alleging that exclusion of women by the national organization violated the Minnesota Human Rights Act, which prohibits discrimination on the basis of gender by a business offering goods or services to the public. The national organization brought suit to enjoin enforcement of the Act against it. The Court held that applying the Minnesota statute to the Jaycees did not violate the Constitution.]

JUSTICE BRENNAN delivered the opinion of the Court.

This case requires us to address a conflict between a State's efforts to eliminate gender-based discrimination against its citizens and the constitutional freedom of association asserted by members of a private organization. In the decision under review, the Court of Appeals for the Eighth Circuit concluded that, by requiring the United State Jaycees to admit women as full voting members, the Minnesota Human Rights Act violates the First and Fourteenth Amendment rights of the organization's members. We noted probable jurisdiction, . . . and now reverse.

. . .

II

Our decisions have referred to constitutionally protected "freedom of association" in two distinct senses. In one line of decisions, the Court has concluded that choices to enter into and maintain certain intimate human relationships must be secured against undue intrusion by the State because of the role of such relationships in safeguarding the individual freedom that is central to our constitutional scheme. In this respect, freedom of association received protection as a fundamental element of personal liberty. In another set of decisions, the Court has recognized a right to associate for the purpose of engaging in those activities protected by the First Amendment—speech, assembly, petition for the redress of grievances, and the exercise of religion. The Constitution guarantees freedom of association of this kind as an indispensable means of preserving other individual liberties.

The intrinsic and instrumental features of constitutionally protected association may, of course, coincide. In particular, when the State interferes with individuals' selection of those with whom they wish to join in a common endeavor, freedom of association in both of its forms may be implicated. The Jaycees contend that this is such a case. Still the nature and degree of constitutional protection afforded freedom of association my vary depending on the extent to which one or the other aspect of the constitutionally protected liberty is at stake in a given case. We therefore find it useful to consider separately the effect of applying the Minnesota statute to the Jaycees on what could be called its members' freedom of intimate association and their freedom of expressive association.

. . .

. . . [As to freedom of intimate association,] the local chapters of the Jaycees are neither small nor selective. Moreover, much of the activity central to the formation and maintenance of the association involves the participation of strangers to that relationship. Accordingly, we conclude that the Jaycees chapters lack the distinctive characteristics that might afford constitutional protection to the decision of its members to exclude women. We turn therefore to consider the extent to which application of the Minnesota statute to compel the Jaycees to accept women infringes the group's freedom of expressive association.

. . .

Government actions that may unconstitutionally infringe upon this freedom can take a number of forms. Among other things, government may seek to impose penalties or withhold benefits from individuals because of their membership in a disfavored group, . . .; it may attempt to require disclosure of the fact of membership in a group seeking anonymity, . . .; and it may try to interfere with the internal organization or affairs of the group, ... By requiring the Jaycees to admit women as full voting members, the Minnesota Act works an infringement of the last type. There can be no clearer example of an intrusion into the internal structure or affairs of an association than a regulation that forces the group to accept members it does not desire. Such a regulation may impair the ability of the original members to express only those views that brought them together. Freedom of association therefore plainly presupposes a freedom not to associate. See Abood v. Detroit Board of Education, ...

The right to associate for expressive purposes is not ... absolute. Infringements on that right may be justified by regulations adopted to serve compelling state interests, unrelated to the suppression of ideas, that cannot be achieved through means significantly less restrictive of associational freedoms.... We are persuaded that Minnesota's compelling interest in eradicating discrimination against its female citizens justifies the impact that application of the statute to the Jaycees may have on the male members' associational freedoms.... We are persuaded that Minnesota's compelling interest in eradicating discrimination against its female citizens justifies the impact that application of the statutes to the Jaycees may have on the male members' associational freedoms.

On its face, the Minnesota Act does not aim at the suppression of speech, does not distinguish between prohibited and permitted activity on the basis of viewpoint, and does not license enforcement authorities to administer the statute on the basis of such constitutionally impermissible criteria.... Nor does the Jaycees contend that the Act has been applied in this case for the purpose of hampering the organization's ability to express its views. Instead, as the Minnesota Supreme Court explained, the Act reflects the State's strong historical commitment to eliminating discrimination and assuring its citizens equal access to publicly available good and services.... That goal, which is unrelated to the suppression of expression, plainly serves compelling state interests of the highest order.

. . .

In applying the Act to the Jaycees, the State has advanced those interests through the least restrictive means of achieving its ends. Indeed, the Jaycees has failed to demonstrate that the Act imposes any serious burdens on the male members' freedom of expressive association.... To be sure, as the Court of Appeals noted, a "not insubstantial part" of the Jaycees' activities constitutes protected expression on political, economic, cultural, and social affairs.... Over the years, the national and local levels of the organization have taken public position on a number of diverse issues, ... and members of the Jaycees regularly engage in a variety of civic, charitable, lobbying, fundraising, and other activities worthy of constitutional protection under the First Amendment.... There is, however, no basis in the record for concluding that admission of women as full voting members will impede the organization's ability to engage in these protected activities or to disseminate its preferred views. The Act requires no change in the Jaycees' creed of promoting the interests of young men, and it imposes no restrictions on the organization's ability to exclude individuals with ideologies or philosophies different from those of its existing members.

. . .

The judgment of the Court of Appeals is reversed.

Justice Rehnquist concurred in the judgment.

JUSTICE O'CONNOR, who concurred in part and concurred in the judgment, wrote a concurring opinion, which is omitted.

The CHIEF JUSTICE and JUSTICE BLACKMUN took no part in the decision of the case.

NOTES

1.   Justice O'Connor's concurring opinion in *Roberts* distinguished the right to expressive association from the right to commercial association. It was only because she viewed the Jaycees as a commercial association that she rejected its constitutional challenge. If she had viewed the Jaycees as an expressive association, she would have decided the case the other way, for she wrote that "an association engaged exclusively in protected expression enjoys First Amendment protection of both the content of its message and the choice of its members. Protection of the message itself is judged by the same standards as protection of speech by an individual. Protection of the association's right to define its membership derives from the recognition that the formation of an expressive association is the creation of a voice, and the selection of members is the definition of that voice.... A ban on specific group voices on public affairs violates the most basic guarantee of the First Amendment—that citizens, not government, control the contest of discussion." 468 U.S., at 634.

2.   The Supreme Court unanimously followed *Roberts* in Board of Directors of Rotary International v. Rotary Club, 481 U.S. 537 (1987). It held that a California statute requiring California Rotary Clubs to admit women did not violate the First Amendment. Even if the statute worked "some slight infringement on Rotary members' right of expressive association," wrote Justice Powell for the Court, "that infringement is justified because it serves the State's compelling interest in eliminating discrimination against women." 483 U.S. at 549.

3.   In Hurley v. Irish–American Gay, Lesbian and Bisexual Group of Boston, 515 U.S. 557 (1995), both parties asserted the right of expressive association: For several years, John J. "Wacko" Hurley and other members of South Boston Allied War Veterans Council, a private organization, organized a St. Patrick's Day parade in Boston. In 1993, the Irish–American Gay, Lesbian, and Bisexual Group of Boston (GLIB) applied to march in the parade. Hurley and the Council rejected GLIB's application. The Council claimed it had no intent to exclude individual homosexuals from the parade, but only GLIB as a parade unit because the Council did not support GLIB's message. GLIB then sued Hurley and the Council under the Massachusetts public accommodation law, which prohibited discrimination on the basis of sexual orientation. The State court decided GLIB's favor and ordered the Council to permit GLIB to participate in the parade. On appeal, the Supreme Court unanimously reversed the State court. "[T]his use of State power," wrote Justice Souter for the Court, "violates the fundamental rule of protection under the First Amendment that a speaker has the autonomy to choose the content of his message." Justice Souter then went on to say: "[The Council's] claim to the benefit of this principle of autonomy to control one's own speech is as sound as the South Boston parade is

expressive. [The] Council clearly decided to exclude a message it did not like from the communication it chose to make, and that is enough to invoke its right as a private speaker to shape its expression by speaking on one subject while remaining silent on another. The message it disfavored is not difficult to identify. Although GLIB's point (like the Council's) is not wholly articulate, a witness to the fact that some Irish are gay, lesbian, or bisexual, and the presence of the organized marchers would suggest their view that people of their sexual orientations have as much claim to unqualified social acceptance as heterosexuals and indeed as members of parade units organized around other identifying characteristics. The parade's organizers may not believe these facts about Irish sexuality to be so or they may object to unqualified social acceptance of gays and lesbians or have some other reason for wishing to keep GLIB's message out of the parade. But whatever the reason, it boils down to the choice of a speaker not to propound a particular point of view, and that choice is presumed to lie beyond the government's power to control."

BOY SCOUTS OF AMERICA v. DALE

United States Supreme Court, 2000.
530 U.S. 640, 120 S.Ct. 2446, 147 L.Ed.2d 554.

CHIEF JUSTICE REHNQUIST delivered the opinion of the Court.

Petitioners are the Boy Scouts of America and the Monmouth Council, a division of the Boy Scouts of America (collectively, Boy Scouts). The Boy Scouts is a private, not-for-profit organization engaged in instilling its system of values in young people. The Boy Scouts asserts that homosexual conduct is inconsistent with the values it seeks to instill. Respondent is James Dale, a former Eagle Scout whose adult membership in the Boy Scouts was revoked when the Boy Scouts learned that he is an avowed homosexual and gay rights activist. The New Jersey Supreme Court held that New Jersey's public accommodations law requires that the Boy Scouts admit Dale. This case presents the question whether applying New Jersey's public accommodations law in this way violates the Boy Scouts' First Amendment right of expressive association. We hold that it does.

I

. . .

II

In Roberts v. United States Jaycees, 468 U.S. 609, 622 (1984), we observed that "implicit in the right to engage in activities protected by the First Amendment" is "a corresponding right to associate with others in pursuit of a wide variety of political, social, economic, educational, religious, and cultural ends.".... Forcing a group to accept certain members may impair the ability of the group to express those views, and only those views, that it intends to express....

The forced inclusion of an unwanted person in a group infringes the group's freedom of expressive association if the presence of that person affects in a significant way the group's ability to advocate public or private viewpoints. New York State Club Assn., Inc. v. City of New York, 487 U.S. 1, 13 (1988). But the freedom of expressive association, like many freedoms, is not absolute. We have held that the freedom could be overridden "by regulations adopted to serve compelling state interests, unrelated to the suppression of ideas, that cannot be achieved through means significantly less restrictive of associational freedoms." . . .

To determine whether a group is protected by the First Amendment's expressive associational right, we must determine whether the group engages in "expressive association." The First Amendment's protection of expressive association is not reserved for advocacy groups. But to come within its ambit, a group must engage in some form of expression, whether it be public or private.

Because this is a First Amendment case where the ultimate conclusions of law are virtually inseparable from findings of fact, we are obligated to independently review the factual record to ensure that the state court's judgment does not unlawfully intrude on free expression. . . . The record reveals the following. The Boy Scouts is a private, nonprofit organization. According to its mission statement:

> "It is the mission of the Boy Scouts of America to serve others by helping to instill values in young people and, in other ways, to prepare them to make ethical choices over their lifetime in achieving their full potential.

> "The values we strive to instill are based on those found in the Scout Oath and Law:

> "On my honor I will do my best to do my duty to God and my country and to obey the Scout Law; to help other people at all times; to keep myself physically strong, mentally awake, and morally straight.

> "Scout Law

> "A Scout is:

> "Trustworthy Obedient Loyal Cheerful Helpful Thrifty Friendly Brave Courteous Clean Kind Reverent."

Thus, the general mission of the Boy Scouts is clear: "[T]o instill values in young people." The Boy Scouts seeks to instill these values by having its adult leaders spend time with the youth members, instructing and engaging them in activities like camping, archery, and fishing. During the time spent with the youth members, the scoutmasters and assistant scoutmasters inculcate them with the Boy Scouts' values—both expressly and by example. It seems indisputable that an association that seeks to transmit such a system of values engages in expressive activity. . . .

Given that the Boy Scouts engages in expressive activity, we must determine whether the forced inclusion of Dale as an assistant scoutmaster would significantly affect the Boy Scouts' ability to advocate public or private viewpoints. This inquiry necessarily requires us first to explore, to a limited extent, the nature of the Boy Scouts' view of homosexuality.

... The Boy Scouts asserts that homosexual conduct is inconsistent with the values embodied in the Scout Oath and Law, particularly with the values represented by the terms "morally straight" and "clean."

Obviously, the Scout Oath and Law do not expressly mention sexuality or sexual orientation. And the terms "morally straight" and "clean" are by no means self-defining. Different people would attribute to those terms very different meanings. For example, some people may believe that engaging in homosexual conduct is not at odds with being "morally straight" and "clean." And others may believe that engaging in homosexual conduct is contrary to being "morally straight" and "clean." The Boy Scouts says it falls within the latter category.

The New Jersey Supreme Court analyzed the Boy Scouts' beliefs and found that the "exclusion of members solely on the basis of their sexual orientation is inconsistent with Boy Scouts' commitment to a diverse and 'representative' membership ... [and] contradicts Boy Scouts' overarching objective to reach 'all eligible youth.'" The court concluded that the exclusion of members like Dale "appears antithetical to the organization's goals and philosophy." But our cases reject this sort of inquiry; it is not the role of the courts to reject a group's expressed values because they disagree with those values or find them internally inconsistent....

The Boy Scouts asserts that it "teach[es] that homosexual conduct is not morally straight," and that it does "not want to promote homosexual conduct as a legitimate form of behavior." We accept the Boy Scouts' assertion. We need not inquire further to determine the nature of the Boy Scouts' expression with respect to homosexuality. But because the record before us contains written evidence of the Boy Scouts' viewpoint, we look to it as instructive, if only on the question of the sincerity of the professed beliefs.

A 1978 position statement to the Boy Scouts' Executive Committee, signed by Downing B. Jenks, the President of the Boy Scouts, and Harvey L. Price, the Chief Scout Executive, expresses the Boy Scouts' "official position" with regard to "homosexuality and Scouting":

"Q. May an individual who openly declares himself to be a homosexual be a volunteer Scout leader?

"A. No. The Boy Scouts of America is a private, membership organization and leadership therein is a privilege and not a right. We do not believe that homosexuality and leadership in Scouting are appropriate. We will continue to select only those who in our judgment meet our standards and qualifications for leadership."

Thus, at least as of 1978—the year James Dale entered Scouting—the official position of the Boy Scouts was that avowed homosexuals were not to be Scout leaders.

A position statement promulgated by the Boy Scouts in 1991 (after Dale's membership was revoked but before this litigation was filed) also supports its current view ...

The Boy Scouts publicly expressed its views with respect to homosexual conduct by its assertions in prior litigation. For example, throughout a California case with similar facts filed in the early 1980's, the Boy Scouts consistently asserted the same position with respect to homosexuality that it asserts today. See Curran v. Mount Diablo Council of Boy Scouts of America, ... 17 Cal. 4th 670, 952 P. 2d 218 (1998). We cannot doubt that the Boy Scouts sincerely holds this view.

We must then determine whether Dale's presence as an assistant scoutmaster would significantly burden the Boy Scouts' desire to not "promote homosexual conduct as a legitimate form of behavior." As we give deference to an association's assertions regarding the nature of its expression, we must also give deference to an association's view of what would impair its expression.... That is not to say that an expressive association can erect a shield against antidiscrimination laws simply by asserting that mere acceptance of a member from a particular group would impair its message. But here Dale, by his own admission, is one of a group of gay Scouts who have "become leaders in their community and are open and honest about their sexual orientation." ... Dale was the copresident of a gay and lesbian organization at college and remains a gay rights activist. Dale's presence in the Boy Scouts would, at the very least, force the organization to send a message, both to the youth members and the world, that the Boy Scouts accepts homosexual conduct as a legitimate form of behavior.

Hurley [v. Irish–American Gay, Lesbian and Bisexual Group of Boston, Inc., 515 U.S. 557 (1995)] is illustrative on this point. There we considered whether the application of Massachusetts' public accommodations law to require the organizers of a private St. Patrick's Day parade to include among the marchers an Irish–American gay, lesbian, and bisexual group, GLIB, violated the parade organizers' First Amendment rights. We noted that the parade organizers did not wish to exclude the GLIB members because of their sexual orientations, but because they wanted to march behind a GLIB banner. We observed:

> "[A] contingent marching behind the organization's banner would at least bear witness to the fact that some Irish are gay, lesbian, or bisexual, and the presence of the organized marchers would suggest their view that people of their sexual orientations have as much claim to unqualified social acceptance as heterosexuals.... The parade's organizers may not believe these facts about Irish sexuality to be so, or they may object to unqualified social acceptance of gays and lesbians or have some other reason for wishing to keep GLIB's message out of the parade. But whatever the reason, it boils down to the choice of a speaker not to propound a particular point of view, and that choice is presumed to lie beyond the government's power to control." ...

Here, we have found that the Boy Scouts believes that homosexual conduct is inconsistent with the values it seeks to instill in its youth members; it will not "promote homosexual conduct as a legitimate form of behavior." As the presence of GLIB in Boston's St. Patrick's Day parade would have interfered with the parade organizers' choice not to propound a particular point of view, the presence of Dale as an assistant scoutmaster would just as surely interfere with the Boy Scout's choice not to propound a point of view contrary to its beliefs.

The New Jersey Supreme Court determined that the Boy Scouts' ability to disseminate its message was not significantly affected by the forced inclusion of Dale as an assistant scoutmaster because of the following findings:

> "Boy Scout members do not associate for the purpose of disseminating the belief that homosexuality is immoral; Boy Scouts discourages its leaders from disseminating any views on sexual issues; and Boy Scouts includes sponsors and members who subscribe to different views in respect of homosexuality."

We disagree with the New Jersey Supreme Court's conclusion drawn from these findings.

First, associations do not have to associate for the "purpose" of disseminating a certain message in order to be entitled to the protections of the First Amendment. An association must merely engage in expressive activity that could be impaired in order to be entitled to protection. For example, the purpose of the St. Patrick's Day parade in *Hurley* was not to espouse any views about sexual orientation, but we held that the parade organizers had a right to exclude certain participants nonetheless.

Second, even if the Boy Scouts discourages Scout leaders from disseminating views on sexual issues—a fact that the Boy Scouts disputes with contrary evidence—the First Amendment protects the Boy Scouts' method of expression. If the Boy Scouts wishes Scout leaders to avoid questions of sexuality and teach only by example, this fact does not negate the sincerity of its belief discussed above.

Third, the First Amendment simply does not require that every member of a group agree on every issue in order for the group's policy to be "expressive association." The Boy Scouts takes an official position with respect to homosexual conduct, and that is sufficient for First Amendment purposes. In this same vein, Dale makes much of the claim that the Boy Scouts does not revoke the membership of heterosexual Scout leaders that openly disagree with the Boy Scouts' policy on sexual orientation. But if this is true, it is irrelevant. The presence of an avowed homosexual and gay rights activist in an assistant scoutmaster's uniform sends a distinctly different message from the presence of a heterosexual assistant scoutmaster who is on record as disagreeing with Boy Scouts policy. The Boy Scouts has a First Amendment right to choose to send one message but not the other. The fact that the organization does not trumpet its views from the housetops, or that it tolerates dissent within its ranks, does not mean that its views receive no First Amendment protection.

Having determined that the Boy Scouts is an expressive association and that the forced inclusion of Dale would significantly affect its expression, we inquire whether the application of New Jersey's public accommodations law to require that the Boy Scouts accept Dale as an assistant scoutmaster runs afoul of the Scouts' freedom of expressive association. We conclude that it does.

State public accommodations laws were originally enacted to prevent discrimination in traditional places of public accommodation—like inns and trains.... Over time, the public accommodations laws have expanded to cover more places. New Jersey's statutory definition of " '[a] place of public accommodation' " is extremely broad. The term is said to "include, but not be limited to," a list of over 50 types of places.... Many on the list are what one would expect to be places where the public is invited. For example, the statute includes as places of public accommodation taverns, restaurants, retail shops, and public libraries. But the statute also includes places that often may not carry with them open invitations to the public, like summer camps and roof gardens. In this case, the New Jersey Supreme Court went a step further and applied its public accommodations law to a private entity without even attempting to tie the term "place" to a physical location. As the definition of "public accommodation" has expanded from clearly commercial entities, such as restaurants, bars, and hotels, to membership organizations such as the Boy Scouts, the potential for conflict between state public accommodations laws and the First Amendment rights of organizations has increased.

. . .

In *Hurley*, we said that public accommodations laws "are well within the State's usual power to enact when a legislature has reason to believe that a given group is the target of discrimination, and they do not, as a general matter, violate the First or Fourteenth Amendments." ... But we went on to note that in that case "the Massachusetts [public accommodations] law has been applied in a peculiar way" because "any contingent of protected individuals with a message would have the right to participate in petitioners' speech, so that the communication produced by the private organizers would be shaped by all those protected by the law who wish to join in with some expressive demonstration of their own.".... So ..., the associational interest in freedom of expression has been set on one side of the scale, and the State's interest on the other.

Dale contends that we should apply the intermediate standard of review enunciated in United States v. O'Brien, 391 U.S. 367 (1968), to evaluate the competing interests. There the Court enunciated a four-part test for review of a governmental regulation that has only an incidental effect on protected speech—in that case the symbolic burning of a draft card. A law prohibiting the destruction of draft cards only incidentally affects the free speech rights of those who happen to use a violation of that law as a symbol of protest. But New Jersey's public accommodations law directly and immediately affects associational rights, in this case associational rights that enjoy First Amendment protection. Thus, *O'Brien* is inapplicable.

In *Hurley*, we applied traditional First Amendment analysis to hold that the application of the Massachusetts public accommodations law to a parade violated the First Amendment rights of the parade organizers. Although we did not explicitly deem the parade in *Hurley* an expressive association, the analysis we applied there is similar to the analysis we apply here. We have already concluded that a state requirement that the Boy Scouts retain Dale as an assistant scoutmaster would significantly burden the organization's right to oppose or disfavor homosexual conduct. The state interests embodied in New Jersey's public accommodations law do not justify such a severe intrusion on the Boy Scouts' rights to freedom of expressive association. That being the case, we hold that the First Amendment prohibits the State from imposing such a requirement through the application of its public accommodations law.

· · ·

We are not, as we must not be, guided by our views of whether the Boy Scouts' teachings with respect to homosexual conduct are right or wrong; public or judicial disapproval of a tenet of an organization's expression does not justify the State's effort to compel the organization to accept members where such acceptance would derogate from the organization's expressive message....

The judgment of the New Jersey Supreme Court is reversed, and the cause remanded for further proceedings not inconsistent with this opinion.

It is so ordered.

JUSTICE STEVENS, with whom JUSTICE SOUTER, JUSTICE GINSBURG and JUSTICE BREYER join, dissenting.

... The New Jersey Supreme Court's construction of the statutory definition of a "place of public accommodation" has given its statute a more expansive coverage than most similar state statutes.... The question in this case is whether that expansive construction trenches on the federal constitutional rights of the Boy Scouts of America (BSA).

· · ·

... New Jersey's law ... does not "impos[e] any serious burdens" on BSA's "collective effort on behalf of [its] shared goals," ... nor does it force BSA to communicate any message that it does not wish to endorse. New Jersey's law, therefore, abridges no constitutional right of the Boy Scouts.

I

· · ·

In this case, Boy Scouts of America contends that it teaches the young boys who are Scouts that homosexuality is immoral. Consequently, it argues, it would violate its right to associate to force it to admit homosexuals as members, as doing so would be at odds with its own shared goals and values. This contention, quite plainly, requires us to look at what, exactly, are the values that BSA actually teaches.

· · ·

To bolster its claim that its shared goals include teaching that homosexuality is wrong, BSA directs our attention to two terms appearing in the Scout Oath and Law. The first is the phrase "morally straight," which appears in the Oath ("On my honor I will do my best ... To keep myself ... morally straight"); the second term is the word "clean," which appears in a list of 12 characteristics together comprising the Scout Law.

. . .

It is plain as the light of day that neither one of these principles—"morally straight" and "clean"—says the slightest thing about homosexuality. Indeed, neither term in the Boy Scouts' Law and Oath expresses any position whatsoever on sexual matters.

. . .

In light of BSA's self-proclaimed ecumenism, furthermore, it is even more difficult to discern any shared goals or common moral stance on homosexuality.... BSA surely is aware that some religions do not teach that homosexuality is wrong.

II

. . .

... BSA's policy statements fail to establish any clear, consistent, and unequivocal position on homosexuality. Nor did BSA have any reason to think Dale's sexual conduct, as opposed to his orientation, was contrary to the group's values.

. . .

III

... [W]e have routinely and easily rejected assertions of this right by expressive organizations with discriminatory membership policies, such as private schools, law firms, and labor organizations. In fact, until today, we have never once found a claimed right to associate in the selection of members to prevail in the face of a State's antidiscrimination law. To the contrary, we have squarely held that a State's antidiscrimination law does not violate a group's right to associate simply because the law conflicts with that group's exclusionary membership policy.

. . .

Several principles are made perfectly clear by *Jaycees* and *Rotary Club*. First, to prevail on a claim of expressive association in the face of a State's antidiscrimination law, it is not enough simply to engage in some kind of expressive activity. Both the Jaycees and the Rotary Club engaged in expressive activity protected by the First Amendment, yet that fact was not dispositive. Second, it is not enough to adopt an openly avowed exclusionary membership policy. Both the Jaycees and the Rotary Club did that as well. Third, it is not sufficient merely to articulate some connection between the group's expressive activities and its exclusionary policy....

. . .

... BSA has, at most, simply adopted an exclusionary membership policy and has no shared goal of disapproving of homosexuality.... In short, Boy Scouts of America is simply silent on homosexuality. There is no shared goal or collective effort to foster a belief about homosexuality at all—let alone one that is significantly burdened by admitting homosexuals.

. . . .

IV

... [T]he majority insists that we must "give deference to an association's assertions regarding the nature of its expression" and "we must also give deference to an association's view of what would impair its expression.". . . .

This is an astounding view of the law. I am unaware of any previous instance in which our analysis of the scope of a constitutional right was determined by looking at what a litigant asserts in his or her brief and inquiring no further. . . .

... An organization can adopt the message of its choice, and it is not this Court's place to disagree with it. But we must inquire whether the group is, in fact, expressing a message (whatever it may be) and whether that message (if one is expressed) is significantly affected by a State's antidiscrimination law. . . .

Surely there are instances in which an organization that truly aims to foster a belief at odds with the purposes of a State's antidiscrimination laws will have a First Amendment right to association that precludes forced compliance with those laws. But that right is not a freedom to discriminate at will, nor is it a right to maintain an exclusionary membership policy simply out of fear of what the public reaction would be if the group's membership were opened up. . . . If this Court were to defer to whatever position an organization is prepared to assert in its briefs, there would be no way to mark the proper boundary between genuine exercises of the right to associate, on the one hand, and sham claims that are simply attempts to insulate nonexpressive private discrimination, on the other hand. . . .

There is, of course, a valid concern that a court's independent review may run the risk of paying too little heed to an organization's sincerely held views. . . .

In this case, no such concern is warranted. It is entirely clear that BSA in fact expresses no clear, unequivocal message burdened by New Jersey's law.

V

Even if BSA's right to associate argument fails, it nonetheless might have a First Amendment right to refrain from including debate and dialogue about homosexuality as part of its mission to instill values in Scouts. . . . BSA cannot be compelled to include a message about homosexuality among the values it actually chooses to teach its Scouts, if it would prefer to remain silent on that subject.

In West Virginia Bd. of Ed. v. Barnette, 319 U. S. 624 (1943), we recognized that the government may not "requir[e] affirmation of a belief and an attitude of mind," nor "force an American citizen publicly to profess any statement of belief," even if doing so does not require the person to "forego any contrary convictions of their own." . . .

In its briefs, BSA implies, even if it does not directly argue, that Dale would use his Scoutmaster position as a "bully pulpit" to convey immoral messages to his troop, and therefore his inclusion in the group would compel BSA to include a message it does not want to impart. . . . Even though the majority does not endorse that argument, I think it is important to explain why it lacks merit, before considering the argument the majority does accept.

BSA has not contended, nor does the record support, that Dale had ever advocated a view on homosexuality to his troop before his membership was revoked.

. . .

. . . [T]here is no basis for BSA to presume that a homosexual will be unable to comply with BSA's policy not to discuss sexual matters any more than it would presume that politically or religiously active members could not resist the urge to proselytize or politicize during troop meetings. . . .

The majority, though, does not rest its conclusion on the claim that Dale will use his position as a bully pulpit. Rather, it contends that Dale's mere presence among the Boy Scouts will itself force the group to convey a message about homosexuality . . .

The majority's argument relies exclusively on *Hurley* . . .

. . .

Dale's inclusion in the Boy Scouts is nothing like the case in *Hurley*. His participation sends no cognizable message to the Scouts or to the world. Unlike GLIB, Dale did not carry a banner or a sign; he did not distribute any fact sheet; and he expressed no intent to send any message. If there is any kind of message being sent, then, it is by the mere act of joining the Boy Scouts. Such an act does not constitute an instance of symbolic speech under the First Amendment.

. . . [I]f merely joining a group did constitute symbolic speech . . ., then the right of free speech effectively becomes a limitless right to exclude for every organization, whether or not it engages in any expressive activities. . . .

The only apparent explanation for the majority's holding, then, is that homosexuals are simply so different from the rest of society that their presence alone—unlike any other individual's—should be singled out for special First Amendment treatment. Under the majority's reasoning, an openly gay male is irreversibly affixed with the label "homosexual." That label, even though unseen, communicates a message that permits his exclusion wherever he goes. His openness is the sole and sufficient justification for his ostracism....

. . .

The State of New Jersey has decided that people who are open and frank about their sexual orientation are entitled to equal access to employment as school teachers, police officers, librarians, athletic coaches, and a host of other jobs filled by citizens who serve as role models for children and adults alike. Dozens of Scout units throughout the State are sponsored by public agencies, such as schools and fire departments, that employ such role models. BSA's affiliation with numerous public agencies that comply with New Jersey's law against discrimination cannot be understood to convey any particular message endorsing or condoning the activities of all these people.

VI

Unfavorable opinions about homosexuals "have ancient roots." ...

That such prejudices are still prevalent and that they have caused serious and tangible harm to countless members of the class New Jersey seeks to protect are established matters of fact that neither the Boy Scouts nor the Court disputes. That harm can only be aggravated by the creation of a constitutional shield for a policy that is itself the product of a habitual way of thinking about strangers....

... I respectfully dissent.

JUSTICE SOUTER, with whom JUSTICE GINSBURG and JUSTICE BREYER join, dissenting.

I join Justice Stevens' dissent but add this further word ...

. . .

The right of expressive association does not, of course, turn on the popularity of the views advanced by a group that claims protection.... I conclude that BSA has not made out an expressive association claim, therefore, not because of what BSA may espouse, but because of its failure to make sexual orientation the subject of any unequivocal advocacy, using the channels it customarily employs to state its message....

If, on the other hand, an expressive association claim has met the conditions Justice Stevens describes as necessary, there may well be circumstances in which the antidiscrimination law must yield, as he says. It is certainly possible for an individual to become so identified with a position as to epitomize it publicly. When that position is at odds with a group's advocated position, applying an antidiscrimination statute to require the group's acceptance of the individual in a position of group leadership could so modify or muddle or frustrate the group's advocacy as to violate the expressive associational right. While it is not our business here to rule on any such hypothetical, it is at least clear that our estimate of the progressive character of the group's position will be irrelevant to the First Amendment analysis if such a case comes to us for decision.

Chapter XVI

THE RIGHT TO SILENCE

I. COMPULSORY DISCLOSURE OF THE SOURCE OF ANONYMOUS PAMPHLETS AND BOOKS*

Anonymous writings have long played an important role in the expression of ideas. Anonymous pamphlets have been used in England since the beginning of printing. The English licensing laws brought forth a series of anonymous religious tracts. John Udall, an Anglican clergyman with Puritan views, was convicted in 1590 for writing unlicensed pamphlets attacking the bishops under the pen name "Martin Marprelate." In 1637 the licensing laws were amended to require that all books bear the name of the author as well as the printer, and to regulate the importing of books. John Lilburn and John Wharton, working men of Puritan views, were convicted of contempt in 1638 for refusing to say whether they had smuggled books from Holland into England. The licensing laws expired in 1694, and the device of anonymous authorship continued to be utilized in English political life; Defoe, Swift and Johnson, as well as many lesser known authors, published anonymous political pamphlets critical of affairs in England. During the early history of the United States prominent persons used anonymous pamphlets and the unsigned letter to the editor to express their views on public issues. William Bradford was brought to trial because he had, in order to inform the people of their rights, anonymously printed and distributed the charter of Pennsylvania. At the time the first amendment was adopted, the device of anonymous political authorship was well known, and utilized by many of the founding fathers. . . .

But throughout history governments have sought to limit or abolish the right of an individual to express himself anonymously, by requiring those engaged in the expression of ideas to register or in some other way to disclose their identity. In 1850 France enacted a requirement that newspaper articles discussing political, philosophical, or religious questions be signed. England in 1881 adopted a requirement that the printers and publishers of unincorporated newspapers file annually the title of the paper and the names of its proprietors. Similarly, in the United States, both the state and federal governments have enacted disclosure provisions. For example, the Post Office Appropriations Act of 1912 required users of second class mailing privileges periodically to file and publish the names of their officers and proprietors. The federal government compels lobbyists and agents of foreign governments to

* Note, The Constitutional Right to Anonymity: Free Speech, Disclosure and the Devil, Yale Law Journal, 1961, vol. 70, p. 1084. Reprinted with permission.

register. Any group which is found by the Security Activities Control Board to be a "communist action group" must submit a membership list. Some organizations have been required by state statutes to disclose to the state the names of their members, persons and groups wishing to use parks and streets for meetings and public speeches have been required to register; and, in some instances, state laws have required authors to sign their works.

In a number of cases such provisions have been challenged in the Supreme Court as violating freedom of expression. While early cases reaching the Court upheld such requirements, in recent years the Court has found some forms of compulsory disclosure invalid under the first and fourteenth amendments.

TALLEY v. CALIFORNIA

Supreme Court of the United States, 1960.
362 U.S. 60, 80 S.Ct. 536, 4 L.Ed.2d 559.

JUSTICE BLACK delivered the opinion of the Court.

The question presented here is whether the provisions of a Los Angeles City ordinance restricting the distribution of [anonymous] handbills "abridge the freedom of speech and of the press secured against state invasion by the Fourteenth Amendment of the Constitution." ...

The petitioner was arrested and tried [and convicted] in a Los Angeles Municipal Court for violating this ordinance. It was stipulated that the petitioner had distributed [anonymous] handbills [that] urged readers to help the organization carry on a boycott against certain merchants and businessmen, whose names were given, on the ground that, as one set of handbills said, they carried products of "manufacturers who will not offer equal employment opportunities to Negroes, Mexicans, and Orientals." ...

In Lovell v. Griffin, 303 U.S. 444, we held void on its face an ordinance that comprehensively forbade any distribution of literature at any time or place in Griffin, Georgia, without a license. Pamphlets and leaflets, it was pointed out, "have been historic weapons in the defense of liberty"[1] and enforcement of the Griffin ordinance "would restore the system of license and censorship in its baldest form." ...

The broad ordinance now before us ... falls precisely under the ban of our prior cases unless this ordinance is saved by the qualification that handbills can be distributed if they have printed on them the names and addresses of the persons who prepared, distributed or sponsored them. For, as in *Griffin,* the ordinance here is not limited to handbills whose content is "obscene or offensive to public morals or that advocates unlawful conduct." Counsel has urged that this ordinance is aimed at

---

1. The Court's entire sentence was: "These [pamphlets and leaflets] indeed have been historic weapons in the defense of liberty, as the pamphlets of Thomas Paine and others in our own history abundantly attest." It has been noted that some of Thomas Paine's pamphlets were signed with pseudonyms. See Bleyer, Main Currents in the History of American Journalism, 1927, pp. 90–93. Illustrations of other anonymous and pseudonymous pamphlets and other writings used to discuss important public questions can be found in this same volume.

providing a way to identify those responsible for fraud, false advertising and libel. Yet the ordinance is in no manner so limited, nor have we been referred to any legislative history indicating such a purpose. Therefore we do not pass on the validity of an ordinance limited to prevent these or any other supposed evils. This ordinance simply bars all handbills under all circumstances anywhere that do not have the names and addresses printed on them in the place the ordinance requires.

There can be no doubt that such an identification requirement would tend to restrict freedom to distribute information and thereby freedom of expression. "Liberty of circulating is as essential to that freedom as liberty of publishing; indeed, without the circulation, the publication would be of little value." Lovell v. Griffin, 303 U.S., at 452.

Anonymous pamphlets, leaflets, brochures and even books have played an important role in the progress of mankind. Persecuted groups and sects from time to time throughout history have been able to criticize oppressive practices and laws either anonymously or not at all. The obnoxious press licensing law of England, which was also enforced on the Colonies was due in part to the knowledge that exposure of the names of printers, writers and distributors would lessen the circulation of literature critical of the government. The old seditious libel cases in England show the lengths to which government had to go to find out who was responsible for books that were obnoxious to the rulers. John Lilburne was whipped, pilloried and fined for refusing to answer questions designed to get evidence to convict him or someone else for the secret distribution of books in England. Two Puritan Ministers, John Penry and John Udal, were sentenced to death on charges that they were responsible for writing, printing or publishing books. Before the Revolutionary War colonial patriots frequently had to conceal their authorship or distribution of literature that easily could have brought down on them prosecutions by English-controlled courts. Along about that time the Letters of Junius were written and the identity of their author is unknown to this day. Even the Federalist Papers, written in favor of the adoption of our Constitution, were published under fictitious names. It is plain that anonymity has sometimes been assumed for the most constructive purposes.

[I]dentification and fear of reprisal might deter perfectly peaceful discussions of public matters of importance. This broad Los Angeles ordinance is subject to the same infirmity. We hold that it, like the Griffin, Georgia, ordinance, is void on its face.

JUSTICE HARLAN, concurring.

In judging the validity of municipal action affecting rights of speech or association protected against invasion by the Fourteenth Amendment, I do not believe that we can escape, as Justice Roberts said in Schneider v. State, 308 U.S. 147, 161, "the delicate and difficult task" of weighing "the circumstances" and appraising "the substantiality of the reasons advanced in support of the regulation of the free enjoyment of" speech. . . .

Here the State says that this ordinance is aimed at the prevention of "fraud, deceit, false advertising, negligent use of words, obscenity, and libel," in that it will aid in the detection of those responsible for spreading material of that character. But the ordinance is not so limited, and I think it will not do for the State simply to say that the circulation of all anonymous handbills must be suppressed in order to identify the distributors of those that may be of an obnoxious character. In the absence of a more substantial showing as to Los Angeles' actual experience with the distribution of obnoxious handbills, such a generality is for me too remote to furnish a constitutionally acceptable justification for the deterrent effect on free speech which this all-embracing ordinance is likely to have.

JUSTICE CLARK, whom JUSTICE FRANKFURTER and JUSTICE WHITTAKER join, dissenting.

TOM C. CLARK—Born on September 23, 1899, in Dallas, Texas, where he grew up in a family of lawyers. Democrat. Presbyterian. University of Texas, A.B., LL.B. Dallas civil district attorney, 1927–1932; special assistant, Justice Department, 1937–1943; assistant U.S. attorney general, 1943–1945; U.S. attorney general, 1945–1949. Active in Democratic politics throughout legal career; supported Harry S. Truman for vice-presidency, 1944. Nominated by President Truman on August 2, 1949, to replace Frank Murphy. Confirmed by the Senate on August 18, 1949, by a 73–8 vote. Retired on June 12, 1967, soon after his son, Ramsey Clark, became U.S. attorney general. Founding director, Federal Judicial Center, 1968–1970. Died on June 13, 1977.

To me, Los Angeles' ordinance cannot be read as being void on its face. Certainly a fair reading of it does not permit a conclusion that it prohibits the distribution of handbills "of any kind at any time, at any place, and in any manner," Lovell v. Griffin, as the Court seems to conclude. In *Griffin,* the ordinance completely prohibited the unlicensed distribution of any handbills. As I read it, the ordinance here merely prohibits the distribution of a handbill which does not carry the identification of the name of the person who "printed, wrote, compiled ... manufactured [or] ... caused" the distribution of it. There could well be a compelling reason for such a requirement. The Court implies as much when it observes that Los Angeles has not "referred to any legislative history indicating" that the ordinance was adopted for the purpose of preventing "fraud, false advertising and libel." ... The Court here, however, makes no appraisal of *the circumstances,* or *the substantiality* of the claims of the litigants, but strikes down the ordinance as being "void on its face...."

Therefore, before passing upon the validity of the ordinance, I would weigh the interests of the public in its enforcement against the claimed right of Talley. The record is barren of any claim, much less proof, that he will suffer any injury whatever by identifying the handbill with his name. Unlike N.A.A.C.P. v. State of Alabama, 1958, 357 U.S. 449, which is relied upon, there is neither allegation nor proof that Talley or any group sponsoring him would suffer economic reprisal, loss of employment, threat of physical coercion [or] other manifestations of public hostility. Id., 357 U.S. at page 462. Talley makes no showing whatever to support his contention that a restraint upon his freedom of speech will result from the enforcement of the ordinance. The existence of such a restraint is necessary before we can strike the ordinance down.

But even if the State had this burden, which it does not, the substantiality of Los Angeles' interest in the enforcement of the ordinance sustains its validity. Its chief law enforcement officer says that the enforcement of the ordinance prevents "fraud, deceit, false advertising, negligent use of words, obscenity, and libel," and, as we have said, that such was its purpose. In the absence of any showing to the contrary by Talley, this appears to me entirely sufficient.

I stand second to none in supporting Talley's right of free speech—but not his freedom of anonymity. . . .

NOTES AND QUESTIONS

1.　The publication of the Junius Letters, mentioned by Justice Black, played an important role in the development of free expression in both Great Britain and United States. The letters, published anonymously in London newspapers between 1769 and 1772, attacked George III and his ministers for abuse of the royal prerogative in denying John Wilkes his seat in Parliament. The Crown, unable to identify the author (now thought to have been Sir Philip Francis), prosecuted two publishers for seditious libel, but juries refused to convict despite Lord Chief Justice Mansfield's instructions interpreting libel law very much in favor of the Crown. "Confronted by popular acclamation of the acquittals," wrote Leonard Levy, "the government quietly dropped the prosecutions of the other publishers against whom information had been filed, but it did not quash alarm that the Crown-libel doctrines menaced the Englishmen's beloved institution, trial by one's peers."* Both the Junius Letters (published in two volumes in 1772) and the Junius trials were well known in the United States at the time of the First Amendment's adoption, which Chafee and Holmes said was intended to make seditious libel unconstitutional. See Chapter 4, pp. 68–69.

2.　Is the Court's opinion in *Talley* another example of the "overbreadth" technique? Does the opinion go further? See Chapter 12, p. 424, note 1. Here are Justice Harlan's views of the opinion as expressed in a letter to Justice Black on February 10, 1960:*

> As I read the opinion it holds, or comes near to holding, that a State cannot prohibit the circulation of anonymous handbills, which is something to which I cannot subscribe, even with your qualification that "there are times and circumstances," etc.
>
> For me the guts of this case is that the State has made no effort to show a subordinating state interest justifying this

---

* Leonard W. Levy, Freedom of Speech and Press in Early American History: Legacy of Suppression, New York, 1963, pp. 160–161.

* Black Papers, Library of Congress, Box 342.

ordinance or its application, still less a "compelling" one. See N.A.A.C.P. v. Alabama, at 463–464. And on this record I would hold the ordinance unconstitutional as applied in this instance.

I realize that I can hardly expect you to meet my difficulties on this score because of your distaste for the "balancing" process in this type of case. Therefore if you get a Court for your opinion, I anticipate that I will be writing separately.

3. Justice Black's opinion does not pass on a disclosure ordinance limited to more particular objectives. Would the ordinance have been valid if it had been limited to leaflets that reflect on an individual's reputation? The Court invalidated a state law forbidding distribution of anonymous political campaign literature in McIntyre v. Ohio Elections Commission, 514 U.S. 334 (1995). An elderly woman had been fined $100 for distributing leaflets she prepared expressing opposition to a forthcoming referendum on a school tax. The state argued that the law was justified to prevent fraudulent and libelous statements. The Court disagreed. Writing for a majority of seven, Justice Stevens said:

> It applies not only to the activities of candidates and their organized supporters, but also to individuals acting independently and using only their own modest resources. It applies not only to elections of public officers, but also to ballot issues that present neither a substantial risk of libel nor any potential appearance of corrupt advantage. It applies not only to leaflets distributed on the eve of an election, when the opportunity for reply is limited, but also to those distributed months in advance. It applies no matter what the character or strength of the author's interest in anonymity. Moreover, as this case also demonstrates, the absence of the author's name on a document does not necessarily protect either that person or a distributor of a forbidden document from being held responsible for compliance with the election code. Nor has the State explained why it can more easily enforce the direct bans on disseminating false documents against anonymous authors and distributors than against wrongdoers who might use false names and addresses in an attempt to avoid detection.

Justice Scalia, joined by Chief Justice Rehnquist, dissented, arguing that "to strike down the Ohio law in its general application—and similar laws of 48 other States and the Federal Government—on the ground that all anonymous communication is in our society traditionally sacrosanct, seems to me a distortion of the past that will lead to a coarsening of the future."

4. Any attempt to limit campaign spending will, in part, require determining the people responsible for particular campaign literature. Would the Los Angeles disclosure ordinance have been valid if limited to leaflets urging the election of a particular candidate, or supporting or opposing any measure on the ballot? On the complex subject of limiting political campaign contributions, a divided Court upheld a requirement that the names of contributors be disclosed. (The Court also upheld the limit on individual campaign contributions, and the provision for public

financing of Presidential campaigns. Provisions limiting candidates' expenditures, and expenditures by third parties on a candidate's behalf, were held to violate the First Amendment.) Buckley v. Valeo, 424 U.S. 1 (1976).

II. COMPULSORY EXPRESSION OF IDEAS

WEST VIRGINIA STATE BOARD OF EDUCATION v. BARNETTE

Supreme Court of the United State, 1943.
319 U.S. 624, 63 S.Ct. 1178, 87 L.Ed. 1628.

[The report of this case appears, at page 36.]

WOOLEY v. MAYNARD

Supreme Court of the United States, 1977.
430 U.S. 705, 97 S.Ct. 1428, 51 L.Ed.2d 752.

CHIEF JUSTICE BURGER delivered the opinion of the Court.

The issue on appeal is whether the State of New Hampshire may constitutionally enforce criminal sanctions against persons who cover the motto "Live Free or Die" on passenger vehicle license plates because that motto is repugnant to their moral and religious beliefs.

Since 1969 New Hampshire has required that noncommercial vehicles bear license plates embossed with the state motto, "Live Free or Die." Another New Hampshire statute makes it a misdemeanor "knowingly [to obscure] ... the figures or letters on any number plate." The term "letters" in this section has been interpreted by the State's highest court to include the state motto. State v. Hoskin, 295 A.2d 454 (1972).

Appellees George Maynard and his wife Maxine are followers of the Jehovah's Witnesses faith. The Maynards consider the New Hampshire State motto to be repugnant to their moral, religious, and political beliefs[1] and therefore assert it objectionable to disseminate this message by displaying it on their automobiles. Pursuant to these beliefs, the Maynards began early in 1974 to cover up the motto on their license plates. . . .

On December 28, 1974, Mr. Maynard was again charged with violating § 262:27-c. He appeared in court on January 31, 1975, and again chose to represent himself; he was found guilty, fined $50, and sentenced to six months in the Grafton County House of Corrections. The court suspended the jail sentence but ordered Mr. Maynard to also pay the $25 fine for the first offense. Maynard informed that court that, as a matter of conscience, he refused to pay the two fines. The court

1. Mr. Maynard described his objections to the state motto:

"[B]y religious training and belief, I believe my 'government'—Jehovah's Kingdom—offers everlasting life. It would be contrary to that belief to give up my life for the state, even if it meant living in bondage. Although I obey all laws of the State not in conflict with my conscience, this slogan is directly at odds with my deep religious convictions.

"I also disagree with the motto on political grounds. I believe that life is more precious than freedom." Affidavit of George Maynard, App. 3.

thereupon sentenced him to jail for a period of 15 days. He has served the full sentence....

On March 4, 1975, appellees brought the present action pursuant to 42 U.S.C. § 1983 in the United States District Court for the District of New Hampshire. They sought injunctive and declaratory relief against enforcement of N.H. Rev. Stat. Ann. § 262:27–c, 263:1, insofar as these required displaying the state motto on their vehicle license plates and made it a criminal offense to obscure the motto....

The District Court held that by covering up the state motto "Live Free or Die" on his automobile license plate, Mr. Maynard was engaging in symbolic speech and that "New Hampshire's interest in the enforcement of its defacement statute is not sufficient to justify the restriction on [appellee's] constitutionally protected expression." We find it unnecessary to pass on the "symbolic speech" issue, since we find more appropriate First Amendment grounds to affirm the judgment of the District Court. We turn instead to what in our view is the essence of appellees' objection to the requirement that they display the motto "Live Free or Die" on their automobile license plates. This is succinctly summarized in the statement made by Mr. Maynard in his affidavit filed with the District Court.

"I refuse to be coerced by the State into advertising a slogan which I find morally, ethically, religiously and politically abhorrent."

We are thus faced with the question of whether the State may constitutionally require an individual to participate in the dissemination of an ideological message by displaying it on his private property in a manner and for the express purpose that it be observed and read by the public. We hold that the State may not do so.

We begin with the proposition that the right of freedom of thought protected by the First Amendment against state action includes both the right to speak freely and the right to refrain from speaking at all. See Board of Education v. Barnette, 319 U.S. 624, 633–634 (1943)....

The Court in *Barnette* was faced with a state statute which required public school students to participate in daily public ceremonies by honoring the flag both with words and traditional salute gestures.... Compelling the affirmative act of a flag salute involved a more serious infringement upon personal liberties than the passive act of carrying the state motto on a license plate, but the difference is essentially one of degree. Here, as in *Barnette*, we are faced with a state measure which forces an individual, as part of his daily life—to be an instrument for fostering public adherence to an ideological point of view he finds unacceptable. In doing so the State "invades the sphere of intellect and spirit which it is the purpose of the First Amendment to our Constitution to reserve from all official control."

New Hampshire's statute in effect requires that appellees use their private property as a "mobile Billboard" for the State's ideological message—or suffer a penalty, as Maynard already has. As a condition to driving an automobile—a virtual necessity for most Americans—the

Maynards must display "Live Free or Die" to hundreds of people each day. The fact that most individuals agree with the thrust of New Hampshire's motto is not the test; most Americans also find the flag salute acceptable. The First Amendment protects the right of individuals to hold a point of view different from the majority and to refuse to foster, in the way New Hampshire commands, an idea they find morally objectionable.

Identifying the Maynards' interests as implicating First Amendment protections does not end our inquiry however. We must also determine whether the State's countervailing interest is sufficiently compelling to justify requiring appellees to display the state motto on their license plates. See, e.g., United States v. O'Brien, 391 U.S. 367, 376–377 (1968). The two interests advanced by the State are that display of the motto (1) facilitates the identification of passenger vehicles, and (2) promotes appreciation of history, individualism, and state pride.

The State first points out that passenger vehicles, but not commercial, trailer, or other vehicles are required to display the state motto. Thus, the argument proceeds, officers of the law are more easily able to determine whether passenger vehicles are carrying the proper plates. However, the record here reveals that New Hampshire passenger license plates normally consist of a specific configuration of letters and numbers, which makes them readily distinguishable from other types of plates, even without reference to the state motto. Even were we to credit the State's reasons and "even though the governmental purpose be legitimate and substantial, that purpose cannot be pursued by means that broadly stifle fundamental personal liberties when the end can be more narrowly achieved. The breadth of legislative abridgment must be viewed in the light of less drastic means for achieving the same basic purpose." Shelton v. Tucker, 364 U.S. 479, 488 (1960).

The State's second claimed interest is not ideologically neutral. The State is seeking to communicate to others an official view as to proper appreciation of history, state pride, and individualism. Of course, the State may legitimately pursue such interests in any number of ways. However, where the State's interest is to disseminate an ideology, no matter how acceptable to some, such interest cannot outweigh an individual's First Amendment right to avoid becoming the courier of such message.

We conclude that the State of New Hampshire may not require appellees to display the state motto[2] upon their vehicle license plates; and accordingly, we affirm the judgement of the District Court.

Affirmed.

---

2. It has been suggested that today's holding be read as sanctioning the obliteration of the national motto, "In God We Trust," from the United States coins and currency. That question is not before us today but we note that currency, which is passed from hand to hand, differs in significant respects from an automobile, which is readily associated with its operator. Currency is generally carried in a purse or pocket and need not be displayed to the public. The bearer of currency is thus not required to publicly advertise the national motto.

Justice Rehnquist, with whom Justice Blackmun joins, dissenting.

. . .

I not only agree with the Court's implicit recognition that there is no protected "symbolic speech" in this case, but I think that that conclusion goes for to undermine the Court's ultimate holding that there is an element of protected expression here. The State has not forced appellees to "say" anything; and it has not forced them to communicate ideas with nonverbal actions reasonably likened to "speech," such as wearing a lapel button promoting a political candidate or waving a flag as a symbolic gesture., The State has simply required that *all* noncommercial automobiles bear license tags with the state motto, "Live Free or Die." Appellees have not been forced to affirm or reject that motto; the are simply required by the State, under its police power, to carry a state auto license tag for identification and registration purposes.

[T]he Court relies almost solely on Board of Education v. Barnette, 319 U.S. 624 (1943). The Court cites Barnette for the proposition that there is a constitutional right in some cases, to "refrain from speaking." What the Court does not demonstrate is that there is any "speech" or "speaking" in the context of this case. The Court also relies upon the "right to decline to foster [religious, political, and ideological] concepts," . . . and treats the state law in this case as if it were forcing appellees to proselytize, or to advocate an ideological point of view. But this begs the question. The issue, confronted by the Court, is whether appellees, in displaying as they are required to do, state license tags, the format of which is known to all as having been prescribed by the State, would be considered to be advocating political or ideological views.

The Court recognizes, as it must, that this case substantially differs from *Barnette*, in which schoolchildren were forced to recite the pledge of allegiance while giving the flag salute. . . . However, the Court states "the difference is essentially one of degree." . . . But having recognized the rather obvious differences between these two cases, the Court does not explain why the same result should obtain. The Court suggests that the test is whether the individual is forced "to be an instrument for fostering public adherence to an ideological point of view he finds unacceptable." . . . But, once again, these are merely conclusory words, barren of analysis. For example, were New Hampshire to erect a multitude of billboards, each proclaiming "Live Free or Die," and tax all citizens for the cost of erection and maintenance, clearly the message would be "fostered" by the individual citizen-taxpayers and just as clearly those individuals would be "instruments" in that communication. Certainly, however, that case would not fall within the ambit of *Barnette*. In that case, as in this case, there is no *affirmation* of belief. For First Amendment principles to be implicated, the State must place the citizen in the position of either apparently or actually "asserting as true" the message. This was the focus of *Barnette*, and clearly distinguishes this case from that one.

. . .

The logic of the Court's opinion leads to startling, and I believe totally unacceptable, results, For example, the mottoes "In God We Trust" and "E Pluribus Unum" appear on the coin and currency of the United States. I cannot imagine that the statutes, proscribing defacement of United States currency, impinge upon the First Amendment rights of an atheist. The fact that an atheist carries and uses United States currency does not, in any meaningful sense, convey any affirmation of belief on his part in the motto, "In God We Trust." Similarly, there is no affirmation of belief involved in the display of state license tags upon the private automobiles involved here.

I would reverse the judgment of the District Court.

NOTES AND QUESTIONS

1. Would the results in Wooley v. Maynard have been the same if he had no religious scruples against the license plate's motto?

2. The Supreme Court relied in part on the flag-salute cases and *Wooley* in Pacific Gas & Electric Co. v. Public Utilities Commission of California, 475 U.S. 1 (1986). The Court decided that, just as the Maynards could not be compelled to carry a message on their license plates, the company could not be required to carry consumer group messages in its monthly billing envelope. Justice Rehnquist's dissent argued that the "negative free speech" recognized in the earlier cases only remotely served one of the interests protected by freedom of speech—the search for truth. Instead, it primarily served an interest in individual freedom of conscience. Because corporations had neither "intellect" nor "mind," it was an interest that simply was not applicable when asserted by a commercial corporation. Justice Powell's opinion, for a plurality, replied that making the utility distribute the message of a consumer group could affect the utility's own affirmative expression. Consumer groups were chosen to have access to the utility's mailing precisely because they expressed a point of view antagonistic to the utility. That could induce the utility to alter its own positions, or to respond to the consumer group's message. "The danger that [the utility] will be required to alter its own message . . . is a proper object of First Amendment solicitude, because the message itself is protected. . . ."

III. COMPULSORY DISCLOSURE OF ASSOCIATION MEMBERSHIP

N.A.A.C.P. v. ALABAMA

Supreme Court of the United States, 1958.
357 U.S. 449, 78 S.Ct. 1163, 2 L.Ed.2d 1488.

[The report of this case appears at page 535.]

IV. COMPULSORY PAYMENT OF DUES FOR IDEOLOGICAL POLITICAL ACTIVITIES

KELLER v. STATE BAR OF CALIFORNIA

Supreme Court of the United States, 1990.
496 U.S. 1, 110 S.Ct. 2228, 110 L.Ed.2d 1.

CHIEF JUSTICE REHNQUIST delivered the opinion of the Court.

Petitioners, members of the State Bar of California, sued that body claiming its use of their membership dues to finance certain ideological or political activities to which they were opposed violated their rights under the First Amendment of the United States Constitution. The Supreme Court of California rejected this challenge on the grounds that respondent State Bar is a state agency, and as such may use the dues for any purpose within its broad statutory authority. We agree that lawyers admitted to practice in the State may be required to join and pay dues to the State Bar, but disagree as to the scope of permissible dues-financed activities in which respondent may engage.

Respondent State Bar is an organization created under California law to regulate the State's legal profession. It is an entity commonly referred to as an "integrated bar"—an association of attorneys in which membership and dues are required as a condition of practicing law in a State.... The association performs a variety of functions ... "[T]he State Bar for many years has lobbied the Legislature and other governmental agencies, filed amicus curiae briefs in pending cases, held an annual conference of delegates at which issues of current interest are debated and resolutions approved, and engaged in a variety of education programs." These activities are financed principally through the use of membership dues.

Petitioners, 21 members of the State Bar, sued in state court claiming that through these activities respondent expends mandatory dues payments to advance political and ideological causes to which they do not subscribe....

. . .

In Lathrop v. Donohue, 367 U.S. 820 (1961), a Wisconsin lawyer claimed that he could not constitutionally be compelled to join and financially support a state bar association which expressed opinions on, and attempted to influence, legislation. Six Members of this Court, relying on Railway Employees v. Hanson, 351 U.S. 225 (1956), rejected this claim....

. . .

The *Lathrop* plurality ... expressly reserved judgment on Lathrop's additional claim that his free speech rights were violated by the Wisconsin Bar's use of his mandatory dues to support objectionable political activities.... Petitioners here present this very claim for decision, contending that the use of their compulsory dues to finance political and ideological activities of the State Bar with which they disagree violates their rights of free speech guaranteed by the First Amendment.

In Abood v. Detroit Board of Education, 431 U.S. 209 (1977), the Court confronted the issue of whether, consistent with the First Amendment, agency-shop dues of nonunion public employees could be used to support political and ideological causes of the union which were unrelated to collective-bargaining activities. We held that while the Constitution did not prohibit a union from spending "funds for the expression of political views . . . or toward the advancement of other ideological causes not germane to its duties as collective-bargaining representative," the Constitution did require that such expenditures be "financed from charges, dues, or assessments paid by employees who [did] not object to advancing those ideas and who [were] not coerced into doing so against their will by the threat of loss of governmental employment." . . . [I]n the later case of Ellis v. Railway Clerks, 466 U.S. 435 (1984), the Court made it clear that the principles of *Abood* apply equally to employees in the private sector. . . .

. . . [T]he California Supreme Court in this case held that respondent's status as a regulated state agency exempted it from any constitutional constraints on the use of its dues. . . . Respondent also urges this position, invoking the so-called "government speech" doctrine [arguing that] "[t]he government must take substantive positions and decide disputed issues to govern. . . . So long as it bases its actions on legitimate goals, government may speak despite citizen disagreement with its message, for government is not required to be content-neutral." . . .

. . . The State Bar of California is a good deal different from most other entities that would be regarded in common parlance as "governmental agencies." Its principal funding comes not from appropriations made to it by the legislature, but from dues levied on its members by the Board of Governors. . . .

There is, by contrast, a substantial analogy between the relationship of the State Bar and its members, on the one hand, and the relation of the employee unions and their members, on the other. The reason behind the legislative enactment of "agency shop" laws is to prevent "free riders" . . . from avoiding their fair share of the cost of a process from which they benefit. The members of the State Bar concededly do not benefit as directly . . ., but the position of the organized bars has generally been that they prefer a large measure of self-regulation to regulation conducted by a government body which has little or no connection with the profession. . . . It is entirely appropriate that all of the lawyers who derive benefit from the unique status of being among those admitted to practice before the courts should be called upon to pay a fair share of the cost of the professional involvement in this effort.

But the very specialized characteristics of the State Bar of California discussed above served to distinguish it from the role of the typical government official or agency. Government officials are expected as a part of the democratic process to represent and to espouse the views of a majority of their constituents. . . . If every citizen were to have a right to insist that no one paid by public funds express a view with which he disagreed, debate over issues of great concern to the public would be limited to those in the private sector, and the process of government as we know it radically transformed. . . .

The State Bar of California was created, not to participate in the general government of the State, but to provide specialized professional advice to those with the ultimate responsibility of governing the legal profession. Its members and officers are such not because they are citizens or voters, but because they are lawyers. We think that these differences between the State Bar, on the one hand, and traditional government agencies and officials, on the other hand, render unavailing respondent's argument that it is not subject to the same constitutional rule with respect to the use of compulsory dues as are labor unions representing public and private employees.

· · ·

Abood held that a union could not expend a dissenting individual's dues for ideological activities not "germane" to the purpose for which compelled association was justified: collective bargaining. Here the compelled association and integrated bar is justified by the State's interest in regulating the legal profession and improving the quality of legal services. The State Bar may therefore constitutionally fund activities germane to those goals out of the mandatory dues of all members. It may not, however, in such manner fund activities of an ideological nature which fall outside of those areas of activity. The difficult question, of course, is to define the latter class of activities.

· · ·

. . . [T]he guiding standard must be whether the challenged expenditures are necessarily or reasonably incurred for the purpose of regulating the legal profession or "improving the quality of the legal service available to the people of the State." . . .

· · ·

Precisely where the line falls between those State Bar activities in which the officials and members of the Bar are acting essentially as professional advisors to those ultimately charged with the regulation of the legal profession, on the one hand, and those activities having political or ideological coloration which are not reasonably related to the advancement of such goals, on the other, will not always be easy to discern. But the extreme ends of the spectrum are clear: Compulsory dues may not be expended to endorse or advance a gun control or nuclear weapons freeze initiative; at the other end of the spectrum petitioners have no valid constitutional objection to their compulsory dues being spent for activities connected with disciplining members of the bar or proposing ethical codes for the profession.

· · ·

In addition to their claim for relief based on respondent's use of their mandatory dues, petitioners' complaint also requested an injunction prohibiting the State Bar from using its name to advance political and ideological causes or beliefs. This request for relief appears to implicate a much broader freedom of association claim than was at issue in *Lathrop*. Petitioners challenge not only their "compelled financial support of group activities," but urge that they cannot be compelled to associate with an organization that engages in political or ideological activities beyond those for which mandatory financial support is justified under the principles of *Lathrop* and *Abood*. The California courts did not address this claim, and we decline to do so in the first instance. The state courts remain free, of course, to consider this issue on remand.

The judgment of the Supreme Court of California is reversed, and the case is remanded for further proceedings not inconsistent with this opinion.

Reversed.

V. COMPULSORY DISCLOSURE OF NEWS SOURCES

BRANZBURG v. HAYES

Supreme Court of the United States, 1972.
408 U.S. 665, 92 S.Ct. 2646, 33 L.Ed.2d 626.

[Three separate cases were consolidated for decision in this opinion. Paul Branzburg, a Kentucky journalist, was ordered by a local grand jury to identify the individuals he had seen using marijuana while he was preparing a story on drug usage. The Kentucky Court of Appeals refused to quash the subpoena, holding that the Kentucky newsman's privilege statute protected a reporter from having to disclose the identity of an informant, but that it did not permit a reporter to refuse to testify about events he had personally observed, including the identities of those persons he had observed.

Paul Pappas, a television newsman, gained entry into the New Bedford, Massachusetts headquarters of the Black Panthers by promising to report only on an anticipated police raid. The raid did not occur and so Pappas made no report of his experiences. A local grand jury subpoenaed him and inquired about what he had observed inside the headquarters. The Supreme Judicial Court of Massachusetts refused to quash the summons, holding that "there exists no constitutional newsman's privilege to refuse to appear and testify before a grand jury."

Earl Caldwell, a New York Times reporter, had been covering Black Panther activities in Oakland, California. A federal grand jury subpoenaed Caldwell, seeking further information about stories he had written. The District Court refused to quash the subpoena, but the Court of Appeals for the Ninth Circuit reversed, holding that Caldwell was privileged to refuse to even attend the grand jury meeting, absent some special showing of necessity by the government.]

JUSTICE WHITE delivered the opinion of the Court.

Petitioners Branzburg and Pappas and respondent Caldwell press First Amendment claims that may be simply put: that to gather news it is often necessary to agree either not to identify the source of information published or to publish only part of the facts revealed, or both; that if the reporter is nevertheless forced to reveal these confidences to a grand jury, the source so identified and other confidential sources of other reporters will be measurably deterred from furnishing publishable information, all to the detriment of the free flow of information protected by the First Amendment. Although the newsmen in these cases do not claim an absolute privilege against official interrogation in all circumstances, they assert that the reporter should not be forced either to appear or to testify before a grand jury or at trial until and unless sufficient grounds are shown for believing that the reporter possesses information relevant to a crime the grand jury is investigating, that the information the reporter has is unavailable from other sources, and that the need for the information is sufficiently compelling to override the claimed invasion of First Amendment interests occasioned by the disclosure. Principally relied upon are prior cases emphasizing the importance of the First Amendment guarantees to individual development and to our system of representative government, decisions requiring that official action with adverse impact on First Amendment rights be justified by a public interest that is "compelling" or "paramount," and those precedents establishing the principle that justifiable governmental goals may not be achieved by unduly broad means having an unnecessary impact on protected rights of speech, press, or association. The heart of the claim is that the burden on news gathering resulting from compelling reporters to disclose confidential information outweighs any public interest in obtaining the information.

BYRON R. WHITE—Born on June 8, 1917, in Fort Collins, Colorado, into a family of modest means. Grew up in Wellington, Colorado, a small town in the sugar beet area of the state. Democrat. Protestant. Colorado, B.A., 1938, graduating first in his class. All American football player whom the press dubbed "Whizzer." Also played varsity basketball and baseball. Played professional football with the Pittsburgh Pirates for one season after graduation from Colorado and led the National Football League in rushing. Oxford, Rhodes Scholar, 1939; Yale, LL.B., magna cum laude, 1946. Played professional football with Detroit Lions while in law school. Law clerk, Chief Justice Fred M. Vinson, 1946–1947; practiced law, 1947–1960; deputy U.S. attorney general, 1961–1962. Nominated associate justice by John F. Kennedy (who had known him since his days as a Rhodes Scholar in England) on March 30, 1962, to replace Charles E. Whittaker. Confirmed by the Senate on April 11, 1962, by voice vote. Retired on June 28, 1993. Died on April 15, 2002.

A number of States have provided newsmen a statutory privilege of varying breadth, but the majority have not done so, and none has been provided by federal statute. Until now the only testimonial privilege for unofficial witnesses that is rooted in the Federal Constitution is the Fifth Amendment privilege against compelled self-incrimination. We are asked to create another by interpreting the First Amendment to grant newsmen a testimonial privilege that other citizens do not enjoy. This we decline to do. Fair and effective law enforcement aimed at providing security for the person and property of the individual is a fundamental function of government, and the grand jury plays an important, constitutionally mandated role in this process. On the records now before us, we perceive no basis for holding that the public interest in law enforcement and in ensuring effective grand jury proceedings is insufficient to override the consequential, but uncertain, burden on news gathering that is said to result from insisting that reporters, like other citizens, respond to relevant questions put to them in the course of a valid grand jury investigation or criminal trial.

This conclusion itself involves no restraint on what newspapers may publish or on the type or quality of information reporters may seek to acquire, nor does it threaten the vast bulk of confidential relationships between reporters and their sources. Grand juries address themselves to the issues of whether crimes have been committed and who committed them. Only where news sources themselves are implicated in crime or possess information relevant to the grand jury's task need they or the reporter be concerned about grand jury subpoenas. Nothing before us indicates that a large number or percentage of *all* confidential news sources falls into either category and would in any way be deterred by our holding that the Constitution does not, as it never has, exempt the newsman from performing the citizen's normal duty of appearing and furnishing information relevant to the grand jury's task.

The argument that the flow of news will be diminished by compelling reporters to aid the grand jury in a criminal investigation is not irrational, nor are the records before us silent on the matter. But we remain unclear how often and to what extent informers are actually deterred from furnishing information when newsmen are forced to testify before a grand jury. The available data indicate that some newsmen rely a great deal on confidential sources and that some informants are particularly sensitive to the threat of exposure and may be silenced if it is held by this Court that, ordinarily, newsmen must testify pursuant to subpoenas, but the evidence fails to demonstrate that there would be a significant constriction of the flow of news to the public if this Court reaffirms the prior common-law and constitutional rule regarding the testimonial obligations of newsmen. Estimates of the inhibiting effect of such subpoenas on the willingness of informants to make disclosures to newsmen are widely divergent and to a great extent speculative. It would be difficult to canvass the views of the informants themselves; surveys of reporters on this topic are chiefly opinions of predicted informant behavior and must be viewed in the light of the professional self-interest of the interviewees. Reliance by the press on confidential informants does not mean that all such sources will in fact dry up because of the later possible appearance of the newsman before a grand jury. The reporter may never be called and if he objects to testifying, the prosecution may not insist. Also, the relationship of many informants to the press is a symbiotic one which is unlikely to be greatly inhibited by the threat of subpoena: quite often, such informants are members of a minority political or cultural group that relies heavily on the media to propagate its views, publicize its aims, and magnify its exposure to the public. Moreover, grand juries characteristically conduct secret proceedings, and law enforcement officers are themselves experienced in dealing with informers, and have their own methods for protecting them without interference with the effective administration of justice. There is little before us indicating that informants whose interest in avoiding exposure is that it may threaten job security, personal safety, or peace of mind, would in fact be in a worse position, or would think they would be, if they risked placing their trust in public officials as well as reporters. We doubt if the informer who prefers anonymity but is sincerely interested in furnishing evidence of crime will always or very often be deterred by the prospect of dealing with those public authorities characteristically charged with the duty to protect the public interest as well as his.

Accepting the fact, however, that an undetermined number of informants not themselves implicated in crime will nevertheless, for whatever reason, refuse to talk to newsmen if they fear identification by a reporter in an official investigation, we cannot accept the argument that the public interest in possible future news about crime from undisclosed, unverified sources must take precedence over the public interest in pursuing and prosecuting those crimes reported to the press by informants and in thus deterring the commission of such crimes in the future.

We are unwilling to embark the judiciary on a long and difficult journey to such an uncertain destination. The administration of a constitutional newsman's privilege would present practical and conceptual difficulties of a high order. Sooner or later, it would be necessary to define those categories of newsmen who qualified for the privilege, a questionable procedure in light of the traditional doctrine that liberty of the press is the right of the lonely pamphleteer who uses carbon paper or a mimeograph just as much as of the large metropolitan publisher who utilizes the latest photocomposition methods. . . . The informative function asserted by representatives of the organized press in the present cases is also performed by lecturers, political pollsters, novelists, academic researchers, and dramatists. Almost any author may quite accurately assert that he is contributing to the flow of information to the public, that he relies on confidential sources of information, and that these sources will be silenced if he is forced to make disclosures before a grand jury.

In each instance where a reporter is subpoenaed to testify, the courts would also be embroiled in preliminary factual and legal determinations with respect to whether the proper predicate had been laid for the reporter's appearance: Is there probable cause to believe a crime has been committed? Is it likely that the reporter has useful information gained in confidence? Could the grand jury obtain the information elsewhere? Is the official interest sufficient to outweigh the claimed privilege?

Thus, in the end, by considering whether enforcement of a particular law served a "compelling" governmental interest, the courts would be inextricably involved in distinguishing between the value of enforcing different criminal laws. By requiring testimony from a reporter in investigations involving some crimes but not in others, they would be making a value judgment that a legislature had declined to make, since in each case the criminal law involved would represent a considered legislative judgment, not constitutionally suspect, of what conduct is liable to criminal prosecution. The task of judges, like other officials outside the legislative branch, is not to make the law but to uphold it in accordance with their oaths.

In addition, there is much force in the pragmatic view that the press has at its disposal powerful mechanisms of communication and is far from helpless to protect itself from harassment or substantial harm. Furthermore, if what the newsmen urged in these cases is true—that law enforcement cannot hope to gain and may suffer from subpoenaing newsmen before grand juries—prosecutors will be loath to risk so much for so little. . . .

Finally, as we have earlier indicated, news gathering is not without its First Amendment protections, and grand jury investigations if instituted or conducted other than in good faith, would pose wholly different issues for resolution under the First Amendment. Official harassment of the press undertaken not for purposes of law enforcement but to disrupt a reporter's relationship with his news sources would have no justification. . . . [The Court reversed the decision in the *Caldwell* case and affirmed the decisions involving Branzburg and Pappas.]

Justice Powell, concurring.

I add this brief statement to emphasize what seems to me to be the limited nature of the Court's holding. The Court does not hold that newsmen, subpoenaed to testify before a grand jury, are without constitutional rights with respect to the gathering of news or in safeguarding their sources. . . .

As indicated in the concluding portion of the opinion, the Court states that no harassment of newsmen will be tolerated. If a newsman believes that the grand jury investigation is not being conducted in good faith he is not without remedy. Indeed, if the newsman is called upon to give information bearing only a remote and tenuous relationship to the subject of the investigation, or if he has some other reason to believe that his testimony implicates confidential source relationships without a legitimate need of law enforcement, he will have access to the court on a motion to quash and an appropriate protective order may be entered. The asserted claim to privilege should be judged on its facts by the striking of a proper balance between freedom of the press and the obligation of all citizens to give relevant testimony with respect to criminal conduct. The balance of these vital constitutional and societal interests on a case-by-case basis accords with the tried and traditional way of adjudicating such questions.

In short, the courts will be available to newsmen under circumstances where legitimate First Amendment interests require protection.

JUSTICE DOUGLAS, dissenting.

Today's decision is more than a clog upon news gathering. It is a signal to publishers and editors that they should exercise caution in how they use whatever information they can obtain. Without immunity they may be summoned to account for their criticism. Entrenched officers have been quick to crash their powers down upon unfriendly commentators.

The intrusion of government into this domain is symptomatic of the disease of this society. As the years pass the power of government becomes more and more pervasive. It is a power to suffocate both people and causes. Those in power, whatever their politics, want only to perpetuate it. Now that the fences of the law and the tradition that has protected the press are broken down, the people are the victims. The First Amendment, as I read it, was designed precisely to prevent that tragedy.

JUSTICE STEWART, with whom JUSTICE BRENNAN and JUSTICE MARSHALL join, dissenting.

The Court's crabbed view of the First Amendment reflects a disturbing insensitivity to the critical role of an independent press in our society. The question whether a reporter has a constitutional right to a confidential relationship with his source is of first impression here, but the principles that should guide our decision are as basic as any to be found in the Constitution. While JUSTICE POWELL's enigmatic concurring opinion gives some hope of a more flexible view in the future, the Court in these cases holds that a newsman has no First Amendment right to protect his sources when called before a grand jury. The Court thus invites state and federal authorities to undermine the historic independence of the press by attempting to annex the journalistic profession as an investigative arm of government. Not only will this decision impair performance of the press' constitutionally protected functions, but it will, I am convinced, in the long run harm rather than help the administration of justice.

I respectfully dissent.

I

The reporter's constitutional right to a confidential relationship with his source stems from the broad societal interest in a full and free flow of information to the public. It is this basic concern that underlies the Constitution's protection of a free press.

The right to gather news implies, in turn, a right to a confidential relationship between a reporter and his source. This proposition follows as a matter of simple logic once three factual predicates are recognized: (1) newsmen require informants to gather news; (2) confidentiality—the promise or understanding that names or certain aspects of communications will be kept off the record—is essential to the creation and maintenance of a news-gathering relationship with informants; and (3) an unbridled subpoena power—the absence of a constitutional right protecting, in *any* way, a confidential relationship from compulsory process—will either deter sources from divulging information or deter reporters from gathering and publishing information.

It is obvious that informants are necessary to the news-gathering process as we know it today. If it is to perform its constitutional mission, the press must do far more than merely print public statements or publish prepared handouts. Familiarity with the people and circumstances involved in the myriad background activities that result in the final product called "news" is vital to complete and responsible journalism, unless the press is to be a captive mouthpiece of "newsmakers."

It is equally obvious that the promise of confidentiality may be a necessary prerequisite to a productive relationship between a newsman and his informants. An officeholder may fear his superior; a member of the bureaucracy, his associates; a dissident, the scorn of majority opinion. All may have information valuable to the public discourse, yet each may be willing to relate that information only in confidence to a reporter whom he trusts, either because of excessive caution or because of a reasonable fear of reprisals or censure for unorthodox views....

Finally, and most important, when governmental officials possess an unchecked power to compel newsmen to disclose information received in confidence, sources will clearly be deterred from giving information, and reporters will clearly be deterred from publishing it, because uncertainty about exercise of the power will lead to "self-censorship." ...

After today's decision, the potential informant can never be sure that his identity or off-the-record communications will not subsequently be revealed through the compelled testimony of a newsman. A public-spirited person inside government, who is not implicated in any crime, will now be fearful of revealing corruption or other governmental wrongdoing, because he will now know he can subsequently be identified by use of compulsory process. The potential source must, therefore, choose between risking exposure by giving information or avoiding the risk by remaining silent.

The reporter must speculate about whether contact with a controversial source or publication of controversial material will lead to a subpoena. In the event of a subpoena, under today's decision, the newsman will know that he must choose between being punished for contempt if he refuses to testify, or violating his profession's ethics and impairing his resourcefulness as a reporter if he discloses confidential information.

The impairment of the flow of news cannot, of course, be proved with scientific precision, as the Court seems to demand. Obviously, not every news-gathering relationship requires confidentiality. And it is difficult to pinpoint precisely how many relationships do require a promise or understanding of nondisclosure. But we have never before demanded that First Amendment rights rest on elaborate empirical studies demonstrating beyond any conceivable doubt that deterrent effects exist; we have never before required proof of the exact number of people potentially affected by governmental action, who would actually be dissuaded from engaging in First Amendment activity.

II

Posed against the First Amendment's protection of the newsman's confidential relationships in these cases is society's interest in the use of the grand jury to administer justice fairly and effectively....

Yet the longstanding rule making every person's evidence available to the grand jury is not absolute. The rule has been limited by the Fifth Amendment, the Fourth Amendment, and the evidentiary privileges of the common law. [Attorney-client, doctor-patient, and husband-wife privileges not to testify are common.] ... [A]ny exemption from the duty to testify before the grand jury "presupposes a very real interest to be protected."

Such an interest must surely be the First Amendment protection of a confidential relationship that I have discussed above in Part I. As noted there, this protection does not exist for the purely private interests of the newsman or his informant, nor even, at bottom, for the First Amendment interests of either partner in the news-gathering relationship. Rather, it functions to insure nothing less than democratic decisionmaking through the free flow of information to the public, ...

In striking the proper balance between the public interest in the efficient administration of justice and the First Amendment guarantee of the fullest flow of information, we must begin with the basic proposition that because of their "delicate and vulnerable" nature, ... and their transcendent importance for the just functioning of our society, First Amendment rights require special safeguards.

This Court has erected such safeguards when government, by legislative investigation or other investigative means, has attempted to pierce the shield of privacy inherent in freedom of association....

I believe the safeguards developed in our decisions involving governmental investigations must apply to the grand jury inquiries in these cases. Surely the function of the grand jury to aid in the enforcement of the law is no more important than the function of the legislature, and its committees, to make the law....

Accordingly, when a reporter is asked to appear before a grand jury and reveal confidences, I would hold that the government must (1) show that there is probable cause to believe that the newsman has information that is clearly relevant to a specific probable violation of law; (2) demonstrate that the information sought cannot be obtained by alternative means less destructive of First Amendment rights; and (3) demonstrate a compelling and overriding interest in the information.

This is not to say that a grand jury could not issue a subpoena until such a showing were made, and it is not to say that a newsman would be in any way privileged to ignore any subpoena that was issued. Obviously, before the government's burden to make such a showing were triggered, the reporter would have to move to quash the subpoena, asserting the basis on which he considered the particular relationship a confidential one.

The error in the Court's absolute rejection of First Amendment interests in these cases seems to me to be most profound. For in the name of advancing the administration of justice, the Court's decision, I think, will only impair the achievement of that goal. People entrusted with law enforcement responsibility, no less than private citizens, need general information relating to controversial social problems. Obviously, press reports have great value to government, even when the newsman cannot be compelled to testify before a grand jury. The sad paradox of the Court's position is that when a grand jury may exercise an unbridled subpoena power, and sources involved in sensitive matters become fearful of disclosing information, the newsman will not only cease to be a useful grand jury witness; he will cease to investigate and punish information about issues of public import. I cannot subscribe to such an anomalous result, for, in my view, the interests protected by the First Amendment are not antagonistic to the administration of justice. Rather, they can, in the long run, only be complementary, and for that reason must be given great "breathing space."

NOTES AND QUESTIONS

1. What exactly does *Branzburg* hold? Does it completely destroy the idea of First Amendment protection for reporters' confidential sources of information? Justice Powell's separate concurrence is obviously important, because he provided the crucial fifth vote. He indicates that a privilege would be appropriate in some situations and he advocates a case-by-case development of this issue.

2. The Supreme Court has not decided another reporter's privilege case since *Branzburg*, but there are several lower federal and state court decisions. Many of these grant a qualified privilege to reporters and cite *Branzburg* as authority. Others cite *Branzburg* as authority for the outright rejection of any reporter's privilege claim.

The lower court cases cannot all be reconciled, but there are some trends that help in analyzing the *Branzburg* decision itself. *Branzburg* seems to have settled the question of appearing before a grand jury. No lower court cases after *Branzburg* have granted a privilege not to appear at all before a grand jury. *Branzburg* also seems to have settled that a reporter who has witnessed a crime can't refuse to testify about what he saw. For example, in Bursey v. United States, 466 F.2d 1059 (9th Cir.1972), the same court that had quashed the Earl Caldwell subpoena held that reporters for a Black Panther newspaper must testify before a grand jury concerning criminal activity they had witnessed. Questions about their news-gathering activities, however, including sources and details of publication, were privileged because the government had not made a sufficient showing of necessity for them.

Other cases have also advocated the use of a balancing test to determine if a privilege should be granted. State v. St. Peter, 132 Vt. 266, 315 A.2d 254 (1974) held that the questions must be relevant and material on the issue of guilt or innocence and the answers not available from any other source before the claim of privilege would be denied in a discovery proceeding before a criminal trial. This test is less arduous for the government to meet than that proposed by Justice Stewart in his *Branzburg* dissent, for it does not require a showing of a compelling state interest in the material. However, even this less stringent test does prevent the kind of "fishing expedition" which Justice Stewart feared and which Justice Powell also seemed to want to avoid.

Thus, many courts still use some sort of a balancing test to decide on claims of privilege under the First Amendment. Only in factual situations that parallel the fact patterns of the three cases decided in *Branzburg* do courts feel obliged to reject a claim of privilege automatically.

3.   *Branzburg* deals only with the claim of *constitutional* protection of newsmen's confidential sources of information. It should be noted that many states have enacted specific "shield" statutes to protect reporters. These statutes vary in their coverage, some protecting only the identity of confidential sources, others also protecting the information received from such sources. These statutes have been difficult to draft, for there are questions as to who qualifies for the privilege, before which bodies it can be invoked, what constitutes waiver of the privilege and when exceptions should be allowed. State courts have tended to construe these provisions narrowly, as demonstrated by the *Branzburg* case itself, where Kentucky's shield statute, which is phrased in absolute terms, was held not to protect observations made by the reporter himself, but only the identity of the sources.

4.   The discussion engendered by the *Branzburg* decision and the problems encountered with the various state shield laws have led to calls for a uniform federal statute protecting newsmen. Congress has given serious consideration to such proposals, but none has yet passed. Is the present uncertain situation in regard to a reporter's privilege so serious as to demand federal legislation? Would it be possible to draft a bill that would adequately deal with all the varied aspects of this problem?

5.   In response to the Court of Appeals decision in *Caldwell,* the United States Justice Department adopted the following set of guidelines regarding subpoenas to the news media.

Department of Justice Guidelines for Subpoenas to the News Media August 10, 1970

FIRST: The Department of Justice recognizes that compulsory process in some circumstances may have a limiting effect on the exercise of First Amendment rights. In determining whether to request issuance of a subpoena to the press, the approach in every case must be to weigh that limiting effect against the public interest to be served in the fair administration of justice.

SECOND: The Department of Justice does not consider the press "an investigative arm of the government." Therefore, all reasonable attempts should be made to obtain information from non-press sources before there is any consideration of subpoenaing the press.

THIRD: It is the policy of the Department to insist that negotiations with the press be attempted in all cases in which a subpoena is contemplated. These negotiations should attempt to accommodate the interests of the grand jury with the interests of the news media. In these negotiations, where the nature of the investigation permits, the government should make clear what its needs are in a particular case as well as its willingness to respond to particular problems of the news media.

FOURTH: If negotiations fail, no Justice Department official should request, or make any arrangements for, a subpoena to the press without the express authorization of the Attorney General. If a subpoena is obtained under such circumstances without this authorization, the Department will—as a matter of course—move to quash the subpoena without prejudice to its rights subsequently to request the subpoena upon the proper authorization.

FIFTH: In requesting the Attorney General's authorization for a subpoena, the following principles will apply: A. There should be sufficient reason to believe that a crime has occurred, from disclosures by non-press sources. The Department does not approve of utilizing the press as a spring board for investigations. B. There should be sufficient reason to believe that the information sought is essential to a successful investigation— particularly with reference to directly establishing guilt or innocence. The subpoena should not be used to obtain peripheral, non-essential or speculative information. C. The government should have unsuccessfully attempted to obtain the information from alternative non-press sources. D. Authorization requests for subpoenas should normally be limited to the verification of published information and to such surrounding circumstances as relate to the accuracy of the published information. E. Great caution should be observed in requesting subpoena authorization by the Attorney General for unpublished information, or where an orthodox First Amendment defense is raised or where a serious claim of confidentiality is alleged. F. Even subpoena authorization requests for publicly disclosed information should be treated with care because, for example, cameramen have recently been subjected to harassment on the grounds that their photographs will become available to the government. G. In any event, subpoenas should, wherever possible, be directed at material information regarding a limited subject matter, should cover a reasonably limited period of time, and should avoid requiring production of a large volume of unpublished material. They should give reasonable and timely notice of the demand for documents. These are general rules designed to cover the great majority of cases. It must always be remembered that emergencies and other unusual situations may develop where a subpoena request to the Attorney General may be submitted which does not exactly conform to these guidelines.

The Justice Department claims that these guidelines have encouraged negotiations between reporters and prosecutors and that subpoenas have only been requested when there is a compelling need for them. Would this kind of voluntary approach be preferable to a statute? Would it ever be possible to get the officials of all fifty states to agree on a voluntary plan?

6.   What happens when a reporter's claim of privilege conflicts with the guarantee of a fair trial for a criminal defendant? The prominent case of New York Times reporter Myron Farber raised some of these issues. Dr. Jascalevich was prosecuted for murdering his patients with curare injections. Since the prosecution resulted in part from articles written by Farber in the New York Times, defense attorneys believed Farber had information that might be vital in defending their client. Farber was ordered to produce his interview notes and other materials, to be inspected by the judge to determine whether they did, in fact, contain material relevant to the defense. Farber was jailed for contempt, and the New York Times fined, when Farber refused to comply. In denying a stay of the contempt order, Justice White remarked that no Supreme Court decision had given reporters any constitutional privilege to refuse to supply information vital to the prosecution or defense of a criminal case. New York Times v. Jascalevich, 439 U.S. 1301 (1978). Farber, incidentally, never complied with the subpoena, but was eventually released after Dr. Jascalevich's trial ended in his acquittal. What if Dr. Jascalevich had been convicted and Myron Farber had withheld information crucial to his defense?

7.   The First Amendment permits a government official or public figure to recover damages for false, defamatory statements, if the statements were deliberately false or made with reckless disregard of truth. (See Chapter 9, Section I.) Suppose, in a libel case, the reporter who wrote the defamatory story claims that he reasonably relied on an informer's tip, but refuses to disclose the informer's name or otherwise identify him. Can the reporter be required, in this case, to identify the informer? A related question was raised in Herbert v. Lando, 441 U.S. 153 (1979). Herbert was a retired Army officer who claimed he was defamed by a CBS documentary on Vietnamese war atrocities. In pretrial proceedings in Herbert's libel suit against CBS, the program's producer was asked what his opinion had been about some of the material gathered by him, and about his conversations with editorial colleagues during preparation of the documentation. The Court held that so long as a relevant question in the libel suit was whether the producer honestly believed statements in the documentary were true, and the questions asked the producer had a bearing on his state of mind, there could be no First Amendment privilege to refuse to answer the questions. Justice White's opinion did, however, indicate that there might be a First Amendment privilege to refuse to answer questions about the editorial process when the questions were asked in a "private or official examination merely to satisfy curiosity or to serve some general end such as the public interest."

Part Three

FREEDOM OF RELIGION

Chapter XVII

HISTORY AND RATIONALE OF THE RELIGION CLAUSES OF THE FIRST AMENDMENT

I. HISTORY OF THE RELIGION CLAUSES

THE SITUATION AT THE TIME THE CONSTITUTION WAS ADOPTED*

Strictly speaking, the American experiment of freedom and separation was not established in the First Amendment command that "Congress shall make no law respecting an establishment of religion or prohibiting the free exercise thereof." That experiment had been launched four years earlier, when the founders of the republic carefully withheld from the new national government any power to deal with religion. As Madison said, the national government had no "jurisdiction" over religion or any "shadow of right to intermeddle" with it.

The First Amendment, then, did not take away or abridge any power of the national government; its intent was to make express the absence of power. The historian George Bancroft, in a letter to Philip Schaff, stated:

> Congress from the beginning was as much without the power to make a law respecting the establishment of religion as it is now that the amendment has passed.

[The situation was very different in the states, however.]

. . .

The relationship of religion to government in the original state constitutions or organic laws at the time of the adoption of the Federal Constitution may be summarized as follows:

> Two out of thirteen, Virginia and Rhode Island, conceded full freedom;

---

* Leo Pfeffer, Church, State, and Freedom, Beacon Press, 1953, pp. 106, 115. Reprinted with permission.

One, New York, gave full freedom except for requiring naturalized citizens to abjure foreign allegiance and subjection in all matters ecclesiastical as well as civil;

Six, New Hampshire, Connecticut, New Jersey, Georgia, North and South Carolina, adhered to religious establishments;

Two, Delaware and Maryland, demanded Christianity;

Four, Pennsylvania, Delaware, North and South Carolina, required assent to the divine inspiration of the Bible;

Two, Pennsylvania and South Carolina, imposed a belief in heaven and hell;

Three, New York, Delaware, and South Carolina, excluded ministers from civil office;

Four, Maryland, Virginia, North Carolina, and Georgia, excluded ministers from the legislature;

Two, Pennsylvania and South Carolina, emphasized belief in one eternal God;

One, Delaware, required assent to the doctrine of the Trinity;

Five, New Hampshire, Massachusetts, Connecticut, Maryland, and South Carolina, insisted on Protestantism;

One, South Carolina, still referred to religious "toleration."

. . .

ADOPTION OF THE FIRST AMENDMENT*

Not simply an established church, but any law respecting an establishment of religion is forbidden. The Amendment was broadly but not loosely phrased. It is the compact and exact summation of its author's views formed during his long struggle for religious freedom. In Madison's own words characterizing Jefferson's Bill for Establishing Religious Freedom, the guaranty he put in our national charter, like the bill he piloted through the Virginia Assembly, was "a Model of technical precision, and perspicuous brevity." Madison could not have confused "church" and "religion," or "an established church" and "an establishment of religion."

The Amendment's purpose was not to strike merely at the official establishment of a single sect, creed or religion, outlawing only a formal relation such as had prevailed in England and some of the colonies. Necessarily it was to uproot all such relationships. But the object was broader than separating church and state in this narrow sense. It was to create a complete and permanent separation of the spheres of religious activity and civil authority by comprehensively forbidding every form of public aid or support for religion. In proof the Amendment's wording and history unite with this Court's consistent utterances whenever attention has been fixed directly upon the question.

---

* Excerpt from the dissenting opinion of Justice Rutledge in Everson v. Board of Education, 330 U.S. 1, 28 (1947).

"Religion" appears only once in the Amendment. But the word governs two prohibitions and governs them alike. It does not have two meanings, one narrow to forbid "an establishment" and another, much broader, for securing "the free exercise thereof." "Thereof" brings down "religion" with its entire and exact content, no more and no less, from the first into the second guaranty, so that Congress and now the states are as broadly restricted concerning the one as they are regarding the other.

No one would claim today that the Amendment is constricted, in "prohibiting the free exercise" of religion, to securing the free exercise of some formal or creedal observance, of one sect or of many. It secures all forms of religious expression, creedal, sectarian or nonsectarian, wherever and however taking place, except conduct which trenches upon the like freedoms of others or clearly and presently endangers the community's good order and security. For the protective purposes of this phase of the basic freedom, street preaching, oral or by distribution of literature, has been given "the same high estate under the First Amendment as ... worship in the churches and preaching from the pulpits." And on this basis parents have been held entitled to send their children to private, religious schools.... Accordingly, daily religious education commingled with secular is "religion" within the guaranty's comprehensive scope. So are religious training and teaching in whatever form. The word connotes the broadest content, determined not by the form or formality of the teaching or where it occurs, but by its essential nature regardless of those details.

"Religion" has the same broad significance in the twin prohibition concerning "an establishment." The Amendment was not duplicitous. "Religion" and "establishment" were not used in any formal or technical sense. The prohibition broadly forbids state support, financial or other, of religion in any guise, form or degree. It outlaws all use of public funds for religious purposes.

No provision of the Constitution is more closely tied to or given content by its generating history than the religious clause of the First Amendment. It is at once the refined product and the terse summation of that history. The history includes not only Madison's authorship and the proceedings before the First Congress, but also the long and intensive struggle for religious freedom in America, more especially in Virginia, of which the Amendment was the direct culmination. In the documents of the times, particularly of Madison, who was leader in the Virginia struggle before he became the Amendment's sponsor, but also in the writings of Jefferson and others and in the issues which engendered them is to be found irrefutable confirmation of the Amendment's sweeping content.

For Madison, as also for Jefferson, religious freedom was the crux of the struggle for freedom in general. Madison was coauthor with George Mason of the religious clause in Virginia's great Declaration of Rights of 1776. He is credited with changing it from a mere statement of the principle of tolerance to the first official legislative pronouncement that freedom of conscience and religion are inherent rights of the individual.

He sought also to have the Declaration expressly condemn the existing Virginia establishment. But the forces supporting it were then too strong.

Accordingly Madison yielded on this phase but not for long. At once he resumed the fight, continuing it before succeeding legislative sessions. As a member of the General Assembly in 1779 he threw his full weight behind Jefferson's historic Bill for Establishing Religious Freedom.* That bill was a prime phase of Jefferson's broad program of democratic reform undertaken on his return from the Continental Congress in 1776 and submitted for the General Assembly's consideration in 1779 as his proposed revised Virginia code. With Jefferson's departure for Europe in 1784, Madison became the Bill's prime sponsor. Enactment failed in successive legislatures from its introduction in June, 1779, until its adoption in January, 1786. But during all this time the fight for religious freedom moved forward in Virginia on various fronts with growing intensity. Madison led throughout, against Patrick Henry's powerful opposing leadership until Henry was elected governor in November, 1784.

The climax came in the legislative struggle of 1784–1785 over the Assessment Bill. This was nothing more nor less than a taxing measure for the support of religion, designed to revive the payment of tithes suspended since 1777. So long as it singled out a particular sect for preference it incurred the active and general hostility of dissentient groups. It was broadened to include them, with the result that some subsided temporarily in their opposition. As altered, the bill gave to each taxpayer the privilege of designating which church should receive his share of the tax. In default of designation the legislature applied it to pious uses. But what is of the utmost significance here, "in its final form the bill left the taxpayer the option of giving his tax to education."

Madison was unyielding at all times, opposing with all his vigor the general and nondiscriminatory as he had the earlier particular and discriminatory assessments proposed. The modified Assessment Bill passed second reading in December, 1784, and was all but enacted. Madison and his followers, however, maneuvered deferment of final consideration until November, 1785. And before the Assembly reconvened in the fall he issued his historic Memorial and Remonstrance.

This is Madison's complete, though not his only, interpretation of religious liberty. It is a broadside attack upon all forms of "establishment" of religion, both general and particular, nondiscriminatory or selective. Reflecting ... the many legislative conflicts over the Assessment Bill and the Bill for Establishing Religious Freedom ... the Remonstrance is at once the most concise and the most accurate state-

---

* This bill provided:

"Well aware that Almighty God hath created the mind free; ... that to compel a man to furnish contributions of money for the propagation of opinions which he disbelieves, is sinful and tyrannical;

"*We, the General Assembly, do enact,* That no man shall be compelled to frequent or support any religious worship, place, or ministry whatsoever, nor shall be enforced, restrained, molested, or burthened in his body or goods, nor shall otherwise suffer, on account of his religious opinions or belief...."

ment of the views of the First Amendment's author concerning what is "an establishment of religion." . . .

The Remonstrance, stirring up a storm of popular protest, killed the Assessment Bill. It collapsed in committee shortly before Christmas, 1785. With this, the way was cleared at last for enactment of Jefferson's Bill for Establishing Religious Freedom. Madison promptly drove it through in January of 1786, seven years from the time it was first introduced. This dual victory substantially ended the fight over establishments, settling the issue against them.

The next year Madison became a member of the Constitutional Convention. Its work done, he fought valiantly to secure the ratification of its great product in Virginia as elsewhere, and nowhere else more effectively. Madison was certain in his own mind that under the Constitution "there is not a shadow of right in the general government to intermeddle with religion" and that "this subject is, for the honor of America, perfectly free and unshackled. The government has no jurisdiction over it. . . ." Nevertheless he pledged that he would work for a Bill of Rights, including a specific guaranty of religious freedom, and Virginia, with other states, ratified the Constitution on this assurance.

Ratification thus accomplished, Madison was sent to the first Congress. There he went at once about performing his pledge to establish freedom for the nation as he had done in Virginia. Within a little more than three years from his legislative victory at home he had proposed and secured the submission and ratification of the First Amendment as the first article of our Bill of Rights.

All the great instruments of the Virginia struggle for religious liberty thus became warp and woof of our constitutional tradition, not simply by the course of history, but by the common unifying force of Madison's life, thought and sponsorship. He epitomized the whole of that tradition in the Amendment's compact, but nonetheless comprehensive, phrasing.

As the Remonstrance discloses throughout, Madison opposed every form and degree of official relation between religion and civil authority. For him religion was a wholly private matter beyond the scope of civil power either to restrain or to support. Denial or abridgment of religious freedom was a violation of rights both of conscience and of natural equality. State aid was no less obnoxious or destructive to freedom and to religion itself than other forms of state interference. "Establishment" and "free exercise" were correlative and coextensive ideas, representing only different facets of the single great and fundamental freedom. The Remonstrance, following the Virginia statute's example, referred to the history of religious conflicts and the effects of all sorts of establishments, current and historical, to suppress religion's free exercise. With Jefferson, Madison believed that to tolerate any fragment of establishment would be by so much to perpetuate restraint upon that freedom. Hence he sought to tear out the institution not partially but root and branch, and to bar its return forever.

In no phase was he more unrelentingly absolute than in opposing state support or aid by taxation. Not even "three pence" contribution was thus to be exacted from any citizen for such a purpose.... Tithes had been the lifeblood of establishment before and after other compulsions disappeared. Madison and his coworkers made no exceptions or abridgments to the complete separation they created. Their objection was not to small tithes. It was to any tithes whatsoever. "If it were lawful to impose a small tax for religion, the admission would pave the way for oppressive levies." Not the amount but "the principle of assessment was wrong." And the principle was as much to prevent "the interference of law in religion" as to restrain religious intervention in political matters. In this field the authors of our freedom would not tolerate "the first experiment on our liberties" or "wait till usurped power had strengthened itself by exercise, and entangled the question in precedents." Nor should we.

. . .

By contrast with the Virginia history, the congressional debates on consideration of the Amendment reveal only sparse discussion, reflecting the fact that the essential issues had been settled. Indeed the matter had become so well understood as to have been taken for granted in all but formal phrasing. Hence, the only enlightening reference shows concern, not to preserve any power to use public funds in aid of religion, but to prevent the Amendment from outlawing private gifts inadvertently by virtue of the breadth of its wording.

NOTE

There are several difficulties in seeking answers to questions about contemporary institutions that were either rudimentary or nonexistent when the Clauses were adopted. For example, most of the problems under the Establishment Clause have involved religious practices in the public schools or public aid to parochial schools. First Amendment history may be an uncertain guide, since the current pattern of universal free public education through high school did not emerge until the Nineteenth Century. Second is the fact that, by its terms, the First Amendment ("Congress shall make no law ...") was applicable only to the federal government. In the Eighteenth Century, that government performed relatively few functions, and almost none that touched the daily lives of citizens.

It can, of course, still be relevant that a particular practice *has* been a long historical tradition. History probably played a large part in the Court's decision that tax exemptions for churches did not violate the Establishment Clause. Walz v. Tax Commission, 397 U.S. 664 (1970). In Marsh v. Chambers, 463 U.S. 783 (1983), Chief Justice Burger's opinion for the Court relied on history to decide that a paid state legislative chaplain did not violate the Establishment Clause. Justice Brennan's dissent objected that "in a wide variety of constitutional contexts that the practices that were in place at the time any particular guarantee was enacted into the Constitution do not necessarily fix forever the meaning" of a constitutional guarantee.

There was remarkably little controversy over the proposition that the Establishment Clause had been "incorporated" as a limitation on the powers of the states by the Fourteenth Amendment. (See Chapter 1, Section V.) Although the Court divided 5–4 on the precise question of paying transportation expenses of parochial school pupils in Everson v. Board of Education, 330 U.S. 1 (1947), the Court was unanimous in concluding that the Fourteenth Amendment had "incorporated" the Establishment Clause. Interestingly, there was almost no discussion of the issue. Was this point decided too summarily?

At the time of the adoption of the Bill of Rights, there were established state churches in the United States. Since the First Amendment applied only to the federal government and did not impose any restrictions on the state governments, can it be argued that a primary purpose of the Establishment Clause was to prevent Congress from interfering with established state churches? (Note the language of the First Amendment. Congress is not forbidden to establish a church, but is forbidden to pass all laws "respecting" establishment of religion.)

IMPACT OF THE FIRST AMENDMENT ON RELIGIOUS ESTABLISHMENTS IN THE STATES*

As the first step towards an analysis of law it seems important that the principal questions of history with which the Court has been concerned should be identified.

The questions are two. The first concerns the interpretation of the religious clause of the First Amendment: "Congress shall make no law respecting an establishment of religion, or prohibiting the free exercise thereof . . ." The second—and in many ways more important—concerns the effect that adoption of the Fourteenth Amendment had on the power of the states. . . .

. . .

The First Amendment [as] interpreted [by Justice Rutledge] would serve two purposes. In the first place, it would protect the individual's conscience from every form of Congressional violation, whether by means of legislation with respect to an establishment of religion or by more direct methods. In the second place, it would impose a disability upon the national government to adopt laws with respect to establishments whether or not their consequence would be to infringe individual rights of conscience.

To find this second purpose in the First Amendment involves, necessarily I think, the admission that the Amendment is something more than a charter of individual liberties. In making that admission one is emphasizing a fact which has too frequently been overlooked—that the Bill of Rights as a whole, and the First Amendment in particular, reflect not only a philosophy of freedom but a theory of federalism. We often forget that the framers were as much concerned with safeguarding the

* Mark DeWolfe Howe, Religion and the Free Society: The Constitutional Question, Center for Democratic Institutions/Fund for the Republic Inc., 1960, pp. 50–55. Reprinted with permission.

powers of the states as they were with protecting the immunities of the people. . . .

. . .

... A few scholars and individual Justices of the Supreme Court have contended that the framers of the Fourteenth Amendment intended that its adoption should transform all the specific limitations on federal power found in the Bill of Rights into rigid limitations on state authority. . . .

A majority of the Court has never been willing to accept such a mechanistic and revolutionary interpretation of the Fourteenth Amendment. Instead the Court has taken the view that though some of the specific prohibitions of the Bill of Rights have become applicable to the states, there are others which the states are not compelled to respect. . . .*

It is not surprising that the Supreme Court, after a period of some uncertainty, came to accept the view that the First Amendment's specific guarantee of freedom of speech and press had been made binding on the states by the Fourteenth Amendment. When that principle was settled it was clear that the free exercise of religion must enjoy similar protection—and it was given that protection with energetic vigor. . . .

... By its re-examination [in *Everson*] of the purposes of the First Amendment the Court imposed, perhaps quite properly, special limitations on the powers of the national government which, as I have said, gain their strength from concepts of federalism rather than from principles of individual liberty. Yet it then proceeded, without discussion, to make those special, non-libertarian limitations on the national government effective against the states as if they were essential to the scheme of ordered liberty prescribed by the due process clause of the Fourteenth Amendment. The Court did not seem to be aware of the fact that some legislative enactments respecting an establishment of religion affect most remotely, if at all, the personal rights of religious liberty.

The Supreme Court of the United States has not yet re-examined its own interpretations of history either as they relate to the original meaning of the First Amendment or as they apply to the incorporation of the non-establishment clause of the Fourteenth. I find it hard to believe that a re-examination of the first matter is of critical importance. I would suggest, however, that public and judicial attention may well be directed to the second issue. If that effort should be made it seems to me that we might find ourselves generally satisfied with the resolution which a respect for history might compel us to adopt. We might find ourselves allowing the states to take such action in aid of religion as does not appreciably affect the religious or other constitutional rights of individuals while condemning all state action which unreasonably restricts the exercise and enjoyment of other constitutional rights.

* There has been considerable change in the law as to how much of the Bill of Rights is "incorporated" into the Fourteenth Amendment since Professor Howe wrote in 1958. (See Chapter 1, Section V.)

NOTE

Another commentator, Leo Pfeffer, stressing the unitary nature of the guarantees of the religion clauses, argued that the states should be equally bound by both the religious freedom and the non-establishment clauses. In support of this analysis, he pointed out:*

Though not required by the First Amendment either to separate church and state or to secure freedom of religion, all the states assumed the dual obligation in their own constitutions. At the time of the adoption of the First Amendment in 1791, all the states guaranteed substantial religious liberty, though some vestiges of colonial intolerance—chiefly political disabilities of Catholics and Jews—remained for a while in a few states. But even in those states the constitutional and statutory restrictions were dead letters for many years before they were formally repealed.

Nor was disestablishment in the states long in coming. When the First Amendment was adopted in 1791, only four of the thirteen States—Massachusetts, Connecticut, New Hampshire, and Maryland—retained any substantial establishment in their basic laws, and in none of these was the establishment exclusive; in each case the taxpayer could choose the religious denomination that was to receive his tax. . . .

Massachusetts was the last state to give up its establishment. It was not until 1833 that a constitutional amendment was adopted which restricted religion to voluntary support.

The evolution of the American principle may, then, be said to have been completed in 1833. The rate of its development was not uniform in all states. Massachusetts arrived in 1833 at the point from which neighboring Rhode Island had started almost two centuries earlier. But by and large a general pattern is discernible: a gradual extension of the areas of religious liberty, first to include all Protestant sects, then all Christians, then all believers in God, and finally elimination of all religious tests. Starting and culminating later, but following more or less the same pattern, was the progress of disestablishment: a gradual extension of the area of tax support, first to include all Protestant sects, then all Christians, then a provision allowing non-Christians to assign their tax to general education or charity (which was the only practicable method in view of the minute number of professed non-Christians), and finally the abolition of all tax support.

It is important to note that in no case did the development end until complete disestablishment was arrived at: no state stopped with according freedom of worship, or indeed with less than complete prohibition of tax support of any and all religions. Moreover, every state that entered the union after the Constitution was adopted incorporated both prohibitions in its

* Leo Pfeffer, Church, State & Freedom, Beacon Press, 1953, pp. 125–127.

constitution or basic laws. In no case was there any attempt to establish any denomination or religion; on the contrary, in varying language but with a single spirit, all states expressly forbade such attempt. This deliberate decision was not motivated by indifference to religion: most of the states had been settled by deeply religious pioneers. Nor was it dictated by purely practical considerations; many of the states had a population far more homogeneous religiously than Canada, Holland, or even England. Nor was the decision required by the Federal government: up to 1868 at least, nothing in the Constitution prevented any state, after its admission to the union, from establishing religion or indeed from restricting freedom of worship. The decision was in all cases voluntary; and it was made because the unitary principle of separation and freedom was as integral a part of American democracy as republicanism, representative government, and freedom of expression.

It is clear, therefore, that by 1868, when the Fourteenth Amendment was adopted, the principle of freedom and separation was firmly established in American life.

In Wallace v. Jaffree, 472 U.S. 38 (1985), the federal trial court concluded that the Supreme Court in *Everson* had been wrong in its assumption that the Establishment Clause operated to bind the states. Predictably, the Supreme Court disagreed. In reaffirming its conclusion that the Establishment Clause imposes identical restraints on state and national governments, the Court emphasized that the Free Exercise Clause and the Establishment Clause were "complementary components of a broader concept of individual freedom of mind" because "the individual's freedom to choose his own creed is the counterpart of his right to refrain from accepting the creed established by the majority." If it was conceded that freedom of religious conscience was a "central liberty" enforceable against the states, the prohibition of establishment was part of that liberty.

In a lengthy dissenting opinion, Justice Rehnquist argued from history in *Wallace* that the Court's conclusion in *Everson* was wrong. He said that James Madison thought that the Establishment Clause was "designed to prohibit the establishment of a national religion, and perhaps to prevent discrimination among sects. He did not see it as requiring neutrality on the part of government between religion and irreligion." In the more than fifty years since the *Everson* decision, Justice Rehnquist has been the only Supreme Court Justice to take that position.

II. THE RATIONALE OF THE RELIGION CLAUSES

The Establishment and Free Exercise Clauses of the First Amendment were not designed to serve contradictory purposes. They have a single goal—to promote freedom of individual religious beliefs and practices. In simplest terms, the Free Exercise Clause prohibits government from inhibiting religious belief with *penalties* for religious beliefs and practice, while the Establishment Clause prohibits government from inhibiting religious belief with *rewards* for religious beliefs and practices. In other words, the two religion clauses were intended to deny government the power to use either the carrot or the stick to influence individual religious beliefs and practices.

There is, however, an uneasy tension between the two clauses, especially if the Free Exercise Clause is interpreted to forbid *all* government penalties or detriments to religious groups while the Establishment Clause is interpreted to forbid *all* government rewards to religious groups. For example, consider the action of city officials who deny the right to use a park to hold a religious meeting. Can the Free Speech and Free Exercise Clauses of the Constitution *require* city officials to allow the use of public property for religious services at the very same time the Establishment Clause *prohibits* city officials from allowing religious groups the use of a public auditorium?

Consider, for example, the decision in Widmar v. Vincent, 454 U.S. 263 (1981). The University of Missouri at Kansas City allowed student groups to meet in University facilities. But it denied a religious group of students permission to meet in University buildings pursuant to a regulation that denied use of University facilities for "religious worship or religious teaching." Despite the University's argument that it was trying to avoid violating the Establishment Clause in the indirect financing of religious worship or training, the Court held that the University had violated the Free Speech Clause by excluding the group from a "public forum" based on the content of the group's intended speech.

What is needed is a theory of the two Religion Clauses that reconciles them. Is there such a theory? Consider the much-debated theory propounded by Professor Philip B. Kurland in the following excerpt.

RECONCILING THE ESTABLISHMENT AND FREE EXERCISE CLAUSES*

Like most commands of our Constitution, the religion clauses of the first amendment are not statements of abstract principles. History, not logic, explains their inclusion in the Bill of Rights; necessity, not merely morality, justifies their presence there....

. . .

Religious toleration, summed up in the second of the two clauses, was ... necessary to preserve the peace. Separation, represented by the first of the two clauses, was necessary to make such religious freedom a reality. But the separation clause had a greater function than the assurance of toleration of dissenting religious beliefs and practices. To suggest but two lessons of the evils resulting from the alliance of church and state, there was abundant evidence of the contributions of the churches to the warfare among nations as well as the conflict within them and equally obvious was the inhibition on scientific endeavor that followed from the acceptance by the state of church dogma.... But admittedly separation was a new concept in practice. Toleration had a

* Philip B. Kurland, Of Church and State and the Supreme Court, University of Chicago Law Review, 1961, vol. 29, pp. 2, 4–6.

long English history; separation—conceived in the English writings of
Roger Williams—had its beginnings as an historical fact only on the
shores of this continent. It is justified in Williams' terms by the necessity
for keeping the state out of the affairs of the church, lest the church be
subordinated to the state; in Jeffersonian terms its function is to keep
the church out of the business of government, lest the government be
subordinated to the church. Limited powers of government were not
instituted to expand the realm of power of religious organizations, but
rather in favor of freedom of action and thought by the people.

Nor were these two concepts closed systems at the time of the
adoption of the first amendment. The objectives of the provisions were
clear, but the means of their attainment were still to be developed and,
indeed, are still in the course of development. Thus, like the other great
clauses of the Constitution, the religion clauses cannot now be confined
to the application they might have received in 1789.

The utilization or application of these clauses in conjunction is
difficult. For if the command is that inhibitions not be placed by the
state on religious activity, it is equally forbidden the state to confer
favors upon religious activity. These commands would be impossible of
effectuation unless they are read ... to mean that religion may not be
used as a basis for classification for purposes of governmental action,
whether that action be the conferring of rights or privileges or the
imposition of duties or obligations.... It must be recognized, however,
that this statement of the "neutral" principle of equality, that religion
cannot supply a basis for classification of governmental action, still
leaves many problems unanswered. Not the least of them flows from the
fact that the actions of the state must be carefully scrutinized to assure
that classifications that purport to relate to other matters are not really
classifications in terms of religion. "[C]lassification in abstract terms can
always be carried to the point at which, in fact, the class singled out
consists only of particular known persons or even a single individual. It
must be admitted that, in spite of many ingenious attempts to solve this
problem, no entirely satisfactory criterion has been found that would
always tell us what kind of classification is compatible with equality
before the law."

... [I]t might be desirable to repeat two propositions. First, the
thesis proposed here as the proper construction of the religion clauses of
the first amendment is that the freedom and separation clauses should
be read as a single precept that government cannot utilize religion as a
standard for action or inaction because these clauses prohibit classification in terms of religion either to confer a benefit or to impose a burden.
Second, the principle offered is meant to provide a starting point for
solutions to problems brought before the Court, not a mechanical answer
to them.

NOTE

Professor Kurland's theory is, simply, that government cannot impose penalties, or give favors, if the basis for doing either of these things
is religion. Consider the case of use of a city park by Jehovah's Witnesses
for a religious meeting. If the city allows all groups to use the parks for

meetings, there is no violation of the Establishment Clause since religion is not the basis for granting or denying permission to use the park. If, however, the park is made available only for use of religious groups, or only for religious meetings, there is a violation of the Establishment Clause since religion is the criterion by which it is decided whether a group will be allowed to use the park. And, finally, if the park is made available for use of all groups *except* those wishing to use the park for religious meetings, under Professor Kurland's theory there is a violation of the Free Exercise Clause since religion is the basis for granting or denying permission.

Debate over the meaning of the Religion Clauses, particularly the Establishment Clause, has not existed in a vacuum. As you are no doubt aware, a major political issue in this country has been public aid to parochial schools. If Professor Kurland's thesis is consistently applied, a program of public funding of all private schools is not rendered unconstitutional merely because some of those private schools are religious schools, since religion is not the criterion by which it is decided whether a school receives aid. (Does it make a difference if *most* of the private schools *are* parochial schools?) On the other hand, a system of aid to private schools that denied aid to parochial schools *would* violate the Free Exercise Clause since religion would be the basis for denying aid to some private schools. It is not surprising that groups promoting aid to religious schools looked upon Professor Kurland's thesis and found it good.

Nor is it surprising that Professor Kurland's thesis came under attack from groups opposing the principle of public aid to religious schools. Mr. Leo Pfeffer, a lawyer and a longtime opponent of aid to religious schools, argued that many laws and practices would violate the Constitution if Professor Kurland's thesis were accepted in interpreting the Free Exercise and Establishment Clauses.

MUST GOVERNMENT BE "RELIGION–BLIND"?*

Let us now see how the religion-blind test would work in actual operation in a number of instances of church-state relationships. I list these in no particular order, but simply as they come to mind.

1.　Polygamy. This one is easy. A state would have to repeal its antipolygamy laws or enforce them equally against all persons irrespective of religious convictions. Since no state has indicated any desire to exempt religiously motivated polygamy from its penal laws, application of the religion-blind principle would have no practical consequence.

2.　Flag saluting. This too is easy. A state may not exempt Jehovah's Witnesses from saluting the flag in the public schools but may make the ceremony voluntary as to all children. . . .

3.　Faith healing. Here we run into trouble. Exemptions of Christian Scientists and other practitioners of faith healing from laws forbidding unlicensed practice of medicine are common among the states. Under Professor Kurland's test the states would be required either to

* Leo Pfeffer, Religion–Blind Government, Stanford Law Review, 1963, vol. 15, pp. 401, 406. Reprinted with permission.

eliminate the exemption or repeal their laws requiring a license to practice the art of healing. . . .

. . .

5. Conscientious objection. Congress has exempted from compulsory military service those whose "religious training and belief" prohibit such participation. If Professor Kurland prevails, exemption must be taken away from religious objectors or granted equally to political and philosophical objectors. Farewell, conscientious objection.

6. Military exemption for ministers and divinity students. Goodbye to this.

7. State aid to sectarian institutions. Practically every state in the union has a constitutional provision that either expressly or impliedly prohibits the appropriation of public money to schools controlled by religious organizations. Some forbid the grant of public funds to any institution not under the control of the state. These would have no problem under the Kurland thesis. Others, however, grant funds to private secular institutions but not to sectarian ones. Professor Kurland would require these states to choose between giving state funds to all private institutions, sectarian as well as secular, or to none. I would guess that most of the states would elect to give funds to none.

8. Tax exemption. Even if the federal government and the states would elect to grant subsidies to religious institutions along with secular ones, the amounts so gained would be minute compared to what would be lost by way of withdrawal of tax exemption. The federal government and every state in the Union exempts from taxation properties owned by religious organizations and used for religious purposes. Even more important, they allow taxpayers to deduct from their reportable income contributions made to religious organizations. American churches have managed to survive without direct subsidies from government. They would find it more difficult to do so if tax exemption and credit for contributions were taken away. Yet this would be required under the religion-blind test unless some broader classification, such as nonprofit, were substituted. The cost to governments, federal and state, if all property owned by nonprofit organizations were tax-exempt and if contributions to them were deductible might well be prohibitive, leaving the governments with no alternative but to withdraw the privilege as to all institutions other than those which are exclusively charitable or educational.

. . .

10. Sunday laws. Some twenty-one states grant some kind of exemption from the operation of their compulsory Sunday laws to persons whose religious convictions require them to abstain from labor or secular business on a day other than Sunday. Here again, Professor Kurland would require the states either to repeal the Sunday laws, eliminate the exemptions entirely, or extend them to anyone who for any reason prefers to abstain from business or labor on a day other than Sunday. Thus ends Sabbatarian exemptions.

11.   Religious practices in the public schools. It need hardly be noted that under the Kurland doctrine no state-sponsored prayers, denominational or nondenominational, voluntary or mandatory, would be permissible in public schools. Nor would devotional Bible reading, singing of religious hymns, or celebration of religious holidays be permissible. . . .

12.   Released time. As was indicated above, the religion-blind mandate would require public schools to drop their programs of released time for religious education off school premises or open them up to nonreligious education. In either case this would mark the end of released time. . . .

. . .

14.   References to God in official documents or proceedings. Outlawed, too, would be all references to God in oaths of office, state constitutions, presidential resolutions, the pledge of allegiance, the national motto, currency and postage stamps, etc. . . .

. . .

18.   Adoption and custody of children. Many states provide that in making orders of adoption or granting custody of children the court must prefer applicants of the same religious faith as the children whose adoption or custody is sought. . . . I do not see how these laws could survive under a religion-blind doctrine.

19.   School absence on holy days. In a number of states, either by statute or regulation, no punishment may be imposed upon a child or his parent if the child absents himself from public school on a day holy to him. This would clearly be an unconstitutional classification based on religion.

20.   Alcoholic beverage sales near churches. Many states, by statute or regulation, forbid the sale of alcoholic beverages within specified distances of churches—again an unconstitutional classification based on religion.

NOTES AND QUESTIONS

1.   Professor Kurland conceded that his "religion-blind" principle was not an easy rule of thumb for the decision of all cases. "[T]he principle . . . is meant to provide a starting point for solutions to problems . . ., not a mechanical answer to them." Mr. Pfeffer replied: "[T]his disclaimer is essentially meaningless or the principle itself is meaningless. If Professor Kurland intends by it that the principle should be applied except where the application leads to undesirable results, then we have no principle at all, and certainly none superior to the subjective . . . weighing test under which the Court evaluates the competing interests of individual conscience and the community's needs."

2.   In the examples given by Mr. Pfeffer, is he correct in the results he says will be required by Professor Kurland's thesis? Are all of those results "undesirable results," or are some of the laws and practices mentioned by Mr. Pfeffer in violation of the Constitution? Is the Kurland

thesis still useful as a starting point, with the qualification that exceptions and refinements have to be worked out? Or, is it flatly wrong?

3. Consider the application of Professor Kurland's thesis to the Massachusetts statute forbidding sale of alcoholic beverages within 500 feet "of a church or school" if the governing body of the church or school objects. The Supreme Court held the statute unconstitutional. Larkin v. Grendel's Den, 459 U.S. 116 (1982). The problem, however, seemed to be that a church was given unilateral power to make the decision whether a liquor license should issue. That, the Court said, "enmeshes churches in the process of government." The Court conceded that an absolute ban on selling liquor within prescribed distances "from churches, schools, hospitals and like institutions" would be valid. Suppose the statute simply talked about churches, and did not control selling liquor near schools or hospitals.

Chapter XVIII

FREE EXERCISE OF RELIGION

I. THE BELIEF—ACTION DISTINCTION

THUGS*

THUGS, a well-organized confederacy of professional assassins, who travelled in gangs through India, wormed themselves into the confidence of wayfarers and when a favourable opportunity occurred, strangled them by throwing a handkerchief or noose round their necks, and then plundered and buried them.... All this was done according to certain ancient and rigidly prescribed forms and after the performance of special religious rites, in which the consecration of the pickaxe and the sacrifice of sugar formed a prominent part. From their using the noose they were also frequently called *Phansigars,* or "noose-operators." Though they themselves traced their origin to seven Mohammedan tribes, Hindus appear to have been associated with them at an early period; at any rate, their religious creed and practices as staunch worshippers of Kali (Devi, Durga), the Hindu goddess of destruction, had certainly no flavour of Islam.

RITUAL MURDER**

An account of a young thug's first killing and some of the religious rites preceding it.

We were all soon assembled, and the gooroo led the way into an adjoining field. He stopped, and turning to the direction in which we were to proceed, raised his hands in a supplicatory manner, and cried, "O Kalee! Maha Kalee! if the traveller now with us should die by the hand of this thy new votary, vouchsafe us the thibaoo!"

All of us stood silently; and wonderful to relate, even at that late hour an ass brayed on the right hand. The gooroo was overjoyed.

"There!" cried he to the others, "was there ever so complete an acceptation of a votary? The omen almost followed the prayer."

"Shookr Alla!" exclaimed my father, "it is now complete; he will go forth and conquer. There only remains for you to tie the knot."

"That I will do when we return," said the gooroo; and when we reached our encampment, he took my handkerchief, and untying the

---

* Encyclopedia Britannica, 14th edition, vol. 22, p. 167. Reprinted with permission.

** From Col. Meadows Taylor, The Confessions of a Thug, Kegan, Paul, Trench, Trobner & Co., Ltd., London, 2d ed., 1873, pp. 57, 59.

knot which had been previously made, he retied it, placing a piece of silver in it. Presenting it to me, he said,—

> "Receive this now sacred weapon; put your trust in it; in the holy name of Kalee I bid it do your will."

I received it in my right hand, and carefully tucked it into my waistband, that I might not lose it, and that it might be ready for action when required.

. . .

I was eagerly waiting the signal; I tightly grasped the fatal handkerchief, and my first victim was within a foot of me! I went behind him as being preferable to one side, and observed one of the other Thugs do the same to a servant. The sahoukar moved a step or two towards the road— I instinctively followed him; I scarcely felt that I stirred, so intensely was I observing him. "Jey Kalee!" shouted my father: it was the signal, and I obeyed it!

As quick as thought the cloth was round his neck; I seemed endued with superhuman strength. I wrenched his neck round—he struggled convulsively for an instant, and fell. I did not quit my hold, I knelt down on him, and strained the cloth till my hand ached; but he moved not—he was dead! I quitted my hold, and started to my feet. I was mad with excitement! My blood boiled, and I felt as though I could have strangled a hundred others, so easy, so simple had the reality been. One turn of my wrists had placed me on an equality with those who had followed the profession for years,—I had taken the first place in the enterprise, for I had killed the principal victim! I should receive the praise of the whole band, many of whom I was confident had looked on me as only a child.

QUESTIONS

1. Would it make sense to start with a principle that the Free Exercise Clause protects all acts done under compulsion of what the defendant saw as a religious duty? (If the ritual murder case doesn't shake your faith in that particular absolute principle, you can probably skip the rest of this chapter.)

2. If the criminal law can punish *some* acts that the individual performs because he was compelled by religious belief, does it follow that the criminal law can punish *any* act even if it is compelled by religion?

REYNOLDS v. UNITED STATES

Supreme Court of the United States, 1878.
98 U.S. 145, 25 L.Ed. 244.

[In the 1870s, while Utah was still a Territory, Reynolds was charged in a territorial court with the crime of bigamy. At his trial, Reynolds testified that Mormon doctrine, to which he adhered, did not simply *permit* plural marriage but *required* it. His testimony was that failing or refusing to practice polygamy "when circumstances would admit," would be punished by "damnation in the life to come." The trial judge refused to instruct the jury that the defendant should be acquitted if he entered into a plural marriage because of religious duty. The Supreme Court affirmed the conviction.]

CHIEF JUSTICE WAITE delivered the opinion of the Court.

MORRISON R. WAITE—Born on November 27, 1816, in Lyme, Connecticut, son of a country lawyer who later became chief justice of the Connecticut Supreme Court. Republican. Episcopalian. Yale, B.A., Phi Beta Kappa, 1837. Read law with his father for a year and then migrated to Ohio. Originally a Whig, he helped organize the Republican Party in Ohio. Practiced law, 1839–1873; unsuccessful candidate for the U.S. House of Representatives, 1846, 1852; Ohio legislator, 1850–1852; member of U.S. delegation to the Geneva Arbitration Tribunal, 1871; Ohio constitutional convention president, 1873–1874. Nominated chief justice of the U.S. by President Ulysses S. Grant on January 19, 1874, to replace Salmon P. Chase. Confirmed by the Senate on January 21, 1874, by a 63–0 vote. Died in office on March 23, 1888.

. . .

Congress cannot pass a law for the government of the Territories which shall prohibit the free exercise of religion. The first amendment to the Constitution expressly forbids such legislation. Religious freedom is guaranteed everywhere throughout the United States, so far as congressional interference is concerned. The question to be determined is, whether the law now under consideration comes within this prohibition.

. . .

. . . [W]e think it may safely be said there never has been a time in any State of the Union when polygamy has not been an offence against society, cognizable by the civil courts and punishable with more or less severity. In the face of all this evidence, it is impossible to believe that the constitutional guaranty of religious freedom was intended to prohibit legislation in respect to this most important feature of social life. Marriage, while from its very nature a sacred obligation, is nevertheless, in most civilized nations, a civil contract, and usually regulated by law. . . .

In our opinion, the statute immediately under consideration is within the legislative power of Congress. It is constitutional and valid as prescribing a rule of action for all those residing in the Territories, and in places over which the United States have exclusive control. This being so, the only question which remains is, whether those who make polygamy a part of their religion are excepted from the operation of the statute. If they are, then those who do not make polygamy a part of their religious belief may be found guilty and punished, while those who do, must be acquitted and go free. This would be introducing a new element into criminal law. Laws are made for the government of actions, and while they cannot interfere with mere religious belief and opinions, they may with practices. Suppose one believed that human sacrifices were a necessary part of religious worship, would it be seriously contended that the civil government under which he lived could not interfere to prevent a sacrifice? Or if a wife religiously believed it was her duty to burn herself upon the funeral pile of her dead husband, would it be beyond the power of the civil government to prevent her carrying her belief into practice?

So here, as a law of the organization of society under the exclusive dominion of the United States, it is provided that plural marriages shall not be allowed. Can a man excuse his practices to the contrary because of his religious belief? To permit this would be to make the professed doctrines of religious belief superior to the law of the land, and in effect to permit every citizen to become a law unto himself. Government could exist only in name under such circumstances.

THE IMPACT OF REYNOLDS

The immediate consequence of Reynolds v. United States, C. Peter Magrath wrote, "was a two-year prison sentence for George Reynolds. Four months after the decision, on a petition for rehearing, the Supreme Court ordered the Utah courts to adjust Reynolds' sentence; he had been wrongly sentenced to 'hard labor in spite of the fact the only penalties of the Morrill Act were fines and imprisonments.' In 1888 Reynolds ... published a book on the subject of holy scripture, *The Story of the Book of Mormon.*" Chief Justice Waite, 18 Vanderbilt Law Review, 533.

NOTES AND QUESTIONS

1.   The conference vote in *Reynolds* was five to four; Chief Justice Waite, joined by Justices Bradley, Field, and Clifford, voted to reverse.* There is no evidence in Waite's papers showing the reasons for the division among the justices. All of the dissenters, except Field, who dissented in part on a nonconstitutional ground, changed their votes. Chief Justice Waite's change of vote permitted him to assign himself the Court's opinion. In preparing to write the opinion, he sought the help of the historian, George Bancroft, who was a neighbor. "As you gave me the information on which the judgment in the later polygamy case rests," the Chief Justice later wrote to Bancroft, "I send you a copy of the opinion that you may see what use has been made of the facts." Waite referred to his opinion as his "sermon on the religion of polygamy" in a letter to Rev. D. Walbridge on Jan. 20, 1879. "I hope you will not find it," he added, tongue in cheek, "poisoned with heterodoxy."**

2.   Chief Justice Waite conceded that the Free Exercise Clause does protect religious belief and opinion. It should follow from that proposition that someone couldn't be punished for entertaining a religious belief in plural marriage if he didn't actually *engage* in polygamy. Could a nineteenth century Mormon be punished for *expressing* his religious belief if he didn't commit bigamy? Could he be punished for being a member of an organization whose members preach and practice polyga-

---

* Docketbook, 1878 Term, Morrison R. Waite Papers, Library of Congress, Box 32.
** Ibid., Box 29.

my? Notice that problems of religious speech and religious association present problems identical to those discussed in the chapters on freedom of speech. Is it significant whether religious belief, speech and association are protected by the Free Speech or the Free Exercise Clause? In any event, in applying Chief Justice Waite's "belief-action" distinction, one should put religious speech on the "belief side," at least to the extent that free speech principles would protect the speech.

3.   The bigamy laws, of course, only punish practicing polygamists. In Davis v. Beason, 133 U.S. 333 (1890), however, a statute of the Territory of Idaho, directed at Mormons, was challenged. The law required voters to take an oath that they were not members of any organization that "teaches, advises, counsels or encourages" its members to commit the crime of bigamy. Davis, a Mormon, took the oath in order to vote, and was convicted of taking a false oath. He argued that the law requiring the oath was unconstitutional. In affirming the conviction, Justice Field's Opinion for the Court treated the problem as if it were identical to the problem in the *Reynolds* case. He said, in part:

> . . . Bigamy and polygamy are crimes by the laws of all civilized and Christian countries. They are crimes by the laws of the United States, and they are crimes by the laws of Idaho. They tend to destroy the purity of the marriage relation, to disturb the peace of families, to degrade woman and to debase man. Few crimes are more pernicious to the best interests of society and receive more general or more deserved punishment. To extend exemption from punishment for such crimes would be to shock the moral judgment of the community. To call their advocacy a tenet of religion is to offend the common sense of mankind. If they are crimes, then to teach, advise and counsel their practice is to aid in their commission, and such teaching and counselling are themselves criminal and proper subjects of punishment, as aiding and abetting crime are in all other cases.

> . . .

> It is assumed by counsel of the petitioner, that because no mode of worship can be established or religious tenets enforced in this country, therefore any form of worship may be followed and any tenets, however destructive of society, may be held and advocated, if asserted to be a part of the religious doctrines of those advocating and practising them. But nothing is further from the truth. Whilst legislation for the establishment of a religion is forbidden, and its free exercise permitted, it does not follow that everything which may be so called can be tolerated. Crime is not the less odious because sanctioned by what any particular sect may designate as religion.

Would it still be true that *all* persons who teach, advise, counsel, or belong to organizations whose members practice plural marriage could be punished by the criminal law? (See Chapter 5, above.)

4.   The most graphic illustration of the relationship between the constitutional protections of speech and religion is the flag salute. See

the opinions in *Gobitis* and *Barnette* in Chapter 2. Justice Frankfurter's opinion for the Court in *Gobitis* approached the problem the way Chief Justice Waite had approached it in *Reynolds*. "The mere possession of religious convictions which contradict the relevant concerns of a political society," wrote Frankfurter, "does not relieve the citizen from the discharge of political responsibilities." When the Court overruled *Gobitis* three years later in *Barnette,* Justice Jackson's opinion for the Court argued that the *Gobitis* opinion had erred in assuming that the problem was whether people with religious scruples had to be excused from the flag salute. Actually, the issue was whether *anyone* could be required to salute the flag—and that was an issue of freedom of expression. The principle that decided the case was that no one could be compelled by government to profess a belief.

> If there is any fixed star in our constitutional constellation, it is that no official, high or petty, can prescribe what shall be orthodox in politics, nationalism, religion, or other matters of opinion or force citizens to confess by word or act their faith therein. If there are any circumstances which permit an exception, they do not now occur to us.

The principle of the flag-salute cases was reaffirmed by the Court in Wooley v. Maynard, 430 U.S. 705 (1977). See p. 573.

5. Notice that, using the belief-action distinction, the Free Exercise Clause becomes superfluous, since all that it protects are those rights fully covered by the Free Speech Clause. Are there any cases where the Free Exercise Clause protects rights not already protected by freedom of speech? Even if religious belief cannot be a defense to *all* criminal charges, are there some cases where religious conscience can excuse compliance with a law?

II. CONSTITUTIONAL PROTECTION OF CONDUCT COMPELLED BY RELIGIOUS BELIEF

SHERBERT v. VERNER

Supreme Court of the United States, 1963.
374 U.S. 398, 83 S.Ct. 1790, 10 L.Ed.2d 965.

[Adell Sherbert worked in a textile mill in Spartanburg, South Carolina. In 1957, she became a member of the Seventh-day Adventist Church. A basic tenet of the Seventh-day Adventists prohibits labor on Saturdays. Sherbert's employer, however, operated the mill on a five-day week, and she was not required to work on Saturdays. In 1959, the work week was changed to six days, including Saturday. Sherbert was discharged because she would not work on Saturday. She was unable to find other employment, because available jobs would also require her to work on Saturday. (There were 150 or more Seventh-day Adventists in the Spartanburg area. Only Sherbert and one other Seventh-day Adventist had been unable to find suitable five-day employment.) She applied for state unemployment compensation. Benefits were denied, because she had refused available work, although the "available" work would have required her to work on Saturday.]

JUSTICE BRENNAN delivered the opinion of the Court.

. . .

Plainly enough, appellant's conscientious objection to Saturday work constitutes no conduct prompted by religious principles of a kind within the reach of state legislation. If, therefore, the decision of the South Carolina Supreme Court is to withstand appellant's constitutional challenge, it must be either because her disqualification as a beneficiary represents no infringement by the State of her constitutional rights of free exercise, or because any incidental burden on the free exercise of appellant's religion may be justified by a "compelling state interest in the regulation of a subject within the State's constitutional power to regulate...."

We turn first to the question whether the disqualification for benefits imposes any burden on the free exercise of appellant's religion. We think it is clear that it does.... The ruling forces her to choose between following the precepts of her religion and forfeiting benefits, on the one hand, and abandoning one of the precepts of her religion in order to accept work, on the other hand. Governmental imposition of such a choice puts the same kind of burden upon the free exercise of religion as would a fine imposed against appellant for her Saturday worship.

. . .

Significantly South Carolina expressly saves the Sunday worshipper from having to make the kind of choice which we here hold infringes the Sabbatarian's religious liberty. When in times of "national emergency" the textile plants are authorized by the State Commissioner of Labor to operate on Sunday, "no employee shall be required to work on Sunday ... who is conscientiously opposed to Sunday work; and if any employee should refuse to work on Sunday on account of conscientious ... objections he or she shall not jeopardize his or her seniority by such refusal or be discriminated against in any other manner." ... The unconstitutionality of the disqualification of the Sabbatarian is thus compounded by the religious discrimination which South Carolina's general statutory scheme necessarily effects.

We must next consider whether some compelling state interest enforced in the eligibility provisions of the South Carolina statute justifies the substantial infringement of appellant's First Amendment right. It is basic that no showing merely of a rational relationship to some colorable state interest would suffice; in this highly sensitive constitutional area, "[o]nly the gravest abuses, endangering paramount interests, give occasion for permissible limitation." No such abuse or danger has been advanced in the present case. The appellees suggest no more than a possibility that the filing of fraudulent claims by unscrupulous claimants feigning religious objections to Saturday work might not only dilute the unemployment compensation fund but also hinder the scheduling by employers of necessary Saturday work. But that possibility is not apposite here because no such objection appears to have been made before the South Carolina Supreme Court, and we are unwilling to assess the importance of an asserted state interest without the views of the state court. Nor, if the contention had been made below, would the record appear to sustain it; there is no proof whatever to warrant such fears of malingering or deceit as those which the respondents now advance. Even if ... the possibility of spurious claims did threaten to dilute the fund and disrupt the scheduling of work, it would plainly be incumbent upon the appellees to demonstrate that no alternative forms of regulation would combat such abuses without infringing First Amendment rights. . . .

. . .

In holding as we do, plainly we are not fostering the "establishment" of the Seventh-day Adventist religion in South Carolina, for the extension of unemployment benefits to Sabbatarians in common with Sunday worshippers reflects nothing more than the governmental obligation of neutrality in the face of religious differences, and does not represent that involvement of religious with secular institutions which it is the object of the Establishment Clause to forestall. Nor does the recognition of the appellant's right to unemployment benefits under the state statute serve to abridge any other person's religious liberties. Nor do we, by our decision today, declare the existence of a constitutional right to unemployment benefits on the part of all persons whose religious convictions are the cause of their unemployment. This is not a case in which an employee's religious convictions serve to make him a nonproductive member of society. Finally, nothing we say today constrains the States to adopt any particular form or scheme of unemployment compensation. Our holding today is only that South Carolina may not constitutionally apply the eligibility provisions so as to constrain a worker to abandon his religious convictions respecting the day of rest. . . .

. . .

[A concurrence by JUSTICE DOUGLAS is omitted.]

JUSTICE STEWART, concurring in the result.

Although fully agreeing with the result which the Court reaches in this case, I cannot join the Court's opinion. This case presents a double-barreled dilemma, which in all candor I think the Court's opinion has not succeeded in papering over. The dilemma ought to be resolved.

. . .

. . . [T]here are many situations where legitimate claims under the Free Exercise Clause will run into head-on collision with the Court's insensitive and sterile construction of the Establishment Clause. The controversy now before us is clearly such a case.

. . .

To require South Carolina to so administer its laws as to pay public money to the appellant under the circumstances of this case is ... clearly to require the State to violate the Establishment Clause as construed by this Court. This poses no problem for me, because I think the Court's mechanistic concept of the Establishment Clause is historically unsound and constitutionally wrong. I think the process of constitutional decision in the area of the relationships between government and religion demands considerably more than the invocation of broad-brushed rhetoric of the kind I have quoted. And I think that the guarantee of religious liberty embodied in the Free Exercise Clause affirmatively requires government to create an atmosphere of hospitality and accommodation to individual belief or disbelief. In short, I think our Constitution commands the positive protection by government of religious freedom—not only for a minority, however small—not only for the majority, however large—but for each of us.

South Carolina would deny unemployment benefits to a mother unavailable for work on Saturdays because she was unable to get a babysitter. Thus, we do not have before us a situation where a State provides unemployment compensation generally, and singles out for disqualification only those persons who are unavailable for work on religious grounds. This is not, in short, a scheme which operates so as to discriminate against religion as such. But the Court nevertheless holds that the State must prefer a religious over a secular ground for being unavailable for work—that state financial support of the appellant's religion is constitutionally required to carry out "the governmental obligation of neutrality in the face of religious differences...."

. . .

[The dissenting opinion of Justices Harlan and White is omitted.]

DRAFTING THE COURT'S OPINION IN SHERBERT*

The April 26, 1963, conference vote was seven-to-two to reverse, with Harlan and White for affirmance. But the division was closer than the vote indicated, as shown by what happened at the opinion-writing stage. Warren assigned the opinion to Brennan on April 30. On May 29, Brennan circulated his first *Sherbert* draft. It was based on the narrow premise that a distinction could be drawn between persons who became unemployed because the employer altered the work schedule to conflict with the exercise of religious beliefs (exactly this case) and workers who had been disqualified because of a religious conversion that might, under the state unemployment compensation law, be deemed a "personal circumstance" barring them from compensation.

The distinction drawn in Brennan's draft was too narrow for the others, except for Clark who agreed to join. Brennan circulated a second draft in which the decision was broadened. But certain reservations remained. These included the suggestion that the statute did not purport to disqualify all persons unemployed for personal reasons, as well as the suggestion that Sherbert's religious practices did not make her unemployable, as shown by the employment of other Sabbatarians in her community. In this form, with minor changes, the opinion proved acceptable to Warren, Black, Clark, and Goldberg.

* Bernard Schwartz, Super Chief, New York, 1983, pp. 468–70. Reprinted with permission.

On June 4, Stewart sent around a sharp concurring opinion that chided the Court for failing to reconcile a "head-on collision" between the Establishment Clause and the Free Exercise Clause of the First Amendment. Stewart asserted that the Court's decision was inconsistent with the 1961 decision upholding Sunday Blue Laws.... In a companion case to that decision, the Court had held that a Sunday Closing Law did not violate the free exercise rights of an orthodox Jewish butcher, who also did not work on Saturday. Now, Stewart urged, the *Sherbert* opinion was effectively overruling that decision, though pretending to distinguish it.

Douglas circulated a milder concurrence the following day. On June 11 Harlan issued a dissent, and White joined him a day later.

Brennan made several changes in his opinion to deal with the points made in the Stewart, Douglas, and Harlan opinions. To answer Stewart's charge that the opinion required the "establishment" of Seventh-day Adventism in order to protect the church member's free exercise right, a paragraph was added to refute the notion that the state was being compelled to pay benefits on religious grounds. Brennan also added a new subsection "E. Religious Considerations in Public Welfare Programs," to Part V of his *Schempp* concurrence, carefully distinguishing between public welfare conditions designed to benefit churches and religions as such, and those designed merely to avoid invidious religious classifications. Despite Brennan's changes in this regard, however, Stewart continued to charge that the Court had "studiously ignored" the asserted conflict between the Establishment and Free Exercise Clauses.

Harlan's dissent stressed that South Carolina had not discriminated against Sherbert because of her religious beliefs, saying she was not "denied benefits *because* she was a Seventh-day Adventist." To answer Harlan, Brennan made two changes in his opinion. The first sought to demonstrate that the state courts had singled out the Sabbatarian for harsher treatment than persons unable to work for other personal reasons. The second was a paragraph to show that the statute contained a built-in discrimination between the Saturday and Sunday worshipper, since the latter could be exempted from Sabbath work in times of emergency while the former could not. The many revisions made by Brennan carried the opinion to six drafts before it was delivered on June 17.

NOTES AND QUESTIONS

1. In the *Sherbert* case, Justice Harlan, joined by Justice White, dissented. One point made by Justice Harlan was that the purpose of the unemployment compensation law was to pay benefits to people who were out of work because economic conditions made work unavailable. Unemployment compensation was thus unavailable to anyone who refused work for any personal reason, no matter how compelling.

> The fact that these personal considerations sprang from her religious convictions was wholly without relevance to the state court's application of the law. Thus in no proper sense can it be said that the State discriminated against the appellant on the

basis of her religious beliefs or that she was denied benefits *because* she was a Seventh-day Adventist. She was denied benefits just as any other claimant would be denied benefits who was not "available for work" for personal reasons.

Justice Brennan's opinion answered this argument in a significant footnote.

> It has been suggested that appellant is not within the class entitled to benefits under the South Carolina statute because her unemployment did not result from discharge or layoff due to lack of work. It is true that unavailability for work for some personal reasons not having to do with matters of conscience or religion has been held to be a basis for disqualification for benefits.... Where the consequence of disqualification so directly affects First Amendment rights, surely we should not conclude that every "personal reason" is a basis for disqualification in the absence of explicit language to that effect in the statute or decisions of the South Carolina Supreme Court.

Suppose the South Carolina statute were amended to contain explicit language that benefits were unavailable to anyone who refused available employment in the area for "personal reasons, no matter how compelling." Does Justice Brennan's footnote mean that someone in Adell Sherbert's position could be denied unemployment compensation if the law were worded that way? Should that be the result?

2.　In Thomas v. Review Board of the Indiana Employment Security Division, 450 U.S. 707 (1981), the Court considered the case of a Jehovah's Witness who quit his job when he was transferred to a department producing turrets for military tanks. Thomas' personal religious belief prevented him from engaging "directly" in production of military arms. The decision to deny unemployment compensation to Thomas was sustained by the state courts. One reason those courts gave in distinguishing Thomas' case from Sherbert v. Verner was that the Ohio law did deny unemployment compensation for people who were out of work for *any* personal reason. Therefore, Thomas did not qualify for benefits because he was not economically unemployed. The Supreme Court disagreed, and held that denial of benefits denied Thomas' free exercise of religion.

3.　Justice Rehnquist was the only dissenter in *Thomas*. He argued that singling out religious personal reasons for unemployment from all other personal reasons required the state to aid religion. He referred to Justice Harlan's dissent in *Sherbert* to argue that it must be wrong to require under the free exercise clause what is forbidden by the establishment clause. On this point, Justice Harlan's dissent in *Sherbert* had said:

> It has been suggested that such singling out of religious conduct for special treatment may violate the constitutional limitations on state action. See Kurland, Of Church and State and The Supreme Court, 29 U. of Chi.L.Rev. 1. My own view, however, is that at least under the circumstances of this case it would be a permissible accommodation of religion for the State, if it *chose* to do so, to create an exception to its eligibility requirements for

persons like the appellant. The constitutional obligation of "neutrality" ... is not so narrow a channel that the slightest deviation from an absolutely straight course leads to condemnation. There are too many instances in which no such course can be chartered....

For very much the same reasons, however, I cannot subscribe to the conclusion that the State is constitutionally *compelled* to carve out an exception to its general rule of eligibility in the present case. Those situations in which the Constitution may require special treatment on account of religion are, in my view, few and far between. Such compulsion in the present case is particularly inappropriate ... in light of the direct financial assistance to religion that today's decision requires.

How does Justice Brennan answer this argument? Does he concede that the result in the *Sherbert* case is to require South Carolina to aid religion, while arguing that this is a case where "aid" is required by the Free Exercise Clause? Or does he deny that the result involves "aid" to religion? The *result* is to require South Carolina to pay unemployment benefits to persons whose religious scruples require they not work on Saturday, while South Carolina denies benefits to those refusing Saturday work for some other "personal" reasons. Are there nonreligious "personal" reasons for refusing Saturday work that are truly comparable to the religious reasons of the Seventh-day Adventists? (See Section III of this chapter, below.)

5. Does Justice Brennan's "compelling state interest" standard mean that the situations where the Constitution requires that there be special treatment on account of religion will *not* be "few and far between" as the dissent argues they should be? Obviously, any process that requires a balancing of state interests against the interests of the individual in free exercise of religion will require, in some cases at least, comparing imponderables. For example, in the *Reynolds* case, how would one compare the state's "interest" in outlawing bigamy with the infringement of the religious freedom of a person whose religion compels plural marriage? In the *Sherbert* case, would the state's interest have been "compelling" if all 150 Seventh-day Adventists in the area were out of work because they turned down jobs requiring Saturday work? In the two principal cases that follow, how would you describe the state interest in enforcing narcotic and compulsory school attendance laws? Can that interest be compared easily with the interest of individuals whose religion required disobedience of the laws?

WISCONSIN v. YODER

Supreme Court of the United States, 1972.
406 U.S. 205, 92 S.Ct. 1526, 32 L.Ed.2d 15.

CHIEF JUSTICE BURGER delivered the opinion of the Court.

On petition of the State of Wisconsin, we granted the writ of certiorari in this case to review a decision of the Wisconsin Supreme Court holding that respondents' convictions of violating the State's compulsory school-attendance law were invalid under the Free Exercise Clause of the First Amendment to the United States Constitution. . . .

. . . Jonas Yoder and Wallace Miller are members of the Old Order Amish religion, and . . . Adin Yutzy is a member of the Conservative Amish Mennonite Church. . . . Wisconsin's compulsory school-attendance law required them to cause their children to attend public or private school until reaching age 16 but the respondents declined to send their children, ages 14 and 15, to public school after they completed the eighth grade. . . .

. . . [They] were charged, tried, and convicted of violating the compulsory-attendance law in Green County Court and were fined the sum of $5 each. . . . They believed that by sending their children to high school, they would not only expose themselves to the danger of the censure of the church community, but, as found by the county court, also endanger their own salvation and that of their children. The State stipulated that respondents' religious beliefs were sincere.

· · ·

. . . Broadly speaking, the Old Order Amish religion pervades and determines the entire mode of life of its adherents. . . .

· · ·

Formal high school education beyond the eighth grade is contrary to Amish beliefs, not only because it places Amish children in an environment hostile to Amish beliefs with increasing emphasis on competition in class work and sports and with pressure to conform to the styles, manners, and ways of the peer group, but also because it takes them away from their community, physically and emotionally, during the crucial and formative adolescent period of life. During this period, the children must acquire Amish attitudes favoring manual work and self-reliance and the specific skills needed to perform the adult role of an Amish farmer or housewife. They must learn to enjoy physical labor. . . .

· · ·

. . . [One expert] testified that compulsory high school attendance could not only result in great psychological harm to Amish children, because of the conflicts it would produce, but would also, in his opinion, ultimately result in the destruction of the Old Order Amish church community as it exists in the United States today. The testimony of [another], an expert witness on education, also showed that the Amish succeed in preparing their high school age children to be productive members of the Amish community. He described their system of learning through doing the skills directly relevant to their adult roles in the Amish community as "ideal" and perhaps superior to ordinary high school education. The evidence also showed that the Amish have an excellent record as law-abiding and generally self-sufficient members of society.

· · ·

There is no doubt as to the power of a State, having a high responsibility for education of its citizens, to impose reasonable regulations for the control and duration of basic education.... [A] State's interest in universal education, however highly we rank it, is not totally free from a balancing process when it impinges on fundamental rights and interests, such as those specifically protected by the Free Exercise Clause of the First Amendment,....

It follows that in order for Wisconsin to compel school attendance beyond the eighth grade against a claim that such attendance interferes with the practice of a legitimate religious belief, it must appear either that the State does not deny the free exercise of religious belief by its requirement, or that there is a state interest of sufficient magnitude to override the interest claiming protection under the Free Exercise Clause....

The essence of all that has been said and written on the subject is that only those interests of the highest order and those not otherwise served can overbalance legitimate claims to the free exercise of religion. We can accept it as settled, therefore, that, however strong the State's interest in universal compulsory education, it is by no means absolute to the exclusion or subordination of all other interests.

We come then to the quality of the claims of the respondents concerning the alleged encroachment of Wisconsin's compulsory school-attendance statute on their rights and the rights of their children to the free exercise of the religious beliefs they and their forebears have adhered to for almost three centuries. In evaluating those claims we must be careful to determine whether the Amish religious faith and their mode of life are, as they claim, inseparable and interdependent. A way of life, however virtuous and admirable, may not be interposed as a barrier to reasonable state regulation of education if it is based on purely secular considerations; to have the protection of the Religion Clauses, the claims must be rooted in religious belief. Although a determination of what is a "religious" belief or practice entitled to constitutional protection may present a most delicate question, the very concept of ordered liberty precludes allowing every person to make his own standards on matters of conduct in which society as a whole has important interests. Thus, if the Amish asserted their claims because of their subjective evaluation and rejection of the contemporary secular values accepted by the majority, much as Thoreau rejected the social values of his time and isolated himself at Walden Pond, their claims would not rest on a religious basis. Thoreau's choice was philosophical and personal rather than religious, and such belief does not rise to the demands of the Religion Clauses.

Giving no weight to such secular considerations, however, we see that the record in this case abundantly supports the claim that the traditional way of life of the Amish is not merely a matter of personal preference, but one of deep religious conviction, shared by an organized group, and intimately related to daily living....

· · ·

As the society around the Amish has become more populous, urban, industrialized, and complex, particularly in this century, government regulation of human affairs has correspondingly become more detailed and pervasive. The Amish mode of life has thus come into conflict increasingly with requirements of contemporary society exerting a hydraulic insistence on conformity to majoritarian standards.... The conclusion is inescapable that secondary schooling, by exposing Amish children to worldly influences in terms of attitudes, goals, and values contrary to beliefs, and by substantially interfering with the religious development of the Amish child and his integration into the way of life of the Amish faith community at the crucial adolescent stage of development, contravenes the basic religious tenets and practice of the Amish faith, both as to the parent and the child.

The impact of the compulsory-attendance law on respondents' practice of the Amish religion is not only severe, but inescapable, for the Wisconsin law affirmatively compels them, under threat of criminal sanction, to perform acts undeniably at odds with fundamental tenets of their religious beliefs. Nor is the impact of the compulsory-attendance law confined to grave interference with important Amish religious tenets from a subjective point of view. It carries with it precisely the kind of objective danger to the free exercise of religion that the First Amendment was designed to prevent. As the record shows, compulsory school attendance to age 16 for Amish children carries with it a very real threat of undermining the Amish community and religious practice as they exist today; they must either abandon belief and be assimilated into society at large, or be forced to migrate to some other and more tolerant region.

In sum, the unchallenged testimony of acknowledged experts in education and religious history, almost 300 years of consistent practice, and strong evidence of a sustained faith pervading and regulating respondents' entire mode of life support the claim that enforcement of the State's requirement of compulsory formal education after the eighth grade would gravely endanger if not destroy the free exercise of respondents' religious beliefs.

. . .

Wisconsin concedes that under the Religion Clauses religious beliefs are absolutely free from the State's control, but it argues that "actions," even though religiously grounded, are outside the protection of the First Amendment. But our decisions have rejected the idea that religiously grounded conduct is always outside the protection of the Free Exercise Clause.... This case, therefore, does not become easier because respondents were convicted for their "actions" in refusing to send their children to the public high school; in this context belief and action cannot be neatly confined in logic-tight compartments.

Nor can this case be disposed of on the grounds that Wisconsin's requirement for school attendance to age 16 applies uniformly to all citizens of the State and does not, on its face, discriminate against religions or a particular religion, or that it is motivated by legitimate secular concerns. A regulation neutral on its face may, in its application, nonetheless offend the constitutional requirement for governmental neutrality if it unduly burdens the free exercise of religion. The Court must not ignore the danger that an exception from a general obligation of citizenship on religious grounds may run afoul of the Establishment Clause, but that danger cannot be allowed to prevent any exception no matter how vital it may be to the protection of values promoted by the right of free exercise. . . .

. . .

The State attacks respondents' position as one fostering "ignorance" from which the child must be protected by the State. No one can question the State's duty to protect children from ignorance but this argument does not square with the facts disclosed in the record. Whatever their idiosyncrasies as seen by the majority, this record strongly shows that the Amish community has been a highly successful social unit within our society, even if apart from the conventional "mainstream." Its members are productive and very law-abiding members of society; they reject public welfare in any of its usual modern forms. The Congress itself recognized their self-sufficiency by authorizing exemption of such groups as the Amish from the obligation to pay social security taxes.

. . .

Insofar as the State's claim rests on the view that a brief additional period of formal education is imperative to enable the Amish to participate effectively and intelligently in our democratic process, it must fall. The Amish alternative to formal secondary school education has enabled them to function effectively in their day-to-day life under self-imposed limitations on relations with the world, and to survive and prosper in contemporary society as a separate, sharply identifiable and highly self-sufficient community for more than 200 years in this country. In itself this is strong evidence that they are capable of fulfilling the social and political responsibilities of citizenship without compelled attendance beyond the eighth grade at the price of jeopardizing their free exercise of religious belief. . . .

. . .

Finally, the State . . . argues that a decision exempting Amish children from the State's requirement fails to recognize the substantive right of the Amish child to a secondary education, and fails to give due regard to the power of the State as parens patriae to extend the benefit of secondary education to children regardless of the wishes of their parents. . . .

. . .

Contrary to the suggestion of the dissenting opinion of Justice Douglas, our holding today in no degree depends on the assertion of the religious interest of the child as contrasted with that of the parents. It is the parents who are subject to prosecution here for failing to cause their children to attend school, and it is their right of free exercise, not that of their children, that must determine Wisconsin's power to impose criminal penalties on the parent. The dissent argues that a child who expresses a desire to attend public high school in conflict with the wishes of his parents should not be prevented from doing so. There is no reason for the Court to consider that point since it is not an issue in the case. The children are not parties to this litigation. The State has at no point tried this case on the theory that respondents were preventing their children from attending school against their expressed desires, and indeed the record is to the contrary. The State's position from the outset has been that it is empowered to apply its compulsory-attendance law to Amish parents in the same manner as to other parents—that is, without regard to the wishes of the child. That is the claim we reject today.

Our holding in no way determines the proper resolution of possible competing interests of parents, children, and the State in an appropriate state court proceeding in which the power of the State is asserted on the theory that Amish parents are preventing their minor children from attending high school despite their expressed desires to the contrary. Recognition of the claim of the State in such a proceeding would, of course, call into question traditional concepts of parental control over the religious upbringing and education of their minor children recognized in this Court's past decisions. It is clear that such an intrusion by a State into family decisions in the area of religious training would give rise to grave questions of religious freedom comparable to those raised here.... On this record we neither reach nor decide those issues.

. . .

For the reasons stated we hold, with the Supreme Court of Wisconsin, that the First and Fourteenth Amendments prevent the State from compelling respondents to cause their children to attend formal high school to age 16.[1] ... It cannot be overemphasized that we are not dealing with a way of life and mode of education by a group claiming to have recently discovered some "progressive" or more enlightened process for rearing children for modern life.

Aided by a history of three centuries as an identifiable religious sect and a long history as a successful and self-sufficient segment of American society, the Amish in this case have convincingly demonstrated the sincerity of their religious beliefs, the interrelationship of belief with their mode of life, the vital role that belief and daily conduct play in the continued survival of Old Order Amish communities and their religious organization, and the hazards presented by the State's enforcement of a statute generally valid as to others.... In light of this convincing showing, one that probably few other religious groups or sects could

1. What we have said should meet the suggestion that the decision of the Wisconsin Supreme Court recognizing an exemption for the Amish from the State's system of compulsory education constituted an impermissible establishment of religion.... Accommodating the religious beliefs of the Amish can hardly be characterized as sponsorship or active involvement. The purpose and effect of such an exemption are not to support, favor, advance, or assist the Amish, but to allow their centuries-old religious society, here long before the advent of any compulsory education, to survive free from the heavy impediment compliance with the Wisconsin compulsory-education law would impose. Such an accommodation "reflects nothing more than the governmental obligation of neutrality in the face of religious differences, and does not represent that involvement of religious with secular institutions which it is the object of the Establishment Clause to forestall." ...

make, and weighing the minimal difference between what the State would require and what the Amish already accept, it was incumbent on the State to show with more particularity how its admittedly strong interest in compulsory education would be adversely affected by granting an exemption to the Amish. Sherbert v. Verner, supra.

· · ·

Affirmed.

Justice Powell and Justice Rehnquist took no part in the consideration or decision of this case.

Justice Stewart, with whom Justice Brennan, joins, concurring.

· · ·

This case in no way involves any questions regarding the right of the children of Amish parents to attend public high schools, or any other institutions of learning, if they wish to do so. As the Court points out, there is no suggestion whatever in the record that the religious beliefs of the children here concerned differ in any way from those of their parents. . . .

· · ·

Justice White, with whom Justice Brennan and Justice Stewart join, concurring.

Cases such as this one inevitably call for a delicate balancing of important but conflicting interests. I join the opinion and judgment of the Court because I cannot say that the State's interest in requiring two more years of compulsory education in the ninth and tenth grades outweighs the importance of the concededly sincere Amish religious practice to the survival of that sect.

This would be a very different case for me if respondents' claim were that their religion forbade their children from attending any school at any time and from complying in any way with the educational standards set by the State. . . .

The importance of the state interest asserted here cannot be denigrated, ...

. . . A State has a legitimate interest not only in seeking to develop the latent talents of its children but also in seeking to prepare them for the life style that they may later choose, or at least to provide them with an option other than the life they have led in the past. In the circumstances of this case, although the question is close, I am unable to say that the State has demonstrated that Amish children who leave school in the eighth grade will be intellectually stultified or unable to acquire new academic skills later. . . .

· · ·

Justice Douglas, dissenting in part.

I agree with the Court that the religious scruples of the Amish are opposed to the education of their children beyond the grade schools, yet I disagree with the Court's conclusion that the matter is within the dispensation of parents alone. The Court's analysis assumes that the only interests at stake in the case are those of the Amish parents on the one hand, and those of the State on the other. The difficulty with this approach is that, despite the Court's claim, the parents are seeking to vindicate not only their own free exercise claims, but also those of their high-school-age children.

NOTES AND QUESTIONS

1. More balancing! In any case where imponderables are being "balanced" against each other, it is possible to argue endlessly that the wrong choice was made because not enough weight was given to the state or individual "interests" on either side. That point has been made over and over again, not only with reference to prior cases in this chapter, but in the free speech chapters as well. Since there is no way to settle the question of how much a particular interest is "worth" it may be more useful to focus on the question of the identity of the interests that are to be taken into account *at all* in striking a balance.

2. Notice, initially, what is *not* involved in the *Yoder* case. Wisconsin is not asserting the right to force Amish children to attend *public* schools. In Pierce v. Society of Sisters, 268 U.S. 510 (1925), the Court held unconstitutional a state law that required all parents to send their children to public schools. While that case was decided on the theory of protecting the property rights of private schools (including military academies as well as religious schools), in later years the *Pierce* case has been viewed as protecting the individual freedom of parents to educate their children in private schools. In the *Yoder* conference, Justice Douglas* took the position that *Pierce* governed the Court's decision. In Griswold v. Connecticut, 381 U.S. 479 (1965), Justice Douglas' opinion for the Court characterized the *Pierce* case as protecting "freedom of inquiry, freedom of thought, and freedom to teach...." The Amish religious beliefs, as described by the Court in *Yoder,* did not allow the Amish to satisfy the compulsory school attendance laws by setting up their own schools beyond the eighth grade. But that was not because Wisconsin forbade the Amish from setting up their own schools. The private schools involved in the *Pierce* case did meet minimal state standards as to the subjects on which instruction must be provided. Here, the Amish objected to exposing their children to that level of education, whether in their own schools or public schools. So, what is at issue in the *Yoder* case is a state requirement that all children be exposed to education with a minimum substantive content through the tenth grade. It is that interest which must be balanced against the Amish interest in free exercise of their religion.

3. Beginning with the individual rights side of the balance, would it be appropriate to judge whether the Amish beliefs about education are "sound" beliefs? It's inconsistent with the rationale of the Free Exercise Clause, isn't it, to have government (whether legislatures or courts) base decisions about religious practice and belief on whether government

* Douglas Papers, Library of Congress, Box 1552.

thinks the religious belief is sensible? Consider United States v. Ballard, 322 U.S. 78 (1944). The defendants were charged with fraudulently collecting money for their religious movement. It was claimed that they falsely represented they had been given divine power to heal the sick. In reversing the convictions, the Court decided that the issues should have been limited to the issue whether the defendants were sincere in their claims that they possessed religious healing powers—that is, whether they honestly *believed* their own claims. The Court explained:

> Heresy trials are foreign to our Constitution. Men may believe what they cannot prove. They may not be put to the proof of their religious doctrines or beliefs. Religious experiences which are as real as life to some may be incomprehensible to others. Yet the fact that they may be beyond the ken of mortals does not mean that they can be made suspect before the law. Many take their gospel from the New Testament. But it would hardly be supposed that they could be tried before a jury charged with the duty of determining whether those teachings contained false representations. The miracles of the New Testament, the Divinity of Christ, life after death, the power of prayer are deep in the religious convictions of many. If one could be sent to jail because a jury in a hostile environment found those teachings false, little indeed would be left of religious freedom. The Fathers of the Constitution were not unaware of the varied and extreme views of religious sects, of the violence of disagreement among them, and of the lack of any one religious creed on which all men would agree. They fashioned a charter of government which envisaged the widest possible toleration of conflicting views. Man's relation to his God was made no concern of the state. He was granted the right to worship as he pleased and to answer to no man for the verity of his religious views. The religious views espoused by respondents might seem incredible, if not preposterous, to most people. But if those doctrines are subject to trial before a jury charged with finding their truth or falsity, then the same can be done with the religious beliefs of any sect. When the triers of fact undertake that task, they enter a forbidden domain.

It may be possible, in cases like *Braunfeld* and *Sherbert,* to balance state interests and religious freedom without considering the soundness of the view that Saturday is the Sabbath and work is forbidden. But is it possible to ignore the soundness of religious views in *Reynolds* and *Yoder?* For example, in *Yoder,* the state's interest is in compulsory education and the relevant religious belief opposes compulsory education. Is it possible to balance the competing considerations while ignoring all questions about whether the Amish objections to education are anti-social?

4.   Even if it's necessary to consider, to some extent, the soundness of Amish views about compulsory education, is it relevant that they are "law-abiding," gainfully employed and don't live on welfare? Justice Douglas, quoting from the dissenting opinion in the Wisconsin Supreme Court, said:

The observation of Justice Heffernan, dissenting below, that the principal opinion in his court portrayed the Amish as leading a life of "idyllic agrarianism," is equally applicable to the majority opinion in this Court. So, too, is his observation that such a portrayal rests on a "mythological basis." Professor Hostetler has noted that "[d]rinking among the youth is common in all the large Amish settlements." Moreover, "[i]t would appear that among the Amish the rate of suicide is just as high, if not higher than for the nation." He also notes an unfortunate Amish "preoccupation with filthy stories," as well as significant "rowdyism and stress." These are not traits peculiar to the Amish, of course. The point is that the Amish are not people set apart and different.

5. Is the Amish objection to compulsory education beyond the eighth grade "religious"? Recall that in *Reynolds,* the defendant believed that failure to engage in plural marriage would result in divine retribution. Isn't the Amish objection a claim to interference with their "way of life" rather than their "religion"? Does the Court's opinion convince you that the Amish "religion" and the Amish "way of life" are indistinguishable? (On the issue of what *is* a religion, see Section III of this chapter, below.)

6. Justice Douglas, in his *Yoder* dissent, argued that the free exercise interest most clearly in point was that of Amish children, not Amish parents. He said:

> It is the future of the student, not the future of the parents, that is imperiled by today's decision. If a parent keeps his child out of school beyond the grade school, then the child will be forever barred from entry into the new and amazing world of diversity that we have today.... It is the student's judgment, not his parents', that is essential if we are to give full meaning to ... the Bill of Rights.... If he is harnessed to the Amish way of life by those in authority over him and if his education is truncated, his entire life may be stunted and deformed.

Suppose an Amish parent insisted that the child leave school after the eighth grade, but the child insisted that he or she wished to continue in school. Would it be a violation of the Free Exercise Clause to punish the parent for taking the child out of school? Would it be a violation of the Free Exercise Clause to allow the parent to take the child out of school, if the state insists that other children attend school?

7. The other justices in *Yoder* argued that Justice Douglas' point about the rights of Amish children was not involved in the case because, at the trial, there was no indication that the children's beliefs were different from their parents' beliefs. Only one of the children testified, and the last two questions asked her when she was cross-examined by the lawyer for Wisconsin were as follows:

> **Q.** So I take it then, Frieda, the only reason you are not going to school, and did not go to school since last September, is because of your religion.

A. Yes.

Q. That is the only reason?

A. Yes.

While Chief Justice Burger's opinion clearly indicates that the issue posed when child and parent disagree was not before the Court, are there intimations as to what the answer would be?

8. Justice Douglas' point was limited to the proposition that each of the children involved in the *Yoder* case was entitled to be heard as to his or her wishes. How could that be worked out? Would each Amish parent have to be criminally prosecuted so that the children could be called to the stand? Would school authorities have to question each child before the child left school in the eighth grade? Brought up in the tightly controlled Amish community, is it possible for eighth grade children to know whether leaving school is a consequence of parental or personal belief?

9. The issue of children's rights lead naturally to one of Wisconsin's major arguments for its "state interest" justifying applying the compulsory education law to Amish children. The argument was that it was important to protect the children's freedom to choose their own way of life—that a child forced to leave school in the eighth grade may not realize the kinds of options alternative to the Amish life style. In other words, if the Amish child is to have freedom of choice, further education is necessary to give the child the information needed when the child is old enough to choose. How does Chief Justice Burger answer the argument? Does the opinion answer the argument to your satisfaction?

10. The balancing process is often employed to decide questions involving issues of individual liberty under the Bill of Rights. So far, we have seen it employed in cases of freedom of speech and free exercise of religion. Even if "balancing" is the appropriate (or even inescapable) approach to a particular problem, there is a recurring difficulty in deciding what to place on the opposing ends of the golden scales. Notice how the answer often depends almost entirely on what question is asked. Most important, the answer may depend on how particularly or generally the individual and state "interests" are described. A free speech case, for example, may be described as a balance between the state's interest in self-preservation on the one hand and the defendant's right to give a particular silly speech on the other; or it might be described as a balance between the defendant's fundamental right of free speech and the state's interest in stopping the particular harmless speech. Compare Prince v. Massachusetts, 321 U.S. 158 (1944). A child's guardian, a Jehovah's Witness, sold religious publications on a public street. The nine year old child stood 20 feet away from her guardian, on the street, holding up copies of the publications. The guardian was convicted for violating a portion of the state's child labor laws that set a minimum age at which children could sell newspapers and magazines in the street. In talking of the state interests involved in the case, Justice Rutledge's opinion for the Court talked about "the interests of society to protect the welfare of children," and its interest "that children be both safeguarded from abuses and given opportunities for growth into free and independent

well-developed men [sic] and citizens." The conviction was affirmed—not surprising if the issue were stated that way. Justice Murphy, dissenting, asked whether permitting the particular child to sell religious tracts in the company of her guardian would adversely affect her health, morals or welfare. Balancing the state's limited interest in prohibiting nine year old Betty Simmons from standing in the street holding up copies of "Watch Tower" and "Consolation" against the most fundamental right of freedom to religion, it was just as easy to conclude that there was a violation of the Free Exercise Clause. Is the Court's approach in the *Yoder* case closer to Justice Rutledge's approach in the *Prince* case or Justice Murphy's approach?

11. How would you put the issue involved in the *Yoder* case? In *Yoder,* we can talk generally about the policies behind Wisconsin's compulsory school laws and balance that against the Amish wishes that their children not take a few extra academic courses. Or, we could argue that Wisconsin's general policies of compulsory education won't be seriously compromised if a handful of Amish children aren't forced to attend the 9th and 10th grades in violation of their fundamental religious beliefs. How do you decide the manner of putting the questions? Does it depend on whether it is likely that the Amish will be the only group seeking exemption on religious grounds? Is it relevant how large the Amish community is?

EMPLOYMENT DIVISION, DEPARTMENT OF HUMAN RESOURCES OF OREGON v. SMITH

Supreme Court of the United States, 1990.
494 U.S. 872, 110 S.Ct. 1595, 108 L.Ed.2d 876.

JUSTICE SCALIA delivered the opinion of the Court.

ANTONIN SCALIA—Born on March 11, 1936, in Trenton, New Jersey, son of an Italian immigrant who taught Romance languages at Brooklyn College and an elementary school teacher whose parents had emigrated from Italy. Republican. Roman Catholic. Grew up in a middle-class neighborhood of Queens, New York. Attended Jesuit schools. Georgetown, A.B., 1957, graduating first in his class; Harvard, LL.B., magna cum laude, 1960. Practiced law, 1961–1967; University of Virginia law professor, 1967–1974; general counsel, Office of Telecommunications Policy, 1971–1972; chairman, U.S. Administrative Conference, 1972–1974; assistant attorney general, U.S. Office of Legal Counsel, 1974–1977; University of Chicago law professor, 1977–1982; visiting law professor at Georgetown, 1977, and Stanford, 1980–81; U.S. Court of Appeals judge (D.C. circuit), 1982–1986. Nominated associate justice by President Ronald Reagan on June 24, 1986, to replace William H. Rehnquist, who was promoted to chief justice. Confirmed by the Senate on September 17, 1986, by a 98–0 vote.

This case requires us to decide whether the Free Exercise Clause of the First Amendment permits the State of Oregon to include religiously inspired peyote use within the reach of its general criminal prohibition on use of that drug, and thus permits the State to deny unemployment benefits to persons dismissed from their jobs because of such religiously inspired use.

I

Oregon law prohibits the knowing or intentional possession of a "controlled substance" ... [including] the drug peyote, a hallucinogen derived from the plant Lophophrawilliamsii Lemaire.

Respondents Alfred Smith and Galen Black were fired from their jobs with a private drug rehabilitation organization because they ingested peyote for sacramental purposes at a ceremony of the Native American Church, of which both are members. When respondents applied to petitioner Employment Division for unemployment compensation, they were determined to be ineligible for benefits because they had been discharged for work-related "misconduct"....

[The Oregon Supreme Court concluded that it would violate the United States Constitution to deny Smith and Black's claims for unemployment compensation. In 1987, the Supreme Court sent the case back to the Oregon courts to decide whether the consumption of peyote was a crime under Oregon law, saying that if Oregon made peyote use a crime, it could also deny unemployment benefits. In its second opinion, the Oregon Supreme Court concluded that consumption of peyote was a crime under Oregon law, but also decided that it would violate the Free Exercise Clause to punish consumption of peyote for religious reasons. The Supreme Court reviewed the case a second time, to decide whether it would violate the Constitution to criminally punish someone for religious use of peyote.]

. . .

II

Respondents' claim for relief rests on our decisions in Sherbert v. Verner, Thomas v. Review Board, Indiana Employment Security Div., and Hobbie v. Unemployment Appeals Comm'n of Florida, 480 U.S. 136 (1987).... As we observed in *Smith I*, however, the conduct at issue in those cases was not prohibited by law.... Now that the Oregon Supreme Court has confirmed that Oregon does prohibit the religious use of peyote, we proceed to consider whether that prohibition is permissible under the Free Exercise Clause.

A

... The free exercise of religion means, first and foremost, the right to believe and profess whatever religious doctrine one desires. Thus, the First Amendment obviously excludes all "governmental regulation of religious *beliefs* as such." ...

But the "exercise of religion" often involves not only belief and profession but the performance of (or abstention from) physical acts: assembling with others for a worship service, participating in sacramental use of bread and wine, proselytizing, abstaining from certain foods or certain modes of transportation. It would be true, we think (though no case of ours has involved the point), that a state would be "prohibiting the free exercise [of religion]" if it sought to ban such acts or abstentions only when they are engaged in for religious reasons, or only because of the religious belief that they display. It would doubtless be unconstitutional, for example, to ban the casting of "statues that are to be used for worship purposes," or to prohibit bowing down before a golden calf.

Respondents in the present case, however, seek to carry the meaning of "prohibiting the free exercise [of religion]" one large step further. They contend that their religious motivation for using peyote places them beyond the reach of a criminal law that is not specifically directed at their religious practice, and that is concededly constitutional as applied to those who use the drug for other reasons. They assert, in other words, that "prohibiting the free exercise [of religion]" includes requiring any individual to observe a generally applicable law that requires (or forbids) the performance of an act that his religious belief forbids (or requires). As a textual matter, we do not think the words must be given that meaning. . . .

. . . We have never held that an individual's religious beliefs excuse him from compliance with an otherwise valid law prohibiting conduct that the State is free to regulate. On the contrary, the record of more than a century of our free exercise jurisprudence contradicts that proposition. As described succinctly by Justice Frankfurter in Minersville School Dist. Bd. of Educ. v. Gobitis, 310 U.S. 586, 594–595 (1940): "Conscientious scruples have not, in the course of the long struggle for religious toleration, relieved the individual from obedience to a general law not aimed at the promotion or restriction of religious beliefs. The mere possession of religious convictions which contradict the relevant concerns of a political society does not relieve the citizen from the discharge of political responsibilities."

We first had occasion to assert that principle in Reynolds v. United States, 98 U.S. 145 (1879), where we rejected the claim that criminal laws against polygamy could not be constitutionally applied to those whose religion commanded the practice. "Laws," we said, "are made for the government of actions, and while they cannot interfere with mere religious belief and opinions, they may with practices. . . . Can a man excuse his practices to the contrary because of his religious belief? To permit this would be to make the professed doctrines of religious belief superior to the law of the land, and in effect to permit every citizen to become a law unto himself." Id., at 166–167.

Subsequent decisions have consistently held that the right of free exercise does not relieve an individual of the obligation to comply with a "valid and neutral law of general applicability on the ground that the law proscribes (or prescribes) conduct that his religion prescribes (or proscribes)." United States v. Lee, 455 U.S. 252, 263, n. 3 (1982)

(Stevens, J., concurring in judgment). In Prince v. Massachusetts, 321 U.S. 158 (1944), we held that a mother could be prosecuted under the child labor laws for using her children to dispense literature in the streets, her religious motivation notwithstanding.... In Braunfeld v. Brown, 366 U.S. 599 (1961) (plurality opinion), we upheld Sunday-closing laws against the claim that they burdened the religious practices of persons whose religions compelled them to refrain from work on other days. In Gillette v. United States, 401 U.S. 437, 461 (1971), we sustained the military selective service system against the claim that it violated free exercise by conscripting persons who opposed a particular war on religious grounds.

Our most recent decision involving a neutral, generally applicable regulatory law that compelled activity forbidden by an individual's religion was United States v. Lee, 455 U.S., at 258–261. There, an Amish employer, on behalf of himself and his employees, sought exemption from collection and payment of Social Security taxes on the ground that the Amish faith prohibited participation in governmental support programs. We rejected the claim that an exemption was constitutionally required. There would be no way, we observed, to distinguish the Amish believer's objection to Social Security taxes from the religious objections that others might have to the collection or use of other taxes. "If, for example, a religious adherent believes war is a sin, and if a certain percentage of the federal budget can be identified as devoted to war-related activities, such individuals would have a similarly valid claim to be exempt from paying that percentage of the income tax. The tax system could not function if denominations were allowed to challenge the tax system because tax payments were spent in a manner that violates their religious belief." Id., at 260.

The only decisions in which we have held that the First Amendment bars application of a neutral, generally applicable law to religiously motivated action have involved not the Free Exercise Clause alone, but the Free Exercise Clause in conjunction with other constitutional protections, such as freedom of speech and of the press, see Cantwell v. Connecticut, 310 U.S., at 304–307 (invalidating a licensing system for religious and charitable solicitations under which the administrator had discretion to deny a license to any cause he deemed nonreligious); Murdock v. Pennsylvania, 319 U.S. 105 (1943) (invalidating a flat tax on solicitation as applied to the dissemination of religious ideas); Follett v. McCormick, 321 U.S. 573 (1944) (same), or the right of parents, acknowledged in Pierce v. Society of Sisters, 268 U.S. 510 (1925), to direct the education of their children, see Wisconsin v. Yoder, 406 U.S. 205 (1972) (invalidating compulsory school-attendance laws as applied to Amish parents who refused on religious grounds to send their children to school). Some of our cases prohibiting compelled expression, decided exclusively upon free speech grounds, have also involved freedom of religion, cf. Wooley v. Maynard, 430 U.S. 705 (1977) (invalidating compelled display of a license plate slogan that offended individual religious beliefs); West Virginia Board of Education v. Barnette, 319 U.S. 624 (1943) (invalidating compulsory flag salute statute challenged by religious objectors)....

The present case does not present such a hybrid situation, but a free exercise claim unconnected with any communicative activity or parental right. Respondents urge us to hold, quite simply, that when otherwise prohibitable conduct is accompanied by religious convictions, not only the convictions but the conduct itself must be free from governmental regulation. We have never held that, and decline to do so now. There being no contention that Oregon's drug law represents an attempt to regulate religious beliefs, the communication of religious beliefs, or the raising of one's children in those beliefs, the rule to which we have adhered ever since *Reynolds* plainly controls....

B

Respondents argue that even though exemption from generally applicable criminal laws need not automatically be extended to religiously motivated actors, at least the claim for a religious exemption must be evaluated under the balancing test set forth in Sherbert v. Verner, 374 U.S. 398 (1963).... We have never invalidated any governmental action on the basis of the *Sherbert* test except the denial of unemployment compensation. Although we have sometimes purported to apply the *Sherbert* test in contexts other than that, we have always found the test satisfied, see United States v. Lee, 455 U.S. 252 (1982); Gillette v. United States, 401 U.S. 437 (1971). In recent years we have abstained from applying the *Sherbert* test (outside the unemployment compensation field) at all. In Bowen v. Roy, 476 U.S. 693 (1986), we declined to apply *Sherbert* analysis to a federal statutory scheme that required benefit applicants and recipients to provide their Social Security numbers. The plaintiffs in that case asserted that it would violate their religious beliefs to obtain and provide a Social Security number for their daughter. We held the statute's application to the plaintiffs valid regardless of whether it was necessary to effectuate a compelling interest. See id., at 699–701. In Lyng v. Northwest Indian Cemetery Protective Assn., 485 U.S. 439 (1988), we declined to apply *Sherbert* analysis to the Government's logging and road construction activities on lands used for religious purposes by several Native American Tribes, even though it was undisputed that the activities "could have devastating effects on traditional Indian religious practices," 485 U.S., at 451. In Goldman v. Weinberger, 475 U.S. 503 (1986), we rejected application of the *Sherbert* test to military dress regulations that forbade the wearing of yarmulkes. In O'Lone v. Estate of Shabazz, 482 U.S. 342 (1987), we sustained, without mentioning the *Sherbert* test, a prison's refusal to excuse inmates from work requirements to attend worship services.

Even if we were inclined to breathe into *Sherbert* some life beyond the unemployment compensation field, we would not apply it to require exemptions from a generally applicable criminal law. The *Sherbert* test, it must be recalled, was developed in a context that lent itself to individualized governmental assessment of the reasons for the relevant conduct. As a plurality of the Court noted in *Roy*, a distinctive feature of unemployment compensation programs is that their eligibility criteria invite consideration of the particular circumstances behind an applicant's unemployment.... As the plurality pointed out in *Roy*, our decisions in the unemployment cases stand for the proposition that where the State has in place a system of individual exemptions, it may not refuse to extend that system to cases of "religious hardship" without compelling reason.

Whether or not the decisions are that limited, they at least have nothing to do with an across-the-board criminal prohibition on a particular form of conduct. Although, as noted earlier, we have sometimes used the *Sherbert* test to analyze free exercise challenges to such laws, we have never applied the test to invalidate one. We conclude today that the sounder approach, and the approach in accord with the vast majority of our precedents, is to hold the test inapplicable to such challenges ..... To make an individual's obligation to obey ... a law contingent upon the law's coincidence with his religious beliefs, except where the State's interest is "compelling" ... contradicts both constitutional tradition and common sense.

The "compelling government interest" requirement seems benign, because it is familiar from other fields. But using it as the standard that must be met before the government may accord different treatment on the basis of race, or before the government may regulate the content of speech, is not remotely comparable to using it for the purpose asserted here. What it produces in those other fields—equality of treatment, and an unrestricted flow of contending speech—are constitutional norms; what it would produce here—a private right to ignore generally applicable laws—is a constitutional anomaly.

Nor is it possible to limit the impact of respondents' proposal by requiring a "compelling state interest" only when the conduct prohibited is "central" to the individual's religion. It is no more appropriate for judges to determine the "centrality" of religious beliefs before applying a "compelling interest" test in the free exercise field, than it would be for them to determine the "importance" of ideas before applying the "compelling interest" test in the free speech field.... Repeatedly and in many different contexts, we have warned that courts must not presume to determine the place of a particular belief in a religion or the plausibility of a religious claim.

If the "compelling interest" test is to be applied at all, then, it must be applied across the board, to all actions thought to be religiously commanded. Moreover, if "compelling interest" really means what it says (and watering it down here would subvert its rigor in the other fields where it is applied), many laws will not meet the test. Any society adopting such a system would be courting anarchy, but that danger increases in direct proportion to the society's diversity of religious beliefs, and its determination to coerce or suppress none of them.... The rule respondents favor would open the prospect of constitutionally required religious exemptions from civic obligations of almost every conceivable kind—ranging from compulsory military service, to the payment of taxes, to health and safety regulation such as manslaughter and child neglect laws, compulsory vaccination laws, drug laws, and traffic laws, to social welfare legislation such as minimum wage laws, child labor laws, animal cruelty laws, environmental protection laws, and laws providing for equality of opportunity for the races. The First Amendment's protection of religious liberty does not require this.

Values that are protected against government interference through enshrinement in the Bill of Rights are not thereby banished from the political process.... It may fairly be said that leaving accommodation to the political process will place at a relative disadvantage those religious practices that are not widely engaged in; but that unavoidable consequence of democratic government must be preferred to a system in which each conscience is a law unto itself or in which judges weigh the social importance of all laws against the centrality of all religious beliefs.

Because respondents' ingestion of peyote was prohibited under Oregon law, and because that prohibition is constitutional, Oregon may, consistent with the Free Exercise Clause, deny respondents unemployment compensation when their dismissal results from use of the drug. The decision of the Oregon Supreme Court is accordingly reversed.

It is so ordered.

JUSTICE O'CONNOR, with whom JUSTICE BRENNAN, JUSTICE MARSHALL, and JUSTICE BLACKMUN join as to Parts I and II, concurring in the judgment.*

Although I agree with the result the Court reaches in this case, I cannot join its opinion. In my view, today's holding dramatically departs from well-settled First Amendment jurisprudence, appears unnecessary to resolve the question presented, and is incompatible with our Nation's fundamental commitment to individual religious liberty.

. . .

II

The Court today extracts from our long history of free exercise precedents the single categorical rule that "if prohibiting the exercise of religion ... is ... merely the incidental effect of a generally applicable and otherwise valid provision, the First Amendment has not been offended." Indeed, the Court holds that where the law is a generally applicable criminal prohibition, our usual free exercise jurisprudence does not even apply. To reach this sweeping result, however, the Court must not only give a strained reading of the First Amendment but must also disregard our consistent application of free exercise doctrine to cases involving generally applicable regulations that burden religious conduct.

A

... Because the First Amendment does not distinguish between religious belief and religious conduct, conduct motivated by sincere religious belief, like the belief itself, must therefore be at least presumptively protected by the Free Exercise Clause.

The Court today, however, interprets the Clause to permit the government to prohibit, without justification, conduct mandated by an individual's religious beliefs, so long as that prohibition is generally

* Although Justice Brennan, Justice Marshall, and Justice Blackmun join Parts I and II of this opinion, they do not concur in the judgment.

applicable. But a law that prohibits certain conduct—conduct that happens to be an act of worship for someone—manifestly does prohibit that person's free exercise of his religion. A person who is barred from engaging in religiously motivated conduct is barred from freely exercising his religion. Moreover, that person is barred from freely exercising his religion regardless of whether the law prohibits the conduct only when engaged in for religious reasons, only by members of that religion, or by all persons. It is difficult to deny that a law that prohibits religiously motivated conduct, even if the law is generally applicable, does not at least implicate First Amendment concerns.

. . .

To say that a person's right to free exercise has been burdened, of course, does not mean that he has an absolute right to engage in the conduct. . . . [W]e have respected both the First Amendment's express textual mandate and the governmental interest in regulation of conduct by requiring the Government to justify any substantial burden on religiously motivated conduct by a compelling state interest and by means narrowly tailored to achieve that interest. . . .

The Court attempts to support its narrow reading of the Clause by claiming that "[w]e have never held that an individual's religious beliefs excuse him from compliance with an otherwise valid law prohibiting conduct that the State is free to regulate." But as the Court later notes, as it must, in cases such as ... *Yoder* we have in fact interpreted the Free Exercise Clause to forbid application of a generally applicable prohibition to religiously motivated conduct. . . .

... Moreover, in each of the other cases cited by the Court to support its categorical rule, we rejected the particular constitutional claims before us only after carefully weighing the competing interests. . . . That we rejected the free exercise claims in those cases hardly calls into question the applicability of First Amendment doctrine in the first place. Indeed, it is surely unusual to judge the vitality of a constitutional doctrine by looking to the win-loss record of the plaintiffs who happen to come before us.

B

. . .

In my view, ... the essence of a free exercise claim is relief from a burden imposed by government on religious practices or beliefs, whether the burden is imposed directly through laws that prohibit or compel specific religious practices, or indirectly through laws that, in effect, make abandonment of one's own religion or conformity to the religious beliefs of others the price of an equal place in the civil community. . . .

Indeed, we have never distinguished between cases in which a State conditions receipt of a benefit on conduct prohibited by religious beliefs and cases in which a State affirmatively prohibits such conduct. The *Sherbert* compelling interest test applies in both kinds of cases. . . .

... Even if, as an empirical matter, a government's criminal laws might usually serve a compelling interest in health, safety, or public order, the First Amendment at least requires a case-by-case determination of the question, sensitive to the facts of each particular claim. Given the range of conduct that a State might legitimately make criminal, we cannot assume, merely because a law carries criminal sanctions and is generally applicable, that the First Amendment *never* requires the State to grant a limited exemption for religiously motivated conduct.

. . .

Finally, the Court today suggests that the disfavoring of minority religions is an "unavoidable consequence" under our system of government and that accommodation of such religions must be left to the political process. In my view, however, the First Amendment was enacted precisely to protect the rights of those whose religious practices are not shared by the majority and may be viewed with hostility. The history of our free exercise doctrine amply demonstrates the harsh impact majoritarian rule has had on unpopular or emerging religious groups such as the Jehovah's Witnesses and the Amish. . . .

III

The Court's holding today not only misreads settled First Amendment precedent; it appears to be unnecessary to this case. I would reach the same result applying our established free exercise jurisprudence.

. . .

. . . [T]he critical question in this case is whether exempting respondents from the State's general criminal prohibition "will unduly interfere with fulfillment of the governmental interest." Although the question is close, I would conclude that uniform application of Oregon's criminal prohibition is "essential to accomplish," its overriding interest in preventing the physical harm caused by the use of a . . . controlled substance. Oregon's criminal prohibition represents that State's judgment that the possession and use of controlled substances, even by only one person, is inherently harmful and dangerous. Because the health effects caused by the use of controlled substances exist regardless of the motivation of the user, the use of such substances, even for religious purposes, violates the very purpose of the laws that prohibit them. Moreover, in view of the societal interest in preventing trafficking in controlled substances, uniform application of the criminal prohibition at issue is essential to the effectiveness of Oregon's stated interest in preventing any possession of peyote.

For these reasons, I believe that granting a selective exemption in this case would seriously impair Oregon's compelling interest in prohibiting possession of peyote by its citizens. Under such circumstances, the Free Exercise Clause does not require the State to accommodate respondents' religiously motivated conduct. . . .

Respondents contend that any incompatibility is belied by the fact that the Federal Government and several States provide exemptions for the religious use of peyote. But other governments may surely choose to grant an exemption without Oregon, with its specific asserted interest in uniform application of its drug laws, being *required* to do so by the First

Amendment. Respondents also note that the sacramental use of peyote is central to the tenets of the Native American Church, but I agree with the Court that ... our determination of the constitutionality of Oregon's general criminal prohibition cannot, and should not, turn on the centrality of the particular religious practice at issue. This does not mean, of course, that courts may not make factual findings as to whether a claimant holds a sincerely held religious belief that conflicts with, and thus is burdened by, the challenged law. The distinction between questions of centrality and questions of sincerity and burden is admittedly fine, but it is one that is an established part of our free exercise doctrine....

I would therefore adhere to our established free exercise jurisprudence and hold that the State in this case has a compelling interest in regulating peyote use by its citizens and that accommodating respondents' religiously motivated conduct "will unduly interfere with fulfillment of the governmental interest." *Lee,* 455 U.S., at 259. Accordingly, I concur in the judgment of the Court.

JUSTICE BLACKMUN, with whom JUSTICE BRENNAN and JUSTICE MARSHALL join, dissenting.

. . .

... I agree with Justice O'Connor's analysis of the applicable free exercise doctrine, and I join parts I and II of her opinion. As she points out, "the critical question in this case is whether exempting respondents from the State's general criminal prohibition 'will unduly interfere with fulfillment of the governmental interest.'" I do disagree, however, with her specific answer to that question.

. . .

... The State's asserted interest ... amounts only to the symbolic preservation of an unenforced prohibition....

. . .

The State proclaims an interest in protecting the health and safety of its citizens from the dangers of unlawful drugs. It offers, however, no evidence that the religious use of peyote has ever harmed anyone. The factual findings of other courts cast doubt on the State's assumption that religious use of peyote is harmful.

. . .

The carefully circumscribed ritual context in which respondents used peyote is far removed from the irresponsible and unrestricted recreational use of unlawful drugs. The Native American Church's internal restrictions on, and supervision of, its members' use of peyote substantially obviate the State's health and safety concerns.

. . .

Finally, the State argues that granting an exception for religious peyote use would erode its interest in the uniform, fair, and certain enforcement of its drug laws. The State fears that, if it grants an exemption for religious peyote use, a flood of other claims to religious exemptions will follow. It would then be placed in a dilemma, it says, between allowing a patchwork of exemptions that would hinder its law enforcement efforts, and risking a violation of the Establishment Clause by arbitrarily limiting its religious exemptions. This argument, however, could be made in almost any free exercise case. . . .

The State's apprehension of a flood of other religious claims is purely speculative. Almost half the States, and the Federal Government, have maintained an exemption for religious peyote use for many years, and apparently have not found themselves overwhelmed by claims to other religious exemptions. . . .

Finally, although I agree with Justice O'Connor that courts should refrain from delving into questions of whether, as a matter of religious doctrine, a particular practice is "central" to the religion, I do not think this means that the courts must turn a blind eye to the severe impact of a State's restrictions on the adherents of a minority religion. . . .

Respondents believe, and their sincerity has *never* been at issue, that the peyote plant embodies their deity, and eating it is an act of worship and communion. Without peyote, they could not enact the essential ritual of their religion.

If Oregon can constitutionally prosecute them for this act of worship, they, like the Amish, may be "forced to migrate to some other and more tolerant region." *Yoder,* 406 U.S., at 218. This potentially devastating impact must be viewed in light of the federal policy—reached in reaction to many years of religious persecution and intolerance—of protecting the religious freedom of Native Americans. See American Indian Religious Freedom Act, 92 Stat. 469, 42 U.S.C. § 1996 ("it shall be the policy of the United States to protect and preserve for American Indians their inherent right of freedom to believe, express, and exercise the traditional religions . . ., including but not limited to access to sites, use and possession of sacred objects, and the freedom to worship through ceremonials and traditional rites"). Congress recognized that certain substances, such as peyote, "have religious significance because they are sacred, they have power, they heal, they are necessary to the exercise of the rites of the religion, they are necessary to the cultural integrity of the tribe, and, therefore, religious survival." H.R.Rep. No. 95–1308, p. 2 (1978).

The American Indian Religious Freedom Act, in itself, may not create rights enforceable against government action restricting religious freedom, but this Court must scrupulously apply its free exercise analysis to the religious claims of Native Americans, however unorthodox they may be. Otherwise, both the First Amendment and the stated policy of Congress will offer to Native Americans merely an unfulfilled and hollow promise.

For these reasons, I conclude that Oregon's interest in enforcing its drug laws against religious use of peyote is not sufficiently compelling to outweigh respondents' right to the free exercise of their religion. Since the State could not constitutionally enforce its criminal prohibition against respondents, the interests underlying the State's drug laws cannot justify its denial of unemployment benefits....

I dissent.

NOTES AND QUESTIONS

1.   The Court concludes that the Mormon polygamy case (Reynolds v. United States) represents the general rule, while the unemployment compensation case (Sherbert v. Verner) and the Amish case (Wisconsin v. Yoder) are narrow exceptions. It is true that the unemployment compensation cases and *Yoder* are the only instances where the Supreme Court has protected religiously-motivated conduct under the free exercise clause. Is Justice O'Connor right that *Sherbert* and *Yoder* represent a rejection of the *Reynolds* approach, and not exceptions to it?

2.   It is not uncommon for court opinions that reject earlier cases to distinguish inconsistent opinions rather than overrule them. (*Sherbert* and *Yoder* did not overrule earlier cases that had denied constitutional protection to religiously-motivated conduct.) Notice the Court's distinction of *Yoder* as resting on two constitutional rights combined—the right of parents to direct the education of their children and the right of free exercise of religion. Under the Court's opinion in *Smith,* the right of free exercise of religion standing alone would not allow Amish parents to disregard the compulsory school attendance law, and under the Court's opinion in *Yoder,* parents whose objection to the law was not religious would also have to obey it. Is it strange that two constitutional claims that will fail alone can combine to prevail? Are there any cases other than *Yoder* itself where a free exercise claim can prevail, when combined with an otherwise insufficient constitutional right?

3.   Does it make sense to limit Sherbert v. Verner to denials of unemployment compensation benefits where the religiously-compelled conduct that leads to job loss is not a violation of the criminal law? Two previous opinions have suggested that there is a difference between criminal punishment for conduct compelled by religious belief, and denial of state benefits for such conduct. Those opinions, however, argued that the religious person was *more* likely to be entitled to constitutional protection when forced to choose between religious conscience and going to jail than when forced to choose between religious conscience and financial loss.

4.   Three of the five justices in the *Smith* majority had previously indicated disagreement with the proposition that it would take a "compelling government interest" to justify state interference with religiously-compelled conduct. Justice White dissented in Sherbert v. Verner, although he treated that opinion as a binding precedent in subsequent unemployment compensation cases. Justice Rehnquist was the sole dissenter in Thomas v. Review Board of the Indiana Employment Security Division when the Court followed *Sherbert* in an unemployment compensation case. In a concurring opinion in United States v. Lee, 455 U.S. 252 (1982), Justice Stevens doubted whether the Court really required a "compelling" state interest in free exercise cases, and argued that free

exercise claims should be rejected unless the religious objector showed "a unique reason for allowing him a special exemption."

5. In recent years, there has been emphasis on protecting individual liberty under state constitutions. Those constitutions have their own bills of rights, and state courts can interpret them to provide broader protection of rights than is available under the United States Constitution. (See note 3, page 225, above.) The Oregon Supreme Court in recent years has followed a consistent practice of deciding federal constitutional questions only after it has first satisfied itself that the Oregon Constitution does not provide constitutional protection. Accordingly, the Oregon Supreme Court seldom discusses the United States Constitution, since in most cases the Oregon Constitution is, at least, as protective of individual liberty as the United States Constitution. In *Smith,* the Oregon Supreme Court twice sustained a free exercise claim under the First Amendment, but this was only after it had examined the Oregon Constitution and rejected any state constitutional protection for religiously-motivated conduct. Justice Hans Linde of that court has been a consistent critic of the technique of balancing competing interests in interpreting the Constitution. "In practice," he has argued "all there is to the 'balancing' to which the Supreme Court has reduced contemporary constitutional law" is the substitution of pragmatic judicial policy-making for law. Linde, E Pluribus—Constitutional Theory and State Courts, Georgia Law Review, 1984, vol. 18, p. 165. Justice Scalia, who wrote the United State Supreme Court's opinion in *Smith* has also been critical of "balancing." In The Rule of Law as a Law of Rules, University of Chicago Law Review, 1989, vol. 56, p. 1175, he said: "We will have totality of the circumstances tests and balancing modes of analysis with us forever—and for my sins, I will probably write some of the opinions that use them. All I urge is that those modes of analysis be avoided where possible; that the *Rule* of Law, the law of *rules,* be extended as far as the nature of the question allows."

6. Despite *Smith*, a unanimous Court found a violation of the Free Exercise Clause in Church of the Lukumi Babalu Aye, Inc. v. City of Hialeah, 508 U.S. 520 (1993). The church practices the Santeria religion, whose rituals include animal sacrifices. When the church proposed to build a house of worship in Hialeah, the city enacted ordinances that targeted the practice of animal sacrifice by the church. One ordinance provided that "[i]t shall be unlawful for any person, persons, corporations or associations to sacrifice any animal within the corporate limits of the City of Hialeah, Florida." "Sacrifice" was defined as "to unnecessarily kill, torment, torture, or mutilate an animal in a public or private ritual or ceremony not for the primary purpose of food consumption." The ordinance contained an exemption for slaughtering by "licensed establishment[s]" of animals "specifically raised for food purposes." The Court held that the ordinances violated the free exercise clause since they were neither "neutral" nor "of general applicability." The ordinances were drafted so that "almost the only conduct subject to [them] is the religious exercise of Santeria church members." All of the asserted governmental purposes (protecting public health and preventing cruelty to animals) were only pursued in the context of Santeria religious

practices. "A law that targets religious conduct for distinctive treatment or advances legitimate governmental interests only against conduct with a religious motivation will survive strict scrutiny only in rare cases."

LOCKE v. DAVEY

540 U.S. 712, 124 S.Ct. 1307, 158 L.Ed.2d 1 (2004).

CHIEF JUSTICE REHNQUIST delivered the opinion of the Court.

The State of Washington established the Promise Scholarship Program to assist academically gifted students with postsecondary education expenses. In accordance with the State Constitution, students may not use the scholarship at an institution where they are pursuing a degree in devotional theology. We hold that such an exclusion from an otherwise inclusive aid program does not violate the Free Exercise Clause of the First Amendment.

. . .

These two Clauses, the Establishment Clause and the Free Exercise Clause, are frequently in tension. . . . Yet we have long said that "there is room for play in the joints" between them. In other words, there are some state actions permitted by the Establishment Clause but not required by the Free Exercise Clause.

. . . [T]here is no doubt that the State could, consistent with the Federal Constitution, permit Promise Scholars to pursue a degree in devotional theology . . . and the State does not contend otherwise. The question before us, however, is whether Washington, pursuant to its own constitution, which has been authoritatively interpreted as prohibiting even indirectly funding religious instruction that will prepare students for the ministry . . .

Davey urges us to answer that question in the negative. He contends that under the rule we enunciated in *Church of Lukumi Babalu Aye, Inc. v. Hialeah*, . . . the program is presumptively unconstitutional because it is not facially neutral with respect to religion. We reject his claim of presumptive unconstitutionality, however; to do otherwise would extend the *Lukumi* line of cases well beyond not only their facts but their reasoning. In *Lukumi*, the city of Hialeah made it a crime to engage in certain kinds of animal slaughter. . . . In the present case, the State's disfavor of religion (if it can be called that) is of a far milder kind. It imposes neither criminal nor civil sanctions on any type of religious service or rite . . . [I]t does not require students to choose between their religious beliefs and receiving a government benefit.[2] The State has merely chosen not to fund a distinct category of instruction.

. . . Because the Promise Scholarship Program funds training for all secular professions, Justice Scalia contends the State must also fund training for religious professions. But training for religious professions and training for secular professions are not fungible. Training someone to lead a congregation is an essentially religious endeavor. . . . [T]he

2. Promise Scholars may still use their scholarship to pursue a secular degree at a different institution from where they are studying devotional theology.

subject of religion is one in which both the United States and state constitutions embody distinct views—in favor of free exercise, but opposed to establishment—that find no counterpart with respect to other callings or professions. That a State would deal differently with religious education for the ministry than with education for other callings is a product of these views, not evidence of hostility toward religion.

Even though the differently worded Washington Constitution draws a more stringent line than that drawn by the United States Constitution, the interest it seeks to further is scarcely novel. In fact, we can think of few areas in which a State's antiestablishment interests come more into play. Since the founding of our country, there have been popular uprisings against procuring taxpayer funds to support church leaders, which was one of the hallmarks of an "established" religion. ...

Most States that sought to avoid an establishment of religion around the time of the founding placed in their constitutions formal prohibitions against using tax funds to support the ministry. ... The plain text of these constitutional provisions prohibited *any* tax dollars from supporting the clergy. We have found nothing to indicate ... that these provisions would not have applied so long as the State equally supported other professions or if the amount at stake was *de minimis*. That early state constitutions saw no problem in explicitly excluding *only* the ministry from receiving state dollars reinforces our conclusion that religious instruction is of a different ilk. ...

Far from evincing the hostility toward religion which was manifest in *Lukumi,* we believe that the entirety of the Promise Scholarship Program goes a long way toward including religion in its benefits. The program permits students to attend pervasively religious schools, so long as they are accredited. ... And under the Promise Scholarship Program's current guidelines, students are still eligible to take devotional theology courses. ...

In short, we find neither in the history or text of Article I, § 11 of the Washington Constitution, nor in the operation of the Promise Scholarship Program, anything that suggests animus towards religion. Given the historic and substantial state interest at issue, we therefore cannot conclude that the denial of funding for vocational religious instruction alone is inherently constitutionally suspect.

Without a presumption of unconstitutionality, Davey's claim must fail. The State's interest in not funding the pursuit of devotional degrees is substantial and the exclusion of such funding places a relatively minor burden on Promise Scholars. If any room exists between the two Religion Clauses, it must be here. We need not venture further into this difficult area in order to uphold the Promise Scholarship Program as currently operated by the State of Washington.

. . .

JUSTICE SCALIA, with whom JUSTICE THOMAS joins, dissenting.

. . .

The Court does not dispute that the Free Exercise Clause places some constraints on public benefits programs, but finds none here, based on a principle of " 'play in the joints.' " I use the term "principle" loosely, for that is not so much a legal principle as a refusal to apply *any* principle when faced with competing constitutional directives. There is nothing anomalous about constitutional commands that abut. A municipality hiring public contractors may not discriminate *against* blacks or *in favor of* them; it cannot discriminate a little bit each way and then plead "play in the joints" when haled into court. If the Religion Clauses demand neutrality, we must enforce them, in hard cases as well as easy ones.

Even if "play in the joints" were a valid legal principle, surely it would apply only when it was a close call whether complying with one of the Religion Clauses would violate the other. ... The establishment question *would not even be close,* as is evident from the fact that this Court's decision in *Witters v. Washington Dept. of Servs. for Blind,* 474 U.S. 481, was unanimous. Perhaps some formally neutral public benefits programs are so gerrymandered and devoid of plausible secular purpose that they might raise specters of state aid to religion, but an evenhanded Promise Scholarship Program is not among them.

In any case, the State already has all the play in the joints it needs. There are any number of ways it could respect both its unusually sensitive concern for the conscience of its taxpayers *and* the Federal Free Exercise Clause. It could make the scholarships redeemable only at public universities (where it sets the curriculum), or only for select courses of study. Either option would replace a program that facially discriminates against religion with one that just happens not to subsidize it. The State could also simply abandon the scholarship program altogether. If that seems a dear price to pay for freedom of conscience, it is only because the State has defined that freedom so broadly that it would be offended by a program with such an incidental, indirect religious effect.

. . .

[T]he interest to which the Court defers is not fear of a conceivable Establishment Clause violation, budget constraints, avoidance of endorsement, or substantive neutrality—none of these. It is a pure philosophical preference: the State's opinion that it would violate taxpayers' freedom of conscience *not* to discriminate against candidates for the ministry. This sort of protection of "freedom of conscience" has no logical limit and can justify the singling out of religion for exclusion from public programs in virtually any context. ...

II

The Court makes no serious attempt to defend the program's neutrality, and instead identifies two features thought to render its discrimination less offensive. The first is the lightness of Davey's burden. The Court offers no authority for approving facial discrimination against religion simply because its material consequences are not severe. I might understand such a test if we were still in the business of reviewing facially neutral laws that merely happen to burden some individual's religious exercise, but we are not. ... The Court has not required proof of "substantial" concrete harm with other forms of discrimination, see, e.g., *Brown v. Board of Education,* ... and it should not do so here.

The other reason the Court thinks this particular facial discrimination less offensive is that the scholarship program was not motivated by animus toward religion. The Court does not explain why the legislature's motive matters, and I fail to see why it should. ...

The Court has not approached other forms of discrimination this way. When we declared racial segregation unconstitutional, we did not ask whether the State had originally adopted the regime, not out of "animus" against blacks, but because of a well-meaning but misguided belief that the races would be better off apart. ... We do sometimes look to legislative intent to smoke out more subtle instances of discrimination, but we do so as a *supplement* to the core guarantee of facially equal treatment, not as a replacement for it. ...

There is no need to rely on analogies, however, because we have rejected the Court's methodology in this very context. In *McDaniel v. Paty,* 435 U.S. 618 (1978), we considered a Tennessee statute that disqualified clergy from participation in the state constitutional convention. That statute, like the one here, was based upon a state constitutional provision—a clause in the 1796 Tennessee Constitution that disqualified clergy from sitting in the legislature. ... The State defended the statute as an attempt to be faithful to its constitutional separation of church and state, and we accepted that claimed benevolent purpose as bona fide. ... Nonetheless, because it did not justify facial discrimination against religion, we invalidated the restriction. ...

. . .

Today's holding is limited to training the clergy, but its logic is readily extendible, and there are plenty of directions to go. What next? Will we deny priests and nuns their prescription-drug benefits on the ground that taxpayers' freedom of conscience forbids medicating the clergy at public expense? This may seem fanciful, but recall that France has proposed banning religious attire from schools, invoking interests in secularism no less benign than those the Court embraces today. ...

JUSTICE THOMAS, dissenting.

I write separately to note that, in my view, the study of theology does not necessarily implicate religious devotion or faith ... [T]he statute itself does not define "theology." And the usual definition of the term "theology" is not limited to devotional studies. "Theology" is defined as "[t]he study of the nature of God and religious truth" and the "rational inquiry into religious questions." American Heritage Dictionary 1794 (4th ed.2000). ... These definitions include the study of theology from a secular perspective as well as from a religious one.

. . .

QUESTIONS

What was the principal basis of the Court's holding in *Locke* that Washington's scholarship program did not violate Davey's right to free exercise of religion? Was it the majority's belief that the program did not penalize Davey for his religious beliefs or practices? Was it that the majority's belief that the state's interest in providing the program was so "substantial" that it outweighed Davey's "relatively minor burden"? Was it the majority's belief that the state's denying Davey a scholarship did not show hostility to religion?

THE RELIGIOUS FREEDOM RESTORATION ACT

On November 16, 1993, President Clinton signed into law the Religious Freedom Restoration Act. The Act had been passed by overwhelming majorities in Congress. It provides, in relevant part:

SEC. 2. CONGRESSIONAL FINDINGS AND DECLARATION OF PURPOSES.

(a) FINDINGS.—The Congress finds that—

(1) the framers of the Constitution, recognizing free exercise of religion as an unalienable right, secured its protection in the First Amendment to the Constitution;

(2) laws "neutral" toward religion may burden religious exercise as surely as laws intended to interfere with religious exercise;

(3) governments should not substantially burden religious exercise without compelling justification;

(4) in Employment Division v. Smith, 494 U.S. 872 (1990) the Supreme Court virtually eliminated the requirement that the government justify burdens on religious exercise imposed by laws neutral toward religion; and

(5) the compelling interest test as set forth in prior Federal court rulings is a workable test for striking sensible balances between religious liberty and competing prior governmental interests.

(b) PURPOSES.—The purposes of this Act are—

(1) to restore the compelling interest test as set forth in Sherbert v. Verner, 374 U.S. 398 (1963) and Wisconsin v. Yoder, 406 U.S. 205 (1972) and to guarantee its application in all cases where free exercise of religion is substantially burdened; and

(2) to provide a claim or defense to persons whose religious exercise is substantially burdened by government.

SEC. 3. FREE EXERCISE OF RELIGION PROTECTED.

(a) IN GENERAL.—Government shall not substantially burden a person's exercise of religion even if the burden results from a rule of general applicability, except as provided in subsection (b).

(b) EXCEPTION.—Government may substantially burden a person's exercise of religion only if it demonstrates that application of the burden to the person—

    (1) is in furtherance of a compelling governmental interest; and

    (2) is the least restrictive means of furthering that compelling governmental interest.

(c) JUDICIAL RELIEF.—A person whose religious exercise has been burdened in violation of this section may assert that violation as a claim or defense in a judicial proceeding and obtain appropriate relief against a government. Standing to assert a claim or defense under this section shall be governed by the general rules of standing under article III of the Constitution.

SEC. 5. DEFINITIONS.

As used in this Act—

(1) the term "government" includes a branch, department, agency, instrumentality, and official (or other person acting under color of law) of the United States, a State, or a subdivision of a State;

(2) the term "State" includes the District of Columbia, the Commonwealth of Puerto Rico, and each territory and possession of the United States;

(3) the term "demonstrates" means meets the burdens of going forward with the evidence and of persuasion; and

(4) the term "exercise of religion" means the exercise of religion under the First Amendment to the Constitution.

SEC. 6. APPLICABILITY.

(a) IN GENERAL.—This Act applies to all Federal and State law, and the implementation of that law, whether statutory or otherwise, and whether adopted before or after the enactment of this Act.

(b) RULE OF CONSTRUCTION.—Federal statutory law adopted after the date of the enactment of this Act is subject to this Act unless such law explicitly excludes such application by reference to this Act.

(c) RELIGIOUS BELIEF UNAFFECTED.—Nothing in this Act shall be construed to authorize any government to burden any religious belief.

NOTES AND QUESTIONS

1. The Act was applicable "to all Federal and State law, and the implementation of that law." In City of Boerne v. Flores, 521 U.S. 507 (1997), RFRA was held to be unconstitutional insofar as it invalidated state and local laws. (The Act had been justified under § 5 of the Fourteenth Amendment as a measure to "enforce" the Free Exercise guarantee. The Court's majority concluded that, to the extent RFRA invalidated laws that were not unconstitutional, it went beyond Congress' power to "enforce" the Constitution. "Laws valid under *Smith*

would fall under RFRA without regard to whether they had the object of stifling or punishing free exercise.")

2. The Court's rationale in *City of Boerne* was directed to the limits on federal power to invalidate state and local law. The Court has not addressed the question whether RFRA can be applied to challenge federal laws and regulations, and it is possible that questions concerning religious autonomy from federal law will be resolved in the future under the statute and not the First Amendment. Notice the stated purpose— "to restore the compelling interest test" as it existed before *Smith* was decided. Re-read Justice Scalia's summary of the cases decided before *Smith*. Would the statute's "restoration" of the compelling interest standard require that any of those cases be decided differently?

CUTTER v. WILKINSON

544 U.S. 709, 125 S.Ct. 2113, 161 L.Ed.2d 1020 (2005).

JUSTICE GINSBURG delivered the opinion of the Court.

Section 3 of the Religious Land Use and Institutionalized Persons Act of 2000 (RLUIPA), 114 Stat. 804, provides in part: "No government shall impose a substantial burden on the religious exercise of a person residing in or confined to an institution," unless the burden furthers "a compelling governmental interest," and does so by "the least restrictive means." Plaintiffs below, petitioners here, are current and former inmates of institutions operated by the Ohio Department of Rehabilitation and Correction and assert that they are adherents of "nonmainstream" religions: the Satanist, Wicca, and Asatru religions, and the Church of Jesus Christ Christian. They complain that Ohio prison officials (respondents here), in violation of RLUIPA, have failed to accommodate their religious exercise "in a variety of different ways, including retaliating and discriminating against them for exercising their nontraditional faiths, denying them access to religious literature, denying them the same opportunities for group worship that are granted to adherents of mainstream religions, forbidding them to adhere to the dress and appearance mandates of their religions, withholding religious ceremonial items that are substantially identical to those that the adherents of mainstream religions are permitted, and failing to provide a chaplain trained in their faith." ...

In response to petitioners' complaints, respondent prison officials have mounted a facial challenge to the institutionalized-persons provision of RLUIPA; respondents contend, *inter alia,* that the Act improperly advances religion in violation of the First Amendment's Establishment Clause. The District Court denied respondents' motion to dismiss petitioners' complaints, but the Court of Appeals reversed that determination. The appeals court held, as the prison officials urged, that the portion of RLUIPA applicable to institutionalized persons, violates the Establishment Clause. We reverse the Court of Appeals' judgment.

"This Court has long recognized that the government may ... accommodate religious practices ... without violating the Establishment Clause." ... But § 3 of RLUIPA, we hold, does not, on its face, exceed the limits of permissible government accommodation of religious practices.

I

A

RLUIPA is the latest of long-running congressional efforts to accord religious exercise heightened protection from government-imposed burdens, consistent with this Court's precedents. Ten years before RLUIPA's enactment, the Court held, in Employment Div., Dept. of Human Resources of Ore. v. Smith, ... that the First Amendment's Free Exercise Clause does not inhibit enforcement of otherwise valid laws of general application that incidentally burden religious conduct. In particular, we ruled that the Free Exercise Clause did not bar Oregon from enforcing its blanket ban on peyote possession with no allowance for sacramental use of the drug. Accordingly, the State could deny unemployment benefits to persons dismissed from their jobs because of their religiously inspired peyote use. The Court recognized, however, that the political branches could shield religious exercise through legislative accommodation, for example, by making an exception to proscriptive drug laws for sacramental peyote use. ...

Responding to *Smith,* Congress enacted the Religious Freedom Restoration Act of 1993 (RFRA) ... In *City of Boerne,* this Court invalidated RFRA as applied to States and their subdivisions, holding that the Act exceeded Congress' remedial powers under the Fourteenth Amendment.[3] ... Congress again responded, this time by enacting RLUIPA. Less sweeping than RFRA, and invoking federal authority under the Spending and Commerce Clauses, RLUIPA targets two areas: Section 2 of the Act concerns land-use regulation, § 3 relates to religious exercise by institutionalized persons, ... Section 3, at issue here, provides that "[n]o [state or local] government shall impose a substantial burden on the religious exercise of a person residing in or confined to an institution," unless the government shows that the burden furthers "a compelling governmental interest" and does so by "the least restrictive means." ... The Act defines "religious exercise" to include "any exercise of religion, whether or not compelled by, or central to, a system of religious belief...." Section 3 applies when "the substantial burden [on religious exercise] is imposed in a program or activity that receives Federal financial assistance," or "the substantial burden affects, or removal of that substantial burden would affect, commerce with foreign nations, among the several States", or with Indian tribes "A person may assert a violation of [RLUIPA] as a claim or defense in a judicial proceeding and obtain appropriate relief against a government."

Before enacting § 3, Congress documented, in hearings spanning three years, that "frivolous or arbitrary" barriers impeded institutionalized persons' religious exercise ... To secure redress for inmates who encountered undue barriers to their religious observances, Congress

---

3. RFRA, Courts of Appeals have held, remains operative as to the Federal Government and federal territories and possessions. ... This Court, however, has not had occasion to rule on the matter.

carried over from RFRA the "compelling governmental interest"/"least restrictive means" standard. . . .

The hearings held by Congress revealed, for a typical example, that "[a] state prison in Ohio refused to provide Moslems with Hallal food, even though it provided Kosher food." . . . Across the country, Jewish inmates complained that prison officials refused to provide sack lunches, which would enable inmates to break their fasts after nightfall. *Id.*, at 39 (statement of Isaac M. Jaroslawicz, Director of Legal Affairs for the Aleph Institute). A priest responsible for communications between Roman Catholic dioceses and corrections facilities in Oklahoma stated that there "was [a] nearly yearly battle over the Catholic use of Sacramental Wine . . . for the celebration of the Mass," and that prisoners' religious possessions, "such as the Bible, the Koran, the Talmud or items needed by Native Americans[,] . . . were frequently treated with contempt and were confiscated, damaged or discarded" by prison officials. . . .

B

Petitioners initially filed suit against respondents asserting claims under the First and Fourteenth Amendments. After RLUIPA's enactment, petitioners amended their complaints to include claims under § 3. Respondents moved to dismiss the statutory claims, . . .

. . .

. . . [T]he District Court rejected the argument that § 3 conflicts with the Establishment Clause. . . .

. . . [T]he Court of Appeals for the Sixth Circuit reversed. [holding] that § 3 of RLUIPA "impermissibly advanc[es] religion by giving greater protection to religious rights than to other constitutionally protected rights." Affording "religious prisoners rights superior to those of nonreligious prisoners," the court suggested, might "encourag[e] prisoners to become religious in order to enjoy greater rights."

We granted certiorari to resolve the conflict among Courts of Appeals on the question whether RLUIPA's institutionalized-persons provision, § 3 of the Act, is consistent with the Establishment Clause of the First Amendment. We now reverse the judgment of the Court of Appeals for the Sixth Circuit.

II

A

While the two [Religion] Clauses express complementary values, they often exert conflicting pressures. . . . ("The Court has struggled to find a neutral course between the two Religion Clauses, both of which are cast in absolute terms, and either of which, if expanded to a logical extreme, would tend to clash with the other.").

Our decisions recognize that "there is room for play in the joints" between the Clauses, . . . some space for legislative action neither compelled by the Free Exercise Clause nor prohibited by the Establishment Clause. . . . On its face, the Act qualifies as a permissible legislative accommodation of religion that is not barred by the Establishment Clause.

Foremost, we find RLUIPA's institutionalized-persons provision compatible with the Establishment Clause because it alleviates exceptional government-created burdens on private religious exercise.... Furthermore, the Act on its face does not founder on shoals our prior decisions have identified: Properly applying RLUIPA, courts must take adequate account of the burdens a requested accommodation may impose on nonbeneficiaries ... and they must be satisfied that the Act's prescriptions are and will be administered neutrally among different faiths ...

... Section 3 covers state-run institutions—mental hospitals, prisons, and the like—in which the government exerts a degree of control unparalleled in civilian society and severely disabling to private religious exercise. ... RLUIPA thus protects institutionalized persons who are unable freely to attend to their religious needs and are therefore dependent on the government's permission and accommodation for exercise of their religion.

In *Goldman v. Weinberger,* 475 U.S. 503, we held that the Free Exercise Clause did not require the Air Force to exempt an Orthodox Jewish officer from uniform dress regulations so that he could wear a yarmulke indoors. In a military community, the Court observed, "there is simply not the same [individual] autonomy as there is in the larger civilian community." Congress responded to *Goldman* by prescribing that "a member of the armed forces may wear an item of religious apparel while wearing the uniform," unless "the wearing of the item would interfere with the performance [of] military duties [or] the item of apparel is not neat and conservative."

We do not read RLUIPA to elevate accommodation of religious observances over an institution's need to maintain order and safety. Our decisions indicate that an accommodation must be measured so that it does not override other significant interests. In *Caldor,* the Court struck down a Connecticut law that "arm[ed] Sabbath observers with an absolute and unqualified right not to work on whatever day they designate[d] as their Sabbath." ... We held the law invalid under the Establishment Clause because it "unyielding[ly] weigh[ted]" the interests of Sabbatarians "over all other interests." ...

We have no cause to believe that RLUIPA would not be applied in an appropriately balanced way, with particular sensitivity to security concerns. While the Act adopts a "compelling governmental interest" standard, Lawmakers supporting RLUIPA were mindful of the urgency of discipline, order, safety, and security in penal institutions. ...

B

The Sixth Circuit misread our precedents to require invalidation of RLUIPA as "impermissibly advancing religion by giving greater protection to religious rights than to other constitutionally protected rights." Our decision in *Amos* counsels otherwise. There, we upheld against an Establishment Clause challenge a provision exempting "religious organizations" from Title VII's prohibition against discrimination in employment on the basis of religion.... Religious accommodations, we held, need not "come packaged with benefits to secular entities."

Were the Court of Appeals' view the correct reading of our decisions, all manner of religious accommodations would fall. Congressional permission for members of the military to wear religious apparel while in uniform would fail,.... Ohio could not, as it now does, accommodate "traditionally recognized" religions The State provides inmates with chaplains "but not with publicists or political consultants," and allows "prisoners to assemble for worship, but not for political rallies."

In upholding RLUIPA's institutionalized-persons provision, we emphasize that respondents "have raised a facial challenge to [the Act's] constitutionality, and have not contended that under the facts of any of [petitioners'] specific cases ... [that] applying RLUIPA would produce unconstitutional results.conflicting assertions on this matter are not before us. It bears repetition, however, that prison security is a compelling state interest, and that deference is due to institutional officials' expertise in this area. ..."

. . .

JUSTICE THOMAS, concurring.

I join the opinion of the Court. I agree with the Court that the Religious Land Use and Institutionalized Persons Act of 2000 (RLUIPA) is constitutional under our modern Establishment Clause case law. I write to explain why a proper historical understanding of the Clause as a federalism provision leads to the same conclusion. ...

III. THE PRINCIPLE OF EQUAL TREATMENT OF RELIGIOUS BELIEF—THE PROBLEM OF DEFINING RELIGION

NOTES AND QUESTIONS

1. As we have seen, in most cases, the state is not compelled by the Free Exercise Clause to allow an exemption to its general laws for religious belief compromised by the law. In Braunfeld v. Brown, 366 U.S. 599 (1961), for example, the Court held that the Free Exercise Clause did not require an exemption to a Sunday closing law for Saturday worshipers. But, the Court just as clearly indicated that Pennsylvania *could* allow the exemption. Pennsylvania could not allow the exemption to Seventh-day Adventists while denying it to orthodox Jews, could it? Once an exemption for religious belief is allowed, the requirement that all religions be treated equally stems from three potential Constitutional sources. The hypothetical law allowing Seventh-day Adventists to open their businesses on Sunday while insisting that orthodox Jews close on Sunday would arguably: violate the Equal Protection Clause of the Fourteenth Amendment because no relevant difference between the two religions justifies the difference in treatment; violate the Establishment Clause since it confers a benefit on one religious group over another; violate the Free Exercise Clause because it discriminates against one religious group.

2. Whether the equal-treatment principle stems from the Equal Protection, Free Exercise, or Establishment Clause, or from two or all three of those Clauses, the problem is whether there are exceptions to the principle. One obvious exception is that religions may be treated in different ways if the content of the religious belief differs in some way that is sufficiently relevant to the policies of the law involved. For example, the state could exempt Saturday worshipers from the Sunday closing laws if their religious beliefs included a belief that work was forbidden on the Sabbath; yet it could insist that even those who recognized Saturday as the Sabbath close on Sundays if their religion did not prohibit work on the Sabbath. Kennedy v. Bureau of Narcotics, 459 F.2d 415 (9th Cir.1972), involved a regulation that exempted from federal control the use of peyote "in bona fide religious ceremonies of the Native American Church." A group called "Church of the Awakening" brought suit, claiming that the Constitution required they be afforded the same exemption. In response, the government argued that differentiating between the Native American Church and the Church of the Awakening was reasonable for two reasons: the use of peyote was "central" to the Native American Church religion and was merely a route to "expanded consciousness" in the religion of the Church of the Awakening; that the Church of the Awakening admitted to membership anyone agreeing with church principles, creating the possibility of people joining the church solely to obtain legal access to the drug, while the Native American Church limited its membership to those of at least one-quarter Indian blood. Do you agree that this justified different treatment of the two groups?*

3. The conscientious objector exemption in the United States Selective Service Act is limited to those with religious objection to *all* wars. Is that an unconstitutional discrimination against those with a sincere religious objection to participation in some, but not all, wars? The Supreme Court held, 8–1, in Gillette v. United States, 401 U.S. 437 (1971), that the distinction did not violate the constitution. Justice Marshall's opinion for the Court concluded the distinction was supported by "neutral and secular" reasons. He began by pointing out that there was no discrimination among those with religious beliefs opposed to *all* wars. The government was entitled, however, to limit the exemption to those whose opposition to war *was* religious. As to those who opposed only particular wars, it would be exceptionally difficult to distinguish objections that were "political" and objections that were "religious." Particularly, there was real danger of discriminating in *favor* of selective war objectors: (a) who were better educated and more able to explain their objections in religious terms: or (b) whose religious beliefs were most conventional.

4. Minnesota required charitable organizations to register and report on their solicitation of funds from nonmembers. Religious organiza-

* Two of the three judges of the United States Court of Appeals *disagreed* with the government's arguments, taking the position that a distinction between the two religions was unjustified. Ironically, since the Church of the Awakening had asked in its lawsuit that the regulation be changed to add their church to the list, the plaintiffs won their point but lost their lawsuit: the suit was dismissed since the majority concluded that adding another church by name to the list would only compound the constitutional problem.

tions were exempted—but only if they solicited less than half their funds from nonmembers. The Court's majority concluded that there was an unconstitutional denominational preference between conventional churches, and those engaging in more extensive fundraising from non-members. Two dissenters (Justices White and Rehnquist) argued there was no denominational preference because the exemption distinguished among religions "on the source of their contributions, not on their brand of religion." Larson v. Valente, 456 U.S. 228 (1982). In the *Larson* case, there was evidence that the statutory exemption had been framed to insure that the Roman Catholic archdiocese would be exempt. The legislative history also included remarks of two legislators that the rule was designed to regulate religious solicitors on the streets who were not "substantial religious institutions," and another who asked "why we're so hot to regulate the Moonies."

5. Do the problems mentioned in Justice Marshall's *Gillette* opinion also exist in granting conscientious objector status to those opposed to *all* war? (That is, isn't it easier for someone with a better education or more conventional religious beliefs to convince his draft board that he *is* a religious conscientious objector?) Would it violate the Free Exercise Clause for Congress to eliminate the conscientious objector exemption entirely? Can the administrative difficulty of distinguishing between religious and non-religious opposition to war, standing alone, be a compelling state interest? The United States Supreme Court has assumed that the conscientious objector exemption to selective service is a matter of legislative grace, and not compelled by the Free Exercise Clause. The cases (collected in Justice Marshall's decision in the *Gillette* case, 401 U.S. at 461, n. 23) were decided when the doctrine of the *Reynolds* case, limiting the Free Exercise Clause to matters of "belief," held sway. Does the decision in *Smith* resolve any doubts About Congress' power to draft people who are conscientious objectors? One reason the question was not resolved is that all selective service laws, from the time of the first draft law during the Civil War, have recognized some exemption for religious objectors.

6. The Civil War draft law limited its conscientious objector exemption to members of religious denominations opposed to the bearing of arms. Similarly, the World War I exemption was limited to those affiliated with a "well-recognized religious sect or organization." Would the limitation to members of organized religions unconstitutionally discriminate against persons who held individual religious objections to all wars, but were not members of groups sharing the belief? Would it be a sufficient justification that the distinction makes it administratively easier to limit the exemption to people whose views are "religious," and to those whose stated religious views are "sincere?" (Actually, the 1917 Act was administered to excuse everyone who had "personal scruples" against war. The history of conscientious objector laws is outlined in United States v. Seeger, 380 U.S. 163, 169–174 (1965).)

7. Since 1940, the policy of the draft laws has been to: (a) extend the conscientious objector exemption to all persons who have religious objections to all wars; and (b) to limit the exemption to those persons whose objections to war are "religious." Whether that policy is com-

pelled by the Free Exercise Clause or not, the Court's opinion in the *Gillette* case makes it clear that the policy is constitutionally permitted. Notice that limiting the exemption to persons whose views are "religious" puts considerable strain on the definition of religion. In 1948, Congress defined "religious training and belief" as including "an individual's belief in a relation to a Supreme Being involving duties superior to those arising from any human relation" and excluding "essentially political, sociological, or philosophic views or a merely personal moral code." (Selective Service Act of 1948, § 6(j).) For purposes of the two Religion Clauses of the First Amendment, would that be an adequate definition of religion?

8.   It was argued that the "Supreme Being clause" of the 1948 Act was unconstitutional because it distinguished between theistic and nontheistic religious beliefs. That is, there are persons whose beliefs do not include the conception of a God literally or physically "up there," but whose views are still religious. Daniel Seeger, when he applied for conscientious objector status in 1957, told his draft board that he was not sure he believed in God, but he did have a "belief in and devotion to goodness and virtue for their own sakes, and a religious faith in a purely ethical creed." He was denied the exemption on the ground that his views were not "religious" as defined in § 6(j) of the 1948 Act. The Supreme Court upheld § 6(j), but only after defining it to include beliefs like Seeger's. Pointing out that the statute read narrowly might exclude Buddhists and Hindus as persons whose views were not religious, the Court decided that Congress had really intended to include nontheistic views within the definition. Thus, a view was religious if it was "a sincere and meaningful belief which occupies in the life of its possessor a place parallel to that filled by the God of those admittedly qualifying for the exemption...." United States v. Seeger, 380 U.S. 163, 176 (1965). Isn't the Court's description of what Congress *meant* in § 6(j) exactly the opposite of what Congress *said*? In 1967, Congress eliminated the reference to a Supreme Being in § 6(j). (Ironically, the 1967 amendment was prompted by Congressional *disagreement* with the Court's decision in the *Seeger* case.)

9.   The Supreme Court returned to the issues of the *Seeger* case five years later, in Welsh v. United States, 398 U.S. 333 (1970). Prior to the 1967 Amendment, when the Supreme Being clause was still part of § 6(j), Welsh's claim for conscientious objector status had been turned down because his views were not religious. Welsh had told his draft board that his views were not religious, but:

> I can only act according to what I am and what I see. And I see that the military complex wastes both human and material resources, that it fosters disregard for (what I consider a paramount concern) human needs and ends; I see that the means we employ to "defend" our "way of life" profoundly change that way of life. I see that in our failure to recognize the political, social and economic realities of the world, we, *as a nation,* fail our responsibility *as a nation.*

Justice Black, writing for himself and Justices Douglas, Brennan and Marshall, thought that Welsh was entitled to an exemption under § 6(j) because his views were "religious" under the test of the *Seeger* case. He said:

> What is necessary under *Seeger* for a registrant's conscientious objection to all war to be "religious" within the meaning of § 6(j) is that this opposition to war stems from the registrant's moral, ethical, or religious beliefs about what is right and wrong and that these beliefs be held with the strength of traditional religious convictions.... If an individual deeply and sincerely holds beliefs that are purely ethical or moral in source and content but that nevertheless impose upon him a duty of conscience to refrain from participating in war at any time, those beliefs certainly occupy in the life of that individual "a place parallel to that filled by ... God" in traditionally religious persons.

Justice Harlan concurred in the result. He thought it was not possible to include Welsh's views as "religious," as that term was used in § 6(j). But, he concluded that it was an unconstitutional "establishment" of religion to distinguish between "religious" and "non-religious" beliefs— that the exemption had to be broad enough to include all persons who held strong beliefs with equal moral conviction, whether those beliefs were "moral, ethical, or philosophical." Justice White, joined by Chief Justice Burger and Justice Stewart, dissented. He agreed with Justice Harlan that Welsh's views were not "religious," and contended there was no constitutional prohibition against distinguishing "religious" from "non-religious" views. He argued that the First Amendment, itself, showed that government did not have to be "neutral" in distinguishing between religious and non-religious beliefs.

> It cannot be ignored that the First Amendment itself contains a religious classification. The Amendment protects belief and speech, but as a general proposition, the free speech provisions stop short of immunizing conduct from official regulation. The Free Exercise Clause, however, has a deeper cut: it protects conduct as well as religious belief and speech.... We should thus not labor to find a violation of the Establishment Clause when free exercise values prompt Congress to relieve religious believers from the burdens of the law....

10. Recall Professor Kurland's views (Chapter 16, pp. 603–604) that the religion clauses prohibit government from making any classification according to religion, and thus one can't read the Free Exercise Clause to require the favoring of religion when the Establishment Clause prohibits aid to religion. In two cases—*Sherbert* and *Yoder*—the Supreme Court has read the Free Exercise Clause to *require* carving out an exception for religious conduct. Could Professor Kurland's argument be answered by adopting the test of the *Seeger* case and the *Welsh* plurality opinion as the definition of "religion" in the First Amendment? Suppose religious views include *all* views that are central and deeply held, and an exemption is made only for those with "religious" views. Are people

whose views are not as central or as deeply held really quite different from people with "religious" views? Or, is it just impossible for atheism to be a "religion?" (Would a program of a local school board, designed to promote atheistic beliefs, and to convince school children that all religions are superstition, be an unconstitutional establishment of *religion*?)

11. Recall that in his *Yoder* opinion, Justice Burger insisted that the Constitution did not require exemption from compulsory school attendance laws of everyone whose "way of life" conflicted with those laws, because an orderly society required that people not disobey each law with which they disagree. Fair enough. But he proceeded to illustrate his point by arguing that, for example, Thoreau's views were "secular," and "philosophical and personal" rather than "religious." Is that consistent with the *Seeger–Welsh* definition of religious belief? Except for Justice Douglas, none of the other Justices in the *Yoder* case objected to this definition of religion. Does that mean that the *Seeger–Welsh* definition is not the constitutional definition? Suppose Wisconsin is confronted with a family that has organized its life around the beliefs of Thoreau, and has concluded that those beliefs require the simple life and prohibit education beyond the eighth grade. Would the *Yoder* case be inapplicable because their beliefs are not religious? (Or would their beliefs be religious if the family was law-abiding, gainfully employed, and didn't live on welfare?)

Chapter XIX

ESTABLISHMENT OF RELIGION:
RELIGION AND SCHOOLS

A significant percentage of the problems in applying the First Amendment's Establishment Clause have arisen in the field of education, involving either (a) religious exercises in the public schools or (b) public financing of religious schools. While this chapter will concentrate on the impact of the Establishment Clause on education, consider whether the appropriate solutions affect other government practices as well. (For example, if prayer is forbidden in elementary schools, is it also unconstitutional to convene sessions of the legislature with prayer or even to stamp "in God we trust" on our coins?)

Before beginning to think about the practices prohibited by the Establishment Clause, a rough description of the major purposes served by the Establishment Clause is necessary. In the first Supreme Court case expounding at any length about the meaning of the Establishment Clause, Justice Black's opinion for the Court described it this way:

> The "establishment of religion" clause of the First Amendment means at least this: Neither a state nor the Federal Government can set up a church. Neither can pass laws which aid one religion, aid all religions, or prefer one religion over another. Neither can force nor influence a person to go to or to remain away from church against his will or force him to profess a belief or disbelief in any religion. No person can be punished for entertaining or professing religious beliefs or disbeliefs, for church attendance or non-attendance. No tax in any amount, large or small, can be levied to support any religious activities or institutions, whatever they may be called, or whatever form they may adopt to teach or practice religion. Neither a state nor the Federal Government can, openly or secretly, participate in the affairs of any religious organizations or groups and *vice versa*. In the words of Jefferson, the clause against establishment of religion by law was intended to erect "a wall of separation between church and State."

Everson v. Board of Education, 330 U.S. 1, 15–16 (1947). While the *Everson* case is a closely divided 5–4 decision, there was no dissent from any of the points in this oft-quoted passage from Justice Black's opinion. The *Everson* case involved the constitutionality of using public funds for transportation of parochial school students to school. The majority opinion went to great length to affirm that there was a "wall of separation" between church and state—but went on to uphold the challenged practice on the ground that it did not "breach" the wall.

660

Where does Aid So — Directly, Indirectly.

Thus, to the extent the four dissenters disagreed, their complaint was that Justice Black had failed to follow through on the implications of his own position.

One reason for Justice Black's "strict-separationist" statement of principle and "accommodationist" conclusion in *Everson* was that he was writing for a divided Court. The conference vote in *Everson* was six to two, with one justice—Murphy—voting "pass." The dissenters— Justices Frankfurter and Rutledge—insisted that the Constitution required "absolute" separation of church and state. The majority split four to two on the grounds for the decision. Only Chief Justice Vinson and Justices Black, Reed, and Douglas agreed that state payment for school transportation was constitutional because the aid was essentially for students rather than religion. Justices Jackson and Burton thought that the constitutionality of the New Jersey law turned on other grounds. In an attempt to hold a majority and win over dissenters, Justice Black conceded in the initial version of his opinion that the Catholic Church derived "an indirect benefit from New Jersey law" and that the law "nears the verge of State support to a religious sect. . . ." He also argued that to deny students such benefits because of their faith would interfere with free exercise of religion. After reading Justice Black's opinion, Justices Jackson and Burton switched their votes. But Justice Black still had a majority, for Justice Murphy, though strongly urged by Justice Frankfurter to do otherwise, agreed to join Justice Black's opinion. Justice Murphy later said that he had done so because of Justice Black's assertion that his opinion protected free exercise of religion. After Justices Jackson and Burton joined the dissenters, Justice Black eliminated the sentence that the New Jersey statute went to "the verge of state support of a religious sect," and he characterized the statute as a general welfare measure for all students regardless of religion. He also added an historical argument based on Madison's and Jefferson's writings supporting his interpretation of the Establishment Clause. The dissenters reacted negatively to the final draft of Justice Black's opinion. The most fitting precedent for the opinion, wrote Justice Jackson in his dissent, "is that of Julia who, according to Byron's reports, 'whispering' I will ne'er consent, '—consented.' " 330 U.S. at 19.

It was immediately apparent that the broad principle upon which *Everson* had been decided was more important than the decision itself. Critics argued that it was historically and semantically indefensible that the Establishment Clause prohibited governmental aid to all religions. Justice Black's interpretation of the provision reflected his understanding of the writings of Madison and Jefferson, but there were other sources, one of which appears to have been the following statement from Charles A. Beard's *The Republic:*

> Congress can make no law respecting an establishment of religion. This means that Congress cannot adopt any form of religion as the national religion. It cannot set up one church as the national church, establish its creed, lay taxes generally to support it, compel people to attend it, and punish them for nonattendance. Nor can Congress any more vote money for the

support of all churches than it can establish one of them as a national church. That would be a form of establishment.

This was Justice Black's initial formulation of his statement in *Everson:*

> The First Amendment according to our prior decisions . . . means that:

> Neither a state nor the Federal Government can set up a state church. Neither can pass laws which prefer one religion over another. Neither can force a person to go to or to remain away from a church against his will or force him to profess a belief or disbelief in any religion. No person can be punished for his religious beliefs or disbeliefs, for church attendance or non-attendance. No tax can be levied to support any institution dedicated to the furtherance or the defeat of religion. Neither the state nor the Federal Government can enter into a partnership, open or secret, with any religious organization or group.

Compare this formulation with the final version in *Everson* quoted on page 655. Note that the prohibition against aid to all religions was not initially present. Note, too, that Justice Black says this formulation is an interpretation of the First Amendment as reflected in the Court's prior decisions, but he does not make that claim in his published opinion in *Everson.* What is the basis of Justice Black's final formulation of his interpretation of the Establishment Clause?*

I. RELEASED TIME PROGRAMS

It's obvious enough that the Establishment Clause prohibits "aid to one religion," or "prefer[ring] one religion over another." Since the *Everson* case, most Supreme Court decisions have begun with the premise that aid to all religions is also prohibited, and have treated the specific problem before them as one of working out the implication of that principle. You should be alert to the continuing question whether the principle makes sense, and whether it needs important qualifications.

Once a general principle is agreed to, there are still problems in applying the principle. If government cannot aid all religions, there are still major uncertainties in knowing what is permitted and prohibited by the Establishment Clause unless we can define "aid." This section will consider that question in the specific context of religious released-time programs involving the *public* schools. It might be useful, before looking at some specific situations, to have a working hypothesis for interpreting the Establishment Clause in that context. Consider Professor Choper's thesis:**

---

* The sources for the above discussion of *Everson* are the papers of Justices Black, Burton, Douglas, Frankfurter, and Rutledge at the Library of Congress; the microfilm copy of Justice Black's marked copy of Charles Beard's The Republic, Viking Press, 1943, p. 165, which is at the U.S. Supreme Court Library; and Sidney Fine, Frank Murphy: The Washington Years, University of Michigan Press, 1984, pp. 567–571.

** Jesse H. Choper, Religion in the Public Schools: A Proposed Constitutional Standard, Minnesota Law Review, 1963, vol. 47, p. 330.

The proposed constitutional standard is that for problems concerning religious intrusion in the public schools, the establishment clause of the first amendment is violated when the state engages in what may be fairly characterized as *solely religious activity* that is likely to result in (1) *compromising* the student's religious or conscientious beliefs or (2) *influencing* the student's freedom of religious or conscientious choice.

In judging whether Professor Choper's proposed constitutional standard is reflected in the decisions that follow, and whether it is a useful standard, consider these questions. How does one determine whether a public school activity is "religious," and, if it is "religious" that it is "solely" religious? Once it is decided that a public school is engaged in a practice that is "solely religious," why doesn't that decide the question? (That is, if a school is engaged in using public employees, money and property in an activity that is "solely religious," doesn't that violate the Establishment Clause whether or not the activity is likely to compromise or influence students' religious beliefs?) If it is relevant whether or not an activity compromises or influences students' religious beliefs, should the issue be whether it *does* so and not whether it is *likely* to do so?

ILLINOIS EX REL. McCOLLUM v. BOARD OF EDUCATION

Supreme Court of the United States, 1948.
333 U.S. 203, 68 S.Ct. 461, 92 L.Ed. 649.

[Vashti McCollum, whose son Terry attended a public elementary school in Champaign, Illinois, brought suit challenging the "released time" program of the Champaign public schools.]

JUSTICE BLACK delivered the opinion of the Court.

In 1940 interested members of the Jewish, Roman Catholic, and a few of the Protestant faiths formed a voluntary association called the Champaign Council on Religious Education. They obtained permission from the Board of Education to offer classes in religious instruction to public school pupils in grades four to nine inclusive. Classes were made up of pupils whose parents signed printed cards requesting that their children be permitted to attend; they were held weekly, thirty minutes for the lower grades, forty-five minutes for the higher. The council employed the religious teachers at no expense to the school authorities, but the instructors were subject to the approval and supervision of the superintendent of schools. The classes were taught in three separate religious groups by Protestant teachers, Catholic priests, and a Jewish rabbi, although for the past several years there have apparently been no classes instructed in the Jewish religion. Classes were conducted in the regular classrooms of the school building. Students who did not choose to take the religious instruction were not released from public school duties; they were required to leave their classrooms and go to some other place in the school building for pursuit of their secular studies. On the other hand, students who were released from secular study for the religious instructions were required to be present at the religious classes. Reports of their presence or absence were to be made to their secular teachers.

The foregoing facts ... show the use of tax-supported property for religious instruction and the close cooperation between the school authorities and the religious council in promoting religious education. The operation of the State's compulsory education system thus assists and is integrated with the program of religious instruction carried on by separate religious sects. Pupils compelled by law to go to school for secular education are released in part from their legal duty upon the condition that they attend the religious classes. This is beyond all question a utilization of the tax-established and tax-supported public school system to aid religious groups to spread their faith. And it falls squarely under the ban of the First Amendment (made applicable to the States by the Fourteenth) as we interpreted it in Everson v. Board of Education.... The majority in the *Everson* case and the minority ... agreed that the First Amendment's language, properly interpreted, had erected a wall of separation between Church and State....

Recognizing that the Illinois program is barred by the First and Fourteenth Amendments if we adhere to the views expressed both by the majority and the minority in the *Everson* case, counsel for the respondents challenge those views as dicta and urge that we reconsider and repudiate them. They argue that historically the First Amendment was intended to forbid only government preference of one religion over another, not an impartial governmental assistance of all religions. In addition they ask that we distinguish or overrule our holding in the *Everson* case that the Fourteenth Amendment made the "establishment of religion" clause of the First Amendment applicable as a prohibition against the States. After giving full consideration to the arguments presented we are unable to accept either of these contentions.

To hold that a state cannot consistently with the First and Fourteenth Amendments utilize its public school system to aid any or all religious faiths or sects in the dissemination of their doctrines and ideals does not, as counsel urge, manifest a governmental hostility to religion or religious teachings. A manifestation of such hostility would be at war with our national tradition as embodied in the First Amendment's guaranty of the free exercise of religion. For the First Amendment rests upon the premise that both religion and government can best work to achieve their lofty aims if each is left free from the other within its respective sphere. Or, as we said in the *Everson* case, the First Amendment has erected a wall between Church and State which must be kept high and impregnable.

Here not only are the State's tax-supported public school buildings used for the dissemination of religious doctrines. The State also affords sectarian groups an invaluable aid in that it helps to provide pupils for their religious classes through use of the State's compulsory public school machinery. This is not separation of Church and State.

. . .

JUSTICE FRANKFURTER delivered the following opinion, in which JUSTICE JACKSON, JUSTICE RUTLEDGE and JUSTICE BURTON join.*

---

* Justice Rutledge and Justice Burton concurred also in the Court's opinion. [A concurring opinion by Justice Jackson is omitted.]

We dissented in Everson v. Board of Education, 330 U.S. 1, because in our view the Constitutional principle requiring separation of Church and State compelled invalidation of the ordinance sustained by the majority. Illinois has here authorized the commingling of sectarian with secular instruction in the public schools. The Constitution of the United States forbids this.

. . .

The substantial differences among arrangements lumped together as "released time" emphasize the importance of detailed analysis of the facts to which the Constitutional test of Separation is to be applied. How does "released time" operate in Champaign? . . .

Religious education conducted on school time and property is patently woven into the working scheme of the school. The Champaign arrangement thus presents powerful elements of inherent pressure by the school system in the interest of religious sects. . . . That a child is offered an alternative may reduce the constraint; it does not eliminate the operation of influence by the school in matters sacred to conscience and outside the school's domain. The law of imitation operates, and non-conformity is not an outstanding characteristic of children. The result is an obvious pressure upon children to attend. . . . As a result, the public school system of Champaign actively furthers inculcation in the religious tenets of some faiths, and in the process sharpens the consciousness of religious differences at least among some of the children committed to its care.

. . .

JUSTICE REED, dissenting.

STANLEY REED—Born on December 31, 1884, in Minerva, Kentucky. His father practiced medicine; his mother, socially and politically active, was registrar general of the National Society of the Daughters of the American Revolution. Grew up in tobacco-rich Mason County, Kentucky. Kentucky Wesleyan, A.B., 1902; Yale, A.B. 1906. Studied law at Virginia and Columbia, 1906–1908, but took no degree. Immediately after his marriage in 1908, he went with his wife to Paris, where he remained for a year, taking graduate courses in civil and international law. Began law practice in Maysville, Kentucky, in 1910. Served as a first lieutenant in the U.S. army during World War I; general counsel of the Federal Farm Board, 1929–1932, and Reconstruction Finance Corporation, 1932–1935; special assistant to U.S. attorney general, 1935; U.S. solicitor general, 1935–1938. Nominated associate justice by President Franklin D. Roosevelt on January 15, 1938, to replace George Sutherland. Confirmed by the Senate on January 25, 1938, by voice vote. Retired on February 25, 1957. Died on April 2, 1980.

. . .

The phrase "an establishment of religion" may have been intended by Congress to be aimed only at a state church. When the First

Amendment was pending in Congress in substantially its present form, "Mr. Madison said, he apprehended the meaning of the words to be, that Congress should not establish a religion, and enforce the legal observation of it by law, nor compel men to worship God in any manner contrary to their conscience." Passing years, however, have brought about acceptance of a broader meaning, although never until today, I believe, has this Court widened its interpretation to any such degree as holding that recognition of the interest of our nation in religion, through the granting, to qualified representatives of the principal faiths, of opportunity to present religion as an optional, extra-curricular subject during released school time in public school buildings, was equivalent to an establishment of religion . . . .

. . .

. . . The Court's opinion quotes the gist of the Court's reasoning in *Everson*. I agree, as there stated, that none of our governmental entities can "set up a church." I agree that they cannot "aid" all or any religions or prefer one "over another." But "aid" must be understood as a purposeful assistance directly to the church itself or to some religious group or organization doing religious work of such a character that it may fairly be said to be performing ecclesiastical functions . . . .

It seems clear to me that the "aid" referred to by the Court in the *Everson* case could not have been those incidental advantages that religious bodies, with other groups similarly situated, obtain as a by-product of organized society. This explains the well-known fact that all churches receive "aid" from government in the form of freedom from taxation. The *Everson* decision itself justified the transportation of children to church schools by New Jersey for safety reasons . . . .

. . .

The practices of the federal government offer many examples of this kind of "aid" by the state to religion. The Congress of the United States has a chaplain for each House who daily invokes divine blessings and guidance for the proceedings. The armed forces have commissioned chaplains from early days. They conduct the public services in accordance with the liturgical requirements of their respective faiths, ashore and afloat, employing for the purpose property belonging to the United States and dedicated to the services of religion . . . .

In the United States Naval Academy and the United States Military Academy, schools wholly supported and completely controlled by the federal government, there are a number of religious activities. Chaplains are attached to both schools. Attendance at church services on Sunday is compulsory at both the Military and Naval Academies. At West Point the Protestant services are held in the Cadet Chapel, the Catholic in the Catholic Chapel, and the Jewish in the Old Cadet Chapel; at Annapolis only Protestant services are held on the reservation, midshipmen of other religious persuasions attend the churches of the city of Annapolis. These facts indicate that both schools since their earliest beginnings have maintained and enforced a pattern of participation in formal worship.

... When actual church services have always been permitted on government property, the mere use of the school buildings by a non-sectarian group for religious education ought not to be condemned as an establishment of religion. For a non-sectarian organization to give the type of instruction here offered cannot be said to violate our rule as to the establishment of religion by the state. . . . Devotion to the great principle of religious liberty should not lead us into a rigid interpretation of the constitutional guarantee that conflicts with accepted habits of our people. This is an instance where, for me, the history of past practices is determinative of the meaning of a constitutional clause, not a decorous introduction to the study of its text. The judgment should be affirmed.

NOTES AND QUESTIONS

1. Justice Frankfurter argued that, the way the Champaign released time program operated, it actively furthered "inculcation in the religious tenets of some faiths" and sharpened the "consciousness of religious differences at least among some of the children." Could a program of religious instruction in the public school buildings during "released time" be fashioned that was not open to these objections? Suppose religious education was offered in public school classrooms after regular school hours, with students not attending religious classes free to go home. Would such a program still violate the Establishment Clause so long as public school property was used for religious teaching?

2. Leo Pfeffer wrote that Justice Black's bare recital of the facts in *McCollum* did not reveal the human element in the case, which involved a "ten-year-old victim of a bitter conflict between a determined atheist mother and an equally determined Godfearing public school board." According to Pfeffer, the facts showed that Mrs. Bess Taylor, Terry's regular teacher, had urged him to enroll in the religion class so there would be 100% class participation. But Terry's mother, Vashti McCollum, absolutely refused to consent. Mrs. Taylor, wrote Pfeffer, "did not quite know what to do with Terry during the religious instruction period. She could not devote her time to him, for that would interfere with her joining in the religious instruction, and she was reluctant to miss that. Searching for a solution, she placed the boy at a desk in the hall outside a classroom, a procedure sometimes employed as a method of punishment. Passing schoolmates teased him, believing he was being punished for being an atheist and for not participating in religious instruction. . . . Mrs. Taylor found nothing wrong with this arrangement and probably would have continued it—at least while the music room was being used. Terry, however, went home crying as a result of the experience, and his mother protested to the school authorities, thereby bringing an end to this practice. When the music room (which was next to the teacher's washroom) was unoccupied, Mrs. Taylor placed him there alone, making certain that the door remained closed. Protests from Mrs. McCollum brought a stop to this practice too; whereupon Mrs. Taylor finally arrived at what was undoubtedly to her the happy solution of depositing him with the other fifth grade teacher during the period of religious instruction, with the result that the latter's pupils also could

observe the consequences of heterodoxy."* Does this statement of facts suggest a different rationale for the Court's decision in *McCollum* than given in Justice Black's opinion?

ZORACH v. CLAUSON

Supreme Court of the United States, 1952.
343 U.S. 306, 72 S.Ct. 679, 96 L.Ed. 954.

JUSTICE DOUGLAS delivered the opinion of the Court.

New York City has a program which permits its public schools to release students during the school day so that they may leave the school buildings and school grounds and go to religious centers for religious instruction or devotional exercises. A student is released on written request of his parents. Those not released stay in the classrooms. The churches make weekly reports to the schools, sending a list of children who have been released from public school but who have not reported for religious instruction.

This "released time" program involves neither religious instruction in public school classrooms nor the expenditure of public funds. All costs, including the application blanks, are paid by the religious organizations. The case is therefore unlike McCollum v. Board of Education, 333 U.S. 203, which involved a "released time" program from Illinois. In that case the classrooms were turned over to religious instructors. We accordingly held that the program violated the First Amendment which (by reason of the Fourteenth Amendment) prohibits the states from establishing religion or prohibiting its free exercise.

. . .

. . . [O]ur problem reduces itself to whether New York by this system has either prohibited the "free exercise" of religion or has made a law "respecting an establishment of religion" within the meaning of the First Amendment.

It takes obtuse reasoning to inject any issue of the "free exercise" of religion into the present case. No one is forced to go to the religious classroom and no religious exercise or instruction is brought to the classrooms of the public schools. A student need not take religious instruction. He is left to his own desires as to the manner or time of his religious devotions, if any.

There is a suggestion that the system involves the use of coercion to get public school students into religious classrooms. There is no evidence in the record before us that supports that conclusion. . . . Hence we put aside that claim of coercion both as respects the "free exercise" of religion and "an establishment of religion" within the meaning of the First Amendment.

Moreover, apart from that claim of coercion, we do not see how New York by this type of "released time" program has made a law respecting an establishment of religion within the meaning of the First Amendment. There is much talk of the separation of Church and State in the

---

* Leo Pfeffer, Church, State, and Freedom, Beacon Press, 1967, pp. 405–406.

history of the Bill of Rights and in the decisions clustering around the First Amendment. See Everson v. Board of Education, ... McCollum v. Board of Education.... There cannot be the slightest doubt that the First Amendment reflects the philosophy that Church and State should be separated. And so far as interference with the "free exercise" of religion and an "establishment" of religion are concerned, the separation must be complete and unequivocal. The First Amendment within the scope of its coverage permits no exception; the prohibition is absolute. The First Amendment, however, does not say that in every and all respects there shall be a separation of Church and State. Rather, it studiously defines the manner, the specific ways, in which there shall be no concert or union or dependency one on the other. That is the common sense of the matter. Otherwise the state and religion would be aliens to each other—hostile, suspicious, and even unfriendly. Churches could not be required to pay even property taxes. Municipalities would not be permitted to render police or fire protection to religious groups. Policemen who helped parishioners into their places of worship would violate the Constitution. Prayers in our legislative halls; the appeals to the Almighty in the messages of the Chief Executive; the proclamations making Thanksgiving Day a holiday; "so help me God" in our courtroom oaths—these and all other references to the Almighty that run through our laws, our public rituals, our ceremonies would be flouting the First Amendment. A fastidious atheist or agnostic could even object to the supplication with which the Court opens each session: "God save the United States and this Honorable Court."

We would have to press the concept of separation of Church and State to these extremes to condemn the present law on constitutional grounds. The nullification of this law would have wide and profound effects. A Catholic student applies to his teacher for permission to leave the school during hours on a Holy Day of Obligation to attend a mass. A Jewish student asks his teacher for permission to be excused for Yom Kippur. A Protestant wants the afternoon off for a family baptismal ceremony. In each case the teacher requires parental consent in writing. In each case the teacher, in order to make sure the student is not a truant, goes further and requires a report from the priest, the rabbi, or the minister. The teacher in other words cooperates in a religious program to the extent of making it possible for her students to participate in it. Whether she does it occasionally for a few students, regularly for one, or pursuant to a systematized program designed to further the religious needs of all the students does not alter the character of the act.

We are a religious people whose institutions presuppose a Supreme Being. We guarantee the freedom to worship as one chooses. We make room for as wide a variety of beliefs and creeds as the spiritual needs of man deem necessary. We sponsor an attitude on the part of government that shows no partiality to any one group and that lets each flourish according to the zeal of its adherents and the appeal of its dogma. When the state encourages religious instruction or cooperates with religious authorities by adjusting the schedule of public events to sectarian needs, it follows the best of our traditions. For it then respects the religious nature of our people and accommodates the public service to their spiritual needs.... The government must be neutral when it comes to competition between sects. It may not thrust any sect on any person. It may not make a religious observance compulsory. It may not coerce anyone to attend church, to observe a religious holiday, or to take religious instruction. But it can close its doors or suspend its operations as to those who want to repair to their religious sanctuary for worship or instruction. No more than that is undertaken here.

. . .

In the *McCollum* case the classrooms were used for religious instruction and the force of the public school was used to promote that instruction. Here, as we have said, the public schools do no more than accommodate their schedules to a program of outside religious instruction. We follow the *McCollum* case. But we cannot expand it to cover the present released time program unless separation of Church and State means that public institutions can make no adjustments of their schedules to accommodate the religious needs of the people. We cannot read into the Bill of Rights such a philosophy of hostility to religion.

JUSTICE BLACK, dissenting.

. . .

I see no significant difference between the invalid Illinois system and that of New York here sustained. Except for the use of the school buildings in Illinois, there is no difference between the systems which I consider even worthy of mention....

I am aware that our *McCollum* decision on separation of Church and State has been subjected to a most searching examination throughout the country. Probably few opinions from this Court in recent years have attracted more attention or stirred wider debate. Our insistence on "a wall between Church and State which must be kept high and impregnable" has seemed to some a correct exposition of the philosophy and a true interpretation of the language of the First Amendment to which we should strictly adhere. With equal conviction and sincerity, others have thought the *McCollum* decision fundamentally wrong and have pledged continuous warfare against it. The opinions in the court below and the briefs here reflect these diverse viewpoints. In dissenting today, I mean to do more than give routine approval to our *McCollum* decision. I mean also to reaffirm my faith in the fundamental philosophy expressed in *McCollum* and Everson v. Board of Education . . .

. . .

JUSTICE JACKSON, dissenting.

This released time program is founded upon a use of the State's power of coercion, which, for me, determines its unconstitutionality. Stripped to its essentials, the plan has two stages: first, that the State compel each student to yield a large part of his time for public secular education; and, second, that some of it be "released" to him on condition that he devote it to sectarian religious purposes.

No one suggests that the Constitution would permit the State directly to require this "released" time to be spent "under the control of a duly constituted religious body." This program accomplishes that forbidden result by indirection. If public education were taking so much of the pupils' time as to injure the public or the students' welfare by encroaching upon their religious opportunity, simply shortening everyone's school day would facilitate voluntary and optional attendance at Church classes. But that suggestion is rejected upon the ground that if they are made free many students will not go to the Church. Hence, they must be deprived of freedom for this period, with Church attendance put to them as one of the two permissible ways of using it.

The greater effectiveness of this system over voluntary attendance after school hours is due to the truant officer who, if the youngster fails to go to the Church school, dogs him back to the public schoolroom. Here schooling is more or less suspended during the "released time" so the nonreligious attendants will not forge ahead of the churchgoing absentees. But it serves as a temporary jail for a pupil who will not go to Church. It takes more subtlety of mind than I possess to deny that this is governmental constraint in support of religion. It is as unconstitutional, in my view, when exerted by indirection as when exercised forthrightly.

As one whose children, as a matter of free choice, have been sent to privately supported Church schools, I may challenge the Court's suggestion that opposition to this plan can only be antireligious, atheistic, or agnostic. My evangelistic brethren confuse an objection to compulsion with an objection to religion. It is possible to hold a faith with enough confidence to believe that what should be rendered to God does not need to be decided and collected by Caesar.

The day that this country ceases to be free for irreligion it will cease to be free for religion—except for the sect that can win political power. The same epithetical jurisprudence used by the Court today to beat down those who oppose pressuring children into some religion can devise as good epithets tomorrow against those who object to pressuring them into a favored religion. And, after all, if we concede to the State power and wisdom to single out "duly constituted religious" bodies as exclusive alternatives for compulsory secular instruction, it would be logical to also uphold the power and wisdom to choose the true faith among those "duly constituted." We start down a rough road when we begin to mix compulsory public education with compulsory godliness.

A number of Justices just short of a majority of the majority that promulgates today's passionate dialectics joined in answering them in Illinois ex rel. McCollum v. Board of Education.... The distinction attempted between that case and this is trivial, almost to the point of cynicism, magnifying its nonessential details and disparaging compulsion which was the underlying reason for invalidity. A reading of the Court's opinion in that case along with its opinion in this case will show such difference of overtones and undertones as to make clear that the *McCollum* case has passed like a storm in a teacup. The wall which the Court was professing to erect between Church and State has become even more warped and twisted than I expected. Today's judgment will be more interesting to students of psychology and of the judicial processes than to students of constitutional law.

[Justice Frankfurter's dissent, which is omitted, agreed generally with Justice Jackson.]

NOTES AND QUESTIONS

1. Is the distinction between released time programs using public school classrooms during class hours, and released time programs where religious education is carried out during school hours off the school premises, really "trivial" as Justice Jackson urges? In terms of financial aid to religious education? In terms of the appearance to children that the public school system "stands behind" the religious education which is given?

2. Even if the distinction between on-school-premises and off-school-premises released time programs is not "trivial," is it *sufficient?* Do you agree with Justice Jackson that *all* programs that meet during school time, keep students who don't attend religious instruction in school, and punish students who elect but don't show up for religious instruction, are *likely* to abridge students' religious freedom? Is "likely" coercion irrelevant if there is no evidence that the particular program *did* operate in that way?

3. Is Justice Douglas correct that there is *no* expenditure of public funds involved? What about the time of school administrators, teachers, and, last but not least, the truant officers. Would you conclude that there is no expenditure because all these people have to be paid their salaries anyway? Or, is there technically an expenditure, but one so small that it should be overlooked? Is the question of whether there has been an expenditure of public funds relevant to solving the problems in the *McCollum* and *Zorach* cases?

4. Is Justice Douglas correct that the arguments for invalidating New York's released time program would also mean that children couldn't be excused from public school for religious holidays?

5. Justice Black's dissent contains an oblique reference to the storm of protest that followed the Court's decision in the *McCollum* case. Justice Jackson's opinion comes close to a direct charge that the Court majority simply backed up from the principle of the *McCollum* case because of the pressure of public opinion. There have been times in the Supreme Court's history where it has changed position because of the intense pressure of public opinion. Was this one of them? How does one determine whether such a charge is true or false? One way is to consider the evidence in the justices' papers bearing on their decisions in *McCollum* and *Zorach*. A study relying on Justice Burton's papers at the Library of Congress shows that Justice Burton played an important role in the *McCollum* decision because he had negotiated a compromise that affected the content of the Court's opinion and the number of justices supporting it.* The compromise also affected the content of Justice

---

* "The Released Time Cases Revisited: A Study of Group Decisionmaking by the Supreme Court," 83 Yale Law Journal, 1974, pp. 1200–1236.

Frankfurter's opinion. One part of the compromise was that Justices Burton and Rutledge would join both Justice Black's and Justice Frankfurter's opinions if they deleted certain references to *Everson*. The result of this part of the compromise was that Justice Black now had six rather than four justices supporting his opinion. The second part of the compromise were assurances that released-time programs like those in *Zorach* were excluded from Justice Black's and Frankfurter's opinions. Burton understood that both justices had given him those assurances. Frankfurter, in fact, included a sentence in his concurring opinion excluding other released-time programs from his opinion. Justice Black, however, refused to put a similar exclusion in his opinion. What did the assurances mean to Justices Black and Frankfurter, and how would they affect the decisions of Chief Justice Vinson and Justices Reed, Burton, and Douglas in *Zorach?* Here are the answers given in the study mentioned above:

> Precisely what Justices Black and Frankfurter meant when they assured Justice Burton was never made clear. There are at least two plausible alternatives. They might have meant that they had not made up their minds about the constitutionality of the New York plan and that their opinions truly left it an open question. On the other hand, they might have meant that their opinions "excluded" the New York plan in a formal sense only, i.e., that no language in their opinions would make it impossible for a Justice who joined them to vote in favor of the New York plan at a later time, or that the New York plan was excluded simply because it was not before the Court at that time.**

The study then went on to discuss the Zorach decision:†

> The opinions in *Zorach* show that the members of the Court were as confused, or at any rate as sharply divided, as the commentators with regard to just what the Court had decided in *McCollum*. Justice Black wrote that he felt that his opinion in *McCollum* made it "categorically clear" that the New York plan was unconstitutional, but six other Justices, including three who had joined his opinion in *McCollum*, disagreed. All three dissenting opinions charged the majority with misreading *McCollum* and Justice Jackson implied that the majority's misinterpretation was purposeful. It seems very likely that at least part of the cause of this disagreement was the ambiguous stipulations which Justice Burton made with Justices Black and Frankfurter just before *McCollum* was handed down. Justices Black and Frankfurter seem to have regarded those stipulations as reserving judgment on the New York plan in a formal sense only, whereas Justices Burton and Douglas and Chief Justice Vinson may well have interpreted them in a broader sense. As a result the interactions among the Justices in *Zorach* were marked by sharp exchanges concerning the meaning of *McCollum*.

** Ibid., p. 1221.

† Ibid., pp. 1227–1229.

After Justice Frankfurter had read Justice Douglas' opinion for the Court, he added a paragraph to his opinion and stated that the majority was breaking faith with the principles which eight Justices had approved in *McCollum*. Justice Douglas responded by adding footnote eight to his opinion. He pointed out that, at the time *McCollum* was decided, Chief Justice Vinson, Justice Burton, and he had felt that the New York plan was not prejudged by that case. As evidence, he quoted Justice Frankfurter's language specifically limiting the holding of his opinion in *McCollum*. And in what may have been a veiled reference to Justice Burton's stipulation, he referred to Justice Frankfurter's limitation of the holding in that case as a "reservation of the question" now before the Court and he pointedly noted that Justice Burton had joined Justice Frankfurter's opinion. Justice Frankfurter responded to this by adding footnote two to his opinion. He stated that his reservation in *McCollum* had not referred to the New York plan or to any other particular released time plan.

In attempting to explain the Court's decision in *Zorach*, a large number of commentators, noting the harsh criticism levied against *McCollum* and the difficulty of reconciling it with *Zorach*, suggested that the pressure of public opinion had caused the Court to switch its position on the issue of released time. Over the years an impressive list of constitutional scholars and experts on the Supreme Court has subscribed to this thesis. Among its adherents were Leo Pfeffer and Professors Philip B. Kurland, Paul G. Kauper, C. Herman Pritchett, and David Fellman. The interactions among the justices in the released time cases, however, strongly suggest that this theory is wrong. Three justices (Burton, Vinson, and Douglas) who had voted to declare the Champaign program unconstitutional later voted to uphold the constitutionality of the New York plan. Justice Burton's communications with Justices Black and Frankfurter during the Court's deliberations on *McCollum* show that he was strongly inclined at that time to find the New York plan constitutional and he relied on stipulations with Justices Black and Frankfurter to preserve that question. As Justice Douglas implied in his exchange of footnotes with Justice Frankfurter in *Zorach*, Chief Justice Vinson and he may also have relied on Justice Burton's stipulations. In any event, since both Justices Black and Frankfurter assured their colleagues in *McCollum* that they had "excluded" the New York program, it is hard to accuse Justice Burton, Justice Douglas, and Chief Justice Vinson of changing positions as a result of public pressure when they later approved the New York plan.

6. Do the *McCollum* and *Zorach* cases, taken together, yield a principle that throws any light on the school prayer cases that follow? Is the *McCollum* case consistent with Professor Choper's proposed constitutional standard? Is the *Zorach* case consistent with Professor Choper's standard? (In *Zorach*, was the "activity" one that was "solely religious"?

Was the "activity" likely to compromise religious beliefs or influence religious choice?)

7. *McCollum* ended the Champaign released-time program. Thereafter, Protestant ministers substituted an after-school program on rented public school premises, but the program soon faltered and died. Frank J. Sorauf, a church-state expert, estimated that from 40 per cent to 50 per cent of the on-premises programs were unaffected by *McCollum*. Sorauf also reported only a slight increase in released-time student attendance one year after *Zorach* (3 million compared to approximately 2.3 million before *McCollum*).* The most significant impact of *Zorach* appears to have been symbolic because of Justice Douglas' statement that "we are a religious people whose institution presuppose a Supreme Being."

II. PRAYER IN THE PUBLIC SCHOOLS

ENGEL v. VITALE

Supreme Court of the United States, 1962.
370 U.S. 421, 82 S.Ct. 1261, 8 L.Ed.2d 601.

JUSTICE BLACK delivered the opinion of the Court.

The ... Board of Education of Union Free School District No. 9, New Hyde Park, New York ... directed the ... following prayer to be said aloud by each class in the presence of a teacher at the beginning of each school day:

> "Almighty God, we acknowledge our dependence upon Thee, and we beg Thy blessings upon us, our parents, our teachers and our Country."

. . .

We think that by using its public school system to encourage recitation of the Regents' prayer, the State of New York has adopted a practice wholly inconsistent with the Establishment Clause. There can, of course, be no doubt that New York's program of daily classroom invocation of God's blessings as prescribed in the Regents' prayer is a religious activity. It is a solemn avowal of divine faith and supplication for the blessings of the Almighty. The nature of such a prayer has always been religious, none of the respondents has denied this and the trial court expressly so found. . . .

. . .

The petitioners contend among other things that the state laws requiring or permitting use of the Regents' prayer must be struck down as a violation of the Establishment Clause because that prayer was composed by governmental officials as a part of a governmental program to further religious beliefs. For this reason, petitioners argue, the State's use of the Regents' prayer in its public school system breaches the constitutional wall of separation between Church and State. We agree

---

* Frank J. Sorauf, "Zorach v. Clause: The Impact of a Supreme Court Decision," *American Political Science Review*, 1953, vol. 53, pp. 777–791.

with that contention since we think that the constitutional prohibition against laws respecting an establishment of religion must at least mean that in this country it is no part of the business of government to compose official prayers for any group of the American people to recite as a part of a religious program carried on by government.

It is a matter of history that this very practice of establishing governmentally composed prayers for religious services was one of the reasons which caused many of our early colonists to leave England and seek religious freedom in America. The Book of Common Prayer, which was created under governmental direction and which was approved by Acts of Parliament in 1548 and 1549, set out in minute detail the accepted form and content of prayer and other religious ceremonies to be used in the established, tax-supported Church of England. The controversies over the Book and what should be its content repeatedly threatened to disrupt the peace of that country.... [Some] groups, lacking the necessary political power to influence the Government on the matter, decided to leave England and its established church and seek freedom in America from England's governmentally ordained and supported religion.

It is an unfortunate fact of history that when some of the very groups which had most strenuously opposed the established Church of England found themselves sufficiently in control of colonial governments in this country to write their own prayers into law, they passed laws making their own religion the official religion of their respective colonies. Indeed, as late as the time of the Revolutionary War, there were established churches in at least eight of the thirteen former colonies and established religions in at least four of the other five. But the successful Revolution against English political domination was shortly followed by intense opposition to the practice of establishing religion by law. This opposition crystallized rapidly into an effective political force in Virginia where the minority religious groups such as Presbyterians, Lutherans, Quakers and Baptists had gained such strength that the adherents to the established Episcopal Church were actually a minority themselves. In 1785–1786, those opposed to the established Church, led by James Madison and Thomas Jefferson, who, though themselves not members of any of these dissenting religious groups, opposed all religious establishments by law on grounds of principle, obtained the enactment of the famous "Virginia Bill for Religious Liberty" by which all religious groups were placed on an equal footing so far as the State was concerned. Similar though less far-reaching legislation was being considered and passed in other States.

By the time of the adoption of the Constitution, our history shows that there was a widespread awareness among many Americans of the dangers of a union of Church and State. These people knew, some of them from bitter personal experience, that one of the greatest dangers to the freedom of the individual to worship in his own way lay in the Government's placing its official stamp of approval upon one particular kind of prayer or one particular form of religious services.... Under [the First] Amendment's prohibition against governmental establishment of religion, as reinforced by the provisions of the Fourteenth Amendment, government in this country, be it state or federal, is without power to prescribe by law any particular form of prayer which is to be used as an official prayer in carrying on any program of governmentally sponsored religious activity.

There can be no doubt that New York's state prayer program officially establishes the religious beliefs embodied in the Regents' prayer.... Neither the fact that the prayer may be denominationally neutral nor the fact that its observance on the part of the students is voluntary can serve to free it from the limitations of the Establishment Clause, as it might from the Free Exercise Clause, of the First Amendment,.... Although these two clauses may in certain instances overlap, they forbid two quite different kinds of governmental encroachment upon religious freedom. The Establishment Clause, unlike the Free Exercise Clause, does not depend upon any showing of direct governmental compulsion and is violated by the enactment of laws which establish an official religion whether those laws operate directly to coerce nonobserving individuals or not. This is not to say, of course, that laws officially prescribing a particular form of religious worship do not involve coercion of such individuals. When the power, prestige and financial support of government is placed behind a particular religious belief, the indirect coercive pressure upon religious minorities to conform to the prevailing officially approved religion is plain. But the purposes underlying the Establishment Clause go much further than that. Its first and most immediate purpose rested on the belief that a union of government and religion tends to destroy government and to degrade religion. The history of governmentally established religion, both in England and in this country, showed that whenever government had allied itself with one particular form of religion, the inevitable result had been that it had incurred the hatred, disrespect and even contempt of those who held contrary beliefs.... The Establishment Clause thus stands as an expression of principle on the part of the Founders of our Constitution that religion is too personal, too sacred, too holy, to permit its "unhallowed perversion" by a civil magistrate. Another purpose of the Establishment Clause rested upon an awareness of the historical fact that governmentally established religions and religious persecutions go hand in hand. The Founders knew that only a few years after the Book of Common Prayer became the only accepted form of religious services in the established Church of England, an Act of Uniformity was passed to compel all Englishmen to attend those services and to make it a criminal offense to conduct or attend religious gatherings of any other kind....

It has been argued that to apply the Constitution in such a way as to prohibit state laws respecting an establishment of religious services in public schools is to indicate a hostility toward religion or toward prayer. Nothing, of course, could be more wrong.... It is neither sacrilegious nor antireligious to say that each separate government in this country should stay out of the business of writing or sanctioning official prayers and leave that purely religious function to the people themselves and to those the people choose to look to for religious guidance.

It is true that New York's establishment of its Regents' prayer as an official approved religious doctrine of that State does not amount to a total establishment of one particular religious sect to the exclusion of all others—that, indeed, the governmental endorsement of that prayer seems relatively insignificant when compared to the governmental encroachments upon religion which were commonplace 200 years ago. To those who may subscribe to the view that because the Regents' official prayer is so brief and general there can be no danger to religious freedom in its governmental establishment, however, it may be appropriate to say in the words of James Madison, the author of the First Amendment:

> "[I]t is proper to take alarm at the first experiment on our liberties.... Who does not see that the same authority which can establish Christianity, in exclusion of all other Religions, may establish with the same ease any particular sect of Christians, in exclusion of all other Sects? That the same authority which can force a citizen to contribute three pence only of his property for the support of any one establishment, may force him to conform to any other establishment in all cases whatsoever?"

· · ·

JUSTICE DOUGLAS, concurring.

It is customary in deciding a constitutional question to treat it in its narrowest form. Yet at times the setting of the question gives it a form and content which no abstract treatment could give. The point for decision is whether the Government can constitutionally finance a religious exercise. Our system at the federal and state levels is presently honeycombed with such financing.[1] Nevertheless, I think it is an unconstitutional undertaking whatever form it takes.

· · ·

Plainly, our Bill of Rights would not permit a State or the Federal Government to adopt an official prayer and penalize anyone who would not utter it. This, however, is not that case, for there is no element of

---

1. "There are many 'aids' to religion in this country at all levels of government. To mention but a few at the federal level, one might begin by observing that the very First Congress which wrote the First Amendment provided for chaplains in both Houses and in the armed services. There is compulsory chapel at the service academies, and religious services are held in federal hospitals and prisons. The President issues religious proclamations. The Bible is used for the administration of oaths. N.Y.A. and W.P.A. funds were available to parochial schools during the depression. Veterans receiving money under the 'G.I.' Bill of 1944 ... could attend denominational schools, to which payments were made directly by the government. During World War II, federal money was contributed to denominational schools for the training of nurses. The benefits of the National School Lunch Act ... are available to students in private as well as public schools. The Hospital Survey and Construction Act of 1946 ... specifically made money available to non-public hospitals. The slogan 'In God We Trust' is used by the Treasury Department, and Congress recently added God to the pledge of allegiance. There is Bible-reading in the schools of the District of Columbia, and religious instruction is given in the District's National Training School for Boys. Religious organizations are exempt from the federal income tax and are granted postal privileges. Up to defined limits—15 per cent of the adjusted gross income of individuals and 5 per cent of the net income of corporations—contributions to religious organizations are deductible for federal income tax purposes. There are no limits to the deductibility of gifts and bequests to religious institutions made under the federal gift and estate tax laws. This list of federal 'aids' could easily be expanded and of course there is a long list in each state." David Fellman, The Limits of Freedom, 1959, pp. 40–41.

compulsion or coercion in New York's regulation requiring that public schools be opened each day with the ... prayer....

· · ·

In short, the only one who need utter the prayer is the teacher; and no teacher is complaining of it. Students can stand mute or even leave the classroom, if they desire.

· · ·

McCollum v. Board of Education ... does not decide this case.... Prayers of course may be so long and of such a character as to amount to an attempt at the religious instruction that was denied the public schools by the *McCollum* case. But New York's prayer is of a character that does not involve any element of proselytizing as in the *McCollum* case.

The question presented by this case is therefore an extremely narrow one. It is whether New York oversteps the bounds when it finances a religious exercise.

What New York does on the opening of its public schools is what we do when we open court. Our Crier has from the beginning announced the convening of the Court and then added "God save the United States and this Honorable Court." That utterance is a supplication, a prayer in which we, the judges, are free to join, but which we need not recite any more than the students need recite the New York prayer.

· · ·

In New York the teacher who leads in prayer is on the public payroll; and the time she takes seems minuscule as compared with the salaries appropriated by state legislatures and Congress for chaplains to conduct prayers in the legislative halls. Only a bare fraction of the teacher's time is given to reciting this short 22–word prayer, about the same amount of time that our Crier spends announcing the opening of our sessions and offering a prayer for this Court. Yet for me the principle is the same, no matter how briefly the prayer is said, for in each of the instances given the person praying is a public official on the public payroll, performing a religious exercise in a governmental institution. It is said that the element of coercion is inherent in the giving of this prayer. If that is true here, it is also true of the prayer with which this Court is convened, and of those that open the Congress. Few adults, let alone children, would leave our courtroom or the Senate or the House while those prayers are being given. Every such audience is in a sense a "captive" audience.

At the same time I cannot say that to authorize this prayer is to establish a religion in the strictly historic meaning of those words. A religion is not established in the usual sense merely by letting those who choose to do so say the prayer that the public school teacher leads. Yet once government finances a religious exercise it inserts a divisive influence into our communities. The New York Court said that the prayer given does not conform to all of the tenets of the Jewish, Unitarian, and Ethical Culture groups. One of the petitioners is an agnostic.

"We are a religious people whose institutions presuppose a Supreme Being." Zorach v. Clauson, 343 U.S. 306, 313. Under our Bill of Rights free play is given for making religion an active force in our lives. But "if a religious leaven is to be worked into the affairs of our people, it is to be done by individuals and groups, not by the Government." . . .

My problem today would be uncomplicated but for Everson v. Board of Education, 330 U.S. 1, 17, which allowed taxpayers' money to be used to pay "the bus fares of parochial school pupils as a part of a general program under which" the fares of pupils attending public and other schools were also paid. The *Everson* case seems in retrospect to be out of line with the First Amendment.

. . .

JUSTICE STEWART, dissenting.

With all respect, I think the Court has misapplied a great constitutional principle. I cannot see how an "official religion" is established by letting those who want to say a prayer say it. On the contrary I think that to deny the wish of these school children to join in reciting this prayer is to deny them the opportunity of sharing in the spiritual heritage of our Nation.

. . .

. . . What [the State of New York] has done has been to recognize and to follow the deeply entrenched and highly cherished spiritual traditions of our Nation—traditions which come down to us from those who almost two hundred years ago avowed their "firm Reliance on the Protection of divine Providence" when they proclaimed the freedom and independence of this brave new world.[1]

I dissent.

SCHOOL DIST. OF ABINGTON TWP., PENNSYLVANIA v. SCHEMPP

Supreme Court of the United States, 1963.
374 U.S. 203, 83 S.Ct. 1560, 10 L.Ed.2d 844.

[Because Justice Black's opinion in the *Engel* case was phrased in terms of a prayer composed by the state, it was inevitable that the Court would be confronted with cases involving school prayers not composed by the state. The following case, reported under one heading is really a consolidation of two cases decided the same day by the Court.

One case involved a Pennsylvania law requiring that "At least ten verses from the Holy Bible shall be read without comment, at the opening of each public school on each school day." Two children of the Schempp family attended high school in the Abington School District, where the practice had been to read selected verses from the King James, Douay, and Revised Standard versions of the Bible, as well as the

---

1. The Declaration of Independence ends with this sentence: "And for the support of this Declaration, with a firm reliance on the protection of divine Providence, we mutually pledge to each other our Lives, our Fortunes and our sacred Honor."

Jewish Holy Scriptures. The Schempps, who were Unitarians, contended that the readings conveyed doctrines contrary to their religious beliefs. While Pennsylvania's law provided that children who objected could be excused from the bible-reading exercises, the father of the Schempp children decided against asking that his children be excused because he was concerned that this would adversely affect the children's relationship with their teachers and classmates.

The second case involved a rule of the Baltimore, Maryland, School Board, which provided for exercises involving "reading, without comment, of a chapter in the Holy Bible and/or the use of the Lord's Prayer." Mrs. Madalyn Murray, a nationally-prominent and evangelical atheist, whose son attended Baltimore city schools, protested the rule. The school board's response was limited to an amendment permitting any child to be excused from the exercise on a parent's request.]

JUSTICE CLARK delivered the opinion of the Court.

Once again we are called upon to consider the scope of the provision of the First Amendment to the United States Constitution which declares that "Congress shall make no law respecting an establishment of religion, or prohibiting the free exercise thereof...." These companion cases present the issues in the context of state action requiring that schools begin each day with readings from the Bible.... [We] hold that the practices at issue and the laws requiring them are unconstitutional under the Establishment Clause, as applied to the States through the Fourteenth Amendment.

. . .

... [T]he Establishment Clause has been directly considered by this Court eight times in the past score of years and, with only one Justice dissenting on the point, it has consistently held that the clause withdrew all legislative power respecting religious belief or the expression thereof. The test may be stated as follows: what are the purpose and the primary effect of the enactment? If either is the advancement or inhibition of religion then the enactment exceeds the scope of legislative power as circumscribed by the Constitution. That is to say that to withstand the strictures of the Establishment Clause there must be a secular legislative purpose and a primary effect that neither advances nor inhibits religion.... The Free Exercise Clause, likewise considered many times here, withdraws from legislative power, state and federal, the exertion of any restraint on the free exercise of religion. Its purpose is to secure religious liberty in the individual by prohibiting any invasions thereof by civil authority. Hence it is necessary in a free exercise case for one to show the coercive effect of the enactment as it operates against him in the practice of his religion. The distinction between the two clauses is apparent—a violation of the Free Exercise Clause is predicated on coercion while the Establishment Clause violation need not be so attended.

Applying the Establishment Clause principles to the cases at bar we find that the States are requiring the selection and reading at the opening of the school day of verses from the Holy Bible and the recitation of the Lord's Prayer by the students in unison. These exercises are prescribed as part of the curricular activities of students who are required by law to attend school. They are held in the school buildings under the supervision and with the participation of teachers employed in those schools. None of these factors, other than compulsory school attendance, was present in the program upheld in Zorach v. Clauson. The trial court in [the *Schempp* case found] that such an opening exercise is a religious ceremony and was intended by the State to be so. We agree with the trial court's finding as to the religious character of the exercises. Given that finding, the exercises and the law requiring them are in violation of the Establishment Clause.

There is no such specific finding as to the religious character of the exercises in [the *Murray* case] and the State contends ... that the program is an effort to extend its benefits to all public school children without regard to their religious belief. Included within its secular purposes, it says, are the promotion of moral values, the contradiction to the materialistic trends of our times, the perpetuation of our institutions and the teaching of literature.... But even if its purpose is not strictly religious, it is sought to be accomplished through readings, without comment, from the Bible. Surely the place of the Bible as an instrument of religion cannot be gainsaid, and the State's recognition of the pervading religious character of the ceremony is evident from the rule's specific permission of the alternative use of the Catholic Douay version as well as the recent amendment permitting nonattendance at the exercises. None of these factors is consistent with the contention that the Bible is here used either as an instrument for nonreligious moral inspiration or as a reference for the teaching of secular subjects.

The conclusion follows that in both cases the laws require religious exercises and such exercises are being conducted in direct violation of the rights of the appellees and petitioners. Nor are these required exercises mitigated by the fact that individual students may absent themselves upon parental request, for that fact furnishes no defense to a claim of unconstitutionality under the Establishment Clause.... Further, it is no defense to urge that the religious practices here may be relatively minor encroachments on the First Amendment. The breach of neutrality that is today a trickling stream may all too soon become a raging torrent and, in the words of Madison, "it is proper to take alarm at the first experiment on our liberties." Memorial and Remonstrance Against Religious Assessments....

It is insisted that unless these religious exercises are permitted a "religion of secularism" is established in the schools. We agree of course that the State may not establish a "religion of secularism" in the sense of affirmatively opposing or showing hostility to religion, thus "preferring those who believe in no religion over those who do believe." Zorach v. Clauson, supra, at 314. We do not agree, however, that this decision in any sense has that effect. In addition, it might well be said that one's education is not complete without a study of comparative religion or the history of religion and its relationship to the advancement of civilization. It certainly may be said that the Bible is worthy of study for its literary and historic qualities. Nothing we have said here indicates that such study of the Bible or of religion, when presented objectively as part of a secular program of education, may not be effected consistently with the First Amendment. But the exercises here do not fall into those categories. They are religious exercises, required by the States in violation of the command of the First Amendment that the Government maintain strict neutrality, neither aiding nor opposing religion.

Finally, we cannot accept that the concept of neutrality, which does not permit a State to require a religious exercise even with the consent of the majority of those affected, collides with the majority's right to free exercise of religion. While the Free Exercise Clause clearly prohibits the use of state action to deny the rights of free exercise to *anyone,* it has never meant that a majority could use the machinery of the State to practice its beliefs....

. . .

JUSTICE DOUGLAS, concurring.

I join the opinion of the Court and add a few words in explanation.

. . .

In these cases we have no coercive religious exercise aimed at making the students conform. The prayers announced are not compulsory, though some may think they have that indirect effect because the nonconformist student may be induced to participate for fear of being called an "oddball." But that coercion, if it be present, has not been shown; so the vices of the present regimes are different.

These regimes violate the Establishment Clause in two different ways. In each case the State is conducting a religious exercise; and, as the Court holds, that cannot be done without violating the "neutrality" required of the State by the balance of power between individual, church and state that has been struck by the First Amendment. But the Establishment Clause is not limited to precluding the State itself from conducting religious exercises. It also forbids the State to employ its facilities or funds in a way that gives any church, or all churches, greater strength in our society than it would have by relying on its members alone. Thus, the present regimes must fall under that clause for the additional reason that public funds, though small in amount, are being used to promote a religious exercise. Through the mechanism of the State, all of the people are being required to finance a religious exercise that only some of the people want and that violates the sensibilities of others.

. . .

JUSTICE BRENNAN, concurring.

I join fully in the opinion and the judgment of the Court. I see no escape from the conclusion that the exercises called in question in these two cases violate the constitutional mandate....

The importance of the issue and the deep conviction with which views on both sides are held seem to me to justify detailing at some length my reasons for joining the Court's judgment and opinion.

. . .

A too literal quest for the advice of the Founding Fathers upon the issues of these cases seems to me futile and misdirected for several reasons: First, on our precise problem the historical record is at best ambiguous, and statements can readily be found to support either side of the proposition. The ambiguity of history is understandable if we recall the nature of the problems uppermost in the thinking of the statesmen who fashioned the religious guarantees; they were concerned with far more flagrant intrusions of government into the realm of religion than any that our century has witnessed. While it is clear to me that the Framers meant the Establishment Clause to prohibit more than the creation of an established federal church such as existed in England, I have no doubt that, in their preoccupation with the imminent question of established churches, they gave no distinct consideration to the particular question whether the clause also forbade devotional exercises in public institutions.

Second, the structure of American education has greatly changed since the First Amendment was adopted. In the context of our modern emphasis upon public education available to all citizens, any views of the eighteenth century as to whether the exercises at bar are an "establishment" offer little aid to decision. . . .

Third, our religious composition makes us a vastly more diverse people than were our forefathers. They knew differences chiefly among Protestant sects. Today the Nation is far more heterogeneous religiously, including as it does substantial minorities not only of Catholics and Jews but as well of those who worship according to no version of the Bible and those who worship no God at all. . . . In the face of such profound changes, practices which may have been objectionable to no one in the time of Jefferson and Madison may today be highly offensive to many persons, the deeply devout and the nonbelievers alike.

. . .

Attendance at the public schools has never been compulsory; parents remain morally and constitutionally free to choose the academic environment in which they wish their children to be educated. The relationship of the Establishment Clause of the First Amendment to the public school system is preeminently that of reserving such a choice to the individual parent, rather than vesting it in the majority of voters of each State or school district. The choice which is thus preserved is between a public secular education with its uniquely democratic values and some form of private or sectarian education, which offers values of its own. In my judgment the First Amendment forbids the State to inhibit that freedom of choice by diminishing the attractiveness of either alternative—either by restricting the liberty of the private schools to inculcate whatever values they wish, or by jeopardizing the freedom of the public schools from private or sectarian pressures....

. . .

I turn now to the cases before us. The religious nature of the exercises here challenged seems plain. Unless Engel v. Vitale is to be overruled, or we are to engage in wholly disingenuous distinction, we cannot sustain these practices....

. . .

[An] element which is said to absolve the practices involved in these cases from the ban of the religious guarantees of the Constitution is the provision to excuse or exempt students who wish not to participate.

... [T]he short, and to me sufficient, answer is that the availability of excusal or exemption simply has no relevance to the establishment question, if it is once found that these practices are essentially religious exercises designed at least in part to achieve religious aims through the use of public school facilities during the school day.

The more difficult question, however, is whether the availability of excusal for the dissenting child serves to refuse challenges to these practices under the Free Exercise Clause. While it is enough to decide these cases to dispose of the establishment questions, questions of free exercise are so inextricably interwoven into the history and present status of these practices as to justify disposition of this second aspect of the excusal issue. The answer is that the excusal procedure itself necessarily operates in such a way as to infringe the rights of free exercise of those children who wish to be excused....

... First, by requiring what is tantamount in the eyes of teachers and schoolmates to a profession of disbelief, or at least of nonconformity, the procedure may well deter those children who do not wish to participate for any reason based upon the dictates of conscience from exercising an indisputably constitutional right to be excused....

Such reluctance to seek exemption seems all the more likely in view of the fact that children are disinclined at this age to step out of line or to flout "peer-group norms." Such is the widely held view of experts who have studied the behaviors and attitudes of children....

. . .

These considerations bring me to a final contention of the school officials in these cases: that the invalidation of the exercises at bar permits this Court no alternative but to declare unconstitutional every vestige, however slight, of cooperation or accommodation between religion and government. I cannot accept that contention. While it is not, of course, appropriate for this Court to decide questions not presently before it, I venture to suggest that religious exercises in the public schools present a unique problem. For not every involvement of religion in public life violates the Establishment Clause. Our decision in these cases does not clearly forecast anything about the constitutionality of other types of interdependence between religious and other public institutions.

... What the Framers meant to foreclose, and what our decisions under the Establishment Clause have forbidden, are those involvements of religious with secular institutions which (a) serve the essentially religious activities of religious institutions; (b) employ the organs of government for essentially religious purposes; or (c) use essentially religious means to serve governmental ends, where secular means would suffice....

The line between permissible and impermissible forms of involvement between government and religion has already been considered by the lower federal and state courts. I think a brief survey of certain of these forms of accommodation will reveal that the First Amendment commands not official hostility toward religion, but only a strict neutrality in matters of religion. Moreover, it may serve to suggest that the scope of our holding today is to be measured by the special circumstances under which these cases have arisen, and by the particular dangers to church and state which religious exercises in the public schools present. It may be helpful for purposes of analysis to group these other practices and forms of accommodations into several rough categories.

A. *The Conflict Between Establishment and Free Exercise.*—There are certain practices, conceivably violative of the Establishment Clause, the striking down of which might seriously interfere with certain religious liberties also protected by the First Amendment. Provisions for churches and chaplains at military establishments for those in the armed services may afford one such example. The like provision by state and federal governments for chaplains in penal institutions may afford another example. It is argued that such provisions may be assumed to contravene the Establishment Clause, yet be sustained on constitutional grounds as necessary to secure to the members of the Armed Forces and prisoners those rights of worship guaranteed under the Free Exercise Clause. Since government has deprived such persons of the opportunity to practice their faith at places of their choice, the argument runs, government may, in order to avoid infringing the free exercise guarantees, provide substitutes where it requires such persons to be. Such a principle might support, for example, the constitutionality of draft exemptions for ministers and divinity students ...; of the excusal of children from school on their respective religious holidays; and of the allowance by government of temporary use of public buildings by religious organizations when their own churches have become unavailable because of a disaster or emergency.

Such activities and practices seem distinguishable from the sponsorship of daily Bible reading and prayer recital. For one thing, there is no element of coercion present in the appointment of military or prison chaplains; the soldier or convict who declines the opportunities for worship would not ordinarily subject himself to the suspicion or obloquy of his peers. Of special significance to this distinction is the fact that we are here usually dealing with adults, not with impressionable children as in the public schools. Moreover, the school exercises are not designed to provide the pupils with general opportunities for worship denied them by the legal obligation to attend school. The student's compelled presence in school for five days a week in no way renders the regular religious facilities of the community less accessible to him than they are to others. The situation of the school child is therefore plainly unlike that of the isolated soldier or the prisoner.

... [H]ostility, not neutrality, would characterize the refusal to provide chaplains and places of worship for prisoners and soldiers cut off by the State from all civilian opportunities for public communion, the withholding of draft exemptions for ministers and conscientious objectors, or the denial of the temporary use of an empty public building to a congregation whose place of worship has been destroyed by fire or flood. I do not say that government *must* provide chaplains or draft exemptions, or that the courts should intercede if it fails to do so.

B. *Establishment and Exercises in Legislative Bodies.*—The saying of invocational prayers in legislative chambers, state or federal, and the appointment of legislative chaplains, might well represent no involvements of the kind prohibited by the Establishment Clause. Legislators, federal and state, are mature adults who may presumably absent themselves from such public and ceremonial exercises without incurring any penalty, direct or indirect....

C. *Non–Devotional Use of the Bible in the Public Schools.*—The holding of the Court today plainly does not foreclose teaching *about* the Holy Scriptures or *about* the differences between religious sects in classes in literature or history. Indeed, whether or not the Bible is involved, it would be impossible to teach meaningfully many subjects in the social sciences or the humanities without some mention of religion....

We do not, ... in my view usurp the jurisdiction of school administrators by holding as we do today that morning devotional exercises in any form are constitutionally invalid. But there is no occasion now to go further and anticipate problems we cannot judge with the material now before us. Any attempt to impose rigid limits upon the mention of God or references to the Bible in the classroom would be fraught with dangers. If it should sometime hereafter be shown that in fact religion can play no part in the teaching of a given subject without resurrecting the ghost of the practices we strike down today, it will then be time enough to consider questions we must now defer.

· · ·

F. *Activities Which, Though Religious in Origin, Have Ceased to Have Religious Meaning.*—As we noted in our *Sunday Law* decisions, nearly every criminal law on the books can be traced to some religious principle or inspiration. But that does not make the present enforcement of the criminal law in any sense an establishment of religion, simply because it accords with widely held religious principles. As we said in McGowan v. Maryland, 366 U.S. 420, 442, "the 'Establishment' Clause does not ban federal or state regulation of conduct whose reason or effect merely happens to coincide or harmonize with the tenets of some or all religions." This rationale suggests that the use of the motto "In God We Trust" on currency, on documents and public buildings and the like may not offend the clause. It is not that the use of these four words can be dismissed as "de minimis"—for I suspect there would be intense opposition to the abandonment of that motto. The truth is that we have simply interwoven the motto so deeply into the fabric of our civil polity that its present use may well not present that type of involvement which the First Amendment prohibits.

This general principle might also serve to insulate the various patriotic exercises and activities used in the public schools and elsewhere which, whatever may have been their origins, no longer have a religious purpose or meaning. The reference to divinity in the revised pledge of allegiance, for example, may merely recognize the historical fact that our Nation was believed to have been founded "under God." Thus reciting the pledge may be no more of a religious exercise than the reading aloud of Lincoln's Gettysburg Address, which contains an allusion to the same historical fact.

· · ·

JUSTICE STEWART, dissenting.

· · ·

The First Amendment declares that "Congress shall make no law respecting an establishment of religion, or prohibiting the free exercise thereof. . . ." It is, I think, a fallacious oversimplification to regard these two provisions as establishing a single constitutional standard of "separation of church and state," which can be mechanically applied in every case to delineate the required boundaries between government and religion. We err in the first place if we do not recognize, as a matter of history and as a matter of the imperatives of our free society, that religion and government must necessarily interact in countless ways. Secondly, the fact is that while in many contexts the Establishment Clause and the Free Exercise Clause fully complement each other, there are areas in which a doctrinaire reading of the Establishment Clause leads to irreconcilable conflict with the Free Exercise Clause.

A single obvious example should suffice to make the point. Spending federal funds to employ chaplains for the armed forces might be said to violate the Establishment Clause. Yet a lonely soldier stationed at some faraway outpost could surely complain that a government which did *not* provide him the opportunity for pastoral guidance was affirmatively prohibiting the free exercise of his religion. And such examples could readily be multiplied. The short of the matter is simply that the two relevant clauses of the First Amendment cannot accurately be reflected in a sterile metaphor which by its very nature may distort rather than illumine the problems involved in a particular case. . . .

· · ·

It is this concept of constitutional protection embodied in our decisions which makes the cases before us such difficult ones for me. For there is involved in these cases a substantial free exercise claim on the part of those who affirmatively desire to have their children's school day open with the reading of passages from the Bible.

. . .

The dangers both to government and to religion inherent in official support of instruction in the tenets of various religious sects are absent in the present cases, which involve only a reading from the Bible unaccompanied by comments which might otherwise constitute instruction. Indeed, since, from all that appears in either record, any teacher who does not wish to do so is free not to participate, it cannot even be contended that some infinitesimal part of the salaries paid by the State are made contingent upon the performance of a religious function.

. . .

. . . I shall for the balance of this dissenting opinion treat the provisions before us as making the variety and content of the exercises, as well as a choice as to their implementation, matters which ultimately reflect the consensus of each local school community. In the absence of coercion upon those who do not wish to participate—because they hold less strong beliefs, other beliefs, or no beliefs at all—such provisions cannot, in my view, be held to represent the type of support of religion barred by the Establishment Clause. For the only support which such rules provide for religion is the withholding of state hostility—a simple acknowledgment on the part of secular authorities that the Constitution does not require extirpation of all expression of religious belief.

. . . [T]he question presented is not whether exercises such as those at issue here are constitutionally compelled, but rather whether they are constitutionally invalid. And that issue, in my view, turns on the question of coercion.

It is clear that the dangers of coercion involved in the holding of religious exercises in a schoolroom differ qualitatively from those presented by the use of similar exercises or affirmations in ceremonies attended by adults. Even as to children, however, the duty laid upon government in connection with religious exercises in the public schools is that of refraining from so structuring the school environment as to put any kind of pressure on a child to participate in those exercises; it is not that of providing an atmosphere in which children are kept scrupulously insulated from any awareness that some of their fellows may want to open the school day with prayer, or of the fact that there exist in our pluralistic society differences of religious belief.

. . .

. . . [C]ertain types of exercises would present situations in which no possibility of coercion on the part of secular officials could be claimed to exist. Thus, if such exercises were held either before or after the official school day, or if the school schedule were such that participation were merely one among a number of desirable alternatives, it could hardly be contended that the exercises did anything more than to provide an opportunity for the voluntary expression of religious belief. On the other hand, a law which provided for religious exercises during the school day and which contained no excusal provision would obviously be unconstitutionally coercive upon those who did not wish to participate. And even under a law containing an excusal provision, if the exercises were held during the school day, and no equally desirable alternative were provided by the school authorities, the likelihood that children might be under at least some psychological compulsion to participate would be great. In a case such as the latter, however, I think we would err if we *assumed* such coercion in the absence of any evidence.

THE IMPACT OF ENGEL AND SCHEMPP

Both the impact of and the reaction to *Engel* and *Schempp* were significant and enduring. The following table dramatically shows the geographical variability of the impact of the Supreme Court prayer decisions.*

USE OF MORNING PRAYERS				
Percentage of 1712 Elementary School Teachers Using Morning Prayers				
Region	Pre–1962	1964–65	Difference	Percentage Reduction
West	14	5	– 9	64
Midwest	38	21	–17	45
East	83	11	–72	87
South	87	64	–23	26

Soon after the Court decided *Schempp,* critics of the decision in Congress introduced constitutional amendments to permit school prayer in public schools. Although they could not muster the necessary two-thirds majority, the issue remained alive. Both the Reagan and Bush administrations supported prayer in public schools.

NOTES AND QUESTIONS

1. In both the *Engel* and *Schempp* cases, school authorities had conceded that those who wished to be excused during school prayer could be excused. Why didn't that concession by the school authorities settle the cases? Do these cases stand for the proposition that any school exercise that compromises a pupil's religious beliefs has to be *stopped?* Reference to the flag-salute cases (which are discussed in more detail, Chapter 2, pp. 22–42) indicates that the answer to the last question is no. In the first flag-salute case, the Court held that religious opposition to saluting the flag didn't even entitle the objectors to be exempted from the exercise. Minersville School Dist. v. Gobitis, 310 U.S. 586 (1940). When the *Gobitis* case was overruled, all the Jehovah's Witness' children received was an exemption from the exercise. West Virginia State Board of Education v. Barnette, 319 U.S. 624 (1943). Why did the plaintiffs in the flag-salute case have a constitutional right, *at most,* to an exemption while the plaintiffs in the prayer cases had the right to insist that the offending exercises be stopped? The short answer is that one exercise

* Kenneth Dolbeare and Phillip E. Hammond, The School Prayer Decision, University of Chicago Press, 1971, p. 32.

was secular and the other was religious. Public school pupils who have a religious objection to exercises that are *secular* have the right, *at most,* to be excused from the requirement. (As to when they have the right to be excused, see Wisconsin v. Yoder, Chapter 17, pp. 620–627.) On the other hand, public school pupils who have an objection to exercises that are *religious* may be entitled to insist that the exercise be stopped. Why is that distinction made? Do the Court's opinion in the prayer cases explain it?

2. Would it have made more sense to draw the line between religious exercises that are *sectarian* and those that are not? That is, shouldn't objecting pupils be entitled to be excused from all religious exercises but not privileged to have the exercises stopped, so long as exercises are non-sectarian? Consider the difficulties of distinguishing between the sectarian and non-sectarian. In the *Schempp* case, the school board had put an "expert witness" on the stand at the trial, to prove that the bible-reading program in the school was non-sectarian. Specifically, he

> stated that the Bible was non-sectarian. He later stated that the phrase "non-sectarian" meant to him non-sectarian within the Christian faiths. [He] stated that his definition of the Holy Bible would include the Jewish Holy Scriptures, but also stated that the "Holy Bible" would not be complete without the New Testament. He stated that the New Testament "conveyed the message of Christians." In his opinion, reading of the Holy Scriptures to the exclusion of the New Testament would be a sectarian practice. . . .

In his concurring opinion in the *Schempp* case, Justice Brennan suggested that the problem went deeper than the difficulty in drawing lines:

> It has been suggested that a tentative solution to these problems may lie in the fashioning of a "common core" of theology tolerable to all creeds but preferential to none. . . . [T]he notion of a "common core" litany or supplication offends many deeply devout worshippers who do not find clearly sectarian practices objectionable. Father Gustave Weigel has recently expressed a widely shared view: "The moral code held by each separate religious community can reductively be unified, but the consistent particular believer wants no such reduction." And, as the American Council on Education warned several years ago, "The notion of a common core suggests a watering down of the several faiths to the point where common essentials appear. This might easily lead to a new sect—a public school sect— which would take its place alongside the existing faiths and compete with them."

Do you agree?

3. Drawing the line between religious and secular exercises was not a major problem in any of the prayer cases. With reference to other exercises and practices in the schools, the line may be difficult, indeed, to draw. In a footnote to Justice Black's opinion for the Court in the *Engel* case, he referred to "patriotic or ceremonial occasions" that incidentally

692 FREEDOM OF RELIGION Pt. 3

involve profession of faith in a Supreme Being. The footnote suggested that these activities were secular. Could someone insist that the words "under God" be deleted from the flag salute? In a footnote to his concurring opinion in the *Engel* case, Justice Douglas said:

> The Pledge of Allegiance, like the prayer, recognizes the existence of a Supreme Being. Since 1954 it has contained the words "one Nation *under God,* indivisible, with liberty and justice for all." ... The House Report recommending the addition of the words "under God" stated that those words in no way run contrary to the First Amendment but recognize "only the guidance of God in our national affairs." ... Senator Ferguson, who sponsored the measure in the Senate, pointed out that the words "In God We Trust" are over the entrance to the Senate Chamber.... He added:

> "I have felt that the Pledge of Allegiance to the Flag which stands for the United States of America should recognize the Creator who we really believe is in control of the destinies of this great Republic.

> "It is true that under the Constitution no power is lodged anywhere to establish a religion. This is not an attempt to establish a religion; it has nothing to do with anything of that kind. It relates to belief in God, in whom we sincerely repose our trust. We know that America cannot be defended by guns, planes, and ships alone. Appropriations and expenditures for defense will be of value only if the God under whom we live believes that we are in the right. We should at all times recognize God's province over the lives of our people and over this great Nation."

And, what of the singing of Christmas carols in music classes? What of decorating classrooms and school buildings during the Christmas holidays?

4. Once it is decided that an exercise in a public school (or before *any* public body, for that matter) is religious, does it necessarily follow that it violates the Establishment Clause? Notice the "test" stated in Justice Clark's opinion for the Court in the *Schempp* case for deciding whether a law violates the Establishment Clause.

> ... what are the purpose and the primary effect of the enactment? If *either* is the advancement or inhibition of religion then the enactment exceeds the scope of legislative power.... [emphasis added.]

Under that test, aren't all the religious practices described in Justice Douglas' concurring opinion in the *Engel* case unconstitutional? Notice in the last part of Justice Brennan's concurring opinion in the *Schempp* case that he lists some practices of public bodies that may be constitutional even if they *are* religious. Do you agree? Did the majority mean, in adopting the "purpose or primary effect" test to foreclose the results suggested by Justice Brennan's opinion?

Notice particularly Justice Brennan's statement that prayers in legislative chambers and the appointment of legislative chaplains "might well represent no involvements ... prohibited by the Establishment Clause" because legislators are mature adults and not a captive audience. In Marsh v. Chambers, 463 U.S. 783 (1983), Justice Brennan confessed that this part of his concurring opinion had been a mistake. Justice Brennan was in dissent in *Marsh,* however, and the Court's majority decided that a paid state legislative chaplain did not violate the Establishment Clause. The Court relied on a long historical tradition to support its conclusion. Is it necessary, to decide this case, that it be viewed as an historical exception to the usual rules? Compare Professor Choper's standard on page 663.

5. Is the *result* in the prayer cases consistent with Professor Choper's thesis—are school prayers *likely* to influence or compromise students' religious beliefs? Would you require, as would Justice Steward (in his dissent in *Schempp*), that the specific school exercise, in its specific setting, be proved to *have* that effect? Notice the distortion created here by the process of trying lawsuits. A lawsuit begins *after* a particular practice has been instituted, and it is tempting to have the result turn on findings of fact at the trial concerning what the actual impact of the challenged practice is. Thus, whether a particular school prayer violated the Constitution, under Justice Stewart's argument, would depend on a number of subtle factors in each case—the makeup of the student body, the attitude of pupils and teachers, community sentiment, the way in which the particular prayers were said, etc. But, with this structure, it would be difficult to predict, in advance of trial, whether a particular school prayer ceremony violated the constitution or not. And, trials are not likely to occur at all unless the objecting parent and child have skins thick enough to stand up to the community displeasure which attends bringing a lawsuit. Compare notes 1–3, above pp. 690–692. Moreover, there may be a need for a predictable rule, applicable to all prayers in public school classrooms during regular school hours, so that school boards, principals, teachers, pupils and parents can know what the Constitution permits and what it forbids. Given these problems, what the Court has done is to condemn all classroom prayers in the public schools during school hours, without reference to nuances in the language of the prayer or the community and classroom setting. Would it have been preferable to have the rule turn on whether, in fact, the specific prayer being challenged compromised or influenced students' religious beliefs? Would it have been preferable to have a flat rule that all public school prayer is constitutional, no matter what its content and setting are, so long as those who object are excused?

6. Do you agree with Justice Douglas that the solution to the problem of whether public prayer violates the Constitution lies in asking whether government is *financing* a religious exercise? In a note to Justice Black on May 28, 1962, Justice Douglas explained what troubled him in *Engel.* "As I see it," he wrote, "there is no penalty for not praying, no coercion; there is, as I read the record, no more compulsion that there is when our marshal says 'God save the United States and

this honorable Court.' The question seems to me to be whether the state or federal government can finance a religious service or exercise. Can they pay ministers to pray for them? Can they start off each session with a prayer? ... No one is being penalized in the slightest—nor compelled to take part. Is it not like the case where by regulation each school day is begun by singing *God Bless America?*" Two weeks later, Justice Douglas wrote Black again saying that he had put his "troubles" on paper—"not for the purpose of filing a concurrence or dissent but in order to define the narrow issue that seems involved." He said he was inclined to reverse if the decision was based on use of public funds to finance a religious exercise. But, he added, if the Court struck down the New York school prayer requirement, "I think we could not consistently open each of our sessions with prayer. That's the kernel of my problem."* Also a problem for Justice Douglas was his vote in *Everson,* which held financing of transportation to parochial schools constitutional. He solved the problem by conceding in his concurring opinion in *Engel* that he was wrong in the *Everson* case when he joined the majority in permitting public funds to be used to transport parochial school students. Do you think that his position in *Engel* and *Schempp* would also require him to recant his majority opinion in the *Zorach* case? (See note 3, p. 691, above.) Notice the citation of the *Zorach* case in Justice Douglas' *Engel* opinion for the proposition that, "We are a religious people whose institutions presuppose a Supreme Being." Would a school board's program be constitutional if it required teachers to recite that sentence from the *Zorach* opinion (giving objectors the option of excusing themselves, of course) each morning just before the flag salute?

7. In his concurring opinion in *Engel,* Justice Douglas said that there is no element of coercion in New York's regulation. Do you agree? Douglas' conference notes in the case record Chief Justice Warren as saying that it would be difficult as a practical matter for little children to refrain from participating in the New York school prayer. Justice Frankfurter said that "there is an inherent compulsion on children to take part." Justice Clark said that "compulsion on the children is present." Douglas Papers, Box 1275.

8. If the validity of a government prayer really turns only on the question whether it is "intended" to serve a religious purpose or whether it has that "effect," it would not seem to be controlling whether the prayer has a tendency to coerce or compromise religious beliefs. In a dissenting opinion in Wallace v. Jaffree, 472 U.S. 38 (1985), Chief Justice Burger mentioned that Congressional sessions open with prayer, and Supreme Court sessions open with the Court's marshal saying "God Save the United States and this honorable Court." He complained that "some wag is bound to say" that prayer in public schools is impermissible, while religious invocations in Congress and the Supreme Court are permissible, "because members of the Judiciary and Congress are more in need of Divine guidance than are schoolchildren." Would it be more appropriate to quip that members of the Judiciary and Congress are beyond redemption?

---

* Black Papers, Library of Congress, Box 354.

9. In Lynch v. Donnelly, 465 U.S. 668 (1984), the Court decided that a Christmas display by the City of Pawtucket, Rhode Island, did not violate the Establishment Clause. Chief Justice Burger's opinion seemed to cast doubt on the "purpose and effect" test of prior cases, saying it was merely a "useful" inquiry in a line-drawing process with "no fixed, *per se* rule." The 5–4 decision was, however, narrowly based on the conclusion that a creche in this particular Christmas display (that included a Santa Claus house, reindeer pulling Santa's sleigh, candy-striped poles, a Christmas tree, carolers, cutout figures of a clown, an elephant, and a teddy bear, colored lights, and a large banner reading "seasons greetings") was intended to depict "the historical origins of this traditional event long recognized as a National Holiday." The display thus had a secular purpose, and did not have the effect of advancing religion.

10. County of Allegheny v. American Civil Liberties Union, 492 U.S. 573 (1989), involved two religious displays on public property in Pittsburgh, Pennsylvania. One was a creche, located on the Grand Staircase of the County Courthouse. The second was an 18–foot tall Chanukah menorah near a 45–foot Christmas tree at the outside entrance of the City–County building, a block away. Four justices (Justice Kennedy, joined by Chief Justice Rehnquist, and Justice White and Scalia) would have permitted both displays. Three justices (Justice Brennan, joined by Justices Marshall and Stevens) would have forbidden both. The outcome was controlled by Justices Blackmun and O'Connor, who voted to permit the menorah, but not the creche. In their view, the display of the menorah, with a Christmas tree and a sign signed by the Mayor proclaiming a "salute to liberty," did not endorse religion. In its setting, unlike the *Lynch* case, the creche standing alone celebrated Christmas as a Christian religious holiday.

11. Justice Kennedy's opinion in the *County of Allegheny* case argued that there should be no violation of the Establishment Clause unless one of two criteria were met:

> government may not coerce anyone to support or participate in any religion or its exercise; and it may not ... give direct benefits to religion in such a degree that it in fact "establishes a [state] religion or religious faith, or tends to do so."

He contended further that, in applying those tests, the Court should be guided, in a very general way, by history.

> Non-coercive government action within the realm of flexible accommodation or passive acknowledgment of existing symbols does not violate the Establishment Clause unless it benefits religion in a way more direct and more substantial than practices that are accepted in our national heritage.

Significantly, a majority of the Court agreed with that portion of Justice Blackmun's opinion rejecting Justice Kennedy's position, because it would "gut the core of the Establishment Clause." Some historical practices represented a "heritage of official discrimination against non-Christians [that] has no place in the jurisprudence of the Establishment Clause." The majority concluded that Justice Kennedy's test was "nothing more than an attempt to lower considerably the level of scrutiny in Establishment Clause cases."

12. The Supreme Court solidly reaffirmed the Court's focus on "purpose" and "effect" of challenged practices in Wallace v. Jaffree, 472 U.S. 38 (1985). The Court invalidated an Alabama statute authorizing a moment of silence in public schools "for meditation or voluntary prayer." The lower federal court had decided that an earlier statute providing a one-minute moment of silence "for meditation" was valid, and that ruling had not been appealed. The invalid statute was different, however, because the language of the statute and its legislative history showed it to be motivated to "endorse" prayer as a favored practice during the moment of silence. In dissent, Chief Justice Burger, echoing his Court opinion in Lynch v. Donnelly, accused the majority of a "naive preoccupation with an easy bright-line approach" to strike down an "innocuous statute."

13. The Court's opinion in Wallace v. Jaffree was premised on the conclusion that if a law has no "secular" purpose, it is invalid, no matter what effect it has. It was irrelevant whether Alabama's moment of silence in its public schools operated in practice in any different way from a moment of silence in public schools in other states. Justice White's dissent raised the question whether laws that operate in an identical manner ought to be struck down because of their choice of language, or their "peculiar legislative history." If it were conceded that a statute could provide for a moment of silence at the beginning of the school day, so long as it did not mention prayer, should a teacher be allowed to give an affirmative answer to a student who asks "May I pray?" Justice White then concluded that it was silly to "invalidate a statute that at the outset provided the legislative answer to the question."

14. Justice O'Connor's concurrence in Wallace v. Jaffree argued that the "purpose and effect" standard needed to be refined to be meaningful. She concluded that government endorsement of religion or religious practices should be invalid if "it sends a message to nonadherents that they are outsiders, not full members of the political community, and an accompanying message to adherents that they are insiders, favored members of the political community." A state sponsored moment of silence in public schools would be valid, she said, under that test. By contrast, the Alabama statute "conveyed to objective observers ... approval of the child who selects prayer over other alternatives during a moment of silence." Does Justice O'Connor's focus on the "message conveyed" by challenged state practices explain the pattern of results in Establishment cases you have seen thus far?

LEE v. WEISMAN

Supreme Court of the United States, 1992.
505 U.S. 577, 112 S.Ct. 2649, 120 L.Ed.2d 467.

JUSTICE KENNEDY delivered the opinion of the Court.

School principals in the public school system of the city of Providence, Rhode Island, are permitted to invite members of the clergy to offer invocation and benediction prayers as part of the formal graduation ceremonies for middle schools and for high schools. The question before us is whether including clerical members who offer prayers as part of the official school graduation ceremony is consistent with the Religion Clauses of the First Amendment. . . .

ANTHONY M. KENNEDY—Born on July 13, 1936, in Sacramento, California, son of a state lobbyist. Republican. Roman Catholic. Grew up in Sacramento in economically comfortable circumstances. Stanford, B.A. 1958; Harvard, LL.B., cum laude, 1961. Practiced law in San Francisco and Sacramento, 1961–1976; part-time constitutional law professor, McGeorge Law School, University of the Pacific, 1965–1988; U.S. Court of Appeals judge (9th Circuit), 1976–1988. Nominated associate justice on November 30, 1987, by President Ronald Reagan, to replace Lewis F. Powell, Jr., after the Senate defeated the nomination of Robert H. Bork, and Reagan withdrew the nomination of Douglas Ginsburg. Confirmed by the Senate on February 3, 1988, by a 97–0 vote. Usually voted with Justice Scalia during his early years on the Court. Voted with the liberal wing of the Court in Lee v. Weisman, Planned Parenthood of Southern Pennsylvania v. Casey and other cases in the 1991 term, leading one writer to comment that Justice Kennedy had been "Blackmunized." (Justice Blackmun had made a similar shift in the mid–1970s.) Hearing of the remark, Justice Blackmun wrote Kennedy, "Don't worry. It's not fatal."

I

A

Deborah Weisman graduated from Nathan Bishop Middle School, a public school in Providence, at a formal ceremony in June 1989. She was about 14 years old. For many years it has been the policy of the Providence School Committee and the Superintendent of Schools to permit principals to invite members of the clergy to give invocations and benedictions at middle school and high school graduations. . . . Deborah's father, Daniel Weisman, objected to any prayers at Deborah's middle school graduation, but to no avail. The school principal, petitioner Robert E. Lee, invited a rabbi to deliver prayers at the graduation exercises for Deborah's class. Rabbi Leslie Gutterman, of the Temple Beth El in Providence, accepted.

It has been the custom of Providence school officials to provide invited clergy with a pamphlet entitled "Guidelines for Civic Occasions," prepared by the National Conference of Christians and Jews. The Guidelines recommend that public prayers at nonsectarian civic ceremonies be composed with "inclusiveness and sensitivity," though they acknowledge that "[p]rayer of any kind may be inappropriate on some civic occasions." The principal gave Rabbi Gutterman the pamphlet before the graduation and advised him the invocation and benediction should be nonsectarian.

Rabbi Gutterman's prayers were as follows:

"INVOCATION

"God of the Free, Hope of the Brave:

"For the legacy of America where diversity is celebrated and the rights of minorities are protected, we thank You. May these young men and women grow up to enrich it.

"For the liberty of America, we thank You. May these new graduates grow up to guard it.

"For the political process of America in which all its citizens may participate, for its court system where all may seek justice we thank You. May those we honor this morning always turn to it in trust.

"For the destiny of America we thank You. May the graduates of Nathan Bishop Middle School so live that they might help to share it.

"May our aspirations for our country and for these young people, who are our hope for the future, be richly fulfilled. AMEN"

"BENEDICTION

"O God, we are grateful to You for having endowed us with the capacity for learning which we have celebrated on this joyous commencement.

"Happy families give thanks for seeing their children achieve an important milestone. Send Your blessings upon the teachers and administrators who helped prepare them.

"The graduates now need strength and guidance for the future, help them to understand that we are not complete with academic knowledge alone. We must each strive to fulfill what You require of us all: To do justly, to love mercy, to walk humbly.

"We give thanks to You, Lord, for keeping us alive, sustaining us and allowing us to reach this special, happy occasion. AMEN"

... In the Providence school system, most high school graduation ceremonies are conducted away from the school, while most middle school ceremonies are held on school premises. Classical High School, which Deborah now attends, has conducted its graduation ceremonies on school premises.... [A]ttendance at graduation ceremonies is voluntary. The graduating students enter as a group in a processional, subject to the direction of teachers and school officials, and sit together, apart from their families. We assume the clergy's participation in any high school graduation exercise would be about what it was at Deborah's middle school ceremony. There the students stood for the Pledge of Allegiance and remained standing during the Rabbi's prayers. Even on the assumption that there was a respectful moment of silence both before and after the prayers, the Rabbi's two presentations must not have extended much beyond a minute each, if that. We do not know whether he remained on stage during the whole ceremony, or whether the students received individual diplomas on stage, or if he helped to congratulate them.

. . .

B

Deborah's graduation was held on the premises of Nathan Bishop Middle School on June 29, 1989. Four days before the ceremony, Daniel Weisman, [brought suit in a federal court] to prohibit school officials from including an invocation or benediction in the graduation ceremony. The court denied [immediate relief for lack of time to consider the issue]. Deborah and her family attended the graduation, where the prayers were recited. In July 1989, Daniel Weisman filed an amended complaint seeking a permanent injunction barring ... the Providence public schools, from inviting the clergy to deliver invocations and benedictions at future graduations. . . .

. . .

II

These dominant facts mark and control the confines of our decision: State officials direct the performance of a formal religious exercise at promotional and graduation ceremonies for secondary schools. Even for those students who object to the religious exercise, their attendance and participation in the state-sponsored religious activity are in a fair and real sense obligatory, though the school district does not require attendance as a condition for receipt of the diploma.

This case does not require us to revisit the difficult questions dividing us in recent cases, questions of the definition and full scope of the principles governing the extent of permitted accommodation by the State for the religious beliefs and practices of many of its citizens. See Allegheny County v. Greater Pittsburgh ACLU, 492 U.S. 573 (1989); Wallace v. Jaffree, 472 U.S. 38 (1985); Lynch v. Donnelly, 465 U.S. 668 (1984). For without reference to those principles in other contexts, the controlling precedents as they relate to prayer and religious exercise in primary and secondary public schools compel the holding here that the policy of the city of Providence is an unconstitutional one. We can decide the case without reconsidering the general constitutional framework by which public schools' efforts to accommodate religion are measured. Thus we do not accept the invitation of petitioners and amicus the United States to reconsider our decision in Lemon v. Kurtzman, supra. The government involvement with religious activity in this case is pervasive, to the point of creating a state-sponsored and state-directed religious exercise in a public school. Conducting this formal religious observance conflicts with settled rules pertaining to prayer exercises for students, and that suffices to determine the question before us.

... [T]he Constitution guarantees that government may not coerce anyone to support or participate in religion or its exercise, or otherwise act in a way which "establishes a [state] religion or religious faith, or tends to do so." ... The State's involvement in the school prayers challenged today violates these central principles.

That involvement is as troubling as it is undenied. A school official, the principal, decided that an invocation and a benediction should be given; this is a choice attributable to the State, and from a constitutional perspective it is as if a state statute decreed that the prayers must occur. The principal chose the religious participant, here a rabbi, and that choice is also attributable to the State. The reason for the choice of a rabbi is not disclosed by the record, but the potential for divisiveness over the choice of a particular member of the clergy to conduct the ceremony is apparent.

Divisiveness, of course, can attend any state decision respecting religions, and neither its existence nor its potential necessarily invalidates the State's attempts to accommodate religion in all cases. The potential for divisiveness is of particular relevance here though, because it centers around an overt religious exercise in a secondary school environment where, as we discuss below, subtle coercive pressures exist and where the student had no real alternative which would have allowed her to avoid the fact or appearance of participation.

The State's role did not end with the decision to include a prayer and with the choice of clergyman. Principal Lee provided Rabbi Gutterman with a copy of the "Guidelines for Civic Occasions," and advised him that his prayers should be nonsectarian. Through these means the principal directed and controlled the content of the prayer. Even if the only sanction for ignoring the instructions were that the rabbi would not be invited back, we think no religious representative who valued his or her continued reputation and effectiveness in the community would incur the State's displeasure in this regard. It is a cornerstone principle of our Establishment Clause jurisprudence that "it is no part of the business of government to compose official prayers for any group of the American people to recite as a part of a religious program carried on by government," Engel v. Vitale, 370 U.S. 421, 425 (1962), and that is what the school officials attempted to do.

Petitioners argue, and we find nothing in the case to refute it, that the directions for the content of the prayers were a good-faith attempt by the school to ensure that the sectarianism which is so often the flashpoint for religious animosity be removed from the graduation ceremony. The concern is understandable, as a prayer which uses ideas or images identified with a particular religion may foster a different sort of sectarian rivalry than an invocation or benediction in terms more neutral. The school's explanation, however, does not resolve the dilemma caused by its participation. The question is not the good faith of the school in attempting to make the prayer acceptable to most persons, but the legitimacy of its undertaking that enterprise at all when the object is to produce a prayer to be used in a formal religious exercise which students, for all practical purposes, are obliged to attend.

We are asked to recognize the existence of a practice of nonsectarian prayer, prayer within the embrace of what is known as the Judeo–Christian tradition, prayer which is more acceptable than one which, for example, makes explicit references to the God of Israel, or to Jesus Christ, or to a patron saint. There may be some support, as an empirical observation, to the statement . . . that there has emerged in this country a civic religion, one which is tolerated when sectarian exercises are not. . . . If common ground can be defined which permits once conflicting faiths to express the shared conviction that there is an ethic and a morality which transcend human invention, the sense of community and purpose sought by all decent societies might be advanced. But though the First Amendment does not allow the government to stifle prayers which aspire to these ends, neither does it permit the government to undertake that task for itself.

The First Amendment's Religion Clauses mean that religious beliefs and religious expression are too precious to be either proscribed or prescribed by the State. The design of the Constitution is that preservation and transmission of religious beliefs and worship is a responsibility and a choice committed to the private sphere, which itself is promised freedom to pursue that mission. It must not be forgotten then, that while concern must be given to define the protection granted to an objector or a dissenting non-believer, these same Clauses exist to protect religion from government interference. James Madison, the principal author of the Bill of Rights, did not rest his opposition to a religious establishment on the sole ground of its effect on the minority. A principal ground for his view was: "[E]xperience witnesseth that ecclesiastical establishments, instead of maintaining the purity and efficacy of Religion, have had a contrary operation." . . .

These concerns have particular application in the case of school officials, whose effort to monitor prayer will be perceived by the students as inducing a participation they might otherwise reject. . . . [O]ur precedents do not permit school officials to assist in composing prayers as an incident to a formal exercise for their students. . . . And these same precedents caution us to measure the idea of a civic religion against the central meaning of the Religion Clauses of the First Amendment, which is that all creeds must be tolerated and none favored. The suggestion that government may establish an official or civic religion as a means of avoiding the establishment of a religion with more specific creeds strikes us as a contradiction that cannot be accepted.

The degree of school involvement here made it clear that the graduation prayers bore the imprint of the State and thus put school-age children who objected in an untenable position. We turn our attention now to consider the position of the students, both those who desired the prayer and she who did not.

To endure the speech of false ideas or offensive content and then to counter it is part of learning how to live in a pluralistic society, a society which insists upon open discourse towards the end of a tolerant citizenry. And tolerance presupposes some mutuality of obligation. It is argued that our constitutional vision of a free society requires confidence in our own ability to accept or reject ideas of which we do not approve, and that prayer at a high school graduation does nothing more than offer a choice. By the time they are seniors, high school students no doubt have been required to attend classes and assemblies and to complete assignments exposing them to ideas they find distasteful or immoral or absurd or all of these. Against this background, students may consider it an odd measure of justice to be subjected during the course of their educations to ideas deemed offensive and irreligious, but to be denied a brief, formal prayer ceremony that the school offers in return. This argument cannot prevail, however. It overlooks a fundamental dynamic of the Constitution.

The First Amendment protects speech and religion by quite different mechanisms. Speech is protected by insuring its full expression even when the government participates, for the very object of some of our most important speech is to persuade the government to adopt an idea as its own.... The method for protecting freedom of worship and freedom of conscience in religious matters is quite the reverse. In religious debate or expression the government is not a prime participant, for the Framers deemed religious establishment antithetical to the freedom of all. The Free Exercise Clause embraces a freedom of conscience and worship that has close parallels in the speech provisions of the First Amendment, but the Establishment Clause is a specific prohibition on forms of state intervention in religious affairs with no precise counterpart in the speech provisions.... The explanation lies in the lesson of history that was and is the inspiration for the Establishment Clause, the lesson that in the hands of government what might begin as a tolerant expression of religious views may end in a policy to indoctrinate and coerce. A state-created orthodoxy puts at grave risk that freedom of belief and conscience which are the sole assurance that religious faith is real, not imposed.

. . .

As we have observed before, there are heightened concerns with protecting freedom of conscience from subtle coercive pressure in the elementary and secondary public schools.... Our decisions ... recognize, among other things, that prayer exercises in public schools carry a particular risk of indirect coercion. The concern may not be limited to the context of schools, but it is most pronounced there.... What to most believers may seem nothing more than a reasonable request that the nonbeliever respect their religious practices, in a school context may appear to the nonbeliever or dissenter to be an attempt to employ the machinery of the State to enforce a religious orthodoxy.

We need not look beyond the circumstances of this case to see the phenomenon at work. The undeniable fact is that the school district's supervision and control of a high school graduation ceremony places public pressure, as well as peer pressure, on attending students to stand as a group or, at least, maintain respectful silence during the Invocation and Benediction. This pressure, though subtle and indirect, can be as real as any overt compulsion. Of course, in our culture standing or remaining silent can signify adherence to a view or simple respect for the views of others. And no doubt some persons who have no desire to join a prayer have little objection to standing as a sign of respect for those who do. But for the dissenter of high school age, who has a reasonable perception that she is being forced by the State to pray in a manner her conscience will not allow, the injury is no less real. There can be no doubt that for many, if not most, of the students at the graduation, the act of standing or remaining silent was an expression of participation in the Rabbi's prayer. That was the very point of the religious exercise. It is of little comfort to a dissenter, then, to be told that for her the act of standing or remaining in silence signifies mere respect, rather than participation. What matters is that, given our social conventions, a reasonable dissenter in this milieu could believe that the group exercise signified her own participation or approval of it.

Finding no violation under these circumstances would place objectors in the dilemma of participating, with all that implies, or protesting. We do not address whether that choice is acceptable if the affected citizens are mature adults, but we think the State may not, consistent with the Establishment Clause, place primary and secondary school children in this position. Research in psychology supports the common assumption that adolescents are often susceptible to pressure from their peers towards conformity, and that the influence is strongest in matters of social convention. Brittain, Adolescent Choices and Parent–Peer Cross–Pressures, 28 Am.Sociological Rev. 385 (June 1963); Clasen & Brown, The Multidimensionality of Peer Pressure in Adolescence, 14 J. of Youth and Adolescence 451 (Dec. 1985); Brown, Clasen, & Eicher, Perceptions of Peer Pressure, Peer Conformity Dispositions, and Self–Reported Behavior Among Adolescents, 22 Developmental Psychology 521 (July 1986). To recognize that the choice imposed by the State constitutes an unacceptable constraint only acknowledges that the government may no more use social pressure to enforce orthodoxy than it may use more direct means.

The injury caused by the government's action, and the reason why Daniel and Deborah Weisman object to it, is that the State, in a school setting, in effect required participation in a religious exercise. It is, we concede, a brief exercise during which the individual can concentrate on joining its message, meditate on her own religion, or let her mind wander. But the embarrassment and the intrusion of the religious exercise cannot be refuted by arguing that these prayers, and similar ones to be said in the future, are of a de minimis character. To do so would be an affront to the Rabbi who offered them and to all those for whom the prayers were an essential and profound recognition of divine authority. And for the same reason, we think that the intrusion is greater than the two minutes or so of time consumed for prayers like these. Assuming, as we must, that the prayers were offensive to the student and the parent who now object, the intrusion was both real and, in the context of a secondary school, a violation of the objectors' rights. That the intrusion was in the course of promulgating religion that sought to be civic or nonsectarian rather than pertaining to one sect does not lessen the offense or isolation to the objectors. At best it narrows their number, at worst increases their sense of isolation and affront.

... [T]he United States, as amicus, [argues] that the option of not attending the graduation excuses any inducement or coercion in the ceremony itself. The argument lacks all persuasion. Law reaches past formalism. And to say a teenage student has a real choice not to attend her high school graduation is formalistic in the extreme. True, Deborah could elect not to attend commencement without renouncing her diploma; but we shall not allow the case to turn on this point. Everyone knows that in our society and in our culture high school graduation is one of life's most significant occasions. A school rule which excuses attendance is beside the point. Attendance may not be required by official decree, yet it is apparent that a student is not free to absent herself from the graduation exercise in any real sense of the term "voluntary," for absence would require forfeiture of those intangible benefits which have motivated the student through youth and all her high school years. Graduation is a time for family and those closest to the student to celebrate success and express mutual wishes of gratitude and respect, all to the end of impressing upon the young person the role that it is his or her right and duty to assume in the community and all of its diverse parts.

The importance of the event is the point the school district and the United States rely upon to argue that a formal prayer ought to be permitted, but it becomes one of the principal reasons why their argument must fail. Their contention, one of considerable force were it not for the constitutional constraints applied to state action, is that the prayers are an essential part of these ceremonies because for many persons an occasion of this significance lacks meaning if there is no recognition, however brief, that human achievements cannot be understood apart from their spiritual essence. We think the Government's position that this interest suffices to force students to choose between compliance or forfeiture demonstrates fundamental inconsistency in its argumentation. It fails to acknowledge that what for many of Deborah's classmates and their parents was a spiritual imperative was for Daniel and Deborah Weisman religious conformance compelled by the State. While in some societies the wishes of the majority might prevail, the Establishment Clause of the First Amendment is addressed to this contingency and rejects the balance urged upon us. The Constitution forbids the State to exact religious conformity from a student as the price of attending her own high school graduation. This is the calculus the Constitution commands.

The Government's argument gives insufficient recognition to the real conflict of conscience faced by the young student. The essence of the Government's position is that with regard to a civic, social occasion of this importance it is the objector, not the majority, who must take unilateral and private action to avoid compromising religious scruples, here by electing to miss the graduation exercise. This turns conventional First Amendment analysis on its head. It is a tenet of the First Amendment that the State cannot require one of its citizens to forfeit his or her rights and benefits as the price of resisting conformance to state-sponsored religious practice. To say that a student must remain apart from the ceremony at the opening invocation and closing benediction is to risk compelling conformity in an environment analogous to the classroom setting, where we have said the risk of compulsion is especially high. Just as in Engel v. Vitale, ... and Abington School District v.

Schempp, ... we found that provisions within the challenged legislation permitting a student to be voluntarily excused from attendance or participation in the daily prayers did not shield those practices from invalidation, the fact that attendance at the graduation ceremonies is voluntary in a legal sense does not save the religious exercise.

Inherent differences between the public school system and a session of a State Legislature distinguish this case from Marsh v. Chambers, 463 U.S. 783 (1983). The considerations we have raised in objection to the invocation and benediction are in many respects similar to the arguments we considered in Marsh. But there are also obvious differences. The atmosphere at the opening of a session of a state legislature where adults are free to enter and leave with little comment and for any number of reasons cannot compare with the constraining potential of the one school event most important for the student to attend. The influence and force of a formal exercise in a school graduation are far greater than the prayer exercise we condoned in *Marsh*. The *Marsh* majority in fact gave specific recognition to this distinction and placed particular reliance on it in upholding the prayers at issue there.... Today's case is different. At a high school graduation, teachers and principals must and do retain a high degree of control over the precise contents of the program, the speeches, the timing, the movements, the dress, and the decorum of the students.... In this atmosphere the state-imposed character of an invocation and benediction by clergy selected by the school combine to make the prayer a state-sanctioned religious exercise in which the student was left with no alternative but to submit. This is different from *Marsh* and suffices to make the religious exercise a First Amendment violation....

We do not hold that every state action implicating religion is invalid if one or a few citizens find it offensive. People may take offense at all manner of religious as well as nonreligious messages, but offense alone does not in every case show a violation. We know too that sometimes to endure social isolation or even anger may be the price of conscience or nonconformity. But, by any reading of our cases, the conformity required of the student in this case was too high an exaction to withstand the test of the Establishment Clause. The prayer exercises in this case are especially improper because the State has in every practical sense compelled attendance and participation in an explicit religious exercise at an event of singular importance to every student, one the objecting student had no real alternative to avoid.

. . .

... We recognize that, at graduation time and throughout the course of the educational process, there will be instances when religious values, religious practices, and religious persons will have some interaction with the public schools and their students.... But these matters, often questions of accommodation of religion, are not before us. The sole question presented is whether a religious exercise may be conducted at a graduation ceremony in circumstances where, as we have found, young graduates who object are induced to conform....

For the reasons we have stated, the judgment of the Court of Appeals is

Affirmed.

Justice Blackmun with whom Justice Stevens and Justice O'Connor join, concurring.

. . .

. . . The question then is whether the government has "plac[ed] its official stamp of approval" on the prayer. . . . [T]here can be no doubt that the government is advancing and promoting religion. As our prior decisions teach us, it is this that the Constitution prohibits.

. . .

I join the Court's opinion today because I find nothing in it inconsistent with the essential precepts of the Establishment Clause developed in our precedents. . . .

. . .

Our decisions have gone beyond prohibiting coercion.

The mixing of government and religion can be a threat to free government, even if no one is forced to participate. When the government puts its imprimatur on a particular religion, it conveys a message of exclusion to all those who do not adhere to the favored beliefs. . . .

. . .

. . . [O]ur cases have prohibited government endorsement of religion, its sponsorship, and active involvement in religion, whether or not citizens were coerced to conform.

I remain convinced that our jurisprudence is not misguided, and that it requires the decision reached by the Court today. . . .

DAVID H. SOUTER—Born on September 17, 1936, in Melrose, Massachusetts, son of a bank loan officer. Grew up in Concord, New Hampshire. Harvard, B.A. 1961; Oxford, Rhodes Scholar, 1961–1962; Harvard, LL.B., 1966. Practiced law, 1966–1968; New Hampshire assistant attorney general, 1968–1971; deputy attorney general, 1971–1976; attorney general, 1976–1978; New Hampshire superior court judge, 1978–1983; New Hampshire Supreme Court justice, 1983–1990. U.S. Court of Appeals judge (First Circuit), 1990. Nominated associate justice by President George Bush on July 25, 1990, to replace William J. Brennan, Jr. Confirmed by the Senate on October 2, 1990, by a 90–9 vote. Very little was known about Justice Souter or his views at the time of his nomination. David Savage of the *Los Angeles Times* wrote that those who knew him said that he was not a political ideologue. Souter's colleagues on the New Hampshire Supreme Court "joked about his drab wardrobe—that it was enlivened by the addition of the black robe." David Savage, Turning Right: The Making of the Rehnquist Court, John Wiley & Sons, 1992, p. 357.

JUSTICE SOUTER, with whom JUSTICE STEVENS and JUSTICE O'CONNOR join, concurring.

I join the whole of the Court's opinion, and fully agree that prayers at public school graduation ceremonies indirectly coerce religious observance. I write separately nonetheless on two issues of Establishment Clause analysis that underlie my independent resolution of this case: whether the Clause applies to governmental practices that do not favor one religion or denomination over others, and whether state coercion of religious conformity, over and above state endorsement of religious exercise or belief, is a necessary element of an Establishment Clause violation.

I

... In barring the State from sponsoring generically Theistic prayers where it could not sponsor sectarian ones, we hold true to a line of precedent from which there is no adequate historical case to depart.

A

Since *Everson,* we have consistently held the Clause applicable no less to governmental acts favoring religion generally than to acts favoring one religion over others. . . .

. . .

Such is the settled law. Here, as elsewhere, we should stick to it absent some compelling reason to discard it. . . .

B

Some have challenged this precedent by reading the Establishment Clause to permit "nonpreferential" state promotion of religion. The challengers argue that, as originally understood by the Framers, "[t]he Establishment Clause did not require government neutrality between religion and irreligion nor did it prohibit the Federal Government from providing nondiscriminatory aid to religion." Wallace, supra, at 106 (Rehnquist, J., dissenting). . . . While a case has been made for this position, it is not so convincing as to warrant reconsideration of our settled law; indeed, I find in the history of the Clause's textual development a more powerful argument supporting the Court's jurisprudence following *Everson.*

When James Madison arrived at the First Congress with a series of proposals to amend the National Constitution, one of the provisions read that "[t]he civil rights of none shall be abridged on account of religious belief or worship, nor shall any national religion be established, nor shall the full and equal rights of conscience be in any manner, or on any pretext, infringed." . . . Madison's language did not last long. It was sent to a Select Committee of the House, which, without explanation, changed it to read that "no religion shall be established by law, nor shall the equal rights of conscience be infringed." . . .

... [T]he House rejected the Select Committee's version, which arguably ensured only that "no religion" enjoyed an official preference over others, and deliberately chose instead a prohibition extending to laws establishing "religion" in general.

The sequence of the Senate's treatment of this House proposal, and the House's response to the Senate, confirm that the Framers meant the Establishment Clause's prohibition to encompass nonpreferential aid to religion.... [T]he Senate ... adopted [narrow language]: "Congress shall make no law establishing articles of faith or a mode of worship, or prohibiting the free exercise of religion." ...

Though it accepted much of the Senate's work on the Bill of Rights, the House rejected the Senate's version of the Establishment Clause and called for a joint conference committee, to which the Senate agreed. The House conferees ultimately won out.... What is remarkable is that, unlike the earliest House drafts or the final Senate proposal, the prevailing language is not limited to laws respecting an establishment of "a religion," "a national religion," "one religious sect," or specific "articles of faith." The Framers repeatedly considered and deliberately rejected such narrow language and instead extended their prohibition to state support for "religion" in general.

Implicit in their choice is the distinction between preferential and nonpreferential establishments, which the weight of evidence suggests the Framers appreciated.... Of particular note, the Framers were vividly familiar with efforts in the colonies and, later, the States to impose general, nondenominational assessments and other incidents of ostensibly ecumenical establishments....

... [O]n balance, history neither contradicts nor warrants reconsideration of the settled principle that the Establishment Clause forbids support for religion in general no less than support for one religion or some.

C

While these considerations are, for me, sufficient to reject the nonpreferentialist position, one further concern animates my judgment. In many contexts, including this one, nonpreferentialism requires some distinction between "sectarian" religious practices and those that would be, by some measure, ecumenical enough to pass Establishment Clause muster. Simply by requiring the enquiry, nonpreferentialists invite the courts to engage in comparative theology. I can hardly imagine a subject less amenable to the competence of the federal judiciary, or more deliberately to be avoided where possible.

This case is nicely in point.... Many Americans who consider themselves religious are not Theistic; some, like several of the Framers, are Deists who would question Rabbi Gutterman's plea for divine advancement of the country's political and moral good. Thus, a nonpreferentialist who would condemn subjecting public school graduates to, say, the Anglican liturgy would still need to explain why the government's preference for Theistic over non-Theistic religion is constitutional.

Nor does it solve the problem to say that the State should promote a "diversity" of religious views; that position would necessarily compel the government and, inevitably, the courts to make wholly inappropriate judgments about the number of religions the State should sponsor and the relative frequency with which it should sponsor each.... [T]he judiciary should not willingly enter the political arena to battle the centripetal force leading from religious pluralism to official preference for the faith with the most votes.

II

Petitioners rest most of their argument on a theory that, whether or not the Establishment Clause permits extensive nonsectarian support for religion, it does not forbid the state to sponsor affirmations of religious belief that coerce neither support for religion nor participation in religious observance. I appreciate the force of some of the arguments supporting a "coercion" analysis of the Clause. See generally *Allegheny County,* ... (opinion of Kennedy, J.).... But we could not adopt that reading without abandoning our settled law....

A

Over the years, this Court has declared the invalidity of many noncoercive state laws and practices conveying a message of religious endorsement. For example, in *Allegheny County,* supra, we forbade the prominent display of a nativity scene on public property; without contesting the dissent's observation that the creche coerced no one into accepting or supporting whatever message it proclaimed, five Members of the Court found its display unconstitutional as a state endorsement of Christianity.... Likewise, in Wallace v. Jaffree, ... we struck down a state law requiring a moment of silence in public classrooms not because the statute coerced students to participate in prayer (for it did not), but because the manner of its enactment "convey[ed] a message of state approval of prayer activities in the public schools." ...

. . .

Our precedents may not always have drawn perfectly straight lines. They simply cannot, however, support the position that a showing of coercion is necessary to a successful Establishment Clause claim.

B

. . .

While some argue that the Framers added the word "respecting" simply to foreclose federal interference with State establishments of religion, ... the language sweeps more broadly than that.... The sweep is broad enough that Madison himself characterized congressional provisions for legislative and military chaplains as unconstitutional "establishments." ... The First Amendment forbids not just laws "respecting an establishment of religion," but also those "prohibiting the free exercise thereof." Yet laws that coerce nonadherents to "support or participate in any religion or its exercise," ... would virtually by definition violate their right to religious free exercise.... Thus, a literal application of the coercion test would render the Establishment Clause a virtual nullity....

. . .

C

Petitioners argue from the political setting in which the Establishment Clause was framed, and from the Framers' own political practices following ratification, that government may constitutionally endorse religion so long as it does not coerce religious conformity. The setting and the practices ... do not reveal [that] degree of consensus in early constitutional thought....

The Framers ... special antipathy to religious coercion did not exhaust their hostility to the features and incidents of establishment....

Petitioners contend that because the early Presidents included religious messages in their inaugural and Thanksgiving Day addresses, the Framers could not have meant the Establishment Clause to forbid noncoercive state endorsement of religion. The argument ignores the fact, however, that Americans today find such proclamations less controversial than did the founding generation, whose published thoughts on the matter belie petitioners' claim. President Jefferson, for example, steadfastly refused to issue Thanksgiving proclamations of any kind, in part because he thought they violated the Religion Clauses....

During his first three years in office, James Madison also refused to call for days of thanksgiving and prayer, though later, amid the political turmoil of the War of 1812, he did so on four separate occasions....

Madison's failure to keep pace with his principles in the face of congressional pressure cannot erase the principles. He admitted to backsliding, and explained that he had made the content of his wartime proclamations inconsequential enough to mitigate much of their impropriety.... While his writings suggest mild variations in his interpretation of the Establishment Clause, Madison was no different in that respect from the rest of his political generation. That he expressed so much doubt about the constitutionality of religious proclamations, however, suggests a brand of separationism stronger even than that embodied in our traditional jurisprudence. So too does his characterization of public subsidies for legislative and military chaplains as unconstitutional "establishments," for the federal courts, however expansive their general view of the Establishment Clause, have upheld both practices....

To be sure, the leaders of the young Republic engaged in some of the practices that separationists like Jefferson and Madison criticized. The First Congress did hire institutional chaplains, ... and Presidents Washington and Adams unapologetically marked days of "public thanksgiving and prayer".... Yet in the face of the separationist dissent, those practices prove, at best, that the Framers simply did not share a common understanding of the Establishment Clause, and, at worst, that they, like other politicians, could raise constitutional ideals one day and turn their backs on them the next....

While we may be unable to know for certain what the Framers meant by the Clause, we do know that, around the time of its ratification, a respectable body of opinion supported a considerably broader reading than petitioners urge upon us. This consistency with the textual considerations is enough to preclude fundamentally reexamining our settled law, and I am accordingly left with the task of considering whether the state practice at issue here violates our traditional understanding of the Clause's proscriptions.

III

While the Establishment Clause's concept of neutrality is not self-revealing, our recent cases have invested it with specific content: the state may not favor or endorse either religion generally over nonreligion or one religion over others.... cf. Lemon v. Kurtzman, 403 U.S. 602, 612–613 (1971). This principle against favoritism and endorsement has become the foundation of Establishment Clause jurisprudence....

A

That government must remain neutral in matters of religion does not foreclose it from ever taking religion into account. The State may "accommodate" the free exercise of religion by relieving people from generally applicable rules that interfere with their religious callings.... [S]uch accommodation does not necessarily signify an official endorsement of religious observance over disbelief.

In everyday life, we routinely accommodate religious beliefs that we do not share. A Christian inviting an Orthodox Jew to lunch might take pains to choose a kosher restaurant; an atheist in a hurry might yield the right of way to an Amish man steering a horse-drawn carriage. In so acting, we express respect for, but not endorsement of, the fundamental values of others. We act without expressing a position on the theological merit of those values or of religious belief in general, and no one perceives us to have taken such a position.

The government may act likewise.... [W]hen enforcement of ... rules cuts across religious sensibilities, as it often does, it puts those affected to the choice of taking sides between God and government. In such circumstances, accommodating religion reveals nothing beyond a recognition that general rules can unnecessarily offend the religious conscience when they offend the conscience of secular society not at all.... Thus, in freeing the Native American Church from federal laws forbidding peyote use, ... the government conveys no endorsement of peyote rituals, the Church, or religion as such; it simply respects the centrality of peyote to the lives of certain Americans....

B

Whatever else may define the scope of accommodation permissible under the Establishment Clause, one requirement is clear: accommodation must lift a discernible burden on the free exercise of religion....

Religious students cannot complain that omitting prayers from their graduation ceremony would, in any realistic sense, "burden" their spiritual callings.... [T]hey may express their religious feelings ... before and after the ceremony. They may even organize a privately sponsored baccalaureate if they desire the company of likeminded students. Because they accordingly have no need for the machinery of the State to affirm their beliefs, the government's sponsorship of prayer at the graduation ceremony is most reasonably understood as an official endorsement of religion and, in this instance, of Theistic religion....

Petitioners would deflect this conclusion by arguing that graduation prayers are no different from presidential religious proclamations and similar official "acknowledgements" of religion in public life. But religious invocations in Thanksgiving Day addresses and the like, rarely noticed, ignored without effort, conveyed over an impersonal medium, and directed at no one in particular, inhabit a pallid zone worlds apart from official prayers delivered to a captive audience of public school students and their families.... When public school officials, armed with the State's authority, convey an endorsement of religion to their students, they strike near the core of the Establishment Clause. However "ceremonial" their messages may be, they are flatly unconstitutional.

JUSTICE SCALIA with whom THE CHIEF JUSTICE, JUSTICE WHITE, and JUSTICE THOMAS join, dissenting.

. . .

... In holding that the Establishment Clause prohibits invocations and benedictions at public-school graduation ceremonies, the Court ... lays waste a tradition that is as old as public-school graduation ceremonies themselves, and that is a component of an even more longstanding American tradition of nonsectarian prayer to God at public celebrations generally. As its instrument of destruction, the bulldozer of its social engineering, the Court invents a boundless, and boundlessly manipulable, test of psychological coercion.... [O]ur Constitution, cannot possibly rest upon the changeable philosophical predilections of the Justices of this Court, but must have deep foundations in the historic practices of our people.

I

. . .

The history and tradition of our Nation are replete with public ceremonies featuring prayers of thanksgiving and petition....

From our Nation's origin, prayer has been a prominent part of governmental ceremonies and proclamations. The Declaration of Independence, the document marking our birth as a separate people, "appeal[ed] to the Supreme Judge of the world for the rectitude of our intentions" and avowed "a firm reliance on the protection of divine Providence." In his first inaugural address, after swearing his oath of office on a Bible, George Washington deliberately made a prayer a part of his first official act as President: "it would be peculiarly improper to omit in this first official act my fervent supplications to that Almighty Being who rules over the universe, who presides in the councils of nations, and whose providential aids can supply every human defect, that His benediction may consecrate to the liberties and happiness of the people of the United States a Government instituted by themselves for these essential purposes." ... Such supplications have been a characteristic feature of inaugural addresses ever since. Thomas Jefferson, for example, prayed in his first inaugural address: "may that Infinite Power which rules the destinies of the universe lead our councils to what is best, and give them a favorable issue for your peace and prosperity." ... In his second inaugural address, Jefferson acknowledged his need for divine guidance and invited his audience to join his prayer.... Similarly, James Madison, in his first inaugural address, placed his confidence "in the guardianship and guidance of that Almighty Being whose power regulates the destiny of nations, whose blessings have been so conspicuously dispensed to this rising Republic, and to whom we are bound to address our devout gratitude for the past, as well as our fervent supplications and best hopes for the future." ... Most recently, President Bush, continuing the tradition established by President Washington, asked those attending his inauguration to bow their heads, and made a prayer his first official act as President....

Our national celebration of Thanksgiving likewise dates back to President Washington.... This tradition of Thanksgiving Proclamations—with their religious theme of prayerful gratitude to God—has been adhered to by almost every President....

The other two branches of the Federal Government also have a long-established practice of prayer at public events. As we detailed in *Marsh,* Congressional sessions have opened with a chaplain's prayer ever since the First Congress.... And this Court's own sessions have opened with the invocation "God save the United States and this Honorable Court" since the days of Chief Justice Marshall....

In addition to this general tradition of prayer at public ceremonies, there exists a more specific tradition of invocations and benedictions at public-school graduation exercises.... [T]he invocation and benediction have long been recognized to be "as traditional as any other parts of the [school] graduation program and are widely established." ...

II

The Court presumably would separate graduation invocations and benedictions from other instances of public "preservation and transmission of religious beliefs" on the ground that they involve "psychological coercion." ... A few citations of "[r]esearch in psychology" that have no particular bearing upon the precise issue here, cannot disguise the fact that the Court has gone beyond the realm where judges know what they are doing. The Court's argument that state officials have "coerced" students to take part in the invocation and benediction at graduation ceremonies is, not to put too fine a point on it, incoherent.

. . .

A

The Court declares that students' "attendance and participation in the [invocation and benediction] are in a fair and real sense obligatory." But what exactly is this "fair and real sense"? ...

... The Court's notion that a student who simply sits in "respectful silence" during the invocation and benediction (when all others are standing) has somehow joined—or would somehow be perceived as having joined—in the prayers is nothing short of ludicrous.... Since ... students exposed to prayer at graduation ceremonies retain (despite "subtle coercive pressures") the free will to sit, there is absolutely no basis for the Court's decision....

But let us assume the very worst, that the nonparticipating graduate is "subtly coerced" ... to stand! Even that ... does not remotely establish a "participation" (or an "appearance of participation") in a religious exercise.... [I]t is a permissible inference that one who is standing is doing so simply out of respect for the prayers of others.... [M]aintaining respect for the religious observances of others is a fundamental civic virtue that government (including the public schools) can and should cultivate ...

... [T]he Court itself has not given careful consideration to its test of psychological coercion. For if it had, how could it observe, with no hint of concern or disapproval, that students stood for the Pledge of Allegiance, which immediately preceded Rabbi Gutterman's invocation? The government can, of course, no more coerce political orthodoxy than religious orthodoxy. West Virginia Board of Education v. Barnette.... Moreover, since the Pledge of Allegiance has been revised since *Barnette* to include the phrase "under God," recital of the Pledge would appear to raise the same Establishment Clause issue as the invocation and benediction. If students were psychologically coerced to remain standing during the invocation, they must also have been psychologically coerced, moments before, to stand for (and thereby, in the Court's view, take part in or appear to take part in) the Pledge. Must the Pledge therefore be barred from the public schools (both from graduation ceremonies and from the classroom)? In *Barnette* we held that a public-school student could not be compelled to recite the Pledge; we did not even hint that she could not be compelled to observe respectful silence—indeed, even to stand in respectful silence—when those who wished to recite it did so. Logically, that ought to be the next project for the Court's bulldozer.

I also find it odd that the Court concludes that high school graduates may not be subjected to this supposed psychological coercion, yet refrains from addressing whether "mature adults" may. I had thought that the reason graduation from high school is regarded as so significant an event is that it is generally associated with transition from adolescence to young adulthood. Many graduating seniors, of course, are old enough to vote. Why, then, does the Court treat them as though they were first-graders? Will we soon have a jurisprudence that distinguishes between mature and immature adults?

B

The other "dominant fac[t]" identified by the Court is that "[s]tate officials direct the performance of a formal religious exercise" at school graduation ceremonies.... All the record shows is that principals ... invited clergy to deliver invocations and benedictions at graduations; and that Principal Lee invited Rabbi Gutterman, provided him a two-page flyer, prepared by the National Conference of Christians and Jews, giving general advice on inclusive prayer for civic occasions, and advised him that his prayers at graduation should be nonsectarian.... [S]chool officials have [never] drafted, edited, screened or censored graduation prayers....

. . .

III

The deeper flaw in the Court's opinion does not lie in its wrong answer to the question whether there was state-induced "peer-pressure" coercion; it lies, rather, in the Court's making violation of the Establishment Clause hinge on such a precious question. The coercion that was a hallmark of historical establishments of religion was coercion of religious orthodoxy and of financial support by force of law and threat of penalty. Typically, attendance at the state church was required; only clergy of the official church could lawfully perform sacraments; and dissenters, if tolerated, faced an array of civil disabilities....

The Establishment Clause was adopted to prohibit such an establishment of religion at the federal level (and to protect state establishments of religion from federal interference)....

... I see no warrant for expanding the concept of coercion beyond acts backed by threat of penalty—a brand of coercion that, happily, is readily discernible ...

... Beyond the fact, stipulated to by the parties, that attendance at graduation is voluntary, there is nothing in the record to indicate that failure of attending students to take part in the invocation or benediction was subject to any penalty or discipline. Contrast this with, for example, the facts of *Barnette:* Schoolchildren were required by law to recite the Pledge of Allegiance; failure to do so resulted in expulsion, threatened the expelled child with the prospect of being sent to a reformatory for criminally inclined juveniles, and subjected his parents to prosecution (and incarceration) for causing delinquency....

The Court relies on our "school prayer" cases.... But whatever the merit of those cases, they do not support, much less compel, the Court's psycho-journey. [They] do not constitute an exception to the rule, distilled from historical practice, that public ceremonies may include prayer ...; rather, they simply do not fall within the scope of the rule (for the obvious reason that school instruction is not a public ceremony). Second, we have made clear our understanding that school prayer occurs within a framework in which legal coercion to attend school (i.e., coercion under threat of penalty) provides the ultimate backdrop.... And finally, our school-prayer cases turn in part on the fact that the classroom is inherently an instructional setting, and daily prayer there—where parents are not present ...—might be thought to raise special concerns regarding state interference with the liberty of parents to direct the religious upbringing of their children.... Voluntary prayer at graduation—a one-time ceremony at which parents, friends and relatives are present—can hardly be thought to raise the same concerns.

IV

Our religion-clause jurisprudence has become bedeviled (so to speak) by reliance on formulaic abstractions that are not derived from, but positively conflict with, our long-accepted constitutional traditions. Foremost among these has been the so-called *Lemon* test.... The Court today demonstrates the irrelevance of *Lemon* by essentially ignoring it, and the interment of that case may be the one happy byproduct of the Court's otherwise lamentable decision. Unfortunately, however, the Court has replaced *Lemon* with its psycho-coercion test, which suffers the double disability of having no roots whatever in our people's historic practice, and being as infinitely expandable as the reasons for psychotherapy itself.

Another happy aspect of the case is that it is only a jurisprudential disaster and not a practical one. Given the odd basis for the Court's decision, invocations and benedictions will be able to be given at public-school graduations next June, as they have for the past century and a half, so long as school authorities make clear that anyone who abstains from screaming in protest does not necessarily participate in the prayers. All that is seemingly needed is an announcement, or perhaps a written insertion at the beginning of the graduation Program, to the effect that, while all are asked to rise for the invocation and benediction, none is compelled to join in them, nor will be assumed, by rising, to have done so. That obvious fact recited, the graduates and their parents may proceed to thank God, as Americans have always done, for the blessings He has generously bestowed on them and on their country.

NOTES AND QUESTIONS

1. While Justice Kennedy writes the opinion for the Court, his emphasis on coercion appears to be rejected by all the other Justices. The four concurring Justices make the point that coercion should not be a necessary element in Establishment Clause cases, and the dissenters criticize the opinion for what they view as an inappropriate conception of what is coercive. For the moment, however, Justice Kennedy's conception of coercion is likely to be controlling concerning religious practices connected to the public schools. If a particular practice is challenged, is the issue whether coercion exists in fact, or whether it is likely to exist? Does each graduation prayer have to be examined to see whether, on the facts in each case, students are coerced? Is Justice Scalia right that prayer at public school graduation ceremonies can proceed without violating the Constitution if there is an announcement that no one is compelled to join and those who stand will not be assumed to have done so? For that matter, is there a constitutional violation if school officials arrange for a graduation prayer and no one objects?

2. Justice Kennedy's opinion is notable because it does not rely on two conventional tests for determining whether there has been an establishment of religion. One is the inquiry whether the challenged government action has the purpose or effect of advancing religion. The other is the inquiry, suggested in a number of Justice O'Connor's opinions, whether government gives the appearance of endorsing religion. In Lamb's Chapel v. Center Moriches Union Free School District,

508 U.S. 384 (1993), Justice White's opinion for the Court mentioned both of these standards, while rejecting an establishment claim. Simply reiterating these standards drew objections from Justices Scalia, Thomas and Kennedy, who argued that they were both inappropriate. Speaking of the purpose or effect test, Justice Scalia argued that the Court's opinions had not really relied on that standard to decide cases. He compared it to a "ghoul in a late-night horror movie that repeatedly sits up in its grave and shuffles abroad, after being repeatedly killed and buried, ... frightening the little children and school attorneys of Center Moriches Union Free School District. Its most recent burial, only last Term, was, to be sure, not fully six-feet under: our decision in Lee v. Weisman, ... conspicuously avoided using the supposed 'test' but also declined the invitation to repudiate it. Over the years, however, no fewer than five of the currently sitting justices have, in their own opinions, personally driven pencils through the creature's heart (the author of today's opinion repeatedly), and a sixth has joined an opinion doing so." Justice White's opinion blandly replied in a footnote: "While we are somewhat diverted by Justice Scalia's evening at the cinema, we return to the reality that there is a proper way to inter an established decision . . ."

3. Santa Fe Independent School District v. Doe, 530 U.S. 290 (2000), followed Lee v. Weisman, and held that a school district violated the Constitution in "permitting," but not "requiring," prayers led by a student at all football home games. The school district argued that there was no coercion because the prayers were the product of "student choice" in electing the student chaplain who delivered the prayer, and because, unlike a graduation ceremony, attendance at football games was voluntary. Justice Stevens' opinion for the Court answered the first argument by emphasizing that the election system, itself, had been chosen by the school board. The Court conceded that "nothing in the Constitution ... prohibits any public school student from voluntarily praying at any time before, during, or after the schoolday,". but "members of the listening audience must perceive the pregame message as a public expression of the views of the majority of the student body delivered with the approval of the school administration."

As to the second argument, the opinion said:

> "Even if we regard every high school student's decision to attend a home football game as purely voluntary, we are nevertheless persuaded that the delivery of a pregame prayer has the improper effect of coercing those present to participate in an act of religious worship.... The constitutional command will not permit the District "to exact religious conformity from a student as the price" of joining her classmates at a varsity football game."

4. In 1954, Congress amended the Flag Salute, adding the words "under God." Under state law, each public school must begin the school day with appropriate patriotic exercises. The Elk Grove School District implemented the law by requiring the flag salute, permitting students who object on religious grounds to abstain. In Elk Grove Unified School

District v. Newdow, 542 U.S. 1 (2004), respondent, whose daughter attends school in the district, brought suit seeking a declaration that the addition of the words "under God" in 1954 violated the Establishment and Free Exercise Clauses. He argued that those words are an endorsement of religion and that they constitute religious indoctrination. Four Justices joined Justice Stevens' opinion for the Court, which concluded that respondent did not have standing to bring the action because he was not the custodial parent, and his daughter did not object to saying the Pledge of Allegiance. Justice Stevens referred to the "deeply rooted commitment 'not to pass on questions of constitutionality' unless adjudication of the constitutional issue is necessary." Chief Justice Rehnquist, joined by Justices O'Connor and Thomas, objected to dismissal of the case on "prudential standing" grounds. Justice O'Connor also wrote that she would sustain the Pledge on the ground that it did not "make a person's religious beliefs relevant to his or her standing in the political community by conveying a message that religion or a particular religious belief is favored or preferred." Justice Thomas also addressed the merits, indicating that he, too, would sustain the Flag Salute. He would substantially rethink the Establishment Clause, however, to permit state "establishment," subject to a requirement that Congress not interfere with state establishments.

III. RELIGION IN THE PUBLIC SCHOOL CURRICULUM

EPPERSON v. ARKANSAS

Supreme Court of the United States, 1968.
393 U.S. 97, 89 S.Ct. 266, 21 L.Ed.2d 228.

JUSTICE FORTAS delivered the opinion of the Court.

This appeal challenges the constitutionality of the "anti-evolution" statute which the State of Arkansas adopted in 1928 to prohibit the teaching in its public schools and universities of the theory that man evolved from other species of life. The statute was a product of the upsurge of "fundamentalist" religious fervor of the twenties. The Arkansas statute was an adaptation of the famous Tennessee "monkey law" which that State adopted in 1925. The constitutionality of the Tennessee law was upheld by the Tennessee Supreme Court in the celebrated *Scopes* case in 1927.[1]

The Arkansas law makes it unlawful for a teacher in any state-supported school or university "to teach the theory or doctrine that mankind ascended or descended from a lower order of animals," or "to adopt or use in any such institution a textbook that teaches" this theory. Violation is a misdemeanor and subjects the violator to dismissal from his position.

---

1. Scopes v. State, 154 Tenn. 105, 289 S.W. 363 (1927). The Tennessee court, however, reversed Scopes' conviction on the ground that the jury and not the judge should have assessed the fine of $100. Since Scopes was no longer in the State's employ, it saw "nothing to be gained by prolonging the life of this bizarre case." It directed that a *nolle prosequi* be entered, in the interests of "the peace and dignity of the State."

The present case concerns the teaching of biology in a high school in Little Rock. According to the testimony, until the events here in litigation, the official textbook furnished for the high school biology course did not have a section on the Darwinian Theory. Then, for the academic year 1965–1966, the school administration, on recommendation of the teachers of biology in the school system, adopted and prescribed a textbook which contained a chapter setting forth "the theory about the origin ... of man from a lower form of animal."

Susan Epperson, a young woman who graduated from Arkansas' school system and then obtained her master's degree in zoology at the University of Illinois, was employed by the Little Rock school system in the fall of 1964 to teach 10th grade biology at Central High School. At the start of the next academic year, 1965, she was confronted by the new textbook (which one surmises from the record was not unwelcome to her). She faced at least a literal dilemma because she was supposed to use the new textbook for classroom instruction and presumably to teach the statutorily condemned chapter; but to do so would be a criminal offense and subject her to dismissal.

She instituted the present action in [an Arkansas state court], seeking a declaration that the Arkansas statute is void....

· · ·

... Only Arkansas and Mississippi have such "anti-evolution" or "monkey" laws on their books. There is no record of any prosecutions in Arkansas under its statute. It is possible that the statute is presently more of a curiosity than a vital fact of life in these States.[2] Nevertheless, the present case was brought, the appeal as of right is properly here, and it is our duty to decide the issues presented.

· · ·

... Arkansas' statute cannot stand. It is of no moment whether the law is deemed to prohibit mention of Darwin's theory, or to forbid any or all of the infinite varieties of communication embraced within the term "teaching." Under either interpretation, the law must be stricken because of its conflict with the constitutional prohibition of state laws respecting an establishment of religion or prohibiting the free exercise thereof. The overriding fact is that Arkansas' law selects from the body of knowledge a particular segment which it proscribes for the sole reason that it is deemed to conflict with a particular religious doctrine; that is, with a particular interpretation of the Book of Genesis by a particular religious group.

The antecedents of today's decision are many and unmistakable. They are rooted in the foundation soil of our Nation. They are fundamental to freedom.

2. Clarence Darrow, who was counsel for the defense in the *Scopes* trial, in his biography published in 1932, somewhat sardonically pointed out that States with anti-evolution laws did not insist upon the fundamentalist theory in all respects. He said: "I understand that the States of Tennessee and Mississippi both continue to teach that the earth is round and that the revolution on its axis brings the day and night, in spite of all opposition." The Story of My Life 247 (1932).

Government in our democracy, state and national, must be neutral in matters of religious theory, doctrine, and practice. It may not be hostile to any religion or to the advocacy of no-religion; and it may not aid, foster, or promote one religion or religious theory against another or even against the militant opposite. The First Amendment mandates governmental neutrality between religion and religion, and between religion and nonreligion.

.   .   .

The earliest cases in this Court on the subject of the impact of constitutional guarantees upon the classroom were decided before the Court expressly applied the specific prohibitions of the First Amendment to the States. But as early as 1923, the Court did not hesitate to condemn under the Due Process Clause "arbitrary" restrictions upon the freedom of teachers to teach and of students to learn. In that year, the Court, in an opinion by Justice McReynolds, held unconstitutional an Act of the State of Nebraska making it a crime to teach any subject in any language other than English to pupils who had not passed the eighth grade. . . .

For purposes of the present case, we need not re-enter the difficult terrain which the Court, in 1923, traversed without apparent misgivings. We need not take advantage of the broad premise which the Court's decision in *Meyer* furnishes, nor need we explore the implications of that decision in terms of the justiciability of the multitude of controversies that beset our campuses today. Today's problem is capable of resolution in the narrower terms of the First Amendment's prohibition of laws respecting an establishment of religion or prohibiting the free exercise thereof.

.   .   .

In the present case, there can be no doubt that Arkansas has sought to prevent its teachers from discussing the theory of evolution because it is contrary to the belief of some that the Book of Genesis must be the exclusive source of doctrine as to the origin of man. No suggestion has been made that Arkansas' law may be justified by considerations of state policy other than the religious views of some of its citizens. It is clear that fundamentalist sectarian conviction was and is the law's reason for existence.[3] Its antecedent, Tennessee's "monkey law," candidly stated its

---

3. The following advertisement is typical of the public appeal which was used in the campaign to secure adoption of the statute:

"THE BIBLE OR ATHEISM, WHICH?

"All atheists favor evolution. If you agree with atheism vote against Act No. 1. If you agree with the Bible vote for Act No. 1. . . . Shall conscientious church members be forced to pay taxes to support teachers to teach evolution which will undermine the faith of their children? The Gazette said Russian Bolshevists laughed at Tennessee. True, and that sort will laugh at Arkansas. Who cares? Vote FOR ACT NO. 1." The Arkansas Gazette, Little Rock, Nov. 4, 1928, p. 12, cols. 4–5.

Letters from the public expressed the fear that teaching of evolution would be "subversive of Christianity," and that it would cause school children "to disrespect the Bible." One letter read: "The cosmogony taught by [evolution] runs contrary to that of Moses and Jesus, and as such is nothing, if anything at all, but atheism. . . . Now let the mothers and fathers of our state that are trying to raise their children in the Christian faith arise in

purpose: to make it unlawful "to teach any theory that denies the story of the Divine Creation of man as taught in the Bible, and to teach instead that man has descended from a lower order of animals." ... [T]here is no doubt that the motivation for the law was the same [as that of the Tennessee statute]: to suppress the teaching of a theory which, it was thought, "denied" the divine creation of man.

Arkansas' law cannot be defended as an act of religious neutrality. Arkansas did not seek to excise from the curricula of its schools and universities all discussion of the origin of man. The law's effort was confined to an attempt to blot out a particular theory because of its supposed conflict with the Biblical account, literally read. Plainly, the law is contrary to the mandate of the First, and in violation of the Fourteenth, Amendment to the Constitution.

. . .

JUSTICE BLACK, concurring.

. . .

... [T]he Court ... leaps headlong into the middle of the very broad problems involved in federal intrusion into state powers to decide what subjects and schoolbooks it may wish to use in teaching state pupils. While I hesitate to enter into the consideration and decision of such sensitive state-federal relationships, I reluctantly acquiesce....

It is plain that a state law prohibiting all teaching of human development or biology is constitutionally quite different from a law that compels a teacher to teach as true only one theory of a given doctrine. It would be difficult to make a First Amendment case out of a state law eliminating the subject of higher mathematics, or astronomy, or biology from its curriculum. And, for all the Supreme Court of Arkansas has said, this particular Act may prohibit that and nothing else. This Court, however, treats the Arkansas Act as though it made it a misdemeanor to teach or to use a book that teaches that evolution is true.* ...

. . .

The Court, not content to strike down this Arkansas Act on the unchallengeable ground of its plain vagueness, chooses rather to invalidate it as a violation of the Establishment of Religion Clause of the First Amendment. I would not decide this case on such a sweeping ground for the following reasons, among others.

1. In the first place I find it difficult to agree with the Court's statement that "there can be no doubt that Arkansas has sought to prevent its teachers from discussing the theory of evolution because it is contrary to the belief of some that the Book of Genesis must be the exclusive source of doctrine as to the origin of man." It may be instead that the people's motive was merely that it would be best to remove this

their might and vote for this anti-evolution bill that will take it out of our tax supported schools. When they have saved the children, they have saved the state."

* The Arkansas Supreme Court held the statute constitutional without deciding "whether the Act in question prohibits any explanation of the theory of evolution or merely prohibits teaching that the theory is true."

controversial subject from its schools; there is no reason I can imagine why a State is without power to withdraw from its curriculum any subject deemed too emotional and controversial for its public schools....

2. A second question that arises for me is whether this Court's decision forbidding a State to exclude the subject of evolution from its schools infringes the religious freedom of those who consider evolution an anti-religious doctrine. If the theory is considered anti-religious, as the Court indicates, how can the State be bound by the Federal Constitution to permit its teachers to advocate such an "anti-religious" doctrine to schoolchildren? The very cases cited by the Court as supporting its conclusion hold that the State must be neutral, not favoring one religious or anti-religious view over another. The Darwinian theory is said to challenge the Bible's story of creation; so too have some of those who believe in the Bible, along with many others, challenged the Darwinian theory. Since there is no indication that the literal Biblical doctrine of the origin of man is included in the curriculum of Arkansas schools, does not the removal of the subject of evolution leave the State in a neutral position toward these supposedly competing religious and anti-religious doctrines? ...

3. I am also not ready to hold that a person hired to teach schoolchildren takes with him into the classroom a constitutional right to teach sociological, economic, political, or religious subjects that the school's managers do not want discussed. This Court has said that the rights of free speech "while fundamental in our democratic society, still do not mean that everyone with opinions or beliefs to express may address a group at any public place and at any time." I question whether it is absolutely certain, as the Court's opinion indicates, that "academic freedom" permits a teacher to breach his contractual agreement to teach only the subjects designated by the school authorities who hired him.

· · ·

JUSTICE HARLAN, concurring.

· · ·

I concur in so much of the Court's opinion as holds that the Arkansas statute constitutes an "establishment of religion" forbidden to the States by the Fourteenth Amendment. I do not understand, however, why the Court finds it necessary to explore at length appellants' contentions that the statutes interfere ... with free speech.... In the process of *not* deciding ... [this], the Court obscures its otherwise straightforward holding, and opens its opinion to possible implications from which I am constrained to disassociate myself.

JUSTICE STEWART, concurring in the result.

The States are most assuredly free "to choose their own curriculums for their own schools." A State is entirely free, for example, to decide that the only foreign language to be taught in its public school system shall be Spanish. But would a State be constitutionally free to punish a teacher for letting his students know that other languages are also spoken in the world? I think not.

It is one thing for a State to determine that "the subject of higher mathematics, or astronomy, or biology" shall or shall not be included in its public school curriculum. It is quite another thing for a State to make it a criminal offense for a public school teacher so much as to mention the very existence of an entire system of respected human thought. That kind of criminal law, I think, would clearly impinge upon the guarantees of free communication contained in the First Amendment, and 0made applicable to the States by the Fourteenth.

NOTES AND QUESTIONS

1. With echoes of the famous *Scopes* trial still heard through the decades, one's first impression of the state law involved in the *Epperson* case is that *of course* it is unconstitutional. If Clarence Darrow, arguing for the invalidity of the Tennessee law in the *Scopes* case didn't win the debate with William Jennings Bryan in the courts of Tennessee, he was the winner by the verdict of history. But why? Is it because Darrow demonstrated the great leaps of faith necessary to believe in the literal Biblical account of creation, and the narrowness of a view that would reject modern scientific evidence? Could a constitutional rule be fashioned around the premise that the Biblical account of creation is false, and evolution is more than a theory—a proven fact? Regardless of your own views as to how solid the evidence is for the theory of evolution as opposed to a theory of creation, it is more than a little difficult to frame any theory under the First Amendment which begins with the premise that one side of the debate is true and the other side is false. Whether the issue is speech or religion, conventional free speech, free exercise of religion, and establishment of religion doctrine all begin with the premise that no doctrine can be labelled "absolutely true" or "absolutely false" by the government for the purpose of forestalling discussion and belief. Isn't it a necessary corollary that no doctrine can be protected by the guarantees of free speech or religion only *because* it is true, and contrary doctrine is false?

2. Would it have been possible to dispose of the *Epperson* case on freedom of speech grounds, without ever reaching the establishment of religion issue? Whether the Arkansas legislature has enjoined teachers from mentioning the theory of evolution, or has told them they can be punished for expressing an honest opinion as to the truth of evolution theory, this *is* a case where the Arkansas legislature has made an official decision as to which dogma is false, and threatens to punish people if they express a contrary view. In other words, the validity of the Arkansas law doesn't turn on whether evolution theory is true or false, but on the admitted fact that the Arkansas legislature has made a decision that evolution is false for the purpose of preventing teachers from discussing the issue. Notice that Justice Fortas' opinion for the Court appears to begin analysis of the issue along these lines, but then abruptly leaves the issue unresolved and turns to the proposition that the law is an unconstitutional establishment of religion. One would guess that there are some difficult, unresolved problems of the freedom of speech rights of public school teachers to teach as they choose. Are these problems similar to selection of books by public libraries?

3. Insofar as a child's parents have the means, and the inclination, to send their children to private schools, the Constitution provides significant protections for their religious and intellectual freedom. The state may not insist that children attend public schools. (That was decided in Pierce v. Society of Sisters, 268 U.S. 510 [1925], discussed in note 2, p. 627, Chapter 18.) And, while the state may insist that private schools meet minimum educational standards, under Meyer v. Nebraska, 262 U.S. 390 (1923), discussed in the Court's *Epperson* opinion, state attempts to prohibit the teaching of offensive doctrines or to insist that subjects be taught with a particular point of view in private schools would be subject to stringent scrutiny under the First Amendment. (The *Meyer* case, like the *Pierce* case, was initially decided under a theory of protecting the economic freedom of private schools. Again, like the *Pierce* case, *Meyer* has been reinterpreted by the Court as protecting freedom of inquiry, freedom of thought, and freedom to teach.) Justice McReynolds' opinion for the Court in *Meyer* said:

> In order to submerge the individual and develop ideal citizens, Sparta assembled the males at seven into barracks and intrusted their subsequent education and training to official guardians. Although such measures have been deliberately approved by men of great genius, their ideas touching the relation between individual and state were wholly different from those upon which our institutions rest; and it hardly will be affirmed that any legislature could impose such restrictions upon the people of a State without doing violence to both letter and spirit of the Constitution.

Under the *Meyer* doctrine, an Arkansas law that prohibited private schools from teaching the subject of evolution, or that required private school teachers to teach that creation was true and evolution false, would probably be invalid under the First Amendment without worrying about whether the law was motivated by religious belief.

4. Thus, under the principle of Meyer v. Nebraska, parents and children who are upset by the point of view and courses taught in the public schools have a safety valve in the constitutional right to attend a more congenial private school. But the right to attend a private school is cold comfort for parents and children who, for financial and other reasons, are unable to avail themselves of the private school option. Justice McReynolds' opinion in the *Meyer* case was careful, however, to indicate that the decision did not touch the state's power to "prescribe a curriculum" in the public schools. Shouldn't a contemporary interpretation of the *Meyer* opinion extend at least some part of its principle to the public schools? Granted, a state has more control over the subject matter in public schools, because it runs them as well as regulates them. In the particular context of the *Meyer* case, it would be difficult to make a strong constitutional argument against a state's decision not to offer foreign languages in the public schools until the ninth grade. On the other hand, limiting the extension of academic freedom to the private schools may have been consistent with an opinion that talked in terms of protecting economic rights, but is hard to square with a theory emphasizing the protection of intellectual freedom. Wouldn't it seem particular-

ly strange to limit an important principle of intellectual freedom in a way that it could only be enjoyed by the well-to-do?

5.   The heart of the problem, nevertheless, lies in defining the scope of the state's admitted power to "prescribe a curriculum" for the public schools. Would it be possible to draw a distinction between state decisions concerning the subjects to be taught in the public schools, and decisions concerning the point of view from which such subjects are taught? There is, of course, the problem of drawing that line. Beyond the line-drawing problem, however, is a more fundamental difficulty. Curriculum planning, at least below the college level, has traditionally involved some centralized decision-making not only about subject matter, and the appropriate grade level, but about values to be inculcated by the instructional program. An obvious example would be education about drugs and alcohol in a public school health class that is consciously designed to teach the evils of drink and drug use. Nor have courses in history, civics or economics in the public schools been designed to be neutral about the values to be taught. Should there be a constitutional principle that the public schools be "neutral" in their teaching of all controversial issues? Suppose a teacher is assigned to a health course that is designed to teach the evils of drug use. Could the teacher be disciplined if he or she stated a firm personal belief in class that the use of marijuana is harmless?

6.   On these questions, re-read Board of Education v. Pico, supra page 156. Despite the sharp 4–4 split among the eight justices addressing the merits of the First Amendment issue concerning removal of books from the school library, all eight of those justices began with the proposition that the First Amendment's Free Speech Clause does not require that the public school's curriculum be value neutral. Indeed, it was Justice Brennan's concession that a public school board could insist that the curriculum actively promote certain values—"be they social, moral or political"—that complicated his attempt to stake out First Amendment limits on the board's decision to ban books from the school library. Was *Pico* a First Amendment victory after all, since it seems to foreclose any argument that the Constitution requires some neutrality in the values that public schools try to instill in their pupils?

7.   The question last asked brings up a second level of complication. The free speech rights involved are not only those of the teachers, but of pupils as well. Moreover, the pupils are a captive audience with little realistic control over the points of view to which they are exposed. Would a constitutional requirement of "neutrality" in presentation of controversial issues bind teachers too? If it did, wouldn't the teacher who loaded discussion of a controversial issue in any direction violate the Constitution? Would the teacher mentioned in the last note, who took a personal stand on the issue of marijuana use, violate the requirement of "neutrality"? On the other hand, if the neutrality requirement bound everyone except teachers, wouldn't that give a fifth grade teacher a constitutional *right* to use the classroom platform to teach pupils to be good Republicans?

8.   One can sympathize with the Supreme Court's desire to avoid broad issues of academic freedom in the public schools—issues it charac-

terized as "difficult terrain." Did the Court successfully avoid that terrain by basing its decision on the Free Exercise and Establishment Clauses of the First Amendment rather than the Free Speech Clause? The Court's rationale strikes down the Arkansas law because it was "motivated" by "fundamentalist sectarian conviction." Are all curriculum decisions motivated by religious views unconstitutional? On the issue of evolution and creation, any decision would have to be a variant or combination of one of four possible positions: leave both views—the general subject—entirely out of the public school curriculum; teach evolution as a sounder theory than creation; teach creation as a sounder theory than evolution; teach both views "neutrally." Are all possible positions unconstitutional so long as the position taken is "motivated" by religious views? Would the Arkansas law have been unconstitutional if it forbade teaching creation as true? Suppose a school board adopts an official text for biology courses stating that evolution is no longer a theory but a fact. Is that a violation of the Constitution? Is the *Epperson* decision limited to laws that make the teaching of certain doctrines in the public schools a criminal offense? Is the decision limited to motives that are not only religious but "sectarian"?

THE IMPACT OF EPPERSON*

Acclaim for the Court's opinion [in Epperson] in the press was virtually unanimous, but one person refused to dance on Bryan's grave. John T. Scopes, living in retirement in Shreveport, Louisiana, sounded a note of caution. "The fight will go on with other actors and other plays," he said. "You don't protect any of your individual liberties by lying down and going to sleep." Savoring victory and disregarding Scopes, evolutionists spent the next decade in slumber. But their opponents burned the midnight oil, devising new legal and legislative strategies which sought to return the Bible to biology. In 1978, a Yale Law School student and fervent creationist, Wendell Bird, published a lengthy student note in *The Yale Law Journal*, "Freedom of Religion and Science Instruction in Public Schools." Bird built his "equal time" case for "scientific creationism" in schools on Supreme Court decisions which recognized the rights of religious minorities like Jehovah's Witnesses and the Amish to practice their beliefs without state interference. The student who rejected evolution, Bird argued, was little different from the Gobitis children who rejected the flag-salute ceremony on religious grounds or the Yoder children who rejected compulsory education after the eighth grade.

Bird's article impressed leaders of the Institute for Creation Research and Creation Science Research Center, separate but sympathetic groups based near San Diego, California. Fueled by the national growth of the Religious Right in the 1970s, which demanded that prayer be returned to schools and abortion banned, the creationist movement took new aim at evolution. After his graduation from Yale, Bird joined the Institute for Creation Research and drafted "equal time" laws which sought an end-run around the Epperson decision. Beginning in 1980, the creationist effort gained support from an increasingly conservative pub-

* Peter Irons, The Courage of Their Convictions, Free Press, 1988, pp. 215–216. Reprinted with permission.

lic. Ronald Reagan, who had encouraged the creationists as California's governor, stated during his successful presidential campaign that he had "a great many questions" about evolution. A national opinion poll in 1981 revealed that 76 percent of the public favored "equal time" for evolution and creationism in the schools. The same year, the legislatures of Arkansas and Louisiana adopted the "equal time" laws that Bird had drafted.

EDWARDS v. AGUILLARD

Supreme Court of the United States, 1987.
482 U.S. 578, 107 S.Ct. 2573, 96 L.Ed.2d 510.

JUSTICE BRENNAN delivered the opinion of the Court.

The question for decision is whether Louisiana's "Balanced Treatment for Creation–Science and Evolution–Science in Public School Instruction" Act (Creationism Act) ... [violates] the Establishment Clause of the First Amendment.

I

The Creationism Act forbids the teaching of the theory of evolution in public schools unless accompanied by instruction in "creation science." ... No school is required to teach evolution or creation science. If either is taught, however, the other must also be taught.... The theories of evolution and creation science are statutorily defined as "the scientific evidences for [creation or evolution] and inferences from those scientific evidences." ...

... [P]arents of children attending Louisiana public schools, Louisiana teachers, and religious leaders, challenged the constitutionality of the Act....

. . .

II

The Establishment Clause forbids the enactment of any law "respecting an establishment of religion." The Court has applied a three-pronged test to determine whether legislation comports with the Establishment Clause. First, the legislature must have adopted the law with a secular purpose. Second, the statute's principal or primary effect must be one that neither advances nor inhibits religion. Third, the statute must not result in an excessive entanglement of government with religion. Lemon v. Kurtzman, 403 U.S. 602, 612–613 (1971). State action violates the Establishment Clause if it fails to satisfy any of these prongs.

In this case, the Court must determine whether the Establishment Clause was violated in the special context of the public elementary and secondary school system. States and local school boards are generally afforded considerable discretion in operating public schools.... "At the same time ... we have necessarily recognized that the discretion of the States and local school boards in matters of education must be exercised in a manner that comports with the transcendent imperatives of the

First Amendment." Board of Education v. Pico, 457 U.S. 853, 864 (1982).

The Court has been particularly vigilant in monitoring compliance with the Establishment Clause in elementary and secondary schools. Families entrust public schools with the education of their children, but condition their trust on the understanding that the classroom will not purposely be used to advance religious views that may conflict with the private beliefs of the student and his or her family. Students in such institutions are impressionable and their attendance is involuntary. . . . The State exerts great authority and coercive power through mandatory attendance requirements, and because of the students' emulation of teachers as role models and the children's susceptibility to peer pressure. . . .

. . .

Therefore, in employing the three-pronged *Lemon* test, we must do so mindful of the particular concerns that arise in the context of public elementary and secondary schools. We now turn to the evaluation of the Act under the *Lemon* test.

III

Lemon's first prong focuses on the purpose that animated adoption of the Act. . . . If the law was enacted for the purpose of endorsing religion, "no consideration of the second or third criteria [of *Lemon*] is necessary." Wallace v. Jaffree, supra, at 56. In this case, the petitioners have identified no clear secular purpose for the Louisiana Act.

True, the Act's stated purpose is to protect academic freedom. . . . This phrase might, in common parlance, be understood as referring to enhancing the freedom of teachers to teach what they will. . . . [T]he Act was not designed to further that goal. . . . [T]he [State argues] that the "legislature may not [have] use[d] the terms 'academic freedom' in the correct legal sense. They might have [had] in mind, instead, a basic concept of fairness; teaching all of the evidence." Even if "academic freedom" is read to mean "teaching all of the evidence" with respect to the origin of human beings, the Act does not further this purpose. The goal of providing a more comprehensive science curriculum is not furthered either by outlawing the teaching of evolution or by requiring the teaching of creation science.

A

While the Court is normally deferential to a State's articulation of a secular purpose, it is required that the statement of such purpose be sincere and not a sham. . . .

It is clear from the legislative history that the purpose of the legislative sponsor, Senator Bill Keith, was to narrow the science curriculum. During the legislative hearings, Senator Keith stated: "My preference would be that neither [creationism nor evolution] be taught." Such a ban on teaching does not promote—indeed, it undermines—the provision of a comprehensive scientific education.

It is equally clear that requiring schools to teach creation science with evolution does not advance academic freedom. The Act does not grant teachers a flexibility that they did not already possess to supplant the present science curriculum with the presentation of theories, besides evolution, about the origin of life.... [N]o law prohibited Louisiana public schoolteachers from teaching any scientific theory....

. . .

Furthermore, the goal of basic "fairness" is hardly furthered by the Act's discriminatory preference for the teaching of creation science and against the teaching of evolution. While requiring that curriculum guides be developed for creation science, the Act says nothing of comparable guides for evolution.... Similarly, research services are supplied for creation science but not for evolution.... Only "creation scientists" can serve on the panel that supplies the resource services.... The Act forbids school boards to discriminate against anyone who "chooses to be a creation-scientist" or to teach "creationism," but fails to protect those who choose to teach evolution or any other non-creation science theory, or who refuse to teach creation science....

If the Louisiana legislature's purpose was solely to maximize the comprehensiveness and effectiveness of science instruction, it would have encouraged the teaching of all scientific theories about the origins of humankind. But under the Act's requirements, teachers who were once free to teach any and all facets of this subject are now unable to do so. Moreover, the Act fails even to ensure that creation science will be taught, but instead requires the teaching of this theory only when the theory of evolution is taught. Thus ... the Act does not serve to protect academic freedom, but has the distinctly different purpose of discrediting "evolution by counterbalancing its teaching at every turn with the teaching of creation science...."

B

. . .

... [W]e need not be blind in this case to the legislature's preeminent religious purpose in enacting this statute. There is a historic and contemporaneous link between the teachings of certain religious denominations and the teaching of evolution. It was this link that concerned the Court in Epperson v. Arkansas, 393 U.S. 97 (1968)....

[The] same historic and contemporaneous antagonisms between the teachings of certain religious denominations and the teaching of evolution are present in this case. The preeminent purpose of the Louisiana legislature was clearly to advance the religious viewpoint that a supernatural being created humankind. The term "creation science" was defined as embracing this particular religious doctrine by those responsible for the passage of the Creationism Act. Senator Keith's leading expert on creation science, Edward Boudreaux, testified at the legislative hearings that the theory of creation science included belief in the existence of a supernatural creator. Senator Keith also cited testimony from other experts to support the creation-science view that "a creator

[was] responsible for the universe and everything in it." The legislative history therefore reveals that the term "creation science," as contemplated by the legislature that adopted this Act, embodies the religious belief that a supernatural creator was responsible for the creation of humankind.

Furthermore, it is not happenstance that the legislature required the teaching of a theory that coincided with this religious view. The legislative history documents that the Act's primary purpose was to change the science curriculum of public schools in order to provide persuasive advantage to a particular religious doctrine that rejects the factual basis of evolution in its entirety. The sponsor of the Creationism Act, Senator Keith, explained during the legislative hearings that his disdain for the theory of evolution resulted from the support that evolution supplied to views contrary to his own religious beliefs. According to Senator Keith, the theory of evolution was consonant with the "cardinal principle[s] of religious humanism, secular humanism, theological liberalism, aetheistism [sic]." The state senator repeatedly stated that scientific evidence supporting his religious views should be included in the public school curriculum to redress the fact that the theory of evolution incidentally coincided with what he characterized as religious beliefs antithetical to his own. The legislation therefore sought to alter the science curriculum to reflect endorsement of a religious view that is antagonistic to the theory of evolution.

In this case, the purpose of the Creationism Act was to restructure the science curriculum to conform with a particular religious viewpoint. Out of many possible science subjects taught in the public schools, the legislature chose to affect the teaching of the one scientific theory that historically has been opposed by certain religious sects. As in *Epperson,* the legislature passed the Act to give preference to those religious groups which have as one of their tenets the creation of humankind by a divine creator. The "overriding fact" that confronted the Court in *Epperson* was "that Arkansas' law selects from the body of knowledge a particular segment which it proscribes for the sole reason that it is deemed to conflict with ... a particular interpretation of the Book of Genesis by a particular religious group." 393 U.S., at 103. Similarly, the Creationism Act is designed either to promote the theory of creation science which embodies a particular religious tenet by requiring that creation science be taught whenever evolution is taught or to prohibit the teaching of a scientific theory disfavored by certain religious sects by forbidding the teaching of evolution when creation science is not also taught. The Establishment Clause, however, "forbids *alike* the preference of a religious doctrine *or* the prohibition of theory which is deemed antagonistic to a particular dogma." Id., at 106–107 (emphasis added). Because the primary purpose of the Creationism Act is to advance a particular religious belief, the Act endorses religion in violation of the First Amendment.

We do not imply that a legislature could never require that scientific critiques of prevailing scientific theories be taught.... [T]eaching a variety of scientific theories about the origins of humankind to schoolchildren might be validly done with the clear secular intent of enhancing the effectiveness of science instruction. But because the primary purpose of the Creationism Act is to endorse a particular religious doctrine, the Act furthers religion in violation of the Establishment Clause.

. . .

V

The Louisiana Creationism Act advances a religious doctrine by requiring either the banishment of the theory of evolution from public school classrooms or the presentation of a religious viewpoint that rejects evolution in its entirety. The Act violates the Establishment Clause of the First Amendment because it seeks to employ the symbolic and financial support of government to achieve a religious purpose....

. . .

JUSTICE POWELL, with whom JUSTICE O'CONNOR joins, concurring.

I write separately to note certain aspects of the legislative history, and to emphasize that nothing in the Court's opinion diminishes the traditionally broad discretion accorded state and local school officials in the selection of the public school curriculum.

I

. . .

C

... My examination of the language and the legislative history of the Balanced Treatment Act confirms that the intent of the Louisiana legislature was to promote a particular religious belief. The legislative history of the Arkansas statute prohibiting the teaching of evolution examined in Epperson v. Arkansas, 393 U.S. 97 (1968), was strikingly similar to the legislative history of the Balanced Treatment Act....

. . .

... The fact that the Louisiana legislature purported to add information to the school curriculum rather than detract from it as in *Epperson* does not affect my analysis. Both legislatures acted with the unconstitutional purpose of structuring the public school curriculum to make it compatible with a particular religious belief: the "divine creation of man."

. . .

II

Even though I find Louisiana's Balanced Treatment Act unconstitutional, I adhere to the view "that the States and locally elected school boards should have the responsibility for determining the educational policy of the public schools." Board of Education v. Pico, 457 U.S. 853, 893 (1982) (Powell, J., dissenting). A decision respecting the subject matter to be taught in public schools does not violate the Establishment Clause simply because the material to be taught " 'happens to coincide or harmonize with the tenets of some or all religions.' " Harris v. McRae,

448 U.S. 297, 319 (1980) (quoting McGowan v. Maryland, 366 U.S. 420, 442 (1961)). In the context of a challenge under the Establishment Clause, interference with the decisions of these authorities is warranted only when the purpose for their decisions is clearly religious.

· · ·

As a matter of history, school children can and should properly be informed of all aspects of this Nation's religious heritage. I would see no constitutional problem if school children were taught the nature of the Founding Father's religious beliefs and how these beliefs affected the attitudes of the times and the structure of our government. Courses in comparative religion of course are customary and constitutionally appropriate. In fact, since religion permeates our history, a familiarity with the nature of religious beliefs is necessary to understand many historical as well as contemporary events. In addition, it is worth noting that the Establishment Clause does not prohibit per se the educational use of religious documents in public school education. . . . The Establishment Clause is properly understood to prohibit the use of the Bible and other religious documents in public school education only when the purpose of the use is to advance a particular religious belief.

III

. . . I concur in the opinion of the Court and its judgment that the Balanced Treatment Act violates the Establishment Clause of the Constitution.

JUSTICE WHITE, concurring in the judgment.

As it comes to us, this is not a difficult case. . . .

· · ·

. . . Unless . . . we are to reconsider the Court's decisions interpreting the Establishment Clause, I agree that the [Louisiana statute is unconstitutional].

JUSTICE SCALIA, with whom THE CHIEF JUSTICE joins, dissenting.

Even if I agreed with the questionable premise that legislation can be invalidated under the Establishment Clause on the basis of its motivation alone, without regard to its effects, I would still find no justification for today's decision. The Louisiana legislators who passed the "Balanced Treatment for Creation–Science and Evolution–Science Act" (Balanced Treatment Act), . . . each of whom had sworn to support the Constitution, were well aware of the potential Establishment Clause problems and considered that aspect of the legislation with great care. . . . [T]he question of its constitutionality cannot rightly be disposed of on the gallop, by impugning the motives of its supporters.

I

. . . [T]he parties are sharply divided over what creation science consists of. Appellants insist that it is a collection of educationally valuable scientific data that has been censored from classrooms by an embarrassed scientific establishment. Appellees insist it is not science at all but thinly veiled religious doctrine. Both interpretations of the intended meaning of that phrase find considerable support in the legislative history.

. . .

II

. . .

B

. . .

The Court cites three provisions of the Act which, it argues, demonstrate a "discriminatory preference for the teaching of creation science" and no interest in "academic freedom." First, the Act prohibits discrimination only against creation scientists and those who teach creation science. . . . Second, the Act requires local school boards to develop and provide to science teachers "a curriculum guide on presentation of creation-science." . . . Finally, the Act requires the governor to designate seven creation scientists who shall, upon request, assist local school boards in developing the curriculum guides. . . . But none of these provisions casts doubt upon the sincerity of the legislators' articulated purpose of "academic freedom"—unless, of course, one gives that term the obviously erroneous meanings preferred by the Court. The Louisiana legislators had been told repeatedly that creation scientists were scorned by most educators and scientists, who themselves had an almost religious faith in evolution. It is hardly surprising, then, that in seeking to achieve a balanced, "nonindoctrinating" curriculum, the legislators protected from discrimination only those teachers whom they thought were *suffering* from discrimination. (Also, the legislators were undoubtedly aware of Epperson v. Arkansas, 393 U.S. 97 (1968), and thus could quite reasonably have concluded that discrimination against evolutionists was already prohibited.) The two provisions respecting the development of curriculum guides are also consistent with "academic freedom" as the Louisiana Legislature understood the term. Witnesses had informed the legislators that, because of the hostility of most scientists and educators to creation science, the topic had been censored from or badly misrepresented in elementary and secondary school texts. In light of the unavailability of works on creation science suitable for classroom use (a fact appellees concede), and the existence of ample materials on evolution, it was entirely reasonable for the Legislature to conclude that science teachers attempting to implement the Act would need a curriculum guide on creation science, but not on evolution, and that those charged with developing the guide would need an easily accessible group of creation scientists. Thus, the provisions of the Act of so much concern to the Court *support* the conclusion that the Legislature acted to advance "academic freedom."

. . .

It is undoubtedly true that what prompted the Legislature to direct its attention to the misrepresentation of evolution in the schools (rather than the inaccurate presentation of other topics) was its awareness of the tension between evolution and the religious beliefs of many children. But even appellees concede that a valid secular purpose is not rendered impermissible simply because its pursuit is prompted by concern for religious sensitivities. If a history teacher falsely told her students that the bones of Jesus Christ had been discovered, or a physics teacher that the Shroud of Turin had been conclusively established to be inexplicable on the basis of natural causes, I cannot believe (despite the majority's implication to the contrary) that legislators or school board members would be constitutionally prohibited from taking corrective action, simply because that action was prompted by concern for the religious beliefs of the misinstructed students.

In sum, even if one concedes, for the sake of argument, that a majority of the Louisiana Legislature voted for the Balanced Treatment Act partly in order to foster (rather than merely eliminate discrimination against) Christian fundamentalist beliefs, our cases establish that that alone would not suffice to invalidate the Act, so long as there was a genuine secular purpose as well. We have, moreover, no adequate basis for disbelieving the secular purpose set forth in the Act itself, or for concluding that it is a sham enacted to conceal the legislators' violation of their oaths of office. I am astonished by the Court's unprecedented readiness to reach such a conclusion, which I can only attribute to an intellectual predisposition created by the facts and the legend of *Scopes v. State,* 154 Tenn. (1 Smith) 105, 289 S.W. 363 (1927)—an instinctive reaction that any governmentally imposed requirements bearing upon the teaching of evolution must be a manifestation of Christian fundamentalist repression. In this case, however, it seems to me the Court's position is the repressive one. The people of Louisiana, including those who are Christian fundamentalists, are quite entitled, as a secular matter, to have whatever scientific evidence there may be against evolution presented in their schools, just as Mr. Scopes was entitled to present whatever scientific evidence there was for it. Perhaps what the Louisiana Legislature has done is unconstitutional because there *is* no such evidence, and the scheme they have established will amount to no more than a presentation of the Book of Genesis. But we cannot say that on the evidence before us in this summary judgment context, which includes ample uncontradicted testimony that "creation science" is a body of scientific knowledge rather than revealed belief. *Infinitely less* can we say (or should we say) that the scientific evidence for evolution is so conclusive that no one could be gullible enough to believe that there is any real scientific evidence to the contrary, so that the legislation's stated purpose must be a lie. Yet that in liberal judgment, that *Scopes-*in-reverse, is ultimately the basis on which the Court's facile rejection of the Louisiana Legislature's purpose must rest.

. . .

Because I believe that the Balanced Treatment Act had a secular purpose, which is all the first component of the *Lemon* test requires, I would reverse the judgment of the Court of Appeals and remand for further consideration.

III

I have to this point assumed the validity of the *Lemon* "purpose" test. In fact, however, I think the pessimistic evaluation that the Chief Justice made of the totality of *Lemon* is particularly applicable to the "purpose" prong: it is "a constitutional theory [that] has no basis in the history of the amendment it seeks to interpret, is difficult to apply and yields unprincipled results." Wallace v. Jaffree, 472 U.S., at 112 (Rehnquist, J., dissenting).

Our cases interpreting and applying the purpose test have made such a maze of the Establishment Clause that even the most conscientious governmental officials can only guess what motives will be held unconstitutional. We have said essentially the following: Government may not act with the purpose of advancing religion, except when forced to do so by the Free Exercise Clause (which is now and then); or when eliminating existing governmental hostility to religion (which exists sometimes); or even when merely accommodating governmentally uninhibited religious practices, except that at some point (it is unclear where) intentional accommodation results in the fostering of religion, which is of course unconstitutional.

But the difficulty of knowing what vitiating purpose one is looking for is as nothing compared with the difficulty of knowing how or where to find it. For while it is possible to discern the objective "purpose" of a statute (i.e., the public good at which its provisions appear to be directed), or even the formal motivation for a statute where that is explicitly set forth (as it was, to no avail, here), discerning the subjective motivation of those enacting the statute is, to be honest, almost always an impossible task. The number of possible motivations, to begin with, is not binary, or indeed even finite. In the present case, for example, a particular legislator need not have voted for the Act either because he wanted to foster religion or because he wanted to improve education. He may have thought the bill would provide jobs for his district, or may have wanted to make amends with a faction of his party he had alienated on another vote, or he may have been a close friend of the bill's sponsor, or he may have been repaying a favor he owed the Majority Leader, or he may have hoped the Governor would appreciate his vote and make a fundraising appearance for him, or he may have been pressured to vote for a bill he disliked by a wealthy contributor or by a flood of constituent mail, or he may have been seeking favorable publicity, or he may have been reluctant to hurt the feelings of a loyal staff member who worked on the bill, or he may have been settling an old score with a legislator who opposed the bill, or he may have been mad at his wife who opposed the bill, or he may have been intoxicated and utterly *un*motivated when the vote was called, or he may have accidentally voted "yes" instead of "no," or, of course, he may have had (and very likely did have) a combination of some of the above and many other motivations. To look for *the sole purpose* of even a single legislator is probably to look for something that does not exist.

Putting that problem aside, however, where ought we to look for the individual legislator's purpose? We cannot of course assume that every member present (if, as is unlikely, we know who or even how many they were) agreed with the motivation expressed in a particular legislator's pre-enactment floor or committee statement.... Can we assume, then, that they all agree with the motivation expressed in the staff-prepared committee reports they might have read—even though we are unwilling to assume that they agreed with the motivation expressed in the very statute that they voted for? Should we consider post-enactment floor statements? Or post-enactment testimony from legislators, obtained expressly for the lawsuit? Should we consider media reports on the realities of the legislative bargaining? All of these sources, of course, are eminently manipulable. Legislative histories can be contrived and sanitized, favorable media coverage orchestrated, and post-enactment recollections conveniently distorted. Perhaps most valuable of all would be more objective indications—for example, evidence regarding the individual legislators' religious affiliations. And if that, why not evidence regarding the fervor or tepidity of their beliefs?

Having achieved, through these simple means, an assessment of what individual legislators intended, we must still confront the question (yet to be addressed in any of our cases) how *many* of them must have the invalidating intent. If a state senate approves a bill by vote of 26 to 25, and only one of the 26 intended solely to advance religion, is the law unconstitutional? What if 13 of the 26 had that intent? What if 3 of the 26 had the impermissible intent, but 3 of the 25 voting against the bill were motivated by religious hostility or were simply attempting to "balance" the votes of their impermissibly motivated colleagues? Or is it possible that the intent of the bill's sponsor is alone enough to invalidate it—on a theory, perhaps, that even though everyone else's intent was pure, what they produced was the fruit of a forbidden tree?

Because there are no good answers to these questions, this Court has recognized from Chief Justice Marshall, see Fletcher v. Peck, 6 Cranch 87, 130 (1810), to Chief Justice Warren, United States v. O'Brien, supra, at 531–532, that determining the subjective intent of legislators is a perilous enterprise. See also Palmer v. Thompson, 403 U.S. 217, 224–225 (1971); Epperson v. Arkansas, 393 U.S., at 113 (Black, J., concurring). It is perilous, I might note, not just for the judges who will very likely reach the wrong result, but also for the legislators who find that they must assess the validity of proposed legislation—and risk the condemnation of having voted for an unconstitutional measure—not on the basis of what the legislation contains, nor even on the basis of what they themselves intend, but on the basis of what *others* have in mind.

Given the many hazards involved in assessing the subjective intent of governmental decisionmakers, the first prong of *Lemon* is defensible, I think, only if the text of the Establishment Clause demands it. That is surely not the case.... It is, in short, far from an inevitable reading of the Establishment Clause that it forbids all governmental action intended to advance religion; and if not inevitable, any reading with such untoward consequences must be wrong.

In the past we have attempted to justify our embarrassing Establishment Clause jurisprudence on the ground that it "sacrifices clarity and predictability for flexibility." Committee for Public Education & Religious Liberty v. Regan, 444 U.S., at 662.... I think it's time that we sacrifice some "flexibility" for "clarity and predictability." Abandoning *Lemon*'s purpose test—a test which exacerbates the tension between the Free Exercise and Establishment Clauses, has no basis in the language or history of the amendment, and, as today's decision shows, has wonderfully flexible consequences—would be a good place to start.

NOTES AND QUESTIONS

1. Despite the sharp dissent by Justice Scalia and Chief Justice Rehnquist, there is no disagreement that the Establishment Clause forbids public schools to teach religious doctrine. (The dissent concedes, for example, that the statute would be unconstitutional if the "scheme they have established will amount to no more than a presentation of the Book of Genesis.") The problem in *Edwards,* as in *Epperson,* was to decide whether curriculum content was religious. Both cases resolve the question whether a law mandating a particular curriculum violates the Establishment Clause by examining the motive of the legislature that enacted it. (As Justice Powell points out, the only difference between the two cases is that in *Epperson* the legislature required that evolution be subtracted from the curriculum and in *Edwards* it required that "creation-science" be added to it.) The point of the dissenters in *Edwards* is that it is not appropriate to decide whether curriculum content is religious by examining the motives of a legislature that required the curriculum. Do you agree? If the motives of the legislature, the school board, and the teacher, are all irrelevant, how would you decide whether public school instruction is inculcating religious doctrine rather than moral or political positions?

2. Michigan passed a law that prohibited advice or information on the subject of birth control to be taught in public school courses on sex and health education. A lower federal court decided that the law was an appropriate exercise of the state's power to control the curriculum of public schools. (Mercer v. Michigan State Board of Education, 379 F.Supp. 580 [E.D.Mich.1974], aff'd 419 U.S. 1081 [1974].) Do you agree? Would it make a difference if the law were motivated by "religious" views? "Sectarian religious" views? How do we find out what motivated the Michigan legislature?

IV.   PRIVATE RELIGIOUS SPEECH ON PUBLIC SCHOOL PROPERTY

GOOD NEWS CLUB v. MILFORD CENTRAL SCHOOL

Supreme Court of the United States, 2001.
533 U.S. 98, 121 S.Ct. 2093, 150 L.Ed.2d 151.

JUSTICE THOMAS delivered the opinion of the Court.

This case presents two questions. The first question is whether Milford Central School violated the free speech rights of the Good News

Club when it excluded the Club from meeting after hours at the school. The second question is whether any such violation is justified by Milford's concern that permitting the Club's activities would violate the Establishment Clause. We conclude that Milford's restriction violates the Club's free speech rights and that no Establishment Clause concern justifies that violation.

I

... In 1992, respondent Milford Central School (Milford) enacted a community use policy adopting seven ... purposes for which its building could be used after school. Two of the stated purposes are relevant here. First, district residents may use the school for "instruction in any branch of education, learning or the arts." Second, the school is available for "social, civic and recreational meetings and entertainment events, and other uses pertaining to the welfare of the community, provided that such uses shall be nonexclusive and shall be opened to the general public."

Stephen and Darleen Fournier reside within Milford's district and therefore are eligible to use the school's facilities as long as their proposed use is approved by the school. Together they are sponsors of the local Good News Club, a private Christian organization for children ages 6 to 12. Pursuant to Milford's policy, ... the Fourniers ... sought permission to hold the Club's weekly afterschool meetings in the school cafeteria.... to have "a fun time of singing songs, hearing a Bible lesson and memorizing scripture," ...

. . .

... [T]he Milford Board of Education adopted a resolution rejecting the Club's request to use Milford's facilities "for the purpose of conducting religious instruction and Bible study."

. . .

II

The standards that we apply to determine whether a State has unconstitutionally excluded a private speaker from use of a public forum depend on the nature of the forum....

. . .

III

... [W]e first address whether the exclusion constituted viewpoint discrimination. We are guided in our analysis by two of our prior opinions, *Lamb's Chapel* [v. Center Moriches Union Free School Dist., 508 U. S. 384 (1993)] and *Rosenberger* [v. Rector and Visitors of Univ. of Va., 515 U. S. 819 (1995)]. In *Lamb's Chapel*, we held that a school district violated the Free Speech Clause of the First Amendment when it excluded a private group from presenting films at the school based solely on the films' discussions of family values from a religious perspective. Likewise, in *Rosenberger*, we held that a university's refusal to fund a student publication because the publication addressed issues from a religious perspective violated the Free Speech Clause. Concluding that Milford's exclusion of the Good News Club based on its religious nature is indistinguishable from the exclusions in these cases, we hold that the exclusion constitutes viewpoint discrimination. Because the restriction is viewpoint discriminatory, we need not decide whether it is unreasonable in light of the purposes served by the forum.

. . .

Like the church in *Lamb's Chapel*, the Club seeks to address a subject otherwise permitted under the rule, the teaching of morals and character, from a religious standpoint.... The only apparent difference between the activity of Lamb's Chapel and the activities of the Good News Club is that the Club chooses to teach moral lessons from a Christian perspective through live storytelling and prayer, whereas Lamb's Chapel taught lessons through films. This distinction is inconsequential. Both modes of speech use a religious viewpoint. Thus, the exclusion of the Good News Club's activities, like the exclusion of Lamb's Chapel's films, constitutes unconstitutional viewpoint discrimination.

Our opinion in *Rosenberger* also is dispositive. In *Rosenberger*, a student organization at the University of Virginia was denied funding for printing expenses because its publication, Wide Awake, offered a Christian viewpoint. Just as the Club emphasizes the role of Christianity in students' morals and character, Wide Awake "challenge[d] Christians to live, in word and deed, according to the faith they proclaim and ... encourage[d] students to consider what a personal relationship with Jesus Christ means." ... Because the university "select[ed] for disfavored treatment those student journalistic efforts with religious editorial viewpoints," we held that the denial of funding was unconstitutional....

. . .

We disagree that something that is "quintessentially religious" or "decidedly religious in nature" cannot also be characterized properly as the teaching of morals and character development from a particular viewpoint.... What matters for purposes of the Free Speech Clause is that we can see no logical difference in kind between the invocation of Christianity by the Club and the invocation of teamwork, loyalty, or patriotism by other associations to provide a foundation for their lessons.... [W]e reaffirm our holdings in *Lamb's Chapel* and *Rosenberger* that speech discussing otherwise permissible subjects cannot be excluded from a limited public forum on the ground that the subject is discussed from a religious viewpoint. Thus, we conclude that Milford's exclusion of the Club from use of the school, pursuant to its community use policy, constitutes impermissible viewpoint discrimination.

IV

Milford argues that, even if its restriction constitutes viewpoint discrimination, its interest in not violating the Establishment Clause outweighs the Club's interest in gaining equal access to the school's facilities.... We disagree.

We have said that a state interest in avoiding an Establishment Clause violation "may be characterized as compelling," and therefore may justify content-based discrimination.... However, it is not clear whether a State's interest in avoiding an Establishment Clause violation would justify viewpoint discrimination.... We need not, however, confront the issue in this case, because we conclude that the school has no valid Establishment Clause interest.

We rejected Establishment Clause defenses similar to Milford's in ... *Lamb's Chapel*.... [W]e explained that "[t]he showing of th[e] film series would not have been during school hours, would not have been sponsored by the school, and would have been open to the public, not just to church members." ...

. . .

Milford attempts to distinguish *Lamb's Chapel* ... by emphasizing that Milford's policy involves elementary school children. According to Milford, children will perceive that the school is endorsing the Club and will feel coercive pressure to participate, because the Club's activities take place on school grounds, even though they occur during nonschool hours. This argument is unpersuasive.

First, we have held that "a significant factor in upholding governmental programs in the face of Establishment Clause attack is their neutrality towards religion." *Rosenberger*, ... Milford's implication that granting access to the Club would do damage to the neutrality principle defies logic. For the "guarantee of neutrality is respected, not offended, when the government, following neutral criteria and evenhanded policies, extends benefits to recipients whose ideologies and viewpoints, including religious ones, are broad and diverse." *Rosenberger* ... The Good News Club seeks nothing more than to be treated neutrally and given access to speak about the same topics as are other groups. Because allowing the Club to speak on school grounds would ensure neutrality, not threaten it, Milford faces an uphill battle in arguing that the Establishment Clause compels it to exclude the Good News Club.

Second, to the extent we consider whether the community would feel coercive pressure to engage in the Club's activities, ... the relevant community would be the parents, not the elementary school children. It is the parents who choose whether their children will attend the Good News Club meetings. Because the children cannot attend without their parents' permission, they cannot be coerced into engaging in the Good News Club's religious activities. Milford does not suggest that the parents of elementary school children would be confused about whether the school was endorsing religion. Nor do we believe that such an argument could be reasonably advanced.

Third, whatever significance we may have assigned in the Establishment Clause context to the suggestion that elementary school children are more impressionable than adults, ... we have never extended our Establishment Clause jurisprudence to foreclose private religious conduct during nonschool hours merely because it takes place on school premises where elementary school children may be present.

None of the cases discussed by Milford persuades us that our Establishment Clause jurisprudence has gone this far. For example, Milford cites Lee v. Weisman ... for the proposition that "there are heightened concerns with protecting freedom of conscience from subtle coercive pressure in the elementary and secondary public schools," ... In *Lee*, however, we concluded that attendance at the graduation exercise was obligatory.... We did not place independent significance on the fact that the graduation exercise might take place on school premises.... Here, where the school facilities are being used for a nonschool function and there is no government sponsorship of the Club's activities, *Lee* is inapposite.

Equally unsupportive is Edwards v. Aguillard, ... in which we held that a Louisiana law that proscribed the teaching of evolution as part of the public school curriculum, unless accompanied by a lesson on creationism, violated the Establishment Clause. In *Edwards*, we mentioned that students are susceptible to pressure in the classroom, particularly given their possible reliance on teachers as role models. But we did not discuss this concern in our application of the law to the facts. Moreover, we did note that mandatory attendance requirements meant that State advancement of religion in a school would be particularly harshly felt by impressionable students. But we did not suggest that, when the school was not actually advancing religion, the impressionability of students would be relevant to the Establishment Clause issue....

. . .

Finally, even if we were to inquire into the minds of schoolchildren in this case, we cannot say the danger that children would misperceive the endorsement of religion is any greater than the danger that they would perceive a hostility toward the religious viewpoint if the Club were excluded from the public forum....

. . .

V

When Milford denied the Good News Club access to the school's limited public forum on the ground that the Club was religious in nature, it discriminated against the Club because of its religious viewpoint in violation of the Free Speech Clause of the First Amendment. Because Milford has not raised a valid Establishment Clause claim, we do not address the question whether such a claim could excuse Milford's viewpoint discrimination.

. . .

JUSTICE SCALIA, concurring.

I join the Court's opinion but write separately to explain further my views ...

. . .

From no other group does respondent require the sterility of speech that it demands of petitioners.... The Club may not ... independently discuss the religious premise on which its views are based—that God exists and His assistance is necessary to morality. It may not defend the premise, and it absolutely must not seek to persuade the children that the premise is true. The children must, so to say, take it on faith. This is blatant viewpoint discrimination.

. . .

The dissenters emphasize that the religious speech used by the Club as the foundation for its views on morals and character is not just any type of religious speech. . . . In Justice Stevens' view, it is speech "aimed principally at proselytizing or inculcating belief in a particular religious faith." This does not . . . distinguish the Club's activities from those of the other groups using respondent's forum—which have not, as Justice Stevens suggests, been restricted to roundtable "discussions" of moral issues. . . .

Justice Souter, while agreeing that the Club's religious speech "may be characterized as proselytizing," thinks that it is even more clearly excludable from respondent's forum because it is essentially "an evangel- ical service of worship." But we have previously rejected the attempt to distinguish worship from other religious speech. . . . If the distinction did have content, it would be beyond the courts' competence to adminis- ter. . . .

. . .

JUSTICE BREYER, concurring in part.

[Justice Breyer argued that the question whether there had been a violation of the Establishment Clause was not procedurally before the Court, and should not have been decided.]

JUSTICE STEVENS, dissenting.

The Milford Central School has invited the public to use its facilities for educational and recreational purposes, but not for "religious pur- poses." Speech for "religious purposes" may reasonably be understood to encompass three different categories. First, there is religious speech that is simply speech about a particular topic from a religious point of view. . . . Second, there is religious speech that amounts to worship, or its equivalent. . . . Third, there is an intermediate category that is aimed principally at proselytizing or inculcating belief in a particular religious faith.

. . .

. . . The novel question that this case . . . is whether a school can, consistently with the First Amendment, create a limited public forum that admits the first type of religious speech without allowing the other two.

. . . If a school decides to authorize after school discussions of current events in its classrooms, it may not exclude people from express- ing their views simply because it dislikes their particular political opin- ions. But must it therefore allow organized political groups—for exam- ple, the Democratic Party, the Libertarian Party, or the Ku Klux Klan— to hold meetings, the principal purpose of which is not to discuss the current-events topic from their own unique point of view but rather to recruit others to join their respective groups? I think not. . . .

School officials may reasonably believe that evangelical meetings designed to convert children to a particular religious faith pose the same risk. And, just as a school may allow meetings to discuss current events from a political perspective without also allowing organized political recruitment, so too can a school allow discussion of topics such as moral development from a religious (or nonreligious) perspective without thereby opening its forum to religious proselytizing or worship. . . .

.   .   .

This case is undoubtedly close. Nonetheless, regardless of whether the Good News Club's activities amount to "worship," it does seem clear, based on the facts in the record, that the school district correctly classified those activities as falling within the third category of religious speech and therefore beyond the scope of the school's limited public forum. . . .

.   .   .

JUSTICE SOUTER, with whom JUSTICE GINSBURG joins, dissenting.

.   .   .

I

.   .   .

It is beyond question that Good News intends to use the public school premises not for the mere discussion of a subject from a particular, Christian point of view, but for an evangelical service of worship calling children to commit themselves in an act of Christian conversion. The majority avoids this reality only by resorting to the bland and general characterization of Good News's activity as "teaching of morals and character, from a religious standpoint." If the majority's statement ignores reality, as it surely does, then today's holding may be understood only in equally generic terms. Otherwise, indeed, this case would stand for the remarkable proposition that any public school opened for civic meetings must be opened for use as a church, synagogue, or mosque.

II

.   .   .

The timing and format of Good News's gatherings ... may well affirmatively suggest the imprimatur of officialdom in the minds of the young children. The club is open solely to elementary students (not the entire community, as in *Lamb's Chapel*), only four outside groups have been identified as meeting in the school, and Good News is, seemingly, the only one whose instruction follows immediately on the conclusion of the official school day. . . . In fact, the temporal and physical continuity of Good News's meetings with the regular school routine seems to be the whole point of using the school. When meetings were held in a community church, 8 or 10 children attended; after the school became the site, the number went up three-fold.

NOTES AND QUESTIONS

1. Is the Court's conclusion—that allowing Good News meetings in the public school at the end of the school day would not violate the Establishment Clause—consistent with the Court's "released time" decisions? Would the decision be different if Good News spent most of the time in worship conducted by ordained clergy?

2. When a religious speaker seeks access to a public forum, there is often a clash between the First Amendment's Speech and Establishment Clauses. The majority in *Good News* concludes that *denying* the religious group's access to school property violated the Free Speech Clause; the dissent concludes that *permitting* access would have violated the Establishment Clause. Is it always true that these are the only possible positions? (In other words, are there some cases where the school board should be able to make either choice—deny or permit access—without violating the Constitution?)

V. AID TO CHURCH–RELATED SCHOOLS

BOWEN v. KENDRICK

Supreme Court of the United States, 1988.
487 U.S. 589, 108 S.Ct. 2562, 101 L.Ed.2d 520.

CHIEF JUSTICE REHNQUIST delivered the Opinion of the Court.

This case involves a challenge to a federal grant program that provides funding for services relating to adolescent sexuality and pregnancy. Considering the federal statute both "on its face" and "as applied," the District Court ruled that the statute violated the Establishment Clause of the First Amendment insofar as it provided for the involvement of religious organizations in the federally funded programs. We conclude, however, that the statute is not unconstitutional on its face, and that a determination of whether any of the grants made pursuant to the statute violate the Establishment Clause requires further proceedings in the District Court.

. . .

II

. . .

. . . As in previous cases involving facial challenges on Establishment Clause grounds, . . . we assess the constitutionality of an enactment by reference to the three factors first articulated in Lemon v. Kurtzman, 403 U.S. 602 (1971). . . .

As we see it, it is clear from the face of the statute that the AFLA [Adolescent Family Life Act] was motivated primarily, if not entirely, by a legitimate secular purpose—the elimination or reduction of social and economic problems caused by teenage sexuality, pregnancy, and parenthood....

· · ·

As usual in Establishment Clause cases, ... the more difficult question is whether the primary effect of the challenged statute is impermissible. Before we address this question, however, it is useful to review ... just what the AFLA sets out to do. Simply stated, it authorizes grants to institutions that are capable of providing certain care and prevention services to adolescents. Because of the complexity of the problems that Congress sought to remedy, potential grantees are required to describe how they will involve other organizations, including religious organizations, in the programs funded by the federal grants.... There is no requirement in the Act that grantees be affiliated with any religious denomination, although the Act clearly does not rule out grants to religious organizations. The services to be provided under the AFLA are not religious in character, nor has there been any suggestion that religious institutions or organizations with religious ties are uniquely well qualified to carry out those services. Certainly it is true that a substantial part of the services listed as "necessary services" under the Act involve some sort of education or counseling, ... but there is nothing inherently religious about these activities and appellees do not contend that, by themselves, the AFLA's "necessary services" somehow have the primary effect of advancing religion. Finally, it is clear that the AFLA takes a particular approach toward dealing with adolescent sexuality and pregnancy—for example, two of its stated purposes are to "promote self discipline and other prudent approaches to the problem of adolescent premarital sexual relations," ... and to "promote adoption as an alternative," ...—but again, that approach is not inherently religious, although it may coincide with the approach taken by certain religions.

Given this statutory framework, there are two ways in which the statute, considered "on its face," might be said to have the impermissible primary effect of advancing religion. First, it can be argued that the AFLA advances religion by expressly recognizing that "religious organizations have a role to play" in addressing the problems associated with teenage sexuality.... In this view, even if no religious institution receives aid or funding pursuant to the AFLA, the statute is invalid under the Establishment Clause because, among other things, it expressly enlists the involvement of religiously affiliated organizations in the federally subsidized programs, it endorses religious solutions to the problems addressed by the Act, or it creates symbolic ties between church and state. Secondly, it can be argued that the AFLA is invalid on its face because it allows religiously affiliated organizations to participate as grantees or subgrantees in AFLA programs. From this standpoint, the Act is invalid because it authorizes direct federal funding of religious organizations which, given the AFLA's educational function and the fact that the AFLA's "viewpoint" may coincide with the grantee's "viewpoint" on sexual matters, will result unavoidably in the impermissible "inculcation" of religious beliefs in the context of a federally funded program.

We consider the former objection first. As noted previously, the AFLA expressly mentions the role of religious organizations in four places. It states (1) that the problems of teenage sexuality are "best approached through a variety of integrated and essential services provided to adolescents and their families by[, among others,] religious organizations," ... (2) that federally subsidized services "should emphasize the provision of support by[, among others,] religious organizations," ... (3) that AFLA programs "shall use such methods as will strengthen the capacity of families ... to make use of support systems such as ... religious ... organizations," ... and (4) that grant applicants shall describe how they will involve religious organizations, among other groups, in the provision of services under the Act....

Putting aside for the moment the possible role of religious organizations as grantees, these provisions of the statute reflect at most Congress' considered judgment that religious organizations can help solve the problems to which the AFLA is addressed.... Nothing in our previous cases prevents Congress from making such a judgment or from recognizing the important part that religion or religious organizations may play in resolving certain secular problems. Particularly when, as Congress found, "prevention of adolescent sexual activity and adolescent pregnancy depends primarily upon developing strong family values and close family ties," ... it seems quite sensible for Congress to recognize that religious organizations can influence values and can have some influence on family life, including parents' relations with their adolescent children. To the extent that this Congressional recognition has any effect of advancing religion, the effect is at most "incidental and remote." ... In addition, although the AFLA does require potential grantees to describe how they will involve religious organizations in the provision of services under the Act, it also requires grantees to describe the involvement of "charitable organizations, voluntary associations, and other groups in the private sector,".... In our view, this reflects the statute's successful maintenance of "a course of neutrality among religions, and between religion and nonreligions,"....

This brings us to the second grounds for objecting to the AFLA: the fact that it allows religious institutions to participate as recipients of federal funds. The AFLA defines an "eligible grant recipient" as a "public or nonprofit private organization or agency" which demonstrates the capability of providing the requisite services.... As this provision would indicate, a fairly wide spectrum of organizations is eligible to apply for and receive funding under the Act, and nothing on the fact of the Act suggests the AFLA is anything but neutral with respect to the grantee's status as a sectarian or purely secular institution.... In this regard, then, the AFLA is similar to other statutes that this Court has upheld against Establishment Clause challenges in the past. In Roemer v. Maryland Board of Public Works, 426 U.S. 736 (1976), for example, we upheld a Maryland statute that provided annual subsidies directly to qualifying colleges and universities in the State, including religiously affiliated institutions.... Similarly, in Tilton v. Richardson, 403 U.S.

672 (1971), we approved the federal Higher Educational Facilities Act, which was intended by Congress to provide construction grants to "all colleges and universities regardless of any affiliation with or sponsorship by a religious body." Id., at 676. And in Hunt v. McNair, 413 U.S. 734 (1973), we rejected a challenge to a South Carolina statute that made certain benefits "available to all institutions of higher education in South Carolina, whether or not having a religious affiliation." Id., at 741. In other cases involving indirect grants of state aid to religious institutions, we have found it important that the aid is made available regardless of whether it will ultimately flow to a secular or sectarian institution. See, e.g., Witters v. Washington Dept. of Services for the Blind, 474 U.S. 481, 487 (1986); Mueller v. Allen, 463 U.S., at 398; Everson v. Board of Education, supra, at 17–18; Walz v. Tax Comm'n, 397 U.S., at 676.

We note in addition that this Court has never held that religious institutions are disabled by the First Amendment from participating in publicly sponsored social welfare programs. To the contrary, in Bradfield v. Roberts, 175 U.S. 291 (1899), the Court upheld an agreement between the Commissioners of the District of Columbia and a religiously affiliated hospital whereby the Federal Government would pay for the construction of a new building on the grounds of the hospital. In effect, the Court refused to hold that the mere fact that the hospital was "conducted under the auspices of the Roman Catholic Church" was sufficient to alter the purely secular legal character of the corporation, . . . particularly in the absence of any allegation that the hospital discriminated on the basis of religion or operated in any way inconsistent with its secular charter. In the Court's view, the giving of federal aid to the hospital was entirely consistent with the Establishment Clause, and the fact that the hospital was religiously affiliated was "wholly immaterial." . . . The propriety of this holding, and the long history of cooperation and interdependency between governments and charitable or religious organizations is reflected in the legislative history of the AFLA. . . .

Of course, even when the challenged statute appears to be neutral on its face, we have always been careful to ensure that direct government aid to religiously affiliated institutions does not have the primary effect of advancing religion. One way in which direct government aid might have that effect is if the aid flows to institutions that are "pervasively sectarian." . . .

The reason for this is that there is a risk that direct government funding, even if it is designated for specific secular purposes, may nonetheless advance the pervasively sectarian institution's "religious mission." . . . Accordingly, a relevant factor in deciding whether a particular statute on its face can be said to have the improper effect of advancing religion is the determination of whether, and to what extent, the statute directs government aid to pervasively sectarian institutions. . . .

In this case, nothing on the face of the AFLA indicates that a significant proportion of the federal funds will be disbursed to "pervasively sectarian" institutions. Indeed, the contention that there is a substantial risk of such institutions receiving direct aid is undercut by the AFLA's facially neutral grant requirements, the wide spectrum of public and private organizations which are capable of meeting the AFLA's requirements, and the fact that, of the eligible religious institutions, many will not deserve the label of "pervasively sectarian." This is not a case like *Grand Rapids,* where the challenged aid flowed almost entirely to parochial schools.... Instead, this case more closely resembles *Tilton* and *Roemer,* where it was foreseeable that some proportion of the recipients of government aid would be religiously affiliated, but that only a small portion of these, if any, could be considered "pervasively sectarian." ... As in *Tilton* and *Roemer,* we do not think the possibility that AFLA grants may go to religious institutions that can be considered "pervasively sectarian" is sufficient to conclude that no grants whatsoever can be given under the statute to religious organizations. We think that the District Court was wrong in concluding otherwise.

Nor do we agree with the District Court that the AFLA necessarily has the effect of advancing religion because the religiously affiliated AFLA grantees will be providing educational and counseling services to adolescents. Of course, we have ... struck down programs that entail an unacceptable risk that government funding would be used to "advance the religious mission" of the religious institution receiving aid. See, e.g., *Meek,* 421 U.S., at 370. But nothing in our prior cases warrants the presumption adopted by the District Court that religiously affiliated AFLA grantees are not capable of carrying out their functions under the AFLA in a lawful, secular manner. Only in the context of aid to "pervasively sectarian" institutions have we invalidated an aid program on the grounds that there was a "substantial" risk that aid to these religious institutions would, knowingly or unknowingly, result in religious indoctrination. E.g., *Grand Rapids,* 473 U.S., at 387–398; *Meek,* supra, at 371. In contrast, when the aid is to flow to religiously affiliated institutions that were not pervasively sectarian, as in *Roemer,* we refused to presume that it would be used in a way that would have the primary effect of advancing religion.... We think that the type of presumption that the District Court applied in this case is simply unwarranted....

We also disagree with the District Court's conclusion that the AFLA is invalid because it authorizes "teaching" by religious grant recipients on "matters [that] are fundamental elements of religious doctrine, such as the harm of premarital sex and the reasons for choosing adoption over abortion...." On an issue as sensitive and important as teenage sexuality, it is not surprising that the government's secular concerns would either coincide or conflict with those of religious institutions. But the possibility or even the likelihood that some of the religious institutions who receive AFLA funding will agree with the message that Congress intended to deliver to adolescents through the AFLA is insufficient to warrant a finding that the statute on its face has the primary effect of advancing religion.... Nor does the alignment of the statute and the religious views of the grantees run afoul of our proscription against "fund[ing] a specifically religious activity in an otherwise substantially secular setting." ... The facially neutral projects authorized by the

AFLA—including pregnancy testing, adoption counseling and referral services, prenatal and postnatal care, educational services, residential care, child care, consumer education, etc.—are not themselves "specifically religious activities," and they are not converted into such activities by the fact that they are carried out by organizations with religious affiliations.

As yet another reason for invalidating parts of the AFLA, the District Court found that the involvement of religious organizations in the Act has the impermissible effect of creating a "crucial symbolic link" between government and religion. If we were to adopt the District Court's reasoning, it could be argued that any time a government aid program provides funding to religious organizations in an area in which the organization also has an interest, an impermissible "symbolic link" could be created, no matter whether the aid was to be used solely for secular purposes. This would jeopardize government aid to religiously affiliated hospitals, for example, on the ground that patients would perceive a "symbolic link" between the hospital—part of whose "religious mission" might be to save lives—and whatever government entity is subsidizing the purely secular medical services provided to the patient. We decline to adopt the District Court's reasoning and conclude that, in this case, whatever "symbolic link" might in fact be created by the AFLA's disbursement of funds to religious institutions is not sufficient to justify striking down the statute on its face.

A final argument that has been advanced for striking down the AFLA on "effects" grounds is the fact that the statute lacks an express provision preventing the use of federal funds for religious purposes.... Clearly, if there were such a provision in this statute, it would be easier to conclude that the statute on its face could not be said to have the primary effect of advancing religion, see, e.g., *Roemer,* supra, at 760, but we have never stated that a *statutory* restriction is constitutionally required.... [T]he Secretary can police the grants that are given out under the Act to ensure that federal funds are not used for impermissible purposes. Unlike some other grant programs, in which aid might be given out in one-time grants without ongoing supervision by the government, the programs established under the authority of the AFLA can be monitored to determine whether the funds are, in effect, being used by the grantees in such a way as to advance religion. Given this statutory scheme, we do not think that the absence of an express limitation on the use of federal funds for religious purposes means that the statute, on its face, has the primary effect of advancing religion.

This, of course, brings us to the third prong of the *Lemon* Establishment Clause "test"—the question whether the AFLA leads to " 'an excessive government entanglement with religion.' " ... There is no doubt that the monitoring of AFLA grants is necessary if the Secretary is to ensure that public money is to be spent in the way that Congress intended and in a way that comports with the Establishment Clause. Accordingly, this case presents us with yet another "Catch–22" argument: the very supervision of the aid to assure that it does not further religion renders the statute invalid.... Most of the cases in which the

Court has divided over the "entanglement" part of the Lemon test have involved aid to parochial schools. . . .

Here, by contrast, there is no reason to assume that the religious organizations which may receive grants are "pervasively sectarian" in the same sense as the Court has held parochial schools to be. There is accordingly no reason to fear that the less intensive monitoring involved here will cause the Government to intrude unduly in the day-to-day operation of the religiously affiliated AFLA grantees. Unquestionably, the Secretary will review the programs set up and run by the AFLA grantees, and undoubtedly this will involve a review of, for example, the educational materials that a grantee proposes to use. The Secretary may also wish to have government employees visit the clinics or offices where AFLA programs are being carried out to see whether they are in fact being administered in accordance with statutory and constitutional requirements. But in our view, this type of grant monitoring does not amount to "excessive entanglement," at least in the context of a statute authorizing grants to religiously affiliated organizations that are not necessarily "pervasively sectarian."[1]

. . .

For the foregoing reasons we conclude that the AFLA does not violate the Establishment Clause "on its face."

III

. . .

. . . [I]t will be open to appellees on remand to show that AFLA aid is flowing to grantees that can be considered "pervasively sectarian" religious institutions, such as we have held parochial schools to be. . . .

The District Court should also consider on remand whether in particular cases AFLA aid has been used to fund "specifically religious activit[ies] in an otherwise substantially secular setting." . . . Here it would be relevant to determine, for example, whether the Secretary has permitted AFLA grantees to use materials that have an explicitly religious content or are designed to inculcate the views of a particular religious faith. . . . [E]vidence that the views espoused on questions such as premarital sex, abortion, and the like happen to coincide with the religious views of the AFLA grantee would not be sufficient to show that the grant funds are being used in such a way as to have a primary effect of advancing religion.

. . .

JUSTICE O'CONNOR, concurring.

. . . I join [the Court's] opinion. I write separately, however, to explain why I do not believe that the Court's approach reflects any

---

1. . . . [A]s we said in Mueller v. Allen, 463 U.S. 388, 404 n. 11 (1983), the question of "political divisiveness" should "be regarded as confined to cases where direct financial subsidies are paid to parochial schools or to teachers in parochial schools."

tolerance for the kind of improper administration that seems to have occurred in the government program at issue here.

. . .

. . . Using religious organizations to advance the secular goals of the AFLA, without thereby permitting religious indoctrination, is inevitably more difficult than in other projects, such as ministering to the poor and the sick. I nonetheless agree with the Court that the partnership between governmental and religious institutions contemplated by the AFLA need not result in constitutional violations, despite an undeniably greater risk than is present in cooperative undertakings that involve less sensitive objectives. If the District Court finds on remand that grants are being made in violation of the Establishment Clause, an appropriate remedy would take into account the history of the program's administration as well as the extent of any continuing constitutional violations.

JUSTICE KENNEDY, with whom JUSTICE SCALIA joins, concurring.

I join the Court's opinion and write this separate concurrence to discuss one feature of the proceedings on remand. The Court states that "it will be open to appellees on remand to show that AFLA aid is flowing to grantees that can be considered 'pervasively sectarian' religious institutions, such as we have held parochial schools to be." In my view, such a showing will not alone be enough, in an as-applied challenge, to make out a violation of the Establishment Clause.

Though I am not confident that the term "pervasively sectarian" is a well-founded juridical category, I recognize the thrust of our previous decisions that a statute which provides for exclusive or disproportionate funding to pervasively sectarian institutions may impermissibly advance religion and as such be invalid on its face. We hold today, however, that the neutrality of the grant requirements and the diversity of the organizations described in the statute before us foreclose the argument that it is disproportionately tied to pervasively sectarian groups. Having held that the statute is not facially invalid, the only purpose of further inquiring whether any particular grantee institution is pervasively sectarian is as a preliminary step to demonstrating that the funds are in fact being used to further religion. In sum, where, as in this case, a statute provides that the benefits of a program are to be distributed in a neutral fashion to religious and non-religious applicants alike, and the program withstands a facial challenge, it is not unconstitutional as applied solely by reason of the religious character of a specific recipient. The question in an as-applied challenge is not whether the entity is of a religious character, but how it spends its grant.

JUSTICE BLACKMUN, with whom JUSTICE BRENNAN, JUSTICE MARSHALL, and JUSTICE STEVENS join, dissenting.

. . .

Whatever Congress had in mind, . . . it enacted a statute that facilitated and, indeed, encouraged the use of public funds for [religious] instruction, by giving religious groups a central pedagogical and counseling role without imposing any restraints on the sectarian quality of the participation.... [F]ederal tax dollars appropriated for AFLA purposes have been used, with Government approval, to support religious teaching.... Because I am firmly convinced that our cases require invalidating this statutory scheme, I dissent.

. . .

II

. . .

The majority first skews the Establishment Clause analysis by adopting a cramped view of what constitutes a pervasively sectarian institution. Perhaps because most of the Court's decisions in this area have come in the context of aid to parochial schools, which traditionally have been characterized as pervasively sectarian, the majority seems to equate the characterization with the institution.... On a continuum of "sectarianism" running from parochial schools at one end to the colleges funded by the statutes upheld in *Tilton, Hunt,* and *Roemer* at the other, the AFLA grantees described by the District Court clearly are much closer to the former than to the latter.

More importantly, the majority also errs in suggesting that the inapplicability of the label is generally dispositive. While a plurality of the Court has framed the inquiry as "whether an institution is so 'pervasively sectarian' that it may receive no direct state aid of any kind," Roemer v. Maryland Public Works Board, 426 U.S., at 758, the Court never has treated the absence of such a finding as a license to disregard the potential for impermissible fostering of religion. The characterization of an institution as "pervasively sectarian" allows us to eschew further inquiry into the use that will be made of direct government aid. In that sense, it is a sufficient, but not a necessary, basis for a finding that a challenged program creates an unacceptable Establishment Clause risk. The label thus serves in some cases as a proxy for a more detailed analysis of the institution, the nature of the aid, and the manner in which the aid may be used.

. . .

III

As is often the case, it is the effect of the statute, rather than its purpose, that creates Establishment Clause problems....

A

The majority's holding that the AFLA is not unconstitutional on its face marks a sharp departure from our precedents. While aid programs providing nonmonetary, verifiably secular aid have been upheld notwithstanding the indirect effect they might have on the allocation of an institution's own funds for religious activities, ... direct cash subsidies have always required much closer scrutiny into the expected and potential uses of the funds, and much greater guarantees that the funds would not be used inconsistently with the Establishment Clause....

Notwithstanding the fact that government funds are paying for religious organizations to teach and counsel impressionable adolescents on a highly sensitive subject of considerable religious significance, often on the premises of a church or parochial school and without any effort to remove religious symbols from the sites, the majority concludes that the AFLA is not facially invalid. . . .

. . .

. . . There is a very real and important difference between running a soup kitchen or a hospital, and counseling pregnant teenagers on how to make the difficult decisions facing them. The risk of advancing religion at public expense, and of creating an appearance that the government is endorsing the medium and the message, is much greater when the religious organization is directly engaged in pedagogy, with the express intent of shaping belief and changing behavior, than where it is neutrally dispensing medication, food, or shelter.

There is also, of course, a fundamental difference between government's employing religion *because* of its unique appeal to a higher authority and the transcendental nature of its message, and government's enlisting the aid of religiously committed individuals or organizations without regard to their sectarian motivation. . . .

. . .

IV

While it is evident that the AFLA does not pass muster under Lemon's "effects" prong, the unconstitutionality of the statute becomes even more apparent when we consider the unprecedented degree of entanglement between Church and State required to prevent subsidizing the advancement of religion with AFLA funds. . . .

. . .

V

. . . I trust . . . that . . . the District Court will not . . . read into the Court's decision a suggestion that the AFLA has been constitutionally implemented by the Government, for the majority deliberately eschews any review of the facts. After . . . further proceedings . . . it may well decide, as I would today, that the AFLA as a whole indeed has been unconstitutionally applied.

NOTES AND QUESTIONS

1. One of the majority's arguments is that, if AFLA was invalid simply because it funded the activities of religious organizations, then government financial aid to hospitals run by religious orders would also be prohibited by the Establishment Clause. Does the majority see no difference "between running a soup kitchen or hospital, and counseling pregnant teenagers"?

2. The majority relies most heavily on the cases involving government funding of institutions of higher learning for the conclusion that the statute is only invalid to the extent it funds grants to "pervasively

sectarian" religious programs. Do you agree that the cases dealing with government fundings of primary and secondary education are different because most of such aid flows to religious schools that are "pervasively sectarian." Do you think that the elementary and high school funding cases are more relevant than the college aid cases because the funds are being used to "teach and counsel impressionable adolescents"?

3. When the case goes back for a new trial, what should the lower court do if the evidence shows that some of the funded programs are being used for "religious indoctrination"? Would a church-affiliated program be "perversely sectarian" if it were conducted on church premises, was staffed by clergy, and consistently counseled pregnant teens not to have abortions under any circumstances because abortions were immoral?

AGOSTINI v. FELTON

Supreme Court of the United States, 1997.
521 U.S. 203, 117 S.Ct. 1997, 138 L.Ed.2d 391.

JUSTICE O'CONNOR delivered the opinion of the Court.

In Aguilar v. Felton, 473 U.S. 402 (1985), this Court held that the Establishment Clause of the First Amendment barred the city of New York from sending public school teachers into parochial schools to provide remedial education to disadvantaged children pursuant to a congressionally mandated program. On remand, the District Court for the Eastern District of New York entered a permanent injunction reflecting our ruling. Twelve years later, petitioners—the parties bound by that injunction—seek relief from its operation. Petitioners maintain that *Aguilar* cannot be squared with our intervening Establishment Clause jurisprudence and ask that we explicitly recognize what our more recent cases already dictate: *Aguilar* is no longer good law. We agree with petitioners that *Aguilar* is not consistent with our subsequent Establishment Clause decisions . . .

I

In 1965, Congress enacted Title I of the Elementary and Secondary Education Act of 1965 . . . to "provid[e] full educational opportunity to every child regardless of economic background." . . . Toward that end, Title I channels federal funds, through the States, to "local educational agencies" (LEA's). . . . The LEA's spend these funds to provide remedial education, guidance, and job counseling to eligible students. . . . Title I funds must be made available to all eligible children, regardless of whether they attend public schools, . . . and the services provided to children attending private schools must be "equitable in comparison to services and other benefits for public school children." . . .

An LEA providing services to children enrolled in private schools is subject to a number of constraints that are not imposed when it provides aid to public schools. Title I services may be provided only to those private school students eligible for aid, and cannot be used to provide services on a "school-wide" basis. . . . In addition, the LEA must retain complete control over Title I funds; retain title to all materials used to provide Title I services; and provide those services through public employees or other persons independent of the private school and any religious institution.... The Title I services themselves must be "secular, neutral, and nonideological," ... and must "supplement, and in no case supplant, the level of services" already provided by the private school....

Petitioner Board of Education of the City of New York (Board), an LEA, first applied for Title I funds in 1966 and has grappled ever since with how to provide Title I services to the private school students within its jurisdiction. Approximately 10% of the total number of students eligible for Title I services are private school students. Recognizing that more than 90% of the private schools within the Board's jurisdiction are sectarian, ... the Board initially arranged to transport children to public schools for after-school Title I instruction. But this enterprise was largely unsuccessful. Attendance was poor, teachers and children were tired, and parents were concerned for the safety of their children.... The Board then moved the after-school instruction onto private school campuses, as Congress had contemplated when it enacted Title I.... After this program also yielded mixed results, the Board implemented the plan we evaluated in Aguilar v. Felton ...

That plan called for the provision of Title I services on private school premises during school hours. Under the plan, only public employees could serve as Title I instructors and counselors.... Assignments to private schools were made on a voluntary basis and without regard to the religious affiliation of the employee or the wishes of the private school....

Before any public employee could provide Title I instruction at a private school, she would be given a detailed set of written and oral instructions emphasizing the secular purpose of Title I and setting out the rules to be followed to ensure that this purpose was not compromised.... All religious symbols were to be removed from classrooms used for Title I services.... The rules acknowledged that it might be necessary for Title I teachers to consult with a student's regular classroom teacher to assess the student's particular needs and progress, but admonished instructors to limit those consultations to mutual professional concerns regarding the student's education....

In 1978, six federal taxpayers ... sued the Board in the District Court for the Eastern District of New York. Respondents sought declaratory and injunctive relief, claiming that the Board's Title I program violated the Establishment Clause.... [T]his Court [held that] the Board's Title I program necessitated an "excessive entanglement of church and state in the administration of [Title I] benefits." ...

The Board, like other LEA's across the United States, modified its Title I program so it could continue serving those students who attended private religious schools. Rather than offer Title I instruction to parochial school students at their schools, the Board reverted to its prior practice of providing instruction at public school sites, at leased sites, and in mobile instructional units (essentially vans converted into classrooms) parked near the sectarian school. The Board also offered computer-aided instruction, which could be provided "on premises" because it did not require public employees to be physically present on the premises of a religious school.

It is not disputed that the additional costs of complying with *Aguilar*'s mandate are significant. Since the 1986–1987 school year, the Board has spent over $100 million providing computer-aided instruction, leasing sites and mobile instructional units, and transporting students to those sites.... These "*Aguilar* costs" ... reduce the amount of Title I money an LEA has available for remedial education, and LEA's have had to cut back on the number of students who receive Title I benefits....

In ... 1995, ... the Board and a new group of parents of parochial school students entitled to Title I services filed motions in the District Court seeking relief ... from the permanent injunction entered ... in *Aguilar*....

II

. . .

[The question is] whether our later Establishment Clause cases have so undermined *Aguilar* that it is no longer good law. We now turn to that inquiry.

III

A

In order to evaluate whether *Aguilar* has been eroded by our subsequent Establishment Clause cases, it is necessary to understand the rationale upon which *Aguilar*, as well as its companion case, School Dist. of Grand Rapids v. Ball, 473 U.S. 373 (1985), rested.

. . .

The Court found that the program violated the Establishment Clause's prohibition against "government-financed or government-sponsored indoctrination into the beliefs of a particular religious faith" in at least three ways.... First, ... the Court observed that "the teachers participating in the programs may become involved in intentionally or inadvertently inculcating particular religious tenets or beliefs." ...

... [A] majority found " 'substantial risk' " that teachers—even those who were not employed by the private schools—might "subtly (or overtly) conform their instruction to the [pervasively sectarian] environment in which they [taught]." ...

The presence of public teachers on parochial school grounds had a second, related impermissible effect: It created a "graphic symbol of the 'concert or union or dependency' of church and state," ...

Third, the Court found that the Shared Time program impermissibly financed religious indoctrination by subsidizing "the primary religious mission of the institutions affected." ... The Court separated its prior decisions evaluating programs that aided the secular activities of religious institutions into two categories: those in which it concluded that the aid resulted in an effect that was "indirect, remote, or incidental" (and upheld the aid); and those in which it concluded that the aid resulted in "a direct and substantial advancement of the sectarian enterprise" (and invalidated the aid).... The *Ball* Court ... placed no weight on the fact that the program was provided to the student rather than to the school. Nor was the impermissible effect mitigated by the fact that the program only supplemented the courses offered by the parochial schools....

The New York City Title I program challenged in *Aguilar* closely resembled the Shared Time program struck down in *Ball*, ...

Distilled to essentials, the Court's conclusion that the Shared Time program in *Ball* had the impermissible effect of advancing religion rested on three assumptions: (i) any public employee who works on the premises of a religious school is presumed to inculcate religion in her work; (ii) the presence of public employees on private school premises creates a symbolic union between church and state; and (iii) any and all public aid that directly aids the educational function of religious schools impermissibly finances religious indoctrination, even if the aid reaches such schools as a consequence of private decisionmaking....

B

Our more recent cases have undermined the assumptions upon which *Ball* and *Aguilar* relied. To be sure, the general principles we use to evaluate whether government aid violates the Establishment Clause have not changed since *Aguilar* was decided. For example, we continue to ask whether the government acted with the purpose of advancing or inhibiting religion, and the nature of that inquiry has remained largely unchanged.... Likewise, we continue to explore whether the aid has the "effect" of advancing or inhibiting religion. What has changed since we decided *Ball* and *Aguilar* is our understanding of the criteria used to assess whether aid to religion has an impermissible effect.

1

As we have repeatedly recognized, government inculcation of religious beliefs has the impermissible effect of advancing religion. Our cases subsequent to *Aguilar* have, however, modified in two significant respects the approach we use to assess indoctrination. First, we have abandoned the presumption ... that the placement of public employees on parochial school grounds inevitably results in the impermissible effect of state-sponsored indoctrination or constitutes a symbolic union between government and religion. In Zobrest v. Catalina Foothills School Dist., 509 U.S. 1 (1993), ... a deaf student ... sought to bring his state-employed sign-language interpreter with him to his Roman Catholic high school. We held that this was permissible, expressly disavowing the notion that "the Establishment Clause [laid] down [an] absolute bar to the placing of a public employee in a sectarian school." ...

. . .

Second, we have departed from the rule relied on in *Ball* that all government aid that directly aids the educational function of religious schools is invalid. In Witters v. Washington Dept. of Servs. for Blind, 474

U.S. 481 (1986), we held that the Establishment Clause did not bar a State from issuing a vocational tuition grant to a blind person who wished to use the grant to attend a Christian college and become a pastor, missionary, or youth director. Even though the grant recipient clearly would use the money to obtain religious education, we observed that the tuition grants were " 'made available generally without regard to the sectarian-nonsectarian, or public-nonpublic nature of the institution benefited.' " ...

Zobrest and *Witters* make clear that, under current law, the Shared Time program in *Ball* and New York City's Title I program in *Aguilar* will not, as a matter of law, be deemed to have the effect of advancing religion through indoctrination. Indeed, each of the premises upon which we relied in *Ball* to reach a contrary conclusion is no longer valid. First, there is no reason to presume that, simply because she enters a parochial school classroom, a full-time public employee such as a Title I teacher will depart from her assigned duties and instructions and embark on religious indoctrination, any more than there was a reason in *Zobrest* to think an interpreter would inculcate religion by altering her translation of classroom lectures....

... *Zobrest* also repudiates *Ball*'s assumption that the presence of Title I teachers in parochial school classrooms will, without more, create the impression of a "symbolic union" between church and state.... We do not see any perceptible (let alone dispositive) difference in the degree of symbolic union between a student receiving remedial instruction in a classroom on his sectarian school's campus and one receiving instruction in a van parked just at the school's curbside....

. . .

2

Although we examined in *Witters* and *Zobrest* the criteria by which an aid program identifies its beneficiaries, we did so solely to assess whether any use of that aid to indoctrinate religion could be attributed to the State. A number of our Establishment Clause cases have found that the criteria used for identifying beneficiaries are relevant in a second respect, apart from enabling a court to evaluate whether the program subsidizes religion. Specifically, the criteria might themselves have the effect of advancing religion by creating a financial incentive to undertake religious indoctrination.... This incentive is not present, however, where the aid is allocated on the basis of neutral, secular criteria that neither favor nor disfavor religion, and is made available to both religious and secular beneficiaries on a nondiscriminatory basis....

In *Ball* and *Aguilar*, the Court gave this consideration no weight. Before and since those decisions, we have sustained programs that provided aid to all eligible children regardless of where they attended school....

. . .

... We ... hold that a federally funded program providing supplemental, remedial instruction to disadvantaged children on a neutral basis is not invalid under the Establishment Clause when such instruction is given on the premises of sectarian schools by government employees pursuant to a program containing safeguards such as those present here.... Accordingly, we must acknowledge that *Aguilar*, as well as the portion of *Ball* addressing Grand Rapids' Shared Time program, are no longer good law.

· · ·

JUSTICE SOUTER with whom JUSTICE STEVENS and JUSTICE GINSBURG join, and with whom JUSTICE BREYER joins as to Part II, dissenting.

· · ·

I

· · ·

... I believe *Aguilar* was a correct and sensible decision.... The State is forbidden to subsidize religion directly and is just as surely forbidden to act in any way that could reasonably be viewed as religious endorsement....

... [T]he flat ban on subsidization ... expresses the hard lesson ... that religions supported by governments are compromised just as surely as the religious freedom of dissenters is burdened when the government supports religion.... The human tendency, of course, is to forget the hard lessons, and to overlook the history of governmental partnership with religion when a cause is worthy, and bureaucrats have programs. That tendency to forget is the reason for having the Establishment Clause (along with the Constitution's other structural and libertarian guarantees), in the hope of stopping the corrosion before it starts.

· · ·

What ... was significant in *Aguilar* and *Ball* about the placement of state-paid teachers into the physical and social settings of the religious schools was not only the consequent temptation of some of those teachers to reflect the schools' religious missions in the rhetoric of their instruction, with a resulting need for monitoring and the certainty of entanglement.... What was so remarkable was that the schemes in issue assumed a teaching responsibility indistinguishable from the responsibility of the schools themselves. The obligation of primary and secondary schools to teach reading necessarily extends to teaching those who are having a hard time at it, and the same is true of math. Calling some classes remedial does not distinguish their subjects from the schools' basic subjects, however inadequately the schools may have been addressing them.

What was true of the Title I scheme as struck down in *Aguilar* will be just as true when New York reverts to the old practices with the Court's approval after today. There is simply no line that can be drawn between the instruction paid for at taxpayers' expense and the instruction in any subject that is not identified as formally religious. While it would be an obvious sham, say, to channel cash to religious schools to be credited only against the expense of "secular" instruction, the line between "supplemental" and general education is likewise impossible to draw. If a State may constitutionally enter the schools to teach in the manner in question, it must in constitutional principle be free to assume, or assume payment for, the entire cost of instruction provided in any ostensibly secular subject in any religious school. This Court explicitly recognized this in *Ball* . . .

It may be objected that there is some subsidy in remedial education even when it takes place off the religious premises, some subsidy, that is, even in the way New York City has administered the Title I program after *Aguilar*. In these circumstances, too, what the State does, the religious school need not do; the schools save money and the program makes it easier for them to survive and concentrate their resources on their religious objectives. This argument may, of course, prove too much, but if it is not thought strong enough to bar even off-premises aid in teaching the basics to religious school pupils (an issue not before the Court in *Aguilar* or today), it does nothing to undermine the sense of drawing a line between remedial teaching on and off-premises. The off-premises teaching is arguably less likely to open the door to relieving religious schools of their responsibilities for secular subjects simply because these schools are less likely (and presumably legally unable) to dispense with those subjects from their curriculums or to make patently significant cut-backs in basic teaching within the schools to offset the outside instruction; if the aid is delivered outside of the schools, it is less likely to supplant some of what would otherwise go on inside them and to subsidize what remains. On top of that, the difference in the degree of reasonably perceptible endorsement is substantial. Sharing the teaching responsibilities within a school having religious objectives is far more likely to telegraph approval of the school's mission than keeping the State's distance would do. . . . When, moreover, the aid goes overwhelmingly to one religious denomination, minimal contact between state and church is the less likely to feed the resentment of other religions that would like access to public money for their own worthy projects.

In sum, if a line is to be drawn short of barring all state aid to religious schools for teaching standard subjects, the *Aguilar–Ball* line was a sensible one capable of principled adherence. It is no less sound, and no less necessary, today.

II

The Court today ignores this doctrine and claims that recent cases rejected the elemental assumptions underlying *Aguilar* and much of *Ball*. But the Court errs. . . .

A

. . .

In *Zobrest* the Court did indeed recognize that the Establishment Clause lays down no absolute bar to placing public employees in a sectarian school . . . but the rejection of such a per se rule was hinged expressly on the nature of the employee's job. . . . The signer could . . . be seen as more like a hearing aid than a teacher, and the signing could not be understood as an opportunity to inject religious content in what was supposed to be secular instruction ... employee's presence in the sectarian school does not violate the Establishment Clause....

. . .

B

. . .

Ball did not establish that "any and all" such aid to religious schools necessarily violates the Establishment Clause. It held that the Shared Time program subsidized the religious functions of the parochial schools by taking over a significant portion of their responsibility for teaching secular subjects....

. . .

... In *Zobrest* and *Witters*, ... individual students were themselves applicants for individual benefits on a scale that could not amount to a systemic supplement. But under Title I, a local educational agency (which in New York City is the Board of Education) may receive federal funding by proposing programs approved to serve individual students who meet the criteria of need, which it then uses to provide such programs at the religious schools; students eligible for such programs may not apply directly for Title I funds. The aid, accordingly, is not even formally aid to the individual students (and even formally individual aid must be seen as aid to a school system when so many individuals receive it that it becomes a significant feature of the system) ...

In sum, nothing since *Ball* and *Aguilar* and before this case has eroded the distinction between "direct and substantial" and "indirect and incidental." That principled line is being breached only here and now.

C

The Court notes that aid programs providing benefits solely to religious groups may be constitutionally suspect, while aid allocated under neutral, secular criteria is less likely to have the effect of advancing religion.... If a scheme of government aid results in support for religion in some substantial degree, or in endorsement of its value, the formal neutrality of the scheme does not render the Establishment Clause helpless or the holdings in *Aguilar* and *Ball* inapposite.

. . .

[A dissenting opinion by Justice Ginsburg has been omitted.]

NOTES AND QUESTIONS

1. The major arguments about aid to church-related schools are simple enough. Proponents of governmental aid have argued that aid to church-related schools does not violate the Establishment Clause because those schools serve an important secular function. They teach mathematics, English, history, government and the like. Just as the government can include church-owned hospitals in a general program of

subsidizing all private hospitals, it can include church-owned schools in a general program of aid to all private schools that teach secular subjects. Opponents of governmental aid have argued that church-related schools do not separate their functions of teaching religious and secular subjects. Any aid to support the educational function of church-related schools involves government in paying for the cost of religious education. Thus aid to church-related schools violates the Establishment Clause because government is paying the cost for propagating sectarian religious views.

2.   The Court has not squarely adopted either of the opposing views of the nature of aid to church-related schools. Since 1947, when the Court sustained a program of paying for transportation to private schools in the *Everson* case, results have often been reached in individual cases by the closest of votes. Wherever the line between permitted and prohibited aid is drawn, it has been difficult to defend the result in cases at the margin. *Aguilar*, for example, permitted the state to provide remedial instruction in mobile classrooms adjacent to the religious school, but not in the religious school itself. Isn't the majority right that it didn't make sense to require New York to "spend millions of dollars on mobile instructional units and leased sites when it could instead be spending that money to give economically disadvantaged children a better chance at success in life"? Would it make sense to *forbid* New York to furnish instructors to religious schools whether on adjacent sites or in the religious school?

3.   In the realm of higher education, the Court has permitted considerably more leeway for aid to church-related schools. This was initially explained on the ground that religious indoctrination did not permeate all areas of education in the colleges as it did in elementary and secondary schools. Would a better explanation be that church-related schools are in the minority among private institutions of higher education and that disputes about aid to private colleges are less divisive along religious lines?

In Roemer v. Board of Public Works, 426 U.S. 736 (1976), a program of aid to private colleges was upheld. Maryland provided for general grants of money to private colleges, including colleges that were religiously affiliated. In granting money to religious colleges, there was a prohibition on using the money for "sectarian purposes." There was no majority opinion. Justice White, joined by Justice Rehnquist, approved the financing program because he would have approved an identical program for financing primary and secondary education. Justice Blackmun, joined by Chief Justice Burger and Justice Powell, found the fact that aid was being given at the college level crucial because, among other things, more than two-thirds of the private colleges were non-religious, creating less danger of political divisiveness when the state legislature decided upon the level of aid. The four dissenters emphasized that the state was giving general broad grants of money to religious schools that would finance their general operation despite the prohibition on use for "sectarian purposes," and that the colleges aided had compulsory courses in theology, so that the state was financing religious education. As is so often true when there is no majority opinion (see footnote

Chapter 5, p. 107), a majority of the Court rejected the crucial distinction—colleges as opposed to other schools—that governed the decision.

ZELMAN v. SIMMONS–HARRIS

536 U.S. 639, 122 S.Ct. 2460, 153 L.Ed.2d 604 (2002).

CHIEF JUSTICE REHNQUIST delivered the opinion of the Court.

The State of Ohio has established a pilot program designed to provide educational choices to families with children who reside in the Cleveland City School District. The question presented is whether this program offends the Establishment Clause of the United States Constitution. We hold that it does not.

There are more than 75,000 children enrolled in the Cleveland City School District. The majority of these children are from low-income and minority families. Few of these families enjoy the means to send their children to any school other than an inner-city public school. For more than a generation, however, Cleveland's public schools have been among the worst performing public schools in the Nation. In 1995, a Federal District Court ... placed the entire Cleveland school district under state control.... The district had failed to meet any of the 18 state standards for minimal acceptable performance. Only 1 in 10 ninth graders could pass a basic proficiency examination, and students at all levels performed at a dismal rate compared with students in other Ohio public schools. More than two-thirds of high school students either dropped or failed out before graduation. Of those students who managed to reach their senior year, one of every four still failed to graduate. Of those students who did graduate, few could read, write, or compute at levels comparable to their counterparts in other cities.

It is against this backdrop that Ohio enacted, among other initiatives, its Pilot Project Scholarship Program ... The program provides financial assistance to families in any Ohio school district that is or has been "under federal court order requiring supervision and operational management of the district by the state superintendent." ... Cleveland is the only Ohio school district to fall within that category.

The program provides two basic kinds of assistance to parents of children in a covered district. First, the program provides tuition aid for students in kindergarten through third grade, expanding each year through eighth grade, to attend a participating public or private school of their parent's choosing.... Second, the program provides tutorial aid for students who choose to remain enrolled in public school....

The tuition aid portion of the program is designed to provide educational choices to parents who reside in a covered district. Any private school, whether religious or nonreligious, may participate in the program and accept program students so long as the school is located within the boundaries of a covered district and meets statewide educational standards.... Participating private schools must agree not to discriminate on the basis of race, religion, or ethnic background, or to "advocate or foster unlawful behavior or teach hatred of any person or group on the basis of race, ethnicity, national origin, or religion." ...

Any public school located in a school district adjacent to the covered district may also participate in the program.... Adjacent public schools are eligible to receive a $2,250 tuition grant for each program student accepted in addition to the full amount of per-pupil state funding attributable to each additional student.... All participating schools, whether public or private, are required to accept students in accordance with rules and procedures established by the state superintendent....

Tuition aid is distributed to parents according to financial need. Families with incomes below 200% of the poverty line are given priority and are eligible to receive 90% of private school tuition up to $2,250.... For these lowest-income families, participating private schools may not charge a parental co-payment greater than $250.... For all other families, the program pays 75% of tuition costs, up to $1,875, with no co-payment cap. ... These families receive tuition aid only if the number of available scholarships exceeds the number of low-income children who choose to participate.... Where tuition aid is spent depends solely upon where parents who receive tuition aid choose to enroll their child. If parents choose a private school, checks are made payable to the parents who then endorse the checks over to the chosen school....

The tutorial aid portion of the program provides tutorial assistance through grants to any student in a covered district who chooses to remain in public school. Parents arrange for registered tutors to provide assistance to their children and then submit bills for those services to the State for payment.... Students from low-income families receive 90% of the amount charged for such assistance up to $360. All other students receive 75% of that amount.... The number of tutorial assistance grants offered to students in a covered district must equal the number of tuition aid scholarships provided to students enrolled at participating private or adjacent public schools....

The program has been in operation within the Cleveland City School District since the 1996–1997 school year. In the 1999–2000 school year, 56 private schools participated in the program, 46 (or 82%) of which had a religious affiliation. None of the public schools in districts adjacent to Cleveland have elected to participate. More than 3,700 students participated in the scholarship program, most of whom (96%) enrolled in religiously affiliated schools. Sixty percent of these students were from families at or below the poverty line. In the 1998–1999 school year, approximately 1,400 Cleveland public school students received tutorial aid. This number was expected to double during the 1999–2000 school year.

· · ·

In July 1999, respondents filed this action in United States District Court, seeking to enjoin the reenacted program on the ground that it violated the Establishment Clause of the United States Constitution.... In December 1999, the District Court granted summary judgment for respondents. In December 2000, a divided panel of the Court of Appeals affirmed the judgment of the District Court ... We ... now reverse the Court of Appeals.

The Establishment Clause of the First Amendment, applied to the States through the Fourteenth Amendment, prevents a State from enacting laws that have the "purpose" or "effect" of advancing or inhibiting religion. *Agostini v. Felton,* 521 U.S. 203, 222–223 (1997) . . . There is no dispute that the program challenged here was enacted for the valid secular purpose of providing educational assistance to poor children in a demonstrably failing public school system. Thus, the question presented is whether the Ohio program nonetheless has the forbidden "effect" of advancing or inhibiting religion.

To answer that question, our decisions have drawn a consistent distinction between government programs that provide aid directly to religious schools . . . and programs of true private choice, in which government aid reaches religious schools only as a result of the genuine and independent choices of private individuals . . . While our jurisprudence with respect to the constitutionality of direct aid programs has "changed significantly" over the past two decades, . . . our jurisprudence with respect to true private choice programs has remained consistent and unbroken. Three times we have confronted Establishment Clause challenges to neutral government programs that provide aid directly to a broad class of individuals, who, in turn, direct the aid to religious schools or institutions of their own choosing. Three times we have rejected such challenges.

In Mueller [v. Allen, 463 U.S. 388 (1983)], we rejected an Establishment Clause challenge to a Minnesota program authorizing tax deductions for various educational expenses, including private school tuition costs, even though the great majority of the program's beneficiaries (96%) were parents of children in religious schools. . . . We . . . found it irrelevant to the constitutional inquiry that the vast majority of beneficiaries were parents of children in religious schools . . . That the program was one of true private choice, with no evidence that the State deliberately skewed incentives toward religious schools, was sufficient for the program to survive scrutiny under the Establishment Clause.

In Witters [v. Washington Dept. of Servs. for Blind, 474 U.S. 481 (1986)], we used identical reasoning to reject an Establishment Clause challenge to a vocational scholarship program that provided tuition aid to a student studying at a religious institution to become a pastor. . . .

Five Members of the Court, in separate opinions, emphasized the general rule from *Mueller* that the amount of government aid channeled to religious institutions by individual aid recipients was not relevant to the constitutional inquiry. . . . Our holding thus rested not on whether few or many recipients chose to expend government aid at a religious school but, rather, on whether recipients generally were empowered to direct the aid to schools or institutions of their own choosing.

Finally, in Zobrest [v. Catalina Foothills School Dist., 509 U.S. 1 (1993)], we applied *Mueller* and *Witters* to reject an Establishment Clause challenge to a federal program that permitted sign-language interpreters to assist deaf children enrolled in religious schools. Reviewing our earlier decisions, we stated that "government programs that neutrally provide benefits to a broad class of citizens defined without reference to religion are not readily subject to an Establishment Clause challenge." ...

. . .

Mueller, Witters, and *Zobrest* thus make clear that where a government aid program is neutral with respect to religion, and provides assistance directly to a broad class of citizens who, in turn, direct government aid to religious schools wholly as a result of their own genuine and independent private choice, the program is not readily subject to challenge under the Establishment Clause. A program that shares these features permits government aid to reach religious institutions only by way of the deliberate choices of numerous individual recipients. The incidental advancement of a religious mission, or the perceived endorsement of a religious message, is reasonably attributable to the individual recipient, not to the government, whose role ends with the disbursement of benefits.... [W]e have never found a program of true private choice to offend the Establishment Clause.

We believe that the program challenged here is a program of true private choice, consistent with *Mueller, Witters,* and *Zobrest*, and thus constitutional. As was true in those cases, the Ohio program is neutral in all respects toward religion. It is part of a general and multifaceted undertaking by the State of Ohio to provide educational opportunities to the children of a failed school district. It confers educational assistance directly to a broad class of individuals defined without reference to religion, *i.e.,* any parent of a school-age child who resides in the Cleveland City School District. The program permits the participation of *all* schools within the district, religious or nonreligious. Adjacent public schools also may participate and have a financial incentive to do so. Program benefits are available to participating families on neutral terms, with no reference to religion. The only preference stated anywhere in the program is a preference for low-income families, who receive greater assistance and are given priority for admission at participating schools.

There are no "financial incentive[s]" that "ske[w]" the program toward religious schools. *Witters, supra,* at 487–488. Such incentives "[are] not present ... where the aid is allocated on the basis of neutral, secular criteria that neither favor nor disfavor religion, and is made available to both religious and secular beneficiaries on a nondiscriminatory basis." *Agostini, supra,* at 231....

Respondents suggest that even without a financial incentive for parents to choose a religious school, the program creates a "public perception that the State is endorsing religious practices and beliefs." ... But we have repeatedly recognized that no reasonable observer would think a neutral program of private choice, where state aid reaches religious schools solely as a result of the numerous independent decisions of private individuals, carries with it the *imprimatur* of government endorsement.... The argument is particularly misplaced here since "the reasonable observer in the endorsement inquiry must be deemed aware" of the "history and context" underlying a challenged program.... Any objective observer familiar with the full history and context of the Ohio program would reasonably view it as one aspect of a broader undertaking to assist poor children in failed schools, not as an endorsement of religious schooling in general.

There also is no evidence that the program fails to provide genuine opportunities for Cleveland parents to select secular educational options for their school-age children. Cleveland schoolchildren enjoy a range of educational choices: They may remain in public school as before, remain in public school with publicly funded tutoring aid, obtain a scholarship and choose a religious school, obtain a scholarship and choose a nonreligious private school, enroll in a community school, or enroll in a magnet school. That 46 of the 56 private schools now participating in the program are religious schools does not condemn it as a violation of the Establishment Clause. The Establishment Clause question is whether Ohio is coercing parents into sending their children to religious schools, and that question must be answered by evaluating *all* options Ohio provides Cleveland schoolchildren, only one of which is to obtain a program scholarship and then choose a religious school.

... It is true that 82% of Cleveland's participating private schools are religious schools, but it is also true that 81% of private schools in Ohio are religious schools. To attribute constitutional significance to this figure, moreover, would lead to the absurd result that a neutral school-choice program might be permissible in some parts of Ohio, such as Columbus, where a lower percentage of private schools are religious schools, but not in inner-city Cleveland, where Ohio has deemed such programs most sorely needed, but where the preponderance of religious schools happens to be greater. Likewise, an identical private choice program might be constitutional in some States, such as Maine or Utah, where less than 45% of private schools are religious schools, but not in other States, such as Nebraska or Kansas, where over 90% of private schools are religious schools.

... The constitutionality of a neutral educational aid program simply does not turn on whether and why, in a particular area, at a particular time, most private schools are run by religious organizations, or most recipients choose to use the aid at a religious school. . . .

. . .

Respondents finally claim that we should look to Committee for Public Ed. & Religious Liberty v. Nyquist, 413 U.S. 756 (1973), to decide these cases. We disagree for two reasons. First, the program in *Nyquist* was quite different from the program challenged here. *Nyquist* involved a New York program that gave a package of benefits exclusively to private schools and the parents of private school enrollees. Although the program was enacted for ostensibly secular purposes, ... we found that its "function" was *"unmistakably* to provide desired financial support for nonpublic, sectarian institutions," ... Its genesis, we said, was that private religious schools faced "increasingly grave fiscal problems." ... The program thus provided direct money grants to religious schools. ...It provided tax benefits "unrelated to the amount of money actually expended by any parent on tuition," ensuring a windfall to parents of children in religious schools. . . . It similarly provided tuition reimbursements designed explicitly to "offe[r] ... an incentive to parents to send their children to sectarian schools." ... Indeed, the program flatly prohibited the participation of any public school, or parent of any public school enrollee.... Ohio's program shares none of these features.

Second, were there any doubt that the program challenged in *Nyquist* is far removed from the program challenged here, we expressly reserved judgment with respect to "a case involving some form of public assistance (*e.g.*, scholarships) made available generally without regard to the sectarian-nonsectarian, or public-nonpublic nature of the institution benefited." ... [W]e now hold that *Nyquist* does not govern neutral educational assistance programs that, like the program here, offer aid directly to a broad class of individual recipients defined without regard to religion.

In sum, the Ohio program is entirely neutral with respect to religion. It provides benefits directly to a wide spectrum of individuals, defined only by financial need and residence in a particular school district. It permits such individuals to exercise genuine choice among options public and private, secular and religious. The program is therefore a program of true private choice. In keeping with an unbroken line of decisions rejecting challenges to similar programs, we hold that the program does not offend the Establishment Clause.

. . .

JUSTICE O'CONNOR, concurring.

... While I join the Court's opinion, I write separately for two reasons. First, although the Court takes an important step, I do not believe that today's decision, when considered in light of other long-standing government programs that impact religious organizations and our prior Establishment Clause jurisprudence, marks a dramatic break from the past. Second, given the emphasis the Court places on verifying that parents of voucher students in religious schools have exercised "true private choice," I think it is worth elaborating on the Court's conclusion that this inquiry should consider all reasonable educational alternatives to religious schools that are available to parents. To do otherwise is to ignore how the educational system in Cleveland actually functions.

I

These cases are different from prior indirect aid cases in part because a significant portion of the funds appropriated for the voucher program reach religious schools without restrictions on the use of these funds. The share of public resources that reach religious schools is not, however, as significant as respondents suggest....

... Even if one assumes that all voucher students came from low-income families and that each voucher student used up the entire $2,250 voucher, at most $8.2 million of public funds flowed to religious schools under the voucher program in 1999–2000....

Although $8.2 million is no small sum, it pales in comparison to the amount of funds that federal, state, and local governments already provide religious institutions. Religious organizations may qualify for exemptions from the federal corporate income tax, ... and property taxes in all 50 States, ... clergy qualify for a federal tax break on income used for housing expenses ... In addition, the Federal Government provides individuals, corporations, trusts, and estates a tax deduction for charitable contributions to qualified religious groups ... Finally, the Federal Government and certain state governments provide tax credits for educational expenses, many of which are spent on education at religious schools....

.   .   .

... Federal dollars also reach religiously affiliated organizations through public health programs such as Medicare, ... and Medicaid, ..., through educational programs such as the Pell Grant program, ... and the G. I. Bill of Rights, ... and through child care programs such as the Child Care and Development Block Grant Program ...

.   .   .

Against this background, the support that the Cleveland voucher program provides religious institutions is neither substantial nor atypical of existing government programs....

II

Nor does today's decision signal a major departure from this Court's prior Establishment Clause jurisprudence. A central tool in our analysis of cases in this area has been the *Lemon* test....

The Court's opinion in these cases focuses on a narrow question related to the *Lemon* test: how to apply the primary effects prong in indirect aid cases? ... Courts are instructed to consider two factors: first, whether the program administers aid in a neutral fashion, without differentiation based on the religious status of beneficiaries or providers of services; second, and more importantly, whether beneficiaries of indirect aid have a genuine choice among religious and nonreligious organizations when determining the organization to which they will direct that aid. If the answer to either query is "no," the program should be struck down under the Establishment Clause.

Justice Souter portrays this inquiry as a departure from *Everson*. A fair reading of the holding in that case suggests quite the opposite.... How else could the Court have upheld a state program to provide students transportation to public and religious schools alike? What the Court clarifies in these cases is that the Establishment Clause also requires that state aid flowing to religious organizations through the hands of beneficiaries must do so only at the direction of those beneficiaries. Such a refinement of the *Lemon* test surely does not betray *Everson*.

III

There is little question in my mind that the Cleveland voucher program is neutral as between religious schools and nonreligious schools....

I do not agree that the nonreligious schools have failed to provide Cleveland parents reasonable alternatives to religious schools in the voucher program. . . .

. . .

In my view the more significant finding in these cases is that Cleveland parents who use vouchers to send their children to religious private schools do so as a result of true private choice. . . .

I find the Court's answer to the question whether parents of students eligible for vouchers have a genuine choice between religious and nonreligious schools persuasive. . . .

. . .

Based on the reasoning in the Court's opinion, which is consistent with the realities of the Cleveland educational system, I am persuaded that the Cleveland voucher program affords parents of eligible children genuine nonreligious options and is consistent with the Establishment Clause.

JUSTICE THOMAS, concurring.

. . .

. . . Today's decision properly upholds the program as constitutional, and I join it in full.

I

. . . I agree with the Court that Ohio's program easily passes muster under our stringent test, but, as a matter of first principles, I question whether this test should be applied to the States.

. . .

. . . When rights are incorporated against the States through the Fourteenth Amendment they should advance, not constrain, individual liberty.

. . . Thus, while the Federal Government may "make no law respecting an establishment of religion," the States may pass laws that include or touch on religious matters so long as these laws do not impede free exercise rights or any other individual religious liberty interest. By considering the particular religious liberty right alleged to be invaded by a State, federal courts can strike a proper balance between the demands of the Fourteenth Amendment on the one hand and the federalism prerogatives of States on the other.

. . . I can accept that the Fourteenth Amendment protects religious liberty rights. But I cannot accept its use to oppose neutral programs of school choice through the incorporation of the Establishment Clause. There would be a tragic irony in converting the Fourteenth Amendment's guarantee of individual liberty into a prohibition on the exercise of educational choice.

II

. . .

While the romanticized ideal of universal public education resonates with the cognoscenti who oppose vouchers, poor urban families just want the best education for their children, who will certainly need it to function in our high-tech and advanced society. . . . If society cannot end racial discrimination, at least it can arm minorities with the education to defend themselves from some of discrimination's effects.

. . . [S]chool choice programs that involve religious schools appear unconstitutional only to those who would twist the Fourteenth Amendment against itself by expansively incorporating the Establishment Clause. Converting the Fourteenth Amendment from a guarantee of opportunity to an obstacle against education reform distorts our constitutional values and disserves those in the greatest need.

. . .

JUSTICE STEVENS, dissenting.

Is a law that authorizes the use of public funds to pay for the indoctrination of thousands of grammar school children in particular religious faiths a "law respecting an establishment of religion" within the meaning of the First Amendment? In answering that question, I think we should ignore three factual matters that are discussed at length by my colleagues.

First, the severe educational crisis that confronted the Cleveland City School District when Ohio enacted its voucher program is not a matter that should affect our appraisal of its constitutionality. . . .

Second, the wide range of choices that have been made available to students *within the public school system* has no bearing on the question whether the State may pay the tuition for students who wish to reject public education entirely and attend private schools that will provide them with a sectarian education. . . .

Third, the voluntary character of the private choice to prefer a parochial education over an education in the public school system seems to me quite irrelevant to the question whether the government's choice to pay for religious indoctrination is constitutionally permissible. Today, however, the Court seems to have decided that the mere fact that a family that cannot afford a private education wants its children educated in a parochial school is a sufficient justification for this use of public funds.

JUSTICE SOUTER, with whom JUSTICE STEVENS, JUSTICE GINSBURG, and JUSTICE BREYER join, dissenting.

. . . If there were an excuse for giving short shrift to the Establishment Clause, it would probably apply here. But there is no excuse. Constitutional limitations are placed on government to preserve constitutional values in hard cases, like these. . . . I therefore respectfully dissent.

The applicability of the Establishment Clause to public funding of benefits to religious schools was settled in *Everson* ..., which inaugurated the modern era of establishment doctrine. The Court stated the principle in words from which there was no dissent:

> "No tax in any amount, large or small, can be levied to support any religious activities or institutions, whatever they may be called, or whatever form they may adopt to teach or practice religion." ...

The Court has never in so many words repudiated this statement, let alone, in so many words, overruled *Everson*.

Today, however, the majority holds that the Establishment Clause is not offended by Ohio's Pilot Project Scholarship Program.... The money will thus pay for eligible students' instruction not only in secular subjects but in religion as well, in schools that can fairly be characterized as founded to teach religious doctrine and to imbue teaching in all subjects with a religious dimension....

How can a Court consistently leave *Everson* on the books and approve the Ohio vouchers? The answer is that it cannot. It is only by ignoring *Everson* that the majority can claim to rest on traditional law in its invocation of neutral aid provisions and private choice to sanction the Ohio law. It is, moreover, only by ignoring the meaning of neutrality and private choice themselves that the majority can even pretend to rest today's decision on those criteria.

I

The majority's statements of Establishment Clause doctrine cannot be appreciated without some historical perspective on the Court's announced limitations on government aid to religious education, and its repeated repudiation of limits previously set.... [D]octrinal bankruptcy has been reached today.

Viewed with the necessary generality, the cases can be categorized in three groups. In the period from 1947 to 1968, the basic principle of no aid to religion through school benefits was unquestioned. Thereafter for some 15 years, the Court termed its efforts as attempts to draw a line against aid that would be divertible to support the religious, as distinct from the secular, activity of an institutional beneficiary. Then, starting in 1983, concern with divertibility was gradually lost in favor of approving aid in amounts unlikely to afford substantial benefits to religious schools, when offered evenhandedly without regard to a recipient's religious character, and when channeled to a religious institution only by the genuinely free choice of some private individual. Now, the three stages are succeeded by a fourth, in which the substantial character of government aid is held to have no constitutional significance, and the espoused criteria of neutrality in offering aid, and private choice in directing it, are shown to be nothing but examples of verbal formalism.

· · ·

... [i]t was not until today that substantiality of aid has clearly been rejected as irrelevant by a majority of this Court, just as it has not been until today that a majority, not a plurality, has held purely formal criteria to suffice for scrutinizing aid that ends up in the coffers of religious schools. Today's cases are notable for their stark illustration of the inadequacy of the majority's chosen formal analysis.

II

Although it has taken half a century since *Everson* to reach the majority's twin standards of neutrality and free choice, the facts show that, in the majority's hands, even these criteria cannot convincingly legitimize the Ohio scheme.

A

Consider first the criterion of neutrality.... [I]n its limited significance, formal neutrality seemed to serve some purpose. Today, however, the majority employs the neutrality criterion in a way that renders it impossible to understand.

Neutrality in this sense refers, of course, to evenhandedness in setting eligibility as between potential religious and secular recipients of public money.... Thus, for example, the aid scheme in *Witters* provided an eligible recipient with a scholarship to be used at any institution within a practically unlimited universe of schools, ...; it did not tend to provide more or less aid depending on which one the scholarship recipient chose, and there was no indication that the maximum scholarship amount would be insufficient at secular schools....

In order to apply the neutrality test, then, it makes sense to ... ask whether the voucher provisions ... were written in a way that skewed the scheme toward benefitting religious schools.

This, however, is not what the majority asks. The majority looks not to the provisions for tuition vouchers, ... but to every provision for educational opportunity....

The illogic is patent. If regular, public schools (which can get no voucher payments) "participate" in a voucher scheme with schools that can, and public expenditure is still predominantly on public schools, then the majority's reasoning would find neutrality in a scheme of vouchers available for private tuition in districts with no secular private schools at all. "Neutrality" as the majority employs the term is, literally, verbal and nothing more....

Why the majority does not simply accept the fact that the challenge here is to the more generous voucher scheme and judge its neutrality in relation to religious use of voucher money seems very odd. It seems odd, that is, until one recognizes that comparable schools for applying the criterion of neutrality are also the comparable schools for applying the other majority criterion, whether the immediate recipients of voucher aid have a genuinely free choice of religious and secular schools to receive the voucher money. And in applying this second criterion, the consideration of "*all* schools" is ostensibly helpful to the majority position.

B

The majority addresses the issue of choice the same way it addresses neutrality, by asking whether recipients or potential recipients of voucher aid have a choice of public schools among secular alternatives to religious schools. Again, however, the majority asks the wrong question and misapplies the criterion. The majority has confused choice in spending scholarships with choice from the entire menu of possible educational placements, most of them open to anyone willing to attend a public school. . . . When the choice test is transformed from where to spend the money to where to go to school, it is cut loose from its very purpose.

Defining choice as choice in spending the money or channeling the aid is, moreover, necessary if the choice criterion is to function as a limiting principle at all. . . .

. . .

. . . [L]eaving the selection of alternatives for choice wide open, as the majority would, virtually guarantees the availability of a "choice" that will satisfy the criterion, limiting the choices to spending choices will not guarantee a negative result in every case. There may, after all, be cases in which a voucher recipient will have a real choice, with enough secular private school desks in relation to the number of religious ones, and a voucher amount high enough to meet secular private school tuition levels. . . .

It is not, of course, that I think even a genuine choice criterion is up to the task of the Establishment Clause when substantial state funds go to religious teaching; the discussion in Part III, *infra*, shows that it is not. The point is simply that if the majority wishes to claim that choice is a criterion, it must define choice in a way that can function as a criterion with a practical capacity to screen something out.

. . .

III

I do not dissent merely because the majority has misapplied its own law, for even if I assumed *arguendo* that the majority's formal criteria were satisfied on the facts, today's conclusion would be profoundly at odds with the Constitution. Proof of this is clear on two levels. The first is circumstantial, in the now discarded symptom of violation, the substantial dimension of the aid. The second is direct, in the defiance of every objective supposed to be served by the bar against establishment.

A

The scale of the aid to religious schools approved today is unprecedented, both in the number of dollars and in the proportion of systemic school expenditure supported. Each measure has received attention in previous cases. On one hand, the sheer quantity of aid, when delivered to a class of religious primary and secondary schools, was suspect on the theory that the greater the aid, the greater its proportion to a religious school's existing expenditures, and the greater the likelihood that public money was supporting religious as well as secular instruction. . . .

On the other hand, the Court has found the gross amount unhelpful for Establishment Clause analysis when the aid afforded a benefit solely to one individual, however substantial as to him, but only an incidental benefit to the religious school at which the individual chose to spend the State's money.... The majority's reliance on the observations of five Members of the Court in *Witters* as to the irrelevance of substantiality of aid in that case is therefore beside the point in the matter before us, which involves considerable sums of public funds systematically distributed through thousands of students attending religious elementary and middle schools in the city of Cleveland.

. . .

B

It is virtually superfluous to point out that every objective underlying the prohibition of religious establishment is betrayed by this scheme, but something has to be said about the enormity of the violation....

. . .

When government aid goes up, so does reliance on it; the only thing likely to go down is independence. If Justice Douglas in *Allen* was concerned with state agencies, influenced by powerful religious groups, choosing the textbooks that parochial schools would use, 392 U.S., at 265 (dissenting opinion), how much more is there reason to wonder when dependence will become great enough to give the State of Ohio an effective veto over basic decisions on the content of curriculums? A day will come when religious schools will learn what political leverage can do, just as Ohio's politicians are now getting a lesson in the leverage exercised by religion.

. . .

STEPHEN G. BREYER—Born August 15, 1938, in San Francisco, California, son of a lawyer and school administrator. Democrat. Jewish. Stanford, A.B., with great distinction, 1959. Oxford, Marshall Scholar, A.B., 1st class honors, 1961. Harvard, LL.B., magna cum laude, 1964. Law clerk to Justice Arthur J. Goldberg, 1964–65. Special assistant, Anti–Trust Division, Department of Justice, 1965–67. Professor, Harvard Law School, 1967–80, Kennedy School of Government, 1977–80. Assistant special prosecutor, Watergate Prosecution Force, 1973. Special counsel, 1974–75, chief counsel, 1979–80, U.S. Senate Judiciary Committee. Judge, U.S. Court of Appeals for the First Circuit, 1980–90, chief judge, 1990–94. Member, U.S. Sentencing Commission, 1985–89. Author of many books and articles on the regulatory process. Nominated to the U.S. Supreme Court by President Bill Clinton on May 13, 1994. Confirmed by the Senate by a 87–to–9 vote on July 9, 1994....

... *Everson*'s statement is still the touchstone of sound law, even though the reality is that in the matter of educational aid the Establishment Clause has largely been read away. True, the majority has not approved vouchers for religious schools alone, or aid earmarked for religious instruction. But no scheme so clumsy will ever get before us, and in the cases that we may see, like these, the Establishment Clause is largely silenced. I do not have the option to leave it silent, and I hope that a future Court will reconsider today's dramatic departure from basic Establishment Clause principle.

JUSTICE BREYER, with whom JUSTICE STEVENS and JUSTICE SOUTER join, dissenting.

I join Justice Souter's opinion, and I agree substantially with Justice Stevens. I write separately, however, to emphasize the risk that publicly financed voucher programs pose in terms of religiously based social conflict. I do so because I believe that the Establishment Clause concern for protecting the Nation's social fabric from religious conflict poses an overriding obstacle to the implementation of this well-intentioned school voucher program. And by explaining the nature of the concern, I hope to demonstrate why, in my view, "parental choice" cannot significantly alleviate the constitutional problem.

I

... The Clauses reflect the Framers' vision of an American Nation free of the religious strife that had long plagued the nations of Europe....

In part for this reason, the Court's 20th century Establishment Clause cases—both those limiting the practice of religion in public schools and those limiting the public funding of private religious education—focused directly upon social conflict, potentially created when government becomes involved in religious education....

. . .

The upshot is the development of constitutional doctrine that reads the Establishment Clause as avoiding religious strife, *not* by providing every religion with an *equal opportunity* (say, to secure state funding or to pray in the public schools), but by drawing fairly clear lines of *separation* between church and state—at least where the heartland of religious belief, such as primary religious education, is at issue.

II

. . .

Consider the voucher program here at issue. That program insists that the religious school accept students of all religions. Does that criterion treat fairly groups whose religion forbids them to do so? The program also insists that no participating school "advocate or foster unlawful behavior or teach hatred of any person or group on the basis of race, ethnicity, national origin, or religion." ...

How are state officials to adjudicate claims that one religion or another is advocating, for example, civil disobedience in response to unjust laws, the use of illegal drugs in a religious ceremony, or resort to force to call attention to what it views as an immoral social practice? What kind of public hearing will there be in response to claims that one religion or another is continuing to teach a view of history that casts members of other religions in the worst possible light? How will the public react to government funding for schools that take controversial religious positions on topics that are of current popular interest—say, the conflict in the Middle East or the war on terrorism? ...

. . .

III

... [V]oucher programs differ ... in both *kind* and *degree* from aid programs upheld in the past. They differ in kind because they direct financing to a core function of the church: the teaching of religious truths to young children.

... History suggests, not that ... private school teaching of religion is undesirable, but that *government funding* of this kind of religious endeavor is far more contentious than providing funding for secular textbooks, computers, vocational training, or even funding for adults who wish to obtain a college education at a religious university....

Vouchers also differ in *degree*. The aid programs recently upheld by the Court involved limited amounts of aid to religion. But the majority's analysis here appears to permit a considerable shift of taxpayer dollars from public secular schools to private religious schools.... [T]he secular aid upheld in *Mitchell* differs dramatically from the present case. Although it was conceivable that minor amounts of money could have, contrary to the statute, found their way to the religious activities of the recipients, ... that case is at worst the camel's nose, while the litigation before us is the camel itself.

IV

I do not believe that the "parental choice" aspect of the voucher program sufficiently offsets the concerns I have mentioned. Parental choice cannot help the taxpayer who does not want to finance the religious education of children. It will not always help the parent who may see little real choice between inadequate nonsectarian public education and adequate education at a school whose religious teachings are contrary to his own. It will not satisfy religious minorities unable to participate because they are too few in number to support the creation of their own private schools. It will not satisfy groups whose religious beliefs preclude them from participating in a government-sponsored program, and who may well feel ignored as government funds primarily support the education of children in the doctrines of the dominant religions. And it does little to ameliorate the entanglement problems or the related problems of social division ... Consequently, the fact that the parent may choose which school can cash the government's voucher check does not alleviate the Establishment Clause concerns associated with voucher programs.

V

The Court, in effect, turns the clock back. It adopts, under the name of "neutrality," an interpretation of the Establishment Clause that this Court rejected more than half a century ago. . . . In a society composed of many different religious creeds, I fear that this present departure from the Court's earlier understanding risks creating a form of religiously based conflict potentially harmful to the Nation's social fabric. Because I believe the Establishment Clause was written in part to avoid this kind of conflict, . . . I respectfully dissent.

VI. RELIGIOUS SPEECH AND DISPLAYS ON PUBLIC PROPERTY

McCREARY COUNTY, KENTUCKY v. AMERICAN CIVIL LIBERTIES UNION OF KENTUCKY

545 U.S. 844, 125 S.Ct. 2722, 162 L.Ed.2d 729 (2005).

JUSTICE SOUTER delivered the opinion of the Court.

Executives of two counties posted a version of the Ten Commandments on the walls of their courthouses. After suits were filed charging violations of the Establishment Clause, the legislative body of each county adopted a resolution calling for a more extensive exhibit meant to show that the Commandments are Kentucky's "precedent legal code." The result in each instance was a modified display of the Commandments surrounded by texts containing religious references as their sole common element. After changing counsel, the counties revised the exhibits again by eliminating some documents, expanding the text set out in another, and adding some new ones.

The issues are whether a determination of the counties' purpose is a sound basis for ruling on the Establishment Clause complaints, and whether evaluation of the counties' claim of secular purpose for the ultimate displays may take their evolution into account. We hold that the counties' manifest objective may be dispositive of the constitutional enquiry, and that the development of the presentation should be considered when determining its purpose.

I

. . .

In November 1999, respondents . . . sued the Counties in Federal District Court . . . and sought a preliminary injunction against maintaining the displays, which the ACLU charged were violations of the prohibition of religious establishment included in the First Amendment of the Constitution. Within a month, and before the District Court had responded to the request for injunction, the legislative body of each County authorized a second, expanded display, by nearly identical resolutions reciting that the Ten Commandments are "the precedent legal code upon which the civil and criminal codes of . . . Kentucky are founded," and stating several grounds for taking that position: that "the Ten Commandments are codified in Kentucky's civil and criminal laws"; that the Kentucky House of Representatives had in 1993 "voted unanimously ... to adjourn ... 'in remembrance and honor of Jesus Christ, the Prince of Ethics' "; that the "County Judge and ... magistrates agree with the arguments set out by Judge [Roy] Moore" in defense of his "display [of] the Ten Commandments in his courtroom"; and that the "Founding Father[s] [had an] explicit understanding of the duty of elected officials to publicly acknowledge God as the source of America's strength and direction."

As directed by the resolutions, the Counties expanded the displays of the Ten Commandments in their locations, presumably along with copies of the resolution, which instructed that it, too, be posted. In addition to the first display's large framed copy of the edited King James version of the Commandments, the second included eight other documents in smaller frames, each either having a religious theme or excerpted to highlight a religious element. The documents were the "endowed by their Creator" passage from the Declaration of Independence; the Preamble to the Constitution of Kentucky; the national motto, "In God We Trust"; a page from the Congressional Record of February 2, 1983, proclaiming the Year of the Bible and including a statement of the Ten Commandments; a proclamation by President Abraham Lincoln designating April 30, 1863, a National Day of Prayer and Humiliation; an excerpt from President Lincoln's "Reply to Loyal Colored People of Baltimore upon Presentation of a Bible," reading that "[t]he Bible is the best gift God has ever given to man"; a proclamation by President Reagan marking 1983 the Year of the Bible; and the Mayflower Compact.

After argument, the District Court entered a preliminary injunction on May 5, 2000, ordering that the "display ... be removed from [each] County Courthouse IMMEDIATELY" and that no county official "erect or cause to be erected similar displays." ... As to governmental purpose, it concluded that the original display "lack[ed] any secular purpose" because the Commandments "are a distinctly religious document, ... " The court found that the second version also "clearly lack[ed] a secular purpose" because the "Count[ies] narrowly tailored [their] selection of foundational documents to incorporate only those with specific references to Christianity."

The Counties ... voluntarily dismissed ... after hiring new lawyers. They then installed another display in each courthouse, the third within a year. No new resolution authorized this one, nor did the Counties repeal the resolutions that preceded the second. The posting consists of nine framed documents of equal size, one of them setting out the Ten Commandments explicitly identified as the "King James Version" at Exodus 20:3–17 and quoted at greater length than before ... Assembled with the Commandments are framed copies of the Magna Carta, the Declaration of Independence, the Bill of Rights, the lyrics of the Star Spangled Banner, the Mayflower Compact, the National Motto, the Preamble to the Kentucky Constitution, and a picture of Lady Justice. The collection is entitled "The Foundations of American Law and Government Display" and each document comes with a statement about its historical and legal significance. The comment on the Ten Commandments reads:

"The Ten Commandments have profoundly influenced the formation of Western legal thought and the formation of our country. That influence is clearly seen in the Declaration of Independence, which declared that 'We hold these truths to be self-evident, that all men are created equal, that they are endowed by their Creator with certain unalienable Rights, that among these are Life, Liberty, and the pursuit of Happiness.' The Ten Commandments provide the moral background of the Declaration of Independence and the foundation of our legal tradition."

The ACLU moved to supplement the preliminary injunction to enjoin the Counties' third display, and the Counties responded with several explanations for the new version, including desires "to demonstrate that the Ten Commandments were part of the foundation of American Law and Government" and "to educate the citizens of the county regarding some of the documents that played a significant role in the foundation of our system of law and government.".... The court, however, took the objective of proclaiming the Commandments' foundational value as "a religious, rather than secular, purpose" ... and found that the assertion that the Counties' broader educational goals are secular "crumble[s] ... upon an examination of the history of this litigation,"

... As requested, the trial court supplemented the injunction, and a divided panel of the Court of Appeals for the Sixth Circuit affirmed. ...

We ... now affirm.

II

Twenty-five years ago in a case prompted by posting the Ten Commandments in Kentucky's public schools, this Court recognized that the Commandments "are undeniably a sacred text in the Jewish and Christian faiths" and held that their display in public classrooms violated the First Amendment's bar against establishment of religion. Stone [v. Graham] 449 U.S., at 41. *Stone* found a predominantly religious purpose in the government's posting of the Commandments, given their prominence as " 'an instrument of religion,' " ... The Counties ask for a different approach here by arguing that official purpose is unknowable and the search for it inherently vain. In the alternative, the Counties would avoid the District Court's conclusion by having us limit the scope of the purpose enquiry so severely that any trivial rationalization would suffice, under a standard oblivious to the history of religious government action like the progression of exhibits in this case.

A

Ever since Lemon v. Kurtzman summarized the three familiar considerations for evaluating Establishment Clause claims, looking to whether government action has "a secular legislative purpose" has been a common, albeit seldom dispositive, element of our cases ... Though we have found government action motivated by an illegitimate purpose only four times since *Lemon*, and "the secular purpose requirement alone may rarely be determinative ..., it nevertheless serves an important function." ...

The touchstone for our analysis is the principle that the "First Amendment mandates governmental neutrality between religion and religion, and between religion and nonreligion." ... When the government acts with the ostensible and predominant purpose of advancing religion, it violates that central Establishment Clause value of official religious neutrality, there being no neutrality when the government's ostensible object is to take sides, ... By showing a purpose to favor religion, the government "sends the ... message to ... nonadherents 'that they are outsiders, not full members of the political community, and an accompanying message to adherents that they are insiders, favored members' " ...

. . .

B

Despite the intuitive importance of official purpose to the realization of Establishment Clause values, the Counties ask us to abandon *Lemon*'s purpose test, or at least to truncate any enquiry into purpose here. Their first argument is that the very consideration of purpose is deceptive: according to them, true "purpose" is unknowable, and its search merely an excuse for courts to act selectively and unpredictably in picking out evidence of subjective intent. The assertions are as seismic as they are unconvincing.

Examination of purpose is a staple of statutory interpretation that makes up the daily fare of every appellate court in the country, ... and governmental purpose is a key element of a good deal of constitutional doctrine, e.g., Washington v. Davis, 426 U.S. 229, ... With enquiries into purpose this common, if they were nothing but hunts for mares' nests deflecting attention from bare judicial will, the whole notion of purpose in law would have dropped into disrepute long ago.

But scrutinizing purpose does make practical sense, as in Establishment Clause analysis, where an understanding of official objective emerges from readily discoverable fact, without any judicial psychoanalysis of a drafter's heart of hearts.... There is, then, nothing hinting at an unpredictable or disingenuous exercise when a court enquires into purpose after a claim is raised under the Establishment Clause.

The cases with findings of a predominantly religious purpose point to the straightforward nature of the test. ... [I]n *Stone*, the Court held that the "[p]osting of religious texts on the wall serve[d] no ... educational function," and found that if "the posted copies of the Ten Commandments [were] to have any effect at all, it [would] be to induce the schoolchildren to read, meditate upon, perhaps to venerate and obey, the Commandments.".....

Nor is there any indication that the enquiry is rigged in practice to finding a religious purpose dominant every time a case is filed. In the past, the test has not been fatal very often, presumably because government does not generally act unconstitutionally, with the predominant purpose of advancing religion. That said, one consequence of the corollary that Establishment Clause analysis does not look to the veiled psyche of government officers could be that in some of the cases in which establishment complaints failed, savvy officials had disguised their religious intent so cleverly that the objective observer just missed it. But that is no reason for great constitutional concern. If someone in the government hides religious motive so well that the " 'objective observer, acquainted with the text, legislative history, and implementation of the statute,' " . . . cannot see it, then without something more the government does not make a divisive announcement that in itself amounts to taking religious sides. A secret motive stirs up no strife and does nothing to make outsiders of nonadherents, and it suffices to wait and see whether such government action turns out to have (as it may even be likely to have) the illegitimate effect of advancing religion.

C

After declining the invitation to abandon concern with purpose wholesale, we also have to avoid the Counties' alternative tack of trivializing the enquiry into it. The Counties would read the cases as if the purpose enquiry were so naive that any transparent claim to secularity would satisfy it, and they would cut context out of the enquiry, to the point of ignoring history, no matter what bearing it actually had on the significance of current circumstances. There is no precedent for the Counties' arguments, or reason supporting them.

1

. . .

. . . [W]e have not made the purpose test a pushover for any secular claim. . . . [I]n those unusual cases where the claim was an apparent sham, or the secular purpose secondary, the unsurprising results have been findings of no adequate secular object, as against a predominantly religious one.

2

The Counties' second proffered limitation can be dispatched quickly. They argue that purpose in a case like this one should be inferred, if at all, only from the latest news about the last in a series of governmental actions, however close they may all be in time and subject. But the world is not made brand new every morning, and the Counties are simply asking us to ignore perfectly probative evidence; they want an absent-minded objective observer, not one presumed to be familiar with the history of the government's actions and competent to learn what history has to show. . . .

III

. . .

We take *Stone* as the initial legal benchmark, our only case dealing with the constitutionality of displaying the Commandments. *Stone* recognized that the Commandments are an "instrument of religion" and that, at least on the facts before it, the display of their text could presumptively be understood as meant to advance religion: although state law specifically required their posting in public school classrooms, their isolated exhibition did not leave room even for an argument that secular education explained their being there.... But *Stone* did not purport to decide the constitutionality of every possible way the Commandments might be set out by the government, and under the Establishment Clause detail is key. ...

A

The display rejected in *Stone* had two obvious similarities to the first one in the sequence here: both set out a text of the Commandments as distinct from any traditionally symbolic representation, and each stood alone, not part of an arguably secular display. *Stone* stressed the significance of integrating the Commandments into a secular scheme to forestall the broadcast of an otherwise clearly religious message, ... and for good reason, the Commandments being a central point of reference in the religious and moral history of Jews and Christians. They proclaim the existence of a monotheistic god (no other gods). They regulate details of religious obligation (no graven images, no sabbath breaking, no vain oath swearing). And they unmistakably rest even the universally accepted prohibitions (as against murder, theft, and the like) on the sanction of the divinity proclaimed at the beginning of the text. Displaying that text is thus different from a symbolic depiction, like tablets with 10 roman numerals, which could be seen as alluding to a general notion of law, not a sectarian conception of faith.... Actually, the posting by the Counties lacked even the *Stone* display's implausible disclaimer that the Commandments were set out to show their effect on the civil law. What is more, at the ceremony for posting the framed Commandments in Pulaski County, the county executive was accompanied by his pastor, who testified to the certainty of the existence of God. The reasonable observer could only think that the Counties meant to emphasize and celebrate the Commandments' religious message.

This is not to deny that the Commandments have had influence on civil or secular law; a major text of a majority religion is bound to be felt. The point is simply that the original text viewed in its entirety is an unmistakably religious statement dealing with religious obligations and with morality subject to religious sanction. When the government initiates an effort to place this statement alone in public view, a religious object is unmistakable.

B

Once the Counties were sued, they modified the exhibits and invited additional insight into their purpose in a display that hung for about six months. This new one was the product of forthright and nearly identical Pulaski and McCreary County resolutions listing a series of American historical documents with theistic and Christian references, which were to be posted in order to furnish a setting for displaying the Ten Commandments and any "other Kentucky and American historical documen[t]" without raising concern about "any Christian or religious references" in them. ... [T]he resolutions expressed support for an Alabama judge who posted the Commandments in his courtroom, and cited the fact the Kentucky Legislature once adjourned a session in honor of "Jesus Christ, Prince of Ethics."

In this second display, unlike the first, the Commandments were not hung in isolation, merely leaving the Counties' purpose to emerge from the pervasively religious text of the Commandments themselves. Instead, the second version was required to include the statement of the government's purpose expressly set out in the county resolutions, and underscored it by juxtaposing the Commandments to other documents with highlighted references to God as their sole common element. The display's unstinting focus was on religious passages, showing that the Counties were posting the Commandments precisely because of their sectarian content. That demonstration of the government's objective was enhanced by serial religious references and the accompanying resolution's claim about the embodiment of ethics in Christ. Together, the display and resolution presented an indisputable, and undisputed, showing of an impermissible purpose.

· · ·

C

1

After the Counties changed lawyers, they mounted a third display, without a new resolution or repeal of the old one. The result was the "Foundations of American Law and Government" exhibit, which placed the Commandments in the company of other documents the Counties thought especially significant in the historical foundation of American government. In trying to persuade the District Court to lift the preliminary injunction, the Counties cited several new purposes for the third version, including a desire "to educate the citizens of the county regarding some of the documents that played a significant role in the foundation of our system of law and government." The Counties' claims did not, however, persuade the court, intimately familiar with the details of this litigation, or the Court of Appeals, neither of which found a legitimizing secular purpose in this third version of the display. " 'When both courts [that have already passed on the case] are unable to discern an arguably valid secular purpose, this Court normally should hesitate to find one.' "

[N]ew statements of purpose were presented only as a litigating position, there being no further authorizing action by the Counties' governing boards. And although repeal of the earlier county authorizations would not have erased them from the record of evidence bearing on current purpose, the extraordinary resolutions for the second display passed just months earlier were not repealed or otherwise repudiated. Indeed, the sectarian spirit of the common resolution found enhanced expression in the third display, which quoted more of the purely religious language of the Commandments than the first two displays had done; . . .

· · ·

2

In holding the preliminary injunction adequately supported by evidence that the Counties' purpose had not changed at the third stage, we do not decide that the Counties' past actions forever taint any effort on their part to deal with the subject matter. We hold only that purpose needs to be taken seriously under the Establishment Clause and needs to be understood in light of context; an implausible claim that governmental purpose has changed should not carry the day in a court of law any more than in a head with common sense. It is enough to say here that district courts are fully capable of adjusting preliminary relief to take account of genuine changes in constitutionally significant conditions. ...

Nor do we have occasion here to hold that a sacred text can never be integrated constitutionally into a governmental display on the subject of law, or American history. We do not forget, and in this litigation have frequently been reminded, that our own courtroom frieze was deliberately designed in the exercise of governmental authority so as to include the figure of Moses holding tablets exhibiting a portion of the Hebrew text of the later, secularly phrased Commandments; in the company of 17 other lawgivers, most of them secular figures, there is no risk that Moses would strike an observer as evidence that the National Government was violating neutrality in religion.

IV

The importance of neutrality as an interpretive guide is no less true now than it was when the Court broached the principle in *Everson* ... and a word needs to be said about the different view taken in today's dissent. We all agree, of course, on the need for some interpretative help. The First Amendment contains no textual definition of "establishment," and the term is certainly not self-defining. No one contends that the prohibition of establishment stops at a designation of a national (or with Fourteenth Amendment incorporation, ... a state) church, but nothing in the text says just how much more it covers. There is no simple answer, for more than one reason.

The prohibition on establishment covers a variety of issues from prayer in widely varying government settings, to financial aid for religious individuals and institutions, to comment on religious questions. In these varied settings, issues of about interpreting inexact Establishment Clause language, like difficult interpretative issues generally, arise from the tension of competing values, each constitutionally respectable, but none open to realization to the logical limit.

The First Amendment has not one but two clauses tied to "religion," the second forbidding any prohibition on the "the free exercise thereof," and sometimes, the two clauses compete: spending government money on the clergy looks like establishing religion, but if the government cannot pay for military chaplains a good many soldiers and sailors would be kept from the opportunity to exercise their chosen religions. ... At other times, limits on governmental action that might make sense as a way to avoid establishment could arguably limit freedom of speech when the speaking is done under government auspices. ... The dissent, then, is wrong to read cases like Walz v. Tax Comm'n of City of New York, 397 U.S. 664, (1970), as a rejection of neutrality on its own terms, for trade-offs are inevitable, and an elegant interpretative rule to draw the line in all the multifarious situations is not be had.

Given the variety of interpretative problems, the principle of neutrality has provided a good sense of direction: the government may not favor one religion over another, or religion over irreligion, religious choice being the prerogative of individuals under the Free Exercise Clause. . . . A sense of the past thus points to governmental neutrality as an objective of the Establishment Clause, and a sensible standard for applying it. To be sure, given its generality as a principle, an appeal to neutrality alone cannot possibly lay every issue to rest, or tell us what issues on the margins are substantial enough for constitutional significance, a point that has been clear from the Founding era to modern times. . . .

The dissent, however, puts forward a limitation on the application of the neutrality principle, with citations to historical evidence said to show that the Framers understood the ban on establishment of religion as sufficiently narrow to allow the government to espouse submission to the divine will. The dissent identifies God as the God of monotheism, all of whose three principal strains (Jewish, Christian, and Muslim) acknowledge the religious importance of the Ten Commandments. On the dissent's view, it apparently follows that even rigorous espousal of a common element of this common monotheism, is consistent with the establishment ban.

But the dissent's argument for the original understanding is flawed from the outset by its failure to consider the full range of evidence showing what the Framers believed. The dissent is certainly correct in putting forward evidence that some of the Framers thought some endorsement of religion was compatible with the establishment ban; the dissent quotes the first President as stating that "national morality [cannot] prevail in exclusion of religious principle," for example, and it cites his first Thanksgiving proclamation giving thanks to God, ... Surely if expressions like these from Washington and his contemporaries were all we had to go on, there would be a good case that the neutrality principle has the effect of broadening the ban on establishment beyond the Framers' understanding of it (although there would, of course, still be the question of whether the historical case could overcome some 60 years of precedent taking neutrality as its guiding principle).

But the fact is that we do have more to go on, for there is also evidence supporting the proposition that the Framers intended the Establishment Clause to require governmental neutrality in matters of religion, including neutrality in statements acknowledging religion. The very language of the Establishment Clause represented a significant departure from early drafts that merely prohibited a single national religion, and, the final language instead "extended [the] prohibition to state support for 'religion' in general." Language. . . .

The historical record, moreover, is complicated beyond the dissent's account by the writings and practices of figures no less influential than

Thomas Jefferson and James Madison. Jefferson, for example, refused to issue Thanksgiving Proclamations because he believed that they violated the Constitution ...

The fair inference is that there was no common understanding about the limits of the establishment prohibition, and the dissent's conclusion that its narrower view was the original understanding, stretches the evidence beyond tensile capacity. What the evidence does show is a group of statesmen, like others before and after them, who proposed a guarantee with contours not wholly worked out, leaving the Establishment Clause with edges still to be determined. And none the worse for that. Indeterminate edges are the kind to have in a constitution meant to endure, and to meet "exigencies which, if foreseen at all, must have been seen dimly, and which can be best provided for as they occur."

While the dissent fails to show a consistent original understanding from which to argue that the neutrality principle should be rejected, it does manage to deliver a surprise. As mentioned, the dissent says that the deity the Framers had in mind was the God of monotheism, with the consequence that government may espouse a tenet of traditional monotheism. This is truly a remarkable view. Other members of the Court have dissented on the ground that the Establishment Clause bars nothing more than governmental preference for one religion over another ..., but at least religion has previously been treated inclusively. Today's dissent, however, apparently means that government should be free to approve the core beliefs of a favored religion over the tenets of others, a view that should trouble anyone who prizes religious liberty. Certainly history cannot justify it; on the contrary, history shows that the religion of concern to the Framers was not that of the monotheistic faiths generally, but Christianity in particular, a fact that no member of this Court takes as a premise for construing the Religion Clauses. ... [T]here is, it seems, no escape from interpretative consequences that would surprise the Framers. Thus, it appears to be common ground in the interpretation of a Constitution "intended to endure for ages to come," ... that applications unanticipated by the Framers are inevitable.

Historical evidence thus supports no solid argument for changing course ... [T]he divisiveness of religion in current public life is inescapable. This is no time to deny the prudence of understanding the Establishment Clause to require the Government to stay neutral on religious belief, which is reserved for the conscience of the individual.

V

Given the ample support for the District Court's finding of a predominantly religious purpose behind the Counties' third display, we affirm the Sixth Circuit in upholding the preliminary injunction.

· · ·

Justice O'Connor, concurring.

I join in the Court's opinion. ...

Reasonable minds can disagree about how to apply the Religion Clauses in a given case. But the goal of the Clauses is clear: to carry out the Founders' plan of preserving religious liberty to the fullest extent possible in a pluralistic society. By enforcing the Clauses, we have kept religion a matter for the individual conscience, not for the prosecutor or bureaucrat. At a time when we see around the world the violent consequences of the assumption of religious authority by government, Americans may count themselves fortunate: Our regard for constitutional boundaries has protected us from similar travails, while allowing private religious exercise to flourish....

. . .

Given the history of this particular display of the Ten Commandments, the Court correctly finds an Establishment Clause violation. The purpose behind the counties' display is relevant because it conveys an unmistakable message of endorsement to the reasonable observer. ...

. . .

Justice Scalia, with Whom the Chief Justice and Justice Thomas join, and with whom Justice Kennedy joins as to Parts II and III, dissenting.

I would uphold McCreary County and Pulaski County, Kentucky's (hereinafter Counties) displays of the Ten Commandments. I shall discuss first, why the Court's oft repeated assertion that the government cannot favor religious practice is false; second, why today's opinion extends the scope of that falsehood even beyond prior cases; and third, why even on the basis of the Court's false assumptions the judgment here is wrong.

I

... That is one model of the relationship between church and state—a model spread across Europe by the armies of Napoleon, and reflected in the Constitution of France, which begins "France is [a] ... secular".... This is not, and never was, the model adopted by America.

Nor have the views of our people on this matter significantly changed. Presidents continue to conclude the Presidential oath with the words "so help me God." Our legislatures, state and national, continue to open their sessions with prayer led by official chaplains. The sessions of this Court continue to open with the prayer "God save the United States and this Honorable Court." Invocation of the Almighty by our public figures, at all levels of government, remains commonplace. Our coinage bears the motto "IN GOD WE TRUST." And our Pledge of Allegiance contains the acknowledgment that we are a Nation "under God." ...

With all of this reality (and much more) staring it in the face, how can the Court *possibly* assert that " 'the First Amendment mandates governmental neutrality between ... religion and nonreligion,' " and that "[m]anifesting a purpose to favor ... adherence to religion generally," is unconstitutional? Who says so? Surely not the words of the Constitution. Surely not the history and traditions that reflect our society's constant understanding of those words. Surely not even the current sense of our society, recently reflected in an Act of Congress adopted *unanimously* by the Senate and with only 5 nays in the House of Representatives, ... criticizing a Court of Appeals opinion that had held "under God" in the Pledge of Allegiance unconstitutional And it is, moreover, a thoroughly discredited say-so. It is discredited, to begin with, because a majority of the Justices on the current Court (including at least one Member of today's majority) have, in separate opinions, repudiated the brain-spun "*Lemon* test" that embodies the supposed principle of neutrality between religion and irreligion. ... And it is discredited because the Court has not had the courage (or the foolhardiness) to apply the neutrality principle consistently.

· · ·

What distinguishes the rule of law from the dictatorship of a shifting Supreme Court majority is the absolutely indispensable requirement that judicial opinions be grounded in consistently applied principle. That is what prevents judges from ruling now this way, now that—thumbs up or thumbs down—as their personal preferences dictate. Today's opinion forthrightly (or actually, somewhat less than forthrightly) admits that it does not rest upon consistently applied principle. ... [T]he Court acknowledges that the "Establishment Clause doctrine" it purports to be applying "lacks the comfort of categorical absolutes." What the Court means by this lovely euphemism is that sometimes the Court chooses to decide cases on the principle that government cannot favor religion, and sometimes it does not. The footnote goes on to say that "[i]n special instances we have found good reason" to dispense with the principle, but "[n]o such reasons present themselves here." *Ibid.* It does not identify all of those "special instances," much less identify the "good reason" for their existence.

· · ·

What ... could be the genuine "good reason" for occasionally the neutrality principle? I suggest the instinct for self-preservation, and the recognition that the Court ... cannot go too far down the road of an enforced neutrality that contradicts both historical fact and current practice without losing all that sustains it: the willingness of he people to accept its interpretation of the Constitution as definitive, in preference to the contrary interpretation of the democratically elected branches.

Besides appealing to the demonstrably false principle that the government cannot favor religion over irreligion, today's opinion suggests that the posting of the Ten Commandments violates the principle that the government cannot favor one religion over another. ... That is indeed a valid principle where public aid or assistance to religion is concerned, ... or where the free exercise of religion is at issue, but it necessarily applies in a more limited sense to public acknowledgment of the Creator. If religion in the public forum had to be entirely nondenominational, there could be no religion in the public forum at all. One cannot say the word "God," or "the Almighty," one cannot offer public supplication or thanksgiving, without contradicting the beliefs of some people that there are many gods, or that God or the gods pay no attention to human affairs. With respect to public acknowledgment of religious belief, it is entirely clear from our Nation's historical practices that the Establishment Clause permits this disregard of polytheists and believers in unconcerned deities, just as it permits the disregard of devout atheists. . . .

Historical practices thus demonstrate that there is a distance between the acknowledgment of a single Creator and the establishment of a religion . . .

B

. . .

II

As bad as the *Lemon* test is, it is worse for the fact that, since its inception, its seemingly simple mandates have been manipulated to fit whatever result the Court aimed to achieve. Today's opinion is no different. In two respects it modifies *Lemon* to ratchet up the Court's hostility to religion. First, the Court justifies inquiry into legislative purpose, not as an end itself, but as a means to ascertain the appearance of the government action to an " 'objective observer.' ". Because in the Court's view the true danger to be guarded against is that the objective observer would feel like an "outside[r]" or "not [a] full membe[r] of the political community," its inquiry focuses not on the *actual purpose* of government action, but the "purpose apparent from government action." Under this approach, even if a government could show that its actual purpose was not to advance religion, it would presumably violate the Constitution as long as the Court's objective observer would think otherwise. . . .

I have remarked before that it is an odd jurisprudence that bases the unconstitutionality of a government practice that does not *actually* advance religion on the hopes of the government that it *would* do so. . . . But that oddity pales in comparison to the one invited by today's analysis: the legitimacy of a government action with a wholly secular effect would turn on the *misperception* of an imaginary observer that the government officials behind the action had the intent to advance religion.

Lemon's more limited requirement . . . finds no support in our cases. In all but one of the five cases in which this Court has invalidated a government practice on the basis of its purpose to benefit religion, it has first declared that the statute was motivated entirely by the desire to advance religion to the result, since the Court rejected the State's only proffered secular purpose as a sham. . . .

III

Even accepting the Court's *Lemon*-based premises, the displays at issue here were constitutional.

A

To any person who happened to walk down the hallway of the McCreary or Pulaski County Courthouse during the roughly nine months when the Foundations Displays were exhibited, the displays must have seemed unremarkable—if indeed they were noticed at all. The walls of both courthouses were already lined with historical documents and other assorted portraits; each Foundations Display was exhibited in the same format as these other displays and nothing in the record suggests that either County took steps to give it greater prominence.

Entitled "The Foundations of American Law and Government Display," each display consisted of nine equally sized documents: the original version of the Magna Carta, the Declaration of Independence, the Bill of Rights, the Star Spangled Banner, the Mayflower Compact of 1620, a picture of Lady Justice, the National Motto of the United States ("In God We Trust"), the Preamble to the Kentucky Constitution, and the Ten Commandments. The displays did not emphasize any of the nine documents in any way: The frame holding the Ten Commandments was of the same size and had the same appearance as that which held each of the other documents.

Posted with the documents was a plaque, identifying the display, and explaining that it "contains documents that played a significant role in the foundation of our system of law and government." *Ibid.* The explanation related to the Ten Commandments was third in the list of nine and did not serve to distinguish it from the other documents. . . .

B

On its face, the Foundations Displays manifested the purely secular purpose that the Counties asserted before the District Court: "to display documents that played a significant role in the foundation of our system of law and government."

. . .

C

In any event, the Court's conclusion that the Counties exhibited the Foundations Displays with the purpose of promoting religion is doubtful. In the Court's view, the impermissible motive was apparent from the initial displays of the Ten Commandments all by themselves: When that occurs, the Court says, "a religious object is unmistakable." Surely that cannot be. If, as discussed above, the Commandments have a proper place in our civic history, even placing them by themselves can be civically motivated—especially when they are placed, not in a school (as they were in the *Stone* case upon which the Court places such reliance), but in a courthouse. . . .

. . .

"No one was compelled to observe or participate in any religious ceremony or activity. [T]he count[ies] [did not] contribut[e] significant amounts of tax money to serve the cause of one religious faith. [The Ten Commandments] are purely passive symbols of [the religious foundation for many of our laws and governmental institutions]. Passersby who disagree with the message conveyed by th[e] displays are free to ignore them, or even to turn their backs, just as they are free to do when they disagree with any other form of government speech.... Nor is it the case that a solo display of the Ten Commandments advances any one faith. They are assuredly a religious symbol, but they are not so closely associated with a single religious belief that their display can reasonably be understood as preferring one religious sect over another. The Ten Commandments are recognized by Judaism, Christianity, and Islam alike as divinely given. ...

. . .

Turning at last to the displays actually at issue in this case, the Court faults the Counties for not *repealing* the resolution expressing what the Court believes to be an impermissible intent. Under these circumstances, the Court says, "no reasonable observer could swallow the claim that the Counties had cast off the objective so unmistakable in the earlier displays." Even were I to accept all that the Court has said before, I would not agree with that assessment. To begin with, of course, it is unlikely that a reasonable observer *would even have been aware* of the resolutions, so there would be nothing to "cast off." The Court implies that the Counties may have been able to remedy the "taint" from the old resolutions by enacting a new one. But that action would have been wholly unnecessary in light of the explanation that the Counties included *with the displays themselves:* A plaque next to the documents informed all who passed by that each display "contains documents that played a significant role in the foundation of our system of law and government." Additionally, there was no reason for the Counties to repeal or repudiate the resolutions adopted with the hanging of the second displays, since they related *only to the second displays.* After complying with the District Court's order to remove the second displays "immediately," and erecting new displays that in content and by express assertion reflected a different purpose from that identified in the resolutions, the Counties had no reason to believe that their previous resolutions would be deemed to be the basis for their actions. After the Counties discovered that the sentiments expressed in the resolutions could be attributed to their most recent displays (in oral argument before this Court), they repudiated them immediately.

In sum: The first displays did not necessarily evidence an intent to further religious practice; nor did the second displays, or the resolutions authorizing them; and there is in any event no basis for attributing whatever intent motivated the first and second displays to the third. Given the presumption of regularity that always accompanies our review of official action, the Court has identified no evidence of a purpose to advance religion in a way that is inconsistent with our cases. The Court may well be correct in identifying the third displays as the fruit of a desire to display the Ten Commandments but neither our cases nor our history support its assertion that such a desire renders the fruit poisonous.

* * *

For the foregoing reasons, I would reverse the judgment of the Court of Appeals.

VAN ORDEN v. PERRY

545 U.S. 677, 125 S.Ct. 2854, 162 L.Ed.2d 607 (2005).

CHIEF JUSTICE REHNQUIST announced the judgment of the Court and delivered an opinion, in which JUSTICE SCALIA, JUSTICE KENNEDY, and JUSTICE THOMAS join.

The question here is whether the Establishment Clause of the First Amendment allows the display of a monument inscribed with the Ten Commandments on the Texas State Capitol grounds. We hold that it does.

The 22 acres surrounding the Texas State Capitol contain 17 monuments and 21 historical markers commemorating the "people, ideals, and events that compose Texan identity.". The monolith challenged here stands 6–feet high and 3 1/2–feet wide. It is located to the north of the Capitol building, between the Capitol and the Supreme Court building. Its primary content is the text of the Ten Commandments. An eagle grasping the American flag, an eye inside of a pyramid, and two small tablets with what appears to be an ancient script are carved above the text of the Ten Commandments. Below the text are two Stars of David and the superimposed Greek letters Chi and Rho, which represent Christ. The bottom of the monument bears the inscription "PRESENT-ED TO THE PEOPLE AND YOUTH OF TEXAS BY THE FRATERNAL ORDER OF EAGLES OF TEXAS 1961.".

The legislative record surrounding the State's acceptance of the monument from the Eagles—a national social, civic, and patriotic organization—is limited to legislative journal entries. After the monument was accepted, the State selected a site for the monument based on the recommendation of the state organization responsible for maintaining the Capitol grounds. The Eagles paid the cost of erecting the monument, the dedication of which was presided over by two state legislators.

Petitioner Thomas Van Orden is a native Texan and a resident of Austin. At one time he was a licensed lawyer, having graduated from Southern Methodist Law School. ...

Forty years after the monument's erection and six years after Van Orden began to encounter the monument frequently, he sued numerous state officials ... seeking both a declaration that the monument's placement violates the Establishment Clause and an injunction requiring its removal. After a bench trial, the District Court held that the monument did not contravene the Establishment Clause. It found that the State had a valid secular purpose in recognizing and commending the Eagles for their efforts to reduce juvenile delinquency. The District Court also determined that a reasonable observer, mindful of the history, purpose, and context, would not conclude that this passive monument conveyed the message that the State was seeking to endorse religion. The Court of Appeals affirmed the District Court's holdings with respect to the monument's purpose and effect. We ... affirm.

Our cases, Januslike, point in two directions in applying the Establishment Clause. One face looks toward the strong role played by religion and religious traditions throughout our Nation's history. . . .

The other face looks toward the principle that governmental intervention in religious matters can itself endanger religious freedom.

This case, like all Establishment Clause challenges, presents us with the difficulty of respecting both faces. Our institutions presuppose a Supreme Being, yet these institutions must not press religious observances upon their citizens. One face looks to the past in acknowledgment of our Nation's heritage, while the other looks to the present in demanding a separation between church and state. Reconciling these two faces requires that we neither abdicate our responsibility to maintain a division between church and state nor evince a hostility to religion by disabling the government from in some ways recognizing our religious heritage ("risk [of] fostering a pervasive bias or hostility to religion, which could undermine the very neutrality the Establishment Clause requires").

These two faces are evident in representative cases both upholding and invalidating laws under the Establishment Clause. Over the last 25 years, we have sometimes pointed to Lemon v. Kurtzman, 403 U.S. 602, (1971), as providing the governing test in Establishment Clause challenges. . . . Others have applied it only after concluding that the challenged practice was invalid under a different Establishment Clause test. . . .

Whatever may be the fate of the *Lemon* test in the larger scheme of Establishment Clause jurisprudence, we think it not useful in dealing with the sort of passive monument that Texas has erected on its Capitol grounds. Instead, our analysis is driven both by the nature of the monument and by our Nation's history.

As we explained in Lynch v. Donnelly, 465 U.S. 668: "There is an unbroken history of official acknowledgment by all three branches of government of the role of religion in American life from at least 1789. . . ."

Recognition of the role of God in our Nation's heritage has also been reflected in our decisions . . .

In this case we are faced with a display of the Ten Commandments on government property outside the Texas State Capitol. Such acknowledgments of the role played by the Ten Commandments in our Nation's heritage are common throughout America. We need only look within our own Courtroom. Since 1935, Moses has stood, holding two tablets that reveal portions of the Ten Commandments written in Hebrew, among other lawgivers in the south frieze. Representations of the Ten Commandments adorn the metal gates lining the north and south sides of the Courtroom as well as the doors leading into the Courtroom. Moses also sits on the exterior east facade of the building holding the Ten Commandments tablets.

Similar acknowledgments can be seen throughout a visitor's tour of our Nation's Capital. . . .

Our opinions, like our building, have recognized the role the Decalogue plays in America's heritage role of the Ten Commandments. . . . These displays and recognitions of the Ten Commandments bespeak the rich American tradition of religious acknowledgments.

Of course, the Ten Commandments are religious—they were so viewed at their inception and so remain. The monument, therefore, has religious significance. According to Judeo–Christian belief, the Ten Commandments were given to Moses by God on Mt. Sinai. But Moses was a lawgiver as well as a religious leader. And the Ten Commandments have an undeniable historical meaning, as the foregoing examples demonstrate. Simply having religious content or promoting a message consistent with a religious doctrine does not run afoul of the Establishment Clause. . . .

There are, of course, limits to the display of religious messages or symbols. For example, we held unconstitutional a Kentucky statute requiring the posting of the Ten Commandments in every public schoolroom. Stone v. Graham, 449 U.S. 39 (1980) *(per curiam)*. In the classroom context, we found that the Kentucky statute had an improper and plainly religious purpose. . . . As evidenced by *Stone*'s almost exclusive reliance upon two of our school prayer cases, it stands as an example of the fact that we have "been particularly vigilant in monitoring compliance with the Establishment Clause in elementary and secondary schools," Neither *Stone* itself nor subsequent opinions have indicated that *Stone*'s holding would extend to a legislative chamber, . . . or to capitol grounds.

The placement of the Ten Commandments monument on the Texas State Capitol grounds is a far more passive use of those texts than was the case in *Stone,* where the text confronted elementary school students every day. Indeed, Van Orden, the petitioner here, apparently walked by the monument for a number of years before bringing this lawsuit. . . . Texas has treated her Capitol grounds monuments as representing the several strands in the State's political and legal history. The inclusion of the Ten Commandments monument in this group has a dual significance, partaking of both religion and government. We cannot say that Texas' display of this monument violates the Establishment Clause of the First Amendment.

The judgment of the Court of Appeals is affirmed.

. . .

JUSTICE SCALIA, concurring.

I join the opinion of the Chief Justice because I think it accurately reflects our current Establishment Clause jurisprudence—or at least the Establishment Clause jurisprudence we currently apply some of the time. I would prefer to reach the same result by adopting an Establishment Clause jurisprudence that is in accord with our Nation's past and present practices, and that can be consistently applied—the central relevant feature of which is that there is nothing unconstitutional in a State's favoring religion generally, honoring God through public prayer and acknowledgment, or, in a nonproselytizing manner, venerating the Ten Commandments. . . .

JUSTICE THOMAS, concurring.

. . . I join the Chief Justice's opinion in full.

This case would be easy if the Court were willing to abandon the inconsistent guideposts it has adopted for addressing Establishment Clause challenges, and return to the original meaning of the Clause. I have previously suggested that the Clause's text and history "resis[t] incorporation" against the States. . . . If the Establishment Clause does not restrain the States, then it has no application here, where only state action is at issue.

Even if the Clause is incorporated, or if the Free Exercise Clause limits the power of States to establish religions, . . . our task would be far simpler if we returned to the original meaning of the word "establishment" than it is under the various approaches this Court now uses. The Framers understood an establishment "necessarily [to] involve actual legal coercion. . . ."

There is no question that, based on the original meaning of the Establishment Clause, the Ten Commandments display at issue here is constitutional. In no sense does Texas compel petitioner Van Orden to do anything. The only injury to him is that he takes offense at seeing the monument as he passes it on his way to the Texas Supreme Court Library. He need not stop to read it or even to look at it, let alone to express support for it or adopt the Commandments as guides for his life. The mere presence of the monument along his path involves no coercion and thus does not violate the Establishment Clause.

Returning to the original meaning would do more than simplify our task. It also would avoid the pitfalls present in the Court's current approach to such challenges. This Court's precedent elevates the trivial to the proverbial "federal case," by making benign signs and postings subject to challenge. Yet even as it does so, the Court's precedent attempts to avoid declaring all religious symbols and words of longstanding tradition unconstitutional, by counterfactually declaring them of little religious significance. . . .

. . .

[T]he very "flexibility" of this Court's Establishment Clause precedent leaves it incapable of consistent application. of Establishment Clause challenges turns on judicial predilections.

Much, if not all, of this would be avoided if the Court would return to the views of the Framers and adopt coercion as the touchstone for our Establishment Clause inquiry. Every acknowledgment of religion would not give rise to an Establishment Clause claim. Courts would not act as theological commissions, judging the meaning of religious matters. Most important, our precedent would be capable of consistent and coherent application. While the Court correctly rejects the challenge to the Ten Commandments monument on the Texas Capitol grounds, a more fundamental rethinking of our Establishment Clause jurisprudence remains in order.

JUSTICE BREYER, concurring in the judgment.

In School Dist. of Abington Township v. Schempp, 374 U.S. 203 (1963), Justice Goldberg, joined by Justice Harlan, wrote, in respect to the First Amendment's Religion Clauses, that there is "no simple and clear measure which by precise application can readily and invariably demark the permissible from the impermissible." One must refer instead to the basic purposes of those Clauses. They seek to "assure the fullest possible scope of religious liberty and tolerance for all." They seek to avoid that divisiveness based upon religion that promotes social conflict, sapping the strength of government and religion alike ... They seek to maintain that "separation of church and state" that has long been critical to the "peaceful dominion that religion exercises in [this] country," ...

Thus, as Justices Goldberg and Harlan pointed out, the Court has found no single mechanical formula that can accurately draw the constitutional line in every case.... Where the Establishment Clause is at issue, tests designed to measure "neutrality" alone are insufficient, both because it is sometimes difficult to determine when a legal rule is "neutral," and because "untutored devotion to the concept of neutrality can lead to invocation or approval of results which partake not simply of that noninterference and noninvolvement with the religious which the Constitution commands, but of a brooding and pervasive devotion to the secular and a passive, or even active, hostility to the religious." ...

Neither can this Court's other tests readily explain the Establishment Clause's tolerance, for example, of the prayers that open legislative meetings, ... certain references to, and invocations of, the Deity in the public words of public officials; the public references to God on coins, decrees, and buildings; or the attention paid to the religious objectives of certain holidays, including Thanksgiving.

If the relation between government and religion is one of separation, but not of mutual hostility and suspicion, one will inevitably find difficult borderline cases. And in such cases, I see no test-related substitute for the exercise of legal judgment. ... That judgment is not a personal judgment. Rather, as in all constitutional cases, it must reflect and remain faithful to the underlying purposes of the Clauses, and it must take account of context and consequences measured in light of those purposes. While the Court's prior tests provide useful guideposts— and might well lead to the same result the Court reaches today,....

The case before us is a borderline case. It concerns a large granite monument bearing the text of the Ten Commandments located on the grounds of the Texas State Capitol. On the one hand, the Commandments' text undeniably has a religious message, invoking, indeed emphasizing, the Diety. On the other hand, focusing on the text of the Commandments alone cannot conclusively resolve this case. Rather, to determine the message that the text here conveys, we must examine how the text is *used*. And that inquiry requires us to consider the context of the display.

In certain contexts, a display of the tablets of the Ten Commandments can convey not simply a religious message but also a secular moral message (about proper standards of social conduct). And in certain contexts, a display of the tablets can also convey a historical message (about a historic relation between those standards and the law)—a fact that helps to explain the display of those tablets in dozens of courthouses throughout the Nation, including the Supreme Court of the United States.

Here the tablets have been used as part of a display that communicates not simply a religious message, but a secular message as well. The circumstances surrounding the display's placement on the capitol grounds and its physical setting suggest that the State itself intended the latter, nonreligious aspects of the tablets' message to predominate. And the monument's 40–year history on the Texas state grounds indicates that that has been its effect.

The group that donated the monument, the Fraternal Order of Eagles, a private civic (and primarily secular) organization, while interested in the religious aspect of the Ten Commandments, sought to highlight the Commandments' role in shaping civic morality as part of that organization's efforts to combat juvenile delinquency. ... The Eagles' consultation with a committee composed of members of several faiths in order to find a nonsectarian text underscores the group's ethics-based motives. The tablets, as displayed on the monument, prominently acknowledge that the Eagles donated the display, a factor which, though not sufficient, thereby further distances the State itself from the religious aspect of the Commandments' message.

. . .

... As far as I can tell, 40 years passed in which the presence of this monument, legally speaking, went unchallenged (until the single legal objection raised by petitioner). And I am not aware of any evidence suggesting that this was due to a climate of intimidation. Hence, those 40 years suggest more strongly than can any set of formulaic tests that few individuals, whatever their system of beliefs, are likely to have understood the monument as amounting, in any significantly detrimental way, to a government effort to favor a particular religious sect, primarily to promote religion over nonreligion, to "engage in" any "religious practic[e]," to "compel" any "religious practice," or to "work deterrence" of any "religious belief." ... Those 40 years suggest that the public visiting the capitol grounds has considered the religious aspect of the tablets' message as part of what is a broader moral and historical message reflective of a cultural heritage.

This case, moreover, is distinguishable from instances where the Court has found Ten Commandments displays impermissible. The display is not on the grounds of a public school, where, given the impressionability of the young, government must exercise particular care in separating church and state. ... This case also differs from *McCreary County*, where the short (and stormy) history of the courthouse Commandments' displays demonstrates the substantially religious objectives of those who mounted them, and the effect of this readily apparent objective upon those who view them. ... That history there indicates a governmental effort substantially to promote religion, not simply an effort primarily to reflect, historically, the secular impact of a religiously inspired document. And, in today's world, in a Nation of so many different religious and comparable nonreligious fundamental beliefs, a more contemporary state effort to focus attention upon a religious text is certainly likely to prove divisive in a way that this longstanding, pre-existing monument has not.

For these reasons, I believe that the Texas display—serving a mixed but primarily nonreligious purpose, not primarily "advanc[ing]" or "in-hibit[ing] religion," and not creating an "excessive government entangle-ment with religion,"—might satisfy this Court's more formal Establish-ment Clause tests. ... But, as I have said, in reaching the conclusion that the Texas display falls on the permissible side of the constitutional line, I rely less upon a literal application of any particular test than upon consideration of the basic purposes of the First Amendment's Religion Clauses themselves. This display has stood apparently uncontested for nearly two generations. That experience helps us understand that as a practical matter of *degree* this display is unlikely to prove divisive. And this matter of degree is, I believe, critical in a borderline case such as this one.

At the same time, to reach a contrary conclusion here, based primarily upon on the religious nature of the tablets' text would, I fear, lead the law to exhibit a hostility toward religion that has no place in our Establishment Clause traditions. Such a holding might well encourage disputes concerning the removal of longstanding depictions of the Ten Commandments from public buildings across the Nation. And it could thereby create the very kind of religiously based divisiveness that the Establishment Clause seeks to avoid. ...

In light of these considerations, I cannot agree with today's plurali-ty's analysis.Nor can I agree with Justice Scalia's dissent in ... *McCreary County* ... I do agree with Justice O'Connor's statement of principles in *McCreary County*, ... though I disagree with her evaluation of the evidence as it bears on the application of those principles to this case.

I concur in the judgment of the Court.

JUSTICE STEVENS, with whom JUSTICE GINSBURG joins, dissenting.

The sole function of the monument on the grounds of Texas' State Capitol is to display the full text of one version of the Ten Command-ments. The monument is not a work of art and does not refer to any event in the history of the State. ...

As the story goes, the program was initiated by the late Judge E.J. Ruegemer, a Minnesota juvenile court judge and then-Chairman of the Eagles National Commission on Youth Guidance. Inspired by a juvenile offender who had never heard of the Ten Commandments, the judge approached the Minnesota Eagles with the idea of distributing paper copies of the Commandments to be posted in courthouses nationwide. The State's Aerie undertook this project and its popularity spread. When

Cecil B. DeMille, who at that time was filming the movie The Ten Commandments, heard of the judge's endeavor, he teamed up with the Eagles to produce the type of granite monolith now displayed in front of the Texas Capitol and at courthouse squares, city halls, and public parks throughout the Nation. Granite was reportedly chosen over DeMille's original suggestion of bronze plaques to better replicate the original Ten Commandments.

The donors were motivated by a desire to "inspire the youth" and curb juvenile delinquency by providing children with a "code of conduct or standards by which to govern their actions." It is the Eagles' belief that disseminating the message conveyed by the Ten Commandments will help to persuade young men and women to observe civilized standards of behavior, and will lead to more productive lives. . . .

The desire to combat juvenile delinquency by providing guidance to youths is both admirable and unquestionably secular. But achieving that goal through biblical teachings injects a religious purpose into an otherwise secular endeavor. By spreading the word of God and converting heathens to Christianity, missionaries expect to enlighten their converts, enhance their satisfaction with life, and improve their behavior. Similarly, by disseminating the "law of God"—directing fidelity to God and proscribing murder, theft, and adultery—the Eagles hope that this divine guidance will help wayward youths conform their behavior and improve their lives. In my judgment, the significant secular by-products that are intended consequences of religious instruction—indeed, of the establishment of most religions—are not the type of "secular" purposes that justify government promulgation of sacred religious messages.

Though the State of Texas may genuinely wish to combat juvenile delinquency, and may rightly want to honor the Eagles for their efforts, it cannot effectuate these admirable purposes through an explicitly religious medium. . . . The State may admonish its citizens not to lie, cheat or steal, to honor their parents and to respect their neighbors' property; and it may do so by printed words, in television commercials, or on granite monuments in front of its public buildings. Moreover, the State may provide its schoolchildren and adult citizens with educational materials that explain the important role that our forebears' faith in God played in their decisions to select America as a refuge from religious persecution, to declare their independence from the British Crown, and to conceive a new Nation. . . . The message at issue in this case, however, is fundamentally different from either a bland admonition to observe generally accepted rules of behavior or a general history lesson.

The reason this message stands apart is that the Decalogue is a venerable religious text. . . . Thankfully, the plurality does not attempt to minimize the religious significance of the Ten Commandments. . . . Attempts to secularize what is unquestionably a sacred text defy credibility and disserve people of faith.

The profoundly sacred message embodied by the text inscribed on the Texas monument is emphasized by the especially large letters that identify its author: "**I AM the LORD thy God**." . . . It commands present worship of Him and no other deity. It directs us to be guided by

His teaching in the current and future conduct of all of our affairs. It instructs us to follow a code of divine law, some of which has informed and been integrated into our secular legal code ("Thou shalt not kill"), but much of which has not ("Thou shalt not make to thyself any graven images.... Thou shalt not covet").

Moreover, despite the Eagles' best efforts to choose a benign nondenominational text ... the Ten Commandments display projects not just a religious, but an inherently sectarian message. There are many distinctive versions of the Decalogue, ascribed to by different religions and even different denominations within a particular faith; to a pious and learned observer, these differences may be of enormous religious significance. ...

Even if, however, the message of the monument, despite the inscribed text, fairly could be said to represent the belief system of all Judeo–Christians, it would still run afoul of the Establishment Clause by prescribing a compelled code of conduct from one God, namely a Judeo–Christian God, that is rejected by prominent polytheistic sects, such as Hinduism, as well as nontheistic religions, such as Buddhism. ... Any of those bases, in my judgment, would be sufficient to conclude that the message should not be proclaimed by the State of Texas on a permanent monument at the seat of its government.

.   .   .

Recognizing the diversity of religious and secular beliefs held by Texans and by all Americans, it seems beyond peradventure that allowing the seat of government to serve as a stage for the propagation of an unmistakably Judeo–Christian message of piety would have the tendency to make nonmonotheists and nonbelievers "feel like [outsiders] in matters of faith, and [strangers] in the political community." ...

.   .   .

Critical examination of the Decalogue's prominent display at the seat of Texas government, rather than generic citation to the role of religion in American life, unmistakably reveals on which side of the "slippery slope," this display must fall. God, as the author of its message, the Eagles, as the donor of the monument, and the State of Texas, as its proud owner, speak with one voice for a common purpose— to encourage Texans to abide by the divine code of a "Judeo–Christian" God. If this message is permissible, then the shining principle of neutrality to which we have long adhered is nothing more than mere shadow.

III

The plurality relies heavily on the fact that our Republic was founded, and has been governed since its nascence, by leaders who spoke then (and speak still) in plainly religious rhetoric. ...

The speeches and rhetoric characteristic of the founding era, however, do not answer the question before us. I have already explained why Texas' display of the full text of the Ten Commandments, given the content of the actual display and the context in which it is situated, sets this case apart from the countless examples of benign government recognitions of religion. But there is another crucial difference. Our leaders, when delivering public addresses, often express their blessings simultaneously in the service of God and their constituents. Thus, when public officials deliver public speeches, we recognize that their words are not exclusively a transmission from *the* government because those oratories have embedded within them the inherently personal views of the speaker as an individual member of the polity. The permanent placement of a textual religious display on state property is different in kind; it amalgamates otherwise discordant individual views into a collective statement of government approval. Moreover, the message never ceases to transmit itself to objecting viewers whose only choices are to accept the message or to ignore the offense by averting their gaze.

The plurality's reliance on early religious statements and proclamations made by the Founders is also problematic because those views were not espoused at the Constitutional Convention in 1787 nor enshrined in the Constitution's text. Thus, the presentation of these religious statements as a unified historical narrative is bound to paint a misleading picture. . . .

· · ·

Ardent separationists aside, there is another critical nuance lost in the plurality's portrayal of history. Simply put, many of the Founders who are often cited as authoritative expositors of the Constitution's original meaning understood the Establishment Clause to stand for a *narrower* proposition than the plurality, for whatever reason, is willing to accept. Namely, many of the Framers understood the word "religion" in the Establishment Clause to encompass only the various sects of Christianity.

· · ·

Unless one is willing to renounce over 65 years of Establishment Clause jurisprudence and cross back over the incorporation bridge, . . . appeals to the religiosity of the Framers ring hollow. But even if there were a coherent way to embrace incorporation with one hand while steadfastly abiding by the Founders' purported religious views on the other, the problem of the selective use of history remains. As the widely divergent views espoused by the leaders of our founding era plainly reveal, the historical record of the preincorporation Establishment Clause is too indeterminate to serve as an interpretive North Star.

· · ·

It is our duty, therefore, to interpret the First Amendment's command that "Congress shall make no law respecting an establishment of religion" not by merely asking what those words meant to observers at the time of the founding, but instead by deriving from the Clause's text and history the broad principles that remain valid today. To reason from the broad principles contained in the Constitution does not, as Justice Scalia suggests, require us to abandon our heritage in favor of unprincipled expressions of personal preference. The task of applying the broad principles that the Framers wrote into the text of the First Amendment is, in any event, no more a matter of personal preference than is one's selection between two (or more) sides in a heated historical debate. We serve our constitutional mandate by expounding the meaning of constitutional provisions with one eye towards our Nation's history and the other fixed on its democratic aspirations. . . .

The principle that guides my analysis is neutrality. The basis for that principle is firmly rooted in our Nation's history and our Constitution's text. I recognize that the requirement that government must remain neutral between religion and irreligion would have seemed foreign to some of the Framers; so too would a requirement of neutrality between Jews and Christians. . . . *McCreary County*, is in my view a direct descendent of the evil of discriminating among Christian sects. The Establishment Clause thus forbids it and, in turn, forbids Texas from displaying the Ten Commandments monument the plurality so casually affirms.

. . .

IV

The Eagles may donate as many monuments as they choose to be displayed in front of Protestant churches, benevolent organizations' meeting places, or on the front lawns of private citizens. The expurgated text of the King James version of the Ten Commandments that they have crafted is unlikely to be accepted by Catholic parishes, Jewish synagogues, or even some Protestant denominations, but the message they seek to convey is surely more compatible with church property than with property that is located on the government side of the metaphorical wall.

The judgment of the Court in this case stands for the proposition that the Constitution permits governmental displays of sacred religious texts. This makes a mockery of the constitutional ideal that government must remain neutral between religion and irreligion. If a State may endorse a particular deity's command to "have no other gods before me," it is difficult to conceive of any textual display that would run afoul of the Establishment Clause.

The disconnect between this Court's approval of Texas's monument and the constitutional prohibition against preferring religion to irreligion cannot be reduced to the exercise of plotting two adjacent locations on a slippery slope. . . . Rather, it is the difference between the shelter of a fortress and exposure to "the winds that would blow" if the wall were allowed to crumble. . . . That wall, however imperfect, remains worth preserving.

I respectfully dissent.

JUSTICE O'CONNOR, dissenting.

For essentially the reasons given by Justice Souter, as well as the reasons given in my concurrence in McCreary County v. American Civil Liberties Union of Ky, I respectfully dissent.

JUSTICE SOUTER, with whom JUSTICE STEVENS and JUSTICE GINSBURG join, dissenting.

Although the First Amendment's Religion Clauses have not been read to mandate absolute governmental neutrality toward religion ... the Establishment Clause requires neutrality as a general rule,.... A governmental display of an obviously religious text cannot be squared with neutrality, except in a setting that plausibly indicates that the statement is not placed in view with a predominant purpose on the part of government either to adopt the religious message or to urge its acceptance by others.

Until today, only one of our cases addressed the constitutionality of posting the Ten Commandments, Stone v. Graham, ... 449 U.S. 39, 41–42 (1980) *(per curiam)*. A Kentucky statute required posting the Commandments on the walls of public school classrooms, and the Court described the State's purpose (relevant under the tripartite test laid out in Lemon v. Kurtzman ... as being at odds with the obligation of religious neutrality). What these observations underscore are the simple realities that the Ten Commandments constitute a religious statement, that their message is inherently religious, and that the purpose of singling them out in a display is clearly the same. ...

[T]he Fraternal Order of Eagles, the group that gave the monument to the State of Texas, donated identical monuments to other jurisdictions, it was seeking to impart a religious message. ...

Thus, a pedestrian happening upon the monument at issue here needs no training in religious doctrine to realize that the statement of the Commandments, quoting God himself, proclaims that the will of the divine being is the source of obligation to obey the rules, including the facially secular ones. In this case, moreover, the text is presented to give particular prominence to the Commandments' first sectarian reference, "I am the Lord thy God." That proclamation is centered on the stone and written in slightly larger letters than the subsequent recitation. To ensure that the religious nature of the monument is clear to even the most casual passerby, the word "Lord" appears in all capital letters (as does the word "am"), so that the most eye-catching segment of the quotation is the declaration "I AM the LORD thy God." What follows, of course, are the rules against other gods, graven images, vain swearing, and Sabbath breaking. And the full text of the fifth Commandment puts forward filial respect as a condition of long life in the land "which the Lord they God giveth thee." ...

To drive the religious point home, and identify the message as religious to any viewer who failed to read the text, the engraved quotation is framed by religious symbols: two tablets with what appears to be ancient script on them, two Stars of David, and the superimposed Greek letters Chi and Rho as the familiar monogram of Christ. Nothing on the monument, in fact, detracts from its religious nature. ...

The monument's presentation of the Commandments with religious text emphasized and enhanced stands in contrast to any number of perfectly constitutional depictions of them, the frieze of our own Courtroom providing a good example, where the figure of Moses stands among history's great lawgivers. While Moses holds the tablets of the Commandments showing some Hebrew text, no one looking at the lines of figures in marble relief is likely to see a religious purpose behind the assemblage or take away a religious message from it. Only one other depiction represents a religious leader, and the historical personages are mixed with symbols of moral and intellectual abstractions like Equity and Authority. . . .

. . .

Texas seeks to take advantage of the recognition that visual symbol and written text can manifest a secular purpose in secular company, when it argues that its monument (like Moses in the frieze) is not alone and ought to be viewed as only 1 among 17 placed on the 22 acres surrounding the state capitol. Texas, indeed, says that the Capitol grounds are like a museum for a collection of exhibits, the kind of setting that several Members of the Court have said can render the exhibition of religious artifacts permissible, even though in other circumstances their display would be seen as meant to convey a religious message forbidden to the State. . . . So, for example, the Government of the United States does not violate the Establishment Clause by hanging Giotto's Madonna on the wall of the National Gallery.

But 17 monuments with no common appearance, history, or esthetic role scattered over 22 acres is not a museum, and anyone strolling around the lawn would surely take each memorial on its own terms without any dawning sense that some purpose held the miscellany together more coherently than fortuity and the edge of the grass. One monument expresses admiration for pioneer women. One pays respect to the fighters of World War II. And one quotes the God of Abraham whose command is the sanction for moral law. The themes are individual grit, patriotic courage, and God as the source of Jewish and Christian morality; there is no common denominator. in the building. . . .

Finally, though this too is a point on which judgment will vary, I do not see a persuasive argument for constitutionality in the plurality's observation that Van Orden's lawsuit comes "[f]orty years after the monument's erection . . .," an observation that echoes the State's contention that one fact cutting in its favor is that "the monument stood . . . in Austin . . . for some forty years without generating any controversy or litigation," It is not that I think the passage of time is necessarily irrelevant in Establishment Clause analysis. We have approved framing-era practices because they must originally have been understood as constitutionally permissible, . . . and we have recognized that Sunday laws have grown recognizably secular over time . . . There is also an analogous argument, not yet evaluated, that ritualistic religious expression can become so numbing over time that its initial Establishment Clause violation becomes at some point too diminished for notice. But I do not understand any of these to be the State's argument, which rather seems to be that 40 years without a challenge shows that as a factual matter the religious expression is too tepid to provoke a serious reaction and constitute a violation. Perhaps, but the writer of Exodus chapter 20 was not lukewarm, and other explanations may do better in accounting for the late resort to the courts. Suing a State over religion puts nothing in a plaintiff's pocket and can take a great deal out, and even with

volunteer litigators to supply time and energy, the risk of social ostracism can be powerfully deterrent. I doubt that a slow walk to the
courthouse, even one that took 40 years, is much evidentiary help in
applying the Establishment Clause.

I would reverse the judgment of the Court of Appeals.

NOTES AND QUESTIONS

1.   There were ten opinions in the Ten Commandments cases, and a
narrow majority agreed with only one of those opinions—Justice Souter's in *McCreary*. What does this suggest about the present state of
Establishment Clause jurisprudence?

2.   In his *McCreary* opinion, Justice Souter quoted Justice O'Connor's previous concurring opinions in Establishment cases seven times.
Why was he so partial to Justice O'Connor's previous concurring opinions?

3.   What was the reason for Justice Breyer's vote in *Van Orden*? It
was apparently not principle but a concern about the consequences of a
contrary holding, which he believed might be "religiously based divisiveness that the Establishment Clause seeks to avoid." Justice Scalia
suggested in *McCreary* that the reason for votes like Breyer's in previous
cases ignoring the neutrality principle was the Court's "instinct for self
preservation and the recognition that the Court ... cannot go too far
down he road of an enforced neutrality that contradicts both historical
fact and current without losing all that sustains it: the willingness of the
people to accept it interpretation of the Constitution as definitive, in
preference to the contrary interpretation of the democratically elected
branches." Is Justice Scalia's suggestion a plausible explanation of
Justice Breyer's vote in *Van Orden*?

Part Four

PRIVACY

During our discussion of the First Amendment, we encountered the right to privacy in four contexts—the possession of obscene material in one's home, the right to damages for media invasions of privacy, freedom of association, and the right to silence.

The next three chapters cover other constitutional guarantees that protect privacy—prohibition on unreasonable search and seizure, restrictions upon compulsory self-incrimination, and constitutional guarantees of autonomy.

As we will see, none of the doctrines that we discuss affords complete protection to the individual's privacy. Rather, each of them protects some aspects of privacy along with certain other values. Indeed, as the following excerpts indicate, the meaning of privacy itself is not too clear. It involves, to be sure, some idea of the control of information about oneself—that certain information is private and is not to be publicized to one's embarrassment, humiliation, or injury. Privacy also has something to do with the prevention of certain kinds of intrusions into the individual's life. Thus a police search of one's home and papers, or even a simple telephone solicitation, at a time when one would rather be doing something else, may cause inconvenience apart from any private information they may gain. Privacy, finally, may also involve the concept of autonomy—the individual's right to make certain decisions free from any regulation.

Chapter XX

THE PROHIBITION OF UNREASONABLE SEARCHES AND SEIZURES

I. HISTORICAL BACKGROUND AND RATIONALE

A. THE ENGLISH DEVELOPMENT*

The Fourth Amendment was not a construct based on abstract considerations of political theory, but was drafted by the framers for the express purpose of providing enforceable safeguards against a recurrence of highhanded search measures which Americans, as well as the people of England, had recently experienced. These abuses, which in the American colonies took place largely in the fifteen years before the American Revolution and which extended over a much longer period of time in England, had done violence to the ancient maxim that "A man's house is his castle." It was to guard against a repetition of these experiences that six of the newly independent American states almost immediately wrote into their own constitutions provisions akin to those of the Fourth Amendment. The antecedent history of the Fourth Amendment, therefore, has two principal sources: the English and American experiences of virtually unrestrained and judicially unsupervised searches, and the action that had already been taken by some of the states to guard constitutionally against a recurrence of this abuse. From these tributaries flowed the Fourth Amendment.

A broad search and seizure power was first introduced into England by the Tudors.[1] This power was continually exercised and expanded as an important instrument in the enforcement of the state licensing system for printed matter. The fight for freedom of the press waged in England for nearly three centuries was thus connected with the issue of the scope of search power.

Within fifty years of the introduction of printing into England in 1476, the control of seditious and nonconformist publications had become a matter of intense state concern. . . .

To help enforce the licensing system, vast powers of search were conferred on those engaged in ferreting out violators and evidence. The Stationers' Company, a private guild organization, was incorporated

---

* Jacob W. Landynski, Search and Seizure and the Supreme Court, Johns Hopkins Press, 1966, pp. 20–30.

1. The use of the search power prior to the Tudors seems to have been sporadic. The first parliamentary legislation on the subject did not appear until the fourteenth century. This legislation, passed in 1335 in the reign of Edward III, required innkeepers in the ports to search guests for imported counterfeit money. As a reward for their trouble they were given one quarter of the seizures. . . .

under Mary in 1557 and, in return for monopoly privileges over printing granted to its members, was instructed "to make search wherever it shall please them in any place ... within our kingdom of England ... and to seize, take hold, burn ... those books and things which are or shall be printed contrary to the form of any statute, act, or proclamation...." ... For nearly a century, until the decline and fall of the monarchy in the 1640's, the Company assumed the main responsibility of enforcement. Its zeal in making the licensing system effective was motivated solely by self-gain; in searching for non-licensed printing its members were, in effect, protecting their own monopoly rights.

. . .

Conditions in seventeenth-century England showed no improvement. James I directed the Court of High Commission "to inquire and search for ... all heretical, schismatical and seditious books, libels and writings, and all other books, pamphlets and portraitures offensive to the state or set forth without sufficient and lawful authority" and to seize the offending materials, together with the presses used to print them. It was in James's reign, apparently, that the writ of assistance (a general warrant for the search and seizure of smuggled goods, so called because it charged all officers of the Crown with assisting those executing the warrant) made its first appearance....

. . .

We have thus far witnessed a virtually uninterrupted growth of the search and seizure power in England over a period of a century and a half. When did limitations eventually come to be placed on the exercise of this power? It seems that, with respect to Parliament's attitude, at least, the Revolution of 1688 marked a turning point of some moment....

It was through efforts to control abusive enforcement of tax laws that limits were first placed on search and seizure. At the urging of the new king, William of Orange, one tax was abolished by Parliament specifically on the ground that the searches required in its enforcement constituted "a badge of slavery upon the whole people, exposing every man's house to be entered into, and searched by persons unknown to him." In 1733 a tobacco and wine tax proposed by Walpole failed of parliamentary enactment because of its search provisions though under its terms only warehouses would have been subject to search on a general warrant; a special warrant would have been required for the search of dwellings. And in 1763 William Pitt proclaimed against the cider tax and its enforcement provisions. In words which have rung out through the centuries, he cried: "The poorest man in his cottage may bid defiance to all the force of the Crown. It may be frail—its roof may shake—the wind may blow through it—the storm may enter—the rain may enter—but the King of England cannot enter; all his force dares not cross the threshold of that ruined tenement!"

Was there any deep-rooted principle in English law that could be set against the galloping search power, and which might be said to be the basis of our Fourth Amendment? ...

More important for our purposes ... was the development of the common law. In disregard of the sweeping arrest and search authorizations by Star Chamber and Parliament, common-law jurists were busy formulating salutary rules of arrest, search, and seizure for everyday crimes either by judicial decision or by recommendation. Foremost among these jurists was Hale, who in his renowned *History of the Pleas of the Crown* charted legal rules, some based on case precedents, which would later be elevated to constitutional principles in the United States.

... Hale ... authorized the use of search warrants on the ground of "necessity, especially in these times, where felonies and robberies are so frequent." Nonetheless, in order to be valid the warrant had to meet certain standards. Hale declared general warrants void, though he admitted there was precedent for them even under common law. They "are not justifiable, for it makes the party to be in effect the judge; and therefore searches made by pretense of such general warrants give no more power to the officer or party, than what they may do by law without them." Even specific warrants, which met the test of particularity in descriptions of persons and premises, were "judicial acts" requiring judicial approval, and were not to be issued unless they followed an examination of the complainant under oath and a finding of probable cause. The following sentence sums up Hale's idea: "They [warrants] are not to be granted without oath made before the justice of a felony committed, and that the party complaining hath probable cause to suspect they are in such a house or place, and do shew his reasons of such suspicion." ...

Such voices as Hale's had gone largely unheeded by King and Parliament. Now, ... it was the judiciary which, in a series of important cases, provided the principal driving force for the abolition of the general warrant. . . .

. . .

The most famous case in the series was Entick v. Carrington, decided in 1765.... Entick, the editor of a critical publication, the *Monitor,* was the victim ... of a general search in which his papers were seized.... Entick ... brought a suit for trespass which won a jury verdict of three hundred pounds.... Lord Camden delivered the opinion of the Court of Common Pleas sustaining the verdict on appeal. "[I]f this point should be determined in favor of the jurisdiction," he declared, "the secret cabinets and bureaus of every subject in this kingdom will be thrown open to the search and inspection of a messenger, whenever the secretary of state shall think fit to charge, or even to suspect, a person to be the author, printer, or publisher of a seditious libel." He rudely dismissed Star Chamber precedent as without authority in a common law court. Such precedent "is null, and nothing but ignorance can excuse the judge that subscribed [to] it."

These judicial decisions, and the popular feeling they aroused, were influential in forcing Parliament to act.... In 1766 the Commons denounced general search warrants as illegal except when their use might specifically be authorized by act of Parliament. The luster of this achievement was, however, somewhat dimmed by the failure of a proposal to abolish the general arrest warrant. It must also be remembered that the power to issue writs of assistance to search for smuggled goods, previously authorized by Parliament, remained unimpaired.

B.   THE DEVELOPMENT IN THE UNITED STATES*

While Englishmen were struggling to free themselves of the bane of indiscriminate searches, important developments concerning the search power were taking place across the Atlantic in England's American colonies. In defense of the mercantile system, Parliament had passed a number of navigation and trade acts which, through the imposition of prohibitive import duties, were designed to prevent the colonies from trading with areas outside the Empire. Before 1760 enforcement was lax and these laws were honored more in the breach than in the observance. Smuggling became rampant in the colonies and was engaged in even by the most respectable persons in order to circumvent laws regarded as oppressive and unjustifiable. In 1760, however, with the French and Indian Wars successfully over, the effort to stamp out smuggling began in earnest. The principal enforcement weapon was the writ of assistance.

In the colonies the writs of assistance ... caused profound resentment. Massachusetts furnishes us with most of the extant historical record concerning colonial writs of assistance, for it was in the Bay province that they were most frequently employed and there that most opposition to their enforcement was encountered. In Massachusetts, as elsewhere in the colonies, it was once the unopposed practice of customs officers to enter and search buildings with no more formal authority than that of their commissions as Crown officers. When opposition to these searches was aroused, the Governor found it necessary to issue writs of assistance to the officers. This practice continued until objections to the propriety of the procedure led the Governor to advise the officers to apply for writs in the Superior Court. Thereafter, the Superior Court took over the function of issuing writs....

... [T]he death of George II [in 1760 set the stage for a court test of the writs.] Since writs of assistance were valid only until six months after the demise of the sovereign in whose reign they were issued, this meant that the writs then in force would expire early in 1761 and new ones would be needed....

Sixty-three Boston merchants, opposed to the issuance of new writs, engaged James Otis, Jr., and Oxenbridge Tatcher to argue their cause....

.   .   .

Otis—"by far the most able, manly and commanding Character of his Age at the Bar," according to John Adams—might have confined himself to challenging the applicability of these statutes to writs of assistance in the colonies.... Otis did argue along this line, but he seized the opportunity to range broadly beyond these limited horizons and, in a stirring argument, on libertarian grounds asserted the princi-

* Ibid., pp. 30–42.

ples of English constitutionalism. He denounced the writ as "the worst instrument of arbitrary power, the most destructive of English liberty and the fundamental principles of law, that was ever found in an English law-book." ...

So impressive was Otis' argument that as [Chief Justice] Hutchinson later acknowledged, "the court seemed inclined to refuse to grant" the writ. The Chief Justice, however, prevailed on his brethren not to render decision immediately but to continue the case while the question was referred to England. Hutchinson wrote for advice ... to the provincial agent, who had once served as a Crown prosecutor in Massachusetts. Upon his favorable reply, the court heard argument once again, in November, 1761, and proceeded to issue the first of the new writs....

·   ·   ·

The controversy over writs of assistance in the colonies continued all the way up to the Revolutionary War. Even after the outbreak of hostilities, the Continental Congress petitioned the King on October 26, 1774, for a redress of grievances, and among those listed was the abuse of the search power: "The officers of the customs are empowered to break open and enter houses, without the authority of any civil magistrate, founded on legal information." It is therefore surprising that the Declaration of Independence, which in its main part consisted of a long list of grievances against the Crown, contained no specific mention of writs of assistance. But that subject may have been alluded to in the remonstrance: "He has ... sent hither swarms of Officers to harass our people...." Even prior to the Declaration, in June of 1776, Virginia had already moved to provide a constitutional guarantee against recurrence of the abuse. Article X of its Declaration of Rights specifically denounced general warrants as "grievous and oppressive." ...

·   ·   ·

In [debates over ratification of the Constitution in] the pivotal state of Virginia, Patrick Henry forcefully urged rejection, and made the absence of a search provision a cardinal point in his argument:

> Any man may be seized, any property may be taken, in the most arbitrary manner, without any evidence or reason. Every thing the most sacred may be searched and ransacked by the strong hand of power. We have infinitely more reason to dread general warrants here than they have in England, because there, if a person be confined, liberty may be quickly obtained by the writ of *habeas corpus*. But here a man living many hundreds of miles from the judges may get in prison before he can get that writ.

Virginia did eventually ratify the Constitution, but not before recommending the adoption of a bill of rights with a search provision even broader than the one in its own Declaration of Rights....

... [Madison, as we have already seen, assumed the leading role in the First Congress' efforts to provide a bill of rights in satisfaction of these and other demands. In the debate he] specifically adverted to the need for search safeguards in the light of the necessary and proper clause: "The General Government has a right to pass all laws which shall be necessary to collect its revenue; the means for enforcing the collection are within the discretion of the Legislature: may not general warrants be considered necessary for this purpose ... ?" Madison's solution to the problem was a clause to read as follows: "The rights of the people to be secure in their persons, their houses, their papers, and their other property, from all unreasonable searches and seizures, shall not be violated by warrants issued without probable cause, supported by oath or affirmation, or not particularly describing the places to be searched, or the persons or things to be seized."

Madison's draft proposal for a bill of rights was referred to committee, where the search provision was altered to read: "The right of the people to be secured in their persons, houses, papers, and effects, shall not be violated by warrants issuing without probable cause, supported by oath or affirmation, and not particularly describing the place to be searched and the persons or things to be seized."

After this version was reported to the House, two errors were noticed by Gerry and were corrected. The word "secured" was altered to read "secure," and the phrase "unreasonable searches and seizures," inadvertently omitted in the committee's draft, was inserted. Benson of New York, objecting to the words "by warrants issuing" as not sufficiently strong, proposed to substitute the words "and no warrant shall issue," but this version was voted down by a substantial majority. Why, might we ask, is Benson's version, the one which failed to carry, embodied today in the Fourth Amendment? For the explanation we are indebted to Lasson. It is possible that Benson, as chairman of a committee to arrange the amendments as passed, instead reported his own version of the amendment as it had been rejected. No one apparently noticed the change.... [T]he amendment *in its present form* was formally passed by the House and the Senate and ratified by the states.

II.   WIRETAPPING, EAVESDROPPING AND THE FOURTH AMENDMENT

OLMSTEAD v. UNITED STATES

Supreme Court of the United States, 1928.
277 U.S. 438, 48 S.Ct. 564, 72 L.Ed. 944.

CHIEF JUSTICE TAFT delivered the opinion of the Court.

. . .

The evidence in the records discloses a conspiracy of amazing magnitude to import, possess and sell liquor unlawfully. It involved the employment of not less than fifty persons, of two seagoing vessels for the transportation of liquor to British Columbia, of smaller vessels for coastwise transportation to the State of Washington, the purchase and use of a ranch beyond the suburban limits of Seattle, with a large underground cache for storage and a number of smaller caches in that city, the maintenance of a central office manned with operators, the employment of executives, salesmen, deliverymen, dispatchers, scouts, bookkeepers, collectors and an attorney. In a bad month sales amounted to $176,000; the aggregate for a year must have exceeded two million dollars.

 WILLIAM HOWARD TAFT—Born on September 15, 1857, in Cincinnati, Ohio, son of a lawyer and state trial judge who became U.S. attorney general, secretary of war, and minister to Vienna and St. Petersburg. Yale, A.B., 1878, graduating second in his class; Cincinnati, LL.B., 1880. Assistant prosecuting attorney, Hamilton County, Ohio, 1881–1883; law practice, 1883–1887; assistant county solicitor, Hamilton County, Ohio, 1885–1887; Cincinnati superior court judge, 1887–1890; U.S. solicitor general, 1890–1891; U.S. Court of Appeals judge (Sixth Circuit), 1892–1900; governor of the Philippines, 1901–1904; secretary of war, 1904–1908; U.S. president, 1909–1913; Yale constitutional law professor, 1913–1921. Nominated chief justice of the U.S. on June 30, 1921, by President Warren G. Harding to replace Edward D. White, whom Taft had promoted to the chief justiceship in 1910. Confirmed by the Senate on June 30, 1921, by voice vote. Retired on February 3, 1930. Died on March 8, 1930. Like his father, Taft aspired to the Supreme Court during most of his professional life and was a serious candidate for the Court as early as 1891.

. . .

The information which led to the discovery of the conspiracy and its nature and extent was largely obtained by intercepting messages on the telephones of the conspirators by four federal prohibition officers. Small wires were inserted along the ordinary telephone wires from the residences of four of the petitioners and those leading from the chief office. The insertions were made without trespass upon any property of the defendants. They were made in the basement of the large office building. The taps from house lines were made in the streets near the houses.

The gathering of evidence continued for many months. Conversations of the conspirators of which refreshing stenographic notes were currently made, were testified to by the government witnesses. They revealed the large business transactions of the partners and their subordinates. Men at the wires heard the orders given for liquor by customers and the acceptances; they became auditors of the conversations between the partners. All this disclosed the conspiracy charged in the indictment. Many of the intercepted conversations were not merely reports but parts of the criminal acts. The evidence also disclosed the difficulties to which the conspirators were subjected, the reported news of the capture of vessels, the arrest of their men and the seizure of cases of liquor in garages and other places. It showed the dealing by Olmstead, the chief conspirator, with members of the Seattle police, the messages to them which secured the release of arrested members of the conspiracy, and also direct promises to officers of payments as soon as opportunity offered.

[The Court discussed the contention made by Olmstead that the wiretapping of "private telephone conversations between the defendants and others ... amounted to a violation of the Fourth Amendment."]

The well known historical purpose of the Fourth Amendment, directed against general warrants and writs of assistance, was to prevent the use of governmental force to search a man's house, his person, his papers and his effects; and to prevent their seizure against his will. . . .

. . .

The Amendment itself shows that the search is to be of material things—the person, the house, his papers or his effects. The description of the warrant necessary to make the proceeding lawful, is that it must specify the place to be searched and the person or *things* to be seized.

. . . It is plainly within the words of the Amendment to say that the unlawful rifling by a government agent of a sealed letter is a search and seizure of the sender's papers or effects. The letter is a paper, an effect, and in the custody of a Government that forbids carriage except under its protection.

The United States takes no such care of telegraph or telephone messages as of mailed sealed letters. The Amendment does not forbid what was done here. There was no searching. There was no seizure. The evidence was secured by the use of the sense of hearing and that only. There was no entry of the houses or offices of the defendants.

By the invention of the telephone, fifty years ago, and its application for the purpose of extending communications, one can talk with another at a far distant place. The language of the Amendment can not be extended and expanded to include telephone wires reaching to the whole world from the defendant's house or office. The intervening wires are not part of his house or office any more than are the highways along which they are stretched.

. . .

. . . [T]he Fourth Amendment [is] to be liberally construed to effect the purpose of the framers of the Constitution in the interest of liberty. But that can not justify enlargement of the language employed beyond the possible practical meaning of houses, persons, papers, and effects, or so to apply the words search and seizure as to forbid hearing or sight.

. . .

Congress may of course protect the secrecy of telephone messages by making them when intercepted inadmissible in evidence in federal criminal trials, by direct legislation, and thus depart from the common law of evidence. But the courts may not adopt such a policy by attributing an enlarged and unusual meaning to the Fourth Amendment. The reasonable view is that one who installs in his house a telephone instrument with connecting wires intends to project his voice to those quite outside, and that the wires beyond his house and messages while passing over them are not within the protection of the Fourth Amendment. Here those who intercepted the projected voices were not in the house of either party to the conversation.

Neither the cases we have cited nor any of the many federal decisions brought to our attention hold the Fourth Amendment to have been violated as against a defendant unless there has been an official search and seizure of his person, or such a seizure of his papers or his tangible material effects, or an actual physical invasion of his house "or curtilage" for the purpose of making a seizure.

We think, therefore, that the wire tapping here disclosed did not amount to a search or seizure within the meaning of the Fourth Amendment.

· · ·

JUSTICE BRANDEIS dissenting.*

· · ·

The government ... concedes that if wiretapping can be deemed a search and seizure within the Fourth Amendment, such wiretapping as was practiced in the case at bar was an unreasonable search and seizure, and that the evidence thus obtained was inadmissible. But it relies on the language of the Amendment; and it claims that the protection given thereby cannot properly be held to include a telephone conversation.

"We must never forget," said Chief Justice Marshall in McCulloch v. Maryland, 4 Wheat. 316, 407, "that it is a constitution we are expounding." Since then, this Court has repeatedly sustained the exercise of power by Congress, under various clauses of that instrument, over objects of which the Fathers could not have dreamed. We have likewise held that general limitations on the powers of Government, like those embodied in the due process clauses of the Fifth and Fourteenth Amendments, do not forbid the United States or the States from meeting modern conditions by regulations which "a century ago, or even half a century ago, probably would have been rejected as arbitrary and oppressive." Clauses guaranteeing to the individual protection against specific abuses of power, must have a similar capacity of adaptation to a changing world. . . .

When the Fourth and Fifth Amendments were adopted, "the form that evil had theretofore taken," had been necessarily simple. Force and violence were then the only means known to man by which a Government could directly effect self-incrimination. It could compel the individual to testify—a compulsion effected, if need be, by torture. It could secure possession of his papers and other articles incident to his private life—a seizure effected, if need be, by breaking and entry. Protection against such invasion of "the sanctities of a man's home and the privacies of life" was provided in the Fourth and Fifth Amendments by specific language. But "time works changes, brings into existence new conditions and purposes." Subtler and more far-reaching means of invading privacy have become available to the Government. Discovery and invention have made it possible for the Government, by means far

* Dissenting opinions by Justices Holmes, Butler, and Stone are omitted.

more effective than stretching upon the rack, to obtain disclosure in court of what is whispered in the closet.

Moreover, "in the application of a constitution, our contemplation cannot be only of what has been but of what may be." The progress of science in furnishing the Government with means of espionage is not likely to stop with wire-tapping. Ways may some day be developed by which the Government, without removing papers from secret drawers, can reproduce them in court, and by which it will be enabled to expose to a jury the most intimate occurrences of the home. Advances in the psychic and related sciences may bring means of exploring unexpressed beliefs, thoughts and emotions. "That places the liberty of every man in the hands of every petty officer" was said by James Otis of much lesser intrusions than these. To Lord Camden, a far slighter intrusion seemed "subversive of all the comforts of society." Can it be that the Constitution affords no protection against such invasions of individual security?

. . .

. . . [A] sealed letter entrusted to the mail is protected by the Amendments. The mail is a public service furnished by the Government. The telephone is a public service furnished by its authority. There is, in essence, no difference between the sealed letter and the private telephone message. As Judge Rudkin said below: "True the one is visible, the other invisible; the one is tangible, the other intangible; the one is sealed and the other unsealed, but these are distinctions without a difference." The evil incident to invasion of the privacy of the telephone is far greater than that involved in tampering with the mails. Whenever a telephone line is tapped, the privacy of the persons at both ends of the line is invaded and all conversations between them upon any subject, and although proper, confidential and privileged, may be overheard. Moreover, the tapping of one man's telephone line involves the tapping of the telephone of every other person whom he may call or who may call him. As a means of espionage, writs of assistance and general warrants are but puny instruments of tyranny and oppression when compared with wiretapping.

Time and again, this Court in giving effect to the principle underlying the Fourth Amendment, has refused to place an unduly literal construction upon it. . . .

. . .

. . . The makers of our Constitution undertook to secure conditions favorable to the pursuit of happiness. They recognized the significance of man's spiritual nature, of his feelings and of his intellect. They knew that only a part of the pain, pleasure and satisfactions of life are to be found in material things. They sought to protect Americans in their beliefs, their thoughts, their emotions and their sensations. They conferred, as against the Government, the right to be let alone—the most comprehensive of rights and the right most valued by civilized men. To protect that right, every unjustifiable intrusion by the Government upon the privacy of the individual, whatever the means employed, must be deemed a violation of the Fourth Amendment.

Applying to the Fourth and Fifth Amendments the established rule of construction, the defendants' objections to the evidence obtained by wiretapping must, in my opinion, be sustained. It is, of course, immaterial where the physical connection with the telephone wires leading into the defendants' premises was made. And it is also immaterial that the intrusion was in aid of law enforcement. Experience should teach us to be most on our guard to protect liberty when the Government's purposes are beneficent. Men born to freedom are naturally alert to repel invasion of their liberty by evil-minded rulers. The greatest dangers to liberty lurk in insidious encroachment by men of zeal, well-meaning but without understanding.

. . .

NOTE ON THE EXCLUSIONARY RULE

Note that both the majority opinion and the dissent in *Olmstead* assumed that, if wiretapping had violated the defendant's Fourth Amendment rights, the evidence so obtained would have been inadmissible in the case. This is a consequence of what is called the "exclusionary rule." This rule, laid down by the Supreme Court in 1914 in Weeks v. United States, 232 U.S. 383, provides—subject to a number of complex exceptions—that, if the government obtains evidence through an unconstitutional search and seizure, it cannot use this evidence in a criminal prosecution. In 1961, the Supreme Court, in Mapp v. Ohio, 367 U.S. 643, extended the exclusionary rule to the state governments.*

The exclusionary rule has been attacked as undesirable on the ground that it can prevent the conviction of criminals simply because police have made an error in search and seizure. Interestingly, the *Olmstead* case contains the classic arguments for an even broader form of the exclusionary rule than now exists. Justices Holmes and Brandeis in their dissents argued that, even apart from whether the federal officials' conduct violated any Fourth Amendment rights, the wiretapped evidence should have been excluded because wiretapping was a crime under the laws of Washington, the state where the events occurred.

Justice Holmes wrote:

... It is desirable that criminals should be detected, and to that end that all available evidence should be used. It also is desirable that the Government should not itself foster and pay for other crimes, when they are the means by which the evidence is to be obtained. If it pays its officers for having got evidence by crime I do not see why it may not as well pay them

* In *Mapp,* Justice Clark wrote for the majority: "Since the Fourth Amendment's right to privacy has been declared enforceable against the States through the Due Process Clause of the Fourteenth Amendment, it is enforceable against them by the same sanction of exclusion as is used against the Federal Government." 367 U.S. at 655. On June 15, 1961, Justice Black wrote Justice Clark saying that the quoted sentence disturbed him. He thought the Fourth Amendment as a whole is applicable to the States and "not some imaginary and unknown fragment designated as 'the right of privacy.'" Clark Papers, University of Texas, Box A115. Justice Clark assured Justice Black that the *Mapp* opinion matched his views; Justice Black then withdrew his objection to the sentence. Cf. Justice Black's statement with his dissenting opinion in Griswold v. Connecticut, 381 U.S. 479 (1965), page 880, et seq. infra.

for getting it in the same way, and I can attach no importance to protestations of disapproval if it knowingly accepts and pays and announces that in future it will pay for the fruits. We have to choose, and for my part I think it a less evil that some criminals should escape than that the Government should play an ignoble part.

For those who agree with me, no distinction can be taken between the Government as prosecutor and the Government as judge. If the existing code does not permit district attorneys to have a hand in such dirty business it does not permit the judge to allow such inequities to succeed.

Justice Brandeis wrote:

Decency, security and liberty alike demand that government officials shall be subjected to the same rules of conduct that are commands to the citizen. In a government of laws, existence of the government will be imperiled if it fails to observe the law scrupulously. Our Government is the potent, the omnipresent teacher. For good or for ill, it teaches the whole people by its example. Crime is contagious. If the Government becomes a lawbreaker, it breeds contempt for law; it invites every man to become a law unto himself; it invites anarchy. To declare that in the administration of the criminal law the end justifies the means—to declare that the Government may commit crimes in order to secure the conviction of a private criminal—would bring terrible retribution. Against that pernicious doctrine this Court should resolutely set its face.

The exclusionary rule is more appropriately studied in a course on criminal justice, and will not be further discussed here.

THE IMPACT OF OLMSTEAD

Both Taft's majority opinion and the dissenters' opinions, particularly those of Brandeis and Holmes, had policy consequences. In 1930, Representative Tinkham of Massachusetts questioned Colonel Amos Woodcock, Director of the Bureau of Prohibition, about wiretapping at an appropriations hearing:*

MR. TINKHAM: Is it your policy to permit the tapping of wires?

MR. WOODCOCK: We do; and the Supreme Court has approved that practice.

MR. TINKHAM: Do you approve of the practice of tapping wires?

MR. WOODCOCK: I do. I have no qualms at all about that, sir. I think the telephone and telegraph franchises are given for the transaction of lawful business and the promotion of lawful commerce. I do not think that the unlawful have any right to use them with impunity. . . .

* Quoted in Walter F. Murphy, Wiretapping on Trial, Random House, 1965, pp. 128–129.

MR. TINKHAM: All right. Just one word. The minority of the Supreme Court called the tapping of wires dirty business and 27 States have made wire tapping a crime.

In 1934, Congress enacted the Federal Communications Act, which provided in Section 605:

> No person not being authorized by the sender shall intercept any communication and divulge or publish the existence, contents, substance, purport, effect or meaning of such intercepted communication to any person....

Another provision of the Act—Section 501—made willful violation punishable by fine and imprisonment.**

In 1940, Congress was considering a bill that would allow wiretapping with consent of agency heads. President Roosevelt sent a letter to Representative Thomas Eliot, giving his opinion of the proposed legislation. Walter F. Murphy reports FDR's views and the Justice Department's interpretation of Section 605 as follows:[†]

> Roosevelt began by noting that he had read the bill and had "no hesitation in saying that it goes entirely too far and that its provisions are unnecessarily broad." The President continued:
>
>> It is more than desirable, it is necessary that criminals be detected and prosecuted vigilantly as possible. It is more necessary that the citizens of a democracy be protected in their rights of privacy from unwarranted snooping. As an instrument for oppression of free citizens, I can think of none worse than indiscriminate wiretapping.... In general, my own personal point of view is close to that of Justice Holmes in his famous dissent in the *Olmstead* case, when he said: "We have to choose, and for my part I think it a less evil that some criminals should escape than that the Government should play an ignoble part."
>
> On the other hand, Roosevelt conceded that the telephone was a particularly valuable instrument to criminals engaged in offenses against national security or in kidnapping and extortion. He suggested, therefore, that a satisfactory bill should limit wiretapping to those classes of crimes, restrict authority to the Department of Justice alone, and require an order personally signed by the Attorney General before officials could tap a telephone.

** It is not clear whether Section 605 resulted from *Olmstead*. The biographers of George F. Vandeveer, who represented Olmstead, believed there was a connection. Lowell S. Hawley and Ralph Bushnell Potts, Counsel for the Damned, New York, 1953, p. 302. But, as Walter F. Murphy points out, the statute "had been pushed through Congress as basically no more than a revision and recodification of existing federal regulations governing radio broadcasting. No mention of wiretapping had been made in the committee hearings, in the committee reports, or in debate in either house of Congress." Murphy, Wiretapping on Trial, p. 133.

† Ibid., pp. 138–139.

In October 1941, with no new legislation yet enacted, Francis Biddle, who had become Attorney General when Robert H. Jackson was appointed to the Supreme Court, announced a new policy. Following Jackson's earlier interpretation of the law, Biddle asserted that Section 605 forbade tapping *plus* disclosure, not merely wiretapping. And, in his opinion, mere reporting by a government agent to his superior of what he had overheard on a wiretap did not constitute disclosure. On the basis of this reasoning, Biddle established a policy—one apparently followed by his successors to date [1965]—allowing FBI agents to tap wires in cases involving national security or in serious crimes such as kidnapping. But FBI agents must first secure the permission of the Director of the FBI and of the Attorney General himself. For obvious reasons, this policy was much the same as that the President had outlined in his letter to Representative Eliot.

NOTE ON THE "EAVESDROPPER" CASES

Note that, in its statement of the facts of the *Olmstead* case, the Court mentioned that the insertions of the wiretaps were "made without trespass upon any property of the defendant." It was assumed by both the majority and the dissent in *Olmstead* that if there had been a trespass on the home or office of the defendant—in other words, if the police had made a physical entry to plant the wiretap—information gathered thereby would have been regarded as the product of an unlawful seizure. This would have been so despite the fact that the evidence obtained would have been intangible.

From *Olmstead,* with roots extending back even further, there developed the eavesdropper line of cases. These held that so long as there had been no entry by the police or by their instruments into the defendant's "protected area," the defendant's rights were not violated by the overhearing of his conversations. The theory of this, one might suppose, was that, if a man talked so loudly in his house that a passerby could hear it, he had no right to complain if he was in fact overheard. Similarly, if he did not bother pulling his shades down or turning out the lights, he could not complain that someone had seen into his home. Nor, apparently, did it make any difference whether some technical aid had helped the spy. Thus, it was thought that the police might use binoculars to spy on an individual in his home, presumably because the citizen could still take reasonable precautions against such eavesdropping, even if it was unlikely that anyone was in the vicinity.

With electronics, however, technology had changed the nature of eavesdropping and spying considerably. Now, using a parabolic microphone, it was possible to hear what went on in someone's home even if he took reasonable precautions and spoke in a whisper. Similarly, using infra-red techniques, one might see into someone's house even though the lights were out. Not only that, but technology threatened even greater and more effective means of completely destroying the privacy of

the individual—all without physically invading his "constitutionally protected area."*

The Supreme Court, faced with this development, could have done
various things. It could have held to the eavesdropper line of cases and
said simply that, so long as the police had made no entry into the
protected area, anything they could discover using any technology was
appropriate. Secondly, it could have held that the eavesdropper line of
cases continued to be appropriate for those invasions using technology
available and known at the time of the passage of the Fourth Amendment. Thus, the police could still use a spy glass, but not a parabolic
microphone. Finally, threatened with the almost total loss of privacy
implicit in the eavesdropper line of cases, the Court could redefine the
entire problem completely. Read Katz v. United States, which follows,
and see what the Court in fact did.

KATZ v. UNITED STATES

Supreme Court of the United States, 1967.
389 U.S. 347, 88 S.Ct. 507, 19 L.Ed.2d 576.

JUSTICE STEWART delivered the opinion of the Court.

The petitioner was convicted in the District Court for the Southern
District of California under an eight-count indictment charging him with
transmitting wagering information by telephone from Los Angeles to
Miami and Boston, in violation of a federal statute. At trial the Government was permitted, over the petitioner's objection, to introduce evidence of the petitioner's end of telephone conversations, overheard by
FBI agents who had attached an electronic listening and recording device
to the outside of the public telephone booth from which he had placed
his calls. In affirming his conviction, the Court of Appeals rejected the
contention that the recordings had been obtained in violation of the
Fourth Amendment, because "[t]here was no physical entrance into the
area occupied by [the petitioner]." . . .

The petitioner has phrased [the Constitutional questions in this
case] as follows:

> "A. Whether a public telephone booth is a constitutionally
> protected area so that evidence obtained by attaching an elec-
> tronic listening recording device to the top of such a booth is
> obtained in violation of the right to privacy of the user of the
> booth."

> "B. Whether physical penetration of a constitutionally pro-
> tected area is necessary before a search and seizure can be said
> to be violative of the Fourth Amendment to the United States
> Constitution."

We decline to adopt this formulation of the issues. In the first place,
the correct solution of Fourth Amendment problems is not necessarily
promoted by incantation of the phrase "constitutionally protected area."

---

* The Court had over the years defined an individual's "constitutionally protected area"
as including his person and clothing, his home, office, automobile and even his back yard, if
it were within the curtilage, or fence surrounding his home.

Secondly, the Fourth Amendment cannot be translated into a general constitutional "right to privacy." That Amendment protects individual privacy against certain kinds of governmental intrusion, but its protections go further, and often have nothing to do with privacy at all.[1] Other provisions of the Constitution protect personal privacy from other forms of governmental invasion. But the protection of a person's *general* right to privacy—his right to be let alone by other people—is, like the protection of his property and of his very life, left largely to the law of the individual States.

Because of the misleading way the issues have been formulated, the parties have attached great significance to the characterization of the telephone booth from which the petitioner placed his calls. The petitioner has strenuously argued that the booth was a "constitutionally protected area." The Government has maintained with equal vigor that it was not. But this effort to decide whether or not a given "area," viewed in the abstract, is "constitutionally protected" deflects attention from the problem presented by this case. For the Fourth Amendment protects people, not places. What a person knowingly exposes to the public, even in his own home or office, is not a subject of Fourth Amendment protection. But what he seeks to preserve as private, even in an area accessible to the public, may be constitutionally protected.

The Government stresses the fact that the telephone booth from which the petitioner made his calls was constructed partly of glass, so that he was as visible after he entered it as he would have been if he had remained outside. But what he sought to exclude when he entered the booth was not the intruding eye—it was the uninvited ear. He did not shed his right to do so simply because he made his calls from a place where he might be seen. No less than an individual in a business office, in a friend's apartment, or in a taxicab, a person in a telephone booth may rely upon the protection of the Fourth Amendment. One who occupies it, shuts the door behind him, and pays the toll that permits him to place a call is surely entitled to assume that the words he utters into the mouthpiece will not be broadcast to the world. To read the Constitution more narrowly is to ignore the vital role that the public telephone has come to play in private communication.

The Government contends, however, that the activities of its agents in this case should not be tested by Fourth Amendment requirements, for the surveillance technique they employed involved no physical penetration of the telephone booth from which the petitioner placed his calls. It is true that the absence of such penetration was at one time thought to foreclose further Fourth Amendment inquiry, Olmstead v. United States, 277 U.S. 438, 457, 464, 466; for that Amendment was thought to limit only searches and seizures of tangible property. But "[t]he premise that property interests control the right of the Government to search and seize has been discredited." Thus, although a closely

---

1. "The average man would very likely not have his feelings soothed any more by having his property seized openly than by having it seized privately and by stealth. . . . And a person can be just as much, if not more, irritated, annoyed and injured by an unceremonious public arrest by a policeman as he is by a seizure in the privacy of his office or home." Griswold v. Connecticut, 381 U.S. 479, 509 (dissenting opinion of Justice Black).

divided Court supposed in *Olmstead* that surveillance without any trespass and without the seizure of any material object fell outside the ambit of the Constitution, we have since departed from the narrow view on which that decision rested. Indeed, we have expressly held that the Fourth Amendment governs not only the seizure of tangible items, but extends as well to the recording of oral statements, overheard without any "technical trespass under ... local property law." Once this much is acknowledged, and once it is recognized that the Fourth Amendment protects people—and not simply "areas"—against unreasonable searches and seizures, it becomes clear that the reach of that Amendment cannot turn upon the presence or absence of a physical intrusion into any given enclosure.

We conclude that the underpinnings of *Olmstead* ... have been so eroded by our subsequent decisions that the "trespass" doctrine there enunciated can no longer be regarded as controlling. The Government's activities in electronically listening to and recording the petitioner's words violated the privacy upon which he justifiably relied while using the telephone booth and thus constituted a "search and seizure" within the meaning of the Fourth Amendment. The fact that the electronic device employed to achieve that end did not happen to penetrate the wall of the booth can have no constitutional significance.

The question remaining for decision, then, is whether the search and seizure conducted in this case complied with constitutional standards. In that regard, the Government's position is that its agents acted in an entirely defensible manner: They did not begin their electronic surveillance until investigation of the petitioner's activities had established a strong probability that he was using the telephone in question to transmit gambling information to persons in other States, in violation of federal law. Moreover, the surveillance was limited, both in scope and in duration, to the specific purpose of establishing the contents of the petitioner's unlawful telephonic communications. The agents confined their surveillance to the brief periods during which he used the telephone booth, and they took great care to overhear only the conversations of the petitioner himself.

Accepting this account of the Government's actions as accurate, it is clear that this surveillance was so narrowly circumscribed that a duly authorized magistrate, properly notified of the need for such investigation, specifically informed of the basis on which it was to proceed, and clearly apprised of the precise intrusion it would entail, could constitutionally have authorized, with appropriate safeguards, the very limited search and seizure that the Government asserts in fact took place....

... [T]his Court has never sustained a search upon the sole ground that officers reasonably expected to find evidence of a particular crime and voluntarily confined their activities to the least intrusive means consistent with that end. Searches conducted without warrants have been held unlawful "notwithstanding facts unquestionably showing probable cause," for the Constitution requires "that the deliberate, impartial judgment of a judicial officer ... be interposed between the citizen and the police...." "Over and again this Court has emphasized that the mandate of the [Fourth] Amendment requires adherence to judicial processes," and that searches conducted outside the judicial process, without prior approval by judge or magistrate, are *per se* unreasonable under the Fourth Amendment—subject only to a few specifically established and well-delineated exceptions.

. . .

... Wherever a man may be, he is entitled to know that he will remain free from unreasonable searches and seizures. The government agents here ignored "the procedure of antecedent justification . . . that is central to the Fourth Amendment," a procedure that we hold to be a constitutional precondition of the kind of electronic surveillance involved in this case. Because the surveillance here failed to meet that condition, and because it led to the petitioner's conviction, the judgment must be reversed.

. . .

[A concurring opinion by Justice Douglas is omitted.]

JUSTICE HARLAN, concurring.

I join the opinion of the Court, which I read to hold only (a) that an enclosed telephone booth is an area where, like a home, and unlike a field, a person has a constitutionally protected reasonable expectation of privacy; (b) that electronic as well as physical intrusion into a place that is in this sense private may constitute a violation of the Fourth Amendment; and (c) that the invasion of a constitutionally protected area by federal authorities is, as the Court has long held, presumptively unreasonable in the absence of a search warrant.

As the Court's opinion states, "the Fourth Amendment protects people, not places." The question, however, is what protection it affords to those people. Generally, as here, the answer to that question requires reference to a "place." My understanding of the rule that has emerged from prior decisions is that there is a twofold requirement, first that a person have exhibited an actual (subjective) expectation of privacy and second, that the expectation be one that society is prepared to recognize as "reasonable." Thus a man's home is, for most purposes, a place where he expects privacy, but objects, activities, or statements that he exposes to the "plain view" of outsiders are not "protected" because no intention to keep them to himself has been exhibited. On the other hand, conversations in the open would not be protected against being overheard, for the expectation of privacy under the circumstances would be unreasonable.

The critical fact in this case is that "[o]ne who occupies it, [a telephone booth] shuts the door behind him, and pays the toll that permits him to place a call is surely entitled to assume" that his conversation is not being intercepted. The point is not that the booth is "accessible to the public" at other times, but that it is a temporarily private place whose momentary occupants' expectations of freedom from intrusion are recognized as reasonable. . . .

. . .

Justice White, concurring.

. . .

In joining the Court's opinion, I note the Court's acknowledgment that there are circumstances in which it is reasonable to search without a warrant.... [T]oday's decision does not reach national security cases. Wiretapping to protect the security of the Nation has been authorized by successive Presidents. The present Administration would apparently save national security cases from restrictions against wiretapping. We should not require the warrant procedure and the magistrate's judgment if the President of the United States or his chief legal officer, the Attorney General, has considered the requirements of national security and authorized electronic surveillance as reasonable.

Justice Black, dissenting.

If I could agree with the Court that eavesdropping carried on by electronic means (equivalent to wiretapping) constitutes a "search" or "seizure," I would be happy to join the Court's opinion....

My basic objection is twofold: (1) I do not believe that the words of the Amendment will bear the meaning given them by today's decision, and (2) I do not believe that it is the proper role of this Court to rewrite the Amendment in order "to bring it into harmony with the times" and thus reach a result that many people believe to be desirable.

While I realize that an argument based on the meaning of words lacks the scope, and no doubt the appeal, of broad policy discussions and philosophical discourses on such nebulous subjects as privacy, for me the language of the Amendment is the crucial place to look in construing a written document such as our Constitution. The Fourth Amendment says that

> "The right of the people to be secure in their persons, houses, papers, and effects, against unreasonable searches and seizures, shall not be violated, and no Warrants shall issue, but upon probable cause, supported by Oath or affirmation, and particularly describing the place to be searched, and the persons or things to be seized."

The first clause protects "persons, houses, papers, and effects, against unreasonable searches and seizures...." These words connote the idea of tangible things with size, form, and weight, things capable of being searched, seized, or both. The second clause of the Amendment still further establishes its Framers' purpose to limit its protection to tangible things by providing that no warrants shall issue but those "particularly describing the place to be searched, and the persons or things to be seized." A conversation overheard by eavesdropping, whether by plain snooping or wiretapping, is not tangible and, under the normally accepted meanings of the words, can neither be searched nor seized. In addition the language of the second clause indicates that the Amendment refers not only to something tangible so it can be seized but to something already in existence so it can be described. Yet the Court's interpretation would have the Amendment apply to overhearing future conversations which by their very nature are nonexistent until they take place. . . . Rather than using language in a completely artificial way, I must conclude that the Fourth Amendment simply does not apply to eavesdropping.

. . .

With this decision the Court has completed, I hope, its rewriting of the Fourth Amendment, which started only recently when the Court began referring incessantly to the Fourth Amendment not so much as a law against *unreasonable* searches and seizures as one to protect an individual's privacy. . . .

The Fourth Amendment protects privacy only to the extent that it prohibits unreasonable searches and seizures of "persons, houses, papers, and effects." No general right is created by the Amendment so as to give this Court the unlimited power to hold unconstitutional everything which affects privacy. Certainly the Framers, well acquainted as they were with the excesses of governmental power, did not intend to grant this Court such omnipotent lawmaking authority as that. The history of governments proves that it is dangerous to freedom to repose such powers in courts.

NOTES AND QUESTIONS

1. According to Justice Douglas' docketbook for the 1967 Term, Chief Justice Warren and Justices Douglas, Brennan, and Fortas voted to grant certiorari in *Katz*. With Justice Marshall not participating, the Court voted four to four on the merits, with the justices who had voted to grant certiorari voting to reverse. Later Justices Harlan, Stewart, and White changed their votes. Do the votes in the case help you understand the multiplicity of opinions and the positions taken in them?

2. If the use of an electronic bugging device on the outside of a phone booth violates a "justifiable expectation of privacy," what about the use of a high power telescope to see in the windows of a twentieth floor apartment? Even if the curtains are open, doesn't one have a reasonable expectation of visual privacy in the twentieth floor of a highrise building? Should the fact that telescopes were available and eavesdropping devices were not at the time the Fourth Amendment was written, affect the constitutionality of their present use? Does the modern technology used in high-power telescopes move them into the same category with electronic bugging devices?

3. Does the use of computerized data banks for purposes other than those for which the information was collected constitute an unreasonable search or seizure under the Fourth Amendment? Isn't there a "reasonable expectation of privacy" when giving out personal information for a restricted purpose, such as to establish a credit rating? Is there not an expectation that the information will be given only to those who have a legitimate interest in the purpose for which the information was revealed? Should the Fourth Amendment protect such partial privacy expectations? Or does this construction simply move too far away from the plain meaning of the words of the Fourth Amendment, as argued by Justice Black in his dissent in *Katz?*

4.   Consider the following excerpt,* which argues that the "reasonable expectations of privacy" formulation unduly restricts the real meaning of *Katz:*

> ... The [Katz] case is, of course now generally recognized as seminal and has rapidly become the basis of a new formula of fourth amendment coverage. The formula is that "wherever an individual may harbor a reasonable 'expectation of privacy,' ... he is entitled to be free from unreasonable governmental intrusion." Notwithstanding the Supreme Court's several repetitions of this formula or variations of it, and notwithstanding even its apparent acceptance by Justice Stewart (the author of the *Katz* opinion), I believe that it destroys the spirit of *Katz* and most of *Katz's* substance.

> ... [L]et us consider the word "expectation" in the "reasonable expectation of privacy" formula to which *Katz* is speedily being reduced. "Expectation" is not a term used in Justice Stewart's majority opinion in *Katz;* it has been lifted by subsequent cases from Justice Harlan's concurring opinion, where it is used to mean "an actual (subjective) expectation of privacy ... that society is prepared to recognize as 'reasonable.' " But Justice Harlan himself later expressed second thoughts about this conception, and rightly so. An actual, subjective expectation of privacy obviously has no place in a statement of what *Katz* held or in a theory of what the fourth amendment protects. It can neither add to, nor can its absence detract from, an individual's claim to fourth amendment protection. If it could, the government could diminish each person's subjective expectation of privacy merely by announcing half-hourly on television that 1984 was being advanced by a decade and that we were all forthwith being placed under comprehensive electronic surveillance.

> I need hardly add that, for many of us, the announcement would be gratuitous. I shall not speak for any of my associates or acquaintances, lest my disclosure of their expectations, or the lack thereof, prejudice their fourth amendment rights. For myself, I have had no actual, subjective expectation of privacy in my telephone, my office or my home since I began handling civil rights cases in the early 1960's. Perhaps the energy crisis will become so bad as to restore that expectation, but it seems unlikely. Even if every police agency in this country reduced its electronic surveillance by 10 or 15 percent to meet general government goals for the reduction of power usage, we would still have an extremely slim basis for much actual expectation of privacy. Fortunately, neither *Katz* nor the fourth amendment asks what we expect of government. They tell us what we should demand of government.

* Anthony G. Amsterdam, Perspectives on the Fourth Amendment, Minnesota Law Review, 1974, vol. 58, pp. 383–385.

Finally, it is plainly wrong to capsulate *Katz* into a comprehensive definition of fourth amendment coverage in terms of "privacy." *Katz* holds that the fourth amendment protects certain privacy interests, but not that those interests are the only interests which the fourth amendment protects. To the contrary, the *Katz* opinion says in so many words that "its protections go further, and often have nothing to do with privacy at all." In short, the common formula for *Katz* fails to capture *Katz* at any point because the *Katz* decision was written to resist captivation in any formula.

5. Does *Katz* apply to dogs—at least dogs trained to sniff out marijuana? The U.S. Court of Appeals for the Second Circuit has held no—though one judge felt that the dog was used because of its keener sense of smell, very much like a microphone or electronic device. A California court, however, has held that one had a reasonable expectation of privacy that could not be defeated by a trained dog's sense of smell.

Would it be different if a police officer happened to have an especially acute sense of smell?

KYLLO v. UNITED STATES

Supreme Court of the United States, 2001.
533 U.S. 27, 121 S.Ct. 2038, 150 L.Ed.2d 94.

JUSTICE SCALIA delivered the opinion of the Court.

This case presents the question whether the use of a thermal-imaging device aimed at a private home from a public street to detect relative amounts of heat within the home constitutes a "search" within the meaning of the Fourth Amendment.

I

In 1991 Agent William Elliott of the United States Department of the Interior came to suspect that marijuana was being grown in the home belonging to petitioner Danny Kyllo, part of a triplex on Rhododendron Drive in Florence, Oregon. Indoor marijuana growth typically requires high-intensity lamps. In order to determine whether an amount of heat was emanating from petitioner's home consistent with the use of such lamps, at 3:20 a.m. on January 16, 1992, Agent Elliott and Dan Haas used an Agema Thermovision 210 thermal imager to scan the triplex. Thermal imagers detect infrared radiation, which virtually all objects emit but which is not visible to the naked eye. The imager converts radiation into images based on relative warmth—black is cool, white is hot, shades of gray connote relative differences; in that respect, it operates somewhat like a video camera showing heat images. The scan of Kyllo's home took only a few minutes and was performed from the passenger seat of Agent Elliott's vehicle across the street from the front of the house and also from the street in back of the house. The scan showed that the roof over the garage and a side wall of petitioner's home were relatively hot compared to the rest of the home and substantially warmer than neighboring homes in the triplex. Agent Elliott concluded that petitioner was using halide lights to grow marijuana in his house, which indeed he was. Based on tips from informants, utility bills, and the thermal imaging, a Federal Magistrate Judge issued a warrant authorizing a search of petitioner's home, and the agents found an indoor growing operation involving more than 100 plants. Petitioner was indicted on one count of manufacturing marijuana, in violation of 21 U.S.C. § 841(a)(1). He unsuccessfully moved to suppress the evidence seized from his home and then entered a conditional guilty plea.

The Court of Appeals for the Ninth Circuit [affirmed].... The court held that petitioner had shown no subjective expectation of privacy because he had made no attempt to conceal the heat escaping from his home, ... and even if he had, there was no objectively reasonable expectation of privacy because the imager "did not expose any intimate details of Kyllo's life," only "amorphous 'hot spots' on the roof and exterior wall." ...

II

The Fourth Amendment provides that "[t]he right of the people to be secure in their persons, houses, papers, and effects, against unreasonable searches and seizures, shall not be violated." "At the very core" of the Fourth Amendment "stands the right of a man to retreat into his own home and there be free from unreasonable governmental intrusion." *Silverman* v. *United States*, 365 U.S. 505, 511 (1961). With few exceptions, the question whether a warrantless search of a home is reasonable and hence constitutional must be answered no....

On the other hand, the antecedent question of whether or not a Fourth Amendment "search" has occurred is not so simple under our precedent. The permissibility of ordinary visual surveillance of a home used to be clear because, well into the 20th century, our Fourth Amendment jurisprudence was tied to common-law trespass.... Visual surveillance was unquestionably lawful because " 'the eye cannot by the laws of England be guilty of a trespass.' " *Boyd* v. *United States*, 116 U.S. 616, 628 (1886) (quoting *Entick* v. *Carrington*, 19 How. St. Tr. 1029, 95 Eng. Rep. 807 (K. B. 1765)). We have since decoupled violation of a person's Fourth Amendment rights from trespassory violation of his property, ... but the lawfulness of warrantless visual surveillance of a home has still been preserved. As we observed in *California* v. *Ciraolo*, 476 U.S. 207, 213 (1986), "[t]he Fourth Amendment protection of the home has never been extended to require law enforcement officers to shield their eyes when passing by a home on public thoroughfares."

One might think that the new validating rationale would be that examining the portion of a house that is in plain public view, while it is a "search" despite the absence of trespass, is not an "unreasonable" one under the Fourth Amendment. But in fact we have held that visual observation is no "search" at all—perhaps in order to preserve somewhat more intact our doctrine that warrantless searches are presumptively unconstitutional.... In assessing when a search is not a search, we have applied somewhat in reverse the principle first enunciated in *Katz* v. *United States*, 389 U.S. 347 (1967). *Katz* involved eavesdropping by means of an electronic listening device placed on the outside of a telephone booth—a location not within the catalog ("persons, houses, papers, and effects") that the Fourth Amendment protects against unreasonable searches. We held that the Fourth Amendment nonetheless protected Katz from the warrantless eavesdropping because he "justifiably relied" upon the privacy of the telephone booth. *Id.*, at 353. As Justice Harlan's oft-quoted concurrence described it, a Fourth Amendment search occurs when the government violates a subjective expectation of privacy that society recognizes as reasonable. See *id.*, at 361. We have subsequently applied this principle to hold that a Fourth Amendment search does *not* occur—even when the explicitly protected location of a *house* is concerned—unless "the individual manifested a subjective expectation of privacy in the object of the challenged search," and "society [is] willing to recognize that expectation as reasonable." *Ciraolo, supra*, at 211. We have applied this test in holding that it is not a search for the police to use a pen register at the phone company to determine what numbers were dialed in a private home, . . . and we have applied the test on two different occasions in holding that aerial surveillance of private homes and surrounding areas does not constitute a search, . . .

III

It would be foolish to contend that the degree of privacy secured to citizens by the Fourth Amendment has been entirely unaffected by the advance of technology. For example, as the cases discussed above make clear, the technology enabling human flight has exposed to public view (and hence, we have said, to official observation) uncovered portions of the house and its curtilage that once were private. . . . The question we confront today is what limits there are upon this power of technology to shrink the realm of guaranteed privacy.

The *Katz* test—whether the individual has an expectation of privacy that society is prepared to recognize as reasonable—has often been criticized as circular, and hence subjective and unpredictable. . . . While it may be difficult to refine *Katz* when the search of areas such as telephone booths, automobiles, or even the curtilage and uncovered portions of residences are at issue, in the case of the search of the interior of homes—the prototypical and hence most commonly litigated area of protected privacy—there is a ready criterion, with roots deep in the common law, of the minimal expectation of privacy that *exists*, and that is acknowledged to be *reasonable*. To withdraw protection of this minimum expectation would be to permit police technology to erode the privacy guaranteed by the Fourth Amendment. We think that obtaining by sense-enhancing technology any information regarding the interior of the home that could not otherwise have been obtained without physical "intrusion into a constitutionally protected area," *Silverman*, 365 U.S., at 512, constitutes a search—at least where (as here) the technology in question is not in general public use. This assures preservation of that degree of privacy against government that existed when the Fourth Amendment was adopted. On the basis of this criterion, the information obtained by the thermal imager in this case was the product of a search.

The Government maintains, however, that the thermal imaging must be upheld because it detected "only heat radiating from the external surface of the house." ... The dissent makes this its leading point, ... contending that there is a fundamental difference between what it calls "off-the-wall" observations and "through-the-wall surveillance." But just as a thermal imager captures only heat emanating from a house, so also a powerful directional microphone picks up only sound emanating from a house—and a satellite capable of scanning from many miles away would pick up only visible light emanating from a house. We rejected such a mechanical interpretation of the Fourth Amendment in *Katz*, where the eavesdropping device picked up only sound waves that reached the exterior of the phone booth. Reversing that approach would leave the homeowner at the mercy of advancing technology—including imaging technology that could discern all human activity in the home. While the technology used in the present case was relatively crude, the rule we adopt must take account of more sophisticated systems that are already in use or in development. The dissent's reliance on the distinction between "off-the-wall" and "through-the-wall" observation is entirely incompatible with the dissent's belief, which we discuss below, that thermal-imaging observations of the intimate details of a home are impermissible. The most sophisticated thermal imaging devices continue to measure heat "off-the-wall" rather than "through-the-wall"; the dissent's disapproval of those more sophisticated thermal-imaging devices, ... is an acknowledgement that there is no substance to this distinction. As for the dissent's extraordinary assertion that anything learned through "an inference" cannot be a search ... that would validate even the "through-the-wall" technologies that the dissent purports to disapprove. Surely the dissent does not believe that the through-the-wall radar or ultrasound technology produces an 8–by–10 Kodak glossy that needs no analysis (*i.e.*, the making of inferences). And, of course, the novel proposition that inference insulates a search is blatantly contrary to *United States* v. *Karo*, 468 U.S. 705 (1984), where the police "inferred" from the activation of a beeper that a certain can of ether was in the home. The police activity was held to be a search, and the search was held unlawful.

. . .

Limiting the prohibition of thermal imaging to "intimate details" would not only be wrong in principle; it would be impractical in application, failing to provide "a workable accommodation between the needs of law enforcement and the interests protected by the Fourth Amendment," *Oliver* v. *United States*, 466 U.S. 170, 181 (1984). To begin with, there is no necessary connection between the sophistication of the surveillance equipment and the "intimacy" of the details that it observes—which means that one cannot say (and the police cannot be assured) that use of the relatively crude equipment at issue here will always be lawful. The Agema Thermovision 210 might disclose, for example, at what hour each night the lady of the house takes her daily sauna and bath—a detail that many would consider "intimate"; and a much more sophisticated system might detect nothing more intimate than the fact that someone left a closet light on. We could not, in other words, develop a rule approving only that through-the-wall surveillance which identifies objects no smaller than 36 by 36 inches, but would have to develop a jurisprudence specifying which home activities are "intimate" and which are not. And even when (if ever) that jurisprudence were fully developed, no police officer would be able to know *in advance* whether his through-the-wall surveillance picks up "intimate" details—and thus would be unable to know in advance whether it is constitutional. . . .

We have said that the Fourth Amendment draws "a firm line at the entrance to the house," *Payton*, 445 U.S., at 590. That line, we think, must be not only firm but also bright—which requires clear specification of those methods of surveillance that require a warrant. While it is certainly possible to conclude from the videotape of the thermal imaging that occurred in this case that no "significant" compromise of the homeowner's privacy has occurred, we must take the long view, from the original meaning of the Fourth Amendment forward.

> "The Fourth Amendment is to be construed in the light of what was deemed an unreasonable search and seizure when it was adopted, and in a manner which will conserve public interests as well as the interests and rights of individual citizens." *Carroll v. United States*, 267 U.S. 132, 149 (1925).

> Where, as here, the Government uses a device that is not in general public use, to explore details of the home that would previously have been unknowable without physical intrusion, the surveillance is a "search" and is presumptively unreasonable without a warrant.

. . .

The judgment of the Court of Appeals is reversed. . . .

JUSTICE STEVENS, with whom THE CHIEF JUSTICE, JUSTICE O'CONNOR, and JUSTICE KENNEDY join, dissenting.

There is, in my judgment, a distinction of constitutional magnitude between "through-the-wall surveillance" that gives the observer or listener direct access to information in a private area, on the one hand, and the thought processes used to draw inferences from information in the public domain, on the other hand. The Court has crafted a rule that purports to deal with direct observations of the inside of the home, but the case before us merely involves indirect deductions from "off-the-wall" surveillance, that is, observations of the exterior of the home. Those observations were made with a fairly primitive thermal imager that gathered data exposed on the outside of petitioner's home but did not invade any constitutionally protected interest in privacy. Moreover, I believe that the supposedly "bright-line" rule the Court has created in response to its concerns about future technological developments is unnecessary, unwise, and inconsistent with the Fourth Amendment.

. . .

The two reasons advanced by the Court as justifications for the adoption of its new rule are both unpersuasive. First, the Court suggests

that its rule is compelled by our holding in *Katz*, because in that case, as in this, the surveillance consisted of nothing more than the monitoring of waves emanating from a private area into the public domain.... Yet there are critical differences between the cases. In *Katz*, the electronic listening device attached to the outside of the phone booth allowed the officers to pick up the content of the conversation inside the booth, making them the functional equivalent of intruders because they gathered information that was otherwise available only to someone inside the private area; it would be as if, in this case, the thermal imager presented a view of the heat-generating activity inside petitioner's home. By contrast, the thermal imager here disclosed only the relative amounts of heat radiating from the house; it would be as if, in *Katz*, the listening device disclosed only the relative volume of sound leaving the booth, which presumably was discernible in the public domain. Surely, there is a significant difference between the general and well-settled expectation that strangers will not have direct access to the contents of private communications, on the one hand, and the rather theoretical expectation that an occasional homeowner would even care if anybody noticed the relative amounts of heat emanating from the walls of his house, on the other. It is pure hyperbole for the Court to suggest that refusing to extend the holding of *Katz* to this case would leave the homeowner at the mercy of "technology that could discern all human activity in the home."
. . .

Second, the Court argues that the permissibility of "through-the-wall surveillance" cannot depend on a distinction between observing "intimate details" such as "the lady of the house [taking] her daily sauna and bath," and noticing only "the nonintimate rug on the vestibule floor" or "objects no smaller than 36 by 36 inches." ... This entire argument assumes, of course, that the thermal imager in this case could or did perform "through-the-wall surveillance" that could identify any detail "that would previously have been unknowable without physical intrusion." ... In fact, the device could not, ... and did not, ... enable its user to identify either the lady of the house, the rug on the vestibule floor, or anything else inside the house, whether smaller or larger than 36 by 36 inches. Indeed, the vague thermal images of petitioner's home that are reproduced ... were submitted by him to the District Court as part of an expert report raising the question whether the device could even take "accurate, consistent infrared images" of the *outside* of his house.... But even if the device could reliably show extraordinary differences in the amounts of heat leaving his home, drawing the inference that there was something suspicious occurring inside the residence—a conclusion that officers far less gifted than Sherlock Holmes would readily draw—does not qualify as "through-the-wall surveillance," much less a Fourth Amendment violation.

. . .

Although the Court is properly and commendably concerned about the threats to privacy that may flow from advances in the technology available to the law enforcement profession, it has unfortunately failed to heed the tried and true counsel of judicial restraint. Instead of concentrating on the rather mundane issue that is actually presented by the case before it, the Court has endeavored to craft an all-encompassing rule for the future. It would be far wiser to give legislators an unimpeded opportunity to grapple with these emerging issues rather than to shackle them with prematurely devised constitutional constraints.

I respectfully dissent.

NOTE ON THE REQUIREMENT OF A SEARCH WARRANT AND SEARCHES WITHOUT WARRANTS

Note that the Fourth Amendment seems to do several things. First, it makes unconstitutional only "unreasonable" searches and seizures. Second, it provides that, for certain kinds of searches and seizures, a warrant is required. One can, it is true, read the amendment as stating that all searches and seizures are unconstitutional unless they are made under a search warrant. The problem with doing this is that this tends to make unnecessary the first part of the amendment. Similarly, one could read the amendment as providing that a warrant was not necessary if the search and seizure were otherwise not unreasonable. Such a reading would render the second part of the Amendment unnecessary. In fact, the Supreme Court, relying in great part on its reading of the history leading up to the Fourth Amendment, has evolved a large and complex body of doctrine as to when a search and seizure requires a search warrant and when "reasonable" searches may be conducted without a warrant. So that the student may have an idea of the complexity of search and seizure laws, it is appropriate that some attention be devoted to the problem.

The classic statement of the purpose of the warrant requirement is that of Justice Robert Jackson in Johnson v. United States, 333 U.S. 10, 13 (1948). The Government defended the search as legally justifiable in that case although there was no search warrant.

> The point of the Fourth Amendment, which often is not grasped by zealous officers, is not that it denies law enforcement the support of the usual inferences which reasonable men draw from evidence. Its protection consists in requiring that those inferences be drawn by a neutral and detached magistrate instead of being judged by the officer engaged in the often competitive enterprise of ferreting out crime. Any assumption that evidence sufficient to support a magistrate's disinterested determination to issue a search warrant will justify the officers in making a search without a warrant would reduce the Amendment to a nullity and leave the people's homes secure only in the discretion of police officers. Crime, even in the privacy of one's own quarters, is, of course, of grave concern to society, and the law allows such crime to be reached on proper showing. The right of officers to thrust themselves into a home is also a grave concern, not only to the individual but to a society which chooses to dwell in reasonable security and freedom from surveillance. When the right of privacy must reasonably yield to the right of search is, as a rule, to be decided by a judicial officer, not by a policeman or government enforcement agent.

There are exceptional circumstances in which, on balancing the need for effective law enforcement against the right of privacy, it may be contended that a magistrate's warrant for search may be dispensed with.

The "exceptional circumstances" referred to by Justice Jackson have been detailed by Amsterdam* as follows:

Exceptions to the warrant requirement fall into three groupings: consent searches, a very limited class of routine searches, and certain searches conducted under circumstances of haste that render the obtaining of a search warrant impracticable. The theory underlying the consent-search exception is unclear, but its substance is that searches without a warrant or probable cause may be made upon the voluntary consent of the party affected or of someone authorized by that party to control access to the places or things searched.

The routine-search category is not as broad as that term suggests: I use the term only as a shorthand description of the rare cases in which unconsented searches may be made without either a warrant or any individuating judgment that the person or place to be searched is connected with criminal activity. These cases include searches of persons and objects entering the United States across an international border, searches of premises licensed for the distribution of such regulated commodities as firearms and liquor, perhaps inventory searches of vehicles properly taken into police custody, and perhaps stoppings of moving vehicles for operator's license, registration and safety checks. Searches in these cases remain subject to the fourth amendment's general requirement of reasonableness; they may not be made, for example, in an abusive or unduly intrusive manner.

The third and most significant group of exceptions involves cases in which an individuating judgment of criminal activity is required but a fast-developing situation precludes resort to a magistrate. Warrantless searches may be made of motor vehicles that are capable of being driven away before a warrant can be procured, if the searching officer has probable cause to believe that the vehicle contains criminally related objects. Apparently, warrantless searches of other highly mobile articles—such as luggage deposited for shipment out of rail or air terminals—are also permissible when there is probable cause to believe that they contain criminally related objects. There is some dictum in Supreme Court cases suggesting a more general class of "exceptional circumstances" in which the imminent removal or destruction of seizable items might permit warrantless searches, but this language has never been applied by the Court to validate an entry into a building without a warrant except in pursuit of a fleeing and dangerous criminal. Warrantless searches incident to a valid arrest—that is, an arrest

---

* Ibid., pp. 358–360.

authorized by law, with or without an arrest warrant, upon probable cause to believe that the arrested person has committed an offense—are allowed within the limited area into which the "arrestee might reach in order to grab a weapon or evidentiary items." Such searches may not ordinarily precede the arrest because their justification rests upon the likelihood that a person taken into custody will attempt to harm the arresting officer or to destroy evidence. However, when a confrontation between an officer and a suspect simultaneously gives the officer probable cause to arrest and alerts the suspect to the officer's suspicions, a warrantless search of the suspect's person may be made prior to arrest, to the restricted extent necessary to prevent him from destroying evidence. A "frisk" of the body of a suspicious person stopped on the street for investigative questioning may also be made if there are reasonable grounds to believe that he is armed and dangerous. The "frisk" may not go beyond what is necessary to detect the presence of a weapon. A line of lower-court cases holds that an officer who has an arrest warrant or probable cause to arrest an individual may make an entry without a search warrant into any premises where he reasonably believes that the person whom he seeks to arrest is located. However, this arrest-entry doctrine is currently undergoing reconsideration, and will probably survive only in "hot pursuit" situations. Searches in the third group of exceptions to the warrant requirement, like those in the second, must be conducted in a reasonable manner, and their scope is generally limited by their specific justifications.

III. WIRETAPPING AND NATIONAL SECURITY

Justice White's concurrence in *Katz* addresses the problem of wiretapping for national security purposes. Should such wiretapping be completely immune from judicial scrutiny? Doesn't the history behind the Fourth Amendment militate against ever allowing the government unfettered discretion in the area of searches and seizures? Should the executive be free to order any wiretap, simply on his conclusion that national security interests were involved? Is it possible that security problems might be created if judicially issued warrants were required for wiretaps or searches where legitimate national defense or security issues were involved? Can these disparate interests be balanced against one another or must someone simply make a value judgment as to whether individual freedom or national security is more important? If a value judgment must be made, is the judiciary the governmental branch to make such a decision? The George W. Bush Administration's openly declared "war on terrorism" during the first decade of the 21st Century brought many of these questions to the forefront of American politics.

Several decades earlier, in United States v. U.S. District Court, 407 U.S. 297 (1972), the Supreme Court held that domestic security cannot be used to justify wiretap activities performed without a warrant. In that case three defendants, who were charged with conspiracy to destroy government property, challenged the validity of a wiretap aimed at "domestic subversion." The tap had been installed without a warrant for the purpose of "gather[ing] intelligence information deemed necessary to protect the nation from attempts of domestic organizations to attack and subvert the existing structure of government." The government argued that the surveillance was lawful as a reasonable exercise of presidential power to protect national security. It also argued that wiretaps involving domestic security should be exempt from the warrant requirement of the Fourth Amendment because of the secrecy necessary for successful intelligence gathering, the importance of domestic security, and the complexity and continuous nature of intelligence gathering. The Court balanced the Government's arguments against the values protected by the Fourth Amendment and held as follows:

> But we do not think a case has been made for the requested departure from Fourth Amendment standards. The circumstances described do not justify complete exemption of domestic security surveillance from prior judicial scrutiny. Official surveillance, whether its purpose be criminal investigation or ongoing intelligence gathering, risks infringement of constitutionally protected privacy of speech. Security surveillances are especially sensitive because of the inherent vagueness of the domestic security concept, the necessarily broad and continuing nature of intelligence gathering, and the temptation to utilize such surveillances to oversee political dissent. We recognize, as we have before, the constitutional basis of the President's domestic security role, but we think it must be exercised in a manner compatible with the Fourth Amendment.

It is still an open question whether or not the President can authorize wiretapping without judicial supervision when national security interests relating to activities of foreign powers are involved. What do you think? Should the FBI be permitted without a warrant to tap the telephone of the Soviet Embassy?

Assuming that the President's power to protect national security interests involving foreign affairs includes the authority to wiretap without judicial supervision, what would limit the President from going beyond wiretapping to gather intelligence? The temptations of such power and the problems of limitation are illustrated in the following excerpts from John D. Ehrlichman's testimony and Senator Talmadge's response before the Senate Watergate Committee.* The excerpts relate to the break-in to the office of Daniel Ellsberg's psychiatrist by a "special unit," known as "the White House Plumbers." Previous to the break-in, Daniel Ellsberg had leaked the "Pentagon Papers," classified documents concerning the Vietnam War, to the press.

> Mr. Ehrlichman.... I considered the special unit's activities to be well within the President's inherent constitutional

---

* Hearings before the Select Committee on Presidential Campaign Activities, United States Congress, 93rd Congress, First Session, July 23, 1973, pp. 2543, 2577, 2600, 2601.

powers, and this particular episode, the break-in in California, likewise to have been within the President's inherent constitutional powers.

. . .

I think that basically you have to take this in context. We had here an unknown quantity in terms of a conspiracy. We had an overt act in the turning over of these secret documents to the Russian Embassy, and moreover we have a technique here in the development of a psychiatric profile which apparently, in the opinion of the experts, is so valuable that the CIA maintains an entire psychiatric section for that purpose.

Now, putting those all together, I submit that certainly there is ... ample constitutional recognition of the President's inherent constitutional powers to form a foundation for what I said to this committee.

Senator Ervin. Well, Mr. Ehrlichman, the Constitution specifies the President's powers to me in the fourth amendment. It says:

> The right of the people to be secure in their persons, houses, papers, and effects, against unreasonable searches and seizures, shall not be violated, and no warrant shall issue, but upon probable cause, supported by oath or affirmation, and particularly describing the place to be searched, and the person or things to be seized.

Nowhere in this does it say the President has the right to suspend the fourth amendment.

. . .

Senator Talmadge. Now, if the President could authorize a covert break-in, and you do not know exactly [to] what [extent] that power would be limited, you do not think it could include murder or other crimes beyond covert break-ins, do you?

Mr. Ehrlichman. I do not know where the line is, Senator.

Senator Talmadge. Where is the check on the Chief Executive's inherent power as to where that power begins and ends? That is what I am trying to determine.

. . .

Do you remember when we were in law school, we studied a famous principle of law that came from England and also is well known in this country, that no matter how humble a man's cottage is, that even the King of England cannot enter without his consent.

Mr. Ehrlichman. I am afraid that has been considerably eroded over the years, has it not?

Senator Talmadge. Down in my country we still think it is a pretty legitimate principle of law. [Applause.]

A NOTE ON THE NSA WARRANTLESS SURVEILLANCE CONTROVERSY

In the wake of the September 11, 2001 terrorist attacks on the United States, President George W. Bush issued an executive order authorizing the National Security Agency (NSA) to conduct surveillance of certain telephone calls conducted by persons in the United States without obtaining a warrant either before or after the surveillance from the Foreign Intelligence Surveillance Court, as required by the Foreign Intelligence Surveillance Act of 1978. On May 22, 2006, it was reported that the NSA had installed monitoring and interception supercomputers capable of listening in on a large proportion of all domestic and international telephone connections, and that officials had utilized this machinery to perform eavesdropping and order investigations of many Americans in connection with the administration's war on terrorism.

One Justice Department official, Assistant Attorney General William Moschella, defended the program in a letter to various Congressional leaders:

> ... the President determined that it was necessary following September 11 to create an early warning detection system. FISA could not have provided the speed and agility required for the early warning detection system. In addition, any legislative change, other than the [original authorization of the president to use military force by congress], that the President might have sought specifically to create such an early warning system would have been public and and would have tipped off our enemies ...

Fourteen constitutional scholars and former government officials[1] responded to this defense. An excerpt from their letter reads as follows:

> ... The DOJ letter fails to offer a plausible legal defense of the NSA domestic spying program. If the Administration felt that FISA was insufficient, the proper course was to seek legislative amendment, as it did with other aspects of FISA in the Patriot Act, and as Congress expressly comtemplated when it enacted the wartime wiretap provision in FISA. One of the crucial features of a constitutional democracy is that it is always open to the president—or anyone else—to seek to change the law ...

Several legal challenges were immediately filed against the NSA's warrantless search program. By late August of 2006, just one court had ruled on the issue. On August 17, 2006, a U.S. District judge in Michigan ruled in *ACLU v. NSA* that the warrantless wiretapping program was unconstitutional, and ordered that it be stopped immediately on the grounds that such activities amounted to violations of the rights to free speech and privacy. More rulings were expected in the months and years that followed.

---

1. The signatories were: Beth Nolan, Curtis Bradley, David Cole, Geoffrey Stone, Harold Hongju Koh, Kathleen M. Sullivan, Laurence H. Tribe, Martin Lederman, Philip B. Heymann, Richard Epstein, Ronald Dworkin, Walter Dellinger, William S. Sessions, and William Van Alstyne.

Chapter XXI

THE PRIVILEGE AGAINST SELF–INCRIMINATION

I. HISTORICAL BACKGROUND AND RATIONALE

A. THE DEVELOPMENT OF THE PRIVILEGE AGAINST SELF–INCRIMINATION IN ENGLAND

The privilege against self-incrimination can only be understood against the background of English history that produced it. In very brief and simplified form, this is what happened:

Early in the reign of Henry VIII, about 450 years ago, England was a Roman Catholic state. Protestants were vigorously persecuted. Then, when Henry broke with the Roman Catholic Church and Parliament established the Church of England, the Protestants reversed the situation and began to persecute the Catholics. This continued until the reign of Bloody Mary when once again the Catholics persecuted the Protestants. This situation was reversed yet again after the death of Mary, when Elizabeth took the throne. From the 1560's moreover Elizabeth's Church began persecuting (in addition to the Catholics) dissident Protestants called Puritans. This continued under James I and Charles I and helped provoke the Revolution in which Puritans and their allies were victorious.

After the Puritan victory, the authorities continued to persecute Catholics, while also persecuting both the Anglican clergy less reform-minded than themselves, and the "left wing" dissenters who broke away from the main body of Puritans. Then, after the accession to power of Oliver Cromwell, the center of the Puritan establishment moved left and began its own campaigns against the "ungodly," persecuting the Catholics, the High Anglicans and the right-wing Puritans. By the time of the Restoration of the monarchy under Charles II, all England was sick of religious persecution and for the most part it ceased.

This history is quite remarkable. In the course of about 150 years, members of every major religious group in England had been both the initiators and the victims of persecution—and the roles had changed with bewildering rapidity.

A major method of these persecutions was the oath. During the persecution of the Puritans by the Church of England under Elizabeth and James, for example, Puritan ministers were called before the High Commission and asked questions under oath about their beliefs. Being men of God, they could not lie—and, if they admitted to their deviant and nonconformist views, they could be very seriously punished. As a result, increasingly, they claimed the right not to answer and the existence or non-existence of such a right gradually became a major issue in 17th century England. One of the most celebrated cases involving the right was that of John Lilburne:*

> In 1637, Lilburne, a Puritan dissenter, was brought before the Star Chamber. Having just returned from Holland, he was charged with sending "factitious and scandalous books" from there to England. Lilburne repeatedly contended that he was entitled to notice, indictment, and court trial under the known laws of England; that he had a right to be represented by counsel; that he had a right to have witnesses summoned in his behalf and be confronted by witnesses against him; and that he could not be compelled to testify against himself.

> For refusing to respond to the questions, Lilburne was fined, was tied to a cart and, his body bared, was whipped through the streets of London. At Westminster he was placed in a pillory—his body bent down, his neck in a hole, and his lacerated back bared to the midday sun; there he stood for two hours and exhorted all who would listen to resist the tyranny of the bishops. Refusing to be quiet, he was gagged so cruelly that his mouth bled. After all this, he was kept in solitary confinement in the Fleet Prison with irons on his hands and legs and without anything to eat for ten days. After Lilburne's release, his cruel treatment and bold resistance had two consequences. The first was the vote of the Long Parliament that his sentence was illegal and that he be paid reparations. The second was the abolition of both the Star Chamber and the Court of the High Commission by the same Parliament.

The development of the privilege was by no means complete at this point. As has been pointed out,**

> [The] objections to compulsory self-incrimination were not, however, aimed at the practice in the regular criminal courts but, rather, at the practice as it was carried out by the Star Chamber and the High Commission. [After the abolition of the Courts of the Star Chamber and of the High Commission,] [q]uestioning of the accused at his trial continued unaltered for nearly two decades; the examination of the prisoner by the committing magistrate continued for as long as two centuries. Nevertheless, a gradual repugnance to compulsory self-incrimination developed. By the end of the reign of Charles II, the privilege was recognized in all courts when claimed by defendant or witness.

* The Bill of Rights, A Source Book for Teachers, California State Department of Education, 1967, pp. 79–80.

** Ibid., p. 80.

B. THE FIFTH AMENDMENT*

The right against self-incrimination was but shakily or unevenly established in America by the close of the seventeenth century. But a perceptible change was occurring in the legal development of all the colonies: the English common law was increasingly becoming American law. The degree to which that was true varied from colony to colony, and the pace was not the same in each. But in all, as their political and economic systems matured, their legal systems, most strikingly in the field of criminal procedure, began more and more to resemble that of England. The consequence was a greater familiarity with and respect for the right against self-incrimination.

The fact must be emphasized that the right in question was a right against *compulsory* self-incrimination, and, excepting rare occasions when judges intervened to protect a witness against incriminating interrogatories, the right had to be claimed by the defendant. Historically it has been a fighting right: unless invoked, it offered no protection. It vested an option to refuse answer but did not bar interrogation nor taint a voluntary confession as improper evidence. Incriminating statements made by a suspect at the preliminary examination or even at arraignment could always be used with devastating effect at his trial. That a man might unwittingly incriminate himself when questioned in no way impaired his legal right to refuse answer. He lacked the right to be warned that he need not answer, for the authorities were under no legal obligation to apprise him of his right. That reform did not come in England until Sir John Jervis' Act in 1848, and in the United States more than a century later the matter was still a subject of acute constitutional controversy. Yet if the authorities in eighteenth-century Britain and in her colonies were not obliged to caution the prisoner, he in turn was not legally obliged to reply....

. . .

As originally proposed by Madison, the Fifth Amendment's self-incrimination clause was part of a miscellaneous article that read: "No person shall be subject, except in cases of impeachment, to more than one punishment or trial for the same offence; nor shall be compelled to be a witness against himself; nor be deprived of life, liberty, or property, without due process of law; nor be obliged to relinquish his property, where it may be necessary for public use, without a just compensation." This proposal reflects the research and novelty that characterized Madison's work.... [N]o state, either in its own constitution or in its recommended amendments, had a self-incrimination clause phrased like that introduced by Madison: "no person ... shall be compelled to be a witness against himself."

Not only was Madison's phrasing original; his placement of the clause was also unusual. In the widely imitated model of his own state, the clause appeared in the midst of an enumeration of the procedural rights of the criminally accused at his trial. Only Delaware and Maryland had departed from this precedent by giving the clause independent

* Leonard W. Levy, Origins of the Fifth Amendment, Oxford University Press, 1968, pp. 368, 375, 422–427, 429–430.

status and applicability in all courts, thereby extending it to witnesses as well as parties and to civil as well as criminal proceedings. In presenting his amendments, Madison said nothing whatever that explained his intentions concerning the self-incrimination clause. Nor do his papers or correspondence illuminate his meaning. We have only the language of his proposal, and that revealed an intent to incorporate into the Constitution the whole scope of the common-law right. From the very meaning of its terms, Madison's proposal seemed as broad as the old *nemo tenetur* maxim in which it had its origins....

Madison's proposal certainly applied to civil as well as criminal proceedings and in principle to any stage of a legal inquiry, from the moment of arrest in a criminal case, to the swearing of a deposition in a civil one. And not being restricted to judicial proceedings, it extended to any other kind of governmental inquiry such as a legislative investigation. Moreover, the unique phrasing, that none could be compelled to be a witness against himself, was far more comprehensive than a prohibition against self-incrimination. By its terms the clause could also apply to any testimony that fell short of making one vulnerable to criminal jeopardy or civil penalty or forfeiture, but that nevertheless exposed him to public disgrace or obloquy, or other injury to name and reputation. Finally, Madison's phrasing protected third parties, those who were merely witnesses called to give testimony for one side or the other, whether in civil, criminal, or equity proceedings. According to customary procedure, witnesses, unlike parties, could in fact be compelled to give evidence, under oath, although they were safeguarded against the necessity of testifying against themselves in any manner that might open them to prosecution for a criminal offense or subject them to a forfeiture or civil penalties.... Madison, going beyond the recommendations of the states and the constitution of his own state, phrased his own proposal to make it coextensive with the broadest practice....

Madison's proposed amendments were sent to a select committee of which he was a member. The committee, when reporting to the House, made no change in the positioning or language of the clause protecting persons from being witnesses against themselves. The report was taken up by the Committee of the Whole after Madison fought off further delaying tactics, and debate followed seriatim on each proposed amendment. There was no debate, however, on the clause in question. Only one speaker, John Laurence, a Federalist lawyer of New York, addressed himself to what he called the proposal that "a person shall not be compelled to give evidence against himself." ... Laurence thought that [the provision] should "be confined to criminal cases," and he moved an amendment for that purpose. The amendment was adopted, apparently without discussion, not even by Madison, and then the clause as amended was adopted unanimously. We do not know whether the House debated Laurence's motion or what the vote on it was. The speed with which the House seems to have acted, without the record showing any controversy over the significant restriction of the scope of the clause, is bewildering. Simple respect for the House's own distinguished select committee, a nonpartisan group that included one member from each state, five of whom had been delegates to the Philadelphia Constitutional

Convention of 1787, ought to have required some explanation. The select committee, following Madison, had intended what Laurence rightly called "a general declaration." Taken literally, the amended clause, "No person shall ... be compelled in any criminal case, to be a witness against himself," excluded from its protection parties and witnesses in civil and equity suits as well as witnesses before nonjudicial governmental proceedings such as legislative investigations. It now applied only to parties and witnesses in criminal cases, presumably to all stages of proceedings from arrest and examination to indictment and trial.

. . .

In the Senate, the House's proposed amendments to the Constitution underwent further change. However, the Senate accepted the self-incrimination clause without change.... The Fifth Amendment, even with the self-incrimination clause restricted to criminal cases, still put its principle broadly enough to apply to witnesses and to any phase of the proceedings.

The clause by its terms also protected against more than just "self-incrimination," a phrase that had never been used in the long history of its origins and development. The "right against self-incrimination" is a short-hand gloss of modern origin that implies a restriction not in the constitutional clause. The right not to be a witness against oneself imports a principle of wider reach, applicable, at least in criminal cases, to the self-production of any adverse evidence, including evidence that made one the herald of his own infamy, thereby publicly disgracing him. The clause extended, in other words, to all the injurious as well as incriminating consequences of disclosure by witness or party....

. . .

Whether the framers of the Fifth Amendment intended it to be fully co-extensive with the common law cannot be proved—or disproved. The language of the clause and its framers' understanding of it may not have been synonymous. The difficulty is that its framers, from Mason to Madison and Laurence, left too few clues. Nothing but passing explication emerged during the process of state ratification of the Bill of Rights from 1789 through 1791. Indeed, in legislative and convention proceedings, in letters, newspapers, and tracts, in judicial opinions and law books, the whole period from 1776 to 1791 reveals neither sufficient explanation of the scope of such a clause nor the reasons for it. That it was a ban on torture and a security for the criminally accused were the most important of its functions, as had been the case historically, but these were not the whole of its functions. Still, nothing can be found of a theoretical nature expressing a rationale or underlying policy for the right in question or its reach.

By 1776 the principle of the *nemo tenetur* maxim was simply taken for granted and so deeply accepted that its constitutional expression had the mechanical quality of a ritualistic gesture in favor of a self-evident truth needing no explanation.... [C]onstitution-makers, in that day at least, did not regard themselves as framers of detailed codes. To them the statement of a bare principle was sufficient, and they were content to put it spaciously, if somewhat ambiguously, in order to allow for its expansion as the need might arise.

C. THE PURPOSES OF THE PRIVILEGE AGAINST SELF–INCRIMINATION

NOTE

One may question whether the privilege against self-incrimination, despite its honorable lineage, has any modern function. After all, most of the practices that led to the establishment of the privilege would now be forbidden by the First Amendment, anyway. A great many justifications, however, have been given for retaining the privilege as an important protection for the individual.

One is that we should still worry whether, in times of national stress, the First Amendment can bear the load of prohibiting governmental intrusion into political beliefs. The Fifth Amendment, by allowing the citizen to frustrate inquiry into such beliefs before anything can be done to him on the basis of his views, beliefs, and thoughts, is, in a sense, a buffer before the First Amendment is ever reached.

In addition, the privilege has been defended as a protection of the right to privacy. It ensures that the government in investigating him cannot force him to give up this privacy in the most coercive form of state action—the criminal process. To be sure, the citizen's privacy can be invaded in various other ways. (If it cannot, it is because other provisions of the Bill of Rights prevent the invasion.) Moreover, the privilege protects only one kind of privacy—being forced to reveal things about one's self. Nonetheless, the privilege at least puts one major method of invading the citizens' privacy beyond the reach of the government. As we will see, the citizen can be forced to answer questions if he is given immunity from criminal prosecution. Nonetheless the very fact that the citizen must be given immunity before he may be compelled to incriminate himself often negates the major reason why the government is pressing the inquiry—punishment of the involuntary witness.

Another defense of the privilege is that it prevents a type of weakening of law enforcement. One would think that the privilege against self-incrimination is a great barrier to law enforcement, and in many senses it is. Nonetheless, some have defended the privilege by pointing out that its neglect by the British Government in India produced the famous comment of one British official that, "It is far easier to sit in the shade rubbing pepper into some poor devil's eyes than it is to go out in the sun hunting evidence." What he meant is that a police force that tends to rely on getting all information out of the mouths of criminal suspects gradually loses the ability to develop information and clues in any other way. The privilege thus prevents this type of debilitation of law enforcement.

An additional justification is that the privilege prevents certain kinds of threats to the dignity and welfare of citizens. The government cannot, consistent with the privilege, subject the citizen to torture to extract information about his criminality because of its effect on the citizen himself. It is true that the privilege historically is far broader than merely a prohibition against torturing confessions out of an accused. Nonetheless, the privilege stands to prevent such governmental conduct.

A related justification for the privilege is that it is basically unseemly to use man, in Justice Frankfurter's words, as "the deluded instrument of his own undoing." The analogy drawn here is that even when we have executed a man, we never made him dig his own grave as well. The privilege has been defended as an impediment to this type of assault upon human dignity—using of men as means rather than ends, and of forcing people to do themselves injury.

Perhaps the most interesting justification for the privilege is as an impediment to "total" law enforcement. When one thinks about armed robbery, mugging, rape and murder, it seems only natural that we would want a society in which everybody obeyed the law. There are, however, all kinds of laws in a society and, according to this view, the only reason we do not have a great many more of them than we do is that the legislature doubts that it can enforce any more—or even those we have. The view implied here is that human government is insatiable and will meddle in its citizens' private lives as much as it can. One author has commented: If we had had a method of perfect law enforcement we would still have Prohibition and we probably would have laws against masturbation, smoking in bed, and 150 other things the legislature would decide were not good for people. It is no coincidence that the countries which come closest to being able to enforce their criminal laws completely are also those which most regiment their citizens, most restrict their behavior and interfere most with their private lives.

Do any of these arguments prove that the prosecutor shouldn't be allowed to ask the defendant in a trial for murder whether he shot the victim?

D.   ACCUSATORIAL AND INQUISITORIAL SYSTEMS OF CRIMINAL TRIALS

There is one additional purpose served by the privilege against self-incrimination. It is at the cornerstone of the accusatorial system of justice as applied in English-speaking countries, as opposed to the continental European "inquisitorial" system. Apart from any other procedural rule, the privilege against self-incrimination theoretically prohibits the most obvious means of starting an investigation of an unsolved crime—calling in the prime suspect and asking him questions. By prohibiting this type of procedure, the privilege against self-incrimination tends to force the process into one where the state has to gather its evidence and then accuse the suspect. It is arguable that in some ways this is not a very rational method of procedure. Isn't the most logical way to begin an investigation of a criminal case to ask the person you think knows most about the crime—that is, the person you think committed it? Consider that question, in connection with the next excerpt, which compares inquisitional and accusatorial systems.

TWO MODELS*

... An accusatorial system assumes a social equilibrium which is not lightly to be disturbed, and assigns great social value to keeping the state out of disputes, especially when stigma and sanction may follow. As a result, the person who charges another with crime cannot rely on his assertion alone to shift to the accused the obligation of proving his innocence. The accuser must, in the first instance, present reasonably persuasive evidence of guilt. It is in this sense that the presumption of innocence is at the heart of an accusatorial system. Until certain procedures and proofs are satisfied, the accused is to be treated by the legal system *as if* he is innocent and need lend no aid to those who would convict him.

An accusatorial system is basically reactive, reflecting its origins in a setting in which enforcement of criminal laws was largely confined to courts. Police and prosecutors had hardly developed; the initiative was left to the complaining party to invoke criminal sanctions by gathering his proofs and presenting them at trial. Before trial, the state played a relatively passive role, doing only what was minimally required to enable the complainant to present his case. If arrests were sought, then probable cause had to be established to the satisfaction of a magistrate, but the magistrate would not investigate on his own. If indictments or informations were sought, the grand jury or prosecutor would approach the matter as a screening agency rather than as an investigator.... In sum, the accusatorial model closely resembles the system of private prosecution which long dominated English criminal justice. It is also reminiscent of a civil case, where the court leaves matters largely to the parties.

.   .   .

Comparativists generally assume that inquisitorial [as distinguished from accusatorial] systems are primarily concerned with enforcing criminal laws and are only incidentally concerned with the manner in which it is done. They point especially to the use of the accused as the primary source of evidence, both during the investigation and at trial. He is ordinarily called as the first witness and is questioned closely by the presiding judge about the facts of his life and his knowledge of the crime. Few rules of evidence inhibit the judge and the state has no explicit burden of proof or persuasion. The judge dominates the proceeding and often appears to move relentlessly toward a predetermined result of conviction....

The inquisitorial trial places little emphasis on oral presentation of evidence or on cross-examination by counsel. Instead, the trial is mainly a public recapitulation of written materials included in a dossier compiled earlier by an investigating magistrate. That dossier, however, is the product of a pretrial process much more formal than ours. Inquisitorial systems explicitly define the relation of the investigating magistrate and

---

* Abraham S. Goldstein, Reflections on Two Models: Inquisitorial Themes in American Criminal Procedures, Stanford Law Review, 1974, vol. 26, pp. 1017–1020.

presiding judge to the investigation and the charge. The applicable legal norms are usually stated in a code, and an investigating magistrate takes over from the moment an arrest is made or a crime is charged. He seeks all logically probative evidence and is bound by almost no restrictions on what he may consider. He is, however, subject to a great many rules on how he must record statements, authenticate documents, and work with experts. He may delegate to the police a good deal of authority to detain or question or search, but records must be kept of each delegation and there must be periodic reviews or renewals.

Throughout, the judiciary as an institution is the central actor and is not expected to subordinate its enforcement of the legal norms to the wishes of counsel, police agencies, or the accused. Little or no discretion is authorized in either prosecutor or judge....

These portraits of accusatorial and inquisitorial systems are, of course, idealized. European criminal procedures are no more purely inquisitorial than ours are purely accusatorial. Europeans too have accusatorial elements and mixed systems; they may tolerate more discretion than their literature concedes and may, in many instances, be moving toward a greater role for counsel and more explicit protection for the accused. Nevertheless, there are central tendencies.

For inquisitorial systems, the dominant mode is state control of the case, usually through the judiciary, rather than party control. The judge, whether as investigating magistrate or at trial, regards himself as more than an umpire. He is expected to take the initiative in amassing evidence and in assuring that the merits of guilt and penalty are correctly assessed. And the judiciary is accustomed to participating in and directing investigative and administrative processes which, in our system, are left largely to police or to counsel.

Similarly, our central tendency has been toward an accusatorial system, but it would blink law and reality to ignore the strong inquisitorial elements in our procedure. From earliest times, grand juries and justices of the peace have served investigative functions, even though they are judicial agencies. In the 16th century, under the statutes of Philip and Mary, the magistrates at preliminary hearings became examining magistrates and conceived of themselves as having an independent obligation to investigate the facts.... Though our magistrates are no longer investigating officials, their contemporary analogues are the one-man grand jury and the expanded role of special and regular grand juries. They take their place alongside other inquisitorial devices which have played an important part in the reality of American law: the use of the accused for interrogation and search [and] the practice of persuading him, directly or indirectly, to waive his rights and immunities by pleading guilty; ...

ANOTHER MODEL

One, of course, might wonder what a society would look like if it had no privilege against self-incrimination at all. The People's Republic of China provides an example of a society with a set of values very different from ours, where self-criticism is the norm and a privilege against self-incrimination would be unthinkable. Traditional Chinese culture, with its strong emphasis on the Confucian virtues of yielding and following the established rites, remains a strong influence in China. Private dispute resolution has traditionally been the norm in China and resorting to the legal system carries with it a certain stigma. The Communists and the Confucians agree on the perfectibility of man and both rely on mass education techniques, including the use of role models, to educate the populace. Thus, in the Chinese system, confession is a necessary first step in the reeducation process.

The first Chinese Constitution, promulgated in 1954, draws heavily on the Soviet model. This constitution reflects the typical European inquisitorial model, with its lack of a strong privilege against self-incrimination. As you read the following excerpt, consider the impact of both traditional culture and the inquisitorial model on the development of modern Chinese practices. Note the difficulty in comparing one specific aspect of a system, such as the lack of a privilege against self-incrimination, when the overall situations are so very different.

CRIMINAL JUSTICE IN CHINA*

"In China, each person is his own lawyer. If he commits a crime, he goes in and makes a confession. By accusing himself as thoroughly as possible, he is defending himself to the best of his ability."

Jean Pasqualini, whose Chinese name is Bao Ruo Wang, in this way summed up a Chinese perspective on criminal justice. A perspective that has its basis in experience: he spent seven years in Chinese prisons for being a counter-revolutionary.

Pasqualini, 49, who is a French citizen although half Chinese, was released after France recognized the People's Republic. . . .

The theme of confession dominated Pasqualini's recollections. He was kept for fifteen months before trial at an interrogation center, where he "wrote 700 pages of everything bad I had done since age eight." (His work for the U.S. Marines and for foreign embassies had been particularly incriminating). He went to interrogation time after time with "confession" after "confession," and after each one was sent back to his cell to think things over. "They would tell me, 'The sooner you make a real confession, the sooner you will go home.'" said Pasqualini.

"I was astonished at first," recalled Pasqualini. "They never threatened, just demanded a frank and full confession. They never forced me, always gave me the opportunity to retract what I had said. The idea was, in confession lies one's salvation. They were just like priests. I think the Chinese Communists learned a great deal from the Catholic missionaries."

Prisoners who were kept in solitary and given minimum rations, recalled Pasqualini, came to look forward to their confession periods as major events in their lives. "It gets so when you meet your interrogator, you feel that he's your best friend in the world," said Pasqualini. "When

* Rob Leflar, Pasqualini Recalls Chinese Prison, Harvard Law Record, 1974, vol. 59, p. 12.

he says, 'We'll stop for the day,' you say, 'No, please! I want to confess for just a half hour more!' And when the day comes when you're allowed to write your own confession, you feel deeply honored—it's a festive occasion!"

After his sentencing, Pasqualini found prison life geared to the inmates' political re-education. "The prisoners were forbidden the use of the word 'comrade,'" he said. "We called each other 'schoolmate.'"

Inmates were expected to report their own and their fellows' "bad actions" to the warden, and to discuss them at nightly sessions. The idea was mutual supervision in a spirit of good will.

The prisoners were never forced to recant their counter-revolutionary ideas, recalled Pasqualini, but were given every incentive to do so. "Our sentences were like rubber bands," he said. "The authorities could stretch or contract them at will, depending on how our attitudes were progressing."

A crucial part of the re-education process was to teach the prisoners that their human relationships with the outside were cut and their former life had no more meaning for them. "They showed me the accusations of my neighbors, of some of my good friends—I had thought they were friends," Pasqualini recalled. "But the crusher was when a warden came up to me and said, 'Congratulations, Wang, your wife is making remarkable improvement in her political development. She has decided to cut off her ties with a counter-revolutionary. You should be proud of her!'" Pasqualini has since remarried.

For all that, Pasqualini, far from being bitter, evaluates the prisons highly....

Asked to sum up his feelings about his experience, Pasqualini responded: "I view my seven years in the camps as a kind of purification process, in which I got rid of a lot of my bad thoughts about the Chinese government...."

II.　EXCHANGING IMMUNITY FROM CRIMINAL PROSECUTION FOR THE PRIVILEGE AGAINST SELF-INCRIMINATION

It might be thought from the simple wording of the Fifth Amendment "[N]or shall [any person] be compelled in any criminal case to be a witness against himself" that the privilege against self-incrimination could only be exercised in a criminal trial. The Fifth Amendment privilege however, like the common law privilege existing at the time of adoption of the Bill of Rights, is broader than this. The privilege developed almost completely as a result of questioning, not in trials, but before investigative bodies. Moreover, the privilege would not be of much value if testimony could be obtained under compulsion by a grand jury or legislative committee and then used against the former witness as an admission or confession in his subsequent criminal trial.

Suppose, then, that the government guaranteed that any information compelled by an investigator's questions would not be used against the witness in a subsequent criminal trial. Would the privilege against self-incrimination still prevent compelling the witness to answer the questions? The first Supreme Court case posing this issue was Counselman v. Hitchcock, 142 U.S. 547 (1892). The Court held that a statute providing that testimony compelled from a witness could not be used against him in any subsequent criminal trial was not an adequate substitute for a privilege not to answer at all. The rationale was that, so long as leads or evidence developed from the compelled testimony might be used against the witness at a later criminal trial, the guarantee of the Fifth Amendment against compulsory self-incrimination was not satisfied. The Court in dictum (a statement of opinion not necessary to decision of the case) stated that the only method of protecting the witness against compulsory self-incrimination was immunity from conviction on any charge relating to the subject-matter of compelled testimony. As a reaction to this Congress passed the broader "transactional" immunity statute at issue in the decision that follows.

BROWN v. WALKER

Supreme Court of the United States, 1896.
161 U.S. 591, 16 S.Ct. 644, 40 L.Ed. 819.

[Brown had pleaded the privilege against self-incrimination and refused to answer certain questions before a grand jury investigating alleged violations of the Interstate Commerce Act by the railroad company for which he worked. Congress had provided that the privilege against self-incrimination would not be available to any witness in an Interstate Commerce Commission investigation. Instead, an immunity from criminal prosecution would be granted for any "transaction, matter or thing concerning which he may testify." The lower courts found Brown in contempt of court for his refusal to testify.]

JUSTICE BROWN ... delivered the opinion of the court.

HENRY BILLINGS BROWN—Born on March 2, 1836, in South Lee, Massachusetts, son of a prosperous businessman. Republican. Protestant. Yale, A.B., 1856; travelled and studied abroad, 1856–1857; read law in a law office for a few months and then briefly attended Yale and Harvard Law Schools. Practiced law, 1868–1875; U.S. deputy marshal, 1861; assistant U.S. attorney, Eastern District, Michigan, 1863–1868, circuit judge, Wayne County, Michigan, 1868; U.S. district judge, Eastern District, Michigan, 1875–1890. Nominated associate justice by President Benjamin Harrison on December 23, 1890, to replace Samuel Miller. Confirmed by the Senate by voice vote on December 29, 1890. Suffered an attack of neuritis in 1890, which blinded him in one eye. Retired on May 28, 1906. Died on September 4, 1916.

· · ·

The clause of the Constitution in question is obviously susceptible of two interpretations. If it be construed literally, as authorizing the witness to refuse to disclose any fact which might tend to incriminate, disgrace or expose him to unfavorable comments, then as he must necessarily to a large extent determine upon his own conscience and responsibility whether his answer to the proposed question will have that tendency, ... the practical result would be, that no one could be compelled to testify to a material fact in a criminal case, unless he chose to do so, or unless it was entirely clear that the privilege was not set up in good faith. If, upon the other hand, the object of the provision be to secure the witness against a criminal prosecution, which might be aided directly or indirectly by his disclosure, then, if no such prosecution be possible—in other words, if his testimony operate as a complete pardon for the offence to which it relates—a statute absolutely securing to him such immunity from prosecution would satisfy the demands of the clause in question.

... It can only be said in general that the clause should be construed, as it was doubtless designed, to effect a practical and beneficent purpose—not necessarily to protect witnesses against every possible detriment which might happen to them from their testimony, nor to unduly impede, hinder or obstruct the administration of criminal justice. That the statute should be upheld, if it can be construed in harmony with the fundamental law, will be admitted....

The maxim *nemo tenetur seipsum accusare* had its origin in a protest against the inquisitorial and manifestly unjust methods of interrogating accused persons.... While the admission or confessions of the prisoner, when voluntarily and freely made, have always ranked high in the scale of incriminating evidence, if an accused person be asked to explain his apparent connection with a crime under investigation, the ease with which the questions put to him may assume an inquisitorial character, the temptation to press the witness unduly, to browbeat him if he be timid or reluctant, to push him into a corner, and to entrap him into fatal contradictions, ... made the system so odious as to give rise to a demand for its total abolition.... So deeply did the iniquities of the ancient system impress themselves upon the minds of the American colonists that the States, with one accord, made a denial of the right to question an accused person a part of their fundamental law, so that a maxim, which in England was a mere rule of evidence, became clothed in this country with the impregnability of a constitutional enactment.

Stringent as the general rule is, however, certain classes of cases have always been treated as not falling within the reason of the rule, and, therefore, constituting apparent exceptions. When examined, these cases will all be found to be based upon the idea that, if the testimony sought cannot possibly be used as a basis for, or in aid of, a criminal prosecution against the witness, the rule ceases to apply, its object being to protect the witness himself and no one else—much less that it shall be made use of as a pretext for securing immunity to others.

1. Thus, if the witness himself elects to waive his privilege, as he may doubtless do, since the privilege is for his protection and not for that of other parties, and discloses his criminal connections, he is not permitted to stop, but must go on and make a full disclosure.

So, under modern statutes permitting accused persons to take the stand in their own behalf, they may be subjected to cross-examination upon their statements.

2.   For the same reason if a prosecution for a crime, concerning which the witness is interrogated, is barred by the statute of limitations, he is compellable to answer....

3.   If the answer of the witness may have a tendency to disgrace him or bring him into disrepute, and the proposed evidence be material to the issue on trial, the great weight of authority is that he may be compelled to answer....

.   .   .

4.   It is almost a necessary corollary of the above propositions that, if the witness has already received a pardon, he cannot longer set up his privilege, since he stands with respect to such offence as if it had never been committed....

.   .   .

All of the [propositions] above cited proceed upon the idea that the prohibition against his being compelled to testify against himself presupposes a legal detriment to the witness arising from the exposure....

The danger of [allowing a witness the absolute privilege of remaining silent under all circumstances] is that the privilege may be put forward for a sentimental reason, or for a purely fanciful protection of the witness against an imaginary danger, and for the real purpose of securing immunity to some third person, who is interested in concealing the facts to which he would testify. Every good citizen is bound to aid in the enforcement of the law, and has no right to permit himself, under the pretext of shielding his own good name, to be made the tool of others, who are desirous of seeking shelter behind his privilege.

.   .   .

It is entirely true that the statute does not purport, nor is it possible for any statute, to shield the witness from the personal disgrace or opprobrium attaching to the exposure of his crime; but, as we have already observed, the authorities are numerous and very nearly uniform to the effect that, if the proposed testimony is material to the issue on trial, the fact that the testimony may tend to degrade the witness in public estimation does not exempt him from the duty of disclosure. A person who commits a criminal act is bound to contemplate the consequences of exposure to his good name and reputation, and ought not to call upon the courts to protect that which he has himself esteemed to be of such little value. The safety and welfare of an entire community should not be put into the scale against the reputation of a self-confessed criminal, who ought not, either in justice or in good morals, to refuse to disclose that which may be of great public utility, in order that his neighbors may think well of him. The design of the constitutional privilege is not to aid the witness in vindicating his character, but to protect him against being compelled to furnish evidence to convict him of a criminal charge. If he secure legal immunity from prosecution, the possible impairment of his good name is a penalty which it is reasonable he should be compelled to pay for the common good. . . .

. . .

. . . While the constitutional provision in question is justly regarded as one of the most valuable prerogatives of the citizen, its object is fully accomplished by the statutory immunity, and we are, therefore, of opinion that the witness was compellable to answer. . . .

. . .

JUSTICE FIELD dissenting.

This court has declared, . . . that "no attempted *substitute* for the constitutional safeguard is sufficient unless it is a *complete* substitute. Such is not the nature and effect of this statute of Congress under consideration. A witness, as observed by counsel, called upon to testify to something which will incriminate him, claims the benefit of the safeguard; he is told that the statute fully protects him against prosecution for his crime; 'but,' he says, 'it leaves me covered with infamy and unable to associate with my fellows;' he is then told that *under the rule of the common law* he would not have been protected against mere infamy, and that the constitutional provision does not assume to protect against infamy *alone,* and that it should not be supposed that its object

STEPHEN J. FIELD—Born on November 4, 1816, in Haddam, Connecticut, to David Dudley Field, a strict Congregational minister, and Submit Dickinson, a member of an old New England Puritan family. Among his brothers were David Dudley Field (renowned lawyer and politician), Cyris West Field (promoter of the Trans–Atlantic Cable), and Henry Martyn Field (leading clergyman). Democrat. Congregationalist. Grew up in Stockbridge, Massachusetts. At the age of 12, went to Turkey to live with his sister and her missionary husband. Lived in Athens and travelled in Europe. Studied Turkish, Greek, Italian, and French. At 17, returned to the U.S. to attend Williams, from which he graduated first in his class in 1837. Read law in the New York office of his brother, David Dudley Field. New York law practice, 1841–1849. Alcalde (mayor-judge) of Marysville, California, 1850; California legislator, 1850–1851; California Supreme Court justice, 1857–1863. Staunch supporter of the Union during the Civil War. Nominated associate justice by President Abraham Lincoln on March 6, 1863, to fill a newly created seat. Confirmed by the Senate on March 10, 1863, by voice vote. Served on the electoral commission that determined that the Republican Rutherford B. Hayes would be president; voted on the losing side of every issue decided in the commission. Served on the Court with his nephew, David B. Brewers, from 1889 to 1897. Though his powers declined in the final years on the Court, he refused to retire until he surpassed Chief Justice Marshall's record for length of service on the Court—34 years and five months. Retired on December 2, 1897. Died on April 9, 1899.

was to protect against infamy even when associated with crime. But he answers: 'I am not claiming any common law privilege, but this particular constitutional safeguard. What its purpose was does not matter. It saves me from infamy, and you furnish me with no *equivalent,* unless by such equivalent I am equally saved from infamy.' " . . .

. . .

The act of Congress [involved here] very materially qualifies the constitutional privilege of exemption of a witness in a criminal case from testifying. . . .

. . . The constitutional safeguards for security and liberty cannot be thus dealt with. They must stand as the Constitution has devised them. They cannot be set aside and replaced by something else on the ground that the substitute will probably answer the same purpose. The citizen, as observed by counsel, is entitled to the very thing which the language of the Constitution assures to him.

. . .

[Justices Shiras, Gray and White also dissented.]

NOTES AND QUESTIONS

1. Although the 5–4 decision in Brown v. Walker was handed down by the slimmest of majorities, it has withstood attack on many subsequent occasions. The most comprehensive attack in recent times came in the dissenting opinion of Justices Douglas and Black in Ullmann v. United States, 350 U.S. 422 (1956). Here, the immunity statute came considerably closer than in *Brown* to the political areas protected by the First Amendment. The statute granting immunity from criminal prosecution authorized the compulsion of testimony in cases involving "national security," "sedition" and the Smith Act (see Chapter 5). The court upheld the statute as constitutional on the authority of Brown v. Walker. Excerpts from Justice Douglas' dissenting opinion follow.

> . . . I would overrule the five-to-four decision of Brown v. Walker, 161 U.S. 591, and adopt the view of the minority in that case that the right of silence created by the Fifth Amendment is beyond the reach of Congress.

> . . . [A]s to Brown v. Walker. The difficulty I have with that decision and with the majority of the Court in the present case is that they add an important qualification to the Fifth Amendment. The guarantee is that no person "shall be compelled in any criminal case to be a witness against himself." The majority does not enforce that guarantee as written but qualifies it; and the qualification apparently reads, "but only if criminal conviction might result." Wisely or not, the Fifth Amendment protects against the compulsory self-accusation of crime without exception or qualification. In Counselman v. Hitchcock . . . Justice Blatchford said, "The privilege is limited to criminal matters, but it is as broad as the mischief against which it seeks to guard."

The "mischief" to be prevented falls under at least three heads.

(1) One "mischief" is not only the risk of conviction but the risk of prosecution. . . .

The risk of prosecution is not a risk which the wise take lightly. As experienced a judge as Learned Hand once said, "I must say that, as a litigant, I should dread a lawsuit beyond almost anything else short of sickness and of death." . . .

. . .

(2) The guarantee against self-incrimination contained in the Fifth Amendment is not only a protection against conviction and prosecution but a safeguard of conscience and human dignity and freedom of expression as well. My view is that the Framers put it beyond the power of Congress to *compel* anyone to confess his crimes. The evil to be guarded against was partly self-accusation under legal compulsion. But that was only a part of the evil. The conscience and dignity of man were also involved. So too was his right to freedom of expression guaranteed by the First Amendment. The Framers, therefore, created the federally protected right of silence and decreed that the law could not be used to pry open one's lips and make him a witness against himself.

. . .

(3) This right of silence, this right of the accused to stand mute serves another high purpose. Justice Field, one of the four dissenters in Brown v. Walker, stated that it is the aim of the Fifth Amendment to protect the accused from all compulsory testimony "which would expose him to infamy and disgrace," as well as that which might lead to a criminal conviction. . . .

. . . The history of infamy as a punishment was notorious. Luther had inveighed against excommunication. The Massachusetts Body of Liberties of 1641 had provided in Article 60: "No church censure shall degrad or depose any man from any Civill dignitie, office, or Authoritie he shall have in the Commonwealth." Loss of office, loss of dignity, loss of face were feudal forms of punishment. Infamy was historically considered to be punishment as effective as fine and imprisonment.

. . . The curse of infamy . . . results from public opinion. Oppression occurs when infamy is imposed on the citizen by the State. . . .

There is great infamy involved in the present case, apart from the loss of rights of citizenship under federal law which I have already mentioned. The disclosure that a person is a Communist practically excommunicates him from society. School boards will not hire him. . . .

It is no answer to say that a witness who exercises his Fifth Amendment right of silence and stands mute may bring himself into disrepute. If so, that is the price he pays for exercising the right of silence granted by the Fifth Amendment. The critical point is that the Constitution places the right of silence *beyond the reach of government*. The Fifth Amendment stands between the citizen and his government. When public opinion casts a person into the outer darkness, as happens today when a person is exposed as a Communist, the government brings infamy on the head of the witness when it compels disclosure. That is precisely what the Fifth Amendment prohibits.

2.   Should the privilege against self-incrimination be available if the disclosed information would incriminate the witness' friends but not the witness himself? What if the disclosed information shows no crime was committed but would provide a reason for firing the witness from his job?

3.   What if the witness is doing a term in prison and is called to testify who his associates were? Should he be released if he answers, or should the immunity merely mean he should not be convicted of additional crimes based on his testimony? What if he will be murdered by other prisoners if he testifies?

4.   In 1972 a new wrinkle was added to the immunity issue. Up to that time the only cases where immunity had been held sufficient to justify compelled testimony were those where the immunity was "transactional." In other words, as in Brown v. Walker, the immunity must extend to any "matter, transaction or thing relating" to the testimony. In the Organized Crime Control Act of 1970, Congress provided an immunity broader than that found insufficient in Counselman v. Hitchcock but narrower than the "transactional" immunity at issue in Brown v. Walker. This "use" immunity provided "that no testimony . . . or other information compelled . . . (or any information directly or indirectly derived from such testimony or other information) may be used against the witness. . . ." In Kastigar v. United States, 406 U.S. 441 (1972) the Supreme Court by a 5–2 majority (Justices Brennan and Rehnquist did not participate) held that such an immunity was sufficient. As a practical matter, how much less advantageous is this kind of "use" immunity to the witness than was the transactional immunity in Brown v. Walker and Ullmann v. United States?

III. APPLICATION OF THE PRIVILEGE AGAINST SELF–INCRIMINATION TO NONVERBAL EVIDENCE AND TO NON–CRIMINAL CASES

The phrasing of the Constitutional privilege against self-incrimination . . . "no person shall be compelled . . . to be a witness against himself" . . . clearly applies to verbal testimony. Should the privilege be extended to include non-verbal evidence, such as blood tests, handwriting analysis and fingerprinting? Does the right of privacy justification for the privilege against self-incrimination apply as much to physical evidence as verbal testimony? Are the state's interests in compelling release of physical evidence stronger than those asserted to justify compulsion of verbal testimony? Are there any alternative methods of obtaining physical evidence? Should the reliability of physical tests such as fingerprint-ing influence the decision as to whether they are privileged or not?

SCHMERBER v. CALIFORNIA

Supreme Court of the United States, 1966.
384 U.S. 757, 86 S.Ct. 1826, 16 L.Ed.2d 908.

[Schmerber was convicted of drunk driving. Evidence that he was intoxicated consisted in part of the analysis of a blood sample withdrawn from him over his protest while he was receiving hospital treatment for injuries in an auto accident.]

JUSTICE BRENNAN delivered the opinion of the Court.

. . .

. . . We . . . must now decide whether the withdrawal of the blood and admission in evidence of the analysis involved in this case violated petitioner's privilege. We hold that the privilege protects an accused only from being compelled to testify against himself, or otherwise provide the State with evidence of a testimonial or communicative nature, and that the withdrawal of blood and use of the analysis in question in this case did not involve compulsion to these ends.

It could not be denied that in requiring petitioner to submit to the withdrawal and chemical analysis of his blood the State compelled him to submit to an attempt to discover evidence that might be used to prosecute him for a criminal offense. . . . The critical question, then, is whether petitioner was thus compelled "to be a witness against himself."

If the scope of the privilege coincided with the complex of values it helps to protect, we might be obliged to conclude that the privilege was violated. . . .

. . . [H]owever, the privilege has never been given the full scope which the values it helps to protect suggest. History and a long line of authorities in lower courts have consistently limited its protection to situations in which the State seeks to submerge those values by obtain-ing the evidence against an accused through "the cruel, simple expedient of compelling it from his own mouth. . . . In sum, the privilege is fulfilled only when the person is guaranteed the right 'to remain silent unless he chooses to speak in the unfettered exercise of his own will.' " The leading case in this Court is Holt v. United States. There the question was whether evidence was admissible that the accused, prior to trial and over his protest, put on a blouse that fitted him. It was contended that compelling the accused to submit to the demand that he model the blouse violated the privilege. Justice Holmes, speaking for the Court, rejected the argument as "based upon an extravagant extension of the Fifth Amendment," and went on to say: "[T]he prohibition of compelling a man in a criminal court to be witness against himself is a prohibition of the use of physical or moral compulsion to extort communications from him, not an exclusion of his body as evidence when it may be material. The objection in principle would forbid a jury to look at a prisoner and compare his features with a photograph. . . ."

It is clear that the protection of the privilege reaches an accused's communications, whatever form they might take, and the compulsion of responses which are also communications, for example, compliance with a subpoena to produce one's papers. On the other hand, ... it offers no protection against compulsion to submit to fingerprinting, photographing, or measurements, to write or speak for identification, to appear in court, to stand, to assume a stance, to walk, or to make a particular gesture. The distinction which has emerged, often expressed in different ways, is that the privilege is a bar against compelling "communications" or "testimony," but that compulsion which makes a suspect or accused the source of "real or physical evidence" does not violate it.

Although we agree that this distinction is a helpful framework for analysis, we are not to be understood to agree with past applications in all instances. There will be many cases in which such a distinction is not readily drawn. Some tests seemingly directed to obtain "physical evidence," for example, lie detector tests measuring changes in body function during interrogation, may actually be directed to eliciting responses which are essentially testimonial. To compel a person to submit to testing in which an effort will be made to determine his guilt or innocence on the basis of physiological responses, whether willed or not, is to evoke the spirit and history of the Fifth Amendment. Such situations call to mind the principle that the protection of the privilege "is as broad as the mischief against which it seeks to guard,"

In the present case, however, no such problem of application is presented. Not even a shadow of testimonial compulsion upon or enforced communication by the accused was involved either in the extraction or in the chemical analysis. Petitioner's testimonial capacities were in no way implicated; indeed, his participation, except as a donor, was irrelevant to the results of the test, which depend on chemical analysis and on that alone. Since the blood test evidence, although an incriminating product of compulsion, was neither petitioner's testimony nor evidence relating to some communicative act or writing by the petitioner, it was not inadmissible on privilege grounds.

· · ·

JUSTICE BLACK with whom JUSTICE DOUGLAS joins, dissenting.

· · ·

... To reach the conclusion that compelling a person to give his blood to help the State convict him is not equivalent to compelling him to be a witness against himself strikes me as quite an extraordinary feat....

... [I]t seems to me that the compulsory extraction of petitioner's blood for analysis so that the person who analyzed it could give evidence to convict him had both a "testimonial" and a "communicative nature." The sole purpose of this project which proved to be successful was to obtain "testimony" from some person to prove that petitioner had alcohol in his blood at the time he was arrested. And the purpose of the project was certainly "communicative" in that the analysis of the blood was to supply information to enable a witness to communicate to the court and jury that petitioner was more or less drunk.

. . .

... How can it reasonably be doubted that the blood test evidence was not in all respects the actual equivalent of "testimony" taken from petitioner when the result of the test was offered as testimony, was considered by the jury as testimony, and the jury's verdict of guilt rests in part on that testimony? The refined, subtle reasoning and balancing process used here to narrow the scope of the Bill of Rights' safeguard against self-incrimination provides a handy instrument for further narrowing of that constitutional protection, as well as others, in the future. Believing with the Framers that these constitutional safeguards broadly construed by independent tribunals of justice provide our best hope for keeping our people free from governmental oppression, I deeply regret the Court's holding. . . .

. . .

JUSTICE DOUGLAS, dissenting.

. . .

... [T]he Fifth Amendment marks "a zone of privacy" which the Government may not force a person to surrender. Likewise the Fourth Amendment recognizes that right when it guarantees the right of the people to be secure "in their persons." ... No clearer invasion of this right of privacy can be imagined than forcible bloodletting of the kind involved here.

[Chief Justice Warren and Justice Fortas also dissented.]

NOTES AND QUESTIONS

1. During the *Schmerber* conference, several justices mentioned Breithaupt v. Abram, 352 U.S. 432 (1957). The facts of the two cases are similar. The principal difference is that in *Breithaupt* the driver was unconscious when the blood had been drawn and he had no opportunity to object to the procedure. The Court had held by a vote of six to three that use of the blood sample in a manslaughter trial did not violate due process. The three dissenters in *Breithaupt*—Chief Justice Warren and Justices Black and Douglas—voted to reverse in *Schmerber*. Justice Fortas, who came to the Court after the *Breithaupt* decision, also voted to reverse. Justice Douglas recorded Justice Stewart as saying that it was a very close case and that he voted "to affirm on *Breithaupt,* though originally he would probably go the other way." Justice Clark said that taking a blood sample was similar to taking fingerprints. Justice Harlan said that a state can require taking of blood samples "in protection of its highways" and that he stood by *Breithaupt.* Chief Warren asked: "Would the principle in *Breithaupt* apply to testing of blood for narcotics?" Justice Harlan answered yes.*

* Douglas Papers, Library of Congress, Box 1370.

2. Note that although both are in part directed at preserving the privacy of the individual from government intrusion, the Fourth Amendment and the Fifth Amendment are very different in their coverage. The Fourth Amendment permits "reasonable" searches if a search warrant is obtained. As a result, if the proper showing is made in advance to the appropriate judicial officer, and if other formalities are observed, the Fourth Amendment imposes no further barrier to the invasion of the citizen's privacy. The Fifth Amendment, on the other hand, erects a complete bar to certain kinds of state impingement on the privacy of the individual. No warrant is available to force a citizen to testify against himself, no matter how great the probable cause.

3. As we have seen, however, the coverage of the Fifth Amendment is by no means complete either. As in *Schmerber,* it does not protect against compulsory disclosure of "non-testimonial" information. This not only applies to the blood-alcohol content and the fingerprints of an individual, but also applies to his handwriting samples and to the quality of his voice. As a result, the Fifth Amendment does not impose any impediment to requiring the citizen to provide these. The restrictions of the Fourth Amendment still apply, however. Indeed, in Davis v. Mississippi, 394 U.S. 721 (1969), the Supreme Court implied that the Fourth Amendment restricted the right of the police to compel fingerprints from a person who was not under valid arrest.

4. The Court says that compulsory application of a lie detector would violate the Fifth Amendment. Is that because the suspect has to speak or because lie detector evidence is more fallible than blood tests and fingerprints? Would it matter if the "lie detector" simply measured involuntary reflexes which somehow showed guilt at the asking of certain questions—without any voluntary action by the "witness"? Would the Fifth Amendment still be at issue if a lie detector were as reliable as a handwriting sample?

5. The privilege against self-incrimination has been restricted in a rather vague set of non-criminal contexts, where the state has other interests than convicting a witness of a crime. The Supreme Court has held that the mere pleading of the privilege against self-incrimination before an investigatory body is not sufficient grounds for non-criminal sanctions such as the firing of a school teacher or a public employee or the disbarring of a lawyer. Presumably, also the state is barred from punishing someone non-criminally for refusing to waive, or give up, the immunity which would otherwise have to be bestowed upon him, before his testimony could be compelled. Thus, in Lefkowitz v. Turley, 414 U.S. 70 (1973), New York State was forbidden to bar a contractor from doing business with the state because he had refused to waive immunity prior to testifying before a grand jury investigating kickbacks to public officials. The Supreme Court reaffirmed this view in Lefkowitz v. Cunningham, 431 U.S. 801 (1977). New York, pursuant to a State statute, attempted to deprive a political party official of his party post for refusing to waive immunity before testifying before a grand jury. The Court decided that this violated the privilege against self-incrimination. Justice Stevens, in dissent, would have distinguished Lefkowitz v. Turley

because the prospective grand jury witness occupied a "sensitive policy-making office."

On the other hand, even if the state can't presume guilt because someone invokes the privilege, should it be able to attach unpleasant consequences for obstructing a legitimate investigation into a person's own misconduct? Thus, if a policeman called in an investigation of police corruption pleads the privilege and refuses to testify should the state be permitted to fire him simply because, criminal prosecution aside, he had a duty to provide relevant information about his job performance and did not do so? Similarly, should an applicant for admission to the bar who refuses, on grounds of self-incrimination, to provide information about his prior conduct, be refused admittance because he has obstructed a relevant, non-criminal investigation?

6. What if the state gives the witness immunity? Take the case where a legislative committee or grand jury calls a public employee before it, gives him immunity, and compels his testimony. What if he is then fired on the basis of the testimony compelled from him? In support of this action one might point to the specific language of the Fifth Amendment—"in any criminal case"—and argue that, since no criminal prosecution can result from the testimony, the privilege has not been infringed. On the other hand, the loss of one's job, especially after a certain age, seems as serious a sanction as conviction of most crimes. Moreover, as government employment has become more common in our society, more people become subject to government pressure to come forth with evidence against themselves. If, as is likely under present Supreme Court decisions, the termination of welfare or other governmental benefits is considered "non-criminal," an even larger percentage of the citizenry becomes vulnerable. Is this in keeping with the purposes of the privilege? The wording?

7. There are a number of situations in which the privilege may not be appropriate, even though compelled testimony may lead to criminal conviction. The most dramatic example of this is the "hit and run" law which requires that a driver involved in an accident give his name and certain information about himself before leaving the scene of the accident. The driver is compelled to admit that it was he who was involved in the accident. Nevertheless, the Supreme Court held in California v. Byers, 402 U.S. 424 (1971), that no immunity is required in such a situation and that the driver's admission may still be used against him in a prosecution for drunken or reckless driving. Similarly, the taxpayer on his tax return may not refuse to divulge his income or other necessary information on grounds that this might incriminate him. In these cases, and several others, the theory seems to be that in an essentially non-criminal statutory regulation, the government has a right to demand certain information of citizens and that if this information is peripherally involved in a criminal prosecution, this does not constitute a violation of the privilege against self-incrimination. Is this in keeping with the purposes of the privilege? Is it simply that it would be terribly inconvenient to apply the privilege to hit and run laws, tax returns etc.?

IV. THE PRIVILEGE AGAINST SELF–INCRIMINATION OF PERSONS IN POLICE CUSTODY

MIRANDA v. ARIZONA

Supreme Court of the United States, 1966.
384 U.S. 436, 86 S.Ct. 1602, 16 L.Ed.2d 694.

[After taking Ernesto Miranda into custody on suspicion of kidnapping and rape, the Phoenix police placed him in a lineup, where the complaining witness identified him. Police officers then interrogated Miranda for two hours, during which he made a confession. In the confession was a typed paragraph saying that Miranda acknowledged his guilt voluntarily, without threats or promises of immunity, with full knowledge of his legal rights, and understanding that what he said might be used against him. Relying primarily on the confession, the jury convicted Miranda of kidnapping and rape, and the judge sentenced him to a prison term of 20 to 30 years on each count. The Arizona Supreme Court upheld the conviction. The U.S. Supreme Court agreed to hear Miranda's application for review with three other similar cases.

Justice Douglas' notes of the *Miranda* conference show that three members of the Court gave their views at some length—Chief Justice Warren and Justices Black and Harlan.

Chief Justice Warren told his colleagues that a person in custody "must be advised of (1) right to remain silent, (2) what he says may be used against him, (3) in time court will appoint a lawyer, (4) he must be given opportunity to get lawyer before he is interrogated unless he waives, (5) burden on government to show waiver, (6) no distinction should be made between one who has a lawyer and one who does not or between one who can have one and one who cannot."

Justice Black said that he agreed largely with the Chief Justice. Referring to the Magna Carta, Black said that an accused "is entitled to all benefits of a def[endant] when government moves against him.... [There is] no right of questioning while he is in custody—when a man is in custody he is a witness against himself."

"What CJ, HLB, WOD have said," Justice Harlan responded, "repudiate all our precedents and history and ABA proposals." Harlan said that he would leave law reform to others. "What we do (if CJ's views obtain)," he concluded, "should be done by constitutional amendment."

When the justices voted, five of them joined Warren—Black, Douglas, Clark, Brennan, and Fortas. Later Justice Clark changed his vote.*]

CHIEF JUSTICE WARREN delivered the opinion of the Court.

The cases before us raise questions which go to the roots of our concepts of American criminal jurisprudence: the restraints society must observe consistent with the Federal Constitution in prosecuting individuals for crime. More specifically, we deal with the admissibility of statements obtained from an individual who is subjected to custodial police

---

* Douglas Papers, Library of Congress, Box 1354.

interrogation and the necessity for procedures which assure that the individual is accorded his privilege under the Fifth Amendment to the Constitution not to be compelled to incriminate himself.

. . .

I.

The constitutional issue we decide in each of these cases is the admissibility of statements obtained from a defendant questioned while in custody or otherwise deprived of his freedom of action in any significant way. In each, the defendant was questioned by police officers, detectives, or a prosecuting attorney in a room in which he was cut off from the outside world. In none of these cases was the defendant given a full and effective warning of his rights at the outset of the interrogation process. In all the cases, the questioning elicited oral admissions, and in three of them, signed statements as well which were admitted at their trials. They all thus share salient features—incommunicado interrogation of individuals in a police-dominated atmosphere, resulting in self-incriminating statements without full warnings of constitutional rights.

An understanding of the nature and setting of this in-custody interrogation is essential to our decisions today. The difficulty in depicting what transpires at such interrogations stems from the fact that in this country they have largely taken place incommunicado. From extensive factual studies undertaken in the early 1930's, including the famous Wickersham Report to Congress by a Presidential Commission, it is clear that police violence and the "third degree" flourished at that time.

. . .

In a series of cases decided by this Court long after these studies, the police resorted to physical brutality—beating, hanging, whipping—and to sustained and protracted questioning incommunicado in order to extort confessions. The Commission on Civil Rights in 1961 found much evidence to indicate that "some policemen still resort to physical force to obtain confessions," 1961 Comm'n on Civil Rights Rep., Justice, pt. 5, 17. The use of physical brutality and violence is not, unfortunately, relegated to the past or to any part of the country. Only recently in Kings County, New York, the police brutally beat, kicked and placed lighted cigarette butts on the back of a potential witness under interrogation for the purpose of securing a statement incriminating a third party. . . .

The examples given above are undoubtedly the exception now, but they are sufficiently widespread to be the object of concern. Unless a proper limitation upon custodial interrogation is achieved—such as these decisions will advance—there can be no assurance that practices of this nature will be eradicated in the foreseeable future. . . .

Again we stress that the modern practice of in-custody interrogation is psychologically rather than physically oriented. As we have stated before, "Since Chambers v. Florida, 309 U.S. 227, this Court has recognized that coercion can be mental as well as physical, and that the blood of the accused is not the only hallmark of an unconstitutional inquisition." Blackburn v. Alabama, 361 U.S. 199, 206 (1960). Interrogation still takes place in privacy. Privacy results in secrecy and this in turn results in a gap in our knowledge as to what in fact goes on in the interrogation rooms.

. . .

II.

We sometimes forget how long it has taken to establish the privilege against self-incrimination, the sources from which it came and the fervor with which it was defended. Its roots go back into ancient times. Perhaps the critical historical event shedding light on its origins and evolution was the trial of one John Lilburn, a vocal anti-Stuart Leveller, who was made to take the Star Chamber Oath in 1637. The oath would have bound him to answer to all questions posed to him on any subject. The Trial of John Lilburn and John Wharton, 3 How.St.Tr. 1315 (1637). He resisted the oath and declaimed the proceedings, stating:

> "Another fundamental right I then contended for, was, that no man's conscience ought to be racked by oaths imposed, to answer to questions concerning himself in matters criminal, or pretended to be so." Haller & Davies, The Leveller Tracts 1647–1653, p. 454 (1944).

On account of the Lilburn Trial, Parliament abolished the inquisitorial Court of Star Chamber and went further in giving him generous reparation. The lofty principles to which Lilburn had appealed during his trial gained popular acceptance in England. These sentiments worked their way over to the Colonies and were implanted after great struggle into the Bill of Rights. Those who framed our Constitution and the Bill of Rights were ever aware of subtle encroachments on individual liberty. They knew that "illegitimate and unconstitutional practices get their first footing ... by silent approaches and slight deviations from legal modes of procedure." Boyd v. United States, 116 U.S. 616, 635 (1886). The privilege was elevated to constitutional status and has always been "as broad as the mischief against which it seeks to guard." Counselman v. Hitchcock, 142 U.S. 547, 562 (1892). We cannot depart from this noble heritage.

Thus we may view the historical development of the privilege as one which groped for the proper scope of governmental power over the citizen. As a "noble principle often transcends its origins," the privilege has come rightfully to be recognized in part as an individual's substantive right, a "right to a private enclave where he may lead a private life. That right is the hallmark of our democracy." United States v. Grunewald, 233 F.2d 556, 579, 581–582 (Frank, J., dissenting), rev'd, 353 U.S. 391 (1957). We have recently noted that the privilege against self-incrimination—the essential mainstay of our adversary system—is founded on a complex of values, Murphy v. Waterfront Comm'n, 378 U.S. 52, 55–57, n. 5 (1964); Tehan v. Shott, 382 U.S. 406, 414–415, n. 12 (1966). All these policies point to one overriding thought: the constitutional foundation underlying the privilege is the respect a government—state or federal—must accord to the dignity and integrity of its citizens.

To maintain a "fair state-individual balance," to require the government "to shoulder the entire load," 8 Wigmore, Evidence 317 (McNaughton rev.1961), to respect the inviolability of the human personality, our accusatory system of criminal justice demands that the government seeking to punish an individual produce the evidence against him by its own independent labors, rather than by the cruel, simple expedient of compelling it from his own mouth. Chambers v. Florida, 309 U.S. 227, 235–238 (1940). In sum, the privilege is fulfilled only when the person is guaranteed the right "to remain silent unless he chooses to speak in the unfettered exercise of his own will." Malloy v. Hogan, 378 U.S. 1, 8 (1964).

The question in these cases is whether the privilege is fully applicable during a period of custodial interrogation. In this Court, the privilege has been accorded a liberal construction. . . . We are satisfied that all the principles embodied in the privilege apply to informal compulsion exerted by law-enforcement officers during in-custody questioning. An individual swept from familiar surroundings into police custody, surrounded by antagonistic forces, and subjected to the techniques of persuasion described above cannot be otherwise than under compulsion to speak. As a practical matter, the compulsion to speak in the isolated setting of the police station may well be greater than in courts or other official investigations, where there are often impartial observers to guard against intimidation or trickery.

This question, in fact, could have been taken as settled in federal courts almost 70 years ago, when, in Bram v. United States, 168 U.S. 532, 542 (1897), this Court held:

> "In criminal trials, in the courts of the United States, wherever a question arises whether a confession is incompetent because not voluntary, the issue is controlled by that portion of the Fifth Amendment ... commanding that no person 'shall be compelled in any criminal case to be a witness against himself.' "

In *Bram,* the Court reviewed the British and American history and case law and set down the Fifth Amendment standard for compulsion which we implement today:

> "Much of the confusion which has resulted from the effort to deduce from the adjudged cases what would be a sufficient quantum of proof to show that a confession was or was not voluntary, has arisen from a misconception of the subject to which the proof must address itself. The rule is not that in order to render a statement admissible the proof must be adequate to establish that the particular communications contained in a statement were voluntarily made, but it must be sufficient to establish that the making of the statement was voluntary; that is to say, that from the causes, which the law treats as legally sufficient to engender in the mind of the accused hope or fear in respect to the crime charged, the accused was not involuntarily impelled to make a statement,

when but for the improper influences he would have remained silent...." 168 U.S., at 549. And see, id., at 542.

The Court has adhered to this reasoning. In 1924, Justice Brandeis wrote for a unanimous Court in reversing a conviction resting on a compelled confession, Wan v. United States, 266 U.S. 1. He stated:

> "In the federal courts, the requisite of voluntariness is not satisfied by establishing merely that the confession was not induced by a promise or a threat. A confession is voluntary in law if, and only if, it was, in fact, voluntarily made. A confession may have been given voluntarily, although it was made to police officers, while in custody, and in answer to an examination conducted by them. But a confession obtained by compulsion must be excluded whatever may have been the character of the compulsion, and whether the compulsion was applied in a judicial proceeding or otherwise. Bram v. United States, 168 U.S. 532." 266 U.S., at 14–15.

In addition to the expansive historical development of the privilege and the sound policies which have nurtured its evolution, judicial precedent thus clearly establishes its application to incommunicado interrogation. In fact, the Government concedes this point as well established in No. 761, Westover v. United States, stating: "We have no doubt ... that it is possible for a suspect's Fifth Amendment right to be violated during in-custody questioning by a law-enforcement officer."

Because of the adoption by Congress of Rule 5(a) of the Federal Rules of Criminal Procedure, and this Court's effectuation of that Rule in McNabb v. United States, 318 U.S. 332 (1943), and Mallory v. United States, 354 U.S. 449 (1957), we have had little occasion in the past quarter century to reach the constitutional issues in dealing with federal interrogations. These supervisory rules, requiring production of an arrested person before a commissioner "without unnecessary delay" and excluding evidence obtained in default of that statutory obligation, were nonetheless responsive to the same considerations of Fifth Amendment policy that unavoidably face us now as to the States. In *McNabb*, 318 U.S., at 343–344, and in *Mallory*, 354 U.S., at 455–456, we recognized both the dangers of interrogation and the appropriateness of prophylaxis stemming from the very fact of interrogation itself.

Our decision in Malloy v. Hogan, 378 U.S. 1 (1964), necessitates an examination of the scope of the privilege in state cases as well. In *Malloy*, we squarely held the privilege applicable to the States, and held that the substantive standards underlying the privilege applied with full force to state court proceedings. There, as in Murphy v. Waterfront Comm'n, 378 U.S. 52 (1964), and Griffin v. California, 380 U.S. 609 (1965), we applied the existing Fifth Amendment standards to the case before us. Aside from the holding itself, the reasoning in *Malloy* made clear what had already become apparent—that the substantive and procedural safeguards surrounding admissibility of confessions in state cases had become exceedingly exacting, reflecting all the policies embedded in the privilege, 378 U.S., at 7–8. The voluntariness doctrine in the state cases, as *Malloy* indicates, encompasses all interrogation practices which are likely to exert such pressure upon an individual as to disable him from making a free and rational choice. The implications of this proposition were elaborated in our decision in Escobedo v. Illinois, 378 U.S. 478, decided one week after *Malloy* applied the privilege to the States.

Our holding there stressed the fact that the police had not advised the defendant of his constitutional privilege to remain silent at the outset of the interrogation, and we drew attention to that fact at several points in the decision, 378 U.S., at 483, 485, 491. This was no isolated factor, but an essential ingredient in our decision. The entire thrust of police interrogation there, as in all the cases today, was to put the defendant in such an emotional state as to impair his capacity for rational judgment. The abdication of the constitutional privilege—the choice on his part to speak to the police—was not made knowingly or competently because of the failure to apprise him of his rights; the compelling atmosphere of the in-custody interrogation, and not an independent decision on his part, caused the defendant to speak.

A different phase of the *Escobedo* decision was significant in its attention to the absence of counsel during the questioning. There, as in the cases today, we sought a protective device to dispel the compelling atmosphere of the interrogation. In *Escobedo,* however, the police did not relieve the defendant of the anxieties which they had created in the interrogation rooms. Rather, they denied his request for the assistance of counsel, 378 U.S., at 481, 488, 491. This heightened his dilemma, and made his later statements the product of this compulsion. Cf. Haynes v. Washington, 373 U.S. 503, 514 (1963). The denial of the defendant's request for his attorney thus undermined his ability to exercise the privilege—to remain silent if he chose or to speak without any intimidation, blatant or subtle. The presence of counsel, in all the cases before us today, would be the adequate protective device necessary to make the process of police interrogation conform to the dictates of the privilege. His presence would insure that statements made in the government-established atmosphere are not the product of compulsion.

It was in this manner that *Escobedo* explicated another facet of the pre-trial privilege, noted in many of the Court's prior decisions: the protection of rights at trial. That counsel is present when statements are taken from an individual during interrogation obviously enhances the integrity of the fact-finding processes in court. The presence of an attorney, and the warnings delivered to the individual, enable the defendant under otherwise compelling circumstances to tell his story without fear, effectively, and in a way that eliminates the evils in the interrogation process. Without the protections flowing from adequate warnings and the rights of counsel, "all the careful safeguards erected around the giving of testimony, whether by an accused or any other witness, would become empty formalities in a procedure where the most compelling possible evidence of guilt, a confession, would have already been obtained at the unsupervised pleasure of the police." Mapp v. Ohio, 367 U.S. 643, 685 (1961) (Harlan, J., dissenting). Cf. Pointer v. Texas, 380 U.S. 400 (1965).

III.

Today, then, there can be no doubt that the Fifth Amendment privilege is available outside of criminal court proceedings and serves to protect persons in all settings in which their freedom of action is curtailed in any significant way from being compelled to incriminate themselves. We have concluded that without proper safeguards the process of in-custody interrogation of persons suspected or accused of crime contains inherently compelling pressures which work to undermine the individual's will to resist and to compel him to speak where he would not otherwise do so freely. In order to combat these pressures and to permit a full opportunity to exercise the privilege against self-incrimination, the accused must be adequately and effectively apprised of his rights and the exercise of those rights must be fully honored.

It is impossible for us to foresee the potential alternatives for protecting the privilege which might be devised by Congress or the States in the exercise of their creative rule-making capacities. Therefore we cannot say that the Constitution necessarily requires adherence to any particular solution for the inherent compulsions of the interrogation process as it is presently conducted. Our decision in no way creates a constitutional straitjacket which will handicap sound efforts at reform, nor is it intended to have this effect. We encourage Congress and the States to continue their laudable search for increasingly effective ways of protecting the rights of the individual while promoting efficient enforcement of our criminal laws. However, unless we are shown other procedures which are at least as effective in apprising accused persons of their right of silence and in assuring a continuous opportunity to exercise it, the following safeguards must be observed.

At the outset, if a person in custody is to be subjected to interrogation, he must first be informed in clear and unequivocal terms that he has the right to remain silent. For those unaware of the privilege, the warning is needed simply to make them aware of it—the threshold requirement for an intelligent decision as to its exercise. More important, such a warning is an absolute prerequisite in overcoming the inherent pressures of the interrogation atmosphere. It is not just the subnormal or woefully ignorant who succumb to an interrogator's imprecations, whether implied or expressly stated, that the interrogation will continue until a confession is obtained or that silence in the face of accusation is itself damning and will bode ill when presented to a jury. Further, the warning will show the individual that his interrogators are prepared to recognize his privilege should he choose to exercise it.

The Fifth Amendment privilege is so fundamental to our system of constitutional rule and the expedient of giving an adequate warning as to the availability of the privilege so simple, we will not pause to inquire in individual cases whether the defendant was aware of his rights without a warning being given. Assessments of the knowledge the defendant possessed, based on information as to his age, education, intelligence, or prior contact with authorities, can never be more than speculation; a warning is a clearcut fact. More important, whatever the background of the person interrogated, a warning at the time of the interrogation is indispensable to overcome its pressures and to insure that the individual knows he is free to exercise the privilege at that point in time.

The warning of the right to remain silent must be accompanied by the explanation that anything said can and will be used against the individual in court. This warning is needed in order to make him aware not only of the privilege, but also of the consequences of forgoing it. It is only through an awareness of these consequences that there can be any assurance of real understanding and intelligent exercise of the privilege. Moreover, this warning may serve to make the individual more acutely aware that he is faced with a phase of the adversary system—that he is not in the presence of persons acting solely in his interest.

The circumstances surrounding in-custody interrogation can operate very quickly to overbear the will of one merely made aware of his privilege by his interrogators. Therefore, the right to have counsel present at the interrogation is indispensable to the protection of the Fifth Amendment privilege under the system we delineate today. Our aim is to assure that the individual's right to choose between silence and speech remains unfettered throughout the interrogation process. A once-stated warning, delivered by those who will conduct the interrogation, cannot itself suffice to that end among those who most require knowledge of their rights. A mere warning given by the interrogators is not alone sufficient to accomplish that end. Prosecutors themselves claim that the admonishment of the right to remain silent without more "will benefit only the recidivist and the professional." Brief for the National District Attorneys Association as *amicus curiae,* p. 14. Even preliminary advice given to the accused by his own attorney can be swiftly overcome by the secret interrogation process. Thus, the need for counsel to protect the Fifth Amendment privilege comprehends not merely a right to consult with counsel prior to questioning, but also to have counsel present during any questioning if the defendant so desires.

The presence of counsel at the interrogation may serve several significant subsidiary functions as well. If the accused decides to talk to his interrogators, the assistance of counsel can mitigate the dangers of untrustworthiness. With a lawyer present the likelihood that the police will practice coercion is reduced, and if coercion is nevertheless exercised the lawyer can testify to it in court. The presence of a lawyer can also help to guarantee that the accused gives a fully accurate statement to the police and that the statement is rightly reported by the prosecution at trial.

An individual need not make a pre-interrogation request for a lawyer. While such request affirmatively secures his right to have one, his failure to ask for a lawyer does not constitute a waiver. No effective waiver of the right to counsel during interrogation can be recognized unless specifically made after the warnings we here delineate have been given. The accused who does not know his rights and therefore does not make a request may be the person who most needs counsel. . . .

Accordingly we hold that an individual held for interrogation must be clearly informed that he has the right to consult with a lawyer and to have the lawyer with him during interrogation under the system for protecting the privilege we delineate today. As with the warnings of the right to remain silent and that anything stated can be used in evidence against him, this warning is an absolute prerequisite to interrogation. No amount of circumstantial evidence that the person may have been aware of this right will suffice to stand in its stead. Only through such a warning is there ascertainable assurance that the accused was aware of this right.

If an individual indicates that he wishes the assistance of counsel before any interrogation occurs, the authorities cannot rationally ignore or deny his request on the basis that the individual does not have or cannot afford a retained attorney. The financial ability of the individual has no relationship to the scope of the rights involved here. The privilege against self-incrimination secured by the Constitution applies to all individuals. The need for counsel in order to protect the privilege exists for the indigent as well as the affluent. In fact, were we to limit these constitutional rights to those who can retain an attorney, our decisions today would be of little significance. The cases before us as well as the vast majority of confession cases with which we have dealt in the past involve those unable to retain counsel. While authorities are not required to relieve the accused of his poverty, they have the obligation not to take advantage of indigence in the administration of justice. Denial of counsel to the indigent at the time of interrogation while allowing an attorney to those who can afford one would be no more supportable by reason or logic than the similar situation at trial and on appeal struck down in Gideon v. Wainwright, 372 U.S. 335 (1963), and Douglas v. California, 372 U.S. 353 (1963).

In order fully to apprise a person interrogated of the extent of his rights under this system then, it is necessary to warn him not only that he has the right to consult with an attorney, but also that if he is indigent a lawyer will be appointed to represent him. Without this additional warning, the admonition of the right to consult with counsel would often be understood as meaning only that he can consult with a lawyer if he has one or has the funds to obtain one. The warning of a right to counsel would be hollow if not couched in terms that would convey to the indigent—the person most often subjected to interrogation—the knowledge that he too has a right to have counsel present. As with the warnings of the right to remain silent and of the general right to counsel, only by effective and express explanation to the indigent of this right can there be assurance that he was truly in a position to exercise it.

Once warnings have been given, the subsequent procedure is clear. If the individual indicates in any manner, at any time prior to or during questioning, that he wishes to remain silent, the interrogation must cease. At this point he has shown that he intends to exercise his Fifth Amendment privilege; any statement taken after the person invokes his privilege cannot be other than the product of compulsion, subtle or otherwise. Without the right to cut off questioning, the setting of in-custody interrogation operates on the individual to overcome free choice in producing a statement after the privilege has been once invoked. If the individual states that he wants an attorney, the interrogation must cease until an attorney is present. At that time, the individual must have an opportunity to confer with the attorney and to have him present during any subsequent questioning. If the individual cannot obtain an attorney and he indicates that he wants one before speaking to police, they must respect his decision to remain silent.

This does not mean, as some have suggested, that each police station must have a "station house lawyer" present at all times to advise prisoners. It does mean, however, that if police propose to interrogate a person they must make known to him that he is entitled to a lawyer and that if he cannot afford one, a lawyer will be provided for him prior to any interrogation. If authorities conclude that they will not provide counsel during a reasonable period of time in which investigation in the field is carried out, they may refrain from doing so without violating the person's Fifth Amendment privilege so long as they do not question him during that time.

If the interrogation continues without the presence of an attorney and a statement is taken, a heavy burden rests on the government to demonstrate that the defendant knowingly and intelligently waived his privilege against self-incrimination and his right to retained or appointed counsel. This Court has always set high standards of proof for the waiver of constitutional rights, Johnson v. Zerbst, 304 U.S. 458 (1938), and we re-assert these standards as applied to in-custody interrogation. Since the State is responsible for establishing the isolated circumstances under which the interrogation takes place and has the only means of making available corroborated evidence of warnings given during incommunicado interrogation, the burden is rightly on its shoulders.

An express statement that the individual is willing to make a statement and does not want an attorney followed closely by a statement could constitute a waiver. But a valid waiver will not be presumed simply from the silence of the accused after warnings are given or simply from the fact that a confession was in fact eventually obtained. . . .

Whatever the testimony of the authorities as to waiver of rights by an accused, the fact of lengthy interrogation or incommunicado incarceration before a statement is made is strong evidence that the accused did not validly waive his rights. In these circumstances the fact that the individual eventually made a statement is consistent with the conclusion that the compelling influence of the interrogation finally forced him to do so. It is inconsistent with any notion of a voluntary relinquishment of the privilege. Moreover, any evidence that the accused was threatened, tricked, or cajoled into a waiver will, of course, show that the defendant did not voluntarily waive his privilege. The requirement of warnings and waiver of rights is fundamental with respect to the Fifth Amendment privilege and not simply a preliminary ritual to existing methods of interrogation.

The warnings required and the waiver necessary in accordance with our opinion today are, in the absence of a fully effective equivalent, prerequisites to the admissibility of any statement made by a defendant. No distinction can be drawn between statements which are direct confessions and statements which amount to "admissions" of part or all of an offense. The privilege against self-incrimination protects the individual from being compelled to incriminate himself in any manner; it does not distinguish degrees of incrimination. Similarly, for precisely the same reason, no distinction may be drawn between inculpatory statements and statements alleged to be merely "exculpatory." If a statement made were in fact truly exculpatory it would, of course, never be used by the prosecution. In fact, statements merely intended to be exculpatory by the defendant are often used to impeach his testimony at trial or to demonstrate untruths in the statement given under interrogation and thus to prove guilt by implication. These statements are incriminating in any meaningful sense of the word and may not be used without the full warnings and effective waiver required for any other statement. In *Escobedo* itself, the defendant fully intended his accusation of another as the slayer to be exculpatory as to himself.

The principles announced today deal with the protection which must be given to the privilege against self-incrimination when the individual is first subjected to police interrogation while in custody at the station or otherwise deprived of his freedom of action in any significant way. It is at this point that our adversary system of criminal proceedings commences, distinguishing itself at the outset from the inquisitorial system recognized in some countries. Under the system of warnings we delineate today or under any other system which may be devised and found effective, the safeguards to be erected about the privilege must come into play at this point.

Our decision is not intended to hamper the traditional function of police officers in investigating crime.... When an individual is in custody on probable cause, the police may, of course, seek out evidence in the field to be used at trial against him. Such investigation may include inquiry of persons not under restraint. General on-the-scene questioning as to facts surrounding a crime or other general questioning of citizens in the fact-finding process is not affected by our holding. It is an act of responsible citizenship for individuals to give whatever information they may have to aid in law enforcement. In such situations the compelling atmosphere inherent in the process of in-custody interrogation is not necessarily present.

In dealing with statements obtained through interrogation, we do not purport to find all confessions inadmissible. Confessions remain a proper element in law enforcement. Any statement given freely and voluntarily without any compelling influences is, of course, admissible in evidence. The fundamental import of the privilege while an individual is in custody is not whether he is allowed to talk to the police without the benefit of warnings and counsel, but whether he can be interrogated. There is no requirement that police stop a person who enters a police station and states that he wishes to confess to a crime, or a person who calls the police to offer a confession or any other statement he desires to make. Volunteered statements of any kind are not barred by the Fifth Amendment and their admissibility is not affected by our holding today.

To summarize, we hold that when an individual is taken into custody or otherwise deprived of his freedom by the authorities in any significant way and is subjected to questioning, the privilege against self-incrimination is jeopardized. Procedural safeguards must be employed to protect the privilege, and unless other fully effective means are adopted to notify the person of his right of silence and to assure that the exercise of the right will be scrupulously honored, the following measures are required. He must be warned prior to any questioning that he has the right to remain silent, that anything he says can be used against him in a court of law, that he has the right to the presence of an attorney, and that if he cannot afford an attorney one will be appointed for him prior to any questioning if he so desires. Opportunity to exercise these rights must be afforded to him throughout the interrogation. After such warnings have been given, and such opportunity afforded him, the individual may knowingly and intelligently waive these rights and agree to answer questions or make a statement. But unless and until such warnings and waiver are demonstrated by the prosecution at trial, no evidence obtained as a result of interrogation can be used against him.

IV.

A recurrent argument made in these cases is that society's need for interrogation outweighs the privilege. This argument is not unfamiliar to this Court. See, e.g., Chambers v. Florida, 309 U.S. 227, 240–241 (1940). The whole thrust of our foregoing discussion demonstrates that the Constitution has prescribed the rights of the individual when confronted with the power of government when it provided in the Fifth Amendment that an individual cannot be compelled to be a witness against himself. That right cannot be abridged. As Justice Brandeis once observed:

> "Decency, security and liberty alike demand that government officials shall be subjected to the same rules of conduct that are commands to the citizen. In a government of laws, existence of the government will be imperilled if it fails to observe the law scrupulously. Our Government is the potent, the omnipresent teacher. For good or for ill, it teaches the whole people by its example. Crime is contagious. If the Government becomes a lawbreaker, it breeds contempt for law; it invites every man to become a law unto himself; it invites anarchy. To declare that in the administration of the criminal law the end justifies the means ... would bring terrible retribution. Against that pernicious doctrine this Court should resolutely set its face." Olmstead v. United States, 277 U.S. 438, 485 (1928) (dissenting opinion).

In this connection, one of our country's distinguished jurists has pointed out: "The quality of a nation's civilization can be largely measured by the methods it uses in the enforcement of its criminal law."

If the individual desires to exercise his privilege, he has the right to do so. This is not for the authorities to decide. An attorney may advise his client not to talk to police until he has had an opportunity to investigate the case, or he may wish to be present with his client during any police questioning. In doing so an attorney is merely exercising the good professional judgment he has been taught. This is not cause for considering the attorney a menace to law enforcement. He is merely carrying out what he is sworn to do under his oath—to protect to the extent of his ability the rights of his client. In fulfilling this responsibility the attorney plays a vital role in the administration of criminal justice under our Constitution.

In announcing these principles, we are not unmindful of the burdens which law enforcement officials must bear, often under trying circumstances. We also fully recognize the obligation of all citizens to aid in enforcing the criminal laws. This Court, while protecting individual rights, has always given ample latitude to law enforcement agencies in the legitimate exercise of their duties. The limits we have placed on the interrogation process should not constitute an undue interference with a proper system of law enforcement. As we have noted, our decision does not in any way preclude police from carrying out their traditional investigatory functions.

. . .

We reverse. From the testimony of the officers and by the admission of respondent, it is clear that Miranda was not in any way apprised of his right to consult with an attorney and to have one present during the interrogation, nor was his right not to be compelled to incriminate himself effectively protected in any other manner. Without these warnings the statements were inadmissible. The mere fact that he signed a statement which contained a typed-in clause stating that he had "full knowledge" of his "legal rights" does not approach the knowing and intelligent waiver required to relinquish constitutional rights.

[A dissenting opinion by Justice Clark has been omitted.]

Justice Harlan, whom Justice Stewart and Justice White join, dissenting.

I believe the decision of the Court represents poor constitutional law and entails harmful consequences for the country at large. How serious these consequences may prove to be only time can tell. But the basic flaws in the Court's justification seem to me readily apparent now once all sides of the problem are considered.

. . .

At the outset, it is well to note exactly what is required by the Court's new constitutional code of rules for confessions.

... [T]he thrust of the new rules is to negate all pressures, to reinforce the nervous or ignorant suspect, and ultimately to discourage any confession at all. The aim in short is toward "voluntariness" in a utopian sense, or to view it from a different angle, voluntariness with a vengeance.

To incorporate this notion into the Constitution requires a strained reading of history and precedent and a disregard of the very pragmatic concerns that alone may on occasion justify such strains. I believe that reasoned examination will show that the Due Process Clauses provide an adequate tool for coping with confessions and that, even if the Fifth Amendment privilege against self-incrimination be invoked, its precedents taken as a whole do not sustain the present rules. Viewed as a choice based on pure policy, these new rules prove to be a highly debatable, if not one-sided, appraisal of the competing interests, imposed over widespread objection, at the very time when judicial restraint is most called for by the circumstances.

... The Court's opinion in my view reveals no adequate basis for extending the Fifth Amendment's privilege against self-incrimination to the police station. Far more important, it fails to show that the Court's new rules are well supported, let alone compelled, by Fifth Amendment precedents. Instead, the new rules actually derive from quotation and analogy drawn from precedents under the Sixth Amendment, which should properly have no bearing on police interrogation.

. . .

Even those who would readily enlarge the privilege must concede some linguistic difficulties since the Fifth Amendment in terms proscribes only compelling any person "in any criminal case to be a witness against himself."

. . .

Though weighty, I do not say these points and similar ones are conclusive, for, as the Court reiterates, the privilege embodies basic principles always capable of expansion. Certainly the privilege does represent a protective concern for the accused and an emphasis upon accusatorial rather than inquisitorial values in law enforcement, although this is similarly true of other limitations such as the grand jury requirement and the reasonable doubt standard. Accusatorial values, however, have openly been absorbed into the due process standard governing confessions; this indeed is why at present "the kinship of the two rules [governing confessions and self-incrimination] is too apparent for denial." McCormick, Evidence 155 (1954). Since extension of the general principle has already occurred, to insist that the privilege applies as such serves only to carry over inapposite historical details and engaging rhetoric and to obscure the policy choices to be made in regulating confessions.

. . .

How much harm this decision will inflict on law enforcement cannot fairly be predicted with accuracy. Evidence on the role of confessions is notoriously incomplete.... We do know that some crimes cannot be solved without confessions, that ample expert testimony attests to their importance in crime control, and that the Court is taking a real risk with society's welfare in imposing its new regime on the country. The social costs of crime are too great to call the new rules anything but a hazardous experimentation.

While passing over the costs and risks of its experiment, the Court portrays the evils of normal police questioning in terms which I think are exaggerated. Albeit stringently confined by the due process standards interrogation is no doubt often inconvenient and unpleasant for the suspect. However, it is no less so for a man to be arrested and jailed, to have his house searched, or to stand trial in court, yet all this may properly happen to the most innocent given probable cause, a warrant, or an indictment. Society has always paid a stiff price for law and order, and peaceful interrogation is not one of the dark moments of the law. . . .

[Justice White's dissenting opinion, with whom Justice Harlan and Justice Stewart joined, is omitted.]

NOTES AND QUESTIONS

1.   Justice Brennan responded to Chief Justice Warren's initial opinion in *Miranda* with a 21–page letter in which he said that he felt "guilty about the extent of the suggestions," but that the *Miranda* opinion "will be one of the most important opinions of our time, and I know that you will want the fullest expression of my views." Justice Brennan made many detailed suggestions, most of which the Chief Justice accepted. Brennan's "major suggestion," he said, "goes to the basic thrust of the approach to be taken. In your very first sentence," wrote Justice Brennan, "you state that the root of the problem is the 'role society must assume, consistent with the federal Constitution, in prosecuting individuals for crime.' I would suggest the root issue is 'the restraints society must observe, consistent with the Federal Constitution, in prosecuting individuals for crime.' "* Chief Justice Warren adopted Justice Brennan's suggestion.

Justice Black also responded to Chief Justice Warren's initial *Miranda* opinion. "I want to congratulate you," Black wrote to Warren, "in doing a fine job in the opinion. . . . It is informative, persuasive, and eloquent." Justice Black had only a few suggestions. One was to eliminate a reference to "southern states," which might suggest erroneously an attack on the South. Another suggestion was to make it clear in the opinion that the Fifth Amendment privilege against self-incrimination as applied to the states through the Fourteenth Amendment was the basis for the Court's decision and not past precedents or "standards of decency." Finally, Justice Black did not believe the Chief Justice's quotation from Justice Brandeis' dissenting opinion in *Olmstead* was necessary or advisable, for Justice Black did not agree with Brandeis. "If you think it necessary to keep the quotation in," wrote Justice Black, "I'd like for you to put a footnote to this effect: 'In quoting the above from the dissenting opinion of Mr. Justice Brandeis, we, of course, do not intend to approve of his views on the constitutional questions in the *Olmstead* cases.' "* Chief Justice Warren retained the Brandeis quotation and added the footnote that Justice Black requested.

2.   *Miranda*'s impact was predominantly symbolic. The decision's critics often cited it in attacking the Supreme Court and congressional debate on the Crime Control Act of 1968. By that time, there were some empirical studies showing that the decision had not significantly affected law enforcement. But these studies had little influence on the debate. As Chief Justice Warren pointed out in his *Memoirs,* congressional reaction appeared to have been based more on a need to find scapegoats and assign blame for a difficult social problem.

* Brennan to Warren, May 16, 1966, Warren Papers, Library of Congress, Box 616.

* Black to Warren, May 18, 1966, ibid., Box 617.

3. Over time, *Miranda* has eroded somewhat as a precedent, but it has never been overruled. In fact, in Dickerson v. United States, 530 U.S. 428 (2000), Chief Justice Rehnquist wrote for the Court majority that *Miranda* remained Supreme Court precedent, as it "has become embedded in routine police practice to the point where the warnings have become part of our national culture . . ."

Chapter XXII

PRIVACY AS AUTONOMY

The idea of privacy as autonomy rests on the premise that there are certain kinds of individual conduct over which government should have no control at all. John Stuart Mill in *On Liberty* provides the classic statement of this philosophy:*

> [T]he sole end for which mankind are warranted, individually or collectively, in interfering with the liberty of action of any of their number is self-protection. That the only purpose for which power can be rightfully exercised over any member of a civilized community, against his will, is to prevent harm to others. His own good, either physical or moral, is not a sufficient warrant. He cannot rightfully be compelled to do or forbear because it will be better for him to do so, because it will make him happier, because, in the opinion of others, to do so would be wise or even right. These are good reasons for remonstrating with him, or reasoning with him or persuading him, or entreating him, but not for compelling him or visiting him with any evil in case he do otherwise. To justify that, the conduct from which it is desired to deter him must be calculated to produce evil to someone else. The only part of the conduct of anyone for which he is amenable to society is that which concerns others. In the part which merely concerns himself, his independence is, of right, absolute. Over himself, over his own body and mind, the individual is sovereign.

To what extent does this philosophy apply to the cases in this chapter?

GRISWOLD v. CONNECTICUT

Supreme Court of the United States, 1965.
381 U.S. 479, 85 S.Ct. 1678, 14 L.Ed.2d 510.

JUSTICE DOUGLAS delivered the opinion of the Court.

Appellant Griswold is Executive Director of the Planned Parenthood League of Connecticut. Appellant Buxton is a licensed physician and a professor at the Yale Medical School who served as Medical Director for the League at its Center in New Haven—a center open and operating from November 1 to November 10, 1961, when appellants were arrested.

They gave information, instruction, and medical advice to *married persons* as to the means of preventing conception. They examined the

---

* John Stuart Mill, *On Liberty*, Bobbs–Merrill Co., Inc., 1956, p. 13.

wife and prescribed the best contraceptive device or material for her use. Fees were usually charged, although some couples were serviced free.

The statutes whose constitutionality is involved in this appeal ... provide

> "Any person who uses any drug, medicinal article or instrument for the purpose of preventing conception shall be fined not less than fifty dollars or imprisoned not less than sixty days nor more than one year or be both fined and imprisoned."

[and]

> "Any person who assists, abets, counsels, causes, hires or commands another to commit any offense [is an accessory and] may be prosecuted and punished as if he were the principal offender."

The appellants were found guilty as accessories [to the use of contraceptives] and fine $100 each....

... [W]e are met with a wide range of questions that implicate the Due Process Clause of the Fourteenth Amendment.... We do not sit as a super-legislature to determine the wisdom, need, and propriety of laws that touch economic problems, business affairs, or social conditions. This law, however, operates directly on an intimate relation of husband and wife and their physician's role in one aspect of that relation.

The association of people is not mentioned in the Constitution nor in the Bill of Rights. The right to educate a child in a school of the parents' choice—whether public or private or parochial—is also not mentioned. Nor is the right to study any particular subject or any foreign language. Yet the First Amendment has been construed to include certain of those rights.

By Pierce v. Society of Sisters, the right to educate one's children as one chooses is made applicable to the States by the force of the First and Fourteenth Amendments. By Meyer v. Nebraska, the same dignity is given the right to study the German language in a private school. In other words, the State may not, consistently with the spirit of the First Amendment, contract the spectrum of available knowledge. The right of freedom of speech and press includes not only the right to utter or to print, but the right to distribute, the right to receive, the right to read and freedom of inquiry, freedom of thought, and freedom to teach— indeed the freedom of the entire university community. Without those peripheral rights the specific rights would be less secure. And so we reaffirm the principle of the *Pierce* and the *Meyer* cases.

.   .   .

... [S]pecific guarantees in the Bill of Rights have penumbras, formed by emanations from those guarantees that help give them life and substance. Various guarantees create zones of privacy. The right of association contained in the penumbra of the First Amendment is one, as we have seen. The Third Amendment in its prohibition against the quartering of soldiers "in any house" in time of peace without the consent of the owner is another facet of that privacy. The Fourth

Amendment explicitly affirms the "right of the people to be secure in their persons, houses, papers, and effects, against unreasonable searches and seizures." The Fifth Amendment in its Self–Incrimination Clause enables the citizen to create a zone of privacy which government may not force him to surrender to his detriment. The Ninth Amendment provides: "The enumeration in the Constitution, of certain rights, shall not be construed to deny or disparage others retained by the people."

The Fourth and Fifth Amendments were described in Boyd v. United States, as protection against all governmental invasions "of the sanctity of a man's home and the privacies of life." We recently referred in Mapp v. Ohio to the Fourth Amendment as creating a "right to privacy, no less important than any other right carefully and particularly reserved to the people."

. . .

The present case, then, concerns a relationship lying within the zone of privacy created by several fundamental constitutional guarantees. And it concerns a law which, in forbidding the *use* of contraceptives rather than regulating their manufacture or sale, seeks to achieve its goals by means having a maximum destructive impact upon that relationship. . . . Would we allow the police to search the sacred precincts of marital bedrooms for telltale signs of the use of contraceptives? The very idea is repulsive to the notions of privacy surrounding the marriage relationship.

We deal with a right of privacy older than the Bill of Rights—older than our political parties, older than our school system. Marriage is a coming together for better or for worse, hopefully enduring, and intimate to the degree of being sacred. It is an association that promotes a way of life, not causes; a harmony in living, not political faiths; a bilateral loyalty, not commercial or social projects. Yet it is an association for as noble a purpose as any involved in our prior decisions.

Reversed.

JUSTICE GOLDBERG, whom THE CHIEF JUSTICE and JUSTICE BRENNAN join, concurring.

I agree with the Court that Connecticut's birth-control law unconstitutionally intrudes upon the right of marital privacy, and I join in its opinion and judgment. Although I have not accepted the view that "due process" as used in the Fourteenth Amendment incorporates all of the first eight Amendments. I do agree that the concept of liberty protects those personal rights that are fundamental, and is not confined to the specific terms of the Bill of Rights. My conclusion that the concept of liberty is not so restricted and that it embraces the right of marital privacy though that right is not mentioned explicitly in the Constitution is supported both by numerous decisions of this Court, referred to in the Court's opinion, and by the language and history of the Ninth Amendment. In reaching the conclusion that the right of marital privacy is protected, as being within the protected penumbra of specific guarantees of the Bill of Rights, the Court refers to the Ninth Amendment. I add these words to emphasize the relevance of that Amendment to the Court's holding.

The Court stated many years ago that the Due Process Clause protects those liberties that are "so rooted in the traditions and conscience of our people as to be ranked as fundamental." . . .

This Court, in a series of decisions, has held that the Fourteenth Amendment absorbs and applies to the States those specifics of the first eight amendments which express fundamental personal rights. The language and history of the Ninth Amendment reveal that the Framers of the Constitution believed that there are additional fundamental rights, protected from governmental infringement, which exist alongside those fundamental rights specifically mentioned in the first eight constitutional amendments.

.   .   .

. . . The Ninth Amendment to the Constitution may be regarded by some as a recent discovery and may be forgotten by others, but since 1791 it has been a basic part of the Constitution which we are sworn to uphold. To hold that a right so basic and fundamental and so deep-rooted in our society as the right of privacy in marriage may be infringed because that right is not guaranteed in so many words by the first eight amendments to the Constitution is to ignore the Ninth Amendment and to give it no effect whatsoever. Moreover, a judicial construction that this fundamental right is not protected by the Constitution because it is not mentioned in explicit terms by one of the first eight amendments or elsewhere in the Constitution would violate the Ninth Amendment, which specifically states that "[t]he enumeration in the Constitution, of certain rights, shall not be *construed* to deny or disparage others retained by the people." (Emphasis added.)

A dissenting opinion suggests that my interpretation of the Ninth Amendment somehow "broaden[s] the powers of this Court." With all due respect, I believe that it misses the import of what I am saying. . . . I do not mean to imply that the Ninth Amendment is applied against the States by the Fourteenth. Nor do I mean to state that the Ninth Amendment constitutes an independent source of rights protected from infringement by either the States or the Federal Government. Rather, the Ninth Amendment shows a belief of the Constitution's authors that fundamental rights exist that are not expressly enumerated in the first eight amendments and an intent that the list of rights included there not be deemed exhaustive. . . . The Ninth Amendment simply shows the intent of the Constitution's authors that other fundamental personal rights should not be denied . . . protection or disparaged in any . . . way simply because they are not specifically listed in the first eight constitutional amendments. I do not see how this broadens the authority of the Court; rather it serves to support what this Court has been doing in protecting fundamental rights.

.   .   .

The Connecticut statutes here involved deal with a particularly important and sensitive area of privacy—that of the marital relation and the marital home. . . .

. . .

Although the Constitution does not speak in so many words of the right of privacy in marriage, I cannot believe that it offers these fundamental rights no protection. The fact that no particular provision of the Constitution explicitly forbids the State from disrupting the traditional relation of the family—a relation as old and as fundamental as our entire civilization—surely does not show that the Government was meant to have the power to do so. Rather, as the Ninth Amendment expressly recognizes, there are fundamental personal rights such as this one, which are protected from abridgment by the Government though not specifically mentioned in the Constitution.

. . .

The logic of the dissents would sanction federal or state legislation that seems to me even more plainly unconstitutional than the statute before us. Surely the Government, absent a showing of a compelling subordinating state interest, could not decree that all husbands and wives must be sterilized after two children have been born to them. Yet by their reasoning such an invasion of marital privacy would not be subject to constitutional challenge because, while it might be "silly," no provision of the Constitution specifically prevents the Government from curtailing the marital right to bear children and raise a family. While it may shock some of my Brethren that the Court today holds that the Constitution protects the right of marital privacy, in my view it is far more shocking to believe that the personal liberty guaranteed by the Constitution does not include protection against such totalitarian limitation of family size, which is at complete variance with our constitutional concepts. Yet, if upon a showing of a slender basis of rationality, a law outlawing voluntary birth control by married persons is valid, then, by the same reasoning, a law requiring compulsory birth control also would seem to be valid. In my view, however, both types of law would unjustifiably intrude upon rights of marital privacy which are constitutionally protected.

. . .

Although the Connecticut birth-control law obviously encroaches upon a fundamental personal liberty, the State does not show that the law serves any "subordinating [state] interest which is compelling" or that it is "necessary ... to the accomplishment of a permissible state policy." The State ... says that preventing the use of birth-control devices by married persons helps prevent the indulgence by some in ... extra-marital relations. The rationality of this justification is dubious, particularly in light of the admitted widespread availability to all persons in the State of Connecticut, unmarried as well as married, of birth-control devices for the prevention of disease, as distinguished from the prevention of conception. . . .

Finally, it should be said of the Court's holding today that it in no way interferes with a State's proper regulation of sexual promiscuity or misconduct. . . .

. . .

JUSTICE HARLAN, concurring in the judgment.

. . .

In my view, the proper constitutional inquiry in this case is whether this Connecticut statute infringes the Due Process Clause of the Fourteenth Amendment because the enactment violates basic values "implicit in the concept of ordered liberty". . . .

. . .

JUSTICE WHITE, concurring in the judgment.

In my view this Connecticut law as applied to married couples deprives them of "liberty" without due process of law, as that concept is used in the Fourteenth Amendment. I therefore concur in the judgment of the Court reversing these convictions under Connecticut's aiding and abetting statute.

. . . [T]he right invoked in this case, to be free of regulation of the intimacies of the marriage relationship, "come[s] to this Court with a momentum for respect lacking when appeal is made to liberties which derive merely from shifting economic arrangements."

The Connecticut anti-contraceptive statute deals rather substantially with this relationship. For it forbids all married persons the right to use birth-control devices, regardless of whether their use is dictated by considerations of family planning, health, or indeed even of life itself. The anti-use statute, together with the general aiding and abetting statute, prohibits doctors from affording advice to married persons on proper and effective methods of birth control. . . .

. . .

. . . [T]he statute is said to serve the State's policy against all forms of promiscuous or illicit sexual relationships, be they premarital or extramarital, concededly a permissible and legitimate legislative goal.

Without taking issue with the premise that the fear of conception operates as a deterrent to such relationships in addition to the criminal proscriptions Connecticut has against such conduct, I wholly fail to see how the ban on the use of contraceptives by married couples in any way reinforces the State's ban on illicit sexual relationships. . . .

JUSTICE BLACK, with whom JUSTICE STEWART joins, dissenting.

. . . I do not to any extent whatever base my view that this Connecticut law is constitutional on a belief that the law is wise or that its policy is a good one. In order that there may be no room at all to doubt why I vote as I do, I feel constrained to add that the law is every bit as offensive to me as it is to my Brethren of the majority. . . . There is no single one of the graphic and eloquent strictures and criticisms fired at the policy of this Connecticut law either by the Court's opinion or by those of my concurring Brethren to which I cannot subscribe—except their conclusion that the evil qualities they see in the law make it unconstitutional.

. . .

The Court talks about a constitutional "right of privacy" as though there is some constitutional provision or provisions forbidding any law ever to be passed which might abridge the "privacy" of individuals. But there is not. There are, of course, guarantees in certain specific constitutional provisions which are designed in part to protect privacy at certain times and places with respect to certain activities. Such, for example, is the Fourth Amendment's guarantee against "unreasonable searches and seizures." But I think it belittles that Amendment to talk about it as though it protects nothing but "privacy." . . .

One of the most effective ways of diluting or expanding a constitutionally guaranteed right is to substitute for the crucial word or words of a constitutional guarantee another word or words, more or less flexible and more or less restricted in meaning. This fact is well illustrated by the use of the term "right of privacy" as a comprehensive substitute for the Fourth Amendment's guarantee against "unreasonable searches and seizures." "Privacy" is a broad, abstract and ambiguous concept which can easily be shrunken in meaning but which can also, on the other hand, easily be interpreted as a constitutional ban against many things other than searches and seizures. . . . I get nowhere in this case by talk about a constitutional "right of privacy" as an emanation from one or more constitutional provisions. I like my privacy as well as the next one, but I am nevertheless compelled to admit that government has a right to invade it unless prohibited by some specific constitutional provision. For these reasons I cannot agree with the Court's judgment and the reasons it gives for holding this Connecticut law unconstitutional.

. . .

My brother Goldberg has adopted the recent discovery that the Ninth Amendment as well as the Due Process Clause can be used by this Court as authority to strike down all state legislation which this Court thinks violates "fundamental principles of liberty and justice," or is contrary to the "traditions and [collective] conscience of our people." . . . That Amendment was passed, not to broaden the powers of this Court or any other department of "the General Government," but, as every student of history knows, to assure the people that the Constitution in all its provisions was intended to limit the Federal Government to the powers granted expressly or by necessary implication. If any broad, unlimited power to hold laws unconstitutional because they offend what this Court conceives to be the "[collective] conscience of our people" is vested in this Court by the Ninth Amendment, the Fourteenth Amendment, or any other provision of the Constitution, it was not given by the Framers, but rather has been bestowed on the Court by the Court. . . .

. . .

... The late Judge Learned Hand, after emphasizing his view that judges should not use the due process formula suggested in the concurring opinions today or any other formula like it to invalidate legislation offensive to their "personal preferences," made the statement, with which I fully agree, that:

"For myself it would be most irksome to be ruled by a bevy of Platonic Guardians, even if I knew how to choose them, which I assuredly do not."

So far as I am concerned, Connecticut's law as applied here is not forbidden by any provision of the Federal Constitution as that Constitution was written, and I would therefore affirm.

JUSTICE STEWART, whom JUSTICE BLACK joins, dissenting.

Since 1879 Connecticut has had on its books a law which forbids the use of contraceptives by anyone. I think this is an uncommonly silly law. As a practical matter, the law is obviously unenforceable, except in the oblique context of the present case. As a philosophical matter, I believe the use of contraceptives in the relationship of marriage should be left to personal and private choice, based upon each individual's moral, ethical, and religious beliefs. As a matter of social policy, I think professional counsel about methods of birth control should be available to all, so that each individual's choice can be meaningfully made. But we are not asked in this case to say whether we think this law is unwise, or even asinine. We are asked to hold that it violates the United States Constitution. And that I cannot do.

In the course of its opinion the Court refers to no less than six Amendments to the Constitution: the First, the Third, the Fourth, the Fifth, the Ninth, and the Fourteenth. But the Court does not say which of these Amendments, if any, it thinks is infringed by this Connecticut law.

·   ·   ·

The Court also quotes the Ninth Amendment, and my Brother Goldberg's concurring opinion relies heavily upon it. But to say that the Ninth Amendment has anything to do with this case is to turn somersaults with history. The Ninth Amendment ... was framed by James Madison and adopted by the States simply to make clear that the adoption of the Bill of Rights did not alter the plan that the *Federal* Government was to be a government of express and limited powers, and that all rights and powers not delegated to it were retained by the people and the individual States. Until today no member of this Court has ever suggested that the Ninth Amendment meant anything else, and the idea that a federal court could ever use the Ninth Amendment to annul a law passed by the elected representatives of the people of the State of Connecticut would have caused James Madison no little wonder.

·   ·   ·

... If, as I should surely hope, the law before us does not reflect the standards of the people of Connecticut, the people of Connecticut can freely exercise their true Ninth and Tenth Amendment rights to persuade their elected representatives to repeal it. That is the constitutional way to take this law off the books.

THE CONFERENCE AND COURT'S OPINION IN GRISWOLD*

In his statement at the April 2, 1965 conference, Warren indicated that, though he favored reversal, he had no clear theory upon which to base that result. "I can't say," the Chief stated, "it affects the First Amendment rights of doctors, nor that the state has no legitimate interest (that could apply to abortion laws). We can't balance, use equal protection, 'shocking' due process, or privacy." Warren did, however, say that reversal might be sustained "on a Yick Wo theory"—referring to the 1886 decision of Yick Wo v. Hopkins, which held that a law might be invalidated, even though fair on its face, if it was administered in an arbitrary manner. Here, Warren said, they could go on the theory "that there is no prohibition on sales. They don't go after doctors as such, but only clinics." Warren said, however, that he preferred the idea that the act was not narrowly enough written. As he put it, "This is the most confidential relationship in our society. It has to be clear-cut and it isn't."

Griswold and Buxton had claimed that the Connecticut law violated their First Amendment right of association. Black, speaking next, rejected this claim. "The right of association," he stated, "is for me a right of assembly and the right of the husband and wife to assemble in bed is a new right of assembly for me." Black also said that he had a hard time saying the law was ambiguous enough to apply the overbreadth doctrine, "which for me is only applicable where the First Amendment is involved. So I can't find why it isn't within state power to enact."

Douglas opposed Black's view, saying that the right of association was more than a right of assembly and that the case should be decided on that right. "We've said the right to travel is in radiation of the First Amendment, and so is this right of association. There's nothing more personal than this relationship and, if on the periphery, it's within First Amendment protection."

Only Stewart supported Black's view. He stated that he could not "find anything [against this law] in the First, Second, Fourth, Fifth, Ninth or other Amendments. So I'd have to affirm." The others agreed that the law should be ruled unconstitutional, but differed in their reasoning. Clark declared, "There's a right to marry, maintain a home, have a family. This is in an area where we have the right to be let alone." Goldberg said, "the state cannot regulate this relationship. There's no compelling state reason in that circumstance justifying the statute."

Warren assigned the opinion to Douglas, who had expressed the clearest theory upon which the Connecticut law might be invalidated. Douglas prepared a draft opinion of the Court of slightly over five printed pages. The draft based the decision on the First Amendment,

---

* Bernard Schwartz, Super Chief, New York, 1983, pp. 577–580. Reprinted with permission.

likening the husband-wife relationship to the forms of association given First Amendment protection.

Most of the Douglas draft was used by him in his final opinion. There were, however, two key portions that were different. After the discussion of the cases on the right to educate one's children and the right to study in German, the draft read, "The family is an instruction unit as much as the school; and husband and wife are both teachers and pupils. And the family, together with its physician, is an instruction unit as much as a school is. To narrow, as does the Connecticut statute, discussion and advice on a problem as important as population and procreation is to introduce a dangerous state influence over the First Amendment right to disseminate knowledge."

The draft also had an entirely different ending that stressed the right of association. After declaring, as does the final Douglas opinion in *Griswold,* that the right of association is necessary to make the First Amendment guarantees meaningful, the Douglas draft concluded as follows:

> The foregoing cases do not decide this case. But they place it in the proper frame of reference. Marriage does not fit precisely any of the categories of First Amendment rights. But it is a form of association as vital in the life of a man or woman as any other, and perhaps more so. We would, indeed, have difficulty protecting the intimacies of one's relations to NAACP and not the intimacies of one's marriage relation. Marriage is the essence of one form of the expression of love, admiration, and loyalty. To protect other forms of such expression and not this, the central one, would seem to us to be a travesty. We deal with a right of association older than the Bill of Rights—older than our political parties, older than our school system. It is a coming together for better or for worse, hopefully enduring, and intimate to the degree of being sacred. This association promotes a way of life, not causes; a harmony in living, not political faiths; a bilateral loyalty, not commercial or social projects. Yet it flourishes on the interchange of ideas. It is the main font of the population problem; and education of each spouse in the ramification of that problem, the health of the wife, and the well-being of the family, is central to family functioning. Those objects are the end products of free expression and these Acts intrude on them.

> If the accessory statute can be enforced as it has been here, so can § 53–32 which also has criminal sanctions. The prospects of police with warrants searching the sacred precincts of marital bedrooms for telltale signs of the use of contraceptives is repulsive to the idea of privacy and of association that make up a goodly part of the penumbra of the Constitution and Bill of Rights. Cf. Rochin v. California, 342 U.S. 165. *Reversed.*

On April 23, Douglas showed a copy of his draft opinion to Brennan and asked for suggestions. The next morning Brennan sent Douglas a letter urging him to abandon his First Amendment approach. Brennan wrote that association under the First Amendment was not meant to protect grouping or coming together as such, but only to protect such activities where essential to fruitful advocacy. In Brennan's view, the "association" of married couples had nothing to do with the advocacy protected by the First Amendment.

To save as much of the Douglas draft as possible, Brennan suggested in his letter that the expansion of the First Amendment to include freedom of association be used as an analogy to justify a similar approach in the area of privacy. Privacy itself could be brought within the zone of constitutional protection by the approach stated in Brennan's concurrence in the already discussed case of Lamont v. Postmaster General. Brennan there had stated that "the protection of the Bill of Rights goes beyond the specific guarantees to protect from congressional abridgement those equally fundamental personal rights necessary to make the express guarantees fully meaningful."

Douglas adopted Brennan's suggested approach in his *Griswold* opinion. . . .

· · ·

Warren felt that the approach was too broad. Like Harlan and White, he preferred to tie the decision to a specific constitutional provision. As late as June 3, he joined a recirculation of White's concurrence. But that would have made the Douglas opinion only that of a plurality, which would have left it uncertain just what the *Griswold* decision meant. When the decision was announced on June 7, the Chief had left White and joined the Goldberg concurrence, which specifically stated that it joined in the opinion, as well as the judgment, of the Court.*

NOTES AND QUESTIONS

1.   The Ninth Amendment states: "The enumeration, in the Constitution, of certain rights, shall not be construed to deny or disparage others retained by the people." It contains a fundamental ambiguity. Was it meant to safeguard certain unnamed individual liberties that are not enumerated in the first Eight Amendments? Does it instead merely protect state governments against the national government's attempt to assume powers not delegated to it by the Constitution? Does the history

---

* When Justice Douglas circulated his second opinion in Griswold, one of Chief Justice Warren's law clerks urged him not to join it because, he said, the Constitution does not explicitly grant a right of privacy, and even if it did, Justice Douglas' opinion did not explain why Connecticut violated the right except to speculate that the state law might lead to police searches of the bedroom. John H. Ely to Earl Warren, April 24, 1965, Warren Papers, Library of Congress, Box 520. Ely took a more favorable view of Justice Goldberg's opinion, but he saw two difficulties—first, the open-ended dimensions of the right of privacy the opinion recognized, and, second, to make its overbreadth argument, the opinion assumed that the statute's purpose was to discourage extramarital relations. Ely to Warren, May 17, 1965, ibid. Ely thought that Justice White's opinion was the best circulated because it did not recognize a right of privacy and made an attempt to explain why the statute should be viewed only in relation to the goal of discouraging extramarital intercourse. Further, it suggested an equal protection argument based on Yick Wo v. Hopkins, which Ely had earlier proposed to the Chief Justice. Chief Justice Warren nonetheless chose to join Justice Douglas' opinion. If he had not, the opinion would not have had the agreement of five justices.

of the Bill of Rights resolve the ambiguity? As we have seen, the Federalists originally argued against the Bill of Rights on the ground that it was unnecessary because the national government had only the powers delegated to it and hence was not authorized to infringe individual liberties. Moreover, they contended in opposition to a Bill of Rights that the enumeration of any rights would be an invitation for the national government to violate other rights not so enumerated. (See Chapter 1.) This latter argument retained force even after it was decided to enact a Bill of Rights.

In presenting the provision that became the Ninth Amendment to the first Congress, James Madison explained:*

> It has been objected also against a bill of rights, that, by enumerating particular exceptions to the grant of power, it would disparage those rights which were not placed in that enumeration; and it might follow by implication, that those rights which were not singled out, were intended to be assigned into the hands of the General Government, and were consequently insecure. This is one of the most plausible arguments I have ever heard urged against the admission of a bill of rights into this system; but, I conceive, that it may be guarded against. I have attempted it, as gentlemen may see by turning to the last clause of the fourth resolution [the Ninth Amendment].

Madison thus did not distinguish between protecting the liberties of the citizens and restricting the powers of the national government vis-a-vis the states. As one commentator has written:**

> [T]here is no reason to believe that those who adopted and ratified the Ninth Amendment had a unitary view of its purpose. Furthermore, any attempt to elucidate the amendment's purposes must deal with some enigmatic data.

> On the one hand, if the Ninth Amendment were concerned primarily with safeguarding individual liberties, one might expect to find similar provisions in some of the bills of rights of contemporary state constitutions; but the Ninth Amendment is unique. On the other hand if the amendment were concerned primarily with safeguarding federalism, it would make surplusage of the Tenth Amendment—which speaks explicitly of the powers "reserved to the States."

Regardless of the meaning intended by its framers, the Ninth Amendment lay virtually unused by the Supreme Court until 1965.

2. Is the Ninth Amendment, as applied by Justice Goldberg in his concurrence, the source of a right of privacy? Or it is merely an answer to the argument that the only rights of privacy guaranteed by the Constitution are those contained in the literal wording of the first eight amendments?

* Annals of Congress, 1789, vol. 1, p. 439.

** Paul Brest, Processes of Constitutional Decision–Making, Little Brown and Co., 1975, p. 708.

3. The Court finds the privacy of married couples invaded by a statute that prevents their use of contraceptives. Which of the many kinds of privacy is at issue? Is it the fact that to discover such crimes would, in the ordinary course of events, require the government to invade the marital bedroom? Is it the privacy of the marital relationship itself? Is it the citizen's right, in certain areas, simply to be let alone by the government? Is it the right not to have the government threaten you with prosecution, even though as a practical matter no such prosecutions are in fact undertaken? Is it the right not to tell the government certain personal information? Is it the right not to have the government know— or even be interested—in one's sexual behavior? Is there support for all of these views in the differing opinions?

4. Justice Douglas' opinion for the Court finds that the "penumbras and emanations" of the original Bill of Rights protect a more generalized right of privacy. Are there penumbras other than privacy that emanate from specific Constitutional guarantees? Are there "penumbras and emanations" from the 26th Amendment (allowing 18–year-olds the right to vote) that require a state to allow 18–year-olds to drink? Compare Chief Justice Burger's plurality opinion in Richmond Newspapers, Inc. v. Virginia, above at p. 518.

If "penumbras and emanations" can increase the rights of the citizen against the government, can they also increase the powers of the government against the citizen? Some commentators have been critical of the "penumbras and emanations" approach, precisely because of this difficulty in limiting its use. Consider the following excerpt,* criticizing the way in which a right of privacy was found in *Griswold*—

> To create the right frame of mind preliminarily, a kaleidoscopic right of privacy is made to appear. This is done by projecting dissimilar senses of "privacy" to create the illusion of a single referent for "privacy." ... Just as a kaleidoscope presents an image for which there is no corresponding object, the *Griswold* opinion presents a word "privacy" for which there is no referent....

>   · · ·

> By this technique of verbal deception the meaning of constitutional provisions as clarified and elaborated through a history of interpretation is in fact ignored.... Regard for interests in privacy which do in some measure underlie the interdictions of the third, fourth, and fifth amendments are obscured by an illogical association with interests of a quite different sort. The word "privacy" is put to torture until it confesses a constitutional guaranty for everything it designates in household parlance....

>   · · ·

* Hyman Gross, The Concept of Privacy, New York University Law Review, 1967, vol. 42, pp. 42–46.

... [To] conceive governmental regulation of this kind of activity as interference with privacy is to lose sight of the fact that privacy is not a matter of restraints or coercions, but rather of security. The third, fourth, and fifth amendments, which are rightly said to protect interests in privacy, are guarantees of security, not freedom. They are not designed to prevent repression of the activities of the people, as the logic of *Griswold* would have it, but rather to set limits upon certain specified governmental activities which are in themselves obnoxious, though necessary. There is no need to stress here the difference between interests in security and interests in freedom ...

· · ·

Griswold, in short, stands on a word which is disembodied from the constitutional provisions that give it meaning and which is used in accordance with some loose habits of everyday speech rather than the logic of constitutional law. If the legislature is indeed to be excluded from the marital bedroom by the Supreme Court, the grounds might well amount to something better than linguistic confusion.

Is the criticism of the Court's approach applicable to any theory that doesn't rest on the "specific" provisions of the Bill of Rights? Is it equally applicable to the concurrences of Justices Harlan and White, which are premised on protecting "liberty" under the Due Process Clause?

5.   Connecticut's birth control law had been enacted a long time ago when the Puritans were in control of state government. In the Twentieth Century, it was politically impossible to repeal the law, in great part because of Catholic opposition to repeal. Would it have been possible to avoid the argument concerning unenumerated constitutional rights by basing decision on the specific prohibition of the First Amendment's Establishment Clause? Is a law invalid because it reflects sectarian religious morality? In Harris v. McRae, 448 U.S. 297 (1980), the Court concluded that the fact that restrictions on public funding of abortion coincided with religious objections to abortion did not, "without more," prove a violation of the Establishment Clause. The Court noted that "it does not follow that a statute violates the Establishment Clause because it 'happens to coincide or harmonize with the tenets of some or all religions.' That the Judaeo–Christian religions oppose stealing does not mean that a State or the Federal Government may not, consistent with the Establishment Clause, enact laws prohibiting larceny." In the *Griswold* case, the State did not argue that that one purpose of the contraceptive law was to enforce a moral prohibition against contraception. If it had made that argument, would the law have done more than "coincide or harmonize" with religious belief? Should the state be prohibited by the Constitution from making any conduct a crime if the only reason for the law is a belief that the prohibited conduct is simply immoral?

6.   The predecessor to the *Griswold* case was Skinner v. Oklahoma, 316 U.S. 535 (1942). The Court held that an Oklahoma law requiring

sterilization of habitual criminals violated the Equal Protection Clause
because it required sterilization of thieves but not embezzlers. The key
to the decision was Justice Douglas' statement, for the Court, that
sterilization legislation "involve[d] one of the basic civil rights of man.
Marriage and procreation are fundamental to the very existence and
survival of the race." Since *Griswold,* the Court has continued to
elaborate the right of autonomy in matters of procreation and family life.
Restrictions on distribution of contraceptives to unmarried persons were
invalidated in Carey v. Population Services International, 431 U.S. 678
(1977), as were restrictions on distribution of contraceptives to persons
under 16. The Court has also extended protection to matters of family
life. In Moore v. City of East Cleveland, 431 U.S. 494 (1977), the Court
invalidated an odd city ordinance that limited occupancy of dwellings to
a single "family," but defined a family in such a way that it did not
include first cousins. (In the *Moore* case, the ordinance would have
prohibited a grandmother from occupying her home with her two grand-
sons, who were cousins rather than brothers.) In Zablocki v. Redhail, 434
U.S. 374 (1978), the Court struck down a Wisconsin law requiring court
permission for marriage of a person under obligation by court order to
support minor children. (The law provided for denial of permission to
marry if support payments were in arrears or the children covered by
the support order were likely to become "public charges.")

7.   The constitutional right of autonomy in family life has been
limited to conventional families and has not been extended to other
forms of intimate association. In Village of Belle Terre v. Boraas, 416
U.S. 1 (1974), Justice Douglas wrote the Court's opinion sustaining a
city ordinance limiting the number of "unrelated" people who could
occupy a house. In a footnote in Carey v. Population Services International, supra note 6, the Court said it had never "definitively answered"
the question whether the Constitution contains a prohibition against
state law regulating private consensual sexual behavior. In dissent,
Justice Rehnquist argued that the Court had indeed decided that the
state has power to prohibit sexual acts by unmarried persons. He relied
on Doe v. Commonwealth's Attorney, 425 U.S. 901 (1976), where the
Court had summarily affirmed a lower court's dismissal of a challenge to
a Virginia law that made homosexual sexual acts a crime. Does it make
sense to limit the constitutional right of family association to conventional families? Should a state law be unconstitutional if it forbids marriage
between first cousins? If it limits marriage to unions of persons of the
opposite sex? If it forbids sexual relations between a parent and an adult
son or daughter?

8.   The Court has also refused to extend the concept of privacy or
constitutionally protected autonomy to a general libertarian freedom to
engage in behavior that does not affect third persons. Should a state law
be unconstitutional if it requires motorcyclists to wear helmets? If it
forbids the ingestion of harmful substances by adults? If it allows state
authorities to close dangerous ski trails to skiers? Contrast the considerably wider definition of constitutionally-protected privacy in Justice
Douglas' concurring opinion in the abortion cases, below at p. 890. How
would Justice Douglas answer the questions in this note?

9. Enumerating the rights of personal autonomy that fall within the zone of constitutionally protected privacy has raised, as has been seen, disturbing questions of constitutional law. Another difficult question is whether some state interests may be so strong that they justify limits on personal autonomy even if the conduct does fall within the protected area. That was not an issue in the *Griswold* case, since the only justification offered by the state was that the law deterred premarital and extramarital sex. Even the dissenters concluded it was "silly" to argue that prohibiting contraceptive use by married couples served that purpose. That justification was also rejected when a state attempted to prohibit use of contraception by minors. Carey v. Population Services International, supra note 6. Concurring in that case Justice Stevens said: "It is as though a State decided to dramatize its disapproval of motorcycles by forbidding the use of safety helmets."

10. In *Troxel v. Granville*, 530 U.S. 57 (2000), a divided Court held a Washington State child visitation statute unconstitutional as applied because it infringed on "the fundamental right of parents to make decisions concerning the care, custody, and control of their children," which "the Due Process Clause of the Fourteenth Amendment protects." Because the Court held the statute unconstitutional as applied, the facts in the case and the precise terms of the statute are important. Brad Troxel and Tommie Graville lived together and had two daughters. They separated, and Brad then lived with his parents, Gary and Jenefer Troxel, and often brought his daughters to his parents' home. In May, 1993, Brad committed suicide. Thereafter, the Troxels continued to see their son's daughters on a regular basis until November, 1993, when Tommie Granville asked them to limit their time with her daughters to one short visit a month. The Troxels then filed a petition for formal visitation rights, which the following Washington statute authorized:

> Any person may petition the court for visitation rights at any time including, but not limited to, custody proceedings. The court may order visitation rights for any person when visitation may serve the best interest of the child whether or not there has been any change of circumstances.

At trial, the Troxels requested two weekends of overnight visitation per month and two weeks visitation each summer. Tommie Granville asked instead that the court order one day of visitation per month with no overnight stay. The trial court granted the Troxels visitations of one weekend a month, one week during the summer, and four hours on the birthdays of the Troxel's granddaughters. Granville appealed to the state appeals court, which reversed the trial court's visitation order. The state supreme court affirmed the appeals court's reversal.

In the Supreme Court, there were six opinions—a plurality opinion by Justice O'Connor, in which Chief Justice Rehnquist and Justices Ginsburg and Breyer joined, concurring opinions by Justices Souter and Thomas, and dissenting opinions by Justices Stevens, Scalia, and Kennedy. Despite the division in the Court, no member, except Justice Scalia indirectly, denied that the Due Process Clause of the Fourteenth Amendment guarantees to parents a fundamental right concerning the upbringing of their children. In Justice Scalia's view that right is among the "inalienable rights" proclaimed in the Declaration of Independence and also among the rights the Ninth Amendment says the Constitution's enumeration of rights "shall not be construed to disparage." But, Justice Scalia stressed, the Declaration of Independence does not confer powers upon courts nor does the Ninth Amendment. "Consequently," he wrote, "while I would think it entirely compatible with the commitment to representative democracy set forth in the founding documents to argue, in legislative chambers or electoral campaigns, that the state has *no power* to interfere with parents' authority over the rearing of their children, I do not believe the power upon me *as a judge* entitles me to deny legal effect to laws that (in my view) infringe upon what is (in my view) that unenumerated right."

LAWRENCE v. TEXAS

539 U.S. 558, 123 S.Ct. 2472, 156 L.Ed.2d 508 (2003).

JUSTICE KENNEDY delivered the opinion of the Court.

Liberty protects the person from unwarranted government intrusions into a dwelling or other private places. In our tradition the State is not omnipresent in the home. And there are other spheres of our lives and existence, outside the home, where the State should not be a dominant presence. Freedom extends beyond spatial bounds. Liberty presumes an autonomy of self that includes freedom of thought, belief, expression, and certain intimate conduct. The instant case involves liberty of the person both in its spatial and more transcendent dimensions.

I

The question before the Court is the validity of a Texas statute making it a crime for two persons of the same sex to engage in certain intimate sexual conduct.

In Houston, Texas, officers ... respon[ding] to a reported weapons disturbance ... entered an apartment where ... Lawrence ... resided [and] observed Lawrence and another man, Tyron Garner, engaging in a sexual act. The two petitioners were arrested ... and [later] convicted....

The complaints described their crime as "deviate sexual intercourse, namely anal sex, with a member of the same sex (man)." ... The applicable state law is Tex. Penal Code Ann. § 21.06(a) (2003). It provides: "A person commits an offense if he engages in deviate sexual intercourse with another individual of the same sex." The statute defines "[d]eviate sexual intercourse" as follows:

"(A) any contact between any part of the genitals of one person and the mouth or anus of another person; or

"(B) the penetration of the genitals or the anus of another person with an object." § 21.01(1).

... The petitioners ... were each fined $200 and assessed court costs of $141.25....

The Court of Appeals for the Texas Fourteenth District ... en banc ..., in a divided opinion, ... affirmed the convictions[,] consider[ing] our decision in *Bowers v. Hardwick,* 478 U.S. 186 (1986), to be controlling on the federal due process aspect of the case....

We granted certiorari....

. . .

II

We conclude the case should be resolved by determining whether the petitioners were free as adults to engage in the private conduct in the exercise of their liberty under the Due Process Clause of the Fourteenth Amendment to the Constitution. For this inquiry we deem it necessary to reconsider the Court's holding in *Bowers.*

. . .

The facts in *Bowers* had some similarities to the instant case.... One difference between the two cases is that the Georgia statute prohibited the conduct whether or not the participants were of the same sex, while the Texas statute ... applies only to participants of the same sex.... [In *Bowers*, t]he Court, in an opinion by Justice White, sustained the Georgia law. Chief Justice Burger and Justice Powell joined the opinion of the Court and filed separate, concurring opinions. Four Justices dissented. 478 U.S., at 199 (opinion of Blackmun, J., joined by Brennan, Marshall, and Stevens, JJ.); *id.*, at 214 (opinion of Stevens, J., joined by Brennan and Marshall, JJ.).

The Court began its substantive discussion in *Bowers* as follows: "The issue presented is whether the Federal Constitution confers a fundamental right upon homosexuals to engage in sodomy and hence invalidates the laws of the many States that still make such conduct illegal and have done so for a very long time." That statement, we now conclude, discloses the Court's own failure to appreciate the extent of the liberty at stake. To say that the issue in *Bowers* was simply the right to engage in certain sexual conduct demeans the claim the individual put forward, just as it would demean a married couple were it to be said marriage is simply about the right to have sexual intercourse. The laws involved in *Bowers* and here are, to be sure, statutes that purport to do no more than prohibit a particular sexual act. Their penalties and purposes, though, have more far-reaching consequences, touching upon the most private human conduct, sexual behavior, and in the most private of places, the home. The statutes do seek to control a personal relationship that, whether or not entitled to formal recognition in the law, is within the liberty of persons to choose without being punished as criminals.

This, as a general rule, should counsel against attempts by the State, or a court, to define the meaning of the relationship or to set its boundaries absent injury to a person or abuse of an institution the law protects. It suffices for us to acknowledge that adults may choose to enter upon this relationship in the confines of their homes and their own private lives and still retain their dignity as free persons. When sexuality finds overt expression in intimate conduct with another person, the conduct can be but one element in a personal bond that is more enduring. The liberty protected by the Constitution allows homosexual persons the right to make this choice.

Having misapprehended the claim of liberty there presented to it, and thus stating the claim to be whether there is a fundamental right to engage in consensual sodomy, the *Bowers* Court said: "Proscriptions against that conduct have ancient roots." ... In academic writings, and in many of the scholarly *amicus* briefs filed to assist the Court in this case, there are fundamental criticisms of the historical premises relied upon by the majority and concurring opinions in *Bowers*. Brief for Cato Institute as *Amicus Curiae* 16–17; Brief for American Civil Liberties Union et al. as *Amici Curiae* 15–21; Brief for Professors of History et al. as *Amici Curiae* 3–10. We need not enter this debate in the attempt to reach a definitive historical judgment, but the following considerations counsel against adopting the definitive conclusions upon which *Bowers* placed such reliance.

[T]here is no longstanding history in this country of laws directed at homosexual conduct as a distinct matter. Beginning in colonial times there were prohibitions of sodomy derived from the English criminal laws passed in the first instance by the Reformation Parliament of 1533. The English prohibition was understood to include relations between men and women as well as relations between men and men. See, *e.g.*, *King v. Wiseman*, 92 Eng. Rep. 774, 775 (K. B. 1718) (interpreting "mankind" in Act of 1533 as including women and girls). Nineteenth-century commentators similarly read American sodomy, buggery, and crime-against-nature statutes as criminalizing certain relations between men and women and between men and men. See, *e.g.*, 2 J. Bishop, Criminal Law § 1028 (1858); 2 J. Chitty, Criminal Law 47–50 (5th Am. ed. 1847); R. Desty, A Compendium of American Criminal Law 143 (1882); J. May, The Law of Crimes § 203 (2d ed. 1893). The absence of legal prohibitions focusing on homosexual conduct may be explained in part by noting that according to some scholars the concept of the homosexual as a distinct category of person did not emerge until the late 19th century. See, *e.g.*, J. Katz, The Invention of Heterosexuality 10 (1995); J. D'Emilio & E. Freedman, Intimate Matters: A History of Sexuality in America 121 (2d ed. 1997) ("The modern terms *homosexuality* and *heterosexuality* do not apply to an era that had not yet articulated these distinctions"). Thus early American sodomy laws were not directed at homosexuals as such but instead sought to prohibit nonprocreative sexual activity more generally. This does not suggest approval of homosexual conduct. It does tend to show that this particular form of conduct was not thought of as a separate category from like conduct between heterosexual persons.

Laws prohibiting sodomy do not seem to have been enforced against consenting adults acting in private. A substantial number of sodomy prosecutions and convictions for which there are surviving records were for predatory acts against those who could not or did not consent, as in the case of a minor or the victim of an assault. As to these, one purpose for the prohibitions was to ensure there would be no lack of coverage if a predator committed a sexual assault that did not constitute rape as defined by the criminal law. Thus the model sodomy indictments presented in a 19th-century treatise, see 2 Chitty, *supra,* at 49, addressed the predatory acts of an adult man against a minor girl or minor boy. Instead of targeting relations between consenting adults in private, 19th-century sodomy prosecutions typically involved relations between men and minor girls or minor boys, relations between adults involving force, relations between adults implicating disparity in status, or relations between men and animals.

... [T]he infrequency of [sodomy] prosecutions ... makes it difficult to say that society approved of a rigorous and systematic punishment of the consensual acts committed in private and by adults. The longstanding criminal prohibition of homosexual sodomy upon which the *Bowers* decision placed such reliance is as consistent with a general condemnation of nonprocreative sex as it is with an established tradition of prosecuting acts because of their homosexual character.

... [F]ar from possessing "ancient roots," *Bowers* ..., American laws targeting same-sex couples did not develop until the last third of the 20th century. The reported decisions concerning the prosecution of consensual, homosexual sodomy between adults for the years 1880–1995 are not always clear in the details, but a significant number involved conduct in a public place....

It was not until the 1970's that any State singled out same-sex relations for criminal prosecution, and only nine States have done so.... Post–*Bowers* even some of these States did not adhere to the policy of suppressing homosexual conduct. Over the course of the last decades, States with same-sex prohibitions have moved toward abolishing them....

In summary, the historical grounds relied upon in *Bowers* are more complex than the majority opinion and the concurring opinion by Chief Justice Burger indicate. Their historical premises are not without doubt and, at the very least, are overstated.

It must be acknowledged, of course, that the Court in *Bowers* was making the broader point that for centuries there have been powerful voices to condemn homosexual conduct as immoral. The condemnation has been shaped by religious beliefs, conceptions of right and acceptable behavior, and respect for the traditional family. For many persons these are not trivial concerns but profound and deep convictions accepted as ethical and moral principles to which they aspire and which thus determine the course of their lives. These considerations do not answer the question before us, however. The issue is whether the majority may use the power of the State to enforce these views on the whole society through operation of the criminal law. "Our obligation is to define the liberty of all, not to mandate our own moral code." *Planned Parenthood of Southeastern Pa. v. Casey,* 505 U.S. 833, 850 (1992).

Chief Justice Burger joined the opinion for the Court in *Bowers* and further explained his views as follows: "Decisions of individuals relating to homosexual conduct have been subject to state intervention throughout the history of Western civilization. Condemnation of those practices is firmly rooted in Judeao–Christian moral and ethical standards." ... As with Justice White's assumptions about history, scholarship casts some doubt on the sweeping nature of the statement by Chief Justice Burger as it pertains to private homosexual conduct between consenting adults.... In all events we think that our laws and traditions in the past half century are of most relevance here. These references show an emerging awareness that liberty gives substantial protection to adult persons in deciding how to conduct their private lives in matters pertaining to sex. "[H]istory and tradition are the starting point but not in all cases the ending point of the substantive due process inquiry." *County of Sacramento v. Lewis*, 523 U.S. 833, 857 (1998) (Kennedy, J., concurring).

This emerging recognition should have been apparent when *Bowers* was decided. In 1955 the American Law Institute promulgated the Model Penal Code and made clear that it did not recommend or provide for "criminal penalties for consensual sexual relations conducted in private." ALI, Model Penal Code § 213.2, Comment 2, p. 372 (1980). It justified its decision on three grounds: (1) The prohibitions undermined respect for the law by penalizing conduct many people engaged in; (2) the statutes regulated private conduct not harmful to others; and (3) the laws were arbitrarily enforced and thus invited the danger of blackmail. ALI, Model Penal Code, Commentary 277–280 (Tent. Draft No. 4, 1955). In 1961 Illinois changed its laws to conform to the Model Penal Code. Other States soon followed....

In *Bowers* the Court referred to the fact that before 1961 all 50 States had outlawed sodomy, and that at the time of the Court's decision 24 States and the District of Columbia had sodomy laws.... Justice Powell pointed out that these prohibitions often were being ignored, however. Georgia, for instance, had not sought to enforce its law for decades....

The sweeping references by Chief Justice Burger to the history of Western civilization and to Judeo–Christian moral and ethical standards did not take account of other authorities pointing in an opposite direction. A committee advising the British Parliament recommended in 1957 repeal of laws punishing homosexual conduct.... Parliament enacted the substance of those recommendations 10 years later....

Of even more importance, almost five years before *Bowers* was decided the European Court of Human Rights considered a case with parallels to *Bowers* and to today's case. An adult male resident in Northern Ireland alleged he was a practicing homosexual who desired to engage in consensual homosexual conduct. The laws of Northern Ireland forbade him that right. He alleged that he had been questioned, his home had been searched, and he feared criminal prosecution. The court held that the laws proscribing the conduct were invalid under the European Convention on Human Rights. *Dudgeon v. United Kingdom*, 45 Eur. Ct. H. R. (1981) & para. 52. Authoritative in all countries that are members of the Council of Europe (21 nations then, 45 nations now), the decision is at odds with the premise in *Bowers* that the claim put forward was insubstantial in our Western civilization.

In our own constitutional system the deficiencies in *Bowers* became even more apparent in the years following its announcement. The 25 States with laws prohibiting the relevant conduct referenced in the *Bowers* decision are reduced now to 13, of which 4 enforce their laws only against homosexual conduct. In those States where sodomy is still proscribed, whether for same-sex or heterosexual conduct, there is a pattern of nonenforcement with respect to consenting adults acting in private. The State of Texas admitted in 1994 that as of that date it had not prosecuted anyone under those circumstances. *State v. Morales*, 869 S. W. 2d 941, 943.

Two principal cases decided after *Bowers* cast its holding into even more doubt. In *Planned Parenthood of Southeastern Pa. v. Casey*, 505 U.S. 833 (1992), the Court reaffirmed ... that our laws and tradition afford constitutional protection to personal decisions relating to marriage, procreation, contraception, family relationships, child rearing, and education.... [W]e stated as follows:

"These matters, involving the most intimate and personal choices a person may make in a lifetime, choices central to personal dignity and autonomy, are central to the liberty protected by the Fourteenth Amendment. At the heart of liberty is the right to define one's own concept of existence, of meaning, of the universe, and of the mystery of human life. Beliefs about these matters could not define the attributes of personhood were they formed under compulsion of the State."

Persons in a homosexual relationship may seek autonomy for these purposes, just as heterosexual persons do. The decision in *Bowers* would deny them this right.

The second post-*Bowers* case of principal relevance is *Romer v. Evans*, 517 U.S. 620 (1996). There the Court struck down class-based legislation directed at homosexuals as a violation of the Equal Protection Clause. *Romer* invalidated an amendment to Colorado's constitution which named as a solitary class persons who were homosexuals, lesbians, or bisexual either by "orientation, conduct, practices or relationships," ..., and deprived them of protection under state antidiscrimination laws. We concluded that the provision was "born of animosity toward the class of persons affected" and further that it had no rational relation to a legitimate governmental purpose....

As an alternative argument in this case, counsel for the petitioners and some *amici* contend that *Romer* provides the basis for declaring the Texas statute invalid under the Equal Protection Clause. That is a tenable argument, but we conclude the instant case requires us to address whether *Bowers* itself has continuing validity. Were we to hold the statute invalid under the Equal Protection Clause some might question whether a prohibition would be valid if drawn differently, say, to prohibit the conduct both between same-sex and different-sex participants.

Equality of treatment and the due process right to demand respect for conduct protected by the substantive guarantee of liberty are linked in important respects, and a decision on the latter point advances both interests. If protected conduct is made criminal and the law which does so remains unexamined for its substantive validity, its stigma might remain even if it were not enforceable as drawn for equal protection reasons. When homosexual conduct is made criminal by the law of the State, that declaration in and of itself is an invitation to subject homosexual persons to discrimination both in the public and in the private spheres. The central holding of *Bowers* has been brought in question by this case, and it should be addressed. Its continuance as precedent demeans the lives of homosexual persons.

The stigma this criminal statute imposes, moreover, is not trivial. The offense, to be sure, is but a class C misdemeanor, a minor offense in the Texas legal system. Still, it remains a criminal offense with all that imports for the dignity of the persons charged[—a] record[, . . . possible] registration [as] sex offenders . . . [in] at least four States [and] the other collateral consequences always following a conviction, such as notations on job application forms. . . .

The foundations of *Bowers* have sustained serious erosion from our recent decisions in *Casey* and *Romer*. When our precedent has been thus weakened, criticism from other sources is of greater significance. In the United States criticism of *Bowers* has been substantial and continuing, disapproving of its reasoning in all respects, not just as to its historical assumptions. See, *e.g.,* C. Fried, Order and Law: Arguing the Reagan Revolution—A Firsthand Account 81–84 (1991); R. Posner, Sex and Reason 341–350 (1992). The courts of five different States have declined to follow it in interpreting provisions in their own state constitutions parallel to the Due Process Clause of the Fourteenth Amendment. . . .

To the extent *Bowers* relied on values we share with a wider civilization, it should be noted that the reasoning and holding in *Bowers* have been rejected elsewhere. The European Court of Human Rights has followed not *Bowers* but its own decision in *Dudgeon v. United Kingdom.* . . . Other nations, too, have taken action consistent with an affirmation of the protected right of homosexual adults to engage in intimate, consensual conduct. . . . The right the petitioners seek in this case has been accepted as an integral part of human freedom in many other countries. There has been no showing that in this country the governmental interest in circumscribing personal choice is somehow more legitimate or urgent.

The doctrine of *stare decisis* is essential to the respect accorded to the judgments of the Court and to the stability of the law. It is not, however, an inexorable command. . . . In *Casey* we noted that when a Court is asked to overrule a precedent recognizing a constitutional liberty interest, individual or societal reliance on the existence of that liberty cautions with particular strength against reversing course. . . . The holding in *Bowers*, however, has not induced detrimental reliance comparable to some instances where recognized individual rights are involved. Indeed, there has been no individual or societal reliance on

Bowers of the sort that could counsel against overturning its holding once there are compelling reasons to do so. *Bowers* itself causes uncertainty, for the precedents before and after its issuance contradict its central holding.

The rationale of *Bowers* does not withstand careful analysis. In his dissenting opinion in *Bowers* Justice Stevens came to these conclusions:

> "Our prior cases make two propositions abundantly clear. First, the fact that the governing majority in a State has traditionally viewed a particular practice as immoral is not a sufficient reason for upholding a law prohibiting the practice; neither history nor tradition could save a law prohibiting miscegenation from constitutional attack. Second, individual decisions by married persons, concerning the intimacies of their physical relationship, even when not intended to produce offspring, are a form of 'liberty' protected by the Due Process Clause of the Fourteenth Amendment. Moreover, this protection extends to intimate choices by unmarried as well as married persons." ...

Justice Stevens' analysis, in our view, should have been controlling in *Bowers* and should control here.

Bowers was not correct when it was decided, and it is not correct today. It ought not to remain binding precedent. *Bowers v. Hardwick* should be and now is overruled.

The present case does not involve minors. It does not involve persons who might be injured or coerced or who are situated in relationships where consent might not easily be refused. It does not involve public conduct or prostitution. It does not involve whether the government must give formal recognition to any relationship that homosexual persons seek to enter. The case does involve two adults who, with full and mutual consent from each other, engaged in sexual practices common to a homosexual lifestyle. The petitioners are entitled to respect for their private lives. The State cannot demean their existence or control their destiny by making their private sexual conduct a crime. Their right to liberty under the Due Process Clause gives them the full right to engage in their conduct without intervention of the government. "It is a promise of the Constitution that there is a realm of personal liberty which the government may not enter." *Casey,* .... The Texas statute furthers no legitimate state interest which can justify its intrusion into the personal and private life of the individual.

Had those who drew and ratified the Due Process Clauses of the Fifth Amendment or the Fourteenth Amendment known the components of liberty in its manifold possibilities, they might have been more specific. They did not presume to have this insight. They knew times can blind us to certain truths and later generations can see that laws once thought necessary and proper in fact serve only to oppress. As the Constitution endures, persons in every generation can invoke its principles in their own search for greater freedom.

[R]eversed ... and ... remanded for further proceedings not inconsistent with this opinion.

JUSTICE O'CONNOR, concurring in the judgment.

... I joined *Bowers*, and do not join the Court in overruling it. Nevertheless, I agree ... that Texas' statute banning same-sex sodomy is unconstitutional.... Rather than relying on the substantive component of the Fourteenth Amendment's Due Process Clause, as the Court does, I base my conclusion on the Fourteenth Amendment's Equal Protection Clause.

.   .   .

... We have consistently held ... that some objectives, such as "a bare ... desire to harm a politically unpopular group," are not legitimate state interests. *Department of Agriculture v. Moreno,*.... See also *Cleburne v. Cleburne Living Center,* ...; *Romer v. Evans,*.... When a law exhibits such a desire to harm a politically unpopular group, we have applied a more searching form of rational basis review to strike down such laws under the Equal Protection Clause.

We have been most likely to apply rational basis review to hold a law unconstitutional under the Equal Protection Clause where, as here, the challenged legislation inhibits personal relationships. In *Department of Agriculture v. Moreno,* for example, we held that a law preventing those households containing an individual unrelated to any other member of the household from receiving food stamps violated equal protection because the purpose of the law was to " 'discriminate against hippies.' " ... The asserted governmental interest in preventing food stamp fraud was not deemed sufficient to satisfy rational basis review.... In *Eisenstadt v. Baird,* 405 U.S. 438, 447–455 (1972), we refused to sanction a law that discriminated between married and unmarried persons by prohibiting the distribution of contraceptives to single persons. Likewise, in *Cleburne v. Cleburne Living Center,* ... we held that it was irrational for a State to require a home for the mentally disabled to obtain a special use permit when other residences—like fraternity houses and apartment buildings—did not have to obtain such a permit. And in *Romer v. Evans,* we disallowed a state statute that "impos[ed] a broad and undifferentiated disability on a single named group"—specifically, homosexuals....

... Sodomy between opposite-sex partners ... is not a crime in Texas. That is, Texas treats the same conduct differently based solely on the participants. Those harmed by this law are people who have a same-sex sexual orientation and thus are more likely to engage in behavior prohibited by § 21.06.

The Texas statute makes homosexuals unequal in the eyes of the law by making particular conduct—and only that conduct—subject to criminal sanction....

... Texas' sodomy law brands all homosexuals as criminals, thereby making it more difficult for homosexuals to be treated in the same manner as everyone else....

Texas attempts to justify its law, and the effects of the law, by arguing that the statute satisfies rational basis review because it furthers the legitimate governmental interest of the promotion of morality. In *Bowers,* we held that a state law criminalizing sodomy as applied to homosexual couples did not violate substantive due process. We rejected the argument that no rational basis existed to justify the law, pointing to the government's interest in promoting morality.... The only question in front of the Court in *Bowers* was whether the substantive component of the Due Process Clause protected a right to engage in homosexual sodomy.... *Bowers* did not hold that moral disapproval of a group is a rational basis under the Equal Protection Clause to criminalize homosexual sodomy when heterosexual sodomy is not punished.

This case raises a different issue than *Bowers:* whether, under the Equal Protection Clause, moral disapproval is a legitimate state interest to justify by itself a statute that bans homosexual sodomy, but not heterosexual sodomy. It is not. Moral disapproval of this group, like a bare desire to harm the group, is an interest that is insufficient to satisfy rational basis review under the Equal Protection Clause.... Indeed, we have never held that moral disapproval, without any other asserted state interest, is a sufficient rationale under the Equal Protection Clause to justify a law that discriminates among groups of persons.

Moral disapproval of a group cannot be a legitimate governmental interest under the Equal Protection Clause because legal classifications must not be "drawn for the purpose of disadvantaging the group burdened by the law." ... Texas' invocation of moral disapproval as a legitimate state interest proves nothing more than Texas' desire to criminalize homosexual sodomy. But the Equal Protection Clause prevents a State from creating "a classification of persons undertaken for its own sake." ... And because Texas so rarely enforces its sodomy law as applied to private, consensual acts, the law serves more as a statement of dislike and disapproval against homosexuals than as a tool to stop criminal behavior. The Texas sodomy law "raise[s] the inevitable inference that the disadvantage imposed is born of animosity toward the class of persons affected." ...

Texas argues, however, that the sodomy law does not discriminate against homosexual persons. Instead, the State maintains that the law discriminates only against homosexual conduct. While it is true that the law applies only to conduct, the conduct targeted by this law is conduct that is closely correlated with being homosexual. Under such circumstances, Texas' sodomy law is targeted at more than conduct. It is instead directed toward gay persons as a class.... When a State makes homosexual conduct criminal, and not "deviate sexual intercourse" committed by persons of different sexes, "that declaration in and of itself is an invitation to subject homosexual persons to discrimination both in the public and in the private spheres."

Indeed, Texas law confirms that the sodomy statute is directed toward homosexuals as a class. In Texas, calling a person a homosexual is slander *per se* because the word "homosexual" "impute[s] the commission of a crime." ... The State has admitted that because of the sodomy law, *being* homosexual carries the presumption of being a criminal. See *State v. Morales*, 826 S. W. 2d, at 202–203 ("[T]he statute brands lesbians and gay men as criminals and thereby legally sanctions discrimination against them in a variety of ways unrelated to the criminal law").

Texas' sodomy law therefore results in discrimination against homosexuals as a class in an array of areas outside the criminal law.... In *Romer v. Evans,* we refused to sanction a law that singled out homosexuals "for disfavored legal status." ... The same is true here. The Equal Protection Clause " 'neither knows nor tolerates classes among citizens.' " ... (quoting *Plessy v. Ferguson,* 163 U.S. 537, 559 (1896) (Harlan, J. dissenting)).

A State can of course assign certain consequences to a violation of its criminal law. But the State cannot single out one identifiable class of citizens for punishment that does not apply to everyone else, with moral disapproval as the only asserted state interest for the law....

Whether a sodomy law that is neutral both in effect and application, see *Yick Wo v. Hopkins,* 118 U.S. 356 (1886), would violate the substantive component of the Due Process Clause is an issue that need not be decided today. I am confident, however, that so long as the Equal Protection Clause requires a sodomy law to apply equally to the private consensual conduct of homosexuals and heterosexuals alike, such a law would not long stand in our democratic society....

That this law as applied to private, consensual conduct is unconstitutional under the Equal Protection Clause does not mean that other laws distinguishing between heterosexuals and homosexuals would similarly fail under rational basis review. Texas cannot assert any legitimate state interest here, such as national security or preserving the traditional institution of marriage. Unlike the moral disapproval of same-sex relations—the asserted state interest in this case—other reasons exist to promote the institution of marriage beyond mere moral disapproval of an excluded group.

A law branding one class of persons as criminal solely based on the State's moral disapproval of that class and the conduct associated with that class runs contrary to the values of the Constitution and the Equal Protection Clause, under any standard of review. I therefore concur in the Court's judgment that Texas' sodomy law banning "deviate sexual intercourse" between consenting adults of the same sex, but not between consenting adults of different sexes, is unconstitutional.

JUSTICE SCALIA, with whom THE CHIEF JUSTICE and JUSTICE THOMAS join, dissenting.

. . .

... [N]owhere does the Court's opinion declare that homosexual sodomy is a "fundamental right" under the Due Process Clause; nor does it subject the Texas law to the standard of review that would be appropriate (strict scrutiny) if homosexual sodomy *were* a "fundamental right." Thus, while overruling the *outcome* of *Bowers,* the Court leaves strangely untouched its central legal conclusion: "[R]espondent would have us announce ... a fundamental right to engage in homosexual sodomy. This we are quite unwilling to do." ... Instead the Court simply describes petitioners' conduct as "an exercise of their liberty"—which it undoubtedly is—and proceeds to apply an unheard-of form of rational-basis review that will have far-reaching implications beyond this case. . . .

I

... I do not myself believe in rigid adherence to *stare decisis* in constitutional cases; but I do believe that we should be consistent rather than manipulative in invoking the doctrine. . . . [T]hree Members of today's majority[,] in *Planned Parenthood v. Casey* . . . when *stare decisis* meant preservation of judicially invented abortion rights, [found] the widespread criticism of *Roe* . . . strong reason to *reaffirm* it. . . .

Today, however, the widespread opposition to *Bowers*, a decision resolving an issue as "intensely divisive" as the issue in *Roe*, is offered as a reason in favor of *overruling* it. . . .

Today's approach to *stare decisis* invites us to overrule an erroneously decided precedent . . . *if:* (1) its foundations have been "eroded" by subsequent decisions; (2) it has been subject to "substantial and continuing" criticism.; and (3) it has not induced "individual or societal reliance" that counsels against overturning. The problem is that *Roe* itself— which today's majority surely has no disposition to overrule—satisfies these conditions to at least the same degree as *Bowers*.

(1) . . .

I do not quarrel with the Court's claim that *Romer v. Evans*, 517 U.S. 620 (1996), "eroded" the "foundations" of *Bowers'* rational-basis holding. See *Romer*, . . . (Scalia, J., dissenting). But *Roe* and *Casey* have been equally "eroded" by *Washington v. Glucksberg*, 521 U.S. 702, 721 (1997), which held that *only* fundamental rights which are " 'deeply rooted in this Nation's history and tradition' " qualify for anything other than rational basis scrutiny under the doctrine of "substantive due process." *Roe* and *Casey*, of course, subjected the restriction of abortion to heightened scrutiny without even attempting to establish that the freedom to abort *was* rooted in this Nation's tradition.

(2) *Bowers*, the Court says, has been subject to "substantial and continuing [criticism], disapproving of its reasoning in all respects, not just as to its historical assumptions." Exactly what those nonhistorical criticisms are, and whether the Court even agrees with them, are left unsaid. . . . Of course, *Roe* too (and by extension *Casey*) had been (and still is) subject to unrelenting criticism, including criticism from the two commentators cited by the Court today. . . .

(3) That leaves, to distinguish the rock-solid, unamendable disposition of *Roe* from the readily overrulable *Bowers*, only the third factor. . . . It seems to me that the "societal reliance" on the principles confirmed in *Bowers* and discarded today has been overwhelming. Countless judicial decisions and legislative enactments have relied on the ancient proposition that a governing majority's belief that certain sexual behavior is "immoral and unacceptable" constitutes a rational basis for regulation. . . . State laws against bigamy, same-sex marriage, adult incest, prostitution, masturbation, adultery, fornication, bestiality, and obscenity are likewise sustainable only in light of *Bowers'* validation of laws based on moral choices. Every single one of these laws is called into

question by today's decision; the Court makes no effort to cabin the
scope of its decision to exclude them from its holding.... The impossibility of distinguishing homosexuality from other traditional "morals"
offenses is precisely why *Bowers* rejected the rational-basis challenge.
"The law," it said, "is constantly based on notions of morality, and if all
laws representing essentially moral choices are to be invalidated under
the Due Process Clause, the courts will be very busy indeed." ...

What a massive disruption of the current social order, therefore, the
overruling of *Bowers* entails. Not so the overruling of *Roe*, which would
simply have restored the regime that existed for centuries before 1973,
in which the permissibility of and restrictions upon abortion were
determined legislatively State-by-State....

. . .

II

. . .

Texas Penal Code Ann. § 21.06(a) (2003) undoubtedly imposes constraints on liberty. So do laws prohibiting prostitution, recreational use
of heroin, and, for that matter, working more than 60 hours per week in
a bakery. But there is no right to "liberty" under the Due Process
Clause, though today's opinion repeatedly makes that claim.... The
Fourteenth Amendment *expressly allows* States to deprive their citizens
of "liberty," *so long as "due process of law" is provided* ....

Our opinions applying the doctrine known as "substantive due
process" hold that the Due Process Clause prohibits States from infringing *fundamental* liberty interests, unless the infringement is narrowly
tailored to serve a compelling state interest. *Washington v. Glucksberg*,
521 U.S., at 721.... All other liberty interests may be abridged or
abrogated pursuant to a validly enacted state law if that law is rationally
related to a legitimate state interest.

Bowers held, first, that criminal prohibitions of homosexual sodomy
are not subject to heightened scrutiny because they do not implicate a
"fundamental right" under the Due Process Clause.... Noting that
"[p]roscriptions against that conduct have ancient roots," ... that
"[s]odomy was a criminal offense at common law and was forbidden by
the laws of the original 13 States when they ratified the Bill of Rights,"
... and that many States had retained their bans on sodomy, ... *Bowers*
concluded that a right to engage in homosexual sodomy was not " 'deeply rooted in this Nation's history and tradition,' " ....

The Court today does not overrule this holding. Not once does it
describe homosexual sodomy as a "fundamental right" or a "fundamental liberty interest," nor does it subject the Texas statute to strict
scrutiny. Instead, ... the Court concludes that the application of Texas's
statute to petitioners' conduct fails the rational-basis test, and overrules
Bowers' holding to the contrary....

. . .

III

. . .

After discussing the history of antisodomy laws, the Court proclaims that, "it should be noted that there is no longstanding history in this country of laws directed at homosexual conduct as a distinct matter." This observation in no way casts into doubt the "definitive [historical] conclusion," ... on which *Bowers* relied: that our Nation has a long-standing history of laws prohibiting *sodomy in general*—regardless of whether it was performed by same-sex or opposite-sex couples:

> "It is obvious to us that neither of these formulations would extend a fundamental right to homosexuals to engage in acts of consensual sodomy. Proscriptions against that conduct have ancient roots. *Sodomy* was a criminal offense at common law and was forbidden by the laws of the original 13 States when they ratified the Bill of Rights. In 1868, when the Fourteenth Amendment was ratified, all but 5 of the 37 States in the Union had *criminal sodomy laws*. In fact, until 1961, all 50 States outlawed *sodomy*, and today, 24 States and the District of Columbia continue to provide criminal penalties for *sodomy* performed in private and between consenting adults. Against this background, to claim that a right to engage in such conduct is 'deeply rooted in this Nation's history and tradition' or 'implicit in the concept of ordered liberty' is, at best, facetious."
> ... (... emphasis added).

It is (as *Bowers* recognized) entirely irrelevant whether the laws in our long national tradition criminalizing homosexual sodomy were "directed at homosexual conduct as a distinct matter." Whether homosexual sodomy was prohibited by a law targeted at same-sex sexual relations or by a more general law prohibiting both homosexual and heterosexual sodomy, the only relevant point is that it *was* criminalized—which suffices to establish that homosexual sodomy is not a right "deeply rooted in our Nation's history and tradition." The Court today agrees that homosexual sodomy was criminalized and thus does not dispute the facts on which *Bowers actually* relied.

Next the Court makes the claim, again unsupported by any citations, that "[l]aws prohibiting sodomy do not seem to have been enforced against consenting adults acting in private." ... The key qualifier here is "acting in private"—since the Court admits that sodomy laws *were* enforced against consenting adults (although the Court contends that prosecutions were "infrequent," ...). I do not know what "acting in private" means; surely consensual sodomy, like heterosexual intercourse, is rarely performed on stage. If all the Court means by "acting in private" is "on private premises, with the doors closed and windows covered," it is entirely unsurprising that evidence of enforcement would be hard to come by. (Imagine the circumstances that would enable a search warrant to be obtained for a residence on the ground that there was probable cause to believe that consensual sodomy was then and there occurring.) Surely that lack of evidence would not sustain the proposition that consensual sodomy on private premises with the doors closed and windows covered was regarded as a "fundamental right," even though all other consensual sodomy was criminalized. There are 203 prosecutions for consensual, adult homosexual sodomy reported in the West Reporting system and official state reporters from the years 1880–1995. See W. Eskridge, *Gaylaw: Challenging Apartheid of the Closet* 375 (1999). There are also records of 20 sodomy prosecutions and 4 executions during the colonial period. J. Katz, *Gay Lesbian Alumni* 29, 58, 669 (1983). *Bowers'* conclusion that homosexual sodomy is not a fundamental right "deeply rooted in this Nation's history and tradition" is utterly unassailable.

Realizing that fact, the Court instead says: "[W]e think that our laws and traditions in the past half century are of most relevance here. These references show *an emerging awareness* that liberty gives substantial protection to adult persons in deciding how to conduct their private lives *in matters pertaining to sex*." (emphasis added). Apart from the fact that such an "emerging awareness" does not establish a "fundamental right," the statement is factually false. States continue to prosecute all sorts of crimes by adults "in matters pertaining to sex": prostitution, adult incest, adultery, obscenity, and child pornography. Sodomy laws, too, have been enforced "in the past half century," in which there have been 134 reported cases involving prosecutions for consensual, adult, homosexual sodomy.... In relying ... upon the American Law Institute's 1955 recommendation not to criminalize " 'consensual sexual relations conducted in private,' " the Court ignores the fact that this recommendation was "a point of resistance in most of the states that considered adopting the Model Penal Code." Gaylaw 159.

In any event, an "emerging awareness" is by definition not "deeply rooted in this Nation's history and tradition[s]," as we have said "fundamental right" status requires. Constitutional entitlements do not spring into existence because some States choose to lessen or eliminate criminal sanctions on certain behavior. Much less do they spring into existence, as the Court seems to believe, because *foreign nations* decriminalize conduct.... The Court's discussion of these foreign views (ignoring, of course, the many countries that have retained criminal prohibitions on sodomy) is therefore meaningless dicta....

IV

I turn now to the ground on which the Court squarely rests its holding: the contention that there is no rational basis for the law here under attack. This proposition is so out of accord with our jurisprudence—indeed, with the jurisprudence of *any* society we know—that it requires little discussion.

The Texas statute undeniably seeks to further the belief of its citizens that certain forms of sexual behavior are "immoral and unacceptable," *Bowers* ...—the same interest furthered by criminal laws against fornication, bigamy, adultery, adult incest, bestiality, and obscenity. *Bowers* held that this *was* a legitimate state interest. The Court today reaches the opposite conclusion.... This effectively decrees the end of all morals legislation. If, as the Court asserts, the promotion of majoritarian sexual morality is not even a *legitimate* state interest, none of the above-mentioned laws can survive rational-basis review.

V

Finally, I turn to petitioners' equal-protection challenge, which no Member of the Court save Justice O'Connor ... embraces: On its face § 21.06(a) applies equally to all persons. Men and women, heterosexuals and homosexuals, are all subject to its prohibition of deviate sexual intercourse with someone of the same sex. To be sure, § 21.06 does distinguish between the sexes insofar as concerns the partner with whom the sexual acts are performed: men can violate the law only with other men, and women only with other women. But this cannot itself be a denial of equal protection, since it is precisely the same distinction regarding partner that is drawn in state laws prohibiting marriage with someone of the same sex while permitting marriage with someone of the opposite sex.

The objection is made, however, that the antimiscegenation laws invalidated in *Loving v. Virginia*, 388 U.S. 1, 8 (1967), similarly were applicable to whites and blacks alike, and only distinguished between the races insofar as the *partner* was concerned. In *Loving*, however, we correctly applied heightened scrutiny, rather than the usual rational-basis review, because the Virginia statute was "designed to maintain White Supremacy." ... A racially discriminatory purpose is always sufficient to subject a law to strict scrutiny.... No purpose to discriminate against men or women as a class can be gleaned from the Texas law, so rational-basis review applies. That review is readily satisfied here by the same rational basis that satisfied it in *Bowers*—society's belief that certain forms of sexual behavior are "immoral and unacceptable,".... This is the same justification that supports many other laws regulating sexual behavior that make a distinction based upon the identity of the partner—for example, laws against adultery, fornication, and adult incest, and laws refusing to recognize homosexual marriage.

Justice O'Connor argues that the discrimination in this law which must be justified is not its discrimination with regard to the sex of the partner but its discrimination with regard to the sexual proclivity of the principal actor....

Of course the same could be said of any law. A law against public nudity targets "the conduct that is closely correlated with being a nudist," and hence "is targeted at more than conduct"; it is "directed toward nudists as a class." But ... [e]ven if the Texas law *does* deny equal protection to "homosexuals as a class," that denial *still* does not need to be justified by anything more than a rational basis, which our cases show is satisfied by the enforcement of traditional notions of sexual morality.

Justice O'Connor simply decrees application of "a more searching form of rational basis review" to the Texas statute. The cases she cites do not recognize such a standard, and reach their conclusions only after finding, as required by conventional rational-basis analysis, that no conceivable legitimate state interest supports the classification at issue.... [She] must at least mean, however, that laws exhibiting " 'a ... desire to harm a politically unpopular group' " are invalid *even though* there may be a conceivable rational basis to support them.

This reasoning leaves on pretty shaky grounds state laws limiting marriage to opposite-sex couples. Justice O'Connor seeks to preserve them by the conclusory statement that "preserving the traditional institution of marriage" is a legitimate state interest. But "preserving the traditional institution of marriage" is just a kinder way of describing the State's *moral disapproval* of same-sex couples. Texas's interest in § 21.06 could be recast in similarly euphemistic terms: "preserving the traditional sexual mores of our society." In the jurisprudence Justice O'Connor has seemingly created, judges can validate laws by characterizing them as "preserving the traditions of society" (good); or invalidate them by characterizing them as "expressing moral disapproval" (bad).

* * *

Today's opinion is the product of a Court, which is the product of a law-profession culture, that has largely signed on to the so-called homosexual agenda, by which I mean the agenda promoted by some homosexual activists directed at eliminating the moral opprobrium that has traditionally attached to homosexual conduct. I noted in a earlier opinion the fact that the American Association of Law Schools (to which any reputable law school *must* seek to belong) excludes from membership any school that refuses to ban from its job-interview facilities a law firm (no matter how small) that does not wish to hire as a prospective partner a person who openly engages in homosexual conduct. (See *Romer, supra,* at 653).

One of the most revealing statements in today's opinion is the Court's grim warning that the criminalization of homosexual conduct is "an invitation to subject homosexual persons to discrimination both in the public and in the private spheres." It is clear from this that the Court has taken sides in the culture war, departing from its role of assuring, as neutral observer, that the democratic rules of engagement are observed. Many Americans do not want persons who openly engage in homosexual conduct as partners in their business, as scoutmasters for their children, as teachers in their children's schools, or as boarders in their home. They view this as protecting themselves and their families from a lifestyle that they believe to be immoral and destructive. The Court views it as "discrimination" which it is the function of our judgments to deter. So imbued is the Court with the law profession's anti-anti-homosexual culture, that it is seemingly unaware that the attitudes of that culture are not obviously "mainstream"; that in most States what the Court calls "discrimination" against those who engage in homosexual acts is perfectly legal; that proposals to ban such "discrimination" under Title VII have repeatedly been rejected by Congress, see Employment Non–Discrimination Act of 1994, S. 2238, 103d Cong., 2d Sess. (1994); Civil Rights Amendments, H. R. 5452, 94th Cong., 1st Sess. (1975); that in some cases such "discrimination" is *mandated* by federal statute, see 10 U. S. C. § 654(b)(1) (mandating discharge from the armed forces of any service member who engages in or intends to engage in homosexual acts); and that in some cases such "discrimination" is a constitutional right, see *Boy Scouts of America v. Dale*, 530 U.S. 640 (2000).

Let me be clear that I have nothing against homosexuals, or any other group, promoting their agenda through normal democratic means. . . . But persuading one's fellow citizens is one thing, and imposing one's views in absence of democratic majority will is something else. I would no more *require* a State to criminalize homosexual acts—or, for that matter, display *any* moral disapprobation of them—than I would *forbid* it to do so. What Texas has chosen to do is well within the range of traditional democratic action, and its hand should not be stayed through the invention of a brand-new "constitutional right" by a Court that is impatient of democratic change. It is indeed true that "later generations can see that laws once thought necessary and proper in fact serve only to oppress"; and when that happens, later generations can repeal those laws. . . .

One of the benefits of leaving regulation of this matter to the people rather than to the courts is that the people, unlike judges, need not carry things to their logical conclusion. The people may feel that their disapprobation of homosexual conduct is strong enough to disallow homosexual marriage, but not strong enough to criminalize private homosexual acts—and may legislate accordingly. The Court today pretends that it possesses a similar freedom of action, so that that we need not fear judicial imposition of homosexual marriage, as has recently occurred in Canada. . . . Do not believe it. . . . Today's opinion dismantles the structure of constitutional law that has permitted a distinction to be made between heterosexual and homosexual unions, insofar as formal recognition in marriage is concerned. If moral disapprobation of homosexual conduct is "no legitimate state interest" for purposes of proscribing that conduct; and if, as the Court coos (casting aside all pretense of neutrality), "[w]hen sexuality finds overt expression in intimate conduct with another person, the conduct can be but one element in a personal bond that is more enduring"; what justification could there possibly be for denying the benefits of marriage to homosexual couples exercising "[t]he liberty protected by the Constitution"? Surely not the encouragement of procreation, since the sterile and the elderly are allowed to marry. This case "does not involve" the issue of homosexual marriage only if one entertains the belief that principle and logic have nothing to do with the decisions of this Court. Many will hope that, as the Court comfortingly assures us, this is so.

. . .

JUSTICE THOMAS, dissenting.

. . . I write separately to note that the law before the Court today "is . . . uncommonly silly." *Griswold v. Connecticut*, 381 U.S. 479, 527 (1965) (Stewart, J., dissenting). If I were a member of the Texas Legislature, I would vote to repeal it. Punishing someone for expressing his sexual preference through noncommercial consensual conduct with another adult does not appear to be a worthy way to expend valuable law enforcement resources.

Notwithstanding this, I recognize that as a member of this Court I am not empowered to help petitioners and others similarly situated.... [J]ust like Justice Stewart, I "can find [neither in the Bill of Rights nor any other part of the Constitution a] general right of privacy," ..., or as the Court terms it today, the "liberty of the person both in its spatial and more transcendent dimensions." ...

NOTES AND QUESTIONS

1. What is the constitutional right protected in *Lawrence*? Is it a fundamental right?

2. In retrospect, two political events—the Senate's rejection of President Reagan's nomination of Judge Robert Bork to replace Justice Powell in 1987 and Bill Clinton's election to the presidency in 1992— appear to be connected to the Supreme Court's decision in *Lawrence*. What are the connections?

3. In his dissent, Justice Scalia warns that we should seriously doubt the majority's claim that the *Lawrence* decision does not logically compel judicial imposition of homosexual marriage. Is Scalia right? Does the recognition of a privacy right in *Lawrence v. Texas* make it impossible to justify denying the benefits of marriage to homosexual couples exercising "the liberty protected by the Constitution?"

ROE v. WADE

Supreme Court of the United States, 1973.
410 U.S. 113, 93 S.Ct. 705, 35 L.Ed.2d 147.

JUSTICE BLACKMUN delivered the opinion of the Court.

This Texas federal appeal and its Georgia companion, Doe v. Bolton, present constitutional challenges to state criminal abortion legislation. The Texas statutes under attack here are typical of those that have been in effect in many States for approximately a century. The Georgia statutes, in contrast, have a modern cast and are a legislative product that, to an extent at least, obviously reflects the influences of recent attitudinal change, of advancing medical knowledge and techniques, and of new thinking about an old issue.

We forthwith acknowledge our awareness of the sensitive and emotional nature of the abortion controversy, of the vigorous opposing views, even among physicians, and of the deep and seemingly absolute convictions that the subject inspires. One's philosophy, one's experiences, one's exposure to the raw edges of human existence, one's religious training, one's attitudes toward life and family and their values, and the moral standards one establishes and seeks to observe, are all likely to influence and to color one's thinking and conclusions about abortion.

In addition, population growth, pollution, poverty, and racial overtones tend to complicate and not to simplify the problem.

Our task, of course, is to resolve the issue by constitutional measurement, free of emotion and of predilection. We seek earnestly to do this, and, because we do, we have inquired into, and in this opinion place some emphasis upon, medical and medical-legal history and what that history reveals about man's attitudes toward the abortion procedure over the centuries. We bear in mind, too, Justice Holmes' admonition in his now-vindicated dissent in Lochner v. New York, ... (1905):

> "[The Constitution] is made for people of fundamentally differing views, and the accident of our finding certain opinions natural and familiar or novel and even shocking ought not to conclude our judgment upon the question whether statutes embodying them conflict with the Constitution of the United States."

. . .

The principal thrust of appellant's attack on the Texas statutes is that they improperly invade a right, said to be possessed by the pregnant woman, to choose to terminate her pregnancy. Appellant would discover this right in the concept of personal "liberty" embodied in the Fourteenth Amendment's Due Process Clause; or in personal, marital, familial, and sexual privacy said to be protected by the Bill of Rights or its penumbras, see Griswold v. Connecticut, or among those rights reserved to the people by the Ninth Amendment, Griswold v. Connecticut (Goldberg, J., concurring). Before addressing this claim, we feel it desirable briefly to survey, in several aspects, the history of abortion, for such insight as that history may afford us, and then to examine the state purposes and interests behind the criminal abortion laws.

It perhaps is not generally appreciated that the restrictive criminal abortion laws in effect in a majority of States today are of relatively recent vintage. Those laws, generally proscribing abortion or its attempt at any time during pregnancy except when necessary to preserve the pregnant woman's life, are not of ancient or even of common-law origin. Instead, they derive from statutory changes effected, for the most part, in the latter half of the 19th century.

. . .

[The Court discusses the history of abortion laws for 10 pages.]

It is thus apparent that at common law, at the time of the adoption of our Constitution, and throughout the major portion of the 19th century, abortion was viewed with less disfavor than under most American statutes currently in effect. Phrasing it another way, a woman enjoyed a substantially broader right to terminate a pregnancy than she does in most States today. At least with respect to the early stage of pregnancy, and very possibly without such a limitation, the opportunity to make this choice was present in this country well into the 19th century. . . .

. . .

Three reasons have been advanced to explain historically the enactment of criminal abortion laws in the 19th century and to justify their continued existence.

It has been argued occasionally that these laws were the product of a Victorian social concern to discourage illicit sexual conduct. Texas, however, does not advance this justification in the present case, and it appears that no court or commentator has taken the argument seriously. The appellants ... contend, moreover, that this is not a proper state purpose at all and suggest that, if it were, the Texas statutes are overbroad in protecting it since the law fails to distinguish between married and unwed mothers.

A second reason is concerned with abortion as a medical procedure. When most criminal abortion laws were first enacted, the procedure was a hazardous one for the woman. This was particularly true prior to the development of antisepsis....

Thus, it has been argued that a State's real concern in enacting a criminal abortion law was to protect the pregnant woman, that is, to restrain her from submitting to a procedure that placed her life in serious jeopardy.

Modern medical techniques have altered this situation.... Mortality rates for women undergoing early abortions, where the procedure is legal, appear to be as low as or lower than the rates for normal childbirth. Consequently, any interest of the State in protecting the woman from an inherently hazardous procedure, except when it would be equally dangerous for her to forgo it, has largely disappeared. Of course, important state interests in the area of health and medical standards do remain. The State has a legitimate interest in seeing to it that abortion, like any other medical procedure, is performed under circumstances that insure maximum safety for the patient. This interest obviously extends at least to the performing physician and his staff, to the facilities involved, to the availability of after-care, and to adequate provision for any complication or emergency that might arise.... Moreover, the risk to the woman increases as her pregnancy continues. Thus, the State retains a definite interest in protecting the woman's own health and safety when an abortion is proposed at a late stage of pregnancy.

The third reason is the State's interest—some phrase it in terms of duty—in protecting prenatal life. Some of the argument for this justification rests on the theory that a new human life is present from the moment of conception. The State's interest and general obligation to protect life then extends, it is argued, to prenatal life. Only when the life of the pregnant mother herself is at stake, balanced against the life she carries within her, should the interest of the embryo or fetus not prevail. Logically, of course, a legitimate state interest in this area need not stand or fall on acceptance of the belief that life begins at conception or at some other point prior to live birth. In assessing the State's interest, recognition may be given to the less rigid claim that as long as at least *potential* life is involved, the State may assert interests beyond the protection of the pregnant woman alone.

· · ·

The Constitution does not explicitly mention any right of privacy.... [H]owever ... the Court has recognized that a right of personal privacy, or a guarantee of certain areas or zones of privacy, does exist under the Constitution.... [Previous] decisions make it clear that the right has some extension to activities relating to marriage; procreation; contraception; family relationships; and child rearing and education.

This right of privacy, whether it be founded in the Fourteenth Amendment's concept of personal liberty and restrictions upon state action, as we feel it is, or as the District Court determined, in the Ninth Amendment's reservation of rights to the people, is broad enough to encompass a woman's decision whether or not to terminate her pregnancy. The detriment that the State would impose upon the pregnant woman by denying this choice altogether is apparent. Specific and direct harm medically diagnosable even in early pregnancy may be involved. Maternity, or additional offspring, may force upon the woman a distressful life and future. Psychological harm may be imminent. Mental and physical health may be taxed by child care. There is also the distress, for all concerned, associated with the unwanted child, and there is the problem of bringing a child into a family already unable, psychologically and otherwise, to care for it. In other cases, as in this one, the additional difficulties and continuing stigma of unwed motherhood may be involved. All these are factors the woman and her responsible physician necessarily will consider in consultation.

On the basis of elements such as these, appellant and some *amici** argue that the woman's right is absolute and that she is entitled to terminate her pregnancy at whatever time, in whatever way, and for whatever reason she alone chooses. With this we do not agree. Appellant's arguments that Texas either has no valid interest at all in regulating the abortion decision, or no interest strong enough to support any limitation upon the woman's sole determination, are unpersuasive. The Court's decisions recognizing a right of privacy also acknowledge that some state regulation in areas protected by that right is appropriate. As noted above, a State may properly assert important interests in safeguarding health, in maintaining medical standards, and in protecting potential life. At some point in pregnancy, these respective interests become sufficiently compelling to sustain regulation of the factors that govern the abortion decision. The privacy right involved, therefore, cannot be said to be absolute.

. . .

Where certain "fundamental rights" are involved, the Court has held that regulation limiting these rights may be justified only by a "compelling state interest," and that legislative enactments must be narrowly drawn to express only the legitimate state interests at stake.

. . .

---

* *Amici* is short for *amici curiae*, friends of the court. An *amicus curiae*, though not a party to a case, may be permitted to file briefs to help the Court (and usually itself) in the decision of a case. In Roe v. Wade and Doe v. Bolton *amicus curiae* briefs were filed by several State Attorneys General, the National Right to Life Committee, Americans United for Life and several other groups in support of the states of Texas and Georgia. *Amicus curiae* briefs supporting the plaintiffs were filed by the American College of Obstetricians and Gynecologists, Planned Parenthood and the American Association of University Women, among others.

The [State of Texas] and certain *amici* argue that the fetus is a "person" within the language and meaning of the Fourteenth Amendment. In support of this, they outline at length and in detail the well-known facts of fetal development. If this suggestion of personhood is established, the appellant's case, of course, collapses, for the fetus' right to life is then guaranteed specifically by the Amendment. The appellant conceded as much on reargument. On the other hand, the appellee conceded on reargument that no case could be cited that holds that a fetus is a person within the meaning of the Fourteenth Amendment.

The Constitution does not define "person" in so many words.... But in nearly all these instances, the use of the word [person in the Constitution] is such that it has application only postnatally. None indicates, with any assurance, that it has any possible pre-natal application.

All this, together with our observation, supra, that throughout the major portion of the 19th century prevailing legal abortion practices were far freer than they are today, persuades us that the word "person," as used in the Fourteenth Amendment, does not include the unborn....

. . .

Texas urges that, apart from the Fourteenth Amendment, life begins at conception and is present throughout pregnancy, and that, therefore, the State has a compelling interest in protecting that life from and after conception. We need not resolve the difficult question of when life begins. When those trained in the respective disciplines of medicine, philosophy, and theology are unable to arrive at any consensus, the judiciary, at this point in the development of man's knowledge, is not in a position to speculate as to the answer.

It should be sufficient to note briefly the wide divergence of thinking on this most sensitive and difficult question. There has always been strong support for the view that life does not begin until live birth. This was the belief of the Stoics. It appears to be the predominant, though not the unanimous, attitude of the Jewish faith.... As we have noted, the common law found greater significance in quickening. Physicians and their scientific colleagues have regarded that event with less interest and have tended to focus either upon conception, upon live birth, or upon the interim point at which the fetus becomes "viable," that is, potentially able to live outside the mother's womb, albeit with artificial aid. Viability is usually placed at about seven months (28 weeks) but may occur earlier, even at 24 weeks.... [Recognition of the existence of life from the moment of conception] is now, of course, the official belief of the Catholic Church.... [T]his is a view strongly held by many non-Catholics as well, and by many physicians. Substantial problems for precise definition of this view are posed, however, by new embryological data that purport to indicate that conception is a "process" over time, rather than an event, and by new medical techniques such as menstrual extraction, [and] the "morning-after" pill....

In areas other than criminal abortion, the law has been reluctant to endorse any theory that life, as we recognize it, begins before live birth or to accord legal rights to the unborn except in narrowly defined situations and except when the rights are contingent upon live birth. For example, the traditional rule of tort law denied recovery for prenatal injuries even though the child was born alive. That rule has been changed in almost every jurisdiction. In most States, recovery is said to be permitted only if the fetus was viable, or at least quick, when the injuries were sustained, though few courts have squarely so held.... Similarly, unborn children have been recognized as acquiring rights or interests by way of inheritance or other devolution of property.... Perfection of the interests involved, again, has generally been contingent upon live birth. In short, the unborn have never been recognized in the law as persons in the whole sense.

In view of all this, we do not agree that, by adopting one theory of life, Texas may override the rights of the pregnant woman that are at stake. We repeat, however, that the State does have an important and legitimate interest in preserving and protecting the health of the pregnant woman, whether she be a resident of the State or a non-resident who seeks medical consultation and treatment there, and that it has still *another* important and legitimate interest in protecting the potentiality of human life. These interests are separate and distinct. Each grows in substantiality as the woman approaches term and, at a point during pregnancy, each becomes "compelling."

With respect to the State's important and legitimate interest in the health of the mother, the "compelling" point, in the light of present medical knowledge, is at approximately the end of the first trimester. This is so because of the now-established medical fact, ... that until the end of the first trimester mortality in abortion may be less than mortality in normal childbirth....

This means, ... that, for the period of pregnancy prior to this "compelling" point, the attending physician, in consultation with his patient, is free to determine, without regulation by the State, that, in his medical judgment, the patient's pregnancy should be terminated. If that decision is reached, the judgment may be effectuated by an abortion free of interference by the State.

With respect to the State's important and legitimate interest in potential life, the "compelling" point is at viability. This is so because the fetus then presumably has the capability of meaningful life outside the mother's womb. State regulation protective of fetal life after viability thus has both logical and biological justifications. If the State is interested in protecting fetal life after viability, it may go so far as to proscribe abortion during that period, except when it is necessary to preserve the life or health of the mother.

Measured against these standards, Art. 1196 of the Texas Penal Code, in restricting legal abortions to those "procured or attempted by medical advice for the purpose of saving the life of the mother," sweeps too broadly. The statute makes no distinction between abortions performed early in pregnancy and those performed later, and it limits to a single reason, "saving" the mother's life, the legal justification for the procedure. The statute, therefore, cannot survive the constitutional attack made upon it here.

. . .

To summarize . . . :

1. A state criminal abortion statute of the current Texas type, that excepts from criminality only a *life-saving* procedure on behalf of the mother, without regard to pregnancy stage and without recognition of the other interests involved, is violative of the Due Process Clause of the Fourteenth Amendment.

(a) For the stage prior to approximately the end of the first trimester, the abortion decision and its effectuation must be left to the medical judgment of the pregnant woman's attending physician.

(b) For the stage subsequent to approximately the end of the first trimester, the State, in promoting its interest in the health of the mother may, if it chooses, regulate the abortion procedure in ways that are reasonably related to maternal health.

(c) For the stage subsequent to viability, the State in promoting its interest in the potentiality of human life may, if it chooses, regulate, and even proscribe, abortion except where it is necessary, in appropriate medical judgment, for the preservation of the life or health of the mother.

2. The State may define the term "physician," . . . to mean only a physician currently licensed by the State, and may proscribe any abortion by a person who is not a physician as so defined.

. . .

JUSTICE DOUGLAS, concurring. . . .

While I join the opinion of the Court, I add a few words.

The questions presented in the present cases . . . involve the right of privacy, one aspect of which we considered in Griswold v. Connecticut, 381 U.S. 479, 484, when we held that various guarantees in the Bill of Rights create zones of privacy.

. . .

The Ninth Amendment obviously does not create federally enforceable rights. It merely says, "The enumeration in the Constitution, of certain rights, shall not be construed to deny or disparage others retained by the people." But a catalogue of these rights includes customary, traditional, and time-honored rights, amenities, privileges, and immunities that come within the sweep of "the Blessings of Liberty" mentioned in the preamble to the Constitution. Many of them, in my view, come within the meaning of the term "liberty" as used in the Fourteenth Amendment.

First is the autonomous control over the development and expression of one's intellect, interests, tastes, and personality.

These are rights protected by the First Amendment and, in my view, they are absolute, permitting of no exceptions....

Second is freedom of choice in the basic decisions of one's life respecting marriage, divorce, procreation, contraception, and the education and upbringing of children.

These rights, unlike those protected by the First Amendment, are subject to some control by the police power. Thus, the Fourth Amendment speaks only of "unreasonable searches and seizures" and of "probable cause." These rights are "fundamental," and we have held that in order to support legislative action the statute must be narrowly and precisely drawn and that a "compelling state interest must be shown in support of the limitation." ...

The liberty to marry a person of one's own choosing, ... the liberty to direct the education of one's own children, ... and the privacy of the marital relation ... are in this category.

. . .

Third is the freedom to care for one's health and person, freedom from bodily restraint or compulsion, freedom to walk, stroll, or loaf.

These rights, though fundamental, are likewise subject to regulation on a showing of "compelling state interests."

. . .

The Georgia statute is as war with the clear message ... that a woman is free to make the basic decision whether to bear an unwanted child....

. . .

... We held in *Griswold* that the States may not preclude spouses from attempting to avoid the joinder of sperm and egg. If this is true, it is difficult to perceive any overriding public necessity which might attach precisely at the moment of conception....

. . .

JUSTICE STEWART, concurring.

. . .

It is clear to me now, that the *Griswold* decision can be rationally understood only as a holding that the Connecticut statute substantively invaded the "liberty" that is protected by the Due Process Clause of the Fourteenth Amendment. As so understood, *Griswold* stands as one in a long line of ... cases decided under the doctrine of substantive due process, and I now accept it as such.

... The Constitution nowhere mentions a specific right of personal choice in matters of marriage and family life, but the "liberty" protected by the Due Process Clause of the Fourteenth Amendment covers more than those freedoms explicitly named in the Bill of Rights. . . .

. . .

Several decisions of this Court make clear that freedom of personal choice in matters of marriage and family life is one of the liberties protected by the Due Process Clause of the Fourteenth Amendment. Pierce v. Society of Sisters; Meyer v. Nebraska. That right necessarily includes the right of a woman to decide whether or not to terminate her pregnancy. . . .

. . .

It is evident that the Texas abortion statute infringes that right directly. Indeed, it is difficult to imagine a more complete abridgment of a constitutional freedom than that worked by the inflexible criminal statute now in force in Texas. The question then becomes whether the state interests advanced to justify this abridgment can survive the "particularly careful scrutiny" that the Fourteenth Amendment here requires.

The asserted state interests are protection of the health and safety of the pregnant woman, and protection of the potential future human life within her. These are legitimate objectives, amply sufficient to permit a State to regulate abortions as it does other surgical procedures, and perhaps sufficient to permit a State to regulate abortions more stringently or even to prohibit them in the late stages of pregnancy. But such legislation is not before us, and I think the Court today has thoroughly demonstrated that these state interests cannot constitutionally support the broad abridgment of personal liberty worked by the existing Texas law. Accordingly, I join the Court's opinion holding that that law is invalid under the Due Process Clause of the Fourteenth Amendment.

CHIEF JUSTICE BURGER, concurring. . . .

I agree that, under the Fourteenth Amendment to the Constitution, the abortion statutes of Georgia and Texas impermissibly limit the performance of abortions necessary to protect the health of pregnant women, using the term health in its broadest medical context. I am somewhat troubled that the Court has taken notice of various scientific and medical data in reaching its conclusion; however, I do not believe that the Court has exceeded the scope of judicial notice accepted in other contexts.

. . .

I do not read the Court's holdings today as having the sweeping consequences attributed to them by the dissenting Justices; the dissenting views discount the reality that the vast majority of physicians observe the standards of their profession, and act only on the basis of carefully deliberated medical judgments relating to life and health.

Plainly, the Court today rejects any claim that the Constitution requires abortions on demand.

. . .

JUSTICE REHNQUIST, dissenting.

The Court's opinion brings to the decision of this troubling question both extensive historical fact and a wealth of legal scholarship. While the opinion thus commands my respect, I find myself nonetheless in fundamental disagreement with those parts of it that invalidate the Texas statute in question, and therefore dissent.

. . .

... I would reach a conclusion opposite to that reached by the Court. I have difficulty in concluding, as the Court does, that the right of "privacy" is involved in this case. Texas, by the statute here challenged, bars the performance of a medical abortion by a licensed physician on a plaintiff such as Roe. A transaction resulting in an operation such as this is not "private" in the ordinary usage of that word. Nor is the "privacy" that the Court finds here even a distant relative of the freedom from searches and seizures protected by the Fourth Amendment to the Constitution, which the Court has referred to as embodying a right to privacy. . . .

If the Court means by the term "privacy" no more than that the claim of a person to be free from unwanted state regulation of consensual transactions may be a form of "liberty" protected by the Fourteenth Amendment, there is no doubt that similar claims have been upheld in our earlier decisions on the basis of that liberty. I agree with the statement of JUSTICE STEWART in his concurring opinion that the "liberty," against deprivation of which without due process the Fourteenth Amendment protects, embraces more than the rights found in the Bill of Rights. But that liberty is not guaranteed absolutely against deprivation, only against deprivation without due process of law. The test traditionally applied in the area of social and economic legislation is whether or not a law such as that challenged has a rational relation to a valid state objective. . . . If the Texas statute were to prohibit an abortion even where the mother's life is in jeopardy, I have little doubt that such a statute would lack a rational relation to a valid state objective. . . . But the Court's sweeping invalidation of any restrictions on abortion during the first trimester is impossible to justify under that standard, and the conscious weighing of competing factors that the Court's opinion apparently substitutes for the established test is far more appropriate to a legislative judgment than to a judicial one.

. . .

JUSTICE WHITE, with whom JUSTICE REHNQUIST joins, dissenting.

At the heart of the controversy in these cases are those recurring pregnancies that pose no danger whatsoever to the life or health of the mother but are, nevertheless, unwanted for any one or more of a variety of reasons—convenience, family planning, economics, dislike of children, the embarrassment of illegitimacy, etc. The common claim before us is that for any one of such reasons, or for no reason at all, and without asserting or claiming any threat to life or health, any woman is entitled to an abortion at her request if she is able to find a medical advisor willing to undertake the procedure.

. . .

With all due respect, I dissent. I find nothing in the language or history of the Constitution to support the Court's judgment. The Court simply fashions and announces a new constitutional right for pregnant mothers and, with scarcely any reason or authority for its action, invests that right with sufficient substance to override most existing state abortion statutes. The upshot is that the people and the legislatures of the 50 States are constitutionally disentitled to weigh the relative importance of the continued existence and development of the fetus, on the one hand, against a spectrum of possible impacts on the mother, on the other hand. As an exercise of raw judicial power, the Court perhaps has authority to do what it does today; but in my view its judgment is an improvident and extravagant exercise of the power of judicial review that the Constitution extends to this Court.

. . .

A RIGHT IN SEARCH OF A THEORY*

Roe v. Wade and Doe v. Bolton had been argued twice. In the conference following the first argument a majority of justices quickly agreed that in some circumstances the Constitution protects a woman's right to an abortion, but they struggled for more than a year in defining that right and developing a constitutional theory to justify it. In presenting *Roe,* Chief Justice Burger spoke of balancing interests: "The balance here is between the state's interest in protecting fetal life and protecting the woman's interest in having children." He concluded that the Texas statute in *Roe* and the Georgia statute in *Doe* were constitutional. Justice Douglas was certain that the Texas statute was unconstitutional. "This is basically a medical problem ...," he said. He thought that the Georgia statute was better drawn, but he wanted to know its practical effects. "Is it weighted on the side of only those who can afford this? What about the poor?" He thought that the case should be remanded to find out the answers. Justice Brennan thought both statutes were unconstitutional and said that the Court should recognize abortion as a constitutionally protected right. Justice Stewart did not disagree, but he thought at some point the state could prohibit abortions. Justice White flatly disagreed with the view that the Constitution protected a right to abortion. He thought both statutes were constitutional. In his remarks on Doe v. Bolton, he said: "The state has the power to protect the unborn child.... I think the state struck the right balance." Justice Marshall said that he agreed with Justice Douglas, but "the time problem" concerned him. He believed the state could not constitutionally prohibit abortions in the early stages of pregnancy. As the constitutional basis for a right to abortion, Marshall said the he would use "liberty" in

* This account is based on Bernard Schwartz, The Unpublished Opinions of the Burger Court, Oxford University Press, 1988, pp. 83–151.

the due process clause of the Fourteenth Amendment. Justice Blackmun was ambivalent. "Can a state," he asked, "properly outlaw all abortions? If we accept fetal life, there is a strong argument that it can. But there are opposing interests: the right of the mother to life and mental and physical health, the right of the parents in case of rape, the right of the state in case of incest. I don't think there's an absolute right to do what you will to [your] body." Yet he concluded that Texas had "a poor statute" that "impinged" on Roe's rights. As for the Georgia statute, he thought that medically it was "perfectly workable," but he recognized that there were competing interests. He said that he wanted the Court to recognize the opposing interests in fetal life and the mother's interest in health and happiness.

Chief Justice Burger's assignment of the opinions in *Roe* and *Doe* to Justice Blackmun surprised Justice Douglas, for he believed that as the senior member of the majority he would assign the cases. When he raised the matter with the Chief Justice, Burger explained that he had not recorded votes in the cases because of the diversity of views expressed. Thus he assigned the cases believing that the vote would be determined by what was written. "That was and still is my view of how to handle these two ... sensitive cases," he told Douglas, and he added that the cases were likely candidates for reargument. Douglas did not press the issue because he and the other members in the majority thought that Blackmun might write an opinion they would find acceptable.

Soon after the conference, Justice Douglas quickly drafted an opinion in the abortion cases. The constitutional right of privacy, he wrote, "covers a wide range [and is] broad enough to encompass the right of a woman to terminate an unwanted pregnancy in its early stages by obtaining an abortion." He acknowledged that the state might qualify the right, but the state must demonstrate a compelling interest. Justice Brennan wrote a 10–page letter agreeing with the main ideas in Douglas' draft opinion and making suggestions for its improvement.

More than five months after the initial conference in abortion cases, Justice Blackmun circulated a memorandum in Roe v. Wade in which he proposed to strike down the Texas statute on the ground of vagueness. Soon thereafter Justice Brennan wrote him saying, "My recollection of the voting on this and the *Georgia* case was that a majority of us felt that the Constitution required the invalidation of abortion statutes save to the extent they required that an abortion be performed by a licensed physician within some limited time after conception. I think essentially this was the view shared by Bill, Potter, Thurgood and me. My notes also indicate that you might support this view at least in this *Texas* case." Justice Brennan went on to say he preferred a disposition of "the core constitutional issue." Justice Douglas then wrote Blackmun to say that his notes confirmed what Justice Brennan had written to Blackmun— "that abortion statutes were invalid save as they required that an abortion be performed by a licensed physician within a limited time after conception." "That," Douglas added, "was the clear view of a majority of the seven who heard the argument ... So I think we should meet what Bill Brennan calls the 'core issue.' "

A few days after receiving Justices Brennan's and Douglas' communications, Justice Blackmun circulated a memorandum in Doe v. Bolton in which he proposed to strike down several provisions of the Georgia statute. In this memorandum, he acknowledged the relevance of the right of privacy in a case. That right, however, did not, in his view, embrace an absolute right to abortion. "The heart of the matter," he wrote, "is that somewhere, either forthwith at conception, or at 'quickening,' or at birth, or at some other point in between, another being becomes involved and the privacy the woman possessed has become dual rather than sole. The woman's right of privacy must be measured accordingly. Thus, the woman's personal right ... is not unlimited. It must be balanced against the state's interest."

At this point, Chief Justice Burger proposed that the abortion cases be reargued before the full Court, which now included the two new Nixon appointees, Lewis F. Powell, Jr., and William H. Rehnquist. Justice Douglas' response was to join in Blackmun's draft opinion in *Roe*. Then, Justice White circulated a dissenting opinion in *Roe* demonstrating the weakness of Blackmun's vagueness approach. There were five votes to issue Justice Blackmun's opinion in *Roe* until Blackmun changed his mind. These were his reasons for re-argument of the cases:

> 1. I believe, on an issue so sensitive and so emotional as this one, the country deserves the conclusion of a nine-man, not a seven-man court, whatever the ultimate decision may be.

> 2. Although I have worked on these cases with some concentration, I am not yet certain about all the details. Should we make the Georgia case the primary opinion and recast Texas in its light? Should we refrain from emasculation of the Georgia statute, and, instead, hold it unconstitutional in its entirety and let the state legislature reconstruct from the beginning? Should we spell out—although it would then necessarily be largely dictum—just what aspects are controllable by the State and to what extent? For example, it has been suggested that ... Georgia's provision as to a licensed hospital should be held unconstitutional, and the Court should approve performance of an abortion in a "licensed medical facility." These are some of the suggestions that have been made and that prompt me to think about a summer's delay.

Justice Douglas strongly opposed reargument of the cases and sent a note to the Chief Justice saying that "[i]f the vote of the conference is to reargue, he would 'file a statement telling what is happening to us and the tragedy it entails.'" When the Court voted to reargue the cases, Justice Douglas did not file a statement.

Reargument did not affect any of the earlier majority's votes. The new appointees—Justices Powell and Rehnquist—split their votes. Justice Powell said that he was "basically in accord with Harry [Blackmun's] position." Justice Rehnquist said that he agreed with Justice White who had said earlier in the conference, "I'm not going to second guess state legislatures in striking the balance in favor of abortion laws." Although the majority justices had not changed their positions, they expressed dissatisfaction with the approach Justice Blackmun had taken in *Roe*. Justice Blackmun told the conference that he had revised both the *Roe* and *Doe* opinions over the summer. The new *Roe* draft was similar to Blackmun's final opinion in the case. Responding to the new draft, Justice Marshall wrote to Blackmun: "I am inclined to agree that drawing the line at viability accommodates the interests at stake better than drawing it at the end of the first trimester. Given the difficulties which many women may have in believing that they are pregnant and in deciding to seek an abortion, I fear that the earlier date may not in practice serve the interests of those women, which your opinion does seek to serve." Marshall suggested that "the opinion state explicitly that, between the end of the first trimester and viability, state regulations directed at health and safety alone were permissible." Marshall acknowledged "that at some point the State's interest in preserving the potential life of the unborn child overrides any individual interests of the women." But, he concluded, "I would be disturbed if that point were set before viability, and I am afraid that the opinion's present focus on the end of the first trimester would lead states to prohibit abortions completely at any later date." Justice Blackmun adopted Justice Marshall's suggestion. Justices Douglas and Brennan raised questions about using the viability approach in determining when the state's interest was compelling, but Justice Blackmun remained firm. Justice Stewart expressed a different criticism of Blackmun's opinion. "One of my concerns with your opinion as presently written," he wrote, "is the specificity of its dictum—particularly in its fixing of the end of the first trimester as the critical point for valid state action. I appreciate the inevitability and indeed wisdom of dicta in the Court's opinion, but I wonder about the desirability of the dicta being quite so inflexibly 'legislative.'"

Thus Justice Blackmun had, with the help of his colleagues—particularly Justices Douglas, Brennan, and Marshall—developed a theory of a right that the majority of the Court wanted to protect from the beginning, and even the Chief Justice finally agreed to join the opinion.

NOTES AND QUESTIONS

1. Note that the Court in *Roe* asserts, "We need not resolve the difficult question of when life begins." Is this, in fact, true? Can the opinion be defended if life, in fact, does begin, as Texas seems to have concluded, at the point of conception? Does the Court decide that life does *not* begin in the first three months of pregnancy? Would that be correct?

2. The Court acknowledges that the state does have a legitimate interest in the *potential* life of the fetus no matter when life begins. Why is it not a compelling interest before viability?

3. What is the relevance of the Court's discussion (10 pages in the original report) leading to the conclusion that "at common law ... abortion was viewed with less disfavor than under most American statutes...."? Is the Court implying that a more liberal attitude toward abortion is therefore fixed in the Constitution?

4.   What is the point of the Court's discussion as to whether a fetus is a "person" within the Fourteenth Amendment? Is anyone arguing, in either of these cases, that the fetus is protected by the Fourteenth Amendment and that hence a more permissive abortion law would be unconstitutional?

5.   In 1974 and 1975, four European constitutional courts considered the subject of abortion. Two of these courts rejected constitutional attacks on recently-enacted abortion laws claimed to permit abortion in too many cases (Austria and France). One court (Italy) held a Mussolini-era law unconstitutional because it permitted too few abortions, but unlike the United States Supreme Court, cautioned that an overly-permissive law might also be unconstitutional. The most interesting decision of all, in contrast to Roe v. Wade, was that of the West German Constitutional Court. That court concluded that a new abortion law permitting abortions on demand during the first three months of pregnancy interfered with the fetus' constitutional right to life, but the court did not refer to the person as a human person. It said that because the fetus is not a "completed" person, it does not enjoy the same rights as human beings generally. None-the-less, the court held that fetal life has "independent legal value" worthy of constitutional protection. The translations of all four cases can be found in M. Cappelletti and W. Cohen, *Comparative Constitutional Law Cases and Materials* 563–622 (1979). The German case is also reprinted and discussed in D. Kommers, *Constitutional Jurisprudence of the Federal Republic of Germany*, 348–362 (1989).

6.   It has been speculated that the United States Supreme Court's 1942 decision striking down Oklahoma's compulsory sterilization law (Skinner v. Oklahoma, note 6, p. 893, above) was influenced by what was already known of the eugenic mass sterilization programs conducted in Nazi Germany, with which the United States was at war. In its abortion decision, the majority of the West German Constitutional Court expressly stated that its result was the product of the "bitter experience" of Hitler's abuse of sterilization, and his mass murder of "unworthy lives." The dissenters in the West German case pointed out that, in the Third Reich, abortion was flatly prohibited by strict criminal laws. (In general, too, the abortion laws of Mussolini's Italy and Vichy France more restrictively prohibited abortion than did contemporary law.) Why would a regime committed to the extinction of "unworthy lives" restrict abortion more than the democratically-elected West German parliament of the 1970's?

7.   It is possible to argue that the decisions of both the West German Constitutional Court and the United States Supreme Court are wrong. Although the two abortion decisions are poles apart in their results, they are in agreement that it was within the province of the judiciary to second-guess legislative judgments about the legality of abortion. Moreover, deciding the issue as one involving the definition of constitutionally protected liberty means that the decisions can't be changed without amending the constitution.

In both *Griswold* and Roe v. Wade, the dissenters' main complaint was that the majority were writing their own notions of morality into the Constitution. In order to understand the background of their complaint, it is necessary to review briefly the development of the doctrine of substantive due process. The Due Process Clause of the Fourteenth Amendment provides that no state shall "deprive any person of life, liberty or property without due process of law." The Fifth Amendment also contains a Due Process Clause which puts similar restraints on the federal government. These Clauses have been interpreted for a long time to require fair procedures. However, for a period of almost fifty years, the Supreme Court interpreted the Due Process Clauses as requiring substantive, as well as procedural, protection of the rights of life, liberty and property. From the turn of the Century until the 1930's, the Supreme Court reviewed economic and social regulation at both the state and federal level and struck down many of these laws. "Liberty" and "property" were both interpreted broadly so as to incorporate laissez-faire economic notions, including freedom of contract and suspicion of government intervention in economic affairs. Lochner v. New York, 198 U.S. 45 (1905), in which the Court struck down a state law limiting bakers to working 10 hours a day and 60 hours a week, is often cited as the epitome of this era of economic substantive due process. Since the mid–1930s the Court has avoided looking at the substantive basis of economic regulations and has refused to use the Due Process Clauses to strike down laws regulating business or labor. In Day–Brite Lighting Inc. v. Missouri, 342 U.S. 421 (1952), Justice Douglas' opinion for the Court summarized the modern decisions as leaving "debatable issues as respects business, economic, and social affairs to legislative decision."

Some legal scholars charge that Roe v. Wade raises the same, serious problem of the judiciary overstepping its power in order to invalidate the judgment of a democratically elected legislature as did the now discredited *Lochner* case. Consider the following argument by Professor Ely* that the rationale of Roe v. Wade is an even more dangerous precedent than *Lochner*:

> Criticism of the *Lochner* philosophy has been virtually universal and will not be rehearsed here. I would, however, like to suggest briefly that although *Lochner* and *Roe* are twins to be sure, they are not identical. While I would hesitate to argue that one is more defensible than the other in terms of judicial style, there *are* differences in that regard that suggest *Roe* may turn out to be the more dangerous precedent.
>
> ... The Court grants that protecting the fetus is an "important and legitimate" governmental goal, and of course it does not deny that restricting abortion promotes it. What it does, instead, is simply announce that that goal is not important enough to sustain the restriction....

* John Hart Ely, The Wages of Crying Wolf. A Comment on Roe v. Wade, Yale Law Journal, 1973, vol. 82, pp. 920, 940–943. Reprinted with permission.

... *Lochner et al.* were thoroughly disreputable decisions, but at least they did us the favor of sowing the seeds of their own destruction. To say that the equalization of bargaining power or the fostering of the labor movement is a goal outside the ambit of a "police power" ... is to say something that is, in a word, wrong. And it is just as obviously wrong to declare ... that restrictions on long working hours cannot reasonably be said to promote health and safety. *Roe*'s "refutation" of the legislative judgment, on the other, is *not* obviously wrong, for the substitution of one nonrational judgment for another concerning the relative importance of a mother's opportunity to live the life she has planned and a fetus's opportunity to live at all, can be labeled neither wrong nor right. The problem with *Roe* is not so much that it bungles the question it sets itself, but rather that it sets itself a question the Constitution has not made the Court's business.

Do you agree with Professor Ely?

PLANNED PARENTHOOD OF SOUTHEASTERN PENNSYLVANIA v. CASEY

Supreme Court of the United States, 1992.
505 U.S. 833, 112 S.Ct. 2791, 120 L.Ed.2d 674.

JUSTICE O'CONNOR, JUSTICE KENNEDY, and JUSTICE SOUTER announced the judgment of the Court and delivered the opinion of the Court with respect to Parts I, II, III, V–A, V–C, and VI, an opinion with respect to Part V–E, in which JUSTICE STEVENS joins, and an opinion with respect to Parts IV, V–B, and V–D.

I

Liberty finds no refuge in a jurisprudence of doubt. Yet 19 years after our holding that the Constitution protects a woman's right to terminate her pregnancy in its early stages, Roe v. Wade, 410 U.S. 113 (1973), that definition of liberty is still questioned.... [T]he United States, as it has done in five other cases in the last decade, again asks us to overrule *Roe*. ...

[Five abortion clinics, and a physician representing doctors who provide abortion services, brought this suit in federal court, challenging five provisions of the Pennsylvania Abortion Control Act: § 3205, which requires that a woman seeking an abortion give her informed consent prior to the procedure, and specifies that she be provided with certain information at least 24 hours before the abortion is performed; § 3206, which mandates the informed consent of one parent for a minor to obtain an abortion, but provides a judicial bypass procedure; § 3209, which commands that, unless certain exceptions apply, a married woman seeking an abortion must sign a statement indicating that she has notified her husband; § 3203, which defines a "medical emergency" that will excuse compliance with the foregoing requirements; and §§ 3207(b), 3214(a), and 3214(f), which impose certain reporting requirements on facilities providing abortion services. The trial court held all the provisions unconstitutional. The appeals court struck down the husband notification provision but upheld the others.]

After considering the fundamental constitutional questions resolved by *Roe,* principles of institutional integrity, and the rule of stare decisis, we are led to conclude this: the essential holding of Roe v. Wade should be retained and once again reaffirmed.

. . . *Roe*'s essential holding, the holding we reaffirm, has three parts. First is a recognition of the right of the woman to choose to have an abortion before viability and to obtain it without undue interference from the State. Before viability, the State's interests are not strong enough to support a prohibition of abortion or the imposition of a substantial obstacle to the woman's effective right to elect the procedure. Second is a confirmation of the State's power to restrict abortions after fetal viability, if the law contains exceptions for pregnancies which endanger a woman's life or health. And third is the principle that the State has legitimate interests from the outset of the pregnancy in protecting the health of the woman and the life of the fetus that may become a child. These principles do not contradict one another; and we adhere to each.

II

. . .

Neither the Bill of Rights nor the specific practices of States at the time of the adoption of the Fourteenth Amendment marks the outer limits of the substantive sphere of liberty which the Fourteenth Amendment protects. . . .

The inescapable fact is that adjudication of substantive due process claims may call upon the Court in interpreting the Constitution to exercise that same capacity which by tradition courts always have exercised: reasoned judgment. Its boundaries are not susceptible of expression as a simple rule. That does not mean we are free to invalidate state policy choices with which we disagree; yet neither does it permit us to shrink from the duties of our office. . . .

Men and women of good conscience can disagree, and we suppose some always shall disagree, about the profound moral and spiritual implications of terminating a pregnancy, even in its earliest stage. Some of us as individuals find abortion offensive to our most basic principles of morality, but that cannot control our decision. Our obligation is to define the liberty of all, not to mandate our own moral code. The underlying constitutional issue is whether the State can resolve these philosophic questions in such a definitive way that a woman lacks all choice in the matter, except perhaps in those rare circumstances in which the pregnancy is itself a danger to her own life or health, or is the result of rape or incest.

. . .

Our law affords constitutional protection to personal decisions relating to marriage, procreation, contraception, family relationships, child rearing, and education. . . . These matters, involving the most intimate and personal choices a person may make in a lifetime, choices central to personal dignity and autonomy, are central to the liberty protected by the Fourteenth Amendment. At the heart of liberty is the right to define one's own concept of existence, of meaning, of the universe, and of the mystery of human life. Beliefs about these matters could not define the attributes of personhood were they formed under compulsion of the State.

These considerations begin our analysis of the woman's interest in terminating her pregnancy but cannot end it, for this reason: though the abortion decision may originate within the zone of conscience and belief, it is more than a philosophic exercise. Abortion is a unique act. It is an act fraught with consequences for others: for the woman who must live with the implications of her decision; for the persons who perform and assist in the procedure; for the spouse, family, and society which must confront the knowledge that these procedures exist, procedures some deem nothing short of an act of violence against innocent human life; and, depending on one's beliefs, for the life or potential life that is aborted. Though abortion is conduct, it does not follow that the State is entitled to proscribe it in all instances. That is because the liberty of the woman is at stake in a sense unique to the human condition and so unique to the law. The mother who carries a child to full term is subject to anxieties, to physical constraints, to pain that only she must bear. That these sacrifices have from the beginning of the human race been endured by woman with a pride that ennobles her in the eyes of others and gives to the infant a bond of love cannot alone be grounds for the State to insist she make the sacrifice. Her suffering is too intimate and personal for the State to insist, without more, upon its own vision of the woman's role, however dominant that vision has been in the course of our history and our culture. The destiny of the woman must be shaped to a large extent on her own conception of her spiritual imperatives and her place in society.

It should be recognized, moreover, that in some critical respects the abortion decision is of the same character as the decision to use contraception, to which Griswold v. Connecticut, Eisenstadt v. Baird, and Carey v. Population Services International, afford constitutional protection. We have no doubt as to the correctness of those decisions. They support the reasoning in *Roe* relating to the woman's liberty because they involve personal decisions concerning not only the meaning of procreation but also human responsibility and respect for it. . . .

. . .

. . . [T]he reservations any of us may have in reaffirming the central holding of *Roe* are outweighed by the explication of individual liberty we have given combined with the force of stare decisis. We turn now to that doctrine.

III

. . .

... *Roe*'s underpinnings [are] unweakened in any way affecting its central holding. While it has engendered disapproval, it has not been unworkable. An entire generation has come of age free to assume *Roe*'s concept of liberty in defining the capacity of women to act in society, and to make reproductive decisions; no erosion of principle going to liberty or personal autonomy has left *Roe*'s central holding a doctrinal remnant; *Roe* portends no developments at odds with other precedent for the analysis of personal liberty; and no changes of fact have rendered viability more or less appropriate as the point at which the balance of interests tips. Within the bounds of normal stare decisis analysis, ... the stronger argument is for affirming *Roe*'s central holding, with whatever degree of personal reluctance any of us may have, not for overruling it.

. . .

The ... comparison that 20th century history invites is with the cases employing the separate-but-equal rule for applying the Fourteenth Amendment's equal protection guarantee. . . .

. . .

... While we think *Plessy* was wrong the day it was decided, ... the *Plessy* Court's explanation for its decision was so clearly at odds with the facts apparent to the Court in 1954 that the decision to reexamine *Plessy* was on this ground alone not only justified but required.

... In constitutional adjudication as elsewhere in life, changed circumstances may impose new obligations, and the thoughtful part of the Nation could accept each decision to overrule a prior case as a response to the Court's constitutional duty.

. . .

... Because neither the factual underpinnings of *Roe*'s central holding nor our understanding of it has changed (and because no other indication of weakened precedent has been shown) the Court could not pretend to be reexamining the prior law with any justification beyond a present doctrinal disposition to come out differently from the Court of 1973. To overrule prior law for no other reason than that would run counter to the view ... that a decision to overrule

. . .

The examination of the conditions justifying the repudiation of *Plessy* by *Brown* is enough to suggest the terrible price that would have been paid if the Court had not overruled as it did. In the present case, however, ... the terrible price would be paid for overruling. . . .

. . .

... [T]he Court's legitimacy depends on making legally principled decisions under circumstances in which their principled character is sufficiently plausible to be accepted by the Nation.

. . .

... [T]he country can accept some correction of error without necessarily questioning the legitimacy of the Court.

. . .

... Where ... the Court decides a case in such a way as to resolve the sort of intensely divisive controversy reflected in *Roe* and those rare, comparable cases, its decision has a dimension that the resolution of the normal case does not carry. It is the dimension present whenever the Court's interpretation of the Constitution calls the contending sides of a national controversy to end their national division by accepting a common mandate rooted in the Constitution.

The Court is not asked to do this very often, having thus addressed the Nation only twice in our lifetime, in the decisions of *Brown* and *Roe*. But when the Court does act in this way, its decision requires an equally rare precedential force to counter the inevitable efforts to overturn it ... [O]nly the most convincing justification ... could suffice to demonstrate that a later decision overruling the first was anything but a surrender to political pressure, and an unjustified repudiation of the principle on which the Court staked its authority in the first instance. So to overrule under fire in the absence of the most compelling reason to reexamine a watershed decision would subvert the Court's legitimacy beyond any serious question. . . .

. . .

... A decision to overrule *Roe*'s essential holding under the existing circumstances would address error, if error there was, at the cost of both profound and unnecessary damage to the Court's legitimacy, and to the Nation's commitment to the rule of law. It is therefore imperative to adhere to the essence of *Roe*'s original decision, and we do so today.

IV

. . .

The woman's right to terminate her pregnancy before viability is the most central principle of Roe v. Wade. It is a rule of law and a component of liberty we cannot renounce.

On the other side of the equation is the interest of the State in the protection of potential life.... We do not need to say whether each of us, ... as an original matter, would have concluded, as the *Roe* Court did, that its weight is insufficient to justify a ban on abortions prior to viability even when it is subject to certain exceptions.... [W]e have concluded that the essential holding of Roe should be affirmed.

Yet it must be remembered that Roe v. Wade speaks with clarity in establishing not only the woman's liberty but also the State's "important and legitimate interest in potential life." ... That portion of the decision in *Roe* has been given too little acknowledgement and implementation by the Court in its subsequent cases. Those cases decided that any regulation touching upon the abortion decision must survive strict scrutiny, to be sustained only if drawn in narrow terms to further a compelling state interest.... Not all of the cases decided under that formulation can be reconciled with the holding in *Roe* itself that the State has legitimate interests in the health of the woman and in protecting the potential life within her. . . .

Roe established a trimester framework to govern abortion regulations. Under this elaborate but rigid construct, almost no regulation at all is permitted during the first trimester of pregnancy; regulations designed to protect the woman's health, but not to further the State's interest in potential life, are permitted during the second trimester; and during the third trimester, when the fetus is viable, prohibitions are permitted provided the life or health of the mother is not at stake. . . .

. . .

The trimester framework no doubt was erected to ensure that the woman's right to choose not become so subordinate to the State's interest in promoting fetal life that her choice exists in theory but not in fact. We do not agree, however, that the trimester approach is necessary to accomplish this objective. A framework of this rigidity was unnecessary and in its later interpretation sometimes contradicted the State's permissible exercise of its powers.

Though the woman has a right to choose to terminate or continue her pregnancy before viability, it does not at all follow that the State is prohibited from taking steps to ensure that this choice is thoughtful and informed. Even in the earliest stages of pregnancy, the State may enact rules and regulations designed to encourage her to know that there are philosophic and social arguments of great weight that can be brought to bear in favor of continuing the pregnancy to full term and that there are procedures and institutions to allow adoption of unwanted children as well as a certain degree of state assistance if the mother chooses to raise the child herself. . . . It follows that States are free to enact laws to provide a reasonable framework for a woman to make a decision that has such profound and lasting meaning. This [is] the inevitable consequence of our holding that the State has an interest in protecting the life of the unborn.

We reject the trimester framework, which we do not consider to be part of the essential holding of *Roe*. . . . Measures aimed at ensuring that a woman's choice contemplates the consequences for the fetus do not necessarily interfere with the right recognized in *Roe*, although those measures have been found to be inconsistent with the rigid trimester framework announced in that case. A logical reading of the central holding in *Roe* itself, and a necessary reconciliation of the liberty of the woman and the interest of the State in promoting prenatal life, require, in our view, that we abandon the trimester framework as a rigid prohibition on all previability regulation aimed at the protection of fetal life. . . .

. . .

The trimester framework . . . does not fulfill *Roe*'s own promise that the State has an interest in protecting fetal life or potential life. *Roe* [used] the trimester framework to forbid any regulation of abortion designed to advance that interest before viability. . . . This treatment is, in our judgment, incompatible with the recognition that there is a substantial state interest in potential life throughout pregnancy....

The very notion that the State has a substantial interest in potential life leads to the conclusion that not all regulations must be deemed unwarranted. Not all burdens on the right to decide whether to terminate a pregnancy will be undue. In our view, the undue burden standard is the appropriate means of reconciling the State's interest with the woman's constitutionally protected liberty.

. . .

A finding of an undue burden is a shorthand for the conclusion that a state regulation has the purpose or effect of placing a substantial obstacle in the path of a woman seeking an abortion of a nonviable fetus. A statute with this purpose is invalid because the means chosen by the State to further the interest in potential life must be calculated to inform the woman's free choice, not hinder it. And a statute which, while furthering the interest in potential life or some other valid state interest, has the effect of placing a substantial obstacle in the path of a woman's choice cannot be considered a permissible means of serving its legitimate ends.... [A] law designed to further the State's interest in fetal life which imposes an undue burden on the woman's decision before fetal viability [is un]constitutional....

Some guiding principles should emerge.... Regulations which do no more than create a structural mechanism by which the State, or the parent or guardian of a minor, may express profound respect for the life of the unborn are permitted, if they are not a substantial obstacle to the woman's exercise of the right to choose. Unless it has that effect on her right of choice, a state measure designed to persuade her to choose childbirth over abortion will be upheld if reasonably related to that goal. Regulations designed to foster the health of a woman seeking an abortion are valid if they do not constitute an undue burden.

Even when jurists reason from shared premises, some disagreement is inevitable.... That is to be expected in the application of any legal standard which must accommodate life's complexity. We do not expect it to be otherwise with respect to the undue burden standard.

. . .

... Our adoption of the undue burden analysis does not disturb the central holding of Roe v. Wade, and we reaffirm that holding. Regardless of whether exceptions are made for particular circumstances, a State may not prohibit any woman from making the ultimate decision to terminate her pregnancy before viability.

... We also reaffirm *Roe*'s holding that "subsequent to viability, the State in promoting its interest in the potentiality of human life may, if it chooses, regulate, and even proscribe, abortion except where it is necessary, in appropriate medical judgment, for the preservation of the life or health of the mother." ...

These principles control our assessment of the Pennsylvania statute, and we now turn to the issue of the validity of its challenged provisions.

V

The Court of Appeals applied what it believed to be the undue burden standard and upheld each of the provisions except for the husband notification requirement. We agree generally with this conclusion, but refine the undue burden analysis in accordance with the principles articulated above. We now consider the separate statutory sections at issue.

A

Because it is central to the operation of various other requirements, we begin with the statute's definition of medical emergency. Under the statute, a medical emergency is "[t]hat condition which, on the basis of the physician's good faith clinical judgment, so complicates the medical condition of a pregnant woman as to necessitate the immediate abortion of her pregnancy to avert her death or for which a delay will create serious risk of substantial and irreversible impairment of a major bodily function." . . .

Petitioners argue that the definition is too narrow, contending that it forecloses the possibility of an immediate abortion despite some significant health risks. If the contention were correct, we would be required to invalidate the restrictive operation of the provision, for the essential holding of *Roe* forbids a State from interfering with a woman's choice to undergo an abortion procedure if continuing her pregnancy would constitute a threat to her health. . . .

[The opinion concludes that, as interpreted by the lower federal court, the definition of medical emergency was sufficiently broad that women would not be required to continue pregnancies threatening to their health.]

B

We next consider the informed consent requirement. . . .

Our prior decisions establish that as with any medical procedure, the State may require a woman to give her written informed consent to an abortion. . . . In this respect, the statute is unexceptional. Petitioners challenge the statute's definition of informed consent because it includes the provision of specific information by the doctor and the mandatory 24-hour waiting period. The conclusions reached by a majority of the Justices in the separate opinions filed today and the undue burden standard adopted in this opinion require us to overrule in part some of the Court's past decisions . . .

In *Akron I,* 462 U.S. 416 (1983), we invalidated an ordinance which required that a woman seeking an abortion be provided by her physician with specific information "designed to influence the woman's informed choice between abortion or childbirth." . . .

To the extent *Akron I* and *Thornburgh* find a constitutional violation when the government requires, as it does here, the giving of truthful, nonmisleading information about the nature of the procedure, the attendant health risks and those of childbirth, and the "probable gestational age" of the fetus, those cases go too far.... In attempting to ensure that a woman apprehend the full consequences of her decision, the State furthers the legitimate purpose of reducing the risk that a woman may elect an abortion, only to discover later, with devastating psychological consequences, that her decision was not fully informed. If the information the State requires to be made available to the woman is truthful and not misleading, the requirement may be permissible.

We also see no reason why the State may not require doctors to inform a woman seeking an abortion of the availability of materials relating to the consequences to the fetus, even when those consequences have no direct relation to her health.... A requirement that the physician make available information similar to that mandated by the statute here was described in *Thornburgh* as "an outright attempt to wedge the Commonwealth's message discouraging abortion into the privacy of the informed-consent dialogue between the woman and her physician." 476 U.S., at 762. We conclude, however, that informed choice need not be defined in such narrow terms that all considerations of the effect on the fetus are made irrelevant.... [W]e depart from the holdings of *Akron I* and *Thornburgh* to the extent that we permit a State to further its legitimate goal of protecting the life of the unborn by enacting legislation aimed at ensuring a decision that is mature and informed, even when in so doing the State expresses a preference for childbirth over abortion.... This requirement cannot be considered a substantial obstacle to obtaining an abortion, and, it follows, there is no undue burden.

Our prior cases also suggest that the "straitjacket," ... of particular information which must be given in each case interferes with a constitutional right of privacy between a pregnant woman and her physician. As a preliminary matter, it is worth noting that the statute now before us does not require a physician to comply with the informed consent provisions "if he or she can demonstrate by a preponderance of the evidence, that he or she reasonably believed that furnishing the information would have resulted in a severely adverse effect on the physical or mental health of the patient." ... In this respect, the statute does not prevent the physician from exercising his or her medical judgment.

... [A] requirement that a doctor give a woman certain information as part of obtaining her consent to an abortion is, for constitutional purposes, no different from a requirement that a doctor give certain specific information about any medical procedure.

· · ·

The Pennsylvania statute also requires us to reconsider the holding in *Akron I* that the State may not require that a physician, as opposed to a qualified assistant, provide information relevant to a woman's informed consent. ...Since there is no evidence on this record that requiring a doctor to give the information as provided by the statute would amount in practical terms to a substantial obstacle to a woman seeking an abortion, we conclude that it is not an undue burden....

Our analysis of Pennsylvania's 24–hour waiting period between the provision of the information deemed necessary to informed consent and the performance of an abortion under the undue burden standard requires us to reconsider the premise behind the decision in *Akron I* invalidating a parallel requirement.... The idea that important decisions will be more informed and deliberate if they follow some period of reflection does not strike us as unreasonable, particularly where the statute directs that important information become part of the background of the decision. The statute, as construed by the Court of Appeals, permits avoidance of the waiting period in the event of a medical emergency and the record evidence shows that in the vast majority of cases, a 24–hour delay does not create any appreciable health risk. In theory, at least, the waiting period is a reasonable measure to implement the State's interest in protecting the life of the unborn, a measure that does not amount to an undue burden.

Whether the mandatory 24–hour waiting period is nonetheless invalid because in practice it is a substantial obstacle to a woman's choice to terminate her pregnancy is a closer question. The [trial court found] that because of the distances many women must travel to reach an abortion provider, the practical effect will often be a delay of much more than a day because the waiting period requires that a woman seeking an abortion make at least two visits to the doctor.... [The trial court concluded] that for those women who have the fewest financial resources, those who must travel long distances, and those who have difficulty explaining their whereabouts to husbands, employers, or others, the 24–hour waiting period will be "particularly burdensome."

These findings are troubling in some respects, but they do not demonstrate that the waiting period constitutes an undue burden. [The trial court] did not conclude that the increased costs and potential delays amount to substantial obstacles. Rather, applying the trimester framework[, it] concluded that the waiting period does not further the state "interest in maternal health" and "infringes the physician's discretion to exercise sound medical judgment." Yet, as we have stated, under the undue burden standard a State is permitted to enact persuasive measures which favor childbirth over abortion, even if those measures do not further a health interest....

We also disagree with the [trial court's] conclusion that the "particularly burdensome" effects of the waiting period on some women require its invalidation. A particular burden is not of necessity a substantial obstacle. Whether a burden falls on a particular group is a distinct inquiry from whether it is a substantial obstacle even as to the women in that group.... [O]n the record before us, and in the context of this facial challenge, we are not convinced that the 24–hour waiting period constitutes an undue burden.

We are left with the argument that the various aspects of the informed consent requirement are unconstitutional because they place barriers in the way of abortion on demand. Even the broadest reading of *Roe*, however, has not suggested that there is a constitutional right to abortion on demand.... Rather, the right protected by *Roe* is a right to decide to terminate a pregnancy free of undue interference by the State. Because the informed consent requirement facilitates the wise exercise of that right it cannot be classified as an interference with the right *Roe* protects. The informed consent requirement is not an undue burden on that right.

C

Section 3209 of Pennsylvania's abortion law provides, except in cases of medical emergency, that no physician shall perform an abortion on a married woman without receiving a signed statement from the woman that she has notified her spouse that she is about to undergo an abortion. The woman has the option of providing an alternative signed statement certifying that her husband is not the man who impregnated her; that her husband could not be located; that the pregnancy is the result of spousal sexual assault which she has reported; or that the woman believes that notifying her husband will cause him or someone else to inflict bodily injury upon her. A physician who performs an abortion on a married woman without receiving the appropriate signed statement will have his or her license revoked, and is liable to the husband for damages.

. . .

. . . In well-functioning marriages, spouses discuss important intimate decisions such as whether to bear a child. But there are millions of women in this country who are the victims of regular physical and psychological abuse at the hands of their husbands. Should these women become pregnant, they may have very good reasons for not wishing to inform their husbands of their decision to obtain an abortion. Many may have justifiable fears of physical abuse, but may be no less fearful of the consequences of reporting prior abuse to the Commonwealth of Pennsylvania. Many may have a reasonable fear that notifying their husbands will provoke further instances of child abuse; these women are not exempt from § 3209's notification requirement. Many may fear devastating forms of psychological abuse from their husbands, including verbal harassment, threats of future violence, the destruction of possessions, physical confinement to the home, the withdrawal of financial support, or the disclosure of the abortion to family and friends. These methods of psychological abuse may act as even more of a deterrent to notification than the possibility of physical violence, but women who are the victims of the abuse are not exempt from § 3209's notification requirement. And many women who are pregnant as a result of sexual assaults by their husbands will be unable to avail themselves of the exception for spousal sexual assault, § 3209(b)(3), because the exception requires that the woman have notified law enforcement authorities within 90 days of the assault, and her husband will be notified of her report once an investigation begins. § 3128(c). If anything in this field is certain, it is that victims of spousal sexual assault are extremely reluctant to report the abuse to the government; hence, a great many spousal rape victims will not be exempt from the notification requirement imposed by § 3209.

The spousal notification requirement is thus likely to prevent a significant number of women from obtaining an abortion. It does not merely make abortions a little more difficult or expensive to obtain; for many women, it will impose a substantial obstacle. We must not blind ourselves to the fact that the significant number of women who fear for their safety and the safety of their children are likely to be deterred from procuring an abortion as surely as if the Commonwealth had outlawed abortion in all cases.

... For the great many women who are victims of abuse inflicted by their husbands, or whose children are the victims of such abuse, a spousal notice requirement enables the husband to wield an effective veto over his wife's decision. Whether the prospect of notification itself deters such women from seeking abortions, or whether the husband, through physical force or psychological pressure or economic coercion, prevents his wife from obtaining an abortion until it is too late, the notice requirement will often be tantamount to [a] veto ... The women most affected by this law—those who most reasonably fear the consequences of notifying their husbands that they are pregnant—are in the gravest danger.

The husband's interest in the life of the child his wife is carrying does not permit the State to empower him with this troubling degree of authority over his wife....

. . .

D

We next consider the parental consent provision. Except in a medical emergency, an unemancipated young woman under 18 may not obtain an abortion unless she and one of her parents (or guardian) provides informed consent.... If neither a parent nor a guardian provides consent, a court may authorize the performance of an abortion upon a determination that the young woman is mature and capable of giving informed consent and has in fact given her informed consent, or that an abortion would be in her best interests.

We have been over most of this ground before. Our cases establish, and we reaffirm today, that a State may require a minor seeking an abortion to obtain the consent of a parent or guardian, provided that there is an adequate judicial bypass procedure....

. . .

E

Under the recordkeeping and reporting requirements of the statute, every facility which performs abortions is required to file a report stating its name and address as well as the name and address of any related entity, such as a controlling or subsidiary organization. In the case of state-funded institutions, the information becomes public.

For each abortion performed, a report must be filed identifying: the physician (and the second physician where required); the facility; the referring physician or agency; the woman's age; the number of prior pregnancies and prior abortions she has had; gestational age; the type of abortion procedure; the date of the abortion; whether there were any pre-existing medical conditions which would complicate pregnancy; medical complications with the abortion; where applicable, the basis for the determination that the abortion was medically necessary; the weight of the aborted fetus; and whether the woman was married, and if so, whether notice was provided or the basis for the failure to give notice. Every abortion facility must also file quarterly reports showing the number of abortions performed broken down by trimester.... In all events, the identity of each woman who has had an abortion remains confidential.

In *Danforth*, 428 U.S., at 80, we held that recordkeeping and reporting provisions "that are reasonably directed to the preservation of maternal health and that properly respect a patient's confidentiality and privacy are permissible." We think that under this standard, all the provisions at issue here except that relating to spousal notice are constitutional....

. . .

Subsection (12) of the reporting provision requires the reporting of, among other things, a married woman's "reason for failure to provide notice" to her husband.... This provision in effect requires women, as a condition of obtaining an abortion, to provide the Commonwealth with the precise information we have already recognized that many women have pressing reasons not to reveal. Like the spousal notice requirement itself, this provision places an undue burden on a woman's choice, and must be invalidated for that reason.

. . .

JUSTICE STEVENS, concurring in part and dissenting in part.

The portions of the Court's opinion that I have joined are more important than those with which I disagree....

. . .

... Contrary to the suggestion of the joint opinion, it is not a "contradiction" to recognize that the State may have a legitimate interest in potential human life and, at the same time, to conclude that that interest does not justify the regulation of abortion before viability (although other interests, such as maternal health, may). The fact that the State's interest is legitimate does not tell us when, if ever, that interest outweighs the pregnant woman's interest in personal liberty....

. . .

Weighing the State's interest in potential life and the woman's liberty interest, I agree with the joint opinion that the State may "expres[s] a preference for normal childbirth," that the State may take steps to ensure that a woman's choice "is thoughtful and informed," and that "States are free to enact laws to provide a reasonable framework for a woman to make a decision that has such profound and lasting meaning." Serious questions arise, however, when a State attempts to "persuade the woman to choose childbirth over abortion." Decisional autonomy must limit the State's power to inject into a woman's most personal deliberations its own views of what is best. The State may promote its preferences by funding childbirth, by creating and maintaining alternatives to abortion, and by espousing the virtues of family; but it must respect the individual's freedom to make such judgments.

. . .

... [T]he Pennsylvania statute require[s] a physician or counselor to provide the woman with a range of materials clearly designed to persuade her to choose not to undergo the abortion. While the State is free ... to produce and disseminate such material, the State may not inject such information into the woman's deliberations just as she is weighing such an important choice.

. . .

The 24–hour waiting period ... raises even more serious concerns. . . .

. . .

... The mandatory delay ... appears to rest on outmoded and unacceptable assumptions about the decisionmaking capacity of women. While there are well-established and consistently maintained reasons for the State to view with skepticism the ability of minors to make decisions, none of those reasons applies to an adult woman's decisionmaking ability. Just as we have left behind the belief that a woman must consult her husband before undertaking serious matters, so we must reject the notion that a woman is less capable of deciding matters of gravity. . . .

In the alternative, the delay requirement may be premised on the belief that the decision to terminate a pregnancy is presumptively wrong. This premise is illegitimate. . . .

. . .

... [W]hile I disagree with Parts IV, V–B, and V–D of the joint opinion, I join the remainder of the Court's opinion.

JUSTICE BLACKMUN, concurring in part, concurring in the judgment in part, and dissenting in part.

I join parts I, II, III, V–A, V–C, and VI of the joint opinion of JUSTICES O'CONNOR, KENNEDY, and SOUTER.

Three years ago, in Webster v. Reproductive Health Serv., 492 U.S. 490 (1989), four Members of this Court appeared poised to "cas[t] into darkness the hopes and visions of every woman in this country" who had come to believe that the Constitution guaranteed her the right to reproductive choice. . . . But now, just when so many expected the darkness to fall, the flame has grown bright.

I do not underestimate the significance of today's joint opinion. Yet I remain steadfast in my belief that the right to reproductive choice is entitled to the full protection [previously] afforded by this Court. And I

fear for the darkness as four Justices anxiously await the single vote
necessary to extinguish the light.

. . .

. . . [W]hile I believe that the joint opinion errs in failing to invalidate the other regulations, I am pleased that the joint opinion has not
ruled out the possibility that these regulations may be shown to impose
an unconstitutional burden. The joint opinion makes clear that its
specific holdings are based on the insufficiency of the record before it. I
am confident that in the future evidence will be produced to show that
"in a large fraction of the cases in which [these regulations are] relevant,
[they] will operate as a substantial obstacle to a woman's choice to
undergo an abortion."

. . .

In one sense, the Court's approach is worlds apart from that of the
Chief Justice and Justice Scalia. And yet, in another sense, the distance
between the two approaches is short—the distance is but a single vote.

I am 83 years old. I cannot remain on this Court forever, and when I
do step down, the confirmation process for my successor well may focus
on the issue before us today. That, I regret, may be exactly where the
choice between the two worlds will be made.

CHIEF JUSTICE REHNQUIST, with whom JUSTICE WHITE, JUSTICE SCALIA,
and JUSTICE THOMAS join, concurring in the judgment in part and dissenting in part.

The joint opinion, following its newly-minted variation on stare
decisis, retains the outer shell of Roe v. Wade, 410 U.S. 113 (1973), but
beats a wholesale retreat from the substance of that case. We believe
that *Roe* was wrongly decided, and that it can and should be overruled
consistently with our traditional approach to stare decisis in constitutional cases. We would adopt the approach of the plurality in Webster v.
Reproductive Health Services, 492 U.S. 490 (1989), and uphold the
challenged provisions of the Pennsylvania statute in their entirety.

. . .

In construing the phrase "liberty" incorporated in the Due Process
Clause of the Fourteenth Amendment, we have recognized that its
meaning extends beyond freedom from physical restraint. . . . But [our
opinions] do not endorse any all-encompassing "right of privacy."

In Roe v. Wade, the Court recognized a "guarantee of personal
privacy" which "is broad enough to encompass a woman's decision
whether or not to terminate her pregnancy." . . . We are now of the view
that, in terming this right fundamental, the Court in *Roe* read the
earlier opinions upon which it based its decision much too broadly.
Unlike marriage, procreation and contraception, abortion "involves the
purposeful termination of potential life." . . . The abortion decision must
therefore "be recognized as sui generis, different in kind from the others
that the Court has protected under the rubric of personal or family
privacy and autonomy." . . .

Nor do the historical traditions of the American people support the view that the right to terminate one's pregnancy is "fundamental." ... 21 of the restrictive abortion laws in effect in 1868 were still in effect in 1973 when *Roe* was decided, and an overwhelming majority of the States prohibited abortion unless necessary to preserve the life or health of the mother....

We think, therefore, both in view of this history and of our decided cases dealing with substantive liberty under the Due Process Clause, that the Court was mistaken in *Roe* when it classified a woman's decision to terminate her pregnancy as a "fundamental right" that could be abridged only in a manner which withstood "strict scrutiny." ...

· · ·

In our view, authentic principles of stare decisis do not require that any portion of the reasoning in *Roe* be kept intact. "Stare decisis is not ... a universal, inexorable command," especially in cases involving the interpretation of the Federal Constitution.... Erroneous decisions in such constitutional cases are uniquely durable, because correction through legislative action, save for constitutional amendment, is impossible. It is therefore our duty to reconsider constitutional interpretations that "depar[t] from a proper understanding" of the Constitution....

· · ·

... [T]he joint opinion's argument is based ... on generalized assertions about the national psyche, on a belief that the people of this country have grown accustomed to the *Roe* decision over the last 19 years and have "ordered their thinking and living around" it. As an initial matter, one might inquire how the joint opinion can view the "central holding" of Roe as so deeply rooted in our constitutional culture, when it so casually uproots and disposes of that same decision's trimester framework. Furthermore, at various points in the past, the same could have been said about this Court's erroneous decisions that the Constitution allowed "separate but equal" treatment of minorities, see Plessy v. Ferguson, 163 U.S. 537 (1896) ...

· · ·

... [W]e doubt that [the joint opinion's] distinction between *Roe,* on the one hand, and *Plessy* ... on the other, withstands analysis. The joint opinion acknowledges that the Court improved its stature by overruling *Plessy* in *Brown* on a deeply divisive issue....

· · ·

There is also a suggestion in the joint opinion that the propriety of overruling a "divisive" decision depends in part on whether "most people" would now agree that it should be overruled. Either the demise of opposition or its progression to substantial popular agreement apparently is required to allow the Court to reconsider a divisive decision. How such agreement would be ascertained, short of a public opinion poll, the joint opinion does not say. But surely even the suggestion is totally at war with the idea of "legitimacy" in whose name it is invoked. The

Judicial Branch derives its legitimacy, not from following public opinion, but from deciding by its best lights whether legislative enactments of the popular branches of Government comport with the Constitution. The doctrine of stare decisis is an adjunct of this duty, and should be no more subject to the vagaries of public opinion than is the basic judicial task.

· · ·

The end result of the joint opinion's paeans of praise for legitimacy is the enunciation of a brand new standard for evaluating state regulation of a woman's right to abortion—the "undue burden" standard. As indicated above, Roe v. Wade adopted a "fundamental right" standard under which state regulations could survive only if they met the requirement of "strict scrutiny." While we disagree with that standard, it at least had a recognized basis in constitutional law at the time *Roe* was decided. The same cannot be said for the "undue burden" standard, which is created largely out of whole cloth by the authors of the joint opinion. It is a standard which even today does not command the support of a majority of this Court. And it will not, we believe, result in the sort of "simple limitation," easily applied, which the joint opinion anticipates. In sum, it is a standard which is not built to last.

· · ·

In evaluating abortion regulations under that standard, judges will have to decide whether they place a "substantial obstacle" in the path of a woman seeking an abortion. In that this standard is based even more on a judge's subjective determinations than was the trimester framework, the standard will do nothing to prevent "judges from roaming at large in the constitutional field" guided only by their personal views.... For example, in the very matter before us now, the authors of the joint opinion would uphold Pennsylvania's 24–hour waiting period, concluding that a "particular burden" on some women is not a substantial obstacle. But the authors would at the same time strike down Pennsylvania's spousal notice provision, after finding that in a "large fraction" of cases the provision will be a substantial obstacle. And, while the authors conclude that the informed consent provisions do not constitute an "undue burden," Justice Stevens would hold that they do.

Furthermore, while striking down the spousal notice regulation, the joint opinion would uphold a parental consent restriction that certainly places very substantial obstacles in the path of a minor's abortion choice. The joint opinion is forthright in admitting that it draws this distinction based on a policy judgment that parents will have the best interests of their children at heart, while the same is not necessarily true of husbands as to their wives. This may or may not be a correct judgment, but it is quintessentially a legislative one. The "undue burden" inquiry does not in any way supply the distinction between parental consent and spousal consent which the joint opinion adopts. Despite the efforts of the joint opinion, the undue burden standard presents nothing more workable than the trimester framework which it discards today. Under the guise of the Constitution, this Court will still impart its own preferences on the States in the form of a complex abortion code.

. . .

[T]he Constitution does not subject state abortion regulations to heightened scrutiny. Accordingly, we think that the correct analysis is that set forth by the plurality opinion in *Webster*. A woman's interest in having an abortion is a form of liberty protected by the Due Process Clause, but States may regulate abortion procedures in ways rationally related to a legitimate state interest.

. . .

. . . Pennsylvania has not imposed a spousal consent requirement of the type the Court struck down in Planned Parenthood of Central Mo. v. Danforth, 428 U.S., at 67–72. Missouri's spousal consent provision was invalidated in that case because of the Court's view that it unconstitutionally granted to the husband "a veto power exercisable for any reason whatsoever or for no reason at all." But this case involves a much less intrusive requirement of spousal notification, not consent. Such a law requiring only notice to the husband "does not give any third party the legal right to make the [woman's] decision for her, or to prevent her from obtaining an abortion should she choose to have one performed." . . . [I]t is not enough for petitioners to show that, in some "worst-case" circumstances, the notice provision will operate as a grant of veto power to husbands. . . . Because they are making a facial challenge to the provision, they must "show that no set of circumstances exists under which the [provision] would be valid." . . . This they have failed to do.

The question before us is therefore whether the spousal notification requirement rationally furthers any legitimate state interests. We conclude that it does. First, a husband's interests in procreation within marriage and in the potential life of his unborn child are certainly substantial ones. . . . The State itself has legitimate interests both in protecting these interests of the father and in protecting the potential life of the fetus, and the spousal notification requirement is reasonably related to advancing those state interests. By providing that a husband will usually know of his spouse's intent to have an abortion, the provision makes it more likely that the husband will participate in deciding the fate of his unborn child, a possibility that might otherwise have been denied him. This participation might in some cases result in a decision to proceed with the pregnancy. . . .

The State also has a legitimate interest in promoting "the integrity of the marital relationship." . . . In our view, the spousal notice requirement is a rational attempt by the State to improve truthful communication between spouses and encourage collaborative decisionmaking, and thereby fosters marital integrity. . . . [I]t is unrealistic to assume that every husband-wife relationship is either (1) so perfect that this type of truthful and important communication will take place as a matter of course, or (2) so imperfect that, upon notice, the husband will react selfishly, violently, or contrary to the best interests of his wife. . . . The spousal notice provision will admittedly be unnecessary in some circumstances, and possibly harmful in others, but "the existence of particular cases in which a feature of a statute performs no function (or is even counterproductive) ordinarily does not render the statute unconstitutional or even constitutionally suspect." ... The Pennsylvania Legislature was in a position to weigh the likely benefits of the provision against its likely adverse effects, and presumably concluded, on balance, that the provision would be beneficial. Whether this was a wise decision or not, we cannot say that it was irrational. We therefore conclude that the spousal notice provision comports with the Constitution....

. . .

JUSTICE SCALIA, with whom THE CHIEF JUSTICE, JUSTICE WHITE, and JUSTICE THOMAS join, concurring in the judgment in part and dissenting in part.

... The States may, if they wish, permit abortion-on-demand, but the Constitution does not require them to do so. The permissibility of abortion, and the limitations upon it, are to be resolved like most important questions in our democracy: by citizens trying to persuade one another and then voting....

... I reach that conclusion not because of anything so exalted as my views concerning the "concept of existence, of meaning, of the universe, and of the mystery of human life." Rather, I reach it ... because of two simple facts: (1) the Constitution says absolutely nothing about it, and (2) the longstanding traditions of American society have permitted it to be legally proscribed....

. . .

To the extent I can discern any meaningful content in the "undue burden" standard as applied in the joint opinion, it appears to be that a State may not regulate abortion in such a way as to reduce significantly its incidence.... Thus, despite flowery rhetoric about the State's "substantial" and "profound" interest in "potential human life," and criticism of Roe for undervaluing that interest, the joint opinion permits the State to pursue that interest only so long as it is not too successful....

. . .

The Court's description of the place of *Roe* in the social history of the United States is unrecognizable. Not only did *Roe* not, as the Court suggests, resolve the deeply divisive issue of abortion; it did more than anything else to nourish it, by elevating it to the national level where it is infinitely more difficult to resolve. National politics were not plagued by abortion protests, national abortion lobbying, or abortion marches on Congress, before Roe v. Wade was decided. Profound disagreement existed among our citizens over the issue—as it does over other issues, such as the death penalty—but that disagreement was being worked out at the state level. As with many other issues, the division of sentiment within each State was not as closely balanced as it was among the population of the Nation as a whole, meaning not only that more people would be satisfied with the results of state-by-state resolution, but also that those results would be more stable. Pre–*Roe*, moreover, political compromise was possible.

Roe's mandate for abortion-on-demand destroyed the compromises of the past, rendered compromise impossible for the future, and required the entire issue to be resolved uniformly, at the national level. At the same time, *Roe* created a vast new class of abortion consumers and abortion proponents by eliminating the moral opprobrium that had attached to the act. ("If the Constitution guarantees abortion, how can it be bad?"—not an accurate line of thought, but a natural one.) Many favor all of those developments, and it is not for me to say that they are wrong. But to portray *Roe* as the statesmanlike "settlement" of a divisive issue, a jurisprudential Peace of Westphalia that is worth preserving, is nothing less than Orwellian. *Roe* fanned into life an issue that has inflamed our national politics in general, and has obscured with its smoke the selection of Justices to this Court in particular, ever since. . . .

. . .

. . . I am as distressed as the Court is . . . about the "political pressure" directed to the Court: the marches, the mail, the protests aimed at inducing us to change our opinions. How upsetting it is, that so many of our citizens . . . think that we Justices should properly take into account their views, as though we were engaged not in ascertaining an objective law but in determining some kind of social consensus. The Court would profit, I think, from giving less attention to the fact of this distressing phenomenon, and more attention to the cause of it. That cause permeates today's opinion: a new mode of constitutional adjudication that relies not upon text and traditional practice to determine the law, but upon what the Court calls "reasoned judgment," which turns out to be nothing but philosophical predilection and moral intuition. All manner of "liberties," the Court tells us, inhere in the Constitution and are enforceable by this Court—not just those mentioned in the text or established in the traditions of our society. . . .

What makes all this relevant to the bothersome application of "political pressure" against the Court are the twin facts that the American people love democracy and the American people are not fools. As long as this Court thought (and the people thought) that we Justices were doing essentially lawyers' work up here—reading text and discerning our society's traditional understanding of that text—the public pretty much left us alone. Texts and traditions are facts to study, not convictions to demonstrate about. But if in reality our process of constitutional adjudication consists primarily of making value judgments; if we can ignore a long and clear tradition clarifying an ambiguous text, . . . if . . . our pronouncement of constitutional law rests primarily on value judgments, then a free and intelligent people's attitude towards us can be expected to be (ought to be) quite different. The people know that their value judgments are quite as good as those taught in any law school—maybe better. If, indeed, the "liberties" protected by the Constitution are, as the Court says, undefined and unbounded, then the people should demonstrate, to protest that we do not implement their values instead of ours. Not only that, but confirmation hearings for new

Justices should deteriorate into question-and-answer sessions in which
Senators go through a list of their constituents' most favored and most
disfavored alleged constitutional rights, and seek the nominee's commitment to support or oppose them. Value judgments, after all, should be
voted on, not dictated; and if our Constitution has somehow accidently
committed them to the Supreme Court, at least we can have a sort of
plebiscite each time a new nominee to that body is put forward. Justice
Blackmun not only regards this prospect with equanimity, he solicits it.

. . .

JUSTICE KENNEDY CROSSES THE RUBICON IN CASEY

On December 13, 1992, David G. Savage published an article on the
front page of the *Los Angeles Times* that discussed the Supreme Court's
decision-making process in *Casey*. According to Savage, the case turned
on Justice Kennedy's vote. The following chronology tells the tale:

January 21, 1992: The Supreme Court agreed to hear Planned
Parenthood of Southeastern Pennsylvania v. Casey, announcing that it
would focus on Pennsylvania's abortion regulations, not on overruling
Roe v. Wade.

April 22, 1992: During oral argument in *Casey*, Solicitor General
Kenneth Starr urged the Court to adopt a rational-relation test for
abortion statutes, which in effect would overrule Roe v. Wade. Questions
by Justices O'Connor and Kennedy indicated that they hoped that *Casey*
might be decided on narrow grounds. Justice Kennedy said that he
thought it would be better for the Court to proceed on a "case-by-case
basis."

April 24, 1992: The views expressed in conference that day by most
of the justices were predictable. Chief Justice Rehnquist and Justices
White and Scalia wanted to overrule Roe v. Wade; Justices Blackmun
and Stevens strongly supported the precedent. Clarence Thomas, the
newest justice, joined Rehnquist, White, and Scalia in voting to uphold
the Pennsylvania regulations. "O'Connor," Savage reported, "was troubled by the provision requiring women to notify their husbands. Certainly most women would do that, but what about an abused and battered
wife? And since when can the government tell married couples what they
must decide? In her view, this provision should be struck down because
it put an undue burden on some women." Justice Souter surprised some
of his colleagues by insisting that the right to abortion be preserved on
grounds of precedent and protection of individual "liberty." "Kennedy,"
wrote Savage, "indicated that he was not prepared to overturn Roe v.
Wade, but the Pennsylvania provisions seemed to be reasonable regulations. He voted to uphold them." So Chief Justice Rehnquist, being in
the majority, would assign the opinion, and he assigned it to himself.

April 26–mid-May, 1992: Early in this period, Justice Kennedy
called on Justice Blackmun in his chambers. To Blackmun, Kennedy
appeared to be going through some "soul searching" in *Casey*. "Still,
Blackmun remained gloomy," reported Savage. "Often Kennedy had
seemed agonized, but in the end, he sided with Rehnquist." But this
time, he would go his own way. Making up his mind in the middle of

May, Justice Kennedy told Justices O'Connor and Souter that he would join them in affirming the core holding of Roe v. Wade. The three then agreed to write a joint opinion, which would be the Court's opinion, for Justices Blackmun and Stevens were sure to join in its essential conclusion. Savage described the efforts of Justices O'Connor, Kennedy, and Souter as follows:

> Souter sat up evenings writing draft after draft on a legal pad. He wanted to stress that the "legitimacy" of the Court depended on the adherence to precedent.

> Kennedy worked at his Virginia home and spelled out an expansive view of "liberty" complete with citations from John Marshall Harlan. "It is the promise of the Constitution that there is a realm of personal liberty which the government may not enter," he wrote.

> O'Connor spelled out her views of women's rights and said that the states may not place any "substantial obstacle in the path of a woman seeking abortions."

Their joint effort, which ran 60 pages, stunned some of their colleagues, and even the law clerks were amazed by the sudden shift of the Court's decision.

June 27, 1992: It was opinion day in *Casey.* Justice Kennedy had invited a reporter from the *California Lawyer* to his chambers for an interview earlier that morning. Looking out the large window of his office at the activists in the plaza waiting for word of the Court's decision in *Casey,* Kennedy said, "Sometimes you don't know if you're Caesar about to cross the Rubicon or Captain Queeg cutting your own tow line. But only history can tell." Approximately 20 minutes later, the Court announced its decision and opinions in *Casey.*

NOTES

1. The reaffirmation of Roe v. Wade—albeit with a rejection of the trimester approach and its replacement with a less demanding "undue burden" standard—was a surprise. In her dissenting opinion in City of Akron v. Akron Center for Reproductive Health, Inc., 462 U.S. 416 (1983), Justice O'Connor had criticized the trimester approach and argued for an undue burden standard. She argued that a state's interest in potential life was "compelling" throughout pregnancy and criticized viability as the criterion for allowing states to forbid abortion. That suggested that she would sustain at least some restrictions on abortion itself, even before viability. Moreover, she said that any restriction on abortion should be valid so long as it did not "infringe substantially" or "heavily burden" abortion. (Justices Rehnquist and White, dissenters here, joined her opinion!) The joint opinion of Justices O'Connor, Kennedy and Souter makes it clear that a State cannot prohibit abortion itself prior to viability, and cannot place a "substantial obstacle in the path of a woman seeking an abortion of a nonviable fetus."

In Webster v. Reproductive Health Services, 492 U.S. 490 (1989), Justice Kennedy joined an opinion of Chief Justice Rehnquist that stopped short of arguing that Roe v. Wade should be overruled, but said that "the goal of constitutional adjudication is surely not to remove 'inexorably divisive' issues from the ambit of the legislative process, whereby the people through their elected representatives deal with matters of concern to them."

In a number of cases decided in June of 1992, Justices O'Connor, Kennedy and Souter formed a moderate bloc, rejecting arguments for major changes in constitutional law. See, for example, Lee v. Weisman, 505 U.S. 577 (1992), page 696, above.

2. While the current members of the Court sit, the "undue burden" standard will control the question whether obstacles to abortion imposed by state law will be sustained. Although the standard is rejected by five members of the Court, the three center justices can form a majority with either the four justices to their right or the two justices to their left. One can predict that abortion restrictions that have been upheld in previous cases will be sustained, but it is hard to make predictions about restrictions that have been invalidated or untested in the past. Moreover, there is the possibility, left open by the joint opinion, that some practices it has sustained might be invalid if a trial demonstrates that the restriction is more burdensome in the State where it is challenged. Note, finally, the statement that, in applying the standard, "[e]ven when jurists reason from shared premises, some disagreement is inevitable." Likely, if any one justice in the middle believes a burden on abortion is not "undue," that justice will form a majority with the four dissenting justices.

3. In Stenberg v. Carhart, 530 U.S. 914 (2000), a bare majority of five—Stevens, O'Connor, Souter, Ginsburg, and Breyer—declared unconstitutional Nebraska's partial-birth abortion statute. Writing for the majority, Justice Breyer applied three principles established in *Casey*: (1) before "viability . . . the woman has a right to choose to terminate her pregnancy"; (2) "a law designed to further the State's interest in fetal life which imposes an undue burden on the woman's decision before viability" is unconstitutional; and (3) "subsequent to viability, the State in promoting its interest in the potentiality of human life may, if it chooses, regulate, and even proscribe, abortion except where it is necessary, in appropriate medical judgment, for the preservation of the life or health of the mother." The Nebraska statute, wrote Breyer, contravened *Casey's* second and third principles.

4. There was much anticipation among pro-life activists in early 2006 when the Supreme Court granted certiorari to decide *Ayotte v. Planned Parenthood*, a case challenging a provision of New Hampshire law requiring that minors who want an abortion first attain parental notification–unlike in many other states, New Hampshire law did not explicitly provide for an exception due to a "medical emergency." Yet rather than deciding the issue on the merits, in *Ayotte v. Planned Parenthood*, ___ U.S. ___, 126 S.Ct. 961 (2006), Justice Sandra Day O'Connor, writing for a unanimous Court, ordered that the case be remanded to the district court to consider whether it could invalidate only that one provision of the law, consistent with the intent of the New Hampshire legislature. The Court thus ducked the larger issue of wheth-

er such a medical emergency exception was even necessary in the first place. This would be Justice O'Connor's final Supreme Court opinion— the possible reconsideration of *Casey* would have to wait for the arrival of Justice O'Connor's successor to the Court, Justice Samuel Alito.

SAMUEL A. ALITO, Jr.—Born April 1, 1950, in San Francisco, California, son of two schoolteachers. Republican. Roman Catholic. Princeton, A.B. 1972; J.D., Yale, 1975. Assistant U.S. Attorney, District of N.J., 1977–1981; Assistant to the Solicitor General, 1981–85; Deputy Assistant to U.S. Attorney General Edwin Meese, 1985–87; U.S. Attorney, District of New Jersey, 1987–90; U.S. Court of Appeals Judge (3rd Cir.), 1990–2006. Nominated Associate Justice by President George W. Bush on October 31, 2005, to replace Sandra Day O'Connor, who had announced her intention to retire. Confirmed by the Senate on January 31, 2006, by a 58–42 vote.

WASHINGTON v. GLUCKSBERG

Supreme Court of the United States, 1997.
521 U.S. 702, 117 S.Ct. 2258, 138 L.Ed.2d 772.

CHIEF JUSTICE REHNQUIST delivered the opinion of the Court.

The question presented in this case is whether Washington's prohibition against "caus[ing]" or "aid[ing]" a suicide offends the fourteenth Amendment to the United States Constitution. We hold that it does not.

It has always been a crime to assist a suicide in the State of Washington.... Today, Washington law provides: "A person is guilty of promoting a suicide attempt when he knowingly causes or aids another person to attempt suicide," Wash. Rev. Code 9A.36.060(1) (1994). "Promoting a suicide attempt" is a felony, punishable by up to five years' imprisonment and up to a $10,000 fine. §§ 9A.36.060(2) and 9A.20.021(1)(c). At the same time, Washington's Natural Death Act, enacted in 1979, states that the "withholding or withdrawal of life-sustaining treatment" at a patient's direction "shall not, for any purpose, constitute a suicide," Wash. Rev. Code § 70.122.070(1)....

... Respondents ... are physicians who practice in Washington[,] occasionally treat terminally ill, suffering patients, and declare that they would assist these patients in ending their lives if not for Washington's assisted-suicide ban. In January 1994, respondents, along with three gravely ill, pseudonymous plaintiffs who have since died and Compassion in Dying, a nonprofit organization that counsels people considering physician-assisted suicide, sued in the United States District Court, seeking a declaration that Wash. Rev. Code 9A.36.060(1) (1994) is, on its face, unconstitutional....

The plaintiffs asserted "the existence of a liberty interest protected by the Fourteenth Amendment which extends to a personal choice by a mentally competent, terminally ill adult to commit physician-assisted suicide," ... Relying primarily on Planned Parenthood v. Casey, 505 U.S. 833 (1992), and Cruzan v. Director, Missouri Dept. Of Health, 497 U.S. 261 (1990), the District Court agreed ... and concluded that Washington's assisted-suicide ban is unconstitutional because it "places an undue burden on the exercise of [that] constitutionally protected liberty interest," ...

The Ninth Circuit ... en banc ... affirmed ...[,] conclud[ing] that "the Constitution encompasses a due process liberty interest in controlling the time and manner of one's death—that there is, in short, a constitutionally-recognized 'right to die.' " ... After "[w]eighing and then balancing" this interest against Washington's various interests, the court held that the State's assisted-suicide ban was unconstitutional "as applied to terminally ill competent adults who wish to hasten their deaths with medication prescribed by their physicians." We ... reverse.

I

We begin, as we do in all due-process cases, by examining our Nation's history, legal traditions, and practices. See, e.g., Casey, 505 U.S., at 849–850; Cruzan, 497 U.S., at 269–279; Moore v. East Cleveland, 431 U.S. 494, 503 (1977) (plurality opinion) (noting importance of "careful 'respect for the teachings of history' "). In almost every State— indeed, in almost every western democracy—it is a crime to assist a suicide. The States' assisted-suicide bans are not innovations. Rather, they are longstanding expressions of the States' commitment to the protection and preservation of all human life.... Indeed, opposition to and condemnation of suicide—and, therefore, of assisting suicide—are consistent and enduring themes of our philosophical, legal, and cultural heritages. See generally ... New York State Task Force on Life and the Law, When Death is Sought: Assisted Suicide and Euthanasia in the Medical Context 77–82 (May 1994) (hereinafter New York Task Force).

More specifically, for over 700 years, the Anglo–American common-law tradition has punished or otherwise disapproved of both suicide and assisting suicide.... [As of] the 13th century, ... "[t]he principle that suicide of a sane person, for whatever reason, was a punishable felony was ... introduced into English common law." ... Blackstone emphasized that "the law has ... ranked [suicide] among the highest crimes," ... although, anticipating later developments, he conceded that the harsh and shameful punishments imposed for suicide "borde[r] a little upon severity." ...

For the most part, the early American colonies adopted the common-law approach....

Over time, however, the American colonies abolished the harsh common-law penalties [of criminal forfeiture] ...

[H]owever, ... the movement away from the common law's harsh sanctions did not represent an acceptance of suicide; rather, ... this change reflected the growing consensus that it was unfair to punish the suicide's family for his wrongdoing.... Nonetheless, ... courts continued to condemn it as a grave public wrong....

That suicide remained a grievous, though nonfelonious, wrong is confirmed by the fact that colonial and early state legislatures and courts did not retreat from prohibiting assisting suicide.... And the prohibitions against assisting suicide never contained exceptions for those who were near death....

The earliest American statute explicitly to outlaw assisting suicide was enacted in New York in 1828, ... and many of the new States and Territories followed New York's example.... By the time the Fourteenth Amendment was ratified, it was a crime in most States to assist a suicide.... In this century, the Model Penal Code also prohibited "aiding" suicide, prompting many States to enact or revise their assisted-suicide bans. The Code's drafters observed that "the interests in the sanctity of life that are represented by the criminal homicide laws are threatened by one who expresses a willingness to participate in taking the life of another, even though the act may be accomplished with the consent, or at the request, of the suicide victim." American Law Institute, Model Penal Code § 210.5, p. 100 (Official Draft and Revised Comments 1980).

Though deeply rooted, the States' assisted-suicide bans have in recent years been reexamined and, generally, reaffirmed. Because of advances in medicine and technology, Americans today are increasingly likely to die in institutions, from chronic illnesses.... Public concern and democratic action are therefore sharply focused on how best to protect dignity and independence at the end of life, with the results there have been many significant changes in state laws and in the attitudes these laws reflect. Many States, for example, now permit "living wills," surrogate health-care decisionmaking, and the withdrawal or refusal of life-sustaining medical treatment.... At the same time, however, voters and legislators continue for the most part to reaffirm their States' prohibitions on assisting suicide.

The Washington statute at issue in this case ... was enacted in 1975 as part of a revision of that State's criminal code. Four years later, Washington passed its Natural Death Act, which specifically stated that the "withholding or withdrawal of life-sustaining treatment ... shall not, for any purpose, constitute a suicide" and "[n]othing in this chapter shall be construed to condone, authorize, or approve mercy killing...."
... In 1991, Washington voters rejected a ballot initiative which, had it passed, would have permitted a form of physician-assisted suicide. Washington then added a provision to the Natural Death Act expressly excluding physician-assisted suicide....

California voters rejected an assisted-suicide initiative similar to Washington's in 1993. On the other hand, in 1994, voters in Oregon enacted, also through ballot initiative, that State's "Death With Dignity Act," which legalized physician-assisted suicide for competent, terminally ill adults. Since the Oregon vote, many proposals to legalize assisted-suicide have been and continue to be introduced in the States' legislatures, but none has been enacted. And just last year, Iowa and Rhode Island joined the overwhelming majority of States explicitly prohibiting assisted suicide.... Also, on April 30, 1997, President Clinton signed the

Federal Assisted Suicide Funding Restriction Act of 1997, which prohibited the use of federal funds in support of physician-assisted suicide. . . .

Thus, the states are currently engaged in serious, thoughtful examinations of physician-assisted suicide and other similar issues. For example, New York State's Task Force on Life and Law—an ongoing, blue-ribbon commission composed of doctors, ethicists, lawyers, religious leaders, and interested laymen—was formed in 1984 and commissioned with "a broad mandate to recommend public policy on issues raised by medical advances." . . . After studying physician-assisted suicide, however, the Task Force unanimously concluded that "[T]he potential dangers of this dramatic change in public policy would outweigh any benefit that might be achieved." . . .

Attitudes toward suicide itself have changed since Bracton, but our laws have consistently condemned, and continue to prohibit, assisting suicide. Despite changes in medical technology and notwithstanding an increased emphasis on the importance of end-of-life decisionmaking, we have not retreated from this prohibition. Against this backdrop of history, tradition, and practice, we now turn to respondents' constitutional claim.

II

The Due Process Clause guarantees more than fair process, and the "Liberty" it protects includes more than the absence of physical restraint. . . . The Clause also provides heightened protection against government interference with certain fundamental rights and liberty interests. . . . We have also assumed, and strongly suggested, that the Due Process Clause protects the traditional right to refuse unwanted lifesaving medical treatment. *Cruzan*, 497 U.S., at 278–279.

But we "ha[ve] always been reluctant to expand the concept of substantive due process because guideposts for responsible decisionmaking in this unchartered area are scarce and open-ended." . . . By extending constitutional protection to an asserted right or liberty interest, we, to a great extent, place the matter outside the arena of public debate and legislative action. We must therefore "exercise the utmost care whenever we are asked to break new ground in this field," . . . lest the liberty protected by the Due Process Clause be subtly transformed into the policy preferences of the members of this Court, *Moore*, 431 U.S., at 502 (plurality opinion).

Our established method of substantive-due-process analysis has two primary features: First, we have regularly observed that the Due Process Clause specially protects those fundamental rights and liberties which are, objectively, "deeply rooted in this Nation's history and tradition," id., at 503 (plurality opinion), Snyder v. Massachusetts, 291 U.S. 97, 105 (1934) ("so rooted in the traditions and conscience of our people as to be ranked as fundamental"), and "implicit in the concept of ordered liberty," such that "neither liberty nor justice would exist if they were sacrificed." Palko v. Connecticut, 302 U.S. 319, 325, 326 (1937). Second, we have required in substantive-due-process cases a "careful description" of the asserted fundamental liberty interest. . . . Our Nation's history, legal traditions, and practices thus provide the crucial "guide-posts for responsible decisionmaking," that direct and restrain our exposition of the Due Process Clause. . . .

Justice Souter, relying on Justice Harlan's dissenting opinion in *Poe v. Ullman*, would largely abandon this restrained methodology, and instead ask "whether [Washington's] statute sets up one of those 'arbi-trary impositions' or 'purposeless restraints' at odds with the Due Process Clause of the Fourteenth Amendment" (quoting Poe, 367 U.S. 497, 543 (1961) (Harlan, J., dissenting)). In our view, however, the development of this Court's substantive-due-process jurisprudence . . . has been a process whereby the outlines of the "liberty" specially protected by the Fourteenth Amendment—never fully clarified, to be sure, and perhaps not capable of being fully clarified—have at least been carefully refined by concrete examples involving fundamental rights found to be deeply rooted in our legal tradition. This approach tends to rein in the subjective elements that are necessarily present in due-process judicial review. In addition, by establishing a threshold require-ment—that a challenged state action implicate a fundamental right—before requiring more than a reasonable relation to a legitimate state interest to justify the action, it avoids the need for complex balancing of competing interests in every case.

. . . [W]e have a tradition of carefully formulating the interest at stake in the substantive-due-process cases. For example, although *Cru-zan* is often described as a "right to die" case, . . . we were, in fact, more precise: we assumed that the constitution granted competent persons a "constitutionally protected right to refuse lifesaving hydration and nutri-tion." . . . The Washington statute at issue in this case prohibits "aid[ing] another person to attempt suicide," . . . and, thus, the question before us is whether the "liberty" specially protected by the Due Process Clause includes a right to commit suicide which itself includes a right to assistance in doing so.

Respondents contend, however, that the liberty interest they assert is consistent with this Court's substantive-due-process line of cases, if not, with this Nation's history and practice. Pointing to *Casey* and *Cruzan* respondents read our jurisprudence in this area as reflecting a general tradition of "self-sovereignty," . . . and as teaching that the "liberty" protected by the Due Process Clause includes "basic and intimate exercises of personal autonomy,". . . . According to respondents, our liberty jurisprudence, and the broad individualistic principles it reflects, protects the "liberty of competent, terminally ill adults to make end-of-life decisions free of undue government interference." . . . The question presented in this case, however, is whether the protections of the Due Process Clause include a right to commit suicide with another's assistance. With this "careful description" of respondents' claim in mind, we turn to *Casey* and *Cruzan*.

In *Cruzan*, we considered whether Nancy Beth Cruzan, who had been severely injured in an automobile accident and was in a persistive vegetative state, "ha[d] a right under the United States Constitution which would require the hospital to withdraw life-sustaining treatment"

at her parents' request.... We began with the observation that "[a]t
common law, even the touching of one person by another without
consent and without legal justification was a battery." ... We then
discussed the related rule that "informed consent is generally required
for medical treatment." ... Nest, we reviewed our own cases on the
subject, and stated that "[t]he principle that a competent person has a
constitutionally protected liberty interest in refusing unwanted medical
treatment may be inferred from our prior decisions." ... We concluded
that, notwithstanding this right, the Constitution permitted Missouri to
require clear and convincing evidence of an incompetent patient's wishes
concerning the withdrawal of life-sustaining treatment....

Respondents contend that in *Cruzan* we "acknowledged that competent, dying persons have the right to direct the removal of life-sustaining
medical treatment and thus hasten death," ... and that "the constitutional principle behind recognizing the patient's liberty to direct the
withdrawal of artificial life support applies at least as strongly to the
choice to hasten impending death by consuming lethal medication,"....
Similarly, the Court of Appeals concluded that "Cruzan, by recognizing a
liberty interest that includes the refusal of artificial provisions of life-
sustaining food and water, necessarily recogniz[d] a liberty interest in
hastening one's own death" ...

The right assumed in *Cruzan,* however, was not simply deduced
from abstract concepts of personal autonomy. Given the common-law
rule that forced medication was a battery, and the long legal tradition
protecting the decision to refuse unwanted medical treatment, our
assumption was entirely consistent with this Nation's history and constitutional traditions. The decision to commit suicide with the assistance of
another may be just as personal and profound as the decision to refuse
unwanted medical treatment, but it has never enjoyed similar legal
protection. Indeed the two acts are widely and reasonably regarded as
quite distinct. See Quill v. Vacco....* In *Cruzan* itself, we recognized

---

* In *Quill*, decided with *Glucksberg*, the Court reversed a decision of the Second Circuit
of Appeals holding that New York's prohibition on assisted suicide violated the Equal
Protection Clause insofar as it prevented prescribing lethal medication for mentally
competent, terminally ill patients, because New York law allowed such patients to refuse
life-sustaining medical treatment, and the distinction was "not rationally related to any
legitimate state interest." Chief Justice Rehnquist's majority opinion concluded that "the
distinction between assisting suicide and withdrawing life-sustaining treatment, a distinction widely recognized and endorsed in the medical profession and in our legal traditions, is
both important and logical; it is certainly rational." The Chief Justice continued:

"The distinction comports with fundamental legal principles of causation and intent.
First, when a patient refuses life-sustaining medical treatment, he dies from an
underlying fatal disease or pathology; but if a patient ingests lethal medication
prescriped by a physician, he is killed by that medication....

"Furthermore, a physician who withdraws, or honors a patient's refusal to begin, life-
sustaining medical treatment purposefully intends, or may so intend, only to respect
his patient's wishes and 'to cease doing useless and futile or degrading things to the
patient when [the patient] no longer stands to benefit from them.' ... The same is
true when a doctor provides aggressive palliative care; in some cases, painkilling drugs
may hasten a patient's death, but the physician's purpose and intent is, or may be,
only to ease his patient's pain. A doctor who assists a suicide, however, 'must,
necessarily and indubitably, intend primarily that the patient be made dead." ...
Similarly, a patient who commits suicide with a doctor's aid necessarily has the specific
intent to end his or her own life, while a patient who refuses or discontinues treatment
might not....

that most States outlawed assisted suicide—and even more do today—
and we certainly gave no intimation that the right to refuse unwanted
medical treatment could be somehow transmuted in a right to assistance
in committing suicide. . . .

Respondents also rely on *Casey*. . . .

The Court of Appeals, like the District Court, found *Casey* " 'highly
instructive' " and " 'almost prescriptive' " for determining " 'what liberty interest may inhere in a terminally ill person's choice to commit
suicide' ":

> "Like the decision of whether or not to have an abortion, the
> decision how and when to die is one of 'the most intimate and
> personal choices a person may make in a lifetime,' a choice
> 'central to personal dignity and autonomy.' " . . .

Similarly, respondents emphasize the statement in *Casey* that:

> "At the heart of liberty is the right to define one's own concept
> of existence, of meaning, of the universe, and of the mystery of
> human life. Beliefs about these matters could not define the
> attributes of personhood were they formed under compulsion of
> the State," . . .

"The law has long used actors' intent or purpose to distinguish between two acts that
may have the same result. . . . Put differently, the law distinguishes actions taken
'because of' a given end from actions taken 'in spite of' their unintended but foreseen
consequences. . . .

"Given these general principles, it is not surprising that many courts, including New
York courts, have carefully distinguished refusing life-sustaining treatment from
suicide. . . .

"Similarly, the overwhelming majority of state legislatures have drawn a clear line
between assisting suicide and withdrawing or permitting the refusal of unwanted
lifesaving medical treatment by prohibiting the former and permitting the latter. . . .

" . . .

"This Court has also recognized, at least implicitly, the distinction between letting a
patient die and making that patient die. In [*Cruzan*], . . . our assumption of a right to
refuse treatment was grounded not, as the Court of Appeals supposed, on the
proposition that patients have a general and abstract 'right to hasten death,' but on
well established, traditional rights to bodily integrity and freedom from unwanted
touching. . . . *Cruzan* therefore provides no support for the notion that refusing life-
sustaining medical treatment is 'nothing more nor less than suicide.'

" . . . Logic and contemporary practice support New York's judgment that the two acts
are different, and New York may therefore, consistent with the Constitution, treat
them differently. . . .

"New York's reasons for recognizing and acting on this distinction . . . are discussed in
greater detail in our opinion in *Glucksberg* [and] easily satisfy the constitutional
requirement that a legislative classification bear a rational relation to some legitimate
end."

Each of the concurring opinions in *Glucksberg* also applied to this case, except that
Justice Souter here said this:

"Even though I do not conclude that assisted suicide is a fundamental right entitled to
recognition at this time, I accord the claims raised by the patients and physicians in this
case and Washington v. Glucksberg (Souter, J., concurring in judgment). The reasons
that lead me to conclude in *Glucksberg* that the prohibition on assisted suicide is not
arbitrary under the due process standard also supports the distinction between assistance to suicide, which is banned, and practices such as termination of artificial life
support and death-hastening pain medication, which are permitted. I accordingly concur
in the judgment of the Court."

By choosing this language, the Court's opinion in *Casey* described, in a general way and in light of our prior cases, those personal activities and decisions that this Court has identified as so deeply rooted in our history and traditions, or so fundamental to our concept of constitutionally ordered liberty, that they are protected by the Fourteenth Amendment.... That many of the rights and liberties protected by the Due Process Clause sound in personal autonomy does not warrant the sweeping conclusion that any and all important, intimate, and personal decisions are so protected, ... and *Casey* did not suggest otherwise.

The history of the law's treatment of assisted suicide in this country has been and continues to be one of the rejection of nearly all efforts to permit it. That being the case, our decisions lead us to conclude that the asserted "right" to assistance in committing suicide is not a fundamental liberty interest protected by the Due Process Clause. The Constitution also requires, however, that Washington's assisted-suicide ban be rationally related to legitimate government interest.... This requirement is unquestionably met here....

First, Washington has an "unqualified interest in the preservation of human life." Cruzan, 497 U.S., at 282. The State's prohibition on assisted suicide, like all homicide laws, both reflects and advances its commitment to this interest....

... The Court of Appeals ... held that the "weight" of this interest depends on the "medical condition and the wishes of the person whose life is at stake," ... Washington, however, ... insisted that all persons' lives, from beginning to end, regardless of physical or mental condition, are under the full protection of the law.... As we have previously affirmed the States "may properly decline to make judgments about the 'quality' of life that a particular individual may enjoy," Cruzan, 497 U.S., at 282. This remains true, as *Cruzan* makes clear, even for those who are near death.

Relatedly, all admit that suicide is a serious public-health problem, especially among persons in otherwise vulnerable groups....

Those who attempt suicide—terminally ill or not—often suffer from depression or other mental disorders.... Research indicates, however, that many people who request physician-assisted suicide withdraw that request if their depression and pain are treated. H. Hendin, Seduced by Death: Doctors, Patients and the Dutch Cure 24–25 (1997) (suicidal, terminally ill patients "usually respond well to treatment for depressive illness and pain medication and are then grateful to be alive"); New York Task Force 177–178. The New York Task Force, however, expressed its concern that, because depression is difficult to diagnose, physicians and medical professionals often fail to respond adequately to seriously ill patients' needs. Id., at 175. Thus, legal physician-assisted suicide could make it more difficult for the State to protect depressed or mentally ill persons, or those who are suffering from untreated pain, from suicidal impulses.

The State also has an interest in protecting the integrity and ethics of the medical profession.... [T]he American Medical Association, like many other medical and physicians' groups, has concluded that "[p]hysician-assisted suicide is fundamentally incompatible with the physician's role as healer." ... And physician-assisted suicide could, it is argued, undermine the trust that is essential to the doctor-patient relationship by blurring the time-honored line between healing and harming....

Next, the State has an interest in protecting vulnerable groups—including the poor, the elderly, and disabled persons—from abuse, neglect, and mistakes.... We have recognized ... the real risk of subtle coercion and undue influence in end-of-life situations. *Cruzan*, 497 U.S., at 281.... If physician-assisted suicide were permitted, many might resort to it to spare their families the substantial financial burden of end-of-life health-care costs.

The State's interest here goes beyond protecting the vulnerable from coercion; it extends to protecting disabled and terminally ill people from prejudice, negative and inaccurate stereotypes, and "societal indifference." ... The State's assisted-suicide ban reflects and reinforces its policy that the lives of terminally ill, disabled, and elderly people must be no less valued than the lives of the young and healthy, and that a seriously disabled person's suicidal impulses should be interpreted and treated the same way as anyone else's....

Finally, the State may fear that permitting assisted suicide will start it down the path to voluntary and perhaps even involuntary euthanasia. The Court of Appeals struck down Washington's assisted-suicide ban only "as applied to competent, terminally ill adults who wish to hasten their deaths by obtaining medication prescribed by their doctors." ... Washington insists, however, that the impact of the court's decision will not and cannot be so limited.... The Court of Appeals' decision, and its expansive reasoning, provide ample support for the State's concerns. The court noted, for example, that the "decision of a duly appointed surrogate decision maker is for all legal purposes the decision of the patient himself," ...; that "in some instances, the patient may be unable to self-administer the drugs and ... administration by the physician ... may be the only way the patient may be able to receive them," ...; and that not only physicians, but also family members and loved ones, will inevitably participate in assisting suicide.... Thus, it turns out that what is couched as a limited right to "physician-assisted suicide" is likely, in effect, a much broader license, which could prove extremely difficult to police and contain. Washington's ban on assisting suicide prevents such erosion.

This concern is further supported by evidence about the practice of euthanasia in the Netherlands ... suggest[ing] that, despite the existence of various reporting procedures, euthanasia in the Netherlands has not been limited to competent, terminally ill adults who are enduring physical suffering, and that regulation of the practice may not have prevented abuses in cases involving vulnerable persons, including severely disabled neonates and elderly persons suffering from dementia.... Washington, like most other States, reasonably ensures against this risk by banning, rather than regulating, assisting suicide....

We need not weigh exactly the relative strengths of these various interests. They are unquestionably important and legitimate, and Washington's ban on assisted suicide is at least reasonably related to their promotion and protection. We therefore hold that Wash. Rev. Code § 9A.36.060(1) (1994) does not violate the Fourteenth Amendment, either on its face or "as applied to competent, terminally ill adults who wish to hasten their deaths by obtaining medication prescribed by their doctors." . . .*

.   .   .

Throughout the Nation, Americans are engaged in an earnest and profound debate about the morality, legality, and practicality of physician-assisted suicide. Our holding permits this debate to continue, as it should in a democratic society. . . .

JUSTICE O'CONNOR, concurring.

.   .   .

. . . I join the Court's opinions because I agree that there is no generalized right to "commit suicide." But respondents urge us to address the narrower question whether a mentally competent person who is experiencing great suffering has a constitutionally cognizable interest in controlling the circumstances of his or her imminent death. I see no need to reach that question in the context of the facial challenges to the New York and Washington laws at issue here. . . . The parties and *amici* agree that in these States a patient who is suffering from a terminal illness and who is experiencing great pain has no legal barriers to obtaining medication, from qualified physicians, to alleviate that suffering, even to the point of causing unconsciousness and hastening death. . . . In this light, even assuming that we would recognize such an interest, I agree that the State's interests in protecting those who are not truly competent or facing imminent death, or those whose decisions to hasten death would not truly be voluntary, are sufficiently weighty to justify a prohibition against physician-assisted suicide.

Every one of us at some point may be affected by our own or a family member's terminal illness. There is no reason to think the democratic process will not strike the proper balance between the interests of terminally ill, mentally competent individuals who would seek to end their suffering and the State's interests in protecting those who might seek to end life mistakenly or under pressure. . . .

In sum, there is no need to address the question whether suffering patients have a constitutionally cognizable interest in obtaining relief from the suffering that they may experience in the last days of their lives. There is no dispute that dying patients in Washington and New York can obtain palliative care, even when doing so would hasten their

---

* . . . We emphasize that we today reject the Court of Appeals' specific holding that the statute is unconstitutional "as applied" to a particular class. . . . Justice Stevens agrees with this holding, but would not "foreclose the possibility that an individual plaintiff seeking to hasten her death, or a doctor whose assistance was sought, could prevail in a more particularized challenge." Our opinion does not absolutely foreclose such a claim. However, given our holding that the Due Process Clause of the Fourteenth Amendment does not provide heightened protection to the asserted liberty interest in ending one's life with a physician's assistance, such a claim would have to be quite different from the ones advanced by respondents here.

deaths. The difficulty in defining terminal illness and the risk that a dying patient's request for assistance in ending his or her life might not be truly voluntary justifies the prohibitions on assisted suicide we uphold here.

JUSTICE STEVENS, concurring in the judgments.

. . .

Today, the Court decides that Washington's statute prohibiting assisted suicide is not invalid "on its face," that is to say, in all or most cases in which it might be applied. That holding, however, does not foreclose the possibility that some applications of the statute might well be invalid.

. . .

History and tradition provide ample support for refusing to recognize an open-ended constitutional right to commit suicide. Much more than the State's paternalistic interest in protecting the individual from the irrevocable consequences of an ill-advised decision motivated by temporary concerns is at stake. . . . The State has an interest in preserving and fostering the benefits that every human being may provide to the community—a community that thrives on the exchange of ideas, expressions of affection, shared memories and humorous incidents as well as on the material contributions that its members create and support. The value to others of a person's life is far too precious to allow the individual to claim a constitutional entitlement to complete autonomy in making a decision to end that life. Thus, I fully agree with the Court that the "liberty" protected by the Due Process Clause does not include a categorical "right to commit suicide which itself includes a right to assistance in doing so."

But just as our conclusion that capital punishment is not always unconstitutional did not preclude later decisions holding that it is sometimes impermissibly cruel, so is it equally clear that a decision upholding a general statutory prohibition of assisted suicide does not mean that every possible application of the statute would be valid. . . .

II

In Cruzan v. Director, Mo. Dept. of Health, 497 U.S. 261 (1990), the Court assumed that the interest in liberty protected by the Fourteenth Amendment encompassed the right of a terminally ill patient to direct the withdrawal of life-sustaining treatment. . . . We have recognized, however, that this common-law right to refuse treatment is neither absolute nor always sufficiently weighty to overcome valid countervailing state interests. . . . In most cases, the individual's constitutionally protected interest in his or her own physical autonomy, including the right to refuse unwanted medical treatment, will give way to the State's interest in preserving human life.

Cruzan, however, was not the normal case. . . . When this Court reviewed the case and upheld Missouri's requirement that there be clear and convincing evidence establishing Nancy Cruzan's intent to have life-sustaining nourishment withdrawn, it made two important assumptions:

(1) that there was a "liberty interest" in refusing unwanted treatment protected by the Due Process Clause; and (2) that this liberty interest did not "end the inquiry" because it might be outweighed by relevant state interests.... I agree with both of those assumptions, but I insist that the source of Nancy Cruzan's right to refuse treatment was not just a common-law rule. Rather, this right is an aspect of a far broader and more basic concept of freedom that is even older than the common law. This freedom embraces, not merely a person's right to refuse a particular kind of unwanted treatment, but also her interest in dignity, and in determining the character of the memories that will survive long after her death....

. . .

The *Cruzan* case demonstrated that some state intrusions on the right to decide how death will be encountered are also intolerable. The now-deceased plaintiffs in this action may in fact have had a liberty interest even stronger than Nancy Cruzan's because, not only were they terminally ill, they were suffering constant and severe pain. Avoiding intolerable pain and the indignity of living one's final days incapacitated and in agony is certainly "[a]t the heart of [the] liberty ... to define one's own concept of existence, of meaning, of the universe, and of the mystery of human life." Casey, 505 U.S., at 851.

... *Cruzan* [gave] recognition, not just to vague, unbridled notions of autonomy, but to the more specific interest in making decisions about how to confront an imminent death. Although there is no absolute right to physician-assisted suicide, *Cruzan* makes it clear that some individuals who no longer have the option of deciding whether to live or to die because they are already on the threshold of death have a constitutionally protected interest that may outweigh the State's interest in preserving life at all costs. The liberty interest at stake in a case like this differs from, and is stronger than, both the common-law right to refuse medical treatment and the unbridled interest in deciding whether to live or die. It is an interest in deciding how, rather than whether, a critical threshold shall be crossed.

III

The state interests supporting a general rule banning the practice of physician-assisted suicide do not have the same force in all cases. First and foremost of these interests is the " 'unqualified interest in the preservation of human life,' ".... Properly viewed, however, this interest is not a collective interest that should always outweigh the interests of a person who because of pain, incapacity, or sedation finds her life intolerable, but rather, an aspect of individual freedom.

... Although as a general matter the State's interest in the contributions each person may make to society outweighs the person's interest in ending her life, this interest does not have the same force for a terminally ill patient faced not with the choice of whether to live, only of how to die. Allowing the individual, rather than the State, to make judgments " 'about the "quality" of life that a particular individual may enjoy,' " does not mean that the lives of terminally-ill, disabled people have less value than the lives of those who are healthy. Rather, it gives proper recognition to the individual's interest in choosing a final chapter that accords with her life story, rather than one that demeans her values and poisons memories of her. . . .

. . . I agree that the State has a compelling interest in preventing persons from committing suicide because of depression, or coercion by third parties. But the State's legitimate interest in preventing abuse does not apply to an individual who is not victimized by abuse, who is not suffering from depression, and who makes a rational and voluntary decision to seek assistance in dying. . . . [P]rofessionals expert in working with dying patients can help patients cope with depression and pain, and help patients assess their options. . . .

Relatedly, the State and *amici* express the concern that patients whose physical pain is inadequately treated will be more likely to request assisted suicide. Encouraging the development and ensuring the availability of adequate pain treatment is of utmost importance; palliative care, however, cannot alleviate all pain and suffering. . . . An individual adequately informed of the care alternatives thus might make a rational choice for assisted suicide. For such an individual, the State's interest in preventing potential abuse and mistake is only minimally implicated.

The final major interest asserted by the State is its interest in preserving the traditional integrity of the medical profession. . . . But for some patients, it would be a physician's refusal to dispense medication to ease their suffering and make their death tolerable and dignified that would be inconsistent with the healing role. . . . Furthermore, because physicians are already involved in making decisions that hasten the death of terminally ill patients—through termination of life support, withholding of medical treatment, and terminal sedation—there is in fact significant tension between the traditional view of the physician's role and the actual practice in a growing number of cases.

. . . Although, as the Court concludes today, the[] potential harms are sufficient to support the State's general public policy against assisted suicide, they will not always outweigh the individual liberty interest of a particular patient. . . . I do not . . . foreclose the possibility that an individual plaintiff seeking to hasten her death, or a doctor whose assistance was sought, could prevail in a more particularized challenge. . . .

IV

In New York, a doctor must respect a competent person's decision to refuse or to discontinue medical treatment even though death will thereby ensue, but the same doctor would be guilty of a felony if she provided her patient assistance in committing suicide. Today we hold that the Equal Protection Clause is not violated by the resulting disparate treatment of two classes of terminally ill people who may have the same interest in hastening death. I agree that the distinction between permitting death to ensue from an underlying fatal disease and causing it to occur by the administration of medication or other means provides a constitutionally sufficient basis for the State's classification. Unlike the

Court, however, I am not persuaded that in all cases there will in fact be a significant difference between the intent of the physicians, the patients or the families in the two situations.

There may be little distinction between the intent of a terminally-ill patient who decides to remove her life-support and one who seeks the assistance of a doctor in ending her life; in both situations, the patient is seeking to hasten a certain, impending death. The doctor's intent might also be the same in prescribing lethal medication as it is in terminating life support. A doctor who fails to administer medical treatment to one who is dying from a disease could be doing so with an intent to harm or kill that patient. Conversely, a doctor who prescribes lethal medication does not necessarily intend the patient's death—rather that doctor may seek simply to ease the patient's suffering and to comply with her wishes. The illusory character of any differences in intent or causation is confirmed by the fact that the American Medical Association unequivo- cally endorses the practice of terminal sedation—the administration of sufficient dosages of pain-killing medication to terminally ill patients to protect them from excruciating pain even when it is clear that the time of death will be advanced. The purpose of terminal sedation is to ease the suffering of the patient and comply with her wishes, and the actual cause of death is the administration of heavy doses of lethal sedatives. This same intent and causation may exist when a doctor complies with a patient's request for lethal medication to hasten her death.

Thus, although the differences the majority notes in causation and intent between terminating life-support and assisting in suicide support the Court's rejection of the respondents' facial challenge, these distinc- tions may be inapplicable to particular terminally ill patients and their doctors. Our holding today in Vacco v. Quill that the Equal Protection Clause is not violated by New York's classification, just like our holding in Washington v. Glucksberg that the Washington statute is not invalid on its face, does not foreclose the possibility that some applications of the New York statute may impose an intolerable intrusion on the patient's freedom.

... In my judgment, ... it is clear that the so-called "unqualified interest in the preservation of human life," ... is not itself sufficient to outweigh the interest in liberty that may justify the only possible means of preserving a dying patient's dignity and alleviating her intolerable suffering.

JUSTICE SOUTER, concurring in the judgment.

... The question is whether the statute sets up one of those "arbitrary impositions" or "purposeless restraints" at odds with the Due Process Clause of the Fourteenth Amendment. Poe v. Ullman, 367 U.S. 497, 543 (1961) (Harlan, J., dissenting)....

. . .

... Justice Harlan's *Poe* dissent ... is important for three things that point to our responsibilities today. The first is Justice Harlan's respect for the tradition of substantive due process review itself, and his acknowledgement of the Judiciary's obligation to carry it on.... The text of the Due Process Clause ... imposes nothing less than an obligation to give substantive content to the words "liberty" and "due process of law."

... The second of the dissent's lessons is a reminder that the business of such review is not the identification of extratextual absolutes but scrutiny of a legislative resolution (perhaps unconscious) of clashing principles, each quite possibly worthy in and of itself, but each to be weighed within the history of our values as a people. It is a comparison of the relative strengths of opposing claims that informs the judicial task, not a deduction from some first premise. Thus informed, judicial review still has no warrant to substitute one reasonable resolution of the contending positions for another, but authority to supplant the balance already struck between the contenders only when it falls outside the realm of the reasonable.... [T]he dissent's third [point] takes the form of an object lesson in the explicit attention to detail that is no less essential to the intellectual discipline of substantive due process review than an understanding of the basic need to account for the two sides in the controversy and to respect legislation within the zone of reasonableness.

III

My understanding of unenumerated rights in the wake of the *Poe* dissent and subsequent cases avoids the absolutist failing of many older cases without embracing the opposite pole of equating reasonableness with past practice described at a very specific level. See Planned Parenthood of Southeastern Pa. v. Casey, 505 U.S. 833, 847–849 (1992). That understanding begins with a concept of "ordered liberty," Poe, 367 U.S., at 549 (Harlan, J.); see also Griswold, 381 U.S., at 500, comprising a continuum of rights to be free from "arbitrary impositions and purposeless restraints," Poe, 367 U.S., at 543 (Harlan, J., dissenting).

"Due Process has not been reduced to any formula; its content cannot be determined by reference to any code. The best that can be said is that through the course of this Court's decisions it has represented the balance which our Nation, built upon postulates of respect for the liberty of the individual, has struck between that liberty and the demands of organized society. If the supplying of content to this Constitutional concept has of necessity been a rational process, it certainly has not been one where judges have felt free to roam where unguided speculation might take them. The balance of which I speak is the balance struck by this country, having regard to what history teaches are the traditions from which it developed as well as the traditions from which it broke. That tradition is a living thing. A decision of this Court which radically departs from it could not long survive, while a decision which builds on what has survived is likely to be sound. No formula could serve as a substitute, in this area, for judgment and restraint." Id., at 542....

. . .

This approach calls for a court to assess the relative "weights" or dignities of the contending interests, and to this extent the judicial method is familiar to the common law. Common law method is subject, however, to two important constraints in the hands of a court engaged in substantive due process review. First, such a court is bound to confine the values that it recognizes to those truly deserving constitutional stature, either to those expressed in constitutional text, or those exemplified by "the traditions from which [the Nation] developed," or revealed by contrast with "the traditions from which it broke." ...

[S]econd[,] ... [i]t is no justification for judicial intervention merely to identify a reasonable resolution of contending values that differs from the terms of the legislation under review. It is only when the legislation's justifying principle, critically valued, is so far from being commensurate with the individual interest as to be arbitrarily or pointlessly applied that the statute must give way. Only if this standard points against the statute can the individual claimant be said to have a constitutional right....

The *Poe* dissent ... reminds us that the process of substantive review by reasoned judgment, ... is one of close criticism going to the details of the opposing interests and to their relationships with the historically recognized principles that lend them weight or value.

... Exact analysis and characterization of any due process claim is critical to the method and to the result.

. . .

... [The *Poe* dissent] points to the importance of evaluating the claims of the parties now before us with comparable detail. For here we are faced with an individual claim not to a right on the part of just anyone to help anyone else commit suicide under any circumstances, but to the right of a narrow class to help others also in a narrow class under a set of limited circumstances. And the claimants are met with the State's assertion, among others, that rights of such narrow scope cannot be recognized without jeopardy to individuals whom the State may concededly protect through its regulations.

IV

A

Respondents claim that a patient facing imminent death, who anticipates physical suffering and indignity, and is capable of responsible and voluntary choice, should have a right to a physician's assistance in providing counsel and drugs to be administered by the patient to end life promptly.... They seek the option to obtain the services of a physician to give them the benefit of advice and medical help, which is said to enjoy a tradition so strong and so devoid of specifically countervailing state concern that denial of a physician's help in these circumstances is arbitrary when physicians are generally free to advise and aid those who exercise other rights to bodily autonomy.

. . .

This liberty interest in bodily integrity was phrased in a general way by then-Judge Cardozo when he said, "[e]very human being of adult years and sound mind has a right to determine what shall be done with his own body" in relation to his medical needs. Schloendorff v. Society of New York Hospital, 211 N.Y. 125, 129, 105 N.E. 92, 93 (1914).... Constitutional recognition of the right to bodily integrity underlies the assumed right, good against the State, to require physicians to terminate artificial life support, *Cruzan*, ... and the affirmative right to obtain medical intervention to cause abortion, see *Casey*, supra, at 857, 896; cf. Roe v. Wade, 410 U.S., at 153.

It is, indeed, in the abortion cases that the most telling recognitions of the importance of bodily integrity and the concomitant tradition of medical assistance have occurred. In Roe v. Wade, ... we stressed the importance of the relationship between patient and physician....

The analogies between the abortion cases and this one are several. Even though the State has a legitimate interest in discouraging abortion, ... the Court recognized a woman's right to a physician's counsel and care. Like the decision to commit suicide, the decision to abort potential life can be made irresponsibly and under the influence of others, and yet the Court has held in the abortion cases that physicians are fit assistants. Without physician assistance in abortion, the woman's right would have too often amounted to nothing more than a right to self-mutilation, and without a physician to assist in the suicide of the dying, the patient's right will often be confined to crude methods of causing death, most shocking and painful to the decedent's survivors.

There is, finally, one more reason for claiming that a physician's assistance here would fall within the accepted tradition of medical care in our society, and the abortion cases are only the most obvious illustration of the further point.... [T]he good physician is not just a mechanic of the human body whose services have no bearing on a person's moral choices, but one who does more than treat symptoms, one who ministers to the patient. This idea of the physician as serving the whole person is a source of the high value traditionally placed on the medical relationship. Its value is surely as apparent here as in the abortion cases, for just as the decision about abortion is not directed to correcting some pathology, so the decision in which a dying patient seeks help is not so limited. The patients here sought not only an end to pain (which they might have had, although perhaps at the price of stupor) but an end to their short remaining lives with a dignity that they believed would be denied them by powerful pain medication, as well as by their consciousness of dependency and helplessness as they approached death. In that period when the end is imminent, they said, the decision to end life is closest to decisions that are generally accepted as proper instances of exercising autonomy over one's own body, instances recognized under the Constitution and the State's own law, instances in which the help of physicians is accepted as falling within the traditional norm.

. . .

The argument supporting respondents' position thus progresses through three steps of increasing forcefulness. First, it emphasizes the decriminalization of suicide ... [as one of] society's occasional choices to reject traditions of the legal past. See Poe v. Ullman, 367 U.S., at 542 (Harlan, J., dissenting). [S]econd[,] the State's own act of decriminalization gives a freedom of choice much like the individual's option in recognized instances of bodily autonomy. One of these, abortion, is a legal right to choose in spite of the interest a State may legitimately invoke in discouraging the practice, just as suicide is now subject to choice, despite a state interest in discouraging it. [T]hird[,] ... [r]espondents base their claim on the traditional right to medical care and counsel, subject to the limiting conditions of informed, responsible choice when death is imminent, conditions that support a strong analogy to rights of care in other situations in which medical counsel and assistance have been available as a matter of course. There can be no stronger claim to a physician's assistance than at the time when death is imminent, a moral judgment implied by the State's own recognition of the legitimacy of medical procedures necessarily hastening the moment of impending death.

In my judgment, the importance of the individual interest here, as within that class of "certain interests" demanding careful scrutiny of the State's contrary claim, see Poe, supra, at 543, cannot be gainsaid. Whether that interest might in some circumstances, or at some time, be seen as "fundamental" to the degree entitled to prevail is not, however, a conclusion that I need draw here, for I am satisfied that the State's interests described in the following section are sufficiently serious to defeat the present claim that its law is arbitrary or purposeless.

B

The State has put forward several interests to justify the Washington law as applied to physicians treating terminally ill patients, even those competent to make responsible choices: protecting life generally, ... discouraging suicide even if knowing and voluntary, ... and protecting terminally ill patients from involuntary suicide and euthanasia, both voluntary and nonvoluntary....

[T]he third is dispositive for me. That third justification is different from the first two, for it addresses specific features of respondents' claim, and it opposes that claim not with a moral judgment contrary to respondents', but with a recognized state interest in the protection of nonresponsible individuals and those who do not stand in relation either to death or to their physicians as do the patients whom respondents describe.... [M]istaken decisions may result from inadequate palliative care or a terminal prognosis that turns out to be error; coercion and abuse may stem from the large medical bills that family members cannot bear or unreimbursed hospitals decline to shoulder. Voluntary and involuntary euthanasia may result once doctors are authorized to prescribe lethal medication in the first instance, for they might find it pointless to distinguish between patients who administer their own fatal drugs and those who wish not to, and their compassion for those who suffer may obscure the distinction between those who ask for death and those who may be unable to request it. The argument is that a progression would occur, obscuring the line between the ill and the dying, and between the responsible and the unduly influenced, until ultimately doctors and perhaps others would abuse a limited freedom to aid suicides by yielding to the impulse to end another's suffering under conditions going beyond the narrow limits the respondents propose. The State thus argues, essentially, that respondents' claim is not as narrow as it sounds, simply because no recognition of the interest they assert could be limited to vindicating those interests and affecting no others. . . .

. . .

The State . . . argue[s] that . . . the lines proposed here (particularly the requirement of a knowing and voluntary decision by the patient) would be more difficult to draw than the lines that have limited other recently recognized due process rights. . . . [T]he knowing and responsible mind is harder to assess. Second, this difficulty could become the greater by combining with another fact within the realm of plausibility, that physicians simply would not be assiduous to preserve the line. They have compassion, and those who would be willing to assist in suicide at all might be the most susceptible to the wishes of a patient, whether the patient were technically quite responsible or not. Physicians, and their hospitals, have their own financial incentives, too, in this new age of managed care. Whether acting from compassion or under some other influence, a physician who would provide a drug for a patient to administer might well go the further step of administering the drug himself; so, the barrier between assisted suicide and euthanasia could become porous, and the line between voluntary and involuntary euthanasia as well. The case for the slippery slope is fairly made out here, not because recognizing one due process right would leave a court with no principled basis to avoid recognizing another, but because there is a plausible case that the right claimed would not be readily containable by reference to facts about the mind that are matters of difficult judgment, or by gatekeepers who are subject to temptation, noble or not.

Respondents propose . . . the answer of state regulation with teeth. . . .

But at least at this moment there are reasons for caution in predicting the effectiveness of the teeth proposed. Respondents' proposals . . . sound much like the guidelines now in place in the Netherlands, the only place where experience with physician-assisted suicide and euthanasia has yielded empirical evidence about how such regulations might affect actual practice. . . . Some commentators marshal evidence that the Dutch guidelines have in practice failed to protect patients from involuntary euthanasia and have been violated with impunity. . . . This evidence is contested. . . . The day may come when we can say with some assurance which side is right, but for now it is the substantiality of the factual disagreement, and the alternatives for resolving it, that matter. They are, for me, dispositive of the due process claim at this time.

. . .

Legislatures . . . have superior opportunities to obtain the facts necessary for a judgment about the present controversy. . . .

. . .

... The experimentation that should be out of the question in constitutional adjudication displacing legislative judgments is entirely proper, as well as highly desirable, when the legislative power addresses an emerging issue like assisted suicide. The Court should accordingly stay its hand to allow reasonable legislative consideration. While I do not decide for all time that respondents' claim should not be recognized, I acknowledge the legislative institutional competence as the better one to deal with that claim at this time.

JUSTICE GINSBURG, concurring in the judgment.

I concur in the Court's judgments in these cases substantially for the reasons stated by Justice O'Connor in her concurring opinion.

JUSTICE BREYER, concurring in the judgment.

I believe that Justice O'Connor's views, which I share, have greater legal significance than the Court's opinion suggests. I join her separate opinion, except insofar as it joins the majority. . . .

I agree with the Court in Vacco v. Quill that the articulated state interests justify the distinction drawn between physician assisted suicide and withdrawal of life-support. I also agree with the Court that the critical question in both of the cases before us is whether "the 'liberty' specially protected by the Due Process Clause includes a right" of the sort that the respondents assert. . . . I do not agree, however, with the Court's formulation of that claimed "liberty" interest. The Court describes it as a "right to commit suicide with another's assistance." But I would not reject the respondents' claim without considering a different formulation, for which our legal tradition may provide greater support. That formulation would use words roughly like a "right to die with dignity." But irrespective of the exact words used, at its core would lie personal control over the manner of death, professional medical assistance, and the avoidance of unnecessary and severe physical suffering—combined.

As Justice Souter points out, Justice Harlan's dissenting opinion in Poe v. Ullman, 367 U.S. 497 (1961), offers some support for such a claim. In that opinion, Justice Harlan referred to the "liberty" that the Fourteenth Amendment protects as including "a freedom from all substantial arbitrary impositions and purposeless restraints" and also as recognizing that "certain interests require particularly careful scrutiny of the state needs asserted to justify their abridgment." . . . The "certain interests" to which Justice Harlan referred may well be similar (perhaps identical) to the rights, liberties, or interests that the Court today, as in the past, regards as "fundamental." . . .

. . . [R]espondents . . . argue that one can find a "right to die with dignity" by examining the protection the law has provided for related, but not identical, interests relating to personal dignity, medical treatment, and freedom from state-inflicted pain. . . .

I do not believe, however, that this Court need or now should decide whether or a not such a right is "fundamental." That is because, in my view, the avoidance of severe physical pain (connected with death) would have to comprise an essential part of any successful claim and because, as Justice O'Connor points out, the laws before us do not force a dying person to undergo that kind of pain. Rather, the laws of New York and of Washington do not prohibit doctors from providing patients with drugs sufficient to control pain despite the risk that those drugs themselves will kill. . . . And under these circumstances the laws of New York and Washington would overcome any remaining significant interests and would be justified, regardless.

. . .

Were the legal circumstances different—for example, were state law to prevent the provision of palliative care, including the administration of drugs as needed to avoid pain at the end of life—then the law's impact upon serious and otherwise unavoidable physical pain (accompanying death) would be more directly at issue. And as Justice O'Connor suggests, the Court might have to revisit its conclusions in these cases.

*

Part Five

EQUALITY

Long before the Fourteenth Amendment's adoption, legal equality was an established principle in the United States. In his first inaugural address, Jefferson told his listeners to keep in mind this "sacred principle"—"that though the will of the majority is in all cases to prevail, that will, to be rightful, must be reasonable; that the minority possess their equal rights, which equal laws must protect, and to violate [those equal rights] would be oppression."* The Fourteenth Amendment's equal protection clause stated that principle without elaboration in 1868. In the next 130 years, The Supreme Court elaborated the principle.

Chapter XXIII

EQUAL PROTECTION OF LAW: FROM PRINCIPLE TO DOCTRINE

The Fourteenth Amendment prohibits the states from denying any person "the equal protection of the laws," and the Fifth Amendment's Due Process Clause extends that guarantee to the federal government. This means that equal protection is a necessary condition for any government action, whether state or federal. But all laws treat different people differently. A criminal law, for example, punishes some people but does not punish others. It is, of course, reasonable to treat differently those people who break the law and those who don't. In general, the equal protection clause permits the states to treat people differently if there is a good enough reason for doing so. A question of primary importance, which runs through this and the next two chapters, is when, if ever, is it reasonable to treat people differently based on their race or gender. Put another way, the question is whether all laws that draw distinctions based on race or gender violate the equal protection clause.

The legality of racial discrimination is a question of primary importance in view of the history of the 14th Amendment. This chapter begins with Supreme Court opinions that draw heavily on that history. Then it considers the scope of the equal protection clause and presents an overview of equal protection doctrine.

* Saul K. Padover, ed., *The Complete Jefferson* (New York, 1943), p. 384.

I. THE ANTI–SLAVERY ORIGINS OF THE FOURTEENTH AMENDMENT

STRAUDER v. WEST VIRGINIA

Supreme Court of the United States, 1879.
100 U.S. 303, 25 L.Ed. 664.

[Strauder, an African American, was convicted of murder in a West Virginia court. A state law which read: "All white male persons who are twenty-one years of age and who are citizens of this State shall be liable to serve as jurors ..." had excluded members of his race from his jury. The controlling question was whether every citizen of the United States has a constitutional right to a trial of an indictment against him by a jury selected and impanelled without discrimination against his race or color, because of race or color.]

JUSTICE STRONG delivered the opinion of the Court.

 WILLIAM STRONG—Born on May 6, 1808, in Somers, Connecticut, into a distinguished New England family that had migrated to Massachusetts in 1630. His father was an eminent Presbyterian clergyman. Democrat. Presbyterian. Yale, B.A., 1828; M.A., 1831. Taught school, read for the bar, and briefly attended Yale Law School. Practiced law, 1832–1846, 1850–1857, 1868–1870; member of the U.S. House of Representatives, 1846–1850; Pennsylvania Supreme Court justice, 1857–1868. Nominated associate justice by President Ulysses S. Grant on February 7, 1870, to replace Robert C. Grier. Confirmed by the Senate on February 18, 1870, by voice vote. While on the Supreme Court, he served as vice-president of the American Bible Society and president of the American Tract Society. Retired on December 14, 1880. Died on August 19, 1895.

[The 14th Amendment] is one of a series of constitutional provisions having a common purpose; namely securing to a race recently emancipated, a race that through many generations had been held in slavery, all the civil rights that the superior race enjoy. The true spirit and meaning of the amendments, as we said in the Slaughter–House Cases ..., cannot be understood without keeping in view the history of the times when they were adopted, and the general objects they plainly sought to accomplish. At the time when they were incorporated into the Constitution, it required little knowledge of human nature to anticipate that those who had long been regarded as an inferior and subject race would, when suddenly raised to the rank of citizenship, be looked upon with jealousy and positive dislike, and that State laws might be enacted or enforced to perpetuate the distinctions that had before existed. Discriminations against them had been habitual. It was well known that in some States laws making such discriminations then existed, and others might well be expected. The colored race, as a race, was abject and ignorant, and in that condition was unfitted to command the respect of those who had superior intelligence. Their training had left them mere children, and as such they needed the protection which a wise government extends to those who are unable to protect themselves. They especially needed protection against unfriendly action in the States where they were resident. It was in view of these considerations the Fourteenth Amendment was framed and adopted. It was designed to assure to the colored race the enjoyment of all the civil rights that under the law are enjoyed by white persons, and to give to that race the protection of the general government, in that enjoyment, whenever it should be denied by the States.... To quote the language used by us in the Slaughter–House Cases, "No one can fail to be impressed with the one pervading purpose found in [the Thirteenth, Fourteenth and Fifteenth] amendments, lying at the foundation of each, and without which none of them would have been suggested,—we mean the freedom of the slave race, the security and firm establishment of that freedom, and the protection of the newly made freeman and citizen from the oppressions of those who had formerly exercised unlimited dominion over them." So again: "The existence of laws in the States where the newly emancipated negroes resided, which discriminated with gross injustice and hardship against them as a class, was the evil to be remedied, and by it [the Fourteenth Amendment] such laws were forbidden. If, however, the States did not conform their laws to its requirements, then, by the fifth section of the article of amendment, Congress was authorized to enforce it by suitable legislation." And it was added, "We doubt very much whether any action of a State, not directed by way of discrimination against the negroes, as a class, will ever be held to come within the purview of [the Equal Protection Clause of the Fourteenth Amendment]."

If this is the spirit and meaning of the amendment, whether it means more or not, it is to be construed liberally, to carry out the purposes of its framers.... [It declares] that the law in the States shall be the same for the black as for the white; that all persons, whether colored or white, shall stand equal before the laws of the States, and, in regard to the colored race, for whose protection the amendment was primarily designed, that no discrimination shall be made against them by law because of their color[.] The words of the amendment, it is true, are prohibitory, but they contain a necessary implication of a positive immunity, or right, most valuable to the colored race,—the right to exemption from unfriendly legislation against them distinctively as colored,—exemption from legal discriminations, implying inferiority in civil society, lessening the security of their enjoyment of the rights which others enjoy, and discriminations which are steps towards reducing them to the condition of a subject race.

That the West Virginia statute respecting juries—the statute that controlled the selection of the grand and petit jury in the case of the plaintiff in error—is such a discrimination ought not to be doubted.... The very fact that colored people are singled out and expressly denied by a statute all right to participate in the administration of the law, as jurors, because of their color, though they are citizens, and may be in other respects fully qualified, is practically a brand upon them, affixed by the law, an assertion of their inferiority, and a stimulant to that race prejudice which is an impediment to securing to individuals of the race that equal justice which the law aims to secure to all others.

. . .

... [I]t is not easy to comprehend how it can be said that while every white man is entitled to a trial by a jury selected from persons of his own race or color, or, rather, selected without discrimination against his color, and a negro is not, the latter is equally protected by the law with the former....

. . .

The Fourteenth Amendment makes no attempt to enumerate the rights it designed to protect. It speaks in general terms, and those are as comprehensive as possible. Its language is prohibitory; but every prohibition implies the existence of rights and immunities, prominent among which is an immunity from inequality of legal protection, either for life, liberty, or property. Any State action that denies this immunity to a colored man is in conflict with the Constitution.

. . .

NOTE AND QUESTIONS

The opinion in *Strauder* cites the Slaughter–House Cases, 83 U.S. 36 (1872), in support of its interpretation of the Fourteenth Amendment. The Court in that case recounted the following history in support of its contention that the Equal Protection Clause of the Fourteenth Amendment probably did not apply to any situation other than racial discrimination:

> ... [W]hatever auxiliary causes may have contributed to bring about [the Civil War], undoubtedly the overshadowing and efficient cause was African slavery.

> In that struggle slavery, as a legalized social relation, perished.... The proclamation of President Lincoln expressed an accomplished fact as to a large portion of the insurrectionary districts, when he declared slavery abolished in them all. But the war being over, those who had succeeded in re-establishing the authority of the Federal government were not content to permit this great act of emancipation to rest on the actual results of the contest or the proclamation of the Executive, both of which might have been questioned in after times, and they determined to place this main and most valuable result in the Constitution of the restored Union as one of its fundamental articles. Hence the thirteenth article of amendment of that instrument....

> [However] [t]he process of restoring to their proper relations with the Federal government and with the other States those which had sided with the rebellion, ... developed the fact that, notwithstanding the formal recognition by those States of the abolition of slavery, the condition of the slave race would, without further protection of the Federal government, be almost as bad as it was before. Among the first acts of legislation adopted by several of the States in the legislative bodies ... were laws which imposed upon the colored race onerous disabilities and burdens, and curtailed their rights in the pursuit of life,

liberty, and property to such an extent that their freedom was of little value, . . .

They were in some States forbidden to appear in the towns in any other character than menial servants. They were required to reside on and cultivate the soil without the right to purchase or own it. They were excluded from many occupations of gain, and were not permitted to give testimony in the courts in any case where a white man was a party. It was said that their lives were at the mercy of bad men, either because the laws for their protection were insufficient or were not enforced.

These circumstances, whatever of falsehood or misconception may have been mingled with their presentation, forced upon the statesmen who had conducted the Federal government in safety through the crisis of the rebellion, and who supposed that by the thirteenth article of amendment they had secured the result of their labors, the conviction that something more was necessary in the way of constitutional protection to the unfortunate race who had suffered so much. They accordingly passed through Congress the proposition for the fourteenth amendment, and they declined to treat as restored to their full participation in the government of the Union the States which had been in insurrection, until they ratified that article by a formal vote of their legislative bodies.

. . . A few years' experience satisfied the thoughtful men who had been the authors of the other two amendments that . . . a race of men distinctively marked as was the negro, living in the midst of another and dominant race, could never be fully secured in their person and their property without the right of suffrage.

Hence the fifteenth amendment. . . . The negro having, by the fourteenth amendment, been declared to be a citizen of the United States, is thus made a voter in every State of the Union.

Is the Court saying in the Slaughter House Cases that framers of the Fourteenth Amendment intended its application only to African Americans? If so, does the language of the amendment support this conclusion? Note the amendment's first sentence reverses Dred Scott v. Sandford, 60 U.S. 393 (1857), which held that African Americans—whether slave or free—could not be state citizens. There is no doubt that the amendment's framers also intended to reverse Chief Justice Taney's statement in *Dred Scott* that African Americans at the time of the Declaration of Independence and making of the Constitution "had . . . been regarded as being of an inferior order; and altogether unfit to associate with the white race, either in social or political relations; and so far inferior, that they had no rights which the white man was bound to respect. . . ."

II. THE SCOPE OF EQUAL PROTECTION

YICK WO v. HOPKINS

Supreme Court of the United States, 1886.
118 U.S. 356, 6 S.Ct. 1064, 30 L.Ed. 220.

[A San Francisco ordinance prohibited the operation of laundries in buildings other than those made of stone or brick unless the board of supervisors granted a waiver. More than 300 of some 320 laundries in San Francisco were wooden structures. With only one exception, the board of supervisors granted waivers to all Caucasian applicants but denied waivers to all Chinese applicants—approximately 200. Yick Wo, Wo Lee, and 150 other Chinese aliens were convicted of violating the ordinance. Yick Wo and Wo Lee appealed.]

JUSTICE MATTHEWS delivered the opinion of the Court.

STANLEY MATTHEWS—Born on July 21, 1824, in Lexington, Kentucky, where his father was a mathematics professor at Transylvania University. Republican. Presbyterian. Kenyon, B.A., 1840, where he was a close friend of Rutherford B. Hayes. Prepared for the bar in a law office. Began practice in Ohio in 1844. Judge of Ohio Court of Common Pleas, 1851–1853. U.S. attorney for Southern District of Ohio, 1858–1861. Joined the Union army with Hayes and served with distinction, 1861–1863. Judge, Superior Court of Cincinnati, 1863–1865. Supported Hayes for the presidency in 1876. Served as counsel to 1877 Electoral Commission and negotiated compromise by which Hayes became president. U.S. senator from Ohio, 1877–1879. Nominated associate justice on January 26, 1881, by President Hayes to replace Noah Haynes Swayne, just before Hayes was to leave office. A storm of protest followed. As a result, the Senate did not act on the nomination. Renominated by President James A. Garfield on March 14, 1881. Confirmed by the Senate on May 12, 1881, by a 24–23 vote. Died in office on March 22, 1898.

. . .

The rights of the petitioners ... are not less because they are aliens. . . .

The Fourteenth Amendment to the Constitution is not confined to the protection of citizens. It says: "Nor shall any State deprive any person of life, liberty, or property without due process of law; nor deny to any person within its jurisdiction the equal protection of the laws." These provisions are universal in their application, to all persons within the territorial jurisdiction, without regard to any differences of race, of color, or of nationality; and the equal protection of the laws is a pledge of the protection of equal laws....

[Petitioners contend that the ordinances] are void on their face, as being within the prohibitions of the Fourteenth Amendment; and, in the alternative, if not so, that they are void by reason of their administration, operating unequally, so as to punish in the present petitioners what is permitted to others as lawful, without any distinction of circumstances—an unjust and illegal discrimination, it is claimed, which, though not made expressly by the ordinances is made possible by them.

When we consider the nature and the theory of our institutions of government, the principles upon which they are supposed to rest, and review the history of their development, we are constrained to conclude that they do not mean to leave room for the play and action of purely personal and arbitrary power. Sovereignty itself is, of course, not subject to law, for it is the author and source of law; but in our system, while sovereign powers are delegated to the agencies of government, sovereignty itself remains with the people, by whom and for whom all government exists and acts. And the law is the definition and limitation of power. It is, indeed, quite true, that there must always be lodged somewhere, and in some person or body, the authority of final decision; and in many cases of mere administration the responsibility is purely political, no appeal lying except to the ultimate tribunal of the public suffrage. But the fundamental rights to life, liberty, and the pursuit of happiness . . . are secured by those maxims of constitutional law which are the monuments showing the victorious progress of the race in securing to men the blessings of civilization under the reign of just and equal laws, so that, in the famous language of the Massachusetts Bill of Rights, the government of the commonwealth "may be a government of laws and not of men." For, the very idea that one man may be compelled to hold his life, or the means of living, or any material right essential to the enjoyment of life, at the mere will of another, seems to be intolerable in any country where freedom prevails, as being the essence of slavery itself.

There are many illustrations that might be given of this truth, which would made manifest that it was self-evident in the light of our system of jurisprudence. The case of the political franchise of voting is one. Though not regarded strictly as a natural right, but as a privilege merely conceded by society according to its will, under certain conditions, nevertheless it is regarded as a fundamental political right, because preservative of all rights. . . .

. . . [T]he cases present the ordinances in actual operation, and the facts establish an administration [of the ordinance] exclusively against a particular class of persons. . . . Though the law itself be fair on its face and impartial in appearance, yet, if it is applied and administered by public authority with an evil eye and an unequal hand, so as practically to make unjust and illegal discriminations between persons in similar circumstances, material to their rights, the denial of equal justice is still within the prohibition of the Constitution. . . .

. . . It appears that both petitioners have complied with every requisite, deemed by the law or by the public officers charged with its administration, necessary for the protection of neighboring property from fire, or as a precaution against injury to the public health. No reason whatever, except the will of the supervisors, is assigned why they should not be permitted to carry on, in the accustomed manner, their harmless and useful occupation, on which they depend for a livelihood. And while this consent of the supervisors is withheld from them and from two hundred others who have also petitioned, all of whom happen to be Chinese subjects, eighty others, not Chinese subjects, are permitted to carry on the same business under similar conditions. The fact of this discrimination is admitted. No reason for it is shown, and the conclusion cannot be resisted, that no reason for it exists except hostility to the race and nationality to which the petitioners belong, and which in the eye of the law is not justified. The discrimination is, therefore, illegal, and the public administration which enforces it is a denial of the equal protection of the laws and a violation of the Fourteenth Amendment of the Constitution. The imprisonment of the petitioners is, therefore, illegal, and they must be discharged.

NOTES AND QUESTIONS

1.   Does *Yick Wo* settle the question whether the equal protection clause applies only to African Americans?

2.   In Plyler v. Doe, 457 U.S. 202 (1982), a closely divided Court, citing *Yick Wo*, held that Texas violated the equal protection clause in denying public education to the children of aliens. Are all aliens entitled to the guarantee of equal protection of the laws? See note 3, p. 998, below.

3.   Note the equal-protection challenge in *Yick Wo* was to the implementation of an ordinance that was nondiscriminatory on its face. Most equal-protection challenges are to statutory classifications.

4.   In Griswold v. Connecticut, 381 U.S. 479 (1965), Chief Justice Warren, citing *Yick Wo,* said in conference that the Connecticut anti-contraception statute could be held unconstitutional as violating equal protection of the laws. Explain his position. Compare his initial conference remarks in Tinker v. Des Moines School Dist., 393 U.S. 503 (1969) (page 281). Was he also relying on *Yick Wo* in *Tinker*?

BOLLING v. SHARPE

Supreme Court of the United States, 1954.
347 U.S. 497, 74 S.Ct. 693, 98 L.Ed. 884.

CHIEF JUSTICE WARREN delivered the opinion of the Court.

This case challenges the validity of segregation in the public schools of the district of Columbia. The petitioners, minors of the Negro race, allege that such segregation deprives them of due process of law under the Fifth Amendment. They were refused admission to a public school attended by white children solely because of their race. . . .

We have this day held that the Equal Protection Clause of the Fourteenth Amendment prohibits the states from maintaining racially segregated public schools. The legal problem in the District of Columbia is somewhat different, however. The Fifth Amendment, which is applicable in the District of Columbia, does not contain an equal protection clause as does the Fourteenth Amendment which applies only to the states. But the concepts of equal protection and due process, both stemming from our American ideal of fairness, are not mutually exclusive. The "equal protection of the laws" is a more explicit safeguard of prohibited unfairness than "due process of law," and, therefore, we do not imply that the two are always interchangeable phrases. But, as this Court has recognized, discrimination may be so unjustifiable as to be violative of due process.

. . .

Although the Court has not assumed to define "liberty" with any great precision, that term is not confined to mere freedom from bodily restraint. Liberty under law extends to the full range of conduct which the individual is free to pursue, and it cannot be restricted except for a proper governmental objective, and thus it imposes on Negro children of the District of Columbia a burden that constitutes an arbitrary deprivation of their liberty in violation of the Due Process Clause.

In view of our decision that the Constitution prohibits the states from maintaining racially segregated public schools, it would be unthinkable that the same Constitution would impose a lesser duty on the Federal Government. We hold that racial segregation in the public schools of the District of Columbia is a denial of the due process of law guaranteed by the Fifth Amendment to the Constitution.

. . .

NOTES AND QUESTIONS

1. Granting that the result achieved by the Court in *Bolling* is beneficent, is not its interpretation of the Fifth Amendment a strained one? Unlike the Fourteenth Amendment, there is absolutely nothing in the text or history of the Fifth Amendment to justify its use in invalidating segregation, and there is no hint that anyone—however radical—who helped adopt the Fifth Amendment thought that, at a time when slavery was lawful, he might be abolishing federally required racial segregation.

2. Is *Bolling* based on the doctrine of substantive due process? If so, is Justice Black's vote in the case consistent with his views of Griswold v. Connecticut, 381 U.S. 479 (1965). See pages 885–888, supra.

3. Has the Supreme Court in *Bolling* incorporated equal protection through the Fifth Amendment's due process clause the way it incorporated guarantees of the Bill of Rights through the Fourteenth Amendment's due process clause?

III. EQUAL PROTECTION DOCTRINE: AN OVERVIEW

Prior to 1938, the Supreme Court seldom used the equal protection clause to secure individual rights. *Strauder* and *Yick Wo* were exceptions. In Buck v. Bell, 274 U.S. 200 (1927), which upheld the constitutionality of eugenic sterilization, Justice Holmes said dismissively that equal protection was "the usual last resort of constitutional arguments."

A. RATIONAL BASIS

In Lindsley v. Natural Carbonic Gas Co., 220 U.S. 61 (1911), Justice Van Devanter set forth as follows the rational-basis approach to deciding equal protection cases:

> 1.   The equal-protection clause of the 14th Amendment does not take from the state the power to classify in the adoption of police laws, but admits of the exercise of a wide scope of discretion in that regard, and avoids what is done only when it is without any reasonable basis, and therefore is purely arbitrary.

> 2.   A classification having some reasonable basis does not offend against that clause merely because it is not made with mathematical nicety. Or because in practice it results in some inequality.

> 3.   When the classification in such a law is called in question, if any state of facts reasonably can be conceived that would sustain it, the existence of that state of facts at the time the law was enacted must be assumed.

> 4.   One who assails the classification in such a law must carry the burden of showing that it does not rest upon any reasonable basis, but is essentially arbitrary.

These propositions applied to all equal protection cases until the late 1930s, and they still apply to cases not involving individual rights.

B. STRICT SCRUTINY

Footnote Four in *Carolene Products* suggested a departure from the rational-basis approach in cases in which there was evidence of "prejudice against discrete and insular minorities." In such cases, statutes would not be accorded the usual presumption of constitutionality, but would be subject to searching judicial inquiry. In Skinner v. Oklahoma, 316 U.S. 535 (1942), Justice Douglas called such judicial inquiry "strict scrutiny."

Skinner involved equal protection and due process challenges to a state statute that authorized sexual sterilization for persons convicted of certain crimes—e.g., larceny—but not others—e.g., embezzlement. Writing for a majority of seven, Justice Douglas said:

> We are dealing here with legislation which involves one of the basic civil rights of man. Marriage and procreation are fundamental to the very existence and survival of the race. The power to sterilize, if exercised, may have subtle, far-reaching and devastating effects. In evil or reckless hands it can cause races or types which are inimical to the dominant groups to wither and disappear. There is no redemption for the individual whom the law touches. Any experiment which the State conducts is to his irreparable injury. He is forever deprived of a basic liberty. We mention these matters not to reexamine the scope of the

police power of the States. We advert to them merely in emphasis of our view that strict scrutiny of the classification which a State makes in a sterilization law is essential, lest unwittingly or otherwise, invidious discriminations are made against groups or types of individuals in violation of the constitutional guaranty of "equal protection of the laws is a pledge of the protection of equal laws." Yick Wo v. Hopkins, 118 U.S. 356, 369. When the law lays an unequal hand on those who have committed intrinsically the same quality of offense and sterilizes one and not the other, it has made as invidious a discrimination as if it had selected a particular race or nationality for oppressive treatment. Yick Wo v. Hopkins, supra; Missouri ex rel. Gaines v. Canada, 305 U.S. 337. Sterilization of those who have thrice committed grand larceny with immunity for those who are embezzlers is a clear, pointed unmistakable discrimination.

In Korematsu v. United States, 323 U.S. 214 (1944), which upheld the constitutionality of internment of American citizens of Japanese ancestry during World War II, Justice Black wrote in the Court's opinion: "[A]ll legal restrictions which curtail the civil rights of a single racial group are immediately suspect. That is not to say that all such restrictions are unconstitutional. It is to say that Courts must subject them to the most rigorous scrutiny. Pressing public necessity may sometimes justify the existence of such restriction; racial antagonism never can."

1. Fundamental Rights

SHAPIRO v. THOMPSON

Supreme Court of the United States, 1969.
394 U.S. 618, 89 S.Ct. 1322, 22 L.Ed.2d 600.

JUSTICE BRENNAN delivered the opinion of the Court.

. . . [This] is an appeal from a decision of a three-judge District Court holding unconstitutional a State or District of Columbia statutory provision which denies welfare assistance to residents of the State or District who have not resided within their jurisdictions for at least one year immediately preceding their application for such assistance. We affirm. . . .

. . .

There is no dispute that the effect of the waiting-period requirement in each case is to create two classes of needy resident families indistinguishable from each other except that one is composed of residents who have resided a year or more, and the second of residents who have resided less than a year, in the jurisdiction. On the basis of this sole difference the first class is granted and the second class is denied welfare aid upon which may depend the ability of the families to obtain the very means to subsist—food, shelter, and other necessities of life. In each case, the District Court found that appellees met the test for residence in their jurisdictions, as well as all other eligibility requirements except the requirement of residence for a full year prior to their applications. On reargument, appellees' central contention is that the statutory prohibition of benefits to residents of less than a year creates a classification which constitutes an invidious discrimination denying them equal protection of the laws. We agree. The interests which appellants assert are promoted by the classification either may not constitutionally be promoted by government or are not compelling governmental interests.

Primarily, appellants justify the waiting-period requirement as a protective device to preserve the fiscal integrity of state welfare assistance during their first year of residence in a State are likely to become continuing burdens on state welfare programs. Therefore, the argument runs, if such people can be deterred from entering the jurisdiction by denying them welfare benefits during the first year, state programs to assist long-time residents will not be impaired by a substantial influx of indigent newcomers.

. . .

We do not doubt that the one-year waiting period device is well suited to discourage the influx of poor families in need of assistance. A indigent who desires to migrate, resettle, find a new job, start a new life will doubtless hesitate if he knows that he must risk making the move without the possibility of falling back on state welfare assistance during his first year of residence, when his need may be most acute. But the purpose of inhibiting migration by needy persons into the State is constitutionally impermissible.

This Court long ago recognized that the nature of our Federal Union and our constitutional concepts of personal liberty unite to require that all citizens be free to travel throughout the length and breadth of our land uninhibited by statutes, rules or regulations which unreasonably burden or restrict this movement....

We have no occasion to ascribe the source of this right to travel interstate to a particular constitutional provision. It suffices that, as Justice Stewart said for the Court in United States v. Guest, 383 U.S. 745, 757–758 (1966):

> "The constitutional right to travel from one State to another ... occupies a position fundamental to the concept of our Federal Union. It is a right that has been firmly established and repeatedly recognized.
>
> "[The] right finds no explicit mention in the Constitution. The reason, it has been suggested, is that a right so elementary was conceived from the beginning to be a necessary concomitant of the stronger Union the Constitution created. In any event, freedom to travel throughout the United States has long been recognized as a basic right under the Constitution."

Thus, the purpose of deterring the in-migration of indigents cannot serve as justification for the classification created by the one-year waiting period, since that purpose is constitutionally impermissible. If a law has "no other purpose ... than to chill the assertion of constitutional rights by penalizing those who choose to exercise them, then it [is] patently unconstitutional." United States v. Jackson, 390 U.S. 570, 581 (1968).

Alternatively, appellants argue that even if it is impermissible for a State to attempt to deter the entry of all indigents, the challenged classification may be justified as a permissible state attempt to discourage those indigents who would enter the State solely to obtain larger benefits. We observe first that none of the statutes before us is tailored to serve that objection. . . .

More fundamentally, a State may no more try to fence out those indigents who seek higher welfare benefits than it may try to fence out indigents generally. Implicit in any such distinction is the notion that indigents who enter a State with the hope of securing higher welfare benefits are somehow less deserving than indigents who do not take this consideration into account. But we do not perceive why a mother who is seeking to make a new life for herself and her children should be regarded as less deserving because she considers, among other factors, the level of a State's public assistance. Surely such a mother is no less deserving than a mother who moves into a particular State in order to take advantage of its better educational facilities.

Appellants argue further that the challenged classification may be sustained as an attempt to distinguish between new and old residents on the basis of the contribution they have made to the community through the payment of taxes. We have difficulty seeing how long-term residents who qualify for welfare are making a greater present contribution to the State in taxes than indigent residents who have recently arrived. If the argument is based on contributions made in the past by the long-term residents, there is some question, as a factual matter, whether this argument is applicable in Pennsylvania where the record suggests that some 40% of those denied public assistance because of the waiting period had lengthy prior residence in the State. But we need not rest on the particular facts of these cases. Appellants' reasoning would logically deprive them of police and fire protection. Indeed, it would permit the State to apportion all benefits and services according to the past tax contributions of its citizens. The Equal Protection Clause prohibits such an apportionment of state services.[1]

We recognize that a State has a valid interest in preserving the fiscal integrity of its programs. It may legitimately attempt to limit its expenditures, whether for public assistance, public education, or any other program. But a State may not accomplish such a purpose by invidious distinctions between classes of its citizens. It could not, for example, reduce expenditures for education by barring indigent children from its schools. Similarly, in the cases before us, appellants must do more than show that denying welfare benefits to new residents saves money. The saving of welfare costs cannot be an independent ground for an invidious classification.

---

1. We are not dealing here with state insurance programs which may legitimately tie the amount of benefits to the individual's contributions.

In sum, neither deterrence of indigents from migrating to the State nor limitation of welfare benefits to those regarded as contributing to the State is a constitutionally permissible state objective.

Appellants next advance as justification certain administrative and related governmental objectives allegedly served by the waiting-period requirement. They argue that the requirement (1) facilitates the planning of the welfare budget; (2) provides an objective test of residence; (3) minimizes the opportunity for recipients fraudulently to receive payments from more than one jurisdiction; and (4) encourages early entry of new residents into the labor force.

At the outset, we reject appellants' argument that a mere showing of a rational relationship between the waiting period and these for admittedly permissible state objectives will suffice to justify the classification. See Lindsley v. Natural Carbonic Gas Co., 220 U.S. 61, 78.... The waiting-period provision denies welfare benefits to otherwise eligible applicants solely because they have recently moved into the jurisdiction. But in moving from State to State or to the District of Columbia appellees were exercising a constitutional right, and any classification which serves to penalize the exercise of that right, unless shown to be necessary to promote a *compelling* governmental interest, is unconstitutional. Cf. Skinner v. Oklahoma, 316 U.S. 535, 541....

The argument that the waiting-period requirement facilitates budget predictability is wholly unfounded. The records in all three cases are utterly devoid of evidence that either State or the District of Columbia in fact uses the one-year requirement as a means to predict the number of people who will require assistance in the budget year....

The argument that the waiting period serves as an administratively efficient rule of thumb for determining residence similarly will not withstand scrutiny. The residence requirement and the one-year waiting-period requirement are distinct and independent prerequisites for assistance under these three statutes, and the fact relevant to the determination of each are directly examined by the welfare authorities. Before granting an application, the welfare authorities investigate the applicant's employment, housing, and family situation and in the course of the inquiry necessarily learn the facts upon which to determine whether the applicant is a resident.

Similarly, there is no need for a State to use the one-year waiting period as a safeguard against fraudulent receipt of benefits; for less drastic means are available, and are employed, to minimize that hazard. Of course, a State has a valid interest in preventing fraud by any applicant, whether a newcomer or a long-time resident. It is not denied, however that the investigations now conducted entail inquiries into facts relevant to that subject. In addition, cooperation among state welfare departments is common. The District of Columbia, for example, provides interim assistance to its former residents who have moved to a State which has a waiting period. As a matter of course, District officials send a letter to the welfare in the recipient's new community "to request the information needed to continue assistance." A like procedure would be an effective safeguard against the hazard of double payments. Since double payments can be prevented by a letter or a telephone call, it is unreasonable to accomplish this objective by the blunderbuss method of denying assistance to all indigent newcomers for an entire year.

Pennsylvania suggests that the one-year waiting period is justified as a means of encouraging new residents to join the labor force promptly. But this logic would also require a similar waiting period for long-term residents of the State. A state purpose to encourage employment provides no rational basis for imposing a one-year waiting period restriction on new residents only.

We conclude therefore that appellants in these cases do not use and have no need to use the one-year requirement for the governmental purposes suggested. Thus, even under traditional equal protection tests a classification of welfare applicants according to whether they have lived in the State for one year would seem irrational and unconstitutional. But, of course, the traditional criteria do not apply in these cases. Since the classification here touches on the fundamental right of interstate movement, its constitutionality must be judged by the stricter standard of whether it promotes a *compelling* state interest. Under this standard, the waiting period requirement clearly violates the Equal Protection Clause.

. . .

JUSTICE STEWART, concurring.

In joining the opinion of the Court, I add a word in response to the dissent of my Brother Harlan, who, I think, has quite misapprehended what the Court's opinion says.

The Court today does *not* "pick out particular human activities, characterize them as 'fundamental,' and give them added protection. . . ." To the contrary, the Court simply recognizes, as it must, an established constitutional right, and gives to that right no less protection than the Constitution itself demands. . . .

CHIEF JUSTICE WARREN, with whom JUSTICE BLACK joins, dissenting.

In my opinion the issue before us can be simply stated: may Congress, acting under one of its enumerated powers, impose minimal nationwide residence requirements or authorize the States to do so? Since I believe that Congress does have this power and has constitutionally exercised it in these cases, I must dissent. . . .

JUSTICE HARLAN, dissenting. . . .

In upholding the equal protection argument, the Court has applied an equal protection doctrine of relatively recent vintage: the rule that statutory classifications which either are based upon certain "suspect" criteria or affect "fundamental rights" will be held to deny equal protection unless justified by a "compelling" governmental interest. . . .

The "compelling interest" doctrine, which today is articulated more explicitly than ever before, constitutes an increasingly significant exception to the long-established rule that a statute does not deny equal protection if it is rationally related to a legitimate governmental objective, The 'compelling interest' doctrine has two branches. The branch which requires that classifications based upon "suspect" criteria be supported by a compelling interest apparently had its genesis in cases involving racial classifications, which have at least since Korematsu v. United States, 323 U.S. 214, 216 (1944), been regarded as inherently "suspect." The criterion of "wealth" apparently was added to the list of "suspects" as an alternative justification for the rationale in Harper v. Virginia Bd. Of Elections, 383 U.S. 663, 668 (1966), in which Virginia's poll tax was struck down. The criterion of political allegiance may have been added in Williams v. Rhodes, 393 U.S. 23 (1968). Today the list apparently has been further enlarged to include classifications based upon recent interstate movement, and perhaps those based upon the exercise of *any* constitutional right . . .

I think that this branch of the "compelling interest" doctrine is sound when applied to racial classifications, for historically the Equal Protection Clause was largely a product of the desire to eradicate legal distinctions founded upon race. However, I believe that the more recent extensions have been unwise. . . .

The second branch of the "compelling interest" principle is even more troublesome. For it has been held that a statutory classification is subject to the "compelling interest" test if the result of the classification may be to affect a "fundamental right," regardless of the basis of the classification. . . .

I think this branch of the "compelling interest" doctrine particularly unfortunate and unnecessary. It is unfortunate because it creates an exception which threatens to swallow the standard equal protection rule. Virtually every state statute affects important rights. This Court has repeatedly held, for example, that the traditional equal protection standard is applicable to statutory classifications affecting such fundamental matters as the right to pursue a particular occupation, the right to receive greater or smaller wages or to work more or less hours, and the right to inherit property. Rights such as these are in principle indistinguishable from those involved here, and to extend the "compelling interest" rule to all cases in which such rights are affected would go far toward making this Court a "super-legislature." This branch of the doctrine is also unnecessary. When the right affected is one assured by the federal Constitution, any infringement can be dealt with under the Due Process Clause. But when a statute affects only matters not mentioned in the federal Constitution and is not arbitrary or irrational, I must reiterate that I know of nothing which entitles this Court to pick out particular human activities, characterize them as "fundamental," and give them added protection under an unusually stringent equal protection test. . . .

NOTES AND QUESTIONS

1. What makes a right fundamental? In Yick Wo v. Hopkins, 118 U.S. 356 (1886), the Supreme Court said that the right to vote was fundamental because it is "preservative of all rights." Why is the right to interstate travel fundamental? Why are the rights to marriage and procreation fundamental? What other fundamental rights are there?

2.   What makes a state interest compelling? If such an interest can be achieved by less restrictive means, is it compelling?

2.   Suspect Classifications

In Bolling v. Sharpe, 347 U.S. 497 (1954), the Supreme Court, citing *Korematsu*, said: "Classifications based solely upon race must be scrutinized with particular care, since they are contrary to our traditions and hence constitutionally suspect." Today the accepted view is that all racial classifications are suspect and thus subject to strict scrutiny. If racial classifications are suspect, are gender classifications also suspect? That ultimately was the issue in the following case.

FRONTIERO v. RICHARDSON

Supreme Court of the United States, 1973.
411 U.S. 677, 93 S.Ct. 1764, 36 L.Ed.2d 583.

JUSTICE BRENNAN announced the judgment of the Court in an opinion in which JUSTICE DOUGLAS, JUSTICE WHITE, and JUSTICE MARSHALL join.

The question before us concerns the right of a female member of the uniformed services to claim her spouse as a "dependent" for the purposes of obtaining increased quarters allowances and medical and dental benefits under 37 U.S.C. §§ 401, 403, and 10 U.S.C. §§ 1072, 1076, on an equal footing with male members. Under these statutes, a serviceman may claim his wife as a "dependent" without regard to whether she is in fact dependent upon him for any part of her support. 37 U.S.C. § 401(1); 10 U.S.C. § 1072(2)(A). A servicewoman, on the other hand, may not claim her husband as a "dependent" under these programs unless he is in fact dependent upon her for over one-half of his support 37 U.S.C. § 401; 10 U.S.C. § 1072(2)(C). Thus, the question for decision is whether this difference in treatment constitutes an unconstitutional discrimination against servicewomen in violation of the Due Process Clause of the Fifth Amendment. A three-judge District Court for the Middle District of Alabama, one judge dissenting, rejected this contention and sustained the constitutionality of the provisions of the statutes making this distinction. . . . We reverse.

· · ·

At the outset, appellants contend that classifications based upon sex, like classifications based upon race, alienage, and national origin, are inherently suspect and must therefore be subjected to close judicial scrutiny. We agree and, indeed, find at least implicit support for such an approach in our unanimous decision only last Term in Reed v. Reed, 404 U.S. 71 (1971).

· · ·

There can be no doubt that our Nation has had a long and unfortunate history of sex discrimination. Traditionally, such discrimination was rationalized by an attitude of "romantic paternalism" which, in practical effect, put women not on a pedestal, but in a cage. Indeed, this paternalistic attitude became so firmly rooted in our national consciousness that, exactly 100 years ago, a distinguished member of this Court was able to proclaim:

> "Man is, or should be, woman's protector and defender. The natural and proper timidity and delicacy which belongs to the female sex evidently unfits it for many of the occupations of civil life. The constitution of the family organization, which is founded in the divine ordinance, as well as in the nature of things, indicates the domestic sphere as that which properly belongs to the domain and functions of womanhood. The harmony, not to say identity, of interests and views which belong, or should belong, to the family institution is repugnant to the ideas of a woman adopting a distinct and independent career from that of her husband. . . .

> " . . . The paramount destiny and mission of women are to fulfil the noble and benign offices of wife and mother. This is the law of the Creator. Bradwell v. Illinois, 83 U.S. [16 Wall.] 130, 141 (1873) (Bradley, J., concurring)."

As a result of notions such as these, our statute books gradually became laden with gross, stereotypical distinctions between the sexes and, indeed, throughout much of the 19th century the position of women in our society was, in many respects, comparable to that of blacks under the pre-Civil War slave codes. Neither slaves nor women could hold office, serve on juries, or bring suit in their own names, and married women traditionally were denied the legal capacity to hold or convey property or to serve as legal guardians of their own children. See generally, L. Kantowitz, Women and the Law: The Unfinished Revolution 5–6 (1969); G. Myrdal, An American Dilemma 1073 (2d ed. 1962). And although blacks were guaranteed the right to vote in 1870, women were denied even that right—which is itself "preservative of other basic civil and political rights"—until the adoption of the Nineteenth Amendment half a century later.

It is true, of course, that the position of women in America has improved markedly in recent decades. Nevertheless, it can hardly be doubted that, in part because of the high visibility of the sex characteristic, women still face pervasive, although at times more subtle, discrimination in our educational institutions, on the job market and, perhaps most conspicuously in the political arena.[1] See generally K. Amundsen, The Silenced Majority: Women and American Democracy (1971); The President's Task Force on Women's Rights and Responsibilities, A Matter of Simple Justice (1970).

Moreover, since sex, like race and national origin, is an immutable characteristic determined solely by the accident of birth, the imposition of special disabilities upon the members of a particular sex because of

---

1. It is true, of course, that when viewed in the abstract, women do not constitute a small and powerless minority. Nevertheless, in part because of past discrimination, women are vastly underrepresented in this Nation's decisionmaking councils. There has never been a female President, nor a female member of this Court. Not a single woman presently sits in the United States Senate, and only 14 women hold seats in the House of Representatives. And, as appellants point out, this underrepresentation is present throughout all levels of our State and Federal Government.

their sex would seem to violate "the basic concept of our system that legal burdens should bear some relationship to individual responsibility ...". Weber v. Aetna Casualty & Surety Co., 406 U.S. 164, 175 (1972). And what differentiates sex from such nonsuspect statuses as intelligence or physical disability, and aligns it with the recognized suspect criteria, is that the sex characteristic frequently bears no relation to ability to perform or contribute to society. As a result, statutory distinctions between the sexes often have the effect of invidiously relegating the entire class of females to inferior legal status without regard to the actual capabilities of its individual members.

. . .

[W]e can only conclude that classifications based upon Sex, like classifications based upon race, alienage, or national origin, are inherently suspect, and must therefore by subjected to strict judicial scrutiny. Applying the analysis mandated by that stricter standard of review, it is clear that the statutory scheme now before us is constitutionally invalid.

The sole basis of the classification established in the challenged statutes is the sex of the individuals involved.

. . .

Reversed.

JUSTICE STEWART concurs in the judgment, agreeing that the statutes before us work an invidious discrimination in violation of the Constitution. Reed v. Reed, 404 U.S. 71.

JUSTICE REHNQUIST dissents for the reason stated by Judge Rives in his opinion for the District Court, Frontiero v. Laird, 341 F.Supp. 201 (1972).

JUSTICE POWELL, with whom THE CHIEF JUSTICE and JUSTICE BLACKMUN join, concurring in the judgment.

I agree that the challenged statutes constitute an unconstitutional discrimination against service women in violation of the Due Process Clause of the Fifth Amendment, but I cannot join the opinion of Justice Brennan, which would hold that all classifications based upon sex, "like classifications based upon race, alienage, and national origin," are "inherently suspect and must therefore be subjected to close judicial scrutiny." ... It is unnecessary for the Court in this case to characterize sex as a suspect classification, with all of the far-reaching implications of such a holding. Reed v. Reed, 404 U.S. 71 (1971), which abundantly supports our decision today, did not add sex to the narrowly limited group of classifications which are inherently suspect. In my view, we can and should decide this case on the authority of *Reed* and reserve for the future any expansion of its rationale.

There is another, and I find compelling, reason for deferring a general categorizing of sex classification as invoking the strictest test of judicial scrutiny. The Equal Rights Amendment, which if adopted will resolve the substance of this precise question, has been approved by the Congress and submitted for ratification by the States. If this Amendment is duly adopted, it will represent the will of the people accomplished in the manner prescribed by the Constitution. By acting prematurely and unnecessarily, as I view it, the Court has assumed a decisional responsibility at the very time when state legislatures, functioning within the traditional democratic process, are debating the proposed Amendment. It seems to me that this reaching out to preempt by judicial action a major political decision which is currently in process of resolution does not reflect appropriate respect for duly prescribed legislative processes.

There are times when this Court, under our system, cannot avoid a constitutional decision on issues which normally should be resolved by the elected representatives of the people. But democratic institutions are weakened, and confidence in the restraint of the Court is impaired, when we appear unnecessarily to decide sensitive issues of broad social and political importance at the very time they are under consideration within the prescribed constitutional processes.

NOTES AND QUESTIONS

1. Because Chief Justice Burger voted originally in *Frontiero* to affirm, Justice Douglas assigned the Court's opinion, and he chose Justice Brennan to speak for the majority. Reflecting the views expressed in the *Frontiero* conference, Justice Brennan's original draft did not address the suspect-classification issue. When responses to his circulation indicated a likely majority for holding gender classifications suspect and requiring strict scrutiny, Justice Brennan restructured his opinion along those lines. Justices Douglas, White, and Marshall readily joined the opinion, but a fifth justice's approval was necessary to make it the Court's opinion. The most likely candidate was Justice Stewart. Although his position was close to Justice Brennan's, Justice Stewart did not join. Instead, he concurred in the result on the ground that the challenged statute worked "an invidious discrimination in violation of the Constitution." This explanation struck commentators as curious, for "invidious discrimination" was the standard term used in racial cases to justify strict scrutiny.

2. Given the special history of the Fourteenth Amendment as applied to race discrimination, is there any historical justification for treating race discrimination and gender discrimination identically under the Equal Protection Clause? Should courts be more willing to find valid the justifications given for different treatment of the sexes than they would be to approve the arguments for different treatment of the races? Is it significant that many women still feel no stigma as a result of classifications based on gender while racial classifications are almost always seen as stigmatic? Does the attitude of the dominant white male group differ in any significant way towards African–Americans and women? Are there any unique aspects of gender classifications making them either more suspect or more benign as a general proposition?

3. In 1971, the Supreme Court said that alien status was also a suspect basis of classification, since aliens were a discrete and politically powerless minority. On that theory, a state law that denied welfare benefits to aliens was struck down. Graham v. Richardson, 403 U.S. 365 (1971). Later cases invalidated other state laws discriminating against

aliens. Sugarman v. Dougall, 413 U.S. 634 (1973) (eligibility for state civil service positions); In re Griffiths, 413 U.S. 717 (1973) (right to practice law); Nyquist v. Mauclet, 432 U.S. 1 (1977) (eligibility for state scholarships, tuition grants and student loans). There was an alternative ground for decision in Graham v. Richardson, however, that may have been as important as the equal protection rationale. The Court noted that the federal government has broad power to decide whether aliens are entitled to stay in this country, and to impose the conditions on which they may remain. State laws imposing disabilities on aliens interfere with decisions by the federal government concerning the status of aliens. It is clear that federal laws disadvantaging aliens may be sustained, even if nearly identical state laws would be invalid. Mathews v. Diaz, 426 U.S. 67 (1976) (aliens ineligible for federal medical insurance); Hampton v. Mow Sun Wong, 426 U.S. 88 (1976) (federal civil service regulation excluding aliens from federal government jobs invalid, but implying that an identical prohibition could be imposed by Congress or the President). And, on the state level, aliens can be denied the rights to vote, run for elected office and hold policy-making government jobs. The Court has also sustained state laws that make aliens ineligible for other state employment. Foley v. Connelie, 435 U.S. 291 (1978) (exclusion of aliens from police force); Ambach v. Norwick, 441 U.S. 68 (1979) (aliens ineligible for certification as public school teachers). It can be argued that the Court has retreated from its 1971 doctrine that aliens are specially protected from discrimination by the equal protection clause, and that future cases will emphasize federal supremacy as the major reason for protecting aliens from discriminatory state laws.

C.　HEIGHTENED SCRUTINY

MISSISSIPPI UNIVERSITY FOR WOMEN v. HOGAN

Supreme Court of the United States, 1982.
458 U.S. 718, 102 S.Ct. 3331, 73 L.Ed.2d 1090.

JUSTICE O'CONNOR delivered the opinion of the Court.

This case presents the narrow issue of whether a state statute that excludes males from enrolling in a state-supported professional nursing school violates the Equal Protection Clause of the Fourteenth Amendment.

I

The facts are not in dispute. In 1884, the Mississippi legislature created the Mississippi Industrial Institute and College for the Education of White Girls of the State of Mississippi, now the oldest state-supported all-female college in the United States. In 1884 Miss.Gen.Laws, Ch. XXX § 6. The school, known today as Mississippi University for Women (MUW), has from its inception limited its enrollment to women.

In 1971, MUW established a School of Nursing, initially offering a two-year associate degree. Three years later, the school instituted a four-year baccalaureate program in nursing and today also offers a graduate program. The School of Nursing has its own faculty and administrative officers and establishes its own criteria for admission.

Respondent, Joe Hogan, is a registered nurse but does not hold a baccalaureate degree in nursing. Since 1974, he has worked as a nursing supervisor in a medical center in Columbus, the city in which MUW is located. In 1979, Hogan applied for admission to the MUW School of Nursing's baccalaureate program. Although he was otherwise qualified, he was denied admission to the School of Nursing solely because of his sex. School officials informed him that he could audit the courses in which he was interested, but could not enroll for credit.

Hogan filed an action in the United States District Court for the Northern District of Mississippi, claiming the single-sex admissions policy of MUW's School of Nursing violated the Equal Protection Clause of the Fourteenth amendment. . . .

[T]he District Court denied preliminary injunctive relief. . . .

The Court of Appeals for the Fifth Circuit reversed, holding that, because the admissions policy discriminates on the basis of gender, the District Court improperly used a "rational relationship" test to judge the constitutionality of the policy. . . .

[We]   . . . affirm. . . .

II

We begin our analysis aided by several firmly-established principles. Because the challenged policy expressly discriminates among applicants on the basis of gender, it is subject to scrutiny under the Equal Protection Clause of the Fourteenth Amendment. Reed v. Reed, 404 U.S. 71, 75 (1971). That this statute discriminates against males rather than against females does not exempt it from scrutiny or reduce the standard of review. Caban v. Mohammed, 441 U.S. 380, 394 (1979); Orr v. Orr, 440 U.S. 268, 279 (1979). Our decisions also establish that the party seeking to uphold a statute that classifies individuals on the basis of their gender must carry the burden of showing an "exceedingly persuasive justification" for the classification. Kirchberg v. Feenstra, 450 U.S. 455, 461 (1981); Personnel Administrator of Massachusetts v. Feeney, 442 U.S. 256, 273 (1979). The burden is met only by showing at least that the classification serves "important governmental objectives and that the discriminatory means employed" are "substantially related to the achievement of those objectives." Wengler v. Druggists Mutual Insurance Co., 446 U.S. 142, 150 (1980).

Although the test for determining the validity of a gender-based classification is straightforward, it must be applied free of fixed notions concerning the roles and abilities of males and females. Care must be taken in ascertaining whether the statutory objective itself reflects archaic and stereotypic notions. Thus, if the statutory objective is to exclude or "protect" members of one gender because they are presumed to suffer from an inherent handicap or to be innately inferior, the objective itself is illegitimate. See Frontiero v. Richardson . . . (1973) (plurality opinion).

If the State's objective is legitimate and important, we next determine whether the requisite direct, substantial relationship between objective and means is present. The purpose of requiring that close relationship is to assure that the validity of a classification is determined through reasoned analysis rather than through the mechanical application of traditional, often inaccurate, assumptions about the proper roles of men and women. The need for the requirement is amply revealed by reference to the broad range of statutes already invalidated by this Court, statutes that relied upon the simplistic, outdated assumption that gender could be used as a "proxy for other, more germane bases of classification," Craig v. Boren, 429 U.S. 190, 198 (1976), to establish a link between objective and classification.

[Applying this framework, Justice O'Connor, writing for a majority of five, concluded that Mississippi had fallen short of establishing the "exceedingly persuasive justification" to sustain a gender-based classification. Hence MUW's policy denying males the right to enroll for credit in its School of Nursing violates equal protection of the law.]

[The dissenting opinions of Chief Justice Burger and Justices Blackmun and Powell are omitted. Justice Rehnquist joined in the latter opinion.]

NOTES AND QUESTIONS

1. The Court's opinion in Mississippi University for Women v. Hogan illustrates heightened scrutiny. Such scrutiny has been also called "middle-tier scrutiny" because it came between the rational-basis and strict-scrutiny tests. The Court decided Mississippi University for Women v. Hogan during Justice O'Connor's first term on the Court. Her vote determined not only the Court's decision in the case but also apparently the Court's adherence to heightened scrutiny in gender cases. If gender classifications are not suspect, they appear to be semi-suspect and hence receive heightened scrutiny.

2. A principle analogous to semi-suspect classification has been applied by the Supreme Court to laws discriminating against children born out of wedlock. The Court has attempted, on a case-by-case basis, to distinguish laws which disadvantage illegitimates for appropriate reasons, such as the difficulties of proof of paternity, and those which disadvantage children because of outmoded moral concepts concerning the status of their birth. The distinctions have often been as close as the Court's vote. In Trimble v. Gordon, 430 U.S. 762 (1977), the Court held an Illinois statute invalid when it provided that an illegitimate child could inherit from a father only if the father had acknowledged the child and married the mother. In Lalli v. Lalli, 439 U.S. 259 (1978), the Court upheld a New York law which denied inheritance rights to illegitimate children unless the father had obtained a court order during his lifetime acknowledging paternity. Both decisions were by 5–4 votes. Eight of the nine justices believed the two cases were indistinguishable. (Four would have held both laws valid; four would have held both laws invalid. Justice Powell, who wrote both opinions, decided that there were legally significant distinctions.)

3.   In Plyler v. Doe, 457 U.S. 202 (1982), the Court relied, in part, on the illegitimacy cases in deciding that Texas could not exclude illegal aliens from public schools. The Court concluded that illegal aliens were not a suspect class, because they entered the country voluntarily, yet had no legal right to be here. Their children, however, had no control over the decision to enter the United States, and "directing the onus of a parent's misconduct against his children does not comport with fundamental conceptions of justice." (The Court's opinion, however, suggested that states could deny other benefits to undocumented alien children, since its rationale also emphasized that education, while not quite a "fundamental" right, was an especially important governmental service.)

4.   Some commentators have argued that there are other minority groups entitled to the same kind of constitutional protection as racial minorities, aliens, women and illegitimate children. Moreover, there are statutes which outlaw some forms of discrimination against older people or the physically handicapped.

The Supreme Court has been unwilling to treat discrimination against other groups as either suspect or semi-suspect. Massachusetts Board of Retirement v. Murgia, 427 U.S. 307 (1976), for example, involved a State law requiring that police officers retire at the age of fifty. It was argued that not all police who reached that age suffered diminished ability to perform their job, and that generalizations about those of advanced age should be subjected to strict scrutiny. The claim was rejected because the treatment of the aged, "while not wholly free of discrimination," had not been marked by a "history of purposeful unequal treatment." The elderly had thus not been "subjected to unique disabilities on the basis of stereotyped characteristics not truly indicative of their abilities." Is the last statement true? The Court also indicated that the aged had not been politically powerless. Does that mean that, as a group gains political power to protect its interests by legislation it forfeits some measure of constitutional protection? Does the history of the civil rights and women's movements suggest that the opposite may be true? (In City of Cleburne v. Cleburne Living Center, 473 U.S. 432 (1985), one reason given by the Court for concluding that the mentally retarded were not a suspect class was that state and federal legislation, in recent years, had "been addressing their difficulties in a manner that belies a continuing antipathy or prejudice." The dissent responded that legislation protecting the rights of the retarded demonstrated an evolving societal consensus that discrimination against them was "inconsistent with fundamental principles upon which American society rests.")

Would it be wiser to have a broad, general constitutional principle that all government decisions have to be based on individual criteria rather than group characteristics? As noted above, in City of Cleburne v. Cleburne Living Center, Inc., the Court's majority concluded that discrimination against the mentally retarded was not to be resolved by applying suspect classification analysis. The Court was unanimous, however, in deciding that it was unconstitutional for a city to prohibit operation of a home for the "feeble minded" in an area where boarding houses, nursing homes, fraternity houses, and dormitories were permitted. The Court's opinion stated that denying permission for the home "appears to us to rest on irrational prejudice" against the mentally retarded. It would be inappropriate for courts to second-guess every decision of every legislative body in the country, and hold laws unconstitutional every time a court decided that distinctions drawn by them were unwise. Is it so easy to identify a distinction that rests on "irrational prejudice" as opposed to one that is very unwise?

Chapter XXIV

RACIAL EQUALITY

I. SEGREGATION

PLESSY v. FERGUSON

Supreme Court of the United States, 1896.
163 U.S. 537, 16 S.Ct. 1138, 41 L.Ed. 256.

[An 1890 Louisiana law required railroads to provide "equal, but separate accommodations" for whites and blacks. Plessy boarded a railroad car reserved for whites. The conductor demanded that he move to the coach assigned to blacks. When Plessy refused to move, he was ejected from the train, and brought to trial for violating the 1890 railroad segregation laws. Ironically, Plessy's original claim seems to be that he was light skinned, and only one eighth black, and was therefore entitled to sit in the white coach. By the time the case reached the Supreme Court, however, the question was considerably broader than whether the conductor had assigned Plessy to the wrong coach. What was involved was the constitutionality of the 1890 law and, inferentially, all other laws segregating the races.]

JUSTICE BROWN ... delivered the opinion of the Court.

· · ·

The constitutionality of this act is attacked upon the ground that it conflicts both with the Thirteenth Amendment of the Constitution, abolishing slavery, and the Fourteenth Amendment, which prohibits certain restrictive legislation on the part of the States.

1. That it does not conflict with the Thirteenth Amendment, which abolished slavery and involuntary servitude, except as a punishment for crime, is too clear for argument. Slavery implies involuntary servitude— a state of bondage....

· · ·

A statute which implies merely a legal distinction between the white and colored races—a distinction which is founded in the color of the two races, and which must always exist so long as white men are distinguished from the other race by color—has no tendency to destroy the legal equality of the two races, or reestablish a state of involuntary servitude. Indeed, we do not understand that the Thirteenth Amendment is strenuously relied upon by the plaintiff in error in this connection.

· · ·

The object of the [Fourteenth Amendment] was undoubtedly to enforce the absolute equality of the two races before the law, but in the nature of things it could not have been intended to abolish distinctions based upon color, or to enforce social, as distinguished from political equality, or a commingling of the two races upon terms unsatisfactory to either. Laws permitting, and even requiring, their separation in places where they are liable to be brought into contact do not necessarily imply the inferiority of either race to the other, and have been generally, if not universally, recognized as within the competency of the state legislatures in the exercise of their police power. The most common instance of this is connected with the establishment of separate schools for white and colored children, which has been held to be a valid exercise of the legislative power even by courts of States where the political rights of the colored race have been longest and most earnestly enforced.

One of the earliest of these cases is that of Roberts v. City of Boston, 5 Cush. (59 Mass.) 198, in which the Supreme Judicial Court of Massachusetts held that the general school committee of Boston had power to make provision for the instruction of colored children in separate schools established exclusively for them, and to prohibit their attendance upon the other schools. "The great principle," said Chief Justice Shaw, p. 206, "advanced by the learned and eloquent advocate for the plaintiff (Mr. Charles Summer) is, that by the constitution and laws of Massachusetts, all persons without distinction of age or sex, birth or color, origin or condition, are equal before the law.... But, when this great principle comes to be applied to the actual various conditions of persons in society, it will not warrant the assertion that men and women are legally clothed with the same civil and political powers, and that children and adults are legally to have the same functions and be subject to the same treatment; but only that the rights of all, as they are settled and regulated by law, are equally entitled to the paternal consideration and protection of the law for their maintenance and security." It was held that the powers of the committee extended to the establishment of separate schools for children of different ages, sexes and colors, and that they might also establish special schools for poor and neglected children, who have become too old to attend the primary school, and yet have not acquired the rudiments of learning, to enable them to enter the ordinary schools. Similar laws have been enacted by Congress under its general power of legislation over the District of Columbia, ... as well as by the legislatures of many of the States, and have been generally, if not uniformly, sustained by the courts. [Cases from Ohio, California, Indiana and Kentucky, among others, are cited here.]

. . .

The distinction between laws interfering with the political equality of the negro and those requiring the separation of the two races in schools, theatres and railway carriages has been frequently drawn by this court. Thus in Strauder v. West Virginia, ... it was held that a law of West Virginia limiting to white male persons, 21 years of age and citizens of the State, the right to sit upon juries, was a discrimination which implied a legal inferiority in civil society, which lessened the security of the right of the colored race, and was a step toward reducing them to a condition of servility. . . .

. . .

. . . [W]e think the enforced separation of the races, as applied to the internal commerce of the State, neither abridges the privileges or immunities of the colored man, deprives him of his property without due process of law, nor denies him the equal protection of the laws, within the meaning of the Fourteenth Amendment. . . .

It is claimed by the plaintiff in error that, in any mixed community, the reputation of belonging to the dominant race, in this instance the white race, is *property,* in the same sense that a right of action, or of inheritance, is property. Conceding this to be so, for the purposes of this case, we are unable to see how this statute deprives him of, or in any way affects his right to, such property. If he be a white man and assigned to a colored coach, he may have his action for damages against the company for being deprived of his so called property. Upon the other hand, if he be a colored man and be so assigned, he has been deprived of no property, since he is not lawfully entitled to the reputation of being a white man.

In this connection, it is also suggested by the learned counsel for the plaintiff in error that the same argument that will justify the state legislature in requiring railways to provide separate accommodations for the two races will also authorize them to require separate cars to be provided for people whose hair is of a certain color, or who are aliens, or who belong to certain nationalities, or to enact laws requiring colored people to walk upon one side of the street, and white people upon the other, or requiring white men's houses to be painted white, and colored men's black, or their vehicles or business signs to be of different colors, upon the theory that one side of the street is as good as the other, or that a house or vehicle of one color is as good as one of another color. The reply to all this is that every exercise of the police power must be reasonable, and extend only to such laws as are enacted in good faith for the promotion for the public good, and not for the annoyance or oppression of a particular class. . . .

So far, then, as a conflict with the Fourteenth Amendment is concerned, the case reduces itself to the question whether the statute of Louisiana is a reasonable regulation, and with respect to this there must necessarily be a large discretion on the part of the legislature. In determining the question of reasonableness it is at liberty to act with reference to the established usages, customs and traditions of the people, and with a view to the promotion of their comfort, and the preservation of the public peace and good order. Gauged by this standard, we cannot say that a law which authorizes or even requires the separation of the two races in public conveyances is unreasonable, or more obnoxious to the Fourteenth Amendment than the acts of Congress requiring separate schools for colored children in the District of Columbia, the constitutionality of which does not seem to have been questioned, or the corresponding acts of state legislatures.

We consider the underlying fallacy of the plaintiff's argument to consist in the assumption that the enforced separation of the two races stamps the colored race with a badge of inferiority. If this be so, it is not by reason of anything found in the act, but solely because the colored race chooses to put that construction upon it. The argument necessarily assumes that if, as has been more than once the case, and is not unlikely to be so again, the colored race should become the dominant power in the state legislature, and should enact a law in precisely similar terms, it would thereby relegate the white race to an inferior position. We imagine that the white race, at least, would not acquiesce in this assumption. The argument also assumes that social prejudices may be overcome by legislation, and that equal rights cannot be secured to the negro except by an enforced commingling of the two races. We cannot accept this proposition. If the two races are to meet upon terms of social equality, it must be the result of natural affinities, a mutual appreciation of each other's merits and a voluntary consent of individuals. . . . Legislation is powerless to eradicate racial instincts or to abolish distinctions based upon physical differences, and the attempt to do so can only result in accentuating the difficulties of the present situation. If the civil and political rights of both races be equal one cannot be inferior to the other civilly or politically. If one race be inferior to the other socially, the Constitution of the United States cannot put them upon the same plane.

It is true that the question of the proportion of colored blood necessary to constitute a colored person, as distinguished from a white person, is one upon which there is a difference of opinion in the different States, some holding that any visible admixture of black blood stamps the person as belonging to the colored race . . .; others that it depends upon the preponderance of blood, . . . and still others that the predominance of white blood must only be in the proportion of three fourths. . . . But these are questions to be determined under the laws of each State and are not properly put in issue in this case. . . .

JUSTICE HARLAN, dissenting.

. . .

It was said in argument that the statute of Louisiana does not discriminate against either race, but prescribes a rule applicable alike to white and colored citizens. But this argument does not meet the difficulty. Every one knows that the statute in question had its origin in the purpose, not so much to exclude white persons from railroad cars occupied by blacks, as to exclude colored people from coaches occupied by or assigned to white persons. . . . The thing to accomplish was, under the guise of giving equal accommodation for whites and blacks to compel the latter to keep to themselves while travelling in railroad passenger coaches. No one would be so wanting in candor as to assert the contrary. The fundamental objection, therefore, to the statute is that it interferes with the personal freedom of citizens. . . . If a white man and a black man choose to occupy the same public conveyance on a public highway, it is their right to do so, and no government, proceeding alone on grounds of race, can prevent it without infringing the personal liberty of each.

JOHN MARSHALL HARLAN I—Born on June 1, 1833, in Boyle County, Kentucky, into a prominent political family. His father was a U.S. Representative and also attorney general and secretary of state of Kentucky. Republican. Presbyterian. Attended Centre College. Studied law with mentors at Transylvania University, his father, and other lawyers. Began practice in 1853. County judge, 1858–1859. Participated in politics throughout his legal career. Though a slaveholder, he remained loyal to the Union and served as a Union officer in the Civil War. Nominated associate justice by President Rutherford B. Hayes, whom he had supported for the presidency, to replace David Davis on October 17, 1877. Confirmed by voice vote on November 29, 1877. Served on the Court until his death on October 14, 1911. Harlan was one of the Court's earliest champions of civil rights and liberties. In the *Civil Rights Cases* (1883) and Plessy v. Ferguson (1896), he wrote eloquent dissenting opinions in defense of racial equality. In the former case, he deliberately used the same pen and inkwell Chief Justice Taney had used in writing the Court's opinion in Dred Scott v. Standford (1857). In Patterson v. Colorado (1907), he argued in dissent that the Fourteenth Amendment protected freedom of speech and press against state action.

. . .

The white race deems itself to be the dominant race in this country. And so it is, in prestige, in achievements, in education, in wealth and in power. So, I doubt not, it will continue to be for all time, if it remains true to its great heritage and holds fast to the principles of constitutional liberty. But in view of the Constitution, in the eye of the law, there is in this country no superior, dominant, ruling class of citizens. There is no caste here. Our Constitution is color-blind, and neither knows nor tolerates classes among citizens. In respect of civil rights, all citizens are equal before the law. The humblest is the peer of the most powerful. The law regards man as man, and takes no account of his surroundings or of his color when his civil rights as guaranteed by the supreme law of the land are involved. It is, therefore, to be regretted that this high tribunal, the final expositor of the fundamental law of the land, has reached the conclusion that it is competent for a State to regulate the enjoyment by citizens of their civil rights solely upon the basis of race.

In my opinion, the judgment this day rendered will, in time, prove to be quite as pernicious as the decision made by this tribunal in the Dred Scott case. It was adjudged in that case that the descendants of Africans who were imported into this country and sold as slaves were not included nor intended to be included under the word "citizens" in the Constitution, and could not claim any of the rights and privileges which that instrument provided for and secured to citizens of the United States; that at the time of the adoption of the Constitution they were "considered as a subordinate and inferior class of beings, who had been subjugated by the dominant race, and, whether emancipated or not, yet remained subject to their authority, and had no rights or privileges but such as those who held the power and the government might choose to grant them." ... The recent amendments of the Constitution, it was supposed, had eradicated these principles from our institutions. But it seems that we have yet, in some of the States, a dominant race—a superior class of citizens, which assumes to regulate the enjoyment of civil rights, common to all citizens, upon the basis of race.... The destinies of the two races, in this country, are indissolubly linked together, and the interests of both require that the common government of all shall not permit the seeds of race hate to be planted under the sanction of law. What can more certainly arouse race hate, what more certainly create and perpetuate a feeling of distrust between these races, than state enactments, which, in fact, proceed on the ground that colored citizens are so inferior and degraded that they cannot be allowed to sit in public coaches occupied by white citizens? That, as all will admit, is the real meaning of such legislation as was enacted in Louisiana....

. . .

... The thin disguise of "equal" accommodations for passengers in railroad coaches will not mislead any one, nor atone for the wrong this day done....

. . .

For the reasons stated, I am constrained to withhold my assent from the opinion and judgment of the majority.

THE IMPACT OF *PLESSY*

Plessy legitimated and encouraged a regime of racial segregation in certain sections of the United States for more than 50 years. In 1946, there were more than 250 statutes in 22 states compelling or permitting racial segregation in schools, colleges, libraries, trains, waiting rooms, buses, street cars, steamboats, ferries, circuses, theaters, public halls, parks, playgrounds, beaches, racetracks, poolrooms, hospitals, mental asylums, prisons, poor houses, orphanages, and homes for the aged. Six states prohibited prisoners of different races to be chained together; one state required separate telephone books; another prohibited interracial boxing.*

NOTES AND QUESTIONS

1. Soon after the Louisiana legislature enacted the separate accommodation law, the law's opponents declared publicly that they would challenge its constitutionality. "Railroad officials," wrote C. Vann Woodward, "proved surprisingly cooperative. The first one approached, however, confessed that his road 'did not enforce the law.' It provided the Jim Crow car and posted the sign required by law, but told its conductors to molest no one who ignored instructions. Officers of two other roads 'said the law was a bad and mean one; they would like to get rid of

---

* This is a partial list. The complete list is in Milton R. Konvitz, The Constitution and Civil Rights, New York, 1946, pp. 230–241.

it,' and asked for time to consult counsel. 'They want to help us,' said [one of the law's opponents], 'but dread public opinion.' The extra expense of separate cars was one reason for railroad opposition to the Jim Crow law."** The first constitutional test of the law involved Daniel F. Desdunes, a young black man who had purchased a ticket from New Orleans to Mobile, Alabama, and took a seat in the white coach. He was arrested, but the case never went to trial, for the Louisiana Supreme Court had just held in another case that the separate-accommodation law was unconstitutional insofar as it applied to interstate passengers. One week later, according to plan, Homer Adolph Plessy, who described himself as "seven-eighths Caucasian and one-eighth African blood," bought a ticket from New Orleans to Covington, Louisiana, entered the white car, and was arrested for violating the law.

2. The major thrust of Justice Brown's opinion in the *Plessy* case is that the Louisiana law did not treat African Americans and Caucasians unequally. Do you think it was true in 1896, as his opinion concluded, that if "the enforced separation of the two races stamps the colored race with a badge of inferiority ... it is not by reason of anything found in the act, but solely because the colored race chooses to put that interpretation on it"?

3. At another point, the opinion states: "If the two races are to meet upon terms of social equality, it must be the result of natural affinities, a mutual appreciation of each other's merits and a voluntary consent of individuals." Is that an argument that the Fourteenth Amendment is inapplicable to laws which impose social inequality? Or is Justice Brown saying that the law requiring segregation doesn't impose inequality of social standing, but the inequality arises from social customs that law is powerless to change? Over half a century later, Chief Justice Warren's opinion in Brown v. Board of Education was severely criticized for relying on social science materials, particularly his citation of Gunnar Myrdal's *An American Dilemma*. The criticism was that the *Brown* decision rested on "sociology" rather than "law." Do you find a hint of sociology in the *Plessy* decision as well, even if Justice Brown didn't cite any sociologists? (Until well into the Twentieth Century, it was the unvarying custom of American courts to cite nothing except court decisions and a few well-recognized legal treatises. Even citation of the most prestigious legal periodicals was frowned on. Certainly, in 1896, one would not dare cite the writings of a sociologist.)

4. A secondary theme of Justice Brown's opinion is that, even if the law treated blacks unequally, it did not violate the Equal Protection Clause because it was "reasonable" to do so. Consider, for example, the hypothetical laws raised in argument by Plessy's counsel that Justice Brown conceded would be unconstitutional—laws requiring the races to walk on different sides of the street, laws requiring that houses occupied by different races be painted different colors, laws requiring separate railroad coaches for aliens or for people with a certain hair color. Do these laws create inequalities that racial segregation in railroad cars does

---

** C. Vann Woodward, The Case of the Louisiana Traveler, in John D. Garraty, ed., Quarrels That Have Shaped the Constitution, Harper & Row, 1964, p. 149.

not? Or would these laws create inequalities which the Court considered to be "unreasonable?"

5. In practice "separate but equal" was rarely a workable doctrine. As described by Charles L. Black, Jr., in the next excerpt, the separate facilities were generally not equal in the area of education:*

> The Negro schools, which were undeniably separate, were generally by no means equal in their most obvious physical characteristics, let alone in more subtle matters such as their quality of education. For instance, in 1950, some 54 years after Plessy v. Ferguson, Mississippi, which had almost equal numbers of white and Negro students, had half again as many teachers in the white schools. Moreover, the widespread belief that from the 1940's on, the Southern states had moved with great energy and rapidity to ease the obvious inequalities in its schools, seems to be refuted by statistics. For instance, in 1952, 56 years after *Plessy,* rather than spending more on the Negro student to close the gap previously created between him and the white student, Mississippi's current educational expenditure per Negro pupil was 30 per cent of that per white pupil; South Carolina's was 60 per cent; Arkansas', 66 per cent; and Georgia's, 68 per cent. Roughly similar figures could be given for the capital expenditures on Negro and white schools. With only two exceptions, Southern states, rather than attempting to make up the deficiency in quality of buildings between white and Negro schools, were still spending more per pupil on the white schools. Georgia was spending 53 per cent as much per pupil on Negro school construction as on white school construction; Alabama, 60 per cent; South Carolina, 46 per cent. Generally, the same type of disparity was noticeable in the salaries paid teachers, the number of books purchased for school libraries, and almost every other characteristic investigated....
>
> The separate but equal doctrine was a failure not only because it was so openly and widely flouted, but because it was impossible to administer rationally. While equality of one railway car with another was susceptible of reasonably accurate measurement, equality of schools was not. For instance, how was a court to balance the fact that a Negro high school was in a newer building against the fact that it was a forty minute bus ride away for Negro students who lived within easy walking distance of a white high school? How could a court balance the availability of fine courses in woodworking in the Negro schools with the absence of a course in trigonometry there? As one district court judge stated, "[The separate but equal doctrine] present[s] problems which are more than judicial and which involve elements of public finance, school administration, politics and sociology.... The federal courts are not school boards;

---

* Charles L. Black, Jr., The Lawfulness of the Segregation Decisions, Yale Law Journal, 1960, vol. 69, pp. 163, 164.

they are not prepared to take over the administration of the public schools of the several states."

6. From 1938 to 1954, the Supreme Court insisted that separate facilities in higher education must be integrated because they did not provide equal education to African American students:*

It was not until 1938, in Missouri ex rel. Gaines v. Canada,[1] that the Supreme Court struck down a state statute providing for segregation in education. Missouri maintained a law school for whites only and no equal, or even unequal, one for Negroes. Rather it offered to pay the tuition of any Missouri Negro at a law school in an adjacent state. In an opinion by Chief Justice Hughes, the Court rejected the state's contention that by paying tuition at equal law schools it had complied with the *Plessy* doctrine. Although Chief Justice Hughes seemed to base his decision entirely on the principle that a state was not providing equal education by requiring resort to another state's facilities, he did avert to the possibility that "equality" under the separate but equal doctrine might mean more than simple parity in physical facilities.

Twelve years after the *Gaines* case, in 1950, the Supreme Court was given an opportunity actually to analyze the ingredients of equality under the *Plessy* doctrine. The Court in two companion opinions, both written by Chief Justice Vinson, examined not only the intangible values associated with a particular school, but also considered the educational process itself. In Sweatt v. Painter,[2] the Court went beyond the mere physical facilities to find Texas' Negro law school inferior to Texas Law School in "those qualities which are incapable of objective measurement." These included the position and influence of the alumni, standing in the community, traditions and prestige. Moreover, for the first time in this context, the Court overtly recognized that in the United States the two races were not on an equal footing. It stated that the segregation deprived the Negro of educational contact with the dominant racial groups, which comprised 85 per cent of the population of the state and included most of the lawyers, jurors, judges, and other officials with whom a lawyer inevitably deals. On the same day that Sweatt v. Painter was decided, the Supreme Court handed down McLaurin v. Oklahoma State Regents,[3] involving a closely related issue. There, Oklahoma, while admitting the Negro petitioner to its graduate school, had insisted that he conform to certain regulations:

> Thus he was required to sit apart at a designated desk in an anteroom adjoining the classroom; to sit at a designated desk on the mezzanine floor of the library,

---

* Ibid., pp. 166–167.

1. 305 U.S. 337 (1938).

2. 339 U.S. 629 (1950).

3. 339 U.S. 637 (1950).

but not to use the desks in the regular reading room; and to sit at a designated table and to eat at a different time from the other students in the school cafeteria.

The Court held that these restrictions "impair and inhibit his ability to study, to engage in discussions, and exchange views with other students and, in general, to learn his profession." Chief Justice Vinson's opinion then struck another blow at the separate but equal doctrine and the rationale of *Plessy* by stating:

> There is a vast difference—a Constitutional difference—between restrictions imposed by the state which prohibit the intellectual commingling of students, and the refusal of individuals to commingle where the state presents no such bar.

BROWN v. BOARD OF EDUCATION

Supreme Court of the United States, 1954.
347 U.S. 483, 74 S.Ct. 686, 98 L.Ed. 873.

[The Segregation Cases were argued twice—first in 1952 and again in 1953. Between the two arguments, Chief Justice Vinson died. Court members immediately realized that Vinson's death was likely to affect, if not the disposition of the cases, at least the Court's votes and opinions in them. Certainly that was Justice Frankfurter's view. Soon after learning of Vinson's death, Frankfurter told his law clerk, Alexander Bickel, "This is the first indication I have ever had that there is a God."* Exactly three months later, Chief Justice Warren presided over the Court when counsel argued the case. Justice Douglas's conference notes, taken five days later, report Warren's views as follows: "[The] separate but equal doctrine rests on [a] basic premise that the Negro race is inferior. [T]hat is [the] only way to sustain Plessy. [The] argument of [N]egro counsel proves they are not inferior. We can't set up one group apart from the rest of us and say they are not entitled to same treatment as all others. [The] 13th, 14th, and 15th Amendments were intended to make equal those who were once slaves. [T]hat view causes trouble perhaps—but [I do] not know how segregation can be justified in this day and age. [I recognize] that [the] time element is important in the deep south. [So] we must act in a tolerant way"* At Warren's request, no formal vote was taken in the Segregation Cases, but it was clear that a majority of the justices supported his views. Warren assigned himself the Court's opinion, and eventually all his colleagues joined the opinion. Justice Reed was the last to give his assent.]

Chief Justice Warren delivered the opinion of the Court.

These cases come to us from the States of Kansas, South Carolina, Virginia, and Delaware. They are premised on different facts and differ-

---

* Alexander Bickel in a conversation with David J. Danelski, 1965. Bickel apparently gave this information to Richard Kluger, who attributes the quoted sentence to "a former law clerk." *Simple Justice*, Knopf, 1976, p. 656.

* Douglas Papers, Library of Congress, Box 1150.

ent local conditions, but a common legal question justifies their consideration together in this consolidated opinion.

In each of the cases, minors of the Negro race, through their legal representatives, seek the aid of the courts in obtaining admission to the public schools of their community on a nonsegregated basis. . . . In each of the cases other than the Delaware case, a three-judge federal district court denied relief to the plaintiffs on the so-called "separate but equal" doctrine announced by this Court in Plessy v. Ferguson. . . . Under that doctrine, equality of treatment is accorded when the races are provided substantially equal facilities, even though these facilities be separate. . . .

The plaintiffs contend that segregated public schools are not "equal" and cannot be made "equal," and that hence they are deprived of the equal protection of the laws. Because of the obvious importance of the question presented, the Court took jurisdiction. Argument was heard in the 1952 Term, and reargument was heard this Term on certain questions propounded by the Court.**

Reargument was largely devoted to the circumstances surrounding the adoption of the Fourteenth Amendment in 1868. It covered exhaustively consideration of the Amendment in Congress, ratification by the states, then existing practices in racial segregation, and the views of proponents and opponents of the Amendment. This discussion and our own investigation convince us that, although these sources cast some light, it is not enough to resolve the problem with which we are faced. At best, they are inconclusive. The most avid proponents of the post-War Amendments undoubtedly intended them to remove all legal distinctions among "all persons born or naturalized in the United States." Their opponents, just as certainly, were antagonistic to both the letter and the spirit of the Amendments and wished them to have the most limited effect. What others in Congress and the state legislatures had in mind cannot be determined with any degree of certainty.

An additional reason for the inconclusive nature of the Amendment's history, with respect to segregated schools, is the status of public education at that time. In the South, the movement toward free common schools, supported by general taxation, had not yet taken hold. Education of white children was largely in the hands of private groups. Education of Negroes was almost nonexistent, and practically all of the

** 1. What evidence is there that the Congress which submitted and the State legislatures and conventions which ratified the Fourteenth Amendment contemplated or did not contemplate, understood or did not understand that it would abolish segregation in public schools?

2. If neither the Congress in submitting nor the States in ratifying the Fourteenth Amendment understood that compliance with it would require the immediate abolition of segregation in public schools, was it nevertheless the understanding of the framers of the Amendment

(a) that future Congresses might, in the exercise of their power under section 5 of the Amendment, abolish such segregation, or

(b) that it would be within the judicial power, in light of future conditions, to construe the Amendment as abolishing such segregation of its own force?

3. On the assumption that the answers to questions 2(a) and (b) do not dispose of the issue, is it within the judicial power, in construing the Amendment, to abolish segregation in public schools? (345 U.S. 972).

race were illiterate. In fact, any education of Negroes was forbidden by law in some states. . . .

. . .

In approaching this problem, we cannot turn the clock back to 1868 when the Amendment was adopted, or even to 1896 when Plessy v. Ferguson was written. We must consider public education in the light of its full development and its present place in American life throughout the Nation. Only in this way can it be determined if segregation in public schools deprives these plaintiffs of the equal protection of the laws.

Today, education is perhaps the most important function of state and local governments. Compulsory school attendance laws and the great expenditures for education both demonstrate our recognition of the importance of education to our democratic society. . . . In these days, it is doubtful that any child may reasonably be expected to succeed in life if he is denied the opportunity of an education. Such an opportunity, where the state has undertaken to provide it, is a right which must be made available to all on equal terms.

We come then to the question presented: Does segregation of children in public schools solely on the basis of race, even though the physical facilities and other "tangible" factors may be equal, deprive the children of the minority group of equal educational opportunities? We believe that it does.

In Sweatt v. Painter, . . . in finding that a segregated law school for Negroes could not provide them equal educational opportunities, this Court relied in large part on "those qualities which are incapable of objective measurement but which make for greatness in a law school." In McLaurin v. Oklahoma State Regents, . . . the Court, in requiring that a Negro admitted to a white graduate school be treated like all other students, again resorted to intangible considerations: ". . . his ability to study, to engage in discussions and exchange views with other students, and, in general, to learn his profession." Such considerations apply with added force to children in grade and high schools. To separate them from others of similar age and qualifications solely because of their race generates a feeling of inferiority as to their status in the community that may affect their hearts and minds in a way unlikely ever to be undone. The effect of this separation on their educational opportunities was well stated by a finding in the Kansas case by a court which nevertheless felt compelled to rule against the Negro plaintiffs:

> "Segregation of white and colored children in public schools has a detrimental effect upon the colored children. The impact is greater when it has the sanction of the law; for the policy of separating the races is usually interpreted as denoting the inferiority of the negro group. A sense of inferiority affects the motivation of a child to learn. Segregation with the sanction of law, therefore, has a tendency to [retard] the educational and mental development of negro children and to deprive them of

some of the benefits they would receive in a racial[ly] integrated school system."[1]

Whatever may have been the extent of psychological knowledge at the time of Plessy v. Ferguson, this finding is amply supported by modern authority.[2] Any language in Plessy v. Ferguson contrary to this finding is rejected.

We conclude that in the field of public education the doctrine of "separate but equal" has no place. Separate educational facilities are inherently unequal. Therefore, we hold that the plaintiffs and others similarly situated for whom the actions have been brought are, by reason of the segregation complained of, deprived of the equal protection of the laws guaranteed by the Fourteenth Amendment. . . .

NOTES AND QUESTIONS

1. In interpreting statutes and the Constitution courts look not only to the history of the times during which the provisions were enacted, but also to the legislative history of the provisions. Legislative histories are useful tools in interpretation but they cannot be considered the final word on the meaning of a statute or constitution. The wording used in a statute or constitutional provision normally means different things to different legislators and one rarely knows the views of every legislator. Constitutional amendments usually provide greater difficulties than statutes since the language used tends to be much more general. An additional difficulty arises because the States, which also must vote on amendments, may have different understandings of an amendment's meaning. Despite these difficulties the Congressional history of a proposed amendment can shed some light on the proper interpretation of the amendment as passed and cannot be lightly cast aside. How did the Court in *Brown* treat the Congressional history of the Fourteenth Amendment?

2. An article by Alexander Bickel* concluded that the Equal Protection clause of the Fourteenth Amendment clearly was "meant to apply neither to jury service nor suffrage, nor antimiscegenation statutes, nor segregation." However, Bickel goes on to provide a rationale for the Court's treatment of the Congressional history of that amendment:

> . . . [M]ay it not be that the Moderates and the Radicals reached a compromise permitting them to go to the country with language which they could, where necessary, defend against damaging alarms raised by the opposition [concerning voting rights, miscegenation, integration, etc.], but which at the

---

1. A similar finding was made in the Delaware case: "I conclude from the testimony that in our Delaware society, State-imposed segregation in education itself results in the Negro children, as a class, receiving educational opportunities which are substantially inferior to those available to white children otherwise similarly situated." 87 A.2d 862, 865.

2. K.B. Clark, Effect of Prejudice and Discrimination on Personality Development (Midcentury White House Conference on Children and Youth, 1950); . . . And see generally Myrdal, An American Dilemma, 1944.

* Alexander M. Bickel, The Original Understanding and the Segregation Decision, Harvard Law Review, 1955, vol. 69, pp. 61–63.

same time was sufficiently elastic to permit reasonable future advances? ... If the [Republican] party was to unite behind a compromise which consisted neither of an exclusive listing of a limited series of rights, nor of a formulation dangerously vulnerable to attacks pandering to the prejudices of the people, [appropriate] language had to be found. Bingham** himself supplied it. It had both sweep and the appearance of a careful enumeration of rights, and it had a right to echo in the national memory of libertarian beginnings.... They could go forth and honestly defend themselves against charges that on the day after ratification Negroes were going to become white men's "social equals," marry their daughters, vote in their elections, sit on their juries, and attend schools with their children. The Radicals ... obtained what early in the session had seemed a very uncertain prize indeed: a firm alliance, under Radical leadership, with the Moderates in the struggle against the President, and thus a good, clear chance at increasing and prolonging their political power. In the future, the Radicals could, in one way or another, put through such further civil rights provisions as they thought the country would take, without being subject to the sort of effective constitutional objections which haunted them when they were forced to operate under the thirteenth amendment.

It is, of course, giving the men of the 39th Congress much more than their due to ennoble them by a comparison of their proceedings with the deliberations of the Philadelphia Convention. Yet if this was the compromise that was struck, then these men emulated the technique of the original framers, who were also responsible to an electorate only partly receptive to the fullness of their principles, and who similarly avoided the explicit grant of some powers without foreclosing their future assumption....

It is such a reading as this of the original understanding, in response to the second of the questions propounded by the Court, that the Chief Justice must have had in mind when he termed the materials "inconclusive." For up to this point they tell a clear story and are anything but inconclusive. From this point on the word is apt, since the interpretation of the evidence ... comes only to this, that the question of giving greater protection ... was deferred, was left open, to be decided another day under a constitutional provision with more scope than the unserviceable thirteenth amendment. Some no doubt felt more certain than others that the new amendment would make possible further strides toward the ideal of equality. That remained to be decided, and there is no indication of the way in which anyone thought the decision would go on any given specific issue....

** Congressman from Ohio and noted abolitionist.

3.   What precisely are the steps in the Court's reasoning in *Brown*? Does the decision rest on the finding by the lower court in the Kansas case that segregation creates a sense of inferiority affecting the ability of African American children to learn? Would segregation by law be constitutional if African American children did as well in segregated schools as integrated schools?

4.   Did the *Brown* decision outlaw segregation in areas other than education? Shortly after *Brown* was decided, the Court, in per curiam decisions unaccompanied by opinions, required the desegregation of public beaches, parks, golf courses, and buses.** If opinions had been written, on what grounds do you think the decisions would have been justified?

HOW SIGNIFICANT WAS CHIEF JUSTICE WARREN'S LEADERSHIP IN BROWN?

The conventional view is that the Vinson Court had been hopelessly deadlocked in the segregation cases in 1952 and that the Court's unanimous vote and opinion in the cases were the result of Chief Justice Warren's astute leadership. Professor Hutchinson calls this view "a myth." At most Chief Justice Warren's achievement in *Brown,* wrote Hutchinson, was to persuade Justice Reed not to dissent and Justice Jackson not to write a concurring opinion. Hutchinson argues that after the Court's decisions in Sweatt v. Painter, 339 U.S. 629 (1950) and McLaurin v. Oklahoma State Regents, 339 U.S. 637 (1950), the Court's decision to overrule Plessy v. Ferguson was a foregone conclusion.* In an interview in 1973, Justice Clark was asked: "What would have happened [in *Brown*] if Vinson had lived?" Justice Clark answered: "The result would have been the same. The opinion may have been written differently. One can hardly surmise how Chief Justice Vinson would have written it. I don't see how any informed person could conclude to the contrary. Indeed, the result was forecast in Sweatt v. Painter."** Milton Konvitz came to a similar conclusion. Challenging the notion that the Court's decision in *Brown* was revolutionary, Konvitz wrote: "The fact is ... that in a series of cases preceding the Brown case the Court showed that it had no intention of lending its great prestige and power to a validation of racial segregation as it continued to accept unquestioningly and dogmatically the doctrine of 'separate but equal.' ... The Brown case undeniably represents a great constitutional leap; but it was a leap for

---

** Attention is usually focused on these inequalities as things in themselves, correctible by detailed decrees. I am more interested in their very clear character as *evidence* of what segregation means to the people who impose it and to the people who are subjected to it. This evidentiary character cannot be erased by one-step-ahead-of-the-marshal correction. Can a system which, in all that can be measured, has practiced the grossest inequality, actually have been "equal" in intent, in total social meaning and in Muir v. Louisville Park Theatrical Assn., 347 U.S. 971 (1954); Mayor of Baltimore v. Dawson, 350 U.S. 877 (1955); Holmes v. City of Atlanta, 350 U.S. 879 (1955); Gayle v. Browder, 352 U.S. 903 (1956).

* Dennis J. Hutchinson, A Scholar's View of the Tom C. Clark Papers, Symposium on the Tom C. Clark Papers, Tarlton Law Library, University of Texas Law School, 1987, pp. 14–16.

** Tom C. Clark interview, Fred M. Vinson Oral History Project, University of Kentucky Library, 1973, pp. 2–3.

which the Justices, like athletes in a sports competition, had prepared themselves by running forward before bounding over the obstacle.''[†]

THE IMPACT OF BROWN

Implementing the command of the *Brown* decision proved, as many had predicted, to be a long and difficult task. In *Brown II v. Board of Education,* 349 U.S. 294 (1955), the Court considered the problem of implementation and decided that desegregation should proceed with "all deliberate speed," that only administrative problems would excuse delay, and that the United States District Courts would have the role of supervising the desegregation process. The judges who sat on the Southern District Courts were Southerners and as a result at least initially, they tended to be sympathetic with those who had favored segregation. Their designation as the source of relief when desegregation proceeded too slowly insured that the emphasis would be on deliberateness rather than speed. Even though the most blatant examples of defiance to the *Brown* decision were struck down, many evasive techniques and excuses for delay were tolerated. Until Congress finally acted and the Supreme Court's patience ended, desegregation proceeded at an extremely slow pace. Ten years after *Brown II,* in 1963–64, 98 percent of black children in eleven Southern states still attended all Black schools.

Then, in 1964, Congress passed the Civil Rights Act which provided that federal funds would be cut off to those school districts still practicing discrimination. Coupled with a massive appropriation in 1965 for educational aid, this act became a spur to desegregation. The Supreme Court was still implementing Brown v. Board of Education as late as 1992.

The most difficult problem in the South, the appropriate remedy for segregated college systems, was not addressed by the Court until 1992, in United States v. Fordice, 505 U.S. 717 (1992). Nearly forty years after *Brown,* Mississippi had five almost completely white and three almost exclusively black universities. The Court rejected Mississippi's argument that it had complied with its constitutional obligations so long as college students were free to choose the institution that they wished to attend. The Court sent the case back to the lower federal courts to decide whether a number of state policies adopted when Mississippi ran a formal dual school system—e.g., requiring higher test scores for admission to the predominantly-white colleges, and duplication of programs at predominantly-white and predominantly-black colleges—contributed to continuing segregation. The Court did not clearly address an obvious tension—between integration as a constitutional goal, and preservation of the historic mission of predominantly black public colleges. On the one hand, the Court explicitly rejected the argument that Mississippi should be ordered to maintain the predominantly black colleges and increase their financing, concluding that Mississippi would not meet "its burden under *Brown* to take affirmative steps to dismantle its prior *de jure* system when it perpetuates a separate, but 'more equal' one." On the other hand, the Court concluded that involuntary student assignment—

[†] Milton Konvitz, Expanding Liberties: Freedom's Gains in Postwar America, Viking Press, 1966, p. 245.

often used to remedy segregation in primary and secondary schools—was inappropriate at the college level. Concurring, Justice Thomas stated that there was a "sound educational justification" to maintain historically black colleges "because of their distinctive histories and traditions." He, therefore, did not read the Court's opinion to forbid the states from continuing to maintain them. "It would be ironic, to say the least, if institutions that sustained blacks during segregation were themselves destroyed in an effort to combat its vestige."

The most significant impact of *Brown was* that it delegitimated de jure racial segregation throughout the United States. The case was also a catalyst for the civil rights movement that resulted in legislation expanding equality for African Americans, women, and others.

II. DISCRIMINATION

KOREMATSU v. UNITED STATES

Supreme Court of the United States, 1944.
323 U.S. 214, 65 S.Ct. 193, 89 L.Ed. 194.

JUSTICE BLACK delivered the opinion of the Court.

The petitioner, an American citizen of Japanese descent, was convicted in a federal district court for remaining in San Leandro, California, a "Military Area," contrary to Civilian Exclusion Order No. 34 of the Commanding General of the Western Command, U.S. Army, which directed that after May 9, 1942, all persons of Japanese ancestry should be excluded from that area. No question was raised as to petitioner's loyalty to the United States. . . .

It should be noted, to begin with, that all legal restrictions which curtail the civil rights of a single racial group are immediately suspect. That is not to say that all such restrictions are unconstitutional. It is to say that courts must subject them to the most rigid scrutiny. Pressing public necessity may sometimes justify the existence of such restrictions; racial antagonism never can.

. . .

Exclusion Order No. 34, which the petitioner knowingly and admittedly violated, . . . was . . . based upon Executive Order No. 9066, . . . [which was in turn authorized by an Act of Congress.] That order, issued after we were at war with Japan, declared that "the successful prosecution of the war requires every possible protection against espionage and against sabotage. . . ."

. . . In Hirabayashi v. United States, 320 U.S. 81, we sustained a conviction obtained for violation of the curfew order [which required all persons of Japanese ancestry in prescribed West Coast military areas to remain in their residences from 8 p.m. to 6 a.m.]

[It was argued] in the Hirabayashi case . . . that to apply the curfew order against none but citizens of Japanese ancestry amounted to a constitutionally prohibited discrimination solely on account of race. . . . We upheld the curfew order as an exercise of the power of the government to take steps necessary to prevent espionage and sabotage in an area threatened by Japanese attack.

In the light of the principles we announced in the *Hirabayashi* case, we are unable to conclude that it was beyond the war power of Congress and the Executive to exclude those of Japanese ancestry from the West Coast war area at the time they did. . . .

In this case the petitioner challenges the assumptions upon which we rested our conclusions in the *Hirabayashi* case. He also urges that by May 1942, when Order No. 34 was promulgated, all danger of Japanese invasion of the West Coast had disappeared. After careful consideration of these contentions we are compelled to reject them.

Here, as in the *Hirabayashi* case, . . . ". . . we cannot reject as unfounded the judgment of the military authorities and of Congress that there were disloyal members of that population, whose number and strength could not be precisely and quickly ascertained. . . ." . . .

. . . To cast this case into outlines of racial prejudice, without reference to the real military dangers which were presented, merely confuses the issue. Korematsu was not excluded from the Military Area because of hostility to him or his race. He *was* excluded because we were at war with the Japanese Empire, because the properly constituted military authorities feared an invasion of our West Coast and felt constrained to take proper security measures, because they decided that the military urgency of the situation demanded that all citizens of Japanese ancestry be segregated from the West Coast temporarily, and finally, because Congress, reposing its confidence in this time of war in our military leaders—as inevitably it must—determined that they should have the power to do just this. There was evidence of disloyalty on the part of some, the military authorities considered that the need for action was great, and time was short. We cannot—by availing ourselves of the calm perspective of hindsight—now say that at that time these actions were unjustified.

JUSTICE ROBERTS, dissenting.

I dissent, because I think the indisputable facts exhibit a clear violation of Constitutional rights.

This is not a case of keeping people off the streets at night as was Hirabayashi v. United States, . . . nor a case of temporary exclusion of a citizen from an area for his own safety or that of the community, nor a case of offering him an opportunity to go temporarily out of an area where his presence might cause danger to himself or to his fellows. On the contrary, it is the case of convicting a citizen as a punishment for not submitting to imprisonment in a concentration camp, based on his ancestry, and solely because of his ancestry, without evidence or inquiry concerning his loyalty and good disposition towards the United States. If this be a correct statement of the facts disclosed by this record, and facts of which we take judicial notice, I need hardly labor the conclusion that Constitutional rights have been violated.

· · ·

JUSTICE MURPHY, dissenting.

OWEN J. ROBERTS—Born on May 7, 1875, in Germantown, Pennsylvania, son of a hardware merchant. Republican. Episcopalian. Pennsylvania, A.B., Phi Beta Kappa, 1895; LL.B., cum laude, law review editor, 1898. Law practice, 1898–1901, 1904–1930; Philadelphia assistant district attorney, 1901–1904; special U.S. attorney to prosecute offenses in Teapot Dome Scandals, 1924–1930. Nominated associate justice by President Herbert Hoover on May 20, 1930, to replace Edward T. Sanford, after Hoover's nomination of Judge John J. Parker failed Senate confirmation. Confirmed by the Senate on May 20, 1930, by voice vote. While on the Court chaired investigation of the Pearl Harbor attack. Resigned on July 31, 1945. Served as dean of the University of Pennsylvania Law School, 1948–1951. Died on May 17, 1955.

This exclusion of "all persons of Japanese ancestry, both alien and non-alien," from the Pacific Coast area on a plea of military necessity in the absence of martial law ought not to be approved. Such exclusion goes over "the very brink of constitutional power" and falls into the ugly abyss of racism.

In dealing with matters relating to the prosecution and progress of a war, we must accord great respect and consideration to the judgments of the military authorities. . . .

At the same time, however, it is essential that there be definite limits to military discretion, especially where martial law has not been declared. Individuals must not be left impoverished of their constitutional rights on a plea of military necessity that has neither substance nor support. . . .

. . .

That this forced exclusion was the result in good measure of an erroneous assumption of racial guilt rather than bona fide military necessity is evidenced by the Commanding General's Final Report on the evacuation from the Pacific Coast area. In it he refers to all individuals of Japanese descent as "subversive," as belonging to "an enemy race" whose "racial strains are undiluted," and as constituting "over 112,000 potential enemies . . . at large today" along the Pacific Coast. In support of this blanket condemnation of all persons of Japanese descent, however, no reliable evidence is cited to show that such individuals were generally disloyal, or had generally so conducted themselves in this area as to constitute a special menace to defense installations or war industries, or had otherwise by their behavior furnished reasonable ground for their exclusion as a group.

Justification for the exclusion is sought, instead, mainly upon questionable racial and sociological grounds not ordinarily within the realm of expert military judgment, supplemented by certain semi-military conclusions drawn from an unwarranted use of circumstantial evidence. Individuals of Japanese ancestry are condemned because they are said to be "a large, unassimilated, tightly knit racial group, bound to an enemy nation by strong ties of race, culture, custom and religion." They are claimed to be given to "emperor worshipping ceremonies" and to "dual citizenship." Japanese language schools and allegedly pro-Japanese organizations are cited as evidence of possible group disloyalty, together with facts as to certain persons being educated and residing at length in Japan. It is intimated that many of these individuals deliberately resided "adjacent to strategic points," thus enabling them "to carry into execution a tremendous program of sabotage on a mass scale should any considerable number of them have been inclined to do so." The need for protective custody is also asserted. The report refers without identity to "numerous incidents of violence" as well as to other admittedly unverified or cumulative incidents. From this, plus certain other events not shown to have been connected with the Japanese Americans, it is concluded that the "situation was fraught with danger to the Japanese population itself" and that the general public "was ready to take matters into its own hands." Finally it is intimated, though not directly charged or proved, that persons of Japanese ancestry were responsible for three minor isolated shellings and bombings of the Pacific Coast area, as well as for unidentified radio transmissions and night signalling.

The main reasons relied upon by those responsible for the forced evacuation, therefore, do not prove a reasonable relation between the group characteristics of Japanese Americans and the dangers of invasion, sabotage and espionage. The reasons appear, instead, to be largely an accumulation of much of the misinformation, half-truths and insinuations that for years have been directed against Japanese Americans by people with racial and economic prejudices—the same people who have been among the foremost advocates of the evacuation.* A military judgment based upon such racial and sociological considerations is not entitled to the great weight ordinarily given the judgments based upon strictly military considerations. . . .

.   .   .

No adequate reason is given for the failure to treat these Japanese Americans on an individual basis by holding investigations and hearings to separate the loyal from the disloyal, as was done in the case of persons of German and Italian ancestry. . . .

I dissent, therefore, from this legalization of racism. Racial discrimination in any form and in any degree has no justifiable part whatever in our democratic way of life. It is unattractive in any setting but it is utterly revolting among a free people who have embraced the principles set forth in the Constitution of the United States. . . .

* Special interest groups were extremely active in applying pressure for mass evacuation. . . . Mr. Austin E. Anson, managing secretary of the Salinas Vegetable Grower–Shipper Association, has frankly admitted that "We're charged with wanting to get rid of the Japs for selfish reasons. . . . We do. It's a question of whether the white man lives on the Pacific Coast or the brown men. They came into this valley to work, and they stayed to take over. . . . They undersell the white man in the markets. . . . They work their women and children while the white farmer has to pay wages for his help. If all the Japs were removed tomorrow, we'd never miss them in two weeks, because the white farmers can take over and produce everything the Jap grows. And we don't want them back when the war ends, either." . . .

Justice Jackson, dissenting.

Korematsu was born on our soil, of parents born in Japan. The Constitution makes him a citizen of the United States by nativity and a citizen of California by residence. No claim is made that he is not loyal to this country.

. . .

Now, if any fundamental assumption underlies our system, it is that guilt is personal and not inheritable. . . . But here is an attempt to make an otherwise innocent act a crime merely because this prisoner is the son of parents as to whom he had no choice, and belongs to a race from which there is no way to resign. . . .

. . .

My duties as a justice as I see them do not require me to make a military judgment as to whether General DeWitt's evacuation and detention program was a reasonable military necessity. I do not suggest that the courts should have attempted to interfere with the Army in carrying out its task. But I do not think they may be asked to execute a military expedient that has no place in law under the Constitution. I would reverse the judgment and discharge the prisoner.

[A concurring opinion by Justice Frankfurter is omitted.]

NOTES AND QUESTIONS

1. In *Hirabayashi,* cited in *Korematsu,* the Court upheld a curfew order imposed on German and Italian aliens, Japanese aliens, and Japanese–American citizens. Why do you suppose that citizens of Japanese descent were included but not citizens of German and Italian descent? Why do you suppose that only the Japanese were included in the exclusion order contested in *Korematsu?*

2. There were three stages to the solution of the Japanese "problem" on the West Coast. At first only a curfew was imposed. Then the Japanese were prohibited from remaining in certain specified areas (most of the West Coast). Finally, they were interned in "relocation centers." Although the Court upheld the curfew in *Hirabayashi* and the exclusion orders in *Korematsu,* it never did rule upon the constitutionality of confining the Japanese in "relocation centers" without benefit of a hearing. However, in Ex parte Endo, 323 U.S. 283 (1944), the Court held that once the loyalty of a Japanese resident had been established, she had to be immediately and unconditionally released from the relocation center in which she was being held. For many this may have been a hollow victory since they were still precluded from returning to the West Coast by the exclusion orders which were not cancelled until after the end of the war. Even if there were a substantial danger of invasion or sabotage as late as 1944, what justification could there be for excluding a concededly loyal citizen from her home town?

3. In judging the *Korematsu* decision one must place the facts of the case in their historical context. Did the situation at the time of the exclusion order constitute "pressing public necessity?" The exclusion

orders which Korematsu was convicted of violating were issued shortly after the Pearl Harbor attack, an attack without warning and one regarded almost unanimously at the time as completely unprovoked. There was indeed a deep public shock and, whether justified, or not, considerable public fear of invasion of the West Coast. The presence of numerous persons on the West Coast who maintained close family cultural ties with the nation which had proved capable of crossing an enormous expanse of ocean to launch an extremely destructive attack, enhanced the fear. The military seemed to believe that there was a substantial threat of imminent invasion and that substantial numbers of Japanese Americans whose identity could not be readily ascertained would assist in a war on their adopted country.

4. The United States was also not alone in taking drastic action against potential fifth column activities. During the summer of 1940, when England most feared a German invasion, all enemy aliens were taken into custody, including some 55,000 Jewish refugees. Some of those taken into custody were even shipped to Canada and Australia. Note, however, that the English relocated aliens only, whereas the United States relocated citizens as well as aliens. Do you believe the outcry against the *Korematsu* case would have been less if the relocation process had excluded citizens? Would it have made a difference in the constitutional analysis?

5. In deciding whether any relocation was necessary, consider the viewpoint expressed in the following excerpt.*

> ... The evacuation went on during the summer of 1942 and actually was not completed until November 1—the date on which the last evacuee entered the relocation centers—close to eleven months after the beginning of the war.
>
> This slow march of events hardly suggests all-engulfing military urgency or acute apprehension of danger emanating from the group being evacuated. While the evacuation proceeded at this leisurely pace, the progress of Japanese arms, swiftly moving across the Pacific, reached its peak and began to decline. The deciphering of the Japanese code in the spring of 1942 was, in Churchill's rumored words, worth ten divisions on the Pacific islands and made it possible to keep closer track of the Japanese fleet. The Battle of Midway on June 6, 1942, decisively disposed of any possibility that the Japanese might marshal the naval effort necessary for an invasion of the West Coast or for sustaining the Japanese toehold on Attu and Kiska. This was the judgment of our military leaders at the time.
>
> Yet evacuation did not then come to an end. The inland removals which had begun on June 2 were relentlessly continued. The last Civilian Exclusion Order, No. 108, was dated July 22, 1942, and fixed August 11 as the deadline for incarceration of the last Pacific Coast Japanese Americans....

---

* Jacobus TenBroek, Edward Barnhard, Floyd Matson, Prejudice, War and the Constitution, University of California Press, 1954, p. 292. Reprinted with permission.

6. Justice Douglas originally dissented in *Korematsu* but later joined the majority. Thirty years later, in looking back at the *Korematsu* case he made the following observation:*

> The decisions were extreme and went to the verge of wartime power; and they have been severely criticized. It is, however, easy in retrospect to denounce what was done, as there actually was no attempted Japanese invasion of our country. While our Joint Chiefs of Staff were worrying about Japanese soldiers landing on the West Coast, they actually were landing in Burma and at Kota Bharu in Malaya. But those making plans for defense of the Nation had no such knowledge and were planning for the worst.

But there was evidence to the contrary. An Office of Naval Intelligence report written by Commander Kenneth Ringle concluded that "less than three percent" of those of Japanese descent on the West Coast posed any potential threat. For that reason, Ringle recommended individual loyalty hearings rather than mass internment. Government counsel in *Hirabayashi* and *Korematsu* were aware of the Ringle report but did not mention it in their briefs. Peter Irons, a lawyer and legal historian, disclosed these facts in his book, *Justice at War,* in 1983. The same year, Irons drafted a *coram nobis* petition that asserted that the government had suppressed evidence in *Korematsu* and asked U.S. District Judge Marilyn Patel in San Francisco to vacate Korematsu's conviction. Responding to the petition, government lawyers called the internment "an unfortunate episode," but did not deny the suppression of evidence. "Judge Patel," Irons later reported, "labeled the government's position as 'tantamount to a confession of error' and erased [Korematsu's] conviction from the Court records."**

7. In 1988, Congress approved the payment of 1.25 billion dollars in reparations to Japanese Americans who had been interned during World War II. Under the legislation, each of approximately 60,000 surviving internees was to receive $20,000. The law authorizing payment stated: "On behalf of the nation, the Congress apologizes."

LOVING v. VIRGINIA

Supreme Court of the United States, 1967.
388 U.S. 1, 87 S.Ct. 1817, 18 L.Ed.2d 1010.

[Mildred Jeter, an African–American woman, and Richard Loving, a white man, both residents of Virginia, were married in the District of Columbia in June 1958. Shortly thereafter, they returned to Virginia to establish a permanent home. In January 1959 the Lovings pleaded guilty to a charge of violating Virginia's ban on interracial marriages. Their jail sentence was suspended on the condition that they leave the State and not return for 25 years.* In 1963, they attempted to set aside the

---

* DeFunis v. Odegaard, 416 U.S. 312, 339 (1974), Justice Douglas dissenting, Ftn. 20.

** Peter Irons, The Courage of Our Convictions, Penguin Books, 1990, pp. 47–48.

* In passing sentence, the judge commented, "Almighty God created the races white, black, yellow, malay and red, and he placed them on separate continents. And but for the

judgment in a Virginia State court on the ground that the Virginia antimiscegenation law violated the equal protection clause of the Fourteenth Amendment. Their motion was denied and two years later the Supreme Court of Appeals of Virginia affirmed this decision. The Lovings then appealed to the United States Supreme Court.]

CHIEF JUSTICE WARREN delivered the opinion of the Court.

This case presents a constitutional question never addressed by this Court: whether a statutory scheme adopted by the State of Virginia to prevent marriages between persons solely on the basis of racial classifications violates the Equal Protection and Due Process Clauses of the Fourteenth Amendment. For reasons which seem to us to reflect the central meaning of those constitutional commands, we conclude that these statutes cannot stand consistently with the Fourteenth Amendment.

. . .

Virginia is now one of 16 States which prohibit and punish marriages on the basis of racial classifications. Penalties for miscegenation arose as an incident to slavery and have been common in Virginia since the colonial period. . . .

. . .

. . . [T]he State argues that the meaning of the Equal Protection Clause, as illuminated by the statements of the Framers, is only that state penal laws containing an interracial element as part of the definition of the offense must apply equally to whites and Negroes in the sense that members of each race are punished to the same degree. Thus, the State contends that, because its miscegenation statutes punish equally both the white and the Negro participants in an interracial marriage, these statutes, despite their reliance on racial classifications, do not constitute an invidious discrimination based upon race. The second argument advanced by the State assumes the validity of its equal application theory. The argument is that, if the Equal Protection Clause does not outlaw miscegenation statutes because of their reliance on racial classifications, the question of constitutionality would thus become whether there was any rational basis for a State to treat interracial marriages differently from other marriages. On this question, the State argues, the scientific evidence is substantially in doubt and, consequently, this Court should defer to the wisdom of the state legislature in adopting its policy of discouraging interracial marriages.

Because we reject the notion that the mere "equal application" of a statute containing racial classifications is enough to remove the classifications from the Fourteenth Amendment's proscription of all invidious racial discriminations, we do not accept the State's contention that these statutes should be upheld if there is any possible basis for concluding that they serve a rational purpose. . . . In . . . cases involving distinctions not drawn according to race, the Court has merely asked whether there

interference with his arrangements there would be no cause for such marriages. The fact that he separated the races shows that he did not intend for the races to mix."

is any rational foundation for the discriminations, and has deferred to the wisdom of the state legislatures. In the case at bar, however, we deal with statutes containing racial classifications, and the fact of equal application does not immunize the statute from the very heavy burden of justification which the Fourteenth Amendment has traditionally required of state statutes drawn according to race.

The State argues that statements in the Thirty-ninth Congress about the time of the passage of the Fourteenth Amendment indicate that the Framers did not intend the Amendment to make unconstitutional state miscegenation laws.... [A]lthough these historical sources "cast some light" they are not sufficient to resolve the problem; "[a]t best, they are inconclusive." ...

. . .

There can be no question but that Virginia's miscegenation statutes rest solely upon distinctions drawn according to race. The statutes proscribe generally accepted conduct if engaged in by members of different races. Over the years, this Court has consistently repudiated "[d]istinctions between citizens solely because of their ancestry" as being "odious to a free people whose institutions are founded upon the doctrine of equality." Hirabayashi v. United States, 320 U.S. 81, 100 (1943). At the very least, the Equal Protection Clause demands that racial classifications, especially suspect in criminal statutes, be subjected to the "most rigid scrutiny," Korematsu v. United States, 323 U.S. 214, 216 (1944), and, if they are ever to be upheld, they must be shown to be necessary to the accomplishment of some permissible state objective, independent of the racial discrimination which it was the object of the Fourteenth Amendment to eliminate....

There is patently no legitimate overriding purpose independent of invidious racial discrimination which justifies this classification.... We have consistently denied the constitutionality of measures which restrict the rights of citizens on account of race. There can be no doubt that restricting the freedom to marry solely because of racial classifications violates the central meaning of the Equal Protection Clause.

JUSTICE STEWART, concurring.

I have previously expressed the belief that "it is simply not possible for a state law to be valid under our Constitution which makes the criminality of an act depend upon the race of the actor." ... Because I adhere to that belief, I concur in the judgment of the Court.

NOTES AND QUESTIONS

1. Since African Americans and whites were treated equally if they violated Virginia's anti-miscegenation law, *Loving* can be viewed as similar to the segregation cases discussed in Part I of this chapter. The law was yet another facet of the pervasive scheme of maintaining racial separation. Interestingly, the law was designed to maintain the integrity only of the white race, since members of any other races were free to intermarry. Would the law have been valid if it had been designed to protect the "integrity" of all races?

2. The penalties for violating the antimiscegenation law applied equally to African Americans and whites. What then, was the classification and the inequality of treatment which the Court found repugnant to the requirements of the Fourteenth Amendment? Did the Court indicate that all racial classifications are per se unconstitutional? Would the Rhode Island statute* which permits the marriage of a Jewish man and his niece while proscribing such marriages for all others be invalid for the same reasons as anti-miscegenation laws are invalid?

PALMORE v. SIDOTI

Supreme Court of the United States, 1984.
466 U.S. 429, 104 S.Ct. 1879, 80 L.Ed.2d 421.

[When Linda Sidoti was divorced from her husband, Anthony, in 1980, she was awarded custody of her three year old daughter. A little more than a year later, Anthony Sidoti filed action in a Florida court to modify the custody award, claiming, among other things that Linda, who was white, was living with an African–American man, Clarence Palmore. By the time of the court hearing, Linda had married Clarence Palmore. The judge noted that the case involved the social consequences of interracial marriage, and Linda "had chosen for herself and for her child, a life style unacceptable to ... society." He granted the change of custody on the ground that the child "will, if allowed to remain in her present situation and attains school age and thus more vulnerable to peer pressures, suffer from the social stigmatization that is sure to come." A state appellate court affirmed the award, and the United States Supreme Court reversed.]

CHIEF JUSTICE BURGER delivered the opinion of the Court.

. . .

The judgment of a state court determining or reviewing a child custody decision is not ordinarily a likely candidate for review by this Court. However, the court's opinion, after stating that the "father's evident resentment of the mother's choice of a black partner is not sufficient" to deprive her of custody, then turns to what it regarded as the damaging impact on the child from remaining in a racially-mixed household. This raises important federal concerns arising from the Constitution's commitment to eradicating discrimination based on race.

The Florida court did not focus directly on the parental qualifications of the natural mother or her present husband, or indeed on the father's qualifications to have custody of the child. The court found that "there is no issue as to either party's devotion to the child, adequacy of housing facilities, or respectability of the new spouse of either parent." This, taken with the absence of any negative finding as to the quality of the care provided by the mother, constitutes a rejection of any claim of petitioner's unfitness to continue the custody of her child.

The court correctly stated that the child's welfare was the controlling factor. But that court was entirely candid and made no effort to

* General Laws of Rhode Island, 15–1–4.

place its holding on any ground other than race. Taking the court's findings and rationale at face value, it is clear that the outcome would have been different had petitioner married a Caucasian male of similar respectability.

A core purpose of the Fourteenth Amendment was to do away with all governmentally imposed discrimination based on race. See Strauder v. West Virginia, 100 U.S. 303, 307–308, 310 (1880). Classifying persons according to their race is more likely to reflect racial prejudice than legitimate public concerns; the race, not the person, dictates the category. Such classifications are subject to the most exacting scrutiny; to pass constitutional muster, they must be justified by a compelling governmental interest and must be "necessary ... to the accomplishment" of their legitimate purpose, McLaughlin v. Florida, 379 U.S. 184, 196 (1964). See Loving v. Virginia, 388 U.S. 1, 11 (1967).

The State, of course, has a duty of the highest order to protect the interests of minor children, particularly those of tender years. In common with most states, Florida law mandates that custody determinations be made in the best interests of the children involved. The goal of granting custody based on the best interests of the child is indisputably a substantial governmental interest for purposes of the Equal Protection Clause.

It would ignore reality to suggest that racial and ethnic prejudices do not exist or that all manifestations of those prejudices have been eliminated. There is a risk that a child living with a stepparent of a different race may be subject to a variety of pressures and stresses not present if the child were living with parents of the same racial or ethnic origin.

The question, however, is whether the reality of private biases and the possible injury they might inflict are permissible considerations for removal of an infant child from the custody of its natural mother. We have little difficulty concluding that they are not. The Constitution cannot control such prejudices but neither can it tolerate them. Private biases may be outside the reach of the law, but the law cannot, directly or indirectly, give them effect....

This is by no means the first time that acknowledged racial prejudice has been invoked to justify racial classifications. In Buchanan v. Warley, 245 U.S. 60 (1917), for example, this Court invalidated a Kentucky law forbidding Negroes to buy homes in white neighborhoods.

> "It is urged that this proposed segregation will promote the public peace by preventing race conflicts. Desirable as this is, and important as is the preservation of the public peace, this aim cannot be accomplished by laws or ordinances which deny rights created or protected by the Federal Constitution."

Whatever problems racially-mixed households may pose for children in 1984 can no more support a denial of constitutional rights than could the stresses that residential integration was thought to entail in 1917. The effects of racial prejudice, however real, cannot justify a racial classification removing an infant child from the custody of its natural mother found to be an appropriate person to have such custody.

. . .

NOTES AND QUESTIONS

1. Suppose a state adoption agency has a policy that, all other things being equal, it will give preference in adoption to parents who are of the same race as the child to be adopted. Would that policy be unconstitutional? Would it make a difference if the policy gave preference to parents, at least one of whom was of the same race as the child?

2. Many laws that are non-discriminatory on their face can be administered in a discriminatory manner. Yick Wo v. Hopkins, 118 U.S. 356 (1886), held that such actions violate the equal protection clause. In Washington v. Davis, 426 U.S. 229 (1976), the Court held that the crucial question in cases where litigants assert governmental discrimination is whether public officials have been moved in their actions by a discriminatory "intent" or "purpose." In Village of Arlington Heights v. Metropolitan Housing Development Corp., 429 U.S. 252 (1977), the Court decided that refusing to rezone property was not unconstitutional if it was motivated by a desire to protect property values and not by a desire to exclude African Americans. The Court's opinion discussed the evidence that would be acceptable to prove that "a discriminatory purpose has been a motivating factor" in the decision:

> The impact of the official action, whether it bears more heavily on one race than another ... may provide an important starting point. Sometimes a clear pattern, unexplainable on grounds other than race, merges from the effect of the state action, even when the governing legislation appears neutral on its face.... [T]he evidentiary inquiry is then relatively easy but such cases are rare ... and the Court must look to other evidence.

> The historical background of the decision is one evidentiary source, particularly if it reveals a series of official actions taken for invidious purposes.... [T]he specific sequence of events leading up to the challenged decision may also shed some light on the decision-makers' purposes.... Departures from the normal procedural sequence also might afford evidence that improper purposes are playing a role. Substantive departures, too, may be relevant, particularly if the factors usually considered important by the decisionmakers strongly favor a decision contrary to the one reached. The legislative or administrative history may be highly relevant, especially where there are contemporary statements by members of the decision-making body, minutes of its meetings or reports. In some extraordinary instances the members may be called to the stand at trial to testify concerning the purpose of the official action....

3. Most protections of personal freedom contained in the Constitution protect the individual only from action taken by the government. It remains true, in general, that private persons who deprive other people

of their rights do not violate the Constitution. The classic statement of
the principle was made in the Civil Rights Cases, 109 U.S. 3 (1883).

> [C]ivil rights, such as are guaranteed by the Constitution
> against State aggression, cannot be impaired by the wrongful
> acts of individuals, unsupported by State authority in the shape
> of laws, customs, or judicial or executive proceedings. The
> wrongful act of an individual, unsupported by any such authori-
> ty, is simply a private wrong, or a crime of that individual. . . .
> An individual cannot deprive a man of his right to vote, to hold
> property, to buy and sell, to sue in the courts, or to be a witness
> or a juror; he may, by force or fraud, interfere with the
> enjoyment of the right in a particular case; he may commit an
> assault against the person, or commit murder, or use ruffian
> violence at the polls, or slander the name of a fellow-citizen;
> but, unless protected in these wrongful acts by some shield of
> State law or State authority, he cannot destroy or injure the
> right. . . .

Since 1883, it has become increasingly difficult to distinguish between denial of constitutional rights by government and private wrongs
by individuals. For constitutional purposes, government consists of more
than just the legislature, the courts and the chief executive. It includes
all subdivisions and agencies of government and all government employees performing their official duties. The areas of private activity which
are untouched by any government policy or action have become fewer
and fewer. As a result, the problem of the search for "state action" has
become pervasive in constitutional law. One aspect of this problem has
already been discussed in some detail—the private forum cases in the
free speech area (Chapter 7).

The Court held in the Civil Rights Cases that private acts of racial
discrimination did not constitute state action, and thus did not violate
the Constitution. For many years, most of the Supreme Court's cases
dealing with the state action problem dealt with the issue of when the
government was sufficiently involved in formally private racial discrimination to constitute a violation of the Constitution. In Shelley v. Kraem-
er, 334 U.S. 1 (1948), the Court decided that judicial enforcement of
"private" racially restrictive covenants forbidding the sale of property to
blacks violated the Fourteenth Amendment. In Terry v. Adams, 345 U.S.
461 (1953), the Court applied the Fifteenth Amendment to an election
held prior to the primary election by an all-white "private club" when
the winners of the club's elections invariably won the Democratic primary and then the general election. In Burton v. Wilmington Parking
Authority, 365 U.S. 715 (1961), the Court decided that it was a violation
of the Fourteenth Amendment to deny service to African Americans in a
"private" restaurant in a "public" parking garage. The implications of
these and other cases was, at one time, a matter of lively debate. It was
questioned whether any significant "private" racial discrimination was

not in some way sanctioned or supported by the government, invoking constitutional prohibitions on racial discrimination.

The controversy, however, has slackened since the mid-to-late 1960's for two reasons. First, since 1964, Congress has passed legislation outlawing private racial discrimination in most significant areas other than the personal and social sphere. The Civil Rights Act of 1964 prohibits any person from discriminating on racial grounds in admission to hotels, restaurants, and places of public amusement. Federal law now broadly prohibits any person from being discriminated against on the basis of race in any program which receives federal financial assistance— a far-reaching provision given the extent of federal expenditures. Employers are prohibited from racial discrimination in hiring, firing, pay, and terms and conditions of employment. Private violence to interfere with people in such activities as voting, running for office, campaigning, and applying for government jobs is a federal crime. Discrimination in the sale, rental, and financing of most housing violates federal law. Thus, Congress has acted to outlaw private racial discrimination in its most significant aspects, including access to restaurants, theatres and hotels, jobs, housing, and education. Second, the Court has recently reinterpreted the Civil Rights Act of 1866 to outlaw additional private discrimination. The 1866 law had been assumed to bar only state-supported racial discrimination. But, over 100 years after its enactment, it was reinterpreted to forbid a wide range of private discrimination.*

As a result of the contemporary federal legislation, and the rediscovery of the 1866 law, constitutional questions which require marking the limits of "state action" are seldom reached in cases involving private racial discrimination. But the problem does occasionally arise in marginal cases beyond the reach of federal and state statutes prohibiting discrimination. Consider Moose Lodge No. 107 v. Irvis, 407 U.S. 163 (1972), where a private club had refused service in its restaurant to an African–American guest of a club member. (Bona fide private clubs are not covered by the provisions of the 1964 Civil Rights Act.) The club held a state liquor license. There was a scarcity of liquor licenses, and only a restaurant or club with a license could serve liquor. Holders of state liquor licenses were also subjected to significant state regulation. A 6–3 decision of the Court held there was not sufficient state action, and the Fourteenth Amendment thus did not prevent the club from discriminating against African Americans. Do you agree? Suppose a city permits the use of city-owned recreational facilities by private athletic teams that practice racial discrimination. If all groups who want to use the athletic facilities are permitted to do so, has there been a violation of the Constitution? (See Gilmore v. City of Montgomery, 417 U.S. 556 [1974].)

4. Are there any state interests that are sufficiently compelling to allow the use of a racial classification? Was the situation in *Korematsu* sufficiently compelling to warrant the exclusion of a whole race from specified areas? Would a state requirement that African Americans be tested before marriage for sickle cell anemia meet a compelling state

---

* The Court held in Jones v. Alfred H. Mayer Co., 392 U.S. 409 (1968), that the 1866 statute was justified under the 13th Amendment as removing a remnant of slavery and hence found no need to reexamine the state action issue.

interest test? Should it be required to meet such a stringent test? What about a law that required African Americans to wear an item of light clothing at night when crossing streets—the better to avoid pedestrian accidents?

Finally, and today most important, should laws using racial classification to benefit minorities rather than harm them be strictly scrutinized by the Court? Chief Justice Warren's answer was "no" in his initial circulation of his opinion in *Loving*. When Justice White questioned the necessity for taking that position in the case because the heavier burden required had not been met by the state, the Chief Justice deleted from his opinion his statement on the matter. White to Warren, May 31, 1969, Warren Papers, Library of Congress, Box 620.

III. AFFIRMATIVE ACTION PROGRAMS

REGENTS OF THE UNIVERSITY OF CALIFORNIA v. BAKKE

Supreme Court of the United States, 1978.
438 U.S. 265, 98 S.Ct. 2733, 57 L.Ed.2d 750.

JUSTICE POWELL announced the judgment of the Court.

LEWIS F. POWELL, JR.—Born on November 19, 1907, in Suffolk, Virginia, into a distinguished family whose roots trace back to an original Jamestown settler in 1607. Democrat. Presbyterian. Lived most of his childhood in Richmond, Virginia. Washington and Lee, B.S., Phi Beta Kappa, 1929; LL.B., 1931. Studied with Professors Felix Frankfurter and Roscoe Pound at the Harvard Law School, LL.M., 1932. Practiced law, 1932–1971; A.B.A. president, 1964–1965; American College of Trial Lawyers president, 1968–1969. Nominated associate justice by President Richard M. Nixon on October 21, 1971, to replace Hugo L. Black. Confirmed by the Senate on December 6, 1971, by an 89–1 vote. Retired on June 21, 1987. Died on August 25, 1998.

This case presents a challenge to the special admissions program of the petitioner, the Medical School of the University of California at Davis, which is designed to assure the admission of a specified number of students from certain minority groups. The Superior Court of California sustained respondent's challenge, holding that petitioner's program violated ... Title VI of the Civil Rights Act of 1964, 42 U.S.C. § 2000d, and the Equal Protection Clause of the Fourteenth Amendment. The court enjoined petitioner from considering respondent's race or the race of any other applicant in making admissions decisions. It refused, however, to order respondent's admission to the Medical School, holding that he had not carried his burden of proving that he would have been admitted but for the constitutional and statutory violations. The Supreme Court of California affirmed those portions of the trial court's judgment [which] declar[ed] the special admissions program unlawful and enjoin[ed] petitioner from considering the race of any applicant. It directed the trial court to order his admission.

For the reasons stated in the following opinion, I believe that so much of the judgment of the California court as holds petitioner's special admissions program unlawful and directs that respondent be admitted to the Medical School must be affirmed. For the reasons expressed in a separate opinion, my Brothers THE CHIEF JUSTICE, JUSTICE STEWART, JUSTICE REHNQUIST, and JUSTICE STEVENS concur in this judgment.

I also conclude for the reasons stated in the following opinion that the portion of the court's judgment enjoining petitioner from according any consideration to race in its admissions process must be reversed. For reasons expressed in separate opinions, my Brothers JUSTICE BRENNAN, JUSTICE WHITE, JUSTICE MARSHALL, and JUSTICE BLACKMUN concur in this judgment.

Affirmed in part and reversed in part.

I

The Medical School of the University of California at Davis opened in 1968 with an entering class of 50 students. In 1971, the size of the entering class was increased to 100 students, a level at which it remains. No admissions program for disadvantaged or minority students existed when the school opened, and the first class contained three Asians but no blacks, no Mexican–Americans, and no American Indians. Over the next two years, the faculty devised a special admissions program to increase the representation of "disadvantaged" students in each medical school class. The special program consisted of a separate admissions system operating in coordination with the regular admissions process.

Under the regular admissions procedure, a candidate could submit his application to the medical school beginning in July of the year preceding the academic year for which admission was sought. Because of the large number of applications, the admissions committee screened each one to select candidates for further consideration. Candidates whose overall undergraduate grade point averages fell below 2.5 on a scale of 4.0 were summarily rejected. About one out of six applicants was invited for a personal interview. Following the interviews, each candidate was rated on a scale of 1 to 100 by his interviewers and four other members of the admissions committee. The rating embraced the interviewers' summaries, the candidate's overall grade point average, grade point average in science courses, and scores on the Medical College Admissions Test (MCAT), letters of recommendation, extracurricular activities, and other biographical data. The ratings were added together to arrive at each candidate's "benchmark" score. Since five committee members rated each candidate in 1973, a perfect score was 500; in 1974, six members rated each candidate, so that a perfect score was 600. The full committee then reviewed the file and scores of each applicant and made offers of admission on a "rolling" basis. The chairman was responsible for placing names on the waiting list. They were not placed in strict numerical order; instead, the chairman had discretion to include persons with "special skills."

The special admissions program operated with a separate committee, a majority of whom were members of minority groups. On the 1973
application form, candidates were asked to indicate whether they wished
to be considered as "economically and/or educationally disadvantaged"
applicants; on the 1974 form the question was whether they wished to be
considered as members of a "minority group," which the medical school
apparently viewed as "Blacks," "Chicanos," "Asians," and "American
Indians." If these questions were answered affirmatively, the application
was forwarded to the special admissions committee. No formal definition
of "disadvantage" was ever produced, but the chairman of the special
committee screened each application to see whether it reflected economic
or educational deprivation. Having passed this initial hurdle, the applications then were rated by the special committee in a fashion similar to
that used by the general admissions committee, except that special
candidates did not have to meet the 2.5 grade point average cut-off
applied to regular applicants. About one-fifth of the total number of
special applicants were invited for interviews in 1973 and 1974. Following each interview, the special committee assigned each special applicant
a benchmark score. The special committee then presented its top choices
to the general admissions committee. The latter did not rate or compare
the special candidates against the general applicants, but could reject
recommended special candidates for failure to meet course requirements
or other specific deficiencies. The special committee continued to recommend special applicants until a number prescribed by faculty vote were
admitted. While the overall class size was still 50, the prescribed number
was eight; in 1973 and 1974, when the class size had doubled to 100, the
prescribed number of special admissions also doubled, to 16.

From the year of the increase in class size—1971—through 1974,
the special program resulted in the admission of 21 black students, 30
Mexican–Americans, and 12 Asians, for a total of 63 minority students.
Over the same period, the regular admissions program produced one
black, six Mexican–Americans, and 37 Asians, for a total of 44 minority
students. Although disadvantaged whites applied to the special program
in large numbers, none received an offer of admission through that
process. Indeed, in 1974, at least, the special committee explicitly considered only "disadvantaged" special applicants who were members of one
of the designated minority groups.

Allan Bakke is a white male who applied to the Davis Medical School
in both 1973 and 1974. In both years Bakke's application was considered
by the general admissions program, and he received an interview. His
1973 interview was with Dr. Theodore H. West, who considered Bakke
"a very desirable applicant to [the] medical school." Despite a strong
benchmark score of 468 out of 500, Bakke was rejected. His application
had come late in the year, and no applicants in the general admissions
process with scores below 470 were accepted after Bakke's application
was completed. There were four special admissions slots unfilled at that
time, however, for which Bakke was not considered. After his 1973
rejection, Bakke wrote to Dr. George H. Lowrey, Associate Dean and
Chairman of the Admissions Committee, protesting that the special
admissions program operated as a racial and ethnic quota.

Bakke's 1974 application was completed early in the year. His student interviewer gave him an overall rating of 94, finding him "friendly, well tempered, conscientious and delightful to speak with." His faculty interviewer was, by coincidence, the same Dr. Lowrey to whom he had written in protest of the special admissions program. Dr. Lowrey found Bakke "rather limited in his approach" to the problems of the medical profession and found disturbing Bakke's "very definite opinions which were based more on his personal viewpoints than upon a study of the total problem." Dr. Lowrey gave Bakke the lowest of his six ratings, an 86; his total was 549 out of 600. Again, Bakke's application was rejected. In neither year did the chairman of the admissions committee, Dr. Lowrey, exercise his discretion to place Bakke on the waiting list. In both years, applicants were admitted under the special program with grade point averages, MCAT scores, and benchmark scores significantly lower than Bakke's.

· · ·

[After his second rejection, Bakke brought suit.]

II

In this Court the parties neither briefed nor argued the applicability of Title VI of the Civil Rights of 1964.[1] Rather, as had the California court, they focused exclusively upon the validity of the special admissions program under the Equal Protection Clause. Because it was possible, however, that a decision on Title VI might obviate resort to constitutional interpretation, we requested supplementary briefing on the statutory issue.

· · ·

[Justice Powell (joined by Justices Brennan, White, Marshall and Blackmun) decided that] ... Title VI ... proscribe[s] only those racial classifications that would violate the Equal Protection Clause or the Fifth Amendment.

III

A

Petitioner does not deny that decisions based on race or ethnic origin by faculties and administrations of state universities are reviewable under the Fourteenth Amendment. For his part, respondent does not argue that all racial or ethnic classifications are per se invalid. The parties do disagree as to the level of judicial scrutiny to be applied to the special admissions program. Petitioner argues that the court below erred in applying strict scrutiny, as this inexact term has been applied in our cases. That level of review, petitioner asserts, should be reserved for classifications that disadvantage "discrete and insular minorities." Respondent, on the other hand, contends that the California court correctly

---

1. Section 601 of Title VI provides as follows:

"No person in the United States shall, on the ground of race, color, or national origin, be excluded from participation in, be denied the benefits of, or be subjected to discrimination under any program or activity receiving Federal financial assistance."

rejected the notion that the degree of judicial scrutiny accorded a particular racial or ethnic classification hinges upon membership in a discrete and insular minority and duly recognized that the "rights established [by the Fourteenth Amendment] are personal rights."

En route to this crucial battle over the scope of judicial review, the parties fight a sharp preliminary action over the proper characterization of the special admissions program. Petitioner prefers to view it as establishing a "goal" of minority representation in the medical school. Respondent, echoing the courts below, labels it a racial quota.[2]

This semantic distinction is beside the point: the special admissions program is undeniably a classification based on race and ethnic background. To the extent that there existed a pool of at least minimally qualified minority applicants to fill the 16 special admissions seats, white applicants could compete only for 84 seats in the entering class, rather than the 100 open to minority applicants. Whether this limitation is described as a quota or a goal, it is a line drawn on the basis of race and ethnic status.[3]

. . .

Nevertheless, petitioner argues that the court below erred in applying strict scrutiny to the special admissions programs because white males, such as respondent, are not a "discrete and insular minority" requiring extraordinary protection from the majoritarian political process. This rationale, however, has never been invoked in our decisions as a prerequisite to subjecting racial or ethnic distinctions to strict scrutiny. Nor has this Court held that discreteness and insularity constitute necessary preconditions to a holding that a particular classification is invidious.... Racial and ethnic distinctions of any sort are inherently suspect and thus call for the most exacting judicial examination.

B

This perception of racial and ethnic distinctions is rooted in our Nation's constitutional and demographic history. The Court's initial view of the Fourteenth Amendment was that its "one pervading purpose" was "the freedom of the slave race, the security and firm establishment of that freedom, and the protection of the newly-made freeman

---

2. Petitioner defines "quota" as a requirement which must be met but can never be exceeded, regardless of the quality of the minority applicants. Petitioner declares that there is no "floor" under the total number of minority students admitted: completely unqualified students will not be admitted simply to meet a "quota." Neither is there a "ceiling," since an unlimited number could be admitted through the general admissions process. On this basis the special admissions program does not meet petitioner's definition of a quota.

The court below found—and petitioner does not deny—that white applicants could not compete for the 16 places reserved solely for the special admissions program. Both courts below characterized this as a "quota" system.

3. Moreover, the University's special admissions program involves a purposeful, acknowledged use of racial criteria. This is not a situation in which the classification on its face is racially neutral, but has a disproportionate racial impact. In that situation, plaintiff must establish an intent to discriminate. Village of Arlington Heights v. Metropolitan Housing Devel. Corp., 429 U.S. 252, 264–265 (1977); Washington v. Davis, 426 U.S. 229, 242 (1976); see Yick Wo v. Hopkins, 118 U.S. 356 (1886).

and citizen from the oppressions of those who had formerly exercised dominion over him." Slaughter–House Cases, 16 Wall. 36, 71 (1873)....

Although many of the Framers of the Fourteenth Amendment conceived of its primary function as bridging the vast distance between members of the Negro race and the white "majority," the Amendment itself was framed in universal terms, without reference to color, ethnic origin, or condition of prior servitude....

Over the past 30 years, this Court has embarked upon the crucial mission of interpreting the Equal Protection Clause with the view of assuring to all persons "the protection of equal laws," ... in a Nation confronting a legacy of slavery and racial discrimination. Because the landmark decisions in this area arose in response to the continued exclusion of Negroes from the mainstream of American society, they could be characterized as involving discrimination by the "majority" white race against the Negro minority. But they need not be read as depending upon that characterization for their results. It suffices to say that "[o]ver the years, this Court consistently repudiated '[d]istinctions between citizens solely because of their ancestry' as being 'odious to a free people whose institutions are founded upon the doctrine of equality.' "

Petitioner urges us to adopt for the first time a more restrictive view of the Equal Protection Clause and hold that discrimination against members of the white "majority" cannot be suspect if its purpose can be characterized as "benign."[4] The clock of our liberties, however, cannot be turned back to 1868. It is far too late to argue that the guarantee of equal protection to *all* persons permits the recognition of special wards entitled to a degree of protection greater than that accorded others.[5] "The Fourteenth Amendment is not directed solely against discrimination due to a 'two-class theory'—that is, based upon differences between 'white' and Negro."

Once the artificial line of a "two-class theory" of the Fourteenth Amendment is put aside, the difficulties entailed in varying the level of

4. In the view of Justice Brennan, Justice White, Justice Marshall, and Justice Blackmun, the pliable notion of "stigma" is the crucial element in analyzing racial classifications. The Equal Protection Clause is not framed in terms of "stigma." Certainly the word has no clearly defined constitutional meaning. It reflects a subjective judgment that is standardless. *All* state-imposed classifications that rearrange burdens and benefits on the basis of race are likely to be viewed with deep resentment by the individuals burdened. The denial to innocent persons of equal rights and opportunities may outrage those so deprived and therefore may be perceived as invidious. These individuals are likely to find little comfort in the notion that the deprivation they are asked to endure is merely the price of membership in the dominant majority and that its imposition is inspired by the supposedly benign purpose of aiding others. One should not lightly dismiss the inherent unfairness of, and the perception of mistreatment that accompanies, a system of allocating benefits and privileges on the basis of skin color and ethnic origin....

5. Professor Bickel noted the self-contradiction of that view:

"The lesson of the great decisions of the Supreme Court and the lesson of contemporary history have been the same for at least a generation: discrimination on the basis of race is illegal, immoral, unconstitutional, inherently wrong, and destructive of democratic society. Now this is to be unlearned and we are told that this is not a matter of fundamental principle but only a matter of whose ox is gored. Those for whom racial equality was demanded are to be more equal than others. Having found support in the Constitution for equality, they now claim support for inequality under the same Constitution." A. Bickel, The Morality of Consent 133 (1975).

judicial review according to a perceived "preferred" status of a particular racial or ethnic minority are intractable. The concepts of "majority" and "minority" necessarily reflect temporary arrangements and political judgments. [T]he white "majority" itself is composed of various minority groups, most of which can lay claim to a history of prior discrimination at the hands of the state and private individuals. Not all of these groups can receive preferential treatment and corresponding judicial tolerance of distinctions drawn in terms of race and nationality, for then the only "majority" left would be a new minority of White Anglo–Saxon Protestants. There is no principled basis for deciding which groups would merit "heightened judicial solicitude" and which would not.[6] Courts would be asked to evaluate the extent of the prejudice and consequent harm suffered by various minority groups. Those whose societal injury is thought to exceed some arbitrary level of tolerability then would be entitled to preferential classifications at the expense of individuals belonging to other groups. Those classifications would be free from exacting judicial scrutiny. As these preferences began to have their desired effect, and the consequences of past discrimination were undone, new judicial rankings would be necessary. The kind of variable sociological and political analysis necessary to produce such rankings simply does not lie within the judicial competence—even if they otherwise were politically feasible and socially desirable.

Moreover, there are serious problems of justice connected with the idea of preference itself. First, it may not always be clear that a so-called preference is in fact benign. Courts may be asked to validate burdens imposed upon individual members of particular groups in order to advance the group's general interest. Nothing in the Constitution supports the notion that individuals may be asked to suffer otherwise impermissible burdens in order to enhance the societal standing of their ethnic groups. Second, preferential programs may only reinforce common stereotypes holding that certain groups are unable to achieve success without special protection based on a factor having no relationship to individual worth. Third, there is a measure of inequity in forcing

6. As I am in agreement with the view that race may be taken into account as a factor in an admissions program, I agree with my Brothers Brennan, White, Marshall, and Blackmun that the portion of the judgment that would proscribe all consideration of race must be reversed. See Part V, infra. But I disagree with much that is said in their opinion.

They would require as a justification for a program such as petitioner's, only two findings: (i) that there has been some form of discrimination against the preferred minority groups "by society at large," (it being conceded that petitioner had no history of discrimination), and (ii) that "there is reason to believe" that the disparate impact sought to be rectified by the program is the "product" of such discrimination....

The breadth of this hypothesis is unprecedented in our constitutional system. The first step is easily taken. No one denies the regrettable fact that there has been societal discrimination in this country against various racial and ethnic groups. The second step, however, involves a speculative leap: but for this discrimination by society at large, Bakke "would have failed to qualify for admission" because Negro applicants—nothing is said about Asians—would have made better scores. Not one word in the record supports this conclusion, and the plurality offers no standard for courts to use in applying such a presumption of causation to other racial or ethnic classifications. This failure is a grave one, since if it may be concluded *on this record* that each of the minority groups preferred by the petitioner's special program is entitled to the benefit of the presumption, it would seem difficult to determine that any of the dozens of minority groups that have suffered "societal discrimination" cannot also claim it, in any area of social intercourse.

innocent persons in respondent's position to bear the burdens of redressing grievances not of their making.

By hitching the meaning of the Equal Protection Clause to these transitory considerations, we would be holding, as a constitutional principle, that judicial scrutiny of classifications touching on racial and ethnic background may vary with the ebb and flow of political forces. Disparate constitutional tolerance of such classifications well may serve to exacerbate racial and ethnic antagonisms rather than alleviate them. Also, the mutability of a constitutional principle, based upon shifting political and social judgments, undermines the chances for consistent application of the Constitution from one generation to the next, a critical feature of its coherent interpretation. In expounding the Constitution, the Court's role is to discern "principles sufficiently absolute to give them roots throughout the community and continuity over significant periods of time, and to lift them above the level of the pragmatic political judgments of a particular time and place." A. Cox, The Role of the Supreme Court in American Government 114 (1976).

If it is the individual who is entitled to judicial protection against classifications based upon his racial or ethnic background because such distinctions impinge upon personal rights, rather than the individual only because of his membership in a particular group, then constitutional standards may be applied consistently. Political judgments regarding the necessity for the particular classification may be weighed in the constitutional balance, Korematsu v. United States, 323 U.S. 214 (1944), but the standard of justification will remain constant. This is as it should be, since those political judgments are the product of rough compromise struck by contending groups within the democratic process. When they touch upon an individual's race or ethnic background, he is entitled to a judicial determination that the burden he is asked to bear on that basis is precisely tailored to serve a compelling governmental interest. The Constitution guarantees that right to every person regardless of his background.

C

Petitioner contends that on several occasions this Court has approved preferential classifications without applying the most exacting scrutiny. Most of the cases upon which petitioner relies are drawn from three areas: school desegregation, employment discrimination, and sex discrimination. Each of the cases cited presented a situation materially different from the facts of this case.

The school desegregation cases are inapposite. Each involved remedies for clearly determined constitutional violations. Racial classifications thus were designed as remedies for the vindication of constitutional entitlement.[7] Here, there was no judicial determination of constitutional violation as a predicate for the formulation of a remedial classification.

7. Respondent's position is wholly dissimilar to that of a pupil bused from his neighborhood school to a comparable school in another neighborhood in compliance with a desegregation decree. Petitioner did not arrange for respondent to attend a different medical school in order to desegregate Davis Medical School; instead, it denied him admission and may have deprived him altogether of a medical education.

The employment discrimination cases also do not advance petitioner's cause. For example, in Franks v. Bowman Transportation Co., 424 U.S. 747 (1976), we approved a retroactive award of seniority to a class of Negro truck drivers who had been the victims of discrimination—not just by society at large, but by the respondent in that case. While this relief imposed some burdens on other employees, it was held necessary " 'to make [the victims] whole for injuries suffered on account of unlawful employment discrimination.' " The courts of appeals have fashioned various types of racial preferences as remedies for constitutional or statutory violations resulting in identified, race-based injuries to individuals held entitled to the preference. Such preferences also have been upheld where a legislative or administrative body charged with the responsibility made determinations of past discrimination by the industries affected, and fashioned remedies deemed appropriate to rectify the discrimination. But we have never approved preferential classifications in the absence of proven constitutional or statutory violations.[8]

. . .

IV

We have held that in "order to justify the use of a suspect classification, a State must show that its purpose or interest is both constitutionally permissible and substantial, and that its use of the classification is 'necessary . . . to the accomplishment' of its purpose or the safeguarding of its interest." The special admissions program purports to serve the purposes of: (i) "reducing the historic deficit of traditionally disfavored minorities in medical schools and the medical profession," (ii) countering the effects of societal discrimination;[10] (iii) increasing the number of

8. This case does not call into question congressionally authorized administrative actions, such as . . . approval of reapportionment plans under § 5 of the Voting Rights Act of 1965. In such cases, there has been detailed legislative consideration of the various indicia of previous constitutional or statutory violations, and particular administrative bodies have been charged with monitoring various activities in order to detect such violations and formulate appropriate remedies.

Furthermore, we are not here presented with an occasion to review legislation by Congress pursuant to its powers under § 2 of the Thirteenth Amendment and § 5 of the Fourteenth Amendment to remedy the effects of prior discrimination. We have previously recognized the special competence of Congress to make findings with respect to the effects of identified past discrimination and its discretionary authority to take appropriate remedial measures.

10. A number of distinct sub-goals have been advanced as falling under the rubric of "compensation for past discrimination." For example, it is said that preferences for Negro applicants may compensate for harm done them personally, or serve to place them at economic levels they might have attained but for discrimination against their forebears. Another view of the "compensation" goal is that it serves as a form of reparation by the "majority" to a victimized group as a whole. That justification for racial or ethnic preference has been subjected to much criticism. Finally, it has been argued that ethnic preferences "compensate" the group by providing examples of success whom other members of the group will emulate, thereby advancing the group's interest and society's interest in encouraging new generations to overcome the barriers and frustrations of the past. For purposes of analysis these sub-goals need not be considered separately.

Racial classifications in admissions conceivably could serve a fifth purpose, one which petitioner does not articulate: fair appraisal of each individual's academic promise in the light of some cultural bias in grading or testing procedures. To the extent that race and ethnic background were considered only to the extent of curing established inaccuracies in predicting academic performance, it might be argued that there is no "preference" at all. Nothing in this record, however, suggests either that any of the quantitative factors

physicians who will practice in communities currently underserved; and (iv) obtaining the educational benefits that flow from an ethnically diverse student body. It is necessary to decide which, if any, of these purposes is substantial enough to support the use of a suspect classification.

A

If petitioner's purpose is to assure within its student body some specified percentage of a particular group merely because of its race or ethnic origin, such a preferential purpose must be rejected not as insubstantial but as facially invalid. Preferring members of any one group for no reason other than race or ethnic origin is discrimination for its own sake. This the Constitution forbids. E.g., Loving v. Virginia; Brown v. Board of Education.

B

The State certainly has a legitimate and substantial interest in ameliorating, or eliminating where feasible, the disabling effects of identified discrimination. The line of school desegregation cases, commencing with *Brown,* attests to the importance of this state goal and the commitment of the judiciary to affirm all lawful means towards its attainment. In the school cases, the States were required by court order to redress the wrongs worked by specific instances of racial discrimination. That goal was far more focused than the remedying of the effects of "societal discrimination," an amorphous concept of injury that may be ageless in its reach into the past.

We have never approved a classification that aids persons perceived as members of relatively victimized groups at the expense of other innocent individuals in the absence of judicial, legislative, or administrative findings of constitutional or statutory violations. After such findings have been made, the governmental interest in preferring members of the injured groups at the expense of others is substantial, since the legal rights of the victims must be vindicated. In such a case, the extent of the injury and the consequent remedy will have been judicially, legislatively, or administratively defined. Also, the remedial action usually remains subject to continuing oversight to assure that it will work the least harm possible to other innocent persons competing for the benefit. Without such findings of constitutional or statutory violations, it cannot be said that the government has any greater interest in helping one individual than in refraining from harming another. Thus, the government has no compelling justification for inflicting such harm.

Petitioner does not purport to have made, and is in no position to make, such findings. Its broad mission is education, not the formulation of any legislative policy or the adjudication of particular claims of illegality. For reasons similar to those stated in Part III of this opinion, isolated segments of our vast governmental structures are not competent

considered by the Medical School were culturally biased or that petitioner's special admissions program was formulated to correct for any such biases. Furthermore, if race or ethnic background were used solely to arrive at an unbiased prediction of academic success, the reservation of fixed numbers of seats would be inexplicable.

to make those decisions, at least in the absence of legislative mandates and legislatively determined criteria.[11] Before relying upon these sorts of findings in establishing a racial classification, a governmental body must have the authority and capability to establish, in the record, that the classification is responsive to identified discrimination. Lacking this capability, petitioner has not carried its burden of justification on this issue.

Hence, the purpose of helping certain groups whom the faculty of the Davis Medical School perceived as victims of "societal discrimination" does not justify a classification that imposes disadvantages upon persons like respondent, who bear no responsibility for whatever harm the beneficiaries of the special admissions program are thought to have suffered. To hold otherwise would be to convert a remedy heretofore reserved for violations of legal rights into a privilege that all institutions throughout the Nation could grant at their pleasure to whatever groups are perceived as victims of societal discrimination. That is a step we have never approved.

C

Petitioner identifies, as another purpose of its program, improving the delivery of health care services to communities currently underserved. It may be assumed that in some situations a State's interest in facilitating the health care of its citizens is sufficiently compelling to support the use of a suspect classification. But there is virtually no evidence in the record indicating that petitioner's special admissions program is either needed or geared to promote that goal.[12] The court below addressed this failure of proof:

> "The University concedes it cannot assure that minority doctors who entered under the program, all of whom express an 'interest' in participating in a disadvantaged community, will actually do so. It may be correct to assume that some of them will carry out this intention, and that it is more likely they will practice in minority communities than the average white doctor. Nevertheless, there are more precise and reliable ways to identify applicants who are genuinely interested in the medical problems of minorities than by race. An applicant of whatever race who has demonstrated his concern for disadvantaged minorities in the past and who declares that practice in such a community is his primary professional goal would be more likely to contribute to alleviation of the medical shortage than one who is chosen entirely on the basis of race and disadvantage. In short, there is [sic] no empirical data to demonstrate that any one race is more selflessly socially oriented or by contrast that another is more selfishly acquisitive."

11. For example, the University is unable to explain its selection of only the three favored groups—Negroes, Mexican–Americans, and Asians—for preferential treatment. The inclusion of the last group is especially curious in light of the substantial numbers of Asians admitted through the regular admissions process.

12. The only evidence in the record with respect to such underservice is a newspaper article.

Petitioner simply has not carried its burden of demonstrating that it must prefer members of particular ethnic groups over all other individuals in order to promote better health care delivery to deprived citizens. Indeed, petitioner has not shown that its preferential classification is likely to have any significant effect on the problem.[13]

D

The fourth goal asserted by petitioner is the attainment of a diverse student body. This clearly is a constitutionally permissible goal for an institution of higher education. Academic freedom, though not a specifically enumerated constitutional right, long has been viewed as a special concern of the First Amendment. The freedom of a university to make its own judgments as to education includes the selection of its student body.... The atmosphere of "speculation, experiment and creation"—so essential to the quality of higher education—is widely believed to be promoted by a diverse student body.[14] As the Court [has] noted, it is not too much to say that the "nation's future depends upon leaders trained through wide exposure" to the ideas and mores of students as diverse as this Nation of many peoples.

. . .

Ethnic diversity, however, is only one element in a range of factors a university properly may consider in attaining the goal of a heterogeneous student body. Although a university must have wide discretion in making the sensitive judgments as to who should be admitted, constitutional limitations protecting individual rights may not be disregarded. Respondent urges—and the courts below have held—that petitioner's dual admissions program is a racial classification that impermissibly infringes his rights under the Fourteenth Amendment. As the interest of diversity is compelling in the context of a university's admissions program, the

---

13. It is not clear that petitioner's two-track system, even if adopted throughout the country, would substantially increase representation of blacks in the medical profession. That is the finding of a recent study by Sleeth & Mishell, Black Under–Representation in United States Medical Schools, New England J. of Med. 1146 (Nov. 24, 1977). Those authors maintain that the cause of black under-representation lies in the small size of the national pool of qualified black applicants. In their view, this problem is traceable to the poor premedical experiences of black undergraduates, and can be remedied effectively only by developing remedial programs for black students before they enter college.

14. The president of Princeton University has described some of the benefits derived from a diverse student body:

"... [A] great deal of learning occurs informally. It occurs through interactions among students of both sexes; of different races, religions, and backgrounds; who come from cities and rural areas, from various states and countries; who have a wide variety of interests and perspectives; and who are able, directly or indirectly, to learn from their differences and to stimulate one another to reexamine even their most deeply held assumptions about themselves and their world. As a wise graduate of ours once observed in commenting on this aspect of the educational process, 'People do not learn very much when they are surrounded only by the likes of themselves.' "

"In the nature of things, it is hard to know how, and when, and even if, this informal 'learning through diversity' actually occurs. It does not occur for everyone. For many, however, the unplanned, casual encounters with roommates, fellow sufferers in an organic chemistry class, student workers in the library, teammates on a basketball squad, or other participants in class affairs or student government can be subtle and yet powerful sources of improved understanding and personal growth."

question remains whether the program's racial classification is necessary to promote this interest.

V

A

It may be assumed that the reservation of a specified number of seats in each class for individuals from the preferred ethnic groups would contribute to the attainment of considerable ethnic diversity in the student body. But petitioner's argument that this is the only effective means of serving the interest of diversity is seriously flawed. In a most fundamental sense the argument misconceives the nature of the state's interest that would justify consideration of race or ethnic background. It is not an interest in simple ethnic diversity, in which a specified percentage of the student body is in effect guaranteed to be members of selected ethnic groups, with the remaining percentage an undifferentiated aggregation of students. The diversity that furthers a compelling state interest encompasses a far broader array of qualifications and characteristics of which racial or ethnic origin is but a single though important element. Petitioner's special admissions program, focused *solely* on ethnic diversity, would hinder rather than further attainment of genuine diversity.

Nor would the state interest in genuine diversity be served by expanding petitioner's two-track system into a multitrack program with a prescribed number of seats set aside for each identifiable category of applicants. Indeed, it is inconceivable that a university would thus pursue the logic of petitioner's two-track program to the illogical end of insulating each category of applicants with certain desired qualifications from competition with all other applicants.

. . .

In [a constitutionally valid] admissions program, race or ethnic background may be deemed a "plus" in a particular applicant's file, yet it does not insulate the individual from comparison with all other candidates for the available seats. The file of a particular black applicant may be examined for his potential contribution to diversity without the factor of race being decisive when compared, for example, with that of an applicant identified as an Italian–American if the latter is thought to exhibit qualities more likely to promote beneficial educational pluralism. Such qualities could include exceptional personal talents, unique work or service experience, leadership potential, maturity, demonstrated compassion, a history of overcoming disadvantage, ability to communicate with the poor, or other qualifications deemed important. In short, an admissions program operated in this way is flexible enough to consider all pertinent elements of diversity in light of the particular qualifications of each applicant, and to place them on the same footing for consideration, although not necessarily according them the same weight. Indeed, the weight attributed to a particular quality may vary from year to year depending upon the "mix" both of the student body and the applicants for the incoming class.

This kind of program treats each applicant as an individual in the admissions process. The applicant who loses out on the last available seat to another candidate receiving a "plus" on the basis of ethnic background will not have been foreclosed from all consideration for that seat simply because he was not the right color or had the wrong surname. It would mean only that his combined qualifications, which may have included similar nonobjective factors, did not outweigh those of the other applicant. His qualifications would have been weighed fairly and competitively, and he would have no basis to complain of unequal treatment under the Fourteenth Amendment.[15]

It has been suggested that an admissions program which considers race only as one factor is simply a subtle and more sophisticated—but no less effective—means of according racial preference than the Davis program. A facial intent to discriminate, however, is evident in petitioner's preference program and not denied in this case. No such facial infirmity exists in an admissions program where race or ethnic background is simply one element—to be weighed fairly against other elements—in the selection process. "A boundary line," as Justice Frankfurter remarked in another connection, "is none the worse for being narrow." And a Court would not assume that a university, professing to employ a facially nondiscriminatory admissions policy, would operate it as a cover for the functional equivalent of a quota system. In short, good faith would be presumed in the absence of a showing to the contrary in the manner permitted by our cases.[16]

B

In summary, it is evident that the Davis special admission program involves the use of an explicit racial classification never before countenanced by this Court. It tells applicants who are not Negro, Asian, or "Chicano" that they are totally excluded from a specific percentage of the seats in an entering class. No matter how strong their qualifications, quantitative and extracurricular, including their own potential for contribution to educational diversity, they are never afforded the chance to compete with applicants from the preferred groups for the special

---

15. The denial to respondent of this right to individualized consideration without regard to his race is the principal evil of petitioner's special admissions program. Nowhere in the opinion of Justice Brennan, Justice White, Justice Marshall, and Justice Blackmun is this denial even addressed.

16. Universities ... may make individualized decisions, in which ethnic background plays a part, under a presumption of legality and legitimate educational purpose. So long as the university proceeds on an individualized, case-by-case basis, there is no warrant for judicial interference in the academic process. If an applicant can establish that the institution does not adhere to a policy of individual comparisons, or can show that a systematic exclusion of certain groups results, the presumption of legality might be overcome, creating the necessity of proving legitimate educational purpose.

There also are strong policy reasons that correspond to the constitutional distinction between petitioner's preference program and one that assures a measure of competition among all applicants. Petitioner's program will be viewed as inherently unfair by the public generally as well as by applicants for admission to state universities. Fairness in individual competition for opportunities, especially those provided by the State, is a widely cherished American ethic. Indeed, in a broader sense, an underlying assumption of the rule of law is the worthiness of a system of justice based on fairness to the individual. As Justice Frankfurter declared in another connection, "[j]ustice must satisfy the appearance of justice."

admission seats. At the same time, the preferred applicants have the opportunity to compete for every seat in the class.

The fatal flaw in petitioner's preferential program is its disregard of individual rights as guaranteed by the Fourteenth Amendment. Such rights are not absolute. But when a State's distribution of benefits or imposition of burdens hinges on the color of a person's skin or ancestry, that individual is entitled to a demonstration that the challenged classification is necessary to promote a substantial state interest. Petitioner has failed to carry this burden. For this reason, that portion of the California court's judgment holding petitioner's special admissions program invalid under the Fourteenth Amendment must be affirmed.

C

In enjoining petitioner from ever considering the race of any applicant, however, the courts below failed to recognize that the State has a substantial interest that legitimately may be served by a properly devised admissions program involving the competitive consideration of race and ethnic origin. For this reason, so much of the California court's judgment as enjoins petitioner from any consideration of the race of any applicant must be reversed.

. . .

Opinion of JUSTICE BRENNAN, JUSTICE WHITE, JUSTICE MARSHALL, and JUSTICE BLACKMUN, concurring in the judgment in part and dissenting.

The Court today, in reversing in part the judgment of the Supreme Court of California, affirms the constitutional power of Federal and State Government to act affirmatively to achieve equal opportunity for all. The difficulty of the issue presented—whether Government may use race-conscious programs to redress the continuing effects of past discrimination—and the mature consideration which each of our Brethren has brought to it have resulted in many opinions, no single one speaking for the Court. But this should not and must not mask the central meaning of today's opinions: Government may take race into account when it acts not to demean or insult any racial group, but to remedy disadvantages cast on minorities by past racial prejudice, at least when appropriate findings have been made by judicial, legislative, or administrative bodies with competence to act in this area.

The Chief Justice and our Brothers Stewart, Rehnquist, and Stevens, have concluded that Title VI of the Civil Rights Act of 1964, prohibits programs such as that at the Davis Medical School. On this statutory theory alone, they would hold that respondent Allan Bakke's rights have been violated and that he must, therefore, be admitted to the Medical School. Our Brother Powell, reaching the Constitution, concludes that, although race may be taken into account in university admissions, the particular special admissions program used by petitioner, which resulted in the exclusion of respondent Bakke, was not shown to be necessary to achieve petitioner's stated goals. Accordingly, these Members of the Court form a majority of five affirming the judgment of the Supreme Court of California insofar as it holds that respondent Bakke "is entitled to an order that he be admitted to the University."

We agree with Justice Powell that, as applied to the case before us, Title VI goes no further in prohibiting the use of race than the Equal Protection Clause of the Fourteenth Amendment itself. We also agree that the effect of the California Supreme Court's affirmance of the judgment of the Superior Court of California would be to prohibit the University from establishing in the future affirmative action programs that take race into account. Since we conclude that the affirmative admissions program at the Davis Medical School is constitutional, we would reverse the judgment below in all respects. Justice Powell agrees that some uses of race in university admissions are permissible and, therefore, he joins with us to make five votes reversing the judgment below insofar as it prohibits the University from establishing race-conscious programs in the future.

I

Our Nation was founded on the principle that "all men are created equal." Yet candor requires acknowledgment that the Framers of our Constitution, to forge the Thirteen Colonies into one Nation, openly compromised this principle of equality with its antithesis: slavery. The consequences of this compromise are well known and have aptly been called our "American Dilemma." Still, it is well to recount how recent the time has been, if it has yet come, when the promise of our principles has flowered into the actuality of equal opportunity for all regardless of race or color.

The Fourteenth Amendment, the embodiment in the Constitution of our abiding belief in human equality, has been the law of our land for only slightly more than half its 200 years. And for half of that half, the Equal Protection Clause of the Amendment was largely moribund so that, as late as 1927, Justice Holmes could sum up the importance of that Clause by remarking that it was "the last resort of constitutional arguments." Worse than desuetude, the Clause was early turned against those whom it was intended to set free, condemning them to a "separate but equal" status before the law, a status always separate but seldom equal. Not until 1954—only 24 years ago—was this odious doctrine interred by our decision in Brown v. Board of Education, 347 U.S. 483 (1954).... [E]ven today officially sanctioned discrimination is not a thing of the past.

Against this background, claims that law must be "color-blind" or that the datum of race is no longer relevant to public policy must be seen as aspiration rather than as description of reality. This is not to denigrate aspiration; for reality rebukes us that race has too often been used by those who would stigmatize and oppress minorities. Yet we cannot—and as we shall demonstrate, need not under our Constitution or Title VI, which merely extends the constraints of the Fourteenth Amendment to private parties who receive federal funds—let color blindness become myopia which masks the reality that many "created equal" have been treated within our lifetimes as inferior both by the law and by their fellow citizens.

II

. . .

In our view, Title VI prohibits only those uses of racial criteria that would violate the Fourteenth Amendment if employed by a State or its agencies; it does not bar the preferential treatment of racial minorities as a means of remedying past societal discrimination to the extent that such action is consistent with the Fourteenth Amendment. . . .

. . .

We turn, therefore, to our analysis of the Equal Protection Clause of the Fourteenth Amendment.

III

A

The assertion of human equality is closely associated with the proposition that differences in color or creed, birth or status, are neither significant nor relevant to the way in which persons should be treated. Nonetheless, the position that such factors must be "[c]onstitutionally an irrelevance," summed up by the shorthand phrase "[o]ur Constitution is color-blind," Plessy v. Ferguson, 163 U.S. 537, 559 (1896) (Harlan, J., dissenting), has never been adopted by this Court as the proper meaning of the Equal Protection Clause. . . .

We conclude, therefore, that racial classifications are not per se invalid under the Fourteenth Amendment. Accordingly, we turn to the problem of articulating what our role should be in reviewing state action that expressly classifies by race.

B

Respondent argues that racial classifications are always suspect and, consequently, that this Court should weigh the importance of the objectives served by Davis' special admissions program to see if they are compelling. In addition, he asserts that this Court must inquire whether, in its judgment, there are alternatives to racial classifications which would suit Davis' purposes. Petitioner, on the other hand, states that our proper role is simply to accept petitioner's determination that the racial classifications used by its program are reasonably related to what it tells us are its benign purposes. We reject petitioner's view, but, because our prior cases are in many respects inapposite to that before us now, we find it necessary to define with precision the meaning of that inexact term, "strict scrutiny."

Unquestionably we have held that a government practice or statute which restricts "fundamental rights" or which contains "suspect classifications" is to be subjected to "strict scrutiny" and can be justified only if it furthers a compelling government purpose and, even then, only if no less restrictive alternative is available. But no fundamental right is involved here. Nor do whites as a class have any of the "traditional indicia of suspectness: the class is not saddled with such disabilities, or subjected to such a history of purposeful unequal treatment, or relegated to such a position of political powerlessness as to command extraordinary protection from the majoritarian political process."

Moreover, if the University's representations are credited, this is not a case where racial classifications are "irrelevant and therefore prohibited." Nor has anyone suggested that the University's purposes contravene the cardinal principle that racial classifications that stigmatize—because they are drawn on the presumption that one race is inferior to another or because they put the weight of government behind racial hatred and separatism—are invalid without more.

On the other hand, the fact that this case does not fit neatly into our prior analytic framework for race cases does not mean that it should be analyzed by applying the very loose rational-basis standard of review that is the very least that is always applied in equal protection cases. " '[T]he mere recitation of a benign, compensatory purpose is not an automatic shield which protects against any inquiry into the actual purposes underlying a statutory scheme.' " Instead, a number of considerations—developed in gender discrimination cases but which carry even more force when applied to racial classifications—lead us to conclude that racial classifications designed to further remedial purposes " 'must serve important governmental objectives and must be substantially related to achievement of those objectives.' "[1]

First, race, like, "gender-based classifications too often [has] been inexcusably utilized to stereotype and stigmatize politically powerless segments of society." While a carefully tailored statute designed to remedy past discrimination could avoid these vices, we nonetheless have recognized that the line between honest and thoughtful appraisal of the effects of past discrimination and paternalistic stereotyping is not so clear and that a statute based on the latter is patently capable of stigmatizing all women with a badge of inferiority. State programs designed ostensibly to ameliorate the effects of past racial discrimination obviously create the same hazard of stigma, since they may promote racial separatism and reinforce the views of those who believe that members of racial minorities are inherently incapable of succeeding on their own.

---

1. We disagree with our Brother Powell's suggestion, that the presence of "rival groups who can claim that they, too, are entitled to preferential treatment," distinguishes the gender cases or is relevant to the question of scope of judicial review of race classifications. We are not asked to determine whether groups other than those favored by the Davis program should similarly be favored. All we are asked to do is to pronounce the constitutionality of what Davis has done.

But, were we asked to decide whether any given rival group—German–Americans for example—must constitutionally be accorded preferential treatment, we do have a "principled basis" for deciding this question, one that is well-established in our cases: The Davis program expressly sets out four classes which receive preferred status. The program clearly distinguishes whites, but one cannot reason from this to a conclusion that German–Americans, as a national group, are singled out for invidious treatment. And even if the Davis program had a differential impact on German–Americans, they would have no constitutional claim unless they could prove that Davis intended invidiously to discriminate against German–Americans. If this could not be shown, then "the principle that calls for the closest scrutiny of distinctions in laws denying fundamental rights ... is inapplicable," and the only question is whether it was rational for Davis to conclude that the groups it preferred had a greater claim to compensation than the groups it excluded.... Thus, claims of rival groups, although they may create thorny political problems, create relatively simple problems for the courts.

Second, race, like gender and illegitimacy, is an immutable characteristic which its possessors are powerless to escape or set aside. While a
classification is not *per se* invalid because it divides classes on the basis
of an immutable characteristic, it is nevertheless true that such divisions
are contrary to our deep belief that "legal burdens should bear some
relationship to individual responsibility or wrongdoing," and that advancement sanctioned, sponsored, or approved by the State should
ideally be based on individual merit or achievement, or at the least on
factors within the control of an individual.

Because this principle is so deeply rooted it might be supposed that
it would be considered in the legislative process and weighed against the
benefits of programs preferring individuals because of their race. But
this is not necessarily so: The "natural consequence of our governing
processes [may well be] that the most 'discrete and insular' of whites ...
will be called upon to bear the immediate, direct costs of benign
discrimination." Moreover, it is clear from our cases that there are limits
beyond which majorities may not go when they classify on the basis of
immutable characteristics. Thus, even if the concern for individualism is
weighed by the political process, that weighing cannot waive the personal rights of individuals under the Fourteenth Amendment.

[B]ecause of the significant risk that racial classifications established
for ostensibly benign purposes can be misused, causing effects not unlike
those created by invidious classifications, it is inappropriate to inquire
only whether there is any conceivable basis that might sustain such a
classification. Instead, to justify such a classification an important and
articulated purpose for its use must be shown. In addition, any statute
must be stricken that stigmatizes any group or that singles out those
least well represented in the political process to bear the brunt of a
benign program. Thus our review under the Fourteenth Amendment
should be strict—not " 'strict' in theory and fatal in fact," because it is
stigma that causes fatality—but strict and searching nonetheless.

IV

Davis' articulated purpose of remedying the effects of past societal
discrimination is, under our cases, sufficiently important to justify the
use of race-conscious admissions programs where there is a sound basis
for concluding that minority underrepresentation is substantial and
chronic, and that the handicap of past discrimination is impeding access
of minorities to the medical school.

· · ·

Properly construed, our prior cases unequivocally show that a state
government may adopt race-conscious programs if the purpose of such
programs is to remove the disparate racial impact its actions might
otherwise have and if there is reason to believe that the disparate impact
is itself the product of past discrimination, whether its own or that of
society at large. There is no question that Davis' program is valid under
this test.

Certainly, on the basis of the undisputed factual submissions before
this Court, Davis had a sound basis for believing that the problem of

underrepresentation of minorities was substantial and chronic and that the problem was attributable to handicaps imposed on minority applicants by past and present racial discrimination. Until at least 1973, the practice of medicine in this country was, in fact, if not in law, largely the prerogative of whites. In 1950, for example, while Negroes comprised 10% of the total population, Negro physicians constituted only 2.2% of the total number of physicians. The overwhelming majority of these, moreover, were educated in two predominantly Negro medical schools, Howard and Meharry. By 1970, the gap between the proportion of Negroes in medicine and their proportion in the population had widened: The number of Negroes employed in medicine remained frozen at 2.2% while the Negro population had increased to 11.1%. The number of Negro admittees to predominantly white medical schools, moreover, had declined in absolute numbers during the years 1955 to 1964.

Moreover, Davis had very good reason to believe that the national pattern of underrepresentation of minorities in medicine would be perpetuated if it retained a single admissions standard. For example, the entering classes in 1968 and 1969, the years in which such a standard was used, included only one Chicano and two Negroes out of 100 admittees. Nor is there any relief from this pattern of underrepresentation in the statistics for the regular admissions program in later years.

Davis clearly could conclude that the serious and persistent underrepresentation of minorities in medicine depicted by these statistics is the result of handicaps under which minority applicants labor as a consequence of a background of deliberate, purposeful discrimination against minorities in education and in society generally, as well as in the medical profession. From the inception of our national life, Negroes have been subjected to unique legal disabilities impairing access to equal educational opportunity. Under slavery, penal sanctions were imposed upon anyone attempting to educate Negroes. After enactment of the Fourteenth Amendment the States continued to deny Negroes equal educational opportunity, enforcing a strict policy of segregation that itself stamped Negroes as inferior, which relegated minorities to inferior educational institutions, and which denied them intercourse in the mainstream of professional life necessary to advancement. . . .

. . .

C

The second prong of our test—whether the Davis program stigmatizes any discrete group or individual and whether race is reasonably used in light of the program's objectives—is clearly satisfied by the Davis program.

. . .

Bakke [was not] in any sense stamped as inferior by the Medical School's rejection of him. Indeed, it is conceded by all that he satisfied those criteria regarded by the School as generally relevant to academic performance better than most of the minority members who were admitted. Moreover, there is absolutely no basis for concluding that Bakke's rejection as a result of Davis' use of racial preference will affect him throughout his life in the same way as the segregation of the Negro school children in *Brown* ... would have affected them....

. . .

In addition, there is simply no evidence that the Davis program discriminates intentionally or unintentionally against any minority group which it purports to benefit. The program does not establish a quota in the invidious sense of a ceiling on the number of minority applicants to be admitted. Nor can the program reasonably be regarded as stigmatizing the program's beneficiaries or their race as inferior. The Davis program does not simply advance less qualified applicants; rather, it compensates applicants, whom it is uncontested are fully qualified to study medicine, for educational disadvantage which it was reasonable to conclude was a product of state-fostered discrimination. Once admitted, these students must satisfy the same degree requirements as regularly admitted students; they are taught by the same faculty in the same classes; and their performance is evaluated by the same standards by which regularly admitted students are judged. Under these circumstances, their performance and degrees must be regarded equally with the regularly admitted students with whom they compete for standing. Since minority graduates cannot justifiably be regarded as less well qualified than nonminority graduates by virtue of the special admissions program, there is no reasonable basis to conclude that minority graduates at schools using such programs would be stigmatized as inferior by the existence of such programs.

D

We disagree with the lower courts' conclusion that the Davis program's use of race was unreasonable in light of its objectives. First, as petitioner argues, there are no practical means by which it could achieve its ends in the foreseeable future without the use of race-conscious measures. With respect to any factor (such as poverty or family educational background) that may be used as a substitute for race as an indicator of past discrimination, whites greatly outnumber racial minorities simply because whites make up a far larger percentage of the total population and therefore far outnumber minorities in absolute terms at every socio-economic level. For example, of a class of recent medical school applicants from families with less than $10,000 income, at least 71% were white. Of all 1970 families headed by a person *not* a high school graduate which included related children under 18, 80% were white and 20% were racial minorities....

Second, the Davis admissions program does not simply equate minority status with disadvantage. Rather, Davis considers on an individual basis each applicant's personal history to determine whether he or she has likely been disadvantaged by racial discrimination. The record makes clear that only minority applicants likely to have been isolated from the mainstream of American life are considered in the special program; other minority applicants are eligible only through the regular admissions program. True, the procedure by which disadvantage is detected is informal, but we have never insisted that educators conduct their affairs through adjudicatory proceedings, and such insistence here is misplaced. A case-by-case inquiry into the extent to which each individual applicant has been affected, either directly or indirectly, by racial discrimination, would seem to be, as a practical matter, virtually impossible, despite the fact that there are excellent reasons for concluding that such effects generally exist. When individual measurement is impossible or extremely impractical, there is nothing to prevent a State from using categorical means to achieve its ends, at least where the category is closely related to the goal. . . .

E

Finally, Davis' special admissions program cannot be said to violate the Constitution simply because it has set aside a predetermined number of places for qualified minority applicants rather than using minority status as a positive factor to be considered in evaluating the applications of disadvantaged minority applicants. For purposes of constitutional adjudication, there is no difference between the two approaches. In any admissions program which accords special consideration to disadvantaged racial minorities, a determination of the degree of preference to be given is unavoidable, and any given preference that results in the exclusion of a white candidate is no more or less constitutionally acceptable than a program such as that at Davis. Furthermore, the extent of the preference inevitably depends on how many minority applicants the particular school is seeking to admit in any particular year so long as the number of qualified minority applicants exceeds that number. There is no sensible, and certainly no constitutional, distinction between, for example, adding a set number of points to the admissions rating of disadvantaged minority applicants as an expression of the preference with the expectation that this will result in the admission of an approximately determined number of qualified minority applicants and setting a fixed number of places for such applicants as was done here.

. . .

IV

Accordingly, we would reverse the judgment of the Supreme Court of California holding the Medical School's special admissions program unconstitutional and directing respondent's admission, as well as that portion of the judgment enjoining the Medical School from according any consideration to race in the admissions process.

[Justices Blackmun, Marshall and White each filed separate opinions, in addition to joining Justice Brennan's opinion. Justice Blackmun's opinion stressed his reasons for agreement with Justice Brennan. Justice White's opinion argued that Title VI did not permit individual suits. Portions of Justice Marshall's opinion follow.]

JUSTICE MARSHALL, dissenting.

. . .

THURGOOD MARSHALL—Born on July 2, 1908, in Baltimore, Maryland, son of a club steward and a primary school teacher, and great grandson of a slave. Named after his paternal grandfather Thoroughgood Marshall, a freeman of Maryland who enlisted in the Union Army during the Civil War. Later shortened his name to Thurgood. Democrat. Episcopalian. Grew up in a comfortable middle-class home in the Druid Hill section of Baltimore. Lincoln, A.B., cum laude, 1930. His application to the University of Maryland Law School was rejected because he was not white. Howard, LL.B., graduating first in his class, 1933. Private practice, 1933–1937; National Association for the Advancement of Colored People counsel, 1934–1961. Argued 32 civil rights cases before the Supreme Court, including the Texas Primary Case (1944), Restrictive Covenant Cases (1948), Texas and Oklahoma Higher Education Cases (1950), and Brown v. Board of Education (1953). U.S. Court of Appeals judge, Second Circuit, 1961–1965; U.S. solicitor general, 1965–1967. Nominated associate justice on June 13, 1967, by President Lyndon B. Johnson to replace Tom C. Clark. Confirmed by the Senate on August 30, 1967, by a 69–11 vote. First African American to serve on the Supreme Court. Retired on October 1, 1991. Died on January 24, 1993. When Regents of the University of California v. Bakke (1978) was before the Court, Marshall and Brennan discussed over lunch the constitutionality of affirmative action programs benefiting upper-middle class African Americans. Asked whether it would be proper for one of his sons to be accorded special consideration in the medical admissions process because of his race, Marshall answered: "Damn right. They owe us." Draft memoir, Brennan Papers, Library of Congress, Box 464.

In light of the sorry history of discrimination and its devastating impact on the lives of Negroes, bringing the Negro into the mainstream of American life should be a state interest of the highest order. To fail to do so is to ensure that America will forever remain a divided society.

. . .

I do not believe that the Fourteenth Amendment requires us to accept that fate. . . .

. . .

While I applaud the judgment of the Court that a university may consider race in its admissions process, it is more than a little ironic that, after several hundred years of class-based discrimination against Negroes, the Court is unwilling to hold that a class-based remedy for that discrimination is permissible. In declining to so hold, today's judgment ignores the fact that for several hundred years Negroes have been discriminated against, not as individuals, but rather solely because of the color of their skins. It is unnecessary in 20th century America to have individual Negroes demonstrate that they have been victims of racial discrimination; the racism of our society has been so pervasive that none, regardless of wealth or position, has managed to escape its impact. The experience of Negroes in America has been different in kind, not just in degree, from that of other ethnic groups. It is not merely the history of slavery alone but also that a whole people were marked as inferior by the law. And that mark has endured. The dream of America as the great melting pot has not been realized for the Negro; because of his skin color he never even made it into the pot.

. . .

I fear that we have come full circle. After the Civil War our government started several "affirmative action" programs. This Court in the Civil Rights Cases and Plessy v. Ferguson destroyed the movement toward complete equality. For almost a century no action was taken, and this nonaction was with the tacit approval of the courts. Then we had Brown v. Board of Education and the Civil Rights Acts of Congress, followed by numerous affirmative action programs. *Now,* we have this Court again stepping in, this time to stop affirmative action programs of the type used by the University of California.

JUSTICE STEVENS, with whom THE CHIEF JUSTICE, JUSTICE STEWART, and JUSTICE REHNQUIST join, concurring in the judgment in part and dissenting in part.

I

[Because this is not a class action and there is no outstanding order that race may not be considered in making an admissions decision it is ...] perfectly clear that the question whether race can ever be used as a factor in an admissions decision is not an issue in this case, and that discussion of that issue is inappropriate.

II

Both petitioner and respondent have asked us to determine the legality of the University's special admissions program by reference to the Constitution. Our settled practice, however, is to avoid the decision of a constitutional issue if a case can be fairly decided on a statutory ground. "If there is one doctrine more deeply rooted than any other in the process of constitutional adjudication, it is that we ought not to pass on questions of constitutionality ... unless such adjudication is unavoidable." ... In this case, we are presented with a constitutional question of undoubted and unusual importance. Since, however, a dispositive statutory claim was raised at the very inception of this case, and squarely decided in the portion of the trial court's judgment affirmed by the California Supreme Court, it is our plain duty to confront it. Only if petitioner should prevail on the statutory issue would it be necessary to decide whether the University's admissions program violated the Equal Protection Clause of the Fourteenth Amendment.

III

Section 601 of the Civil Rights Act of 1964 provides:

"No person in the United States shall, on the ground of race, color, or national origin, be excluded from participation in, be denied the benefits of, or be subjected to discrimination under any program or activity receiving Federal financial assistance."

The University, through its special admissions policy, excluded Bakke from participation in its program of medical education because of his race. The University also acknowledges that it was, and still is, receiving federal financial assistance. The plain language of the statute therefore requires affirmance of the judgment below.

NOTES AND QUESTIONS

1. What does the *Bakke* case decide? Because there is no majority opinion, and the prevailing opinion of Justice Powell expresses only his own views, that is a complicated question. Four justices (those joining Justice Stevens' opinion) never reach the constitutional questions. Of course the opinions of Justice Powell and Justice Brennan range broadly over a series of questions under the Fourteenth Amendment. They disagree, however, about a number of those issues. Can you list, in light of their disagreements, the constitutional issues that are not decided?

2. Focusing on Justice Powell's opinion, can you state the precise reason why he thinks the University of California at Davis Medical School program is impermissible? Isn't it true, whether or not a specified number of places are set aside for minorities, that if race is taken into account, non-minorities will be excluded because of their race?

It is arguable that Justice Powell's opinion, in its distinction between permissible and impermissible affirmative action programs, has the advantage of political compromise—reaching the solution most acceptable to the largest number of people. Is the distinction sound in principle? Is it fortunate that his opinion—although it controls because his is the "swing" vote—is not expressly adopted by a majority of the Court?

Would Justice Powell's rationale permit admissions decisions that disfavor minorities, if they are for the purpose of increasing diversity? Suppose a University's graduate department of physics discovers that all of the best applicants for its Ph.D. program are Asians. Would it be permissible to prefer non-Asians? How would Justice Brennan treat racial decisions that disfavor minorities?

3. Some affirmative action programs give favorable treatment to some racial minorities but not to others. Do African Americans have to be among the groups given favorable treatment? What about Mexican Americans? Native Americans? Puerto Ricans? Persons with Spanish surnames who are not Mexican Americans? Asians? Economically disadvantaged Caucasians? Women? How would Justice Powell treat a university's affirmative action program that left out one or more of the above groups? Justice Brennan? Justice Marshall?

On the other side of the question, would those justices approve the *inclusion* of any ethnic minority in the list of favored groups so long as that minority is under-represented in the student body? Does it make a difference if that group has been subjected to past societal discrimination? Whether that discrimination has anything to do with under-representation?

4. Important Supreme Court decisions concerning individual rights often revolve around difficult moral questions. Two important moral

issues involved in the *Bakke* case are these: should all decisions affecting individuals be made on the basis of individual merit rather than group identification? Are some decisions based on group identification less morally reprehensible than others? Is the use of race in admissions policies for the purpose of achieving integration more morally reprehensible than using such nonquantifiable criteria as athletic ability, or leadership ability? Is it more morally reprehensible than giving preferences to the physically handicapped, children of faculty members, children of alumni, military veterans, or applicants from specific geographic areas? If race is relevant, is it more morally reprehensible to disfavor racial minorities on the basis of their race than it is to favor them?

On the first question, consider United Jewish Organizations v. Carey, 430 U.S. 144 (1977). There, race was taken into account in drawing up legislative districts, to maximize representation of blacks in the legislature. Can it be argued that representation of groups is the essence of the process of electing a legislature, and that there is nothing wrong with government taking affirmative action to see that some groups—including racial groups—are proportionally represented? Could the same argument be made about appointment of government officials, such as judges? If one has to be a lawyer before one can be a judge, would the argument apply to admission to a law school? In short, the problem is whether there are some decisions that are appropriately made on the basis of notions of proportional representation, and some that should be made on the basis of individual merit.

With reference to the second question, is the use of race in admissions policies for the purpose of achieving integration more morally reprehensible than using such nonquantifiable criteria as athletic ability, or leadership ability? Is it more morally reprehensible than giving preferences to the physically handicapped, children of faculty members, children of alumni, military veterans or applicants from specific geographic areas? If race is relevant, is it more morally reprehensible to disfavor racial minorities on the basis of their race than it is to favor them?

GRUTTER v. BOLLINGER

539 U.S. 306, 123 S.Ct. 2325, 156 L.Ed.2d 304 (2003).

Justice O'Connor delivered the opinion of the Court.

This case requires us to decide whether the use of race as a factor in student admissions by the University of Michigan Law School ... is unlawful.

I

A

The Law School['s admissions policy seeks an academically capable, diverse student body through efforts that sought to] compl[y] with this Court's most recent ruling on the use of race in university admissions. See *Regents of Univ. of Cal. v. Bakke,* 438 U.S. 265 (1978)....

The hallmark of that policy is its focus on academic ability coupled with a flexible assessment of applicants' talents, experiences, and potential "to contribute to the learning of those around them." ... The policy requires admissions officials to evaluate each applicant based on all the information available in the file, including a personal statement, letters of recommendation, and an essay describing the ways in which the applicant will contribute to the life and diversity of the Law School.... In reviewing an applicant's file, admissions officials must consider the applicant's undergraduate grade point average (GPA) and Law School Admissions Test (LSAT) score because they are important (if imperfect) predictors of academic success in law school.... The policy stresses that "no applicant should be admitted unless we expect that applicant to do well enough to graduate with no serious academic problems." ...

The policy makes clear, however, that even the highest possible score does not guarantee admission.... Nor does a low score automatically disqualify an applicant.... Rather, the policy requires admissions officials to look beyond grades and test scores to other criteria that are important to the Law School's educational objectives.... So-called " 'soft' variables" such as "the enthusiasm of recommenders, the quality of the undergraduate institution, the quality of the applicant's essay, and the areas and difficulty of undergraduate course selection" are all brought to bear in assessing an "applicant's likely contributions to the intellectual and social life of the institution." ...

The policy aspires to "achieve that diversity which has the potential to enrich everyone's education and thus make a law school class stronger than the sum of its parts." ... The policy does not restrict the types of diversity contributions eligible for "substantial weight" in the admissions process, but instead recognizes "many possible bases for diversity admissions." ... The policy does, however, reaffirm the Law School's longstanding commitment to "one particular type of diversity," that is, "racial and ethnic diversity with special reference to the inclusion of students from groups which have been historically discriminated against, like African–Americans, Hispanics and Native Americans, who without this commitment might not be represented in our student body in meaningful numbers." ... By enrolling a " 'critical mass' of [underrepresented] minority students," the Law School seeks to "ensur[e] their ability to make unique contributions to the character of the Law School." ...

The policy does not define diversity "solely in terms of racial and ethnic status." ... Nor is the policy "insensitive to the competition among all students for admission to the [L]aw [S]chool." ... Rather, the policy seeks to guide admissions officers in "producing classes both diverse and academically outstanding, classes made up of students who promise to continue the tradition of outstanding contribution by Michigan Graduates to the legal profession." ...

B

Petitioner Barbara Grutter is a white Michigan resident who applied to the Law School in 1996 with a 3.8 grade point average and 161 LSAT score. The Law School [eventually] rejected her application [and she sued,] ... alleg[ing] that respondents discriminated against her on the basis of race in violation of the Fourteenth Amendment; Title VI of the Civil Rights Act of 1964, ... 42 U.S.C. § 2000d; and ... 42 U.S.C. § 1981.

Petitioner further alleged that her application was rejected because the Law School uses race as a "predominant" factor, giving applicants who belong to certain minority groups "a significantly greater chance of admission than students with similar credentials from disfavored racial groups." ...

. . .

... The District Court ... conduct[ed] a bench trial on the extent to which race was a factor in the Law School's admissions decisions, and whether the Law School's consideration of race in admissions decisions constituted a race-based double standard.

... [The] Director of Admissions ... testified that he did not direct his staff to admit a particular percentage or number of minority students, but rather to consider an applicant's race along with all other factors. ... [He] testified that at the height of the admissions season, he would frequently consult the so-called "daily reports" that kept track of the racial and ethnic composition of the class (along with other information such as residency status and gender) ... to ensure that a critical mass of underrepresented minority students would be reached so as to realize the educational benefits of a diverse student body. ... [He] stressed, however, that he did not seek to admit any particular number or percentage of underrepresented minority students. ...

[A successor] Director of Admissions ... testified that " 'critical mass' " means " 'meaningful numbers' " or " 'meaningful representation,' " which she understood to mean a number that encourages underrepresented minority students to participate in the classroom and not feel isolated. ... [She] stated there is no number, percentage, or range of numbers or percentages that constitute critical mass [and] that she must consider the race of applicants because a critical mass of underrepresented minority students could not be enrolled if admissions decisions were based primarily on undergraduate GPAs and LSAT scores. ...

The ... Dean of the Law School ... indicated that critical mass means numbers such that underrepresented minority students do not feel isolated or like spokespersons for their race. ... In some cases, [he testified,] an applicant's race may play no role, while in others it may be a " 'determinative' " factor. ...

. . .

In an attempt to quantify the extent to which the Law School actually considers race in making admissions decisions, the parties introduced voluminous evidence at trial. [P]etitioner's expert ... generated and analyzed "admissions grids" for ... 1995–2000 ... show[ing] the number of applicants and the number of admittees for all combinations of GPAs and LSAT scores. ... He concluded that membership in certain minority groups " 'is an extremely strong factor in the decision for acceptance,' " and that applicants from these minority groups " 'are given an extremely large allowance for admission' " as compared to applicants who are members of nonfavored groups.... [He] conceded, however, that race is not the predominant factor in the Law School's admissions calculus....

[T]he Law School's expert ... focused on the predicted effect of eliminating race as a factor in the Law School's admission process [and concluded that] a race-blind admissions system would have a " 'very dramatic,' " negative effect on underrepresented minority admissions.... He testified that in 2000, 35 percent of underrepresented minority applicants were admitted [and] predicted that if race were not considered, only 10 percent of those applicants would have been admitted.... Under this scenario, underrepresented minority students would have comprised 4 percent of the entering class in 2000 instead of the actual figure of 14.5 percent....

In the end, the District Court concluded that the Law School's use of race as a factor in admissions decisions was unlawful....

Sitting en banc, the Court of Appeals reversed[, four judges dissenting.] ...

. . .

We granted certiorari ... to resolve the disagreement among the Courts of Appeals on a question of national importance: Whether diversity is a compelling interest that can justify the narrowly tailored use of race in selecting applicants for admission to public universities. ...

II

A

We last addressed the use of race in public higher education over 25 years ago. In the landmark *Bakke* case, we reviewed a racial set-aside program that reserved 16 out of 100 seats in a medical school class for members of certain minority groups. 438 U.S. 265 (1978). The decision produced six separate opinions, none of which commanded a majority of the Court. Four Justices would have upheld the program against all attack on the ground that the government can use race to "remedy disadvantages cast on minorities by past racial prejudice." *Id.*, at 325 (joint opinion of Brennan, White, Marshall, and Blackmun, JJ., concurring in judgment in part and dissenting in part). Four other Justices avoided the constitutional question altogether and struck down the program on statutory grounds. *Id.*, at 408 (opinion of Stevens, J., joined by Burger, C. J., and Stewart and Rehnquist, JJ., concurring in judgment in part and dissenting in part). Justice Powell provided a fifth vote not only for invalidating the set-aside program, but also for reversing the state court's injunction against any use of race whatsoever. The only holding for the Court in *Bakke* was that a "State has a substantial interest that legitimately may be served by a properly devised admissions program involving the competitive consideration of race and ethnic origin." ... Thus, we reversed that part of the lower court's judgment that enjoined the university "from any consideration of the race of any applicant." . . .

Since this Court's splintered decision in *Bakke*, Justice Powell's opinion announcing the judgment of the Court has served as the touchstone for constitutional analysis of race-conscious admissions policies. Public and private universities across the Nation have modeled their own admissions programs on Justice Powell's views on permissible race-conscious policies. . . . We therefore discuss Justice Powell's opinion in some detail.

Justice Powell began by stating that "[t]he guarantee of equal protection cannot mean one thing when applied to one individual and something else when applied to a person of another color. If both are not accorded the same protection, then it is not equal." . . . In Justice Powell's view, when governmental decisions "touch upon an individual's race or ethnic background, he is entitled to a judicial determination that the burden he is asked to bear on that basis is precisely tailored to serve a compelling governmental interest." . . . Under this exacting standard, only one of the interests asserted by the university survived Justice Powell's scrutiny.

First, Justice Powell rejected an interest in " 'reducing the historic deficit of traditionally disfavored minorities in medical schools and in the medical profession' " as an unlawful interest in racial balancing. . . . Second, Justice Powell rejected an interest in remedying societal discrimination because such measures would risk placing unnecessary burdens on innocent third parties "who bear no responsibility for whatever harm the beneficiaries of the special admissions program are thought to have suffered." . . . Third, Justice Powell rejected an interest in "increasing the number of physicians who will practice in communities currently underserved," concluding that even if such an interest could be compelling in some circumstances the program under review was not "geared to promote that goal." . . .

Justice Powell approved the university's use of race to further only one interest: "the attainment of a diverse student body." . . . With the important proviso that "constitutional limitations protecting individual rights may not be disregarded," Justice Powell grounded his analysis in the academic freedom that "long has been viewed as a special concern of the First Amendment." . . . Justice Powell emphasized that nothing less than the " 'nation's future depends upon leaders trained through wide exposure' to the ideas and mores of students as diverse as this Nation of many peoples." . . . In seeking the "right to select those students who will contribute the most to the 'robust exchange of ideas,' " a university seeks "to achieve a goal that is of paramount importance in the fulfillment of its mission." . . . Both "tradition and experience lend support to the view that the contribution of diversity is substantial." . . .

Justice Powell was, however, careful to emphasize that in his view race "is only one element in a range of factors a university properly may consider in attaining the goal of a heterogeneous student body." . . . For Justice Powell, "[i]t is not an interest in simple ethnic diversity, in which a specified percentage of the student body is in effect guaranteed to be members of selected ethnic groups," that can justify the use of race.... Rather, "[t]he diversity that furthers a compelling state interest encompasses a far broader array of qualifications and characteristics of which racial or ethnic origin is but a single though important element." ...

. . .

... [F]or the reasons set out below, today we endorse Justice Powell's view that student body diversity is a compelling state interest that can justify the use of race in university admissions.

B

... Because the Fourteenth Amendment "protect[s] *persons*, not *groups*," all "governmental action based on race—a *group* classification long recognized as in most circumstances irrelevant and therefore prohibited—should be subjected to detailed judicial inquiry to ensure that the *personal* right to equal protection of the laws has not been infringed." *Adarand Constructors, Inc. v. Pea,* 515 U.S. 200, 227 (1995) (emphasis in original ...)....

We have held that all racial classifications imposed by government "must be analyzed by a reviewing court under strict scrutiny." ... This means that such classifications are constitutional only if they are narrowly tailored to further compelling governmental interests. "Absent searching judicial inquiry into the justification for such race-based measures," we have no way to determine what "classifications are 'benign' or 'remedial' and what classifications are in fact motivated by illegitimate notions of racial inferiority or simple racial politics." *Richmond v. J. A. Croson Co.,* 488 U.S. 469, 493 (1989) (plurality opinion). We apply strict scrutiny to all racial classifications to " 'smoke out' illegitimate uses of race by assuring that [government] is pursuing a goal important enough to warrant use of a highly suspect tool." ...

Strict scrutiny is not "strict in theory, but fatal in fact." *Adarand* ... Although all governmental uses of race are subject to strict scrutiny, not all are invalidated by it. ...When race-based action is necessary to further a compelling governmental interest, such action does not violate the constitutional guarantee of equal protection so long as the narrow-tailoring requirement is also satisfied.

Context matters when reviewing race-based governmental action under the Equal Protection Clause.... Not every decision influenced by race is equally objectionable and strict scrutiny is designed to provide a framework for carefully examining the importance and the sincerity of the reasons advanced by the governmental decisionmaker for the use of race in that particular context.

III

A

With these principles in mind, we turn to the question whether the Law School's use of race is justified by a compelling state interest. [R]espondents assert only one justification for their use of race in the admissions process: obtaining "the educational benefits that flow from a diverse student body." ... In other words, the Law School asks us to recognize, in the context of higher education, a compelling state interest in student body diversity.

We first wish to dispel the notion that the Law School's argument has been foreclosed, either expressly or implicitly, by our affirmative-action cases decided since *Bakke*. It is true that some language in those opinions might be read to suggest that remedying past discrimination is the only permissible justification for race-based governmental action. See, *e.g.*, *Richmond v. J. A. Croson Co., supra*, at 493 (plurality opinion) (stating that unless classifications based on race are "strictly reserved for remedial settings, they may in fact promote notions of racial inferiority and lead to a politics of racial hostility"). But we have never held that the only governmental use of race that can survive strict scrutiny is remedying past discrimination. Nor, since *Bakke*, have we directly addressed the use of race in the context of public higher education. Today, we hold that the Law School has a compelling interest in attaining a diverse student body.

The Law School's educational judgment that such diversity is essential to its educational mission is one to which we defer. The Law School's assessment that diversity will, in fact, yield educational benefits is substantiated by respondents and their *amici*. Our scrutiny of the interest asserted by the Law School is no less strict for taking into account complex educational judgments in an area that lies primarily within the expertise of the university. Our holding today is in keeping with our tradition of giving a degree of deference to a university's academic decisions, within constitutionally prescribed limits. . . .

We have long recognized that, given the important purpose of public education and the expansive freedoms of speech and thought associated with the university environment, universities occupy a special niche in our constitutional tradition. . . . In announcing the principle of student body diversity as a compelling state interest, Justice Powell invoked our cases recognizing a constitutional dimension, grounded in the First Amendment, of educational autonomy: "The freedom of a university to make its own judgments as to education includes the selection of its student body." *Bakke* ... From this premise, Justice Powell reasoned that by claiming "the right to select those students who will contribute the most to the 'robust exchange of ideas,' a university 'seek[s] to achieve a goal that is of paramount importance in the fulfillment of its mission.'" ... Our conclusion that the Law School has a compelling interest in a diverse student body is informed by our view that attaining a diverse student body is at the heart of the Law School's proper institutional mission, and that "good faith" on the part of a university is "presumed" absent "a showing to the contrary." ...

As part of its goal of "assembling a class that is both exceptionally academically qualified and broadly diverse," the Law School seeks to "enroll a 'critical mass' of minority students." ... The Law School's interest is not simply "to assure within its student body some specified percentage of a particular group merely because of its race or ethnic origin." *Bakke*, ... (opinion of Powell, J.). That would amount to outright racial balancing, which is patently unconstitutional.... Rather, the Law School's concept of critical mass is defined by reference to the educational benefits that diversity is designed to produce.

These benefits are substantial. As the District Court emphasized, the Law School's admissions policy promotes "cross-racial understanding," helps to break down racial stereotypes, and "enables [students] to better understand persons of different races." ... These benefits are "important and laudable," because "classroom discussion is livelier, more spirited, and simply more enlightening and interesting" when the students have "the greatest possible variety of backgrounds." ...

The Law School's claim of a compelling interest is further bolstered by its *amici*, who point to the educational benefits that flow from student body diversity. In addition to the expert studies and reports entered into evidence at trial, numerous studies show that student body diversity promotes learning outcomes, and "better prepares students for an increasingly diverse workforce and society, and better prepares them as professionals." Brief for American Educational Research Association et al. as *Amici Curiae* 3; see, *e.g.*, W. Bowen & D. Bok, The Shape of the River (1998); Diversity Challenged: Evidence on the Impact of Affirmative Action (G. Orfield & M. Kurlaender eds. 2001); Compelling Interest: Examining the Evidence on Racial Dynamics in Colleges and Universities (M. Chang, D. Witt, J. Jones, & K. Hakuta eds. 2003).

These benefits are not theoretical but real, as major American businesses have made clear that the skills needed in today's increasingly global marketplace can only be developed through exposure to widely diverse people, cultures, ideas, and viewpoints. Brief for 3M et al. as *Amici Curiae* 5; Brief for General Motors Corp. as *Amicus Curiae* 3–4. What is more, high-ranking retired officers and civilian leaders of the United States military assert that, "[b]ased on [their] decades of experience," a "highly qualified, racially diverse officer corps ... is essential to the military's ability to fulfill its principle mission to provide national security." Brief for Julius W. Becton, Jr. et al. as *Amici Curiae* 27. The primary sources for the Nation's officer corps are the service academies and the Reserve Officers Training Corps (ROTC), the latter comprising students already admitted to participating colleges and universities.... At present, "the military cannot achieve an officer corps that is *both* highly qualified *and* racially diverse unless the service academies and the ROTC used limited race-conscious recruiting and admissions policies." *Ibid.* (emphasis in original). To fulfill its mission, the military "must be selective in admissions for training and education for the officer corps, *and* it must train and educate a highly qualified, racially diverse officer corps in a racially diverse setting." ... (emphasis in original). We agree that "[i]t requires only a small step from this analysis to conclude that our country's other most selective institutions must remain both diverse and selective." *Ibid*.

We have repeatedly acknowledged the overriding importance of preparing students for work and citizenship, describing education as pivotal to "sustaining our political and cultural heritage" with a fundamental role in maintaining the fabric of society. *Plyler v. Doe*, 457 U.S. 202, 221 (1982). This Court has long recognized that "education ... is the very foundation of good citizenship." *Brown v. Board of Education*, 347 U.S. 483, 493 (1954). For this reason, the diffusion of knowledge and opportunity through public institutions of higher education must be accessible to all individuals regardless of race or ethnicity. The United States, as *amicus curiae*, affirms that "[e]nsuring that public institutions are open and available to all segments of American society, including people of all races and ethnicities, represents a paramount government objective." ... And, "[n]owhere is the importance of such openness more acute than in the context of higher education." ... Effective participation by members of all racial and ethnic groups in the civic life of our Nation is essential if the dream of one Nation, indivisible, is to be realized.

Moreover, universities, and in particular, law schools, represent the training ground for a large number of our Nation's leaders. *Sweatt v. Painter*, 339 U.S. 629, 634 (1950) (describing law school as a "proving ground for legal learning and practice"). Individuals with law degrees occupy roughly half the state governorships, more than half the seats in the United States Senate, and more than a third of the seats in the United States House of Representatives.... The pattern is even more striking when it comes to highly selective law schools. A handful of these schools accounts for 25 of the 100 United States Senators, 74 United States Courts of Appeals judges, and nearly 200 of the more than 600 United States District Court judges....

In order to cultivate a set of leaders with legitimacy in the eyes of the citizenry, it is necessary that the path to leadership be visibly open to talented and qualified individuals of every race and ethnicity. All members of our heterogeneous society must have confidence in the openness and integrity of the educational institutions that provide this training. [L]aw schools "cannot be effective in isolation from the individuals and institutions with which the law interacts." See *Sweatt v. Painter*.... Access to legal education (and thus the legal profession) must be inclusive of talented and qualified individuals of every race and ethnicity, so that all members of our heterogeneous society may participate in the educational institutions that provide the training and education necessary to succeed in America.

The Law School does not premise its need for critical mass on "any belief that minority students always (or even consistently) express some characteristic minority viewpoint on any issue." ... To the contrary, diminishing the force of such stereotypes is both a crucial part of the Law School's mission, and one that it cannot accomplish with only token numbers of minority students. Just as growing up in a particular region or having particular professional experiences is likely to affect an individual's views, so too is one's own, unique experience of being a racial minority in a society, like our own, in which race unfortunately still matters. The Law School has determined, based on its experience and expertise, that a "critical mass" of underrepresented minorities is necessary to further its compelling interest in securing the educational benefits of a diverse student body.

B

Even in the limited circumstance when drawing racial distinctions is permissible to further a compelling state interest, government is still "constrained in how it may pursue that end: [T]he means chosen to accomplish the [government's] asserted purpose must be specifically and narrowly framed to accomplish that purpose." *Shaw v. Hunt,* 517 U.S. 899, 908 (1996).... The purpose of the narrow tailoring requirement is to ensure that "the means chosen 'fit' ... th[e] compelling goal so closely that there is little or no possibility that the motive for the classification was illegitimate racial prejudice or stereotype." *Richmond v. J. A. Croson Co.,* 488 U.S., at 493 (plurality opinion).

Since *Bakke,* we have had no occasion to define the contours of the narrow-tailoring inquiry with respect to race-conscious university admissions programs. That inquiry must be calibrated to fit the distinct issues raised by the use of race to achieve student body diversity in public higher education. Contrary to Justice Kennedy's assertions, we do not "abandon[] strict scrutiny." Rather, ... we adhere to *Adarand*'s teaching that the very purpose of strict scrutiny is to take such "relevant differences into account." ...

To be narrowly tailored, a race-conscious admissions program cannot use a quota system—it cannot "insulat[e] each category of applicants with certain desired qualifications from competition with all other applicants." *Bakke,* ... (opinion of Powell, J.). Instead, a university may consider race or ethnicity only as a " 'plus' in a particular applicant's file," without "insulat[ing] the individual from comparison with all other candidates for the available seats." ... In other words, an admissions program must be "flexible enough to consider all pertinent elements of diversity in light of the particular qualifications of each applicant, and to place them on the same footing for consideration, although not necessarily according them the same weight." ...

We find that the Law School's admissions program bears the hallmarks of a narrowly tailored plan. As Justice Powell made clear in *Bakke,* truly individualized consideration demands that race be used in a flexible, nonmechanical way. It follows from this mandate that universities cannot establish quotas for members of certain racial groups or put members of those groups on separate admissions tracks.... Nor can universities insulate applicants who belong to certain racial or ethnic groups from the competition for admission.... Universities can, however, consider race or ethnicity more flexibly as a "plus" factor in the context of individualized consideration of each and every applicant....

We are satisfied that the Law School's admissions program, like the Harvard plan described by Justice Powell, does not operate as a quota. Properly understood, a "quota" is a program in which a certain fixed number or proportion of opportunities are "reserved exclusively for certain minority groups." ... Quotas " 'impose a fixed number or percentage which must be attained, or which cannot be exceeded,' " ... and "insulate the individual from comparison with all other candidates for the available seats." ... In contrast, "a permissible goal ... require[s] only a good-faith effort ... to come within a range demarcated by the goal itself," ... and permits consideration of race as a "plus" factor in any given case while still ensuring that each candidate "compete[s] with all other qualified applicants,".....

Justice Powell's distinction between the medical school's rigid 16–seat quota and Harvard's flexible use of race as a "plus" factor is instructive. Harvard certainly had minimum *goals* for minority enrollment, even if it had no specific number firmly in mind. See *Bakke,* ... (opinion of Powell, J.) ("10 or 20 black students could not begin to bring to their classmates and to each other the variety of points of view, backgrounds and experiences of blacks in the United States"). What is more, Justice Powell flatly rejected the argument that Harvard's program was "the functional equivalent of a quota" merely because it had some " 'plus' " for race, or gave greater "weight" to race than to some other factors, in order to achieve student body diversity. ...

The Law School's goal of attaining a critical mass of underrepresented minority students does not transform its program into a quota. As the Harvard plan described by Justice Powell recognized, there is of course "some relationship between numbers and achieving the benefits to be derived from a diverse student body, and between numbers and providing a reasonable environment for those students admitted." ... "[S]ome attention to numbers," without more, does not transform a flexible admissions system into a rigid quota.... Nor, as Justice Kennedy posits, does the Law School's consultation of the "daily reports," which keep track of the racial and ethnic composition of the class (as well as of residency and gender), "suggest [] there was no further attempt at individual review save for race itself" during the final stages of the admissions process. To the contrary, the Law School's admissions officers testified without contradiction that they never gave race any more or less weight based on the information contained in these reports. ... Moreover, as Justice Kennedy concedes, between 1993 and 2000, the number of African–American, Latino, and Native–American students in each class at the Law School varied from 13.5 to 20.1 percent, a range inconsistent with a quota.

The Chief Justice believes that the Law School's policy conceals an attempt to achieve racial balancing, and cites admissions data to contend that the Law School discriminates among different groups within the critical mass. But, as the Chief Justice concedes, the number of underrepresented minority students who ultimately enroll in the Law School differs substantially from their representation in the applicant pool and varies considerably for each group from year to year....

That a race-conscious admissions program does not operate as a quota does not, by itself, satisfy the requirement of individualized consideration. When using race as a "plus" factor in university admissions, a university's admissions program must remain flexible enough to ensure that each applicant is evaluated as an individual and not in a way that makes an applicant's race or ethnicity the defining feature of his or her application. The importance of this individualized consideration in the context of a race-conscious admissions program is paramount....

Here, the Law School engages in a highly individualized, holistic review of each applicant's file, giving serious consideration to all the ways an applicant might contribute to a diverse educational environment. The Law School affords this individualized consideration to applicants of all races. There is no policy, either *de jure* or *de facto*, of automatic acceptance or rejection based on any single "soft" variable. Unlike the program at issue in *Gratz v. Bollinger*, [539 U.S. __ (2003),] the Law School awards no mechanical, predetermined diversity "bonuses" based on race or ethnicity. See [*Gratz*] (distinguishing a race-conscious admissions program that automatically awards 20 points based on race from the Harvard plan, which considered race but "did not contemplate that any single characteristic automatically ensured a specific and identifiable contribution to a university's diversity"). Like the Harvard plan, the Law School's admissions policy "is flexible enough to consider all pertinent elements of diversity in light of the particular qualifications of each applicant, and to place them on the same footing for consideration, although not necessarily according them the same weight." ...

We also find that, like the Harvard plan Justice Powell referenced in *Bakke*, the Law School's race-conscious admissions program adequately ensures that all factors that may contribute to student body diversity are meaningfully considered alongside race in admissions decisions. With respect to the use of race itself, all underrepresented minority students admitted by the Law School have been deemed qualified. By virtue of our Nation's struggle with racial inequality, such students are both likely to have experiences of particular importance to the Law School's mission, and less likely to be admitted in meaningful numbers on criteria that ignore those experiences....

The Law School does not, however, limit in any way the broad range of qualities and experiences that may be considered valuable contributions to student body diversity. To the contrary, the [admissions] policy makes clear "[t]here are many possible bases for diversity admissions," and provides examples of admittees who have lived or traveled widely abroad, are fluent in several languages, have overcome personal adversity and family hardship, have exceptional records of extensive community service, and have had successful careers in other fields.... The Law School seriously considers each "applicant's promise of making a notable contribution to the class by way of a particular strength, attainment, or characteristic—*e.g.*, an unusual intellectual achievement, employment experience, nonacademic performance, or personal background." ... All applicants have the opportunity to highlight their own potential diversity contributions through the submission of a personal statement, letters of recommendation, and an essay describing the ways in which the applicant will contribute to the life and diversity of the Law School.

What is more, the Law School actually gives substantial weight to diversity factors besides race. The Law School frequently accepts nonminority applicants with grades and test scores lower than underrepresented minority applicants (and other nonminority applicants) who are rejected.... This shows that the Law School seriously weighs many other diversity factors besides race that can make a real and dispositive difference for nonminority applicants as well. By this flexible approach, the Law School sufficiently takes into account, in practice as well as in theory, a wide variety of characteristics besides race and ethnicity that contribute to a diverse student body. Justice Kennedy speculates that "race is likely outcome determinative for many members of minority groups" who do not fall within the upper range of LSAT scores and grades.... But the same could be said of the Harvard plan discussed approvingly by Justice Powell in *Bakke*, and indeed of any plan that uses race as one of many factors....

Petitioner and the United States argue that the Law School's plan is not narrowly tailored because race-neutral means exist to obtain the educational benefits of student body diversity that the Law School seeks. We disagree. Narrow tailoring does not require exhaustion of every conceivable race-neutral alternative. Nor does it require a university to choose between maintaining a reputation for excellence or fulfilling a commitment to provide educational opportunities to members of all racial groups.... Narrow tailoring does, however, require serious, good faith consideration of workable race-neutral alternatives that will achieve the diversity the university seeks....

We agree with the Court of Appeals that the Law School sufficiently considered workable race-neutral alternatives. The District Court took the Law School to task for failing to consider race-neutral alternatives such as "using a lottery system" or "decreasing the emphasis for all applicants on undergraduate GPA and LSAT scores." ... But these alternatives would require a dramatic sacrifice of diversity, the academic quality of all admitted students, or both.

The Law School's current admissions program considers race as one factor among many, in an effort to assemble a student body that is diverse in ways broader than race. Because a lottery would make that kind of nuanced judgment impossible, it would effectively sacrifice all other educational values, not to mention every other kind of diversity. So too with the suggestion that the Law School simply lower admissions standards for all students, a drastic remedy that would require the Law School to become a much different institution and sacrifice a vital component of its educational mission. The United States advocates "percentage plans," recently adopted by public undergraduate institutions in Texas, Florida, and California to guarantee admission to all students above a certain class-rank threshold in every high school in the State.... The United States does not, however, explain how such plans could work for graduate and professional schools. Moreover, even assuming such plans are race-neutral, they may preclude the university from conducting the individualized assessments necessary to assemble a student body that is not just racially diverse, but diverse along all the qualities valued by the university. We are satisfied that the Law School adequately considered race-neutral alternatives currently capable of producing a critical mass without forcing the Law School to abandon the academic selectivity that is the cornerstone of its educational mission.

We acknowledge that "there are serious problems of justice connected with the idea of preference itself." *Bakke,* ... (opinion of Powell, J.).

Narrow tailoring, therefore, requires that a race-conscious admissions program not unduly harm members of any racial group. . . .

We are satisfied that the Law School's admissions program does not. Because the Law School considers "all pertinent elements of diversity," it can (and does) select nonminority applicants who have greater potential to enhance student body diversity over underrepresented minority applicants. . . . As Justice Powell recognized in *Bakke*, so long as a race-conscious admissions program uses race as a "plus" factor in the context of individualized consideration, a rejected applicant

> "will not have been foreclosed from all consideration for that seat simply because he was not the right color or had the wrong surname. . . . His qualifications would have been weighed fairly and competitively, and he would have no basis to complain of unequal treatment under the Fourteenth Amendment." . . .

We agree that, in the context of its individualized inquiry into the possible diversity contributions of all applicants, the Law School's race-conscious admissions program does not unduly harm nonminority applicants.

We are mindful, however, that "[a] core purpose of the Fourteenth Amendment was to do away with all governmentally imposed discrimination based on race." *Palmore v. Sidoti*, 466 U.S. 429, 432 (1984). Accordingly, race-conscious admissions policies must be limited in time. This requirement reflects that racial classifications, however compelling their goals, are potentially so dangerous that they may be employed no more broadly than the interest demands. Enshrining a permanent justification for racial preferences would offend this fundamental equal protection principle. We see no reason to exempt race-conscious admissions programs from the requirement that all governmental use of race must have a logical end point. The Law School, too, concedes that all "race-conscious programs must have reasonable durational limits." . . .

In the context of higher education, the durational requirement can be met by sunset provisions in race-conscious admissions policies and periodic reviews to determine whether racial preferences are still necessary to achieve student body diversity. Universities in California, Florida, and Washington State, where racial preferences in admissions are prohibited by state law, are currently engaged in experimenting with a wide variety of alternative approaches. Universities in other States can and should draw on the most promising aspects of these race-neutral alternatives as they develop. . . .

The requirement that all race-conscious admissions programs have a termination point "assure[s] all citizens that the deviation from the norm of equal treatment of all racial and ethnic groups is a temporary matter, a measure taken in the service of the goal of equality itself." *Richmond v. J. A. Croson Co.,* . . . .

We take the Law School at its word that it would "like nothing better than to find a race-neutral admissions formula" and will terminate its race-conscious admissions program as soon as practicable. . . . It has been 25 years since Justice Powell first approved the use of race to further an interest in student body diversity in the context of public higher education. Since that time, the number of minority applicants with high grades and test scores has indeed increased.... We expect that 25 years from now, the use of racial preferences will no longer be necessary to further the interest approved today.

IV

In summary, the Equal Protection Clause does not prohibit the Law School's narrowly tailored use of race in admissions decisions to further a compelling interest in obtaining the educational benefits that flow from a diverse student body. Consequently, petitioner's statutory claims based on Title VI and 42 U.S.C. § 1981 also fail. See *Bakke, supra,* at 287 (opinion of Powell, J.) ("Title VI ... proscribe[s] only those racial classifications that would violate the Equal Protection Clause or the Fifth Amendment"); *General Building Contractors Assn., Inc. v. Pennsylvania,* 458 U.S. 375, 389–391 (1982) (the prohibition against discrimination in § 1981 is co-extensive with the Equal Protection Clause). The judgment of the Court of Appeals for the Sixth Circuit, accordingly, is affirmed.

. . .

JUSTICE GINSBURG, with whom JUSTICE BREYER joins, concurring.

. . .

The Court ... observes that "[i]t has been 25 years since Justice Powell [in *Regents of Univ. of Cal. v. Bakke,* 438 U.S. 265 (1978)] first approved the use of race to further an interest in student body diversity in the context of public higher education." For at least part of that time, however, the law could not fairly be described as "settled," and in some regions of the Nation, overtly race-conscious admissions policies have been proscribed.... Moreover, it was only 25 years before *Bakke* that this Court declared public school segregation unconstitutional, a declaration that, after prolonged resistance, yielded an end to a law-enforced racial caste system, itself the legacy of centuries of slavery....

It is well documented that conscious and unconscious race bias, even rank discrimination based on race, remain alive in our land, impeding realization of our highest values and ideals.... As to public education, data for the years 2000–2001 show that 71.6% of African–American children and 76.3% of Hispanic children attended a school in which minorities made up a majority of the student body. ...And schools in predominantly minority communities lag far behind others measured by the educational resources available to them....

However strong the public's desire for improved education systems may be, ... it remains the current reality that many minority students encounter markedly inadequate and unequal educational opportunities. Despite these inequalities, some minority students are able to meet the high threshold requirements set for admission to the country's finest undergraduate and graduate educational institutions. As lower school education in minority communities improves, an increase in the number of such students may be anticipated. From today's vantage point, one may hope, but not firmly forecast, that over the next generation's span, progress toward nondiscrimination and genuinely equal opportunity will make it safe to sunset affirmative action.

CHIEF JUSTICE REHNQUIST, with whom JUSTICE SCALIA, JUSTICE KENNEDY, and JUSTICE THOMAS join, dissenting.

... I do not believe ... that the University of Michigan Law School's ... means are narrowly tailored to the interest it asserts. The Law School claims it must take the steps it does to achieve a " 'critical mass' " of underrepresented minority students.... But its actual program bears no relation to this asserted goal. Stripped of its "critical mass" veil, the Law School's program is revealed as a naked effort to achieve racial balancing.

... Our cases establish that ... respondents must demonstrate that their methods of using race " 'fit' " a compelling state interest "with greater precision than any alternative means." ...

Before the Court's decision today, we consistently applied the same strict scrutiny analysis regardless of the government's purported reason for using race and regardless of the setting in which race was being used.... Indeed, even in the specific context of higher education, we emphasized that "constitutional limitations protecting individual rights may not be disregarded." *Bakke*, ...

Although the Court recites the language of our strict scrutiny analysis, its application of that review is unprecedented in its deference.

. . .

In practice, the Law School's program bears little or no relation to its asserted goal of achieving "critical mass." Respondents explain that the Law School seeks to accumulate a "critical mass" of *each* underrepresented minority group.... But the record demonstrates that the Law School's admissions practices with respect to these groups differ dramatically and cannot be defended under any consistent use of the term "critical mass."

From 1995 through 2000, the Law School admitted between 1,130 and 1,310 students. Of those, between 13 and 19 were Native American, between 91 and 108 were African–Americans, and between 47 and 56 were Hispanic. If the Law School is admitting between 91 and 108 African–Americans in order to achieve "critical mass," thereby preventing African–American students from feeling "isolated or like spokespersons for their race," one would think that a number of the same order of magnitude would be necessary to accomplish the same purpose for Hispanics and Native Americans. Similarly, even if all of the Native American applicants admitted in a given year matriculate, which the record demonstrates is not at all the case, how can this possibly constitute a "critical mass" of Native Americans in a class of over 350 students? In order for this pattern of admission to be consistent with the Law School's explanation of "critical mass," one would have to believe that the objectives of "critical mass" offered by respondents are achieved with only half the number of Hispanics and one-sixth the number of Native Americans as compared to African–Americans. But respondents offer no race-specific reasons for such disparities. Instead, they simply emphasize the importance of achieving "critical mass," without any explanation of why that concept is applied differently among the three underrepresented minority groups.

These different numbers, moreover, come only as a result of substantially different treatment among the three underrepresented minority groups, as is apparent in an example offered by the Law School and highlighted by the Court: The school asserts that it "frequently accepts nonminority applicants with grades and test scores lower than underrepresented minority applicants (and other nonminority applicants) who are rejected." ... Specifically, the Law School states that "[s]ixty-nine minority applicants were rejected between 1995 and 2000 with at least a 3.5 [Grade Point Average (GPA)] and a [score of] 159 or higher on the [Law School Admissions Test (LSAT)]" while a number of Caucasian and Asian–American applicants with similar or lower scores were admitted. . . .

Review of the record reveals only 67 such individuals. Of these 67 individuals, *56* were Hispanic, while only 6 were African–American, and only 5 were Native American. This discrepancy reflects a consistent practice. For example, in 2000, 12 Hispanics who scored between a 159–160 on the LSAT and earned a GPA of 3.00 or higher applied for admission and only 2 were admitted. . . . Meanwhile, 12 African–Americans in the same range of qualifications applied for admission and all 12 were admitted. . . . Likewise, that same year, 16 Hispanics who scored between a 151–153 on the LSAT and earned a 3.00 or higher applied for admission and only 1 of those applicants was admitted. . . . Twenty-three similarly qualified African–Americans applied for admission and 14 were admitted. . . .

These statistics have a significant bearing on petitioner's case. Respondents have *never* offered any race-specific arguments explaining why significantly more individuals from one underrepresented minority group are needed in order to achieve "critical mass" or further student body diversity. They certainly have not explained why Hispanics, who they have said are among "the groups most isolated by racial barriers in our country," should have their admission capped out in this manner. . . . [T]he Law School's disparate admissions practices with respect to these minority groups demonstrate that its alleged goal of "critical mass" is simply a sham. . . . Surely strict scrutiny cannot permit these sort of disparities without at least some explanation.

Only when the "critical mass" label is discarded does a likely explanation for these numbers emerge. . . .

[T]he correlation between the percentage of the Law School's pool of applicants who are members of the three minority groups and the percentage of the admitted applicants who are members of these same groups is far too precise to be dismissed as merely the result of the school paying "some attention to [the] numbers." ... [F]rom 1995 through 2000 the percentage of admitted applicants who were members of these minority groups closely tracked the percentage of individuals in the school's applicant pool who were from the same groups.

. . .

For example, in 1995, when 9.7% of the applicant pool was African–American, 9.4% of the admitted class was African–American. By 2000, only 7.5% of the applicant pool was African–American, and 7.3% of the admitted class was African–American. This correlation is striking. Respondents themselves emphasize that the number of underrepresented minority students admitted to the Law School would be significantly smaller if the race of each applicant were not considered. . . . But, as the examples above illustrate, the measure of the decrease would differ dramatically among the groups. The tight correlation between the percentage of applicants and admittees of a given race, therefore, must result from careful race based planning by the Law School. It suggests a formula for admission based on the aspirational assumption that all applicants are equally qualified academically, and therefore that the proportion of each group admitted should be the same as the proportion of that group in the applicant pool. . . .

Not only do respondents fail to explain this phenomenon, they attempt to obscure it. . . . ("The Law School's minority enrollment percentages . . . diverged from the percentages in the applicant pool by as much as 17.7% from 1995–2000"). But the divergence between the percentages of underrepresented minorities in the applicant pool and in the *enrolled* classes is not the only relevant comparison. In fact, it may not be the most relevant comparison. The Law School cannot precisely control which of its admitted applicants decide to attend the university. But it can and, as the numbers demonstrate, clearly does employ racial preferences in extending offers of admission. Indeed, the ostensibly flexible nature of the Law School's admissions program that the Court finds appealing appears to be, in practice, a carefully managed program designed to ensure proportionate representation of applicants from selected minority groups.

I do not believe that the Constitution gives the Law School such free rein in the use of race. The Law School has offered no explanation for its actual admissions practices and, unexplained, we are bound to conclude that the Law School has managed its admissions program, not to achieve a "critical mass," but to extend offers of admission to members of selected minority groups in proportion to their statistical representation in the applicant pool. But this is precisely the type of racial balancing that the Court itself calls "patently unconstitutional."

Finally, I believe that the Law School's program fails strict scrutiny because it is devoid of any reasonably precise time limit on the Law School's use of race in admissions. . . .

The Court suggests a possible 25–year limitation on the Law School's current program. Respondents, on the other hand, remain more ambiguous, explaining that "the Law School of course recognizes that race-conscious programs must have reasonable durational limits, and the Sixth Circuit properly found such a limit in the Law School's resolve to cease considering race when genuine race-neutral alternatives become available." ... These discussions of a time limit are the vaguest of assurances. In truth, they permit the Law School's use of racial preferences on a seemingly permanent basis. Thus, an important component of strict scrutiny—that a program be limited in time—is casually subverted.

The Court, in an unprecedented display of deference under our strict scrutiny analysis, upholds the Law School's program despite its obvious flaws. We have said that when it comes to the use of race, the connection between the ends and the means used to attain them must be precise. But here the flaw is deeper than that; it is not merely a question of "fit" between ends and means. Here the means actually used are forbidden by the Equal Protection Clause of the Constitution.

JUSTICE KENNEDY, dissenting.

The separate opinion by Justice Powell in *Regents of Univ. of Cal. v. Bakke* is based on the principle that a university admissions program may take account of race as one, nonpredominant factor in a system designed to consider each applicant as an individual, provided the program can meet the test of strict scrutiny by the judiciary. ... This is a unitary formulation. If strict scrutiny is abandoned or manipulated to distort its real and accepted meaning, the Court lacks authority to approve the use of race even in this modest, limited way. The opinion by Justice Powell, in my view, states the correct rule for resolving this case. The Court, however, does not apply strict scrutiny. By trying to say otherwise, it undermines both the test and its own controlling precedents.

Justice Powell's approval of the use of race in university admissions reflected a tradition, grounded in the First Amendment, of acknowledging a university's conception of its educational mission.... Our precedents provide a basis for the Court's acceptance of a university's considered judgment that racial diversity among students can further its educational task, when supported by empirical evidence....

It is unfortunate, however, that the Court takes the first part of Justice Powell's rule but abandons the second. Having approved the use of race as a factor in the admissions process, the majority proceeds to nullify the essential safeguard Justice Powell insisted upon as the precondition of the approval [—] rigorous judicial review, with strict scrutiny as the controlling standard.... The Court confuses deference to a university's definition of its educational objective with deference to the implementation of this goal. In the context of university admissions the objective of racial diversity can be accepted based on empirical data known to us, but deference is not to be given with respect to the methods by which it is pursued....

The Court, in a review that is nothing short of perfunctory, accepts the University of Michigan Law School's assurances that its admissions process meets with constitutional requirements. The majority fails to confront the reality of how the Law School's admissions policy is implemented. The dissenting opinion by the Chief Justice, which I join in full, demonstrates beyond question why the concept of critical mass is a delusion used by the Law School to mask its attempt to make race an automatic factor in most instances and to achieve numerical goals indistinguishable from quotas.... It remains to point out how critical mass becomes inconsistent with individual consideration in some more specific aspects of the admissions process.

About 80 to 85 percent of the places in the entering class are given to applicants in the upper range of Law School Admissions Test scores and grades. An applicant with these credentials likely will be admitted without consideration of race or ethnicity. With respect to the remaining 15 to 20 percent of the seats, race is likely outcome determinative for many members of minority groups. That is where the competition becomes tight and where any given applicant's chance of admission is far smaller if he or she lacks minority status. At this point the numerical concept of critical mass has the real potential to compromise individual review.

The Law School has not demonstrated how individual consideration is, or can be, preserved at this stage of the application process given the instruction to attain what it calls critical mass. In fact the evidence shows otherwise. There was little deviation among admitted minority students during the years from 1995 to 1998. The percentage of enrolled minorities fluctuated only by 0.3%, from 13.5% to 13.8%. The number of minority students to whom offers were extended varied by just a slightly greater magnitude of 2.2%, from the high of 15.6% in 1995 to the low of 13.4% in 1998.

The District Court relied on this uncontested fact to draw an inference that the Law School's pursuit of critical mass mutated into the equivalent of a quota.... Admittedly, there were greater fluctuations among enrolled minorities in the preceding years, 1987–1994, by as much as 5 or 6%. The percentage of minority offers, however, at no point fell below 12%, historically defined by the Law School as the bottom of its critical mass range. The greater variance during the earlier years, in any event, does not dispel suspicion that the school engaged in racial balancing. The data would be consistent with an inference that the Law School modified its target only twice, in 1991 (from 13% to 19%), and then again in 1995 (back from 20% to 13%). The intervening year, 1993, when the percentage dropped to 14.5%, could be an aberration, caused by the school's miscalculation as to how many applicants with offers would accept or by its redefinition, made in April 1992, of which minority groups were entitled to race-based preference....

The narrow fluctuation band raises an inference that the Law School subverted individual determination, and strict scrutiny requires the Law School to overcome the inference....

... At the very least, the constancy of admitted minority students and the close correlation between the racial breakdown of admitted minorities and the composition of the applicant pool ... require the Law School either to produce a convincing explanation or to show it has taken adequate steps to ensure individual assessment. The Law School does neither.

The obvious tension between the pursuit of critical mass and the requirement of individual review increased by the end of the admissions season. Most of the decisions where race may decide the outcome are made during this period. . . .

The consultation of daily reports during the last stages in the admissions process suggests there was no further attempt at individual review save for race itself. The admissions officers could use the reports to recalibrate the plus factor given to race depending on how close they were to achieving the Law School's goal of critical mass. The bonus factor of race would then become divorced from individual review; it would be premised instead on the numerical objective set by the Law School.

The Law School made no effort to guard against this danger. It provided no guidelines to its admissions personnel on how to reconcile individual assessment with the directive to admit a critical mass of minority students. The admissions program could have been structured to eliminate at least some of the risk that the promise of individual evaluation was not being kept. The daily consideration of racial breakdown of admitted students is not a feature of affirmative-action programs used by other institutions of higher learning. . . .

To be constitutional, a university's compelling interest in a diverse student body must be achieved by a system where individual assessment is safeguarded through the entire process. There is no constitutional objection to the goal of considering race as one modest factor among many others to achieve diversity, but an educational institution must ensure, through sufficient procedures, that each applicant receives individual consideration and that race does not become a predominant factor in the admissions decisionmaking. . . .

. . . By deferring to the law schools' choice of minority admissions programs, the courts will lose the talents and resources of the faculties and administrators in devising new and fairer ways to ensure individual consideration. Constant and rigorous judicial review forces the law school faculties to undertake their responsibilities as state employees in this most sensitive of areas with utmost fidelity to the mandate of the Constitution. . . . Prospective students, the courts, and the public can demand that the State and its law schools prove their process is fair and constitutional in every phase of implementation.

It is difficult to assess the Court's pronouncement that race-conscious admissions programs will be unnecessary 25 years from now. If it is intended to mitigate the damage the Court does to the concept of strict scrutiny, neither petitioners nor other rejected law school applicants will find solace in knowing the basic protection put in place by Justice Powell will be suspended for a full quarter of a century. Deference is antithetical to strict scrutiny, not consistent with it.

As to the interpretation that the opinion contains its own self-destruct mechanism, the majority's abandonment of strict scrutiny undermines this objective. Were the courts to apply a searching standard to race-based admissions schemes, that would force educational institutions to seriously explore race-neutral alternatives. The Court, by contrast, is willing to be satisfied by the Law School's profession of its own good faith. . . .

If universities are given the latitude to administer programs that are tantamount to quotas, they will have few incentives to make the existing minority admissions schemes transparent and protective of individual review. The unhappy consequence will be to perpetuate the hostilities that proper consideration of race is designed to avoid. The perpetuation, of course, would be the worst of all outcomes. Other programs do exist which will be more effective in bringing about the harmony and mutual respect among all citizens that our constitutional tradition has always sought. They, and not the program under review here, should be the model, even if the Court defaults by not demanding it.

It is regrettable the Court's important holding allowing racial minorities to have their special circumstances considered in order to improve their educational opportunities is accompanied by a suspension of the strict scrutiny which was the predicate of allowing race to be considered in the first place. If the Court abdicates its constitutional duty to give strict scrutiny to the use of race in university admissions, it negates my authority to approve the use of race in pursuit of student diversity. The Constitution cannot confer the right to classify on the basis of race even in this special context absent searching judicial review. For these reasons, though I reiterate my approval of giving appropriate consideration to race in this one context, I must dissent in the present case.

JUSTICE SCALIA, with whom JUSTICE THOMAS joins, concurring in part and dissenting in part.

I join the opinion of the Chief Justice. As he demonstrates, the University of Michigan Law School's mystical "critical mass" justification for its discrimination by race challenges even the most gullible mind. The admissions statistics show it to be a sham to cover a scheme of racially proportionate admissions.

I also join Parts I through VII of Justice Thomas's opinion. I find particularly unanswerable his central point: that the allegedly "compelling state interest" at issue here is not the incremental "educational benefit" that emanates from the fabled "critical mass" of minority students, but rather Michigan's interest in maintaining a "prestige" law school whose normal admissions standards disproportionately exclude blacks and other minorities. If that is a compelling state interest, everything is.

I add the following: The "educational benefit" that the University of Michigan seeks to achieve by racial discrimination consists, according to the Court, of " 'cross-racial understanding,' " and " 'better prepar[ation of] students for an increasingly diverse workforce and society,' " all of which is necessary not only for work, but also for good "citizenship." . . . If it is appropriate for the University of Michigan Law School to use racial discrimination for the purpose of putting together a "critical mass" that will convey generic lessons in socialization and good citizenship, surely it is no less appropriate—indeed, *particularly* appropriate— for the civil service system of the State of Michigan to do so. . . . And surely private employers cannot be criticized—indeed, should be praised—if they also "teach" good citizenship to their adult employees through a patriotic, all-American system of racial discrimination in hiring. The nonminority individuals who are deprived of a legal education, a civil service job, or any job at all by reason of their skin color will surely understand.

Unlike a clear constitutional holding that racial preferences in state educational institutions are impermissible, or even a clear anticonstitutional holding that racial preferences in state educational institutions are OK, today's *Grutter–Gratz* split double header seems perversely designed to prolong the controversy and the litigation. Some future lawsuits will presumably focus on whether the discriminatory scheme in question contains enough evaluation of the applicant "as an individual" and sufficiently avoids "separate admissions tracks" to fall under *Grutter* rather than *Gratz*. Some will focus on whether a university has gone beyond the bounds of a " 'good faith effort' " and has so zealously pursued its "critical mass" as to make it an unconstitutional *de facto* quota system, rather than merely " 'a permissible goal.' " ... Other lawsuits may focus on whether, in the particular setting at issue, any educational benefits flow from racial diversity.... Still other suits may challenge the bona fides of the institution's expressed commitment to the educational benefits of diversity that immunize the discriminatory scheme in *Grutter*.... And still other suits may claim that the institution's racial preferences have gone below or above the mystical *Grutter*-approved "critical mass." Finally, litigation can be expected on behalf of minority groups intentionally short changed in the institution's composition of its generic minority "critical mass." I do not look forward to any of these cases. The Constitution proscribes government discrimination on the basis of race, and state-provided education is no exception.

JUSTICE THOMAS, with whom JUSTICE SCALIA joins as to Parts I–VII, concurring in part and dissenting in part.

... I believe blacks can achieve in every avenue of American life without the meddling of university administrators....

No one would argue that a university could set up a lower general admission standard and then impose heightened requirements only on black applicants. Similarly, a university may not maintain a high admission standard and grant exemptions to favored races. The Law School, of its own choosing, and for its own purposes, maintains an exclusionary admissions system that it knows produces racially disproportionate results. Racial discrimination is not a permissible solution to the self-inflicted wounds of this elitist admissions policy.

. . .

I

The majority agrees that the Law School's racial discrimination should be subjected to strict scrutiny....

... A majority of the Court has validated only two circumstances where "pressing public necessity" or a "compelling state interest" can possibly justify racial discrimination by state actors. First, the lesson of *Korematsu* is that national security constitutes a "pressing public necessity," though the government's use of race to advance that objective must be narrowly tailored. Second, the Court has recognized as a compelling state interest a government's effort to remedy past discrimination for which it is responsible. *Richmond v. J. A. Croson Co.,* 488 U.S. 469, 504 (1989).

. . .

... In *Palmore v. Sidoti,* 466 U.S. 429 (1984), the Court held that even the best interests of a child did not constitute a compelling state interest that would allow a state court to award custody to the father because the mother was in a mixed-race marriage....

. . .

Where the Court has accepted only national security, and rejected even the best interests of a child, as a justification for racial discrimination, I conclude that only those measures the State must take to provide a bulwark against anarchy, or to prevent violence, will constitute a "pressing public necessity." ...

. . .

II

Unlike the majority, I seek to define with precision the interest being asserted by the Law School before determining whether that interest is so compelling as to justify racial discrimination....

... Attaining "diversity," whatever it means, is the mechanism by which the Law School obtains educational benefits, not an end of itself. ...

... It is the *educational benefits* that are the end, or allegedly compelling state interest, not "diversity."

One must also consider the Law School's refusal to entertain changes to its current admissions system that might produce the same educational benefits. The Law School adamantly disclaims any race-neutral alternative that would reduce "academic selectivity," which would in turn "require the Law School to become a very different institution, and to sacrifice a core part of its educational mission." ... In other words, the Law School seeks to improve marginally the education it offers without sacrificing too much of its exclusivity and elite status.[22]

The proffered interest that the majority vindicates today, then, is not simply "diversity." Instead the Court upholds the use of racial discrimination as a tool to advance the Law School's interest in offering a marginally superior education while maintaining an elite institution. Unless each constituent part of this state interest is of pressing public necessity, the Law School's use of race is unconstitutional. I find each of them to fall far short of this standard.

---

22. The Law School believes both that the educational benefits of a racially engineered student body are large and that adjusting its overall admissions standards to achieve the same racial mix would require it to sacrifice its elite status. If the Law School is correct that the educational benefits of "diversity" are so great, then achieving them by altering admissions standards should not compromise its elite status. The Law School's reluctance to do this suggests that the educational benefits it alleges are not significant or do not exist at all.

III

A

A close reading of the Court's opinion reveals that all of its legal work is done through one conclusory statement: The Law School has a "compelling interest in securing the educational benefits of a diverse student body." . . .

Justice Powell's opinion in *Bakke* and the Court's decision today rest on the fundamentally flawed proposition that racial discrimination can be contextualized so that a goal, such as classroom aesthetics, can be compelling in one context but not in another. This "we know it when we see it" approach to evaluating state interests is not capable of judicial application. Today, the Court insists on radically expanding the range of permissible uses of race to something as trivial (by comparison) as the assembling of a law school class. I can only presume that the majority's failure to justify its decision by reference to any principle arises from the absence of any such principle. See Part VI, *infra*.

B

Under the proper standard, there is no pressing public necessity in maintaining a public law school at all and, it follows, certainly not an elite law school. Likewise, marginal improvements in legal education do not qualify as a compelling state interest.

1

While legal education at a public university may be good policy or otherwise laudable, it is obviously not a pressing public necessity. . . .

2

. . . Michigan has no compelling interest in having a law school at all, much less an *elite* one. Still, even assuming that a State may, under appropriate circumstances, demonstrate a cognizable interest in having an elite law school, Michigan has failed to do so here.

. . .

. . . The only interests that can satisfy the Equal Protection Clause's demands are those found within a State's jurisdiction.

The only cognizable state interests vindicated by operating a public law school are, therefore, the education of that State's citizens and the training of that State's lawyers. . . .

The Law School today, however, does precious little training of those attorneys who will serve the citizens of Michigan. In 2002, graduates of the University of Michigan Law School made up less than 6% of applicants to the Michigan bar. . . .

In sum, the Law School trains few Michigan residents and overwhelmingly serves students, who, as lawyers, leave the State of Michigan. By contrast, Michigan's other public law school, Wayne State University Law School, sends 88% of its graduates on to serve the people of Michigan. . . . It does not take a social scientist to conclude that it is precisely the Law School's status as an elite institution that causes it to be a way-station for the rest of the country's lawyers, rather than a training ground for those who will remain in Michigan. The Law School's decision to be an elite institution does little to advance the welfare of the people of Michigan or any cognizable interest of the State of Michigan.

[Also,] that few States choose to maintain elite law schools raises a strong inference that there is nothing compelling about elite status....

3

Finally, even if the Law School's racial tinkering produces tangible educational benefits, a marginal improvement in legal education cannot justify racial discrimination where the Law School has no compelling interest in either its existence or in its current educational and admissions policies.

IV

The interest in remaining elite and exclusive that the majority thinks so obviously critical requires the use of admissions "standards" that, in turn, create the Law School's "need" to discriminate on the basis of race. The Court validates these admissions standards by concluding that alternatives that would require "a dramatic sacrifice of ... the academic quality of all admitted students" need not be considered before racial discrimination can be employed....

With the adoption of different admissions methods, such as accepting all students who meet minimum qualifications, see Brief for United States as *Amicus Curiae* 13–14, the Law School could achieve its vision of the racially aesthetic student body without the use of racial discrimination.... [E]ven if its "academic selectivity" must be maintained at all costs along with racial discrimination, the Court ignores the fact that other top law schools have succeeded in meeting their aesthetic demands without racial discrimination.

·   ·   ·

The Court's deference to the Law School's conclusion that its racial experimentation leads to educational benefits will, if adhered to, have serious collateral consequences. The Court relies heavily on social science evidence to justify its deference.... The Court never acknowledges, however, the growing evidence that racial (and other sorts) of heterogeneity actually impairs learning among black students. See, *e.g.*, Flowers & Pascarella, Cognitive Effects of College Racial Composition on African American Students After 3 Years of College, 40 J. of College Student Development 669, 674 (1999) (concluding that black students experience superior cognitive development at Historically Black Colleges (HBCs) and that, even among blacks, "a substantial diversity moderates the cognitive effects of attending an HBC"); Allen, The Color of Success: African–American College Student Outcomes at Predominantly White and Historically Black Public Colleges and Universities, 62 Harv. Educ. Rev. 26, 35 (1992) (finding that black students attending HBCs report higher academic achievement than those attending predominantly white colleges).

. . .

The majority grants deference to the Law School's "assessment that diversity will, in fact, yield educational benefits." It follows, therefore, that an HBC's assessment that racial homogeneity will yield educational benefits would similarly be given deference. An HBC's rejection of white applicants in order to maintain racial homogeneity seems permissible, therefore, under the majority's view of the Equal Protection Clause. . . .

Moreover one would think, in light of the Court's decision in *United States v. Virginia,* 518 U.S. 515 (1996), that before being given license to use racial discrimination, the Law School would be required to radically reshape its admissions process, even to the point of sacrificing some elements of its character. In *Virginia,* a majority of the Court, without a word about academic freedom, accepted the all-male Virginia Military Institute's (VMI) representation that some changes in its "adversative" method of education would be required with the admission of women, . . . but did not defer to VMI's judgment that these changes would be too great. Instead, the Court concluded that they were "manageable." . . . That case involved sex discrimination, which is subjected to intermediate, not strict, scrutiny. . . . So in *Virginia,* where the standard of review dictated that greater flexibility be granted to VMI's educational policies than the Law School deserves here, this Court gave no deference. Apparently where the status quo being defended is that of the elite establishment—here the Law School—rather than a less fashionable Southern military institution, the Court will defer without serious inquiry and without regard to the applicable legal standard.

. . .

Virginia is also notable for the fact that the Court relied on the "experience" of formerly single-sex institutions, such as the service academies, to conclude that admission of women to VMI would be "manageable." . . . Today, however, the majority ignores the "experience" of those institutions that have been forced to abandon explicit racial discrimination in admissions.

The sky has not fallen at Boalt Hall at the University of California, Berkeley, for example. Prior to Proposition 209's adoption of Cal. Const., Art. 1, § 31(a), which bars the State from "grant[ing] preferential treatment . . . on the basis of race . . . in the operation of . . . public education," Boalt Hall enrolled 20 blacks and 28 Hispanics in its first-year class for 1996. In 2002, without deploying express racial discrimination in admissions, Boalt's entering class enrolled 14 blacks and 36 Hispanics. . . . Total underrepresented minority student enrollment at Boalt Hall now exceeds 1996 levels. Apparently [Michigan] Law School cannot be counted on to be as resourceful. The Court is willfully blind to the very real experience in California and elsewhere, which raises the inference that institutions with "reputation[s] for excellence" rivaling the Law School's have satisfied their sense of mission without resorting to prohibited racial discrimination.

V

. . .

[T]here is nothing ancient, honorable, or constitutionally protected about "selective" admissions....

... Since its inception, selective admissions has been the vehicle for racial, ethnic, and religious tinkering and experimentation by university administrators. The initial driving force for the relocation of the selective function from the high school to the universities was the same desire to select racial winners and losers that the Law School exhibits today. Columbia, Harvard, and others infamously determined that they had "too many" Jews, just as today the Law School argues it would have "too many" whites if it could not discriminate in its admissions process....

Columbia employed intelligence tests precisely because Jewish applicants, who were predominantly immigrants, scored worse on such tests.... In other words, the tests were adopted with full knowledge of their disparate impact. Cf. *DeFunis v. Odegaard,* 416 U.S. 312, 335 (1974) *(per curiam)* (Douglas, J., dissenting).

Similarly no modern law school can claim ignorance of the poor performance of blacks, relatively speaking, on the Law School Admissions Test (LSAT). Nevertheless, law schools continue to use the test and then attempt to "correct" for black underperformance by using racial discrimination in admissions so as to obtain their aesthetic student body. The Law School's continued adherence to measures it knows produce racially skewed results is not entitled to deference by this Court....

Having decided to use the LSAT, the Law School must accept the constitutional burdens that come with this decision. The Law School may freely continue to employ the LSAT and other allegedly merit-based standards in whatever fashion it likes. What the Equal Protection Clause forbids, but the Court today allows, is the use of these standards hand-in-hand with racial discrimination....

The Court will not even deign to make the Law School try other methods, however, preferring instead to grant a 25–year license to violate the Constitution....

VI

... I believe what lies beneath the Court's decision today are the benighted notions that one can tell when racial discrimination benefits (rather than hurts) minority groups, ... and that racial discrimination is necessary to remedy general societal ills. This Court's precedents supposedly settled both issues, but clearly the majority still cannot commit to the principle that racial classifications are *per se* harmful and that almost no amount of benefit in the eye of the beholder can justify such classifications.

Putting aside what I take to be the Court's implicit rejection of *Adarand*'s holding that beneficial and burdensome racial classifications are equally invalid, I must contest the notion that the Law School's discrimination benefits those admitted as a result of it.... [N]owhere in any of the filings in this Court is any evidence that the purported "beneficiaries" of this racial discrimination prove themselves by performing at (or even near) the same level as those students who receive no preferences. Cf. Thernstrom & Thernstrom, Reflections on the Shape of the River, 46 UCLA L. Rev. 1583, 1605–1608 (1999) (discussing the failure of defenders of racial discrimination in admissions to consider the fact that its "beneficiaries" are underperforming in the classroom).

The silence in this case is deafening to those of us who view higher education's purpose as imparting knowledge and skills to students, rather than a communal, rubber-stamp, credentialing process. The Law School is not looking for those students who, despite a lower LSAT score or undergraduate grade point average, will succeed in the study of law. The Law School seeks only a facade—it is sufficient that the class looks right, even if it does not perform right.

. . .

Beyond the harm the Law School's racial discrimination visits upon its test subjects, no social science has disproved the notion that this discrimination "engender[s] attitudes of superiority or, alternatively, provoke[s] resentment among those who believe that they have been wronged by the government's use of race." *Adarand*, . . . (Thomas, J., concurring in part and concurring in judgment). "These programs stamp minorities with a badge of inferiority and may cause them to develop dependencies or to adopt an attitude that they are 'entitled' to preferences." . . .

. . . The majority of blacks are admitted to the Law School because of discrimination, and because of this policy all are tarred as undeserving. This problem of stigma does not depend on determinacy as to whether those stigmatized are actually the "beneficiaries" of racial discrimination. When blacks take positions in the highest places of government, industry, or academia, it is an open question today whether their skin color played a part in their advancement. The question itself is the stigma—because either racial discrimination did play a role, in which case the person may be deemed "otherwise unqualified," or it did not, in which case asking the question itself unfairly marks those blacks who would succeed without discrimination. Is this what the Court means by "visibly open"?

Finally, the Court's disturbing reference to the importance of the country's law schools as training grounds meant to cultivate "a set of leaders with legitimacy in the eyes of the citizenry" through the use of racial discrimination deserves discussion. [T]he Court has soundly rejected the remedying of societal discrimination as a justification for governmental use of race. *Wygant*, 476 U.S., at 276 (plurality opinion); *Croson*, 488 U.S., at 497 (plurality opinion); *id.*, at 520–521 (Scalia, J., concurring in judgment). For those who believe that every racial disproportionality in our society is caused by some kind of racial discrimination, there can be no distinction between remedying societal discrimination and erasing racial disproportionalities in the country's leadership caste. And if the lack of proportional racial representation among our leaders is not caused by societal discrimination, then "fixing" it is even less of a pressing public necessity.

. . .

VII

As the foregoing makes clear, I believe the Court's opinion to be, in most respects, erroneous. I do, however, find two points on which I agree.

A

First, I note that the issue of unconstitutional racial discrimination among the groups the Law School prefers is not presented in this case, because petitioner has never argued that the Law School engages in such a practice, and the Law School maintains that it does not. . . . I join the Court's opinion insofar as it confirms that this type of racial discrimination remains unlawful. . . . [T]he Law School may not discriminate in admissions between similarly situated blacks and Hispanics, or between whites and Asians. This is so because preferring black to Hispanic applicants, for instance, does nothing to further the interest recognized by the majority today.[23] Indeed, the majority describes such racial balancing as "patently unconstitutional." Like the Court, I express no opinion as to whether the Law School's current admissions program runs afoul of this prohibition.

B

The Court also holds that racial discrimination in admissions should be given another 25 years before it is deemed no longer narrowly tailored to the Law School's fabricated compelling state interest. While I agree that in 25 years the practices of the Law School will be illegal, they are, for the reasons I have given, illegal now. . . . No one can seriously contend, and the Court does not, that the racial gap in academic credentials will disappear in 25 years. Nor is the Court's holding that racial discrimination will be unconstitutional in 25 years made contingent on the gap closing in that time.

. . .

I . . . understand the imposition of a 25–year time limit only as a holding that the deference the Court pays to the Law School's educational judgments and refusal to change its admissions policies will itself expire. . . . The Court defines this time limit in terms of narrow tailoring, but I believe this arises from its refusal to define rigorously the

---

23. That interest depends on enrolling a "critical mass" of underrepresented minority students, as the majority repeatedly states. . . . As it relates to the Law School's racial discrimination, the Court clearly approves of only one use of race—the distinction between underrepresented minority applicants and those of all other races. A relative preference awarded to a black applicant over, for example, a similarly situated Native American applicant, does not lead to the enrollment of even one more underrepresented minority student, but only balances the races within the "critical mass."

broad state interest vindicated today. ... With these observations, I join the last sentence of Part III of the opinion of the Court.

* * *

For the immediate future, ... the majority has placed its *imprimatur* on a practice that can only weaken the principle of equality embodied in the Declaration of Independence and the Equal Protection Clause. "Our Constitution is color-blind, and neither knows nor tolerated classes among citizens." *Plessy v. Ferguson*, 163 U.S. 556, 559 (1896) (Harlan J., dissenting). It has been nearly 140 years since Frederick Douglass asked the intellectual ancestors of the Law School to "[d]o nothing with us!" and the nation adopted the Fourteenth Amendment. Now we must wait another 25 years to see this principle of equality vindicated. I therefore respectfully dissent from the remainder of the Court's opinion and the judgment.

NOTE

The same day the Supreme Court decided *Grutter* it also decided *Gratz v. Bollinger*, 539 U.S. 244 (2003) by a 6–to–3 vote, with Justices Stevens, Souter, and Ginsburg dissenting. In an opinion by Chief Justice Rehnquist, the Court held that the University of Michigan's undergraduate affirmative-action policy violated the Equal Protection Clause of the Fourteenth Amendment because it was not narrowly tailored to achieve the University's asserted compelling interest in diversity. The policy took race into account by awarding 20 points of the 100 needed for admission to all minority candidates—African Americans, Hispanics, and Native Americans. As a result, virtually all qualified candidates from those groups were admitted. In a concurring opinion, Justice O'Connor explained that Michigan's undergraduate affirmative-action policy was unconstitutional because its automatic assignment of a 20–point bonus on the basis of race denied applicants meaningful individualized review. By contrast, she wrote, the law school admission policy in *Grutter* "required consideration of each applicant's individual qualifications, including the contribution each individual's race or ethnic identity would make to the diversity of the student body, taking into account diversity within and among all racial and ethnic groups."

AFFIRMATIVE ACTION IN EMPLOYMENT

In recent years, the question of affirmative action in hiring, promotion, and layoffs has been central in several Supreme Court decisions.

Employment-related affirmative action plans can raise constitutional questions in two contexts. First, a government agency or a court can order an employer to adopt an affirmative action plan, raising the question whether the government or court order meets constitutional standards. Second, a government employer can voluntarily adopt an affirmative action plan, raising the question whether the government, as an employer, has violated the constitution. An affirmative action plan voluntarily adopted by a private employer does not technically raise any question of constitutional law, since the constitution limits only the authority of government. An affirmative action program of a private employer can raise similar legal questions, however, under federal and state laws that prohibit discrimination on the basis of race and gender. The federal fair employment practice law, prohibiting both racial and gender discrimination, is contained in Title VII of the Civil Rights Act of 1964. That statute was originally limited to private sector employment, but was extended to cover government employers by a 1972 amendment.

In 1986 and 1987, the Supreme Court decided three cases dealing with constitutional questions concerning affirmative action in employment. (As in other cases involving these constitutional questions, no position was accepted by a majority of the Court.) In Local 28 of Sheet Metal Workers' v. Equal Employment Opportunity Commission, 478 U.S. 421 (1986), the Court upheld an order of the Commission requiring a union, found to have discriminated in the past against African Americans and Hispanics, to achieve a goal of 29.23% nonwhite members. A majority of the justices rejected an argument by the Solicitor General of the United States that it violated the Constitution to require the union to prefer a nonwhite who had not personally been a victim of discrimination by the union over a white who had not participated in that discrimination. In United States v. Paradise, 480 U.S. 149 (1987), the Court affirmed the temporary order of lower federal courts requiring that 50 percent of the promotions in the Alabama highway patrol go to African Americans. The Alabama Department's employment practices had been constantly in litigation since a decision by a federal court in 1972 that it had systematically refused to hire blacks as state troopers.

Sheet Metal Workers' and Paradise thus affirmed the power of government agencies and courts to order employers and unions clearly guilty of employment discrimination to adopt affirmative action programs. In Wygant v. Jackson Board of Education, 476 U.S. 267 (1986), however, the Court held that a public school board violated the Constitution when it voluntarily adopted a policy to protect junior African American teachers from layoffs. The school board policy was that, when teachers were laid off, it would not release "a greater percentage of minority personnel ... than the current percentage of minority personnel employed."

One of the issues central in the Wygant case was the question whether a government employer not guilty of past discrimination could justify a program of affirmative action. Some of the justices in the majority emphasized that the school board had not engaged in racial discrimination, and concluded that racial discrimination in society generally could not justify affirmative action. Other justices emphasized the distinction between affirmative action in firing people, and affirmative action in hiring decisions.

One of the constitutional questions that remained after the Wygant decision was whether all voluntary programs for affirmative action by government employers had to be based on past employment discrimination by that employer. (For example, did it make a difference whether the program dealt with hiring or promotions, rather than layoffs as in Wygant? Did it make a difference whether the program used softer numerical standards than the invalid policy in Wygant?) In Johnson v.

Transportation Agency, Santa Clara County, 480 U.S. 616 (1987), the Court sustained a voluntary affirmative action program by a government employer as it applied to the promotion of women. In doing so, however, the Court did not decide whether the program met *constitutional* standards. The complaining party had litigated only the question whether the failure to promote him had violated the federal fair employment practice act, Title VII, and had not raised the question whether his government employer had violated the Constitution. Relying on an earlier decision (United Steelworkers v. Weber, 443 U.S. 193 (1979)), the Court stated that Title VII did not subject voluntary affirmative programs to all of the same restraints imposed by constitutional decisions. (As noted, until 1972 Title VII did not even apply to government employers. Even after the 1972 amendment, its restraints applied to private employers, who are not subject to constitutional limits, as well as government employers, who are.) The Court decided that, *under Title VII,* a voluntary program of affirmative action can be justified by "conspicuous imbalance in traditionally segregated job categories," even if the employer did not concede that it had engaged in past discrimination.

As noted, the question remains open whether the voluntary affirmative action program in *Johnson* would have been approved if it had been attacked on constitutional grounds. Another potential constitutional question in cases like *Johnson* is whether the constitutional standards for affirmative action programs advantaging women are the same as for affirmative action programs advantaging racial minorities. That issue is discussed in the next chapter.

NOTES

1. In his plurality opinion in the *Wygant* case, Justice Powell rejected the argument that the layoff plan was designed to remedy prior discrimination against minorities in hiring of teachers on the ground that the lower courts had not found that such discrimination had ever happened. Indeed, in prior litigation, the board had contended, and the trial judge found, that the low number of minority teachers was the result of "general societal discrimination" and not employment discrimination by the school board. Contrast the handling of this issue in the *Johnson* case. Justice Brennan's opinion for the Court started with the proposition that Title VII had the purpose of eliminating the effects of employment discrimination, and thus provided employers some flexibility to adopt affirmative action plans to remedy past discrimination. He stated that requiring an employer to admit past discrimination to justify an affirmative action plan would be a major disincentive to adoption of those plans because the admission might subject it to potential liability. (To underscore the possibility that there may be differences between the requirements of Title VII and the Constitution, it should be noted that Justice Powell joined Justice Brennan's opinion in *Johnson.*)

2. Justice Powell's plurality opinion in *Wygant* rejected the argument that racial preference in layoffs could be justified because minority students needed more minority teachers as "role models." Carried to its logical extreme, the idea that African–American students are better off

with African–American teachers could lead to employing all African–American faculties in schools with predominantly African–American students. Justice Stevens, in his dissent, argued at length that there were other concerns beyond the question whether an employer had discriminated in the past. He argued that the school board could have decided that an integrated faculty is important for students' education, even if its all-white faculty had not been produced by discrimination. Other examples he gave of cases where race might be relevant were a decision to use an African–American undercover police officer to investigate crime in an African–American neighborhood, and a decision by a superintendent of police in a racially troubled city that an integrated police force would do a more effective job of maintaining order.

3. Another factor discussed in the employment affirmative action cases is the burden on "innocent employees." Justice Powell's plurality opinion in *Wygant* emphasized the distinction between layoff policies and hiring policies. "In cases involving valid *hiring* goals, the burden to be borne by an innocent individual is diffused to a considerable extent among society generally. Though hiring goals may burden some innocent individuals, they simply do not impose the same kind of injury that layoffs impose. Denial of a future employment opportunity is not as intrusive as loss of an existing job." Justice White's concurrence was even more pointed. He said he could not "believe that in order to integrate a work force, it would be permissible to discharge whites and hire African Americans until the latter comprised a suitable percentage of the work force." Justice Brennan's opinion in *Johnson* contrasted the position of the male employee who had not been promoted, but "retained his employment with the Agency, at the same salary and with the same seniority, and remained eligible for other promotions."

4. Another important factor in determining the validity of affirmative action plans in employment is how flexible the program is. The program held invalid in *Wygant* used strict numerical standards to determine who would be laid off. The plan upheld in *Johnson* did not require the promotion of specific numbers of women or minorities, but set "goals" and required more generally that "consideration be given to affirmative action concerns when evaluating prospective applicants." The Court noted that a plan that failed to take into account the qualifications of persons applying for promotion, and required the promotion of specific numbers of minorities or women, would "dictate mere blind hiring by the numbers" and "its validity fairly could be called into question."

ADARAND CONSTRUCTORS, INC. v. PENA

Supreme Court of the United States, 1995.
515 U.S. 200, 115 S.Ct. 2097, 132 L.Ed.2d 158.

JUSTICE O'CONNOR announced the judgment of the Court and delivered an opinion with respect to Parts I, II, III–A, III–B, III–D, and IV, which is for the Court except insofar as it might be inconsistent with the views expressed in JUSTICE SCALIA's concurrence, and an opinion with respect to Part III–C in which JUSTICE KENNEDY joins.

Petitioner Adarand Constructors, Inc., claims that the Federal Government's practice of giving general contractors on government projects a financial incentive to hire subcontractors controlled by "socially and economically disadvantaged individuals," and in particular, the Government's use of race-based presumptions in identifying such individuals, violates the equal protection component of the Fifth Amendment's Due Process Clause. The Court of Appeals rejected Adarand's claim. We conclude, however, that courts should analyze cases of this kind under a different standard of review than the one the Court of Appeals applied. We therefore vacate the Court of Appeals' judgment and remand the case for further proceedings.

I

[In 1989, Adarand was the low bidder for a subcontract to build guardrails on a highway. The prime contractor awarded the contract to a minority-owned company, although it submitted a higher bid. The highway was financed by federal funds, and federal law requires that prime contractors be given additional compensation for hiring subcontractors controlled by "socially and economically disadvantaged individuals," who are assumed to be "Black Americans, Hispanic Americans, Native Americans, Asian Pacific Americans, and other minorities, or any other individual found to be disadvantaged by the [Small Business] Administration ..."] Adarand claims that the presumption set forth in that statute discriminates on the basis of race in violation of the Federal Government's Fifth Amendment obligation not to deny anyone equal protection of the laws.

· · ·

III

· · ·

Adarand's claim arises under the Fifth Amendment [Due Process Clause.] Although this Court has always understood that Clause to provide some measure of protection against arbitrary treatment by the Federal Government, it is not as explicit a guarantee of equal treatment as the Fourteenth Amendment [Equal Protection Clause].... Our cases have accorded varying degrees of significance to the difference in the language of those two Clauses....

A

Through the 1940s, this Court had routinely taken the view in non-race-related cases that, "[u]nlike the Fourteenth Amendment, the Fifth contains no equal protection clause and it provides no guaranty against discriminatory legislation by Congress.".... When the Court first faced a Fifth Amendment equal protection challenge to a federal racial classification, it adopted a similar approach, with most unfortunate results. In Hirabayashi v. United States, 320 U.S. 81 (1943), the Court considered a curfew applicable only to persons of Japanese ancestry. The Court observed—correctly—that "[d]istinctions between citizens solely because of their ancestry are by their very nature odious to a free people whose institutions are founded upon the doctrine of equality," and that "racial discriminations are in most circumstances irrelevant and therefore prohibited." ... But it ... upheld the curfew....

. . .

... [I]n 1975, the Court stated explicitly that "[t]his Court's approach to Fifth Amendment equal protection claims has always been precisely the same as to equal protection claims under the Fourteenth Amendment." ...

Most of the cases discussed above involved classifications burdening groups that have suffered discrimination in our society. In 1978, the Court confronted the question whether race-based governmental action designed to benefit such groups should also be subject to "the most rigid scrutiny." Regents of Univ. of California v. Bakke ... did not produce an opinion for the Court....

Two years after *Bakke*, the Court faced another challenge to remedial race-based action, this time involving action undertaken by the Federal Government. In Fullilove v. Klutznick, 448 U.S. 448 (1980), the Court upheld Congress' inclusion of a 10% set-aside for minority-owned businesses in the Public Works Employment Act of 1977. As in *Bakke*, there was no opinion for the Court. Chief Justice Burger, in an opinion joined by Justices White and Powell, observed that "[a]ny preference based on racial or ethnic criteria must necessarily receive a most searching examination to make sure that it does not conflict with constitutional guarantees." ... That opinion, however, "d[id] not adopt, either expressly or implicitly, the formulas of analysis articulated in such cases as [*Bakke*]." ... It employed instead a two-part test which asked, first, "whether the objectives of th[e] legislation are within the power of Congress," and second, "whether the limited use of racial and ethnic criteria, in the context presented, is a constitutionally permissible means for achieving the congressional objectives." ... It then upheld the program under that test, adding at the end of the opinion that the program also "would survive judicial review under either 'test' articulated in the several *Bakke* opinions." ... Justice Powell wrote separately to express his view that the plurality opinion had essentially applied "strict scrutiny" as described in his *Bakke* opinion—i.e., it had determined that the set-aside was "a necessary means of advancing a compelling governmental interest"—and had done so correctly.... Justice Stewart (joined by then-Justice Rehnquist) dissented, arguing that the Constitution required the Federal Government to meet the same strict standard as the States when enacting racial classifications, ... and that the program before the Court failed that standard. Justice Stevens also dissented, arguing that "[r]acial classifications are simply too pernicious to permit any but the most exact connection between justification and classification," ... and that the program before the Court could not be characterized "as a 'narrowly tailored' remedial measure." ... Justice Marshall (joined by Justices Brennan and Blackmun) concurred in the judgment, reiterating the view of four Justices in *Bakke* that any race-based governmental action designed to "remed[y] the present effects of past racial discrimination" should be upheld if it was "substantially related" to the achievement of an "important governmental objective"—i.e., such action should be subjected only to what we now call "intermediate scrutiny." ...

In Wygant v. Jackson Board of Ed., 476 U.S. 267 (1986), the Court considered ... whether a school board could adopt race-based preferences in determining which teachers to lay off. . . .

The Court's failure to produce a majority opinion in *Bakke*, *Fullilove*, and *Wygant* left unresolved the proper analysis for remedial race-based governmental action. . . .

The Court resolved the issue, at least in part, in 1989. Richmond v. J.A. Croson Co., 488 U.S. 469 (1989), concerned a city's determination that 30% of its contracting work should go to minority-owned businesses. A majority of the Court in *Croson* held that "the standard of review under the Equal Protection Clause is not dependent on the race of those burdened or benefited by a particular classification," and that the single standard of review for racial classifications should be "strict scrutiny." . . .

With *Croson*, the Court finally agreed that the Fourteenth Amendment requires strict scrutiny of all race-based action by state and local governments. But *Croson* of course had no occasion to declare what standard of review the Fifth Amendment requires for such action taken by the Federal Government. *Croson* observed simply that the Court's "treatment of an exercise of congressional power in *Fullilove* cannot be dispositive here," because *Croson*'s facts did not implicate Congress' broad power under § 5 of the Fourteenth Amendment. . . .

Despite lingering uncertainty in the details, however, the Court's cases through *Croson* had established three general propositions with respect to governmental racial classifications. First, skepticism: " '[a]ny preference based on racial or ethnic criteria must necessarily receive a most searching examination,' " ... Second, consistency: "the standard of review under the Equal Protection Clause is not dependent on the race of those burdened or benefited by a particular classification," *Croson* ..., i.e., all racial classifications reviewable under the Equal Protection Clause must be strictly scrutinized. And third, congruence: "[e]qual protection analysis in the Fifth Amendment area is the same as that under the Fourteenth Amendment,". . . . Taken together, these three propositions lead to the conclusion that any person, of whatever race, has the right to demand that any governmental actor subject to the Constitution justify any racial classification subjecting that person to unequal treatment under the strictest judicial scrutiny. . . .

A year later, however, the Court took a surprising turn. Metro Broadcasting, Inc. v. FCC, 497 U.S. 547 (1990), involved a Fifth Amendment challenge to two race-based policies of the Federal Communications Commission. In *Metro Broadcasting*, the Court ... [held] that "benign" federal racial classifications need only satisfy intermediate scrutiny, even though *Croson* had recently concluded that such classifications enacted by a State must satisfy strict scrutiny. "[B]enign" federal racial classifications, the Court said, "... are constitutionally permissible to the extent that they serve important governmental objectives within the

power of Congress and are substantially related to achievement of those objectives." ... The Court did not explain how to tell whether a racial classification should be deemed "benign," other than to express "confiden[ce] that an 'examination of the legislative scheme and its history' will separate benign measures from other types of racial classifications."
...

Applying this test, the Court first noted that the FCC policies at issue did not serve as a remedy for past discrimination.... Proceeding on the assumption that the policies were nonetheless "benign," it concluded that they served the "important governmental objective" of "enhancing broadcast diversity," ... and that they were "substantially related" to that objective.... It therefore upheld the policies.

By adopting intermediate scrutiny as the standard of review for congressionally mandated "benign" racial classifications, *Metro Broadcasting* departed from prior cases in two significant respects. First, it turned its back on *Croson*'s explanation of why strict scrutiny of all governmental racial classifications is essential:

> "Absent searching judicial inquiry into the justification for such race-based measures, there is simply no way of determining what classifications are 'benign' or 'remedial' and what classifications are in fact motivated by illegitimate notions of racial inferiority or simple racial politics. Indeed, the purpose of strict scrutiny is to 'smoke out' illegitimate uses of race by assuring that the legislative body is pursuing a goal important enough to warrant use of a highly suspect tool. The test also ensures that the means chosen 'fit' this compelling goal so closely that there is little or no possibility that the motive for the classification was illegitimate racial prejudice or stereotype." ...

We adhere to that view today, despite the surface appeal of holding "benign" racial classifications to a lower standard, because "it may not always be clear that a so-called preference is in fact benign,"....

Second, *Metro Broadcasting* squarely rejected one of the three propositions established by the Court's earlier equal protection cases, namely, congruence between the standards applicable to federal and state racial classifications, and in so doing also undermined the other two—skepticism of all racial classifications, and consistency of treatment irrespective of the race of the burdened or benefited group.... Under *Metro Broadcasting*, certain racial classifications ("benign" ones enacted by the Federal Government) should be treated less skeptically than others; and the race of the benefited group is critical to the determination of which standard of review to apply. *Metro Broadcasting* was thus a significant departure from much of what had come before it.

The three propositions undermined by *Metro Broadcasting* all derive from the basic principle that the Fifth and Fourteenth Amendments to the Constitution protect persons, not groups. It follows from that principle that all governmental action based on race ... should be subjected to detailed judicial inquiry to ensure that the personal right to equal protection of the laws has not been infringed. These ideas have long been central to this Court's understanding of equal protection, and holding "benign" state and federal racial classifications to different standards does not square with them. . . . Accordingly, we hold today that all racial classifications, imposed by whatever federal, state, or local governmental actor, must be analyzed by a reviewing court under strict scrutiny. In other words, such classifications are constitutional only if they are narrowly tailored measures that further compelling governmental interests. To the extent that *Metro Broadcasting* is inconsistent with that holding, it is overruled.

In dissent, Justice Stevens['s] . . . criticisms reflect a serious misunderstanding of our opinion.

. . . What he fails to recognize is that strict scrutiny does take "relevant differences" into account—indeed, that is its fundamental purpose. The point of carefully examining the interest asserted by the government in support of a racial classification, and the evidence offered to show that the classification is needed, is precisely to distinguish legitimate from illegitimate uses of race in governmental decisionmaking. . . . Strict scrutiny does not "trea[t] dissimilar race-based decisions as though they were equally objectionable"; to the contrary, it evaluates carefully all governmental race-based decisions in order to decide which are constitutionally objectionable and which are not. By requiring strict scrutiny of racial classifications, we require courts to make sure that a governmental classification based on race . . . is legitimate, before permitting unequal treatment based on race to proceed.

Justice Stevens chides us for our "supposed inability to differentiate between 'invidious' and 'benign' discrimination," because it is in his view sufficient that "people understand the difference between good intentions and bad." But . . . the point of strict scrutiny is to "differentiate between" permissible and impermissible governmental use of race. . . .

Perhaps it is not the standard of strict scrutiny itself, but our use of the concepts of "consistency" and "congruence" in conjunction with it, that leads Justice Stevens to dissent. . . . The principle of consistency simply means that whenever the government treats any person unequally because of his or her race, that person has suffered an injury that falls squarely within the language and spirit of the Constitution's guarantee of equal protection. It says nothing about the ultimate validity of any particular law; that determination is the job of the court applying strict scrutiny. The principle of consistency explains the circumstances in which the injury requiring strict scrutiny occurs. The application of strict scrutiny, in turn, determines whether a compelling governmental interest justifies the infliction of that injury.

Consistency does recognize that any individual suffers an injury when he or she is disadvantaged by the government because of his or her race, whatever that race may be. . . .

. . .

C

. . .

... *Metro Broadcasting* undermined important principles of this Court's equal protection jurisprudence....

. . .

... *Metro Broadcasting*'s untenable distinction between state and federal racial classifications lacks support in our precedent, and undermines the fundamental principle of equal protection as a personal right. In this case, as between that principle and "its later misapplications," the principle must prevail.

D

Our action today makes explicit what Justice Powell thought implicit in the *Fullilove* lead opinion: federal racial classifications, like those of a State, must serve a compelling governmental interest, and must be narrowly tailored to further that interest.... [I]t follows that to the extent (if any) that *Fullilove* held federal racial classifications to be subject to a less rigorous standard, it is no longer controlling. But we need not decide today whether the program upheld in *Fullilove* would survive strict scrutiny as our more recent cases have defined it.

Some have questioned the importance of debating the proper standard of review of race-based legislation.... But we agree with Justice Stevens that, "[b]ecause racial characteristics so seldom provide a relevant basis for disparate treatment, and because classifications based on race are potentially so harmful to the entire body politic, it is especially important that the reasons for any such classification be clearly identified and unquestionably legitimate," and that "[r]acial classifications are simply too pernicious to permit any but the most exact connection between justification and classification." *Fullilove* ... (dissenting opinion).... We think that requiring strict scrutiny is the best way to ensure that courts will consistently give racial classifications that kind of detailed examination, both as to ends and as to means. *Korematsu* demonstrates vividly that even "the most rigid scrutiny" can sometimes fail to detect an illegitimate racial classification.... Any retreat from the most searching judicial inquiry can only increase the risk of another such error occurring in the future.

Finally, we wish to dispel the notion that strict scrutiny is "strict in theory, but fatal in fact." ... The unhappy persistence of both the practice and the lingering effects of racial discrimination against minority groups in this country is an unfortunate reality, and government is not disqualified from acting in response to it. As recently as 1987, for example, every Justice of this Court agreed that the Alabama Department of Public Safety's "pervasive, systematic, and obstinate discriminatory conduct" justified a narrowly tailored race-based remedy. See United States v. Paradise, 480 U.S., at 167 (plurality opinion of Brennan, J.); id., at 190 (Stevens, J., concurring in judgment); id., at 196 (O'Connor, J., dissenting). When race-based action is necessary to further a compelling interest, such action is within constitutional constraints if it satisfies the "narrow tailoring" test this Court has set out in previous cases.

IV

Because our decision today alters the playing field in some important respects, we think it best to remand ... for further consideration in light of the principles we have announced. The Court of Appeals, following *Metro Broadcasting* and *Fullilove*, analyzed the case in terms of intermediate scrutiny. It ... did not decide ... whether the interests served by the use of subcontractor compensation clauses are properly described as "compelling." It also did not address the question of narrow tailoring in terms of our strict scrutiny cases, by asking, for example, whether there was "any consideration of the use of race-neutral means to increase minority business participation" in government contracting, *Croson* ..., or whether the program was appropriately limited such that it "will not last longer than the discriminatory effects it is designed to eliminate," *Fullilove* ... (Powell, J., concurring).

Moreover, unresolved questions remain concerning the details of the complex regulatory regimes implicated by the use of subcontractor compensation clauses.... The question whether any of the ways in which the Government uses subcontractor compensation clauses can survive strict scrutiny, and any relevance distinctions such as these may have to that question, should be addressed in the first instance by the lower courts.

· · ·

JUSTICE SCALIA, concurring in part and concurring in the judgment.

I join the opinion of the Court, except Part III–C, and except insofar as it may be inconsistent with the following: In my view, government can never have a "compelling interest" in discriminating on the basis of race in order to "make up" for past racial discrimination in the opposite direction.... Individuals who have been wronged by unlawful racial discrimination should be made whole; but under our Constitution there can be no such thing as either a creditor or a debtor race. That concept is alien to the Constitution's focus upon the individual ... and its rejection of dispositions based on race, see Amdt. 15, § 1 (prohibiting abridgment of the right to vote "on account of race") or based on blood, see Art. III, § 3 ("[N]o Attainder of Treason shall work Corruption of Blood"); Art. I, § 9 ("No Title of Nobility shall be granted by the United States"). To pursue the concept of racial entitlement—even for the most admirable and benign of purposes—is to reinforce and preserve for future mischief the way of thinking that produced race slavery, race privilege and race hatred. In the eyes of government, we are just one race here. It is American.

It is unlikely, if not impossible, that the challenged program would survive under this understanding of strict scrutiny, but I am content to leave that to be decided on remand.

JUSTICE THOMAS, concurring in part and concurring in the judgment.

I agree with the majority's conclusion that strict scrutiny applies to all government classifications based on race. I write separately, however, to express my disagreement with the premise underlying Justice Stevens' and Justice Ginsburg's dissents: that there is a racial paternalism exception to the principle of equal protection. I believe that there is a "moral [and] constitutional equivalence" (Stevens, J., dissenting) between laws designed to subjugate a race and those that distribute benefits on the basis of race in order to foster some current notion of equality. Government cannot make us equal; it can only recognize, respect, and protect us as equal before the law.

That these programs may have been motivated, in part, by good intentions cannot provide refuge from the principle that under our Constitution, the government may not make distinctions on the basis of race. As far as the Constitution is concerned, it is irrelevant whether a government's racial classifications are drawn by those who wish to oppress a race or by those who have a sincere desire to help those thought to be disadvantaged. There can be no doubt that the paternalism that appears to lie at the heart of this program is at war with the principle of inherent equality that underlies and infuses our Constitution. . . .

These programs . . . also undermine the moral basis of the equal protection principle. Purchased at the price of immeasurable human suffering, the equal protection principle reflects our Nation's understanding that such classifications ultimately have a destructive impact on the individual and our society. . . . [T]here can be no doubt that racial paternalism and its unintended consequences can be as poisonous and pernicious as any other form of discrimination. So-called "benign" discrimination teaches many that because of chronic and apparently immutable handicaps, minorities cannot compete with them without their patronizing indulgence. Inevitably, such programs engender attitudes of superiority or, alternatively, provoke resentment among those who believe that they have been wronged by the government's use of race. These programs stamp minorities with a badge of inferiority and may cause them to develop dependencies or to adopt an attitude that they are "entitled" to preferences. . . .

In my mind, government-sponsored racial discrimination based on benign prejudice is just as noxious as discrimination inspired by malicious prejudice. In each instance, it is racial discrimination, plain and simple.

JUSTICE STEVENS, with whom JUSTICE GINSBURG joins, dissenting.

Instead of deciding this case in accordance with controlling precedent, the Court today delivers a disconcerting lecture about the evils of governmental racial classifications. . . . I believe this Court has a duty to affirm. . . .

I

The Court's concept of skepticism is, at least in principle, a good statement of law and of common sense. Undoubtedly, a court should be wary of a governmental decision that relies upon a racial classification. . . . [B]ecause uniform standards are often anything but uniform, we should evaluate the Court's comments on "consistency," "congruence," and stare decisis with the same type of skepticism that the Court advocates for the underlying issue.

II

The Court's concept of "consistency" assumes that there is no significant difference between a decision by the majority to impose a special burden on the members of a minority race and a decision by the majority to provide a benefit to certain members of that minority notwithstanding its incidental burden on some members of the majority. [T]hat assumption is untenable. There is no moral or constitutional equivalence between a policy that is designed to perpetuate a caste system and one that seeks to eradicate racial subordination. Invidious discrimination is an engine of oppression, subjugating a disfavored group to enhance or maintain the power of the majority. Remedial race-based preferences reflect the opposite impulse: a desire to foster equality in society. No sensible conception of the Government's constitutional obligation to "govern impartially" . . . should ignore this distinction.

. . .

The consistency that the Court espouses would disregard the difference between a "No Trespassing" sign and a welcome mat. It would treat a Dixiecrat Senator's decision to vote against Thurgood Marshall's confirmation in order to keep African Americans off the Supreme Court as on a par with President Johnson's evaluation of his nominee's race as a positive factor. It would equate a law that made black citizens ineligible for military service with a program aimed at recruiting black soldiers. An attempt by the majority to exclude members of a minority race from a regulated market is fundamentally different from a subsidy that enables a relatively small group of newcomers to enter that market. An interest in "consistency" does not justify treating differences as though they were similarities.

The Court's explanation for treating dissimilar race-based decisions as though they were equally objectionable is a supposed inability to differentiate between "invidious" and "benign" discrimination. But the term "affirmative action" is common and well understood. Its presence in everyday parlance shows that people understand the difference between good intentions and bad. As with any legal concept, some cases may be difficult to classify, but our equal protection jurisprudence has identified a critical difference between state action that imposes burdens on a disfavored few and state action that benefits the few "in spite of" its adverse effects on the many. . . .

. . .

Nothing is inherently wrong with applying a single standard to fundamentally different situations, as long as that standard takes relevant differences into account. . . . But a single standard that purports to equate remedial preferences with invidious discrimination cannot be defended in the name of "equal protection."

Moreover, the Court may find that its new "consistency" approach to race-based classifications is difficult to square with its insistence upon rigidly separate categories for discrimination against different classes of individuals. For example, as the law currently stands, the Court will apply "intermediate scrutiny" to cases of invidious gender discrimination and "strict scrutiny" to cases of invidious race discrimination, while applying the same standard for benign classifications as for invidious ones. If this remains the law, then today's lecture about "consistency" will produce the anomalous result that the Government can more easily enact affirmative-action programs to remedy discrimination against women than it can enact affirmative-action programs to remedy discrimination against African Americans—even though the primary purpose of the Equal Protection Clause was to end discrimination against the former slaves.... When a court becomes preoccupied with abstract standards, it risks sacrificing common sense at the altar of formal consistency.

. . .

III

The Court's concept of "congruence" assumes that there is no significant difference between a decision by the Congress of the United States to adopt an affirmative-action program and such a decision by a State or a municipality. [T]hat assumption ... ignores important practical and legal differences between federal and state or local decision-makers.

These differences have been identified repeatedly and consistently both in opinions of the Court and in separate opinions authored by members of today's majority. Thus, in Metro Broadcasting, Inc. v. FCC, 497 U.S. 547 (1990), ... we identified the special "institutional competence" of our National Legislature....

. . .

An additional reason for giving greater deference to the National Legislature than to a local law-making body is that federal affirmative-action programs represent the will of our entire Nation's elected representatives, whereas a state or local program may have an impact on nonresident entities who played no part in the decision to enact it. Thus, in the state or local context, individuals who were unable to vote for the local representatives who enacted a race-conscious program may nonetheless feel the effects of that program....

. . .

... [I]t is one thing to say (as no one seems to dispute) that the Fifth Amendment encompasses a general guarantee of equal protection as broad as that contained within the Fourteenth Amendment. It is another thing entirely to say that Congress' institutional competence and constitutional authority entitles it to no greater deference when it enacts a program designed to foster equality than the deference due a State legislature....

Our opinion in *Metro Broadcasting* relied on several constitutional provisions to justify the greater deference we owe to Congress when it acts with respect to private individuals.... In the programs challenged in this case, Congress has acted both with respect to private individuals and, as in *Fullilove*, with respect to the States themselves. When Congress does this, it draws its power directly from § 5 of the Fourteenth Amendment.... The Fourteenth Amendment directly empowers Congress at the same time it expressly limits the States. This is no accident. It represents our Nation's consensus, achieved after hard experience throughout our sorry history of race relations, that the Federal Government must be the primary defender of racial minorities against the States, some of which may be inclined to oppress such minorities. A rule of "congruence" that ignores a purposeful "incongruity" so fundamental to our system of government is unacceptable.

. . .

IV

The Court's concept of stare decisis treats some of the language we have used in explaining our decisions as though it were more important than our actual holdings....

This is the third time in the Court's entire history that it has considered the constitutionality of a federal affirmative-action program. On each of the two prior occasions, the first in 1980, Fullilove v. Klutznick, 448 U.S. 448, and the second in 1990, Metro Broadcasting, Inc. v. FCC, 497 U.S. 547, the Court upheld the program....

In the Court's view, our decision in *Metro Broadcasting* was inconsistent with the rule announced in Richmond v. J.A. Croson Co., 488 U.S. 469 (1989). But two decisive distinctions separate those two cases. First, *Metro Broadcasting* involved a federal program, whereas *Croson* involved a city ordinance....

Second, *Metro Broadcasting*'s holding rested on more than its application of "intermediate scrutiny." ... What truly distinguishes *Metro Broadcasting* from our other affirmative-action precedents is the distinctive goal of the federal program in that case. Instead of merely seeking to remedy past discrimination, the FCC program was intended to achieve future benefits in the form of broadcast diversity....

[P]rior to *Metro Broadcasting*, the interest in diversity had been mentioned in a few opinions, but it is perfectly clear that the Court had not yet decided whether that interest had sufficient magnitude to justify a racial classification. *Metro Broadcasting*, of course, answered that question in the affirmative. The majority today overrules *Metro Broadcasting* only insofar as it is "inconsistent with [the] holding" that strict scrutiny applies to "benign" racial classifications promulgated by the Federal Government. The proposition that fostering diversity may provide a sufficient interest to justify such a program is not inconsistent with the Court's holding today—indeed, the question is not remotely presented in this case—and I do not take the Court's opinion to diminish that aspect of our decision in *Metro Broadcasting*.

The Court's suggestion that it may be necessary in the future to overrule *Fullilove* in order to restore the fabric of the law is even more disingenuous than its treatment of *Metro Broadcasting*.... As was true of *Metro Broadcasting*, the Court in *Fullilove* decided an important, novel, and difficult question. Providing a different answer to a similar question today cannot fairly be characterized as merely "restoring" previously settled law.

V

The Court's holding in *Fullilove* surely governs the result in this case. The Public Works Employment Act of 1977 (1977 Act) ... is different in several critical respects from the portions of the Small Business Act (SBA) ... and STURAA [Surface Transportation and Uniform Relocation Assistance Act of 1987] ... challenged in this case. Each of those differences makes the current program ... significantly less objectionable than the 1977 categorical grant of $400 million in exchange for a 10% set-aside in public contracts....

Unlike the 1977 Act, the present statutory scheme does not make race the sole criterion of eligibility for participation in the program. Race does give rise to a rebuttable presumption of social disadvantage which, at least under STURAA, gives rise to a second rebuttable presumption of economic disadvantage.... But a small business may qualify as a DBE [Disadvantaged Business Enterprise], by showing that it is both socially and economically disadvantaged, even if it receives neither of these presumptions.... Thus, the current preference is more inclusive than the 1977 Act because it does not make race a necessary qualification.

More importantly, race is not a sufficient qualification. Whereas a millionaire with a long history of financial successes ... would have qualified for a preference under the 1977 Act merely because he was an Asian American or an African American, ... neither the SBA nor STURAA creates any such anomaly. The DBE program excludes members of minority races who are not, in fact, socially or economically disadvantaged.... The presumption of social disadvantage reflects the unfortunate fact that irrational racial prejudice—along with its lingering effects—still survives. The presumption of economic disadvantage embodies a recognition that success in the private sector of the economy is often attributable, in part, to social skills and relationships. Unlike the 1977 set-asides, the current preference is designed to overcome the social and economic disadvantages that are often associated with racial characteristics. If, in a particular case, these disadvantages are not present, the presumptions can be rebutted.... The program is thus designed to allow race to play a part in the decisional process only when there is a meaningful basis for assuming its relevance.

[I]t is particularly significant that the current program targets the negotiation of subcontracts between private firms. The 1977 Act applied entirely to the award of public contracts, an area of the economy in which social relationships should be irrelevant and in which proper supervision of government contracting officers should preclude any discrimination against particular bidders on account of their race. [Here], the program seeks to overcome barriers of prejudice between private parties—specifically, between general contractors and subcontractors. The SBA and STURAA embody Congress' recognition that such barriers may actually handicap minority firms seeking business as subcontractors from established leaders in the industry that have a history of doing business with their golfing partners. Indeed, minority subcontractors may face more obstacles than direct, intentional racial prejudice: they may face particular barriers simply because they are more likely to be new in the business and less likely to know others in the business. Given such difficulties, Congress could reasonably find that a minority subcontractor is less likely to receive favors from the entrenched businesspersons who award subcontracts only to people with whom—or with whose friends—they have an existing relationship. This program, then, if in part a remedy for past discrimination, is most importantly a forward-looking response to practical problems faced by minority subcontractors.

The current program contains another forward-looking component that the 1977 set-asides did not share. Section 8(a) of the SBA provides for periodic review of the status of DBE's, ... and DBE status can be challenged by a competitor at any time under any of the routes to certification.... Such review prevents ineligible firms from taking part in the program solely because of their minority ownership, even when those firms were once disadvantaged but have since become successful. The emphasis on review also indicates the Administration's anticipation that after their presumed disadvantages have been overcome, firms will "graduate" into a status in which they will be able to compete for business, including prime contracts, on an equal basis.... As with other phases of the statutory policy of encouraging the formation and growth of small business enterprises, this program is intended to facilitate entry and increase competition in the free market.

Significantly, the current program, unlike the 1977 set-aside, does not establish any requirement—numerical or otherwise—that a general contractor must hire DBE subcontractors. The program we upheld in *Fullilove* required that 10% of the federal grant for every federally funded project be expended on minority business enterprises. In contrast, the current program contains no quota. Although it provides monetary incentives to general contractors to hire DBE subcontractors, it does not require them to hire DBE's, and they do not lose their contracts if they fail to do so. The importance of this incentive to general contractors (who always seek to offer the lowest bid) should not be underestimated; but the preference here is far less rigid, and thus more narrowly tailored, than the 1977 Act....

Finally, the record shows a dramatic contrast between the sparse deliberations that preceded the 1977 Act ... and the extensive hearings conducted in several Congresses before the current program was developed.... If the 1977 program of race-based set-asides satisfied the strict scrutiny dictated by Justice Powell's vision of the Constitution—a vision the Court expressly endorses today—it must follow as night follows the day that the Court of Appeals' judgment upholding this more carefully crafted program should be affirmed.

· · ·

JUSTICE SOUTER, with whom JUSTICE GINSBURG and JUSTICE BREYER join, dissenting

· · ·

... The statutory scheme must be treated as constitutional if Fullilove v. Klutznick, 448 U.S. 448 (1980), is applied, and petitioners did not identify any of the factual premises on which *Fullilove* rested as having disappeared since that case was decided.

. . .

The Court ... does not reach the application of *Fullilove* ..., and on remand ... the Government and petitioner [must] address anew the facts upon which statutes like these must be judged on the Government's remedial theory of justification: facts about the current effects of past discrimination, the necessity for a preferential remedy, and the suitability of this particular preferential scheme.... [I]t seems fair to ask whether the statutes will meet a different fate from what *Fullilove* would have decreed. The answer is, quite probably not, though of course there will be some interpretive forks in the road before the significance of strict scrutiny for congressional remedial statutes becomes entirely clear.

... Indeed, the Court's very recognition today that strict scrutiny can be compatible with the survival of a classification so reviewed demonstrates that our concepts of equal protection enjoy a greater elasticity than the standard categories might suggest....

. . .

Finally, ... I do not understand that today's decision will necessarily have any effect on the ... long accepted ... view that constitutional authority to remedy past discrimination is not limited to the power to forbid its continuation, but extends to eliminating those effects that would otherwise persist and skew the operation of public systems even in the absence of current intent to practice any discrimination.... This is so whether the remedial authority is exercised by a court, ... the Congress, ... or some other legislature.... Indeed, a majority of the Court today reiterates that there are circumstances in which Government may, consistently with the Constitution, adopt programs aimed at remedying the effects of past invidious discrimination....

When the extirpation of lingering discriminatory effects is thought to require a catch-up mechanism, like the racially preferential inducement under the statutes considered here, the result may be that some members of the historically favored race are hurt by that remedial mechanism, however innocent they may be of any personal responsibility for any discriminatory conduct. When this price is considered reasonable, it is in part because it is a price to be paid only temporarily; if the justification for the preference is eliminating the effects of a past practice, the assumption is that the effects will themselves recede into the past, becoming attenuated and finally disappearing....

. . .

JUSTICE GINSBURG, with whom JUSTICE BREYER joins, dissenting.

For the reasons stated by Justice Souter, and in view of the attention the political branches are currently giving the matter of affirmative action, I see no compelling cause for the intervention the Court has made in this case. I further agree with Justice Stevens that ... large deference is owed by the Judiciary to "Congress' institutional competence and constitutional authority to overcome historic racial subjugation." I write separately to underscore ... the considerable field of agreement ... revealed in opinions that together speak for a majority of the Court.

I

. . .

The divisions in this difficult case should not obscure the Court's recognition of the persistence of racial inequality and a majority's acknowledgement of Congress' authority to act affirmatively, not only to end discrimination, but also to counteract discrimination's lingering effects.... Those effects, reflective of a system of racial caste only recently ended, are evident in our workplaces, markets, and neighborhoods. Job applicants with identical resumes, qualifications, and interview styles still experience different receptions, depending on their race. White and African–American consumers still encounter different deals. People of color looking for housing still face discriminatory treatment by landlords, real estate agents, and mortgage lenders. Minority entrepreneurs sometimes fail to gain contracts though they are the low bidders, and they are sometimes refused work even after winning contracts. Bias both conscious and unconscious, reflecting traditional and unexamined habits of thought, keeps up barriers that must come down if equal opportunity and nondiscrimination are ever genuinely to become this country's law and practice.

Given this history and its practical consequences, Congress surely can conclude that a carefully designed affirmative action program may help to realize, finally, the "equal protection of the laws" the Fourteenth Amendment has promised since 1868.

II

The lead opinion uses one term, "strict scrutiny," to describe the standard of judicial review for all governmental classifications by race. But that opinion's elaboration strongly suggests that the strict standard announced is indeed "fatal" for classifications burdening groups that have suffered discrimination in our society. That seems to me, and, I believe, to the Court, the enduring lesson one should draw from Korematsu v. United States, 323 U.S. 214 (1944).... A *Korematsu*-type classification, as I read the opinions in this case, will never again survive scrutiny....

For a classification made to hasten the day when "we are just one race," (Scalia, J., concurring in part and concurring in judgment), however, the lead opinion has dispelled the notion that "strict scrutiny" is " 'fatal in fact.' " ... Properly, a majority of the Court calls for review that is searching, in order to ferret out classifications in reality malign, but masquerading as benign. The Court's once lax review of sex-based classifications demonstrates the need for such suspicion....

Close review also is in order for this further reason.... [S]ome members of the historically favored race can be hurt by catch-up mechanisms designed to cope with the lingering effects of entrenched racial subjugation. Court review can ensure that preferences are not so large as to trammel unduly upon the opportunities of others or interfere too harshly with legitimate expectations of persons in once-preferred groups. . . .

While I would not disturb the programs challenged in this case, and would leave their improvement to the political branches, I see today's decision as one that allows our precedent to evolve, still to be informed by and responsive to changing conditions.

NOTES AND QUESTIONS

1. The Court's opinion rests, in large part, on the concept of "consistency"—"the standard of review under the Equal Protection Clause is not dependent on the race of those burdened or benefited by a particular classification." Does this mean that the Court accepts the proposition advanced by Justice Scalia's concurring opinion—that government can never use race to "make up" for past racial discrimination in the opposite direction? Does it accept Justice Thomas' position that all racial preferences are "racial discrimination, plain and simple."

2. Justice Stevens suggests that the insistence on a single standard because of the concept of consistency can produce anomalous results. As the cases in the next chapter will show, the Court has not judged distinctions based on sex by the same strict standard as distinctions based on race. They are governed by "heightened scrutiny" rather than "strict scrutiny." One of the arguments for a lesser standard to judge discrimination against women has been that discrimination against women has not been as severe as discrimination against racial minorities. Does it follow that affirmative action programs that benefit women should be easier to justify than affirmative action programs that benefit racial minorities?

3. The Court's 1989 *Croson* decision (discussed in the *Adarand* case) established the principle of "consistency." A 5–4 decision held that affirmative action programs at the state and local level were to be judged by "strict scrutiny." The next year, a 5–4 majority in the *Metro Broadcasting* case held that federal affirmative action programs were to be judged by a more lenient "heightened scrutiny." *Metro Broadcasting* is overruled by *Adarand*, establishing the principle of "congruence." Do you agree with the Court that the principle of "consistency" necessarily requires the principle of "congruence," and that *Croson* and *Metro Broadcasting* were inconsistent? (Actually 8 of the 9 Justices who participated in both *Croson* and *Metro Broadcasting* believed they were inconsistent, dissenting in one case or the other. Only Justice White was in both majorities.)

4. Suppose that Congress adopts a program awarding some federal public construction contracts to minority-owned businesses, and the city council of a large city adopts an identical program for city-financed construction contracts. Are there good reasons to give Congress more flexibility in designing affirmative action programs than the city council?

5. The Court's opinion states that not all racial affirmative action programs will be invalid, even under "strict scrutiny." The issue will

turn on a substantial variety of factors, including: (a) the nature of the government objective sought to be achieved; (b) the ability or inability to achieve that objective without drawing racial lines; (c) the flexibility or inflexibility of the racial lines that are drawn; (d) the extent of the injury to those excluded by the racial lines that are drawn. Can you predict whether the program in *Adarand*, as its details are described in Justice Stevens' dissent, will be upheld in the end? (Despite the statement in the Court's opinion that an affirmative action program will be upheld if it is "narrowly tailored" to meet a "compelling government interest," no member of the majority has ever voted to uphold a challenged affirmative action program. On the other hand, one can guess that the present Court will uphold a challenged program if any member of the *Adarand* majority joins with the four *Adarand* dissenters.)

6. Another significant factor involved in deciding affirmative action cases concerns the nature of the benefit or burden at stake. Most of the Supreme Court cases have involved admission to graduate schools, government jobs, and government contracts. In these cases, the Court has rejected the argument that it is a permissible government goal to provide "representation"—to allocate government benefits in a way that mimics the racial makeup of the population. The standard argument has been that the equal protection clause treats people as "individuals" and not as members of "groups." In one situation, however,—representation in elected government bodies—the name of the game is to provide representation for groups of people. Should the Constitution permit the use of voters' race in drawing the lines between electoral districts? That issue is discussed in Chapter 26, Section 3.

Chapter XXV

GENDER EQUALITY

I. THE CONSTITUTIONAL STATUS OF GENDER CLASSIFICATIONS

A. RACE DISCRIMINATION AND GENDER DISCRIMINATION*

In every society there are at least two groups of people, besides the Negroes, who are characterized by high social visibility expressed in physical appearance, dress, and patterns of behavior, and who have been "suppressed." We refer to women and children. Their present status, as well as their history and their problems in society, reveal striking similarities to those of the Negroes. . . .

In the historical development of these problem groups in America there have been much closer relations than is now ordinarily recorded. In the earlier common law, women and children were placed under the jurisdiction of the paternal power. When a legal status had to be found for the imported Negro servants in the seventeenth century, the nearest and most natural analogy was the status of women and children. The ninth commandment—linking together women, servants, mules, and other property—could be invoked, as well as a great number of other passages of Holy Scripture.

There was, of course, even in the beginning, a tremendous difference both in actual status of these different groups and in the tone of sentiment in the respective relations. In the decades before the Civil War, in the conservative and increasingly antiquarian ideology of the American South, woman was elevated as an ornament and looked upon with pride, while the Negro slave became increasingly a chattel and a ward. The paternalistic construction came, however, to good service when the South had to build up a moral defense for slavery, and it is found everywhere in the apologetic literature up to the beginning of the Civil War . . .

The parallel goes, however, considerably deeper than being only a structural part in the defense ideology built up around slavery. Women at that time lacked a number of rights otherwise belonging to all free white citizens of full age.

So chivalrous, indeed, was the ante-bellum South that its women were granted scarcely any rights at all. Everywhere they were subjected to political, legal, educational, and social and economic restrictions. They

---

* Abridgement of A Parallel to the Negro Problem, in Gunnar Myrdal, An American Dilemma, Harper & Row, 1962, pp. 1073–1078.

1106

took no part in governmental affairs, were without legal rights over their property or the guardianship of their children, were denied adequate educational facilities, and were excluded from business and the professions.

The same was very much true of the rest of the country and of the rest of the world. But there was an especially close relation in the South between the subordination of women and that of Negroes. This is perhaps best expressed in a comment attributed to Dolly Madison, that the Southern wife was "the chief slave of the harem."

From the very beginning, the fight in America for the liberation of the Negro slaves was, therefore, closely coordinated with the fight for women's emancipation. . . .

.   .   .

The Union's victory [in the Civil War], however, brought disappointment to the women suffragists. The arguments "the Negro's hour" and "a political necessity" met and swept aside all their arguments for leaving the word "male" out of the 14th Amendment and putting "sex" alongside "race" and "color" in the 15th Amendment. . . . The War and Reconstruction Amendments had thus sharply divided the women's problem from the Negro problem in actual politics. The deeper relation between the two will, however, be recognized up till this day. . . .

This close relation is no accident. The ideological and economic forces behind the two movements—the emancipation of women and children and the emancipation of Negroes—have much in common and are closely interrelated. Paternalism was a pre-industrial scheme of life, and was gradually becoming broken in the nineteenth century. Negroes and women, both of whom had been under the yoke of the paternalistic system, were both strongly and fatefully influenced by the Industrial Revolution. For neither group is the readjustment process yet consummated. Both are still problem groups. The women's problem is the center of the whole complex of problems of how to reorganize the institution of the family to fit the new economic and ideological basis. . . .

As in the Negro problem, most men have accepted as self-evident, until recently, the doctrine that women had inferior endowments in most of those respects which carry prestige, power, and advantages in society, but that they were, at the same time, superior in some other respects. The arguments, when arguments were used, have been about the same: smaller brains, scarcity of geniuses and so on. The study of women's intelligence and personality has had broadly the same history as the one we record for Negroes. As in the case of the Negro, women themselves have often been brought to believe in their inferiority of endowment. As the Negro was awarded his "place" in society, so there was a "women's place." In both cases the rationalization was strongly believed that men, in confining them to this place, did not act against the true interest of the subordinate groups. The myth of the "contented women," who did not want to have suffrage or other civil rights and equal opportunities, had the same social function as the myth of the "contented Negro." In both cases there was probably—in a static sense—often some truth behind the myth.

. . .

Political franchise was not granted to women until recently. Even now there are, in all countries, great difficulties for a woman to attain public office. The most important disabilities still affecting her status are those barring her attempt to earn a living and to attain promotion in her work. As in the Negro's case, there are certain "women's jobs," traditionally monopolized by women. They are regularly in the low salary bracket and do not offer much of a career. All over the world men have used the trade unions to keep women out of competition. Woman's competition has, like the Negro's, been particularly obnoxious and dreaded by men because of the low wages women, with their few earning outlets, are prepared to work for. Men often dislike the very idea of having women on an equal plane as coworkers and competitors, and usually they find it even more "unnatural" to work under women. White people generally hold similar attitudes toward Negroes. On the other hand, it is said about women that they prefer men as bosses and do not want to work under another woman. Negroes often feel the same way about working under other Negroes.

In personal relations with both women and Negroes, white men generally prefer a less professional and more human relation, actually a more paternalistic and protective position. . . .

In drawing a parallel between the position of, and feeling toward, women and Negroes we are uncovering a fundamental basis of our culture. Although it is changing, atavistic elements sometimes unexpectedly break through even in the most emancipated individuals. The similarities in the women's and the Negroes' problems are not accidental. They were, as we have pointed out, originally determined in a paternalistic order of society. The problems remain, even though paternalism is gradually declining as an ideal and is losing its economic basis. In the final analysis, women are still hindered in their competition by the function of procreation; Negroes are laboring under the yoke of the doctrine of unassimilability which has remained although slavery is abolished. The second barrier is actually much stronger than the first in America today. But the first is more eternally inexorable.

QUESTIONS

Are you convinced that, in our culture, there is a "parallel between the position of, and feeling toward, women and Negroes?" Are there, in any event, great differences too? To the extent that there is a parallel, does that suggest that the same constitutional standard should govern the validity of government distinctions drawn between African Americans and whites and government distinctions drawn between men and women?

B. THE CONSTITUTIONALITY OF GENDER DISTINCTIONS

REED v. REED

Supreme Court of the United States, 1971.
404 U.S. 71, 92 S.Ct. 251, 30 L.Ed.2d 225.

[When Richard Reed, a minor, died, both his parents, who were separated, applied for appointment as administrator of the son's estate. Idaho law provided that "of several persons claiming and equally entitled to administer, males must be preferred to females...." Thus, Cecil Reed, the father, was appointed administrator. Sally Reed appealed from this decision, arguing that the law violated the Equal Protection Clause by giving a mandatory preference to males over females, without regard to their individual qualifications as potential administrators.]

CHIEF JUSTICE BURGER delivered the opinion of the Court.

. . .

... We have concluded that the arbitrary preference established in favor of males ... cannot stand in the face of the Fourteenth Amendment's command that no State deny the equal protection of the laws to any person within its jurisdiction.

. . .

In applying that clause, this Court has consistently recognized that the Fourteenth Amendment does not deny to States the power to treat different classes of persons in different ways. The Equal Protection Clause of that amendment does, however, deny to States the power to legislate that different treatment be accorded to persons placed by a statute into different classes on the basis of criteria wholly unrelated to the objective of that statute. A classification "must be reasonable, not arbitrary, and must rest upon some ground of difference having a fair and substantial relation to the object of the legislation, so that all persons similarly circumstanced shall be treated alike." The question presented by this case, then, is whether a difference in the sex of competing applicants for letters of administration bears a rational relationship to a state objective that is sought to be advanced....

In upholding the [statute], the Idaho Supreme Court concluded that its objective was to eliminate one area of controversy when two or more persons, equally entitled, seek letters of administration and thereby present the probate court "with the issue of which one should be named." The court also concluded that where such persons are not of the same sex, the elimination of females from consideration "is neither an illogical nor arbitrary method devised by the legislature to resolve an issue that would otherwise require a hearing as to the relative merits ... of the two or more petitioning relatives...."

Clearly the objective of reducing the workload on probate courts by eliminating one class of contests is not without some legitimacy. The crucial question, however, is whether [the preference for males] advances that objective in a manner consistent with the command of the

Equal Protection Clause. We hold that it does not. To give a mandatory preference to members of either sex over members of the other, merely to accomplish the elimination of hearings on the merits, is to make the very kind of arbitrary legislative choice forbidden by the Equal Protection Clause of the Fourteenth Amendment; and whatever may be said as to the positive values of avoiding intrafamily controversy, the choice in this context may not lawfully be mandated solely on the basis of sex.

. . .

NOTES AND QUESTIONS

1. The Court in Reed v. Reed appears to be applying a rational basis standard. This test requires only that the challenged classification (that between men and women) bear a rational relationship to some legitimate state objective in order to be upheld. Traditionally this standard has been a very lenient one and has amounted to no review at all. Even if the state government failed to suggest a legitimate objective for the legislation, the Court often postulated some possible purpose and sustained the regulation on that basis.

2. In the *Reed* case the state of Idaho asserted several seemingly legitimate objectives of the statute. The primary ground asserted was administrative efficiency. The statutory preference for males would eliminate the need to hold hearings on the qualifications of the parties to be administrators. Moreover, the classification was asserted to be rational because men traditionally have greater knowledge of business affairs than do women.

3. Laws often use general standards to avoid the problem of making difficult case-by-case decisions. Suppose, for example, a law preferred parents of the deceased to siblings as administrators. Would the law be *unconstitutional* if it preferred the deceased's aged mother to a son who was a professional estate manager? If not, are distinctions based on gender to be treated differently? Was the Court then applying some heightened scrutiny to the challenged classification?

Perhaps the Court's failure to acknowledge that gender discrimination was a special kind of problem was caused by the fact that Reed v. Reed was the first legislative sex classification struck down on equal protection grounds. By the time the next gender classification case had reached the Court the issue of whether gender like race was a "suspect classification" had surfaced more clearly in the justices' deliberations.

4. In San Antonio Independent School District v. Rodriguez, 411 U.S. 1 (1973), Justice Marshall interpreted the meaning of the *Reed* decision. He acknowledged in a dissenting opinion that the Court had said it had in fact used the rational-basis test in *Reed,* but he went on to say that it had "resorted to a more stringent standard of equal protection review than employed in cases involving commercial matters. . . . This Court . . . was unwilling to consider a theoretical and unsubstantiated basis for distinction—however reasonable it might appear to be—sufficient to sustain a statute discriminating on the basis of sex." 411 U.S. at 107. When Frontiero v. Richardson, 411 U.S. 677 (1973), was before the Court, Justice White wrote Justice Brennan: "Thurgood is

right about this. If moving beyond the lesser test means that there is a suspect classification, then *Reed* has already determined that." Justice Brennan agreed and told Justice Powell: "Thurgood's discussion of *Reed* in his dissent to your *Rodriguez* convinces me that the only rational explication of *Reed* is that it rests upon the 'suspect' approach." Chief Justice Burger wrote Justice Brennan that he had been watching the "shuttlecock" memos about "suspect" classification and Reed v. Reed. "Some may construe *Reed* as supporting the 'suspect' view," he wrote, "but I do not. The author of *Reed* never remotely contemplated such a broad concept but, then, a lot of people sire offspring unintended!" Douglas Papers, Library of Congress, Box 1576.

FRONTIERO v. RICHARDSON

Supreme Court of the United States, 1973.
411 U.S. 677, 93 S.Ct. 1764, 36 L.Ed.2d 583.

[The report in this case appears at page 991.]

CRAIG v. BOREN

Supreme Court of the United States, 1976.
429 U.S. 190, 97 S.Ct. 451, 50 L.Ed.2d 397.

JUSTICE BRENNAN delivered the opinion of the Court.

[In 1972, Oklahoma provided that the age of majority, and the age of criminal responsibility, for both men and women, was 18. At the same time, however, Oklahoma re-enacted an earlier law dealing with the sale of "nonintoxicating" 3.2% beer. Under that law, sale to males under the age of 21, and females under the age of 18, was prohibited. This suit was brought by a male between 18 and 21 years of age, complaining that the 3.2% beer law discriminated against males in his age group. The lower court declared that the law was constitutional.]

. . .

Analysis may appropriately begin with the reminder that Reed v. Reed emphasized that statutory classifications that distinguish between males and females are "subject to scrutiny under the Equal Protection Clause." To withstand constitutional challenge, previous cases establish that classifications by gender must serve important governmental objectives and must be substantially related to achievement of those objectives. Thus, in *Reed,* the objectives of "reducing the workload on probate courts," and "avoiding intra-family controversy," were deemed of insufficient importance to sustain use of an overt gender criterion in the appointment of intestate administrators. Decisions following *Reed* similarly have rejected administrative ease and convenience as sufficiently important objectives to justify gender-based classifications. . . .

Reed v. Reed has also provided the underpinning for decisions that have invalidated statutes employing gender as an inaccurate proxy for other, more germane bases of classification. . . . Similarly, increasingly outdated misconceptions concerning the role of females in the home rather than in the "marketplace and world of ideas" were rejected as loose-fitting characterizations incapable of supporting state statutory schemes that were premised upon their accuracy. In light of the weak congruence between gender and the characteristic or trait that gender purported to represent, it was necessary that the legislatures choose either to realign their substantive laws in a gender-neutral fashion, or to adopt procedures for identifying those instances where the sex-centered generalization actually comported to fact.

In this case, too, "*Reed* we feel is controlling . . .". We turn then to the question whether, under *Reed,* the difference between males and females with respect to the purchase of 3.2% beer warrants the differential in age drawn by the Oklahoma statute. We conclude that it does not.

The District Court recognized that Reed v. Reed was controlling. In applying the teachings of that case, the Court found the requisite important governmental objective in the traffic-safety goal proffered by the Oklahoma Attorney General. It then concluded that the statistics introduced by the appellees established that the gender-based distinction was substantially related to achievement of that goal.

. . . Clearly, the protection of public health and safety represents an important function of state and local governments. However, appellees' statistics in our view cannot support the conclusion that the gender-based distinction closely serves to achieve that objective and therefore the distinction cannot under *Reed* withstand equal protection challenge.

The appellees introduced a variety of statistical surveys. . . .

Even were this statistical evidence accepted as accurate, it nevertheless offers only a weak answer to the equal protection question presented here. The most focused and relevant of the statistical surveys, arrests of 18–20–year–olds for alcohol-related driving offenses, exemplifies the ultimate unpersuasiveness of this evidentiary record. Viewed in terms of the correlation between sex and the actual activity that Oklahoma seeks to regulate—driving while under the influence of alcohol—the statistics broadly establish that .18% of females and 2% of males in that age group were arrested for that offense. While such a disparity is not trivial in a statistical sense, it hardly can form the basis for employment of a gender line as a classifying device. Certainly if maleness is to serve as a proxy for drinking and driving, a correlation of 2% must be considered an unduly tenuous "fit." Indeed, prior cases have consistently rejected the use of sex as a decisionmaking factor even though the statutes in question certainly rested on far more predictive empirical relationships than this.

. . .

. . . [P]roving broad sociological propositions by statistics is a dubious business, and one that inevitably is in tension with the normative philosophy that underlies the Equal Protection Clause. Suffice to say that the showing offered by the appellees does not satisfy us that sex represents a legitimate, accurate proxy for the regulation of drinking and driving. In fact, when it is further recognized that Oklahoma's statute prohibits only the selling of 3.2% beer to young males and not their drinking the beverage once acquired (even after purchase by their 18–

20–year–old female companions), the relationship between gender and traffic safety becomes far too tenuous to satisfy *Reed's* requirement that the gender-based difference be substantially related to achievement of the statutory objective.

We hold, therefore, that under *Reed,* Oklahoma's 3.2% beer statute invidiously discriminates against males 18–20 years of age.

. . .

JUSTICE POWELL, concurring.

I join the opinion of the Court as I am in general agreement with it. I do have reservations as to some of the discussion concerning the appropriate standard for equal protection analysis and the relevance of the statistical evidence. Accordingly, I add this concurring statement.

With respect to the equal protection standard, I agree that Reed v. Reed is the most relevant precedent. But I find it unnecessary, in deciding this case, to read that decision as broadly as some of the Court's language may imply. *Reed* and subsequent cases involving gender-based classifications make clear that the Court subjects such classifications to a more critical examination than is normally applied when "fundamental" constitutional rights and "suspect classes" are not present.

I view this as a relatively easy case. . . .

It seems to me that the statistics offered by the State and relied upon by the District Court do tend generally to support the view that young men drive more, possibly are inclined to drink more, and—for various reasons—are involved in more accidents than young women. Even so, I am not persuaded that these facts and the inferences fairly drawn from them justify this classification based on a three-year age differential between the sexes, and especially one that it so easily circumvented as to be virtually meaningless. Putting it differently, this gender-based classification does not bear a fair and substantial relation to the object of the legislation.

JUSTICE STEVENS, concurring.

There is only one Equal Protection Clause. It requires every State to govern impartially. It does not direct the courts to apply one standard of review in some cases and a different standard in other cases. Whatever criticism may be levelled at a judicial opinion implying that there are at least three such standards applies with the same force to a double standard.

I am inclined to believe that what has become known as the two-tiered analysis of equal protection claims does not describe a completely logical method of deciding cases, but rather is a method the Court has employed to explain decisions that actually apply a single standard in a reasonably consistent fashion. I also suspect that a careful explanation of the reasons motivating particular decisions may contribute more to an identification of that standard than an attempt to articulate it in all-encompassing terms. It may therefore be appropriate for me to state the principal reasons which persuaded me to join the Court's opinion.

In this case, the classification is not as obnoxious as some the Court has condemned, nor as inoffensive as some the Court has accepted. It is objectionable because it is based on an accident of birth, because it is a mere remnant of the now almost universally rejected tradition of discriminating against males in this age bracket, and because, to the extent it reflects any physical difference between males and females, it is actually perverse. The question then is whether the traffic safety justification put forward by the State is sufficient to make an otherwise offensive classification acceptable.

The classification is not totally irrational. For the evidence does indicate that there are more males than females in this age bracket who drive and also more who drink. Nevertheless, there are several reasons why I regard the justification as unacceptable. It is difficult to believe that the statute was actually intended to cope with the problem of traffic safety, since it has only a minimal effect on access to a not-very-intoxicating beverage and does not prohibit its consumption. Moreover, the empirical data submitted by the State accentuates the unfairness of treating all 18–21–year–old males as inferior to their female counterparts. The legislation imposes a restraint on one hundred percent of the males in the class allegedly because about 2% of them have probably violated one or more laws relating to the consumption of alcoholic beverages. It is unlikely that this law will have a significant deterrent effect either on that 2% or on the law-abiding 98%. But even assuming some such slight benefit, it does not seem to me that an insult to all of the young men of the State can be justified by visiting the sins of the 2% on the 98%.

JUSTICE STEWART, concurring in the judgment.

. . .

The disparity created by these Oklahoma statutes amounts to total irrationality. For the statistics upon which the State now relies, whatever their other shortcomings, wholly fail to prove or even suggest that 3.2% beer is somehow more deleterious when it comes into the hands of a male aged 18–20 than of a female of like age. The disparate statutory treatment of the sexes here, without even a colorably valid justification or explanation, thus amounts to invidious discrimination.

CHIEF JUSTICE BURGER, dissenting.

I am in general agreement with JUSTICE REHNQUIST's dissent, but even at the risk of compounding the obvious confusion created by those voting to reverse the District Court, I will add a few words.

. . .

. . . Though today's decision does not go so far as to make gender-based classifications "suspect," it makes gender a disfavored classification. Without an independent constitutional basis supporting the right asserted or disfavoring the classification adopted, I can justify no substantive constitutional protection other than the normal protection afforded by the Equal Protection Clause.

The means employed by the Oklahoma Legislature to achieve the objectives sought may not be agreeable to some judges, but since eight Members of the Court think the means not irrational, I see no basis for striking down the statute as violative of the Constitution simply because we find it unwise, unneeded, or possibly even a bit foolish.

With JUSTICE REHNQUIST, I would affirm the judgment of the District Court.

JUSTICE REHNQUIST, dissenting.

... I think the Oklahoma statute challenged here need pass only the "rational basis" equal protection analysis ... and I believe that it is constitutional under that analysis.

I

In Frontiero v. Richardson, the opinion for the plurality sets forth the reasons of four Justices for concluding that sex should be regarded as a suspect classification for purposes of equal protection analysis....

Subsequent to *Frontiero,* the Court has declined to hold that sex is a suspect class, and no such holding is imported by the Court's resolution of this case. However, the Court's application here of an elevated or "intermediate" level scrutiny, like that invoked in cases dealing with discrimination against females, raises the question of why the statute here should be treated any differently than countless legislative classifications unrelated to sex which have been upheld under a minimum rationality standard.

Most obviously unavailable to support any kind of special scrutiny in this case, is a history or pattern of past discrimination, such as was relied on by the plurality in *Frontiero* to support its invocation of strict scrutiny. There is no suggestion in the Court's opinion that males in this age group are in any way peculiarly disadvantaged, subject to systematic discriminatory treatment, or otherwise in need of special solicitude from the courts.

. . .

It is true that a number of our opinions contain broadly phrased dicta implying that the same test should be applied to all classifications based on sex, whether affecting females or males. However, before today, no decision of this Court has applied an elevated level of scrutiny to invalidate a statutory discrimination harmful to males, except where the statute impaired an important personal interest protected by the Constitution. There being no such interest here, and there being no plausible argument that this is a discrimination against females,[1] the Court's reliance on our previous sex-discrimination cases is ill-founded. It treats gender classification as a talisman which—without regard to the rights involved or the persons affected—calls into effect a heavier burden of judicial review.

---

1. I am not unaware of the argument from time to time advanced, that all discriminations between the sexes ultimately redound to the detriment of females, because they tend to reinforce "old notions" restricting the roles and opportunities of women.

The Court's conclusion that a law which treats males less favorably than females "must serve important governmental objectives and must be substantially related to achievement of those objectives" apparently comes out of thin air. The Equal Protection Clause contains no such language, and none of our previous cases adopt that standard. I would think we have had enough difficulty with the two standards of review which our cases have recognized—the norm of "rational basis," and the "compelling state interest" required where a "suspect classification" is involved—so as to counsel weightily against the insertion of still another "standard" between those two. How is this Court to divine what objectives are important? How is it to determine whether a particular law is "substantially" related to the achievement of such objective, rather than related in some other way to its achievement? Both of the phrases used are so diaphanous and elastic as to invite subjective judicial preferences or prejudices relating to particular types of legislation, masquerading as judgments whether such legislation is directed at "important" objectives or, whether the relationship to those objectives is "substantial" enough.

. . .

II

. . .

Our decisions indicate that application of the Equal Protection Clause in a context not justifying an elevated level of scrutiny does not demand "mathematical nicety" or the elimination of all inequality. Those cases recognize that the practical problems of government may require rough accommodations of interests, and hold that such accommodations should be respected unless no reasonable basis can be found to support them. . . .

. . .

The Oklahoma Legislature could have believed that 18–20–year–old males drive substantially more, and tend more often to be intoxicated than their female counterparts; that they prefer beer and admit to drinking and driving at a higher rate than females; and that they suffer traffic injuries out of proportion to the part they make up of the population. Under the appropriate rational basis test for equal protection, it is neither irrational nor arbitrary to bar them from making purchases of 3.2% beer, which purchases might in many cases be made by a young man who immediately returns to his vehicle with the beverage in his possession. The record does not give any good indication of the true proportion of males in the age group who drink and drive (except that it is no doubt greater than the 2% who are arrested), but whatever it may be I cannot see that the mere purchase right involved could conceivably raise a due process question. There being no violation of either equal protection or due process, the statute should accordingly be upheld.

NOTES AND QUESTIONS

1. Most commentators read the decision in Craig v. Boren in the same way as the dissenting and concurring justices—that classifications

based on gender are "semi-suspect" and require heightened scrutiny. Later cases, however, confused the question of the proper verbal standard for judging the constitutional validity of gender classifications. In Michael M. v. Superior Court, 450 U.S. 464 (1981), the Court divided 5–4 in sustaining California's statutory rape law. The law made intercourse with a female under 18 a crime. Thus, in a case where there was intercourse between two juveniles, only the male was guilty of a crime. (Other states have "gender neutral" statutory rape laws, making it a crime for older persons to have intercourse with younger persons. California's law was enacted in 1859; those states with gender-neutral laws have enacted them in the last two decades.)

There was no opinion for the Court in *Michael M.* Justice Rehnquist's opinion for himself and three other justices summarized the Court's earlier cases as invalidating laws that "make overbroad generalizations based on sex which are entirely unrelated to any differences between men or women or which demean the ability or social status of the affected class," and sustaining laws where gender classification "is not invidious, but rather realistically reflects the fact that the sexes are not similarly situated." California's law met that standard, he said, because California could legitimately treat the young female as the victim of the crime. Only the female could become pregnant. California could decide that since males were not deterred by the fear of pregnancy, there was a need for criminal penalties to deter their behavior. Moreover, young females would be more likely to report offenses if they were not made criminals, and young males could be punished since they were as capable of inflicting the harm as older males. Justice Blackmun's concurrence in the result was cryptic. Referring to cases involving abortion, he emphasized the importance of the problem of teenage pregnancy, and summarily concluded that the California law was a "sufficiently reasoned and constitutional effort to control the problem at its inception." The four dissenters argued that the California law was not based on a concern for teenage pregnancy, but reflected an outmoded stereotype that males were always the aggressors in sexual encounters. Moreover, the fact that only females could become pregnant did not explain their exemption from criminal penalty even if the state was concerned with their pregnancy. It still was rational to limit punishment to the male only if one added the stereotype that the male was more blameworthy.

2. In Rostker v. Goldberg, 453 U.S. 57 (1981), the Court divided 6–3 in sustaining draft registration limited to males. This time, Justice Rehnquist wrote the opinion of the Court. Speaking of the standards for judging the validity of gender classifications, he disparaged the usefulness of previous verbal formulations. "We do not think that the substantive guarantee of due process or certainty in the law will be advanced by any further 'refinement' in the applicable tests.... Announced degrees of 'deference' to legislative judgments, just as levels of 'scrutiny' which this Court announces that it applies to particular classifications made by a legislative body, may all too readily become facile abstractions used to justify a result." Viewing registration as the prelude to actual conscription in an emergency, and conscription as primarily designed to produce

combat troops, drafting only men was permissible if it was permissible to exempt women from combat. As to the validity of the exemption of women from combat, Justice Rehnquist quoted from a United States Senate report: "The principle that women should not intentionally and routinely engage in combat is fundamental, and enjoys wide support among our people." The three dissenters did not directly contradict the proposition that women should not serve in combat roles. Justice White, joined by Justice Brennan, argued that the record did not demonstrate that all noncombatant military personnel needs would be filled by volunteers and thus, to some extent, an all-male draft would conscript some men, but no women, for noncombat positions. Justice Marshall, also joined by Justice Brennan, emphasized that the challenged statute dealt with registration and not conscription, and there were no solid reasons for exempting women from the registration requirement.

3. None of the justices writing in the *Rostker* case questioned the constitutional validity of a practice of reserving combat military roles to men. The dissenters' positions turned on arguments that it was unconstitutional to limit selective service registration to men even if combat was limited to men. And, while Justice Rehnquist's opinion for the Court rests on the proposition that women can be excused from combat, his only support for that position is a Senate report that concludes that the proposition is "fundamental and enjoys wide support." Doubtless, the Senate report is correct in concluding that many people strongly believe that women should never be used in military combat positions. Why is that? Is it a stereotype? Is it outmoded? Is it "demeaning"?

4. Many of the cases that have struck down gender distinctions in laws can be explained on the ground that the challenged laws were based on a stereotype that men had a role in the workforce and a woman's place was in the home. Should other gender stereotypes (such as sexual roles, as in *Michael M.*, and military assignments, as in *Rostker*) be viewed as less invidious?

5. Consider the 5–4 decision in Mississippi University for Women v. Hogan, 458 U.S. 718 (1982), where the Court, applying the heightened-scrutiny test, held that it was unconstitutional for a state women's university to limit enrollment in its nursing program to women. For the dissenters, the issue was whether it was constitutional for a state to honor the preference of women for a "traditionally popular and respected choice" to attend a single-sex college rather than a coeducational institution. The majority did not reach the broad question whether all state-run single-sex schools were unconstitutional, nor did it decide whether the Mississippi University for Women could limit enrollment to females in schools other than its nursing school. One point made in Justice O'Connor's opinion for the Court was that the nursing school's policy was based on "the stereotyped view of nursing as an exclusively woman's job."

6. A number of the cases in this chapter were argued in the Supreme Court by *Professor* Ruth Ginsburg, taking the position that all gender distinctions should be treated by the Supreme Court in all cases in the same way as analogous racial distinctions. One case where race

and gender distinctions *are* treated alike is that of jury selection. In civil and criminal cases, lawyers for both sides are customarily allowed to remove a number of jurors without giving any explicit reason for doing so. These challenges—peremptory challenges—allow lawyers to use hunches or irrational stereotypes—to pick a sympathetic jury. In Batson v. Kentucky, 476 U.S. 79 (1986), however, the Court held that peremptory challenges of jurors intended to remove jurors of one race violated the Equal Protection Clause. In J.E.B. v. Alabama ex rel. T.B., 511 U.S. 127 (1994), the Court extended that principle to peremptory challenges intended to remove jurors of one gender. Justice Ruth Ginsburg joined the Court's opinion, written by Justice Blackmun, which said, in a footnote, that the Court had never decided whether or not "classifications based on gender are inherently suspect." The opinion did acknowledge that "[w]hile the prejudicial attitudes toward women in this country have not been identical to those held toward racial minorities, the similarities between the experiences of racial minorities and women, in some contexts, 'overpower those differences.'"

UNITED STATES v. VIRGINIA

Supreme Court of the United States, 1996.
518 U.S. 515, 116 S.Ct. 2264, 135 L.Ed.2d 735.

JUSTICE GINSBURG delivered the opinion of the Court.

Virginia's public institutions of higher learning include an incomparable military college, Virginia Military Institute (VMI). The United States maintains that the Constitution's equal protection guarantee precludes Virginia from reserving exclusively to men the unique educational opportunities VMI affords. We agree.

RUTH BADER GINSBURG—Born on March 15, 1933, in Brooklyn, New York, daughter of a haberdasher. Her mother greatly influenced her by stressing achievement and independence. Jewish. Democrat. Educated in Brooklyn's public schools. Cornell, B.A., Phi Beta Kappa, 1954. After marrying and having a child, she entered the Harvard Law School in 1956—one of nine women in a class of 500. Accompanying her husband to New York in 1958, she transferred to Columbia Law School, where she was a Kent Scholar and where she received an LL.B., in 1959, graduating at the top of her class. Reportedly rejected for a clerkship with Justice Frankfurter because she was a woman and unable to obtain employment with leading New York law firms, which she attributed to being a woman, a Jew, and a mother, she clerked with U.S. District Judge Edmund L. Palmieri. She then did research at Columbia Law School, 1961–63, and taught at Rutgers Law School, 1963–72. In 1972, she became the first tenured woman at Columbia Law School. Thereafter, she participated as counsel in several leading gender equality cases—Reed v. Reed (1971), Frontiero v. Richardson (1972), Weinberger v. Wiesenfeld (1975), and Califano v. Goldfarb (1977). Judge, U.S. Court of Appeals (D.C.Circuit), 1980–1993. Nominated on June 14, 1993, by President Bill Clinton to replace Byron White. Confirmed by the Senate on August 3, 1993, by a 97–3 vote.

I

Founded in 1839, VMI is today the sole single-sex school among Virginia's 15 public institutions of higher learning. VMI's distinctive mission is to produce "citizen-soldiers," men prepared for leadership in civilian life and in military service. VMI pursues this mission through pervasive training of a kind not available anywhere else in Virginia. Assigning prime place to character development, VMI uses an "adversative method" modeled on English public schools and once characteristic of military instruction. VMI constantly endeavors to instill physical and mental discipline in its cadets and impart to them a strong moral code. The school's graduates leave VMI with heightened comprehension of their capacity to deal with duress and stress, and a large sense of accomplishment for completing the hazardous course.

VMI has notably succeeded in its mission to produce leaders; among its alumni are military generals, Members of Congress, and business executives. The school's alumni overwhelmingly perceive that their VMI training helped them to realize their personal goals. VMI's endowment reflects the loyalty of its graduates; VMI has the largest per-student endowment of all undergraduate institutions in the Nation.

Neither the goal of producing citizen-soldiers nor VMI's implementing methodology is inherently unsuitable to women. And the school's impressive record in producing leaders has made admission desirable to some women. Nevertheless, Virginia has elected to preserve exclusively for men the advantages and opportunities a VMI education affords.

II

A

From its establishment in 1839 as one of the Nation's first state military colleges, ... VMI has remained financially supported by Virginia and "subject to the control of the [Virginia] General Assembly," ...

VMI today enrolls about 1,300 men as cadets. Its academic offerings in the liberal arts, sciences, and engineering are also available at other public colleges and universities in Virginia. But VMI's mission is special. It is the mission of the school " 'to produce educated and honorable men, prepared for the varied work of civil life, imbued with love of learning, confident in the functions and attitudes of leadership, possessing a high sense of public service, advocates of the American democracy and free enterprise system, and ready as citizen-soldiers to defend their country in time of national peril.' " ... In contrast to the federal service academies, ... VMI's program "is directed at preparation for both military and civilian life"; "[o]nly about 15% of VMI cadets enter career military service."

VMI produces its "citizen-soldiers" through "an adversative, or doubting, model of education" which features "[p]hysical rigor, mental stress, absolute equality of treatment, absence of privacy, minute regulation of behavior, and indoctrination in desirable values." ...

VMI cadets live in spartan barracks where surveillance is constant and privacy nonexistent; they wear uniforms, eat together in the mess hall, and regularly participate in drills. Entering students are incessantly exposed to the rat line, "an extreme form of the adversative model," comparable in intensity to Marine Corps boot camp. Tormenting and punishing, the rat line bonds new cadets to their fellow sufferers and, when they have completed the 7–month experience, to their former tormentors.

VMI's "adversative model" is further characterized by a hierarchical "class system" of privileges and responsibilities, a "dyke system" for assigning a senior class mentor to each entering class "rat," and a stringently enforced "honor code," which prescribes that a cadet " 'does not lie, cheat, steal nor tolerate those who do.' "

VMI attracts some applicants because of its reputation as an extraordinarily challenging military school, and "because its alumni are exceptionally close to the school." ... "[W]omen have no opportunity anywhere to gain the benefits of [the system of education at VMI]."

B

In 1990, prompted by a complaint filed with the Attorney General by a female high-school student seeking admission to VMI, the United States sued the Commonwealth of Virginia and VMI, alleging that VMI's exclusively male admission policy violated the Equal Protection Clause of the Fourteenth Amendment....

[The United States District Court ruled that there was no constitutional violation. The Court of Appeals reversed and, in response, Virginia proposed a parallel program for women: Virginia Women's Institute for Leadership (VWIL), located at Mary Baldwin College, a private liberal arts women's college. The District Court decided that the program for women satisfied the requirement of equal protection, and the Court of Appeals affirmed. VMI appealed from the first Court of Appeals ruling, and the United States appealed from the second.]

III

The cross-petitions in this case present two ultimate issues. First, does Virginia's exclusion of women from the educational opportunities provided by VMI ... deny to women ... the equal protection of the laws guaranteed by the Fourteenth Amendment? Second, if VMI's "unique" situation—as Virginia's sole single-sex public institution of higher education—offends the Constitution's equal protection principle, what is the remedial requirement?

IV

... Parties who seek to defend gender-based government action must demonstrate an "exceedingly persuasive justification" for that action.

Today's skeptical scrutiny of official action denying rights or opportunities based on sex responds to volumes of history. As a plurality of this Court acknowledged a generation ago, "our Nation has had a long and unfortunate history of sex discrimination." Frontiero v. Richardson, 411 U.S. 677, 684 (1973). Through a century plus three decades and more of that history, women did not count among voters composing "We the People"; not until 1920 did women gain a constitutional right to the franchise. And for a half century thereafter, it remained the prevailing doctrine that government, both federal and state, could withhold from women opportunities accorded men so long as any "basis in reason" could be conceived for the discrimination. . . .

. . .

Without equating gender classifications for all purposes to classifications based on race or national origin, the Court, in post-*Reed* decisions, has carefully inspected official action that closes a door or denies opportunity to women (or to men). . . .

The heightened review standard our precedent establishes does not make sex a proscribed classification. Supposed "inherent differences" are no longer accepted as a ground for race or national origin classifications. See Loving v. Virginia, 388 U.S. 1 (1967). Physical differences between men and women, however, are enduring . . .

"Inherent differences" between men and women, we have come to appreciate, remain cause for celebration, but not for denigration of the members of either sex or for artificial constraints on an individual's opportunity. Sex classifications . . . may not be used, as they once were, . . . to create or perpetuate the legal, social, and economic inferiority of women.

Measuring the record in this case against the review standard just described, we conclude that Virginia has shown no "exceedingly persuasive justification" for excluding all women from the citizen-soldier training afforded by VMI. We therefore affirm the Fourth Circuit's initial judgment, which held that Virginia had violated the Fourteenth Amendment's Equal Protection Clause. Because the remedy proffered by Virginia—the Mary Baldwin VWIL program—does not cure the constitutional violation, i.e., it does not provide equal opportunity, we reverse the Fourth Circuit's final judgment in this case.

V

. . . Virginia . . . asserts two justifications in defense of VMI's exclusion of women. First, the Commonwealth contends, "single-sex education provides important educational benefits," and the option of single-sex education contributes to "diversity in educational approaches," Second, the Commonwealth argues, "the unique VMI method of character development and leadership training," the school's adversative approach, would have to be modified were VMI to admit women. We consider these two justifications in turn.

A

. . . [D]iversity among public educational institutions can serve the public good. But Virginia has not shown that VMI was established, or has been maintained, with a view to diversifying, by its categorical exclusion of women, educational opportunities within the State. In cases of this genre, our precedent instructs that "benign" justifications proffered in defense of categorical exclusions will not be accepted automatically; a tenable justification must describe actual state purposes, not rationalizations for actions in fact differently grounded....

Mississippi Univ. for Women is immediately in point. There the State asserted, in justification of its exclusion of men from a nursing school, that it was engaging in "educational affirmative action" by "compensat[ing] for discrimination against women." ... Undertaking a "searching analysis," ... the Court found no close resemblance between "the alleged objective" and "the actual purpose underlying the discriminatory classification," ... Pursuing a similar inquiry here, we reach the same conclusion.

Neither recent nor distant history bears out Virginia's alleged pursuit of diversity through single-sex educational options. In 1839, when the State established VMI, a range of educational opportunities for men and women was scarcely contemplated. Higher education at the time was considered dangerous for women; reflecting widely held views about women's proper place, the Nation's first universities and colleges—for example, Harvard in Massachusetts, William and Mary in Virginia— admitted only men.... VMI was not at all novel in this respect: In admitting no women, VMI followed the lead of the State's flagship school, the University of Virginia, founded in 1819.

. . .

Virginia eventually provided for several women's seminaries and colleges. Farmville Female Seminary became a public institution in 1884.... Two women's schools, Mary Washington College and James Madison University, were founded in 1908; another, Radford University, was founded in 1910. By the mid–1970's, all four schools had become coeducational.

Debate concerning women's admission as undergraduates at the main university continued well past the century's midpoint. Familiar arguments were rehearsed. If women were admitted, it was feared, they "would encroach on the rights of men; there would be new problems of government, perhaps scandals; the old honor system would have to be changed; standards would be lowered to those of other coeducational schools; and the glorious reputation of the university, as a school for men, would be trailed in the dust." ...

Ultimately, in 1970, ... the University of Virginia, introduced coeducation and, in 1972, began to admit women on an equal basis with men....

Virginia describes the current absence of public single-sex higher education for women as "an historical anomaly." But the historical record indicates action more deliberate than anomalous: First, protection of women against higher education; next, schools for women far from equal in resources and stature to schools for men; finally, conversion of the separate schools to coeducation....

. . .

In sum, we find no persuasive evidence in this record that VMI's male-only admission policy "is in furtherance of a state policy of 'diversity.'" No such policy ... can be discerned from the movement of all other public colleges and universities in Virginia away from single-sex education.... A purpose genuinely to advance an array of educational options, as the Court of Appeals recognized, is not served by VMI's historic and constant plan—a plan to "affor[d] a unique educational benefit only to males." However "liberally" this plan serves the State's sons, it makes no provision whatever for her daughters. That is not equal protection.

B

Virginia next argues that VMI's adversative method of training provides educational benefits that cannot be made available, unmodified, to women. Alterations to accommodate women would necessarily be "radical," so "drastic," Virginia asserts, as to transform, indeed "destroy," VMI's program. Neither sex would be favored by the transformation, Virginia maintains: Men would be deprived of the unique opportunity currently available to them; women would not gain that opportunity because their participation would "eliminat[e] the very aspects of [the] program that distinguish [VMI] from ... other institutions of higher education in Virginia."

... [I]t is uncontested that women's admission would require accommodations, primarily in arranging housing assignments and physical training programs for female cadets. It is also undisputed, however, that "the VMI methodology could be used to educate women." ... The parties, furthermore, agree that "some women can meet the physical standards [VMI] now impose[s] on men." ...

. . .

It may be assumed, for purposes of this decision, that most women would not choose VMI's adversative method.... [I]t is also probable that "many men would not want to be educated in such an environment." ... The issue, however, is not whether "women—or men—should be forced to attend VMI"; rather, the question is whether the State can constitutionally deny to women who have the will and capacity, the training and attendant opportunities that VMI uniquely affords.

The notion that admission of women would downgrade VMI's stature, destroy the adversative system and, with it, even the school, is a judgment hardly proved—a prediction hardly different from other "self-fulfilling prophec[ies]," ... once routinely used to deny rights or opportunities. When women first sought admission to the bar and access to legal education, concerns of the same order were expressed. For example, in 1876, the Court of Common Pleas of Hennepin County, Minnesota, explained why women were thought ineligible for the practice of law. Women train and educate the young, the court said, which "forbids that they shall bestow that time (early and late) and labor, so essential in attaining to the eminence to which the true lawyer should ever aspire. It cannot therefore be said that the opposition of courts to the admission of females to practice ... is to any extent the outgrowth of ... 'old fogyism[.]' ... [I]t arises rather from a comprehension of the magnitude of the responsibilities connected with the successful practice of law, and a desire to grade up the profession." ... A like fear, according to a 1925 report, accounted for Columbia Law School's resistance to women's admission, although "[t]he faculty ... never maintained that women could not master legal learning.... No, its argument has been ... more practical. If women were admitted to the Columbia Law School, [the faculty] said, then the choicer, more manly and red-blooded graduates of our great universities would go to the Harvard Law School!" ...

Medical faculties similarly resisted men and women as partners in the study of medicine.... More recently, women seeking careers in policing encountered resistance based on fears that their presence would "undermine male solidarity," ... deprive male partners of adequate assistance, ... and lead to sexual misconduct ...

Women's successful entry into the federal military academies, and their participation in the Nation's military forces, indicate that Virginia's fears for the future of VMI may not be solidly grounded. The State's justification for excluding all women from "citizen-soldier" training for which some are qualified, in any event, cannot rank as "exceedingly persuasive," as we have explained and applied that standard.

. . .

VI

In the second phase of the litigation, Virginia presented its remedial plan—maintain VMI as a male-only college and create VWIL as a separate program for women.... [T]he Court of Appeals concluded that Virginia had arranged for men and women opportunities "sufficiently comparable" to survive equal protection evaluation. The United States challenges this "remedial" ruling as pervasively misguided.

A

A remedial decree, this Court has said, must closely fit the constitutional violation; it must be shaped to place persons unconstitutionally denied an opportunity or advantage in "the position they would have occupied in the absence of [discrimination]." ... The constitutional violation in this case is the categorical exclusion of women from an extraordinary educational opportunity afforded men....

... Virginia was obliged to show that its remedial proposal "directly address[ed] and relate[d] to" the violation, ... i.e., the equal protection denied to women ready, willing, and able to benefit from educational opportunities of the kind VMI offers.... If the VWIL program could not "eliminate the discriminatory effects of the past," could it at least "bar like discrimination in the future"? ... A comparison of the programs said to be "parallel" informs our answer....

VWIL affords women no opportunity to experience the rigorous military training for which VMI is famed....

VWIL students receive their "leadership training" in seminars, externships, and speaker series, episodes and encounters lacking the "[p]hysical rigor, mental stress, ... minute regulation of behavior, and indoctrination in desirable values" made hallmarks of VMI's citizen-soldier training. Kept away from the pressures, hazards, and psychological bonding characteristic of VMI's adversative training, VWIL students will not know the "feeling of tremendous accomplishment" commonly experienced by VMI's successful cadets.

Virginia maintains that these methodological differences are "justified pedagogically," based on "important differences between men and women in learning and developmental needs," "psychological and sociological differences" Virginia describes as "real" and "not stereotypes." The Task Force charged with developing the leadership program for women, drawn from the staff and faculty at Mary Baldwin College, "determined that a military model and, especially VMI's adversative method, would be wholly inappropriate for educating and training most women."

... [G]eneralizations about "the way women are," estimates of what is appropriate for most women, no longer justify denying opportunity to women whose talent and capacity place them outside the average description. Notably, Virginia never asserted that VMI's method of education suits most men. . . .

In contrast to the generalizations about women on which Virginia rests, we note again these dispositive realities: VMI's "implementing methodology" is not "inherently unsuitable to women," "some women ... do well under [the] adversative model," "some women, at least, would want to attend [VMI] if they had the opportunity," "some women are capable of all of the individual activities required of VMI cadets," and "can meet the physical standards [VMI] now impose[s] on men." It is on behalf of these women that the United States has instituted this suit, and it is for them that a remedy must be crafted . . .

B

In myriad respects other than military training, VWIL does not qualify as VMI's equal. VWIL's student body, faculty, course offerings, and facilities hardly match VMI's. Nor can the VWIL graduate anticipate the benefits associated with VMI's 157–year history, the school's prestige, and its influential alumni network.

Mary Baldwin College, whose degree VWIL students will gain, enrolls first-year women with an average combined SAT score about 100 points lower than the average score for VMI freshmen. The Mary Baldwin faculty holds "significantly fewer Ph.D.'s," and receives substantially lower salaries than the faculty at VMI.

Mary Baldwin does not offer a VWIL student the range of curricular choices available to a VMI cadet. VMI awards baccalaureate degrees in liberal arts, biology, chemistry, civil engineering, electrical and computer engineering, and mechanical engineering. . . . VWIL students attend a school that "does not have a math and science focus"; they cannot take at Mary Baldwin any courses in engineering or the advanced math and physics courses VMI offers.

For physical training, Mary Baldwin has "two multi-purpose fields" and "[o]ne gymnasium." VMI has "an NCAA competition level indoor track and field facility; a number of multi-purpose fields; baseball, soccer and lacrosse fields; an obstacle course; large boxing, wrestling and martial arts facilities; an 11–laps-to-the-mile indoor running course; an indoor pool; indoor and outdoor rifle ranges; and a football stadium that also contains a practice field and outdoor track."

Although Virginia has represented that it will provide equal financial support for in-state VWIL students and VMI cadets, and the VMI Foundation has agreed to endow VWIL with $5.4625 million, the difference between the two schools' financial reserves is pronounced. Mary Baldwin's endowment, currently about $19 million, will gain an additional $35 million based on future commitments; VMI's current endowment, $131 million—the largest per-student endowment in the Nation—will gain $220 million.

The VWIL student does not graduate with the advantage of a VMI degree. Her diploma does not unite her with the legions of VMI "graduates [who] have distinguished themselves" in military and civilian life. "[VMI] alumni are exceptionally close to the school," and that closeness accounts, in part, for VMI's success in attracting applicants. A VWIL graduate cannot assume that the "network of business owners, corporations, VMI graduates and non-graduate employers ... interested in hiring VMI graduates," will be equally responsive to her search for employment.

Virginia, in sum, while maintaining VMI for men only, has failed to provide any "comparable single-gender women's institution." Instead, the Commonwealth has created a VWIL program fairly appraised as a "pale shadow" of VMI in terms of the range of curricular choices and faculty stature, funding, prestige, alumni support and influence.

Virginia's VWIL solution is reminiscent of the remedy Texas proposed 50 years ago, in response to a state trial court's 1946 ruling that, given the equal protection guarantee, African Americans could not be denied a legal education at a state facility. See Sweatt v. Painter, 339 U.S. 629 (1950). Reluctant to admit African Americans to its flagship University of Texas Law School, the State set up a separate school for Herman Sweatt and other black law students.... As originally opened, the new school had no independent faculty or library, and it lacked accreditation.... Nevertheless, the state trial and appellate courts were satisfied that the new school offered Sweatt opportunities for the study of law "substantially equivalent to those offered by the State to white students at the University of Texas." ...

Before this Court considered the case, the new school had gained "a faculty of five full-time professors; a student body of 23; a library of some 16,500 volumes serviced by a full-time staff; a practice court and legal aid association; and one alumnus who ha[d] become a member of the Texas Bar." ... This Court contrasted resources at the new school with those at the school from which Sweatt had been excluded. The University of Texas Law School had a full-time faculty of 16, a student body of

850, a library containing over 65,000 volumes, scholarship funds, a law review, and moot court facilities....

More important than the tangible features, the Court emphasized, are "those qualities which are incapable of objective measurement but which make for greatness" in a school, including "reputation of the faculty, experience of the administration, position and influence of the alumni, standing in the community, traditions and prestige." ... Facing the marked differences reported in the Sweatt opinion, the Court unanimously ruled that Texas had not shown "substantial equality in the [separate] educational opportunities" the State offered....

C

. . .

The Fourth Circuit plainly erred in exposing Virginia's VWIL plan to a deferential analysis, for "all gender-based classifications today" warrant "heightened scrutiny." ... Valuable as VWIL may prove for students who seek the program offered, Virginia's remedy affords no cure at all for the opportunities and advantages withheld from women who want a VMI education and can make the grade. In sum, Virginia's remedy does not match the constitutional violation; the State has shown no "exceedingly persuasive justification" for withholding from women qualified for the experience premier training of the kind VMI affords . . .*

CHIEF JUSTICE REHNQUIST, concurring in judgment.

... While I agree with [its] conclusions, I disagree with the Court's analysis and so I write separately.

. . .

Long after the adoption of the Fourteenth Amendment, and well into this century, legal distinctions between men and women were thought to raise no question under the Equal Protection Clause....

. . .

... In Mississippi Univ. for Women v. Hogan, 458 U.S. 718 (1982), a case actually involving a single-sex admissions policy in higher education, the Court held that the exclusion of men from a nursing program violated the Equal Protection Clause. This holding did place Virginia on notice that VMI's men-only admissions policy was open to serious question.

. . .

... [U]nlike the majority, I would consider only evidence that postdates our decision in *Hogan*, and would draw no negative inferences from the State's actions before that time. I think that after *Hogan*, the State was entitled to reconsider its policy with respect to VMI, and to not have earlier justifications, or lack thereof, held against it.

---

* Justice Thomas did not participate in the decision because his son was attending VMI.

Even if diversity in educational opportunity were the State's actual objective, the State's position would still be problematic. The difficulty with its position is that the diversity benefited only one sex; there was single-sex public education available for men at VMI, but no corresponding single-sex public education available for women.... Was there something else the State could have done to avoid an equal protection violation? Since the State did nothing, we do not have to definitively answer that question.

I do not think, however, that the State's options were as limited as the majority may imply.... VMI had been in operation for over a century and a half, and had an established, successful and devoted group of alumni. No legislative wand could instantly call into existence a similar institution for women; and it would be a tremendous loss to scrap VMI's history and tradition.... [T]he State faced a condition ... that had been brought about, not through defiance of decisions construing gender bias under the Equal Protection Clause, but, until the decision in *Hogan*, a condition which had not appeared to offend the Constitution. Had Virginia made a genuine effort to devote comparable public resources to a facility for women, and followed through on such a plan, it might well have avoided an equal protection violation. I do not believe the State was faced with the stark choice of either admitting women to VMI, on the one hand, or abandoning VMI and starting from scratch for both men and women, on the other.

But, as I have noted, neither the governing board of VMI nor the State took any action after 1982....

. . .

II

The Court defines the constitutional violation in this case as "the categorical exclusion of women from an extraordinary educational opportunity afforded to men." By defining the violation in this way, and by emphasizing that a remedy for a constitutional violation must place the victims of discrimination in " 'the position they would have occupied in the absence of [discrimination],' " the Court necessarily implies that the only adequate remedy would be the admission of women to the all-male institution. As the foregoing discussion suggests, I would not define the violation in this way; it is not the "exclusion of women" that violates the Equal Protection Clause, but the maintenance of an all-men school without providing any—much less a comparable—institution for women.

Accordingly, the remedy should not necessarily require either the admission of women to VMI, or the creation of a VMI clone for women....

. . .

In the end, the women's institution Virginia proposes, VWIL, fails as a remedy, because it is distinctly inferior to the existing men's institution and will continue to be for the foreseeable future....

JUSTICE SCALIA, dissenting.

Today the Court shuts down an institution that has served the people of the Commonwealth of Virginia with pride and distinction for over a century and a half. To achieve that desired result, it ... drastically revises our established standards for reviewing sex-based classifications. And as to history: it counts for nothing the long tradition, enduring down to the present, of men's military colleges supported by both States and the Federal Government.

Much of the Court's opinion is devoted to deprecating the closed-mindedness of our forebears with regard to women's education, and even with regard to the treatment of women in areas that have nothing to do with education. Closed-minded they were—as every age is, including our own, with regard to matters it cannot guess, because it simply does not consider them debatable. The virtue of a democratic system with a First Amendment is that it readily enables the people, over time, to be persuaded that what they took for granted is not so, and to change their laws accordingly. That system is destroyed if the smug assurances of each age are removed from the democratic process and written into the Constitution.... Today [the Court] enshrines the notion that no substantial educational value is to be served by an all-men's military academy.... Since it is entirely clear that the Constitution of the United States—the old one—takes no sides in this educational debate, I dissent.

I

... [T]he Court's ... current equal-protection jurisprudence ... regards this Court as free to evaluate everything under the sun by applying one of three tests: "rational basis" scrutiny, intermediate scrutiny, or strict scrutiny.... Strict scrutiny, we have said, is reserved for state "classifications based on race or national origin and classifications affecting fundamental rights,".... It is my position that the term "fundamental rights" should be limited to "interest[s] traditionally protected by our society," ... but the Court has not accepted that view, so that strict scrutiny will be applied to the deprivation of whatever sort of right we consider "fundamental." We have no established criterion for "intermediate scrutiny" either, but essentially apply it when it seems like a good idea to load the dice. So far it has been applied to content-neutral restrictions that place an incidental burden on speech, to disabilities attendant to illegitimacy, and to discrimination on the basis of sex....

... [I]n my view the function of this Court is to preserve our society's values ..., not to revise them.... For that reason it is my view that, whatever abstract tests we may choose to devise, they cannot supersede—and indeed ought to be crafted so as to reflect—those constant and unbroken national traditions that embody the people's understanding of ambiguous constitutional texts. More specifically, it is my view that "when a practice not expressly prohibited by the text of the Bill of Rights bears the endorsement of a long tradition of open, widespread, and unchallenged use that dates back to the beginning of the Republic, we have no proper basis for striking it down." ...

The all-male constitution of VMI comes squarely within such a governing tradition....

And the same applies, more broadly, to single-sex education in general, which, as I shall discuss, is threatened by today's decision with the cut-off of all state and federal support....

· · ·

II

To reject the Court's disposition today, however, it is not necessary to accept my view that the Court's made-up tests cannot displace longstanding national traditions.... It is only necessary to apply honestly the test the Court has been applying to sex-based classifications for the past two decades.... [W]e evaluate a statutory classification based on sex under a standard that lies "[b]etween th[e] extremes of rational basis review and strict scrutiny." ... We have denominated this standard "intermediate scrutiny" and under it have inquired whether the statutory classification is "substantially related to an important governmental objective."

... [T]he United States urged us to hold in this case "that strict scrutiny is the correct constitutional standard for evaluating classifications that deny opportunities to individuals based on their sex." ... The Court, while making no reference to the Government's argument, effectively accepts it.

Although the Court in two places recites the test as stated in *Hogan*, which asks whether the State has demonstrated "that the classification serves important governmental objectives and that the discriminatory means employed are substantially related to the achievement of those objectives," ... the Court never answers the question presented in anything resembling that form. When it engages in analysis, the Court instead prefers the phrase "exceedingly persuasive justification" from *Hogan*. The Court's nine invocations of that phrase ... would be unobjectionable if the Court acknowledged that whether a "justification" is "exceedingly persuasive" must be assessed by asking "[whether] the classification serves important governmental objectives and [whether] the discriminatory means employed are substantially related to the achievement of those objectives." Instead, however, the Court proceeds to interpret "exceedingly persuasive justification" in a fashion that contradicts the reasoning of *Hogan* and our other precedents.

· · ·

Only the amorphous "exceedingly persuasive justification" phrase, and not the standard elaboration of intermediate scrutiny, can be made to yield [the] conclusion that VMI's single-sex composition is unconstitutional because there exist several women (or, one would have to conclude under the Court's reasoning, a single woman) willing and able to undertake VMI's program....

Not content to execute a de facto abandonment of the intermediate scrutiny that has been our standard for sex-based classifications for some two decades, the Court purports to reserve the question whether, even in principle, a higher standard (i.e., strict scrutiny) should apply. "The Court has," it says, "thus far reserved most stringent judicial scrutiny for classifications based on race or national origin ...," ... and it describes our earlier cases as having done no more than decline to "equat[e] gender classifications, for all purposes, to classifications based on race or national origin". The wonderful thing about these statements is that they are not actually false.... But the statements are misleading, insofar as they suggest that we have not already categorically held strict scrutiny to be inapplicable to sex-based classifications....

... [I]f the question of the applicable standard of review for sex-based classifications were to be regarded as an appropriate subject for reconsideration, the stronger argument would be not for elevating the standard to strict scrutiny, but for reducing it to rational-basis review.... It is hard to consider women a "discrete and insular minorit[y]" unable to employ the "political processes ordinarily to be relied upon," when they constitute a majority of the electorate. And the suggestion that they are incapable of exerting that political power smacks of the same paternalism that the Court so roundly condemns....

· · ·

IV

As is frequently true, the Court's decision today will have consequences that extend far beyond the parties to the case. What I take to be the Court's unease with these consequences, and its resulting unwillingness to acknowledge them, cannot alter the reality.

A

· · ·

... [T]he Court's rationale ... ensures that single-sex public education is functionally dead. The costs of litigating the constitutionality of a single-sex education program, and the risks of ultimately losing that litigation, are simply too high to be embraced by public officials....

This is especially regrettable.... Until quite recently, some public officials have attempted to institute new single-sex programs, at least as experiments. In 1991, for example, the Detroit Board of Education announced a program to establish three boys-only schools for inner-city youth; it was met with a lawsuit, a preliminary injunction was swiftly entered by a District Court that purported to rely on Hogan, see Garrett v. Board of Education of School Dist. of Detroit, 775 F.Supp. 1004, 1006 (E.D.Mich.1991), and the Detroit Board of Education voted to abandon the litigation and thus abandon the plan.... Today's opinion assures that no such experiment will be tried again.

B

There are few extant single-sex public educational programs. The potential of today's decision for widespread disruption of existing institutions lies in its application to private single-sex education. Government support is immensely important to private educational institutions ..... Charitable status under the tax laws is also highly significant for private educational institutions, and it is certainly not beyond the Court that rendered today's decision to hold that a donation to a single-sex college should be deemed contrary to public policy and therefore not deductible if the college discriminates on the basis of sex. See ... Bob Jones Univ. v. United States, 461 U.S. 574 (1983).

... The Government, in its briefs to this Court, ... contends that private colleges which are the direct or indirect beneficiaries of government funding are not thereby necessarily converted into state actors to which the Equal Protection Clause is then applicable ... (discussing Rendell–Baker v. Kohn, 457 U.S. 830 (1982), and Blum v. Yaretsky, 457 U.S. 991 (1982)). That is true. It is also virtually meaningless.

The issue will be not whether government assistance turns private colleges into state actors, but whether the government itself would be violating the Constitution by providing state support to single-sex colleges. For example, in Norwood v. Harrison, 413 U.S. 455 (1973), we saw no room to distinguish between state operation of racially segregated schools and state support of privately run segregated schools....

The only hope for state-assisted single-sex private schools is that the Court will not apply in the future the principles of law it has applied today.... It will certainly be possible for this Court to write a future opinion that ignores the broad principles of law set forth today, and that characterizes as utterly dispositive the opinion's perceptions that VMI was a uniquely prestigious all-male institution, conceived in chauvinism, etc., etc. I will not join that opinion.

. . .

NOTES AND QUESTIONS

1. The immediate impact of this decision was limited. The only single-sex *public* institutions of higher learning were VMI in Virginia and the Citadel in South Carolina. There are, however, a number of single-sex *private* colleges. Does the decision raise serious questions, as Justice Scalia suggests, about their legality?

2. As previously indicated, the commands of the Fourteenth Amendment are addressed to government, and not private actors. Federal civil rights laws dealing with racial discrimination apply the same constraints to state educational institutions that receive federal funds. Thus, a decision by the Supreme Court that a state university's program of racial affirmative action admissions violates the Constitution would also mean that an identical program by private universities would violate federal law. Title IX of the Education Amendments of 1972 prohibits gender discrimination by education programs receiving federal funds. It exempts admissions policies, however, of institutions "that traditionally and continually from [their] establishment [have] had a policy of admitting only students of one sex." It is for this reason that the VMI litigation focused not on violation of Title IX but on the constitutional command. The exemption also means that private single-sex colleges do not violate Title IX because they receive federal funds and limit admission to members of one sex.

3. The Supreme Court has settled the proposition that private educational institutions are not subject to constitutional limitations merely because they receive substantial public funding. Thus, teachers

discharged from a public school are entitled to fair hearings under the Fourteenth Amendment's Due Process Clause. Private school teachers were not guaranteed procedural due process when they were discharged, even though their school received 90 to 99% of its funds from the city and state. Rendell–Baker v. Kohn, 457 U.S. 830 (1982). As Justice Scalia notes, however, the issue becomes more difficult if one treats gender discrimination as being identical to racial discrimination. In Norwood v. Harrison, 413 U.S. 455 (1973), a state violated the Constitution by furnishing textbooks to private schools that practiced racial discrimination in admission. If state and federal governments would violate the Constitution by financial support to single-race private schools, would they also violate the Constitution by financing single-sex private schools? Does that turn on whether Justice Scalia is correct that the Court is really following the constitutional standard used in racial discrimination cases?

4. Finally, if one is comparing the race and gender cases, is Justice Rehnquist right that separate public education for men and women would be constitutional if, although separate, the education provided was more nearly equal? Would the Court's opinion invalidate the Detroit public school program described in Justice Scalia's dissent?

NGUYEN v. IMMIGRATION AND NATURALIZATION SERVICE

Supreme Court of the United States, 2001.
533 U.S. 53, 121 S.Ct. 2053, 150 L.Ed.2d 115.

JUSTICE KENNEDY delivered the opinion of the Court.

... Title 8 U.S.C. § 1409 governs the acquisition of United States citizenship by persons born to one United States citizen parent and one noncitizen parent when the parents are unmarried and the child is born outside of the United States or its possessions. The statute imposes different requirements for the child's acquisition of citizenship depending upon whether the citizen parent is the mother or the father. The question before us is whether the statutory distinction is consistent with the equal protection guarantee embedded in the Due Process Clause of the Fifth Amendment.

I

Petitioner Tuan Ahn Nguyen was born in Saigon, Vietnam, on September 11, 1969, to copetitioner Joseph Boulais and a Vietnamese citizen. Boulais and Nguyen's mother were not married. Boulais always has been a citizen of the United States, and he was in Vietnam under the employ of a corporation. After he and Nguyen's mother ended their relationship, Nguyen lived for a time with the family of Boulais' new Vietnamese girlfriend. In June 1975, Nguyen, then almost six years of age, came to the United States. He became a lawful permanent resident and was raised in Texas by Boulais.

In 1992, when Nguyen was 22, he pleaded guilty in a Texas state court to two counts of sexual assault on a child. He was sentenced to eight years in prison on each count. Three years later, the United States Immigration and Naturalization Service (INS) initiated deportation proceedings against Nguyen as an alien who had been convicted of two crimes involving moral turpitude, as well as an aggravated felony.... Though later he would change his position and argue he was a United States citizen, Nguyen testified at his deportation hearing that he was a citizen of Vietnam. The Immigration Judge found him deportable.

Nguyen appealed to the Board of Immigration of Appeals, ... [which] dismissed [his] appeal, rejecting his claim to United States citizenship because he had failed to establish compliance with 8 U.S.C. § 1409(a), which sets forth the requirements for one who was born out of wedlock and abroad to a citizen father and a noncitizen mother.

Nguyen ... [then] appealed to the Court of Appeals for the Fifth Circuit, arguing that § 1409 violates equal protection by providing different rules for attainment of citizenship by children born abroad and out of wedlock depending upon whether the one parent with American citizenship is the mother or the father. The court rejected the constitutional challenge to § 1409(a)....

II

The general requirement for acquisition of citizenship by a child born outside the United States and its outlying possessions and to parents who are married, one of whom is a citizen and the other of whom is an alien, is set forth in 8 U.S.C. § 1401(g). The statute provides that the child is also a citizen if, before the birth, the citizen parent had been physically present in the United States for a total of five years, at least two of which were after the parent turned 14 years of age.

As to an individual born under the same circumstances, save that the parents are unwed, § 1409(a) sets forth the following requirements where the father is the citizen parent and the mother is an alien:

"(1) a blood relationship between the person and the father is established by clear and convincing evidence,

"(2) the father had the nationality of the United States at the time of the person's birth,

"(3) the father (unless deceased) has agreed in writing to provide financial support for the person until the person reaches the age of 18 years, and

"(4) while the person is under the age of 18 years—

"(A) the person is legitimated under the law of the person's residence or domicile,

"(B) the father acknowledges paternity of the person in writing under oath, or

"(C) the paternity of the person is established by adjudication of a competent court."

In addition, § 1409(a) incorporates by reference, as to the citizen parent, the residency requirement of § 1401(g).

When the citizen parent of the child born abroad and out of wedlock is the child's mother, the requirements for the transmittal of citizenship are described in § 1409(c):

"(c) Notwithstanding the provision of subsection (a) of this section, a person born, after December 23, 1952, outside the United States and out of wedlock shall be held to have acquired at birth the nationality status of his mother, if the mother had the nationality of the United States at the time of such person's birth, and if the mother had previously been physically present in the United States or one of its outlying possessions for a continuous period of one year."

Section 1409(a) thus imposes a set of requirements on the children of citizen fathers born abroad and out of wedlock to a noncitizen mother that are not imposed under like circumstances when the citizen parent is the mother. All concede the requirements of §§ 1409(a)(3) and (a)(4), relating to a citizen father's acknowledgment of a child while he is under 18, were not satisfied in this case.

III

For a gender-based classification to withstand equal protection scrutiny, it must be established " 'at least that the [challenged] classification serves important governmental objectives and that the discriminatory means employed' are 'substantially related to the achievement of those objectives.' " *United States v. Virginia,* 518 U.S. 515, 533 (1996) (quoting *Mississippi Univ. for Women v. Hogan,* 458 U.S. 718, 724 (1982) in turn quoting *Wengler v. Druggists Mut. Ins. Co.,* 446 U.S. 142, 150 (1980)). For reasons to follow, we conclude § 1409 satisfies this standard....

A

The first governmental interest to be served is the importance of assuring that a biological parent-child relationship exists. In the case of the mother, the relation is verifiable from the birth itself. The mother's status is documented in most instances by the birth certificate or hospital records and the witnesses who attest to her having given birth.

In the case of the father, the uncontestable fact is that he need not be present at the birth. If he is present, furthermore, that circumstance is not incontrovertible proof of fatherhood.... Fathers and mothers are not similarly situated with regard to the proof of biological parenthood. The imposition of a different set of rules for making that legal determination with respect to fathers and mothers is neither surprising nor troublesome from a constitutional perspective.... Section 1409(a)(4)'s provision of three options for a father seeking to establish paternity— legitimation, paternity oath, and court order of paternity—is designed to ensure an acceptable documentation of paternity.

... The requirement of § 1409(a)(4) represents a reasonable conclusion by the legislature that the satisfaction of one of several alternatives will suffice to establish the blood link between father and child required as a predicate to the child's acquisition of citizenship.... Given the proof of motherhood that is inherent in birth itself, it is unremarkable that Congress did not require the same affirmative steps of mothers.

Finally, to require Congress to speak without reference to the gender of the parent with regard to its objective of ensuring a blood tie between parent and child would be to insist on a hollow neutrality....

Congress could have required both mothers and fathers to prove parenthood within 30 days or, for that matter, 18 years, of the child's birth. . . . Given that the mother is always present at birth, but that the father need not be, the facially neutral rule would sometimes require fathers to take additional affirmative steps which would not be required of mothers, whose names will appear on the birth certificate as a result of their presence at the birth, and who will have the benefit of witnesses to the birth to call upon. The issue is not the use of gender specific terms instead of neutral ones. Just as neutral terms can mask discrimination that is unlawful, gender specific terms can mark a permissible distinction. The equal protection question is whether the distinction is lawful. Here, the use of gender specific terms takes into account a biological difference between the parents. The differential treatment is inherent in a sensible statutory scheme, given the unique relationship of the mother to the event of birth.

B

1

The second important governmental interest furthered in a substantial manner by § 1409(a)(4) is the determination to ensure that the child and the citizen parent have some demonstrated opportunity or potential to develop not just a relationship that is recognized, as a formal matter, by the law, but one that consists of the real, everyday ties that provide a connection between child and citizen parent and, in turn, the United States. . . . In the case of a citizen mother and a child born overseas, the opportunity for a meaningful relationship between citizen parent and child inheres in the very event of birth, an event so often critical to our constitutional and statutory understandings of citizenship. The mother knows that the child is in being and is hers and has an initial point of contact with him. There is at least an opportunity for mother and child to develop a real, meaningful relationship.

The same opportunity does not result from the event of birth, as a matter of biological inevitability, in the case of the unwed father. Given the 9–month interval between conception and birth, it is not always certain that a father will know that a child was conceived, nor is it always clear that even the mother will be sure of the father's identity. This fact takes on particular significance in the case of a child born overseas and out of wedlock. One concern in this context has always been with young people, men for the most part, who are on duty with the Armed Forces in foreign countries. . . .

When we turn to the conditions which prevail today, we find that the passage of time has produced additional and even more substantial grounds to justify the statutory distinction. The ease of travel and the willingness of Americans to visit foreign countries have resulted in numbers of trips abroad that must be of real concern when we contemplate the prospect of accepting petitioners' argument, which would mandate, contrary to Congress' wishes, citizenship by male parentage subject to no condition save the father's previous length of residence in this country. . . .

Principles of equal protection do not require Congress to ignore this reality. To the contrary, these facts demonstrate the critical importance of the Government's interest in ensuring some opportunity for a tie between citizen father and foreign born child which is a reasonable substitute for the opportunity manifest between mother and child at the time of birth. Indeed, especially in light of the number of Americans who take short sojourns abroad, the prospect that a father might not even know of the conception is a realistic possibility.... Even if a father knows of the fact of conception, moreover, it does not follow that he will be present at the birth of the child. Thus, unlike the case of the mother, there is no assurance that the father and his biological child will ever meet. Without an initial point of contact with the child by a father who knows the child is his own, there is no opportunity for father and child to begin a relationship. Section 1409 takes the unremarkable step of ensuring that such an opportunity, inherent in the event of birth as to the mother-child relationship, exists between father and child before citizenship is conferred upon the latter.

. . .

Petitioners and their *amici* argue in addition that, rather than fulfilling an important governmental interest, § 1409 merely embodies a gender-based stereotype. Although the above discussion should illustrate that, contrary to petitioners' assertions, § 1409 addresses an undeniable difference in the circumstance of the parents at the time a child is born, it should be noted, furthermore, that the difference does not result from some stereotype, defined as a frame of mind resulting from irrational or uncritical analysis. There is nothing irrational or improper in the recognition that at the moment of birth—a critical event in the statutory scheme and in the whole tradition of citizenship law—the mother's knowledge of the child and the fact of parenthood have been established in a way not guaranteed in the case of the unwed father. This is not a stereotype....

2

Having concluded that facilitation of a relationship between parent and child is an important governmental interest, the question remains whether the means Congress chose to further its objective—the imposition of certain additional requirements upon an unwed father—substantially relate to that end. Under this test, the means Congress adopted must be sustained.

First, it should be unsurprising that Congress decided to require that an opportunity for a parent-child relationship occur during the formative years of the child's minority. In furtherance of the desire to ensure some tie between this country and one who seeks citizenship, various other statutory provisions concerning citizenship and naturalization require some act linking the child to the United States to occur before the child reaches 18 years of age....

Second, petitioners argue that § 1409(a)(4) is not effective. In particular, petitioners assert that, although a mother will know of her child's birth, "knowledge that one is a parent, no matter how it is acquired, does not guarantee a relationship with one's child." ... They thus maintain that the imposition of the additional requirements of § 1409(a)(4) only on the children of citizen fathers must reflect a stereotype that women are more likely than men to actually establish a relationship with their children....

This line of argument misconceives the nature of both the governmental interest at issue and the manner in which we examine statutes alleged to violate equal protection. As to the former, Congress would of course be entitled to advance the interest of ensuring an actual, meaningful relationship in every case before citizenship is conferred. Or Congress could excuse compliance with the formal requirements when an actual father-child relationship is proved. It did neither here, perhaps because of the subjectivity, intrusiveness, and difficulties of proof that might attend an inquiry into any particular bond or tie. Instead, Congress enacted an easily administered scheme to promote the different but still substantial interest of ensuring at least an opportunity for a parent-child relationship to develop. Petitioners' argument confuses the means and ends of the equal protection inquiry; § 1409(a)(4) should not be invalidated because Congress elected to advance an interest that is less demanding to satisfy than some other alternative.

Even if one conceives of the interest Congress pursues as the establishment of a real, practical relationship of considerable substance between parent and child in every case, as opposed simply to ensuring the potential for the relationship to begin, petitioners' misconception of the nature of the equal protection inquiry is fatal to their argument. A statute meets the equal protection standard we here apply so long as it is "substantially related to the achievement of" the governmental objective in question. *Virginia, supra,* at 533 (quoting *Hogan,* 458 U.S., at 724 (in turn quoting *Wengler,* 446 U.S., at 150)). It is almost axiomatic that a policy which seeks to foster the opportunity for meaningful parent-child bonds to develop has a close and substantial bearing on the governmental interest in the actual formation of that bond. None of our gender-based classification equal protection cases have required that the statute under consideration must be capable of achieving its ultimate objective in every instance.

In this difficult context of conferring citizenship on vast numbers of persons, the means adopted by Congress are in substantial furtherance of important governmental objectives. The fit between the means and the important end is "exceedingly persuasive." See *Virginia,* 518 U.S., at 533. We have explained that an "exceedingly persuasive justification" is established "by showing at least that the classification serves 'important governmental objectives and that the discriminatory means employed' are 'substantially related to the achievement of those objectives.'" *Hogan, supra,* at 724 (citations omitted). Section 1409 meets this standard.

. . .

To fail to acknowledge even our most basic biological differences— such as the fact that a mother must be present at birth but the father need not be—risks making the guarantee of equal protection superficial, and so disserving it. Mechanistic classification of all our differences as stereotypes would operate to obscure those misconceptions and prejudices that are real. The distinction embodied in the statutory scheme here at issue is not marked by misconception and prejudice, nor does it show disrespect for either class. The difference between men and women in relation to the birth process is a real one, and the principle of equal protection does not forbid Congress to address the problem at hand in a manner specific to each gender.

The judgment of the Court of Appeals is

Affirmed.

A concurring opinion by Justice Scalia, with whom Justice Thomas joined, is omitted.

JUSTICE O'CONNOR, with whom JUSTICE SOUTER, JUSTICE GINSBURG, and JUSTICE BREYER join, dissenting.

In a long line of cases spanning nearly three decades, this Court has applied heightened scrutiny to legislative classifications based on sex. The Court today confronts another statute that classifies individuals on the basis of their sex. While the Court invokes heightened scrutiny, the manner in which it explains and applies this standard is a stranger to our precedents. Because the Immigration and Naturalization Service (INS) has not shown an exceedingly persuasive justification for the sex-based classification embodied in 8 U.S.C. § 1409(a)(4)—*i.e.,* because it has failed to establish at least that the classification substantially relates to the achievement of important governmental objectives—I would reverse the judgment of the Court of Appeals.

I

Sex-based statutes, even when accurately reflecting the way most men or women behave, deny individuals opportunity. Such generalizations must be viewed not in isolation, but in the context of our Nation's "long and unfortunate history of sex discrimination." *J. E. B. v. Alabama ex rel. T. B.,* 511 U.S. 127, 136 (1994) (quoting *Frontiero v. Richardson,* 411 U.S. 677, 684 (1973) (plurality opinion)). Sex-based generalizations both reflect and reinforce "fixed notions concerning the roles and abilities of males and females." *Mississippi Univ. for Women v. Hogan,* 458 U.S. 718, 725 (1982).

For these reasons, a party who seeks to defend a statute that classifies individuals on the basis of sex "must carry the burden of showing an 'exceedingly persuasive justification' for the classification." *Id.,* at 724 (quoting *Kirchberg v. Feenstra,* 450 U.S. 455, 461 (1981)); see also *United States v. Virginia,* 518 U.S. 515, 531 (1996). The defender of the classification meets this burden "only by showing at least that the classification serves 'important governmental objectives and that the discriminatory means employed' are 'substantially related to the achievement of those objectives.'" *Mississippi Univ. for Women, supra,* at 724 (quoting *Wengler v. Druggists Mut. Ins. Co.,* 446 U.S. 142, 150 (1980)); see also *Virginia, supra,* at 533.

Our cases provide significant guidance concerning the meaning of this standard and how a reviewing court is to apply it. This Court's instruction concerning the application of heightened scrutiny to sex-based classifications stands in stark contrast to our elucidation of the rudiments of rational basis review. To begin with, under heightened scrutiny, "[t]he burden of justification is demanding and it rests entirely on [the party defending the classification]." *Virginia, supra,* at 533. Under rational basis scrutiny, by contrast, the defender of the classification "has no obligation to produce evidence to sustain the rationality of a statutory classification." *Heller v. Doe,* 509 U.S. 312, 320 (1993). Instead, "[t]he burden is on the one attacking the legislative arrangement to negative every conceivable basis which might support it, whether or not the basis has a foundation in the record." *Id.,* at 320–321. . . .

Further, a justification that sustains a sex-based classification "must be genuine, not hypothesized or invented *post hoc* in response to litigation." *Virginia, supra,* at 533. "[T]he mere recitation of a benign, compensatory purpose is not an automatic shield which protects against any inquiry into the actual purposes underlying a statutory scheme." *Weinberger v. Wiesenfeld,* 420 U.S. 636, 648 (1975). Under rational basis review, by contrast, it is "constitutionally irrelevant [what] reasoning in fact underlay the legislative decision." *Railroad Retirement Bd. v. Fritz,* 449 U.S. 166, 179 (1980) (quoting *Flemming v. Nestor,* 363 U.S. 603, 612 (1960)).

Heightened scrutiny does not countenance justifications that "rely on overbroad generalizations about the different talents, capacities, or preferences of males and females." *Virginia, supra,* at 533. Rational basis review, by contrast, is much more tolerant of the use of broad generalizations about different classes of individuals, so long as the classification is not arbitrary or irrational. . . .

Moreover, overbroad sex-based generalizations are impermissible even when they enjoy empirical support. . . . Under rational basis scrutiny, however, empirical support is not even necessary to sustain a classification. . . .

The different burdens imposed by these equal protection standards correspond to the different duties of a reviewing court in applying each standard. The court's task in applying heightened scrutiny to a sex-based classification is clear: "Focusing on the differential treatment or denial of opportunity for which relief is sought, the reviewing court must determine whether the proffered justification is 'exceedingly persuasive.'" *Virginia,* 518 U.S., at 532–533. In making this determination, the court must inquire into the actual purposes of the discrimination, for "a tenable justification must describe actual state purposes, not rationalizations for actions in fact differently grounded." *Id.,* at 535–536; see also *id.,* at 533; *Wiesenfeld, supra,* at 648; *Califano v. Goldfarb,* 430 U.S. 199, 212–217 (1977) (plurality opinion); *id.,* at 219–221 (Stevens, J., concurring in judgment). The rational basis standard, on the other hand, instructs that "a classification 'must be upheld against equal protection challenge if there is any reasonably conceivable state of facts that could provide a rational basis for the classification.'" *Heller, supra,* at 320. . . .

This standard permits a court to hypothesize interests that might support legislative distinctions, whereas heightened scrutiny limits the realm of justification to demonstrable reality.

These different standards of equal protection review also set different bars for the magnitude of the governmental interest that justifies the statutory classification. Heightened scrutiny demands that the governmental interest served by the classification be "important," ... whereas rational basis scrutiny requires only that the end be "legitimate." ...

The most important difference between heightened scrutiny and rational basis review, of course, is the required fit between the means employed and the ends served. Under heightened scrutiny, the discriminatory means must be "substantially related" to an actual and important governmental interest. See, e.g., *Virginia, supra,* at 533. Under rational basis scrutiny, the means need only be "rationally related" to a conceivable and legitimate state end....

The fact that other means are better suited to the achievement of governmental ends therefore is of no moment under rational basis review.... But because we require a much tighter fit between means and ends under heightened scrutiny, the availability of sex-neutral alternatives to a sex-based classification is often highly probative of the validity of the classification....

II

The Court recites the governing substantive standard for heightened scrutiny of sex-based classifications, ... but departs from the guidance of our precedents concerning such classifications in several ways. In the first sentence of its equal protection analysis, the majority glosses over the crucial matter of the burden of justification.... In other circumstances, the Court's use of an impersonal construction might represent a mere elision of what we have stated expressly in our prior cases. Here, however, the elision presages some of the larger failings of the opinion.

For example, the majority hypothesizes about the interests served by the statute and fails adequately to inquire into the actual purposes of § 1409(a)(4). The Court also does not always explain adequately the importance of the interests that it claims to be served by the provision. The majority also fails carefully to consider whether the sex-based classification is being used impermissibly "as a 'proxy for other, more germane bases of classification,'" *Mississippi Univ. for Women,* 458 U.S., at 726 (quoting *Craig [v. Boren]*), 429 U.S. 199, 198 [(1976)], and instead casually dismisses the relevance of available sex-neutral alternatives. And, contrary to the majority's conclusion, the fit between the means and ends of § 1409(a)(4) is far too attenuated for the provision to survive heightened scrutiny. In all, the majority opinion represents far less than the rigorous application of heightened scrutiny that our precedents require.

A

According to the Court, "[t]he first governmental interest to be served is the importance of assuring that a biological parent-child relationship exists." ... The majority does not elaborate on the importance of this interest, which presumably lies in preventing fraudulent conveyances of citizenship. Nor does the majority demonstrate that this is one of the actual purposes of § 1409(a)(4)....

The gravest defect in the Court's reliance on this interest, however, is the insufficiency of the fit between § 1409(a)(4)'s discriminatory means and the asserted end. Section 1409(c) imposes no particular burden of proof on mothers wishing to convey citizenship to their children. By contrast, § 1409(a)(1), which petitioners do not challenge before this Court, requires that "a blood relationship between the person and the father [be] established by clear and convincing evidence." ...

It is also difficult to see how § 1409(a)(4)'s limitation of the time allowed for obtaining proof of paternity substantially furthers the assurance of a blood relationship. Modern DNA testing, in addition to providing accuracy unmatched by other methods of establishing a biological link, essentially negates the evidentiary significance of the passage of time. Moreover, the application of § 1409(a)(1)'s "clear and convincing evidence" requirement can account for any effect that the passage of time has on the quality of the evidence.

In our prior cases, the existence of comparable or superior sex-neutral alternatives has been a powerful reason to reject a sex-based classification.... The majority, however, turns this principle on its head by denigrating as "hollow" the very neutrality that the law requires.... While the majority trumpets the availability of superior sex-neutral alternatives as confirmation of § 1409(a)(4)'s validity, our precedents demonstrate that this fact is a decided strike *against* the law. Far from being "hollow," the avoidance of gratuitous sex-based distinctions is the hallmark of equal protection....

The majority's acknowledgment of the availability of sex-neutral alternatives scarcely confirms the point that "[t]he differential treatment is inherent in a sensible statutory scheme." ... The discussion instead demonstrates that, at most, differential *impact* will result from the fact that "[f]athers and mothers are not similarly situated with regard to the proof of biological parenthood." ... In other words, it will likely be easier for mothers to satisfy a sex-neutral proof of parentage requirement. But facially neutral laws that have a disparate impact are a different animal for purposes of constitutional analysis than laws that specifically provide for disparate treatment. We have long held that the differential impact of a facially neutral law does not trigger heightened scrutiny, see, e.g., *Washington v. Davis*, 426 U.S. 229 (1976), whereas we apply heightened scrutiny to laws that facially classify individuals on the basis of their sex....

If rational basis scrutiny were appropriate in this case, then the claim that "[t]he Constitution ... does not require that Congress elect one particular mechanism from among many possible methods of establishing paternity," ... would have much greater force. So too would the claim that "[t]he requirement of § 1409(a)(4) represents a reasonable conclusion...." But fidelity to the Constitution's pledge of equal protection demands more when a facially sex-based classification is at issue.

This is not because we sit in judgment of the wisdom of laws in one instance but not the other, ... but rather because of the potential for "injury ... to personal dignity" J. E. B., *supra,* at 153 (Kennedy, J., concurring in judgment), that inheres in or accompanies so many sex-based classifications.

B

The Court states that "[t]he second important governmental interest furthered in a substantial manner by § 1409(a)(4) is the determination to ensure that the child and the citizen parent have some demonstrated opportunity or potential to develop not just a relationship that is recognized, as a formal matter, by the law, but one that consists of the real, everyday ties that provide a connection between child and citizen parent and, in turn, the United States." ... The Court again fails to demonstrate that this was Congress' actual purpose in enacting § 1409(a)(4). The majority's focus on "some demonstrated opportunity or potential to develop ... real, everyday ties," in fact appears to be the type of hypothesized rationale that is insufficient under heightened scrutiny. . . .

The majority later ratchets up the interest, for the sake of argument, to "the establishment of a real, practical relationship of considerable substance between parent and child in every case, as opposed simply to ensuring the potential for the relationship to begin." ... But the majority then dismisses the distinction between opportunity and reality as immaterial to the inquiry in this case. . . . The majority rests its analysis of the means-end fit largely on the following proposition: "It is almost axiomatic that a policy which seeks to foster the opportunity for meaningful parent-child bonds to develop has a close and substantial bearing on the governmental interest in the actual formation of that bond." ... A bare assertion of what is allegedly "almost axiomatic," however, is no substitute for the "demanding" burden of justification borne by the defender of the classification. *Virginia, supra,* at 533.

Moreover, the Court's reasoning hardly conforms to the tailoring requirement of heightened scrutiny. The fact that a discriminatory policy embodies the good intention of "seek[ing] to foster" the opportunity for something beneficial to happen is of little relevance in itself to whether the policy substantially furthers the desired occurrence. Whether the classification indeed "has a close and substantial bearing" on the actual occurrence of the preferred result depends on facts and circumstances and must be proved by the classification's defender. Far from being a virtual axiom, the relationship between the intent to foster an opportunity and the fruition of the desired effect is merely a contingent proposition. The majority's sweeping claim is no surrogate for the careful application of heightened scrutiny to a particular classification.

The question that then remains is the sufficiency of the fit between § 1409(a)(4)'s discriminatory means and the goal of "establish[ing] ... a real, practical relationship of considerable substance." ... If Congress wishes to advance this end, it could easily do so by employing a sex-neutral classification that is a far "more germane bas[i]s of classification" than sex, *Craig,* 429 U. S., at 198. For example, Congress could require some degree of regular contact between the child and the citizen parent over a period of time. . . .

The majority again raises this possibility of the use of sex-neutral means only to dismiss it as irrelevant. The Court admits that "Congress could excuse compliance with the formal requirements when an actual father-child relationship is proved," but speculates that Congress did not do so "perhaps because of the subjectivity, intrusiveness, and difficulties of proof that might attend an inquiry into any particular bond or tie." . . . We have repeatedly rejected efforts to justify sex-based classifications on the ground of administrative convenience. See, e.g., *Wengler,* 446 U.S., at 152; *Frontiero,* 411 U.S., at 690–691. There is no reason to think that this is a case where administrative convenience concerns are so powerful that they would justify the sex-based discrimination, cf. *Wengler, supra,* at 152, especially where the use of sex as a proxy is so ill fit to the purported ends as it is here. And to the extent Congress might seek simply to ensure an "opportunity" for a relationship, little administrative inconvenience would seem to accompany a sex-neutral requirement of presence at birth, knowledge of birth, or contact between parent and child prior to a certain age.

The claim that § 1409(a)(4) substantially relates to the achievement of the goal of a "real, practical relationship" thus finds support not in biological differences but instead in a stereotype—*i.e.,* "the generalization that mothers are significantly more likely than fathers . . . to develop caring relationships with their children." *Miller, supra,* at 482–483 (Breyer, J., dissenting). Such a claim relies on "the very stereotype the law condemns," *J. E. B.,* 511 U.S., at 138 . . . , "lends credibility" to the generalization, *Mississippi Univ. for Women,* 458 U.S., at 730, and helps to convert that "assumption" into "a self-fulfilling prophecy," *ibid.* . . . Indeed, contrary to this stereotype, Boulais has reared Nguyen, while Nguyen apparently has lacked a relationship with his mother.

The majority apparently tries to avoid reliance on this stereotype by characterizing the governmental interest as a "demonstrated opportunity" for a relationship and attempting to close the gap between opportunity and reality with a dubious claim about what is "almost axiomatic." But the fact that one route is wisely forgone does not mean that the other is plausibly taken. The inescapable conclusion instead is that § 1409(a)(4) lacks an exceedingly persuasive justification.

In denying petitioner's claim that § 1409(a)(4) rests on stereotypes, the majority articulates a misshapen notion of "stereotype" and its significance in our equal protection jurisprudence. The majority asserts that a "stereotype" is "defined as a frame of mind resulting from irrational or uncritical analysis." . . . This Court has long recognized, however, that an impermissible stereotype may enjoy empirical support and thus be in a sense "rational." . . . Indeed, the stereotypes that underlie a sex-based classification "may hold true for many, even most, individuals." *Miller* [v. *Albright*], 523 U.S. [420], 460 [(1998)] (Ginsburg, J., dissenting). But in numerous cases where a measure of truth has inhered in the generalization, "the Court has rejected official actions that classify unnecessarily and overbroadly by gender when more accurate and impartial functional lines can be drawn." *Ibid.*

Nor do stereotypes consist only of those overbroad generalizations that the reviewing court considers to "show disrespect" for a class.... The hallmark of a stereotypical sex-based classification under this Court's precedents is not whether the classification is insulting, but whether it "relie[s] upon the simplistic, outdated assumption that gender could be used as a 'proxy for other, more germane bases of classification.'" *Mississippi Univ. for Women, supra,* at 726 (quoting *Craig, supra,* at 198).

It is also important to note that, while our explanations of many decisions invalidating sex-based classifications have pointed to the problems of "stereotypes" and "overbroad generalizations," these explanations certainly do not mean that the burden is on the challenger of the classification to prove legislative reliance on such generalizations. Indeed, an arbitrary distinction between the sexes may rely on no identifiable generalization at all but may simply be a denial of opportunity out of pure caprice. Such a distinction, of course, would nonetheless be a classic equal protection violation. The burden of proving that use of a sex-based classification substantially relates to the achievement of an important governmental interest remains unmistakably and entirely with the classification's defender. See, e.g., *Virginia,* 518 U.S., at 532–533.

· · ·

No one should mistake the majority's analysis for a careful application of this Court's equal protection jurisprudence concerning sex-based classifications. Today's decision instead represents a deviation from a line of cases in which we have vigilantly applied heightened scrutiny to such classifications to determine whether a constitutional violation has occurred. I trust that the depth and vitality of these precedents will ensure that today's error remains an aberration. I respectfully dissent.

C.   GENDER DISTINCTIONS DISADVANTAGING MALES

KAHN v. SHEVIN

Supreme Court of the United States, 1974.
416 U.S. 351, 94 S.Ct. 1734, 40 L.Ed.2d 189.

[Florida had provided tax exemptions for widows since 1885. Kahn, a widower, applied for the current $500 property tax exemption. When his application was denied, he sought a court decision that the law was unconstitutional because it did not treat widows and widowers alike. The Florida Supreme Court decided that the law was valid because there was a "disparity between the economic capabilities of a man and a woman." The United States Supreme Court agreed.]

Justice Douglas delivered the opinion of the Court.

· · ·

There can be no dispute that the financial difficulties confronting the lone woman in Florida or in any other State exceed those facing the man. Whether from overt discrimination or from the socialization process of a male-dominated culture, the job market is inhospitable to the woman seeking any but the lowest paid jobs.... [I]n 1972 a woman working full time had a median income which was only 57.9% of the median for males—a figure actually six points lower than had been achieved in 1955.... The disparity is likely to be exacerbated for the widow. While the widower can usually continue in the occupation which preceded his spouse's death, in many cases the widow will find herself suddenly forced into a job market with which she is unfamiliar, and in which, because of her former economic dependency, she will have fewer skills to offer.

There can be no doubt, therefore, that Florida's differing treatment of widows and widowers " 'rest[s] upon some ground of difference having a fair and substantial relation to the object of the legislation.' " Reed v. Reed.

This is not a case like Frontiero v. Richardson, where the Government denied its female employees both substantive and procedural benefits granted males "*solely* ... for administrative convenience."[1] We deal here with a state tax law reasonably designed to further the state policy of cushioning the financial impact of spousal loss upon the sex for which that loss imposes a disproportionately heavy burden....

JUSTICE BRENNAN, with whom JUSTICE MARSHALL joins, dissenting.

... In my view, ... a legislative classification that distinguishes potential beneficiaries solely by reference to their gender-based status as widows or widowers, like classifications based upon race, alienage, and national origin, must be subjected to close judicial scrutiny, because it focuses upon generally immutable characteristics over which individuals have little or no control, and also because gender-based classifications too often have been inexcusably utilized to stereotype and stigmatize politically powerless segments of society. See Frontiero v. Richardson. The Court is not, therefore, free to sustain the statute on the ground that it rationally promotes legitimate governmental interests; rather, such suspect classifications can be sustained only when the State bears the burden of demonstrating that the challenged legislation serves overriding or compelling interests that cannot be achieved either by a more carefully tailored legislative classification or by the use of feasible, less drastic means. While, in my view, the statute serves a compelling governmental interest by "cushioning the financial impact of spousal loss upon the sex for which that loss imposes a disproportionately heavy burden," I think that the statute is invalid because the State's interest can be served equally well by a more narrowly drafted statute.

... Florida's justification of [the statute] is not that it serves administrative convenience or helps to preserve the public fisc. Rather, the asserted justification is that [it] is an affirmative step toward alleviating the effects of past economic discrimination against women.

1. And in *Frontiero* the plurality opinion also noted that the statutes there were "not in any sense designed to rectify the effects of past discrimination against women. On the contrary, these statutes seize upon a group—women—who have historically suffered discrimination in employment, and rely on the effects of this past discrimination as a justification for heaping on additional economic disadvantages."

... [But] the $500 property tax exemption may be obtained by a financially independent heiress as well as by an unemployed widow with dependent children. The State has offered nothing to explain why inclusion of widows of substantial economic means was necessary to advance the State's interest in ameliorating the effects of past economic discrimination against women.

... By merely ... exclud[ing] widows who earn annual incomes, or possess assets, in excess of specified amounts, the State could readily narrow the class of beneficiaries to those widows for whom the effects of past economic discrimination against women have been a practical reality.

JUSTICE WHITE, dissenting.

... [T]here are many widowers who are needy and who are in more desperate financial straits and have less access to the job market than many widows. Yet none of them qualifies for the exemption.

I find the discrimination invidious and violative of the Equal Protection Clause. There is merit in giving poor widows a tax break, but gender-based classifications are suspect and require more justification than the State has offered.

I perceive no purpose served by the exemption other than to alleviate current economic necessity, but the State extends the exemption to widows who do not need the help and denies it to widowers who do. It may be administratively inconvenient to make individual determinations of entitlement and to extend the exemption to needy men as well as needy women, but administrative efficiency is not an adequate justification for discriminations based purely on sex. Frontiero v. Richardson; Reed v. Reed.

It may be suggested that the State is entitled to prefer widows over widowers because their assumed need is rooted in past and present economic discrimination against women. But this is not a credible explanation of Florida's tax exemption; for if the State's purpose was to compensate for past discrimination against females, surely it would not have limited the exemption to women who are widows. Moreover, even if past discrimination is considered to be the criterion for current tax exemption, the State nevertheless ignores all those widowers who have felt the effects of economic discrimination, whether as a member of a racial group or as one of the many who cannot escape the cycle of poverty. It seems to me that the State in this case is merely conferring an economic benefit in the form of a tax exemption and has not adequately explained why women should be treated differently from men.

. . .

NOTES AND QUESTIONS

1. Justice Douglas joined Justice Brennan's opinion in *Frontiero* (which argued that sex is a suspect classification). The other two justices who joined the Brennan *Frontiero* opinion (Justices Marshall and White) along with Justice Brennan himself, all thought the Florida law in Kahn

v. Shevin was unconstitutional. Is there any way to reconcile Justice Douglas' opinion for the majority in *Kahn* with Justice Brennan's opinion in *Frontiero?*

2. Are there differences in the positions taken in the two dissenting opinions? What if a state law provided that all widows (but no widowers) who had incomes under $10,000 a year were entitled to the tax exemption. Would Justice Brennan sustain that law? Would Justice White?

3. Not every law that discriminates in favor of women can be justified as designed to make up for past discrimination suffered by women. Justice Stevens regarded the 3.2% beer law in Craig v. Boren as a remnant of a tradition of discrimination *against* young males. A footnote to Justice Brennan's decision in *Craig* remarked: "Needless to say, in this case Oklahoma does not suggest that the age-sex differential was enacted to ensure the availability of 3.2% beer for women as compensation for previous deprivations." Would it have made a difference if Oklahoma had "suggested" that the purpose of the law *was* compensation for past discrimination?

4. One context in which it has been difficult to say whether a law discriminates against women or favors disadvantaged women is in connection with social security benefits. Until recently, it had been traditional to view men as the primary source of support for their families, even when their wives were also gainfully employed. Based on that stereotype, a number of provisions of the Social Security Act were drafted on the assumption that workers' widows were more needy than workers' widowers. Weinberger v. Wiesenfeld, 420 U.S. 636 (1975), involved such a provision. After a two-year marriage, Stephen Wiesenfeld's wife died in childbirth, leaving him with sole responsibility for care of their infant son. During their brief marriage, Paula Wiesenfeld had earned substantially more than Stephen. Under the law, Stephen received substantially less in social security benefits than Paula would have received if Stephen had died. Is this a law protecting widows who have poorer employment prospects than widowers? The Supreme Court did not think so. It described the law as discriminating against women workers who were given less than men workers for the protection of their families. Thus, the discrimination could not be explained "as an attempt to provide for the special problems of women," and the law was held unconstitutional. A similar issue arose two years later in Califano v. Goldfarb, 430 U.S. 199 (1977). Another provision of the Social Security Act provided benefits to all widows of deceased workers, but provided benefits for widowers of deceased workers only if the widower had been receiving at least half his support from his deceased wife. Four justices concluded that the law was unconstitutional because it discriminated against women workers. Four justices argued that the law favored widows, and was constitutional. Justice Stevens cast the fifth vote to declare the law unconstitutional, although he agreed with the dissenters that the law favored widows. He argued that the *Wiesenfeld* case established that it was not always constitutional to favor widows over widowers. The problem arose again, in the context of survivors' benefits under a state workers' compensation law, in the following case.

D. DISTINCTIONS BASED ON SEX–
SPECIFIC CHARACTERISTICS

The classic case of gender discrimination involves a situation in which men and women otherwise similarly qualified are treated differently solely because of their gender. What if people are treated differently on the basis of a trait which only one gender possesses? Is that the same thing as discrimination based on gender? Classifications based on the fact of pregnancy have been the focus of controversy involving "sex-specific characteristics." The Supreme Court in Geduldig v. Aiello, 417 U.S. 484 (1974), was called on to determine if the exclusion of normal pregnancy from the California state disability insurance program constituted an unconstitutional gender discrimination. The California program provided compensation for most medical and accidental disabilities. Pregnancy-related disabilities were excluded because that would have significantly raised the costs of the program. The Court, through Justice Stewart, held that there was no gender discrimination involved at all.

> . . . This case is a far cry from cases like Reed v. Reed, . . . and Frontiero v. Richardson, . . . involving discrimination based upon gender as such. The California insurance program does not exclude anyone from benefit eligibility because of gender but merely removes one physical condition—pregnancy—from the list of compensable disabilities. While it is true that only women can become pregnant, it does not follow that every legislative classification concerning pregnancy is a sex-based classification like those considered in *Reed,* and *Frontiero.* Normal pregnancy is an objectively identifiable physical condition with unique characteristics. Absent a showing that distinctions involving pregnancy are mere pretexts designed to effect an invidious discrimination against the members of one sex or the other, lawmakers are constitutionally free to include or exclude pregnancy from the coverage of legislation such as this on any reasonable basis, just as with respect to any other physical condition.

> The lack of identity between the excluded disability and gender as such under this insurance program becomes clear upon the most cursory analysis. The program divides potential recipients into two groups—pregnant women and nonpregnant persons. While the first group is exclusively female, the second includes members of both sexes. The fiscal and actuarial benefits of the program thus accrue to members of both sexes.

Justice Brennan in a dissenting opinion joined by Justices Douglas and Marshall saw the problem quite differently.

> . . . [Under the California program] compensation is paid for virtually all disabling conditions without regard to cost, voluntariness, uniqueness, predictability, or "normalcy" of the disability. Thus, for example, workers are compensated for costly disabilities such as heart attacks, voluntary disabilities

such as cosmetic surgery or sterilization, disabilities unique to sex or race such as prostatectomies or sickle-cell anemia, pre-existing conditions inevitably resulting in disability such as degenerative arthritis or cataracts, and "normal" disabilities such as removal of irritating wisdom teeth or other orthodontia.

Despite the Act's broad goals and scope of coverage, compensation is denied for disabilities suffered in connection with a "normal" pregnancy—disabilities suffered only by women. Disabilities caused by pregnancy, however, like other physically disabling conditions covered by the Act, require medical care, often include hospitalization, anesthesia and surgical procedures, and may involve genuine risk to life. Moreover, the economic effects caused by pregnancy-related disabilities are functionally indistinguishable from the effects caused by any other disability: wages are lost due to a physical inability to work, and medical expenses are incurred for the delivery of the child and for postpartum care. In my view, by singling out for less favorable treatment a gender-linked disability peculiar to women, the State has created a double standard for disability compensation: a limitation is imposed upon the disabilities for which women workers may recover, while men receive full compensation for all disabilities suffered, including those that affect only or primarily their sex, such as prostatectomies, circumcision, hemophilia, and gout. In effect, one set of rules is applied to females and another to males. Such dissimilar treatment of men and women, on the basis of physical characteristics inextricably linked to one sex, inevitably constitutes sex discrimination.

NOTES AND QUESTIONS

1. If sickle-cell anemia (a disease suffered almost exclusively by African Americans) were very expensive to treat, could a state constitutionally omit it from the coverage of the state disability insurance program?

2. Notice that Justice Stewart supported his argument that a distinction based on pregnancy was not the same as a distinction based on gender by saying that the distinction was, instead, one between pregnant women and "nonpregnant persons." Is that consistent with the statutory rape case, *Michael M.,* where a distinction that *was* based on gender was upheld because only women can become pregnant?

II. THE EQUAL RIGHTS AMENDMENT

In response to charges that legislative and judicial remedies for sex discrimination were too slow and too piecemeal to solve the problem, Congress approved the Equal Rights Amendment in March, 1972, and submitted it for ratification by the states. (Congress had taken no action to submit similar proposals for ratification before that, although they had been introduced in every session since 1923.) The proposed amendment provided:

Section 1. Equality of rights under the law shall not be denied or abridged by the United States or by any State on account of sex.

Section 2. The Congress shall have the power to enforce, by appropriate legislation, the provisions of this article.

Section 3. This amendment shall take effect two years after the date of ratification.

The Congressional resolution referring the ERA to the states for ratification required that the process be completed within 7 years. As the March 22, 1979, deadline approached, only 35 of the necessary 38 states had ratified. In October of 1978, Congress extended the time for ratification until June 30, 1982, by which date a sufficient number of states had not ratified the amendment to make it a part of the Constitution.

Part Six

THE RIGHT TO VOTE

Chapter XXVI

THE CONSTITUTION AND THE ELECTORAL PROCESS

I. THE FIFTEENTH AMENDMENT

A. ENFORCING THE FIFTEENTH AMENDMENT IN COURT

The Fifteenth Amendment, ratified in 1870, says simply that the "right of citizens of the United States to vote shall not be denied or abridged by the United States or by any State on account of race, color, or previous condition of servitude." It should not take an elaborate theory of constitutional interpretation to conclude that denial of the right to vote to adult African Americans violated the Constitution. Yet within a few years of ratification of the Fifteenth Amendment, through the first two-thirds of the twentieth century, African Americans were effectively denied the right to vote by the former Confederate States.

Part of the story involves private retaliation and violence directed at African American voters, since the Fifteenth Amendment was directed only to government. A larger part of the story involves a series of state laws designed to deny the franchise to African Americans. The Supreme Court invalidated many of these laws—but often decades after they had been enacted and used to close the ballot box. Each victory enforcing the Fifteenth Amendment was met by a new evasion and more litigation, with no effective enforcement of the Amendment.

One of the early devices was the "Grandfather Clause," limiting the right to vote to those who were entitled to vote, or whose ancestors were entitled to vote, before the Fifteenth Amendment was ratified. The Supreme Court held an Oklahoma provision of this kind invalid, but the decision was not rendered until 1915. Guinn v. United States, 238 U.S. 347 (1915). Oklahoma responded by providing that Oklahoma voters who had previously voted were automatically registered, and that new voters were permanently disenfranchised unless they registered from April 30 to May 11, 1916. The Supreme Court invalidated this law, too, but nearly one quarter of a century later. Lane v. Wilson, 307 U.S. 268 (1939).

In the one-party South, the most effective tool for practical disenfranchisement was the "white primary." If the States could not lawfully prevent African Americans from voting in the official elections, the Democratic party would bar them from party membership, and from voting in party primaries. Since victory in the Democratic primary meant automatic election, African Americans were theoretically allowed to vote in a general election whose outcome was preordained. Litigation over the Texas white primary is instructive. In 1927, the Court invalidated a Texas statute that explicitly denied African Americans the right to vote in Democratic primaries. Nixon v. Herndon, 273 U.S. 536 (1927). Texas repealed the offending statute, and enacted new laws that authorized the Democratic Party to prescribe qualifications for party membership. When the Party predictably excluded African Americans, the Court held that it had been authorized to do so by the statute, and was acting unconstitutionally as an agent of the State. Nixon v. Condon, 286 U.S. 73 (1932). (Both *Herndon* and *Condon* were decided under the Equal Protection Clause of the Fourteenth Amendment. This made it unnecessary to decide whether primary elections involved the "right ... to vote" protected by the Fifteenth Amendment.) Texas again repealed the unconstitutional statute, and this time the Democratic Party voted to restrict party membership to whites without formal authorization by the State. The Court concluded that the Texas Democratic Party was a private organization, and could determine its own membership. Grovey v. Townsend, 295 U.S. 45 (1935). Nine years later, the Court overruled Grovey v. Townsend, and held that exclusion of African Americans from the only Texas elections that counted violated the Fifteenth Amendment. Smith v. Allwright, 321 U.S. 649 (1944). The final chapter was written another nine years later, in Terry v. Adams, 345 U.S. 461 (1953). One Texas county had a "Jaybird Democratic Association," which selected candidates for county offices. Its candidates ran unopposed in the Democratic primary, and invariably won the general election. The Court concluded that excluding African Americans from voting in the "Jaybird primary" was also a violation of the Fifteenth Amendment.

In many of these election cases, the political implications of the Court's decisions concerned the Justices. In Smith v. Allwright, for example, some Justices questioned the wisdom of Chief Justice Stone's assignment of the opinion to Justice Frankfurter. Justice Jackson wrote the Chief Justice on January 17, 1944:

> It is a delicate matter. We must reverse a recent, well considered and unanimous decision [Grovey v. Townsend]. We deny the entire South the right to a white primary, which is one of its most cherished rights. It seems to me very important that the strength which an all but unanimous decision [only Justice Roberts dissented] would have may be greatly weakened if the voice that utters it is the one that grates on Southern sensibilities. Mr. Justice Frankfurter unites in a rare degree factors which unhappily excite prejudice. In the first place he is a Jew. In the second place, he is from New England, the seat of the abolition movement. In the third place, he has not been thought of a person particularly sympathetic with the Democratic Party

in the past. I know that every one of these things is a consideration that to you is distasteful and they are things which I mention only with the greatest reluctance and fear of being misunderstood. I have told Mr. Justice Frankfurter that in my opinion it is best for this Court and for him that he not be its spokesman in this matter and that I intend to bring my view of it to your attention. With all humility I suggest that the Court's decision, bound to arouse bitter resentment, will be much less apt to stir ugly reactions if the news that the white primary is dead, is broken to it, if possible, by a Southerner who has been a Democrat and is not a member of one of the minorities which stir prejudices kindred to those against the Negro. (Stone Papers, Library of Congress Box 75.)

Chief Justice Stone reassigned the *Smith* opinion to Justice Reed, who was from Kentucky.

The death of the white primary resulted in a non-trivial increase in voting by African Americans, but the vast majority still were not registered and did not vote. Beyond private threats, some of the explanation could be found in the poll tax. Payment of the poll tax as a requirement to register to vote had been upheld by the Supreme Court in Breedlove v. Suttles, 302 U.S. 277 (1937), and did not violate the Fifteenth Amendment because it disenfranchised poor people of all races. Butler v. Thompson, 341 U.S. 937 (1951). The Twenty-fourth Amendment, ratified in 1964, eliminated the poll tax in elections for federal office. Two years later, the Court overruled Breedlove v. Suttles and held that poll taxes for local office violated the Equal Protection Clause of the Fourteenth Amendment. (See Harper v. Virginia State Board of Elections, below at page 1166.)

Finally, there were literacy tests. As late as 1959, a unanimous Supreme Court decided that states could require literacy tests as a prerequisite to voter registration. Lassiter v. Northampton County Board of Elections, 360 U.S. 45. Discriminatory application of literacy tests was widespread, however. Lawsuits could be brought, proving that voting registrars applied more rigorous tests for African Americans, and after much delay, a court could order appropriate relief. Often, this was met by registrars deserting their offices and refusing to register any new voters. (White voters, who were already registered, could continue to vote.)

The most recent case of Court enforcement of the Fifteenth Amendment is Rice v. Cayetano, 528 U.S. 495 (2000). In that case, the Supreme Court held unconstitutional a provision of the Hawaii Constitution that limited voting rights in state-wide elections of trustees to the Office of Hawaiian Affairs (OHA), a state agency that administers programs benefitting descendants of the people inhabiting the Hawaiian Islands in 1778. Only Hawaiians with such ancestry were entitled to vote for OHA trustees. The Court mentioned in its opinion the subtle and indirect means that had been used to limit voting rights based on race in Guinn v. United States, Smith v. Allwright, Terry v. Adams, and other cases. The voting structure [in *Rice*], it said, "is neither subtle nor indirect. It is specific in granting the vote to persons of defined ancestry." Since ancestry in this case is "a proxy for race," the Court held that the Fifteenth Amendment, which is "self-executing," invalidates the Hawaii constitutional provision limiting voting rights.

B. CONGRESS AND THE FIFTEENTH AMENDMENT

Nearly a century after ratification of the Fifteenth Amendment, and after decades of court decisions attempting to enforce it, African Americans were effectively disenfranchised in most of the former Confederate States. Section 2 of the Fifteenth Amendment authorizes Congress to enforce its provisions by "appropriate legislation." Truly effective legislation was enacted as the Voting Rights Act of 1965. The problem of literacy tests was solved by suspending their use in states where they were used to disenfranchise substantial numbers of voters. (Later, Congress would suspend the use of literacy tests for voters permanently in all States.) The absent voter registrars could be replaced by federal registrars appointed by the Attorney General. The most controversial provision, and the most effective, was designed to deal with the past history of evasion of the Fifteenth Amendment. "Covered jurisdictions"—states or political subdivisions that had used literacy tests and where less than half the adult population voted—could not adopt new laws relating to voting unless the United States Attorney General certified that the new law "does not have the purpose and will not have the effect of denying or abridging the right to vote on account of race or color." The requirement that affected states "preclear" their new electoral laws was upheld by the Supreme Court in South Carolina v. Katzenbach, 383 U.S. 301 (1966) and in City of Rome v. United States, 446 U.S. 156 (1980).

II. APPLICATION OF THE FOURTEENTH AMENDMENT'S EQUAL PROTECTION CLAUSE TO DENIALS OF VOTING RIGHTS

A. ONE PERSON, ONE VOTE

REYNOLDS v. SIMS

Supreme Court of the United States, 1964.
377 U.S. 533, 84 S.Ct. 1362, 12 L.Ed.2d 506.

CHIEF JUSTICE WARREN delivered the opinion of the Court.

. . . .

I.

[Alabama voters claimed that the apportionment of the Alabama Senate and House violated the Equal Protection Clause of the Fourteenth Amendment. In the House, the largest district had 5 times the population of the smallest; in the Senate, the population disparity between the largest and smallest districts was 59 to 1.]

II.

Undeniably the Constitution of the United States protects the right of all qualified citizens to vote, in state as well as in federal elections. A consistent line of decisions by this Court in cases involving attempts to deny or restrict the right of suffrage has made this indelibly clear. It has been repeatedly recognized that all qualified voters have a constitutionally protected right to vote.... As the Court stated in [United States v.] Classic, [313 U.S. 299 (1941)] "Obviously included within the right to choose, secured by the Constitution, is the right of qualified voters within a state to cast their ballots and have them counted." And history has seen a continuing expansion of the scope of the right of suffrage in this country. The right to vote freely for the candidate of one's choice is of the essence of a democratic society, and any restrictions on that right strike at the heart of representative government. And the right of suffrage can be denied by a debasement or dilution of the weight of a citizen's vote just as effectively as by wholly prohibiting the free exercise of the franchise.

In Baker v. Carr, 369 U.S. 186, we held that a claim asserted under the Equal Protection Clause challenging the constitutionality of a State's apportionment of seats in its legislature ... presented a justiciable controversy subject to adjudication by federal courts.... In *Baker*, ... [w]e intimated no view as to the proper constitutional standards for evaluating the validity of a state legislative apportionment scheme. Nor did we give any consideration to the question of appropriate remedies....

. . .

In Gray v. Sanders, 372 U.S. 368, we held that the Georgia county unit system, applicable in statewide primary elections, was unconstitutional since it resulted in a dilution of the weight of the votes of certain Georgia voters merely because of where they resided....

. . .

In Wesberry v. Sanders, 376 U.S. 1, decided earlier this Term, we ... determined that the constitutional test for the validity of congressional districting schemes was one of substantial equality of population among the various districts established by a state legislature for the election of members of the Federal House of Representatives.

In that case we ... concluded that the constitutional prescription for election of members of the House of Representatives "by the People," construed in its historical context, "means that as nearly as is practicable one man's vote in a congressional election is to be worth as much as another's." ...

... Admittedly, those decisions, in which we held that, in statewide and in congressional elections, one person's vote must be counted equally with those of all other voters in a State, were based on different constitutional considerations and were addressed to rather distinct problems.... Our problem, then, is to ascertain, in the instant cases, whether there are any constitutionally cognizable principles which would justify departures from the basic standard of equality among voters in the apportionment of seats in state legislatures.

A predominant consideration in determining whether a State's legislative apportionment scheme constitutes an invidious discrimination violative of rights asserted under the Equal Protection Clause is that the rights allegedly impaired are individual and personal in nature.... Undoubtedly, the right of suffrage is a fundamental matter in a free and democratic society. Especially since the right to exercise the franchise in a free and unimpaired manner is preservative of other basic civil and political rights, any alleged infringement of the right of citizens to vote must be carefully and meticulously scrutinized....

Legislators represent people, not trees or acres. Legislators are elected by voters, not farms or cities or economic interests. As long as ours is a representative form of government, and our legislatures are those instruments of government elected directly by and directly representative of the people, the right to elect legislators in a free and unimpaired fashion is a bedrock of our political system. It could hardly be gainsaid that a constitutional claim had been asserted by an allegation that certain otherwise qualified voters had been entirely prohibited from voting for members of their state legislature. And, if a State should provide that the votes of citizens in one part of the State should be given two times, or five times, or 10 times the weight of votes of citizens in another part of the State, it could hardly be contended that the right to vote of those residing in the disfavored areas had not been effectively diluted. It would appear extraordinary to suggest that a State could be constitutionally permitted to enact a law providing that certain of the State's voters could vote two, five, or 10 times for their legislative representatives, while voters living elsewhere could vote only once. And it is inconceivable that a state law to the effect that, in counting votes for legislators, the votes of citizens in one part of the State would be multiplied by two, five, or 10, while the votes of persons in another area would be counted only at face value, could be constitutionally sustainable. Of course, the effect of state legislative districting schemes which give the same number of representatives to unequal numbers of constituents is identical. Overweighting and overvaluation of the votes of those living here has the certain effect of dilution and undervaluation of the votes of those living there. The resulting discrimination against those individual voters living in disfavored areas is easily demonstrable mathematically. Their right to vote is simply not the same right to vote as that of those living in a favored part of the State. Two, five, or 10 of them must vote before the effect of their voting is equivalent to that of their favored neighbor. Weighting the votes of citizens differently, by any method or means, merely because of where they happen to reside, hardly seems justifiable....

Logically, in a society ostensibly grounded on representative government, it would seem reasonable that a majority of the people of a State could elect a majority of that State's legislators. To conclude differently, and to sanction minority control of state legislative bodies, would appear to deny majority rights in a way that far surpasses any possible denial of minority rights that might otherwise be thought to result. Since legislatures are responsible for enacting laws by which all citizens are to be governed, they should be bodies which are collectively responsive to the popular will.... Since the achieving of fair and effective representation for all citizens is concededly the basic aim of legislative apportionment, we conclude that the Equal Protection Clause guarantees the opportunity for equal participation by all voters in the election of state legislators. Diluting the weight of votes because of place of residence impairs basic constitutional rights under the Fourteenth Amendment just as much as invidious discriminations based upon factors such as race, Brown v. Board of Education, 347 U.S. 483, or economic status, Griffin v. Illinois, 351 U.S. 12, Douglas v. California, 372 U.S. 353. Our constitutional system amply provides for the protection of minorities by means other than giving them majority control of state legislatures. And the democratic ideals of equality and majority rule, which have served this Nation so well in the past, are hardly of any less significance for the present and the future.

We are told that the matter of apportioning representation in a state legislature is a complex and many-faceted one. We are advised that States can rationally consider factors other than population in apportioning legislative representation. We are admonished not to restrict the power of the States to impose differing views as to political philosophy on their citizens. We are cautioned about the dangers of entering into political thickets and mathematical quagmires. Our answer is this: a denial of constitutionally protected rights demands judicial protection; our oath and our office require no less of us....

To the extent that a citizen's right to vote is debased, he is that much less a citizen. The fact that an individual lives here or there is not a legitimate reason for overweighting or diluting the efficacy of his vote. The complexions of societies and civilizations change, often with amazing rapidity. A nation once primarily rural in character becomes predominantly urban. Representation schemes once fair and equitable become archaic and outdated. But the basic principle of representative government remains, and must remain, unchanged—the weight of a citizen's vote cannot be made to depend on where he lives. Population is, of necessity, the starting point for consideration and the controlling criterion for judgment in legislative apportionment controversies. A citizen, a qualified voter, is no more nor no less so because he lives in the city or on the farm. This is the clear and strong command of our Constitution's Equal Protection Clause. This is an essential part of the concept of a government of laws and not men. This is at the heart of Lincoln's vision of "government of the people, by the people, (and) for the people." The Equal Protection Clause demands no less than substantially equal state legislative representation for all citizens, of all places as well as of all races.

IV.

We hold that, as a basic constitutional standard, the Equal Protection Clause requires that the seats in both houses of a bicameral state legislature must be apportioned on a population basis. Simply stated, an individual's right to vote for state legislators is unconstitutionally impaired when its weight is in a substantial fashion diluted when compared with votes of citizens living on other parts of the State. Since, under neither the existing apportionment provisions nor either of the proposed plans was either of the houses of the Alabama Legislature apportioned on a population basis, the District Court correctly held that all three of these schemes were constitutionally invalid. . . .

. . .

V.

Since neither of the houses of the Alabama Legislature, under any of the three plans considered by the District Court, was apportioned on a population basis, we would be justified in proceeding no further. However, one of the proposed plans, that contained in the so-called 67–Senator Amendment, at least superficially resembles the scheme of legislative representation followed in the Federal Congress. Under this plan, each of Alabama's 67 counties is allotted one senator, and no counties are given more than one Senate seat. . . .

Much has been written since our decision in Baker v. Carr about the applicability of the so-called federal analogy to state legislative apportionment arrangements. We . . . find the federal analogy inapposite and irrelevant to state legislative districting schemes. Attempted reliance on the federal analogy appears often to be little more than an after-the-fact rationalization offered in defense of maladjusted state apportionment arrangements. The original constitutions of 36 of our States provided that representation in both houses of the state legislatures would be based completely, or predominantly, on population. And the Founding Fathers clearly had no intention of establishing a pattern or model for the apportionment of seats in state legislatures when the system of representation in the Federal Congress was adopted. Demonstrative of this is the fact that the Northwest Ordinance, adopted in the same year, 1787, as the Federal Constitution, provided for the apportionment of seats in territorial legislatures solely on the basis of population.

The system of representation in the two Houses of the Federal Congress is one ingrained in our Constitution, as part of the law of the land. It is one conceived out of compromise and concession indispensable to the establishment of our federal republic. Arising from unique historical circumstances, it is based on the consideration that in establishing our type of federalism a group of formerly independent States bound themselves together under one national government. . . .

Political subdivisions of States—counties, cities, or whatever—never were and never have been considered as sovereign entities. Rather, they have been traditionally regarded as subordinate governmental instrumentalities created by the State to assist in the carrying out of state governmental functions. . . .

. . .

Since we find the so-called federal analogy inapposite to a consideration of the constitutional validity of state legislative apportionment schemes, we necessarily hold that the Equal Protection Clause requires both houses of a state legislature to be apportioned on a population basis. The right of a citizen to equal representation and to have his vote weighted equally with those of all other citizens in the election of members of one house of a bicameral state legislature would amount to little if States could effectively submerge the equal-population principle in the apportionment of seats in the other house. . . .

We do not believe that the concept of bicameralism is rendered anachronistic and meaningless when the predominant basis of representation in the two state legislative bodies is required to be the same— population. A prime reason for bicameralism, modernly considered, is to insure mature and deliberate consideration of, and to prevent precipitate action on, proposed legislative measures. Simply because the controlling criterion for apportioning representation is required to be the same in both houses does not mean that there will be no differences in the composition and complexion of the two bodies. Different constituencies can be represented in the two houses. One body could be composed of single-member districts while the other could have at least some multi-member districts. The length of terms of the legislators in the separate bodies could differ. The numerical size of the two bodies could be made to differ, even significantly, and the geographical size of districts from which legislators are elected could also be made to differ. And apportionment in one house could be arranged so as to balance off minor inequities in the representation of certain areas in the other house. In summary, these and other factors could be, and are presently in many States, utilized to engender differing complexions and collective attitudes in the two bodies of a state legislature, although both are apportioned substantially on a population basis.

VI.

By holding that as a federal constitutional requisite both houses of a state legislature must be apportioned on a population basis, we mean that the Equal Protection Clause requires that a State make an honest and good faith effort to construct districts, in both houses of its legislature, as nearly of equal population as is practicable. . . .

. . .

History indicates, however, that many States have deviated, to a greater or lesser degree, from the equal-population principle in the apportionment of seats in at least one house of their legislatures. So long as the divergences from a strict population standard are based on legitimate considerations incident to the effectuation of a rational state policy, some deviations from the equal-population principle are constitutionally permissible with respect to the apportionment of seats in either or both of the two houses of a bicameral state legislature. But neither history alone, nor economic or other sorts of group interests, are permissible factors in attempting to justify disparities from population-based representation. Citizens, not history or economic interests, cast votes. Considerations of area alone provide an insufficient justification for deviations from the equal-population principle. Again, people, not land or trees or pastures, vote. . . .

A consideration that appears to be of more substance in justifying some deviations from population-based representation in state legislatures is that of insuring some voice to political subdivisions, as political subdivisions.... However, permitting deviations from population-based representation does not mean that each local governmental unit or political subdivision can be given separate representation, regardless of population. Carried too far, a scheme of giving at least one seat in one house to each political subdivision (for example, to each county) could easily result, in many States, in a total subversion of the equal-population principle in that legislative body. This would be especially true in a State where the number of counties is large and many of them are sparsely populated, and the number of seats in the legislative body being apportioned does not significantly exceed the number of counties. Such a result, we conclude, would be constitutionally impermissible.... [I]f, even as a result of a clearly rational state policy of according some legislative representation to political subdivisions, population is submerged as the controlling consideration in the apportionment of seats in the particular legislative body, then the right of all of the State's citizens to cast an effective and adequately weighted vote would be unconstitutionally impaired.

. . .

VIII.

That the Equal Protection Clause requires that both houses of a state legislature be apportioned on a population basis does not mean that States cannot adopt some reasonable plan for periodic revision of their apportionment schemes. Decennial reapportionment appears to be a rational approach to readjustment of legislative representation in order to take into account population shifts and growth. Reallocation of legislative seats every 10 years coincides with the prescribed practice in 41 of the States, often honored more in the breach than the observance, however. Illustratively, the Alabama Constitution requires decennial reapportionment, yet the last reapportionment of the Alabama Legislature, when this suit was brought, was in 1901.... While we do not intend to indicate that decennial reapportionment is a constitutional requisite, compliance with such an approach would clearly meet the minimal requirements for maintaining a reasonably current scheme of legislative representation. And we do not mean to intimate that more frequent reapportionment would not be constitutionally permissible or practicably desirable. But if reapportionment were accomplished with less frequency, it would assuredly be constitutionally suspect.

. . .

JUSTICE CLARK, concurring in the affirmance.

The Court goes much beyond the necessities of this case in laying down a new "equal population" principle for state legislative apportionment....

It seems to me that all that the Court need say in this case is that each plan considered by the trial court is "a crazy quilt," clearly revealing invidious discrimination ...

I, therefore, do not reach the question of the so-called "federal analogy." But in my view, if one house of the State Legislature meets the population standard, representation in the other house might include some departure from it so as to take into account, on a rational basis, other factors in order to afford some representation to the various elements of the State. . . .

JUSTICE STEWART . . .

All of the parties have agreed with the District Court's finding that legislative inaction for some 60 years in the face of growth and shifts in population has converted Alabama's legislative apportionment plan enacted in 1901 into one completely lacking in rationality. Accordingly, . . . I would affirm the judgment of the District Court holding that this apportionment violated the Equal Protection Clause.

. . .

JUSTICE HARLAN, dissenting.

. . . These decisions . . . have the effect of placing basic aspects of state political systems under the pervasive overlordship of the federal judiciary. . . .

. . .

. . . Whatever may be thought of this holding as a piece of political ideology . . . I think it demonstrable that the Fourteenth Amendment does not impose this political tenet on the States or authorize this Court to do so.

The Court's constitutional discussion . . . is remarkable . . . for its failure to address itself at all to the Fourteenth Amendment as a whole or to the legislative history of the Amendment pertinent to the matter at hand. Stripped of aphorisms, the Court's argument boils down to the assertion that appellees' right to vote has been invidiously "debased" or "diluted" by systems of apportionment which entitle them to vote for fewer legislators than other voters, an assertion which is tied to the Equal Protection Clause only by the constitutionally frail tautology that "equal" means "equal."

Had the Court paused to probe more deeply into the matter, it would have found that the Equal Protection Clause was never intended to inhibit the States in choosing any democratic method they pleased for the apportionment of their legislatures. This is shown by the language of the Fourteenth Amendment taken as a whole, by the understanding of those who proposed and ratified it, and by the political practices of the States at the time the Amendment was adopted. It is confirmed by numerous state and congressional actions since the adoption of the Fourteenth Amendment, and by the common understanding of the Amendment as evidenced by subsequent constitutional amendments and decisions of this Court before Baker v. Carr, supra, made an abrupt break with the past in 1962.

. . .

I.

. . .

The Court relies exclusively on that portion of § 1 of the Fourteenth Amendment which provides that no State shall "deny to any person within its jurisdiction the equal protection of the laws," and disregards entirely the significance of § 2, which reads: "Representatives shall be apportioned among the several States according to their respective numbers, counting the whole number of persons in each State, excluding Indians not taxed. But when the right to vote at any election for the choice of electors for President and Vice President of the United States, Representatives in Congress, the Executive and Judicial officers of a State, or the members of the Legislature thereof, is denied to any of the male inhabitants of such State, being twenty-one years of age, and citizens of the United States, or in any way abridged, except for partic- ipation in rebellion, or other crime, the basis of representation therein shall be reduced in the proportion which the number of such male citizens shall bear to the whole number of male citizens twenty-one years of age in such State."

. . . I am unable to understand the Court's utter disregard of the second section which expressly recognizes the States' power to deny "or in any way" abridge the right of their inhabitants to vote for "the members of the (State) Legislature," and its express provision of a remedy for such denial or abridgment. The comprehensive scope of the second section and its particular reference to the state legislatures preclude the suggestion that the first section was intended to have the result reached by the Court today. . . .

. . .

The history of the adoption of the Fourteenth Amendment provides conclusive evidence that neither those who proposed nor those who ratified the Amendment believed that the Equal Protection Clause limited the power of the States to apportion their legislatures as they saw fit. Moreover, the history demonstrate that the intention to leave this power undisturbed was deliberate and was widely believed to be essential to the adoption of the Amendment.

. . .

. . . As of 1961, the Constitutions of all but 11 States, roughly 20% of the total, recognized bases of apportionment other than geographic spread of population, and to some extent favored sparsely populated areas by a variety of devices, ranging from straight area representation or guaranteed minimum area representation to complicated schemes . . .

. . .

. . . [N]ote should be taken of the Fifteenth and Nineteenth Amend- ments.

. . .

... If constitutional amendment was the only means by which all men and, later, women, could be guaranteed the right to vote at all, even for federal officers, how can it be that the far less obvious right to a particular kind of apportionment of state legislatures ... can be conferred by judicial construction of the Fourteenth Amendment? ...

. . .

... In my judgment, today's decisions are refuted by the language of the Amendment which they construe and by the inference fairly to be drawn from subsequently enacted Amendments. They are unequivocally refuted by history and by consistent theory and practice from the time of the adoption of the Fourteenth Amendment until today.

II.

The Court's elaboration of its new "constitutional" doctrine indicates how far—and how unwisely—it has strayed from the appropriate bounds of its authority. The consequence of today's decision is that ... the local District Court or, it may be, the state courts, are given blanket authority and the constitutional duty to supervise apportionment of the State Legislatures. It is difficult to imagine a more intolerable and inappropriate interference by the judiciary with the independent legislatures of the States.

. . .

These decisions also cut deeply into the fabric of our federalism.... [T]he aftermath of these cases, however desirable it may be thought in itself, will have been achieved at the cost of a radical alteration in the relationship between the States and the Federal Government, more particularly the Federal Judiciary....

Finally, these decisions give support to a current mistaken view of the Constitution and the constitutional function of this Court. This view, in a nutshell, is that every major social ill in this country can find its cure in some constitutional "principle," and that this Court should "take the lead" in promoting reform when other branches of government fail to act. The Constitution is not a panacea for every blot upon the public welfare, nor should this Court, ordained as a judicial body, be though of as a general haven for reform movements. The Constitution is an instrument of government, fundamental to which is the premise that in a diffusion of governmental authority lies the greatest promise that this Nation will realize liberty for all its citizens. This Court, limited in function in accordance with that premise, does not serve its high purpose when it exceeds its authority, even to satisfy justified impatience with the slow workings of the political process. For when, in the name of constitutional interpretation, the Court adds something to the Constitution that was deliberately excluded from it, the Court in reality substitutes its view of what should be so for the amending process.

. . .

NOTES AND QUESTIONS

1.   There has been considerable controversy, in recent years, whether the Court should be limited, in interpreting the Constitution, to its

text and "original meaning." Does Justice Harlan convince you that Section One of the Fourteenth Amendment was understood in 1868 to be inapplicable to all issues concerning denial of the right to vote?* (Notice his argument that Section Two of the Fourteenth Amendment contains an explicit remedy for denials of the right to vote, implying that denials of the right to vote do not violate Section 1.) If so, does that establish that the Court's decision in Reynolds v. Sims was wrong?

2. Justice Harlan, at the end of his dissent, mentions "justified impatience with the slow workings of the political process." In some reapportionment cases, the problem was that the malapportioned legislature could block its reapportionment. As Chief Justice Warren mentions, the Alabama constitution required reapportionment every ten years, but it had not been done, despite major population shifts, in more than sixty years. The same situation existed in Tennessee, as described in the 1962 decision in Baker v. Carr. Consider an argument suggested by a famous footnote by Justice (later Chief Justice) Harlan Stone in United States v. Carolene Products Co., 304 U.S. 144 (1938). Justice Stone mentioned the possibility that there should be "more exacting judicial scrutiny" when a challenged law "restricts those political processes which can ordinarily be expected to bring about repeal of undesirable legislation." Is that the situation in Reynolds v. Sims? If so, would that justify invalidating the Alabama and Tennessee apportionments even if Section One of the Fourteenth Amendment was originally meant to be inapplicable to voting?

3. Finally, even if one assumes that the Equal Protection Clause applies to issues of legislative apportionment, there remains the question of the appropriate standard. Justices Stewart and Clark reject the Court's one-person-one-vote standard, and would permit substantial difference in the population of districts so long as the apportionment was "rational" or was not a "crazy quilt." In subsequent cases, the one-person-one-vote standard has been applied to permit only small deviations in population in either house of a state legislature. The Court has been even more insistent on population equality with reference to Congressional districts—in Karcher v. Daggett, 462 U.S. 725 (1983), it invalidated New Jersey's 1982 apportionment of congressional districts even though the difference between the largest and smallest district was less than one percent of the population of an average district. Is the real advantage of a relatively strict one-person-one-vote standard that it is more manageable for courts to apply?

B. WHO CAN VOTE

HARPER v. VIRGINIA STATE BOARD OF ELECTIONS

Supreme Court of the United States, 1966.
383 U.S. 663, 86 S.Ct. 1079, 16 L.Ed.2d 169.

JUSTICE DOUGLAS delivered the opinion of the Court.

[In 1964, the Twenty-fourth Amendment was ratified, abolishing poll taxes in federal elections. By 1966, all but four states had abolished poll taxes with respect to state elections.]

---

* For an extensive rebuttal to Justice Harlan's position, see Van Alstyne, *The Fourteenth Amendment, the "Right" to Vote, and the Understanding of the Thirty–Ninth Congress*, 1965 THE SUPREME COURT REVIEW 33.

These are suits by Virginia residents to have declared unconstitutional Virginia's poll tax. The three-judge District Court, feeling bound by our decision in Breedlove v. Suttles, 302 U.S. 277, dismissed the complaint. . . .

While the right to vote in federal elections is conferred by Art. I, § 2, of the Constitution . . ., the right to vote in state elections is nowhere expressly mentioned. It is argued that the right to vote in state elections is implicit, particularly by reason of the First Amendment and that it may not constitutionally be conditioned upon the payment of a tax or fee. . . . We do not stop to canvass the relation between voting and political expression. For it is enough to say that once the franchise is granted to the electorate, lines may not be drawn which are inconsistent with the Equal Protection Clause of the Fourteenth Amendment. [In Lassiter v. Northampton County Board of Elections, 360 U.S. 45, 51 (1959) the Court sustained a state literacy test.] But the *Lassiter* case does not govern the result here, because, unlike a poll tax, the "ability to read and write . . . has some relation to standards designed to promote intelligent use of the ballot." . . .

We conclude that a State violates the Equal Protection Clause of the Fourteenth Amendment whenever it makes the affluence of the voter or payment of any fee an electoral standard. Voter qualifications have no relation to wealth nor to paying or not paying this or any other tax. Our cases demonstrate that the Equal Protection Clause of the Fourteenth Amendment restrains the States from fixing voter qualifications which invidiously discriminate. Thus without questioning the power of a State to impose reasonable residence restrictions on the availability of the ballot . . ., we held in Carrington v. Rash, 380 U.S. 89, that a State may not deny the opportunity to vote to a bona fide resident merely because he is a member of the armed services. . . .

. . . Recently in Reynolds v. Sims, 377 U.S. 533, 561–562, we said, ". . . The Equal Protection Clause demands no less than substantially equal state legislative representation for all citizens, of all places as well as of all races." . . .

We say the same whether the citizen, otherwise qualified to vote, has $1.50 in his pocket or nothing at all, pays the fee or fails to pay it. The principle that denies the State the right to dilute a citizen's vote on account of his economic status or other such factors by analogy bars a system which excludes those unable to pay a fee to vote or who fail to pay.

It is argued that a State may exact fees from citizens for many different kinds of licenses; that if it can demand from all an equal fee for a driver's license, it can demand from all an equal poll tax for voting. But we must remember that the interest of the State, when it comes to voting, is limited to the power to fix qualifications. Wealth, like race, creed, or color, is not germane to one's ability to participate intelligently in the electoral process. Lines drawn on the basis of wealth or property, like those of race (Korematsu v. United States, 323 U.S. 214), are traditionally disfavored. See Edwards v. California, 314 U.S. 160, 184–185 (Jackson, J., concurring); Griffin v. Illinois, 351 U.S. 12; Douglas v. California, 372 U.S. 353. To introduce wealth or payment of a fee as a measure of a voter's qualifications is to introduce a capricious or irrelevant factor. The degree of the discrimination is irrelevant. In this context—that is, as a condition of obtaining a ballot—the requirement of fee paying causes an "invidious" discrimination ... that runs afoul of the Equal Protection Clause. Levy "by the poll," as stated in Breedlove v. Suttles, ... is an old familiar form of taxation; and we say nothing to impair its validity so long as it is not made a condition to the exercise of the franchise. Breedlove v. Suttles sanctioned its use as "a prerequisite of voting." ... To that extent the *Breedlove* case is overruled.

. . .

JUSTICE BLACK, dissenting.

In Breedlove v. Suttles, 302 U.S. 277, decided December 6, 1937, a few weeks after I took my seat as a member of this Court, we unanimously upheld the right of the State of Georgia to make payment of its state poll tax a prerequisite to voting in state elections.... I joined the Court's judgment and opinion. Later, May 28, 1951, I joined the Court's judgment in Butler v. Thompson, 341 U.S. 937, upholding, over the dissent of. Justice Douglas, the Virginia state poll tax law challenged here against the same equal protection challenges. Since the *Breedlove* and *Butler* cases were decided the Federal Constitution has not been amended in the only way it could constitutionally have been, that is, as provided in Article V of the Constitution. I would adhere to the holding of those cases. The Court, however, overrules *Breedlove* in part, but its opinion reveals that it does so not by using its limited power to interpret the original meaning of the Equal Protection Clause, but by giving that clause a new meaning which it believes represents a better governmental policy. From this action I dissent.

. . .

JUSTICE HARLAN, whom JUSTICE STEWART joins, dissenting.

The final demise of state poll taxes ... is perhaps in itself not of great moment. But that fact that the coup de grace has been administered by this Court instead of being left to the affected States or to the federal political process should be a matter of continuing concern to all interested in maintaining the proper role of this tribunal under our scheme of government.

. . .

Property qualifications and poll taxes have been a traditional part of our political structure. In the Colonies the franchise was generally a restricted one. Over the years these and other restrictions were gradually lifted, primarily because popular theories of political representation had changed. Often restrictions were lifted only after wide public debate.

The issue of woman suffrage, for example, raised question of family relationships, of participation in public affairs, of the very nature of the type of society in which Americans wished to live; eventually a consensus was reached, which culminated in the Nineteenth Amendment no more than 45 years ago.

Similarly with property qualifications, it is only by fiat that it can be said, especially in the context of American history, that there can be no rational debate as to their advisability. Most of the early Colonies had them; many of the States have had them during much of their histories; and, whether one agrees or not, arguments have been and still can be made in favor of them. For example, it is certainly a rational argument that payment of some minimal poll tax promotes civic responsibility, weeding out those who do not care enough about public affairs to pay $1.50 or thereabouts a year for the exercise of the franchise. It is also arguable, indeed it was probably accepted as sound political theory by a large percentage of Americans through most of our history, that people with some property have a deeper stake in community affairs, and are consequently more responsible, more educated, more knowledgeable, more worthy of confidence, than those without means, and that the community and Nation would be better managed if the franchise were restricted to such citizens. . . .

These viewpoints, to be sure, ring hollow on most contemporary ears. Their lack of acceptance today is evidenced by the fact that nearly all of the States, left to their own devices, have eliminated property or poll-tax qualifications; by the cognate fact that Congress and three-quarters of the States quickly ratified the Twenty–Fourth Amendment; and by the fact that rules such as the "pauper exclusion" in Virginia law, . . . have never been enforced.

Property and poll-tax qualifications, very simply, are not in accord with current egalitarian notions of how a modern democracy should be organized. It is of course entirely fitting that legislatures should modify the law to reflect such changes in popular attitudes. However, it is all wrong, in my view, for the Court to adopt the political doctrines popularly accepted at a particular moment of our history and to declare all others to be irrational and invidious, barring them from the range of choice by reasonably minded people acting through the political process. . . .

NOTES AND QUESTIONS

1. If one simply read the Constitution to see what it said about voting, it would be hard to come to the conclusion that Virginia was not permitted to condition voting on payment of a poll tax. These provisions of the Constitution deal explicitly with the franchise: Art. I, sec. 2; Amendments XII, XIV (sec. 2), XV, XVII, XIX, XXIV, and XXVI. Notice that none of these provisions specify who can vote, but place limits on the bases for denying the franchise. Does that suggest a negative corollary—that denial of the right to vote on other bases is permissible? Is that particularly true in *Harper*, given the specific terms of the

Twenty-fourth Amendment, which had been ratified only two years earlier?

2. As Justice Black points out, the Court had decided in 1937 and 1951 that poll taxes were constitutional, and Justice Douglas dissented in the 1951 case. (*Butler* was a decision without opinion, and Justice Douglas was the sole dissenter—also without opinion.) Justice Douglas, however, wrote the 1959 *Lassiter* decision, which sustained nondiscriminatory literacy tests for voters. In his opinion in that case, he wrote that "States have long been held to have broad powers to determine the conditions under which the right of suffrage may be exercised ... absent of course the discrimination which the Constitution condemns." Was the Virginia poll tax racially discriminatory? Chief Justice Warren and Justice Douglas thought so. Justice Fortas recorded Warren saying in conference that the poll tax was "Discrimination v. Poor & Negroes," and Douglas saying that the "poll tax is [an] engine for racial discrimination." Fortas Papers, Yale University.

3. *Lassiter* assumed that the "discrimination which the Constitution condemns" were those specifically prohibited, such as race (Fifteenth Amendment) and sex (Nineteenth Amendment). *Harper* was the first of a series of decisions that invalidated voter qualifications not specifically prohibited by the Constitution. These included residency requirements longer than 50 days before the election (Dunn v. Blumstein, 405 U.S. 330 (1972)), and property ownership qualifications (Kramer v. Union Free School District, 395 U.S. 621 (1969); Cipriano v. City of Houma, 395 U.S. 701 (1969)). In short, the Court has required universal adult suffrage, with only two modest exceptions. Voters may be disqualified who have committed crimes. (This was based on the specific reference in Section 2 of the Fourteenth Amendment to exclusion of felons from the vote. Richardson v. Ramirez, 418 U.S. 24 (1974).) In "special interest" elections—such as by a street light district which erects street lights financed by assessing adjoining property owners— voting may be based on property ownership. (For example, in Ball v. James, 451 U.S. 355 (1981), the Court upheld a system for electing directors of an "agricultural improvement and irrigation district" where votes were apportioned on the basis of acres owned within the district.)

4. It can be argued that the Court's post-*Harper* voting cases were the inevitable outcome of the earlier decision in Reynolds v. Sims. If the Equal Protection Clause of the Fourteenth Amendment protected voters from dilution of their votes by unequal districts, then it must also protect them from state laws that deny them the right to cast any vote at all. If Justice Black dissented in *Harper* because, the Court has "limited power to interpret the original meaning of the Equal Protection Clause," but has no power to give "that clause a new meaning which it believes represents a better governmental policy," why did he join the Court's opinion in Reynolds v. Sims?

C. UNIFORM STANDARDS IN COUNTING VOTES

BUSH v. GORE

Supreme Court of the United States, 2000.
531 U.S. 98, 121 S.Ct. 525, 148 L.Ed.2d 388.

[The following chronology of events led up to the Court's decision in this case, which is also known as *Bush* II:

November 7. Election day.

November 8. The 2000 presidential election is too close to call. It appears that Florida's 25 electoral votes will determine the election. The Florida Division of Elections reports that George W. Bush leads Albert Gore by 1,784 votes out of a total of 5,816,486 votes cast.

November 9. Unofficial returns show that Gore leads Bush nationally by more than 200,000 votes. Machine recounts required by Florida law because of the closeness of the election reduce Bush's lead to 327 votes. Gore seeks manual recounts in four Florida Counties: Broward, Miami–Dade, Palm Beach, and Volusia. Secretary of State Katherine Harris announces that all vote totals must be submitted by the general statutory deadline, November 14.

November 18. Overseas ballot returns increase Bush's lead to 930 votes.

November 21. The Florida Supreme Court unanimously orders in *Palm Beach County Canvassing Bd.* v. *Harris* and two companion cases that manual recounts proceed in selected counties. The Court also interprets two conflicting provisions of the Florida elections law—one stating that the secretary of state "shall" ignore returns received after the statutory deadline, and the other that the secretary "may" ignore such returns—and concludes the latter provision controls. Finally, the Court, relying upon the right to vote guaranteed by the Declaration of Rights in the Florida Constitution, holds that late manual returns may be rejected by the secretary only in limited circumstances, and invoking its equitable powers, the Court extends the deadline for all ballot returns to November 26 at 5 p.m.

November 22. Bush petitions the U.S. Supreme Court to review the Florida Supreme Court's decision. His petition presents two questions: (1) Did the Florida Supreme Court change the state's election procedure after the election in violation of the Due Process Clause or 3 U.S.C.§ 5?[1] (2) Did the Florida

---

1. 3 U.S.C. § 5 provides: "If any State shall have provided, by laws enacted prior to the day fixed for the appointment of the electors, for its final determination of any controversy or contest concerning the appointment of all or any of the electors of such State, by judicial or other methods or procedures, and such determination shall have been made at least six days before the time fixed for the meeting of the electors, such determination made pursuant to such law so existing on said day, and made at least six days prior to said time of meeting of the electors, shall be conclusive, and shall govern in the counting of the

Supreme Court change the manner of the state election in violation of the state legislature's power to designate the manner for selection under Art II, § 1, cl. 2?[2]

November 24. The U.S. Supreme Court grants Bush's petition.

December 1. Counsel for Bush and Gore argue *Bush* I before the U.S. Supreme Court.

December 4. The U.S. Supreme Court, in a *per curiam* opinion, unanimously vacates the Florida Supreme Court in *Bush* I. But the U.S. Supreme Court declines to answer the questions presented in Bush's petition because, it says, the grounds for the state court's actions are unclear, specifically "as to the extent to which the Florida Supreme Court saw the Florida constitution as circumscribing the legislature's authority under Art. II, § 1, cl. 2 [and] as to the consideration the Florida Court accorded to 3 U.S.C. § 5."

December 8. The Florida Supreme Court holds in *Gore* v. *Harris* (which would become *Bush* II) that 9,000 ballots in Miami–Dade County must be manually counted and orders the Circuit Court to include in the certified results of the election 215 votes in Palm Beach County and 168 votes in Miami–Dade County for Gore. It also orders the Circuit Court to resolve Bush's assertion that Gore's net gain in Palm Beach County totals 176 votes. Further, the Florida Supreme Court holds that relief requires manual recounts in all Florida counties where "undervotes" had been subject to manual tabulation, and the standard to be used in determining a legal vote is the one provided by the legislature—"one in which there is a clear indication of the intent of the voter." Bush immediately applies to the U.S. Supreme Court for a stay of the Florida Supreme Court's orders.

December 9. The U.S. Supreme Court, by a five-to-four vote, stays the Florida Supreme Court's orders. Justice Stevens issues a dissenting opinion, joined by Justices Souter, Ginsberg, and Breyer, in which he says:

> To stop the counting of legal votes, the majority today departs from three venerable rules of judicial restraint that have guided the Court throughout its history. On questions of state law, we have consistently respected the opinions of the highest courts of the States. On questions whose resolution is committed at least in large measure to another branch of the Federal

electoral votes as provided in the Constitution, and as hereinafter regulated, so far as the ascertainment of the electors appointed by such State is concerned."

2. Art. II, § 1, cl. 2 provides: "Each State shall appoint, in such Manner as the Legislature thereof may direct, a Number of Electors, equal to the whole Number of Senators and Representatives to which the State may be entitled in the Congress: but no Senator or Representative, or Person holding an Office of Trust or Profit under the United States, shall be appointed an Elector."

Government, we have construed our own jurisdiction narrowly and exercised it cautiously. On federal constitutional questions that were not fairly presented to the court whose judgment is being reviewed, we have prudently declined to express an opinion. The majority has acted unwisely.

Time does not permit a full discussion of the merits. It is clear, however, that a stay should not be granted unless an applicant makes a substantial showing of a likelihood of irreparable harm. In this case, applicants have failed to carry that heavy burden. Counting every legally cast vote cannot constitute irreparable harm. On the other had, there is a danger that a stay may cause irreparable harm to the respondents—and, more importantly, the public at large—because of the risk that "the entry of the stay would be tantamount to a decision on the merits in favor of the applicants."

Justice Scalia responds as follows in a concurring opinion:

... The issue is not, as the dissent puts it, whether "[c]ounting every legally cast vote ca[n] constitute irreparable harm." One of the principal issues in the appeal we have accepted is precisely whether that votes that have been ordered to be counted are, under a reasonable interpretation of Florida law, "legally cast vote[s]." The counting of votes that are of questionable legality does in my view threaten irreparable harm to petitioner, and to the country, by casting a cloud upon what he claims to be the legitimacy of his election. Count first, and rule upon legality afterwards, is not a recipe for producing election results that have the public acceptance democratic stability requires. Another issue in the case, moreover, is the propriety, indeed the constitutionality, of letting the standard for determination of voters' intent—dimpled chads, hanging chads, etc.—vary from county to county, as the Florida Supreme Court opinion, as interpreted by the Circuit Court, permits. If the petitioner is correct that counting in this fashion is unlawful, permitting the count to proceed on that erroneous basis will prevent an accurate recount from being conducted on a proper basis later, since it is generally agreed that each manual recount produces a degradation of the ballots, which renders a subsequent count inaccurate.

December 11. Counsel for Bush and Gore argues *Bush* II before the U.S. Supreme Court.

December 12. The U.S. Supreme Court decides *Bush* v. *Gore* (*Bush* II).

December 13, Gore concedes the election.

December 18, the Electoral College votes. Bush receives 271 votes, and Gore receives 266.]

Per Curiam.

I

. . .

The petition presents the following questions: whether the Florida Supreme Court established new standards for resolving Presidential election contests, thereby violating Art. II, § 1, cl. 2, of the United States Constitution and failing to comply with 3 U.S.C. § 5 and whether the use of standardless manual recounts violates the Equal Protection and Due Process Clauses. With respect to the equal protection question, we find a violation of the Equal Protection Clause.

II

A

The closeness of this election, and the multitude of legal challenges which have followed in its wake, have brought into sharp focus a common, if heretofore unnoticed, phenomenon. Nationwide statistics reveal that an estimated 2% of ballots cast do not register a vote for President for whatever reason, including deliberately choosing no candidate at all or some voter error, such as voting for two candidates or insufficiently marking a ballot.... In certifying election results, the votes eligible for inclusion in the certification are the votes meeting the properly established legal requirements.

This case has shown that punch card balloting machines can produce an unfortunate number of ballots which are not punched in a clean, complete way by the voter. After the current counting, it is likely legislative bodies nationwide will examine ways to improve the mechanisms and machinery for voting.

B

The individual citizen has no federal constitutional right to vote for electors for the President of the United States unless and until the state legislature chooses a statewide election as the means to implement its power to appoint members of the Electoral College. U.S. Const., Art. II, § 1. This is the source for the statement in *McPherson* v. *Blacker*, 146 U.S. 1, 35 (1892), that the State legislature's power to select the manner for appointing electors is plenary; it may, if it so chooses, select the electors itself, which indeed was the manner used by State legislatures in several States for many years after the Framing of our Constitution.... History has now favored the voter, and in each of the several States the citizens themselves vote for Presidential electors. When the state legislature vests the right to vote for President in its people, the right to vote as the legislature has prescribed is fundamental; and one source of its fundamental nature lies in the equal weight accorded to each vote and the equal dignity owed to each voter. The State, of course, after granting the franchise in the special context of Article II, can take back the power to appoint electors. . . .

The right to vote is protected in more than the initial allocation of the franchise. Equal protection applies as well to the manner of its exercise. Having once granted the right to vote on equal terms, the State may not, by later arbitrary and disparate treatment, value one person's vote over that of another. . . .

There is no difference between the two sides of the present controversy on these basic propositions. . . . The question before us, however, is whether the recount procedures the Florida Supreme Court has adopted are consistent with its obligation to avoid arbitrary and disparate treatment of the members of its electorate.

Much of the controversy seems to revolve around ballot cards designed to be perforated by a stylus but which, either through error or deliberate omission, have not been perforated with sufficient precision for a machine to count them. In some cases a piece of the card—a chad— is hanging, say by two corners. In other cases there is no separation at all, just an indentation.

The Florida Supreme Court has ordered that the intent of the voter be discerned from such ballots. For purposes of resolving the equal protection challenge, it is not necessary to decide whether the Florida Supreme Court had the authority under the legislative scheme for resolving election disputes to define what a legal vote is and to mandate a manual recount implementing that definition. The recount mechanisms implemented in response to the decisions of the Florida Supreme Court do not satisfy the minimum requirement for non-arbitrary treatment of voters necessary to secure the fundamental right. Florida's basic command for the count of legally cast votes is to consider the "intent of the voter." . . . This is unobjectionable as an abstract proposition and a starting principle. The problem inheres in the absence of specific standards to ensure its equal application. The formulation of uniform rules to determine intent based on these recurring circumstances is practicable and, we conclude, necessary.

· · ·

The want of those rules here has led to unequal evaluation of ballots in various respects. . . . As seems to have been acknowledged at oral argument, the standards for accepting or rejecting contested ballots might vary not only from county to county but indeed within a single county from one recount team to another.

The record provides some examples. A monitor in Miami–Dade County testified at trial that he observed that three members of the county canvassing board applied different standards in defining a legal vote. . . . And testimony at trial also revealed that at least one county changed its evaluative standards during the counting process. Palm Beach County, for example, began the process with a 1990 guideline which precluded counting completely attached chads, switched to a rule that considered a vote to be legal if any light could be seen through a chad, changed back to the 1990 rule, and then abandoned any pretense of a *per se* rule, only to have a court order that the county consider dimpled chads legal. This is not a process with sufficient guarantees of equal treatment.

. . .

The State Supreme Court ratified this uneven treatment. It mandated that the recount totals from two counties, Miami–Dade and Palm Beach, be included in the certified total. The court also appeared to hold *sub silentio* that the recount totals from Broward County, which were not completed until after the original November 14 certification by the Secretary of State, were to be considered part of the new certified vote totals even though the county certification was not contested by Vice President Gore. Yet each of the counties used varying standards to determine what was a legal vote. Broward County used a more forgiving standard than Palm Beach County, and uncovered almost three times as many new votes, a result markedly disproportionate to the difference in population between the counties.

In addition, the recounts in these three counties were not limited to so-called undervotes but extended to all of the ballots. The distinction has real consequences. A manual recount of all ballots identifies not only those ballots which show no vote but also those which contain more than one, the so-called overvotes. Neither category will be counted by the machine. This is not a trivial concern. At oral argument, respondents estimated there are as many as 110,000 overvotes statewide. As a result, the citizen whose ballot was not read by a machine because he failed to vote for a candidate in a way readable by a machine may still have his vote counted in a manual recount; on the other hand, the citizen who marks two candidates in a way discernable by the machine will not have the same opportunity to have his vote count, even if a manual examination of the ballot would reveal the requisite indicia of intent. Furthermore, the citizen who marks two candidates, only one of which is discernable by the machine, will have his vote counted even though it should have been read as an invalid ballot. The State Supreme Court's inclusion of vote counts based on these variant standards exemplifies concerns with the remedial processes that were under way.

That brings the analysis to yet a further equal protection problem. The votes certified by the court included a partial total from one county, Miami–Dade. The Florida Supreme Court's decision thus gives no assurance that the recounts included in a final certification must be complete. Indeed, it is respondent's submission that it would be consistent with the rules of the recount procedures to include whatever partial counts are done by the time of final certification, and we interpret the Florida Supreme Court's decision to permit this.... This accommodation no doubt results from the truncated contest period established by the Florida Supreme Court in *Bush I*, at respondents' own urging. The press of time does not diminish the constitutional concern. A desire for speed is not a general excuse for ignoring equal protection guarantees.

In addition to these difficulties the actual process by which the votes were to be counted under the Florida Supreme Court's decision raises further concerns. That order did not specify who would recount the ballots. The county canvassing boards were forced to pull together ad hoc teams comprised of judges from various Circuits who had no previous training in handling and interpreting ballots. Furthermore, while others were permitted to observe, they were prohibited from objecting during the recount.

The recount process, in its features here described, is inconsistent with the minimum procedures necessary to protect the fundamental right of each voter in the special instance of a statewide recount under the authority of a single state judicial officer. Our consideration is limited to the present circumstances, for the problem of equal protection in election processes generally presents many complexities.

The question before the Court is not whether local entities, in the exercise of their expertise, may develop different systems for implementing elections. Instead, we are presented with a situation where a state court with the power to assure uniformity has ordered a statewide recount with minimal procedural safeguards. When a court orders a statewide remedy, there must be at least some assurance that the rudimentary requirements of equal treatment and fundamental fairness are satisfied.

Given the Court's assessment that the recount process underway was probably being conducted in an unconstitutional manner, the Court stayed the order directing the recount so it could hear this case and render an expedited decision. The contest provision, as it was mandated by the State Supreme Court, is not well calculated to sustain the confidence that all citizens must have in the outcome of elections. The State has not shown that its procedures include the necessary safeguards. The problem, for instance, of the estimated 110,000 overvotes has not been addressed, although Chief Justice Wells called attention to the concern in his dissenting opinion....

Upon due consideration of the difficulties identified to this point, it is obvious that the recount cannot be conducted in compliance with the requirements of equal protection and due process without substantial additional work. It would require not only the adoption (after opportunity for argument) of adequate statewide standards for determining what is a legal vote, and practicable procedures to implement them, but also orderly judicial review of any disputed matters that might arise....

The Supreme Court of Florida has said that the legislature intended the State's electors to "participat[e] fully in the federal electoral process," as provided in 3 U.S.C. § 5.... That statute, in turn, requires that any controversy or contest that is designed to lead to a conclusive selection of electors be completed by December 12. That date is upon us, and there is no recount procedure in place under the State Supreme Court's order that comports with minimal constitutional standards. Because it is evident that any recount seeking to meet the December 12 date will be unconstitutional for the reasons we have discussed, we reverse the judgment of the Supreme Court of Florida ordering a recount to proceed.

Seven Justices of the Court agree that there are constitutional problems with the recount ordered by the Florida Supreme Court that demand a remedy.... The only disagreement is as to the remedy. Because the Florida Supreme Court has said that the Florida Legislature intended to obtain the safe-harbor benefits of 3 U.S.C. § 5 Justice Breyer's proposed remedy—remanding to the Florida Supreme Court for its ordering of a constitutionally proper contest until December 18— contemplates action in violation of the Florida election code, and hence could not be part of an "appropriate" order authorized by Fla. Stat. § 102.168(8) (2000).

. . .

The judgment of the Supreme Court of Florida is reversed, and the case is remanded for further proceedings not inconsistent with this opinion.

CHIEF JUSTICE REHNQUIST, with whom JUSTICE SCALIA and JUSTICE THOMAS join, concurring.

We join the *per curiam* opinion. We write separately because we believe there are additional grounds that require us to reverse the Florida Supreme Court's decision.

I

We deal here not with an ordinary election, but with an election for the President of the United States....

In most cases, comity and respect for federalism compel us to defer to the decisions of state courts on issues of state law. That practice reflects our understanding that the decisions of state courts are definitive pronouncements of the will of the States as sovereigns.... Of course, in ordinary cases, the distribution of powers among the branches of a State's government raises no questions of federal constitutional law, ... But there are a few exceptional cases in which the Constitution imposes a duty or confers a power on a particular branch of a State's government. This is one of them. Article II, § 1, cl. 2, provides that "[e]ach State shall appoint, in such Manner as the *Legislature* thereof may direct," electors for President and Vice President. (Emphasis added.) Thus, the text of the election law itself, and not just its interpretation by the courts of the States, takes on independent significance.

In *McPherson* v. *Blacker,* 146 U.S. 1 (1892), we explained that Art. II, § 1, cl. 2, "convey[s] the broadest power of determination" and "leaves it to the legislature exclusively to define the method" of appointment.... A significant departure from the legislative scheme for appointing Presidential electors presents a federal constitutional question.

3 U.S.C. § 5 informs our application of Art. II, § 1, cl. 2, to the Florida statutory scheme, which, as the Florida Supreme Court acknowledged, took that statute into account. Section 5 provides that the State's selection of electors "shall be conclusive, and shall govern in the counting of the electoral votes" if the electors are chosen under laws enacted prior to election day, and if the selection process is completed six days prior to the meeting of the electoral college. As we noted in *Bush* v. *Palm Beach County Canvassing Bd.,* ...

"Since § 5 contains a principle of federal law that would assure finality of the State's determination if made pursuant to a state law in effect before the election, a legislative wish to take advantage of the 'safe harbor' would counsel against any construction of the Election Code that Congress might deem to be a change in the law."

If we are to respect the legislature's Article II powers, therefore, we must ensure that postelection state-court actions do not frustrate the legislative desire to attain the "safe harbor" provided by § 5.

In Florida, the legislature has chosen to hold statewide elections to appoint the State's 25 electors. Importantly, the legislature has delegated the authority to run the elections and to oversee election disputes to the Secretary of State (Secretary) ... and to state circuit courts.... [T]he general coherence of the legislative scheme may not be altered by judicial interpretation so as to wholly change the statutorily provided apportionment of responsibility among these various bodies. In any election but a Presidential election, the Florida Supreme Court can give as little or as much deference to Florida's executives as it chooses, so far as Article II is concerned, and this Court will have no cause to question the court's actions. But, with respect to a Presidential election, the court must be both mindful of the legislature's role under Article II in choosing the manner of appointing electors and deferential to those bodies expressly empowered by the legislature to carry out its constitutional mandate.

In order to determine whether a state court has infringed upon the legislature's authority, we necessarily must examine the law of the State as it existed prior to the action of the court. Though we generally defer to state courts on the interpretation of state law ... there are of course areas in which the Constitution requires this Court to undertake an independent, if still deferential, analysis of state law.

.   .   .

II

Acting pursuant to its constitutional grant of authority, the Florida Legislature has created a detailed, if not perfectly crafted, statutory scheme that provides for appointment of Presidential electors by direct election.... The legislature has designated the Secretary of State as the "chief election officer," with the responsibility to "[o]btain and maintain uniformity in the application, operation, and interpretation of the election laws." ... The state legislature has delegated to county canvassing boards the duties of administering elections.... Those boards are responsible for providing results to the state Elections Canvassing Commission, comprising the Governor, the Secretary of State, and the Director of the Division of Elections....

After the election has taken place, the canvassing boards receive returns from precincts, count the votes, and in the event that a candidate was defeated by .5% or less, conduct a mandatory recount.... The county canvassing boards must file certified election returns with the

Department of State by 5 p.m. on the seventh day following the election....

. . .

In its first decision, ... the Florida Supreme Court extended the 7-day statutory certification deadline established by the legislature. This modification of the code, by lengthening the protest period, necessarily shortened the contest period for Presidential elections. Underlying the extension of the certification deadline and the shortchanging of the contest period was, presumably, the clear implication that certification was a matter of significance: The certified winner would enjoy presumptive validity, making a contest proceeding by the losing candidate an uphill battle. In its latest opinion, however, the court empties certification of virtually all legal consequence during the contest, and in doing so departs from the provisions enacted by the Florida Legislature.

... Moreover, the Florida court held that all late vote tallies arriving during the contest period should be automatically included in the certification regardless of the certification deadline, ... thus virtually eliminating both the deadline and the Secretary's discretion to disregard recounts that violate it.

Moreover, the court's interpretation of "legal vote," and hence its decision to order a contest-period recount, plainly departed from the legislative scheme. Florida statutory law cannot reasonably be thought to *require* the counting of improperly marked ballots.... The scheme that the Florida Supreme Court's opinion attributes to the legislature is one in which machines are *required* to be "capable of correctly counting votes," ... but which nonetheless regularly produces elections in which legal votes are predictably *not* tabulated, so that in close elections manual recounts are regularly required. This is of course absurd. The Secretary of State, who is authorized by law to issue binding interpretations of the election code, ... rejected this peculiar reading of the statutes.... The Florida Supreme Court, although it must defer to the Secretary's interpretations, ... rejected her reasonable interpretation and embraced the peculiar one....

But as we indicated in our remand of the earlier case, in a Presidential election the clearly expressed intent of the legislature must prevail. And there is no basis for reading the Florida statutes as requiring the counting of improperly marked ballots ...

III

The scope and nature of the remedy ordered by the Florida Supreme Court jeopardizes the "legislative wish" to take advantage of the safe harbor provided by 3 U.S.C. § 5.... December 12, 2000, is the last date for a final determination of the Florida electors that will satisfy § 5. Yet in the late afternoon of December 8th—four days before this deadline—the Supreme Court of Florida ordered recounts of tens of thousands of so-called "undervotes" spread through 64 of the State's 67 counties. This was done in a search for elusive—perhaps delusive—certainty as to the exact count of 6 million votes. But no one claims that these ballots have not previously been tabulated; they were initially read by voting machines at the time of the election, and thereafter reread by virtue of Florida's automatic recount provision. No one claims there was any fraud in the election. The Supreme Court of Florida ordered this additional recount under the provision of the election code giving the circuit judge the authority to provide relief that is "appropriate under such circumstances." . . .

Surely when the Florida Legislature empowered the courts of the State to grant "appropriate" relief, it must have meant relief that would have become final by the cut-off date of 3 U.S.C. § 5 . . . . Although the Florida Supreme Court has on occasion taken over a year to resolve disputes over local elections, . . . it has heard and decided the appeals in the present case with great promptness. But the federal deadlines for the Presidential election simply do not permit even such a shortened process.

. . .

Given all these factors, and in light of the legislative intent identified by the Florida Supreme Court to bring Florida within the "safe harbor" provision of 3 U.S.C. § 5 the remedy prescribed by the Supreme Court of Florida cannot be deemed an "appropriate" one . . .

For these reasons, in addition to those given in the *per curiam*, we would reverse.

Justice Stevens, with whom Justice Ginsburg and Justice Breyer join, dissenting.

The Constitution assigns to the States the primary responsibility for determining the manner of selecting the Presidential electors. See Art. II, § 1, cl. 2. When questions arise about the meaning of state laws, including election laws, it is our settled practice to accept the opinions of the highest courts of the States as providing the final answers. On rare occasions, however, either federal statutes or the Federal Constitution may require federal judicial intervention in state elections. This is not such an occasion.

The federal questions that ultimately emerged in this case are not substantial. Article II . . . does not create state legislatures out of whole cloth, but rather takes them as they come—as creatures born of, and constrained by, their state constitutions. . . . The legislative power in Florida is subject to judicial review pursuant to Article V of the Florida Constitution, and nothing in Article II of the Federal Constitution frees the state legislature from the constraints in the state constitution that created it. Moreover, the Florida Legislature's own decision to employ a unitary code for all elections indicates that it intended the Florida Supreme Court to play the same role in Presidential elections that it has historically played in resolving electoral disputes. The Florida Supreme Court's exercise of appellate jurisdiction therefore was wholly consistent with, and indeed contemplated by, the grant of authority in Article II.

It hardly needs stating that Congress, pursuant to 3 U.S.C. § 5 did not impose any affirmative duties upon the States that their governmental branches could "violate." Rather, § 5 provides a safe harbor for States to select electors in contested elections "by judicial or other methods" established by laws prior to the election day . . . .

Nor are petitioners correct in asserting that the failure of the Florida Supreme Court to specify in detail the precise manner in which the "intent of the voter" ... is to be determined rises to the level of a constitutional violation.... [W]e have never before called into question the substantive standard by which a State determines that a vote has been legally cast....

... We must remember that the machinery of government would not work if it were not allowed "a little play in its joints." ... If it were otherwise, Florida's decision to leave to each county the determination of what balloting system to employ—despite enormous differences in accuracy—might run afoul of equal protection. So, too, might the similar decisions of the vast majority of state legislatures to delegate to local authorities certain decisions with respect to voting systems and ballot design.

Even assuming that aspects of the remedial scheme might ultimately be found to violate the Equal Protection Clause, I could not subscribe to the majority's disposition of the case.... Under their own reasoning, the appropriate course of action would be to remand to allow more specific procedures for implementing the legislature's uniform general standard to be established.

In the interest of finality, however, the majority effectively orders the disenfranchisement of an unknown number of voters whose ballots reveal their intent—and are therefore legal votes under state law—but were for some reason rejected by ballot-counting machines. It does so on the basis of the deadlines set forth in Title 3 of the United States Code.... But, as I have already noted, those provisions merely provide rules of decision for Congress to follow when selecting among conflicting slates of electors.... They do not prohibit a State from counting what the majority concedes to be legal votes until a bona fide winner is determined....

Finally, neither in this case, nor in its earlier opinion ... did the Florida Supreme Court make any substantive change in Florida electoral law. Its decisions were rooted in long-established precedent and were consistent with the relevant statutory provisions, taken as a whole. It did what courts do—it decided the case before it in light of the legislature's intent to leave no legally cast vote uncounted....

What must underlie petitioners' entire federal assault on the Florida election procedures is an unstated lack of confidence in the impartiality and capacity of the state judges who would make the critical decisions if the vote count were to proceed. Otherwise, their position is wholly without merit. The endorsement of that position by the majority of this Court can only lend credence to the most cynical appraisal of the work of judges throughout the land. It is confidence in the men and women who administer the judicial system that is the true backbone of the rule of law. Time will one day heal the wound to that confidence that will be inflicted by today's decision. One thing, however, is certain. Although we may never know with complete certainty the identity of the winner of this year's Presidential election, the identity of the loser is perfectly clear. It is the Nation's confidence in the judge as an impartial guardian of the rule of law.

I respectfully dissent.

JUSTICE SOUTER, with whom JUSTICE BREYER joins and with whom JUSTICE STEVENS and JUSTICE GINSBURG join with regard to all but Part C, dissenting.

The Court should not have reviewed either *Bush* v. *Palm Beach County Canvassing Bd.,* ... or this case, and should not have stopped Florida's attempt to recount all undervote ballots ... by issuing a stay of the Florida Supreme Court's orders during the period of this review.... The case being before us, however, its resolution by the majority is another erroneous decision.

As will be clear, I am in substantial agreement with the dissenting opinions of Justice Stevens, Justice Ginsburg and Justice Breyer. I write separately only to say how straightforward the issues before us really are.

There are three issues: whether the State Supreme Court's interpretation of the statute providing for a contest of the state election results somehow violates 3 U.S.C. § 5; whether that court's construction of the state statutory provisions governing contests impermissibly changes a state law from what the State's legislature has provided, in violation of Article II, § 1, cl. 2, of the national Constitution; and whether the manner of interpreting markings on disputed ballots failing to cause machines to register votes for President (the undervote ballots) violates the equal protection or due process guaranteed by the Fourteenth Amendment. None of these issues is difficult to describe or to resolve.

A

The 3 U.S.C. § 5 issue is not serious.... [T]he sanction for failing to satisfy the conditions of § 5 is simply loss of what has been called its "safe harbor." And even that determination is to be made, if made anywhere, in the Congress.

B

The second matter here goes to the State Supreme Court's interpretation of certain terms in the state statute governing election "contests," ... The issue is whether the ... law as declared by the court [is] different from the provisions made by the legislature, to which the national Constitution commits responsibility for determining how each State's Presidential electors are chosen.... [T]he contention, is that the interpretation of § 102.168 was so unreasonable as to transcend the accepted bounds of statutory interpretation, to the point of being a nonjudicial act and producing new law untethered to the legislative act in question.

. . .

... As Justice Ginsburg has persuasively explained in her own dissenting opinion, our customary respect for state interpretations of state law counsels against rejection of the Florida court's determinations in this case.

C

It is only on the third issue before us that there is a meritorious argument for relief, as this Court's *Per Curiam* opinion recognizes. It is an issue that might well have been dealt with adequately by the Florida courts if the state proceedings had not been interrupted, and if not disposed of at the state level it could have been considered by the Congress in any electoral vote dispute....

Petitioners have raised an equal protection claim.... It is true that the Equal Protection Clause does not forbid the use of a variety of voting mechanisms within a jurisdiction, even though different mechanisms will have different levels of effectiveness in recording voters' intentions; local variety can be justified by concerns about cost, the potential value of innovation, and so on. But evidence in the record here suggests that a different order of disparity obtains under rules for determining a voter's intent that have been applied (and could continue to be applied) to identical types of ballots used in identical brands of machines and exhibiting identical physical characteristics (such as "hanging" or "dimpled" chads).... I can conceive of no legitimate state interest served by these differing treatments of the expressions of voters' fundamental rights. The differences appear wholly arbitrary.

. . .

Unlike the majority, I see no warrant for this Court to assume that Florida could not possibly comply with this requirement before the date set for the meeting of electors, December 18.... To recount these manually would be a tall order, but before this Court stayed the effort to do that the courts of Florida were ready to do their best to get that job done. There is no justification for denying the State the opportunity to try to count all disputed ballots now.

I respectfully dissent.

JUSTICE GINSBURG, with whom JUSTICE STEVENS joins, and with whom JUSTICE SOUTER and JUSTICE BREYER join as to Part I, dissenting.

I

The Chief Justice acknowledges that provisions of Florida's Election Code "may well admit of more than one interpretation." ... But instead of respecting the state high court's province to say what the State's Election Code means, The Chief Justice maintains that Florida's Supreme Court has veered so far from the ordinary practice of judicial review that what it did cannot properly be called judging.... But disagreement with the Florida court's interpretation of its own State's law does not warrant the conclusion that the justices of that court have legislated....

. . .

The extraordinary setting of this case has obscured the ordinary principle that dictates its proper resolution: Federal courts defer to state high courts' interpretations of their state's own law.... Were the other members of this Court as mindful as they generally are of our system of dual sovereignty, they would affirm the judgment of the Florida Supreme Court.

II

I agree with Justice Stevens that petitioners have not presented a substantial equal protection claim. Ideally, perfection would be the appropriate standard for judging the recount. But we live in an imperfect world, one in which thousands of votes have not been counted. I cannot agree that the recount adopted by the Florida court, flawed as it may be, would yield a result any less fair or precise than the certification that preceded that recount....

Even if there were an equal protection violation, I would agree with Justice Stevens, Justice Souter, and Justice Breyer that the Court's concern about "the December 12 deadline," ... is misplaced. Time is short in part because of the Court's entry of a stay on December 9.... In sum, the Court's conclusion that a constitutionally adequate recount is impractical is a prophecy the Court's own judgment will not allow to be tested. Such an untested prophecy should not decide the Presidency of the United States.

I dissent.

JUSTICE BREYER, with whom JUSTICE STEVENS and JUSTICE GINSBURG join except as to Part I—A—1, and with whom JUSTICE SOUTER joins as to Part I, dissenting.

The Court was wrong to take this case. It was wrong to grant a stay. It should now vacate that stay and permit the Florida Supreme Court to decide whether the recount should resume.

I

The political implications of this case for the country are momentous. But the federal legal questions presented, with one exception, are insubstantial.

A

I

The majority raises three Equal Protection problems with the Florida Supreme Court's recount order: first, the failure to include overvotes in the manual recount; second, the fact that *all* ballots, rather than simply the undervotes, were recounted in some, but not all, counties; and third, the absence of a uniform, specific standard to guide the recounts. As far as the first issue is concerned, petitioners presented no evidence, to this Court or to any Florida court, that a manual recount of overvotes would identify additional legal votes. The same is true of the second, and, in addition, the majority's reasoning would seem to invalidate any state provision for a manual recount of individual counties in a statewide election.

The majority's third concern does implicate principles of fundamental fairness. The majority concludes that the Equal Protection Clause requires that a manual recount be governed not only by the uniform general standard of the "clear intent of the voter," but also by uniform subsidiary standards (for example, a uniform determination whether indented, but not perforated, "undervotes" should count).... In light of our previous remand, the Florida Supreme Court may have been reluctant to adopt a more specific standard than that provided for by the legislature for fear of exceeding its authority under Article II. However, since the use of different standards could favor one or the other of the candidates, since time was, and is, too short to permit the lower courts to iron out significant differences through ordinary judicial review, and since the relevant distinction was embodied in the order of the State's highest court, I agree that, in these very special circumstances, basic principles of fairness may well have counseled the adoption of a uniform standard to address the problem. In light of the majority's disposition, I need not decide whether, or the extent to which, as a remedial matter, the Constitution would place limits upon the content of the uniform standard.

2

Nonetheless, there is no justification for the majority's remedy, which is simply to reverse the lower court and halt the recount entirely. An appropriate remedy would be, instead, to remand this case with instructions that, even at this late date, would permit the Florida Supreme Court to require recounting *all* undercounted votes in ... accordance with a single-uniform substandard.

The majority justifies stopping the recount entirely on the ground that there is no more time.... Whether there is time to conduct a recount prior to December 18, when the electors are scheduled to meet, is a matter for the state courts to determine. And whether, under Florida law, Florida could or could not take further action is obviously a matter for Florida courts, not this Court, to decide....

By halting the manual recount, and thus ensuring that the uncounted legal votes will not be counted under any standard, this Court crafts a remedy out of proportion to the asserted harm. And that remedy harms the very fairness interests the Court is attempting to protect. The manual recount would itself redress a problem of unequal treatment of ballots.... [I]n a system that allows counties to use different types of voting systems, voters already arrive at the polls with an unequal chance that their votes will be counted. I do not see how the fact that this results from counties' selection of different voting machines rather than a court order makes the outcome any more fair. Nor do I understand why the Florida Supreme Court's recount order, which helps to redress this inequity, must be entirely prohibited based on a deficiency that could easily be remedied.

B

The remainder of petitioners' claims, which are the focus of the Chief Justice's concurrence, raise no significant federal questions....

II

... With one exception, petitioners' claims do not ask us to vindicate a constitutional provision designed to protect a basic human right....

Of course, the selection of the President is of fundamental national importance. But that importance is political, not legal....

The Constitution and federal statutes themselves make clear that restraint is appropriate. They set forth a road map of how to resolve disputes about electors, even after an election as close as this one. That road map foresees resolution of electoral disputes by *state* courts.... But it nowhere provides for involvement by the United States Supreme Court.

To the contrary, the Twelfth Amendment commits to Congress the authority and responsibility to count electoral votes. A federal statute, the Electoral Count Act, enacted after the close 1876 Hayes–Tilden Presidential election, specifies that, after States have tried to resolve disputes (through "judicial" or other means), Congress is the body primarily authorized to resolve remaining disputes....

The legislative history of the Act makes clear its intent to commit the power to resolve such disputes to Congress, rather than the courts:

> "The two Houses are, by the Constitution, authorized to make the count of electoral votes. They can only count legal votes, and in doing so must determine, from the best evidence to be had, what are legal votes.... The power to determine rests with the two Houses, and there is no other constitutional tribunal." H. Rep. No. 1638, 49th Cong., 1st Sess., 2 (1886) (report submitted by Rep. Caldwell, Select Committee on the Election of President and Vice–President).

The Member of Congress who introduced the Act added:

> "The power to judge of the legality of the votes is a necessary consequent of the power to count. The existence of this power is of absolute necessity to the preservation of the Government. The interests of all the States in their relations to each other in the Federal Union demand that the ultimate tribunal to decide upon the election of President should be a constituent body, in which the States in their federal relationships and the people in their sovereign capacity should be represented." 18 Cong. Rec. 30 (1886).

> "Under the Constitution who else could decide? Who is nearer to the State in determining a question of vital importance to the whole union of States than the constituent body upon whom the Constitution has devolved the duty to count the vote?" *Id.*, at 31.

The Act goes on to set out rules for the congressional determination of disputes about those votes. If, for example, a state submits a single slate of electors, Congress must count those votes unless both Houses agree that the votes "have not been ... regularly given." ... If, as occurred in 1876, one or more states submits two sets of electors, then

Congress must determine whether a slate has entered the safe harbor of § 5, in which case its votes will have "conclusive" effect.... If, as also occurred in 1876, there is controversy about "which of two or more of such State authorities ... is the lawful tribunal" authorized to appoint electors, then each House shall determine separately which votes are "supported by the decision of such State so authorized by its law." ... If the two Houses of Congress agree, the votes they have approved will be counted. If they disagree, then "the votes of the electors whose appointment shall have been certified by the executive of the State, under the seal thereof, shall be counted." ...

Given this detailed, comprehensive scheme for counting electoral votes, there is no reason to believe that federal law either foresees or requires resolution of such a political issue by this Court....

The decision by both the Constitution's Framers and the 1886 Congress to minimize this Court's role in resolving close federal presidential elections is as wise as it is clear. However awkward or difficult it may be for Congress to resolve difficult electoral disputes, Congress, being a political body, expresses the people's will far more accurately than does an unelected Court. And the people's will is what elections are about.

Moreover, Congress was fully aware of the danger that would arise should it ask judges, unarmed with appropriate legal standards, to resolve a hotly contested Presidential election contest. Just after the 1876 Presidential election, Florida, South Carolina, and Louisiana each sent two slates of electors to Washington. Without these States, Tilden, the Democrat, had 184 electoral votes, one short of the number required to win the Presidency. With those States, Hayes, his Republican opponent, would have had 185. In order to choose between the two slates of electors, Congress decided to appoint an electoral commission composed of five Senators, five Representatives, and five Supreme Court Justices. Initially the Commission was to be evenly divided between Republicans and Democrats, with Justice David Davis, an Independent, to possess the decisive vote. However, when at the last minute the Illinois Legislature elected Justice Davis to the United States Senate, the final position on the Commission was filled by Supreme Court Justice Joseph P. Bradley.

The Commission divided along partisan lines, and the responsibility to cast the deciding vote fell to Justice Bradley. He decided to accept the votes by the Republican electors, and thereby awarded the Presidency to Hayes.

Justice Bradley immediately became the subject of vociferous attacks. Bradley was accused of accepting bribes, of being captured by railroad interests, and of an eleventh-hour change in position after a night in which his house "was surrounded by the carriages" of Republican partisans and railroad officials. C. Woodward, Reunion and Reaction 159–160 (1966). Many years later, Professor Bickel concluded that Bradley was honest and impartial. He thought that " 'the great question' for Bradley was, in fact, whether Congress was entitled to go behind election returns or had to accept them as certified by state authorities," an "issue of principle." The Least Dangerous Branch 185 (1962). Nonetheless, Bickel points out, the legal question upon which Justice Bradley's decision turned was not very important in the contemporaneous political context. . . .

For present purposes, the relevance of this history lies in the fact that the participation in the work of the electoral commission by five Justices, including Justice Bradley, did not lend that process legitimacy. Nor did it assure the public that the process had worked fairly, guided by the law. Rather, it simply embroiled Members of the Court in partisan conflict, thereby undermining respect for the judicial process. And the Congress that later enacted the Electoral Count Act knew it.

This history may help to explain why I think it not only legally wrong, but also most unfortunate, for the Court simply to have terminated the Florida recount. . . .

. . .

I respectfully dissent.

III.   GERRYMANDERS

The Court's decision in Reynolds v. Sims meant that a voter's influence could not be diluted by placing her in a district with too many voters. That left the possibility, however, that her influence could be diluted by the way that lines were drawn to define districts of equal population. Voters from one party could be divided among districts in a way that—given the tradition of winner-take-all elections—few members of that party were elected. No Supreme Court case, however, has provided relief against partisan political gerrymanders. In Davis v. Bandemer, 478 U.S. 109 (1986), a majority of the Justices agreed that an extreme political gerrymander was unconstitutional, but were unable to agree on the appropriate standard. Three Justices, in an opinion by Justice O'Connor, argued that all claims of political gerrymandering should be rejected because there were no defensible standards that would distinguish the permissible from the impermissible.

The Court's experience with racial gerrymanders is more complex.

GOMILLION v. LIGHTFOOT

Supreme Court of the United States, 1960.
364 U.S. 339, 81 S.Ct. 125, 5 L.Ed.2d 110.

JUSTICE FRANKFURTER delivered the opinion of the Court.

[A 1957 Alabama statute altered the boundaries of the City of Tuskegee from a square to "an uncouth twenty-eight-sided figure that removed all but four or five of its 400 African–American voters while not removing a single white voter." This is a suit by African–American voters who had lived within the city.]

... Act 140 was not an ordinary geographic redistricting measure even within familiar abuses of gerrymandering. . . . [T]he legislation is solely concerned with segregating white and colored voters by fencing

Negro citizens out of town so as to deprive them of their pre-existing municipal vote.

... "The (Fifteenth) Amendment nullifies sophisticated as well as simple-minded modes of discrimination." Lane v. Wilson, 307 U.S. 268.

The complaint amply alleges a claim of racial discrimination. Against this claim the respondents have never suggested, either in their brief or in oral argument, any countervailing municipal function which Act 140 is designed to serve. The respondents invoke generalities expressing the State's unrestricted power—unlimited, that is, by the United States Constitution—to establish, destroy, or reorganize by contraction or expansion its political subdivisions, to wit, cities, counties, and other local units. We freely recognize the breadth and importance of this aspect of the State's political power. To exalt this power into an absolute is to misconceive the reach and rule of this Court's decisions ...

. . .

... [T]he Court has never acknowledged that the States have power to do as they will with municipal corporations regardless of consequences. Legislative control of municipalities, no less than other state power, lies within the scope of relevant limitations imposed by the United States Constitution....

... [S]uch power, extensive though it is, is met and overcome by the Fifteenth Amendment to the Constitution of the United States, which forbids a State from passing any law which deprives a citizen of his vote because of his race. The opposite conclusion, urged upon us by respondents, would sanction the achievement by a State of any impairment of voting rights whatever so long as it was cloaked in the garb of the realignment of political subdivisions....

. . .

When a State exercises power wholly within the domain of state interest, it is insulated from federal judicial review. But such insulation is not carried over when state power is used as an instrument for circumventing a federally protected right. This principle has had many applications. It has long been recognized in cases which have prohibited a State from exploiting a power acknowledged to be absolute in an isolated context to justify the imposition of an "unconstitutional condition." What the Court has said in those cases is equally applicable here, viz., that "Acts generally lawful may become unlawful when done to accomplish an unlawful end, ... and a constitutional power cannot be used by way of condition to attain an unconstitutional result." ...

. . .

JUSTICE WHITTAKER, concurring.

I concur in the Court's judgment, but not in the whole of its opinion. It seems to me that the decision should be rested not on the Fifteenth Amendment, but rather on the Equal Protection Clause of the Fourteenth Amendment to the Constitution.... [T]he "right * * * to vote" that is guaranteed by the Fifteenth Amendment is but the same right to vote as is enjoyed by all others within the same election precinct, ward or other political division. And, inasmuch as no one has the right to vote in a political division, or in a local election concerning only an area in which he does not reside, it would seem to follow that one's right to vote in Division A is not abridged by a redistricting that places his residence in Division B . . .

But . . . accomplishment of a State's purpose . . . is an unlawful segregation of races of citizens, in violation of the Equal Protection Clause of the Fourteenth Amendment, Brown v. Board of Education . . .

NOTES AND QUESTIONS

1.   The decision was predictable in its outcome. Given the history of evasion of the command of the Fifteenth Amendment, a decision allowing Tuskegee to legislate all of its African–American families out of town would have invited an unknown number of Southern cities and towns to follow suit. Still, as in Smith v. Allwright, there was concern for political reaction to the decision. According to Justice Douglas' notes, Justice Black said in Conference: "Our opinion will be received with as much hostility as Brown v. Bd. of Educ. [I]f political considerations are to keep us from adjudicating a case, this should be the one. All cities in the South do this."

2.   Despite the Court's unanimity, the case was more difficult to decide than it would appear today. A major issue not resolved in 1960 was the reapportionment issue—whether the Constitution afforded a judicial remedy against electoral districts of different sizes. In Colegrove v. Green, 328 U.S. 549 (1946), the Court dismissed a suit complaining about an 8–1 variance in the population of Illinois Congressional districts. There was no opinion for the Court, but Justice Frankfurter wrote for himself and two other Justices that any constitutional commands relevant to the case were not judicially enforceable because they would require the courts to enter a "political thicket." During the conference to decide *Gomillion*, Justices Black and Frankfurter debated the relevance of *Colegrove*. Justice Black argued that the two cases were indistinguishable, to which Justice Frankfurter replied that "Colegrove [was] not remotely relevant here—Colegrove is irrelevant because the Const[itution] gives Congress express power to redistrict—here Negroes are fenced out because they are Negroes." Douglas Papers, Library of Congress, Box 1232.

Justice Frankfurter obviously tried to write a narrow opinion in *Gomillion* that would not require courts to enter the "political thicket" of reapportionment cases. When Baker v. Carr, 369 U.S. 186, held reapportionment cases justiciable two years later, Justice Frankfurter predictably dissented. Justice Whittaker had attempted to treat *Gomillion* as not a voting case at all. He did not participate in the final phase of the Court's decision in Baker v. Carr, because doctors at Walter Reed Hospital told him that he was completely exhausted and that resumption of the work on the Court would endanger his life. According to Bernard Schwartz, Whittaker had joined Frankfurter's draft dissent in Baker v. Carr, but "his vote had never been firm, and he was subjected to constant pressure from Frankfurter to prevent him from wavering."

Schwartz concludes that stress over Baker v. Carr was a major factor leading to Whittaker's collapse and his retirement at the age of 61. Schwartz, *Super Chief: Earl Warren and his Supreme Court—A Judicial Biography* 428 (1983).

3. The combination of Davis v. Bandemer and Gomillion v. Lightfoot suggested that gerrymanders intended to disenfranchise racial minorities were unconstitutional and could be undone by courts, although there was no realistic judicial remedy against partisan political gerrymanders. It was also thought that it was permissible to use gerrymanders as a remedy to increase the voting power of racial minorities.

4. That understanding was the result of the decision in United Jewish Organizations v. Carey, 430 U.S. 144 (1977). As indicated at the beginning of this chapter, the Voting Rights Act of 1965 provides that "covered jurisdictions" cannot enact new laws related to voting without approval of the United States Attorney General who must determine whether the new law has the purpose or effect of abridging the right to vote on account of race. In Allen v. State Board of Elections, 393 U.S. 544 (1969), the Court decided that the Act required "preclearance" not only of laws that dealt with registration and voting, but also with a wide range of electoral practices—including reapportionment. Portions of New York were, in the 1970s, "covered jurisdictions," and the Attorney General refused to approve the reapportionment of the New York legislature. In response, New York's legislature drew new lines in Brooklyn, splitting the Hasidic Jewish community into two districts in order to maintain certain percentages of white and nonwhite voters in those two districts. In a case brought by Hasidic Jews, who claimed that their voting strength had been diluted by the drawing of lines based on race, the Court sustained the reapportionment. There was no opinion for the Court, however, despite the Court's approval of explicit consideration of race to draw electoral lines in this case.

MILLER v. JOHNSON

Supreme Court of the United States, 1995.
515 U.S. 900, 115 S.Ct. 2475, 132 L.Ed.2d 762.

JUSTICE KENNEDY delivered the opinion of the Court.

The constitutionality of Georgia's congressional redistricting plan is at issue here. In Shaw v. Reno, 509 U.S. 630 (1993), we held that a plaintiff states a claim under the Equal Protection Clause by alleging that a state redistricting plan, on its face, has no rational explanation save as an effort to separate voters on the basis of race. The question we now decide is whether Georgia's new Eleventh District gives rise to a valid equal protection claim under the principles announced in *Shaw*, and, if so, whether it can be sustained nonetheless as narrowly tailored to serve a compelling governmental interest.

I

A

The Equal Protection Clause['s] ... central mandate is racial neutrality in governmental decisionmaking.... Laws classifying citizens on the basis of race cannot be upheld unless they are narrowly tailored to achieving a compelling state interest. See, e.g., *Adarand* ...

In Shaw v. Reno ... we recognized that these equal protection principles govern a State's drawing of congressional districts, though, as our cautious approach there discloses, application of these principles to electoral districting is a most delicate task. Our analysis began from the premise that "[l]aws that explicitly distinguish between individuals on racial grounds fall within the core of [the Equal Protection Clause's] prohibition." ... Applying this basic Equal Protection analysis in the voting rights context, we held that "redistricting legislation that is so bizarre on its face that it is 'unexplainable on grounds other than race,' ... demands the same close scrutiny that we give other state laws that classify citizens by race." ...

This case requires us to apply the principles articulated in *Shaw* to the most recent congressional redistricting plan enacted by the State of Georgia.

B

In 1965, the Attorney General designated Georgia a covered jurisdiction under § 4(b) of the Voting Rights Act.... In consequence, § 5 of the Act requires Georgia to obtain ... administrative preclearance by the Attorney General.... "[T]he purpose of § 5 has always been to insure that no voting-procedure changes would be made that would lead to a retrogression in the position of racial minorities with respect to their effective exercise of the electoral franchise." ...

Between 1980 and 1990, one of Georgia's 10 congressional districts was a majority-black district, that is, a majority of the district's voters were black. The 1990 Decennial Census indicated that Georgia's population of 6,478,216 persons, 27% of whom are black, entitled it to an additional eleventh congressional seat, ... prompting Georgia's General Assembly to redraw the State's congressional districts....

[Two successive redistricting plans submitted to the Attorney General for preclearance, each containing two majority-minority districts, were rejected because the Justice Department, "relying on alternative plans proposing three majority-minority districts"—one alternative being "the so-called 'max-black' plan ... drafted by the American Civil Liberties Union (ACLU) for the General Assembly's black caucus"— "concluded that Georgia had 'failed to explain adequately' its failure to create a third majority-minority district."]

Twice spurned, the General Assembly set out to create three majority-minority districts to gain preclearance.... Using the ACLU's "max-black" plan as its benchmark, ... the General Assembly enacted a plan that "bore all the signs of [the Justice Department's] involvement...." The Eleventh District lost the black population of Macon, but picked up Savannah, thereby connecting the black neighborhoods of metropolitan Atlanta and the poor black populace of coastal Chatham County, though 260 miles apart in distance and worlds apart in culture.... Georgia's plan included three majority-black districts, though, and received Justice Department preclearance ...

Elections were held under the new congressional redistricting plan on November 4, 1992, and black candidates were elected to Congress from all three majority-black districts.... [F]ive white voters from the Eleventh District [sued,] ... alleg[ing] that Georgia's Eleventh District was a racial gerrymander and so a violation of the Equal Protection Clause as interpreted in Shaw v. Reno. A three-judge [federal district] court was convened [and held] the Eleventh District ... invalid under *Shaw*, with one judge dissenting....

II

A

... [Appellants] contend that evidence of a legislature's deliberate classification of voters on the basis of race cannot alone suffice to state a claim under *Shaw*. They argue that ... a plaintiff must demonstrate that a district's shape is so bizarre that it is unexplainable other than on the basis of race, and that appellees failed to make that showing here. Appellants' conception of the constitutional violation misapprehends our holding in *Shaw* ...

Shaw recognized a claim "analytically distinct" from a vote dilution claim.... Whereas a vote dilution claim alleges that the State has enacted a particular voting scheme as a purposeful device "to minimize or cancel out the voting potential of racial or ethnic minorities," Mobile v. Bolden, 446 U.S. 55, 66 (1980) ..., an action disadvantaging voters of a particular race, the essence of the equal protection claim recognized in *Shaw* is that the State has used race as a basis for separating voters into districts. Just as the State may not, absent extraordinary justification, segregate citizens on the basis of race in its public parks, ... buses, ... golf courses, ..., beaches, ... and schools, ... so did we recognize in *Shaw* that it may not separate its citizens into different voting districts on the basis of race.... As we concluded in *Shaw*: "Racial classifications with respect to voting carry particular dangers. Racial gerrymandering, even for remedial purposes, may balkanize us into competing racial factions; it threatens to carry us further from the goal of a political system in which race no longer matters—a goal that the Fourteenth and Fifteenth Amendments embody, and to which the Nation continues to aspire. It is for these reasons that race-based districting by our state legislatures demands close judicial scrutiny." ...

Our observation in *Shaw* of the consequences of racial stereotyping was not meant to suggest that a district must be bizarre on its face before there is a constitutional violation.... Shape is relevant not because bizarreness is ... the constitutional wrong ..., but because it may be persuasive circumstantial evidence that race for its own sake, and not other districting principles, was the legislature's dominant and controlling rationale in drawing its district lines....

... [In prior cases,] the presumed racial purpose of state action, not its stark manifestation, [was] the constitutional violation....

Shaw applied these same principles to redistricting. "In some exceptional cases, a reapportionment plan may be so highly irregular that, on its face, it rationally cannot be understood as anything other than an effort to 'segregat[e] ... voters' on the basis of race." ... In other cases, where the district is not so bizarre on its face that it discloses a racial design, the proof will be more "difficul[t]." ...

Appellants and some of their amici argue that the Equal Protection Clause's general proscription on race-based decisionmaking does not obtain in the districting context because redistricting by definition involves racial considerations. Underlying their argument are the very stereotypical assumptions the Equal Protection Clause forbids. It is true that redistricting in most cases will implicate a political calculus in which various interests compete for recognition, but it does not follow from this that individuals of the same race share a single political interest. The view that they do is "based on the demeaning notion that members of the defined racial groups ascribe to certain 'minority views' that must be different from those of other citizens," ... the precise use of race as a proxy the Constitution prohibits. Nor can the argument that districting cases are excepted from standard equal protection precepts be resuscitated by United Jewish Organizations of Williamsburgh, Inc. v. Carey, 430 U.S. 144 (1977), where the Court addressed a claim that New York violated the Constitution by splitting a Hasidic Jewish community in order to include additional majority-minority districts.... To the extent any of the opinions in that "highly fractured decision" ... can be interpreted as suggesting that a State's assignment of voters on the basis of race would be subject to anything but our strictest scrutiny, those views ought not be deemed controlling.

In sum, we make clear that parties alleging that a State has assigned voters on the basis of race are neither confined in their proof to evidence regarding the district's geometry and makeup nor required to make a threshold showing of bizarreness. Today's case requires us further to consider the requirements of the proof necessary to sustain this equal protection challenge.

B

Federal court review of districting legislation represents a serious intrusion on the most vital of local functions.... Electoral districting is a most difficult subject for legislatures, and so the States must have discretion to exercise the political judgment necessary to balance competing interests.... The courts, in assessing the sufficiency of a challenge to a districting plan, must be sensitive to the complex interplay of forces that enter a legislature's redistricting calculus. Redistricting legislatures will, for example, almost always be aware of racial demographics; but it does not follow that race predominates in the redistricting process.... The distinction between being aware of racial considerations and being motivated by them may be difficult to make. This evidentiary difficulty, together with the sensitive nature of redistricting and the presumption of good faith that must be accorded legislative enactments, requires courts to exercise extraordinary caution in adjudicating claims that a state has drawn district lines on the basis of race. The plaintiff's burden is to show, either through circumstantial evidence of a district's shape and demographics or more direct evidence going to legislative purpose, that race was the predominant factor motivating the legislature's decision to place a significant number of voters within or without a particular district. To make this showing, a plaintiff must prove that the legislature subordinated traditional race-neutral districting principles, including but not limited to compactness, contiguity, respect for political subdivisions or communities defined by actual shared interests, to racial considerations. Where these or other race-neutral considerations are the basis for redistricting legislation, and are not subordinated to race, a state can "defeat a claim that a district has been gerrymandered on racial lines." . . .

In our view, the District Court applied the correct analysis, and its finding that race was the predominant factor motivating the drawing of the Eleventh District was not clearly erroneous. The court found it was "exceedingly obvious" from the shape of the Eleventh District, together with the relevant racial demographics, that the drawing of narrow land bridges to incorporate within the District outlying appendages containing nearly 80% of the district's total black population was a deliberate attempt to bring black populations into the district. . . . The District Court had before it considerable additional evidence showing that the General Assembly was motivated by a predominant, overriding desire to assign black populations to the Eleventh District and thereby permit the creation of a third majority-black district in the Second. . . .

· · ·

Race was, as the District Court found, the predominant, overriding factor explaining the General Assembly's decision to attach to the Eleventh District various appendages containing dense majority-black populations. . . . As a result, Georgia's congressional redistricting plan cannot be upheld unless it satisfies strict scrutiny, our most rigorous and exacting standard of constitutional review.

III

To satisfy strict scrutiny, the State must demonstrate that its districting legislation is narrowly tailored to achieve a compelling interest. . . . The State does not argue, however, that it created the Eleventh District to remedy past discrimination, and with good reason: there is little doubt that the State's true interest in designing the Eleventh District was creating a third majority-black district to satisfy the Justice Department's preclearance demands. . . . Whether or not in some cases compliance with the Voting Rights Act, standing alone, can provide a compelling interest independent of any interest in remedying past discrimination, it cannot do so here. . . . The congressional plan challenged here was not required by the Voting Rights Act under a correct reading of the statute.

· · ·

Georgia's drawing of the Eleventh District was not required under the Act because there was no reasonable basis to believe that Georgia's earlier enacted plans violated § 5. . . . Georgia's first and second proposed plans increased the number of majority-black districts from 1 out of 10 (10%) to 2 out of 11 (18.18%). These plans were "ameliorative" and could not have violated § 5's non-retrogression principle.... Acknowledging as much, ... the United States [objects] that Georgia failed to proffer a nondiscriminatory purpose for its refusal in the first two submissions to take the steps necessary to create a third majority-minority district.

The Government's position is insupportable.... The State's policy of adhering to other districting principles instead of creating as many majority-minority districts as possible does not support an inference that the plan "so discriminates on the basis of race or color as to violate the Constitution," ... and thus cannot provide any basis under § 5 for the Justice Department's objection.

Instead of grounding its objections on evidence of a discriminatory purpose, it would appear the Government was driven by its policy of maximizing majority-black districts. Although the Government now disavows having had that policy, ... and seems to concede its impropriety, the District Court's well-documented factual finding was that the Department did adopt a maximization policy ...

Section 5 was directed at preventing a particular set of invidious practices ...

... "[T]he purpose of § 5 has always been to insure that no voting-procedure changes would be made that would lead to a retrogression in the position of racial minorities with respect to their effective exercise of the electoral franchise." ... The Justice Department's maximization policy seems quite far removed from this purpose. We are especially reluctant to conclude that § 5 justifies that policy given the serious constitutional concerns it raises. In South Carolina v. Katzenbach, 383 U.S. 301 (1966), we upheld § 5 as a necessary and constitutional response to some states' "extraordinary stratagem[s] of contriving new rules of various kinds for the sole purpose of perpetuating voting discrimination in the face of adverse federal court decrees." ... But our belief in *Katzenbach* that the federalism costs exacted by § 5 preclearance could be justified by those extraordinary circumstances does not mean they can be justified in the circumstances of this case. And the Justice Department's implicit command that States engage in presumptively unconstitutional race-based districting brings the Voting Rights Act, once upheld as a proper exercise of Congress' authority under § 2 of the Fifteenth Amendment, *Katzenbach* ..., into tension with the Fourteenth Amendment....

IV

The Voting Rights Act, and its grant of authority to the federal courts to uncover official efforts to abridge minorities' right to vote, has been of vital importance in eradicating invidious discrimination from the electoral process and enhancing the legitimacy of our political institutions.... It takes a shortsighted and unauthorized view of the Voting Rights Act to invoke that statute, which has played a decisive role in redressing some of our worst forms of discrimination, to demand the very racial stereotyping the Fourteenth Amendment forbids.

· · ·

The judgment of the District Court is affirmed, and the case is remanded for further proceedings consistent with this decision.

It is so ordered.

Justice O'Connor, concurring.

I understand the threshold standard the Court adopts—"that the legislature subordinated traditional race-neutral districting principles ... to racial considerations"—to be a demanding one. To invoke strict scrutiny, a plaintiff must show that the State has relied on race in substantial disregard of customary and traditional districting practices. Those practices provide a crucial frame of reference and therefore constitute a significant governing principle in cases of this kind. The standard would be no different if a legislature had drawn the boundaries to favor some other ethnic group; certainly the standard does not treat efforts to create majority-minority districts less favorably than similar efforts on behalf of other groups. Indeed, the driving force behind the adoption of the Fourteenth Amendment was the desire to end legal discrimination against blacks.

Application of the Court's standard does not throw into doubt the vast majority of the Nation's 435 congressional districts, where presumably the States have drawn the boundaries in accordance with their customary districting principles. That is so even though race may well have been considered in the redistricting process.... But application of the Court's standard helps achieve *Shaw*'s basic objective of making extreme instances of gerrymandering subject to meaningful judicial review. I therefore join the Court's opinion.

Justice Stevens, dissenting.

... I believe the respondents in these cases ... have not suffered any legally cognizable injury.

In Shaw v. Reno, 509 U.S. 630 (1993), the Court crafted a new cause of action with two novel, troubling features. First, the Court misapplied the term "gerrymander," previously used to describe grotesque line-drawing by a dominant group to maintain or enhance its political power at a minority's expense, to condemn the efforts of a majority (whites) to share its power with a minority (African Americans). Second, the Court dispensed with its previous insistence in vote dilution cases on a showing of injury to an identifiable group of voters, but it failed to explain adequately what showing a plaintiff must make to establish standing to litigate the newly minted *Shaw* claim. Neither in *Shaw* itself nor in the cases decided today has the Court coherently articulated what injury this cause of action is designed to redress....

. . .

The Court's equation of *Shaw* claims with our desegregation decisions is inappropriate.... In each of those cases, legal segregation frustrated the public interest in diversity and tolerance by barring African Americans from joining whites in the activities at issue. The districting plan here, in contrast, serves the interest in diversity and tolerance by increasing the likelihood that a meaningful number of black representatives will add their voices to legislative debates.... That racial integration of the sort attempted by Georgia now appears more vulnerable to judicial challenge than some policies alleged to perpetuate racial bias ... is anomalous, to say the least.

Equally distressing is the Court's equation of traditional gerrymanders, designed to maintain or enhance a dominant group's power, with a dominant group's decision to share its power with a previously underrepresented group....

. . .

JUSTICE GINSBURG, with whom JUSTICES STEVENS and BREYER join, and with whom JUSTICE SOUTER joins except as to Part III–B, dissenting.

. . .

I

. . .

... [T]he fact that the Georgia General Assembly took account of race in drawing district lines—a fact not in dispute—does not render the State's plan invalid. To offend the Equal Protection Clause, all agree, the legislature had to do more than consider race. How much more, is the issue that divides the Court today.

A

. . .

... District lines are drawn to accommodate a myriad of factors— geographic, economic, historical, and political—and state legislatures, as arenas of compromise and electoral accountability, are best positioned to mediate competing claims; courts, with a mandate to adjudicate, are ill equipped for the task.

B

Federal courts have ventured into the political thicket of apportionment when necessary to secure to members of racial minorities equal voting rights—rights denied in many States, including Georgia, until not long ago.

. . .

It was against this backdrop that the Court, construing the Equal Protection Clause, undertook to ensure that apportionment plans do not dilute minority voting strength.... By enacting the Voting Rights Act of 1965, Congress heightened federal judicial involvement in apportionment, and also fashioned a role for the Attorney General....

These Court decisions and congressional directions significantly reduced voting discrimination against minorities. In the 1972 election, Georgia gained its first black Member of Congress since Reconstruction, and the 1981 apportionment created the State's first majority-minority district....

II

A

Before Shaw v. Reno, 509 U.S. 630 (1993), this Court invoked the Equal Protection Clause to justify intervention in the quintessentially political task of legislative districting in two circumstances: to enforce the one-person-one-vote requirement, see Reynolds v. Sims, 377 U.S. 533 (1964); and to prevent dilution of a minority group's voting strength. . . .

In *Shaw*, the Court recognized a third basis for an equal protection challenge to a State's apportionment plan. . . .

B

The record before us does not show that race ... overwhelmed traditional districting practices in Georgia. Although the Georgia General Assembly prominently considered race in shaping the Eleventh District, race did not crowd out all other factors, as the Court found it did in North Carolina's delineation of the *Shaw* district.

In contrast to the snake-like North Carolina district inspected in *Shaw*, Georgia's Eleventh District is hardly "bizarre," "extremely irregular," or "irrational on its face." . . .

. . .

C

The Court suggests that it was not Georgia's legislature, but the U.S. Department of Justice, that effectively drew the lines, and that Department officers did so with nothing but race in mind. Yet the "Max–Black" plan advanced by the Attorney General was not the plan passed by the Georgia General Assembly. . . .

. . .

D

. . .

To accommodate the reality of ethnic bonds, legislatures have long drawn voting districts along ethnic lines. Our Nation's cities are full of districts identified by their ethnic character—Chinese, Irish, Italian, Jewish, Polish, Russian, for example. . . . The creation of ethnic districts reflecting felt identity is not ordinarily viewed as offensive or demeaning to those included in the delineation.

III

... [A] federal case can be mounted whenever plaintiffs plausibly allege that other factors carried less weight than race. This invitation to litigate against the State seems to me neither necessary nor proper.

A

. . .

In adopting districting plans, ... States do not treat people as individuals. Apportionment schemes, by their very nature, assemble people in groups. States do not assign voters to districts based on merit or achievement, standards States might use in hiring employees or engaging contractors. . . .

That ethnicity defines some of these groups is a political reality. . . . Until now, no constitutional infirmity has been seen in districting Irish or Italian voters together, for example, so long as the delineation does not abandon familiar apportionment practices. . . . If Chinese–Americans and Russian–Americans may seek and secure group recognition in the delineation of voting districts, then African–Americans should not be dissimilarly treated. Otherwise, in the name of equal protection, we would shut out "the very minority group whose history in the United States gave birth to the Equal Protection Clause."

B

Under the Court's approach, judicial review of the same intensity, i.e., strict scrutiny, is in order once it is determined that an apportionment is predominantly motivated by race. It matters not at all, in this new regime, whether the apportionment dilutes or enhances minority voting strength. As very recently observed, however, "[t]here is no moral or constitutional equivalence between a policy that is designed to perpetuate a caste system and one that seeks to eradicate racial subordination." Adarand Constructors, Inc. v. Pena, . . . (Stevens, J., dissenting).

Special circumstances justify vigilant judicial inspection to protect minority voters—circumstances that do not apply to majority voters. A history of exclusion from state politics left racial minorities without clout to extract provisions for fair representation in the lawmaking forum. . . . The equal protection rights of minority voters thus could have remained unrealized absent the Judiciary's close surveillance. Cf. United States v. Carolene Products Co., 304 U.S. 144, 153, n. 4 (1938) (referring to the "more searching judicial inquiry" that may properly attend classifications adversely affecting "discrete and insular minorities"). The majority, by definition, encounters no such blockage. White voters in Georgia do not lack means to exert strong pressure on their state legislators. The force of their numbers is itself a powerful determiner of what the legislature will do that does not coincide with perceived majority interests.

NOTES AND QUESTIONS

1.   Did the *Gomillion* decision dictate the decisions in Shaw v. Reno and Miller v. Johnson? Recall the discussion in Adarand Constructors, Inc. v. Pena, above p. 1088, concerning the concept of "consistency." (The dissenters in Miller v. Johnson are the same Justices who dissented in *Adarand*.) Is there a stronger case for rejecting "consistency" in the context of gerrymanders disadvantaging minority voters and gerrymanders advantaging minority voters?

2.   Suppose that a state legislature defines a voting district so that it will be composed primarily of Irish–Americans. In other contexts, the Court has treated lines drawn on the basis of race and those drawn on the basis of national origin identically. (In the *Korematsu* case, discussed

above on pages 1016–1022, the decision to intern people of Japanese origin was technically one based on national origin rather than race.) Is Justice O'Connor correct that the principle that the State cannot rely "on *race* in substantial disregard of customary and traditional districting practices" applies, not just to lines drawn on the basis of race, but lines drawn to favor any ethnic group?

3.   Suppose that the legislature can demonstrate that it created a district where Irish–Americans were in the majority primarily to benefit the political party that a substantial majority of Irish–Americans usually voted for. Given the Court's political gerrymander cases, is a political gerrymander one that is "in substantial disregard of customary and traditional districting practices"?

4.   The distinction between racial and political gerrymanders was at the center of the decision in Bush v. Vera, 517 U.S. 952 (1996). The Court held that three majority-minority Texas Congressional districts were unconstitutional racial gerrymanders. One district had been described as resembling "a sacred Mayan bird, with its body running eastward along the Ship Channel from downtown Houston until the tail terminates in Baytown. Spindly legs reach south to Hobby Airport, while the plumed head rises northward almost to Intercontinental. In the western extremity of the district, an open beak appears to be searching for worms in Spring Branch. Here and there, ruffled feathers jut out at odd angles." (M. Barone & G. Ujifusa, ALMANAC OF AMERICAN POLITICS 1996, p. 1335 (1995).) Justice Stevens' dissent argued that Texas Congressional districts resulting from partisan political gerrymandering were equally bizarre. Justice O'Connor's plurality opinion explained that racial gerrymanders were different from political gerrymanders because the Fourteenth Amendment "evinces a commitment to eliminate unnecessary and excessive government use and reinforcement of racial stereotypes." Justice Stevens dissent responded: "While any racial classification may risk some stereotyping, the risk of true 'discrimination' in this case is extremely tenuous in light of the remedial purpose ... and the long history of resistance to giving minorities a full voice in the political process."

5.   A racial gerrymander is subject to "strict scrutiny" which means that it is permitted if it is "narrowly tailored to achieve a compelling state interest." Justice O'Connor wrote a separate opinion in Bush v. Vera, suggesting when strict scrutiny might be satisfied—"where voting is racially polarized" and "(i) the minority group is sufficiently large and geographically compact to constitute a majority in a single-member district, (ii) it is politically cohesive, and (iii) the white majority votes sufficiently as a bloc to enable it usually to defeat the minority's preferred candidate." With the votes of the 4 dissenters, her position is likely to control. If it is conceded that race was the predominant factor used to draw a majority-minority district, will the constitutional issue turn on the district's shape? Justice O'Connor conceded that drawing the constitutional lines—if not the district lines—"sometimes requires difficult exercises of judgment."

6. Under the Court's approach, consideration of race in drawing political district lines does not invite "strict scrutiny" if "race-neutral, traditional districting considerations predominated over racial ones." The Court in Bush v. Vera conceded that it would be appropriate to draw an irregularly-shaped district, even one composed of a majority of minority voters, if that were done for the purpose of protecting political incumbents. Defenders of the three districts at issue in that case argued that this is what *had* been done in Texas. There was a "substantial case" for the claim that "incumbency protection rivaled race" in determining the shape of some of the challenged districts. The Court concluded, however, that "racially motivated gerrymandering had a qualitatively greater influence on the drawing of district lines than politically motivated gerrymandering, and that political gerrymandering was accomplished in large part by the use of race as a proxy." Justice Souter's dissent argued that distinguishing a permissible political gerrymander from an impermissible racial gerrymander would be difficult.

7. In Easley v. Cromartie, 532 U.S. 234 (2001), the Court decided, 5–4, that North Carolina Congressional Districts had been drawn with the permissible purpose of creating a safe Democratic district rather than the unconstitutional objective of creating a safe minority district. Justice Breyer's opinion for the Court quoted Justice O'Connor's opinion in Bush v. Vera. "If district lines merely correlate with race because they are drawn on the basis of political affiliation, which correlates with race, there is no racial consideration to justify."

LEAGUE OF UNITED LATIN AMERICAN CITIZENS v. RICK PERRY, GOVERNOR OF TEXAS, *et al.*

___ U.S. ___, 126 S.Ct. 2594, 165 L.Ed.2d 609 (2006).

JUSTICE KENNEDY announced the judgment of the Court and delivered the opinion of the Court with respect to Parts II–A and III, an opinion with respect to Parts I and IV, in which THE CHIEF JUSTICE and JUSTICE ALITO join, an opinion with respect to Parts II–B and II–C, and an opinion with respect to Part II–D, in which JUSTICE SOUTER and JUSTICE GINSBURG join.

These four consolidated cases are appeals from a judgment entered by the United States District Court for the Eastern District of Texas.... Appellants [ ] contend that the use of race and politics in drawing lines of specific districts violates the First Amendment and the Equal Protection Clause of the Fourteenth Amendment ...

I

... The 1990 census resulted in a 30–seat congressional delegation for Texas, an increase of 3 seats over the 27 representatives allotted to the State in the decade before. See *Bush* v. *Vera,* 517 U.S. 952, 956–957 (1996). In 1991 the Texas Legislature drew new district lines. At the time, the Democratic Party controlled both houses in the state legislature, the governorship, and 19 of the State's 27 seats in Congress. Yet change appeared to be on the horizon. In the previous 30 years the Democratic Party's post-Reconstruction dominance over the Republican

Party had eroded, and by 1990 the Republicans received 47% of the statewide vote, while the Democrats received 51%.... Faced with a Republican opposition that could be moving toward majority status, the state legislature drew a congressional redistricting plan designed to favor Democratic candidates ... Using then-emerging computer technology to draw district lines with artful precision, the legislature enacted a plan later described as the "shrewdest gerrymander of the 1990s." ... The 1991 plan "carefully constructs democratic districts 'with incredibly convoluted lines' and packs 'heavily Republican' suburban areas into just a few districts." ... despite carrying 59% of the vote in statewide elections in 2000, the Republicans only won 13 congressional seats to the Democrats' 17....

... After a protracted partisan struggle, during which Democratic legislators left the State for a time to frustrate quorum requirements, the legislature enacted a new congressional districting map in October 2003. It is called Plan 1374C. The 2004 congressional elections did not disappoint the plan's drafters. Republicans won 21 seats to the Democrats' 11, while also obtaining 58% of the vote in statewide races against the Democrats' 41%.

III

Plan 1374C made changes to district lines in south and west Texas that appellants challenge as violations of § 2 of the Voting Rights Act and the Equal Protection Clause of the Fourteenth Amendment. The most significant changes occurred to District 23, which—both before and after the redistricting—covers a large land area in west Texas, and to District 25, which earlier included Houston but now includes a different area, a north-south strip from Austin to the Rio Grande Valley.

After the 2002 election, it became apparent that District 23 as then drawn had an increasingly powerful Latino population that threatened to oust the incumbent Republican, Henry Bonilla. Before the 2003 redistricting, the Latino share of the citizen voting-age population was 57.5%, and Bonilla's support among Latinos had dropped with each successive election since 1996.... Faced with this loss of voter support, the legislature acted to protect Bonilla's incumbency by changing the lines—and hence the population mix—of the district. To begin with, the new plan divided Webb County and the city of Laredo, on the Mexican border, that formed the county's population base. Webb County, which is 94% Latino, had previously rested entirely within District 23; under the new plan, nearly 100,000 people were shifted into neighboring District 28.... The rest of the county, approximately 93,000 people, remained in District 23. To replace the numbers District 23 lost, the State added voters in counties comprising a largely Anglo, Republican area in central Texas.... In the newly drawn district, the Latino share of the citizen voting-age population dropped to 46%, though the Latino share of the total voting-age population remained just over 50%....

These changes required adjustments elsewhere, of course, so the State inserted a third district between the two districts to the east of District 23, and extended all three of them farther north. New District 25 is a long, narrow strip that winds its way from McAllen and the

Mexican border towns in the south to Austin, in the center of the State and 300 miles away.... The Latinos in District 25, comprising 55% of the district's citizen voting-age population, are also mostly divided between the two distant areas, north and south.... The Latino communities at the opposite ends of District 25 have divergent "needs and interests," [ ] owing to "differences in socio-economic status, education, employment, health, and other characteristics," ... The District Court summed up the purposes underlying the redistricting in south and west Texas: "The change to Congressional District 23 served the dual goal of increasing Republican seats in general and protecting Bonilla's incumbency in particular, with the additional political nuance that Bonilla would be reelected in a district that had a majority of Latino voting age population—although clearly not a majority of citizen voting age population and certainly not an effective voting majority" ...

A

The question we address is whether Plan 1374C violates § 2 of the Voting Rights Act. A State violates § 2

"if, based on the totality of circumstances, it is shown that the political processes leading to nomination or election in the State or political subdivision are not equally open to participation by members of [a racial group] in that its members have less opportunity than other members of the electorate to participate in the political process and to elect representatives of their choice." 42 U.S.C. § 1973(b).

The Court has identified three threshold conditions for establishing a § 2 violation: (1) the racial group is " 'sufficiently large and geographically compact to constitute a majority in a single-member district' "; (2) the racial group is " 'politically cohesive' "; and (3) the majority " 'vot[es] sufficiently as a bloc to enable it ... usually to defeat the minority's preferred candidate.' " *Johnson* v. *De Grandy,* 512 U.S. 997, 1006–1007 (1994) ... (quoting *Growe,* 507 U.S., at 40 (in turn quoting *Thornburg* v. *Gingles,* 478 U.S. 30, 50–51 (1986))). These are the so-called *Gingles* requirements.

If all three *Gingles* requirements are established, the statutory text directs us to consider the "totality of circumstances" to determine whether members of a racial group have less opportunity than do other members of the electorate....

B

Appellants argue that the changes to District 23 diluted the voting rights of Latinos who remain in the district. Specifically, the redrawing of lines in District 23 caused the Latino share of the citizen voting-age population to drop from 57.5% to 46%. The District Court recognized that "Latino voting strength in Congressional District 23 is, unquestionably, weakened under Plan 1374C." *Session,* 298 F.Supp.2d, at 497. The question is whether this weakening amounts to vote dilution.

To begin the *Gingles* analysis, it is evident that the second and third *Gingles* preconditions—cohesion among the minority group and bloc voting among the majority population—are present in District 23. The District Court found "racially polarized voting" in south and west Texas, and indeed "throughout the State." ... The polarization in District 23 was especially severe: 92% of Latinos voted against Bonilla in 2002, while 88% of non-Latinos voted for him.... Furthermore, the projected results in new District 23 show that the Anglo citizen voting-age majority will often, if not always, prevent Latinos from electing the candidate of their choice in the district ... ... [I]n the congressional race, Bonilla could not have prevailed without some Latino support, limited though it was. State legislators changed District 23 specifically because they worried that Latinos would vote Bonilla out of office....

... [T]he concomitant rise in Latino voting power in each successive election, the near-victory of the Latino candidate of choice in 2002, and the resulting threat to the Bonilla incumbency, were the very reasons that led the State to redraw the district lines. Since the redistricting prevented the immediate success of the emergent Latino majority in District 23, there was a denial of opportunity in the real sense of that term.... In sum, appellants have established that Latinos could have had an opportunity district in District 23 had its lines not been altered and that they do not have one now.

... The State argues, nonetheless, that it met its § 2 obligations by creating new District 25 as an offsetting opportunity district. It is true, of course, that "States retain broad discretion in drawing districts to comply with the mandate of § 2." *Shaw* v. *Hunt,* 517 U.S. 899, 917, n. 9 (1996) *(Shaw II).* This principle has limits, though. The Court has rejected the premise that a State can always make up for the less-than-equal opportunity of some individuals by providing greater opportunity to others. See *id.,* at 917.... As set out below, these conflicting concerns are resolved by allowing the State to use one majority-minority district to compensate for the absence of another only when the racial group in each area had a § 2 right and both could not be accommodated.

... The noncompact district cannot [ ] remedy a violation elsewhere in the State.... Simply put, the State's creation of an opportunity district for those without a § 2 right offers no excuse for its failure to provide an opportunity district for those with a § 2 right....

While no precise rule has emerged governing § 2 compactness, the "inquiry should take into account 'traditional districting principles such as maintaining communities of interest and traditional boundaries.'" ... The recognition of nonracial communities of interest reflects the principle that a State may not "assum[e] from a group of voters' race that they 'think alike, share the same political interests, and will prefer the same candidates at the polls.'" ... In the absence of this prohibited assumption, there is no basis to believe a district that combines two far-flung segments of a racial group with disparate interests provides the opportunity that § 2 requires or that the first *Gingles* condition contemplates. "The purpose of the Voting Rights Act is to prevent discrimination in the exercise of the electoral franchise and to foster our transformation to a society that is no longer fixated on race." ... We do a disservice to these important goals by failing to account for the differences between people of the same race. . . .

C

We proceed now to the totality of the circumstances, and first to the proportionality inquiry, comparing the percentage of total districts that are Latino opportunity districts with the Latino share of the citizen voting-age population. . . . We conclude the answer in these cases is to look at proportionality statewide. . . . the State's seven-district area is arbitrary. It just as easily could have included six or eight districts. . . . District 23's Latino voters were poised to elect their candidate of choice. They were becoming more politically active, with a marked and continuous rise in Spanish-surnamed voter registration. . . . In successive elections Latinos were voting against Bonilla in greater numbers, and in 2002 they almost ousted him. . . . In response to the growing participation that threatened Bonilla's incumbency, the State divided the cohesive Latino community in Webb County, moving about 100,000 Latinos to District 28, which was already a Latino opportunity district, and leaving the rest in a district where they now have little hope of electing their candidate of choice.

The changes to District 23 undermined the progress of a racial group that has been subject to significant voting-related discrimination and that was becoming increasingly politically active and cohesive. . . . Based on the foregoing, the totality of the circumstances demonstrates a § 2 violation. Even assuming Plan 1374C provides something close to proportional representation for Latinos, its troubling blend of politics and race—and the resulting vote dilution of a group that was beginning to achieve § 2's goal of overcoming prior electoral discrimination—cannot be sustained.

D

Because we hold Plan 1374C violates § 2 in its redrawing of District 23, we do not address appellants' claims that the use of race and politics in drawing that district violates the First Amendment and equal protection. We also need not confront appellants' claim of an equal protection violation in the drawing of District 25. The districts in south and west Texas will have to be redrawn to remedy the violation in District 23, and we have no cause to pass on the legitimacy of a district that must be changed. . . .

. . . We do hold that the redrawing of lines in District 23 violates § 2 of the Voting Rights Act. The judgment of the District Court is affirmed in part, reversed in part, and vacated in part, and the cases are remanded for further proceedings.

It is so ordered.

NOTES AND QUESTIONS

1. In the words of *New York Times* writer Linda Greenhouse, Justice Kennedy in *LALUC v. Perry* has once again "deserted the conservatives." Yet this time Kennedy's alliance with the more liberal

members of the Court seemed particularly surprising given that it was Kennedy who authored the Court's opinion in *Miller v. Johnson, supra.* Moreover, Justice Kennedy had provided a reliably conservative vote in redistricting cases dating all the way back to *Shaw v. Reno,* 509 U.S. 630 (1993). Is there something about *LALUC v. Perry* that distinguishes it from the other high profile redistricting cases? In dissent, Chief Justice Roberts made it clear where his sympathies lie: "It is a sordid business, this divvying up by race."

2.   In sections of the *LALUC v. Perry* case not excerpted above, the Supreme Court also considered the question of whether the Court went too far in its efforts to gerrymander along partisan lines: the Texas legislature controlled by Republicans had revisited the Congressional map and redrawn the district lines mid-decade (i.e. without an intervening census count) specifically to benefit Republican candidates. In an especially splintered opinion, a plurality of the Court rejected that challenge and upheld the partisan gerrymander.

IV.   THE FIRST AMENDMENT AND THE ELECTORAL PROCESS

A.   RUNNING FOR OFFICE

REPUBLICAN PARTY OF MINNESOTA v. WHITE

536 U.S. 765, 122 S.Ct. 2528, 153 L.Ed.2d 694 (2002).

Justice Scalia delivered the opinion of the Court.

The question presented in this case is whether the First Amendment permits the Minnesota Supreme Court to prohibit candidates for judicial election in that State from announcing their views on disputed legal and political issues.

I

Since Minnesota's admission to the Union in 1858, the State's Constitution has provided for the selection of all state judges by popular election. ... Since 1912, those elections have been nonpartisan.... Since 1974, they have been subject to a legal restriction which states that a "candidate for a judicial office, including an incumbent judge, 'shall not' announce his or her views on disputed legal or political issues." ... This prohibition, promulgated by the Minnesota Supreme Court and based on Canon 7(B) of the 1972 American Bar Association (ABA) Model Code of Judicial Conduct, is known as the "announce clause." Incumbent judges who violate it are subject to discipline, including removal, censure, civil penalties, and suspension without pay.... Lawyers who run for judicial office also must comply with the announce clause.... Those who violate it are subject to, *inter alia,* disbarment, suspension, and probation....

In 1996, one of the petitioners, Gregory Wersal, ran for associate justice of the Minnesota Supreme Court. In the course of the campaign, he distributed literature criticizing several Minnesota Supreme Court decisions on issues such as crime, welfare, and abortion. A complaint against Wersal challenging, among other things, the propriety of this literature was filed with the Office of Lawyers Professional Responsibility, the agency which, under the direction of the Minnesota Lawyers Professional Responsibility Board, investigates and prosecutes ethical violations of lawyer candidates for judicial office. The Lawyers Board dismissed the complaint; with regard to the charges that his campaign materials violated the announce clause, it expressed doubt whether the clause could constitutionally be enforced. Nonetheless, fearing that further ethical complaints would jeopardize his ability to practice law, Wersal withdrew from the election. In 1998, Wersal ran again for the same office. Early in that race, he sought an advisory opinion from the Lawyers Board with regard to whether it planned to enforce the announce clause. The Lawyers Board responded equivocally, stating that, although it had significant doubts about the constitutionality of the provision, it was unable to answer his question because he had not submitted a list of the announcements he wished to make.

Shortly thereafter, Wersal filed this lawsuit in Federal District Court against respondents, seeking, *inter alia*, a declaration that the announce clause violates the First Amendment and an injunction against its enforcement. Wersal alleged that he was forced to refrain from announcing his views on disputed issues during the 1998 campaign, to the point where he declined response to questions put to him by the press and public, out of concern that he might run afoul of the announce clause. Other plaintiffs in the suit, including the Minnesota Republican Party, alleged that, because the clause kept Wersal from announcing his views, they were unable to learn those views and support or oppose his candidacy accordingly. The ... District Court found in favor of respondents, holding that the announce clause did not violate the First Amendment. ... [T]he United States Court of Appeals for the Eighth Circuit affirmed. ...

II

Before considering the constitutionality of the announce clause, we must be clear about its meaning. Its text says that a candidate for judicial office shall not "announce his or her views on disputed legal or political issues." ...

We know that "announc[ing] ... views" on an issue covers much more than *promising* to decide an issue a particular way. The prohibition extends to the candidate's mere statement of his current position, even if he does not bind himself to maintain that position after election. ...

There are, however, some limitations that the Minnesota Supreme Court has placed upon the scope of the announce clause that are not (to put it politely) immediately apparent from its text. The statements that formed the basis of the complaint against Wersal in 1996 included criticism of past decisions of the Minnesota Supreme Court. ... The Judicial Board issued an opinion stating that judicial candidates may criticize past decisions ... The Eighth Circuit relied on the Judicial Board's opinion in upholding the announce clause, and the Minnesota

Supreme Court recently embraced the Eighth Circuit's interpretation....

There are yet further limitations upon the apparent plain meaning of the announce clause: In light of the constitutional concerns, the District Court construed the clause to reach only disputed issues that are likely to come before the candidate if he is elected judge.... The Eighth Circuit accepted this limiting interpretation by the District Court, and in addition construed the clause to allow general discussions of case law and judicial philosophy.... The Supreme Court of Minnesota adopted these interpretations as well when it ordered enforcement of the announce clause in accordance with the Eighth Circuit's opinion....

It seems to us, however, that—like the text of the announce clause itself—these limitations upon the text of the announce clause are not all that they appear to be. First, respondents acknowledged at oral argument that statements critical of past judicial decisions are *not* permissible if the candidate also states that he is against *stare decisis*. Thus, candidates must choose between stating their views critical of past decisions and stating their views in opposition to *stare decisis*. Or, to look at it more concretely, they may state their view that prior decisions were erroneous only if they do not assert that they, if elected, have any power to eliminate erroneous decisions. Second, limiting the scope of the clause to issues likely to come before a court is not much of a limitation at all.... [T]he "disputed legal or political issues" raised in the course of a state judicial election ... will be those legal or political disputes that are the proper (or by past decisions have been made the improper) business of the state courts. And within that relevant category, "[t]here is almost no legal or political issue that is unlikely to come before a judge of an American court, state or federal, of general jurisdiction." ... Third, construing the clause to allow "general" discussions of case law and judicial philosophy turns out to be of little help in an election campaign....

In any event, it is clear that the announce clause prohibits a judicial candidate from stating his views on any specific nonfanciful legal question within the province of the court for which he is running, except in the context of discussing past decisions—and in the latter context as well, if he expresses the view that he is not bound by *stare decisis*.

Respondents contend that this still leaves plenty of topics for discussion on the campaign trail. These include a candidate's "character," "education," "work habits," and "how [he] would handle administrative duties if elected." Indeed, the Judicial Board has printed a list of preapproved questions which judicial candidates are allowed to answer. These include how the candidate feels about cameras in the courtroom, how he would go about reducing the caseload, how the costs of judicial administration can be reduced, and how he proposes to ensure that minorities and women are treated more fairly by the court system. Whether this list of preapproved subjects, and other topics not prohibited by the announce clause, adequately fulfill the First Amendment's guarantee of freedom of speech is the question to which we now turn.

III

As the Court of Appeals recognized, the announce clause both prohibits speech on the basis of its content and burdens a category of speech that is "at the core of our First Amendment freedoms"—speech about the qualifications of candidates for public office. . . .

The Court of Appeals concluded that respondents had established two interests as sufficiently compelling to justify the announce clause: preserving the impartiality of the state judiciary and preserving the appearance of the impartiality of the state judiciary. Respondents reassert these two interests before us, arguing that the first is compelling because it protects the due process rights of litigants, and that the second is compelling because it preserves public confidence in the judiciary. Respondents are rather vague, however, about what they mean by "impartiality." . . . Clarity on this point is essential before we can decide whether impartiality is indeed a compelling state interest, and, if so, whether the announce clause is narrowly tailored to achieve it.

A

One meaning of "impartiality" in the judicial context—and of course its root meaning—is the lack of bias for or against either *party* to the proceeding. . . . This is the traditional sense in which the term is used. . . .

We think it plain that the announce clause is not narrowly tailored to serve impartiality (or the appearance of impartiality) in this sense. Indeed, the clause is barely tailored to serve that interest *at all*, inasmuch as it does not restrict speech for or against particular *parties*, but rather speech for or against particular *issues*. . . .

B

It is perhaps possible to use the term "impartiality" in the judicial context (though this is certainly not a common usage) to mean lack of preconception in favor of or against a particular *legal view*. . . . A judge's lack of predisposition regarding the relevant legal issues in a case has never been thought a necessary component of equal justice, and with good reason. For one thing, it is virtually impossible to find a judge who does not have preconceptions about the law. . . . Indeed, even if it were possible to select judges who did not have preconceived views on legal issues, it would hardly be desirable to do so. . . . And since avoiding judicial preconceptions on legal issues is neither possible nor desirable, pretending otherwise by attempting to preserve the "appearance" of that type of impartiality can hardly be a compelling state interest either.

C

A third possible meaning of "impartiality" (again not a common one) might be described as openmindedness. This quality in a judge demands, not that he have no preconceptions on legal issues, but that he be willing to consider views that oppose his preconceptions, and remain open to persuasion, when the issues arise in a pending case. . . .

Respondents argue that the announce clause serves the interest in openmindedness, or at least in the appearance of openmindedness, because it relieves a judge from pressure to rule a certain way in order to maintain consistency with statements the judge has previously made. The problem is, however, that statements in election campaigns are such an infinitesimal portion of the public commitments to legal positions that judges (or judges-to-be) undertake, that this object of the prohibition is implausible. Before they arrive on the bench (whether by election or otherwise) judges have often committed themselves on legal issues that they must later rule upon. . . .

. . . In Minnesota, a candidate for judicial office may not say "I think it is constitutional for the legislature to prohibit same-sex marriages." He may say the very same thing, however, up until the very day before he declares himself a candidate, and may say it repeatedly (until litigation is pending) after he is elected. As a means of pursuing the objective of openmindedness that respondents now articulate, the announce clause is so woefully underinclusive as to render belief in that purpose a challenge to the credulous. . . .

· · ·

Moreover, the notion that the special context of electioneering justifies an *abridgment* of the right to speak out on disputed issues sets our First Amendment jurisprudence on its head. "[D]ebate on the qualifications of candidates" is "at the core of our electoral process and of the First Amendment freedoms," not at the edges. . . . We have never allowed the government to prohibit candidates from communicating relevant information to voters during an election.

· · ·

. . . Justice Ginsburg greatly exaggerates the difference between judicial and legislative elections. . . . [C]omplete separation of the judiciary from the enterprise of "representative government" might have some truth in those countries where judges neither make law themselves nor set aside the laws enacted by the legislature. It is not a true picture of the American system. . . .

IV

To sustain the announce clause, the Eighth Circuit relied heavily on the fact that a pervasive practice of prohibiting judicial candidates from discussing disputed legal and political issues developed during the last half of the 20th century. It is true that a "universal and long-established" tradition of prohibiting certain conduct creates "a strong presumption" that the prohibition is constitutional: "Principles of liberty fundamental enough to have been embodied within constitutional guarantees are not readily erased from the Nation's consciousness." *McIntyre v. Ohio Elections Comm'n*, 514 U.S. 334, 375–377 (1995) (Scalia, J., dissenting). The practice of prohibiting speech by judicial candidates on disputed issues, however, is neither long nor universal.

. . . We know of no restrictions upon statements that could be made by judicial candidates (including judges) throughout the 19th and the

first quarter of the 20th century. Indeed, judicial elections were generally partisan during this period, the movement toward nonpartisan judicial
elections not even beginning until the 1870's.... Thus, not only were
judicial candidates (including judges) discussing disputed legal and political issues on the campaign trail, but they were touting party affiliations
and angling for party nominations all the while.

* * *

There is an obvious tension between the article of Minnesota's
popularly approved Constitution which provides that judges shall be
elected, and the Minnesota Supreme Court's announce clause which
places most subjects of interest to the voters off limits.... If the State
chooses to tap the energy and the legitimizing power of the democratic
process, it must accord the participants in that process ... "the First
Amendment rights that attach to their roles." ...

The Minnesota Supreme Court's canon of judicial conduct prohibiting candidates for judicial election from announcing their views on
disputed legal and political issues violates the First Amendment. Accordingly, we reverse the grant of summary judgment to respondents and
remand the case for proceedings consistent with this opinion.

It is so ordered.

JUSTICE O'CONNOR, concurring.

I join the opinion of the Court but write separately to express my
concerns about judicial elections generally....

We of course want judges to be impartial, in the sense of being free
from any personal stake in the outcome of the cases to which they are
assigned. But if judges are subject to regular elections they are likely to
feel that they have at least some personal stake in the outcome of every
publicized case. Elected judges cannot help being aware that if the public
is not satisfied with the outcome of a particular case, it could hurt their
reelection prospects. ... Even if judges were able to suppress their
awareness of the potential electoral consequences of their decisions and
refrain from acting on it, the public's confidence in the judiciary could be
undermined simply by the possibility that judges would be unable to do
so.

Moreover, contested elections generally entail campaigning. And
campaigning for a judicial post today can require substantial funds....
Even if judges were able to refrain from favoring donors, the mere
possibility that judges' decisions may be motivated by the desire to repay
campaign contributors is likely to undermine the public's confidence in
the judiciary....

. . .

Minnesota has chosen to select its judges through contested popular
elections instead of through an appointment system or a combined
appointment and retention election system along the lines of the Missouri Plan. In doing so the State has voluntarily taken on the risks to
judicial bias described above. As a result, the State's claim that it needs

to significantly restrict judges' speech in order to protect judicial impartiality is particularly troubling. If the State has a problem with judicial impartiality, it is largely one the State brought upon itself by continuing the practice of popularly electing judges.

JUSTICE KENNEDY, concurring.

I agree with the Court that Minnesota's prohibition on judicial candidates' announcing their legal views is an unconstitutional abridgment of the freedom of speech. There is authority for the Court to apply strict scrutiny analysis to resolve some First Amendment cases, ... and the Court explains in clear and forceful terms why the Minnesota regulatory scheme fails that test. So I join its opinion.

I adhere to my view, however, that content-based speech restrictions that do not fall within any traditional exception should be invalidated without inquiry into narrow tailoring or compelling government interests. The speech at issue here does not come within any of the exceptions to the First Amendment recognized by the Court.... The political speech of candidates is at the heart of the First Amendment, and direct restrictions on the content of candidate speech are simply beyond the power of government to impose.

· · ·

Minnesota may choose to have an elected judiciary. It may strive to define those characteristics that exemplify judicial excellence. It may enshrine its definitions in a code of judicial conduct. It may adopt recusal standards more rigorous than due process requires, and censure judges who violate these standards. What Minnesota may not do, however, is censor what the people hear as they undertake to decide for themselves which candidate is most likely to be an exemplary judicial officer....

· · ·

If Minnesota believes that certain sorts of candidate speech disclose flaws in the candidate's credentials, democracy and free speech are their own correctives....

· · ·

... This case does not present the question whether a State may restrict the speech of judges because they are judges—for example, as part of a code of judicial conduct; the law at issue here regulates judges only when and because they are candidates. Whether the rationale of *Pickering v. Board of Ed. of Township High School Dist. 205, Will Cty.,* 391 U.S. 563, 568 (1968), and *Connick v. Myers,* 461 U.S. 138 (1983), could be extended to allow a general speech restriction on sitting judges—regardless of whether they are campaigning—in order to promote the efficient administration of justice, is not an issue raised here.

Petitioner Gregory Wersal was not a sitting judge but a challenger; he had not voluntarily entered into an employment relationship with the State or surrendered any First Amendment rights. His speech may not be controlled or abridged in this manner. Even the undoubted interest of the State in the excellence of its judiciary does not allow it to restrain candidate speech by reason of its content. Minnesota's attempt to regulate campaign speech is impermissible.

JUSTICE STEVENS, with whom JUSTICE SOUTER, JUSTICE GINSBURG, and JUSTICE BREYER join, dissenting.

... I ... join [Justice Ginsburg's] opinion without reservation. I add these comments to emphasize the force of her arguments and to explain why I find the Court's reasoning even more troubling than its holding. The limits of the Court's holding are evident: Even if the Minnesota Lawyers Professional Responsibility Board (Board) may not sanction a judicial candidate for announcing his views on issues likely to come before him, it may surely advise the electorate that such announcements demonstrate the speaker's unfitness for judicial office. If the solution to harmful speech must be more speech, so be it. The Court's reasoning, however, will unfortunately endure beyond the next election cycle. By obscuring the fundamental distinction between campaigns for the judiciary and the political branches, and by failing to recognize the difference between statements made in articles or opinions and those made on the campaign trail, the Court defies any sensible notion of the judicial office and the importance of impartiality in that context.

. . .

The disposition of this case on the flawed premise that the criteria for the election to judicial office should mirror the rules applicable to political elections is profoundly misguided. I therefore respectfully dissent.

JUSTICE GINSBURG, with whom JUSTICE STEVENS, JUSTICE SOUTER, and JUSTICE BREYER join, dissenting.

... Unlike their counterparts in the political branches, judges are expected to refrain from catering to particular constituencies or committing themselves on controversial issues in advance of adversarial presentation. . . .

. . .

The ability of the judiciary to discharge its unique role rests to a large degree on the manner in which judges are selected. . . .

The question this case presents is whether the First Amendment stops Minnesota from furthering its interest in judicial integrity through this precisely targeted speech restriction.

I

. . .

... I would differentiate elections for political offices, in which the First Amendment holds full sway, from elections designed to select those whose office it is to administer justice without respect to persons. . . .

Legislative and executive officials serve in representative capacities. . . .

Judges, however, are not political actors. They do not sit as representatives of particular persons, communities, or parties; they serve no faction or constituency.... They must strive to do what is legally right, all the more so when the result is not the one "the home crowd" wants....

Thus, the rationale underlying unconstrained speech in elections for political office—that representative government depends on the public's ability to choose agents who will act at its behest—does not carry over to campaigns for the bench....

. . .

... The balance the State sought to achieve—allowing the people to elect judges, but safeguarding the process so that the integrity of the judiciary would not be compromised—should encounter no First Amendment shoal.

. . .

This Court has recognized in the past, as Justice O'Connor does today, a "fundamental tension between the ideal character of the judicial office and the real world of electoral politics." ... We have no warrant to resolve that tension, however, by forcing States to choose one pole or the other. Judges are not politicians, and the First Amendment does not require that they be treated as politicians simply because they are chosen by popular vote. Nor does the First Amendment command States who wish to promote the integrity of their judges in fact and appearance to abandon systems of judicial selection that the people, in the exercise of their sovereign prerogatives, have devised.

For more than three-quarters of a century, States like Minnesota have endeavored, through experiment tested by experience, to balance the constitutional interests in judicial integrity and free expression within the unique setting of an elected judiciary.... I would uphold it as an essential component in Minnesota's accommodation of the complex and competing concerns in this sensitive area....

ANDERSON v. CELEBREZZE

Supreme Court of the United States, 1983.
460 U.S. 780, 103 S.Ct. 1564, 75 L.Ed.2d 547.

JUSTICE STEVENS delivered the opinion of the Court.

On April 24, 1980, petitioner John Anderson announced that he was an independent candidate for the office of President of the United States. Thereafter, his supporters—by gathering the signatures of registered voters, filing required documents, and submitting filing fees—were able to meet the substantive requirements for having his name placed on the ballot for the general election in November 1980 in all 50 States and the District of Columbia. On April 24, however, it was already too late for Anderson to qualify for a position on the ballot in Ohio and certain other states because the statutory deadlines for filing a statement of candidacy had already passed. The question presented by this case is whether Ohio's early filing deadline placed an unconstitutional burden on the voting and associational rights of Anderson's supporters.

... On May 16, 1980, Anderson's supporters tendered a nominating petition containing approximately 14,500 signatures and a statement of candidacy to respondent Celebrezze, the Ohio Secretary of State. These documents would have entitled Anderson to a place on the ballot if they had been filed on or before March 20, 1980. Respondent refused to accept the petition solely because it had not been filed within the time required by [Ohio law]. . . .

. . .

I

After a date toward the end of March, even if intervening events create unanticipated political opportunities, no independent candidate may enter the Presidential race and seek to place his name on the Ohio general election ballot. Thus the direct impact of Ohio's early filing deadline falls upon aspirants for office. Nevertheless, as we have recognized, "the rights of voters and the rights of candidates do not lend themselves to neat separation; laws that affect candidates always have at least some theoretical, correlative effect on voters." . . .

The impact of candidate eligibility requirements on voters implicates basic constitutional rights. . . . In our first review of Ohio's electoral scheme, Williams v. Rhodes, 393 U.S. 23, 30–31 (1968), this Court explained the interwoven strands of "liberty" affected by ballot access restrictions:

> "In the present situation the state laws place burdens on two different, although overlapping, kinds of rights—the right of individuals to associate for the advancement of political beliefs, and the right of qualified voters, regardless of their political persuasion, to cast their votes effectively. Both of these rights, of course, rank among our most precious freedoms."

As we have repeatedly recognized, voters can assert their preferences only through candidates or parties or both. . . . The right to vote is "heavily burdened" if that vote may be cast only for major-party candidates at a time when other parties or other candidates are "clamoring for a place on the ballot." . . . The exclusion of candidates also burdens voters' freedom of association, because an election campaign is an effective platform for the expression of views on the issues of the day, and a candidate serves as a rallying-point for like-minded citizens.

Although these rights of voters are fundamental, not all restrictions imposed by the States on candidates' eligibility for the ballot impose constitutionally-suspect burdens on voters' rights to associate or to choose among candidates. We have recognized that, "as a practical matter, there must be a substantial regulation of elections if they are to be fair and honest and if some sort of order, rather than chaos, is to accompany the democratic processes." . . . To achieve these necessary objectives, States have enacted comprehensive and sometimes complex election codes. Each provision of these schemes, whether it governs the registration and qualifications of voters, the selection and eligibility of candidates, or the voting process itself, inevitably affects—at least to some degree—the individual's right to vote and his right to associate with others for political ends. Nevertheless, the state's important regulatory interests are generally sufficient to justify reasonable, nondiscriminatory restrictions.

Constitutional challenges to specific provisions of a State's election laws therefore cannot be resolved by any "litmus-paper test" that will separate valid from invalid restrictions.... Instead, a court ... must first consider the character and magnitude of the asserted injury to the rights protected by the First and Fourteenth Amendments that the plaintiff seeks to vindicate. It then must identify and evaluate the precise interests put forward by the State as justifications for the burden imposed by its rule.... Only after weighing all these factors is the reviewing court in a position to decide whether the challenged provision is unconstitutional....

II

An early filing deadline may have a substantial impact on independent-minded voters. In election campaigns, particularly those which are national in scope, the candidates and the issues simply do not remain static over time. Various candidates rise and fall in popularity; domestic and international developments bring new issues to center stage and may affect voters' assessments of national problems. Such developments will certainly affect the strategies of candidates who have already entered the race; they may also create opportunities for new candidacies.... Yet Ohio's filing deadline prevents persons who wish to be independent candidates from entering the significant political arena established in the State by a Presidential election campaign—and creating new political coalitions of Ohio voters—at any time after mid-to-late March. At this point developments in campaigns for the major-party nominations have only begun, and the major parties will not adopt their nominees and platforms for another five months. Candidates and supporters within the major parties thus have the political advantage of continued flexibility; for independents, the inflexibility imposed by the March filing deadline is a correlative disadvantage because of the competitive nature of the electoral process.

If the State's filing deadline were later in the year, a newly-emergent independent candidate could serve as the focal point for a grouping of Ohio voters who decide, after mid-March, that they are dissatisfied with the choices within the two major parties....

. . .

A burden that falls unequally on new or small political parties or on independent candidates impinges, by its very nature, on associational choices protected by the First Amendment. It discriminates against those candidates and—of particular importance—against those voters whose political preferences lie outside the existing political parties.... Historically political figures outside the two major parties have been fertile sources of new ideas and new programs; many of their challenges to the status quo have in time made their way into the political mainstream.... In short, the primary values protected by the First Amendment ... are served when election campaigns are not monopolized by the existing political parties.

Furthermore, in the context of a Presidential election, state-imposed restrictions implicate a uniquely important national interest. For the President and the Vice President of the United States are the only elected officials who represent all the voters in the Nation. Moreover, the impact of the votes cast in each State is affected by the votes cast for the various candidates in other States. Thus in a Presidential election a State's enforcement of more stringent ballot access requirements, including filing deadlines, has an impact beyond its own borders. Similarly, the State has a less important interest in regulating Presidential elections than statewide or local elections, because the outcome of the former will be largely determined by voters beyond the State's boundaries....

III

. . .

Ohio's asserted interest in political stability amounts to a desire to protect existing political parties from competition—competition for campaign workers, voter support, and other campaign resources—generated by independent candidates who have previously been affiliated with the party....

... [P]rotecting the Republican and Democratic parties from external competition cannot justify the virtual exclusion of other political aspirants from the political arena....

On the other hand, in Storer v. Brown [415 U.S. 724 (1974)] we upheld two California statutory provisions that restricted access by independent candidates to the general election ballot. Under California law, a person could not run as an independent in November if he had been defeated in a party primary that year or if he had been registered with a political party within one year prior to that year's primary election....

Thus in *Storer* we recognized the legitimacy of the State's interest in preventing "splintered parties and unrestrained factionalism." ... By requiring a candidate to remain in the intraparty competition once the disaffiliation deadline had passed, and by giving conclusive effect to the winnowing process performed by party members in the primary election, the challenged provisions were an essential part of "a general state policy aimed at maintaining the integrity of the various routes to the ballot." Moreover, we pointed out that the policy "involves no discrimination against independents." ...

Ohio's challenged restriction is substantially different from the California provisions upheld in *Storer*. As we have noted, the early filing deadline does discriminate against independents. And the deadline is neither a "sore loser" provision nor a disaffiliation statute. Furthermore, it is important to recognize that *Storer* upheld the State's interest in avoiding political fragmentation in the context of elections wholly within the boundaries of California. The State's interest in regulating a nationwide Presidential election is not nearly as strong; no State could single-handedly assure "political stability" in the Presidential context. The Ohio deadline does not serve any state interest in "maintaining the integrity of the various routes to the ballot" for the Presidency, because Ohio's Presidential preference primary does not serve to narrow the field for the general election. A major party candidate who loses the Ohio primary, or who does not even run in Ohio, may nonetheless appear on the November general election ballot as the party's nominee. In addition, the national scope of the competition for delegates at the Presidential nominating conventions assures that "intraparty feuding" will continue until August.

More generally, the early filing deadline is not precisely drawn to protect the parties from "intraparty feuding," whatever legitimacy that state goal may have in a Presidential election.... [T]he early deadline applies broadly to independent candidates who have not been affiliated in the recent past with any political party. On the other hand, as long as the decision to run is made before the March deadline, Ohio does not prohibit independent candidacies by persons formerly affiliated with a political party, or currently participating in intraparty competition in other States—regardless of the effect on the political party structure.

. . .

IV

... Under any realistic appraisal, the "extent and nature" of the burdens Ohio has placed on the voters' freedom of choice and freedom of association, in an election of nationwide importance, unquestionably outweigh the State's minimal interest in imposing a March deadline.

. . .

JUSTICE REHNQUIST, with whom JUSTICE WHITE, JUSTICE POWELL, and JUSTICE O'CONNOR join, dissenting.

Article II of the Constitution provides that "[e]ach State shall appoint, in such Manner as the Legislature thereof may direct, a Number of Electors" who shall select the President of the United States. U.S. Const., art. II, § 1, cl. 2. This provision, one of few in the Constitution that grants an express plenary power to the States, conveys "the broadest power of determination" ...

. . .

... [T]he Constitution does not require that a State allow any particular Presidential candidate to be on its ballot, and so long as the Ohio ballot access laws are rational and allow nonparty candidates reasonable access to the general election ballot, this Court should not interfere with Ohio's exercise of its Article II, § 1, cl. 2 power. Since I believe that the Ohio laws meet these criteria, I dissent.

. . .

... [T]he effect of the Ohio filing deadline is quite easily summarized: it requires that a candidate, who has already decided to run for President, decide by March 20 which route his candidacy will take. He can become a nonparty candidate by filing a nominating petition with

5,000 signatures and assure himself a place on the general election ballot. Or, he can become a party candidate and take his chances in securing a position on the general election ballot by seeking the nomination of a party's national convention. Anderson chose the latter route and submitted in a timely fashion his nominating petition for Ohio's Republican Primary. Then, realizing that he had no chance for the Republican nomination, Anderson sought to change the form of this candidacy. The Ohio filing deadline prevented him from making this change. Quite clearly, rather than prohibiting him from seeking the Presidency, the filing deadline only prevented Anderson from having two shots at it in the same election year.

. . .

Refusing to own up to the conflict its opinion creates with Storer [v. Brown], the Court tries to distinguish it. . . . What the Ohio filing deadline prevents is a candidate such as Anderson from seeking a party nomination and then, finding that he is rejected by the party, bolting from the party to form an independent candidacy. This is precisely the same behavior that California sought to prevent by the disaffiliation statute this Court upheld in *Storer*.

. . .

The Court further notes that "*Storer* upheld the State's interest in avoiding political fragmentation in the context of elections wholly within the boundaries of California. The State's interest in regulating a nation-wide Presidential election is not nearly as strong." The Court's characterization of the election simply is incorrect. The Ohio general election in 1980, among other things, was for the appointment of Ohio's representatives to the Electoral College. U.S. Const., art. II, § 1, cl. 2. The Court throughout its opinion fails to come to grips with this fact. While Ohio may have a lesser interest in who is ultimately selected by the Electoral College, its interest in who is supported by its own Presidential electors must be at least as strong as its interest in electing other representatives. . . .

. . .

The Court's opinion protects this particular kind of candidate—an individual who decides well in advance to become a Presidential candidate, decides which route to follow in seeking a position on the general election ballot, and, after seeing his hopes turn to ashes, wants to try another route. The Court's opinion draws no line; I presume that a State must wait until all party nominees are chosen and then allow all unsuccessful party candidates to refight their party battles by forming an "independent" candidacy. I find nothing in the Constitution which requires this result. . . .

NOTES AND QUESTIONS

1. As the Court indicates, restrictions on access to the ballot implicate constitutional rights of both the candidate and the voter. These rights are, moreover, described as "most precious freedoms." Can you find the place in the Constitution where these "precious freedoms" are

located? (Justice Brennan's memorandum to the conference, prior to the justices' initial vote after the case was argued, argued that the early "filing deadline implicates core First Amendment interests" that included the rights of independent candidates to run for office and the right of their supporters to vote for them. Brennan Papers, Library of Congress, Box 624).

2. As "precious" as the right to ballot access is, it is a right that can be denied to some. The Court describes the decision-making process as involving a balance—between the voters' and candidates' rights on the one hand, and various state interests on the other. As the close division of the justices in this case indicates, it is often difficult to predict in advance how courts will strike the balance. In Williams v. Rhodes, 393 U.S. 23 (1968), the Court invalidated a requirement that a political party seeking access to the Presidential ballot file a nominating petition signed by fifteen percent of the number of voters participating in the last gubernatorial election, and file that petition nine months before the election. In holding that George Wallace was entitled to a place on the 1968 Ohio ballot, the Court noted that Ohio's law made it "virtually impossible" for any new political party to obtain a place on the ballot. On the other hand, in Jenness v. Fortson, 403 U.S. 431 (1971), the Court upheld a Georgia law that required independent candidates to file a petition signed by five percent of the voters participating in the previous election. American Party v. White, 415 U.S. 767 (1974), sustained a Texas law denying a place on the ballot to political parties who had neither received two percent of the votes in the previous general election nor filed petitions signed by registered voters numbering one percent of the votes cast in the previous general election.

3. The asserted state interest served by requiring that candidates submit signed petitions, or that parties have received a minimum number of votes in previous elections, is elimination of frivolous candidacies. A requirement that candidates pay a filing fee serves the same purpose. In Lubin v. Panish, 415 U.S. 709 (1974), however, the Court held that a filing fee could not constitutionally be required of an indigent candidate. (An indigent could be required to file a petition with a reasonable number of signatures.)

4. The state interest most implicated in *Anderson* is that of preventing "splintered parties and unrestrained factionalism," an interest that all the Justices assume to be valid. The earlier *Storer* case sustained a California law that denied independents a position on the ballot if they had been defeated in the party primary for that office, or if they had been a party member within a year. Is the Ohio law struck down in this case different because the early filing deadline applies even if a candidate had not been defeated in the previous party primary and had not been registered as a member of a party?

5. Is the real difference between the *Storer* case and this one the difference between ballot access for election to state office and ballot access for independent candidates for president and vice president? On this issue, the majority and dissent take strikingly different positions. For the majority, state interests are discounted by the "uniquely nation-

al interest" in the only election to fill offices that represent all the nation's voters. For the dissent, choice of the president and vice president involves the provisions of art. II, § 1, cl. 2, governing the choice of electors, which the dissent characterizes as giving "the broadest power of determination" to the states. Who has the better of this argument?

CALIFORNIA DEMOCRATIC PARTY v. JONES

Supreme Court of the United States, 2000.
530 U.S. 567, 120 S.Ct. 2402, 147 L.Ed.2d 502.

JUSTICE SCALIA delivered the opinion of the Court.

This case presents the question whether the State of California may, consistent with the First Amendment to the United States Constitution, use a so-called "blanket" primary to determine a political party's nominee for the general election.

I

Under California law, a candidate for public office has two routes to gain access to the general ballot for most state and federal elective offices. He may receive the nomination of a qualified political party by winning its primary, ... or he may file as an independent by obtaining (for a statewide race) the signatures of one percent of the State's electorate or (for other races) the signatures of three percent of the voting population of the area represented by the office in contest ...

Until 1996, to determine the nominees of qualified parties California held what is known as a "closed" partisan primary, in which only persons who are members of the political party—i.e., who have declared affiliation with that party when they register to vote ...—can vote on its nominee.... In 1996 the citizens of California adopted by initiative Proposition 198. Promoted largely as a measure that would "weaken party hard-liners" and ease the way for "moderate problem-solvers," Proposition 198 changed California's partisan primary from a closed primary to a blanket primary. Under the new system, "[a]ll persons entitled to vote, including those not affiliated with any political party, shall have the right to vote ... for any candidate regardless of the candidate's political affiliation." ... Whereas under the closed primary each voter received a ballot limited to candidates of his own party, as a result of Proposition 198 each voter's primary ballot now lists every candidate regardless of party affiliation and allows the voter to choose freely among them. It remains the case, however, that the candidate of each party who wins the greatest number of votes "is the nominee of that party at the ensuing general election." ...

Petitioners in this case are four political parties—the California Democratic Party, the California Republican Party, the Libertarian Party of California, and the Peace and Freedom Party—each of which has a rule prohibiting persons not members of the party from voting in the party's primary....

II

Respondents rest their defense of the blanket primary upon the proposition that primaries play an integral role in citizens' selection of public officials. As a consequence, they contend, primaries are public rather than private proceedings, and the States may and must play a role in ensuring that they serve the public interest. Proposition 198, respondents conclude, is simply a rather pedestrian example of a State's regulating its system of elections.

We have recognized, of course, that States have a major role to play in structuring and monitoring the election process, including primaries....

What we have not held, however, is that the processes by which political parties select their nominees are, as respondents would have it, wholly public affairs that States may regulate freely. To the contrary, we have continually stressed that when States regulate parties' internal processes they must act within limits imposed by the Constitution.... In this regard, respondents' reliance on Smith v. Allwright, 321 U.S. 649 (1944), and Terry v. Adams, 345 U.S. 461 (1953), is misplaced. In *Allwright*, we invalidated the Texas Democratic Party's rule limiting participation in its primary to whites; in *Terry*, we invalidated the same rule promulgated by the Jaybird Democratic Association, a "self-governing voluntary club," ... These cases held only that, when a State prescribes an election process that gives a special role to political parties, ... the parties' discriminatory action becomes state action under the Fifteenth Amendment.... They do not stand for the proposition that party affairs are public affairs, free of First Amendment protections ...

· · ·

In no area is the political association's right to exclude more important than in the process of selecting its nominee. That process often determines the party's positions on the most significant public policy issues of the day, and even when those positions are predetermined it is the nominee who becomes the party's ambassador to the general electorate in winning it over to the party's views....

Unsurprisingly, our cases vigorously affirm the special place the First Amendment reserves for, and the special protection it accords, the process by which a political party "select[s] a standard bearer who best represents the party's ideologies and preferences." ...

· · ·

In [Democratic Party of United States v. Wisconsin ex rel. La Follette, 450 U.S. 107], the State of Wisconsin conducted an open presidential preference primary.[6] Although the voters did not select the delegates to the Democratic Party's National Convention directly—they were chosen later at caucuses of party members—Wisconsin law required these delegates to vote in accord with the primary results. Thus allowing

---

6. An open primary differs from a blanket primary in that, although as in the blanket primary any person, regardless of party affiliation, may vote for a party's nominee, his choice is limited to that party's nominees for all offices. He may not, for example, support a Republican nominee for Governor and a Democratic nominee for attorney general.

nonparty members to participate in the selection of the party's nominee conflicted with the Democratic Party's rules. We held that, whatever the strength of the state interests supporting the open primary itself, they could not justify this "substantial intrusion into the associational freedom of members of the National Party."[7] ...

California's blanket primary violates the principles set forth in these cases. Proposition 198 forces political parties to associate with—to have their nominees, and hence their positions, determined by—those who, at best, have refused to affiliate with the party, and, at worst, have expressly affiliated with a rival. In this respect, it is qualitatively different from a closed primary. Under that system, even when it is made quite easy for a voter to change his party affiliation the day of the primary, and thus, in some sense, to "cross over," at least he must formally become a member of the party; and once he does so, he is limited to voting for candidates of that party.[8]

The evidence in this case demonstrates that under California's blanket primary system, the prospect of having a party's nominee determined by adherents of an opposing party is far from remote—indeed, it is a clear and present danger. For example, in one 1997 survey of California voters 37 percent of Republicans said that they planned to vote in the 1998 Democratic gubernatorial primary, and 20 percent of Democrats said they planned to vote in the 1998 Republican United States Senate primary. Those figures are comparable to the results of studies in other States with blanket primaries.... The impact of voting by nonparty members is much greater upon minor parties, such as the Libertarian Party and the Peace and Freedom Party. In the first primaries these parties conducted following California's implementation of Proposition 198, the total votes cast for party candidates in some races was more than double the total number of registered party members....

The record also supports the obvious proposition that these substantial numbers of voters who help select the nominees of parties they have chosen not to join often have policy views that diverge from those of the party faithful.... One expert went so far as to describe it as "inevitable [under Proposition 198] that parties will be forced in some circumstances to give their official designation to a candidate who's not preferred by a majority or even plurality of party members."

. . .

In any event, the deleterious effects of Proposition 198 are not limited to altering the identity of the nominee. Even when the person favored by a majority of the party members prevails, he will have prevailed by taking somewhat different positions—and, should he be elected, will continue to take somewhat different positions in order to be renominated. As respondents' own expert concluded, "[t]he policy posi-

---

7. ... Of course *La Follette* involved the burden a state regulation imposed on a national party, but that factor affected only the weight of the State's interest, and had no bearing upon the existence vel non of a party's First Amendment right to exclude ...

8. In this sense, the blanket primary also may be constitutionally distinct from the open primary, see n. 6, supra, in which the voter is limited to one party's ballot.... This case does not require us to determine the constitutionality of open primaries.

tions of Members of Congress elected from blanket primary states are ... more moderate, both in an absolute sense and relative to the other party, and so are more reflective of the preferences of the mass of voters at the center of the ideological spectrum." It is unnecessary to cumulate evidence of this phenomenon, since, after all, the whole purpose of Proposition 198 was to favor nominees with "moderate" positions....

Nor can we accept the Court of Appeals' contention that the burden imposed by Proposition 198 is minor because petitioners are free to endorse and financially support the candidate of their choice in the primary. The ability of the party leadership to endorse a candidate is simply no substitute for the party members' ability to choose their own nominee.... [P]arty-leadership endorsements are not always effective.... In any event, the ability of the party leadership to endorse a candidate does not assist the party rank and file, who may not themselves agree with the party leadership, but do not want the party's choice decided by outsiders.

We are similarly unconvinced by respondents' claim that the burden is not severe because Proposition 198 does not limit the parties from engaging fully in other traditional party behavior, such as ensuring orderly internal party governance, maintaining party discipline in the legislature, and conducting campaigns. The accuracy of this assertion is highly questionable, at least as to the first two activities. That party nominees will be equally observant of internal party procedures and equally respectful of party discipline when their nomination depends on the general electorate rather than on the party faithful seems to us improbable.... In the end, however, the effect of Proposition 198 on these other activities is beside the point.... There is simply no substitute for a party's selecting its own candidates.

In sum, Proposition 198 forces petitioners to adulterate their candidate-selection process—the "basic function of a political party," ...—by opening it up to persons wholly unaffiliated with the party. Such forced association has the likely outcome—indeed, in this case the intended outcome—of changing the parties' message. We can think of no heavier burden on a political party's associational freedom. Proposition 198 is therefore unconstitutional unless it is narrowly tailored to serve a compelling state interest.... It is to that question which we now turn.

III

Respondents proffer ... state interests they claim are compelling. Two of them—producing elected officials who better represent the electorate and expanding candidate debate beyond the scope of partisan concerns—are simply circumlocution for producing nominees and nominee positions other than those the parties would choose if left to their own devices.... Both of these supposed interests, therefore, reduce to nothing more than a stark repudiation of freedom of political association: Parties should not be free to select their own nominees because those nominees, and the positions taken by those nominees, will not be congenial to the majority.

. . .

Respondents' remaining four asserted state interests—promoting fairness, affording voters greater choice, increasing voter participation, and protecting privacy—are not . . . compelling . . .

The aspect of fairness addressed by Proposition 198 is presumably the supposed inequity of not permitting nonparty members in "safe" districts to determine the party nominee. If that is unfair at all (rather than merely a consequence of . . . majority [rule]), it seems to us less unfair than permitting nonparty members to hijack the party. As for affording voters greater choice, it is obvious that the net effect of this scheme—indeed, its avowed purpose—is to reduce the scope of choice, by assuring a range of candidates who are all more "centrist." This . . . is hardly a compelling state interest, if indeed it is even a legitimate one. The interest in increasing voter participation is just a variation on the same theme (more choices favored by the majority will produce more voters), and suffers from the same defect. As for the protection of privacy: The specific privacy interest at issue is . . . confidentiality of one's party affiliation . . . . . [T]he State's interest in assuring the privacy of this piece of information in all cases can conceivably be considered a "compelling" one. . . .

Finally, we may observe that even if all these state interests were compelling ones, Proposition 198 is not a narrowly tailored means of furthering them. Respondents could protect them all by resorting to a nonpartisan blanket primary. Generally speaking, under such a system, the State determines what qualifications it requires for a candidate to have a place on the primary ballot—which may include nomination by established parties and voter-petition requirements for independent candidates. Each voter, regardless of party affiliation, may then vote for any candidate, and the top two vote getters (or however many the State prescribes) then move on to the general election. This system has all the characteristics of the partisan blanket primary, save the constitutionally crucial one: Primary voters are not choosing a party's nominee. Under a nonpartisan blanket primary, a State may ensure more choice, greater participation, increased "privacy," and a sense of "fairness"—all without severely burdening a political party's First Amendment right of association.

* * *

Respondents' legitimate state interests and petitioners' First Amendment rights are not inherently incompatible. To the extent they are in this case, the State of California has made them so by forcing political parties to associate with those who do not share their beliefs. And it has done this at the "crucial juncture" at which party members traditionally find their collective voice and select their spokesman. . . . The burden Proposition 198 places on petitioners' rights of political association is both severe and unnecessary. The judgment for the Court of Appeals for the Ninth Circuit is reversed.

It is so ordered.

JUSTICE KENNEDY, concurring.

. . .

... [T]here is much to be said in favor of California's law; and I might find this to be a close case if it were simply a way to make elections more fair and open or addressed matters purely of party structure.

The true purpose of this law, however, is to force a political party to accept a candidate it may not want and, by so doing, to change the party's doctrinal position on major issues.... I agree with the Court's opinion.

I add this separate concurrence to say that Proposition 198 is doubtful for a further reason. In justification of its statute California tells us a political party has the means at hand to protect its associational freedoms.... The important additional point ... is that, by reason of the Court's denial of First Amendment protections to a political party's spending of its own funds and resources in cooperation with its preferred candidate, see Colorado Republican Federal Campaign Comm. v. Federal Election Comm'n, 518 U.S. 604 (1996), the Federal Government or the State has the power to prevent the party from using the very remedy California now offers up to defend its law.

. . .

Were the views of those who would uphold both California's blanket primary system and limitations on coordinated party expenditures to become prevailing law, the State could control political parties at two vital points in the election process. First, it could mandate a blanket primary to weaken the party's ability to defend and maintain its doctrinal positions by allowing nonparty members to vote in the primary. Second, it could impose severe restrictions on the amount of funds and resources the party could spend in efforts to counteract the State's doctrinal intervention. In other words, the First Amendment injury done by the Court's ruling in *Colorado Republican* would be compounded were California to prevail in the instant case.

... With these observations, I join the opinion of the Court.

JUSTICE STEVENS, with whom JUSTICE GINSBURG joins as to Part I, dissenting.

... I am convinced that California's adoption of a blanket primary pursuant to Proposition 198 does not violate the First Amendment, and that its use in primary elections for state offices is therefore valid. The application of Proposition 198 to elections for United States Senators and Representatives, however, raises a more difficult question under the Elections Clause of the United States Constitution, Art. I, § 4, cl. 1. I shall first explain my disagreement with the Court's resolution of the First Amendment issue and then comment on the Elections Clause issue.

I

A State's power to determine how its officials are to be elected is a quintessential attribute of sovereignty ..... In my view, principles of federalism require us to respect the policy choice made by the State's voters in approving Proposition 198.

The blanket primary system instituted by Proposition 198 does not abridge "the ability of citizens to band together in promoting among the electorate candidates who espouse their political views." ... [T]he Court blurs two distinctions that are critical: (1) the distinction between a private organization's right to define itself and its messages, on the one hand, and the State's right to define the obligations of citizens and organizations performing public functions, on the other; and (2) the distinction between laws that abridge participation in the political process and those that encourage such participation.

When a political party defines the organization and composition of its governing units, when it decides what candidates to endorse, and when it decides whether and how to communicate those endorsements to the public, it is engaged in the kind of private expressive associational activity that the First Amendment protects.... A political party could, if a majority of its members chose to do so, adopt a platform advocating white supremacy and opposing the election of any non-Caucasians. Indeed, it could decide to use its funds and oratorical skills to support only those candidates who were loyal to its racist views. Moreover, if a State permitted its political parties to select their candidates through conventions or caucuses, a racist party would also be free to select only candidates who would adhere to the party line.

... [T]he associational rights of political parties are neither absolute nor as comprehensive as the rights enjoyed by wholly private associations.... I think it clear—though the point has never been decided by this Court—"that a State may require parties to use the primary format for selecting their nominees." The reason a State may impose this significant restriction on a party's associational freedoms is that both the general election and the primary are quintessential forms of state action. It is because the primary is state action that an organization—whether it calls itself a political party or just a "Jaybird" association—may not deny non-Caucasians the right to participate in the selection of its nominees. Terry v. Adams, 345 U.S. 461 (1953); Smith v. Allwright, 321 U.S. 649, 663–664 (1944). The Court is quite right in stating that those cases "do not stand for the proposition that party affairs are [wholly] public affairs, free of First Amendment protections." They do, however, stand for the proposition that primary elections, unlike most "party affairs," are state action. The protections that the First Amendment affords to the "internal processes" of a political party, do not encompass a right to exclude nonmembers from voting in a state-required, state-financed primary election.

The so-called "right not to associate" that the Court relies upon, then, is simply inapplicable to participation in a state election. A political party, like any other association, may refuse to allow non-members to participate in the party's decisions when it is conducting its own affairs; California's blanket primary system does not infringe this principle. But an election, unlike a convention or caucus, is a public affair. Although it is true that we have extended First Amendment protection to a party's right to invite independents to participate in its primaries, Tashjian v. Republican Party of Conn., 479 U.S. 208 (1986), neither that case nor any other has held or suggested that the "right not to associate" imposes a limit on the State's power to open up its primary elections to all voters eligible to vote in a general election. In my view, while state rules abridging participation in its elections should be closely scrutinized, the First Amendment does not inhibit the State from acting to broaden voter access to state-run, state-financed elections. When a State acts not to limit democratic participation but to expand the ability of individuals to participate in the democratic process, it is acting not as a foe of the First Amendment but as a friend and ally.

. . .

The Court's reliance on a political party's "right not to associate" as a basis for limiting a State's power to conduct primary elections will inevitably require it either to draw unprincipled distinctions among various primary configurations or to alter voting practices throughout the Nation in fundamental ways. Assuming that a registered Democrat or independent who wants to vote in the Republican gubernatorial primary can do so merely by asking for a Republican ballot, the Republican Party's constitutional right "not to associate" is pretty feeble if the only cost it imposes on that Democrat or independent is a loss of his right to vote for non-Republican candidates for other offices. . . .

. . . Given that open primaries are supported by essentially the same state interests that the Court disparages today and are not as "narrow" as nonpartisan primaries, there is surely a danger that open primaries will fare no better against a First Amendment challenge than blanket primaries have.

. . . 3 States presently have blanket primaries, while an additional 21 States have open primaries and 8 States have semi-closed primaries in which independents may participate. . . . This Court's willingness to invalidate the primary schemes of 3 States and cast serious constitutional doubt on the schemes of 29 others at the parties' behest is, as the District Court rightly observed, "an extraordinary intrusion into the complex and changing election laws of the States [that] . . . remove[s] from the American political system a method for candidate selection that many States consider beneficial and which in the uncertain future could take on new appeal and importance."

. . .

II

The Elections Clause of the United States Constitution, Art. I, § 4, cl. 1, provides that "[t]he Times, Places and Manner of holding Elections for Senators and Representatives, shall be prescribed in each State by the Legislature thereof" (emphasis added). This broad constitutional grant of power to state legislatures is "matched by state control over the election process for state offices." Tashjian, 479 U.S., at 217. For the reasons given in Part I, supra, I believe it would be a proper exercise of these powers and would not violate the First Amendment for the California Legislature to adopt a blanket primary system. This particular blanket primary system, however, was adopted by popular initiative. Although this distinction is not relevant with respect to elections for state offices, it is unclear whether a state election system not adopted by the legislature is constitutional insofar as it applies to the manner of electing United States Senators and Representatives.

NOTES AND QUESTIONS

1. As indicated in the debate between the Court's majority and dissent, the Court's treatment of party primary elections has been schizophrenic. In cases decided in the 1940s and 1950s the Court held that political parties violated the Constitution when they denied African American citizens the right to vote in their primaries. Those cases reasoned from the fact that party primaries (particularly in the one-party politics of the South) played a crucial role in elections, and were "public functions." Thus a party's autonomy in selection of its members was *limited* by the Constitution. On the other hand, cases decided in the 1970s and 1980s held that States violated the Constitution in imposing some limits on the election procedures by which the parties chose convention delegates and candidates for public office. Those cases reasoned from the fact that parties were voluntary political associations whose processes were private affairs. Thus a party's autonomy in selection of its members was *protected* by the Constitution.

2. The Court's opinion, in footnote 8, says that the "case does not require us to determine the question of open primaries." Is the dissent correct that the Court's First Amendment rationale is equally applicable to open primaries?

3. Would you prefer the nonpartisan blanket primary, discussed near the end of the Court's opinion to a closed partisan primary? Would it "ensure more choice, greater participation, increased 'privacy,' and a sense of 'fairness'—all without severely burdening a political party's First Amendment right of association." If the nonpartisan blanket primary regularly resulted in a runoff between candidates of the two major parties, would this be a denial of ballot access to other parties' candidates?

CLINGMAN v. BEAVER

544 U.S. 581, 125 S.Ct. 2029, 161 L.Ed.2d 920 (2005).

JUSTICE THOMAS delivered the opinion of the Court, except as to Part II–A.

Oklahoma has a semiclosed primary system, in which a political party may invite only its own party members and voters registered as Independents to vote in the party's primary. The Court of Appeals held that this system violates the right to freedom of association of the Libertarian Party of Oklahoma (LPO) and several Oklahomans who are registered members of the Republican and Democratic parties. We hold that it does not.

I

Oklahoma's election laws provide that only registered members of a political party may vote in the party's primary unless the party opens its primary to registered Independents as well, ... In May 2000, the LPO notified the secretary of the Oklahoma State Election Board that it wanted to open its upcoming primary to all registered Oklahoma voters, without regard to their party affiliation. ... [T]he secretary agreed as to Independent voters, but not as to voters registered with other political parties. The LPO and several Republican and Democratic voters then sued for declaratory and injunctive relief in the United States District Court for the Western District of Oklahoma, alleging that Oklahoma's semiclosed primary law unconstitutionally burdens their First Amendment right to freedom of political association. ... The District Court ... upheld the semiclosed primary statute as constitutional.

. . .

On appeal, the Court of Appeals for the Tenth Circuit reversed the judgment of the District Court. The Court of Appeals concluded that the State's semiclosed primary statute imposed a severe burden on respondents' associational rights, ... Finding none of Oklahoma's interests compelling, the Court of Appeals enjoined Oklahoma from using its semiclosed primary law. Because the Court of Appeals' decision not only prohibits Oklahoma from using its primary system but also casts doubt on the semiclosed primary laws of 23 other States, we granted certiorari. ...

II

The Constitution grants States "broad power to prescribe the 'Time, Places and Manner of holding Elections for Senators and Representatives,' Art 1, § 4, cl. 1, which power is matched by state control over the election process for state offices." ... We have held that the First Amendment, among other things, protects the right of citizens "to band together in promoting among the electorate candidates who espouse their political views." California Democratic Party v. Jones, 530 U.S. 567. Regulations that impose severe burdens on associational rights must be narrowly tailored to serve a compelling state interest. ... However, when regulations impose lesser burdens, "a State's important regulatory interests will usually be enough to justify reasonable, nondiscriminatory restrictions." ... This case presents a question ... whether a State may prevent a political party from inviting registered voters of other parties to vote in its primary.... We are persuaded that any burden Oklahoma's semiclosed primary imposes is minor and justified by legitimate state interests....

A

At the outset, we note that Oklahoma's semiclosed primary system is unlike other laws this Court has held to infringe associational rights. Oklahoma has not sought through its electoral system to ... compel the LPO's association with unwanted members or voters, see *Jones*, supra, ... The LPO is free to canvass the electorate, enroll or exclude potential members, nominate the candidate of its choice, and engage in the same electoral activities as every other political party in Oklahoma. Oklahoma merely prohibits the LPO from leaving the selection of its candidates to people who are members of another political party. ...

In other words, the Republican and Democratic voters who have brought this action do not want to associate with the LPO, at least not in any formal sense. They wish to remain registered with the Republican, Democratic, or Reform parties, and yet to assist in selecting the Libertarian Party's candidates for the general election. Their interest is in casting a vote for a Libertarian candidate in a particular primary election, rather than in banding together with fellow citizens committed to the LPO's political goals and ideas. . . . And the LPO is happy to have their votes, if not their membership on the party rolls.

However, a voter who is unwilling to disaffiliate from another party to vote in the LPO's primary forms little "association" with the LPO—nor the LPO with him . . .

. . .

. . . Oklahoma's law does not regulate the LPO's internal processes, its authority to exclude unwanted members, or its capacity to communicate with the public. . . . Oklahoma conditions the party's ability to welcome a voter into its primary on the voter's willingness to dissociate from his current party of choice. If anything, it is "[t]he moment of choosing the party's nominee" that matters far more, . . . for that is "the crucial juncture at which the appeal to common principles may be translated into concerted action, and hence to political power in the community,". . . . If a party may be prevented from associating with the candidate of its choice . . . because that candidate refuses to disaffiliate from another political party, a party may also be prevented from associating with a voter who refuses to do the same. . . .

. . .

B

. . .

. . . To deem ordinary and widespread burdens like these severe would subject virtually every electoral regulation to strict scrutiny, hamper the ability of States to run efficient and equitable elections, and compel federal courts to rewrite state electoral codes. The Constitution does not require that result, for it is beyond question "that States may, and inevitably must, enact reasonable regulations of parties, elections, and ballots to reduce election-and campaign-related disorder." . . . .

C

When a state electoral provision places no heavy burden on associational rights, "a State's important regulatory interests will usually be enough to justify reasonable, nondiscriminatory restrictions." . . . Here, Oklahoma's semiclosed primary advances a number of regulatory interests that this Court recognizes as important: It "preserv[es] [political] parties as viable and identifiable interest groups," . . . enhances parties' electioneering and party-building efforts, . . . and guards against party raiding and "sore loser" candidacies by spurned primary contenders. . . . It does not matter that the LPO is willing to risk the surrender of its identity in exchange for electoral success. Oklahoma's interest is independent and concerns the integrity of its primary system. The State wants to "avoid primary election outcomes which would tend to confuse or mislead the general voting population to the extent [it] relies on party labels as representative of certain ideologies." ... Oklahoma reasonably has concluded that opening the LPO's primary to all voters regardless of party affiliation would undermine the crucial role of political parties in the primary process. Cf. *Jones*, 530 U.S., at 574.

* * *

Oklahoma remains free to allow the LPO to invite registered voters of other parties to vote in its primary. But the Constitution leaves that choice to the democratic process, not to the courts.

JUSTICE O'CONNOR, with whom JUSTICE BREYER joins except as to Part III, concurring in part and concurring in the judgment.

I join the Court's opinion except for Part II–A. Although I agree with most of the Court's reasoning, I write separately to emphasize two points. First, I think respondents' claim implicates important associational interests, and I see no reason to minimize those interests to dispose of this case. Second, I agree with the Court that only Oklahoma's semiclosed primary law is properly before us, that standing alone it imposes only a modest, nondiscriminatory burden on respondents' associational rights, and that this burden is justified by the State's legitimate regulatory interests. I note, however, that there are some grounds for concern that other state laws may unreasonably restrict voters' ability to change party registration so as to participate in the Libertarian Party of Oklahoma's (LPO) primary. A realistic assessment of regulatory burdens on associational rights would, in an appropriate case, require examination of the cumulative effects of the State's overall scheme governing primary elections; and any finding of a more severe burden would trigger more probing review of the justifications offered by the State.

. . .

... [W]here a party invites a voter to participate in its primary and the voter seeks to do so, we should begin with the premise that there are significant associational interests at stake. From this starting point, we can then ask to what extent and in what manner the State may justifiably restrict those interests ...

. . .

JUSTICE STEVENS, with whom JUSTICE GINSBURG joins, and with whom JUSTICE SOUTER joins as to Parts I, II, and III, dissenting.

The Court's decision today diminishes the value of two important rights protected by the First Amendment: the individual citizen's right to vote for the candidate of her choice and a political party's right to define its own mission. No one would contend that a citizen's membership in either the Republican or the Democratic Party could disqualify her from attending political functions sponsored by another party, or from voting for a third party's candidate in a general election. If a third party invites her to participate in its primary election, her right to support the candidate of her choice merits constitutional protection, whether she elects to make a speech, to donate funds, or to cast a ballot. The importance of vindicating that individual right far outweighs any public interest in punishing registered Republicans or Democrats for acts of disloyalty. The balance becomes even more lopsided when the individual right is reinforced by the right of the Libertarian Party of Oklahoma (LPO) to associate with willing voters.

In concluding that the State's interests override those important values, the Court focuses on interests that are not legitimate. States do not have a valid interest in manipulating the outcome of elections, in protecting the major parties from competition, or in stunting the growth of new parties. While States do have a valid interest in conducting orderly elections and in encouraging the maximum participation of voters, neither of these interests overrides (or, indeed, even conflicts with) the valid interests of both the LPO and the voters who wish to participate in its primary.

In the final analysis, this case is simple. . . . Oklahoma . . . denies a party the right to invite willing voters to participate in its primary elections. I would therefore affirm the Court of Appeals' judgment.

B.   FINANCING THE CAMPAIGN

Money talks! For some, that is the core of the problem with contemporary political campaigns—given the high costs of mounting successful political campaigns, contributions insure that elected officials will be unduly influenced by moneyed interests even if they do not buy outright corruption. For a majority of the Supreme Court, however, it is because money talks that there are serious constitutional limits under the First Amendment when government attempts to control expenditures in political campaigns.

BUCKLEY v. VALEO

Supreme Court of the United States, 1976.
424 U.S. 1, 96 S.Ct. 612, 46 L.Ed.2d 659.

Per Curiam.

These appeals present constitutional challenges to key provisions of the Federal Election Campaign Act of 1971 . . . as amended in 1974.

[Plaintiffs, including political candidates, contributors to candidates, party organizations, and other organizations, brought suit in the district court in the District of Columbia pursuant to a special statutory review procedure. Defendants were relevant federal officials. Plaintiffs sought a declaration of unconstitutionality and an injunction against the enforcement of the Act.]

I.   CONTRIBUTION AND EXPENDITURE LIMITATIONS

The intricate statutory scheme adopted by Congress to regulate federal election campaigns includes restrictions on political contributions and expenditures that apply broadly to all phases of and all participants in the election process. The major contribution and expenditure limitations in the Act prohibit individuals from contributing more than $25,000 in a single year or more than $1,000 to any single candidate for an election campaign and from spending more than $1,000 a year "relative to a clearly identified candidate." Other provisions restrict a candidate's use of personal and family resources in his campaign and limit the overall amount that can be spent by a candidate in campaigning for federal office.

· · ·

A. General Principles

The Act's contribution and expenditure limitations operate in an area of the most fundamental First Amendment activities. Discussion of public issues and debate on the qualifications of candidates are integral to the operation of the system of government established by our Constitution. . . .

The First Amendment protects political association as well as political expression. . . .

It is with these principles in mind that we consider the primary contentions of the parties with respect to the Act's limitations upon the giving and spending of money in political campaigns. Those conflicting contentions could not more sharply define the basic issues before us. Appellees contend that what the Act regulates is conduct, and that its effect on speech and association is incidental at most. Appellants respond that contributions and expenditures are at the very core of political speech, and that the Act's limitations thus constitute restraints on First Amendment liberty that are both gross and direct.

· · ·

We cannot share the view that the present Act's contribution and expenditure limitations are comparable to the restrictions on conduct upheld in *O'Brien*. The expenditure of money simply cannot be equated with such conduct as destruction of a draft card. Some forms of communication made possible by the giving and spending of money involve speech alone, some involve conduct primarily, and some involve a combination of the two. Yet this Court has never suggested that the dependence of a communication on the expenditure of money operates itself to introduce a nonspeech element or to reduce the exacting scrutiny required by the First Amendment. . . .

· · ·

Nor can the Act's contribution and expenditure limitations be sustained, as some of the parties suggest, by reference to the constitutional principles reflected in such decisions as Cox v. Louisiana, supra, Adderley v. Florida, 385 U.S. 39 (1966), and Kovacs v. Cooper, 336 U.S. 77 (1949). . . . The critical difference between this case and those time, place, and manner cases is that the present Act's contribution and expenditure limitations impose direct quantity restrictions on political communication and association by persons, groups, candidates, and political parties in addition to any reasonable time, place, and manner regulations otherwise imposed.

A restriction on the amount of money a person or group can spend on political communication during a campaign necessarily reduces the quantity of expression by restricting the number of issues discussed, the depth of their exploration, and the size of the audience reached. This is because virtually every means of communicating ideas in today's mass society requires the expenditure of money....

The expenditure limitations contained in the Act represent substantial rather than merely theoretical restrains on the quantity and diversity of political speech. The $1,000 ceiling on spending "relative to a clearly identified candidate," 18 U.S.C. § 608(e)(1) ... would appear to exclude all citizens and groups except candidates, political parties, and the institutional press from any significant use of the most effective modes of communication. Although the Act's limitations on expenditures by campaign organizations and political parties provide substantially greater room for discussion and debate, they would have required restrictions in the scope of a number of past congressional and Presidential campaigns and would operate to constrain campaigning by candidates who raise sums in excess of the spending ceiling.

By contrast with a limitation upon expenditures for political expression, a limitation upon the amount that any one person or group may contribute to a candidate or political committee entails only a marginal restriction upon the contributor's ability to engage in free communication. A contribution serves as a general expression of support for the candidate and his views, but does not communicate the underlying basis for the support.... While contributions may result in political expression if spent by a candidate or an association to present views to the voters, the transformation of contributions into political debate involves speech by someone other than the contributor.

Given the important role of contributions in financing political campaigns, contribution restrictions could have a severe impact on political dialogue if the limitations prevented candidates and political committees from amassing the resources necessary for effective advocacy. There is no indication, however, that the contribution limitations imposed by the Act would have any dramatic adverse effect on the funding of campaigns and political associations. The overall effect of the Act's contribution ceilings is merely to require candidates and political committees to raise funds from a greater number of persons and to compel people who would otherwise contribute amounts greater than the statutory limits to expend such funds on direct political expression, rather than to reduce the total amount of money potentially available to promote political expression.

The Act's contribution and expenditure limitations also impinge on protected associational freedoms. Making a contribution, like joining a political party, serves to affiliate a person with a candidate. In addition, it enables like-minded persons to pool their resources in furtherance of common political goals. The Act's contribution ceilings thus limit one important means of associating with a candidate or committee, but leave the contributor free to become a member of any political association and to assist personally in the association's efforts on behalf of candidates.

And the Act's contribution limitations permit associations and candidates to aggregate large sums of money to promote effective advocacy. By contrast, the Act's $1,000 limitation on independent expenditures "relative to a clearly identified candidate" precludes most associations from effectively amplifying the voice of their adherents, the original basis for the recognition of First Amendment protection of the freedom of association. . . .

In sum, although the Act's contribution and expenditure limitations both implicate fundamental First Amendment interests, its expenditure ceilings impose significantly more severe restrictions on protected freedoms of political expression and association than do its limitations of financial contributions.

B.   Contribution Limitations

1.   The $1,000 Limitation of Contributions by Individuals and Groups to Candidates and Authorized Campaign Committees

. . .

(a)

As the general discussion in Part I–A, supra, indicated, the primary First Amendment problem raised by the Act's contribution limitations is their restriction of one aspect of the contributor's freedom of political association. . . .

. . .

The Act's $1,000 contribution limitation focuses precisely on the problem of large campaign contributions—the narrow aspect of political association where the actuality and potential for corruption have been identified—while leaving persons free to engage in independent political expression, to associate actively through volunteering their services, and to assist to a limited but nonetheless substantial extent in supporting candidates and committees with financial resources. Significantly, the Act's contribution limitations in themselves do not undermine to any material degree the potential for robust and effective discussion of candidates and campaign issues by individual citizens, associations, the institutional press, candidates, and political parties.

We find that, under the rigorous standard of review established by our prior decisions, the weighty interests served by restricting the size of financial contributions to political candidates are sufficient to justify the limited effect upon First Amendment freedoms caused by the $1,000 ceiling.

. . .

(c)

Apart from these First Amendment concerns, appellants argue that the contribution limitations work such an invidious discrimination between incumbents and challengers that the statutory provisions must be declared unconstitutional on their face. In considering this contention, it is important at the outset to note that the Act applies the same limitations on contributions to all candidates regardless of their present occupations, ideological views, or party affiliations. Absent record evidence of invidious discrimination against challengers as a class, a court should generally be hesitant to invalidate legislation which on its face imposes evenhanded restriction....

. . .

The charge of discrimination against minor-party and independent candidates is more troubling, but the record provides no basis for concluding that the Act invidiously disadvantages such candidates. As noted above, the Act on its face treats all candidates equally with regard to contribution limitations. And the restriction would appear to benefit minor-party and independent candidates relative to their major-party opponents because major-party candidates receive far more money in large contributions. Although there is some force to appellants' response that minor-party candidates are primarily concerned with their ability to amass the resources necessary to reach the electorate rather than with their funding position relative to their major-party opponents, the record is virtually devoid of support for the claim that the $1,000 contribution limitation will have a serious effect on the initiation and scope of minor-party and independent candidacies. Moreover, any attempt to exclude minor parties and independents en masse from the Act's contribution limitations overlooks the fact that minor-party candidates may win elective office or have a substantial impact on the outcome of an election.

In view of these considerations, we conclude that the impact of the Act's $1,000 contribution limitation on major-party challengers and on minor-party candidates does not render the provision unconstitutional on its face.

[The Court also upheld the $5,000 limit on contributions by political committees, limitations on volunteers' incidental expenses, and the $25,000 limitation on total contributions during any calendar year.]

. . .

C. Expenditure Limitations

The Act's expenditure ceilings impose direct and substantial restraints on the quantity of political speech.... It is clear that a primary effect of these expenditure limitations is to restrict the quantity of campaign speech by individuals, groups, and candidates. The restrictions, while neutral as to the ideas expressed, limit political expression "at the core of our electoral process and of the First Amendment freedoms." Williams v. Rhodes, 393 U.S. 23, 32 (1968).

1. The $1,000 Limitation on Expenditures "Relative to a Clearly Identified Candidate"

. . .

... [T]he constitutionality of § 608(e)(1) turns on whether the governmental interests advanced in its support satisfy the exacting scrutiny applicable to limitations on core First Amendment rights of political expression.

We find that the governmental interest in preventing corruption and the appearance of corruption is inadequate to justify § 608(e)(1)'s ceiling on independent expenditures....

. . .

It is argued, however, that the ancillary governmental interest in equalizing the relative ability of individuals and groups to influence the outcome of elections serves to justify the limitation on express advocacy of the election or defeat of candidates imposed by § 608(e)(1)'s expenditure ceiling. But the concept that government may restrict the speech of some elements of our society in order to enhance the relative voice of others is wholly foreign to the First Amendment.... The First Amendment's protection against governmental abridgment of free expression cannot properly be made to depend on a person's financial ability to engage in public discussion....

. . .

For the reasons stated, we conclude that § 608(e)(1)'s independent expenditure limitation is unconstitutional under the First Amendment.

2. Limitation on Expenditures by Candidates from Personal or Family Resources

. . .

The ceiling on personal expenditures by candidates on their own behalf, like the limitations on independent expenditures contained in § 608(e)(1), imposes a substantial restraint on the ability of persons to engage in protected First Amendment expression. The candidate, no less than any other person, has a First Amendment right to engage in the discussion of public issues and vigorously and tirelessly to advocate his own election and the election of other candidates. Indeed, it is of particular importance that the candidates have the unfettered opportunity to make their views known so that the electorate may intelligently evaluate the candidates' personal qualities and their positions on vital public issues before choosing among them on election day. Mr. Justice Brandeis' observation that in our country "public discussion is a political duty," applies with special force to candidates for public office. Section 608(a)'s ceiling on personal expenditures by a candidate in furtherance of his own candidacy thus clearly and directly interferes with constitutionally protected freedoms.

The primary governmental interest served by the Act—the prevention of actual and apparent corruption of the political process—does not support the limitation on the candidate's expenditure of his own personal funds. As the Court of Appeals concluded: "[M]anifestly, the core problem of avoiding undisclosed and undue influence on candidates from outside interests has lesser application when the monies involved come from the candidate himself or from his immediate family." Indeed, the use of personal funds reduces the candidate's dependence on outside contributions and thereby counteracts the coercive pressures and attendant risks of abuse to which the Act's contribution limitations are directed.

The ancillary interest in equalizing the relative financial resources of candidates competing for elective office, therefore, provides the sole relevant rationale for § 608(a)'s expenditure ceiling. That interest is clearly not sufficient to justify the provision's infringement of fundamental First Amendment rights. First, the limitation may fail to promote financial equality among candidates. A candidate who spends less of his personal resources on his campaign may nonetheless outspend his rival as a result of more successful fundraising efforts. Indeed, a candidate's personal wealth may impede his efforts to persuade others that he needs their financial contributions or volunteer efforts to conduct an effective campaign. Second, and more fundamentally, the First Amendment simply cannot tolerate § 608(a)'s restriction upon the freedom of a candidate to speak without legislative limit on behalf of his own candidacy. We therefore hold that § 608(a)'s restriction on a candidate's personal expenditures is unconstitutional.

3.   Limitations on Campaign Expenditures

Section 608(c) places limitations on overall campaign expenditures by candidates seeking nomination for election and election to federal office....

No Governmental interest that has been suggested is sufficient to justify the restriction on the quantity of political expression imposed by § 608(c)'s campaign expenditure limitations. The major evil associated with rapidly increasing campaign expenditures is the danger of candidate dependence on large contributions. The interest in alleviating the corrupting influence of large contributions is served by the Act's contribution limitations and disclosure provisions rather than by § 608(c)'s campaign expenditure ceilings....

The interest in equalizing the financial resources of candidates competing for federal office is no more convincing a justification for restricting the scope of federal election campaigns....

The campaign expenditure ceilings appear to be designed primarily to serve the governmental interests in reducing the allegedly skyrocketing costs of political campaigns.... The First Amendment denies government the power to determine that spending to promote one's political views is wasteful, excessive, or unwise. In the free society ordained by our Constitution it is not the government but the people—individually as citizens and candidates and collectively as associations and political committees—who must retain control over the quantity and range of debate on public issues in a political campaign.

For these reasons we hold that § 608(c) is constitutionally invalid.

In sum, the provisions of the Act that impose a $1,000 limitation on contributions to a single candidate, § 608(b)(1), a $5,000 limitation on contributions by a political committee to a single candidate, § 608(b)(2), and a $25,000 limitation on total contributions by an individual during any calendar year, § 608(b)(3), are constitutionally valid. These limitations, along with the disclosure provisions, constitute the Act's primary weapons against the reality or appearance of improper influence stemming from the dependence of candidates on large campaign contribu-

tions. The contribution ceilings thus serve the basic governmental interest in safeguarding the integrity of the electoral process without directly
impinging upon the rights of individual citizens and candidates to engage
in political debate and discussion. By contrast, the First Amendment
requires the invalidation of the Act's independent expenditure ceiling,
§ 608(e)(1), its limitations on a candidate's expenditures from his own
personal funds, § 608(a), and its ceilings on overall campaign expenditures, § 608(c). These provisions place substantial and direct restrictions
on the ability of candidates, citizens, and associations to engage in
protected political expression, restriction that the First Amendment
cannot tolerate.

[Five justices dissented but went in different directions. Justice
White argued that the expenditure limitations ought to be valid, because
limiting the amount that can be spent would "ease the candidate's
understandable obsession with fundraising," and "dispel the impression
that federal elections are purely and simply a function of money." Chief
Justice Burger agreed with Justice White that expenditures and contributions should be treated in the same way, but argued that both the
expenditure and contribution limits ought to be *invalid*. He pointed out
that "contributions and expenditures are two sides of the same First
Amendment coin." Justice Blackmun agreed that there was no "principled distinction" between the contribution limitations and the expenditure limitations. Justice Marshall dissented from a portion of the opinion
invalidating limits on expenditures from a candidate's personal funds.
Justice Rehnquist dissented from a portion of the opinion upholding
disparities in public funding of presidential campaigns between the two
major parties, on one hand, and minor parties, on the other.]

NOTES AND QUESTIONS

1.   Chief Justice Burger appointed a six-justice "drafting team"—
himself, Brennan, Stewart, Powell, White, and Rehnquist—to write the
per curiam opinion in Buckley v. Valeo. Burger drafted the statement of
the case, Powell wrote on the Federal Election Campaign Act's disclosure
provisions, Brennan on its public funding provisions, Stewart on its
provisions dealing with contribution and expenditure limitations, and
White and Rehnquist on the provision dealing with the Election Commission. Burger to Brennan, Nov. 18, 1975, Box 396, Brennan Papers,
Library of Congress. Brennan played a major role in uniting the Court to
the extent possible. Late in the circulation of the opinion, Powell sent
Brennan the following handwritten note: "Bill—we are indebted to you
for your firm leadership in guiding and moving this case forward—as
was so urgently needed." Ibid. Part of Brennan's leadership was the
suppression of his dissenting views on the limits of candidates' personal
contributions. Originally he had joined Marshall on this issue, for he
wrote to his colleagues on January 2, 1976: "I personally adhere to my
vote in conference to sustain the limits on expenditures from personal or
family funds." Ibid.

2.   In his dissenting opinion, Justice Marshall disagreed with the
majority that the equalization of relative financial resources of the
candidates was an insufficient interest to justify upholding the constitu-

tionality of limitations on candidates' personal contributions. Marshall maintained the "the wealthy candidate's immediate access to a substantial personal fortune may give him an initial advantage that his less wealthy opponent may never overcome. And even if the advantage can be overcome, the perception that personal wealth wins elections may not only discourage potential candidates without significant personal wealth from entering the political arena, but also undermine public confidence in the integrity of the electoral process." In a footnote, Marshall pointed out that in 1970, 11 of 15 major senatorial candidates in the nation's seven largest states were millionaires and that the four who were not millionaires lost their bids for election. Does Marshall's argument persuade you that there was a sufficient interest for the Court to uphold the limitations of personal and family funds in federal elections?

3. The First Amendment law concerning the regulation of campaign financing and expenditures has become extremely complex, with the Court often sharply divided about the outcome of particular cases. Still, the distinction between campaign contributions and expenditures is the starting point. Do you agree that it is inconsistent to permit government to limit campaign contributions but not expenditures? If so, do you agree with Justice White or Chief Justice Burger and Justice Blackmun?

4. The distinction between contribution limits and spending limits was central in Colorado Republican Federal Campaign Committee v. Federal Election Commission, 518 U.S. 604 (1996). The Federal Election Campaign Act of 1971 imposes dollar limits on political party "expenditure[s] in connection with the general election campaign of a [congressional] candidate." After the Colorado Republican Party selected its 1986 candidate for United States Senate, it bought radio advertisements attacking the likely Democratic Party candidate. While seven justices agreed that the Constitution precluded enforcement of the Act in this case, there was no opinion for the Court. Three justices (Breyer, O'Connor and Souter) concluded that the Party Expenditure Provision was unconstitutional as applied to "independent" party expenditures that were not an "indirect campaign contribution" to a candidate. Justice Breyer's opinion took no position concerning the validity of party expenditure limitations as applied to a party expenditure "in cooperation, consultation, or concert with ... a candidate." Four justices (Kennedy, Rehnquist, Scalia and Thomas) would have held the Party Expenditure Provision unconstitutional on its face, even in the latter context. Justice Kennedy (joined by the Chief Justice and Justice Scalia) argued that all party expenditures fell within the rationale of Buckley v. Valeo, which forbids limitation on spending money on one's own speech. Justice Thomas (also joined by the Chief Justice and Justice Scalia) argued that *Buckley*'s corruption rationale was inapplicable to contributions by a party to its own candidate. In a portion of his opinion where he spoke only for himself, Justice Thomas argued that *Buckley*'s distinction between contribution limits and spending limits should be rejected. Justice Stevens (joined by Justice Ginsburg) dissented, arguing that spending limits for political parties were constitutional, serving "an important

interest in leveling the electoral field by constraining the cost of federal campaigns."

5. Not all limits on campaign expenditures are invalid. A significant holding in Buckley v. Valeo was that legislatures could limit campaign expenditures by candidates who accepted public funding. Unlike candidates for Congressional office, candidates for president were offered public financing in the 1974 Act, with limitations on expenditures by those candidates who accepted public financing. Ironically, the Act's expenditure limits for presidential candidates who had accepted public financing, which the Court upheld, were identical to expenditure limits for presidential candidates who had not accepted public financing, which the Court invalidated. Does allowing the government to use public funding as a carrot to limit campaign expenditures demonstrate the inconsistency between the Court's treatment of expenditures and contributions? Does it soften the distinction between expenditures and contributions by giving government a way to control expenditures. (Since Buckley v. Valeo, Congress has not extended public financing to Congressional campaigns, nor have many states provided public financing for campaigns for state offices.)

6. Austin v. Michigan Chamber of Commerce, 494 U.S. 652 (1990), sustained a state law forbidding the use of corporate funds to support the election of any candidate for state office. The Court reasoned that corporations possessed "the special benefits conferred by the corporate structure" and had "the potential for distorting the political process." Justice Scalia's angry dissent argued that this reasoning was equivalent to this "Orwellian announcement":

> Attention all citizens. To assure the fairness of elections by preventing disproportionate expression of the views of any single group, your Government has decided that the following associations of persons shall be prohibited from speaking or writing in support of any candidate.

7. Not all limitations on contributions are valid. In Citizens Against Rent Control/Coalition For Fair Housing v. Berkeley, 454 U.S. 290 (1981), the Court invalidated a city ordinance limiting contributions to committees supporting or opposing ballot measures. Contribution limits had been approved in Buckley v. Valeo because of the interest in preventing corruption. It was not possible to corrupt a ballot measure. Any interest in allowing voters to identify who was speaking through ballot measure committees was served by disclosure requirements.

8. The Court sustained requirements that candidates disclose contributions of as little as ten dollars in Buckley v. Valeo. Disclosure requirements provided voters with information as to the base of a candidate's support, deterred corruption or the appearance of corruption, and helped to enforce contribution limitations. The Court put to one side the possible case of an unpopular minor party candidate where a disclosure requirement would unduly deter potential contributors. In Brown v. Socialist Workers '74 Campaign Committee, 459 U.S. 87 (1982), the Court held that a state law requiring disclosure of campaign

contributions was invalid as applied to candidates of the Socialist Workers Party.

9. In Nixon v. Shrink, 528 U.S. 377 (2000), the Court upheld a Missouri statute that limited campaign contributions to state political candidates. Specifically the case held that Buckley v. Valeo was authority for such limits and that the federal limits in *Buckley* without adjustment for inflation were permissible even without adjustment for inflation....

Justice Thomas wrote a dissenting opinion joined by Justice Scalia, arguing that the Court's decision in *Buckley* should be overruled. He asserted that the Court's reasoning in *Buckley* was flawed because campaign contributions as well as expenditures are speech protected by the First Amendment. "[T]he constitution leaves it entirely to citizens and candidates to determine who shall speak, the means they will use, and the amount of speech sufficient to inform and persuade. *Buckley*'s ratification of the government's attempt to wrest this fundamental right from the citizens was error."

Justice Kennedy dissented, leaving:

"open the possibility that Congress, or a state legislature, might devise a system in which there are some limits on both expenditures and contributions, thus permitting officeholders to concentrate their time and efforts on official duties, rather than on fundraising.... [T]here are serious constitutional questions to be confronted in enacting any such scheme, but I would not foreclose it at the outset. I would overrule *Buckley* and then free Congress or state legislatures to attempt some new reform, if, based upon their own considered view of the First Amendment, it is possible to do so. Until any reexamination takes place, however, the existing distortion of speech caused by the halfway house we created in *Buckley* ought to be eliminated. The First Amendment ought to be allowed to take its own course without further obstruction from the artificial system we have imposed. It suffices here to say that the law in question does not come even close to passing any serious scrutiny."

Justice Stevens' answer to the dissenters was: "Money is property; it is not speech."

"Speech has the power to inspire volunteers to perform a multitude of tasks on a campaign trail, on a battleground, or even on a football field. Money, meanwhile, has the power to pay hired laborers to perform the same tasks. It does not follow, however, that the First Amendment provides the same measure of protection to the use of money to accomplish such goals as it provides to the use of ideas to achieve the same results.

"Our Constitution and our heritage properly protect the individual's interest in making decisions about the use of his or her own property. Governmental regulation of such decisions can sometimes be viewed either as 'deprivations of liberty' or as 'deprivations of property.' ... Telling a grandmother that she may not use her own property to provide shelter to a grandchild—or to hire mercenaries to work in that grandchild's campaign for public office—raises important constitutional concerns that are unrelated to the First Amendment. . . .

"Reliance on the First Amendment to justify the invalidation of campaign finance regulations is the functional equivalent of the Court's candid reliance on the doctrine of substantive due process. . . . The right to use one's own money to hire gladiators, or to fund 'speech by proxy,' certainly merits significant constitutional protection. These property rights, however, are not entitled to the same protection as the right to say what one pleases."

Justice Breyer also responded to the dissenters in an opinion joined by Justice Ginsburg. He wrote:

". . . [T]his is a case where constitutionally protected interests lie on both sides of the legal equation. For that reason, there is no place for a strong presumption against constitutionality . . .

" . . .

"On the one hand, a decision to contribute money to a campaign is a matter of First Amendment concern not because money is speech (it is not), but because it enables speech. Through contributions, the contributor associates himself with the candidate's cause, helps the candidate communicate a political message with which the contributor agrees, and helps the candidate win by attracting the votes of similarly minded voters. . . . Both political association and political communication are at stake. . . .

"On the other hand, restrictions upon the amount any one individual can contribute to a particular candidate seek to protect the integrity of the electoral process—the means through which a free society democratically translates political speech into concrete governmental action. . . . Moreover, by limiting the size of the largest contributions, such restrictions aim to democratize the influence that money itself may bring to bear upon the electoral process. . . . In doing so, they seek to build public confidence in that process and broaden the base of a candidate's meaningful financial support, encouraging the public participation and open discussion that the First Amendment itself presupposes.

" . . .

"In such circumstances—where a law significantly implicates competing constitutionally protected interests in complex ways—the Court has closely scrutinized the statute's impact on those interests, but refrained from employing a simple test that effectively presumes unconstitutionality. Rather, it has balanced interests. And in practice that has meant asking whether the statute burdens one such interest in a manner out of proportion to the statute's salutary effects upon the others (perhaps, but not necessarily, because of the existence of a clearly superior, less restrictive alternative). Where a legislature has significantly greater institutional expertise, as, for example, in the field of election regulation, the Court in practice defers to empirical legislative judgments—at least where that deference does not risk such constitutional evils as, say, permitting incumbents to insulate themselves from effective electoral challenge. This approach is that taken in fact by *Buckley* for contributions, and is found generally where competing constitutional interests are implicated. . . .

"But what if I am wrong about *Buckley*? Suppose *Buckley* denies the political branches sufficient leeway to enact comprehensive solutions to the problems posed by campaign finance. If so, like Justice Kennedy, I believe the Constitution would require us to reconsider *Buckley*."

McCONNELL v. FEDERAL ELECTION COMMISSION

540 U.S. 93, 124 S.Ct. 619, 157 L.Ed.2d 491 (2003).

JUSTICE STEVENS and JUSTICE O'CONNOR delivered the opinion of the Court with respect to BCRA Titles I and II.*

The Bipartisan Campaign Reform Act of 2002 (BCRA) . . . contains a series of amendments to the Federal Election Campaign Act of 1971 (FECA) . . . and other portions of the United States Code . . . that are challenged in these cases. In this opinion we discuss Titles I and II of BCRA. The opinion of the Court delivered by the Chief Justice discusses Titles III and IV, and the opinion of the Court delivered by Justice Bryer discusses Title V.

I

More than a century ago the "sober-minded Elihu Root" advocated legislation that would prohibit political contributions by corporations in order to prevent "the great aggregations of wealth, from using their corporate funds, directly or indirectly," to elect legislators who would "vote for their protection and the advancement of their interests as against those of the public". . . .   In Root's opinion, such legislation would "strik[e] at a constantly growing evil which has done more to shake the confidence of the plain people of small means of this country in our political institutions than any other practice which has ever obtained since the foundation of our Government" . . . The Congress of the United States has repeatedly enacted legislation endorsing Root's judgment.

. . . [T]he first such enactment responded to President Theodore Roosevelt's call for legislation forbidding all contributions by corporations "to any political committee or for any political purpose." . . . The resulting 1907 statute completely banned corporate contributions of "money . . . in connection with" any federal election. . . .

---

* Justice Souter, Justice Ginsburg, and Justice Breyer join this opinion in its entirety.

In 1925 Congress extended the prohibition of "contributions" to include "anything of value", and made acceptance of a corporate contribution as well as the giving of such a contribution a crime. ... We upheld the amended statute against a constitutional challenge, observing that "[t]he power of Congress to protect the election of President and Vice President from corruption being clear, the choice of means to that end presents a question primarily addressed to the judgment of Congress." Burroughs v. United States, 290 U.S. 534, 547 (1934).

Congress' historical concern with the "political potentialities of wealth" and their "untoward consequences for the democratic process," ... has long reached beyond corporate money. During and shortly after World War II, Congress reacted to the "enormous financial outlays" made by some unions in connection with national elections. ... Congress first restricted union contributions in the Hatch Act ... and it later prohibited "union contributions in connection with federal elections ... altogether." ... Congress subsequently extended that prohibition to cover unions' election-related expenditures as well as contributions, and it broadened the coverage of federal campaigns to include both primary and general elections. ...

In early 1972 Congress continued its steady improvement of the national election laws by enacting FECA ... As first enacted, that statute required disclosure of all contributions exceeding $100 and of expenditures by candidates and political committees that spent more than $1,000 per year. ...

As the 1972 presidential elections made clear, however, FECA's passage did not deter unseemly fundraising and campaign practices. Evidence of those practices persuaded Congress to enact the Federal Election Campaign Act Amendments of 1974 ...

The 1974 amendments closed the loophole that had allowed candidates to use an unlimited number of political committees for fundraising purposes and thereby to circumvent the limits on individual committees' receipts and disbursements. They also limited individual political contributions to any single candidate to $1,000 per election, with an overall annual limitation of $25,000 by any contributor; imposed ceilings on spending by candidates and political parties for national conventions; required reporting and public disclosure of contributions and expenditures exceeding certain limits; and established the Federal Election Commission (FEC) to administer and enforce the legislation. ...

. . .

... This Court ... concluded that each set of limitations raised serious—though different—concerns under the First Amendment. *Buckley v. Valeo*, 424 U.S. 1, 14–23 (1976) *(per curiam)*. We treated the limitations on candidate and individual expenditures as direct restraints on speech, but we observed that the contribution limitations, in contrast, imposed only "a marginal restriction upon the contributor's ability to engage in free communication." ... Considering the "deeply disturbing examples" of corruption related to candidate contributions discussed in the Court of Appeals' opinion, we determined that limiting contributions served an interest in protecting "the integrity of our system of representative democracy." ... [T]he Act's primary purpose—"to limit the actuality and appearance of corruption resulting from large individual financial contributions"—provided "a constitutionally sufficient justification for the $1,000 contribution limitation." ...

We prefaced our analysis of the $1,000 limitation on expenditures by observing that it broadly encompassed every expenditure " 'relative to a clearly identified candidate.' " ... To avoid vagueness concerns we construed that phrase to apply only to "communications that in express terms advocate the election or defeat of a clearly identified candidate for federal office." ... We concluded, however, that as so narrowed, the provision would not provide effective protection against the dangers of *quid pro quo* arrangements, because persons and groups could eschew expenditures that expressly advocated the election or defeat of a clearly identified candidate while remaining "free to spend as much as they want to promote the candidate and his views." ... We also rejected the argument that the expenditure limits were necessary to prevent attempts to circumvent the Act's contribution limits, because FECA already treated expenditures controlled by or coordinated with the candidate as contributions, and we were not persuaded that independent expenditures posed the same risk of real or apparent corruption as coordinated expenditures. ... We therefore held that Congress' interest in preventing real or apparent corruption was inadequate to justify the heavy burdens on the freedoms of expression and association that the expenditure limits imposed.

. . .

Three important developments in the years after our decision in *Buckley* persuaded Congress that further legislation was necessary to regulate the role that corporations, unions, and wealthy contributors play in the electoral process. As a preface to our discussion of the specific provisions of BCRA, we comment briefly on the increased importance of "soft money," the proliferation of "issue ads," and the disturbing findings of a Senate investigation into campaign practices related to the 1996 federal elections.

Soft Money

Under FECA, "contributions" must be made with funds that are subject to the Act's disclosure requirements and source and amount limitations. Such funds are known as "federal" or "hard" money. FECA defines the term "contribution," however, to include only the gift or advance of anything of value "made by any person for the purpose of influencing any election for *Federal* office." ... Donations made solely for the purpose of influencing state or local elections are therefore unaffected by FECA's requirements and prohibitions. As a result, prior to the enactment of BCRA, federal law permitted corporations and unions, as well as individuals who had already made the maximum permissible contributions to federal candidates, to contribute "nonfederal money"—also known as "soft money"—to political parties for activities intended to influence state or local elections.

Shortly after *Buckley* was decided, questions arose concerning the treatment of contributions intended to influence both federal and state elections. Although a literal reading of FECA's definition of "contribution" would have required such activities to be funded with hard money, the FEC ruled that political parties could fund mixed-purpose activities—including get-out-the-vote drives and generic party advertising—in part with soft money. In 1995 the FEC concluded that the parties could also use soft money to defray the costs of "legislative advocacy media advertisements," even if the ads mentioned the name of a federal candidate, so long as they did not expressly advocate the candidate's election or defeat. . . .

As the permissible uses of soft money expanded, the amount of soft money raised and spent by the national political parties increased exponentially. . . .

Many contributions of soft money were dramatically larger than the contributions of hard money permitted by FECA. For example, in 1996 the top five corporate soft-money donors gave, in total, more than $9 million in nonfederal funds to the two national party committees. In the most recent election cycle the political parties raised almost $300 million—60% of their total soft-money fundraising—from just 800 donors, each of which contributed a minimum of $120,000. Moreover, the largest corporate donors often made substantial contributions to both parties. Such practices corroborate evidence indicating that many corporate contributions were motivated by a desire for access to candidates and a fear of being placed at a disadvantage in the legislative process relative to other contributors, rather than by ideological support for the candidates and parties.

. . .

The solicitation, transfer, and use of soft money thus enabled parties and candidates to circumvent FECA's limitations on the source and amount of contributions in connection with federal elections.

Issue Advertising

In *Buckley* we construed FECA's disclosure and reporting requirements, as well as its expenditure limitations, "to reach only funds used for communications that expressly advocate the election or defeat of a clearly identified candidate." . . . As a result of that strict reading of the statute, the use or omission of "magic words" such as "Elect John Smith" or "Vote Against Jane Doe" marked a bright statutory line separating "express advocacy" from "issue advocacy." . . . So-called issue ads . . . not only could be financed with soft money, but could be aired without disclosing the identity of, or any other information about, their sponsors.

While the distinction between "issue" and express advocacy seemed neat in theory, the two categories of advertisements proved functionally identical in important respects. . . . Little difference existed, for example, between an ad that urged viewers to "vote against Jane Doe" and one that condemned Jane Doe's record on a particular issue before exhorting viewers to "call Jane Doe and tell her what you think." . . . [T]he conclusion that such ads were specifically intended to affect election results was confirmed by the fact that almost all of them aired in the 60 days immediately preceding a federal election. ... Indeed, the ads were attractive to organizations and candidates precisely because they were beyond FECA's reach, enabling candidates and their parties to work closely with friendly interest groups to sponsor so-called issue ads when the candidates themselves were running out of money.

. . .

... As with soft-money contributions, political parties and candidates used the availability of so-called issue ads to circumvent FECA's limitations, asking donors who contributed their permitted quota of hard money to give money to nonprofit corporations to spend on "issue" advocacy.

Senate Committee Investigation

In 1998 the Senate Committee on Governmental Affairs issued a six-volume report summarizing the results of an extensive investigation into the campaign practices in the 1996 federal elections. The report gave particular attention to the effect of soft money on the American political system, including elected officials' practice of granting special access in return for political contributions.

The committee's principal findings relating to Democratic Party fundraising were set forth in the majority's report, while the minority report primarily described Republican practices. The two reports reached consensus, however, on certain central propositions. They agreed that the "soft money loophole" had led to a "meltdown" of the campaign finance system that had been intended "to keep corporate, union and large individual contributions from influencing the electoral process." One Senator stated that "the hearings provided overwhelming evidence that the twin loopholes of soft money and bogus issue advertising have virtually destroyed our campaign finance laws, leaving us with little more than a pile of legal rubble."

. . .

The report discussed potential reforms, including a ban on soft money at the national and state party levels and restrictions on sham issue advocacy by nonparty groups. The majority expressed the view that a ban on the raising of soft money by national party committees would effectively address the use of union and corporate general treasury funds in the federal political process only if it required that candidate-specific ads be funded with hard money. The minority similarly recommended the elimination of soft-money contributions to political parties from individuals, corporations, and unions, as well as "reforms addressing candidate advertisements masquerading as issue ads."

II

In BCRA, Congress enacted many of the committee's proposed reforms. BCRA's central provisions are designed to address Congress' concerns about the increasing use of soft money and issue advertising to influence federal elections. Title I regulates the use of soft money by political parties, officeholders, and candidates. Title II primarily prohibits corporations and labor unions from using general treasury funds for communications that are intended to, or have the effect of, influencing the outcome of federal elections.

Section 403 of BCRA provides special rules for actions challenging the constitutionality of any of the Act's provisions. ... Eleven such actions were filed promptly after the statute went into effect in March 2002. As required by § 403, those actions were filed in the District Court for the District of Columbia and heard by a three-judge court. ... The court ... ultimately delivered a decision embodied in a two-judge *per curiam* opinion and three separate, lengthy opinions, ... [holding] some parts of BCRA unconstitutional and [holding other parts constitutional]. ...

. . .

III

Title I is Congress' effort to plug the soft-money loophole. The cornerstone of Title I is new FECA § 323(a), which prohibits national party committees and their agents from soliciting, receiving, directing, or spending any soft money. ... In short, § 323(a) takes national parties out of the soft-money business.

The remaining provisions of new FECA § 323 largely reinforce the restrictions in § 323(a). ...

Plaintiffs mount a facial First Amendment challenge to new FECA § 323, as well as challenges based on the Elections Clause, U.S. Const., Art. I, § 4, principles of federalism, and the equal protection component of the Due Process Clause. We address these challenges in turn.

A

In *Buckley* and subsequent cases, we have subjected restrictions on campaign expenditures to closer scrutiny than limits on campaign contributions. In these cases we have recognized that contribution limits, unlike limits on expenditures, "entai[l] only a marginal restriction upon the contributor's ability to engage in free communication." ...

Because the communicative value of large contributions inheres mainly in their ability to facilitate the speech of their recipients, we have said that contribution limits impose serious burdens on free speech only if they are so low as to "preven[t] candidates and political committees from amassing the resources necessary for effective advocacy." *Ibid.*

... The "overall effect" of dollar limits on contributions is "merely to require candidates and political committees to raise funds from a greater number of persons." ...

Our treatment of contribution restrictions ... also reflects the importance of the interests that underlie contribution limits—interests in preventing "both the actual corruption threatened by large financial contributions and the eroding of public confidence in the electoral process through the appearance of corruption." ... The less rigorous standard of review we have applied to contribution limits ... shows proper deference to Congress' ability to weigh competing constitutional interests in an area in which it enjoys particular expertise. It also provides Congress with sufficient room to anticipate and respond to concerns about circumvention of regulations designed to protect the integrity of the political process.

Our application of this less rigorous degree of scrutiny has given rise to significant criticism in the past from our dissenting colleagues. [citing dissenting opinions of Justices Kennedy and Thomas] ... [I]n its lengthy deliberations leading to the enactment of BCRA, Congress properly relied on the recognition of its authority contained in *Buckley* and its progeny. Considerations of *stare decisis,* buttressed by the respect that the Legislative and Judicial Branches owe to one another, provide additional powerful reasons for adhering to the analysis of contribution limits that the Court has consistently followed since *Buckley* ...

Like the contribution limits we upheld in *Buckley,* § 323's restrictions have only a marginal impact on the ability of contributors, candidates, officeholders, and parties to engage in effective political speech. ...

Plaintiffs contend that we must apply strict scrutiny to § 323 because many of its provisions restrict not only contributions but also the spending and solicitation of funds raised outside of FECA's contribution limits. But for purposes of determining the level of scrutiny, it is irrelevant that Congress chose in § 323 to regulate contributions on the demand rather than the supply side. ... The relevant inquiry is whether the mechanism adopted to implement the contribution limit, or to prevent circumvention of that limit, burdens speech in a way that a direct restriction on the contribution itself would not. That is not the case here.

For example, while § 323(a) prohibits national parties from receiving or spending nonfederal money, and § 323(b) prohibits state party committees from spending nonfederal money on federal election activities, neither provision in any way limits the total amount of money parties can spend. ... Rather, they simply limit the source and individual amount of donations. That they do so by prohibiting the spending of soft money does not render them expenditure limitations.

Similarly, the solicitation provisions of § 323(a) and § 323(e), which restrict the ability of national party committees, federal candidates, and federal officeholders to solicit nonfederal funds, leave open ample opportunities for soliciting federal funds on behalf of entities subject to FECA's source and amount restrictions. ...

Section 323 thus shows "due regard for the reality that solicitation is characteristically intertwined with informative and perhaps persuasive speech seeking support for particular causes or for particular views." ... The fact that party committees and federal candidates and officeholders must now ask only for limited dollar amounts or request that a corporation or union contribute money through its PAC in no way alters or impairs the political message "intertwined" with the solicitation. ... And rather than chill such solicitations, ... the restriction here tends to increase the dissemination of information by forcing parties, candidates, and officeholders to solicit from a wider array of potential donors. As with direct limits on contributions, therefore, § 323's spending and solicitation restrictions have only a marginal impact on political speech. . . .

Finally, plaintiffs contend that the type of associational burdens that § 323 imposes are fundamentally different from the burdens that accompanied *Buckley*'s contribution limits, and merit the type of strict scrutiny we have applied to attempts to regulate the internal processes of political parties. . . . In making this argument, plaintiffs greatly exaggerate the effect of § 323, contending that it precludes *any* collaboration among national, state, and local committees of the same party in fundraising and electioneering activities. We do not read the provisions in that way. Section 323 merely subjects a greater percentage of contributions to parties and candidates to FECA's source and amount limitations. . . . The modest impact that § 323 has on the ability of committees within a party to associate with each other does not independently occasion strict scrutiny. None of this is to suggest that the alleged associational burdens imposed on parties by § 323 have no place in the First Amendment analysis; it is only that we account for them in the application, rather than the choice, of the appropriate level of scrutiny.

With these principles in mind, we apply the less rigorous scrutiny applicable to contribution limits to evaluate the constitutionality of new FECA § 323. . . .

New FECA § 323(a)'s Restrictions on National Party Committees

The core of Title I is new FECA § 323(a), which provides that "national committee[s] of a political party . . . may not solicit, receive, or direct to another person a contribution, donation, or transfer of funds or any other thing of value, or spend any funds, that are not subject to the limitations, prohibitions, and reporting requirements of this Act." . . .

The main goal of § 323(a) is modest. In large part, it simply effects a return to the scheme that was approved in *Buckley* and that was subverted by the creation of the FEC's allocation regime, which permitted the political parties to fund federal electioneering efforts with a combination of hard and soft money. . . .

1. *Governmental Interests Underlying New FECA § 323(a)*

The Government defends § 323(a)'s ban on national parties' involvement with soft money as necessary to prevent the actual and apparent corruption of federal candidates and officeholders. . . . We have not limited that interest to the elimination of cash-for-votes exchanges. . . .

Of "almost equal" importance has been the Government's interest in combating the appearance or perception of corruption engendered by large campaign contributions. . . . And because the First Amendment does not require Congress to ignore the fact that "candidates, donors, and parties test the limits of the current law," . . . these interests have been sufficient to justify not only contribution limits themselves, but laws preventing the circumvention of such limits, ...

... The idea that large contributions to a national party can corrupt or, at the very least, create the appearance of corruption of federal candidates and officeholders is neither novel nor implausible. ... [C]ontributions to a federal candidate's party in aid of that candidate's campaign threaten to create—no less than would a direct contribution to the candidate—a sense of obligation. ... This is particularly true of contributions to national parties, with which federal candidates and officeholders enjoy a special relationship and unity of interest. ...

The question for present purposes is whether large *soft-money* contributions to national party committees have a corrupting influence or give rise to the appearance of corruption. Both common sense and the ample record in these cases confirm Congress' belief that they do. ... [C]orporate, union, and wealthy individual donors have been free to contribute substantial sums of soft money to the national parties, which the parties can spend for the specific purpose of influencing a particular candidate's federal election. It is not only plausible, but likely, that candidates would feel grateful for such donations and that donors would seek to exploit that gratitude.

... Thus, despite FECA's hard-money limits on direct contributions to candidates, federal officeholders have commonly asked donors to make soft-money donations ...

· · ·

Plaintiffs argue that without concrete evidence of an instance in which a federal officeholder has actually switched a vote (or, presumably, evidence of a specific instance where the public believes a vote was switched), Congress has not shown that there exists real or apparent corruption. But the record is to the contrary. The evidence connects soft money to manipulations of the legislative calendar, leading to Congress' failure to enact, among other things, generic drug legislation, tort reform, and tobacco legislation. ... To claim that such actions do not change legislative outcomes surely misunderstands the legislative process.

More importantly, plaintiffs conceive of corruption too narrowly. Our cases have firmly established that Congress' legitimate interest extends beyond preventing simple cash-for-votes corruption to curbing "undue influence on an officeholder's judgment, and the appearance of such influence." ...

The record in the present case is replete with ... examples of national party committees peddling access to federal candidates and officeholders in exchange for large soft-money donations. ...

Despite this evidence ..., Justice Kennedy would limit Congress' regulatory interest *only* to the prevention of the actual or apparent *quid pro quo* corruption "inherent in" contributions made directly to, contributions made at the express behest of, and expenditures made in coordination with, a federal officeholder or candidate. Regulation of any other donation or expenditure—regardless of its size, the recipient's relationship to the candidate or officeholder, its potential impact on a candidate's election, its value to the candidate, or its unabashed and explicit intent to purchase influence—would, according to Justice Kennedy, simply be out of bounds. This crabbed view of corruption, and particularly of the appearance of corruption, ignores precedent, common sense, and the realities of political fundraising exposed by the record in this litigation.

Justice Kennedy's interpretation of the First Amendment would render Congress powerless to address more subtle but equally dispiriting forms of corruption. Just as troubling to a functioning democracy as classic *quid pro quo* corruption is the danger that officeholders will decide issues not on the merits or the desires of their constituencies, but according to the wishes of those who have made large financial contributions valued by the officeholder. . . .

Justice Kennedy likewise takes too narrow a view of the appearance of corruption. . . . In our view, however, Congress is not required to ignore historical evidence regarding a particular practice or to view conduct in isolation from its context. To be sure, mere political favoritism or opportunity for influence alone is insufficient to justify regulation. As the record demonstrates, it is the manner in which parties have *sold* access to federal candidates and officeholders that has given rise to the appearance of undue influence. Implicit (and, as the record shows, sometimes explicit) in the sale of access is the suggestion that money buys influence. It is no surprise then that purchasers of such access unabashedly admit that they are seeking to purchase just such influence. It was not unwarranted for Congress to conclude that the selling of access gives rise to the appearance of corruption.

· · ·

2. *New FECA § 323(a)'s Restriction on Spending and Receiving Soft Money*

Plaintiffs and the Chief Justice contend that § 323(a) is impermissibly overbroad because it subjects *all* funds raised and spent by national parties to FECA's hard-money source and amount limits, including, for example, funds spent on purely state and local elections in which no federal office is at stake. . . . As the record demonstrates, it is the close relationship between federal officeholders and the national parties, as well as the means by which parties have traded on that relationship, that have made all large soft-money contributions to national parties suspect.

· · ·

. . . [N]ational parties [are] in a position to sell access to federal officeholders in exchange for soft-money contributions that the party can then use for its own purposes. Access to federal officeholders is the most valuable favor the national party committees are able to give in exchange for large donations. . . . [L]arge soft-money donations to national party committees are likely to buy donors preferential access to federal officeholders no matter the ends to which their contributions are eventually put. . . .

3. *New FECA § 323(a)'s Restriction on Soliciting or Directing Soft Money*

Plaintiffs also contend that § 323(a)'s prohibition on national parties' soliciting or directing soft-money contributions is substantially overbroad. The reach of the solicitation prohibition, however, is limited. It bars only solicitations of soft money by national party committees and by party officers in their official capacities. The committees remain free to solicit hard money on their own behalf, as well as to solicit hard money on behalf of state committees and state and local candidates. ...

This limited restriction on solicitation follows sensibly from the prohibition on national committees' receiving soft money. ...

4. *New FECA § 323(a)'s Application to Minor Parties*

The McConnell and political party plaintiffs contend that § 323(a) is substantially overbroad and must be stricken on its face because it impermissibly infringes the speech and associational rights of minor parties ... which, owing to their slim prospects for electoral success and the fact that they receive few large soft-money contributions from corporate sources, pose no threat of corruption comparable to that posed by the RNC and DNC. In *Buckley,* we rejected a similar argument ... [T]he relevance of the interest in avoiding actual or apparent corruption is not a function of the number of legislators a given party manages to elect. It applies as much to a minor party that manages to elect only one of its members to federal office as it does to a major party whose members make up a majority of Congress. It is therefore reasonable to require that all parties and all candidates follow the same set of rules designed to protect the integrity of the electoral process.

We add that ... [o]nly when an organization has gained official status, which carries with it significant benefits for its members, will the proscriptions of § 323(a) apply. Even then, a nascent or struggling minor party can bring an as-applied challenge if § 323(a) prevents it from "amassing the resources necessary for effective advocacy."

. . .

New FECA § 323(b)'s Restrictions on State and Local Party Committees

In constructing a coherent scheme of campaign finance regulation, Congress recognized that, given the close ties between federal candidates and state party committees, BCRA's restrictions on national committee activity would rapidly become ineffective if state and local committees remained available as a conduit for soft-money donations. Section 323(b) ... prevents donors from contributing nonfederal funds to state and local party committees to help finance "Federal election activity." ... The term "Federal election activity" encompasses four distinct categories of electioneering: (1) voter registration activity during the 120 days preceding a regularly scheduled federal election; (2) voter identification, get-out-the-vote (GOTV), and generic campaign activity that is "conducted in connection with an election in which a candidate for Federal office appears on the ballot"; (3) any "public communication" that "refers to a

clearly identified candidate for Federal office" and "promotes," "supports," "attacks," or "opposes" a candidate for that office; and (4) the
services provided by a state committee employee who dedicates more
than 25% of his or her time to "activities in connection with a Federal
election." ... All activities that fall within the statutory definition must
be funded with hard money. ...

Section 323(b)(2), the so-called Levin Amendment, carves out an
exception to this general rule ... [that] allows state and local party
committees to pay for certain types of federal election activity with an
allocated ratio of hard money and "Levin funds"—that is, funds raised
within an annual limit of $10,000 per person. ...

The scope of the Levin Amendment is limited in two ways. First,
state and local parties can use Levin money to fund only activities that
fall within categories (1) and (2) of the statute's definition of federal
election activity—namely, voter registration activity, voter identification
drives, GOTV drives, and generic campaign activities. ... And not all of
these activities qualify: Levin funds cannot be used to pay for any
activities that refer to "a clearly identified candidate for Federal office";
they likewise cannot be used to fund broadcast communications unless
they refer "solely to a clearly identified candidate for State or local
office." ...

Second, both the Levin funds and the allocated portion of hard
money used to pay for such activities must be raised entirely by the state
or local committee that spends them. § 441i(b)(2)(B)(iv). This means
that a state party committee cannot use Levin funds transferred from
other party committees to cover the Levin funds portion of a Levin
Amendment expenditure. It also means that a state party committee
cannot use hard money transferred from other party committees to cover
the hard-money portion of a Levin Amendment expenditure. Furthermore, national committees, federal candidates, and federal officeholders
generally may not solicit Levin funds on behalf of state committees, and
state committees may not team up to raise Levin funds. ... They can,
however, jointly raise the hard money used to make Levin expenditures.

1. *Governmental Interests Underlying New FECA § 323(b)*

. . .

... Having been taught the hard lesson of circumvention by the
entire history of campaign finance regulation, Congress knew that soft-
money donors would react to § 323(a) by scrambling to find another way
to purchase influence. ...

2. *New FECA § 323(b)'s Tailoring*

Plaintiffs argue that even if some legitimate interest might be
served by § 323(b), the ... provision is substantially overbroad because
it federalizes activities that pose no conceivable risk of corrupting or
appearing to corrupt federal officeholders. Second, they argue that the
Levin Amendment imposes an unconstitutional burden on the associational rights of political parties. Finally, they argue that the provision

prevents them from amassing the resources they need to engage in effective advocacy. We address these points in turn.

a. *§ 323(b)'s Application to Federal Election Activity*

Plaintiffs assert that § 323(b) ... goes well beyond Congress' concerns about the corruption of the federal electoral process. We disagree.

It is true that § 323(b) captures some activities that affect state campaigns for nonfederal offices. But these are the same sorts of activities that already were covered by the FEC's pre-BCRA allocation rules, and thus had to be funded in part by hard money, because they affect federal as well as state elections. ...

Like the rest of Title I, § 323(b) is premised on Congress' judgment that if a large donation is capable of putting a federal candidate in the debt of the contributor, it poses a threat of corruption or the appearance of corruption. ... § 323(b) is narrowly focused on regulating ... contributions to state and local parties that can be used to benefit federal candidates directly. Further, these regulations all are reasonably tailored, with various temporal and substantive limitations designed to focus the regulations on the important anti-corruption interests to be served. We conclude that § 323(b) is a closely-drawn means of countering both corruption and the appearance of corruption.

The first two categories of "Federal election activity," voter registration efforts ... and generic campaign activities conducted in connection with a federal election, ... clearly capture activity that benefits federal candidates. Common sense dictates ... that a party's efforts to register voters sympathetic to that party directly assist the party's candidates for federal office. ... It is equally clear that federal candidates reap substantial rewards from any efforts that increase the number of like-minded registered voters who actually go to the polls. ...

. . .

Because voter registration, voter identification, GOTV, and generic campaign activity all confer substantial benefits on federal candidates, the funding of such activities creates a significant risk of actual and apparent corruption. ... The prohibition on the use of soft money in connection with these activities is therefore closely drawn to meet the sufficiently important governmental interests of avoiding corruption and its appearance.

. . .

IV

. . .

BCRA § 201's Definition of "Electioneering Communication"

... § 201, comprehensively amends FECA § 304, which requires political committees to file detailed periodic financial reports with the FEC. The amendment coins a new term, "electioneering communication," to replace the narrowing construction ... in *Buckley*, ... [which] limited the coverage of FECA's disclosure requirement to communications expressly advocating the election or defeat of particular candidates. By contrast, the term "electioneering communication" is not so limited, but is defined to encompass any "broadcast, cable, or satellite communication" that

"(I) refers to a clearly identified candidate for Federal office;

"(II) is made within—

"(aa) 60 days before a general, special, or runoff election for the office sought by the candidate; or

"(bb) 30 days before a primary or preference election, or a convention or caucus of a political party that has authority to nominate a candidate, for the office sought by the candidate; and

"(III) in the case of a communication which refers to a candidate other than President or Vice President, is targeted to the relevant electorate." ...

New FECA § 304(f)(3)(C) further provides that a communication is "targeted to the relevant electorate" if it "can be received by 50,000 or more persons" in the district or State the candidate seeks to represent. ...

... BCRA's use of this new term is not limited to the disclosure context. A later section ... restricts corporations' and labor unions' funding of electioneering communications. Plaintiffs challenge the constitutionality of the new term as it applies in both the disclosure and the expenditure contexts.

The major premise of plaintiffs' challenge to BCRA's use of the term "electioneering communication" is that *Buckley* drew a constitutionally mandated line between express advocacy and so-called issue advocacy, and that speakers possess an inviolable First Amendment right to engage in the latter category of speech. Thus, plaintiffs maintain, Congress cannot constitutionally require disclosure of, or regulate expenditures for, "electioneering communications" without making an exception for those "communications" that do not meet *Buckley*'s definition of express advocacy.

... [T]he express advocacy restriction was an endpoint of statutory interpretation, not a first principle of constitutional law. ...

· · ·

... In narrowly reading the FECA provisions in *Buckley* to avoid problems of vagueness and overbreadth, we nowhere suggested that a statute that was neither vague nor overbroad would be required to toe the same express advocacy line. ...

... *Buckley* ... in no way drew a constitutional boundary that forever fixed the permissible scope of provisions regulating campaign-related speech.

Nor are we persuaded, independent of our precedents, that the First Amendment erects a rigid barrier between express advocacy and so-called issue advocacy. That notion cannot be squared with our longstanding recognition that the presence or absence of magic words cannot meaningfully distinguish electioneering speech from a true issue ad. ... *Buckley's* express advocacy line, in short, has not aided the legislative effort to combat real or apparent corruption, and Congress enacted BCRA to correct the flaws it found in the existing system.

Finally we observe that new FECA § 304(f)(3)'s definition of "electioneering communication" raises none of the vagueness concerns that drove our analysis in *Buckley*. ...

BCRA § 201's Disclosure Requirements

... [W]henever any person makes disbursements totaling more than $10,000 during any calendar year for the direct costs of producing and airing electioneering communications, he must file a statement with the FEC identifying the pertinent elections and all persons sharing the costs of the disbursements. ... If the disbursements are made from a corporation's or labor union's segregated account, or by a single individual who has collected contributions from others, the statement must identify all persons who contributed $1,000 or more to the account or the individual during the calendar year. ... The statement must be filed within 24 hours of each "disclosure date"—a term defined to include the first date and all subsequent dates on which a person's aggregate undisclosed expenses for electioneering communications exceed $10,000 for that calendar year. ...

... [P]laintiffs challenge [these] disclosure requirements as unnecessarily ... requiring disclosure of the names of persons who contributed $1,000 or more to the individual or group that paid for a communication ...

... [T]he important state interests that prompted the *Buckley* Court to uphold FECA's disclosure requirements—providing the electorate with information, deterring actual corruption and avoiding any appearance thereof, and gathering the data necessary to enforce more substantive electioneering restrictions—apply in full ...

... *Buckley* forecloses a facial attack on the new provision in § 304 that requires disclosure of the names of persons contributing $1,000 or more to segregated funds or individuals that spend more than $10,000 in a calendar year on electioneering communications. ... *Buckley* rejected the contention that FECA's disclosure requirements could not constitutionally be applied to minor parties and independent candidates because the Government's interest in obtaining information from such parties was minimal and the danger of infringing their rights substantial. In *Buckley*, ... we found no evidence that any party had been exposed to economic reprisals or physical threats as a result of the compelled disclosures. ... We acknowledged that such a case might arise in the future, however, and addressed the standard of proof that would then apply ...

A few years later we used that standard to resolve a minor party's challenge to the constitutionality of the State of Ohio's disclosure requirements. We held that the First Amendment prohibits States from compelling disclosures that would subject identified persons to "threats, harassment, and reprisals," and that the District Court's findings had established a "reasonable probability" of such a result. Brown v. Socialist Workers '74 Campaign Comm. (Ohio), 459 U.S. 87, 100 (1982).

. . .

BCRA § 202's Treatment of "Coordinated Communications" as Contributions

Section 202 of BCRA ... provide[s] that disbursements for "electioneering communication[s]" that are coordinated with a candidate or party will be treated as contributions to, and expenditures by, that candidate or party. ... The amendment clarifies the scope of the preceding subsection, ... which states more generally that "expenditures made by any person in cooperation, consultation, or concert, with, or at the request or suggestion of" a candidate or party will constitute contributions. ... In *Buckley* we construed the statutory term "expenditure" to reach only spending for express advocacy. ... BCRA § 202 preempts a possible claim that ... coordinated expenditures for communications that avoid express advocacy cannot be counted as contributions. As we explained above, *Buckley*'s narrow interpretation of the term "expenditure" was not a constitutional limitation on Congress' power to regulate federal elections. Accordingly, there is no reason why Congress may not treat coordinated disbursements for electioneering communications in the same way it treats all other coordinated expenditures. ...

BCRA § 203's Prohibition of Corporate and Labor Disbursements for Electioneering Communications

Since our decision in *Buckley,* Congress' power to prohibit corporations and unions from using funds in their treasuries to finance advertisements expressly advocating the election or defeat of candidates in federal elections has been firmly embedded in our law. The ability to form and administer separate segregated funds authorized by FECA § 316 ... has provided corporations and unions with a constitutionally sufficient opportunity to engage in express advocacy. That has been this Court's unanimous view, and it is not challenged in this litigation.

Section 203 of BCRA ... extend[s] this rule, which previously applied only to express advocacy, to all "electioneering communications" ... Because corporations can still fund electioneering communications with PAC money, it is "simply wrong" to view the provision as a "complete ban" on expression rather than a regulation. ...

. . .

In light of our precedents, plaintiffs do not contest that the Government has a compelling interest in regulating advertisements that expressly advocate the election or defeat of a candidate for federal office. Nor do they contend that the speech involved in so-called issue advocacy is any more core political speech than are words of express advocacy. ... Rather, plaintiffs argue that the justifications that adequately support the regulation of express advocacy do not apply to significant quantities of speech encompassed by the definition of electioneering communications.

... The precise percentage of issue ads that clearly identified a candidate and were aired during those relatively brief preelection time spans but had no electioneering purpose is a matter of dispute between the parties ... Nevertheless, the vast majority of ads clearly had such a purpose. ... Moreover, whatever the precise percentage may have been in the past, in the future corporations and unions may finance genuine issue ads during those time frames by simply avoiding any specific reference to federal candidates, or in doubtful cases by paying for the ad from a segregated fund.

... Even if we assumed that BCRA will inhibit some constitutionally protected corporate and union speech, that assumption would not "justify prohibiting all enforcement" of the law unless its application to protected speech is substantial, "not only in an absolute sense, but also relative to the scope of the law's plainly legitimate applications." ...

Plaintiffs also argue that FECA § 316(b)(2)'s segregated-fund requirement for electioneering communications is underinclusive because it does not apply to advertising in the print media or on the Internet. ... As we held in *Buckley,* "reform may take one step at a time, addressing itself to the phase of the problem which seems most acute to the legislative mind." ... One might just as well argue that the electioneering communication definition is underinclusive because it leaves advertising 61 days in advance of an election entirely unregulated. The record amply justifies Congress' line drawing.

In addition to arguing that § 316(b)(2)'s segregated-fund requirement is underinclusive, some plaintiffs contend that it unconstitutionally discriminates in favor of media companies [by excluding] from the definition of electioneering communications any "communication appearing in a news story, commentary, or editorial distributed through the facilities of any broadcasting station, unless such facilities are owned or controlled by any political party, political committee, or candidate." ... Plaintiffs argue this provision gives free rein to media companies to engage in speech without resort to PAC money. [The] effect, however, is much narrower than plaintiffs suggest. The provision excepts news items and commentary only; it does not afford *carte blanche* to media companies generally to ignore FECA's provisions. The statute's narrow exception is wholly consistent with First Amendment principles. "A valid distinction ... exists between corporations that are part of the media industry and other corporations that are not involved in the regular business of imparting news to the public." ...

. . .

V

Many years ago we observed that "[t]o say that Congress is without power to pass appropriate legislation to safeguard ... an election from the improper use of money to influence the result is to deny to the nation in a vital particular the power of self protection." ... We abide by that conviction in considering Congress' most recent effort to confine the ill effects of aggregated wealth on our political system. We are under no illusion that BCRA will be the last congressional statement on the matter. Money, like water, will always find an outlet. What problems will arise, and how Congress will respond, are concerns for another day. In the main we uphold BCRA's two principal, complementary features: the control of soft money and the regulation of electioneering communications. . . .

CHIEF JUSTICE REHNQUIST delivered the opinion of the Court with respect to BCRA Titles III and IV.*

This opinion addresses issues involving miscellaneous Title III and IV provisions . . .

BCRA § 305

BCRA § 305 amends the federal Communications Act of 1934, . . . which requires that, 45 days before a primary or 60 days before a general election, broadcast stations must sell a qualified candidate the "lowest unit charge of the station for the same class and amount of time for the same period," . . . Section 305's amendment, in turn, denies a candidate the benefit of that lowest unit charge unless the candidate "provides written certification to the broadcast station that the candidate (and any authorized committee of the candidate) shall not make any direct reference to another candidate for the same office," or the candidate, in the manner prescribed in BCRA § 305(a)(3), clearly identifies herself at the end of the broadcast and states that she approves of the broadcast. . . .

The McConnell plaintiffs challenge § 305. They argue that Senator McConnell's testimony that he plans to run advertisements critical of his opponents in the future and that he had run them in the past is sufficient to establish standing. We think not.

. . .

. . . § 305 amended the Communication Act's requirements with respect to the lowest unit charge for broadcasting time. But this price is not available to qualified candidates until 45 days before a primary election or 60 days before a general election. Because Senator McConnell's current term does not expire until 2009, the earliest day he could be affected by § 305 is 45 days before the Republican primary election in 2008. This alleged injury in fact is too remote temporally to satisfy Article III standing. . . .

[The opinion concluded that plaintiffs similarly lacked standing to challenge a number of provisions in Titles III and IV.]

BCRA § 318

BCRA § 318 . . . prohibits individuals "17 years old or younger" from making contributions to candidates and contributions or donations to political parties. . . . The McConnell and Echols plaintiffs . . . argue that § 318 violates the First Amendment rights of minors. We agree.

---

* Justice O'Connor, Justice Scalia, Justice Kennedy, and Justice Souter join this opinion in its entirety. Justice Stevens, Justice Ginsburg, and Justice Breyer join this opinion, except with respect to BCRA § 305. Justice Thomas joins this opinion with respect to BCRA §§ 304, 305, 307, 316, 319, and 403(b). [Justice Stevens wrote a dissenting opinion with respect to BCRA § 305 in which Justices Ginsburg and Breyer joined. That opinion is omitted.]

Minors enjoy the protection of the First Amendment. ... Limitations on the amount that an individual may contribute to a candidate or political committee impinge on the protected freedoms of expression and association. ... The Government asserts that the provision protects against corruption by conduit; that is, donations by parents through their minor children to circumvent contribution limits applicable to the parents. But the Government offers scant evidence of this form of evasion. ... Absent a more convincing case of the claimed evil, this interest is simply too attenuated for § 318 to withstand heightened scrutiny. ...

Even assuming, *arguendo,* the Government advances an important interest, the provision is overinclusive. The States have adopted a variety of more tailored approaches—*e.g.,* counting contributions by minors against the total permitted for a parent or family unit, imposing a lower cap on contributions by minors, and prohibiting contributions by very young children. Without deciding whether any of these alternatives is sufficiently tailored, we hold that the provision here sweeps too broadly. ...

. . .

Justice Breyer delivered the opinion of the Court with respect to BCRA Title V.*

We consider here the constitutionality of § 504 of [BICRA, which] requires broadcasters to keep publicly available records of politically related broadcasting requests. ... The McConnell plaintiffs, who include the National Association of Broadcasters, argue that § 504 imposes onerous administrative burdens, lacks any offsetting justification, and consequently violates the First Amendment. ... We disagree ...

I

BCRA § 504's key requirements are the following:

(1) A "candidate request" requirement calls for broadcasters to keep records of broadcast requests "made by or on behalf of" any "legally qualified candidate for public office." ...

(2) An "election message request" requirement calls for broadcasters to keep records of requests (made by anyone) to broadcast "message[s]" that refer either to a "legally qualified candidate" or to "any election to Federal office." ...

(3) An "issue request" requirement calls for broadcasters to keep records of requests (made by anyone) to broadcast "message[s]" related to a "national legislative issue of public importance," ... or otherwise relating to a "political matter of national importance," ...

---

* Justice Stevens, Justice O'Connor, Justice Souter, and Justice Ginsburg join this opinion in its entirety. [Chief Justice Rehnquist wrote a dissenting opinion with respect to BCRA Titles I and V in which Justices Scalia and Kennedy joined. That opinion is omitted.]

II

BCRA § 504's "candidate request" requirements are virtually identical to those contained in a regulation that the Federal Communications Commission (FCC) promulgated as early as 1938 ...

. . .

... Because we cannot, on the present record, find the longstanding FCC regulation unconstitutional, we likewise cannot strike down the "candidate request" provision in BCRA § 504; for the latter simply embodies the regulation in a statute, thereby blocking any agency attempt to repeal it.

III

BCRA § 504's "election message request" requirements call for broadcasters to keep records of requests (made by any member of the public) to broadcast a "message" about "a legally qualified candidate" or "any election to Federal office." ...

Given the nature of many of the messages, recordkeeping can help both the regulatory agencies and the public evaluate broadcasting fairness, and determine the amount of money that individuals or groups, supporters or opponents, intend to spend to help elect a particular candidate. ...

. . .

... If, as we have held, the "candidate request" requirements are constitutional, the "election message" requirements, which serve similar governmental interests and impose only a small incremental burden, must be constitutional as well.

IV

The "issue request" requirements call for broadcasters to keep records of requests (made by any member of the public) to broadcast "message [s]" about "a national legislative issue of public importance" or "any political matter of national importance." ... These recordkeeping requirements seem likely to help the FCC determine whether broadcasters are carrying out their "obligations to afford reasonable opportunity for the discussion of conflicting views on issues of public importance," ... and whether broadcasters are too heavily favoring entertainment, and discriminating against broadcasts devoted to public affairs ...

. . .

The regulatory burden, in practice, will depend on how the FCC interprets and applies this provision. The FCC has adequate legal authority to write regulations that may limit, and make more specific, the provision's potential linguistic reach. ... The parties remain free to challenge the provisions, as interpreted by the FCC in regulations, or as otherwise applied. Any such challenge will likely provide greater information about the provisions' justifications and administrative burdens. Without that additional information, we cannot now say that the burdens are so great, or the justifications so minimal, as to warrant finding the provisions unconstitutional on their face.

The McConnell plaintiffs and the Chief Justice make one final claim. They say that the "issue request" requirement will force them to disclose information that will reveal their political strategies to opponents, perhaps prior to a broadcast. We are willing to assume that the Constitution includes some form of protection against premature disclosure of campaign strategy—though, given the First Amendment interest in free and open discussion of campaign issues, we make this assumption purely for argument's sake. Nonetheless, even on that assumption we do not see how BCRA § 504 can be unconstitutional on its face.

. . .

JUSTICE KENNEDY, concurring in the judgment in part and dissenting in part with respect to BCRA Titles I and II.*

The First Amendment guarantees our citizens the right to judge for themselves the most effective means for the expression of political views and to decide for themselves which entities to trust as reliable speakers. Significant portions of Titles I and II . . . constrain that freedom. . . .

Today's decision upholding these laws purports simply to follow Buckley v. Valeo, . . . but the majority, to make its decision work, must abridge free speech where *Buckley* did not. . . . In so doing, it replaces discrete and respected First Amendment principles with new, amorphous, and unsound rules, rules which dismantle basic protections for speech.

. . . BCRA would have imposed felony punishment on Ross Perot's 1996 efforts to build the Reform Party. . . . BCRA makes it a felony for an environmental group to broadcast an ad, within 60 days of an election, exhorting the public to protest a Congressman's impending vote to permit logging in national forests. . . .

To the majority, all this is . . . part of Congress' "steady improvement of the national election laws." We should make no mistake. . . . It is an effort by Congress to ensure that civic discourse takes place only through the modes of its choosing. And BCRA is only the beginning . . .

. . . Government cannot be trusted to moderate its own rules for suppression of speech. The dangers posed by speech regulations have led the Court to insist upon principled constitutional lines and a rigorous standard of review. The majority now abandons these distinctions and limitations.

With respect, I dissent from the majority opinion upholding BCRA Titles I and II. . . .

I. TITLE I AND COORDINATION PROVISIONS

. . . Even a cursory review of the speech and association burdens these laws create makes their First Amendment infirmities obvious:

---

* The Chief Justice joins this opinion in its entirety. Justice Scalia joins this opinion except to the extent it upholds new FECA § 323(e) and BCRA § 202. Justice Thomas joins this opinion with respect to BCRA § 213.

Title I bars individuals with shared beliefs from pooling their money above limits set by Congress to form a new third party ... Title I bars national party officials from soliciting or directing soft money to state parties for use on a state ballot initiative. ... Title I compels speech. Party officials who want to engage in activity such as fundraising must now speak magic words to ensure the solicitation cannot be interpreted as anything other than a solicitation for hard, not soft, money. ... Title I prohibits the national parties from giving any sort of funds to nonprofit entities, even federally regulated hard money ... By express terms, Title I imposes multiple different forms of spending caps on parties, candidates, and their agents. ...

Until today ... the Court has accepted but two principles to use in determining the validity of campaign finance restrictions. First is the anticorruption rationale. ... Second, the Court ... has said that the willing adoption of the entity form by corporations and unions justifies regulating them differently. ...

... Most of the regulations at issue, notably all of the Title I soft money bans and the Title II coordination provisions, do not draw distinctions based on corporate or union status. ... [T]he focus must be on *Buckley*'s anticorruption rationale and the First Amendment rights of individual citizens.

A. Constitutionally Sufficient Interest

In *Buckley,* the Court held that one, and only one, interest justified the significant burden on the right of association involved there: eliminating, or preventing, actual corruption or the appearance of corruption stemming from contributions to candidates. ...

. . .

Thus, though *Buckley* subjected expenditure limits to strict scrutiny and contribution limits to less exacting review, it held neither could withstand constitutional challenge unless it was shown to advance the anticorruption interest. ... If the interest is not advanced, the regulations cannot comport with the Constitution, quite apart from the standard of review.

Buckley made clear, by its express language and its context, that the corruption interest only justifies regulating candidates' and officeholders' receipt of what we can call the *"quids"* in the *quid pro quo* formulation. ...

. . .

[T]he perception of corruption that the majority now asserts is somehow different from the *quid pro quo* potential ... created by ... contributions directly to a candidate.

. . .

The Court ... interprets the anticorruption rationale to allow regulation not just of "actual or apparent *quid pro quo* arrangements," but of any conduct that wins goodwill from or influences a Member of Congress. . . .

. . .

Access in itself, however, shows only that in a general sense an officeholder favors someone or that someone has influence on the officeholder. . . .

The generic favoritism or influence theory articulated by the Court is at odds with standard First Amendment analyses because it is unbounded and susceptible to no limiting principle. Any given action might be favored by any given person, so by the Court's reasoning political loyalty of the purest sort can be prohibited. There is no remaining principled method for inquiring whether a campaign finance regulation does in fact regulate corruption in a serious and meaningful way. We are left to defer to a congressional conclusion that certain conduct creates favoritism or influence.

. . .

The majority attempts to mask its extension of *Buckley* under claims that BCRA prevents the appearance of corruption, even if it does not prevent actual corruption . . . [T]he inquiry does not turn on whether some persons assert that an appearance of corruption exists. . . . Instead, the Court asked whether the Government had proved that the regulated conduct, the expenditures, posed inherent *quid pro quo* corruption potential. . . .

. . .

1.   New FECA §§ 323(a), (b), (d), and (f)

Sections 323(a), (b), (d), and (f) . . . cannot stand because they do not add regulation to conduct that poses a demonstrable *quid pro quo* danger. They do not further *Buckley*'s corruption interest.

On its face § 323(a) does not regulate federal candidates' or officeholders' receipt of *quids* because it does not regulate contributions to, or conduct by, candidates or officeholders. . . .

. . .

. . . The record confirms that soft money party contributions, without more, do not create *quid pro quo* corruption potential. As a conceptual matter, generic party contributions may engender good will from a candidate or officeholder . . . Still, no Member of Congress testified this favoritism changed voting behavior.

. . .

None of [the] other sections has an independent justifying interest. Section 323(b), for example, adds regulation only to activity undertaken by a state party. In the District Court two of the three judges found as fact that particular state and local parties exist primarily to participate in state and local elections, that they spend the majority of their resources on those elections, and that their voter registration and Get

Out The Vote (GOTV) activities, in particular, are directed primarily at state and local elections. . . .

. . .

When one recognizes that §§ 323(a), (b), (d), and (f) do not serve the interest the anticorruption rationale contemplates, Title I's entirety begins to look very much like an incumbency protection plan. . . . That impression is worsened by the fact that Congress exempted its office-holders from the more stringent prohibitions imposed on party officials. Compare new FECA § 323(a) with new FECA § 323(e). Section 323(a) raises an inflexible bar against soft money solicitation, in any way, by parties or party officials. Section 323(e), in contrast, enacts exceptions to the rule for federal officeholders (the very centerpiece of possible corruption), and allows them to solicit soft money for various uses and organizations.

. . .

2. New FECA § 323(e)

Ultimately, only one of the challenged Title I provisions satisfies *Buckley*'s anticorruption rationale and the First Amendment's guarantee. It is § 323(e). This provision is the sole aspect of Title I that is a direct and necessary regulation of federal candidates' and officeholders' receipt of *quids*. Section 323(e) . . . and the regulations that follow, limit candidates' and their agents' solicitation of soft money. The regulation of a candidate's receipt of funds furthers a constitutionally sufficient interest. More difficult, however, is the question whether regulation of a candidate's solicitation of funds also furthers this interest if the funds are given to another.

I agree with the Court that the broader solicitation regulation does further a sufficient interest. The making of a solicited gift is a *quid* both to the recipient of the money and to the one who solicits the payment (by granting his request). Rules governing candidates' or officeholders' solicitation of contributions are, therefore, regulations governing their receipt of *quids*. This regulation fits under *Buckley*'s anticorruption rationale.

. . .

B. Standard of Review

. . . In *Buckley*, we applied "closely drawn" scrutiny to contribution limitations and strict scrutiny to expenditure limitations. . . . [T]he majority assumes that because *Buckley* applied the rationale in the context of contribution and expenditure limits, its application gives Congress and the Court the capacity to classify any challenged campaign finance regulation as either a contribution or an expenditure limit. . . .

Title I's provisions prohibit the receipt of funds; and in most instances, but not all, this can be defined as a contribution limit. . . . They prohibit the giving of funds to nonprofit groups; and this falls within neither definition as we have ever defined it. Finally, they prohibit fundraising activity; and the parties dispute the classification of this regulation (the challengers say it is core political association, while the Government says it ultimately results only in a limit on contribution receipts).

. . .

Even if the laws could be classified in broad terms as only contribution limits, ... that still leaves the question what "contribution limits" can include if they are to be upheld under *Buckley*. *Buckley*'s application of a less exacting review to contribution limits must be confined to the narrow category of money gifts that are directed, in some manner, to a candidate or officeholder. Any broader definition of the category contradicts *Buckley*'s *quid pro quo* rationale ...

The Court, it must be acknowledged, both in *Buckley* and on other occasions, has described contribution limits due some more deferential review in less than precise terms. At times it implied that donations to political parties would also qualify as contributions whose limitation too would be subject to less exacting review. ...

Buckley's underlying rationale is this: Less exacting review applies to Government regulations that "significantly interfere" with First Amendment rights of association. But any regulation of speech or associational rights creating "markedly greater interference" than such significant interference receives strict scrutiny. Unworkable and ill advised though it may be, *Buckley* unavoidably sets forth this test: Even a "significant interference" with protected rights of political association' may be sustained if the State demonstrates [1] a sufficiently important interest and [2] employs means closely drawn to avoid unnecessary abridgment of associational freedoms. ...

. . .

The majority makes *Buckley*'s already awkward and imprecise test all but meaningless in its application. ...

. . .

Congress has undertaken this comprehensive reordering of association and speech rights in the name of enforcing contribution limitations. Here, however, as in *Buckley*, "[t]he markedly greater burden on basic freedoms caused by [BCRA's pervasive regulation] cannot be sustained simply by invoking the interest in maximizing the effectiveness of the less intrusive contribution limitations." ... BCRA fundamentally alters, and thereby burdens, protected speech and association throughout our society. Strict scrutiny ought apply to review of its constitutionality. (Under strict scrutiny, the congressional scheme, for the most part, cannot survive.) ...

. . .

Compared to the narrowly tailored effort of § 323(e), which addresses in direct and specific terms federal candidates' and officeholders' quest for dollars, these sections cast a wide net not confined to the critical categories of federal candidate or officeholder involvement. They are not narrowly tailored; they are not closely drawn; they flatly violate the First Amendment; and even if they do encompass some speech that poses a regulable *quid pro quo* danger, that little assurance does not justify or permit a regime which silences so many legitimate voices in this protected sphere.

. . .

The final aspect of BCRA that implicates *Buckley*'s anticorruption rationale is § 213, the forced choice provision. The majority concludes § 213 violates the Constitution. I agree and write on this aspect of the case to point out that the section's unlawfulness flows . . . from its raw suppression of constitutionally protected speech.

Section 213 unconstitutionally forces the parties to surrender one of two First Amendment rights. I continue to believe . . . that even under *Buckley* a political party has a protected right to make coordinated expenditures with its candidates. . . . Our well-established constitutional tradition respects the role parties play in the electoral process and in stabilizing our representative democracy. . . . Section 213's command that the parties abandon one First Amendment right or the other offends the Constitution.

II. TITLE II PROVISIONS

A. Disclosure Provisions

. . . I agree with the Court's judgment upholding the disclosure provisions contained in § 201 of Title II, with one exception.

Section 201's advance disclosure requirement—the aspect of the provision requiring those who have contracted to speak to disclose their speech in advance—is, in my view, unconstitutional. Advance disclosure imposes real burdens on political speech that *post hoc* disclosure does not. It forces disclosure of political strategy by revealing where ads are to be run and what their content is likely to be (based on who is running the ad). It also provides an opportunity for the ad buyer's opponents to dissuade broadcasters from running ads. . . . Against those tangible additional burdens, the Government identifies no additional interest uniquely served by advance disclosure. If Congress intended to ensure that advertisers could not flout these disclosure laws by running an ad before the election, but paying for it afterwards, then Congress should simply have required the disclosure upon the running of the ad. Burdening the First Amendment further by requiring advance disclosure is not a constitutionally acceptable alternative. To the extent § 201 requires advance disclosure, it finds no justification in its subordinating interests and imposes greater burdens than the First Amendment permits.

. . .

B. BCRA § 203

The majority permits a new and serious intrusion on speech when it upholds § 203, the key provision in Title II that prohibits corporations and labor unions from using money from their general treasury to fund electioneering communications. The majority compounds the error made in Austin v. Michigan Chamber of Commerce, 494 U.S. 652 (1990) . . .

Instead of extending *Austin* to suppress new and vibrant voices, I would overrule it and return our campaign finance jurisprudence to principles consistent with the First Amendment.

1.

The Government and the majority are right about one thing: The express-advocacy requirement, with its list of magic words, is easy to circumvent. . . . What the Court and the Government call sham, however, are the ads speakers find most effective. Unlike express ads that leave nothing to the imagination, the record shows that issues ads are preferred by almost all candidates, even though politicians, unlike corporations, can lawfully broadcast express ads if they so choose. It is a measure of the Government's disdain for protected speech that it would label as a sham the mode of communication sophisticated speakers choose because it is the most powerful.

The Government's use of the pejorative label should not obscure § 203's practical effect: It prohibits a mass communication technique favored in the modern political process for the very reason that it is the most potent. That the Government would regulate it for this reason goes only to prove the illegitimacy of the Government's purpose. . . . The problem is that the majority uses *Austin,* a decision itself unfaithful to our First Amendment precedents, to justify banning a far greater range of speech. This has it all backwards. If protected speech is being suppressed, that must be the end of the inquiry.

· · ·

Austin was the first and, until now, the only time our Court had allowed the Government to exercise the power to censor political speech based on the speaker's corporate identity. The majority's contrary contention is simply incorrect. . . . The distinction . . . between independent expenditures for commenting on issues, on the one hand, and supporting or opposing a candidate, on the other, has no First Amendment significance apart from *Austin*'s arbitrary line.

Austin was based on a faulty assumption. . . . [T]here is a general recognition now that discussions of candidates and issues are quite often intertwined in practical terms. . . . Just as arguments about immense aggregations of corporate wealth and concerns about protecting shareholders and union members do not justify a ban on issue ads, they cannot sustain a ban on independent expenditures for express ads. . . .

· · ·

I surmise that even the majority . . . appreciates these problems with *Austin.* That is why it invents a new justification. We are now told that "the government also has a compelling interest in insulating federal elections from the type of corruption arising from the real or apparent creation of political debts." . . .

This rationale has no limiting principle. Were we to accept it, Congress would have the authority to outlaw even pure issue ads, because they, too, could endear their sponsors to candidates who adopt the favored positions. Taken to its logical conclusion, the alleged Government interest "in insulating federal elections from ... the real or apparent creation of political debts" also conflicts with *Buckley*. ... The Government's position would eviscerate the line between expenditures and contributions and subject both to the same "complaisant review under the First Amendment." ...

. . .

5.

Title II's vagueness and overbreadth demonstrate Congress' fundamental misunderstanding of the First Amendment. The Court, it must be said, succumbs to the same mistake. The majority begins with a denunciation of direct campaign contributions by corporations and unions. It then uses this rhetorical momentum as its leverage to uphold the Act. The problem, however, is that Title II's ban on electioneering communications covers general commentaries on political issues and is far removed from laws prohibiting direct contributions from corporate and union treasuries. The severe First Amendment burden of this ban on independent expenditures requires much stronger justifications than the majority offers. ...

The hostility toward corporations and unions that infuses the majority opinion is inconsistent with the viewpoint neutrality the First Amendment demands of all Government actors, including the members of this Court. Corporations, after all, are the engines of our modern economy. They facilitate complex operations on which the Nation's prosperity depends. ... Unions are also an established part of the national economic system. They, too, have their own unique insights to contribute to the political debate, but the law's impact on them is just as severe. The costs of the majority's misplaced concerns about the "corrosive and distorting effects of immense aggregations of wealth," ... moreover, will weigh most heavily on budget-strapped nonprofit entities upon which many of our citizens rely for political commentary and advocacy. These groups must now choose between staying on the sidelines in the next election or establishing a PAC against their institutional identities. PACs are a legal construct sanctioned by Congress. They are not necessarily the means of communication chosen and preferred by the citizenry.

. . .

CONCLUSION

. . .

The First Amendment ... cannot be read to allow Congress to provide for the imprisonment of those who attempt to establish new political parties and alter the civic discourse. Our pluralistic society is filled with voices expressing new and different viewpoints, speaking through modes and mechanisms that must be allowed to change in response to the demands of an interested public. ... The Court, upholding multiple laws that suppress both spontaneous and concerted speech, leaves us less free than before. Today's decision breaks faith with our tradition of robust and unfettered debate.

For the foregoing reasons, with respect, I dissent from the Court's decision upholding the main features of Titles I and II.

JUSTICE SCALIA, concurring with respect to BCRA Titles III and IV, dissenting with respect to BCRA Titles I and V, and concurring in the judgment in part and dissenting in part with respect to BCRA Title II.

... I cannot avoid adding to the many writings a few words of my own.

This is a sad day for the freedom of speech. Who could have imagined that the same Court which, within the past four years, has sternly disapproved of restrictions upon such inconsequential forms of expression as virtual child pornography, ... tobacco advertising, ... dissemination of illegally intercepted communications, ... and sexually explicit cable programming, ... would smile with favor upon a law that cuts to the heart of what the First Amendment is meant to protect: the right to criticize the government. For that is what the most offensive provisions of this legislation are all about. ...

. . .

I wish to address three fallacious propositions that might be thought to justify some or all of the provisions of this legislation—only the last of which is explicitly embraced by the principal opinion for the Court, but all of which underlie, I think, its approach to these cases.

(a) Money is Not Speech

It was said by congressional proponents of this legislation, ... that since this legislation regulates nothing but the expenditure of money for speech, as opposed to speech itself, the burden it imposes is not subject to full First Amendment scrutiny ... Until today, however, that view has been categorically rejected by our jurisprudence. ...

... [T]oday's cavalier attitude toward regulating the financing of speech (the "exacting scrutiny" test of *Buckley* is not uttered in any majority opinion, and is not observed in the ones from which I dissent) frustrates the fundamental purpose of the First Amendment. ...

. . .

... [A] law limiting the amount a person can spend to broadcast his political views is a direct restriction on speech. That is no different from a law limiting the amount a newspaper can pay its editorial staff or the amount a charity can pay its leafletters. It is equally clear that a limit on the amount a candidate can *raise* from any one individual for the purpose of speaking is also a direct limitation on speech. ...

(b) Pooling Money is Not Speech

Another proposition which could explain at least some of the results of today's opinion is that the First Amendment right to spend money for speech does not include the right to combine with others in spending money for speech. ...

We have said that "implicit in the right to engage in activities protected by the First Amendment" is "a corresponding right to associate with others in pursuit of a wide variety of political, social, economic, educational, religious, and cultural ends." ... That "right to associate ... in pursuit" includes the right to pool financial resources.

. . .

(c) Speech by Corporations Can Be Abridged

. . .

... The First Amendment does not in my view permit the restriction of ... political speech. And the same holds true for corporate electoral speech: A candidate should not be insulated from the most effective speech that the major participants in the economy and major incorporated interest groups can generate.

... The premise of the First Amendment is that the American people are neither sheep nor fools, and hence fully capable of considering both the substance of the speech presented to them and its proximate and ultimate source. If that premise is wrong, our democracy has a much greater problem to overcome than merely the influence of amassed wealth. Given the premises of democracy, there is no such thing as *too much* speech.

... [C]orporate (like noncorporate) allies will have greater access to the officeholder, and ... he will tend to favor the same causes as those who support him (which is usually *why* they supported him). That is the nature of politics—if not indeed human nature—and how this can properly be considered "corruption" (or "the appearance of corruption") with regard to corporate allies and not with regard to other allies is beyond me. ...

. . .

... This litigation is about preventing criticism of the government. ... Having abandoned that approach to a limited extent in *Buckley,* we abandon it much further today.

We will unquestionably be called upon to abandon it further still in the future. ...

. . .

... The federal election campaign laws ... can be expected to grow more voluminous, more detailed, and more complex in the years to come—and always, always, with the objective of reducing the excessive amount of speech.

JUSTICE THOMAS, concurring ... in part and dissenting in part with respect to BCRA Title II, and dissenting with respect to BCRA Titles I, V, and 311.

. . .

The joint opinion not only continues the errors of Buckley v. Valeo, by applying a low level of scrutiny to contribution ceilings, but also builds upon these errors by expanding the anticircumvention rationale beyond reason. . . .

. . .

I must now address an issue on which I differ from all of my colleagues: the disclosure provisions . . . The Court now [allows] the established right to anonymous speech to be stripped away based on the flimsiest of justifications.

. . .

I have long maintained that *Buckley* was incorrectly decided and should be overturned. . . .

. . . The chilling endpoint of the Court's reasoning is not difficult to foresee: outright regulation of the press. None of the rationales offered by the defendants, and none of the reasoning employed by the Court, exempts the press. . . .

. . .

NOTE AND QUESTION

Justices Stevens and O'Connor jointly wrote one of the Court's opinions in *McConnell*. Joint opinions for the Court are unusual but not unprecedented. For example, Justices O'Connor, Kennedy, and Souter jointly wrote the Court's opinion in Planned Parenthood of Southeastern Pennsylvania v. Casey (1992). As the senior associate justice voting in the majority on most of the issues in *McConnell*, Justices Stevens could have assigned the Court's opinion on those issues to himself solely or to any other justice in the majority. What are the likely reasons for Stevens assigning that Court's opinion to himself and Justice O'Connor?

RANDALL v. SORRELL, *et al.* VERMONT REPUBLICAN STATE COMMITTEE, *et al.*

___ U.S. ___, 126 S.Ct. 2479, 165 L.Ed.2d 482 (2006).

JUSTICE BREYER announced the judgment of the Court, and delivered an opinion in which THE CHIEF JUSTICE joins, and in which JUSTICE ALITO joins except as to Parts II–B–1 and II–B–2.

We here consider the constitutionality of a Vermont campaign finance statute that limits both (1) the amounts that candidates for state office may spend on their campaigns (expenditure limitations) and (2) the amounts that individuals, organizations, and political parties may contribute to those campaigns (contribution limitations) Vt. Stat. Ann., Tit. 17, § 2801 *et seq.* (2002). We hold that both sets of limitations are inconsistent with the First Amendment. . . .

I

In 1997, Vermont enacted a more stringent campaign finance law, Pub. Act No. 64, codified at Vt. Stat. Ann., Tit. 17, § 2801 *et seq.* (2002) (hereinafter Act or Act 64), the statute at issue here. Act 64, which took effect immediately after the 1998 elections, imposes mandatory expendi-

RIGHT TO VOTE Pt. 6

ture limits on the total amount a candidate for state office can spend during a "two-year general election cycle," *i.e.*, the primary plus the general election, in approximately the following amounts: governor, $300,000; lieutenant governor, $100,000; other statewide offices, $45,000; state senator, $4,000 (plus an additional $2,500 for each additional seat in the district); state representative (two-member district), $3,000; and state representative (single member district), $2,000. § 2805a(a). These limits are adjusted for inflation in odd-numbered years based on the Consumer Price Index. § 2805a(e). Incumbents seeking reelection to statewide office may spend no more than 85% of the above amounts, and incumbents seeking reelection to the State Senate or House may spend no more than 90% of the above amounts. § 2805a(c). The Act defines "[e]xpenditure" broadly to mean the

> "payment, disbursement, distribution, advance, deposit, loan or gift of money or anything of value, paid or promised to be paid, for the purpose of influencing an election, advocating a position on a public question, or supporting or opposing one or more candidates." § 2801(3)....

... Act 64 also imposes strict contribution limits. The amount any single individual can contribute to the campaign of a candidate for state office during a "two-year general election cycle" is limited as follows: governor, lieutenant governor, and other statewide offices, $400; state senator, $300; and state representative, $200. § 2805(a). Unlike its expenditure limits, Act 64's contribution limits are not indexed for inflation ... A political committee is subject to these same limits. *Ibid.* So is a political party, *ibid.* ... The Act also imposes a limit of $2,000 upon the amount any individual can give to a political party during a 2–year general election cycle. § 2805(a).

The Act defines "contribution" broadly in approximately the same way it defines "expenditure." § 2801(2). Any expenditure made on a candidate's behalf counts as a contribution to the candidate if it is "intentionally facilitated by, solicited by or approved by" the candidate. §§ 2809(a), (c). And a party expenditure that "primarily benefits six or fewer candidates who are associated with the" party is "presumed" to count against the party's contribution limits. §§ 2809(a), (d) ...

The District Court agreed with the petitioners that the Act's expenditure limits violate the First Amendment. See *Buckley,* 424 U.S. 1. The court also held unconstitutional the Act's limits on the contributions of political parties to candidates. At the same time, the court found the Act's other contribution limits constitutional. *Landell v. Sorrell,* 118 F. Supp. 2d 470 (Vt. 2000).... A divided panel of the Court of Appeals for the Second Circuit held that *all* of the Act's contribution limits are constitutional. It also held that the Act's expenditure limits may be constitutional....

The petitioners and respondents all sought certiorari. They asked us to consider the constitutionality of Act 64's expenditure limits, its contribution limits, and a related definitional provision. We agreed to do so. 545 U.S. ___ (2005).

II

We turn first to the Act's expenditure limits. Do those limits violate the First Amendment's free speech guarantees? ...

In *Buckley v. Valeo, supra,* the Court considered the constitutionality of the Federal Election Campaign Act of 1971 (FECA), 86 Stat. 3, as amended, 2 U.S.C. § 431 *et seq.,* a statute that, much like the Act before us, imposed both expenditure and contribution limitations on campaigns for public office. The Court, while upholding FECA's contribution limitations as constitutional, held that the statute's expenditure limitations violated the First Amendment ... *Buckley* stated that both kinds of limitations "implicate fundamental First Amendment interests." 424 U.S., at 23. ... Over the last 30 years, in considering the constitutionality of a host of different campaign finance statutes, this Court has repeatedly adhered to *Buckley*'s constraints, including those on expenditure limits. ...

The respondents recognize that, in respect to expenditure limits, *Buckley* appears to be a controlling—and unfavorable—precedent. They seek to overcome that precedent in two ways. First, they ask us in effect to overrule *Buckley.* Post-*Buckley* experience, they believe, has shown that contribution limits (and disclosure requirements) alone cannot effectively deter corruption or its appearance; hence experience has undermined an assumption underlying that case. Indeed, the respondents have devoted several pages of their briefs to attacking *Buckley*'s holding on expenditure limits. ... Second, in the alternative, they ask us to limit the scope of *Buckley* significantly by distinguishing *Buckley* from the present case. They advance as a ground for distinction a justification for expenditure limitations that, they say, *Buckley* did not consider, namely that such limits help to protect candidates from spending too much time raising money rather than devoting that time to campaigning among ordinary voters. We find neither argument persuasive.

The Court has often recognized the "fundamental importance" of *stare decisis,* the basic legal principle that commands judicial respect for a court's earlier decisions and the rules of law they embody ... The Court has pointed out that *stare decisis* " 'promotes the evenhanded, predictable, and consistent development of legal principles, fosters reliance on judicial decisions, and contributes to the actual and perceived integrity of the judicial process.' " ... *Stare decisis* thereby avoids the instability and unfairness that accompany disruption of settled legal expectations. For this reason, the rule of law demands that adhering to our prior case law be the norm. Departure from precedent is exceptional, and requires "special justification." *Arizona v. Rumsey,* 467 U.S. 203, 212 (1984). This is especially true where, as here, the principle has become settled through iteration and reiteration over a long period of time.

We can find here no such special justification that would require us to overrule *Buckley.* Subsequent case law has not made *Buckley* a legal anomaly or otherwise undermined its basic legal principles ... We cannot find in the respondents' claims any demonstration that circumstances have changed so radically as to undermine *Buckley's* critical factual assumptions. The respondents have not shown, for example, any dramatic increase in corruption or its appearance in Vermont; nor have they shown that expenditure limits are the only way to attack that problem.... At the same time, *Buckley* has promoted considerable reliance. Congress and state legislatures have used *Buckley* when drafting campaign finance laws. And, as we have said, this Court has followed *Buckley,* upholding and applying its reasoning in later cases. Overruling *Buckley* now would dramatically undermine this reliance on our settled precedent.

For all these reasons, we find this a case that fits the *stare decisis* norm. And we do not perceive the strong justification that would be necessary to warrant overruling so well established a precedent. We consequently decline the respondents' invitation to reconsider *Buckley.*

The respondents also ask us to distinguish these cases from *Buckley.* But we can find no significant basis for that distinction. Act 64's expenditure limits are not substantially different from those at issue in *Buckley.* In both instances the limits consist of a dollar cap imposed upon a candidate's expenditures. Nor is Vermont's primary justification for imposing its expenditure limits significantly different from Congress' rationale for the *Buckley* limits: preventing corruption and its appearance.

The sole basis on which the respondents seek to distinguish *Buckley* concerns a further supporting justification. They argue that expenditure limits are necessary in order to reduce the amount of time candidates must spend raising money.... In our view, it is highly unlikely that fuller consideration of this time protection rationale would have changed *Buckley*'s result. The *Buckley* Court was aware of the connection between expenditure limits and a reduction in fundraising time.... And, in any event, the connection between high campaign expenditures and increased fundraising demands seems perfectly obvious ... Under these circumstances, the respondents' argument amounts to no more than an invitation so to limit *Buckley's* holding as effectively to overrule it. For the reasons set forth above, we decline that invitation as well. And, given *Buckley's* continued authority, we must conclude that Act 64's expenditure limits violate the First Amendment.

III

We turn now to a more complex question, namely the constitutionality of Act 64's contribution limits. The parties, while accepting *Buckley's* approach, dispute whether, despite *Buckley's* general approval of statutes that limit campaign contributions, Act 64's contribution limits are so severe that in the circumstances its particular limits violate the First Amendment.

A

... Following *Buckley,* we must determine whether Act 64's contribution limits prevent candidates from "amassing the resources necessary for effective [campaign] advocacy," 424 U.S., at 21; whether they magnify the advantages of incumbency to the point where they put challengers to a significant disadvantage; in a word, whether they are too low and too strict to survive First Amendment scrutiny. In answering these questions, we recognize, as *Buckley* stated, that we have "no scalpel to probe" each possible contribution level. *Id.*, at 30. We cannot determine with any degree of exactitude the precise restriction necessary to carry out the statute's legitimate objectives. In practice, the legislature is better equipped to make such empirical judgments, as legislators have "particular expertise" in matters related to the costs and nature of running for office. *McConnell*, 540 U.S., at 137. Thus ordinarily we have deferred to the legislature's determination of such matters.

Nonetheless, as *Buckley* acknowledged, we must recognize the existence of some lower bound. At some point the constitutional risks to the democratic electoral process become too great. After all, the interests underlying contribution limits, preventing corruption and the appearance of corruption, "directly implicate the integrity of our electoral process." ... We find those danger signs present here. As compared with the contribution limits upheld by the Court in the past, and with those in force in other States, Act 64's limits are sufficiently low as to generate suspicion that they are not closely drawn. The Act sets its limits per election cycle, which includes both a primary and a general election. Thus, in a gubernatorial race with both primary and final election contests, the Act's contribution limit amounts to $200 per election per candidate (with significantly lower limits for contributions to candidates for State Senate and House of Representatives, see *supra*, at 3). These limits apply both to contributions from individuals and to contributions from political parties, whether made in cash or in expenditures coordinated (or presumed to be coordinated) with the candidate.... These limits are well below the limits this Court upheld in *Buckley* ...

... Moreover, considered as a whole, Vermont's contribution limits are the lowest in the Nation .... Act 64's contribution limits are substantially lower than both the limits we have previously upheld and comparable limits in other States. These are danger signs that Act 64's contribution limits may fall outside tolerable First Amendment limits. We consequently must examine the record independently and carefully to determine whether Act 64's contribution limits are "closely drawn" to match the State's interests....

... Our examination of the record convinces us that, from a constitutional perspective, Act 64's contribution limits are too restrictive. We reach this conclusion based not merely on the low dollar amounts of the limits themselves, but also on the statute's effect on political parties and on volunteer activity in Vermont elections. *Taken together*, Act 64's substantial restrictions on the ability of candidates to raise the funds necessary to run a competitive election, on the ability of political parties to help their candidates get elected, and on the ability of individual citizens to volunteer their time to campaigns show that the Act is not closely drawn to meet its objectives. In particular, five factors together lead us to this decision.

First, the record suggests, though it does not conclusively prove, that Act 64's contribution limits will significantly restrict the amount of funding available for challengers to run competitive campaigns.... *Second,* Act 64's insistence that political parties abide by *exactly* the same low contribution limits that apply to other contributors threatens harm to a particularly important political right, the right to associate in a political party ... *Third,* the Act's treatment of volunteer services aggravates the problem. Like its federal statutory counterpart, the Act excludes from its definition of "contribution" all "services provided without compensation by individuals volunteering their time on behalf of a candidate." ... *Fourth,* ... Act 64's contribution limits are not adjusted for inflation .... *Fifth,* we have found nowhere in the record any special justification that might warrant a contribution limit so low or so restrictive as to bring about the serious associational and expressive problems that we have described. Rather, the basic justifications the State has advanced in support of such limits are those present in *Buckley.* ...

... These five sets of considerations, taken together, lead us to conclude that Act 64's contribution limits are not narrowly tailored ...

IV

We conclude that Act 64's expenditure limits violate the First Amendment as interpreted in *Buckley v. Valeo.* We also conclude that the specific details of Act 64's contribution limits require us to hold that those limits violate the First Amendment, for they burden First Amendment interests in a manner that is disproportionate to the public purposes they were enacted to advance. Given our holding, we need not, and do not, examine the constitutionality of the statute's presumption that certain party expenditures are coordinated with a candidate. Vt. Stat. Ann., Tit. 17, § 2809(d) (2002). Accordingly, the judgment of the Court of Appeals is reversed, and the cases are remanded for further proceedings.

It is so ordered.

JUSTICE THOMAS, with whom JUSTICE SCALIA joins, concurring in the judgment.

Although I agree with the plurality that Vt. Stat. Ann., Tit. 17, § 2801 *et seq.* (2002) (Act 64), is unconstitutional, I disagree with its rationale for striking down that statute. Invoking *stare decisis,* the plurality rejects the invitation to overrule *Buckley v. Valeo,* 424 U.S. 1 (1976) (per curiam). It then applies *Buckley* to invalidate the expenditure limitations and, less persuasively, the contribution limitations. I continue to believe that *Buckley* provides insufficient protection to political speech, the core of the First Amendment. The illegitimacy of *Buckley* is further underscored by the continuing inability of the Court (and the plurality here) to apply *Buckley* in a coherent and principled fashion. As a result, *stare decisis* should pose no bar to overruling *Buckley* and replacing it with a standard faithful to the First Amendment. Accordingly, I concur only in the judgment.

... [T]the plurality's determination that this statute clearly lies on the *impermissible* side of the constitutional line gives no assistance in drawing this line, and it is clear that no such line can be drawn rationally. There is simply no way to calculate just how much money a person would need to receive before he would be corrupt or perceived to be corrupt (and such a calculation would undoubtedly vary by person). Likewise, there is no meaningful way of discerning just how many resources must be lost before speech is "disproportionately burden[ed]." *Ante*, at 28. *Buckley*, as the plurality has applied it, gives us license to simply strike down any limits that just *seem* to be too stringent, and to uphold the rest. The First Amendment does not grant us this authority. *Buckley* provides no consistent protection to the core of the First Amendment, and must be overruled.

For these reasons, I concur only in the judgment.

C. THE SPOILS SYSTEM AND THE CIVIL SERVICE SYSTEM

Particularly in the case of big city "political machines," there was an alternative to soliciting donations from private citizens or groups to run a political campaign. Government employees owed their jobs to political parties, and could be counted on to contribute a portion of their salary or their time, or both, to support the party. Interestingly, both the "spoils system"—which denies continued employment to members of the losing party—and the civil service system—which seeks to distance public employees from the election process—have raised First Amendment issues.

UNITED PUBLIC WORKERS v. MITCHELL

Supreme Court of the United States, 1947.
330 U.S. 75, 67 S.Ct. 556, 91 L.Ed. 754.

JUSTICE REED delivered the opinion of the Court.

The Hatch Act, enacted in 1940, declares unlawful certain specified political activities of federal employees. Section 9 forbids officers and employees in the executive branch of the Federal Government, with exceptions, from taking "any active part in political management or in political campaigns." . . .

. . . [George P.] Poole has been charged by the Commission with political activity and a proposed order for his removal from his position adopted subject to his right under Commission procedure to reply to the charges and to present further evidence in refutation. [Poole was an employee of the Philadelphia mint, and served as Democratic Ward Executive Committeeman in that city.] . . .

. . .

. . . Poole's stated offense is taking an "active part in political management or in political campaigns." He was a ward executive committeeman of a political party and was politically active on election day as a worker at the polls and a paymaster for the services of other party workers. . . .

. . .

... The right claimed as inviolate may be stated as the right of a citizen to act as a party official or worker to further his own political views. Thus we have a measure of interference by the Hatch Act ... with what otherwise would be the freedom of the civil servant under the First, [Amendment]....

We do not find persuasion in appellants' argument that such activities during free time are not subject to regulation even though admittedly political activities cannot be indulged in during working hours. The influence of political activity by government employees, if evil in its effects on the service, the employees or people dealing with them, is hardly less so because that activity takes place after hours. Of course, the question of the need for this regulation is for other branches of government rather than the courts. Our duty in this case ends if the Hatch Act provision under examination is constitutional.

Of course, it is accepted constitutional doctrine that these fundamental human rights are not absolutes. The requirements of residence and age must be met. The essential rights of the First Amendment in some instances are subject to the elemental need for order without which the guarantees of civil rights to others would be a mockery.... Again this Court must balance the extent of the guarantees of freedom against a congressional enactment to protect a democratic society against the supposed evil of political partisanship by classified employees of government.

... [T]he practice of excluding classified employees from party offices and personal political activity at the polls has been in effect for several decades. Some incidents similar to those that are under examination here have been before this Court and the prohibition against certain types of political activity by office holders has been upheld. The leading case was decided in 1882. Ex parte Curtis, 106 U.S. 371. There a subordinate United States employee was indicted for violation of an act that forbade employees who were not appointed by the President and confirmed by the Senate from giving or receiving money for political purposes from or to other employees of the government on penalty of discharge and criminal punishment. Curtis urged that the statute was unconstitutional. This Court upheld the right of Congress to punish the infraction of this law. The decisive principle was the power of Congress, within reasonable limits, to regulate, so far as it might deem necessary, the political conduct of its employees. A list of prohibitions against acts by public officials that are permitted to other citizens was given. This Court said, 106 U.S. at page 373:

> "The evident purpose of congress in all this class of enactments has been to promote efficiency and integrity in the discharge of official duties, and to maintain proper discipline in the public service. Clearly such a purpose is within the just scope of legislative power, and it is not easy to see why the act now under consideration does not come fairly within the legitimate means to such an end."

The right to contribute money through fellow employees to advance the contributor's political theories was held not to be protected by any

Constitutional provision. It was held subject to regulation. A dissent by Justice Bradley emphasized the broad basis of the Court's opinion. He contended that a citizen's right to promote his political views could not be so restricted merely because he was an official of government.

No other member of the Court joined in this dissent. The conclusion of the Court, that there was no constitutional bar to regulation of such financial contributions of public servants as distinguished from the exercise of political privileges such as the ballot, has found acceptance in the subsequent practice of Congress and the growth of the principle of required political neutrality for classified public servants as a sound element for efficiency. The conviction that an actively partisan governmental personnel threatens good administration has deepened since Ex parte Curtis. Congress recognizes danger to the service in that political rather than official effort may earn advancement and to the public in that governmental favor may be channeled through political connections.

In United States v. Wurzbach, 280 U.S. 396, the doctrine of legislative power over actions of governmental officials was held valid when extended to members of Congress. The members of Congress were prohibited from receiving contributions for "any political purpose whatever" from any other federal employees. Private citizens were not affected. The argument of unconstitutionality because of interference with the political rights of a citizen by that time was dismissed in a sentence....

The provisions of § 9 of the Hatch Act ... are not dissimilar in purpose from the statutes against political contributions of money. The prohibitions now under discussion are directed at political contributions of energy by Government employees. These contributions, too, have a long background of disapproval. Congress and the President are responsible for an efficient public service. If, in their judgment, efficiency may be best obtained by prohibiting active participation by classified employees in politics as party officers or workers, we see no constitutional objection.

Another Congress may determine that on the whole, limitations on active political management by federal personnel are unwise. The teaching of experience has evidently led Congress to enact the Hatch Act provisions. The declare that the present supposed evils of political activity are beyond the power of Congress to redress would leave the nation impotent to deal with what many sincere men believe is a material threat to the democratic system. Congress is not politically naive or regardless of public welfare or that of the employees. It leaves untouched full participation by employees in political decisions at the ballot box and forbids only the partisan activity of federal personnel deemed offensive to efficiency. With that limitation only, employees may make their contributions to public affairs or protect their own interests, as before the passage of the act.

The argument that political neutrality is not indispensable to a merit system for federal employees may be accepted. But because it is not indispensable does not mean that it is not desirable or permissible. Modern American politics involves organized political parties. Many classifications of Government employees have been accustomed to work in politics—national, state and local—as a matter of principle or to assure their tenure. Congress may reasonably desire to limit party activity of federal employees so as to avoid a tendency toward a one-party system. It may have considered that parties would be more truly devoted to the public welfare if public servants were not over active politically.

　　... A reading of the Act ... shows the wide range of public activities with which there is no interference by the legislation. It is only partisan political activity that is interdicted. It is active participation in political management and political campaigns. Expressions, public or private, on public affairs, personalities and matters of public interest, not an objective of party action, are unrestricted by law so long as the Government employee does not direct his activities toward party success.

　　It is urged, however, that Congress has gone further than necessary in prohibiting political activity to all types of classified employees. It is pointed out by appellants "that the impartiality of many of these is a matter of complete indifference to the effective performance" of their duties. Mr. Poole would appear to be a good illustration for appellants' argument. The complaint states that he is a roller in the Mint. We take it this is a job calling for the qualities of a skilled mechanic and that it does not involve contact with the public. Nevertheless, if in free time he is engaged in political activity, Congress may have concluded that the activity may promote or retard his advancement or preferment with his superiors. Congress may have thought that Government employees are handy elements for leaders in political policy to use in building a political machine. For regulation of employees it is not necessary that the act regulated be anything more than an act reasonably deemed by Congress to interfere with the efficiency of the public service. There are hundreds of thousands of United States employees with positions no more influential upon policy determination than that of Mr. Poole. Evidently what Congress feared was the cumulative effect on employee morale of political activity by all employees who could be induced to participate actively. It does not seem to us an unconstitutional basis for legislation.

　　There is a suggestion that administrative workers may be barred, constitutionally, from political management and political campaigns while the industrial workers may not be barred, constitutionally, without an act "narrowly drawn to define and punish specific conduct." ... Congress has determined that the presence of government employees, whether industrial or administrative, in the ranks of political party workers is bad. Whatever differences there may be between administrative employees of the Government and industrial workers in its employ are differences in detail so far as the constitutional power under review is concerned. Whether there are such differences and what weight to attach to them, are all matters of detail for Congress. We do not know whether the number of federal employees will expand or contract; whether the need for regulation of their political activities will increase or diminish. The use of the constitutional power of regulation is for Congress, not for the courts.

We have said that Congress may regulate the political conduct of Government employees "within reasonable limits," even though the regulation trenches to some extent upon unfettered political action. The determination of the extent to which political activities of governmental employees shall be regulated lies primarily with Congress. Courts will interfere only when such regulation passes beyond the general existing conception of governmental power. That conception develops from practice, history, and changing educational, social and economic conditions. The regulation of such activities as Poole carried on has the approval of long practice by the Commission, court decisions upon similar problems and a large body of informed public opinion. Congress and the administrative agencies have authority over the discipline and efficiency of the public service. When actions of civil servants in the judgment of Congress menace the integrity and the competency of the service, legislation to forestall such danger and adequate to maintain its usefulness is required. The Hatch Act is the answer of Congress to this need. We cannot say with such a background that these restrictions are unconstitutional.

. . .

JUSTICE MURPHY and JUSTICE JACKSON took no part in the consideration or decision of this case.

JUSTICE RUTLEDGE dissents as to Poole for the reasons stated by JUSTICE BLACK. . . .

JUSTICE BLACK, dissenting.

The sentence in § 9 of the statute, here upheld, makes it unlawful for any person employed in the executive branch of the Federal Government, with minor numerical exceptions, to "take any active part in political management or in political campaigns." . . . The number of federal employees thus barred from political action is approximately three million. . . . No one of all these millions of citizens can, without violating this law, "take any active part" in any campaign for a cause or for a candidate if the cause or candidate is "specifically identified with any National or State political party." Since under our common political practices most causes and candidates are espoused by political parties, the result is that, because they are paid out of the public treasury, all these citizens who engage in public work can take no really effective part in campaigns that may bring about changes in their lives, their fortunes, and their happiness.

. . .

Had this measure deprived five million farmers, or a million businessmen of all right to participate in elections, because Congress thought that federal farm or business subsidies might prompt some of them to exercise, or be susceptible to, a corrupting influence on politics or government, I would not sustain such an Act on the ground that it could be interpreted so as to apply only to some of them. Certainly laws which restrict the liberties guaranteed by the First Amendment should be narrowly drawn to meet the evil aimed at and to affect only the minimum number of people imperatively necessary to prevent a grave and imminent danger to the public....

The right to vote and privately to express an opinion on political matters, important though they be, are but parts of the broad freedoms which our Constitution has provided as the bulwark of our free political institutions. Popular government, to be effective, must permit and encourage much wider political activity by all the people.... Legislation which muzzles several million citizens threatens popular government, not only because it injures the individuals muzzled, but also, because of its harmful effect on the body politic in depriving it of the political participation and interest of such a large segment of our citizens. Forcing public employees to contribute money and influence can well be proscribed in the interest of "clean politics" and public administration. But I think the Constitution prohibits legislation which prevents millions of citizens from contributing their arguments, complaints, and suggestions to the political debates which are the essence of our democracy; prevents them from engaging in organizational activity to urge others to vote and take an interest in political affairs; bars them from performing the interested citizen's duty of insuring that his and his fellow citizens' votes are counted. Such drastic limitations on the right of all the people to express political opinions and take political action would be inconsistent with the First Amendment's guaranty of freedom of speech, press, assembly, and petition....

There is nothing about federal and state employees as a class which justifies depriving them or society of the benefits of their participation in public affairs. They, like other citizens, pay taxes and serve their country in peace and in war. The taxes they pay and the wars in which they fight are determined by the elected spokesmen of all the people. They come from the same homes, communities, schools, churches, and colleges as do the other citizens. I think the Constitution guarantees to them the same right that other groups of good citizens have to engage in activities which decide who their elected representatives shall be.

. . .

It is argued that it is in the interest of clean politics to suppress political activities of federal and state employees. It would hardly seem to be imperative to muzzle millions of citizens because some of them, if left their constitutional freedoms, might corrupt the political process....

It may be true, as contended, that some higher employees, unless restrained, might coerce their subordinates or that Government employees might use their official position to coerce other citizens.... [It does not] seem plausible that all of the millions of public employees whose rights to free expression are here stifled, might, if they participate in elections, coerce other citizens not employed by the Government or the States. Poole, one of the petitioners here, is a roller in a government printing office. His job is about on a par in terms of political influence with that of most other state, federal, and private business employees. Such jobs generally do not give such employees who hold them sufficient authority to enable them to wield a dangerous or coercive influence on the political world. If the possibility exists that some other public employees may, by reason of their more influential positions, coerce other public employees or other citizens, laws can be drawn to punish the coercers. It hardly seems consistent with our system of equal justice to all to suppress the political and speaking freedom of millions of good citizens because a few bad citizens might engage in coercion.

It may also be true, as contended, that if public employees are permitted to exercise a full freedom to express their views in political campaigns, some public officials will discharge some employees and grant promotion to others on a political rather than on a merit basis. For the same reasons other public officials, occupying positions of influence, may use their influence to have their own political supporters appointed or promoted. But here again, if the practice of making discharges, promotions or recommendations for promotions on a political basis is so great an evil as to require legislation, the law could punish those public officials who engage in the practice. To punish millions of employees and to deprive the nation of their contribution to public affairs, in order to remove temptation from a proportionately small number of public officials, seems at the least to be a novel method of suppressing what is thought to be an evil practice.

. . .

The section of the Act here held valid reduces the constitutionally protected liberty of several million citizens to less than a shadow of its substance. It relegates millions of federal, state, and municipal employees to the role of mere spectators of events upon which hinge the safety and welfare of all the people, including public employees. It removes a sizable proportion of our electorate from full participation in affairs destined to mold the fortunes of the Nation. . . . Laudable as its purpose may be, it seems to me to hack at the roots of a Government by the people themselves; and consequently I cannot agree to sustain its validity.

JUSTICE DOUGLAS, dissenting . . .

. . .

. . . Poole is not in the administrative category of civil service. He is an industrial worker—a roller in the mint, a skilled laborer or artisan whose work or functions in no way affect the policy of the agency nor involve relationships with the public. There is a marked difference in the British treatment of administrative and industrial employees under civil service. And the difference between the two is for me relevant to the problem we have here.

The civil service system has been called "the one great political invention" of nineteenth century democracy. The intricacies of modern government, the important and manifold tasks it performs, the skill and expertise required, the vast discretionary powers vested in the various agencies, and the impact of their work on individual claimants as well as on the general welfare have made the integrity, devotion, and skill of the men and women who compose the system a matter of deep concern of many thoughtful people. Political fortunes of parties will ebb and flow; top policy men in administrations will come and go; new laws will be passed and old ones amended or repealed. But those who give continuity to administration, those who contribute the basic skill and efficiency to the daily work of government, and those on whom the new as well as the old administration is dependent for smooth functioning of the complicated machinery of modern government are the core of the civil service. If they are beneficiaries of political patronage rather than professional careerists, serious results might follow—or so Congress could reasonably believe. Public confidence in the objectivity and integrity of the civil service system might be so weakened as to jeopardize the effectiveness of administrative government. Or it might founder on the rocks of incompetency, if every change in political fortunes turned out the incumbents, broke the continuity of administration, and thus interfered with the development of expert management at the technical levels. Or if the incumbents were political adventurers or party workers, partisanship might color or corrupt the processes of administration of law with which most of the administrative agencies are entrusted.

The philosophy is to develop a civil service which can and will serve loyally and equally well any political party which comes into power.

Those considerations might well apply to the entire group of civil servants in the administrative category—whether they are those in the so-called expert classification or are clerks, stenographers and the like. They are the ones who have access to the files, who meet the public, who arrange appointments, who prepare the basic data on which policy decisions are made. Each may be a tributary, though perhaps a small one, to the main stream which we call policy making or administrative action. If the element of partisanship enters into the official activities of any member of the group it may have its repercussions or effect throughout the administrative process. Thus in that type of case there would be much to support the view of the Court that Congress need not undertake to draw the line to include only the more important offices but can take the precaution of protecting the whole by insulating even the lowest echelon from partisan activities.

So, I think that if the issues tendered by Poole were tendered by an administrative employee, we would have quite a different case. For Poole claims the right to work as a ward executive committeeman, i.e., as an office holder in a political party.

But Poole, being an industrial worker, is as remote from contact with the public or from policy making or from the functioning of the administrative process as a charwoman. The fact that he is in the classified civil service is not, I think, relevant to the question of the degree to which his political activities may be curtailed. He is in a position not essentially different from one who works in the machine shop of a railroad or steamship which the Government runs, or who rolls aluminum in a manufacturing plant which the Government owns and operates. Can all of those categories of industrial employees constitutionally be insulated from American political life? If at some future time it should come to pass in this country, as it has in England, that a broad policy of state ownership of basic industries is inaugurated, does this decision mean that all of the hundreds of thousands of industrial workers affected could be debarred from the normal political activity which is one of our valued traditions?

The evils of the "spoils" system do not, of course, end with the administrative group of civil servants. History shows that the political regimentation of government industrial workers produces its own crop of abuses. Those in top policy posts or others in supervisory positions might seek to knit the industrial workers in civil service into a political machine. As a weapon they might seek to make the advancement of industrial workers dependent on political loyalty, on financial contributions, or on other partisan efforts. Or political activities of these workers might take place on government premises, on government time, or otherwise at government expense. These are specific evils which would require a specific treatment.

There is, however, no showing of any such abuse here. What Poole did, he did on his own without compulsion or suggestion or invitation from any one higher up. Nor does it appear that what he did was done on government time or on government premises. . . .

. . . The difficulty lies in attempting to preserve our democratic way of life by measures which deprive a large segment of the population of all political rights except the right to vote. Absent coercion, improper use of government position or government funds, or neglect or inefficiency in the performance of duty, federal employees have the same rights as other citizens under the Constitution. They are not second class citizens. If, in exercise of their rights, they find common political interests and join with each other or other groups in what they conceive to be their interests or the interests of the nation, they are simply doing what any other group might do. In other situations where the balance was between constitutional rights of individuals and a community interest which sought to qualify those rights, we have insisted that the statute be "narrowly drawn to define and punish specific conduct as constituting a clear and present danger to a substantial interest" of government. . . .

. . . It seems plain to me that that [substantial interest] has its roots in the coercive activity of those in the hierarchy who have the power to regiment the industrial group or who undertake to do so. To sacrifice the political rights of the industrial workers goes far beyond any demonstrated or demonstrable need. Those rights are too basic and fundamental in our democratic political society to be sacrificed or qualified for anything short of a clear and present danger to the civil service system. . . .

NOTES AND QUESTIONS

1.   Like Buckley v. Valeo, *Mitchell* balanced competing interests to resolve the First Amendment issue. The Court in *Mitchell*, however, deferred to Congressional judgment about how the competing interests should be weighed and resolved. The Court in *Buckley*, nearly three decades later, used a first amendment formula that talked about the necessity that the governmental interests used to justify abridgment of speech be "compelling," and deferred much less to legislative judgments about the balance. The difference in tone is the result of thirty years of gradual development of First Amendment doctrine. Would the *Mitchell*

case have been decided differently if the Court had insisted that the restriction be "closely drawn to avoid unnecessary abridgment" of First Amendment freedoms?

2. Another problem in *Mitchell*, was the conception that public employment was a "privilege"—public employees had no "right" to their jobs, and could not complain if the government imposed conditions on their continued employment. In an 1892 case, when Justice Holmes was on the Massachusetts Supreme Judicial Court, he wrote an opinion dispatching the claim of a policeman who had been fired for his political activities. In a famous quote, he said: "The petitioner may have a constitutional right to talk politics, but he has no constitutional right to be a policeman." McAuliffe v. Mayor of New Bedford, 155 Mass. 216, 220, 29 N.E. 517, 517 (1892). *Mitchell* didn't respond to George Poole's case that bruskly, conceding that Poole had First Amendment rights that must be weighed against competing government interests. The older tradition, represented by *McAuliffe*, could be seen in *Mitchell*, however, in the deference given to the government interests. Later cases, beginning two decades after *Mitchell*, have explicitly rejected the older view that public employment is a "privilege" and that public employees' speech can lead to loss of their jobs. In Pickering v. Board of Education, 391 U.S. 563 (1968), the Court held that the Board of Education had violated the First Amendment when it fired a teacher for writing a letter to the editor criticizing the Board.

3. Despite the fact that First Amendment law had changed greatly in the intervening years, the Court reaffirmed *Mitchell* in United States Civil Service Commission v. National Association of Letter Carriers, 413 U.S. 548 (1973). Justice Douglas—the only remaining member of the Court that decided *Mitchell*—wrote a dissent joined by Justices Brennan and Marshall. He argued that *Mitchell*'s "rational basis standard" was out of line with later cases that established that government employment was not a "privilege" that could be taken away for constitutionally protected speech.

4. In 1993, Congress amended the Hatch Act, removing its restrictions from about 97 percent of federal employees. The provisions of analogous state laws, applicable to state employees, vary considerably from state to state.

ELROD v. BURNS

Supreme Court of the United States, 1976.
427 U.S. 347, 96 S.Ct. 2673, 49 L.Ed.2d 547.

JUSTICE BRENNAN announced the judgment of the Court and delivered an opinion in which JUSTICE WHITE and JUSTICE MARSHALL joined.

This case presents the question whether public employees who allege that they were discharged or threatened with discharge solely because of their partisan political affiliation or nonaffiliation state a claim for deprivation of constitutional rights secured by the First and Fourteenth Amendments.

I

Respondents ... alleged that they were discharged or threatened with discharge solely for the reason that they were not affiliated with or sponsored by the Democratic Party....

II

In December 1970, the Sheriff of Cook County, a Republican, was replaced by Richard Elrod, a Democrat. At that time, respondents, all Republicans, were employees of the Cook County Sheriff's Office. They were non-civil-service employees and, therefore, not covered by any statute, ordinance, or regulation protecting them from arbitrary discharge. One respondent, John Burns, was Chief Deputy of the Process Division and supervised all departments of the Sheriff's Office working on the seventh floor of the building housing that office. Frank Vargas was a bailiff and security guard at the Juvenile Court of Cook County. Fred L. Buckley was employed as a process server in the office. Joseph Dennard was an employee in the office.

It has been the practice of the Sheriff of Cook County, when he assumes office from a Sheriff of a different political party, to replace non-civil-service employees of the Sheriffs' Office with members of his own party when the existing employees lack or fail to obtain requisite support from, or fail to affiliate with, that party. Consequently, subsequent to Sheriff Elrod's assumption of office, respondents, with the exception of Buckley, were discharged from their employment solely because they did not support and were not members of the Democratic Party and had failed to obtain the sponsorship of one of its leaders. Buckley is in imminent danger of being discharged solely for the same reasons. Respondents allege that the discharges were ordered by Sheriff Elrod under the direction of the codefendants in this suit.

IV

The Cook County Sheriff's practice of dismissing employees on a partisan basis is but one form of the general practice of political patronage. The practice also includes placing loyal supporters in government jobs that may or may not have been made available by political discharges. Non-office holders may be the beneficiaries of lucrative government contracts for highway construction, buildings, and supplies. Favored wards may receive improved public services. Members of the judiciary may even engage in the practice through the appointment of receiverships, trusteeships, and refereeships. Although political patronage comprises a broad range of activities, we are here concerned only with the constitutionality of dismissing public employees for partisan reasons.

Patronage practice is not new to American politics. It has existed at the federal level at least since the Presidency of Thomas Jefferson, although its popularization and legitimation primarily occurred later, in the Presidency of Andrew Jackson.... More recent times have witnessed a strong decline in its use, particularly with respect to public employment. Indeed, only a few decades after Andrew Jackson's administration, strong discontent with the corruption and inefficiency of the patronage system of public employment eventuated in the Pendleton Act, the foundation of modern civil service. And on the state and local levels, merit systems have increasingly displaced the practice. This trend led the Court to observe in CSC v. National Association of Letter Carriers, 413 U.S. 548, 564 (1973), that "the judgment of Congress, the Executive, and the country appears to have been that partisan political activities by federal employees must be limited if the Government is to operate effectively and fairly, elections are to play their proper part in representative government, and employees themselves are to be sufficiently free from improper influences."

The decline of patronage employment is not, of course relevant to the question of its constitutionality. It is the practice itself, not the magnitude of its occurrence, the constitutionality of which must be determined....

V

The cost of the practice of patronage is the restraint it places on freedoms of belief and association. In order to maintain their jobs, respondents were required to pledge their political allegiance to the Democratic Party, work for the election of other candidates of the Democratic Party, contribute a portion of their wages to the Party, or obtain the sponsorship of a member of the Party, usually at the price of one of the first three alternatives. Regardless of the incumbent party's identity, Democratic or otherwise, the consequences for association and belief are the same. An individual who is a member of the out-party maintains affiliation with his own party at the risk of losing his job. He works for the election of his party's candidates and espouses its policies at the same risk. The financial and campaign assistance that he is induced to provide to another party furthers the advancement of that party's policies to the detriment of his party's views and ultimately his own beliefs, and any assessment of his salary is tantamount to coerced belief....

It is not only belief and association which are restricted where political patronage is the practice. The free functioning of the electoral process also suffers. Conditioning public employment on partisan support prevents support of competing political interests. Existing employees are deterred from such support, as well as the multitude seeking jobs. As government employment, state or federal, becomes more pervasive, the greater the dependence on it becomes, and therefore the greater becomes the power to starve political opposition by commanding partisan support, financial and otherwise. Patronage thus tips the electoral process in favor of the incumbent party, and where the practice's scope is substantial relative to the size of the electorate, the impact on the process can be significant.

Our concern with the impact of patronage on political believe and association does not occur in the abstract, for political belief and association constitute the core of those activities protected by the First Amendment....

... Patronage, ... to the extent it compels or restrains belief and association is inimical to the process which undergirds our system of government and is "at war with the deeper traditions of democracy embodied in the First Amendment." ...

. . .

Particularly pertinent to the constitutionality of the practice of patronage dismissals are Keyishian v. Board of Regents, 385 U.S. 589 (1967), and Perry v. Sindermann, 408 U.S. 593 (1972). In *Keyishian*, the Court invalidated New York statutes barring employment merely on the basis of membership in "subversive" organizations. *Keyishian* squarely held that political association alone could not, consistently with the First Amendment, constitute an adequate ground for denying public employment. In *Perry*, the Court broadly rejected the validity of limitations on First Amendment rights as a condition to the receipt of a governmental benefit ...

Patronage practice falls squarely within the prohibitions of *Keyishian* and *Perry*. Under that practice, public employees hold their jobs on the condition that they provide, in some acceptable manner, support for the favored political party. The threat of dismissal for failure to provide that support unquestionably inhibits protected belief and association, and dismissal for failure to provide support only penalizes its exercise. The belief and association which government may not ordain directly are achieved by indirection. . . .

VI

Although the practice of patronage dismissals clearly infringes First Amendment interests, our inquiry is not at an end, for the prohibition on encroachment of First Amendment protections is not an absolute. Restraints are permitted for appropriate reasons. *Keyishian* and *Perry*, however, ... dispose of ... the notion that because there is no right to a government benefit, such as public employment, the benefit may be denied for any reason.

While the right-privilege distinction furnishes no ground on which to justify patronage, petitioners raise several other justifications requiring consideration. Before examining those justifications, however, it is necessary to have in mind the standards according to which their sufficiency is to be measured. It is firmly established that a significant impairment of First Amendment rights must survive exacting scrutiny. . . . Thus encroachment "cannot be justified upon a mere showing of a legitimate state interest." ... The interest advanced must be paramount, one of vital importance, and the burden is on the government to show the existence of such an interest. . . . In the instant case, care must be taken not to confuse the interest of partisan organizations with governmental interests. Only the latter will suffice. Moreover, it is not enough that the means chosen in furtherance of the interest be rationally related to that end. . . . The gain to the subordinating interest provided by the means must outweigh the incurred loss of protected rights, ... and the government must "emplo[y] means closely drawn to avoid unnecessary abridgment. . . ." ... In short, if conditioning the retention of public employment on the employee's support of the in-party is to survive constitutional challenge, it must further some vital government end by a means that is least restrictive of freedom of belief and association in achieving that end, and the benefit gained must outweigh the loss of constitutionally protected rights.

One interest which has been offered in justification of patronage is the need to insure effective government and the efficiency of public employees. It is argued that employees of political persuasions not the same as that of the party in control of public office will not have the incentive to work effectively and may even be motivated to subvert the incumbent administration's efforts to govern effectively. We are not persuaded. The inefficiency resulting from the wholesale replacement of large numbers of public employees every time political office changes hands belies this justification. And the prospect of dismissal after an election in which the incumbent party has lost is only a disincentive to good work. Further, it is not clear that dismissal in order to make room for a patronage appointment will result in replacement by a person more qualified to do the job since appointment often occurs in exchange for the delivery of votes, or other party service, not job capability. More fundamentally, however, the argument does not succeed because it is doubtful that the mere difference of political persuasion motivates poor performance; nor do we think it legitimately may be used as a basis for imputing such behavior.... Specifically, employees may always be discharged for good cause, such as insubordination or poor job performance, when those bases in fact exist.

Even if the first argument that patronage serves effectiveness and efficiency be rejected, it still may be argued that patronage serves those interests by giving the employees of an incumbent party the incentive to perform well in order to insure their party's incumbency and thereby their jobs. Patronage, according to the argument, thus makes employees highly accountable to the public. But the ability of officials more directly accountable to the electorate to discharge employees for cause and the availability of merit systems, growth in the use of which has been quite significant, convince us that means less intrusive than patronage still exist for achieving accountability in the public work force and, thereby, effective and efficient government. The greater effectiveness of patronage over these less drastic means, if any, is at best marginal, a gain outweighed by the absence of intrusion on protected interests under the alternatives.

The lack of any justification for patronage dismissals as a means of furthering government effectiveness and efficiency distinguishes this case from CSC v. Letter Carriers, 413 U.S. 548 (1973), and United Public Workers v. Mitchell, 330 U.S. 75 (1947). In both of those cases, legislative restraints on political management and campaigning by public employees were upheld despite their encroachment on First Amendment rights because, inter alia, they did serve in a necessary manner to foster and protect efficient and effective government. Interestingly, the activities that were restrained by the legislation involved in those cases are characteristic of patronage practices....

A second interest advanced in support of patronage is the need for political loyalty of employees, not to the end that effectiveness and efficiency be insured, but to the end that representative government not be undercut by tactics obstructing the implementation of policies of the new administration, policies presumably sanctioned by the electorate. The justification is not without force, but is nevertheless inadequate to validate patronage wholesale. Limiting patronage dismissals to policy-making positions is sufficient to achieve this governmental end. Nonpolicymaking individuals usually have only limited responsibility and are therefore not in a position to thwart the goals of the in-party.

No clear line can be drawn between policymaking and nonpolicymaking positions. While nonpolicymaking individuals usually have limited responsibility, that is not to say that one with a number of responsibilities is necessarily in a policymaking position. The nature of the responsibilities is critical. Employee supervisors, for example, may have many responsibilities, but those responsibilities may have only limited and well-defined objectives. An employee with responsibilities that are not well defined or are of broad scope more likely functions in a policymaking position. In determining whether an employee occupies a policymaking position, consideration could also be given to whether the employee acts as an adviser or formulates plans for the implementation of broad goals.... Since ... it is the government's burden to demonstrate an overriding interest in order to validate an encroachment on protected interests, the burden of establishing this justification as to any particular respondent will rest on the petitioners on remand, cases of doubt being resolved in favor of the particular respondent.

It is argued that a third interest supporting patronage dismissals is the preservation of the democratic process.... The argument is ... premised on the centrality of partisan politics to the democratic process.

... [H]owever important preservation of the two-party system or any system involving a fixed number of parties may or may not be, ... we are not persuaded that the elimination of patronage practice or, as is specifically involved here, the interdiction of patronage dismissals, will bring about the demise of party politics. Political parties existed in the absence of active patronage practice prior to the administration of Andrew Jackson, and they have survived substantial reduction in their patronage power through the establishment of merit systems.

Patronage dismissals thus are not the least restrictive alternative to achieving the contribution they may make to the democratic process. The process functions as well without the practice, perhaps even better, for patronage dismissals clearly also retard that process. Patronage can result in the entrenchment of one or a few parties to the exclusion of others. And most indisputably, as we recognized at the outset, patronage is a very effective impediment to the associational and speech freedoms which are essential to a meaningful system of democratic government. Thus, if patronage contributes at all to the elective process, that contribution is diminished by the practice's impairment of the same. Indeed, unlike the gain to representative government provided by the Hatch Act in CSC v. Letter Carriers, supra, and United Public Workers v. Mitchell, supra, the gain to representative government provided by the practice of patronage, if any, would be insufficient to justify its sacrifice of First Amendment rights.

To be sure, *Letter Carriers* and *Mitchell* upheld Hatch Act restraints sacrificing political campaigning and management, activities themselves protected by the First Amendment. But in those cases it was the Court's judgment that congressional subordination of those activities was permissible to safeguard the core interests of individual belief and association. Subordination of some First Amendment activity was permissible to protect other such activity. Today, we hold that subordination of other First Amendment activity, that is, patronage dismissals, not only is permissible, but also is mandated by the First Amendment. . . .

It is apparent that at bottom we are required to engage in the resolution of conflicting interests under the First Amendment. The constitutional adjudication called for by this task is well within our province. . . .

In summary, patronage dismissals severely restrict political belief and association. Though there is a vital need for government efficiency and effectiveness, such dismissals are on balance not the least restrictive means for fostering that end. There is also a need to insure that policies which the electorate has sanctioned are effectively implemented. That interest can be fully satisfied by limiting patronage dismissals to policy-making positions. Finally, patronage dismissals cannot be justified by their contribution to the proper functioning of our democratic process through their assistance to partisan politics since political parties are nurtured by other, less intrusive and equally effective methods. More fundamentally, however, any contribution of patronage dismissals to the democratic process does not suffice to override their severe encroachment on First Amendment freedoms. We hold, therefore, that the practice of patronage dismissals is unconstitutional under the First and Fourteenth Amendments, and that respondents thus stated a valid claim for relief.

· · ·

JUSTICE STEVENS did not participate in the consideration or decision of this case.

JUSTICE STEWART, with whom JUSTICE BLACKMUN joins, concurring in the judgment.

Although I cannot join the plurality's wide-ranging opinion, I can and do concur in its judgment.

This case does not require us to consider the broad contours of the so-called patronage system, with all its variations and permutations. In particular, it does not require us to consider the constitutional validity of a system that confines the hiring of some governmental employees to those of a particular political party, and I would intimate no views whatever on that question.

The single substantive question involved in this case is whether a nonpolicymaking, nonconfidential government employee can be discharged or threatened with discharge from a job that he is satisfactorily performing upon the sole ground of his political beliefs. I agree with the plurality that he cannot.

JUSTICE POWELL, with whom THE CHIEF JUSTICE and JUSTICE REHNQUIST join, dissenting.

The Court holds unconstitutional a practice as old as the Republic, a practice which has contributed significantly to the democratization of American politics. This decision is urged on us in the name of First Amendment rights, but in my view the judgment neither is constitutionally required nor serves the interest of a representative democracy. It also may well disserve rather than promote core values of the First Amendment. I therefore dissent.

· · ·

II

As the plurality opinion recognizes, patronage practices of the sort under consideration here have a long history in America. . . . The observation that patronage employment received its primary popularization and legitimation during Jackson's Presidency, understates the historical antecedents of the practice, which stretch back to Washington's presidency.

Partisan politics, as we now know them, did not assume a prominent role in national politics immediately after the adoption of the Constitution. Nonetheless, Washington tended to confine appointments even of customs officials and postmasters to Federalists, as opposed to anti-Federalists. As the role of parties expanded, partisan considerations quickly influenced employment decisions. John Adams removed some Republicans from minor posts, and Jefferson, the first President to succeed a President of an opposing party, made significant patronage use of the appointment and removal powers. The administrations of Madison, Monroe, and John Quincy Adams provided no occasion for conspicuous patronage practice in employment, as each succeeded a copartisan. Jackson, of course, used patronage extensively when he became the first President since Jefferson to succeed an antagonistic administration.

It thus appears that patronage employment practices emerged on the national level at an early date, and that they were conspicuous during Jackson's Presidency largely because of their necessary dormancy during the long succession of Republican Presidents. During that period, however, patronage in hiring was practiced widely in the States, especially in New York and Pennsylvania. This afforded a theoretical and popular legitimacy to patronage, helping to lay the groundwork for acceptance of Jackson's actions on the national level.

It recognized that patronage in employment played a significant role in democratizing American politics. . . . Before patronage practices developed fully, an "aristocratic" class dominated political affairs, a tendency that persisted in areas where patronage did not become prevalent. . . . Patronage practices broadened the base of political participation by providing incentives to take part in the process, thereby increasing the volume of political discourse in society. Patronage also strengthened

parties, and hence encouraged the development of institutional responsibility to the electorate on a permanent basis. Parties became "instru-
ment(s) through which discipline and responsibility may be achieved
within the Leviathan." . . .

   In many situations patronage employment practices also entailed
costs to government efficiency. These costs led eventually to reforms
placing most federal and state civil service employment on a nonpatro-
nage basis. But the course of such reform is of limited relevance to the
task of constitutional adjudication in this case. It is pertinent to note,
however, that a perceived impingement on employees' political beliefs by
the patronage system was not a significant impetus to such reform. Most
advocates of reform were concerned primarily with the corruption and
inefficiency that patronage was thought to induce in civil service and the
power that patronage practices were thought to give the "professional"
politicians who relied on them. . . . Moreover, it generally was thought
that elimination of these evils required the imposition both of a merit
system and of restrictions on First Amendment activities by government
employees. . . .

III

   It might well be possible to dispose of this case on the ground that it
implicates no First Amendment right of the respondents. . . . We . . .
have complaining employees who apparently accepted patronage jobs
knowingly and willingly, while fully familiar with the "tenure" practices
long prevailing in the Sheriff's Office. Such employees have benefited
from their political beliefs and activities; they have not been penalized
for them. In these circumstances, I am inclined to agree . . . that
beneficiaries of a patronage system may not be heard to challenge it
when it comes their turn to be replaced. . . .

                              . . .

IV

   . . . It is difficult to disagree with the view, as an abstract proposition, that government employment ordinarily should not be conditioned
upon one's political beliefs or activities. But we deal here with a highly
practical and rather fundamental element of our political system, not the
theoretical abstractions of a political science seminar. In concluding that
patronage hiring practices are unconstitutional, the plurality seriously
underestimates the strength of the government interest especially at the
local level in allowing some patronage hiring practices, and it exaggerates the perceived burden on First Amendment rights.

A

   As indicated above, patronage hiring practices have contributed to
American democracy by stimulating political activity and by strengthening parties, thereby helping to make government accountable. . . .

                              . . .

   . . . In the States, and especially in the thousands of local communities, there are large numbers of elective offices, and many are as

relatively obscure as that of the local sheriff or constable. Despite the importance of elective offices to the ongoing work of local governments, election campaigns for lesser offices in particular usually attract little attention from the media, with consequent disinterest and absence of intelligent participation on the part of the public. Unless the candidates for these offices are able to dispense the traditional patronage that has accrued to the offices, they also are unlikely to attract donations of time or money from voluntary groups. In short, the resource pools that fuel the intensity of political interest and debate in "important" elections frequently "could care less" about who fills the offices deemed to be relatively unimportant. Long experience teaches that at this local level traditional patronage practices contribute significantly to the democratic process. The candidates for these offices derive their support at the precinct level, and their modest funding for publicity, from cadres of friends and political associates who hope to benefit if their "man" is elected. The activities of the latter are often the principal source of political information for the voting public. The "robust" political discourse that the plurality opinion properly emphasizes is furthered not restricted by the time-honored system.

Patronage hiring practices also enable party organizations to persist and function at the local level. Such organizations become visible to the electorate at large only at election time, but the dull periods between elections require ongoing activities: precinct organizations must be maintained; new voters registered; and minor political "chores" performed for citizens who otherwise may have no practical means of access to officeholders. In some communities, party organizations and clubs also render helpful social services.

It is naive to think that these types of political activities are motivated at these levels by some academic interest in "democracy" or other public service impulse. For the most part, as every politician knows, the hope of some reward generates a major portion of the local political activity supporting parties. It is difficult to overestimate the contributions to our system by the major political parties, fortunately limited in number compared to the fractionalization that has made the continued existence of democratic government doubtful in some other countries. Parties generally are stable, high-profile, and permanent institutions. When the names on a long ballot are meaningless to the average voter, party affiliation affords a guidepost by which voters may rationalize a myriad of political choices.... Voters can and do hold parties to long-term accountability, and it is not too much to say that, in their absence, responsive and responsible performance in low-profile offices, particularly, is difficult to maintain.

It is against decades of experience to the contrary, then, that the plurality opinion concludes that patronage hiring practices interfere with the "free functioning of the electoral process." ...

. . .

B

I thus conclude that patronage hiring practices sufficiently serve important state interests, including some interests sought to be advanced by the First Amendment, to justify a tolerable intrusion on the First Amendment interests of employees or potential employees.

. . .

... I would hold that a state or local government may elect to condition employment on the political affiliation of a prospective employee and on the political fortunes of the hiring incumbent. History and long-prevailing practice across the country support the view that patronage hiring practices make a sufficiently substantial contribution to the practical functioning of our democratic system to support their relatively modest intrusion on First Amendment interests. The judgment today unnecessarily constitutionalizes another element of American life an element certainly not without its faults but one which generations have accepted on balance as having merit. . . .

NOTES AND QUESTIONS

1.　Justice Brennan's opinion is a "plurality" opinion that did not secure the agreement of a majority. His position prevailed only with the votes of Justices Stewart and Blackmun who disassociated themselves from Justice Brennan's "wide-ranging opinion." Justice Stevens wrote for a majority of the Court, however, in Branti v. Finkel, 445 U.S. 507 (1980), holding that it was unconstitutional for a Democratic public defender to fire Republican assistant public defenders. Justice Stevens' opinion quoted extensively from Justice Brennan's *Elrod opinion.* He interpreted *Elrod* to stand for the proposition that public employment can not be conditioned on political party allegiance except in those cases where "party affiliation is an appropriate requirement for the effective performance of the public office involved." (As an example, Justice Stevens mentioned the speech-writer for an elected official.)

2.　Justice Stewart dissented in Branti v. Finkel, arguing that there was a "close professional and necessarily confidential association" between the public defender and his assistants. Justice Stevens responded that the primary responsibility of lawyers in a public defender's office was to represent individuals charged with crime. Making their tenure depend on political allegiance would undermine that responsibility. Suppose that a new Democratic *prosecutor* fired all the Republican prosecutors in her office. Would that violate the Constitution?

3.　The Court also relied on *Elrod* in Rutan v. Republican Party of Illinois, 497 U.S. 62 (1990). This time Justice Brennan wrote for a majority of the Court, extending the *Elrod* principle from discharges to failures to hire, failures to recall laid-off employees, and failures to promote, based on political affiliation. He broadly stated the applicable principle: "conditioning hiring decisions on political belief and association plainly constitutes an unconstitutional condition, unless the government has a vital interest in doing so." Justice Scalia's dissent, joined by Chief Justice Rehnquist and Justice Kennedy, argued that *Elrod* and *Branti* should be overruled. Political patronage was an "unbroken tradition" that should not be regarded as violating an "ambiguous constitutional text." Justice O'Connor also dissented.

4.   Despite the bare 5–4 majority in *Rutan*, the Court reaffirmed *Branti* and *Elrod*, with only Justices Scalia and Thomas dissenting, in O'Hare Truck Service, Inc. v. City of Northlake, 518 U.S. 712 (1996). Moreover, the Court extended the proposition—that discharges for political affiliation violate the First Amendment unless political affiliation is an appropriate requirement for the position—to the discharge of an independent contractor. O'Hare's company had been on a list of approved city towing services, but was removed after he refused to contribute to the mayor's reelection campaign and supported the mayor's opponent.

5.   Is the distinction between the Hatch Act cases and the political patronage cases a distinction between the relative merits of the civil service and patronage systems? Is it easier to explain them by the differences in First Amendment law in 1947 and 1976?

*

APPENDIX A

THE CONSTITUTION OF THE UNITED STATES OF AMERICA

We the People of the United States, in Order to form a more perfect Union, establish Justice, insure domestic Tranquility, provide for the common defence, promote the general Welfare, and secure the Blessings of Liberty to ourselves and our Posterity, do ordain and establish this Constitution for the United States of America.

ARTICLE I.

SECTION 1. All legislative Powers herein granted shall be vested in a Congress of the United States, which shall consist of a Senate and House of Representatives.

SECTION 2. The House of Representatives shall be composed of Members chosen every second Year by the People of the several States, and the Electors in each State shall have the Qualifications requisite for Electors of the most numerous Branch of the State Legislature.

No Person shall be a Representative who shall not have attained to the Age of twenty five Years, and been seven Years a Citizen of the United States, and who shall not, when elected, be an Inhabitant of that State in which he shall be chosen.

Representatives and direct Taxes shall be apportioned among the several States which may be included within this Union, according to their respective Numbers, which shall be determined by adding to the whole Number of free Persons, including those bound to Service for a Term of Years, and excluding Indians not taxed, three fifths of all other Persons. The actual Enumeration shall be made within three Years after the first Meeting of the Congress of the United States, and within every subsequent Term of ten Years, in such Manner as they shall by Law direct. The Number of Representatives shall not exceed one for every thirty Thousand, but each State shall have at Least one Representative; and until such enumeration shall be made, the State of New Hampshire shall be entitled to chuse three, Massachusetts eight, Rhode Island and Providence Plantations one, Connecticut five, New York six, New Jersey four, Pennsylvania eight, Delaware one, Maryland six, Virginia ten, North Carolina five, South Carolina five, and Georgia three.

When vacancies happen in the Representation from any State, the Executive Authority thereof shall issue Writs of Election to fill such Vacancies.

The House of Representatives shall chuse their Speaker and other Officers; and shall have the sole Power of Impeachment.

SECTION 3. The Senate of the United States shall be composed of two Senators from each State, chosen by the Legislature thereof, for six Years; and each Senator shall have one Vote.

Immediately after they shall be assembled in Consequence of the first Election, they shall be divided as equally as may be into three Classes. The Seats of the Senators of the first Class shall be vacated at the Expiration of the second Year, of the second Class at the Expiration of the fourth Year, and of the third Class at the Expiration of the sixth Year, so that one third may be chosen every second Year; and if Vacancies happen by Resignation, or otherwise, during the Recess of the Legislature of any State, the Executive thereof may make temporary Appointments until the next Meeting of the Legislature, which shall then fill such Vacancies.

No Person shall be a Senator who shall not have attained to the Age of thirty Years, and been nine Years a Citizen of the United States, and who shall not, when elected, be an Inhabitant of that State for which he shall be chosen.

The Vice President of the United States shall be President of the Senate, but shall have no Vote, unless they be equally divided.

The Senate shall chuse their other Officers, and also a President pro tempore, in the Absence of the Vice President, or when he shall exercise the Office of President of the United States.

The Senate shall have the sole Power to try all Impeachments. When sitting for that Purpose, they shall be on Oath or Affirmation. When the President of the United States is tried the Chief Justice shall preside: And no Person shall be convicted without the Concurrence of two thirds of the Members present.

Judgment in Cases of Impeachment shall not extend further than to removal from Office, and disqualification to hold and enjoy any Office of honor, Trust or Profit under the United States: but the Party convicted shall nevertheless be liable and subject to Indictment, Trial, Judgment and Punishment, according to Law.

SECTION 4. The Times, Places and Manner of holding Elections for Senators and Representatives, shall be prescribed in each State by the Legislature thereof; but the Congress may at any time by Law make or alter such Regulations, except as to the Places of chusing Senators.

The Congress shall assemble at least once in every Year, and such Meeting shall be on the first Monday in December, unless they shall by Law appoint a different Day.

SECTION 5. Each House shall be the Judge of the Elections, Returns and Qualifications of its own Members, and a Majority of each shall constitute a Quorum to do Business; but a smaller Number may adjourn from day to day, and may be authorized to compel the Attendance of absent Members, in such Manner, and under such Penalties as each House may provide.

Each House may determine the Rules of its Proceedings, punish its Members for disorderly Behaviour, and, with the Concurrence of two thirds, expel a Member.

Each House shall keep a Journal of its Proceedings, and from time to time publish the same, excepting such Parts as may in their Judgment require Secrecy; and the Yeas and Nays of the Members of either House on any question shall, at the Desire of one fifth of those Present, be entered on the Journal.

Neither House, during the Session of Congress, shall, without the Consent of the other, adjourn for more than three days, nor to any other Place than that in which the two Houses shall be sitting.

SECTION 6. The Senators and Representatives shall receive a Compensation for their Services, to be ascertained by Law, and paid out of the Treasury of the United States. They shall in all Cases, except Treason, Felony and Breach of the Peace, be privileged from Arrest during their Attendance at the Session of their respective Houses, and in going to and returning from the same; and for any Speech or Debate in either House, they shall not be questioned in any other Place.

No Senator or Representative shall, during the Time for which he was elected, be appointed to any civil Office under the Authority of the United States, which shall have been created, or the Emoluments whereof shall have been encreased during such time; and no Person holding any Office under the United States, shall be a Member of either House during his Continuance in Office.

SECTION 7. All Bills for raising Revenue shall originate in the House of Representatives; but the Senate may propose or concur with amendments as on other Bills.

Every Bill which shall have passed the House of Representatives and the Senate, shall, before it become a Law, be presented to the President of the United States; If he approve he shall sign it, but if not he shall return it, with his Objections to that House in which it shall have originated, who shall enter the Objections at large on their Journal, and proceed to reconsider it. If after such Reconsideration two thirds of that House shall agree to pass the Bill, it shall be sent, together with the Objections, to the other House, by which it shall likewise be reconsidered, and if approved by two thirds of that House, it shall become a Law. But in all such Cases the Votes of both Houses shall be determined by Yeas and Nays, and the Names of the Persons voting for and against the Bill shall be entered on the Journal of each House respectively. If any Bill shall not be returned by the President within ten Days (Sunday excepted) after it shall have been presented to him, the Same shall be a Law, in like Manner as if he had signed it, unless the Congress by their Adjournment prevent its Return, in which Case it shall not be a Law.

Every Order, Resolution, or Vote to which the Concurrence of the Senate and House of Representatives may be necessary (except on a question of Adjournment) shall be presented to the President of the United States; and before the Same shall take Effect, shall be approved by him, or being disapproved by him, shall be repassed by two thirds of the Senate and House of Representatives, according to the Rules and Limitations prescribed in the Case of a Bill.

SECTION 8. The Congress shall have Power To lay and collect Taxes, Duties, Imposts and Excises, to pay the Debts and provide for the common Defence and general Welfare of the United States; but all Duties, Imposts and Excises shall be uniform throughout the United States;

To borrow Money on the credit of the United States;

To regulate Commerce with foreign Nations, and among the several States, and with the Indian Tribes;

To establish an uniform Rule of Naturalization, and uniform Laws on the subject of Bankruptcies throughout the United States;

To coin Money, regulate the Value thereof, and of foreign Coin, and fix the Standard of Weights and Measures;

To provide for the Punishment of counterfeiting the Securities and current Coin of the United States;

To establish Post Offices and post Roads;

To promote the Progress of Science and useful Arts, by securing for limited Times to Authors and Inventors the exclusive Right to their respective Writings and Discoveries;

To constitute Tribunals inferior to the supreme Court;

To define and punish Piracies and Felonies committed on the high Seas, and Offences against the Law of Nations;

To declare War, grant Letters of Marque and Reprisal, and make Rules concerning Captures on Land and Water;

To raise and support Armies, but no Appropriation of Money to that Use shall be for a longer Term than two Years;

To provide and maintain a Navy;

To make Rules for the Government and Regulation of the land and naval Forces;

To provide for calling forth the Militia to execute the Laws of the Union, suppress Insurrections and repel Invasions;

To provide for organizing, arming, and disciplining, the Militia, and for governing such Part of them as may be employed in the Service of the United States, reserving to the States respectively, the Appointment of the Officers, and the Authority of training the Militia according to the discipline prescribed by Congress;

To exercise exclusive Legislation in all Cases whatsoever, over such District (not exceeding ten Miles square) as may, by Cession of particular States, and the Acceptance of Congress, become the Seat of the Government of the United States, and to exercise like Authority over all Places purchased by the Consent of the Legislature of the State in which the Same shall be, for the Erection of Forts, Magazines, Arsenals, dock-Yards, and other needful Buildings;—And

To make all Laws which shall be necessary and proper for carrying into Execution the foregoing Powers, and all other Powers vested by this Constitution in the Government of the United States, or in any Department or Officer thereof.

SECTION 9. The Migration or Importation of such Persons as any of the States now existing shall think proper to admit, shall not be prohibited by the Congress prior to the Year one thousand eight hundred and eight, but a Tax or duty may be imposed on such Importation, not exceeding ten dollars for each Person.

The Privilege of the Writ of Habeas Corpus shall not be suspended, unless when in Cases of Rebellion or Invasion the public Safety may require it.

No Bill of Attainder or ex post facto Law shall be passed.

No Capitation, or other direct, Tax shall be laid, unless in Proportion to the Census or Enumeration herein before directed to be taken.

No Tax or Duty shall be laid on Articles exported from any State.

No Preference shall be given by any Regulation of Commerce or Revenue to the Ports of one State over those of another; nor shall Vessels bound to, or from, one State, be obliged to enter, clear or pay Duties in another.

No Money shall be drawn from the Treasury, but in Consequence of Appropriations made by Law; and a regular Statement and Account of the Receipts and Expenditures of all public Money shall be published from time to time.

No Title of Nobility shall be granted by the United States: And no Person holding any Office of Profit or Trust under them, shall, without the Consent of the Congress, accept of any present, Emolument, Office, or Title, of any kind whatever, from any King, Prince or foreign State.

SECTION 10. No State shall enter into any Treaty, Alliance, or Confederation; grant Letters of Marque and Reprisal; coin Money; emit Bills of Credit; make any Thing but gold and silver Coin a Tender in Payment of Debts; pass any Bill of Attainder, ex post facto Law, or Law impairing the Obligation of Contracts, or grant any Title of Nobility.

No State shall, without the Consent of the Congress, lay any Imposts or Duties on Imports or Exports, except what may be absolutely necessary for executing its inspection Laws: and the net Produce of all Duties and Imposts, laid by any State on Imports or Exports, shall be for the Use of the Treasury of the United States; and all such Laws shall be subject to the Revision and Controul of the Congress.

No State shall, without the Consent of Congress, lay any Duty of Tonnage, keep Troops, or Ships of War in time of Peace, enter into any Agreement or Compact with another State, or with a foreign Power, or engage in War, unless actually invaded, or in such imminent Danger as will not admit of delay.

ARTICLE II.

SECTION 1. The executive Power shall be vested in a President of the United States of America. He shall hold his Office during the Term of four Years, and, together with the Vice President, chosen for the same Term, be elected, as follows

Each State shall appoint, in such Manner as the Legislature thereof may direct, a Number of Electors, equal to the whole Number of Senators and Representatives to which the State may be entitled in the Congress: but no Senator or Representative, or Person holding an Office of Trust or Profit under the United States, shall be appointed an Elector.

The Electors shall meet in their respective States, and vote by Ballot for two Persons, of whom one at least shall not be an Inhabitant of the same State with themselves. And they shall make a List of all the Persons voted for, and of the Number of Votes for each; which List they shall sign and certify, and transmit sealed to the Seat of the Government of the United States, directed to the President of the Senate. The President of the Senate shall, in the Presence of the Senate and House of Representatives, open all the Certificates, and the Votes shall then be counted. The Person having the greatest Number of Votes shall be the President, if such Number be a Majority of the whole Number of Electors appointed; and if there be more than one who have such Majority, and have an equal Number of Votes, then the House of Representatives shall immediately chuse by Ballot one of them for President; and if no Person have a Majority, then from the five highest on the List the said House shall in like Manner chuse the President. But in chusing the President, the Votes shall be taken by States, the Representation from each State having one Vote; a quorum for this Purpose shall consist of a Member or Members from two thirds of the States, and a Majority of all the States shall be necessary to a Choice. In every Case, after the Choice of the President, the Person having the greatest Number of Votes of the Electors shall be the Vice President. But if there should remain two or more who have equal Votes, the Senate shall chuse from them by Ballot the Vice President.

The Congress may determine the Time of chusing the Electors, and the Day on which they shall give their Votes; which Day shall be the same throughout the United States.

No Person except a natural born Citizen, or a Citizen of the United States, at the time of the Adoption of this Constitution, shall be eligible to the Office of President; neither shall any Person be eligible to that Office who shall not have attained to the Age of thirty five Years, and been fourteen Years a Resident within the United States.

In Case of the Removal of the President from Office, or of his Death, Resignation, or Inability to discharge the Powers and Duties of the said Office, the Same shall devolve on the Vice President, and the Congress may by Law provide for the Case of Removal, Death, Resignation or Inability, both of the President and Vice President, declaring what Officer shall then act as President, and such Officer shall act accordingly, until the Disability be removed, or a President shall be elected.

The President shall, at stated Times, receive for his Services, a Compensation, which shall neither be encreased nor diminished during the Period for which he shall have been elected, and he shall not receive within that Period any other Emolument from the United States, or any of them.

Before he enter on the Execution of his Office, he shall take the following Oath or Affirmation:—"I do solemnly swear (or affirm) that I will faithfully execute the Office of President of the United States, and will to the best of my Ability, preserve, protect and defend the Constitution of the United States."

SECTION 2. The President shall be Commander in Chief of the Army and Navy of the United States, and of the Militia of the several States, when called into the actual Service of the United States; he may require the Opinion, in writing, of the principal Officer in each of the executive Departments, upon any Subject relating to the Duties of their respective Offices, and he shall have Power to grant Reprieves and Pardons for Offences against the United States, except in Cases of Impeachment.

He shall have Power, by and with the Advice and Consent of the Senate, to make Treaties, provided two thirds of the Senators present concur; and he shall nominate, and by and with the Advice and Consent of the Senate, shall appoint Ambassadors, other public Ministers and Consuls, Judges of the supreme Court, and all other Officers of the United States, whose Appointments are not herein otherwise provided for, and which shall be established by Law: but the Congress may by Law vest the Appointment of such inferior Officers, as they think proper, in the President alone, in the Courts of Law, or in the Heads of Departments.

The President shall have Power to fill up all Vacancies that may happen during the Recess of the Senate, by granting Commissions which shall expire at the End of their next Session.

SECTION 3. He shall from time to time give to the Congress Information of the State of the Union, and recommend to their Consideration such Measures as he shall judge necessary and expedient; he may, on extraordinary Occasions, convene both Houses, or either of them, and in Case of Disagreement between them, with Respect to the Time of Adjournment, he may adjourn them to such Time as he shall think proper; he shall receive Ambassadors and other public Ministers; he shall take Care that the Laws be faithfully executed, and shall Commission all the Officers of the United States.

SECTION 4. The President, Vice President and all Civil Officers of the United States, shall be removed from Office on Impeachment for, and Conviction of, Treason, Bribery, or other high Crimes and Misdemeanors.

ARTICLE III.

SECTION 1. The judicial Power of the United States, shall be vested in one supreme Court, and in such inferior Courts as the Congress may from time to time ordain and establish. The Judges, both of the supreme and inferior Courts, shall hold their Offices during good Behaviour, and shall, at stated Times, receive for their Services, a Compensation, which shall not be diminished during their Continuance in Office.

SECTION 2. The judicial Power shall extend to all Cases, in Law and Equity, arising under this Constitution, the Laws of the United States, and Treaties made, or which shall be made, under their Authority;—to all Cases affecting Ambassadors, other public Ministers and Consuls;—to all Cases of admiralty and maritime Jurisdiction;—to Controversies to which the United States shall be a Party;—to Controversies between two or more States;—between a State and Citizens of another State;—between Citizens of different States;—between Citizens of the same State claiming Lands under Grants of different States, and between a State, or the Citizens thereof, and foreign States, Citizens or Subjects.

In all Cases affecting Ambassadors, other public Ministers and Consuls, and those in which a State shall be Party, the Supreme Court shall have original Jurisdiction. In all the other Cases before mentioned, the supreme Court shall have appellate Jurisdiction, both as to Law and Fact, with such Exceptions, and under such Regulations as the Congress shall make.

The Trial of all Crimes, except in Cases of Impeachment, shall be by Jury; and such Trial shall be held in the State where the said Crimes shall have been committed; but when not committed within any State, the Trial shall be at such Place or Places as the Congress may by Law have directed.

SECTION 3. Treason against the United States, shall consist only in levying War against them, or in adhering to their Enemies, giving them Aid and Comfort. No Person shall be convicted of Treason unless on the Testimony of two Witnesses to the same overt Act, or on Confession in open Court.

The Congress shall have Power to declare the Punishment of Treason, but no Attainder of Treason shall work Corruption of Blood, or Forfeiture except during the Life of the Person attainted.

ARTICLE IV.

SECTION 1. Full Faith and Credit shall be given in each State to the public Acts, Records, and judicial Proceedings of every other State. And the Congress may by general Laws prescribe the Manner in which such Acts, Records and Proceedings shall be proved, and the Effect thereof.

SECTION 2. The Citizens of each State shall be entitled to all Privileges and Immunities of Citizens in the several States.

A Person charged in any State with Treason, Felony, or other Crime, who shall flee from Justice, and be found in another State, shall on Demand of the executive Authority of the State from which he fled, be delivered up, to be removed to the State having Jurisdiction of the Crime.

No Person held to Service or Labour in one State, under the Laws thereof, escaping into another, shall, in Consequence of any Law or Regulation therein, be discharged from such Service or Labour, but shall be delivered up on Claim of the Party to whom such Service or Labour may be due.

SECTION 3. New States may be admitted by the Congress into this Union; but no new State shall be formed or erected within the Jurisdiction of any other State; nor any State be formed by the Junction of two or more States, or Parts of States, without the Consent of the Legislatures of the States concerned as well as of the Congress.

The Congress shall have Power to dispose of and make all needful Rules and Regulations respecting the Territory or other Property belonging to the United States; and nothing in this Constitution shall be so construed as to Prejudice any Claims of the United States, or of any particular State.

SECTION 4. The United States shall guarantee to every State in this Union a Republican Form of Government, and shall protect each of them against Invasion; and on Application of the Legislature, or of the Executive (when the Legislature cannot be convened) against domestic Violence.

ARTICLE V.

The Congress, whenever two thirds of both Houses shall deem it necessary, shall propose Amendments to this Constitution, or, on the Application of the Legislatures of two thirds of the several States, shall call a Convention for proposing Amendments, which, in either Case, shall be valid to all Intents and Purposes, as Part of this Constitution, when ratified by the Legislatures of three fourths of the several States, or by Conventions in three fourths thereof, as the one or the other Mode of Ratification may be proposed by the Congress; Provided that no Amendment which may be made prior to the Year One thousand eight hundred and eight shall in any Manner affect the first and fourth Clauses in the Ninth Section of the first Article; and that no State, without its Consent, shall be deprived of its equal Suffrage in the Senate.

ARTICLE VI.

All Debts contracted and Engagements entered into, before the Adoption of this Constitution, shall be as valid against the United States under this Constitution, as under the Confederation.

This Constitution, and the Laws of the United States which shall be made in Pursuance thereof; and all Treaties made, or which shall be made, under the Authority of the United States, shall be the supreme Law of the Land; and the Judges in every State shall be bound thereby, any Thing in the Constitution or Laws of any State to the Contrary notwithstanding.

The Senators and Representatives before mentioned, and the Members of the several State Legislatures, and all executive and judicial Officers, both of the United States and of the several States, shall be bound by Oath or Affirmation, to support this Constitution; but no religious Test shall ever be required as a Qualification to any Office or public Trust under the United States.

ARTICLE VII.

The Ratification of the Conventions of nine States, shall be sufficient for the Establishment of this Constitution between the States so ratifying the Same.

. . .

ARTICLES IN ADDITION TO, AND AMENDMENT OF, THE CONSTITUTION OF THE UNITED STATES OF AMERICA, PROPOSED BY CONGRESS, AND RATIFIED BY THE SEVERAL STATES, PURSUANT TO THE FIFTH ARTICLE OF THE ORIGINAL CONSTITUTION.

AMENDMENT I [1791].

Congress shall make no law respecting an establishment of religion, or prohibiting the free exercise thereof; or abridging the freedom of speech, or of the press; or the right of the people peaceably to assemble, and to petition the Government for a redress of grievances.

AMENDMENT II [1791].

A well regulated Militia, being necessary to the security of a free State, the right of the people to keep and bear Arms, shall not be infringed.

AMENDMENT III [1791].

No Soldier shall, in time of peace be quartered in any house, without the consent of the Owner, nor in time of war, but in a manner to be prescribed by law.

AMENDMENT IV [1791].

The right of the people to be secure in their persons, houses, papers, and effects, against unreasonable searches and seizures, shall not be violated, and no Warrants shall issue, but upon probable cause, supported by Oath or affirmation, and particularly describing the place to be searched, and the persons or things to be seized.

AMENDMENT V [1791].

No person shall be held to answer for a capital, or otherwise infamous crime, unless on a presentment or indictment of a Grand Jury, except in cases arising in the land or naval forces, or in the Militia, when in actual service in time of War or public danger; nor shall any person be subject for the same offence to be twice put in jeopardy of life or limb; nor shall be compelled in any criminal case to be a witness against himself, nor be deprived of life, liberty, or property, without due process of law; nor shall private property be taken for public use, without just compensation.

AMENDMENT VI [1791].

In all criminal prosecutions, the accused shall enjoy the right to a speedy and public trial, by an impartial jury of the State and district wherein the crime shall have been committed, which district shall have been previously ascertained by law, and to be informed of the nature and cause of the accusation; to be confronted with the witnesses against him; to have compulsory process for obtaining Witnesses in his favor, and to have the Assistance of Counsel for his defence.

AMENDMENT VII [1791].

In Suits at common law, where the value in controversy shall exceed twenty dollars, the right of trial by jury shall be preserved, and no fact tried by a jury, shall be otherwise re-examined in any Court of the United States, than according to the rules of the common law.

AMENDMENT VIII [1791].

Excessive bail shall not be required, nor excessive fines imposed, nor cruel and unusual punishments inflicted.

AMENDMENT IX [1791].

The enumeration in the Constitution, of certain rights, shall not be construed to deny or disparage others retained by the people.

AMENDMENT X [1791].

The powers not delegated to the United States by the Constitution, nor prohibited by it to the States, are reserved to the States respectively, or to the people.

AMENDMENT XI [1798].

The Judicial power of the United States shall not be construed to extend to any suit in law or equity, commenced or prosecuted against one of the United States by Citizens of another State, or by Citizens or Subjects of any Foreign State.

AMENDMENT XII [1804].

The Electors shall meet in their respective states and vote by ballot for President and Vice–President, one of whom, at least, shall not be an inhabitant of the same state with themselves; they shall name in their ballots the person voted for as President, and in distinct ballots the person voted for as Vice–President, and they shall make distinct lists of all persons voted for as President, and of all persons voted for as Vice–President, and of the number of votes for each, which lists they shall sign and certify, and transmit sealed to the seat of the government of the United States, directed to the President of the Senate;—The President of the Senate shall, in the presence of the Senate and House of Representatives, open all the certificates and the votes shall then be counted;—The person having the greatest number of votes for President, shall be the President, if such number be a majority of the whole number of Electors appointed; and if no person have such majority, then from the persons having the highest numbers not exceeding three on the list of those voted for as President, the House of Representatives shall choose immediately, by ballot, the President. But in choosing the President, the votes shall be taken by states, the representation from each state having one vote; a quorum for this purpose shall consist of a member or members from two-thirds of the states, and a majority of all the states shall be necessary to a choice. And if the House of Representatives shall not choose a President whenever the right of choice shall devolve upon them, before the fourth day of March next following, then the Vice–President shall act as President, as in the case of the death or other constitutional disability of the President—The person having the greatest number of votes as Vice–President, shall be the Vice–President, if such number be a majority of the whole number of Electors appointed, and if no person have a majority, then from the two highest numbers on the list, the Senate shall choose the Vice–President; a quorum for the purpose shall consist of two-thirds of the whole number of Senators, and a majority of the whole number shall be necessary to a choice. But no person constitutionally ineligible to the office of President shall be eligible to that of Vice–President of the United States.

AMENDMENT XIII [1865].

SECTION 1. Neither slavery nor involuntary servitude, except as a punishment for crime whereof the party shall have been duly convicted, shall exist within the United States, or any place subject to their jurisdiction.

SECTION 2. Congress shall have power to enforce this article by appropriate legislation.

AMENDMENT XIV [1868].

SECTION 1. All persons born or naturalized in the United States and subject to the jurisdiction thereof, are citizens of the United States and of the State wherein they reside. No State shall make or enforce any law which shall abridge the privileges or immunities of citizens of the United States; nor shall any State deprive any person of life, liberty, or property, without due process of law; nor deny to any person within its jurisdiction the equal protection of the laws.

SECTION 2. Representatives shall be apportioned among the several States according to their respective numbers, counting the whole number of persons in each State, excluding Indians not taxed. But when the right to vote at any election for the choice of electors for President and Vice President of the United States, Representatives in Congress, the Executive and Judicial officers of a State, or the members of the Legislature thereof, is denied to any of the male inhabitants of such State, being twenty-one years of age, and citizens of the United States, or in any way abridged, except for participation in rebellion, or other crime, the basis of representation therein shall be reduced in the proportion which the number of such male citizens shall bear to the whole number of male citizens twenty-one years of age in such State.

SECTION 3. No person shall be a Senator or Representative in Congress, or elector of President and Vice President, or hold any office, civil or military, under the United States, or under any State, who, having previously taken an oath, as a member of Congress, or as an officer of the United States, or as a member of any State legislature, or as an executive or judicial officer of any State, to support the Constitution of the United States, shall have engaged in insurrection or rebellion against the same, or given aid or comfort to the enemies thereof. But Congress may by a vote of two-thirds of each House, remove such disability.

SECTION 4. The validity of the public debt of the United States, authorized by law, including debts incurred for payment of pensions and bounties for services in suppressing insurrection or rebellion, shall not be questioned. But neither the United States nor any State shall assume or pay any debt or obligation incurred in aid of insurrection or rebellion against the United States, or any claim for the loss or emancipation of any slave; but all such debts, obligations and claims shall be held illegal and void.

SECTION 5. The Congress shall have power to enforce, by appropriate legislation, the provisions of this article.

AMENDMENT XV [1870].

SECTION 1. The right of citizens of the United States to vote shall not be denied or abridged by the United States or by any State on account of race, color, or previous condition of servitude.

SECTION 2. The Congress shall have power to enforce this article by appropriate legislation.

AMENDMENT XVI [1913].

The Congress shall have power to lay and collect taxes on incomes, from whatever source derived, without apportionment among the several States, and without regard to any census or enumeration.

AMENDMENT XVII [1913].

The Senate of the United States shall be composed of two Senators from each State, elected by the people thereof, for six years; and each Senator shall have one vote. The electors in each State shall have the qualifications requisite for electors of the most numerous branch of the State legislatures.

When vacancies happen in the representation of any State in the Senate, the executive authority of such State shall issue writs of election to fill such vacancies: Provided, That the legislature of any State may empower the executive thereof to make temporary appointments until the people fill the vacancies by election as the legislature may direct.

This amendment shall not be so construed as to affect the election or term of any Senator chosen before it becomes valid as part of the Constitution.

AMENDMENT XVIII [1919].

SECTION 1. After one year from the ratification of this article the manufacture, sale, or transportation of intoxicating liquors within, the importation thereof into, or the exportation thereof from the United States and all territory subject to the jurisdiction thereof for beverage purposes is hereby prohibited.

SECTION 2. The Congress and the several States shall have concurrent power to enforce this article by appropriate legislation.

SECTION 3. This article shall be inoperative unless it shall have been ratified as an amendment to the Constitution by the legislatures of the several States, as provided in the Constitution, within seven years from the date of the submission hereof to the States by the Congress.

AMENDMENT XIX [1920].

The right of citizens of the United States to vote shall not be denied or abridged by the United States or by any State on account of sex.

Congress shall have power to enforce this article by appropriate legislation.

AMENDMENT XX [1933].

SECTION 1. The terms of the President and Vice President shall end at noon on the 20th day of January, and the terms of Senators and Representatives at noon on the 3d day of January, of the years in which such terms would have ended if this article had not been ratified; and the terms of their successors shall then begin.

SECTION 2. The Congress shall assemble at least once in every year, and such meeting shall begin at noon on the 3d day of January, unless they shall by law appoint a different day.

SECTION 3. If, at the time fixed for the beginning of the term of the President, the President elect shall have died, the Vice President elect shall become President. If a President shall not have been chosen before the time fixed for the beginning of his term, or if the President elect shall have failed to qualify, then the Vice President elect shall act as President until a President shall have qualified; and the Congress may by law provide for the case wherein neither a President elect nor a Vice President elect shall have qualified, declaring who shall then act as President, or the manner in which one who is to act shall be selected, and such person shall act accordingly until a President or Vice President shall have qualified.

SECTION 4. The Congress may by law provide for the case of the death of any of the persons from whom the House of Representatives may choose a President whenever the right of choice shall have devolved upon them, and for the case of the death of any of the persons from whom the Senate may choose a Vice President whenever the right of choice shall have devolved upon them.

SECTION 5. Sections 1 and 2 shall take effect on the 15th day of October following the ratification of this article.

SECTION 6. This article shall be inoperative unless it shall have been ratified as an amendment to the Constitution by the legislatures of three-fourths of the several States within seven years from the date of its submission.

AMENDMENT XXI [1933].

SECTION 1. The eighteenth article of amendment to the Constitution of the United States is hereby repealed.

SECTION 2. The transportation or importation into any State, Territory, or possession of the United States for delivery or use therein of intoxicating liquors, in violation of the laws thereof, is hereby prohibited.

SECTION 3. This article shall be inoperative unless it shall have been ratified as an amendment to the Constitution by conventions in the several States, as provided in the Constitution, within seven years from the date of the submission hereof to the States by the Congress.

AMENDMENT XXII [1951].

SECTION 1. No person shall be elected to the office of the President more than twice, and no person who has held the office of President, or acted as President, for more than two years of a term to which some other person was elected President shall be elected to the office of the President more than once. But this Article shall not apply to any person holding the office of President when this Article was proposed by the Congress, and shall not prevent any person who may be holding the office of President, or acting as President, during the term within which this Article becomes operative from holding the office of President or acting as President during the remainder of such term.

SECTION 2. This article shall be inoperative unless it shall have been ratified as an amendment to the Constitution by the legislatures of three-fourths of the several States within seven years from the date of its submission to the States by the Congress.

AMENDMENT XXIII [1961].

SECTION 1. The District constituting the seat of Government of the United States shall appoint in such manner as the Congress may direct:

A number of electors of President and Vice President equal to the whole number of Senators and Representatives in Congress to which the District would be entitled if it were a State, but in no event more than the least populous State; they shall be in addition to those appointed by the States, but they shall be considered, for the purposes of the election of President and Vice President, to be electors appointed by a State; and they shall meet in the District and perform such duties as provided by the twelfth article of amendment.

SECTION 2. The Congress shall have power to enforce this article by appropriate legislation.

AMENDMENT XXIV [1964].

SECTION 1. The right of citizens of the United States to vote in any primary or other election for President or Vice President, for electors for President or Vice President, or for Senator or Representative in Congress, shall not be denied or abridged by the United States or any State by reason of failure to pay any poll tax or other tax.

SECTION 2. The Congress shall have power to enforce this article by appropriate legislation.

AMENDMENT XXV [1967].

SECTION 1. In case of the removal of the President from office or of his death or resignation, the Vice President shall become President.

SECTION 2. Whenever there is a vacancy in the office of the Vice President, the President shall nominate a Vice President who shall take office upon confirmation by a majority vote of both Houses of Congress.

SECTION 3. Whenever the President transmits to the President pro tempore of the Senate and the Speaker of the House of Representatives his written declaration that he is unable to discharge the powers and duties of his office, and until he transmits to them a written declaration to the contrary, such powers and duties shall be discharged by the Vice President as Acting President.

SECTION 4. Whenever the Vice President and a majority of either the principal officers of the executive departments or of such other body as Congress may by law provide, transmit to the President pro tempore of the Senate and the Speaker of the House of Representatives their written declaration that the President is unable to discharge the powers and duties of his office, the Vice President shall immediately assume the powers and duties of the office as Acting President.

Thereafter, when the President transmits to the President pro tempore of the Senate and the Speaker of the House of Representatives his written declaration that no inability exists, he shall resume the powers and duties of his office unless the Vice President and a majority of either the principal officers of the executive department or of such other body as Congress may by law provide, transmit within four days to the President pro tempore of the Senate and the Speaker of the House of Representatives their written declaration that the President is unable to discharge the powers and duties of his office. Thereupon Congress shall decide the issue, assembling within forty-eight hours for that purpose if not in session. If the Congress, within twenty-one days after receipt of the latter written declaration, or, if Congress is not in session, within twenty-one days after Congress is required to assemble, determines by two-thirds vote of both Houses that the President is unable to discharge the powers and duties of his office, the Vice President shall continue to discharge the same as Acting President; otherwise, the President shall resume the powers and duties of his office.

AMENDMENT XXVI [1971].

SECTION 1. The right of citizens of the United States, who are eighteen years of age or older, to vote shall not be denied or abridged by the United States or by any State on account of age.

SECTION 2. The Congress shall have power to enforce this article by appropriate legislation.

AMENDMENT XXVII [1992].

No law, varying the compensation for the services of the Senators and Representatives, shall take effect, until an election for Representatives shall have intervened.

*

APPENDIX B

THE UNITED STATES SUPREME COURT

A Chart

1789–2006*

The following chart is designed to provide a means of identifying the composition of the Court at any specified date, and thereby to help the student follow the relationship between changes in the personnel and doctrines of the Court.

If the student is concerned with a decision bearing a date which approximates a change in the Court's personnel it will be necessary to consult the footnotes. These notes show, following the dates of birth and death, political affiliation, and home state at the time of appointment, each justice's dates of commission and termination of service. Of course, members do not always participate in decisions rendered during their term of service; the fact of participation must be independently verified. Large X's indicate vacancies.

The information reflected in the chart and footnotes has been gathered primarily from the Dictionary of American Biography,[1] Warren, The Supreme Court in United States History[2] and for dates of commission and termination of service, the Senate Manual, and the Official Reports of the Supreme Court.

---

* This chart was originally prepared by Paul Gay, and has been updated by the editors.

1. New York, Scribner, 1928–37. 20 v. Supplement one, 1944; Supplement two, 1959.

2. Boston, Little Brown, 1922.

Washington 1789–1797	Adams 1797–1801	Jefferson 1801–1809	Madison 1809–1817

Jay[1] 1789– –1795 | **2 Ellsworth[10]** 1796–1800 | **Marshall[13]** 1801–

Rutledge 2 | **Johnson 7** | **Paterson[8]** 1793– –1806 | **Livingston[15]** 1806–

Cushing[3] 1789– –1810 | **Story[17]** 1811–

Wilson[4] 1789– –1798 | **Washington[11]** 1798–

Blair[5] 1789– –1796 | **Chase[9]** 1796– –1811 | **Duvall[18]** 1811–

Iredell[6] 1790– –1799 | **Moore[12]** 1799– –1804 | **Johnson[14]** 1804–

Todd[16] 1807–

1. John Jay, 1745–1829. Fed., N. Y. 9–26–1789 to 6–29–1795.

2. John Rutledge, 1739–1800. Fed., S. C. 9–26–1789 to 3–5–1791. Comm. C.J. 7–1–1795 (recess appoint.) pres. August term 1795, rejected by Senate 12–15–1795.

3. William Cushing, 1732–1810. Fed., Mass. 9–27–1789 to 9–13–1810.

4. James Wilson, 1742–1798. Fed., Pa. 9–29–1789 to 8–21–1798.

5. John Blair, 1732–1800. Fed., Va. 9–30–1789 to 1–27–1796.

6. James Iredell, 1751–1799. Fed., N. C. 2–10–1790 to 10–20–1799.

7. Thomas Johnson, 1732–1819. Fed., Md. 11–7–1791 to 2–1–1793.

8. William Paterson, 1745–1806. Fed., N. J. 3–4–1793 to 9–9–1806.

9. Samuel Chase, 1741–1811. Fed., Md. 1–27–1796 to 6–19–1811.

10. Oliver Ellsworth, 1745–1807. Fed., Conn. 3–4–1796 to 12–15–1800.

11. Bushrod Washington, 1762–1829. Fed., Va. 12–20–1798 to 11–26–1829.

12. Alfred Moore, 1755–1810. Fed., N. C. 12–10–1799 to 1–26–1804.

13. John Marshall, 1755–1835. Fed., Va. 1–31–1801 to 7–6–1835.

14. William Johnson, 1771–1834. Rep., S. C. 3–26–1804 to 8–4–1834.

15. [Henry] Brockholst Livingston, 1757–1823. Rep., N. Y. 11–10–1806 to 3–18–1823.

16. Thomas Todd, 1765–1826. Rep., Ky. 3–3–1807 to 2–7–1826. Post created by Congress by Act February 24, 1807.

17. Gabriel Duvall, 1752–1844. Rep., Md. 11–18–1811 to 1–14–1835.

18. Joseph Story, 1779–1845. Rep., Mass. 11–18–1811 to 9–10–1845.

Monroe 1817–1825	J. Q. Adams 1825–1829	Jackson 1829–1837	Van Buren 1837–1841	Harrison 3/4–4/4 Tyler 1841–1845

Marshall		–1835	Taney[24] 1836–	
Livingston –1823	Thompson[19] 1823–		–1843	X N[29]
Story				

Washington	–1829	Baldwin[22] 1830–	–1844	X
Duvall		–1835	Barbour[25] 1836– –1841	Daniel[23] 1841–
Johnson		–1834	Wayne[23] 1835–	
Todd	–1826	Trimble[20] '26–8	McLean[21] 1829–	

Catron[26] 1837–

McKinley[27] 1837–

19. Smith Thompson, 1768–1843. Rep., N. Y. 12–9–1823 to 12–18–1843.

20. Robert Trimble, 1777–1828. Rep., Ky. 5–9–1826 to 8–25–1828.

21. John McLean, 1785–1861. Dem./Rep., Ohio 3–7–1829 to 4–4–1861.

22. Henry Baldwin, 1780–1844. Dem., Pa. 1–6–1830 to 4–21–1844.

23. James Moore Wayne, 1790–1867. Dem., Ga. 1–9–1835 to 7–5–1867.

24. Roger Brooke Taney, 1777–1864. Dem., Md. 3–15–1836 to 10–12–1864.

25. Philip Pendleton Barbour, 1783–1841. Dem., Va. 3–15–1836 to 2–25–1841.

26. John Catron, ca. (1778–86) 1865. Dem., Tenn. 3–8–1837 to 5–30–1865. Post created by Congress by Act of March 3, 1837 and abolished by Congress by Act of July 23, 1866.

27. John McKinley, 1780–1852. Dem., Ky./Ala. 9–25–1837 to 7–19–1852. Post created by Congress by Act of March 3, 1837.

28. Peter Vivian Daniel, 1784–1860. Dem., Va. 3–3–1841 to 5–31–1860.

29. Samuel Nelson, 1792–1873. Dem., N. Y. 2–13–1845 to 11–28–1872.

Polk 1845–1849	Taylor 1849–1850 Fillmore 1850–1853	Pierce 1853–1857	Buchanan 1857–1861	Lincoln 1861– 4/15/65	Johnson 1865–1869	Grant 1869–

Taney —1864 | **Chase[39]** 1864– —1873

Nelson[29] —1872

| S | **Woodbury[30]** 1845– —1851 | **Curtis[32]** 1851– —1857 | **Clifford[34]** 1858– |

Grier[31] 1846– —1870 | **S[40]** 1870–

Daniel —1860 | **Miller[36]** 1862–

Wayne —1867 | **B[41]** 1870–

McLean —1861 | **Swayne[35]** 1862–

Catron —1865*

McKinley —1852 | **Campbell[33]** 1853– —1861 | **Davis[37]** 1862–

Field[38] 1863–

30. Levi Woodbury, 1789–1851. Dem., N. H. 9–20–1845 to 9–4–1851.

31. Robert Cooper Grier, 1794–1870. Dem., Pa. 8–4–1846 to 1–31–1870.

32. Benjamin Robbins Curtis, 1809–1874. Whig, Mass. 12–20–1851 to 9–30–1857.

33. John Archibald Campbell, 1811–1889. Dem., Ala. 3–22–1853 to 4–30–1861.

34. Nathan Clifford, 1803–1881. Dem., Me. 1–12–1858 to 7–25–1881.

35. Noah Haynes Swayne, 1804–1884. Rep., Ohio 1–24–1862 to 1–24–1881.

36. Samuel Freeman Miller, 1816–1890. Rep., Iowa 7–16–1862 to 10–13–1890.

37. David Davis, 1815–1886. Rep./Dem., Ill. 12–8–1862 to 3–4–1877.

38. Stephen Johnson Field, 1816–1899. Dem., Cal. 3–10–1863 to 12–1–1897. Post created by Congress by Act of March 3, 1863.

39. Salmon Portland Chase, 1808–1873. Rep., Ohio 12–6–1864 to 5–7–1873.

40. William Strong, 1808–1895. Dem./Rep., Pa. 2–18–1870 to 12–14–1880.

41. Joseph P. Bradley, 1813–1892. Whig/Rep., N. J. 3–21–1870 to 1–22–1892.

* Post abolished by Congress by Act of July 23, 1866.

Grant –1877	Hayes 1877–1881	Garfield 3/4–9/19 Arthur 1881–1885	Cleveland 1885–1889	Harrison 1889–1893	Cleveland 1893–1897	McKinley 1897– 9/14/1901
Waite[43] 1874–			–1888	**Fuller**[50] 1888–		
Hunt[42] 1872–	–1882	**Blatchford**[48] 1882–		–1893	**White**[55] 1894–	
Clifford –1881	**Gray**[47] 1881–					
Strong –1880	**Woods**[45] 1880–	–1887	**Lamar**[49] 1888–	–1893	**Jackson**[54] 1893–5	**Peckham**[56] 1895–
Miller			–1890	**Brown**[52] 1890–		
Bradley				–1892	**Shiras**[53] 1892–	
Swayne –1881	**Matthews**[46] 1881–		–1889	**Brewer**[51] 1889–		
Davis –1877	**Harlan**[44] 1877–					
Field					–1897	**McKenna**[57] 1898–

42. Ward Hunt, 1810–1886. Rep., N. Y. 12–11–1872 to 1–27–1882.

43. Morrison Remick Waite, 1816–1888. Rep., Ohio 1–21–1874 to 3–23–1888.

44. John Marshall Harlan, 1833–1911. Rep., Ky. 11–29–1877 to 10–14–1911.

45. William Burnham Woods, 1824–1887. Rep., Ga. 12–21–1880 to 5–14–1887.

46. [Thomas] Stanley Matthews, 1824–1889. Rep., Ohio 5–12–1881 to 3–22–1889.

47. Horace Gray, 1828–1902. Rep., Mass. 12–20–1881 to 9–15–1902.

48. Samuel Blatchford, 1820–1893. Rep., N. Y. 3–22–1882 to 7–7–1893.

49. Lucius Quintus Cincinnatus Lamar, 1825–1893. Dem., Miss. 1–16–1888 to 1–23–1893.

50. Melville Weston Fuller, 1833–1910. Dem., Ill. 7–20–1888 to 7–4–1910.

51. David Josiah Brewer, 1837–1910. Rep., Kan. 12–18–1889 to 3–28–1910.

52. Henry Billings Brown, 1836–1913. Rep., Mich. 12–29–1890 to 5–28–1906.

53. George Shiras, 1832–1924. Rep., Pa. 7–26–1892 to 2–23–1903.

54. Howell Edmunds Jackson, 1832–1895. Whig/Dem., Tenn. 2–18–1893 to 8–8–1895.

55. Edward Douglass White, 1845–1921. Dem., La. Asso. Just. 2–19–1894 to 12–18–1910; C. J. 12–12–1910 to 5–19–1921.

56. Rufus Wheeler Peckham, 1838–1909. Dem., N. Y. 12–9–1895 to 10–24–1909.

57. Joseph McKenna, 1843–1926. Rep., Cal. 1–21–1898 to 1–5–1925.

T. Roosevelt 1901–1909	Taft 1909–1913	Wilson 1913–1921	Harding 1921– 8/2 /23	Coolidge 1923–1929

Fuller	White[55]		Taft[69]	
–1910	1910–	–1921	1921–	–1930

White	Van Devanter[63]			
–1910	1910–			

Gray	Holmes[58]			
–1902	1902–			

Peckham	Lurton[61]	McReynolds[66]		
–1909	1909– –1914	1914–		

Brown	Moody[60]	Lamar[64]	Brandeis[67]	
–1906	1906– –1910	1910– –1916	1916–	

Shiras	Day[59]		Butler[71]	
–1903	1903–	–1922	1922–	

Brewer	Hughes[62]	Clark[68]	Sutherland[70]	
–1910	1910– –1916	1916– –1922	1922–	

Harlan	Pitney[65]		Sanford[72]	
–1911	1912–	–1922	1923–	

McKenna			Stone[73]	
		–1925	1925–	

58. Oliver Wendell Holmes, 1841–1935. Rep., Mass. 12–4–1902 to 1–12–1932.

59. William Rufus Day, 1849–1923. Rep., Ohio 2–23–1903 to 11–13–1922.

60. William Henry Moody, 1853–1917. Rep., Mass. 12–12–1906 to 11–20–1910.

61. Horace Harmon Lurton, 1844–1914. Dem., Tenn. 12–20–1909 to 7–12–1914.

62. Charles Evans Hughes, 1862–1948. Rep., N. Y. Asso. Just. 5–2–1910 to 6–10–1916; C. J. 2–13–1930 to 6–30–1941.

63. Willis Van Devanter, 1859–1941. Rep., Wyo. 12–16–1910 to 6–2–1937.

64. Joseph Rucker Lamar, 1857–1916. Dem., Ga. 12–17–1910 to 1–2–1916.

65. Mahlon Pitney, 1858–1924. Rep., N. J. 3–13–1912 to 12–31–1922.

66. James Clark McReynolds, 1862–1946. Dem., Tenn. 8–29–1914 to 1–31–1941.

67. Louis Dembitz Brandeis, 1856–1941. Dem., Mass. 6–1–1916 to 2–13–1939.

68. John Hessin Clarke, 1857–1945. Dem., Ohio 7–24–1916 to 9–18–1922.

69. William Howard Taft, 1857–1930. Rep., Conn. 6–30–1921 to 2–3–1930.

70. George Sutherland, 1862–1942. Rep., Utah 9–5–1922 to 1–17–1938.

71. Pierce Butler, 1866–1939. Dem., Minn. 12–21–1922 to 11–16–1939.

72. Edward Terry Sanford, 1865–1930. Rep., Tenn. 1–29–1923 to 3–8–1930.

Hoover 1929–1933	F. D. Roosevelt 1933–4/12/1945	Truman 1945–1953

T. '30	Hughes[62] 1930–	–1941	Stone[73] 1941–	–1946	Vinson[85] 1946–	–1953
Van Devanter		–1937	Black[76] 1937–			
Holmes –1932	Cardozo[75] 1932–	–1938	Frankfurter[78] 1939–			
McReynolds		–1941	B.[81] '41–2	Rutledge[83] 1943– –1949	Minton[87] 1949–	
Brandeis		–1939	Douglas[79] 1939–			
Butler		–1939	Murphy[80] 1940–	–1949	Clark[86] 1949–	
Sutherland		–1938	Reed[77] 1938–			
S. '30	Roberts[74] 1930–			–1945	Burton[84] 1945–	
Stone		(To C. J.) –1941	Jackson[82] 1941–			

73. Harlan Fiske Stone, 1872–1946. Rep., N. Y. Asso. Just. 2–5–1925 to 7–2–1941; C. J. 7–3–1941 to 4–22–1946.

74. Owen Josephus Roberts, 1875–1955. Rep., Pa. 5–20–1930 to 7–31–1945.

75. Benjamin Nathan Cardozo, 1870–1938. Dem., N. Y. 3–2–1932 to 7–9–1938.

76. Hugo Lafayette Black, 1886–1971. Dem., Ala. 8–18–1937 to 9–17–1971.

77. Stanley Forman Reed, 1884–1980. Dem., Ky. 1–27–1938 to 2–25–1957.

78. Felix Frankfurter, 1882–1965. Ind., Mass. 1–20–1939 to 8–28–1962.

79. William Orville Douglas, 1898–1980. Dem., Conn. 4–15–1939 to 11–12–1975.

80. Frank Murphy, 1890–1949. Dem., Mich. 1–18–1940 to 7–19–1949.

81. James Francis Byrnes, 1879–1972. Dem., S. C. 6–25–1941 to 10–3–1942.

82. Robert Hougwout Jackson, 1892–1954. Dem., N. Y. 7–11–1941 to 10–9–1954.

83. Wiley Blount Rutledge, 1894–1949. Dem., Iowa 2–11–1943 to 9–10–1949.

84. Harold Hitz Burton, 1888–1964. Rep., Ohio 9–22–1945 to 10–13–1958.

85. Frederick Moore Vinson, 1890–1953. Dem., Ky. 6–21–1946 to 9–8–1953.

86. Thomas Campbell Clark, 1899–1977. Dem., Texas 8–19–1949 to 6–12–1967.

87. Sherman Minton, 1890–1965. Dem., Ind. 10–5–1949 to 10–15–1956.

Eisenhower 1953–1961	Kennedy 1961–1963	Johnson 1963–1969

Warren[88]
1953–

Black

Frankfurter		Goldberg[94]		Fortas[95]
	–1962	1962–	–1965	1965–

Minton	Brennan[90]
–1956	1956–

Douglas

Clark		Marshall[96]
	–1967	1967–

Reed		Whittaker[91]		White[93]
	–1957	1957–	–1962	1962–

Burton		Stewart[92]
	–1958	1958–

J	Harlan[89]
'54	1954–

---

88. Earl Warren, 1891–1974, Rep., Cal. 10–2–1953 to 6–23–1969.
89. John Marshall Harlan, 1899–1971. Rep., N. Y. 3–17–1955 to 9–23–1971.
90. William Joseph Brennan, 1906–1997. Dem., N. J. 10–15–1956 to 7–20–1990.
91. Charles Evans Whittaker, 1901–1973. Rep., Mo. 3–19–1957 to 4–1–1962.
92. Potter Stewart, 1915–1985. Rep., Ohio 10–13–1958 to 7–7–1981.
93. Byron R. White, 1917–2002. Dem., Colo. 4–16–1962 to 6–28–1993.
94. Arthur Joseph Goldberg, 1908–1990. Dem., Ill. 10–1–1962 to 7–26–1965.
95. Abe Fortas, 1910–1982. Dem., Tenn. 10–4–1965 to 5–15–1969.
96. Thurgood Marshall, 1908–1993. Dem., N. Y. 10–2–1967 to 10–7–1991.

Nixon 1969–1974	Ford 1974–1977	Carter 1977–1981	Reagan 1981–1989

Warren −1969	**Burger**[97] 1969–	−1986	**Rehnquist**[100] 1986–2005
Black −1971	**Powell**[99] 1971–	−1987	**Kennedy**[104] 1988–2005
Fortas −1969	**Blackmun**[98] 1970–		

Brennan

Douglas −1975	**Stevens**[101] 1975–*

Marshall

White

Stewart −1981	**O'Connor**[102] 1981–2006
Harlan −1971	**Rehnquist**[100] 1971–	(To C. J.) −1986	**Scalia**[103] 1986–*

97. Warren Earl Burger, 1907–1995. Rep., Va. 6–23–1969 to 9–26–1986.

98. Harry Andrew Blackmun, 1908–1999. Rep., Minn. 5–14–1970 to 6–30–1994.

99. Lewis Franklin Powell, Jr., 1907–1998. Dem., Va. 12–19–1971 to 6–26–1987.

100. William Hubbs Rehnquist, 1924–2005. Rep., Ariz. Asso. Just. 12–15–1971 to 9–26–1986; C.J. 9–26–1986 to 9–3–2005.

101. John Paul Stevens, 1920–. Rep., Ill. 12–19–1975 to–.

102. Sandra Day O'Connor, 1930–. Rep., Ariz. 9–25–1981 to 1–31–2006.

103. Antonin Scalia, 1936–. Rep., Washington, D.C. 9–26–1986 to–.

104. Anthony M. Kennedy, 1936–. Rep., Cal. 2–18–1988 to–.

Bush 1989–1993	Clinton 1993–2001	G. W. Bush 2001–*

Rehnquist		Roberts[109]
	–2005	2005–*

Kennedy

Blackmun	Breyer[108]	
	–1994	1994–*

Brennan	Souter[105]	
–1990	1990–*	

Stevens

Marshall	Thomas[106]	
	–1991	1991–*

White	Ginsburg[107]	
	–1993	1993–*

O'Connor		Alito[110]
	– 2006	2006–*

Scalia

105. David H. Souter, 1939–. Rep., N.H. 10–19–1990 to–.

106. Clarence Thomas, 1945–. Rep., Washington, D.C. 10–23–1991 to–.

107. Ruth B. Ginsburg, 1933–. Dem., Washington, D.C. 8–10–1993 to–.

108. Stephen G. Breyer, 1938–. Dem., Mass. 8–14–1994 to–.

109. John G. Roberts, Jr., 1955–. Rep., Washington D.C. 9–29–2005 to–.

110. Samuel A. Alito, Jr., 1950–. Rep., Pa. 1–31–2006 to–.

* This table represents the composition of the Court to August 25, 2006.

INDEX

References are to pages.

†